The Bare Facts Video Guide

Third Edition

Craig Hosoda

Second Edition owners: This Third Edition
is physically thinner because thinner paper
was used. (Even though it has almost 200
more pages than the Second Edition!)

Additional copies of this book (volume purchases also available)
can be purchased from:

The Bare Facts
P.O. Box 3255
Santa Clara, CA 95055-3255
(408) 249-2021

Cover Design: Robert Steven Pawlak Design
                San Francisco, California.

ISBN 0-9625474-3-3

HOW TO USE THIS BOOK

The book is divided into three sections: Actresses, Actors and Titles. In the People sections, everyone is listed alphabetically by last name. If a • appears in front of someone's name, it means they are new to this edition. Under each name are films, TV shows and magazines that a person has appeared in. The non-nudity titles are listed to help you remember who a particular person is. If they have appeared nude in a film or magazine, the title is in bold face. Following the title is the year the film was released, then the character name or article title. "n.a." for the character name is an abbreviation for "not available." Under the title is a • to ••• rating and the time or the page number the nudity occurs. Lastly, is a brief description of how the person appears in the scene.

In the Title section, Films or Made for Cable TV Movies that have nude scenes (of someone in the People section) are listed. Under each entry, are the cast and character names. All the nude scenes for each cast member are listed under their names. If a person is listed in the Title section, they have a listing in the Actor or Actress section. Note that a film can have more nude scenes than are listed—I only list nude scenes of people who are in the Actress or Actor section.

Time definitions:
Very, very brief:	Need to use PAUSE to see one frame
Very brief:	Use SLOW MOTION to see under 1 second
Brief:	About 1 second
No comment:	2 to 15 seconds
Long scene:	Longer than 15 seconds

Rating definitions:
•	Yawn. Usually too brief or hard to see for some reason.
••	Okay. Check it out if you are interested in the person.
•••	Wow! Don't miss it. The scene usually lasts for a while.

The ratings are approximate guides to how much nudity an actor or actress has in a scene. More weight is given on how famous a person is, how well lit and clear the scene is, if it's a close shot and the length of time they stay still so you can see clearly. So if someone has an erotic love scene but they don't show any skin or they are topless but their backs are toward the camera, it won't get rated.

To help you find the nude scenes quickly and accurately, the location on video tape is specified in hours and minutes rather than counter numbers since different VCR's have different counters. The time starts at 0:00 after the last film company logo disappears (Universal, Paramount, etc.). It's easier to locate the scenes if you have a VCR that has a real-time counter.

In the descriptions, "topless" means you see both breasts, "full frontal nudity" means you see both breasts and the pubic area, "lower frontal nudity" means you see the pubic area and "nude" means you see both breasts, the pubic area and the buns.

Actresses that have appeared nude in only one film and are never seen anywhere else are not included because this book helps you locate someone unclothed that you've seen somewhere else before. "One timer" actors are listed though, because without them, the Actors section would be woefully thin!

Some film titles have bold type with no descriptions and others have bold type with descriptions and no time. These are video tapes that readers have sent as additions that aren't on video tape or I haven't had time to verify. These titles are listed so as not to waste people's time sending me duplicate additions.

INTRODUCTION

It used to be that people did nude scenes in films at the beginning of their careers trying to get their "big break." Once they established themselves, they announced they would not be doing any more nudity and hoped that everybody would forget their earlier performances. Phoebe Cates and Sherilyn Fenn for example. But more and more actors and actresses are surprising us and doing nudity in films later in their careers (Sigourney Weaver and Julie Andrews). Fortunately, there are a few who do nudity in just about every film they are in. Sylvia Kristel and Marilyn Chambers for example. This book compiles all of these unbashful actors and actresses into one reference to help you locate their nude scenes on video tape to save you time and money. I have listed a few close calls like Janine Turner in *Monkey Shines* and Christina Applegate in *Streets*.

Some actresses that have done *Playboy* and *Penthouse* pictorials are included because not all actresses do nude scenes in films. Unrevealing pictorials that would be rated PG are not listed (Janet Jones and Jayne Kennedy for example). I've started to include *Playboy* Special Edition magazines, like the *Book of Lingerie*, because there are some actresses who appear nude in them who are also in films. I haven't finished reviewing all of the magazine back issues in this edition but I will in future editions. I'm slow on the magazines because this is a guide for nude scenes on video tape, so magazines are not really supposed to be the focus.

Actresses that *look* like they have done nudity in films, but have used body doubles instead, are also noted. A body double is another person who is used for nude scenes when an actor or actress is too modest. You can usually spot a body double in a movie when there is a nude body without seeing a face.

Some filmographies (Marilyn Monroe, Elizabeth Taylor) are incomplete. Everyone knows who there actress are, so I try to save space by just listing the important things for them. For everyone else, I try to list all of their most recent work. Older, less well known films might get left off a person's filmography. If you need complete filmographies for people, please consult *The Motion Picture Guide* or some of the other reference books listed in the back of this book.

I have spent my time concentrating on getting the greatest *number* of people into this book as possible. Therefore, you'll find the entries for some people like Laura Gemser or Claudia Jennings, incomplete since it's relatively easy to locate films they have nude scenes in. Obviously, I haven't been able to view all the movies ever made (yet), so there will be films with nude scenes that I have missed. (I haven't even started looking at Russ Meyers' films!)

I realize that I don't always use the best English in my descriptions, "Right breast making love." Please try not to laugh out loud too much! I'd rather be succinct and to the point, because I know this book ain't gonna win a Pulitzer Prize.

If you find any mistakes or have additions, please write to me and they will be corrected in the next edition. I have a long list of nude scenes compiled from letters sent in by readers. I need to verify each nude scene because occasionally, readers send me scenes they have incorrectly remembered. There is no need to send *Playboy* and *Penthouse* magazine information, I have a friend who has back issues and I'll eventually include them.

I only review video tapes, not the theatrical release in movie theaters, so you won't see times for *Basic Instinct* or *Body of Evidence* in this edition because they weren't on video tape when this book was being prepared. But you can be assured that they will be in the next edition!

Enjoy!

THANKS, THANKS AND MORE THANKS!

First of all, I need to thank my wife, Marie, for her help and patience putting up with all my video tape viewing. I also need to thank my children, Christopher and Melanie, for taking their naps so I can watch video tapes. Thanks also to my parents and parents in-laws and the rest of my family for all their help and support.

Thank you to Sam Kattuah and his wife, Christa, who not only provide me with free and low cost video tape rentals from their store, Video Land Inc. in Santa Clara, but have also become close friends with me and my family.

Thank you to Dave Dell'Aquila of Rae Technology in Cupertino, California, who is my 4th Dimension Consultant. Without his help, I couldn't have set up the database, imported the data or generated the Title cross reference section of this book. Also thank you to Ron Dell'Aquila who programmed the export from 4th Dimension into FrameMaker.

Thanks to Greg Romankiw & Kevin Rose/Roman Video, Kenny Preston/LaserForce and Irv Slifkin for letting me borrow some of their hard-to-find video tapes and laser discs.

Thanks to the personalities who have provided information or answered questions: Stephanie Blake, Tricia Brown, Emilia Crow, Deborah Dutch, Todd Field, Annie Gaybis, Cuba Gooding Jr., Tab Hunter, Zalman King, Becky LeBeau, Shelley Michelle, Melissa Moore, Susan Napoli, Joan Severance, Nina Siemaszko and Brinke Stevens.

Thanks to friends and business relations who have helped: Tony Borg/Playboy Video, David Brandt, Allen Brody, John Cross, S. C. Dacy, Cindy Farello, Donald Farmer, Dean Goldfarb, Heather King, Holly King, Bruce Kluger/Playboy Magazine, Leila Lavassani, Bob Leighton/HBO, Deborah Meyer/Playboy Video, Pat Moran, Mark Ouimet, Jim Pehling, Jack Qualman, Ed Rasen, Fred Olen Ray, Bert Rhine, Mike Santomauro, Andy & Arlene Sidaris, Rick Sloane, Stuart Wall, Steve Williams and Monica Zadworski.

Thanks to all the media people who have enabled me to spread word about *The Bare Facts* through newspapers, magazines, radio and television: D. Scott Apel/San Jose Mercury News, John Battelle/MacWEEK, Joe Bob Briggs, Richard Corliss/Film Comment, Alex Duvall/The Guardian, George L. George/American Cinematographer, Al Goldstein/Penthouse, George Hackett/Newsweek, Andrea Hill, Daryl Jevens/Chicago Sun Times, Bob Katerzynske/VideoMania, Craig Ledbetter/European Trash Cinema, Steven Levy/Macworld, Jerry D. Mead/The Wine Trader, Mary Ann Meyer/Video, Irv O. Neal/Fox, Dan O'Day, Joao Primo, Steven Puchalski/Shock Cinema, Dawn Reshen/Media Management, Neil Reshen/Media Management, Debbie Richard/Entertainment Tonight, William Rodamor, Gene Ross/Adult Video News, Jeff Smith/Wet Paint, Owen Whetzel/San Jose Mercury News and Andy Wickstrom.

THANKS TO MY CONTRIBUTORS

Thanks to all the people who have sent me additions and corrections:

These individuals have gone beyond the call of duty:
Matt Bear, Marc Benson, Ben A. Braden, Bruce Chapman, David L. Clark, Wallace C. Clopton, Steve Draper, Mark S. Duemmel, Steven L. Edford, Joseph P. Falco, Ray Finocchiaro, Tony Gyngell, F. Hillman, Bill Hunt, Dan Leone, Charles Lipscomb, Jerry E. May, Erich Mees, Paul R. Mewborn, Richard S. Paisley, Dave Parker, John E. Robertson, Gordon Rose, John Schurr, Stephen Seyer and George M. St. George.

A big thank you also to:
Ben Albright-Cassel, Doug Anderson, Tim Bamford, Nicholas Barbano, Garrett Belcher, Garrett Belcher, Jim Bereza, Tom Berry, Meg Birdseye, Larry Blackman, Mark Brookes, Paul Cipriano, Kris Clark, Timothy Coyne, Tom Dawson, Ken Delong, James M. Dempsey, Robert T. Dolsay, Don Douglas, C. Ehrmann, J. K. Embree, Joseph P. Falco, P. R. Finn, Gabriel Flores A., Frederick D. Floreth, W. T. Furgerson, Michael Furl, Norman E. Gaines, Jr., Ward Gambrell, Brian Gari, Michael Goalen, Rodney Eric Griffith, Scott F. Hall, Mark Hammon, Hansjürgen Hellwig, D.A. Helser, Daniel Hill, Edmond E. Hodge, Jr., Randall J. Hole, Jim Jenkins, J. P. Jones, William Kaminsky, James Killian, R. Kunkel, Santo A. LaNasa III, Joseph Lobosco, Joseph Lobosco, Philip Long, Bill Luhman, Keith Markum, James Marshall, Tony Martin, Scott McDonald, Shawn Melton, Dominique Miller, John Miller, Chris Munson, Robert Neill, Duane Oyen, Matt Pachosa, Jerry Palenik, Robin Phillips, Kyle T. Pope, Steve Rakobowchuk, Dr. Bud Rankin, John Reeks, James W. Renner, Mark J. Repp, Dan Rondello, Ricky Rosenholm, T.R. Rouff, T.L. Ruppe, Keith Sabin, Alan W. Shader, Roy Songer, Alan Soprych, Steven Stone, Walter Emil Teague III, Lee Thompson, Chuck Walker, John H. Weimer, Dave Werner, Richard A. White, Bill Williams and Patrick S. Young.

Actresses

Aames, Angela
Films:
Fairytales (1979). . . . . Little Bo Peep
••• 0:14—Nude with The Prince in the woods.
H.O.T.S. (1979) . . . . Boom-Boom Bangs
• 0:21—Topless parachuting into pool.
• 0:39—Topless in bathtub playing with a seal.
• 1:33—Topless playing football.
...All the Marbles (1981). . . . . Louise
a.k.a. The California Dolls
•• 0:20—Topless in Peter Falk's motel room talking with Iris, then sitting on the bed.
The Best of Sex and Violence (1981). . Little Bo Peep
• 0:18—Brief topless in scene from *Fairytales*.
• 0:20—Brief right breast in scene from *Fairytales*.
Famous T & A (1982) . . . . Little Bo Peep
(No longer available for purchase, check your video store for rental.)
•• 0:50—Topless scene from *Fairytales*.
The Lost Empire (1983) . . . . Heather McClure
••• 0:31—Topless and buns taking a shower while Angel and White Star talk to her.
Scarface (1983). . . . . Woman at the Babylon Club
Bachelor Party (1984) . . . . Mrs. Klupner
Basic Training (1984). . . . . Cheryl
• 0:19—Brief topless in bathtub.
Chopping Mall (1986) . . . . Miss Vanders

Abigail
Films:
Alvin Purple (1973; Australian) . . . . Girl in See-Through
0:01—On bus in see-through top. Hard to see anything.
Alvin Rides Again (1974; Australian) . . . . Mae
••• 0:12—Topless in store with Alvin.
The Adventures of Eliza Fraser (1976; Australian)
. . . . Buxom Girl
• 0:01—Topless when Martin pulls the sheets off her.
Breaking Loose (1988; Australian) . . . . Helen

• Able, Sheri
Films:
The Evil Below (1991) . . . . Tracy
• 0:10—Buns, in two piece swimsuit on boat.
0:16—In wet T-shirt getting on boat after diving.
• 0:21—Right breast, with Max behind curtain. Hard to see.
Ultimate Desires (1991). . . . . Carlos' Girlfriend

Abril, Victoria
Films:
Comin' At Ya! (1982) . . . . Abilene
The Moon in the Gutter (1983; French/Italian) . . . . Bella
On the Line (1984; Spanish) . . . . Engracia
••• 0:16—Topless getting undressed to make love with Mitch.
• 0:29—Very brief topless, making love in bed with Mitch.
0:54—In white lingerie getting dressed.

L'Addition (1985; French). . . . . Patty
Padre Nuestro (1987) . . . . n.a.
Tie Me Up! Tie Me Down! (1990; Spanish)
. . . . Marina Osorio
••• 0:24—Full frontal nudity playing with a frogman toy in the bathtub.
• 0:34—Buns and brief side of right breast, getting dressed.
•• 0:44—Topless changing clothes, then on TV while Maximo watches.
•• 1:09—Topless changing clothes.
••• 1:16—Right breast, then topless in bed making love with Ricky.
High Heels (1991; Spanish) . . . . Rebecca
Magazines:
Playboy (Nov 1987) . . . . Sex in Cinema 1987
• 143—Topless in bed from *Padre Nuestro*.
Playboy (Nov 1992) . . . . Sex in Cinema 1992
• 147—Buns, from *Amantes (Lovers)*.

Ackerman, Leslie
Films:
The First Nudie Musical (1979) . . . . Susie
Hardcore (1979) . . . . Felice
• 0:44—Topless in porno house with George C. Scott.
Blame It on the Night (1984). . . . . Shelly
TV:
Skag (1980) . . . . Barbara Skagska

Adams, Brooke
Films:
Shock Wave (1977) . . . . Rose
Days of Heaven (1978). . . . . Abby
Invasion of the Body Snatchers (1978)
. . . . Elizabeth Driscoll
0:49—All covered in pod gunk in her bedroom when Donald Sutherland discovers her. Don't really see anything.
•• 1:43—Brief topless behind plants when Sutherland sees her change into a pod person. Hard to see because plants are in the way.
• 1:48—Topless walking through the pod factory pointing out Sutherland to everybody. Long shot, hard to see.
Cuba (1979) . . . . Alexandra Pulido
Tell Me a Riddle (1980) . . . . Jeannie
The Dead Zone (1983). . . . . Sarah Bracknell
Utilities (1983). . . . . Marion
Almost You (1984) . . . . Erica Boyer
Key Exchange (1985) . . . . Lisa
0:10—Nude on bicycle with her boyfriend, but you can't see anything because of his strategically placed arms.
• 0:45—Very brief right breast getting into the shower with her boyfriend, then hard to see behind the shower curtain.
The Unborn (1991) . . . . Virginia Marshall
• 1:12—Right breast, while breast feeding her baby creature.

Gas Food Lodging (1992) .Nora
Miniseries:
Lace (1984). . . . . .Pagan
Lace II (1985) . . . . .Pagan
Made for TV Movies:
Bridesmaids (1989) . . . . Pat
Stephen King's "Sometimes They Come Back" (1991)
. . . . Sally
TV:
O.K. Crackerby (1965-66) . . . . Cynthia Crackerby

Adams, Maud

Films:
The Christian Licorice Store (1971) . . . Cynthia Vicstrom
The Girl in Blue (1973; Canadian) . . . . . . .Paula/Tracy
a.k.a. U-turn
• 1:16—Side view of right breast, while sitting on bed
with Scott.
1:19—In two piece swimsuit getting out of lake.
The Man with the Golden Gun (1974; British)
. . . . Andrea Anders
Killer Force (1975; Swiss/Irish) . . . . . . .Claire Chambers
Rollerball (1975) . . . . Ella
Laura (1979) . . . . Sarah
a.k.a. Shattered Innocence
Tattoo (1981) . . . . Maddy
• 0:22—Very brief topless taking off clothes and putting a bathrobe on.
•• 0:23—Topless opening bathrobe so Bruce Dern can
start painting.
•• 0:25—Brief topless getting into the shower to take
off body paint.
•• 0:58—Brief topless and buns getting out of bed.
•• 1:04—Topless, knocked out on table before Dern
starts tattooing her.
••• 1:07—Topless looking at herself in the mirror with a
few tattoos on.
•• 1:24—Topless lying on table masturbating while
Dern watches through peep hole in the door.
••• 1:36—Full frontal nudity taking off robe then making love with Dern (her body is covered with tattoos).
Target Eagle (1982) . . . . Carmen
Octopussy (1983; British) . . . . Octopussy
1:06—Very brief nude getting out of swimming pool
while Bond watches. Long, long shot.
Hell Hunters (1985). . . . . Amanda Hoffman
Nairobi Affair (1986) . . . . Anne Malone
Jane and the Lost City (1987; British) . . . . . .Lola Pagola
The Women's Club (1987) . . . . .Angie Blake
0:17—In black panties, garter belt and stockings
making out with Michael Paré.
Angel III: The Final Chapter (1988) . . . . Nadine
Intimate Power (1989) . . . . Sineperver
The Kill Reflex (1990) . . . . Crystal Tarver
Silent Night, Deadly Night 4: Initiation (1990) . . . .Fima
Made for TV Movies:
Playing for Time (1980) . . . . .Mala

TV:
Chicago Story (1982) . . . . Dr. Judith Bergstrom
Emerald Point N.A.S. (1983-84) . . . . Maggie Farrell
Magazines:
Playboy (Oct 1981) . . . . Tattooed Woman
••• 100-107—Topless photos from *Tattoo.*
Playboy (Dec 1981) . . . . Sex Stars of 1981
238—Right breast, holding pink robe against her-
self.
Playboy (Aug 1983) . . . . . .The Spy They Love To Love
92—Topless on pier.
Playboy (Sep 1987) . . . . .25 Years of James Bond
•• 131—Left breast.

Adjani, Isabelle

Films:
Story of Adele H. (1975; French) . . . . .Adele Hugo
The Tenant (1976; French) . . . . .Stella
The Driver (1978). . . . . .The Player
The Bronte Sisters (1979; French). . . . . .Emily
Nosferatu, The Vampire (1979; French/German)
. . . . Lucy Harker
Possession (1981; French/German) . . . . . .Anna/Helen
• 0:04—Topless in bed.
• 0:16—Topless lying in bed when Sam Neill pulls the
covers over her.
••• 0:47—Right breast, then topless lying in bed with
Neill.
• 1:08—Right breast, while lying on the floor with
Neill, then sitting up.
Quartet (1981; British/French) . . . . Marya Zelli
•• 1:06—Topless in bed with Alan Bates.
Next Year if All Goes Well (1983; French). . . Isabelle
• 0:27—Brief right breast, lying in bed with Maxime.
One Deadly Summer (1984; French) . . . . .Eliane
•• 0:21—Brief topless changing in the window for Florimond.
••• 0:32—Nude, walking in and out of the barn.
• 0:36—Brief left breast lying in bed when Florimond
gets up.
• 0:40—Buns and topless taking a bath.
• 1:41—Part of right breast, getting felt up by an old
guy, then right breast then brief topless.
•• 1:47—Topless in bedroom with Florimond.
1:49—In white bra and panties talking with Florimond.
Subway (1985; French) . . . . .Helena
Ishtar (1987) . . . . Shirra Assel
• 0:27—Very brief left breast flashing herself to Dustin
Hoffman at the airport while wearing sunglasses.
Camille Claudel (1989; French) . . . . Camille Claudel

Agbayani, Tetchie

Films:
The Emerald Forest (1985). . . . . Caya
• 1:48—Topless in the river when Kachiri is match
making all the couples together.
Gymkata (1985). . . . . .Princess Rubali
The Money Pit (1986) . . . . .Florinda

Rikky & Pete (1988; Australian) . . . . .Flossie
- 0:58—Brief upper half of left breast in bed with Pete when Rikky accidentally sees them in bed.
- ••• 1:30—Topless in black panties dancing outside the jail while Pete watches from inside.

Mission Manila (1989) . . . . Maria
Indio 2: The Revolt (1990) . . . . .Gabriel's Mother

• Ager, Suzanne
Films:
Crocodile Dundee II (1988). . . . . Hooker
Mob Boss (1990). . . . . Pool Girl
Shock 'Em Dead (1990) . . . . Groupie 3
Smoothtalker (1990) . . . . Candy (The 976-GIRL)
- 0:23—Left breast and partial buns, while lying on the floor dead.
- 0:24—More left breast, while lying dead on the floor. Lit with red light.
- 0:35—Left breast, while lying dead on the floor. Very brief buns in G-string.

The Alien Within (1991) . . . . .n.a.
Angel Eyes (1991). . . . . .n.a.
Buford's Beach Bunnies (1991) . . . . .n.a.
Evil Toons (1991) . . . . .Terry
- ••• 0:31—Topless and buns in G-string, taking off clothes to put on her pajamas.
- •• 1:09—Right breast, while on the floor getting her pajamas ripped open by Roxanne.
- •• 1:10—Brief topless when Roxanne rips the pajamas all the way down.

Inner Sanctum (1991). . . . . .Maureen
Little Devils (1991). . . . . .n.a.
Millenium Countdown (1991). . . . . .n.a.

Agutter, Jenny
Films:
East of Sudan (1964; British) . . . . .Asua
Gates to Paradise (1968; British/German) . . . . Maud
I Started Counting (1970; British) . . . . Wynne
The Railway Children (1971; British) . . . . Bobbie
Walkabout (1971; Australian/U.S.) . . . . .Girl
(Hard to find this video tape.)
Nude several times.
Logan's Run (1976) .Jessica
- 1:05—Very brief topless and buns changing into fur coat in ice cave with Michael York.

The Eagle Has Landed (1977; British) . . . . . . Molly Prior
Equus (1977). . . . . .Jill Mason
- ••• 2:00—Nude in loft above the horses in orange light, then making love with Alan.

China 9, Liberty 37 (1978; Italian). . . . . Catherine
a.k.a. Gunfire
(Hard to find this video tape.)
Gunfire has the nude scenes cut out.
Dominique is Dead (1978; British). . . . . Miss Ballard
a.k.a. Dominique
Survivor (1980; Australian) . . . . .Hobbs

Sweet William (1980; British) . . . . .Ann
0:27—Buns, while standing on balcony with Sam Waterston.
- •• 0:28—Topless sitting on edge of the bed while talking with Waterston.
- 0:44—Brief left breast when Waterston takes her blouse off in the living room.

An American Werewolf in London (1981)
. . . . .Alex Price
- 0:41—Brief right breast in bed with David Naughton. Dark, hard to see.

Riddle of the Sands (1984; British) . . . . . . Clara Dollman
Secret Places (1984; British) . . . . Miss Lowrie
Dark Tower (1987). . . . . .Carolyn Page
0:05—In black teddy in her office while a window washer watches from outside.
Child's Play 2 (1990) . . . . .Joanne Simpson
Darkman (1990) . . . . .Uncredited Doctor
Made for TV Movies:
The Man in the Iron Mask (1977). . . Louise de la Valliere
Beulah Land (1980) . . . . Lizzie Corlay
Silas Marner (1985; British) . . . . .Nancy Lammeter

• Aiton, Lisa Bradford
See: Bradford-Aiton, Lisa.

• Akesson, Monica
Films:
Novel Desires (1991). Model
- ••• 0:17—Buns, then topless while making love outside during story.
- ••• 0:18—Topless making love on picnic table with Eric.

The Swindle (1991). . . . . Tom's Last Hurrah
- ••• 1:17—Topless, then full frontal nudity, posing on couch for Tom.

Last Dance (1992) . . . . Body Double

Albert, Laura
Films:
Angel III: The Final Chapter (1988) . . .Nude Dancer
- 0:00—Brief topless dancing in a casino. Wearing red G-string.
- 0:01—Brief topless dancing in background.
- 0:06—Side view of left breast and buns, while yelling at Molly for taking her picture.

Bloodstone . . . . Kim Chi
- 0:05—Very brief side view of left breast turning around in pool to look at a guy.

Glitch (1988) . . . . Topless
- 0:35—Brief topless auditioning for two guys by taking off her top.

The Jigsaw Murders (1988) . . . . Blonde Stripper
- ••• 0:19—Topless and buns in black G-string, stripping during bachelor party in front of a group of policemen.

Party Plane (1988) . . Uncredited Auditioning Woman
- •• 0:30—Topless, taking off blue dress during audition. She's wearing a white ribbon in her ponytail.

The Unnameable (1988) . . . . Wendy Barnes
•• 0:46—Left breast while lying on floor kissing John, then brief buns when he pulls her panties down.
Blood Games (1989) . . . . Babe
0:03—Pitching in baseball game in braless T-shirt.
0:16—In white bra and black shorts in locker room.
Dr. Alien (1989) . . . . Rocker Chick #3
a.k.a. I Was a Teenage Sex Mutant
••• 0:21—Topless in black outfit during dream sequence with two other rocker chicks.
Dr. Caligari (1989) . . . . Mrs. Van Houten
••• 0:05—Topless taking off yellow towel, then sitting in bathtub.
•• 0:07—Lying down, making love with guy wearing a mask.
••• 0:10—Topless taking orange bra off, then lying back and playing with herself.
•• 0:11—More topless, lying on the floor.
•• 0:12—More topless, lying on the floor again.
• 0:30—Brief left breast with big tongue.
Roadhouse (1989) . . . . Strip Joint Girl
•• 0:45—Topless and buns dancing on stage, wearing a hat.
Stone Cold (1991) . . . . Joe's Girlfriend
• 0:11—Buns, in bed when waking up. Very brief right breast.
Made for Cable TV:
Tales From the Crypt: The Man Who was Death (1989; HBO) . . . . Go-Go Dancer
• 0:20—Brief topless a couple of times dancing in a cage in a nightclub.
Dream On: The First Episode (1990; HBO) . . . . Whipped Cream Girl
0:22—Covered with whipped cream in bed with Martin.
Dream On: Pants on Fire (1991; HBO) . . . . Tanya
•• 0:16—Topless sitting up on the couch, talking to Martin.
Magazines:
Playboy (Nov 1989) . . . . Sex in Cinema 1989
•• 136—Right breast in still from *Roadhouse.*

Alessandrini, Toni

Films:
Bachelor Party (1984) . . . Woman Dancing with Donkey
Hell Squad (1986) . . . . Night Club Waitress
Vice Academy, Part 2 (1990) . . . . Aphrodisia
• 0:33—Topless in dressing room.
••• 0:34—Topless and buns in G-string, dancing in club.
Vice Academy, Part 3 (1991) . . . . Stripper
•• 0:26—Topless taking off dress on stage.
•• 0:27—More topless on stage (about five times).
• 0:28—More topless giving away her money.
• 0:34—Buns in G-string, dancing on stage.

Alexander, Jane

Films:
A Gunfight (1971). . . . . Nora Tenneray
The New Centurions (1972) . . . . Dorothy

The Betsy (1978) . . . . Alicia Hardeman
Kramer vs. Kramer (1979) . . . . Margaret Phelps
Brubaker (1980). . . . . Lillian
Night Crossing (1981) . . . . Doris Strelzyks
Testament (1983). . . . . Carol Wetherly
City Heat (1984) . . . . Addy
Sweet Country (1985). . . . . Anna
• 1:39—Brief side view of left breast after getting out of bed.
Square Dance (1987) . . . . Juanelle
a.k.a. Home is Where the Heart Is
Made for TV Movies:
Playing for Time (1980) . . . . Alma Rose
Stay the Night (1992) . . . . Blanche Kettmann

Alexander, Nina

See: Parton, Julie.

Alhanti, Iris

Films:
Kramer vs. Kramer (1979) . . . . n.a.
Partners (1982) . . . . Jogger
•• 0:21—Topless in the shower when Ryan O'Neal opens the shower curtain.

Aliff, Lisa

Films:
Dragnet (1987) . . . . April
Remote Control (1987) . . . . Heroine
Playroom (1989) . . . . Jenny
a.k.a. Schizo
•• 0:23—Topless making love on top of Christopher.
Damned River (1990) . . . . Anne
0:28—Silhouette topless undressing in tent.
• 0:32—Very, very brief top of right breast in open blouse, then half of right breast in wet blouse washing her hair.
• 0:50—Very brief topless struggling with Ray when he rips her top open. Don't see her face.

Alise, Esther

a.k.a. Esther Elise.
Films:
Deathrow Game Show (1988) . . . . Groupie
•• 0:08—Topless in bed with Chuck.
Hollywood Chainsaw Hookers (1988) . . . . Lisa
••• 0:25—Topless playing with a baseball bat while a John photographs her.
Vampire at Midnight (1988) . . . . Lucia Giannini
••• 1:01—In black lingerie, then topless and buns while taking off clothes to wish Roger a happy birthday.

Allen, Ginger Lynn

Former adult film actress.
Films:
Vice Academy (1988). . . . . Holly
1:20—Buns, in white lingerie outfit when graduation robe gets torn off.

Wild Man (1988) .Dawn Hall
•• 0:24—Topless taking off her dress in front of Eric,
then making love with him.
Cleo/Leo (1989) . . . . Karen
••• 0:39—Full frontal nudity getting out of the shower,
getting dried with a towel by Jane Hamilton, then in
nightgown.
••• 0:57—Full frontal nudity getting out of the shower
and dried off again.
Dr. Alien (1989) . . . . Rocker Chick #1
a.k.a. I Was a Teenage Sex Mutant
••• 0:21—Topless in red panties during dream sequence
with two other rocker chicks.
Edgar Allan Poe's "Buried Alive" (1989). . . . Debbie
• 0:12—Very, very brief left breast, while struggling
with the other girls in the kitchen.
Hollywood Boulevard II (1989) . . . . Candy Chandler
•• 0:33—Topless in screening room with Woody, the
writer.
Vice Academy, Part 2 (1990) . . . . .Holly
• 0:44—Buns in black bra, panties, garter belt and
stockings.
•• 1:04—Buns in G-string, then topless dancing with
Linnea Quigley on stage at club.
Young Guns II (1990) . . . . Dove
Vice Academy, Part 3 (1991) . . . . .Holly
Whore (1991) .Wounded Girl
a.k.a. If you're afraid to say it... Just see it
Mind, Body & Soul (1992) . . . . .n.a.
TV:
SuperForce (1991-) . . . . Crystal
Magazines:
Playboy (Nov 1985) . . . . Sex in Cinema 1985
• 131—Buns in still from *New Wave Hookers*.
Playboy (Jul 1989). . . . . B-Movie Bimbos
••• 137—Full frontal nudity, standing in a car.

Allen, India

Wife of TV sportscaster Bill Macatee.
Video Tapes:
Playboy Video Centerfold: India Allen
. . . . Playmate of the Year 1988
Playboy Video Calendar 1989 (1988) . . . . . .January
••• 0:01—Nude.
Playboy's Playmates of the Year: The '80s (1989)
. . . . Playmate of the Year 1988
••• 0:03—Nude, posing in chair.
••• 0:04—Nude, exercising and dancing around the
house.
••• 0:06—Nude in bed.
•• 0:52—Topless in chair. Full frontal nudity in bed.
Playmates at Play (1990) . . . . . . .Hoops, Hardbodies
Magazines:
Playboy (Dec 1987). . . . . Playmate
Playboy's Nudes (Oct 1990). . . . . Herself
••• 98-99—Full frontal nudity.

Allen, Karen

Films:
Animal House (1978) . . . . Katherine "Katy" Fuller
1:21—Brief buns putting on shirt when Boone visits
her at her house.
Manhattan (1979) . . . . TV Actor
The Wanderers (1979) . . . . Nina
Cruising (1980) . . . . Nancy
A Small Circle of Friends (1980) . . . . Jessica
• 0:47—Brief topless in bathroom with Brad Davis.
Don't see her face.
• 0:48—Very brief topless, pushing Davis off her. Then
very, very brief half of left breast turning around to
walk to the mirror.
Raiders of the Lost Ark (1981) . . . . . Marion Ravenwood
Shoot the Moon (1982) . . . . Sandy
Split Image (1982) . . . . .Rebecca
Starman (1984) . . . . Jenny Hayden
Until September (1984) . . . . Mo Alexander
•• 0:41—Topless in bed making love with Thierry Lher-
mitte.
•• 1:13—Topless and buns walking from bed to Lher-
mitte.
• 1:25—Brief topless jumping out of bathtub.
Backfire (1987) . . . . Mara
• 0:48—Lots of buns, then brief topless with Keith
Carradine in the bedroom.
• 1:00—Brief topless in the shower.
The Glass Menagerie (1987). . . . . .Laura
Scrooged (1988) . . . . .Claire Phillips
Sweet Talker (1991; Australian) . . . . .Julie
Made for Cable Movies:
Secret Weapon (1990) . . . . Ruth
Made for TV Movies:
Challenger (1990) . . . . .Christa McAuliffe
TV:
East of Eden (1981) . . . . Abra

Allen, Nancy

Films:
The Last Detail (1973) . . . . Nancy
Forced Entry (1975) . . . . Hitchhiker
• 0:44—Topless and buns tied up by Carl on the
beach.
Carrie (1976) . . . . Chris Hargenson
•• 0:01—Nude, in slow motion in girls' locker room behind Amy Irving.
I Wanna Hold Your Hand (1978) . . . . .Pam
1941 (1979). . . . . .Donna
0:17—Wearing red bra in cockpit of airplane with
Tim Matheson.
1:12—In red bra again with Matheson in the airplane.
Dressed to Kill (1980). . . . . Liz Blake
1:21—In black bra, panties and stockings in Michael
Caine's office.
• 1:36—Topless (from above), buns and brief right
breast in shower.
Home Movies (1980) . . . . Kristina

Blow Out (1981) . . . . Sally
- 0:58—Brief upper half of right breast with the sheet pulled up in B&W photograph that John Travolta examines.

Strange Invaders (1983) . . . . Betty Walker
The Buddy System (1984). . . . . Carrie
Not for Publication (1984) . . . . Lois Thorndyke
The Philadelphia Experiment (1984) . . . . Allison
Terror in the Aisles (1984) . . . . Hostess
Robocop (1987) . . . . Ann Lewis
Sweet Revenge (1987) . . . . Jillian Grey
Poltergeist III (1988) . . . . Patricia Gardner
Limit Up (1989) . . . . Casey Falls
Robocop 2 (1990). . . . . Anne Lewis
Made for Cable Movies:
Memories of Murder (1990; Lifetime) . . . . .n.a.

• Allen, Rosalind

Films:
Three Men and a Little Lady (1990) . . . . .Pretty Girl
To Die For 2 (1991) . . . . Nina
- 0:37—Topless a few times in bed, making love with Max.

Alley, Kirstie

Wife of actor Parker Stevenson.
Films:
Star Trek II: The Wrath of Kahn (1982) . . . . . . Lt. Saavik
Blind Date (1984). . . . . Claire Parker
(Not the same 1987 *Blind Date* with Bruce Willis.)
- 0:12—Brief topless making love in bed with Joseph Bottoms. Dark, hard to see anything.

Runaway (1984) . . . . Jackie
1:04—Briefly in white bra getting scanned at the police station for bugging devices.
Summer School (1987) . . . . Robin Bishop
Shoot to Kill (1988). . . . . Sarah
Look Who's Talking (1989) . . . . Mollie
Loverboy (1989) . . . . Joyce Palmer
Look Who's Talking Too (1990) . . . . .Mollie
Madhouse (1990) . . . . Jessie
0:02—In white slip in bedroom with John Laroquette.
0:18—Brief bra shots while doing a sexy strip tease for Laroquette.
1:16—In bra under blazer throwing everybody out of her house.
Sibling Rivalry (1990) . . . . .Marjorie Turner
Made for Cable TV:
The Hitchhiker: Out of the Night (1985; HBO)
. . . . Angelica
Miniseries:
North and South (1985) . . . . Virgilia Hazard
North and South, Book II (1986). . . . . . . Virgilia Hazard
Made for TV Movies:
Sins of the Past (1984) . . . . Patrice
A Bunny's Tale (1985) . . . . Gloria Steinem
Stark: Mirror Images (1986) . . . . .Maggie

TV:
Masquerade (1983-84) . . . . .Casey Collins
Cheers (1987-) . . . . .Rebecca Howe

Almgren, Susan

Films:
Separate Vacations (1985). . . . . .Helene Gilbert
•• 1:05—Topless and buns before getting into bed and then in bed with David Naughton.
• 1:07—Topless in bathroom with Naughton.
Shades of Love: Lilac Dream (1987) . . . . n.a.
Made for Cable Movies:
Deadly Survallance (1991; Showtime) . . . . Rachel
0:00—Very, very brief right breast, while getting dressed. Don't see her face. B&W.
• 0:12—Topless in the shower. Long shot.
•• 0:34—Topless in the shower with Nickels.
••• 0:54—Buns, in black panties and bra, then topless in room with Michael Ironside.
Twin Sisters (1992) . . . . .Sophie
•• 0:06—Topless and buns, making love in bed with a guy.

Alonso, Maria Conchita

Miss Teen World 1975 and Miss Venezuela 1981.
Films:
Fear City (1984) . . . . Silver Chavez
Moscow on the Hudson (1984) . . . . .Lucia Lombardo
•• 1:17—Topless in bathtub with Robin Williams.
Touch and Go (1984). . . . . .Denise
A Fine Mess (1986) . . . . Claudia Pazzo
Extreme Prejudice (1987) . . . . Sarita Cisneros
•• 0:27—Brief topless in the shower while Nick Nolte is in the bathroom talking to her.
The Running Man (1987). . . . . Amber Mendez
0:16—In black body suit, exercising in her apartment.
0:20—In black body suit, tied up to weight machine in her apartment, talking to Arnold Schwarzenegger.
Colors (1988) . . . . Louisa Gomez
••• 0:48—Topless making love in bed with Sean Penn.
Con el Corazón en la Mano (1988; Mexican) . . . n.a.
• 0:38—Very, very brief right breast, while turning over in bed with her husband.
• 0:39—Topless several times, taking a bath.
•• 1:15—Topless ripping off her dress. Long shot, side view, standing while kissing a guy.
Vampire's Kiss (1989) . . . . .Alva
0:47—In white bra, ironing her clothes in her living room.
0:59—In white bra getting attacked by Nicholas Cage.
Predator 2 (1990) . . . . Leona
McBain (1991). . . . . Cristine
Made for Cable Movies:
Blood Ties (1986; Italian; Showtime) . . . . .Caterina
•• 0:35—Brief topless when Vincent Spano rips her dress off.

Alphen, Corinne

a.k.a. Corinne Wahl.
Films:
Hot T-Shirts (1980). . . . . Judy
   0:55—In braless T-shirt as a car hop.
  • 1:10—In yellow outfit dancing in wet T-shirt contest.
   Brief topless flashing her breasts at the crowd.
New York Nights (1981) . . . . The Debutante
  •• 0:10—Topless, making love in the back seat of a limousine with the rock star.
  ••• 1:38—Topless dancing in the bedroom while the
   Financier watches from the bed.
Brainwaves (1983) . . . . Lelia Adams
  • 0:03—Brief side of right breast, reaching out to turn
   off the water faucets in the bathtub.
  • 0:05—Full frontal nudity, getting electrocuted in the
   bubble bath.
  • 0:50—Brief right breast, during Kaylie's vision.
C.O.D. (1983). . . . . Cheryl Westwood
  • 0:21—Brief topless changing clothes in dressing
   room while talking to Zacks.
  • 1:25—Brief topless taking off her blouse in dressing
   room scene.
   1:26—In green bra, talking to Albert.
   1:28—In green bra during fashion show.
Spring Break (1983; Canadian) . . . . Joan
   0:32—Taking a shower in a two piece bathing suit in
   an outdoor shower at the beach.
Equalizer 2000 (1986). Karen
Amazon Women on the Moon (1987) . . . . . . .Shari
  ••• 1:13—In black bra, then topless on TV while Ray
   watches.
Screwball Hotel (1988) . . . . .Cherry Amour
  • 0:46—Buns, in black outfit on bed with Norman.
Magazines:
Penthouse (Jun 1978). . . . . Pet
Penthouse (Aug 1981) . . . . Pet
Penthouse (Nov 1982) . . . . Pet of the Year
  ••• 123-139—Nude.
Penthouse (Sep 1983) . . . . . . .Pet of the Year Play-Off
  ••• 60-61—Topless and buns.

Alt, Carol

Supermodel.
Films:
Portfolio (1983) . . . . Herself
  • 0:28—Brief right breast, while adjusting black, see-
   through blouse.
   0:31—Brief side view of a little bit of right breast
   while changing clothes backstage at a fashion show.
Bye Bye Baby (1989; Italian) . . . . Sandra
   0:09—Part of right breast, while in the shower.
   0:22—Wearing a white bra, while taking off her
   blouse in the doctor's office.
A Family Matter (1990) . . . . .Nancy
  •• 1:08—Buns, in panties. Brief side view of left breast
   with Eric Roberts.
Millions (1990) . . . . Beta

Sports Illustrated's 25th Anniversary Swimsuit Video
   (1989) . . . . .Herself
   (The version shown on HBO left out two music video
   segments at the end. If you like buns, definitely watch
   the video tape!)
   0:40—Briefly in wet white swimsuit.

Always, Julie

Films:
Hardbodies (1984) . . . . Photo Session Hardbody
  •• 0:40—Topless with other girls posing topless getting
   pictures taken by Rounder. She's wearing blue dress
   with a white belt.
The Rosebud Beach Hotel (1985) . . . . Bellhop
  •• 0:22—Topless, in open blouse, undressing with two
   other bellhops. She's the blonde on the left.
  •• 0:44—Topless, playing spin the grenade, with two
   guys and the two other bellhops. She's on the left.

• Ames, Denise

Films:
Slash Dance (1989) . . . . Dancer
Danger Zone III: Steel Horse War (1991) . . . . n.a.
The Last Boy Scout (1991) . . . . Jacuzzi Party Girl
  • 0:11—Brief topless getting out of the Jacuzzi.

Amis, Suzy

Films:
Fandango (1985). . . . . .The Girl
The Big Town (1987) . . . . .Aggie Donaldson
Plain Clothes (1988). . . . . Robin Torrence
Rocket Gibraltar (1988) . . . . .Aggie
Twister (1989) . . . . Maureen
Where the Heart Is (1990). . . . . Chloe McBain
  • 0:08—Topless during her art film. Artfully covered
   with paint, with a bird. Topless again in the third
   segment.
  • 0:09—Topless during the film again. Hard to see because of the paint. Last segment while she narrates.

Amore, Gianna

Films:
Screwball Hotel (1988). . . . . Mary Beth
Nothing But Trouble (1991). . . . . .Party Girl
Video Tapes:
Wet and Wild (1989) . . . . Model
Playmates at Play (1990) Free Wheeling, Gotta Dance
Playboy Video Calendar 1992 (1991). . . . . . January
  ••• 0:01—Nude in Italian restaurant fantasy.
  ••• 0:02—Nude in classical music fantasy in warehouse.
Magazines:
Playboy (Aug 1989) . . . . Playmate
Playboy's Nudes (Oct 1990) . . . . .Herself
  •• 71—Side of left breast and buns.
Playboy's Book of Lingerie (Jan 1991) . . . . . .Herself
  •• 52—Right breast.
Playboy's Book of Lingerie (Mar 1991). . . . . .Herself
  •• 92—Topless and lower frontal nudity.

Playboy's Book of Lingerie (Mar 1992) . . . . . Herself
••• 14-15—Left breast and lower frontal nudity.
Playboy's Book of Lingerie (Jul 1992) . . . . . . Herself
•• 36-37—Side of right breast and buns.

Amy-Rochelle

See: Weiss, Amy-Rochelle.

• Anders, Avalon

a.k.a. Sheila Stronegger.
Films:
Bikini Summer II (1992) .n.a.
Video Tapes:
California Girl Fox Hunt Bikini Competition #6
. . . . Avalon
••• 0:02—Buns in sexy one piece swimsuit.
0:47—Buns during review.
Magazines:
Playboy (Jan 1992) . . . . .The Swedish Bikini Team
Uma Thorensen.
••• 78-85—Right breast, while holding squirt gun. Topless lying in inflatable lounge in pool. Buns, while
holding up surfboard (first one on the left). Right
breast in green bikini bottoms. Topless, kneeling
and holding suspender with her left hand. Buns and
side of right breast, while climbing cliff. Partial left
breast, while holding swimsuit string with both
hands.

Anderson, Erika

Films:
The Nightmare on Elm Street 5: The Dream Child
(1989) . . . . Greta
Zandalee (1991) . . . . .Zandalee Martin
••• 0:02—Nude, taking off robe and dancing around
the room.
••• 0:21—Nude, undressing, then in bed with Judge Reinhold. Long scene.
••• 0:30—Right breast, then topless making love in bed
with Nicholas Cage.
•• 0:32—Topless as Cage paints on her with his finger.
••• 0:45—Left breast, then topless and lower frontal nudity on floor with Cage.
•• 0:47—Nude, getting massaged by Cage with an oil
and cocaine mixture.
• 0:48—Brief topless getting into bed with Reinhold.
Slightly out of focus.
•• 1:09—Topless opening her dress for Reinhold while
lying on a river bank, then making love with him at
night in bed.
Made for Cable TV:
Dream On: B.S. Elliot (1992; HBO) . . . . Marina
TV:
Twin Peaks (1990-91) . . . . Emerald/Jade
Magazines:
Playboy (Nov 1991) . . . . Sex in Cinema 1991
• 144—Full frontal nudity in mirror. From *Zandalee*.
Playboy (Dec 1991). . . . . Sex Stars 1991
• 185—Right breast in B&W photo.

• Anderson, Kim

Films:
Small Time (1991) . . . . Woman on Street
Video Tapes:
Swimwear Illustrated: On Location (1986)
. . . . .Swimsuit Model
(Blonde hair.)
Rock Video Girls (1991) . . . . .Herself
(Brunette hair.)
• 0:02—Dancing in wet T-shirt. Buns and brief topless
on the beach (some in B&W).
Magazines:
Inside Sports (Apr 1992) . . . . .Journey to St. John
39—Buns, while sitting in two piece swimsuit.
• 46-47—Buns, while lying in the surf in a two piece
swimsuit.

Anderson, Melody

Films:
Flash Gordon (1980) . . . . Dale Arden
Dead and Buried (1981). . . . . Janet
The Boy in Blue (1986; Canadian). . . . . Dulcie
• 0:07—Brief cleavage while making love with Nicho-
las Cage, then very brief top half of right breast
when a policeman scares her.
Firewalker (1986) . . . . Patricia Goodwyn
Final Notice (1989) . . . . Kate Davis
Made for Cable Movies:
Hitler's Daughter (1990). . . . . n.a.
Made for TV Movies:
Policewoman Centerfold (1983). . . . . Jan Oaks
0:51—Very brief partial side of right breast kneeling
on bed during photo shoot.
Ladies of the Night (1986) . . . . Claudia
TV:
Manimal (1983) . . . . .Brooke McKenzie

Anderson, Pamela

Films:
The Taking of Beverly Hills (1991) . . . . .Cheerleader
TV:
Home Improvement (1991-) . . . . Lisa the Tool Time Girl
Baywatch (1992-) . . . . .C. J. Parker
Video Tapes:
Playboy Video Calendar 1991 (1990). . . . . July
••• 0:26—Nude.
Sexy Lingerie II (1990) . . . . Model
Sexy Lingerie III (1991). . . . . Model
Wet and Wild III (1991) . . . . Model
Playboy Video Centerfold: Pamela Anderson
(1992) . . . . Playmate
••• 0:00—Nude throughout.
Magazines:
Playboy (Feb 1990) . . . . Playmate
••• 102-113—Nude.
Playboy's Book of Lingerie (Sep 1991) . . . . . .Herself
••• 44-45—Nude.
••• 57—Full frontal nudity.

Playboy's Book of Lingerie (Nov 1991) . . . . . Herself
• 26-27—Right breast.
Playboy's Book of Lingerie (Mar 1992) . . . . . Herself
••• 80-81—Full frontal nudity.
•• 93—Buns and partial right breast.
Playboy's Book of Lingerie (May 1992) . . . . . Herself
••• 79—Full frontal nudity.
Playboy's Book of Lingerie (Jul 1992) . . . . . . Herself
••• 38—Topless.
Playboy (Jul 1992). . . . . Getting Kicks on Route 66
••• 67-73—Nude.
Playboy's Career Girls (Aug 1992)
. . . . Baywatch Playmates
••• 5—Full frontal nudity.

• *Anderson, Pat*

Films:
Dirty O'Neil (1974). . . . . .Lisa
Newman's Law (1974) . . . . Sharon
Summer School Teachers (1975) . . . . Sally
•• 0:52—Topless and buns, posing for photos, then in
bed with Bob.
• 1:05—Side view of right breast in photo in maga-
zine.
TNT Jackson (1975). . . . . .n.a.
Magazines:
Playboy (Nov 1974) . . . . Sex in Cinema 1974
•• 152—Topless sitting in bed from *Newman's Law*.

Andersson, Bibi

Films:
The Seventh Seal (1956; Swedish). . . . . .Mia
Brink of Life (1957; Swedish). . . . . Hjordis
Wild Strawberries (1957; Swedish) . . . . Sara
The Magician (1959). . . . . Sara
Duel at Diablo (1966) . . . . .Ellen Grange
Persona (1966; Swedish). . . . . .Nurse Alma
The Touch (1971; U.S./Swedish). . . . . . Karen Vergerus
• 0:31—Topless in bed with Elliott Gould.
••• 0:56—Topless kissing Gould.
1:13—Very, very brief right breast washing Gould's
hair in the sink.
Scenes from a Marriage (1973; Swedish). . . . . . Katarina
I Never Promised You a Rose Garden (1977) . . . Dr. Fried
Quintet (1979) . . . . Ambrosia
Twice a Woman (1979) . . . . Laura
• 0:05—Topless taking off her bra and putting a
blouse on.
• 0:06—Brief side view of left breast, getting into bed,
brief left breast lying back in bed.
Exposed (1983). Margaret
Babette's Feast (1987; Danish)
. . . . .Swedish Court Lady-in-Waiting
a.k.a. Babettes Gaestebud
Made for TV Movies:
Wallenberg: A Hero's Story (1985) . . . . .Maj

Andreeff, Starr

Films:
Dance of the Damned (1988) . . . . .Jodi
•• 0:03—Topless dancing in black bikini bottoms on
stage in a club.
1:06—In black bra, panties, garter belt and stock-
ings dancing in bar just for the vampire.
•• 1:08—Topless in the bar with the vampire.
Ghoulies II (1988) . . . . Alice
Out of the Dark (1988) . . . . Camille
The Terror Within (1988) . . . . Sue
Streets (1989) . . . . Policewoman on Horse
Syngenor (1990) . . . . .Susan
Driving Me Crazy (1991) . . . . .Legs

Andress, Ursula

Films:
Dr. No (1962; British). . . . . .Honey
1:19—Almost very, very brief topless after going
through shower to remove radioactivity.
Four for Texas (1963). . . . . Maxine Richter
Fun in Acapulco (1963) . . . . Margarita Douphine
Nightmare in the Sun (1964). . . . . .Marsha Wilson
What's New, Pussycat? (1965; U.S./French) . . . . Rita
The Blue Max (1966). . . . . Countess Kasti
1:46—Almost right breast, several times, in room
with George Peppard (towel around her neck gets in
the way).
1:48—Very brief half of left breast, while lying on the
bed.
Casino Royale (1967; British) . . . . .Vesper Lynd
Anyone Can Play (1968; Italian). . . . . .Norma
The Southern Star (1969; French/British) . . Erica Kramer
Perfect Friday (1970; British) . . . . . .Lady Britt Dorsett
Red Sun (1972; French/Italian/Spanish) . . . . . . Cristina
1:12—Almost side view of right breast, then left
breast while changing tops in room while Charles
Bronson watches.
Loaded Guns (1975) .Laura
0:32—Buns, lying in bed with a guy.
••• 0:33—Topless and buns getting out of bed. Full
frontal nudity in elevator.
•• 0:40—Nude getting out of bed and putting dress
on.
••• 0:48—Nude getting into bathtub, topless in tub,
nude getting out and drying herself off.
1:00—Buns while getting undressed and hopping in
to bed.
• 1:02—Brief side view of right breast while getting
dressed.
The Sensuous Nurse (1975; Italian) . . . . Anna
•• 0:16—Topless and buns in bed after making love
with Benito.
•• 0:22—Nude swimming in pool while Adonais
watches.
••• 0:50—Nude slowly stripping and getting in bed
with Adonais.
••• 1:10—Nude getting into bed.

Stateline Motel (1975; Italian) . . . . . . Michelle Nolton
a.k.a. Last Chance for a Born Loser
••• 0:34—Left breast, then topless on bed with Oleg.
The Loves and Times of Scaramouche (1976; Italian)
. . . . Josephine
Slave of the Cannibal God (1979; Italian) . . . . . . n.a.
•• 0:33—Topless taking off shirt and putting on a T-shirt.
••• 1:07—Nude getting tied to a pole by the Cannibal
  People and covered with red paint.
  1:20—Brief peek at buns under her skirt when running away from the Cannibal People.
Tigers in Lipstick (1979)
. . . . The Stroller and The Widow
  0:02—In black bra, panties and garter belt and
  stockings opening her fur coat to cause an accident.
  0:48—In slip posing for photographer.
• 0:50—Very brief topless when top of slip accidentally falls down.
• 0:51—More topless with the photographer.
Clash of the Titans (1981) . . . . Aphrodite
Famous T & A (1982) . . . . Herself
  (No longer available for purchase, check your video
  store for rental.)
••• 0:15—Full frontal nudity scenes from *Slave of the
  Cannibal God*.
The Chinatown Murders: Man Against the Mob (1989)
. . . . Betty Starr
Video Tapes:
Playboy Video Magazine, Volume 1 (1982)
. . . . Herself
•• 0:58—Topless in still photos from *Playboy* pictorial.
Magazines:
Playboy (Nov 1973) . . . . Encore
••• 102-109—Topless and buns.
Playboy (Jan 1974) . . . . Twenty Years of Playboy
••• 206—Topless in water from *She is Ursula Andress* pic-
  torial.
Playboy (Nov 1974) . . . . Sex in Cinema 1974
•• 145—Topless from *Last Chance For a Born Loser*.
Playboy (Apr 1976) . . . . Incomparably Ursula
••• 91-95—Photos from the film *The Loves and Times of
  Scaramouche*. Full frontal nudity.
Playboy (Jan 1979) . . . . 25 Beautiful Years
•• 158—Topless in a stream.
Playboy (Jan 1989) . . . . Women of the Sixties
••• 163—Topless running her fingers through her hair
  sitting by a pond.
Playboy's Nudes (Oct 1990) . . . . Herself
••• 18-19—Topless.

Andrews, Julie

Films:
Americanization of Emily (1964) . . . . Emily
Mary Poppins (1964) . . . . Mary Poppins
  (Academy Award for Best Actress.)
The Sound of Music (1965) . . . . Maria
Hawaii (1966) . . . . Jerusha Bromley
Thoroughly Modern Millie (1967) . . . . . Millie Dillmount

Darling Lili (1970) . . . . Lili Smith
Very, very brief left breast, when doing strip tease and
tossing aside yellow outfit to duck behind curtain. I
couldn't tell the time because I saw this on TNT. I don't
think this film available on video tape.
The Tamarind Seed (1974; British) . . . . Judith Farrow
10 (1979) . . . . Sam
Little Miss Marker (1980) . . . . Amanda
S.O.B. (1981) . . . . Sally Miles
•• 1:19—Topless pulling the top off her red dress during the filming of a movie.
Victor/Victoria (1982) . . . . Victor/Victoria
The Man Who Loved Women (1983) . . . . Marianna
That's Life! (1986) . . . . Gillian Fairchild
Duet for One (1987) . . . . Stephanie Anderson
• 0:28—Very brief left breast in gaping blouse in bathroom splashing water on her face because she feels
  sick, then wet T-shirt.
••• 1:06—Topless stretching, lying in bed.
• 1:07—Very brief buns and very brief right breast,
  when she rolls off the bed onto the floor.
  1:30—In wet white blouse from perspiring after taking an overdose of pills.
Made for TV Movies:
Our Sons (1991) . . . . Audrey Grant
TV:
The Julie Andrews Hour (1972-73) . . . . Hostess
Julie (1992) . . . . Julie Carlisle

Angel, Vanessa

Films:
Spies Like Us (1985) . . . . . . Russian Rocket Crewmember
  1:31—In bra, putting on her snow outfit, coming
  out of tent after Dan Aykroyd.
Another Chance (1989) . . . . Jacky Johanssen
• 0:26—Sort of topless under water in spa. Hard to see
  because of the bubbles.
King of New York (1990) . . . . British Female
Stop! Or My Mom Will Shoot (1992) . . . . . . Stewardess
TV:
Baywatch (1992-) . . . . Megan

• Ann, Tiffany

Video Tapes:
Hot Body International: #2 Miss Puerto Vallarta
  (1990) . . . . Contestant
•• 0:29—Topless wearing pasties and buns, in G-string.
•• 0:57—1st place.
•• 0:58—Buns, posing in wet, green two piece swimsuit.
Hot Body International: #4 Spring Break (1992)
. . . . Contestant
  0:07—Dancing in two piece swimsuit on stage.
  0:15—5th place winner.
• 0:36—Barely there wet T-shirt. Brief right breast,
  when bending over.
  0:58—Winning 4th place in wet T-shirt contest.

Ann-Margret

Films:

Pocketful of Miracles (1961) . . . . .Louise
State Fair (1962) . . . . Emily Porter
Bye Bye Birdie (1963) . . . . Kim McAfee
The Pleasure Seekers (1964) . . . . .Fran Hobson
Viva Las Vegas (1964) . . . . .Rusty Martin
Bus Riley's Back in Town (1965). . . . . Laurel
The Cincinnati Kid (1965) . . . . .Melba
Murderer's Row (1966) . . . . Suzie Solaris
The Swinger (1966) . . . . Kelly Olsson
Tiger and the Pussycat (1967; U.S./Italian) . . . . Carolina
C. C. & Company (1970) . . . . Ann
R.P.M. (1970). . . . . .Rhoda
　•• 0:07—Brief left breast and buns getting out of bed
　　talking with Anthony Quinn.
　　0:30—In fishnet top.
Carnal Knowledge (1971) . . . . Bobbie
　•• 0:48—Topless and buns making love in bed with
　　Jack Nicholson, then getting out of bed and into
　　shower with Jack.
　• 1:07—Brief side view of left breast putting a bra on
　　in the bedroom.
The Outside Man (1973; U.S./French) . . . . .Nancy
The Train Robbers (1973) . . . . .Mrs. Lowe
Tommy (1975; British) . . . . Nora Walker
The Twist (1976). . . . . Charlie Minerva
　　0:24—Left breast when Claire daydreams someone
　　is sticking a pin into Ann-Margret's breast. A little
　　bloody. Body double.
　　1:24—Very, very brief left breast during Bruce Dern's
　　daydream. Seen from above, body double again.
Joseph Andrews (1977; British/French) . . . . .Lady Boaby
The Last Remake of Beau Geste (1977)
　. . . . . Lady Flavia Geste
The Cheap Detective (1978) . . . . .Jezebel Desire
Magic (1978). . . . . Peggy Ann Snow
　••• 0:44—Right breast, lying on her side in bed talking
　　to Anthony Hopkins.
The Villain (1979) . . . . Charming Jones
Middle Age Crazy (1980; Canadian) . . . . Sue Ann
I Ought to be in Pictures (1982) . . . . .Stephanie
Return of the Soldier (1983; British) . . . . Jenny
Twice in a Lifetime (1985) . . . . Audrey
52 Pick-Up (1986). . . . . Barbara Mitchell
A New Life (1988) . . . . Jackie
A Tiger's Tale (1988) .Rose
　• 0:45—Side view of left breast in bra, then topless
　　jumping up after fire ants start biting her. Brief buns
　　running along a hill. Long shot, probably a body
　　double.
Made for TV Movies:
Our Sons (1991) . . . . Luanne Barnes
Magazines:
Playboy (Feb 1981) . . . . The Year in Sex
　•• 146—Left breast in still from *Magic*.

Annen, Glory

Films:

Felicity (1978; Australian) . . . . .Felicity
　•• 0:02—Topless taking off leotard in girl's shower
　　room, then nude taking a shower.
　• 0:05—Buns, then left breast, then right breast un-
　　dressing to go skinny dipping.
　•• 0:10—Topless and buns at night at the girl's dormi-
　　tory.
　•• 0:15—Topless undressing in room with Christine.
　• 0:16—Left breast, while touching herself in bed.
　••• 0:20—Lots of lower frontal nudity trying on clothes,
　　bras and panties in dressing room. Brief topless.
　••• 0:25—Buns and topless taking a bath. Full frontal
　　nudity when Steve peeks in at her.
　• 0:31—Brief full frontal nudity losing her virginity on
　　car with Andrew.
　••• 0:38—Full frontal nudity in bath with Mei Ling and
　　two other girls. Long scene. Hot!
　••• 0:58—Full frontal nudity in bed with Miles.
　••• 1:13—Full frontal nudity with Mei Ling making love
　　on bed. Long scene.
　• 1:20—Left breast, while making love standing up.
　•• 1:21—Topless and buns making love with Miles.
　•• 1:27—Nude making love again with Miles.
　　1:29—Buns, in the water with Miles.
Spaced Out (1980; British) . . . . .Cosia
　••• 0:23—Topless talking to the other two space wom-
　　en. Long scene.
　• 0:31—Very brief topless changing clothes while
　　dancing.
　•• 0:43—Topless in bed with Willy.
　••• 1:08—Topless lying down.
The Lonely Lady (1983) . . . . Marion
　• 0:07—Brief left breast in back seat of car with Joe.
　　Dark, hard to see.
Alien Prey (1984; British) . . . . .Jessica
　• 0:22—Topless unbuttoning blouse to sunbathe.
　•• 0:34—Topless taking off top, getting into bed with
　　Josephine, then making love with her.
　　0:36—Buns, rolling on top of Josephine.
　••• 0:38—More topless when Josephine is playing with
　　her.
　　0:39—More buns in bed. Long shot.
　• 0:46—Left breast and buns standing up in bathtub.
　•• 1:05—Topless getting out of bed and putting a dress
　　on.
　•• 1:19—Topless in bed with Anders. Brief buns when
　　he rips her panties off.
Supergirl (1984; British) . . . . Midvale Protestor

• Annesley, Imogen

Films:

Playing Beatie Bow (1986; Australian) . . . . .Abigail
Howling III: The Marsupials (1987) . . . . Jerboa
　• 0:42—Very brief topless taking off dress in barn to
　　give birth. Breasts are covered with makeup.
Kiss the Night (1988; Australian) . . . . Sacha
Strapless (1990) . . . . .Imogen

Annis, Francesca

Films:
Macbeth (1972) . . . . .Lady Macbeth
• 1:41—Buns, walking around after the bad guys have attacked and looted the castle. Side view of left breast, hard to see because it's covered by her hair.
Dune (1984) . . . . .Lady Jessica
Under the Cherry Moon (1986) . . . . . . Mrs. Wellington
Miniseries:
Masterpiece Theatre: Lilli (1979) . . . . .Lilli Langtree
Made for TV Movies:
The Richest Man in the World: The Story of Aristotle Onassis (1988) . . . . Jacqueline Kennedy Onassis
Parnell & The Englishwoman (1991) . . Katharine O'Shea
Magazines:
Playboy (Feb 1972) . . . . The Making of "Macbeth"
Playboy (Nov 1972) . . . . Sex in Cinema 1972
• 167—Right breast, sticking out of hair. Photo from *MacBeth.*

Anspach, Susan

Films:
Five Easy Pieces (1970) . . . . .Catherine Van Oost
The Landlord (1970) . . . . Susan
Play It Again, Sam (1972) . . . . .Nancy
Blume in Love (1973) . . . . Nina Blume
The Big Fix (1978). . . . . Lila
Running (1979). . . . . Janet Andropolis
Gas (1981; Canadian). . . . . .Jane Beardsley
Montenegro (1981; British/Swedish) . . Marilyn Jordan
•• 1:08—Full frontal nudity taking a shower.
• 1:28—Right breast making love with Montenegro.
Blood Red (1988) . . . . Widow
Into the Fire (1988) . . . . Rosalind Winfield
a.k.a. Legend of Lone Wolf
•• 0:22—Left breast, under trench coat when she first comes into the house, briefly again in the kitchen.
•• 0:31—Topless in bedroom standing up with Wade.
Back to Back (1990) . . . . Madeline Hix
The Rutanga Tapes (1991) . . . . Kate Simpson
Made for Cable Movies:
Gone Are the Days (1984; Disney) . . . . .n.a.
Made for Cable TV:
The Hitchhiker: Dead Man's Curve . . . . .Claudia
(Available on *The Hitchhiker, Volume 2.*)
0:14—Buns (probably a body double) in a hotel room with a guy.
TV:
The Yellow Rose (1983). . . . . Grace McKenzie

Anthony, Lysette

Films:
Krull (1983). . . . . .Lyssa
Looking for Eileen (1988; Dutch)
. . . . Marjan/Eileen/Karnen
(Not available on video tape.)
Topless.
Without a Clue (1988) . . . . Fake Leslie
The Pleasure Principal (1991; British). . . . . . . Charlotte

Switch (1991). . . . . .Liz
• 0:05—Brief topless in spa with JoBeth Williams and Felicia, trying to kill Steve.
Made for Cable Movies:
A Ghost in Monte Carlo (1990) . . . . n.a.
Made for TV Movies:
Ivanhoe (1982) .Lady Rowena
Jack the Ripper (1988) . . . . Mary Jane Kelly
The Lady and the Highwayman (1989)
. . . . Lady Panthea Vyne
TV:
Dark Shadows (1991). . . . . Angelique
Magazines:
Playboy (Dec 1988) . . . . .Lysette
• 166-173—Topless B&W photos.
Playboy's Nudes (Oct 1990) . . . . Herself
•• 9—Topless.

Antonelli, Laura

Films:
Dr. Goldfoot and the Girl Bombs (1966; Italian)
. . . . .Rosanna
Man Called Sledge (1971; Italian) . . . . Ria
Docteur Popaul (1972; French) . . . . Martine
Without Apparent Motive (1972; French)
. . . . Juliette Vaudreuil
How Funny Can Sex Be? (1973)
. . . . Miscellaneous Personalities
• 0:01—Brief topless taking off swimsuit.
• 0:04—Brief topless in bathtub covered with bubbles.
0:13—Lying in bed in sheer nightgown.
0:18—Lying in bed again.
• 0:26—Topless getting into bed.
• 0:36—Topless making love in elevator behind frosted glass. Shot at fast speed.
• 1:08—In sheer white nun's outfit during fantasy sequence. Brief topless and buns. Nice slow motion.
1:16—In black nightie.
• 1:24—In black bra and panties, then topless while changing clothes.
Malicious (1974; Italian). . . . . .Angela
• 1:14—Topless after undressing while two boys watch from above.
•• 1:27—Topless, undressing under flashlight. Hard to see because the light is moving around a lot.
• 1:29—Topless and buns running around the house.
Till Marriage Do Us Part (1974; Italian). . . . . Eugenia
•• 0:58—Topless in the barn lying on hay after guy takes off her clothes.
•• 1:02—Full frontal nudity standing up in bathtub while maid washes her.
•• 1:07—Right breast with chauffeur in barn.
•• 1:36—Topless surrounded by feathers on the bed while priest is talking.
The Innocent (1976; Italian) . . . . Julianna
••• 0:41—Topless in bed with her husband.
••• 0:53—Full frontal nudity in bed when her husband lifts her dress up.

The Divine Nymph (1977; Italian)
. . . . Manoela Roderighi
•• 0:10—Full frontal nudity reclining in chair.
• 0:18—Right breast in open blouse sitting in bed.
Lower frontal nudity while getting up.
Wifemistress (1977; Italian) . . . . Antonia De Angelis
0:50—In lacy nightgown in her bedroom.
1:22—Brief upper half of left breast in bed with Clara and her husband.
1:25—In sheer lacy nightgown leaning out the window.
1:29—Almost right breast making love with a guy in bed.
Tigers in Lipstick (1979) . . . . The Pick Up
0:24—In brown lingerie lying in bed, then getting dressed.
0:34—In same lingerie, getting undressed, then in bed.
High Heels (1980). Martine
0:35—Topless undressing while Jean-Paul Belmondo watches. Long, long shot.
• 0:36—Briefly nude when Belmondo watches through opera glasses.
••• 0:53—Topless and buns, getting out of bed and walking around.
• 0:55—Buns, getting a shot while lying on examination table.
•• 0:56—Topless, twice, sitting naked on examination table.
• 1:30—Brief side of right breast during flashback of 0:56 scene.
1:31—Brief full frontal nudity, running around her house while Mia Farrow watches. Long shot.
Secret Fantasy (1981) . . . . Costanza Vivaldi
(Topless a lot. Only the best are listed.)
••• 0:16—In black bra in Doctor's office, then left breast, then topless getting examined.
•• 0:18—In black bra and panties in another Doctor's office. Topless and buns.
•• 0:19—Topless getting X-rayed. Brief topless lying down.
•• 0:32—Topless and buns when Nicolo drugs her and takes Polaroid photos of her.
•• 0:49—Topless and buns posing around the house for Nicolo while he takes Polaroid photos.
•• 0:53—Topless and buns during Nicolo's dream.
••• 1:12—Topless in Doctor's office.
•• 1:14—Topless and buns in room with another guy.
•• 1:16—Topless on train while workers "accidentally" see her.
•• 1:20—Topless on bed after being carried from bathtub.
•• 1:25—Topless dropping dress during opera.
•• 1:27—More topless scenes from 0:49.
Passion of Love (1982) .Clara
a.k.a. Passion D'Amor
0:05—Brief side of right breast, undressing by the fire. Long shot.
La Venexiana (1986) . . . . Angela

Collector's Item (1988). . . . . Marie Colbert
a.k.a. The Trap
0:18—In white lingerie with Tony Musante.
• 0:20—Lower frontal nudity, then right breast making love with Musante. Dark.
0:37—In black bra, garter belt and stockings in open robe undressing for Musante.
0:41—In the same lingerie again dropping robe and getting dressed.
Magazines:
Playboy (Dec 1974) . . . . .Sex Stars of 1974
••• 209—Topless.
Playboy (Dec 1979) . . . . .Sex Stars of 1979
••• 250—Topless.
Playboy (Nov 1980) . . . . Sex in Cinema 1980
••• 179—Full frontal nudity.

Antonia
See: Dorian, Antonia.

Anulka
See: Dziubinska, Anulka.

Apollonia
Real name is Patty Kotero.
Singer.
Films:
Amor Ciego (1980; Mexican). . . . . Patty
• 0:32—Topless getting out of hammock.
••• 0:52—Right breast, standing up, then topless kissing Daniel. More topless in bed.
••• 0:59—Buns, making love in bed, then topless afterwards.
•• 1:11—Topless, taking off her towel and putting Daniel's hand on her left breast.
•• 1:15—Topless, turning over, then lying in bed.
Heartbreaker (1983). . . . . Rose
Purple Rain (1984) . . . . .Apollonia
•• 0:20—Brief topless taking off jacket before jumping into lake.
0:41—In lingerie making love with Prince.
1:06—In black lingerie and stockings singing on stage.
Ministry of Vengeance (1989) . . . . .Zarah
Back to Back (1990). . . . . Jesse Duro
Black Magic Woman (1990) . . . . .Cassandra Perry
0:18—Brief side of left breast with Mark Hamill. Don't see her face.
0:25—Very brief upper half of left breast, while in shower with Hamill.
TV:
Falcon Crest (1985-86). . . . . .Apollonia
Magazines:
Playboy (Jan 1985). . . . . The Girls of Rock 'n' Roll
98—In leather bikini, rated PG.

Applegate, Christina

Films:

Streets (1989) . . . . Dawn
    1:09—Very, very brief almost side view of left breast,
    while kissing her boyfriend. His hand is over her
    breast. Not really a nude scene, but I'm including it
    because people might send this in as an addition.
Don't Tell Mom the Babysitter's Dead (1991) . . . . . Swell

TV:

Heart of the City (1986-87) . . . . Robin Kennedy
Married ...with Children (1987-) . . . . Kelly Bundy

Applegate, Colleen

a.k.a. Adult film actress Shauna Grant.

Video Tapes:

Nudes in Limbo (1983) . . . . Model
Penthouse Love Stories (1986)
  . . . . Service Station Woman
••• 0:10—Nude, making love in a bedroom. Long
    scene.
Penthouse: On the Wild Side (1988) . . . . Colleen
••• 0:39—Topless in lingerie on bed. Nude on the floor.

• Archer, Anne

Daughter of actor John Archer and actress Marjorie Lord.

Films:

Cancel My Reservation (1972) . . . . Crazy
The All-American Boy (1973) . . . . Drenna Valentine
Lifeguard (1975) . . . . Cathy
  • 1:04—Very brief nipple while kissing Sam Elliott.
    Need to crank the brightness on your TV to the max-
    imum. It appears in the lower right corner of the
    screen as the camera pans from right to left.
Paradise Alley (1978) . . . . Annie
Good Guys Wear Black (1979) . . . . Margaret
Hero at Large (1980) . . . . J. Marsh
Raise the Titanic (1980; British) . . . . Dana Archibald
Green Ice (1981; British) . . . . Holbrook
The Naked Face (1984) . . . . Ann Blake
Too Scared to Scream (1985) . . . . Kate
The Check is in the Mail (1986) . . . . Peggy Jackson
Fatal Attraction (1987) . . . . Ellen Gallagher
  0:51—In white bra, sitting in front of mirror, getting
    ready for a party.
Love at Large (1990) . . . . Miss Dolan
Narrow Margin (1990) . . . . Hunnicut
Eminent Domain (1991) . . . . Mita

Made for Cable Movies:

The Last of His Tribe (1992; HBO) . . . . Henriette Kroeber
Nails (1992; Showtime) . . . . Mary Niles
•• 0:16—Topless and buns, several times during love
    scene with Dennis Hopper. Probably a body double
    because you never see her face.

Miniseries:

Seventh Avenue (1977) . . . . Myrna Gold

TV:

Bob & Carol & Ted & Alice (1973) . . . . . . Carol Sanders
The Family Tree (1983) . . . . Annie Benjamin Nichols
Falcon Crest (1985) . . . . Cassandra Wilder

• Argo, Allison

Films:

Between the Lines (1977) . . . . Dancer
  • 0:28—Topless dancing on stage.
Cry From the Mountain (1986) . . . . . . Laurie Matthews

TV:

Ladies' Man (1980-81) . . . . Susan

Ariane

Model.
Full name is Ariane Koizumi.

Films:

The Year of the Dragon (1985) . . . . Tracy Tzu
  • 0:59—Very brief topless when Mickey Rourke rips
    her blouse off in her apartment.
  •• 1:14—Nude, taking a shower in her apartment.
  •• 1:18—Topless straddling Rourke, while making love
    on the bed.
King of New York (1990) . . . . Dinner Guest

Made for Cable Movies:

Women & Men 2: Three Short Stories (1991; HBO)
  . . . . Alice

• Aries, Anna

Films:

The Omega Man (1971) . . . Woman in Cemetary Crypt
Rage (1972) . . . . n.a.
Invasion of the Bee Girls (1973) . . . . Cora Kline
  •• 0:55—Buns and topless getting transformed into a
    Bee Girl.
  ••• 1:00—Topless getting out of the bee transformer.

Armstrong, Bess

Films:

Four Seasons (1981) . . . . Ginny Newley
    0:26—In two piece swimsuit on boat putting lotion
    on herself.
  • 0:38—Brief buns twice skinny dipping in the water
    with Nick.
    0:40—In one piece swimsuit.
Jekyll & Hyde... Together Again (1982) . . . . Mary
High Road to China (1983) . . . . Eve
Jaws 3 (1983) . . . . Kathryn Morgan
The House of God (1984) . . . . Dr. Worthington
  (Not available on video tape.)
  Topless.
Nothing in Common (1986) . . . . Donna Mildred Martin
Second Sight (1989) . . . . Sister Elizabeth

Made for Cable TV:

Tales From the Crypt: What's Cookin' (1992; HBO)
  . . . . Erma

Made for TV Movies:

The Lakeside Killer (1979) . . . . n.a.

TV:

On Our Own (1977-78) . . . . Julia Peters
All Is Forgiven (1986) . . . . Paula Russell
Married People (1990-91) . . . . Elizabeth Meyers

• *Armstrong, Katherine*
Films:
The Arrival (1990) . . . . .n.a.
Crash and Burn (1990) . . . . .Christine
••• 1:00—Topless taking a shower before being killed.
Ambition (1991) . . . . Roseanne
••• 1:13—Buns in G-string, then topless in Clancy
　　Brown's apartment.
Street Soldiers (1991) . . . . Julie

• *Armstrong, Kerry*
Films:
Key Exchange (1985) . . . . The Beauty
Hunting (1990; Australian) . . . . Michelle Harris
• 0:29—Side view of left breast in steamy shower.
•• 0:35—Topless, making love with John Savage in
　　bed. Seen on video monitors.
• 1:00—Topless and upper half of buns, making love
　　with Savage.
• 1:02—Brief buns, turning over in bed.
• 1:26—Very, very brief topless, getting her dress top
　　yanked down. Topless, long shot, getting raped on
　　dining table. Left breast, lying on the floor after-
　　wards.

• *Armstrong, Melinda*
Films:
In the Cold of the Night (1989) . . . . .Laser Model 2
Bikini Summer (1991) . . . . Cheryl
• 0:07—Very brief topless and partial buns, in bath-
　　room when Chet interrupts her.
0:25—Close-up of buns, bending over while wear-
　　ing a swimsuit.
••• 0:35—Nude in swimming pool and talking to Burt.
　　Nice, long scene.
•• 0:49—Topless and buns, trying on swimsuits, then
　　having a water fight with Shelley Michelle.
0:51—Buns, in swimsuit at the beach.
••• 1:17—Full frontal nudity in swimming pool flash-
　　back.
Bikini Summer II (1992) .n.a.
Magazines:
Playboy (May 1992) . . . . .Grapevine
•• 167—Buns in G-string. Lower half of right breast.

Armstrong, Rebekka
Films:
Mortuary Academy (1988) . . . . Nurse
Hider in the House (1989). . . . . . . .Attractive Woman
• 0:47—Brief topless in bed with Mimi Roger's hus-
　　band when she surprises them.
Immortalizer (1990) . . . . June
• 0:16—Topless getting blouse taken off by nurse.
••• 0:29—Topless when a worker fondles her while she's
　　asleep.
Instant Karma (1990) . . . . Jamie
Video Tapes:
Playboy Video Centerfold: Rebekka Armstrong
. . . . Playmate

Playboy Video Calendar 1987 (1986). . . . . Playmate
Playboy Video Magazine, Volume 10 (1986)
. . . . Playmate
••• 0:40—Nude in song and dance number in car repair
　　shop.
Sexy Lingerie (1988). Model
Wet and Wild (1989) . . . . Model
Playboy Video Centerfold: Kerri Kendall (1990)
. . . . Playmate
••• 0:33—Nude.
Playmates at Play (1990) . . . . Gotta Dance
Wet and Wild II (1990). . . . . Model
Sexy Lingerie III (1991). . . . . Model
Wet and Wild III (1991) . . . . Model
Intimate Workout For Lovers (1992)
. . . . .Sensual Exercise
••• 0:11—Nude, exercising in living room and exercise
　　room.
Magazines:
Playboy (Sep 1986) . . . . Playmate
Playboy's Book of Lingerie (Jan 1991) . . . . . .Herself
••• 32—Full frontal nudity.
Playboy's Book of Lingerie (May 1992) . . . . .Herself
•• 43—Topless.

Arnett, Sherry
Video Tapes:
Playboy Video Centerfold: Sherry Arnett
. . . . Playmate
Playboy Video Calendar 1987 (1986). . . . . Playmate
Playboy Video Calendar 1988 (1987). . . . . Playmate
Magazines:
Playboy (Jan 1986) . . . . Playmate

• *Arnold, Caroline*
Films:
Vindicator (1986; Canadian) . . . . Lisa
a.k.a. Frankenstein '88
•• 0:40—Topless in bed with a jerk, then putting her
　　blouse on.
Meatballs III (1987) . . . . .Ida (Girl in VW Bug)

Aronson, Judie
Films:
Friday the 13th, Part IV—The Final Chapter
(1984) . . . . Samantha
• 0:26—Brief topless and very brief buns taking
　　clothes off to go skinny dipping.
• 0:29—Brief topless under water pretending to be
　　dead.
•• 0:39—Topless and brief buns taking off her T-shirt to
　　go skinny dipping at night.
American Ninja (1985). . . . . Patricia
Weird Science (1985). .Hilly
After Midnight (1989) . . . . Jennifer
Cool Blue (1990) . . . . Cathy
•• 1:03—Topless in bed on top of Woody Harrelson.

The Sleeping Car (1990) . . . . Kim
 •• 0:42—Brief topless on top of David Naughton making love. Brief topless three times after he hallucinates.
TV:
Pursuit of Happiness (1987-88) . . . . Sara Duncan

Arquette, Rosanna

Sister of actress Patricia Arquette.
Daughter of actor/director Lewis Arquette.
Films:
Gorp (1980) . . . . Judy
S.O.B. (1981) . . . . Babs
 • 0:21—Brief topless taking off white T-shirt on the deck of the house. Long shot, hard to see.
The Executioner's Song (1982) . . . . Nicole Baker
(European Version reviewed.)
 ••• 0:30—Brief topless in bed, then getting out of bed. Buns, walking to kitchen.
 ••• 0:41—Topless in bed with Tommy Lee Jones.
 ••• 0:48—Topless on top of Jones making love.
 •• 1:36—Right breast and buns, standing up getting strip searched before visiting Jones in prison.
Off the Wall (1982) . . . . Pam
Baby, It's You (1983) . . . . Jill
 •• 1:17—Left breast, making love in bed with Vincent Spano.
The Aviator (1984) . . . . Tilly Hansen
After Hours (1985) . . . . Marcy
 0:48—In bed, dead, in panties. Arm covers breasts.
Desperately Seeking Susan (1985) . . . Roberta Glass
 • 0:46—Topless getting dressed when Aidan Quinn sees her through the fish tank. Long shot, hard to see.
Silverado (1985) . . . . Hannah
8 Million Ways to Die (1986). . . . . Sarah
 1:00—In a bra in Jeff Bridges' apartment.
Nobody's Fool (1986) . . . . Cassie
Amazon Women on the Moon (1987). . . . . Karen
The Big Blue (1988) . . . . Johana
 1:00—Brief right breast in bra in water when Jacques helps her out of the dolphin tank and her sweater gets pulled up.
Black Rainbow (1989; British) . . . . Martha Travis
 0:48—In black bra, panties, garter belt and stockings in while talking to Tom Hulce.
 ••• 0:50—Topless in bed with Hulce, then walking to bathroom.
New York Stories (1989) . . . . Paulette
...Almost (1990; Australian) . . . . Wendy
Flight of the Intruder (1991) . . . . Callie
Made for Cable Movies:
Sweet Revenge (1990) . . . . Kate
Miniseries:
Son of Morning Star (1991) . . . . Libbie Custer
Magazines:
Playboy (Sep 1990) . . . . Rosanna
 ••• 126-137—B&W and color photos nude in the surf. Some are out of focus.

Arth, Emily

Video Tapes:
Playboy Video Calendar 1990 (1989). . . . . May
 ••• 0:23—Nude.
Playboy Video Playmate Six-Pack 1992 (1992)
. . . . Playmate
Magazines:
Playboy (Jun 1988). . . . . Playmate

• Arthur, Sean'a

a.k.a. Shana Arthur.
Films:
Body Waves (1991) . . . . .Dream Girl
 •• 0:02—Brief buns in swimsuit, walking into office.
 ••• 0:03—Topless, taking off her bathing suit top during Rick's dream.
 •• 0:07—Topless and side view of buns in swimsuit bottom, during Dooner's fantasy.
Dance with Death (1991). . . . . Sherilyn
 • 0:42—Buns, while dancing on stage with Lola.
Uncaged (1991) . . . . Dancer
a.k.a. Angel in Red
 •• 0:44—Buns in lingerie. Topless dancing on stage.
Black Belt (1992) . . . . Reporter

• Arthur, Stacy

Mrs. Ohio 1990.
Video Tapes:
Playboy Video Calendar 1992 (1991). . . . . .October
 ••• 0:39—Buns in lingerie. Full frontal nudity fantasizing in bed.
 ••• 0:41—Nude in various locations around the house.
Playboy's Playmate Review 1992 (1992)
. . . . Miss January
 ••• 0:18—Nude, dancing on back of truck, then using a pottery wheel.
Sexy Lingerie IV (1992) . . . . Model
Magazines:
Playboy (Jan 1991). . . . . Playmate
 ••• 118-129—Nude.

• Ashbrook, Daphne

Films:
Gimme an "F" (1981) . . . . Phoebe Willis
Sunset Heat (1991) . . . . Julie
(Unrated version reviewed.)
 • 1:06—Brief topless silhouette, making love with Michael Paré. Dark.
 •• 1:07—More topless, on top of Paré, then lying down.
Made for TV Movies:
Daughters of Privilege (1990). . . . . Mary Hope
Intruders (1992). Lesley Hahn
TV:
Our Family Honor (1985-86) . . . . .Officer Liz McKay
Fortune Dane (1986) . . . . Kathy "Speed" Davenport

Ashley, Elizabeth

Films:
The Carpetbaggers (1964) . . . . Monica Winthrop
The Marriage of a Young Stockbroker (1971) . . . . . Nan
Paperback Hero (1973; Canadian). . . . . Loretta
••• 0:37—Nude in shower with Keir Dullea. Long scene.
••• 0:39—Topless, straddling Dullea in the shower.
Rancho Deluxe (1975) . . . . Cora Brown
The Great Scout and Cathouse Thursday (1976)
. . . . Nancy Sue
Coma (1978) . . . . Mrs. Emerson
Paternity (1981) . . . . Sophia Thatcher
Split Image (1982) . . . . Diana
Dragnet (1987). . . . . Police Commissioner Jane Kilpatrick
Vampire's Kiss (1989) . . . . Dr. Glaser
Made for Cable TV:
The Hitchhiker: Out of the Night (1985; HBO)
. . . . .Woman
Made for TV Movies:
In the Best Interest of the Children (1992). . . Carla Scott
TV:
Evening Shade (1990-). . . . . Frieda Evans

Ashley, Jennifer

Films:
Your Three Minutes Are Up (1973) . . . . . Teenage Driver
The Centerfold Girls (1974) . . . . .Charly
  • 0:34—Topless taking off blouse while changing
    clothes.
  •• 0:49—Topless and buns posing for photographer
    outside with Glory.
The Pom Pom Girls (1976) . . . . Laurie
Tintorera (1977) . . . . .n.a.
Horror Planet (1980; British) . . . . .Holly
  a.k.a. Inseminoid
Partners (1982) . . . . Secretary
Chained Heat (1983; U.S./German) . . . . .Grinder
The Man Who Loved Women (1983) . . .David's Mother
Magazines:
Playboy (Nov 1978) . . . . Sex in Cinema 1978
  • 187—Topless above the water.

• Ashley, Susan

Made for Cable TV:
Dream On: What I Did for Lust (1991; HBO)
. . . . Marsha
  •• 0:01—Topless in Eddie's dressing room with a
    sweater over her head.
Video Tapes:
Rock Video Girls (1991). . . . . Herself

• Assan, Ratna

Films:
Papillon (1973) . . . . Zoraima
Magazines:
Playboy (Feb 1974) . . . . "Butterfly" Girl
  ••• 151-153—Full frontal nudity.

• Asti, Adrianna

Films:
Before the Revolution (1964; Italian) . . . . Gina
Ludwig (1973; Italian) . . . . Lila Von Buliowski
Down the Ancient Staircase (1975; Italian). . . . . .Gianna
The Inheritance (1978; Italian) . . . . Teta Ferramonti
Caligula (1980) . . . . .Ennia
  (X-rated, 147 minute version.)
    • 0:27—Topless at side of bed with Malcolm McDow-
      ell when he feels her breasts.
    •• 0:54—Topless lying down surrounded by slaves.
      Mostly her right breast.
Chimere (1989; French). . . . . Alice's Mother

Astley, Pat

Films:
Playbirds (1978; British). . . . . .Doreen Hamilton
  •• 0:00—Topless posing for photo session.
Don't Open 'Till Christmas (1984; British) . . . . . .Sharon

Austin, Julie

Films:
Elves (1989) . . . . .Kirsten
Night of the Wilding (1990) . . . . Betty
    0:13—In bra and panties, undressing in bedroom.
  •• 0:14—Side of left breast, taking off bra in bathroom.
    Topless in shower.
    • 0:16—More topless in the shower.
    0:17—Topless behind shower door.
Smoothtalker (1990) . . . . Ms. Weston
Twisted Justice (1990) . . . . .Andrea Leyton

Austin, Lynne

Video Tapes:
Playboy Video Centerfold: Lynne Austin
. . . . Playmate
Playboy Video Calendar 1989 (1988). . . . . .May
  ••• 0:17—Nude.
Sexy Lingerie (1988). . . . . Model
Wet and Wild (1989) . . . . Model
Playboy's Fantasies II (1990) . . . . n.a.
Magazines:
Playboy (Jul 1986) . . . . Playmate
Playboy's Book of Lingerie (Mar 1991). . . . . .Herself
  ••• 8—Topless.

Austin, Teri

Films:
Terminal Choice (1985; Canadian) . . . . Lylah Crane
    0:14—Full frontal nudity, covered with blood on op-
      erating table. Long shot.
    0:21—Right breast, on table being examined by
      Ellen Barkin. Dead, covered with dried blood.
    0:26—Very brief left breast under plastic on table,
      hard to see.

Vindicator (1986; Canadian) . . . . . . .Lauren Lehman
a.k.a. Frankenstein '88
  • 0:30—Very brief left breast and buns in mirror get-
    ting out of the bubble bath covered with bubbles.
    Long shot, hard to see anything.
Dangerous Love (1988). . . . . Dominique
Made for TV Movies:
Laura Lansing Slept Here (1988) . . . . Melody Gomphers
False Witness (1989) . . . . Sandralee
TV:
Knots Landing (1985-89) . . . . Jill Bennett

• *Austine, Nicola*

Films:
Suburban Wives (1973; British) . . . . Jean
The Adventures of a Private Eye (1974; British)
. . . . Wife in Bed
  •• 0:00—Topless and buns, getting out of bed to take
    a shower.
Old Dracula (1975; British) . . . . Playboy Bunny

• *Avery, Belle*

Films:
Repossessed (1990). . . . . Gym Receptionist
Made for Cable Movies:
Sketch Artist (1992; Showtime) . . . . Krista
  • 1:11—Right breast, while making love with Paul by
    swimming pool. Long shot, don't see her face very
    well.

• *Avery, Margaret*

Films:
Cool Breeze (1972) . . . . .Lark/Mercer's Mistress
Terror House (1972) . . . . Edwina
Hell Up in Harlem (1973) . . . . Sister Jennifer
  ••• 0:42—Topless in bed, while making love with Fred
    Williamson.
Magnum Force (1973) . . . . Prostitute
Which Way Is Up? (1977) . . . . Annie Mae
The Fish That Saved Pittsburgh (1979) . . . Toby Millman
The Color Purple (1985) . . . . Shug Avery
Riverbend (1990) . . . . Bell Coleman

• *Axelrod, Lisa*

Films:
Click: Calendar Girl Killer (1989) . . . . .Jennifer
Night Angel (1989). . . . . Double
Roadhouse (1989). . . . . Party Girl
Coldfire (1990) . . . . Dancer
  •• 0:11—Topless, twice, dancing on stage.
  • 0:13—Brief topless, getting pushed off the stage.

Axelrod, Nina

Films:
Roller Boogie (1979) . . . . Bobby's Friend
Motel Hell (1980) . . . . .Terry
  0:58—In wet white T-shirt, tubin' with Ida.
  •• 1:01—Topless sitting up in bed to kiss Vincent.

  • 1:04—Very brief topless in tub when Bruce breaks
    the door down, then getting out of tub.
Time Walker (1982) . . . . Susie
Brainstorm (1983) . . . . Simulator Technician
Cross Country (1983; Canadian) . . . . Lois Hayes
  0:28—Brief buns and sort of topless, getting fondled
    by Richard.
  1:05—Very, very brief topless fighting outside the
    motel in the rain with Johnny.
Cobra (1986). . . . . .Waitress
Critters 3 (1991) . . . . Mrs. Briggs

Ayer, Lois

a.k.a. Adult film actress Lois Ayers or Sondra Stilman.
Films:
Wet Water T's (1987) . . . . .Herself
  ••• 0:55—Topless during boxing match. Long scene.
Tougher Than Leather (1988). . . . . .Charlotte
Video Tapes:
In Search of the Perfect 10 (1986) . . . Perfect Girl #2
  ••• 0:08—In swimsuit, then topless exercising by the
    pool.

Ayres-Hamilton, Leah

Films:
All That Jazz (1979) . . . . .Nurse Capobianco
The Burning (1981) . . . . .Michelle
Eddie Macon's Run (1983) . . . . Chris
Bloodsport (1987) . . . . Janice
Hot Child in the City (1987) . . . . Rachel
  0:38—In braless white T-shirt walking out by the
    pool and inside her sister's house.
  • 1:12—Very brief topless in the shower with a guy.
    Long shot, hard to see anything.
TV:
9 to 5 (1983) .Linda Bowman

Bach, Barbara

Wife of singer/former *Beatles* drummer Ringo Starr.
Films:
Black Belly of the Tarantula (1972; Italian) . . . . . . .Jenny
Stateline Motel (1975; Italian) . . . . Emily
  a.k.a. Last Chance for a Born Loser
The Spy Who Loved Me (1977; British)
  . . . . .Major Anya Amosova
  1:21—Brief side view of right breast in shower on
    submarine. Don't see her face.
Force Ten from Navarone (1978) . . . . Maritza
  • 0:32—Brief topless taking a bath in the German of-
    ficer's room.
Screamers (1978; Italian) . . . . .Amanda
  a.k.a. The Island of the Fishmen
  a.k.a. Something Waits in the Dark
The Humanoid (1979; Italian) . . . . n.a.
Jaguar Lives (1979). . . . . Anna
Great Alligator (1980; Italian). . . . . n.a.
Caveman (1981) . . . . Lana
The Unseen (1981) . . . . Jennifer
Up the Academy (1981). . . . . Bliss

Give My Regards to Broad Street (1984; British)
. . . . Journalist
Miniseries:
Princess Daisy (1983) . . . . .n.a.
Magazines:
Playboy (Jun 1977) . . . . Bonded Barbara
•• 106-109—In lingerie, partial buns and topless.
Playboy (Jan 1981) . . . . Barbara Bach
••• 120-127—Full frontal nudity.
Playboy (Sep 1987) . . . . .25 Years of James Bond
•• 130—Left breast.
Playboy (Jan 1989) . . . . Women of the Seventies
212-213—Buns.

• Bach, Catherine
Films:
Nicole (1972). . . . . .Sue
a.k.a. The Widow's Revenge
•• 1:01—Brief topless, twice, undressing to put on
nightgown on boat. Nice shots, but too brief.
•• 1:10—Very brief side view of breasts, three times,
getting felt by Leslie Caron. Don't see either Bach's
or Caron's face.
The Midnight Man (1974) . . . . Natalie
Thunderbolt and Lightfoot (1974) . . . . .Melody
Hustle (1975) . . . . Peggy Summers
Cannonball Run II (1984) . . . . Marcie
Street Justice (1988) . . . . Tamarra
Driving Force (1990). . . . . Harry
Masters of Menace (1990) . . . . Kitty Wheeler
TV:
The Dukes of Hazzard (1979-85) . . . . Daisy Duke
Magazines:
Playboy (Mar 1980). . . . . .Grapevine
• 259—Right nipple sticking out of dress top. B&W.

• Bach, Pamela
Films:
Appointment with Fear (1988) . . . . Samantha
• 0:56—Topless getting into the spa. Long shot, hard
to see.
Nudity Required (1989) . . . . Dee Dee
TV:
Baywatch (1991-). . . . . Kay Morgan

• Bachman, Cheryl
Video Tapes:
Playboy Video Calendar 1993 (1992) . . . . April
Playboy's Playmate Review 1992 (1992)
. . . . Miss October
••• 0:30—Nude on rooftop and then outside in a field.
Magazines:
Playboy (Oct 1991) . . . . Playmate
••• 110-121—Nude.
Playboy's Book of Lingerie (Jul 1992) . . . . . . Herself
• 15—Lower frontal nudity.
Playboy's Book of Lingerie (Sep 1992) . . . . . Herself
• 23—In wet bra and panties.

Bagdasarian, Carol
Films:
The Strawberry Statement (1970) . . . . . . Telephone Girl
Charge of the Model T's (1979) . . . . n.a.
The Octagon (1980) . . . . Aura
• 1:18—Brief side view of right breast, while sitting on
bed next to Chuck Norris and taking her blouse off.
The Aurora Encounter (1985). . . . . Alain

Baker, Carroll
Films:
Baby Doll (1956) . . . . .Baby Doll
Giant (1956) . . . . .Luz Benedict II
How the West was Won (1963) . . . . .Eve Prescott
The Carpetbaggers (1964). . . . . .Rina
Harlow (1965) . . . . .Jean Harlow
Sylvia (1965) . . . . Sylvia West
Orgasmo (1968) . . . . n.a.
The Sweet Body of Deborah (1968) . . . . . . Deborah
(Not available on video tape.)
Topless.
My Father's Wife (1976; Italian) . . . . .Lara
• 0:03—Right breast making love in bed with her hus-
band, Antonio.
•• 0:06—Topless standing in front of bed talking to An-
tonio.
••• 0:18—Topless kneeling in bed, then getting out and
putting a robe on while wearing beige panties.
Andy Warhol's Bad (1977; Italian) . . . . n.a.
The World is Full of Married Men (1979; British)
. . . . .Linda Cooper
• 0:19—Brief left breast, while sitting up in bathtub
covered with bubbles.
The Watcher in the Woods (1981) . . . . .Helen Curtis
Star 80 (1983) . . . . Dorothy's Mother
The Secret Diary of Sigmund Freud (1984)
. . . . Mama Freud
Ironweed (1987) . . . . Annie Phelan
Kindergarten Cop (1990). . . . . Eleanor Crisp
Magazines:
Playboy (Jun 1980). . . . . Grapevine
• 300—Left breast in bathtub in B&W still from *The
World is Full of Married Men.*

Baker, Cheryl
Films:
Lethal Weapon (1987) . . . . .Girl in Shower #1
Die Hard (1988). . . . . Woman with Man
• 0:22—Brief topless in office with a guy when the ter-
rorists first break into the building.
Roadhouse (1989) . . . . Well-Endowed Wife
L.A. Story (1991) . . . . Changing Room Woman
• 0:18—Brief topless in dressing room, when Steve
Martin sees her.

Baker, Cynthia
Films:
Sector 13 (1982) . . . . n.a.
Risky Business (1983) . . . . .Test Teacher

Blood Diner (1987). . . . . Cindy
••• 0:44—Nude outside by fire with her boyfriend, then fighting a guy with an axe.

Baker, Kirsten

Films:
California Dreaming (1978). . . . . Karen
Teen Lust (1978). . . . . Carol Hill
a.k.a. Girls Next Door
• 0:45—Brief side view of left breas, while changing clothes in her bedroom.
Friday the 13th, Part II (1981). . . . . .Terry
•• 0:45—Topless and buns taking off clothes to go skinny dipping.
• 0:47—Very brief topless jumping up in the water.
• 0:48—Full frontal nudity and buns getting out of the water. Long shot.
Terror in the Aisles (1984) . . . . .Terry
•• 1:03—Topless and buns, undressing to go skinny dipping from *Friday the 13th, Part II.*
Mr. Frost (1990; French/British). . . . . Dr. Sara Day
TV:
James at 15 (1978) . . . . Christina Kollberg

Baker, LeeAnne

Films:
Breeders (1986) . . . . .Kathleen
••• 0:28—Nude, undressing from her nurse outfit in the kitchen, then taking a shower.
• 0:59—Brief topless in alien nest. (She's the blonde in front.)
•• 1:08—Topless in alien nest.
•• 1:09—Topless in alien nest again. (Behind Alec.)
• 1:11—Topless behind Alec again. Then long shot when nest is electrocuted. (On the left.)
Mutant Hunt (1987) . . . . Pleasure Droid
Necropolis (1987). . . . . Eva
• 0:04—Right breast, while dancing in skimpy black outfit during vampire ceremony.
• 0:38—Brief topless in front of three evil things. (Before she has special make up to make it look like she has six breasts).
Galactic Gigolo (1989) . . . . Lucy
a.k.a. Club Earth

Baker, Marina

Video Tapes:
Playboy Video Calendar 1988 (1987) . . . . Playmate
Wet and Wild (1989). . . . . .Model
Playboy Video Playmate Six-Pack 1992 (1992)
. . . . Playmate
Magazines:
Playboy (Mar 1987). . . . . Playmate

Baker, Penny

Films:
Real Genius (1985) . . . . .Ick's Girl at Party
The Men's Club (1986). . . . . Lake
•• 1:13—Topless in bed with Treat Williams.

Million Dollar Mystery (1987). . . . . Charity
Video Tapes:
Playboy Video Magazine, Volume 4 (1983)
. . . . Playmate
Playboy Video Magazine, Volume 5 (1983)
. . . . Playmate
••• 1:03—Full frontal nudity, in outdoor bathtub.
•• 1:04—Full frontal nudity on a chair in a field.
•• 1:09—Miscellaneous topless shots.
••• 1:11—Full frontal nudity in an Asian-themed bedroom set.
Wet and Wild (1989) . . . . Model
Magazines:
Playboy (Sep 1980)
. . . . Girls of the Southwest Conference
••• 146-147—Full frontal nudity.
Playboy (Jan 1984). . . . . Playmate
Playboy (Nov 1986). . . . . Sex in Cinema 1986
• 126—Topless in bed with Treat Williams.
Playboy (Jan 1989). . . . . .Women of the Eighties
••• 253—Full frontal nudity.
Playboy's Nudes (Oct 1990) . . . . .Herself
••• 31—Full frontal nudity.

• Baker, Sylvia

Films:
Roadhouse (1989) . . . . Table Dancer
Video Tapes:
Centerfold Screen Test, Take 3 (1988). . . . . .Herself
••• 0:38—Nude after taking off dress during audition.
Starlet Screen Test II (1991) . . . . .Herself
••• 0:01—Nude on couch (same segment from *Centerfold Screen Test, Take 3.*)

Bakke, Brenda

Films:
Last Resort (1985). . . . . Veroneeka
•• 0:36—Topless in the woods with Charles Grodin.
Hardbodies 2 (1986). . . . . Morgan
•• 0:34—Buns, getting into bathtub, then topless, taking a bath.
Death Spa (1987) . . . . .Laura
••• 0:05—Very brief lower frontal nudity, while taking off pants in locker room. Don't see her face. Then nude, in steam room.
Dangerous Love (1988) . . . . Chris
Scavengers (1988) . . . . .Kimberly Blake
Fist Fighter (1989) . . . . Ellen
Nowhere to Run (1989). . . . . Joanie
Made for TV Movies:
Danielle Steel's "Secrets" (1992) . . . . . . Sandy Warwick

• Bako, Brigitte

Films:
One Good Cop (1991) . . . . Mrs. Garrett
Made for Cable Movies:
Red Shoe Diaries (1992; Showtime). . . . . Alex
(Most of the scenes where you don't see her face are a body double.)
- 0:26—Buns and topless, getting out of bathtub with Jake.
- 0:35—Very brief buns when Tom rips off her panties.
- • 0:36—Several brief topless shots while making love with Tom in bed.
- 0:40—Brief topless, leaning back on bed with Tom.

Balaski, Belinda

Films:
Bobbie Jo and the Outlaw (1976) . . .Essie Beaumont
- • • 0:29—Topless in pond with Marjoe Gortner and Lynda Carter.
- 0:43—Very brief topless, when Gortner pushes her into a pond.
Cannonball (1976; U.S./Hong Kong). . . . . . .Maryanne
Food of the Gods (1976). . . . . .Rita
Piranha (1978) . . . . Betsy
Till Death (1978). . . . . .n.a.
The Howling (1981) . . . . .Terry Fisher
Amazon Women on the Moon (1987). . . . Bernice Pitnik
Gremlins 2: The New Batch (1990)
. . . . .Movie Theatre Mom
Made for TV Movies:
Deadly Care (1987). .Terry

Baldwin, Janit

Films:
Prime Cut (1972) . . . . Violet
- 0:25—Very brief nude, being swung around when Gene Hackman lifts her up to show to Lee Marvin.
- 0:41—Brief topless putting on a red dress.
Gator Bait (1973) . . . . .n.a.
- • 0:27—Topless and buns walking into a pond, then getting out and getting dressed.
- 0:35—Very brief right breast, twice, popping out of her dress when the bad guys hold her.
- 0:40—Brief left breast struggling against two guys on the bed.
Ruby (1977) . . . . Leslie Claire
Where the Buffalo Roam (1980) . . . . .n.a.
Humongous (1982; Canadian) . . . . Carla Simmons

Baldwin, Judy

Films:
The Seven Minutes (1971) . . . . Fremont's Girlfriend
Evel Knievel (1972) . . . . Sorority Girl
No Small Affair (1984). . . . . Stephanie
- • • 0:36—In white bra, panties and garter belt, then topless in Jon Cryer's bedroom trying to seduce him.
Talking Walls (1987) . . . . .n.a.
Made in U.S.A. (1988). . . . . Dorie
Pretty Woman (1990) . . . . Susan

TV:
The Bold and the Beautiful (1987) . . . . Beth Logan

• Baltron, Donna

Films:
Hide and Go Shriek (1988). . . . . Judy Ramerize
- • 0:56—Topless after undressing in front of her boyfriend.
Shallow Grave (1988). . . . . Rose

• Bang, Joy

Films:
Cisco Pike (1971). . . . . Lynn
Pretty Maids All in a Row (1971) . . . . Rita
- 0:57—Brief topless in car with Rock Hudson.
- 1:01—Right breast, in car with Hudson. Dark. More right breast, while getting dressed.
Red Sky at Morning (1971) . . . . Corky
Play It Again, Sam (1972). . . . . .Julie
Dead People (1974). Toni
Night of the Cobra Woman (1974; U.S./Philippines)
. . . . .Joanna

Barbeau, Adrienne

Ex-wife of director John Carpenter.
Films:
The Fog (1980) . . . . .Stevie Wayne
The Cannonball Run (1981) . . . . .Marcie
Escape from New York (1981) . . . . Maggie
Swamp Thing (1981) . . . . Alice Cable
- 1:03—Side view of left breast washing herself off in the swamp. Long shot.
Creepshow (1982) . . . . Wilma Northrup
The Next One (1983). . . . . .Andrea Johnson
Back to School (1986) . . . . Vanessa
Open House (1987) . . . . Lisa Grant
- 0:27—In black lace lingerie, then very brief half of left breast making love with Joseph Bottoms on the floor.
- • 1:15—Brief side view of right breast getting out of bed at night to look at something in her briefcase.
- • • 1:16—Brief topless taking off bathrobe and getting back into bed. Kind of dark.
Cannibal Women in the Avocado Jungle of Death (1988)
. . . . Dr. Kurtz
Two Evil Eyes (1991) . . . . .Jessica
Made for Cable Movies:
Doublecrossed (1991; HBO). . . . . .Debbie Seal
Made for Cable TV:
Dream On: Bad Girls (1992; HBO) . . . . Gloria Gantz
Miniseries:
The Burden of Proof (1992) . . . . .Silvia Hartnell
TV:
Maude (1972-78). . . . . Carol

• Barber, Frances

Films:
The Missionary (1982; British) . . . . .Mission Girl
Acceptable Levels (1983; British) . . . . Jill

A Zed and Two Noughts (1985; British)
. . . . Venus de Milo
••• 0:22—Topless, sitting in bed, talking to Oliver, then
   nude while getting thrown out of his place.
Castaway (1986). . . . . Sister Saint Winifred
Prick Up Your Ears (1987; British) . . . . . . Leonie Orton
Sammy and Rosie Get Laid (1987; British)
. . . . Rosie Hobbs
We Think the World of You (1988; British). . . . . . Megan
Young Soul Rebels (1991; British) . . . . Ann

Barber, Glynnis

Films:
Terror (1979; British). . . . . Carol
Yesterday's Hero (1979; British). . . . . Susan
The Hound of the Baskervilles (1983; British). . . . . . .n.a.
The Wicked Lady (1983; British) . . . . Caroline
••• 0:58—Topless and buns making love with Kitt in the
   living room. Possible body double.
Edge of Sanity (1988) . . . . Elisabeth Jekyll
TV:
Blake's 7 (1981) . . . . Soolin
Dempsey and Makepeace (1984-86)
. . . . Detective Sergeant Harriet Makepeace

Bardot, Brigitte

Films:
Head Over Heels. . . . . Cecile
Doctor at Sea (1955; British). . . . . Helene Colbert
...and God created woman (1957; French)
. . . . Juliette
• 0:40—Very brief side view of right breast getting out
   of bed.
A Very Private Affair (1962; French/Italian) . . . . Jill
Contempt (1963; French/Italian). . . . . . . Camille Javal
   0:04—Buns.
   0:52—Almost buns walking through door after
   bath.
   0:54—Buns, while lying on rug.
   1:30—Buns, while lying on beach. Long shot.
Dear Brigitte (1965) . . . . Herself
Shalako (1968; British) . . . . Countess Irini Lazaar
Ms. Don Juan (1973) . . . . Joan
• 0:19—Left breast in bathtub.
•• 1:19—Topless through fish tank. Buns and left
   breast, then brief topless in mirror with Paul.
Famous T & A (1982) . . . . Joan
(No longer available for purchase, check your video
   store for rental.)
• 0:25—Buns, then brief topless in scene from *Ms. Don
   Juan.*

Barkin, Ellen

Wife of actor Gabriel Byrne.
Films:
Diner (1982). . . . . Beth
Daniel (1983) . . . . Phyllis Isaacson
Eddie and the Cruisers (1983) . . . . Maggie
Tender Mercies (1983) . . . . Sue Anne

The Adventures of Buckaroo Banzai, Across the 8th
   Dimension (1984) . . . . Penny Priddy
Harry and Son (1984) . . . . Katie
Terminal Choice (1985; Canadian). . . . . Mary O'Connor
Desert Bloom (1986) . . . . Starr
Down by Law (1986) . . . . Laurette
The Big Easy (1987) . . . . Anne Osborne
   0:21—White panties in lifted up dress in bed with
   Dennis Quaid.
   0:32—Brief buns jumping up in kitchen after pinch-
   ing a guy who she thinks is Quaid.
Made in Heaven (1987) . . . . Lucille
Siesta (1987) . . . . Diane
••• 0:03—Brief full frontal nudity long shot taking off
   red dress, topless, brief buns standing up, then full
   frontal nudity lying down.
   1:22—Right nipple sticking out of dress while imag-
   ining she's with Gabriel Byrne instead of the reality
   of getting raped by taxi driver.
• 1:23—Brief lower frontal nudity, very brief silhouette
   of a breast, then brief buns some more while with
   Byrne. Dark, hard to see.
• 1:24—Lower frontal nudity, with torn dress while lying in bed after the taxi driver gets up.
   1:26—Very brief lower frontal nudity, while running
   down road and her dress flies up as police cars pass
   by.
   1:28—Very brief side view of right breast putting on
   dress in bed just before Isabella Rossellini comes into
   the bedroom to attack her. Long distance shot.
Johnny Handsome (1989) . . . . Sunny Boyd
Sea of Love (1989) . . . . Helen Cruger
   0:56—Side view of left breast of body double, then
   buns standing up making out with Al Pacino in his
   apartment.
   0:59—Back view wearing panties, putting blouse on
   in bathroom.
   1:13—Brief upper half of buns, lying in bed with
   Pacino.
Switch (1991) . . . . Amanda Brooks/Steve
Man Trouble (1992). . . . . Joan Spruance
Made for Cable Movies:
Blood Money: The Story of Clinton and Nadine
   (1988; HBO). . . . . n.a.
Original title: *Clinton and Nadine.*

Barnes, Priscilla

Films:
Delta Fox (1977) . . . . Karen
   0:36—Left breast undressing in room for David. Very
   dark, hard to see.
• 0:38—Very brief topless struggling with a bad guy
   and getting slammed against the wall.
   0:39—Very brief blurry left breast running in front of
   the fireplace.
• 0:40—Topless sneaking out of house. Brief topless
   getting into Porsche.

- 0:49—Brief right breast reclining onto bed with David. Side view of left breast several times while making love.
  1:29—Very brief side view of left breast in David's flashback.
- **Texas Detour** (1977) . . . . Claudia Hunter
  - ••• 1:03—Topless, changing clothes and walking around in bedroom. Wearing white panties. This is her best topless scene.
  - • 1:11—Topless sitting up in bed with Patrick Wayne.
- **Tintorera** (1977). . . . . .n.a.
  - • 1:12—Very brief topless dropping her beer into the water.
  - • 1:14—Topless, on the beach after the shark attack (on the left).
- **Seniors** (1978). . . . . Sylvia
  - •• 0:18—Topless at the top of the stairs while Arnold climbs up the stairs while the rest of the guys watch.
  The Last Married Couple in America (1980)
  . . . . Helena Dryden
  Sunday Lovers (1980; Italian/French) . . . . Donna
  Traxx (1988) . . . . Mayor Alexandria Cray
  License to Kill (1989). . . . . Della Churchill
  Lords of the Deep (1989) . . . . Claire
  Little Devils (1991) . . . . .n.a.
- **Stepfather III: Father's Day** (1992) . . Christine Davis
  - • 1:27—Very brief buns, sitting down in bubble bath.
  Made for TV Movies:
  Perry Mason: The Case of the Reckless Romeo (1992)
  . . . . Brenda Kingsley
  TV:
  The American Girls (1978) . . . . Rebecca Tomkins
  Three's Company (1981-84) . . . . Terri Alden
  Magazines:
  Penthouse (Mar 1976) . . . . Pet
  (Used the name Joann Witty.)

•Baron, Carla
Films:
  Necromancer (1988) . . . . .Gail
  - • 0:42—Brief topless getting out of bed with Paul. Dark.
  Sorority Babes in the Slimeball Bowl-O-Rama (1988)
  . . . . Frankie

Barrault, Marie-Christine
Films:
  My Night at Maud's (1970; French) . . . . Francoise
  Cousin, Cousine (1975; French) . . . . Marthe
  - •• 1:05—Topless in bed with her lover, cutting his nails.
  - • 1:07—Brief side view of right breast, while giving him a bath.
  - ••• 1:16—Topless with penciled tattoos all over her body.
    1:33—Braless in see-through white blouse saying "good bye" to everybody.
  The Daydreamer (1975; French) . . . . .Lisa
  The Medusa Touch (1978; British). . . . . .Patricia
  Stardust Memories (1980). . . . . Isabel

Table for Five (1983) . . . . .Marie
A Love in Germany (1984; French/German)
. . . . .Maria Wyler
  - • 0:23—Right breast, in bed with her lover when Pauline peeks from across the way.
  - •• 0:28—Right breast in bedroom with Karl. Very brief lower frontal nudity getting back into bed. Long scene.
  - ••• 0:43—Topless in bedroom with Karl. Subtitles get in the way! Long scene.
  Swann in Love (1984; French/German)
  . . . . Madame Verdunn
  a.k.a. Un Amour de Swann

Barrese, Katherine
Films:
  Homer & Eddie (1989). . . . . .Waitress
  Jezebel's Kiss (1990) .Jezebel
  - •• 0:36—Full frontal nudity washing herself off in kitchen after having sex with the sheriff.
  - • 0:42—Brief buns, going for a swim in the ocean. Dark.
  - ••• 0:48—Topless taking off her robe in front of Hunt, then making love with him.
  - • 0:58—Brief right breast and buns while Malcolm McDowell watches through slit in curtain. Long shot.
  - • 1:09—Right breast and buns getting undressed. Long shot. Closer shot of buns, putting robe on.
  - ••• 1:12—Topless making love with McDowell. More topless after.

•Barrett, Alice
Films:
  Incoming Freshman (1979) . . . . Boxing Student
  - •• 0:43—Topless answering a question during Professor Bilbo's fantasy.
  - • 0:55—Topless in another of Bilbo's fantasy.
  - • 1:18—Topless during end credits.
  Mission Hill (1982). . . . . n.a.

Barrett, Jamie
Films:
  Club Life (1987). . . . . Sissy
  House of the Rising Sun (1987). . . . . .Janet
  - • 1:04—Very brief topless making love with Louis.

Barrett, Nitchie
Films:
  Preppies (1984) . . . . Roxanne
  - • 0:11—Brief topless changing into waitress costumes with her two friends.
  She-Devil (1989) . . . . Bob's Secretary
  A Time to Die (1991) . . . . Sheila
  - • 0:12—Buns, getting out of bed.
  - •• 0:16—Topless making love in bed with Sam.

Barrett, Victoria

Films:
Hot Resort (1984) . . . . Jane
Hot Chili (1985) . . . . Victoria Stevenson
  • 0:55—Very brief close up shot of right breast when
    it pops out of her dress. Don't see her face.
Three Kinds of Heat (1987) . . . . .Terry O'Shea

Barrington, Rebecca

Films:
Dance or Die (1988) . . . . .n.a.
The Newlydeads (1988) . . . . .n.a.
Living to Die (1990). . . . . Married Woman
  • 0:23—In red bra, blindfolded and tied to a lounge
    chair, then topless while getting photographed.
  • 0:27—Topless in chair when Wings Hauser talks to
    her.

Barry, Wendy

Films:
3:15—The Moment of Truth (1986) . . . . Lora
Knights of the City (1986). . . . . .Jasmine
Young Lady Chatterley II (1986)
  . . . . Sybil "Maid in Hot House"
  • 0:12—Topless in hot house with the Gardener.

• Basil, Toni

Singer and Choreographer.
Films:
Pajama Party (1964) . . . . .Pajama Girl
Easy Rider (1969) . . . . .Mary
  • 1:24—Brief right breast (her hair gets in the way)
    and very, very brief buns, taking off clothes in grave-
    yard during hallucination sequence.
    1:26—Very brief buns, climbing on something (seen
    through fish-eye lens).
  • 1:27—Buns, while lying down (seen through fish-
    eye lens).
Sweet Charity (1969)
  . . . . .Dancer in "Rhythm of Life" Number
Five Easy Pieces (1970) . . . . Terry Grouse
The Last Movie (1971) . . . . Rose
Mother, Jugs & Speed (1976) . . . . Addict
Angel III: The Final Chapter (1988) . . . . .Hillary
Slaughterhouse Rock (1988) . . . . Sammy Mitchell
Rockula (1990) . . . . .Phoebe
Eating (1991) . . . . Jackie

Basinger, Kim

Films:
Hard Country (1981) . . . . .Jodie Lynn Palmer
Motherlode (1982) . . . . .Andrea Spalding
The Man Who Loved Women (1983) . . . . Louise "Lulu"
Never Say Never Again (1983) . . . . .Domino Vitale
The Natural (1984) . . . . Memo Paris
Fool For Love (1985) . . . . May

9 1/2 Weeks (1986) . . . . Elizabeth
  • 0:27—Blindfolded while Mickey Rourke plays with
    an ice cube on her. Brief right breast.
    0:36—Masturbating while watching slides of art.
    0:41—Playing with food at the refrigerator with
    Rourke. Messy, but erotic.
  • 0:54—Very brief left breast, while rolling over in bed.
    0:58—Making love with Rourke in clock tower.
  ••• 1:11—In wet lingerie, then topless making love in a
    wet stairwell with Rourke.
  • 1:19—Doing a sexy dance for Rourke in a white slip.
  • 1:22—Buns, showing off to Rourke on building.
  • 1:44—Brief buns, putting on pants and getting out
    of bed.
No Mercy (1986) . . . . Michel Duval
Blind Date (1987). . . . . .Nadia Gates
Nadine (1987) . . . . .Nadine Hightower
My Stepmother Is An Alien (1988) . . . . . .Celeste Martin
  0:40—Dancing very seductively in a white slip in
    front of Dan Aykroyd while he lies in bed. No nudity,
    but still very exciting.
Batman (1989). . . . . Vicki Vale
The Marrying Man (1991) . . . . .Vicki Anderson
  a.k.a. Too Hot to Handle
Cool World (1992) . . . . Holli Would
Final Analysis (1992). . . . . Heather Evans
  •• 0:21—Right breast, while making love in bed under
    Richard Gere.
Miniseries:
From Here to Eternity (1979) . . . . Lorene Rogers
Made for TV Movies:
Katie: Portrait of a Centerfold (1978) . . . . n.a.
TV:
Dog and Cat (1977). . . . . Officer J.Z. Kane
From Here to Eternity (1980) . . . . Lorene Rogers
Video Tapes:
Playboy Video Magazine, Volume 10 (1986)
  . . . . 9 1/2 Weeks
  • 0:32—Brief right breast in ice cube scene.
  • 0:34—Brief right breast during slide show scene.
  • 0:37—Brief topless in wet stairwell scene.
Magazines:
Playboy (Feb 1983) . . . . Betting on Kim
  ••• 82-89—Nude.
Playboy (Dec 1983) . . . . .Sex Stars of 1983
  •• 211—Topless.
Playboy (Dec 1984) . . . . .Sex Stars of 1984
  ••• 208—Topless walking in water.
Playboy (Sep 1987) . . . . 25 Years of James Bond
  •• 130—Topless.
Playboy (Jan 1988). . . . . Kim
  ••• 78-85—Topless and buns from Feb 1983.
Playboy (Jan 1989). . . . . .Women of the Eighties
  256—Buns.
Playboy (Dec 1990) . . . . .Sex Stars of 1990
  • 173—Buns, lying in water. B&W.
Playboy (Dec 1991) . . . . .Sex Stars 1991
  • 180—Left breast under sheer dress top. B&W.

Bates, Jo Anne

Films:
Perfect Timing (1984) . . . . Karen
   ••• 0:21—Nude, getting ready to get her picture taken.
Heavenly Bodies (1985) . . . . Girl in Locker Room
Immediate Family (1989) . . . . Home Buyer

• Bates, Kathy

Films:
Straight Time (1978) . . . . Selma Darin
Come Back to the Five and Dime, Jimmy Dean, Jimmy
  (1982) . . . . Stella May
Two of a Kind (1983) . . . . Furniture Man's Wife
The Morning After (1986) . . . . . Woman on Mateo Street
Summer Heat (1987) . . . . Ruth Stanton
Arthur 2 On the Rocks (1988) . . . . Mrs. Canby
High Stakes (1989) . . . . Jill
Men Don't Leave (1989) . . . . Lisa Coleman
Dick Tracy (1990) . . . . Mrs. Green
Misery (1990) . . . . Annie Wilkes
  (Academy Award for Best Actress.)
White Palace (1990) . . . . Rosemary Powers
At Play in the Fields of the Lord (1991)
  . . . . Hazel Quarrier
  • 2:22—(0:52 into tape 2) Nude, covered with mud
    and leaves, going crazy outside after her son dies.
Fried Green Tomatoes (1991) . . . . Evelyn Couch
  a.k.a. Fried Green Tomatoes at the Whistle Stop Café
Shadows and Fog (1992) . . . . n.a.

Bauer, Belinda

Films:
The American Success Company (1979) . . . . Sarah
Winter Kills (1979) . . . . Yvette Malone
  •• 0:46—Topless making love in bed with Jeff Bridges,
    then getting out of bed.
  • 1:25—Topless, dead as a corpse when sheet uncov-
    ers her body.
Flashdance (1983) . . . . Katie Hurley
Timerider (1983) . . . . Clair Cygne
The Rosary Murders (1987) . . . . Pat Lennon
UHF (1989) . . . . Mud Wrestler
Act of Piracy (1990) . . . . Sandy Andrews
Robocop 2 (1990) . . . . Juliette Faxx
Made for Cable TV:
The Hitchhiker: Love Sounds . . . . . Veronica Hoffman
  • 0:15—Brief topless, making love in the house with
    Kerry.
  •• 0:22—Topless, making love in the boat.
Made for TV Movies:
Starcrossed (1985) . . . . Mary

Bauer, Jaime Lyn

(Yes, her name is spelled Jaime.)
Films:
The Centerfold Girls (1974) . . . . Jackie
  •• 0:04—Topless getting out of bed and walking
    around the house.
  ••• 0:14—Topless getting undressed in the bathroom.

  •• 0:15—Brief topless and buns putting on robe and
    getting out of bed, three times.
Young Doctors in Love (1982) . . . . Cameo
TV:
The Young and the Restless (1973-82)
  . . . . Lauralee (Laurie) Brooks Prentiss
Bare Essence (1983) . . . . Barbara Fisher
The Young and the Restless (1984)
  . . . . Lauralee (Laurie) Brooks Prentiss
Magazines:
Penthouse (May 1974) . . . . Jessica
  (Used the name Jessica Len.)
  ••• 48-55—Nude.

Bauer, Michelle

a.k.a. Michelle McClellan briefly when her ex-husband
  threatened to sue for using "Bauer."
a.k.a. Former adult film actress Pia Snow.
The easiest adult video tape to find is *Cafe Flesh*.
Films:
Homework (1982) . . . . Uncredited Dream Groupie
  ••• 1:01—Topless with two other groupies, groping
    Tommy while he sings. (She has a flower in her hair
    and is the only brunette.)
Cave Girl (1985) . . . . Locker Room Student
  •• 0:05—Topless with four other girls in the girls' locker
    room undressing, then running after Rex. She's the
    first to take her top off, wearing white panties, run-
    ning and carrying a tennis racket.
Armed Response (1986) . . . . Stripper
  • 0:41—Topless, dancing on stage.
Cyclone (1986) . . . . Uncredited Shower Girl
  • 0:06—Very brief buns and side of left breast walking
    around in locker room. (Passes several times in front
    of camera.)
Reform School Girls (1986) . . Uncredited Shower Girl
  •• 0:25—Topless, then nude in the shower.
Roller Blade (1986) . . . . Bod Sister
  • 0:11—Topless, being held by Satacoy's Devils.
  ••• 0:13—More topless and buns in G-string during
    fight. Long scene.
  • 0:16—Brief topless twice, getting saved by the Sis-
    ters.
  •• 0:33—Topless during ceremony with the other two
    Bod Sisters. Buns also.
  ••• 0:35—Full frontal nudity after dip in hot tub. (Sec-
    ond to leave the tub.)
  •• 0:40—Nude, on skates with the other two Bod Sis-
    ters. (She's on the left.)
Screen Test (1986) . . . . Dancer/Ninja Girl
  •• 0:04—Topless dancing on stage.
  ••• 0:42—Nude, with Monique Gabrielle, making love
    in a boy's dream.
Nightmare Sisters (1987) . . . . Mickey
  ••• 0:39—Topless standing in panties with Melody and
    Marci after transforming from nerds to sexy women.
  ••• 0:40—Topless in the kitchen with Melody and Mar-
    ci.

••• 0:44—Full frontal nudity in the bathtub with Melody and Marci. Excellent, long scene.

••• 0:47—Topless in the bathtub. Nice close up.

••• 0:48—Still more topless in the bathtub.

•• 0:53—Topless in bed with J.J.

Phantom Empire (1987) . . . . Cave Bunny
0:32—Running around in the cave a lot in two piece loincloth swimsuit.

•• 1:13—Finally topless after losing her top during a fight, stays topless until Andrew puts his jacket on her.

The Tomb (1987) . . . . Nefartis

Demonwarp (1988) . . . . Betsy

•• 0:41—Topless, taking off her T-shirt to get a tan in the woods.

•• 0:43—Left breast, lying down, then brief topless getting up when the creature attacks.

•• 0:47—Topless putting blood-stained T-shirt back on.

•• 1:19—Topless, strapped to table, getting ready to be sacrificed.

• 1:22—Topless on stretcher, dead.

Hollywood Chainsaw Hookers (1988) . . . . Mercedes

••• 0:09—Nude in motel room with a John just before chainsawing him to pieces.

The Jigsaw Murders (1988) . . . . Cindy Jakulski
0:20—Brief buns on cover of puzzle box during bachelor party.

• 0:21—Brief topless in puzzle on underside of glass table after the policemen put the puzzle together.

• 0:29—Very brief topless when the police officers show the photographer the puzzle picture.

• 0:43—Very brief topless long shots in some pictures that the photographer is watching on a screen.

Sorority Babes in the Slimeball Bowl-O-Rama
(1988). . . . . Lisa
0:07—In panties getting spanked with Brinke Stevens.

••• 0:12—Topless brushing herself in the front of mirror while Stevens takes a shower.

• 0:14—Brief full frontal nudity when the three nerds fall into the bathroom.
0:33—In black bra, panties, garter belt and stockings asking for Keith.
0:35—Wearing the same lingerie, on top of Keith in the locker room.

••• 0:40—Topless taking off her bra.

••• 0:43—More topless undoing garter belt.

•• 0:46—More topless in locker room.

•• 0:47—More topless taking off stockings.

• 1:04—Full frontal nudity sitting on the floor by herself.

•• 1:05—Full frontal nudity getting up after the lights go out. Kind of dark.

Warlords (1988) . . . . Harem Girl

••• 0:14—Topless, getting her top ripped off, then shot by a bad guy.

Wild Man (1988) . . . . Trisha Collins
1:02—In sheer white lingerie with Eric. Buns also.

••• 1:06—Topless on couch making love with Eric. Brief lower frontal nudity.

Assault of the Party Nerds (1989) . . . . Muffin

• 0:16—Side view of left breast kissing Bud.

••• 0:20—Topless lying in bed seen from Bud's point of view, then sitting up by herself.

• 1:15—Brief right breast, then topless in bed with Scott.

Beverly Hills Vamp (1989) . . . . Kristina

• 0:12—Buns and brief side view of right breast in bed biting a guy.
0:33—In red slip, with Kyle.

•• 0:38—Topless trying to get into Kyle's pants.
1:09—In black lingerie attacking Russell in bed with Debra Lamb and Jillian Kesner.
1:19—In black lingerie enticing Mr. Pendleton into bedroom.
1:22—In black lingerie, getting killed as a vampire by Kyle.

Deadly Embrace (1989) . . . . Female Spirit of Sex

•• 0:22—Topless caressing herself during fantasy sequence.

••• 0:28—Topless taking off tube top and caressing herself.

••• 0:40—Topless and buns kissing blonde guy. Nice close up of him kissing her breasts.

• 0:42—Side of left breast lying down with the guy.

• 1:03—Buns and side of right breast with the guy.

Dr. Alien (1989) . . . . Coed #1
a.k.a. I Was a Teenage Sex Mutant

••• 0:53—Topless taking off her top (she's on the left) in the women's locker room after another coed takes hers off in front of Wesley.

Murder Weapon (1989) . . . . Girl in Shower on TV

• 1:00—Brief left breast on TV that the guys are watching. Scene from *Nightmare Sisters*.

Puppet Master III: Toulon's Revenge (1990) Lili

• 0:15—Brief topless bringing the phone to the General while he takes a bath.

•• 0:43—Topless, twice, making love on top of the General.

Virgin High (1990) . . . . Miss Bush

The Dwelling (1991) . . . . n.a.

Evil Toons (1991) . . . . Mrs. Burt

•• 0:48—Topless opening her lingerie for Burt. Buns, while walking away in G-string.

Inner Sanctum (1991)
. . . . Body Double for Margaux Hemingway

• 0:09—Left breast, body double in office for Margaux Hemingway.

•• 0:23—Topless body double for Hemingway, while in bed with Joseph Bottoms.

Lady Avenger (1991). . . . . Annalee

••• 0:30—Topless, making love in bed on top of J.C.

••• 0:52—Topless, making love in bed on top of Ray.

Little Devils (1991) . . . . n.a.

Spirits (1991) . . . . Sister Mary
••• 0:21—Topless, taking off nun's habit, trying to seduce Erik Estrada. Brief lower frontal nudity and buns also. Long scene.
Terror Night (1991) . . . . .n.a.
Chickboxer (1992) . . . . Greta "Chickboxer" Holtz
0:39—In sexy pink outfit.
••• 0:57—Full frontal nudity, making love with a guy in bed.
Hellroller (1992) . . . . .Michelle Novak
0:26—Undressing in motel room down to white body suit, then exercising.
••• 0:30—Topless taking a bath.
0:35—Dead in bathroom, covered with blood and with her guts hanging out.

Video Tapes:
Nudes in Limbo (1983) .Model
Best Chest in the West (1984) . . . . Michelle
••• 0:24—In two piece swimsuit, then topless and buns.
Love Skills: A Guide to the Pleasures of Sex (1984)
. . . . .Model
••• 0:34—Full frontal nudity, caressing herself in front of a mirror.
Candid Candid Camera, Volume 4 (1985) . . .Model
••• 0:08—Full frontal nudity, undressing while complaining about a bad tan from a tanning salon.
••• 0:50—Nude, posing in front of a guy, asking his opinion on her poses. Long scene.
Terror on Tape (1985)
. . . . .Unsatisfied Video Store Customer
Candid Candid Camera, Volume 5 (1986)
. . . . Debbie White
••• 0:34—Buns, pulling down her pants while a guy rubs purple paint on her rear.
Centerfold Screen Test, Take 2 (1986) . . . . . Marsha
••• 0:12—Topless taking off her dress for Mr. Johnson. Then full frontal nudity. Nice, long scene.
In Search of the Perfect 10 (1986)
. . . . Perfect Girl #10
••• 0:53—In yellow outfit stripping in office. Topless and buns in G-string bottom.
Penthouse Love Stories (1986) . . . .Therapist's Patient
••• 0:45—Nude, making love in Therapist's office with his assistant.
Night of the Living Babes (1987) . . . . .Sue
•• 0:44—Topless chained up with Chuck and Buck.
••• 0:46—More topless chained up.
• 0:50—Topless getting rescued with Lulu.
Playboy Video Magazine, Volume 12 (1987)
. . . . Candid Candid Camera
•• 0:35—Lower nudity when her skirt falls down whenever she sneezes.
Penthouse: On the Wild Side (1988)
. . . . Punk or Bust Hairdresser
• 0:32—Topless in black leather outfit.
••• 0:34—Nude while wearing black leather outfit, making love with Julie Parton.

Scream Queen Hot Tub Party (1991) . . . . . . .Herself
•• 0:00—Full frontal nudity during opening credits.
•• 0:07—Topless taking off pink outfit and putting on red teddy.
• 0:12—Buns, while walking up the stairs.
••• 0:33—Nude, stripping out of blue dress in scene from *Hollywood Chainsaw Hookers*. Long scene.
••• 0:38—In black lingerie, then stripping to topless to demonstrate the proper Scream Queen use of a chainsaw.
••• 0:44—Topless taking off her swimsuit top and soaping up with the other girls.
•• 0:46—Topless in still shot during the end credits.

Magazines:
Penthouse (Nov 1980) . . . . .Swept Away
••• 142-151—Nude with a blonde woman.
Penthouse (Jul 1981) . . . . .Pet
Playboy (Jul 1989) . . . . B-Movie Bimbos
•• 138—Topless and buns lying in a car that looks like a shark.
Playboy (Nov 1991) . . . . Grapevine
••• 183—Topless, kneeling. B&W.

Baxter, Amy Lynn

Films:
Summer's Games (1987). . .Boxer/Girl from Penthouse
•• 0:04—Topless opening her swimsuit top after contest. (1st place winner.)
•• 0:18—Topless during boxing match.
Wet Water T's (1987) . . . . .Herself
••• 0:33—Topless in black lingerie bottoms, then buns in G-string, dancing on stage in a contest.
•• 0:38—Topless during judging.
•• 0:39—Topless during semi-finals.
••• 0:40—Topless dancing with the other women during semi-final judging.
••• 0:43—Topless during finals.
•• 0:47—Topless during final judging.
•• 0:48—Topless dancing after winning first place.
Spring Fever USA (1988) . . . . Amy (Car Wash Girl)
a.k.a. Lauderdale
Summer Job (1989) . . . . .Susan
•• 0:10—Topless changing in room with the other three girls. More topless sitting on bed.
0:15—In white bra, looking at herself in mirror.
• 0:34—Brief topless when her swimsuit top pops off after saving a guy in swimming pool.
• 0:45—In white lingerie, brief topless on stairs, flashing her breasts (wearing curlers).
1:00—Brief buns in two piece swimsuit turning around.
• 1:23—Topless pulling her top down talking to Mr. Burns.
Affairs of the Heart (1992) . . . . .Josie Hart
Private Screenings
•• 0:00—Topless during opening credits.
•• 0:02—Topless and buns in G-string, while posing for photos.

••• 1:09—Topless posing in santa cap during photo session.
•• 1:13—Topless with Richard during smoky dream scene.

Video Tapes:
Penthouse Passport to Paradise/Hawaii (1991)
. . . . .Model
••• 0:49—Undressing on boat in white swimsuit top and white panties, then full frontal nudity.

Beacham, Stephanie

Films:
The Games (1970) . . . . .Angela Simmonds
The Nightcomers (1971; British)
. . . . Miss Margaret Jessel
• 0:13—Brief left breast lying in bed having her breasts fondled.
••• 0:30—Topless in bed with Marlon Brando while a little boy watches through the window.
•• 0:55—Topless in bed pulling the sheets down.
The Devil's Widow (1972; British) . . . . .Janet
Dracula A.D. 1972 (1972; British) . . . Jessica Van Helsing
And Now the Screaming Starts (1973; British)
. . . . Catherine Fengrifen
The Confessional (1977; British) . . . . .Vanessa
Schizo (1977; British) . . . . Beth
a.k.a. Amok
a.k.a. Blood of the Undead
Horror Planet (1980; British) . . . . Kate
a.k.a. Inseminoid
Troop Beverly Hills (1989) . . . . .Vicki Sprantz
Miniseries:
Napolean and Josephine (1987) . . . . .Therese
Made for TV Movies:
Danielle Steel's "Secrets" (1992) . . . . Sabina Quarles
To Be The Best (1992). . . . . Arabella
TV:
The Colbys (1985-87). . . . . Sable Scott Colby
Sister Kate (1989-90) . . . . Sister Katherine Lambert
Magazines:
Playboy (Nov 1972) . . . . Sex in Cinema 1972
•• 160—Right breast, B&W photo from *The Nightcomers*.
Playboy (Feb 1987). .n.a.
•• 112-121—Color photos taken in 1972.

Beal, Cindy

Films:
My Chauffeur (1986) .Beebop
Slavegirls from Beyond Infinity (1987). . . . . . . .Tisa
(Wearing skimpy outfits during most of the movie.)
0:25—Walking around in white bra and panties.
••• 0:36—Topless on beach wearing white panties.
• 1:05—Left breast leaning back on table while getting attacked by Zed.

Beall, Sandra

Films:
Easy Money (1983) . . . . .Maid of Honor
A Night in Heaven (1983) . . . . .Slick
• 1:09—Brief close up of left breast in shower with Christopher Atkins.
The Cotton Club (1984). . . . . Myrtle Fay
Birdy (1985). . . . . Shirley
Key Exchange (1985) . . . . Marcy
••• 1:14—Topless on bed taking off her clothes and talking to Daniel Stern.
Loverboy (1989) . . . . .Robin
State of Grace (1990). . . . . .Steve's Date

Beals, Jennifer

Films:
Flashdance (1983) . . . . .Alex
The Bride (1985) . . . . Eva
0:21—Lower frontal nudity and buns of body double coming down stairs and to kneel down and talk to Sting.
0:53—Standing in wet white nightgown in the rain talking to Sting.
Split Decisions (1988) . . . . Barbara Uribe
Vampire's Kiss (1989) . . . . Rachel
0:14—Almost topless in bed with Nicholas Cage. Squished left breast against Cage while she bites him. In one shot, you can see the beige pastie she put over her left nipple.
0:27—In bed again with Cage.
0:41—In black lingerie taking her dress off for Cage.
Club Extinction (1990) . . . . Sonja Vogler
a.k.a. Doctor M
• 1:16—Brief side of left breast rolling over in bed with Hartmann. Don't see her face, but probably her.
•• 1:17—Brief topless in bed with Hartmann when he kisses her right breast, then brief right breast.
Blood & Concrete: A Love Story (1991). . . . . Mona
• 0:10—Buns, in pulled up slip on bed with Billy Zane. Brief, out-of-focus shot of her left breast. Don't see her face.
TV:
2000 Malibu Road (1992) . . . . .Perry Quinn

•Beaman, Lee Anne

Films:
Mirror Images (1991) . . . . .Rebecca
••• 1:11—Buns in G-string, then topless in conference room, undressing in front of Jeff Conaway and Carter.
The Other Woman (1992) . . . . .Jessica Mathews
(Unrated version reviewed.)
••• 0:17—Nude, undressing and getting into the shower.
•• 0:40—Topless in the bathtub.
•• 0:51—Buns, while lying in bed in the fetal position.
••• 1:09—Nude, on the floor making love with Traci. Interesting camera angles.

••• 1:13—Nude, getting up and out of bed, taking a shower, then making love with Carl. Long scene.
•• 1:23—Topless on floor with Traci during video play-back on TV.
••• 1:34—Buns, in long shot, taking off robe to greet Zmed. Topless and buns in bed with him.

Béart, Emmanuelle

Model for *Borghese* cosmetics.
Films:
Date with an Angel (1987) . . . . Angel
Manon of the Spring (1987; French) . . . . Manon
  • 0:11—Brief nude dancing around a spring playing a harmonica.
La Belle Noiseuse (1992; French) . . . . Marianne
Magazines:
Playboy (Nov 1992) . . . . Sex in Cinema 1992
•• 146—Left breast and partial buns, lying down from *La Belle Noiseuse*.

Beck, Kimberly

Films:
Massacre at Central High (1976) . . . . .Theresa
  • 0:32—Nude romping in the ocean with David. Long shot, dark, hard to see anything.
  •• 0:42—Topless on the beach making love with An-drew Stevens after a hang glider crash.
Roller Boogie (1979) . . . . Lana
Friday the 13th, Part IV—The Final Chapter (1984)
  . . . . Trish
Maid to Order (1987) . . . . Kim
Adventures in Dinosaur City (1992). . . . . Chanteuse
TV:
Peyton Place (1965) . . . . Kim Schuster
Lucas Tanner (1974-75) . . . . .Terry Klitsner
General Hospital (1975) . . . . Samantha Chandler
Rich Man, Poor Man—Book II (1976-77) . . Diane Porter
Capitol (1982-83) . . . . Julie Clegg

Becker, Desiree

Films:
Good Morning, Babylon (1987; Italian/French)
  . . . . .Mabel
  • 1:06—Brief topless in the woods making love.
Made for Cable TV:
The Hitchhiker: Out of the Night (1985; HBO)
  . . . . Kathy
  •• 0:12—Brief topless lying in the steam room talking to Peter, then close up topless.

Bedelia, Bonnie

Films:
The Gypsy Moths (1969). . . . . Annie Burke
  (Not available on video tape.)
Lovers and Other Strangers (1970) . . . Susan Henderson
The Big Fix (1978). . . . . Suzanne
Heart Like a Wheel (1983). . . . . .Shirley Muldowney
The Boy Who Could Fly (1986) . . . . .Charlene

The Stranger (1986) . . . . Alice Kildee
  • 0:15—Brief right breast sticking up from behind her lover's arm making love in bed during flashback sequence (B&W).
  • 0:19—Brief left breast turning over in hospital bed when a guy walks in. Long shot, hard to see.
  •• 0:38—Right breast again making love (B&W).
Violets Are Blue (1986). . . . . Ruth Squires
Die Hard (1988). . . . . .Holly McClane
The Prince of Pennsylvania (1988) . . . . . Pam Marshetta
  0:12—In black bra in open blouse in kitchen. Long scene.
Fat Man and Little Boy (1989) . . . . . Kitty Oppenheimer
Die Hard 2 (1990) . . . . .Holly McClane
Presumed Innocent (1990). . . . . .Barbara Sabich
Made for Cable Movies:
Somebody Has to Shoot the Picture (1990; HBO)
  . . . . .Hannah McGrath
  1:15—Upper half of left breast, lying in bed with Roy Scheider.
Made for TV Movies:
Memorial Day (1983). . . . . n.a.
Switched at Birth (1991) . . . . .Regina Twigg
TV:
The New Land (1974) . . . . .Anna Larsen

• Bega, Leslie

Films:
For Keeps (1988) . . . . Carlita
Mobsters (1991) . . . . Anna Lansky
  a.k.a. Mobsters—The Evil Empire
Uncaged (1991). . . . . Micki
  a.k.a. Angel in Red
  •• 0:02—Topless on top of a customer, in bed.
  •• 0:16—Topless in bed with Evan.
  • 0:42—Brief topless with Evan on the floor.
  0:51—In white lingerie outfit with a customer and Ros.
TV:
Head of the Class (1986-89). . . . . Maria Borges

• Beldam, Lia

Films:
The Shining (1980) . . . . Young Woman in Bath
  ••• 1:12—Full frontal nudity getting out of bathtub while Jack Nicholson watches.
Magazines:
Playboy (Nov 1980) . . . . Sex in Cinema 1980
  •• 174—Side view of left breast.

Bell, Jeannie

Films:
Black Gunn (1972). . . . . Lisa
Mean Streets (1973) .Diane
  • 0:07—Topless dancing on stage with pasties on.
  • 1:00—Topless backstage wearing pasties.
The Klansman (1974). . . . . .Mary Anne
Policewoman (1974) . . . . n.a.
Three the Hard Way (1974) . . . . Polly

TNT Jackson (1975) . . . . TNT Jackson
Sex on the Run (1979; German/French/Italian)
. . . . Slave Girl
a.k.a. Some Like It Cool
a.k.a. Casanova and Co.
••• 0:01—Topless, reading book in large bath with
Marisa Berenson.
••• 0:24—Topless, giving Berenson a back massage.
Bloodfist III: Forced to Fight (1991) . . . TNT Jackson
•• 0:55—Topless several times in movie *TNT Jackson*
that the inmates watch while Diddler gets stabbed
to death.
Magazines:
Playboy (Oct 1969) . . . . Playmate
Playboy (Dec 1980) . . . . Bunny Birthday
••• 153—Topless.

Beller, Kathleen
Films:
The Godfather, Part II (1974) . . . . Girl in "Senza Mama"
The Betsy (1978) . . . . Betsy Hardeman
••• 0:12—Brief nude getting into swimming pool.
•• 1:14—Topless in bed with Tommy Lee Jones.
Movie Movie (1978) . . . . Angie Popchik
Promises in the Dark (1979) . . . . Buffy Koenig
Surfacing (1980) . . . . Kate
0:22—Very brief buns, pulling down pants to
change. Dark, hard to see.
0:23—Very brief right breast undressing. Dark, hard
to see.
• 0:24—Very, very brief topless turning over in bed.
0:25—Buns, standing next to bed.
••• 1:23—Topless washing herself in the water. One
long shot, one side view of right breast.
Fort Apache, The Bronx (1981) . . . . Theresa
The Sword and the Sorcerer (1982) . . . . Alana
• 0:54—Side view of buns, lying face down getting oil
rubbed all over her.
Touched (1982) . . . . Jennifer
Cloud Waltzing (1986) . . . . n.a.
Time Trackers (1989) . . . . R. J. Craig
Miniseries:
Blue and the Gray (1982) . . . . Kathy Reynolds
Made for TV Movies:
Mary White (1977) . . . . n.a.
Are You in the House Alone? (1978) . . . . Gail
TV:
Search for Tomorrow (1971-74) . . . . Liza Walton
Dynasty (1982-84) . . . . Kirby Anders
Bronx Zoo (1987-88) . . . . Callahan

Belli, Agostina
Films:
Bluebeard (1972) . . . . Caroline
• 1:31—Brief left breast lying on grass getting a tan.
•• 1:32—Topless taking off clothes and lying on the
couch.
Blood in the Streets (1974; French/Italian) . . . . . . Maria
The Seduction of Mimi (1974; Italian) . . . . n.a.

The Purple Taxi (1977; French/Italian/Irish)
. . . . Anne Taubelman
Holocaust 2000 (1978) . . . . Sara Golen
•• 0:50—Topless in bed making love with Kirk Douglas.

Bellwood, Pamela
Films:
Two-Minute Warning (1976) . . . . Peggy Ramsay
Airport '77 (1977) . . . . Lisa
Hanger 18 (1980) . . . . Sarah
Serial (1980) . . . . Carol
The Incredible Shrinking Woman (1981)
. . . . Sandra Dyson
Cellar Dweller (1987) . . . . Amanda
Made for TV Movies:
Double Standard (1988) . . . . Joan
TV:
W.E.B. (1978) . . . . Ellen Cunningham
Dynasty (1981-86) . . . . Claudia Blaisdel
Magazines:
Playboy (Apr 1983) . . . . Going Native
• Covered with mud and body paint.

Bening, Annette
Films:
The Great Outdoors (1988) . . . . Kate Craig
Valmont (1989) . . . . Marquise de Merteuil
0:10—Very brief, hard to see right breast, reaching
up to kiss Jeffrey Jones.
The Grifters (1990) . . . . Myra Langtry
•• 0:36—In bra and panties in her apartment, then
topless lying in bed "paying" her rent. Kind of dark.
••• 1:06—Nude, walking down the hall to the bedroom
and into bed.
1:30—Very brief right breast, dead in morgue. Long
shot.
Postcards from the Edge (1990) . . . . Evelyn Ames
Bugsy (1991) . . . . Virginia Hill
Guilty by Suspicion (1991) . . . . Ruth Merrill
1:01—In white bra and slip getting dressed.
Regarding Henry (1991) . . . . Sarah Turner
Magazines:
Playboy (Nov 1991) . . . . Sex in Cinema 1991
• 143—Topless, lying in bed, in scene from *The Grifters.*

Bennett, Angela
Films:
Fatal Games (1984) . . . . Sue Allen Baines
•• 0:21—Full frontal nudity in the sauna with Teal Roberts.
• 0:23—Nude, running around the school, trying to
get away from the killer. Dark.
Punchline (1988) . . . . Nurse

Benson, Vickie

Films:

Private Resort (1985) . . . . Bikini Girl
- 0:28—In blue two piece swimsuit, showing her buns, then brief topless with Reeves.
  1:11—Buns, in locker room, trying to slap Reeves.

Las Vegas Weekend (1986) .n.a.
My Chauffeur (1986) . . . . Party Girl
The Wraith (1986) . . . . Waitress
- 0:59—Topless in bed with Packard when Loomis interrupts them.

Cheerleader Camp (1987). . . . . .Miss Tipton
a.k.a. Bloody Pom Poms
- 0:27—Brief topless undressing in her bedroom.

Blue Movies (1988). . . . . Andrea
Mortuary Academy (1988) . . . . Salesgirl

Bentley Konkel, Dana

Films:

Bad Girls from Mars (1990) . . . . Martine
- •• 0:28—Topless taking off her blouse in office.
- •• 0:59—Topless several times wrestling with Edy Williams.

Death Merchant (1990). . . . . .Jason's Girlfriend
- 0:35—Brief topless undressing for shower during dream.

Invisible Maniac (1990). . . . . .Newscaster
- 1:22—Brief topless on monitor doing the news.

Repo Jake (1990). . . . . Jenny
Sorority House Massacre 2 (1990). . . . . Janey
- ••• 0:23—Topless in bedroom talking to Suzanne and looking in the mirror. Buns, while getting dressed in black bodysuit.
  0:48—Left breast, sticking out of bodysuit, covered with blood, when the girls discover her dead.

Benton, Barbi

Films:

Hospital Massacre (1982) . . . . Susan Jeremy
a.k.a. X-Ray
  0:29—Undressing behind a curtain while the Doctor watches her silhouette.
- ••• 0:31—Topless getting examined by the Doctor. First sitting up, then lying down.
- ••• 0:34—Great close up shot of breasts while the Doctor uses stethoscope on her.

Deathstalker (1983). . . . . Codille
- •• 0:39—Topless struggling while chained up and everybody is fighting.
- 0:47—Right breast, struggling on the bed with Deathstalker.

TV:

Hee Haw (1971-76) .Regular
Sugar Time! (1977-78) . . . . Maxx

Video Tapes:

Playboy Video Magazine, Volume 9. . . . . Herself

Magazines:

Playboy (Dec 1973). . . . . Barbi's Back!
- ••• 143-149—Nude.

Playboy (Jan 1989). . . . . Women of the Seventies
- ••• 210—Topless.

Benton, Suzanne

Films:

That Cold Day in the Park (1969). . . . . Nina
- 0:38—Side view of left breast putting top on. Long shot.
- 1:05—Topless taking off her clothes and getting into the bathtub. Another long shot.

Catch-22 (1970) . . . . .Dreedle's WAC
Best Friends (1975) . . . . .Kathy
A Boy and His Dog (1976) . . . . .Quilla June
- •• 0:29—Nude, getting dressed while Don Johnson watches.
- 0:45—Right breast lying down with Johnson after making love with him.

Bentzen, Jane

Films:

Nightmare at Shadow Woods (1983). . . . . .Julie
a.k.a. Blood Rage
  0:38—In red lingerie, black stockings and garter belt in her apartment with Phil.

Made for Cable Movies:

A Breed Apart (1984; HBO) . . . . Reporter
- ••• 0:55—Left breast in bed with Powers Booth, then full frontal nudity getting out of bed and putting her clothes on.

Benz, Donna Kei

Films:

Looker (1981) . . . . Ellen
The Challenge (1982) .Akiko
- 1:23—Topless making love with Scott Glenn in motel room. Could be a body double. Dark, hard to see anything.

Pray for Death (1986) . . . . Aiko Saito
Moon in Scorpio (1987). . . . . .Nurse Mitchell

Magazines:

Playboy (Nov 1982) . . . . Sex in Cinema 1982
- 161—Topless.

Berenson, Marisa

Films:

Death in Venice (1971; Italian/French)
. . . . Frau Von Aschenbach
Cabaret (1972) . . . . Natalia Landauer
Barry Lyndon (1975; British) . . . . Lady Lyndon
  Topless in bathtub.
Killer Fish (1979; Italian/Brazilian). . . . . .Ann
Sex on the Run (1979; German/French/Italian) . . . . n.a.
a.k.a. Some Like It Cool
a.k.a. Casanova and Co.
  1:23—Almost right breast, while in bed with Tony Curtis when she rolls over him.
S.O.B. (1981) . . . . .Mavis
- •• 1:20—Topless in bed with Robert Vaughn.
Night of the Cyclone (1990) . . . . .Francoise

White Hunter Black Heart (1990). . . . . Kay Gibson
Made for Cable Movies:
Notorious (1992; Lifetime) . . . . Katarina
Miniseries:
Sins (1986) . . . . .n.a.
Made for TV Movies:
Playing for Time (1980). . . . . .n.a.
Magazines:
Playboy (Dec 1973). . . . . Sex Stars of 1973
• 210—Right breast.
Playboy (Nov 1976) . . . . Sex in Cinema 1976
• 114—Left breast in a shot that wasn't used in *Barry Lyndon.*

Berg, Carmen

Video Tapes:
Playboy Video Calendar 1989 (1988) . . . . July
••• 0:25—Nude.
Sexy Lingerie (1988) .Model
Wet and Wild (1989). . . . . .Model
Magazines:
Playboy (Jul 1987). . . . . Playmate
Playboy's Book of Lingerie (Mar 1991) . . . . . Herself
• 83—Left breast.
Playboy's Book of Lingerie (Sep 1991) . . . . . Herself
••• 74—Topless.
Playboy's Book of Lingerie (Mar 1992) . . . . . Herself
• 60—Partial left breast.

Bergen, Candice

Wife of French director Louis Malle.
Films:
The Group (1966). . . . . .Lakey Eastlake
The Adventurers (1970) . . . . Sue Ann
Getting Straight (1970). . . . . Jan
Soldier Blue (1970) . . . . Cresta Marybelle Lee
Carnal Knowledge (1971). . . . . Susan
The Hunting Party (1971; British) . . . . Melissa Ruger
T. R. Baskin (1971) . . . . T.R. Baskin
Bite the Bullet (1975) . . . . .Miss Jones
The Wind and the Lion (1975) . . . . Eden Pedecaris
A Night Full of Rain (1978; Italian) . . . . .Lizzy
(Not available on video tape.)
Topless.
Oliver's Story (1978) . . . . Marcie Bonwit
Starting Over (1979) . . . . Jessica Potter
1:01—In a sheer blouse sitting on couch talking to
Burt Reynolds.
• 1:29—Very, very brief left breast in bed with Reynolds when he undoes her top. You see her breast just before the scene dissolves into the next one. Long shot, hard to see.
Rich and Famous (1981) . . . . Merry Noel Blake
Gandhi (1982) . . . . Margaret Bourke-White
Made for TV Movies:
Mayflower Madam (1987) . . . . . Sydney Biddle Barrows
TV:
Murphy Brown (1988-) . . . . Murphy Brown

• Berger, Senta

Films:
Ambushers (1967) . . . . .Francesca
If It's Tuesday, This Must Be Belgium (1969) . . . . n.a.
When Women Had Tails (1970; Italian) . . . . Felli
• 0:22—Buns, while lying in pit.
• 1:08—Buns, while getting carried around.
• 1:30—Buns, after her boyfriend gets caught in tree.
Cross Of Iron (1977) . . . . Eva
Killing Cars (1986) . . . . .Marie

Berger, Sophie

Films:
Emmanuelle IV (1984) . . . . .Maria
•• 0:46—Full frontal nudity putting on robe.
0:49—Buns, taking off robe in front of Mia Nygren.
Love Circles Around the World (1984) . . . .Dagmar
••• 0:38—Topless in women's restroom in casino making love with a guy in a tuxedo.
••• 0:43—Topless in steam room wearing a towel around her waist, then making love.

Bergman, Sandahl

Films:
All That Jazz (1979) .Sandra
•• 0:52—Topless dancing on scaffolding during a dance routine.
Xanadu (1980). . . . . A Muse
Airplane II: The Sequel (1982) . . . . .Officer
Conan the Barbarian (1982) . . . . Valeria
•• 0:49—Brief left breast making love with Arnold Schwarzenegger.
She (1983) . . . . She
•• 0:22—Topless getting into a pool of water to clean her wounds after sword fight.
Red Sonja (1985) . . . . .Queen Gedren
Hell Comes to Frogtown (1987). . . . . Spangle
Kandyland (1987) . . . . Harlow Divine
Programmed to Kill (1987) . . . . .Samira
a.k.a. The Retaliator
• 0:11—Brief side view of right breast taking off T-shirt and leaning over to kiss a guy. Don't see her face.
Stewardess School (1987) . . . . Wanda Polanski
Raw Nerve (1991) . . . . Gloria Freedman
Made for TV Movies:
Getting Physical (1984) . . . . n.a.
In the Arms of a Killer (1992) . . . . Nurse Henninger
Video Tapes:
The Firm Aerobic Workout With Weights, Vol. 3
. . . . .Instructor
Magazines:
Playboy (Mar 1980) . . . . .All That Fosse
••• 174-175—Topless stills from *All That Jazz.*
Playboy (Dec 1981) . . . . .Sex Stars of 1981
•• 239—Topless.

Bernard, Sue

Films:
Faster, Pussycat! Kill! Kill! (1966) . . . . Linda
Russ Meyer film.
The Killing Kind (1973) . . . . Tina
• 0:00—Topless during gang rape.
• 0:19—Topless again during flashback.
• 1:12—Brief topless again several times during flashbacks.
The Witching (1983) . . . . .Nancy
a.k.a. Necromancy
(Originally filmed in 1971 as *Necromancy*, additional
scenes were added and re-released in 1983.)
• 1:03—Brief topless in bed with Michael Ontkean.
Magazines:
Playboy (Dec 1966). . . . . Playmate

Bernhard, Sandra

Comedienne.
Films:
King of Comedy (1983) . . . . Masha
Track 29 (1988; British) . . . . .Nurse Stein
Heavy Petting (1989) . . . . .Herself/Comedienne
Without You I'm Nothing (1990)
. . . . Miscellaneous Characters
••• 1:20—Dancing in very small pasties and very small
G-string on stage for a long time. Rear shots of her
buns.
Hudson Hawk (1991) . . . . .Minerva Mayflower
Truth or Dare (1991). . . . . Herself
Made for Cable TV:
The Hitchhiker: O. D. Feeling . . . . .n.a.
Tales From the Crypt: Top Billing (1991)
. . . . Sheila Winters
Sandra After Dark (1992; HBO) . . . . .Hostess
••• 0:47—Topless and buns, taking off bra and panties
and getting into bed.
TV:
Roseanne (1992-). . . . . .Nancy
Magazines:
Playboy (May 1991) . . . . .Grapevine
• 182—Upper half of right breast in open dress. B&W.
Playboy (Aug 1992). . . . . Next Month
• 166—Partial right breast.
Playboy (Sep 1992) . . . . . .Not Just Another Pretty Face
•• 70-77—Full frontal nudity in B&W and color photos.

Berridge, Elizabeth

Films:
The Funhouse (1981) . . . . Amy
•• 0:03—Brief topless taking off robe to get into the
shower, then very brief topless getting out to chase
Joey.
Amadeus (1984) . . . . Constanze
Five Corners (1988). . . . . Melanie
TV:
The Powers That Be (1992) . . . . Charlotte

•Bertinelli, Valerie

Wife of singer Eddie Van Halen.
Made for TV Movies:
Young Love, First Love (1979) . . . . .n.a.
Ordinary Heroes (1986) . . . . .Maria Pezzo
• 0:28—Brief silhouette of breast in darkened room
backlit by window, when she takes off her blouse
while on top of Richard Dean Anderson in bed.
Pancho Barnes (1988) . . . . .Pancho Barnes
Taken Away (1989) . . . . .n.a.
In a Child's Name (1991) . . . . .Angela
TV:
One Day at a Time (1975-84). . . . Barbara Cooper Royer
Sydney (1990) . . . . Sydney

Besch, Bibi

Mother of actress Samantha Mathis.
Films:
The Long Dark Night (1977) . . . . Marge
a.k.a. The Pack
Hardcore (1979) . . . . Mary
The Beast Within (1982) . . . . Caroline MacCleary
•• 0:06—Topless, getting her blouse torn off by the
beast while she is unconscious. Dark, hard to see her
face.
Star Trek II: The Wrath of Kahn (1982)
. . . . Dr. Carol Marcus
The Lonely Lady (1983) . . . . Veronica
Who's That Girl? (1987). . . . . Mrs. Worthington
Kill Me Again (1989) . . . . Jack's Secretary
Steel Magnolias (1989) . . . . .Belle Marmillion
Tremors (1989) . . . . Megan - The Doctor's Wife
Betsy's Wedding (1990) . . . . Nancy Lovell
Made for TV Movies:
Doing Time on Maple Drive (1992) . . . . Lisa
TV:
Secrets of Midland Heights (1980-81)
. . . . Dorothy Wheeler
The Hamptons (1983) . . . . .Adrienne Duncan Mortimer
Freshman Dorm (1992-) . . . . Mrs. Flynn

Beswick, Martine

Films:
From Russia with Love (1963; British) . . . . Zora
Saturday Night Out (1963; British). . . . . n.a.
Thunderball (1965; British). . . . . Paula Caplan
One Million Years B.C. (1966; U.S./British) . . . . Nupondi
Dr. Jekyll and Sister Hyde (1971) . . . . . . Sister Hyde
• 0:25—Topless, opening her blouse and examining
her breasts after transforming from a man.
• 0:27—Left breast, feeling herself.
• 0:44—Brief buns, taking off coat to put on a dress.
The Happy Hooker Goes Hollywood (1980)
. . . . Xaviera Hollander
•• 0:05—Brief topless in bedroom with Policeman.
••• 0:22—Brief buns, jumping into the swimming pool,
then topless next to the pool with Adam West.
• 0:27—Topless in bed with West, then topless waking
up.

Melvin and Howard (1980) . . . . Real Estate Woman
Cyclone (1986) . . . . Waters
The Offspring (1986) . . . . Katherine White
Miami Blues (1990) . . . . Noira
Evil Spirits (1991) . . . . Vanya
Trancers II (1991) . . . . Nurse Trotter
TV:
Aspen (1977) . . . . Joan Carolinian

• Beyer, Tanya
Video Tapes:
Playboy Playmates in Paradise (1992) . . . Playmate
Playboy Video Calendar 1993 (1992) . . . . . . .March
Wet and Wild IV (1992) . . . . .Model
Magazines:
Playboy (Feb 1992) . . . . Playmate
••• 90-101—Nude.

• Biffignani, Monique
Video Tapes:
Rock Video Girls 2 (1992) . . . . Herself
0:00—Brief right breast in gauze during opening
credits.
0:47—In pink bra, in dressing room.
• 0:49—Right breast under gauze and buns in G-
string after being unwrapped as a mummy.
0:53—Briefly in pink bra and gauze again during
end credits.
0:54—Briefly in gauze again during end credits.
Sexy Lingerie IV (1992) . . . . .Model
Magazines:
Playboy's Book of Lingerie (Sep 1992) . . . . . Herself
••• 3-7—Full frontal nudity.
•• 11—Left breast.

Binoche, Juliette
Films:
Hail Mary (1985) . . . . Juliette
Rendez-Vous (1986; French) . . . . . Anne "Nina" Larrieu
• 0:07—Brief topless in dressing room when Paulot
surprises her and Fred.
••• 0:25—Side of left breast, then topless and buns in
empty apartment with Paulot.
•• 0:32—Full frontal nudity in bed with Quentin.
•• 0:35—Buns, then brief topless in bed with Paulot
and Quentin. Full frontal nudity getting out.
•• 1:08—Topless taking off her top in front of Paulot in
the dark, then topless lying on the floor.
• 1:11—Right breast, making love on the stairs. Dark.
The Unbearable Lightness of Being (1988)
. . . . .Tereza
0:22—In white bra in Tomas' apartment.
• 1:33—Brief topless jumping onto couch.
1:36—Buns, sitting in front of fire being photographed, then running around, trying to hide.
• 2:18—Left breast in The Engineer's apartment.
Made for Cable Movies:
Women & Men 2: Three Short Stories (1991; HBO)
. . . . .Mara

Magazines:
Playboy (Nov 1987) . . . . Sex in Cinema 1987
• 143—Side view of right breast from *Rendez-vous*.

Bird, Minah
Films:
Oh, Alfiel (1975; British) . . . . Gloria
a.k.a. Alfie Darling
The Stud (1978; British) . . . . .Molly
•• 0:26—Topless in bed when Tony is talking on the
telephone.

Birkin, Jane
Films:
Blow-Up (1966; British/Italian) . . . . Teenager
Nude.
Ms. Don Juan (1973) . . . . Clara
0:58—Lower frontal nudity lying in bed with Brigitte
Bardot.
1:00—Brief topless in bed with Bardot. Long shot.
•• 1:01—Full frontal nudity getting dressed. Brief topless in open blouse.
Dark Places (1974; British) . . . . Alta
Catherine & Co. (1975; French) . . . . Catherine
• 0:07—Topless, standing up in the bathtub to open
the door for another woman.
•• 0:09—Side view of left breast, while taking off her
blouse in bed.
••• 0:10—Topless, sitting up and turning the light on,
smoking a cigarette.
•• 0:17—Right breast, while making love in bed.
•• 0:24—Topless taking off her dress, then buns jumping into bed.
•• 0:36—Buns and left breast posing for a painter.
• 0:45—Topless taking off dress, walking around the
house. Left breast, inviting the neighbor in.
Stuntwoman (1981) . . . . n.a.
Dust (1985; French/Belgian) . . . . .Magda
1:17—Brief topless and buns, taking off robe and
pounding the wall. Very dark.
Kung Fu Master (1989; French) . . . . Mary-Jane
a.k.a. Le Petit Amour
Daddy Nostalgie (1991; French) . . . . .Caroline
La Belle Noiseuse (1992; French) . . . . Liz

• Bishop, Stephanie
a.k.a. Adult film actress Viper.
Films:
Vice Academy (1988) . . . . Desiree/Redhead

Bisignano, Jeannine
Films:
Body Rock (1984) . . . . Girl
My Chauffeur (1986) . . . . .Party Girl
• 1:23—Topless, several times, taking off her white
blouse in the back of the limousine. (She's the only
brunette.)

Ruthless People (1986) . . . . Hooker in Car
    0:17—Topless, hanging out of the car. Long, long
    shot, don't see anything.
    • 0:40—Topless in the same scene three times on TV
    while Danny De Vito watches.
    • 0:49—Left breast hanging out of the car when the
    Chief of Police watches on TV. Closest shot.
    1:15—Same scene again in department store TV's.
    Long shot, hard to see.
Stripped to Kill II (1988) . . . . Sonny
    0:06—Buns, while wearing a black bra in dressing
    room.
    ••• 0:38—Topless and buns during strip dance routine
    in white lingerie.
License to Kill (1989) . . . . Stripper
Made for Cable Movies:
Lies of the Twins (1991; USA) . . . . Biker Girl
Magazines:
Playboy (Nov 1986) . . . . Sex in Cinema 1986
    •• 131—Topless in a photo from *Ruthless People*, lean-
    ing out of the car.

Bisset, Jacqueline

Films:
Cul-de-sac (1966) . . . . Jacqueline
Casino Royale (1967; British) . . . . Miss Goodthighs
Two for the Road (1967; British) . . . . Jackie
Bullitt (1968) . . . . Cathy
The Detective (1968) . . . . Norma McIver
The Sweet Ride (1968) . . . . Vicki Cartwright
    (Not available on video tape.)
    Topless.
The Secret World (1969; French) . . . . Wendy
Airport (1970) . . . . Gwen Meighen
The Grasshopper (1970) . . . . Christine Adams
    a.k.a. The Passing of Evil
    0:21—In flesh colored Las Vegas-style showgirl cos-
    tume. Dark, hard to see.
    0:27—More showgirl shots.
    1:14—In black two piece swimsuit.
    1:16—Almost left breast while squished against Jay
    in the shower.
Believe in Me (1971) . . . . Pamela
The Mephisto Waltz (1971) . . . . Paula Clarkson
    • 0:48—Very brief right and side view of left breast in
    bed with Alan Alda.
    1:36—Sort of left breast getting undressed for
    witchcraft ceremony. Long shot side views of right
    breast, but you can't see her face.
    •• 1:45—Very brief topless twice under bloody water in
    blood covered bathtub, dead. Discovered by Kath-
    leen Widdoes.
Secrets (1971) . . . . Jenny
    0:49—Very brief lower frontal nudity, putting pant-
    ies on while wearing a black dress.
    ••• 1:02—Brief buns and a lot of topless on bed making
    love with Raoul.
The Life and Times of Judge Roy Bean (1972)
    . . . . Rose Bean

The Thief Who Came to Dinner (1973) . . . . Laura
The Magnificent One (1974; French/Italian)
    . . . . Tatiana/Christine
Murder on the Orient Express (1974; British)
    . . . . Countess Andrenyi
The Spiral Staircase (1975; British) . . . . Helen
St. Ives (1976) . . . . Janet Whistler
The Deep (1977) . . . . Gail Berke
    ••• 0:01—Scuba diving underwater in a wet T-shirt.
    • 0:08—More wet T-shirt, getting out of water, onto
    boat.
The Greek Tycoon (1978) . . . . Liz Cassidy
Who is Killing the Great Chefs of Europe? (1978)
    . . . . Natasha
When Time Ran Out! (1980) . . . . Kay Kirby
Inchon (1981) . . . . Barbara Hallsworth
Rich and Famous (1981) . . . . Liz Hamilton
Famous T & A (1982) . . . . Jenny
    (No longer available for purchase, check your video
    store for rental.)
    ••• 0:31—Topless scene from *Secrets*.
Class (1983) . . . . Ellen
Under the Volcano (1984) . . . . Yvonne Firmin
High Season (1988; British) . . . . Katherine Shaw
    • 0:56—Brief topless doing the backstroke in the wa-
    ter with Rick, then left breast while lying down. Hard
    to see, everything is lit with blue light.
Scenes from the Class Struggle in Beverly Hills (1989)
    . . . . Clare
The Maid (1990) . . . . Nicole Chantrelle
    0:47—In lingerie, changing clothes in front of Mar-
    tin Sheen while talking to him.
    1:13—Very, very brief side of left breast shadow on
    wall, leaping out of bed with Sheen.
Wild Orchid (1990) . . . . Claudia
    1:21—Dancing in braless white tank top during car-
    nival.
Made for Cable Movies:
Forbidden (1985) . . . . Nina von Halder
    0:25—In bra and slip in villa with her Jewish lover.
    0:47—Squished breasts against Jurgen Prochnow in
    bed making love.
Miniseries:
Anna Karenina (1985) . . . . Anna Karenina
Napolean and Josephine (1987)
    . . . . Josephine de Beauharnais
    Lots of cleavage.

• Bissett, Josie

Films:
All-American Murder (1991) . . . . Tally Fuller
    1:01—Brief topless in Polaroid photographs that
    Charlie Schlatter looks at. Hard to see.
    • 1:07—Very brief topless several times during B&W
    flashbacks.
    • 1:12—Topless on top of the Dean during Joanna
    Cassidy's B&W flashbacks. Quick cuts.
The Book of Love (1991) . . . . Lily
The Doors (1991) . . . . Robby Krieger's Girlfriend

I Posed for Playboy (1991) . . . . Claire Baywood
a.k.a. Posing: Inspired by Three Real Stories
(Shown on network TV without the nudity.)
- 0:09—Close-up of left breast, while on couch with
  Nick. Don't see her face.
Mikey (1992) . . . . .n.a.
Made for TV Movies:
Danielle Steel's "Secrets" (1992) . . . . Gaby Smith
TV:
Hogan Family (1990-91) . . . . Cara
Melrose Place (1992-) . . . . .Jane Mancini

Black, Karen

Films:
Easy Rider (1969) . . . . Karen
Five Easy Pieces (1970) . . . . Rayette Dipesto
   0:48—In sheer black nightie in bathroom, then
   walking to bedroom with Jack Nicholson.
Cisco Pike (1971) . . . . .Sue
Drive, He Said (1972). .Olive
- 1:05—Brief topless screaming in the bathtub when
  she gets scared when a bird flies in.
   1:19—Brief lower frontal nudity running out of the
   house in her bathrobe.
Little Laura and Big John (1972) . . . . Laura
Portnoy's Complaint (1972) . . . . The Monkey
Airport 1975 (1974) .Nancy
The Great Gatsby (1974). . . . . Myrtle Wilson
The Day of the Locust (1975) . . . . Faye
Nashville (1975) . . . . Connie White
Burnt Offerings (1976) . . . . Marion
Capricorn One (1978). . . . . Judy Drinkwater
In Praise of Older Women (1978; Canadian)
. . . . Maya
   •• 0:35—Topless in bed with Tom Berenger.
Separate Ways (1979) . . . . Valentine Colby
- 0:04—Topless and in panties changing while her
  husband talks on the phone, then in bra. Long shot.
   •• 0:18—Topless in bed, while making love with Tony
   Lo Bianco.
   •• 0:36—Topless taking a shower, then getting out.
Chanel Solitaire (1981) . . . . .Emilienne D'Alencon
Killing Heat (1981). . . . . Mary Turner
   •• 0:41—Full frontal nudity giving herself a shower in
   the bedroom.
Come Back to the Five and Dime, Jimmy Dean, Jimmy
(1982). . . . . .Joanne
Can She Bake a Cherry Pie? (1983) . . . . .Zee
   0:40—Sort of left breast squished against a guy,
   while kissing him in bed.
- 1:02—Very brief upper half of left breast in bed
  when she reaches up to touch her hair.
Cut and Run (1985; Italian). . . . . .Karin
Invaders from Mars (1986) . . . . Linda
Dixie Lanes (1987) . . . . .Zelma
Eternal Evil (1987). . . . . .n.a.
Miss Right (1987; Italian) . . . . Amy
- 0:47—Brief topless jumping out of bed and running
  to get a bucket of water to put out a fire.

The Invisible Kid (1988) . . . . .Mom
It's Alive III: Island of the Alive (1988) . . . . . . Ellen Jarvis
Out of the Dark (1988) . . . . Ruth
Bad Manners (1989) . . . . Mrs. Fitzpatrick
Homer & Eddie (1989). . . . . Belle
Night Angel (1989) . . . . Rita
The Children (1990). . . . . Sybil Lollmer
Club Fed (1990). .Sally Rich
Haunting Fear (1990). . . . . .Dr. Julia Harcourt
Mirror Mirror (1990) . . . . Mrs. Gordon
Overexposed (1990) . . . . Mrs. Trowbridge
Twisted Justice (1990) . . . . .Mrs. Granger
Blood Money (1991) . . . . .Barrett
   a.k.a. The Killers Edge
Evil Spirits (1991) . . . . .Mrs. Purdy
Hitz (1992). . . . . Tiffany Powers
   a.k.a. Judgment
Made for Cable TV:
The Hitchhiker: Hired Help (1985; HBO)
. . . . .Mrs. Kay Mason
   (Available on *The Hitchhiker, Volume 1*.)
Made for TV Movies:
Trilogy of Terror (1974) . . . . .n.a.
TV:
The Second Hundred Years (1967-68)
. . . . Marcia Garroway
Magazines:
Playboy (Dec 1973) . . . . .Sex Stars of 1973
- 207—Half of left breast under gaping blouse.
Playboy (Dec 1976) . . . . .Sex Stars of 1976
   •• 185—In pink see-through night gown.

Black, Nicole

a.k.a. Adult film actress Nicole Noir.
Films:
Simply Irresistible (1983). . . . . Mata Hari
(R-rated version. *Irresistible* is the X-rated version.)
   1:07—Pulling up her dress, then stripping in front of
   two guys in prison.
   •• 1:14—Full frontal nudity tied to a chair.
Video Tapes:
Nudes in Limbo (1983) . . . . Model

Blackburn, Greta

Films:
48 Hrs. (1982) . . . . Lisa
   •• 0:13—Topless and buns in bathroom in hotel room
   with James Remar.
The Concrete Jungle (1982) . . . . Lady in Bar
Time Walker (1982) .Sherri
Chained Heat (1983; U.S./German) . . . . .Lulu
Yellowbeard (1983) . . . . .Mr. Prostitute
Party Line (1988) . . . . .Angelina
Death Feud (1989). .Jenny
   0:29—In sexy black dress talking to Frank Stallone.
   1:04—In black lingerie on couch.
Under the Boardwalk (1989) . . . . Mrs. Vorpin
My Blue Heaven (1990) . . . . Stewardess

Miniseries:
V: The Final Battle (1984) . . . . Lorraine

• *Blacklinie, Susan*
Films:
1941 (1979). . . . . .Polar Bear Girl
- 0:02—Brief topless and buns of woman taking off robe and running into the ocean. Dark, hard to see.
0:05—Buns, while hanging on submarine periscope.
0:06—Very, very brief left breast when getting back into the water.
Magazines:
Penthouse (Jan 1973) . . . . The Lady and the Lion
••• 80-85—Nude posing with a lion.

Blackman, Joan
Films:
Vengeance of Virgo (1972) . . . . .n.a.
Macon County Line (1974) . . . . .Carol Morgan
Pets (1974) . . . . Geraldine Mills
- 0:46—Brief side view of left breast, while getting out of bed after making love with Bonnie.
Moonrunners (1975). .Reba
One Man (1979; Canadian) . . . . .n.a.
Return to Waterloo (1986) . . . . .n.a.

Blackwood, Nina
Films:
Vice Squad (1982). . . . . Ginger
TV:
Entertainment Tonight . . . . Music Correspondent
Music Television . . . . .Video Jockey
Magazines:
Playboy (Aug 1978). . . . . .The Girls in the Office
••• 142—Full frontal nudity (with brunette hair).

Blair, Linda
Films:
Dead Sleep . . . . .n.a.
Way We Live Now (1970) . . . . Sara Aldridge
The Sporting Club (1971) . . . . Barby
The Exorcist (1973). .Regan
Airport 1975 (1974) . . . . Janice Abbott
Exorcist II: The Heretic (1977) . . . . .Regan
Roller Boogie (1979) . . . . .Terry Barkley
Hell Night (1981) . . . . Marti
Chained Heat (1983; U.S./German) . . . . Carol
••• 0:30—Topless in the shower.
•• 0:56—In bra, then topless in the Warden's office when he rapes her.
Night Patrol (1985) . . . . .Sue
- 1:19—Brief left breast, in bed with The Unknown Comic.
Savage Island (1985). Daly
Savage Streets (1985) . . . . Brenda
••• 1:05—Topless sitting in the bathtub thinking.
Night Force (1986) . . . . .n.a.
Grotesque (1987) . . . . .Lisa

Red Heat (1987; U.S./German) . . . . .Chris Carlson
0:09—In blue nightgown in the bedroom with her boyfriend, almost topless.
••• 0:56—Topless in shower room scene.
••• 1:01—Brief topless getting raped by Sylvia Kristel while the male guard watches.
Silent Assassins (1988) . . . . .Sara
0:48—Very brief, wearing light blue bra struggling on couch with a masked attacker.
Up Your Alley (1988) . . . . Vickie Adderly
W. B., Blue and the Bean (1988). . . . . Nettie
a.k.a. Bail Out
Witchery (1988). Jane Brooks
Bedroom Eyes II (1989) . . . . Sophie Stevens
0:31—Buns, in bed with Wings Hauser.
- 0:33—Brief left breast under bubbles in the bathtub. Don't see her face.
A Woman Obsessed (1989) . . . . Evie Barnes
Repossessed (1990) . . . . .Nancy Aglet
The Chilling (1991) . . . . .n.a.
Made for TV Movies:
Born Innocent (1974). n.a.
Sarah T.: Portrait of a Teenage Alcoholic (1975) . . .Sarah
Calendar Girl, Cop, Killer? The Bambi Bembenek Story (1992) . . . . Jane Mader
Magazines:
Playboy (Dec 1983) . . . . .Sex Stars of 1983
••• 209—Topless.
Playboy (Dec 1984) . . . . .Sex Stars of 1984
••• 207—Topless in the water up to her breasts.

Blaisdell, Deborah
a.k.a. Adult film actress Tracey Adams.
Films:
The Lost Empire (1983) . . . . Girl Recruit
Screen Test (1986). . . . . Dancer
- 1:20—Brief topless, twice, dancing on stage. Long shot.
Student Affairs (1987) . . . . Kelly
••• 0:26—Topless sitting up in bed talking to a guy.
Wildest Dreams (1987). . . . . Joan Peabody
- 1:10—Brief topless during fight on floor with two other women.
Wimps (1987) . . . . Roxanne Chandless
- 1:22—Brief topless and buns taking off clothes and getting into bed with Francis in bedroom.
Enrapture (1989). Martha
••• 0:10—Topless undressing in her apartment with Keith.
•• 0:17—Left breast, in bed with Keith, then brief topless.

Blake, Stephanie
a.k.a. Stella Blalack and Cimmaron.
Films:
The Big Bet (1985) . . . . Mrs. Roberts
••• 0:04—Topless sitting on bed, then making love with Chris.

•• 0:37—Nude on bed with Chris. Shot at fast speed, he runs between bedrooms.

•• 0:59—Full frontal nudity in bed again. Shot at fast speed.

The Sure Thing (1985) . . . . Barmaid
Ferris Bueller's Day Off (1986) . . . . Singing Nurse
Over the Top (1987) . . . . Ticket Agent
Danger Zone II: Reaper's Revenge (1988)
. . . . Tattooed Topless Dancer
••• 0:47—Topless, dancing on stage in bikini bottoms.
Invisible Maniac (1990) . . . . Mrs. Cello
•• 0:42—Topless opening her blouse for Chet.
•• 0:52—Topless in her office trying to seduce Dr. Smith. Nice close up of right breast.
Whore (1991) . . . . Stripper in Big T's
a.k.a. If you're afraid to say it... Just see it
• 0:35—Buns, in G-string on stage.
••• 0:36—Topless, dancing on stage in a club.
The Mambo Kings (1992) . . . . Stripper

Blakely, Susan

Films:
Savages (1972) . . . . Cecily
The Way We Were (1973) . . . . Judianne
The Lords of Flatbush (1974) . . . . Jane Bradshaw
The Towering Inferno (1974) . . . . Patty Simmons
Capone (1975) . . . . Iris Crawford
(Not available on video tape.)
Topless.
Report to the Commissioner (1975) . . . . . . Patty Butler
Airport '79: The Concorde (1979) . . . . Maggie
Over the Top (1987) . . . . Christine Hawk
Blackmail (1991) . . . . Lucinda Sullivan
Made for Cable Movies:
Wildflower (1991; Lifetime) . . . . Ada
Made for Cable TV:
The Hitchhiker: Remembering Melody
(1984; HBO) . . . . Melody
••• 0:17—Right breast in shower with Ted and brief topless in the bathtub.
Miniseries:
Rich Man, Poor Man (1976)
. . . . Julie Prescott Abbott Jordache
Made for TV Movies:
Broken Angel (1988) . . . . Catherine Coburn
Murder Times Seven (1990) . . . . Gert Kiley
And the Sea Will Tell (1991) . . . . Gail Bugliosi
Intruders (1992) . . . . Leigh Holland
Magazines:
Playboy (Mar 1972) . . . . Savages
• 142—Topless.
• 145—Topless.

Blanchard, Vanessa

Films:
Witchfire (1986) . . . . Liz
•• 0:52—Brief topless in bed and then the shower.
Uphill All the Way (1987) . . . . Velma

Blee, Debra

Films:
The Beach Girls (1982) . . . . Sarah
••• 1:22—Brief topless opening her swimsuit top on the beach.
Sloane (1984) . . . . Cynthia Thursby
• 0:15—Very brief topless during attempted rape.
The Malibu Bikini Shop (1985) . . . . Jane
Savage Streets (1985) . . . . Rachel
0:20—In a bra in the girls locker room.
Hamburger—The Motion Picture (1986) . . . . . Mia Vunk
0:25—Briefly in wet dress in the swimming pool.

• Blondi

a.k.a. Adult film actress Blondie or Blondi Bee.
a.k.a. Marjorie Miller.
Films:
Party Favors (1987) . . . . Bobbi
•• 0:04—Topless in dressing room, taking off red top and putting on black one.
• 0:23—Brief topless when blouse pops off while delivering pizza.
••• 0:27—Topless and buns in G-string doing a strip routine outside.
• 0:31—Brief topless flapping her blouse to cool off.
••• 1:04—Topless doing a strip routine in a little girl outfit. Buns, in G-string. More topless after.
• 1:16—Nude taking off swimsuit next to pool during final credits.
Video Tapes:
High Society Centerspread Video #3: Blondi
. . . . Herself
The Girls of Malibu (1986) . . . . Marjorie
••• 0:06—In two piece swimsuit. Topless riding a motorcycle. Full frontal nudity posing on it. Nude outside.
In Search of the Perfect 10 (1986) . . . Perfect Girl #3
••• 0:14—Topless in back of car.
Best Buns on the Beach (1987) . . . . Blondi
••• 0:06—Topless, stripping on stage during dance routine. Buns, in G-string.
•• 0:52—Topless and buns with all the contestants during review.
••• 0:53—Topless and buns in final pose-off.
•• 0:57—Topless and buns winning the contest.
••• 0:58—More slow motion topless and bun shots during the final credits.
Night of the Living Babes (1987)
. . . . Mondo Zombie Girl Darlene
••• 0:12—Topless wearing dark purple wig and long gloves, with the other Mondo Zombie Girls.
••• 0:16—More topless and buns in bed with Buck.
• 0:50—Topless on the couch with the other Zombie Girls.
• 0:52—Topless on the couch again.
The Perfect Body Contest (1987) . . . . Jennifer
••• 0:46—Buns, in two piece swimsuit, then topless.
• 0:50—Topless on stage with the other contestants.

Bloom, Claire

Films:
The Illustrated Man (1969) . . . . .Felicia
Three into Two Won't Go (1969; British)
. . . . Frances Howard
A Severed Head (1971; British) . . . . Honor Klein
• 1:10—Topless leaning up then right beast while sitting up in bed with Richard Attenborough.
A Doll's House (1973; British) . . . . .Nora Helmer
Islands in the Stream (1977) . . . . Audrey
Clash of the Titans (1981) . . . . Hera
Deja Vu (1984) . . . . .n.a.
Queenie (1987). . . . . .Vicky Kelley
Sammy and Rosie Get Laid (1987; British) . . . . . . .Alice
Miniseries:
Brideshead Revisited (1981; British). . . .Lady Marchmain
Made for TV Movies:
Promises to Keep (1985) . . . . Sally

Bloom, Lindsay

Films:
Six Pack Annie (1975) . . . . Annie
Texas Detour (1977) . . . . Sugar McCarthy
French Quarter (1978)
. . . . "Big Butt" Annie/Policewoman in Bar
H.O.T.S. (1979) . . . . Melody Ragmore
• 0:28—Very brief right breast on balcony.
• 1:34—Brief topless during football game throwing football as quarterback.
The Main Event (1979) . . . . Girl in Bed
The Happy Hooker Goes Hollywood (1980) . . . . . .Chris
TV:
Dallas (1982) . . . . .Bonnie Robertson
Mike Hammer (1984-87) . . . . Velda

Blount, Lisa

Films:
9/30/55 (1977). . . . . Billie Jean
Dead and Buried (1981) . . . . Girl on the Beach
• 0:06—Brief topless on the beach getting her picture taken by a photographer.
An Officer and a Gentleman (1982) . . Lynette Pomeroy
1:25—In a red bra and tap pants in a motel room with David Keith.
Radioactive Dreams (1984) . . . . Miles Archer
Cease Fire (1985) . . . . .Paula Murphy
Cut and Run (1985; Italian). . . . . .Fran Hudson
What Waits Below (1986) . . . . Leslie Peterson
Nightflyers (1987). . . . . Audrey
Prince of Darkness (1987) . . . . Catherine
South of Reno (1987) . . . . Anette Clark
1:02—In black bra getting blouse torn open while lying down.
Great Balls of Fire (1989) . . . . Lois Brown
Out Cold (1989) . . . . Phyllis
Blind Fury (1990) . . . . Annie Winchester
Femme Fatale (1990) . . . . Jenny

Made for Cable TV:
The Hitchhiker: One Last Prayer . . . . .Miranda
0:06—Briefly in a black bra putting a new homemade outfit on.
Made for TV Movies:
Unholy Matrimony (1988) . . . . .Karen Stockwell
In Sickness and in Health (1992) . . . . .Carmen
TV:
Sons and Daughters (1990-91) . . . . .Mary Ruth

• Blueberry

Films:
One Man Force (1989). . . . . .Santiago's Girlfriend
Video Tapes:
Rock Video Girls 2 (1992) . . . . .Herself
• 0:28—Buns in G-string under sheer body stocking.

Bockrath, Tina

Films:
Totally Exposed (1991). . . . . Lillian Tucker
•• 0:00—Buns and topless, turning over on tanning table during opening credits.
• 0:01—Brief full frontal nudity, lying on tanning table.
•• 0:03—Brief nude, getting out of bed and putting on towel while talking to Bill.
••• 1:01—Full frontal nudity, turning over in tanning table. Full frontal nudity, dropping her towel in reception area.
••• 1:02—Buns, walking back to the room. Nude, taking off towel and lying on massage table.
••• 1:04—Nude, sitting up on table and standing up with Bill.
Made for Cable TV:
Tales From the Crypt: Abra Cadaver (1991)
. . . . Paula/Cadaver
• 0:04—Topless (in B&W) pretending to be a corpse during practical joke.
Video Tapes:
Playboy Video Calendar 1991 (1990). . . . . . January
••• 0:01—Nude.
Sexy Lingerie II (1990) . . . . Model
Magazines:
Playboy (May 1990). . . . . .Playmate
Playboy's Book of Lingerie (Sep 1991) . . . . . .Herself
•• 61—Left breast and lower frontal nudity.
Playboy's Book of Lingerie (Nov 1991) . . . . .Herself
•• 22—Side view of right breast and lower frontal nudity.
Playboy's Book of Lingerie (Mar 1992) . . . . .Herself
Playboy's Book of Lingerie (Jul 1992) . . . . . . .Herself
••• 69—Topless.
Playboy's Career Girls (Aug 1992)
. . . . Baywatch Playmates
••• 9—Full frontal nudity.
Playboy's Book of Lingerie (Sep 1992) . . . . . .Herself
• 71—Tip of left breast.

Bohrer, Corinne
Films:
The Beach Girls (1982) . . . . .Champagne Girl
I, the Jury (1982). . . . . .Soap Opera Actress
My Favorite Year (1982) . . . . .n.a.
Zapped! (1982). . . . . Cindy
Joysticks (1983). . . . . Patsy Rutter
Surf II (1984). . . . . .Cindy Lou
Police Academy 4: Citizens on Patrol (1987) . . . . . Laura
Stewardess School (1987) . . . . Cindy Adams
Vice Versa (1988) . . . . Sam
Made for Cable Movies:
Dead Solid Perfect (1988; HBO) . . . . . . Janie Rimmer
 ••• 0:31—Nude, getting out of bed to get some ice for
    Randy Quaid. Nice scene!
Made for Cable TV:
Dream On: What I Did for Lust (1991; HBO) . . . . . Chloe
TV:
E/R (1984-85) . . . . .Nurse Cory Smith
Free Spirit (1989-90). . . . . .Winnie Goodwin
Man of the People (1991) . . . . Constance

•Boisson, Christine
Films:
Emmanuelle (1974) . . . . .Marie-Ange
 (R-rated version reviewed.)
 •• 0:16—Full frontal nudity diving into swimming
    pool. Also buns, under water.
 ••• 0:19—Topless outside in hanging chair with Sylvia
    Kristel.
Identification of a Woman (1983; Italian) . . . . Ida
Le Passage (1986; French). . . . . Catherine Diez
Dreamers (1987). . . . . .Sima
Sandra (1989; French). . . . . Sandra

Bolling, Tiffany
Films:
Tony Rome (1967) . . . . .Photo Girl
The Marriage of a Young Stockbroker (1971)
 . . . . Girl in the Rain
Bonnie's Kids (1973) . . . . .Ellie
 •• 0:21—Topless, modeling in office.
 • 1:16—Brief right breast making love in bed.
Wicked, Wicked (1973) . . . . .Lisa James
The Centerfold Girls (1974) . . . . Vera
 • 1:02—Brief topless in photograph.
 ••• 1:12—Topless in the shower.
 • 1:21—Brief topless in motel bed getting raped by
    two guys after they drug her beer.
The Wild Party (1975) . . . . Kate
Kingdom of the Spiders (1977) . . . . .Diane Ashley
The Vals (1982) . . . . Valley Attorney and Parent
Love Scenes (1984). . . . . Val
a.k.a. Ecstacy
 •• 0:01—Side view of left breast in bed with Peter.
 ••• 0:06—Topless getting photographed by Britt Ekland
    in the house.
 • 0:09—Brief topless opening her bathrobe to show
    Peter.

• 0:12—Topless in bathtub with Peter.
••• 0:19—Topless lying in bed talking with Peter, then
   making love.
•• 0:43—Topless acting in a movie when Rick opens
   her blouse.
•• 0:57—Nude behind shower door, then topless getting out and talking to Peter.
•• 0:59—Topless making love tied up on bed with Rick
   during filming of movie.
• 1:07—Topless, then full frontal nudity acting with
   Elizabeth during filming of movie.
•• 1:17—Full frontal nudity getting out of pool.
•• 1:26—Topless with Peter on the bed.
Open House (1987) . . . . Judy Roberts
Made for TV Movies:
Key West (1973). . . . . Ruth
TV:
The New People (1969-70) . . . . Susan Bradley
Magazines:
Playboy (Apr 1972) . . . . Tiffany's A Gem
Playboy (Dec 1972) . . . . .Sex Stars of 1972
 ••• 210—Topless.
Playboy (Nov 1973) . . . . Sex in Cinema 1973
 •• 152—Left breast in red light.
Playboy (Dec 1973) . . . . .Sex Stars of 1973
 •• 208—Left breast.
Playboy (Dec 1974) . . . . .Sex Stars of 1974
 ••• 211—Topless.

Bonet, Lisa
Ex-wife of singer Lenny Kravitz.
Films:
Angel Heart (1987) . . . . .Epiphany Proudfoot
 (Original Unedited Version reviewed.)
    0:53—In wet top, talking with Mickey Rourke out-
    side.
 • 1:01—Brief left breast, twice, in open dress during
    vodoo ceremony.
 ••• 1:27—Topless in bed with Rourke. It gets kind of
    bloody.
 • 1:32—Topless in bathtub.
 • 1:48—Topless in bed, dead. Covered with a bloody
    sheet.
TV:
The Cosby Show (1984-87) . . . . Denise Huxtable
A Different World (1987-89). . . . . Denise Huxtable
The Cosby Show (1989-92) . . . Denise Huxtable-Kendall

Bonet, Nai
Films:
The Greatest (1977; U.S./British) . . . . Suzie Gomez
Fairytales (1979) . . . . Sheherazade
 • 0:29—Buns and very brief left breast doing a belly
    dance and rubbing oil on herself.
Nocturna (1979) . . . . .Nocturna

Bonham-Carter, Helena

Films:

A Room with a View (1986; British) . . Lucy Honeychurch
Lady Jane (1987; British) . . . . Lady Jane Grey
 • 1:19—Topless kneeling on the bed with Guilford.
 • 2:09—Side view of right breast and very, very brief
  topless sitting by fire with Guilford.
Maurice (1987; British) . . . Young Lady at Cricket Match
Getting It Right (1989) . . . . Minerva Munday
 •• 0:18—Topless a couple of times in bed talking to
  Gavin. It's hard to recognize her because she has lots
  of makeup on her face.
Hamlet (1990) . . . . Ophelia
Howards End (1992) . . . . Helen Schlegel
Where Angels Fear to Tread (1992) . . . . Caroline Abbott
Made for TV Movies:
A Hazard of Hearts (1987). . . . . .n.a.

Bonnaire, Sandrine

Films:

A Nos Amours (1984; French) . . . . Suzanne
 • 0:17—Brief topless, pulling dress top down to put
  on nightgown.
 •• 0:34—Topless sitting up in bed talking to Bernard.
  Brief side view of buns.
 • 0:42—Very brief side view of left breast while waking
  up in bed.
 • 0:57—Very brief lower frontal nudity, while getting
  out of bed with Martine and her boyfriend. Long
  shot of buns, while hugging Bernard in the background (out of focus).
Police (1985; French). Lydie
 ••• 0:49—Full frontal nudity, undressing in front of
  Gérard Depardieu, then getting out of the shower.
Monsieur Hire (1990; French) . . . . Alice

Boorman, Katrine

Films:

Excalibur (1981; British) . . . . .Igrayne
 • 0:14—Right breast, then topless in front of the fire
  when Uther tricks her into thinking that he is her
  husband and makes love to her.
Dream One (1984; British/French)
 . . . . Duchka/Nemo's Mother
Marche A L'Hombre (1984; French) . . . . Katrina
Hope and Glory (1987; British) . . . . Charity
Camille Claudel (1989; French). . . . . Jessie

Botsford, Sara

Films:

By Design (1982; Canadian) . . . . Angie
 • 0:23—Full frontal nudity in the ocean. Long shot,
  hard to see anything.
 • 1:08—Brief side view of left breast making love in
  bed while talking on the phone.
Deadly Eyes (1982; Canadian) . . . . Kelly Leonard
 • 0:42—Topless several times, making love with Paul.
Still of the Night (1982) . . . . .Gail Phillips

Bouche, Sugar

Films:

Heavenly Bodies (1985) . . . . .Stripper
 • 0:16—Topless doing stripper-gram for Steve.
Graveyard Shift (1987). . . . . Fabulous Frannie
 ••• 0:12—Topless doing a stripper routine on stage.
 • 0:24—Brief topless in the shower.

Bouchet, Barbara

Films:

A Global Affair (1964) . . . . Girl
Good Neighbor Sam (1964). . . . . .Receptionist
Sex and the Single Girl (1964) . . . . Frannie
What a Way to Go (1964) . . . . Girl on Plane
In Harm's Way (1965). . . . . Liz Eddington
 • 0:05—Very, very brief right breast waving to a guy
  from the water.
Agent for H.A.R.M. (1966) . . . . .Ava Vestak
Casino Royale (1967; British) . . . . .Moneypenny
Danger Route (1968; British) . . . . Mari
Sweet Charity (1969) . . . . Ursula
Black Belly of the Tarantula (1972; Italian) . . .Maria Zani
Cry of a Prostitute: Love Kills (1975; Italian)
 . . . . .Margie
 • 0:30—Brief left breast, lying in bed with Rico.
 • 0:31—Brief topless in bed, with Rico when he starts
  making love with her.
 •• 0:50—Topless in panties and robe, walking angrily
  around her room.
  0:56—In braless blouse in Bedroom with Tony.
Down the Ancient Staircase (1975; Italian) . . . . Carla
Blood Feast (1976; Italian) . . . . n.a.
Duck in Orange Sauce (1976; Italian) . . . . Patty
Sex with a Smile (1976; Italian)
 . . . . "One for the Money" segment
 ••• 0:50—Topless sitting up in bed with a guy in bed,
  then lying down, wearing glasses.
Death Rage (1978; Italian) . . . . n.a.
Maniac Mansion (1978; Italian) . . . . n.a.
Magazines:
Playboy (Nov 1972) . . . . Sex in Cinema 1972
 • 161—Buns.

Boulting, Ingrid

Films:

The Last Tycoon (1976) . . . . .Kathleen Moore
Deadly Passion (1985) . . . . Martha Greenwood
 • 0:46—Brief buns taking off clothes and jumping into
  pool. Long shot.
 •• 0:47—Topless getting out of pool and kissing Brent
  Huff. Right breast in bed.
 • 0:54—Topless in whirlpool bath with Huff.
 ••• 1:02—Topless, wearing white panties and massaging herself in front of a mirror.
 •• 1:31—Topless taking off clothes and jumping into
  bed with Huff.

Bouquet, Carole

Model for *Chanel* cosmetics.
Films:
That Obscure Object of Desire
(1977; French/Spanish) . . . . .Conchita
••• 0:53—Topless in bedroom.
••• 1:01—Topless in bed with Fernando Rey.
For Your Eyes Only (1981). . . . . Melina Havelock
Bingo Bongo (1983) . . . . Laura
Dream One (1984; British/French) . . . . Rals-Akrai
Too Beautiful for You (1990; French)
. . . . .Florence Barthelemy

Boushel, Joy

Films:
Pick-Up Summer (1979; Canadian) . . . . Sally
••• 0:56—Topless playing pinball, then running around.
Terror Train (1980; Canadian) . . . . Pet
•• 0:49—Topless wearing panties in sleeper room on
train with Mo.
Quest For Fire (1981) . . . . .Tribe Member
Humongous (1982; Canadian) . . . . .Donna Blake
•• 0:09—Topless looking out the window. More topless
in the room in the mirror.
• 0:48—Topless undoing her top to warm up Bert.
Thrillkill (1984) . . . . .Maggie
The Fly (1986) . . . . .Tawny
• 0:54—Very brief topless viewed from below when
Jeff Goldblum pulls her by the arm to get her out of
bed.
Keeping Track (1988) . . . . Judy
Look Who's Talking (1989) . . . . Melissa

• Bowker, Judi

Films:
Brother Sun, Sister Moon (1973). . . . . .Clare
East of Elephant Rock (1976; British) . . . . .n.a.
Clash of the Titans (1981) . . . . Andromeda
• 1:41—Buns and partial side view of right breast get-
ting out of bath. Don't see her face.
The Shooting Party (1985; British). . . . . . . Olivia Lilburn
Miniseries:
Ellis Island (1984) . . . . Georgiana O'Donnell
Anna Karenina (1985). Kitty
Sins (1986) . . . . Natalie Junot
Made for TV Movies:
In This House of Brede (1975). . . . . Joanne

Bowser, Sue

Films:
Stripes (1981) . . . . Mud Wrestler
Doctor Detroit (1983). . . . . Dream Girl
Into the Night (1985) . . . . Girl on Boat
•• 0:24—Topless taking off blouse with Jake on his boat
after Michelle Pfeiffer leaves.
Magazines:
Playboy (Nov 1985) . . . . Sex in Cinema 1985
••• 130—Topless in still from *Into the Night*.

Boyd, Tanya

Films:
Black Shampoo (1976). . . . . .Brenda
Ilsa, Harem Keeper of the Oil Sheiks (1978) . . . . . . Satin
The Happy Hooker Goes Hollywood (1980)
. . . . .Sylvie
• 0:39—Brief topless in jungle room when an older
customer accidentally comes in.
Wholly Moses! (1980) . . . . Princess
Jo Jo Dancer, Your Life Is Calling (1986) . . . . Alicia

Bracci, Teda

Films:
C. C. & Company (1970) .Pig
R.P.M. (1970). . . . . n.a.
The Big Bird Cage (1972) . . . . .Bull Jones
•• 0:15—Topless in front of the guard, Rocco.
• 0:51—Very brief right breast, then left breast during
fight with Pam Grier. Brief left breast standing up in
rice paddy.
The Centerfold Girls (1974). . . . . Rita
• 0:18—Topless taking off her clothes in the living
room in front of everybody.
The Trial of Billy Jack (1974) . . . . Teda
The World's Greatest Lover (1977) . . . . n.a.

• Brackett, Sarah

Films:
The Third Secret (1964; British) . . . . Nurse
Battle Beneath the Earth (1968; British) . . .Meg Webson
Emily (1976; British) . . . . .Margaret
• 0:09—Buns, while looking out the window at Koo
Stark.
The Lords of Discipline (1983) . . . . Mrs. Durrell

• Bradford-Aiton, Lisa

Films:
Screwball Hotel (1988). . . . . Punk Singer
Magazines:
Penthouse (Nov 1987). .Pet
Penthouse (Aug 1988). .Pet

Brady, Janelle

Films:
Class of Nuke 'Em High (1986) . . . . .Chrissy
•• 0:26—Topless sitting on bed in the attic with Warren.
• 0:31—Brief topless scene from 0:26 superimposed
over Warren's nightmare.
Teen Wolf Too (1987). . . . . History Student

Braga, Sonia

Films:
Dona Flor and Her Two Husbands (1978; Brazilian)
. . . . Flor
• 0:13—Buns and brief topless with her husband.
•• 0:15—Topless lying on the bed.
0:17—Buns, getting out of bed.

••• 0:54—Topless making love on the bed with her husband.

•• 0:57—Topless lying on the bed.

••• 1:41—Topless kissing her first husband.

Lady on the Bus (1978; Brazilian) . . . . .n.a.

• 0:11—Brief left breast.

••• 0:12—Topless, then buns, then full frontal nudity in bed getting her slip torn off by her newlywed husband. Long struggle scene.

•• 0:39—Right breast standing with half open dress, then topless lying in bed, then getting into the pool.

••• 0:48—Topless and buns on the beach after picking up a guy on the bus.

• 0:54—Brief topless in bed dreaming.

• 1:02—Brief topless in waterfall with bus driver.

•• 1:05—Topless in cemetery after picking up another guy on the bus.

• 1:13—Topless on the ground with another guy from a bus.

• 1:16—Left breast sitting on sofa while her husband talks.

I Love You (1982; Brazilian). . . . . Maria

a.k.a. Eu Te Amo

••• 0:34—Full frontal nudity making love with Paulo.

•• 0:36—Topless sitting on the edge of the bed.

• 0:49—Topless running around the house teasing Paulo.

•• 0:50—Brief nude in blinking light. Don't see her face.

• 0:53—Topless eating fruit with Paulo.

••• 0:54—Topless wearing white panties in front of windows with Paulo. Long scene.

• 1:03—Left breast standing talking to Paulo.

• 1:10—Left breast talking to Paulo.

• 1:15—Very brief full frontal nudity, several times, in Paulo's flashback in blinking light scene.

••• 1:23—Topless with Paulo during an argument. Dark, but long scene.

•• 1:28—Topless walking around Paulo's place with a gun. Dark.

•• 1:33—Various topless scenes.

Gabriela (1984; Brazilian) . . . . Gabriela

• 0:26—Topless leaning back out the window making love on a table with Marcello Mastroianni.

••• 0:27—Nude, taking a shower outside and cleaning herself up.

• 0:32—Right breast in bed.

•• 0:38—Nude, making love with Mastroianni on the kitchen table.

•• 0:45—Nude, getting in bed with Mastroianni.

1:13—Full frontal nudity, on bed with another man, then getting beat up by Mastroianni.

••• 1:17—Nude, changing clothes in the bedroom.

•• 1:32—Topless and buns making love outside with Mastroianni. Lots of passion!

Kiss of the Spider Woman (1985; U.S./Brazilian)

. . . . Leni/Marta/Spider Woman

The Milagro Beanfield War (1988). . . . . . Ruby Archuleta

Moon Over Parador (1988). . . . . Madonna Mendez

The Rookie (1990) . . . . .Liesl

Made for Cable Movies:

The Last Prostitute (1991; Lifetime) . . . . Loah

Made for Cable TV:

Tales From the Crypt: This'll Kill Ya (1992; HBO) . . . n.a.

Magazines:

Playboy (May 1979). . . . . .Foreign Sex Stars

•• 165—Topless.

Playboy (Nov 1983) . . . . Sex in Cinema 1983

••• 149—Topless.

Playboy (Oct 1984) . . . . The Girls from Brazil

••• 86-91—Nude.

Playboy (Dec 1984) . . . . .Sex Stars of 1984

••• 205—Full frontal nudity leaning against bed.

Playboy (Nov 1985) . . . . Sex in Cinema 1985

• 132—Side view of right breast in scene not used in *Kiss of the Spider Woman*.

Playboy (Dec 1987) . . . . .Sex Stars of 1987

••• 153—Full frontal nudity.

Playboy (Dec 1988) . . . . .Sex Stars of 1988

••• 183—Full frontal nudity leaning against bed.

Playboy's Nudes (Oct 1990) . . . . .Herself

••• 26-27—Full frontal nudity.

Playboy (Sep 1992) . . . . Grapevine

•• 162—Topless under sheer blouse. B&W.

•*Brahms, Penny*

Films:

The Wrong Box (1966; British)

. . . . .Twitering Female on Moor

2001: A Space Odyssey (1968; British/U.S.)

. . . . Stewardess Girl

Hammerhead (1968) . . . . Frieda

Games That Lovers Play (1970). . . . . Constance

Private Screenings.

•• 0:08—Topless outside with a customer.

•• 0:10—Topless again putting dress back on.

Brandt, Brandi

Films:

Wedding Band (1989) . . . . Serena (Gypsy Wedding)

Video Tapes:

Playboy Video Calendar 1989 (1988). . . . November

••• 0:41—Nude.

Glamour Through Your Lens—Outdoor Techniques (1989) . . . . .Herself

0:42—In white lingerie on couch.

Playmates at Play (1990) . . . . Easy Rider

Magazines:

Playboy (Oct 1987) . . . . Playmate

Playboy's Book of Lingerie (Jan 1991) . . . . . .Herself

•• 74—Side of right breast and buns.

•• 98—Topless.

•*Brandy*

Stage name is Jisél.

Video Tapes:

Penthouse Satin & Lace: An Erotic History of Lingerie (1992) . . . . Model

Magazines:
Penthouse (Jan 1992) . . . . Pet of the Year
••• 123-137—Nude.
Penthouse (Sep 1992) . . . . Brandy
••• 150-159—Nude.
Penthouse (Oct 1992) . . . . . .The Seduction of Brandy
••• 99-107—Nude with adult film actress Tori Welles.

Bremmer, Leslee

Films:
Hardbodies (1984) . . . . .Photo Session Hardbody
• 0:02—Topless in the surf when her friends take off her swimsuit top during the opening credits.
•• 0:40—Topless with other topless girls posing for photographs taken by Rounder. She takes off her dress and is wearing a black G-string.
Paradise Motel (1985)
. . . . Uncredited Girl Leaving Room
• 0:38—Topless buttoning her pink sweater, leaving motel room.
School Spirit (1985) . . . . Sandy
• 1:18—Topless on a guy's shoulder in pool. (She's on the right, wearing red swimsuit bottoms.)
My Chauffeur (1986) . . . . Party Girl
1:19—Dancing in yellow outfit at a club. Most of buns.
• 1:24—Buns and brief topless in back of the limousine, taking off her yellow outfit.
• 1:25—Topless sleeping when Penn and Teller leave the limousine.
Reform School Girls (1986)
. . . . Uncredited Shower Girl
•• 0:25—Brief topless in the shower three times. Walking from left to right in the background, full frontal nudity by herself with wet hair, topless walking from left to right.
Another Chance (1989). . . . .Girl in Womanizer's Meeting
Video Tapes:
Best Chest in the West (1984) . . . . Leslee
••• 0:29—In black, two piece swimsuit, then topless and buns.
• 0:32—More topless during judging and winning the 2nd round.
Centerfold Screen Test (1985) . . . . Herself
0:22—Topless under fishnet top. (Practically see-through top.)
•• 0:24—Dancing, wearing the fishnet top and black G-string.
••• 0:28—Closer shot, dancing, while wearing the top.
Best Chest in the West II (1986) . . . . Herself
0:49—Dancing in pink top. Buns, in G-string.
The Girls of Malibu (1986) . . . . Leslee
••• 0:01—In two piece swimsuit, then nude, posing outside.
Starlet Screen Test (1986). . . . . Leslee
••• 0:11—Nude, taking off towel in hot tub.
Best Chest in the U.S. (1987) . . . . Bernadette
• 0:25—Buns in G-string.

Hot Body International: #1 Miss Cancun (1990)
. . . . .Contestant
•• 0:25—Buns in two piece swimsuit.
Starlet Screen Test II (1991) . . . . .Lauren
••• 0:41—Topless and buns, in swimsuit bottom, dancing on stage.
Starlets Exposed! Volume II (1991) . . . . Leslee
(Same as *The Girls of Malibu*.)
••• 0:40—Topless, then nude, taking off two piece swimsuit in garden.

Brennan, Eileen

Films:
The Last Picture Show (1971). . . . . Genevieve
Scarecrow (1973) . . . . Darlene
• 0:27—Brief topless in bed when Gene Hackman takes off her bra and grabs her breasts.
The Sting (1973) . . . . Billie
Daisy Miller (1974) . . . . Mrs. Walker
Hustle (1975). . . . . Paula Hollinger
The Great Smokey Roadblock (1976) . . . . Penelope
Murder by Death (1976) . . . . .Tess Skeffington
The Cheap Detective (1978) . . . . Betty DeBoop
FM (1978) . . . . Mother
Private Benjamin (1980). . . . . Captain Doreen Lewis
Clue (1985) . . . . Mrs. Peacock
The New Adventures of Pippi Longstocking (1988)
. . . . Miss Bannister
Texasville (1990) . . . . Genevieve Morgan
White Palace (1990). . . . . .Judy
I Don't Buy Kisses Anymore (1992) . . . . n.a.
Made for TV Movies:
Deadly Intentions...Again? (1991) . . . . .Charlotte
Taking Back My Life: The Nancy Ziegenmeyer Story
(1992) . . . . Vicky Martin

Brentano, Amy

Films:
Blood Sisters (1986) . . . . .Linda
••• 0:12—Topless, getting out of bed.
•• 0:14—Topless, walking around. Right breast, in bed with Russ. Brief upper half of buns.
Breeders (1986). . . . . Gail
• 0:59—Long shot of buns, getting into the nest.
• 1:07—Topless in nest, throwing her head back.
•• 1:08—Brief topless, writhing around in the nest, then topless, arching her back.
• 1:11—Topless, long shot, just before the nest is destroyed.
Robot Holocaust (1986). . . . . .Irradiated Female
Prime Evil (1987). . . . . Brett
••• 1:13—Topless removing her gown (she's in the middle) with Cathy and Judy.

Bresee, Bobbie

Films:

Mausoleum (1983) . . . . Susan Farrell
- ••• 0:25—Topless and buns wrapping a towel around herself in her bedroom.
- •• 0:26—Topless on the balcony showing herself to the gardener.
- • 0:29—Topless in the garage with the gardener. Brief, dark, hard to see.
- • 0:32—Brief left breast, while kissing Marjoe Gortner.
- • 1:10—Topless in the bathtub talking to Gortner. Long shot.

Armed Response (1986) .Anna
Star Slammer—The Escape (1986) . . . . Marai
Surf Nazis Must Die (1986) . . . . Smeg's Mom
Evil Spawn (1987) . . . . Lynn Roman
- 0:14—Very brief half of right breast in bed with a guy.
- 0:26—In red one piece swimsuit.
- ••• 0:36—Topless in bathroom looking at herself in the mirror, then taking a shower.

Magazines:

Playboy (Jul 1989) . . . . B-Movie Bimbos
- ••• 133—Full frontal nudity leaning on a car.

Brighton, Connie

Video Tapes:

Playboy's Playmate Review 3 (1985) . . . . . Playmate
Playboy Video Centerfold: Kerri Kendall (1990)
. . . . Playmate
- ••• 0:31—Nude.

Magazines:

Playboy (Sep 1982) . . . . Playmate

Brimhall, Cynthia

Films:

Hard Ticket to Hawaii (1987) . . . . .Edy
- •• 0:47—Topless changing out of a dress into a blouse and pants.
- •• 1:33—Topless during the end credits.

Picasso Trigger (1989) .Edy
- •• 0:59—Topless in weight room with a guy.

Guns (1990). . . . . Edy Stark
- 0:26—Buns, in G-string singing and dancing at club.
- •• 0:27—Topless in dressing room.
- 0:53—Buns, in black one piece outfit and stockings, singing in club. Nice legs!

Do or Die (1991). . . . . Edy Stark
- • 0:31—Most of buns, wearing white lingerie outfit, singing and dancing at night.
- ••• 0:36—Topless and buns, making love with Lucas on floor in front of fire.

Video Tapes:

Playboy Video Calendar 1987 (1986) . . . . Playmate
Playboy Video Magazine, Volume 10 (1986)
. . . . Playmate
- ••• 0:53—Nude in still photos, then in the woods after riding motorcycle and then in the desert.

Sexy Lingerie (1988) . . . . Model
Playmates at Play (1990) . . . . Easy Rider

Magazines:

Playboy (Oct 1985) .Playmate
Playboy's Nudes (Oct 1990) . . . . .Herself
- ••• 22—Full frontal nudity.

Playboy's Book of Lingerie (Mar 1991) . . . . .Herself
- • 32—Left breast.

Playboy (Nov 1992) . . . . Sex in Cinema 1992
- ••• 145—Topless in bed with Tony Peck from *Hard Hunted*.

• Brin, Michele

Films:

Secret Games (1991) .Julianne
(Unrated version reviewed.)
(Nude a lot, only the best are listed.)
- •• 0:03—Left breast, while lying in bed with Billy Drago.
- ••• 0:08—Topless and buns, while taking a shower.
- •• 0:09—Topless under sheer white robe, trying to entice Drago.
- ••• 0:34—Topless, sunbathing with the other girls. (She's wearing brown framed sunglasses.)
- ••• 0:38—Topless in bed, making love with Martin Hewitt.
- ••• 0:43—Buns and topless making love in bed with Drago.
- ••• 0:48—Topless, while tied to the bed.
- ••• 0:54—In white bra and panties, then nude taking them off and putting new ones on.
- ••• 1:10—Topless, while lying in bed with Hewitt.
- ••• 1:13—Topless and buns, making love with Hewitt in bathtub.
- •• 1:15—Topless under sheer robe.
- •• 1:32—Buns in G-string, then topless, getting into bed and making love with Drago.

Made for Cable TV:

Dream On: Up All Night (1992; HBO) . . . . .Ariel
- ••• 0:14—Topless, taking off her dress and walking down hallway during Martin's dream.

Brisebois, Danielle

Films:

The Premonition (1976) . . . . Janie
King of the Gypsies (1978) . . . . .Young Tita
Big Bad Mama II (1987) . . . . Billy Jean McClatchie
- ••• 0:12—Topless with Julie McCullough playing in a pond underneath a waterfall.
- 0:36—In a white slip standing at the door talking to McCullough, then talking to Angie Dickinson.

Kill Crazy (1989) . . . . .Libby
- •• 0:39—Topless taking off top to go skinny dipping with Rachel.

TV:

All In the Family (1978-83) . . . . Stephanie Mills
Knots Landing (1983-84) . . . . Mary-Frances Sumner

Brittany, Tally

See: Chanel, Tally.

Broady, Eloise

Films:
Dangerous Love (1988) . . . . Bree
••• 0:06—Topless changing into lingerie in the mirror.
To Die For (1988) . . . . Girl at Party
Troop Beverly Hills (1989) . . . . Starlet at Party
Weekend at Bernie's (1989). . . . . .Tawny
  a.k.a. Hot and Cold
    0:35—Buns in two piece swimsuit, coming into
    Bernie's house to get the keys to the ski boat.
Video Tapes:
Playboy Video Calendar 1989 (1988) . . . .December
••• 0:45—Nude.
Wet and Wild III (1991). . . . . .Model
Playboy Video Playmate Six-Pack 1992 (1992)
. . . . Playmate
Magazines:
Playboy (Apr 1988) . . . . Playmate

Brooke, Sandy

Films:
Bits and Pieces (1985) . . . . Mrs. Talbot
••• 1:03—Topless in bathtub washing herself before the
  killer drowns her. Very brief right breast when struggling.
• 1:09—Brief topless under water in bathtub, dead.
Star Slammer—The Escape (1986) . . . . Taura
••• 0:21—Topless in jail putting a new top on. In braless
  white T-shirt for most of the rest of the film.
•• 1:09—Topless changing into a clean top.
The Terror on Alcatraz (1986) . . . . Mona
• 0:05—Right breast on bed getting burned with a
  cigarette by Frank.
Nightmare Sisters (1987) . . . . Amanda Detweiler
Deep Space (1988) . . . . Woman in House

•Brooks, Cindy

Films:
The Money Pit (1986). . . . . Benny's Girl Friend
It Takes Two (1988). . . . . Leslie
Pass the Ammo (1988) . . . . Debbie
Steel and Lace (1990) . . . . Girl in T-bird
Martial Law (1991) . . . . .Foster's Girl
Magazines:
Playboy (Apr 1985) . . . . Playmate

Brooks, Elisabeth

Films:
The Howling (1981) . . . . Marsha
•• 0:46—Full frontal nudity taking off her robe in front
  of a campfire.
• 0:48—Topless sitting on Bill by the fire.
Deep Space (1988) . . . . Mrs. Ridley
The Forgotten One (1989) . . . . .Carla

TV:
  Doctors' Hospital (1975-76). . Nurse Connie Kimbrough
Magazines:
Playboy (Nov 1980) . . . . Sex in Cinema 1980
••• 174—Full frontal nudity.

Brooks, Randi

Films:
Looker (1981) . . . . .Girl in Bikini
Deal of the Century (1983) . . . . .Ms. Della Rosa
The Man with Two Brains (1983) . . . . .Fran
•• 1:11—Brief topless showing Steve Martin her breasts
  in front of the hotel. Buns, changing in the hotel
  room, then wearing black see-through negligee.
Tightrope (1984). . . . . .Jamie Cory
••• 0:20—Topless taking off her robe and getting into
  the spa.
  0:24—Buns, dead in the spa while Clint Eastwood
  looks at her.
Hamburger—The Motion Picture (1986)
. . . . Mrs. Vunk
•• 0:52—Brief topless in helicopter with a guy.
Cop (1988) . . . . Jeanie Pratt
  0:32—In a bra making love in her kitchen with James
  Woods.
TV:
Wizards and Warriors (1983) . . . . Witch Bethel
The Last Precinct (1986). . . . . Officer Mel Brubaker
Magazines:
Playboy (Nov 1983) . . . . Sex in Cinema 1983
• 150—See-through negligee.
Playboy (Dec 1983) . . . . .Sex Stars of 1983
• 210—Side view of right breast and buns.

Brown, Blair

Films:
The Choirboys (1977) . . . . Mrs. Lyles
Altered States (1980) . . . . .Emily Jessup
• 0:10—Brief left breast making love with William Hurt
  in red light from an electric heater.
•• 0:34—Topless lying on her stomach during Hurt's
  mushroom induced hallucination.
  1:39—Buns, sitting in hallway with Hurt after the
  transformations go away.
One Trick Pony (1980) . . . . Marion
Continental Divide (1981) . . . . Nell
A Flash of Green (1984) . . . . .Catherine "Kat" Hubble
• 1:30—Very brief right breast moving around in bed
  with Ed Harris.
Strapless (1990) . . . . Dr. Lillian Hempel
Made for Cable TV:
Days and Nights of Molly Dodd . . . . Molly Dodd
Miniseries:
Wheels (1978) . . . . .Barbara Lipton
Space (1985) . . . . .Penny Hardesty Pope
Made for TV Movies:
Hands of a Stranger (1987) . . . . Diane Benton
Extreme Close-Up (1990). . . . . n.a.
Those Secrets (1992) . . . . n.a.

TV:
Captains and the Kings (1976)
. . . . Elizabeth Healey Hennessey
Days and Nights of Molly Dodd (1987-88)
. . . . Molly Dodd

• *Brown, Juanita*

Films:
Caged Heat (1974) . . . . .Maggie
  a.k.a. Renegade Girls
   • 0:25—Topless in shower scene.
Foxy Brown (1974) . . . . .Claudia

Brown, Julie

Comedienne.
Singer–"The Homecoming Queen's Got a Gun."
Not to be confused with MTV Video Jockey "Downtown"
Julie Brown.
Films:
Any Which Way You Can (1980) . . . . .Candy
Bloody Birthday (1980) . . . . Beverly
  ••• 0:13—Dancing in red bra, then topless while two
    boys peek through hole in the wall, then buns. Nice,
    long scene.
    0:48—In bedroom wearing red bra.
    1:03—In bedroom again in the red bra.
Police Academy II: Their First Assignment (1985)
. . . . Chloe
Earth Girls are Easy (1989). . . . . .Candy
Timebomb (1990). . . . Uncredited Waitress at Al's Diner
The Spirit of '76 (1991). . . . . Ms. Liberty
Shakes the Clown (1992) . . . . .n.a.
Made for Cable Movies:
Medusa: Dare to be Truthful (1991; Showtime)
. . . . Medusa
Made for Cable TV:
Just Say Julie . . . . .Hostess
TV:
The Edge (1992-) . . . . Cast Member

• *Brown, Tricia*

Films:
Vamp (1986) . . . . Candi
   • 0:32—Brief topless doing strip tease.
Phantom Empire (1987) . . . . Cavegirl
Hollywood Chainsaw Hookers (1988) . . . . Ilsa
  •• 0:37—Topless while Jack is tied up in bed.

• *Browne, Suzanne*

Films:
The Last Boy Scout (1991) . . . . Dancer
   • 0:19—Brief topless and buns while dancing in club.
The Bikini Carwash Company (1992) . . . . . . .Sunny
(Unrated version reviewed.)
   • 0:15—Brief topless when Stanley steals her bikini
    top.
  •• 0:25—Topless, washing windshield and side win-
    dow.
  ••• 0:26—More topless while window washing.

  •• 0:30—Topless during water fight.
  •• 0:31—Topless at car wash.
  •• 0:35—Topless running after a guy who stole her bi-
    kini top.
  ••• 0:46—Topless and buns in G-string, hand washing a
    customer with Rita.
  ••• 0:47—Topless and buns, dancing inside car wash.
  •• 0:53—Topless outside at car wash.
  ••• 1:02—Nude, soaped up in car wash with Melissa
    and Rita.
  ••• 1:12—Topless, posing for photos.
  •• 1:15—Topless when Stanley takes her top off.

Bruce, Andi

Films:
Summer's Games (1987). . . . . .News Anchor
    0:12—Brief right breast, while turning around to
    look at monitor.
   • 0:42—Topless turning around to look at the moni-
    tor.
Screwball Hotel (1988). . . . . .Bobbi Jo
Magazines:
Penthouse (Aug 1987) . . . . .Pet

• *Bryant, D'Andrea*

Films:
Nothing But Trouble (1991) . . . . .Party Girl
Video Tapes:
Sexy Lingerie II (1990) . . . . Model
Magazines:
Playboy's Book of Lingerie (Mar 1991) . . . . .Herself
  •• 11—Buns.
  ••• 79—Topless.
Playboy's Book of Lingerie (Sep 1991) . . . . . .Herself
   • 20-21—Buns.
Playboy's Book of Lingerie (Nov 1991) . . . . .Herself
  ••• 62-63—Topless.
Playboy's Book of Lingerie (Jan 1992) . . . . .Herself
Playboy's Book of Lingerie (Mar 1992). . . . . .Herself
  ••• 28—Buns and left breast.
Playboy's Book of Lingerie (May 1992) . . . . .Herself
  ••• 73—Topless.

Bryant, Pamela Jean

Films:
Don't Answer the Phone (1979) . . . . Sue Ellen
  •• 0:28—Topless in the killer's photo studio when he
    rips her jacket off and kills her.
H.O.T.S. (1979) . . . . Teri Lynn
   • 1:33—Topless during football game.
Separate Ways (1979) . . . . Cocktail Waitress
Looker (1981) .Reston Girl
Lunch Wagon (1981) . . . . Marcy
  •• 0:04—Topless changing tops in room in gas station
    with Rosanne Katon while a guy watches through
    key hole.
   • 0:55—Left breast, several times, in van with Bif.

Private Lessons (1981)................... Joyce
- • 0:03—Very brief right breast, changing in the house while Billy and his friend peep from outside.

Made for TV Movies:
B.J. and the Bear (1978) ....n.a.

Magazines:
Playboy (Sep 1977)............. Girls of the Big Ten
- •• 148—Topless.

Playboy (Apr 1978)................... Playmate
Playboy (Nov 1980) .... The World of Playboy
- ••• 12—Full frontal nudity.

• *Buchanan, Yvette*

Films:
Night Eyes (1990)..................... Baby Doll
(Unrated version reviewed.)
- • 0:07—Brief left breast, then topless making love in bathroom with Ronee.

The Malibu Beach Vampires (1991)
.... The Rocket Scientist
Roots of Evil (1991)...................... Hooker
(Unrated version reviewed.)

• *Buchfellner, Ursula*

Films:
Popcorn and Ice Cream (1978; West German)
.............................Yvonne
- ••• 0:30—Nude with the hotel manager, Vivi and Bea.
- • 0:40—Topless in open dress at the disco.

Magazines:
Playboy (Oct 1979)................... Playmate
Playboy's Nudes (Oct 1990).............. Herself
- ••• 77—Full frontal nudity.

Buckman, Tara

Films:
Rollercoaster (1977) .... Coaster Attendant
Hooper (1978) ....Debbie
The Cannonball Run (1981) ....Jill
Silent Night, Deadly Night (1984) .... Mother (Ellie)
- • 0:12—Brief right breast twice when the killer dressed as Santa Claus, rips her blouse open. Topless lying dead with slit throat.
- • 0:18—Very, very brief topless during Billy's flashback.
- • 0:43—Brief topless a couple of times again in another of Billy's flashbacks.

Never Too Young to Die (1986)..... Sacrificed Punkette
Silent Night, Deadly Night, Part 2 (1986)
.............................Mother
- • 0:09—Very brief right breast, with Santa Claus during flashback.
- • 0:14—Very brief topless on ground during flashback.
- • 0:22—Very, very brief blurry topless during flashback.
- • 0:47—Very, very brief topless during flashback.

Terminal Exposure (1988) ....n.a.

The Loves of a Wall Street Woman (1989)
.... Brenda Baxter
Private Screenings.
- • 0:00—Topless taking a shower, opening the door and getting a towel.
- •• 0:06—Topless changing clothes in locker room in black panties. Nice legs!
- ••• 0:18—Topless in bed making love with Alex.
- •• 0:31—Topless in bed with Alex making love.
- •• 0:40—Topless in black panties dressing in locker room.
- • 0:46—Brief topless lying in bed, talking to her lover, side view of buns. Long shot.
- ••• 1:16—Topless making love in bed with Alex.

The Marilyn Diaries (1990) ....Jane
Private Screenings.
- •• 0:53—Topless and buns, taking off robe and getting into bathtub. Left breast, in tub reading diary.
- •• 0:54—Topless in and getting out of tub. Very brief lower frontal nudity.
- •• 1:27—Topless in bathtub talking with John.

Object of Desire (1991) ....Angie
Private Screenings.
- • 0:12—Topless, leaning up on massage table.
- •• 0:14—Topless, getting dressed so Derrick can see.
- •• 0:23—Topless, making love with Derrick in her dressing room.
- ••• 0:28—Topless in bathtub with Derrick.
- • 0:43—Right breast, while making love in bed with Derrick.
- • 0:50—Side view of buns, while lying in bed.
- •• 0:51—Right breast, while sitting up in bed, then full frontal nudity.
- ••• 0:55—Topless, opening her blouse in Steve's office in front of him.
- ••• 1:09—Full frontal nudity, posing for photographer in studio. Also side view of his buns.
- • 1:12—Brief topless in magazine photos.
- ••• 1:18—Topless changing clothes in dressing room.

Xtro 2, The Second Encounter (1991)
.... Dr. Julie Casserly
Round Trip to Heaven (1992)............... Phyllis

Bujold, Genevieve

Films:
King of Hearts (1966; French/Italian) ...... Colombine
The Thief of Paris (1967; French/Italian)..... Charlotte
Anne of the Thousand Days (1969; British)
.... Anne Boleyn
The Trojan Women (1972)............... Cassandra
Kamouraska (1973; Canadian/French) ..... Elisabeth
Nude in long shot.
Earthquake (1974) ....Denise
Obsession (1976)
.... Elizabeth Courtland/Sandra Portinari
Swashbuckler (1976) .... Jane Barnet
- • 1:00—Very brief side view nude, diving from the ship into the water. Long shot, don't really see anything.

• 1:01—Buns and brief side of left breast seen from under water.
Coma (1978) . . . . Dr. Susan Wheeler
0:03—Nude behind frosted glass shower door, so you can't see anything.
Murder by Decree (1979) . . . . Annie Crook
Last Flight of Noah's Ark (1980) . . . . Bernadette Lafleur
Monsignor (1982) . . . . .Clara
••• 1:05—Topless getting undressed and climbing into bed while talking to Christopher Reeve.
Choose Me (1984) . . . . Dr. Love
Tightrope (1984) . . . . Beryl Thibodeaux
Trouble in Mind (1986) . . . . Wanda
Dead Ringers (1988) . . . . Claire Niveau
•• 0:49—Very brief right breast in bed with Jeremy Irons, then brief topless reaching for pills and water. Dark, hard to see.
The Moderns (1988) . . . . .Libby Valentin
Paper Wedding (1991; Canadian) . . . . Claire
Made for TV Movies:
Red Earth, White Earth (1989) . . . . Madeline

•Burch, Tracey
Films:
Marked for Death (1990) . . . . Sexy Girl #1
• 0:39—Brief topless on bed with Jimmy when Steven Seagal bursts into the room. (She's the blonde.)
Dance with Death (1991) . . . . Whitney
••• 0:03—Topless and buns in G-string, dancing on stage.
••• 0:05—More topless and buns while dancing.

Burger, Michele
Films:
Party Plane (1988) . . . . Carol
• 0:31—Topless, squirting whipped cream on herself for her audition.
•• 0:38—Topless doing a strip tease routine on the plane.
••• 1:02—Topless mud wrestling with Renee on the plane.
• 1:09—Topless in the cockpit, covered with mud.
•• 1:17—Topless in serving cart.
Payback (1988) . . . . Laura
• 0:08—Brief topless sitting up in bed just before getting shot, then brief topless twice, dead in bed.
Roadhouse (1989) . . . . .Strip Joint Girl
Ninja Academy (1990) . . . . Nudist

•Burgoyne, Victoria
Films:
Death Ship (1980; Canadian) . . . . .Lori
Stealing Heaven (1988; British/Yugoslavian)
. . . . Prostitute
• 0:28—Left breast, taking off her top. Side view of right breast and buns.
•• 0:29—Topless lying in bed.

Burkett, Laura
Films:
Avenging Angel (1985) . . . . .Blonde Hooker
Daddy's Boys (1988) . . . . Christie
••• 0:17—Topless in room with Jimmy.
•• 0:20—Left breast, while making love with Jimmy in bed again.
• 0:21—Brief topless during Jimmy's nightmare.
• 0:43—Brief topless in bed again, then getting dressed.
• 0:53—Brief topless in bed consoling Jimmy.
• 1:11—Left breast, while in bed with Jimmy.
Rush Week (1989) . . . . Rebecca Winters
•• 0:43—Topless in the shower, talking to Jonelle.
• 0:55—Brief topless getting dressed after modeling session.

Burns, Bobbi
Films:
New York Nights (1981) . . . . The Authoress
•• 0:16—Topless on the couch outside with the rock star, then topless in bed.
I, the Jury (1982) .Sheila Kyle
Q (1982) . . . . Sunbather
•• 0:06—Topless taking off swimsuit top and rubbing lotion on herself.

•Burns, Catherine
Films:
Last Summer (1969) . . . . Rhoda
• 1:31—Very brief topless struggling with Stacy, Peter and Dan. Long shot.
Me, Natalie (1969) . . . . .Hester
Red Sky at Morning (1971) . . . . Marcia Davidson

•Burns, Janell
Video Tapes:
Hot Body International: #3 Lingerie Special (1992) . . . . .Contestant
•• 0:31—Buns in one piece body suit.
Hot Body International: #5 Miss Acapulco (1992) . . . . .Contestant
••• 0:14—Topless and buns in swimsuit in pool. Topless applying flowers to her breasts, then taking them off.
•• 0:16—Topless taking off bikini top outside next to pool.

•Burrell, Gretchen
Films:
Pretty Maids All in a Row (1971) . . . . .Marjorie
• 0:05—Partial side of right breast, in office with Rock Hudson.
• 0:07—Topless on the couch in Hudson's office.
Magazines:
Playboy (Apr 1971) . . . . Vadim's "Pretty Maids"
••• 154—Topless.

Burstyn, Ellen

Films:
Goodbye Charlie (1964) . . . . .n.a.
The Last Picture Show (1971) . . . . .Lois Farrow
King of Marvin Gardens (1972) . . . . Sally
• 0:50—Brief topless, while kneeling on the floor and
turning around to shoot squirt guns.
The Exorcist (1973) .Chris
Harry and Tonto (1974) . . . . Shirley
Alice Doesn't Live Here Anymore (1975) . . . . Alice Hyatt
(Academy Award for Best Actress.)
A Dream of Passion (1978) . . . . Brenda
Same Time Next Year (1978). . . . . .Doris
Resurrection (1980). . . . . .Edna McCauley
The Ambassador (1984) . . . . Alex Hacker
••• 0:06—Topless opening her robe to greet her lover.
••• 0:07—Brief topless making love in bed.
••• 0:29—Topless in a movie while her husband, Robert
Mitchum, watches.
Twice in a Lifetime (1985). . . . . Kate
Hanna's War (1988) . . . . Katalin Senesh
Dying Young (1991) . . . . .Mrs. O'Neil
Made for TV Movies:
Pack of Lies (1987) . . . . .n.a.
Taking Back My Life: The Nancy Ziegenmeyer Story
(1992). . . . . .Wilma
TV:
The Iron Horse (1967-68) . . . . .Julie Parsons
The Ellen Burstyn Show (1986-88) . . . . Ellen Brewer

• Bush, Jovita

Films:
The Cheerleaders (1973). . . . . .n.a.
Fox Style (1974) . . . . Bonnie
• 1:02—Brief right breast while in dressing room,
changing clothes.

• Butler, Bridget

Films:
Sunset Heat (1991) . . . . Lady in New York
(Unrated version reviewed.)
• 0:00—Buns, lying in bed.
• 0:01—Buns, when Michael Paré takes off her shirt.
Buns and partial left breast lying on him in bed.
Sunset Strip (1992) . . . . Candice

Butler, Cher

Video Tapes:
Wet and Wild (1989). . . . . .Model
Playmates at Play (1990) . . . . .Bareback
Magazines:
Playboy (Aug 1985) . . . . Playmate

• Buxbaum, Ingrid

Films:
Stars and Bars (1988) . . . . Photographer
Made for Cable Movies:

Traveling Man (1989; HBO) . . . . .Uncredited Salesgirl
••• 0:05—Topless and buns while wearing G-string,
dancing during sales meeting.

Byrd-Nethery, Miriam

Films:
Lies (1984; British) . . . . n.a.
The Offspring (1986) . . . . Eileen Burnside
• 0:26—Topless in bathtub filled with ice while her
husband tries to kill her with an ice pick.
• 0:29—Very brief right breast, dead in bathtub while
her husband is downstairs.
Summer Heat (1987) . . . . Aunt Patty
Walk Like a Man (1987) . . . . Toy Store Clerk
Stepfather 2 (1989) . . . . .Sally Jenkins
Leatherface: The Texas Chainsaw Massacre III (1990)
. . . . Mama
The Raven Red Kiss-Off (1990) . . . . Motel Manager
TV:
Mr. T and Tina (1976) . . . . Miss Llewellyn

Byrne, Patti T.

Films:
Fuzz (1972) . . . . .Abigail
Night Call Nurses (1972) . . . . Barbara
a.k.a. Young LA Nurses 2
•• 0:59—Topless several times in bed with the Doctor.

• Byrnes, Maureen

Films:
Hurry Up, Or I'll Be 30 (1973) . . . . .Flo
Sugar Cookies (1973) . . . . Dola
•• 0:37—Right breast while Gus is on top of her, then
topless and buns.
Goin' South (1978) . . . . .Mrs. Warren

• Byun, Susan

Films:
Crime Lords (1990) . . . . .Monahan
•• 1:06—Left breast, then right breast, while making
out with Wayne Crawford on the couch.
Video Tapes:
Inside Out 4 (1992) . . . . . .Lee Anne/Three on a Match
(Unrated version reviewed.)
••• 0:58—Topless, changing blouse in the bathroom.

• Cabasa, Lisa Ann

Films:
Wild at Heart (1990) . . . . Reindeer Dancer
•• 0:30—Topless standing while Mr. Reindeer talks on
the phone. More topless dancing in front of him.
Made for Cable Movies:
Lies of the Twins (1991; USA). . . . . Caryn

Cable, Tawnni

Video Tapes:
Playboy Video Calendar 1990 (1989). . . . . . . March
••• 0:13—Nude.

Playboy Video Centerfold: Tawnni Cable (1990)
. . . . Playmate
••• 0:00—Nude throughout.
Playmates at Play (1990) . . . . Gotta Dance
Playboy Playmates in Paradise (1992) . . . Playmate
Magazines:
Playboy (Jun 1989) . . . . Playmate
Playboy's Nudes (Oct 1990). . . . . Herself
••• 70—Full frontal nudity.
Playboy's Book of Lingerie (Jan 1991) . . . . . . Herself
••• 13—Full frontal nudity.
Playboy's Book of Lingerie (Mar 1991) . . . . . Herself
••• 12—Full frontal nudity.
Playboy's Book of Lingerie (May 1992) . . . . . Herself
••• 59—Topless.
Playboy's Book of Lingerie (Jul 1992) . . . . . . Herself
•• 59—Topless.

Cadell, Ava
Films:
Happy Housewives . . . . Schoolgirl
　0:39—Buns, getting caught by the Squire and get-
　ting spanked.
Spaced Out (1980; British) . . . . Partha
•• 0:41—Left breast making love on bed with Cliff.
•• 0:42—Nude wrestling on bed with Cliff.
• 0:43—Brief left breast lying in bed alone.
•• 1:08—Topless sitting on bed.
Smokey and the Bandit III (1983) . . . . Blond
Commando (1985). . . . . Girl in Bed
• 0:46—Very brief topless three times in bed when Ar-
　nold Schwarzenegger knocks a guy through the mo-
　tel door into her room.
Jungle Warriors (1985) . . . . Didi Belair
• 0:50—Brief topless getting yellow top ripped open
　by a bad guy.
Not of This Earth (1988) . . . . Second Hooker
•• 0:41—Topless in cellar with Paul just before getting
　killed with two other hookers. Wearing a gold dress.
Do or Die (1991). . . . . Ava
•• 0:20—Buns and brief topless, getting dressed in mo-
　tor home. Lots of buns shots, wearing swimsuit.
Made for Cable TV:
Pillow Previews . . . . Hostess
Magazines:
Playboy (Jun 1989) . . . . Grapevine
　187—Buns, on bear skin rug in B&W photo.

Caffaro, Cheri
Films:
Ginger (1970). . . . . Ginger
The Abductors (1971). Ginger
A Place Called Today (1972) . . . . . . Cindy Cartwright
•• 0:14—Full frontal nudity covered with oil or some-
　thing writhing around on the bed.
• 1:21—Brief side view of right breast undressing in
　the bathroom.
• 1:23—Brief full frontal nudity getting kidnapped by
　two guys.

•• 1:30—Nude when they take off the blanket.
• 1:35—Brief topless just before getting killed.
Girls Are For Loving (1973) . . . . Ginger
Savage Sisters (1974) . . . . Jo Turner
Too Hot To Handle (1975) . . . . Samantha Fox
•• 0:06—Topless wearing a black push-up bra and
　buns in black G-string.
• 0:13—Full frontal nudity lying on boat.
••• 0:39—Topless making love in bed with Dominco.
••• 0:55—Full frontal nudity taking off clothes and lying
　in bed.
• 1:06—Brief left breast in bed with Dominco.
Magazines:
Playboy (Nov 1972) . . . . Sex in Cinema 1972
• 168—Left breast, lit with red light in a photo from *A
　Place Called Today.*
Playboy (Dec 1972) . . . . Sex Stars of 1972
••• 216—Frontal nudity.
Playboy (Nov 1973) . . . . Sex in Cinema 1973
••• 156-157—Full frontal nudity.

• Cagan, Andrea
Films:
Captain Milkshake (1970) . . . . Melissa
The Hot Box (1972). Bunny
•• 0:16—Topless cleaning herself off in stream behind
　Ellie and getting out.
• 0:21—Topless sleeping in hammock. (She's the third
　girl from the front, stretching.)
••• 0:45—Topless in stream while bathing with the oth-
　er three girls.
Teenager (1975). . . . . n.a.

Calabrese, Gina
Films:
Goin' All the Way (1981) . . . . n.a.
•• 0:12—Left breast, in the girls' locker room shower.
　Standing on the left.
The Vals (1982) . . . . Annie
• 0:04—Topless changing clothes in bedroom with
　three of her friends. Long shot, hard to see.
• 0:15—Right breast, while making love with a guy at
　a party.
　0:32—In black bra with her friends in a store dress-
　ing room.

Cameron, Cissie
See: Colpitts-Cameron, Cissie.

Cameron, Joanna
Films:
B.S. I Love You (1971) . . . . Marilyn Michele
　(Not available on video tape.)
Pretty Maids All in a Row (1971) . . . . Yvonne
TV:
　Isis (1975-78). . . . . Isis

51

Camp, Colleen

Films:
Smile (1974) . . . . Connie Thompson
    0:47—Side profile of right breast and buns in dress-
    ing room while Little Bob is outside taking pictures.
The Swinging Cheerleaders (1974) . . . . Mary Ann
Fox Fire (1976) . . . . .n.a.
a.k.a. Fox Force
Death Game, The Seducers (1977) . . . . Donna
a.k.a. Mrs. Manning's Weekend
    0:16—Buns, in spa with Sondra Locke trying to get
    George in with them.
    • 0:47—Brief topless jumping up and down on the
    bed while George is tied up.
    •• 1:16—Topless behind stained glass door taunting
    George. Hard to see.
Cat in the Cage (1978) . . . . Gilda Riener
    • 0:36—Very brief left breast twice, while making love
    in bed with Bruce.
Apocalypse Now (1979) . . . . Playmate
The Game of Death (1979) . . . . Anne Morris
Cloud Dancer (1980) . . . . Cindy
    1:02—In bra, driving a convertible car while Joseph
    Bottoms flies a plane over her.
The Deadly Games (1980). . . . . Randy
They All Laughed (1981) . . . . Christy Miller
The Seduction (1982) . . . . Robin
Smokey and the Bandit III (1983) . . . . Dusty Trails
Valley Girl (1983) . . . . Sarah Richman
Doin' Time (1984). . . . . Catlett
The Joy of Sex (1984) . . . . Liz Sampson
Clue (1985). . . . . Yvette
D.A.R.Y.L. (1985). . . . . Elaine
Police Academy II: Their First Assignment (1985)
    . . . . Kirkland
The Rosebud Beach Hotel (1985) . . . . Tracy
    0:07—In white lingerie in hotel room with Peter Sco-
    lari.
    0:28—In black one piece swimsuit on lounge chair,
    then walking on the beach.
Police Academy 4: Citizens on Patrol (1987)
    . . . . Mrs. Kirkland-Tackleberry
Walk Like a Man (1987). . . . . .Rhonda
Illegally Yours (1988). . . . . Molly Gilbert
Track 29 (1988; British) . . . . .Arlanda
Wicked Stepmother (1989) . . . . Jenny
My Blue Heaven (1990). . . . . .Margaret Snow
Wayne's World (1992). . . . . Mrs. Vanderhoff
Made for TV Movies:
Addicted to his Love (1988) . . . . .Ellie Snyder
Backfield in Motion (1991) . . . . Laurie
Magazines:
Playboy (Oct 1979) . . . ."Apocalypse" Finally
    ••• 118-119—Topless.
Playboy (Nov 1979) . . . . Sex in Cinema 1979
    • 175—Side view of right breast.

• Campbell, Nell

Films:
Lisztomania (1975; British) . . . . Olga
    ••• 1:04—Topless in bed several times with Roger Dal-
    trey when Ringo Starr comes in.
    •• 1:06—Topless in bed, sitting up and drinking.
    ••• 1:07—More topless in bed with a gun after Starr
    leaves.
The Rocky Horror Picture Show (1975; British)
    . . . . .Columbia
    • 1:17—Top of breasts popping out of her blouse dur-
    ing song and dance on stage.
Journey Among Women (1977; Australian) . . . . . . Meg
Pink Floyd The Wall (1982). . . . . .Groupie

Cannon, Dyan

Films:
Such Good Friends (1971) . . . . Julie Messinger
    (Not available on video tape.)
    Dyan's head was composited over a different nude body
    for a close-up of a Polaroid photograph.

• Cantrell, Cady

Video Tapes:
Playboy Video Calendar 1993 (1992). . . . . . . .May
Playboy Video Centerfold: Cady Cantrell (1992)
    . . . . Playmate
Playboy Video Playmate Six-Pack 1992 (1992)
    . . . . Playmate
Wet and Wild IV (1992) . . . . Model
Magazines:
Playboy's Book of Lingerie (Mar 1991). . . . . .Herself
    ••• 26—Topless.
Playboy (Apr 1992) . . . . Playmate
    ••• 90-101—Nude.

Capri, Ahna

Films:
Company of Killers (1970) . . . . Mary Jane Smythe
Darker than Amber (1970). . . . . Del
Payday (1972) . . . . Mayleen
    • 0:20—Left breast in bed sleeping, then right breast
    with Rip Torn.
    ••• 0:21—Topless sitting up in bed smoking a cigarette
    and talking to Torn. Long scene.
Enter the Dragon (1973) . . . . Tania
    • 0:47—Very brief left breast three times in open
    blouse in bed with John Saxon.
The Specialist (1975) . . . . Londa Wyeth
    ••• 0:10—Topless, while in bed, talking on the phone.
    ••• 0:28—Topless on couch, posing for Bert.
    •• 1:09—Topless, sitting up in bed and putting robe
    on.

Cara, Irene

Films:
Aaron Loves Angela (1975) . . . . Angela
Sparkle (1976) . . . . Sparkle

Fame (1980) . . . . Coco
   1:16—In leotard, dancing and talking to Hillary.
   • 1:57—Brief topless during "audition" on a B&W TV
    monitor.
D.C. Cab (1983) . . . . Herself
City Heat (1984) . . . . Ginny Lee
Certain Fury (1985) . . . . Tracy
   0:32—Getting undressed to take a shower. Very brief
   side views of left breast.
   0:35—Very brief topless in shower after Tatum
   O'Neal turns on the kitchen faucet. Hard to see because of the shower door.
   •• 0:36—Frontal nudity and side view of buns, behind
   shower door while Sniffer comes into the bathroom.
   •• 0:39—Topless several times when Sniffer tries to
   rape her and she fights back.
   • 0:41—Buns, kneeling on floor. Overhead view.
Killing 'Em Softly (1985) . . . . n.a.
Caged in Paradiso (1989) . . . . Eva
   In two piece swimsuit a lot.
Miniseries:
Roots: The Next Generation (1979)
. . . . Bertha Palmer Haley

Cardan, Christina
Films:
Chained Heat (1983; U.S./German) . . . . Miss King
Glitch (1988) . . . . Non SAG
   • 0:47—Brief topless in spa taking off her swimsuit
   top.

• Cardone, Nathalie
Films:
Drole D'Endroit Pour Une Recontre (1988; French)
. . . . Sylvie
The Little Thief (1989; French) . . . . Mauricette
a.k.a. La Petite Voleuse
   •• 1:19—Topless in convent arguing with a nun, then
   getting a shot.

• Carides, Gia
Films:
Bliss (1985; Australian) . . . . Lucy Joy
   • 1:25—Brief topless during nightmare. Cockroaches
   crawl out of cut between her breasts. Pretty gross.
   (The cockroaches—not her.)
Backlash (1986; Australian) . . . . Nikki Iceton
TV:
Ultraman: Towards the Future
   (1990; Australian/Japanese) . . . . Jean Echo

Carl, Kitty
Films:
Your Three Minutes Are Up (1973) . . . . Susan
The Centerfold Girls (1974) . . . . Sandi
   •• 0:45—Topless taking off her top while sitting on the
   bed with Perry.
   0:51—Topless on the beach, dead. Long shot, hard
   to see.

Kitty Can't Help It (1975) . . . . n.a.
Carhops (1980) . . . . n.a.

Carlisi, Olimpia
Films:
Catch-22 (1970) . . . . Luciana
   • 1:04—Topless lying in bed talking with Alan Arkin.
Casanova (1976; Italian). . . . . Isabella
The Tragedy of a Ridiculous Man (1981; Italian)
. . . . Chiromat
Rendez-Vous (1986; French). . . . . n.a.

Carlisle, Anne
Films:
Liquid Sky (1984). . . . . Margaret/Jimmy
Perfect Strangers (1984) . . . . .Sally
   • 0:34—Left breast, while making love in bed with
   Johnny.
Desperately Seeking Susan (1985) . . . . Victoria
Suicide Club (1988) . . . . Catherine
Magazines:
Playboy (Sep 1984) . . . . Cult Queen
   •• 80-85—Nude.
Playboy (Dec 1984) . . . . .Sex Stars of 1984
   • 203—Right breast and lower frontal nudity, stand-
   ing in bra, garter belt and stockings.

Carlson, Karen
Films:
Shame, Shame, Everybody Knows Her Name (1969)
. . . . Susan Barton
The Student Nurses (1970) . . . . .Phred
  a.k.a. Young LA Nurses
   • 0:08—Topless in bed with the wrong guy.
   0:19—In bra, on sofa with Dr. Jim Casper.
   ••• 0:50—In bed with Jim, topless and buns getting out,
   then topless sitting in chair. Long scene.
   • 1:02—Brief topless in bed.
The Candidate (1972) . . . . Nancy McKay
Black Oak Conspiracy (1977) . . . . Lucy
Matilda (1978). . . . . Kathleen Smith
The Octagon (1980) . . . . .Justine
Fleshburn (1984) . . . . Shirley Pinter
TV:
Dallas (1987) . . . . Mrs. Scottfield

Carlton, Hope Marie
Films:
Hard Ticket to Hawaii (1987) . . . . .Taryn
   •• 0:07—Topless taking a shower outside while talking
   to Dona Speir.
   ••• 0:23—Topless in the spa with Speir looking at diamonds they found.
   ••• 0:40—Topless and buns on the beach making love
   with her boyfriend, Jimmy John.
   •• 1:33—Topless during the end credits.
A Nightmare on Elm Street 4: The Dream Master
   (1988) . . . . .Pin-Up Girl
   • 0:21—Brief topless swimming in a waterbed.

Slaughterhouse Rock (1988) . . . . . . .Krista Halpern
- 0:09—Brief right breast, taking off her top in bedroom with her boyfriend.
- •• 0:49—Topless, getting raped by Richard as he turns into a monster.

Terminal Exposure (1988). . . . . .Christie
- ••• 1:11—Topless in bathtub licking ice cream off a guy.

How I Got Into College (1989) . . . .Game Show Hostess

Picasso Trigger (1989). . . . . Taryn
0:17—In white lingerie on boat with Dona Speir.
- ••• 0:56—Topless and buns in spa with a guy.

Savage Beach (1989) . . . . Taryn
0:06—Almost topless in spa with the three other women.
- 0:32—Topless changing clothes in airplane with Dona Speir.
- •• 0:48—Nude, going for a swim on the beach with Speir.

Round Numbers (1990) .Mitzi
Side Out (1990) . . . . .Vanna
Bloodmatch (1991). . . . . Connie Angel
Ghoulies III, Ghoulies Go To College (1991) . . . . . . .n.a.
Video Tapes:
Playboy Video Magazine, Volume 9 . . . . . Playmate
Playmate Playoffs . . . . Playmate
Playboy Video Centerfold: Teri Weigel (1986)
. . . . Playmate
Sexy Lingerie (1988) . . . . .Model
Playmates at Play (1990) . . . . .Flights of Fancy
Magazines:
Playboy (Jul 1985). . . . . Playmate
Playboy's Book of Lingerie (Mar 1991) . . . . . Herself
- 34—Right breast.
Playboy's Book of Lingerie (Sep 1991) . . . . . Herself
- 8—Side of right breast.
Playboy's Book of Lingerie (Jul 1992) . . . . . . Herself
- •• 32-33—Lower nudity.

• *Carmack, Cody*
Films:
Affairs of the Heart (1992). . . . . .Itchy
Private Screenings.
- ••• 0:45—Topless taking off her bikini top with her husband.
Magazines:
Penthouse (May 1981) . . . . Pet

• *Carney, Bridget*
Films:
Sorority House Massacre 2 (1990). . . . . .Candy
- ••• 0:40—Topless and buns in G-string, dancing in club.
Night of the Warrior (1991) . . . . Sarah
Tower of Terror (1991) . . . . .n.a.
Video Tapes:
Scream Queen Hot Tub Party (1991). . . . . .n.a.
- ••• 0:17—Topless and buns in shower from *Tower of Terror.*

• *Carnon, Angela*
Films:
Guess What Happened to Count Dracula (1970)
. . . . Nurse
Innocent Sally (1973) . . . . n.a.
a.k.a. The Dirty Mind of Young Sally
Video Vixens (1973) . . . . Mrs. Gordon
- •• 1:13—Full frontal nudity making love with Mr. Gordon in bed in various positions. Shot at fast speed.
Young and Wild (1975) . . . . n.a.

Carol, Jean
a.k.a. Jeannie Daly.
Films:
Payback (1988) . . . . .Donna Nathan
- ••• 0:24—Topless opening her pink robe for Jason while reclining on couch.
TV:
The Guiding Light . . . . Nadine Cooper

Carol, Linda
Films:
School Spirit (1985) .Hogette
Reform School Girls (1986) . . . . Jennifer Williams
- •• 0:05—Nude in the shower.
- 0:56—Topless in the back of a truck with Norton.
- •• 1:13—Topless getting hosed down by Edna.
Future Hunters (1987) . . . . n.a.
Carnal Crimes (1991) . . . . .Elise
- 0:01—Very brief left breast, while rolling over in bed.
- 0:05—In wet lingerie and very brief side view of right breast in shower fantasy.
- 0:07—Topless in B&W photo collage.
- 0:09—Full frontal nudity under sheer nightie, trying to get Stanley into bed.
- 0:11—Topless in B&W photo again.
- 0:24—Brief right breast outside window opening her top while watching Renny & Mia make out.
- 0:26—Brief upper half of right breast when bum molests her.
- ••• 0:28—Topless posing for Renny with Mia.
- ••• 0:29—Full frontal nudity making love with Renny and Mia.
- 0:30—Brief buns, sleeping in bed.
- ••• 0:38—Topless making love with the baker. Long scene.
- 0:49—Topless in B&W photo again.
- 1:02—Brief side view of right breast in gaping blouse.
- 1:33—Side view of buns in dominatrix outfit.
Fear of Scandal (1992). .n.a.
Made for Cable Movies:
Prey of the Chameleon (1992; Showtime) . . . . Nurse
- 0:00—Topless several times, making love with a guy in restroom. Dark.

Video Tapes:
Inside Out 2 (1992) . . . The Hitchhiker/The Hitchhiker (Unrated version reviewed.)
- ••• 1:17—Topless undressing in room, while a guy watches from across the way. Long scene. B&W.

Carpenter, Linda
a.k.a. Playboy Playmate Linda Beatty.
Films:
Apocalypse Now (1979). . . . . Playmate
- • 1:01—Topless in centerfold photo, hung up for display. Long shot.

A Different Story (1979) . . . . Chastity
(R-rated version reviewed.)
- • 1:33—Very brief topless in shower, shutting the door when Meg Foster discovers her with Perry King.

Magazines:
Playboy (Aug 1976). . . . . Playmate

Carr, Laurie Ann
Films:
Mortuary Academy (1988) . . . . Nurse
Video Tapes:
Wet and Wild (1989) . . . . .Model
Magazines:
Playboy (Dec 1986). . . . . Playmate
Playboy's Book of Lingerie (Jan 1991) . . . . . . Herself
- ••• 16—Full frontal nudity.
- • 108—Partial right breast and partial lower frontal nudity.

Playboy's Book of Lingerie (Mar 1991) . . . . . Herself
- •• 27—Topless.
- ••• 36-37—Topless.
- • 56—Left breast.

Playboy's Book of Lingerie (May 1992) . . . . . Herself
- • 11—Partial left breast.

• Carr, Tanya
Video Tapes:
Hot Body International: #2 Miss Puerto Vallarta (1990). . . . . Contestant
- • 0:15—Very, very brief topless, flashing her breasts.
- •• 0:24—Buns, in two piece swimsuit, then topless wearing pasties.
- •• 0:56—Wearing pasties.

Hot Body International: #4 Spring Break (1992)
. . . . Contestant
0:08—Dancing in two piece swimsuit on stage.
0:15—4th place winner.
- ••• 0:42—Topless popping out of wet T-shirt, quite a few times. Buns in G-string.
0:58—Brief topless several times winning 3rd place in wet T-shirt contest.

Carrera, Barbara
Films:
Embryo (1976) . . . . .Victoria
0:36—Almost topless meeting Rock Hudson for the first time. Hair covers breasts.

1:09—In see through top in bedroom with Hudson.
- •• 1:10—Brief buns and topless in the mirror after making love with Hudson.
- • 1:11—Left breast sticking out of bathrobe.

The Island of Dr. Moreau (1977) . . . . .Maria
When Time Ran Out! (1980) . . . . .Iolani
Condorman (1981) . . . . .Natalia
I, the Jury (1982) . . . . .Dr. Charolette Bennett
- ••• 1:02—Nude on bed making love with Armand Assante. Very sexy.
- • 1:46—Brief topless in hallway kissing Assante.

Lone Wolf McQuade (1983). . . . . .Lola
Never Say Never Again (1983) . . . . Fatima Blush
Wild Geese II (1985; British) . . . . .Kathy
The Underachievers (1987) . . . . .Katherine
Love at Stake (1988) . . . . Faith Stewart
Loverboy (1989) . . . . .Alex Barnett
Wicked Stepmother (1989) . . . . Priscilla
- • 1:14—Very, very brief upper half of right breast peeking out of the top of her dress when she flips her head back while seducing Steve.

Miniseries:
Masada (1981). . . . . Sheva
TV:
Centennial (1978-79). . . . . Clay Basket
Dallas (1985-89) . . . . Angelica Nero
Video Tapes:
Playboy Video Magazine, Volume 1 (1982)
. . . . .Herself
- •• 0:01—Nude in still photos. Nude in scenes from *I, the Jury.*
- •• 0:30—Topless in still photos.
- ••• 0:32—Nude in scenes from *I, the Jury.*

Magazines:
Playboy (Jul 1977) . . . . Acting Beastly
- ••• 93-97—Topless.

Playboy (Apr 1980) . . . . Grapevine
- • 294—Topless under wet, white blouse in B&W photo.

Playboy (Mar 1982) . . . . Aye, Barbara
- ••• 148-155—Nude, also photos from *I, the Jury.*

Playboy (Sep 1987) . . . . 25 Years of James Bond
- •• 129—Topless.

Carrere, Tia
Films:
Aloha Summer (1988) . . . . Lani Kepoo
Fatal Mission (1990) . . . . Mai Chang
- • 0:22—Side view of right breast while changing tops. Dark.

Harley Davidson and The Marlboro Man (1991)
. . . . .Kimiko
Little Sister (1991) . . . . Adrienne
Showdown in Little Tokyo (1991) . . . . Minako
- • 0:50—Buns and side view of left breast, taking off robe and getting into outdoor tub with Dolph Lundgren. Don't see her face.
- • 0:52—Left breast, while making love in bed with Lundgren. Don't see her face again.

Wayne's World (1992)...................Cassandra
Made for Cable Movies:
Intimate Strangers (1991; Showtime)........ Mino
  • 0:34—In black lingerie in Nick's apartment. Very
    brief side of right breast in bed with him.
Made for Cable TV:
Tales From the Crypt: On a Dead Man's Chest
  (1992; HBO)........................Scarlett
TV:
General Hospital (1986-87)..............Jade Sung
Music Videos:
Ballroom Blitz/Wayne's World (1992)........ Herself

• Carrico, Monica
Films:
Lucky 13 (1984).............. Charlene Andrews
  a.k.a. Running Hot
  a.k.a. Highway to Hell
    0:09—Lying on bed in white bra and open dress top.
    0:18—Walking around in panties and a blouse.
  •• 0:49—Topless sitting on a rock after skinny dipping
    with Eric Stoltz.
  •• 0:51—Topless and buns after getting out of water
    and picking up clothes.
  •• 1:03—Topless in bed making love with Stoltz.
  ••• 1:15—Topless lying in bed with Stoltz.
Guilty by Suspicion (1991)............ Nelly Lesser

Carrillo, Elpidia
Films:
The Border (1982)...................... Maria
  • 1:19—Right breast, opening her blouse in shack
    with Jack Nicholson.
Beyond the Limit (1983)..................Clara
  •• 0:31—Topless making love with Richard Gere. Long
    scene.
  •• 1:08—Topless talking to Gere. Another long scene.
Under Fire (1983)...............Sandanista (Leon)
Let's Get Harry (1986)...................Veronica
Salvador (1986)...................... Maria
  • 0:21—Very brief right breast, lying in a hammock
    with James Woods.
Predator (1987) ....Anna
The Assassin (1989).......................Elena
Predator 2 (1990).......................Anna
Made for TV Movies:
Dangerous Passion (1990)................ Angela

Carroll, Jill
Films:
The Vals (1982)......................... Sam
The Man Who Loved Women (1983)
  .... Sue the Baby Sitter
The Unholy (1988)...................... Millie
  • 1:10—Very brief upper half of left breast, while talk-
    ing in the courtyard with Ben Cross.
Made for TV Movies:
American Harvest (1987)............ Calla Bergstrom

Carroll, Regina
Films:
Brain of Blood (1971; Philippines) .... n.a.
Blazing Stewardesses (1975) .... n.a.
Jessi's Girls (1976).....................Claire
  •• 0:58—Topless and buns in hay with Indian guy.
    Don't see her face.

• Carson, Rachelle
Films:
Kill Crazy (1989) .... Rachel
  •• 0:39—Topless taking off top to go skinny dipping
    with Libby.
  • 0:46—Very brief right breast, while lying on ground
    with a bad guy while getting raped. Buns, getting
    turned over before being shot.
Eating (1991)........................... Cathy

Carter, Lynda
Miss World U.S.A. 1973.
Films:
Bobbie Jo and the Outlaw (1976)
  .... Bobbie Jo Baker
    0:10—Partial side of left breast, changing blouses in
    her bedroom.
  ••• 0:17—Left breast, several times, while making love
    with Marjoe Gortner.
  •• 0:27—Brief left breast, making love with Gortner
    again at night.
  • 0:31—Very brief left breast, then very brief topless in
    pond with Gortner experimenting with mushrooms.
I Posed for Playboy (1991)........Meredith Lanahan
  a.k.a. Posing: Inspired by Three Real Stories
  (Shown on network TV without the nudity.)
Made for TV Movies:
Rita Hayworth: The Love Goddess (1983)
  .... Rita Hayworth
Mickey Spillane's Mike Hammer: Murder Takes All
  (1989) ....Helen Durant
Danielle Steel's "Daddy" (1991).... Charlotte Sampson
TV:
Wonder Woman (1976-79)
  .... Yeoman Diana Prince/Wonder Woman
Partners in Crime (1984) .... Carole Stanwyck

Cartwright, Nancy
Films:
Flesh + Blood (1985)................... Kathleen
  • 0:28—Brief topless showing Jennifer Jason Leigh
    how to make love. Long shot.
Going Undercover (1988; British)......... Stephanie

Cartwright, Veronica
Films:
Inserts (1976)........................ Harlene
  •• 0:16—Topless sitting on bed with Richard Dreyfuss.
  ••• 0:31—Nude on bed with Stephen Davies making a
    porno movie for Dreyfuss. Long scene.
Goin' South (1978) .... Hermine

Invasion of the Body Snatchers (1978) . . Nancy Bellicec
Alien (1979) . . . . Lambert
Nightmares (1983) . . . . Claire
The Right Stuff (1983). . . . . Betty Grissom
Flight of the Navigator (1986). . . . . Helen Freeman
My Man Adam (1986) . . . . Elaine Swit
• 1:09—Side view of right breast lying on tanning table when Adam steals her card keys. Long shot, hard to see.
Wisdom (1986). . . . . Samantha Wisdom
The Witches of Eastwick (1987). . . . . Felicia Alden
Valentino Returns (1988) . . . . Pat Gibbs
••• 0:33—Topless sitting in bed with Frederic Forrest. Fairly long scene.
Made for Cable Movies:
Hitler's Daughter (1990) . . . . n.a.
Dead In the Water (1991) . . . . Victoria Haines
TV:
Daniel Boone (1964-66) . . . . Jenima Boone

Case, Catherine
Films:
The Jigsaw Murders (1988). . . . . Stripper #2
• 0:27—Brief topless in black peek-a-boo bra posing for photographer.
Dr. Caligari (1989) . . . . . . Patient with Extra Hormones

Cash, Rosalind
Films:
Klute (1971) . . . . Pat
The Omega Man (1971). . . . . Lisa
•• 1:09—Side view of left breast and upper half of buns getting out of bed. Buns and topless sitting in bed.
• 1:21—Side view topless in beige underwear while trying on clothes.
Hickey and Boggs (1972) . . . . Nyona
The New Centurions (1972) . . . . Lorrie
The All-American Boy (1973). . . . . Poppy
Uptown Saturday Night (1974). . . . . Sarah Jackson
Wrong is Right (1982). . . . . Mrs. Ford
The Adventures of Buckaroo Banzai, Across the 8th Dimension (1984) . . . . John Emdall
Go Tell It On the Mountain (1984) . . . . . . Aunt Florence
Death Spa (1987) . . . . Sgt. Stone

• Casini, Stefania
Films:
Andy Warhol's Bad (1977; Italian) . . . . n.a.
Suspiria (1977; Italian) . . . . Sara
The Belly of an Architect (1987; British/Italian)
. . . . Flavia Speckler
••• 1:15—Lower frontal nudity, in open robe with Brian Dennehy. Then buns and topless on couch. Kind of a long shot.

Cassidy, Joanna
Films:
Bank Shot (1974) . . . . El
The Laughing Policeman (1974) . . . . Monica

The Stepford Wives (1975). . . . . n.a.
Stay Hungry (1976) . . . . Joe Mason
The Late Show (1977) . . . . Laura Birdwell
Stunts (1977) . . . . Patti Johnson
Our Winning Season (1978) . . . . Sheila
The Glove (1980). . . . . Sheila Michaels
Night Games (1980) . . . . Julie Miller
0:44—Buns, skinny dipping in the pool with Cindy Pickett.
•• 0:45—Brief full frontal nudity sitting up.
Blade Runner (1982). . . . . Zhora
•• 0:54—Topless getting dressed after taking a shower while talking with Harrison Ford.
Under Fire (1983). . . . . Claire
Club Paradise (1986) . . . . Terry Hamlin
The Fourth Protocol (1987; British) . . . . Vassilieva
• 1:39—Brief left breast. She's lying dead in Pierce Brosnan's bathtub.
• 1:49—Same thing, different angle.
1969 (1988). . . . . Ev
Who Framed Roger Rabbit (1988) . . . . Dolores
May Wine (1990; French). . . . . Lorraine
Where the Heart Is (1990) . . . . Jean McBain
All-American Murder (1991). . . . . Erica Darby
Don't Tell Mom the Babysitter's Dead (1991). . . . . Rose
Lonely Hearts (1991) . . . . n.a.
Made for Cable Movies:
Wheels of Terror (1990) . . . . Laura
Miniseries:
Hollywood Wives (1988) . . . . Maralee Gray
Grass Roots (1992) . . . . Ann Heath
Made for TV Movies:
Pleasures (1986). . . . . n.a.
LIVE! From Death Row (1992) . . . . Alana Powers
Taking Back My Life: The Nancy Ziegenmeyer Story (1992) . . . . Geneva Overholser
TV:
Shields and Yarnell (1977) . . . . Regular
The Roller Girls (1978) . . . . Selma "Books" Cassidy
240 Robert (1979-80) . . . . Deputy Morgan Wainwright
Buffalo Bill (1983-84) . . . . JoJo White
Falcon Crest (1983) . . . . Katherine Demery
The Family Tree (1983) . . . . Elizabeth Nichols
Codename: Foxfire (1985) . . . Elizabeth "Foxfire" Towne

Castle, Martina
Films:
Hollywood Hot Tubs 2—Educating Crystal (1989)
. . . . Hardie
Death Merchant (1990) . . . . Martina
Total Exposure (1991) . . . . Cissy
• 1:06—Topless in spa being questioned by a guy with a gun.

Cates, Phoebe

Wife of actor Kevin Kline.
Films:
Paradise (1981). . . . . Sarah
- •• 0:23—Buns and topless taking a shower in a cave while Willie Aames watches.
- 0:36—In wet white dress in a pond with Aames.
- • 0:40—Very brief left breast caressing herself while looking at her reflection in the water.
- • 0:43—Buns, getting out of bed to check out Aames' body while he sleeps.
- • 0:46—Buns, washing herself in a pond at night.
- •• 0:55—Side view of her silhouette at the beach at night. Nude swimming in the water, viewed from below.
- •• 1:10—Topless making love with Aames. It looks like a body double. Don't see her face.
- ••• 1:12—Nude swimming under water with Aames.
- •• 1:16—Topless making love with Aames again. It looks like the body double again.

Fast Times at Ridgemont High (1982)
. . . . Linda Barrett
- ••• 0:50—Topless getting out of swimming pool during Judge Reinhold's fantasy.

Private School (1983) . . . . Christine
- 1:21—Brief buns lying in sand with Mathew Modine.
- 1:24—Upper half of buns flashing with the rest of the girls during graduation ceremony.

Gremlins (1984) . . . . Kate
Date with an Angel (1987) . . . . Patty Winston
Bright Lights, Big City (1988) . . . . Amanda
Heart of Dixie (1989) . . . . Aiken
Shag (1989) . . . . Carson McBride
Gremlins 2: The New Batch (1990) . . . . Kate Beringer
I Love You to Death (1990) . . . . . . Uncredited Girl in Bar
Drop Dead Fred (1991). . . . . Elizabeth
Miniseries:
Lace (1984). Lili
Lace II (1985) Lili

Cattrall, Kim

Films:
Rosebud (1975) . . . . Joyce
Tribute (1980; Canadian) . . . . Sally Haines
Porky's (1981; Canadian) . . . . Honeywell
- • 0:58—Brief buns, then very brief lower frontal nudity after removing skirt to make love in the boy's locker room.

Ticket to Heaven (1981; Canadian) . . . . Ruthie
City Limits (1984). Wickings
- •• 1:02—Right breast, while sitting up in bed with a piece of paper stuck to her.

Police Academy (1984) . . . . Karen Thompson
Turk 182 (1985) . . . . Danny Boudreau
Big Trouble in Little China (1986) . . . . Gracie Law
Mannequin (1987) . . . . Emmy

Masquerade (1988). . . . . Mrs. Brooke Morrison
- ••• 0:04—Topless in bed with Rob Lowe.
- 0:47—In white teddy after having sex with Lowe.

Midnight Crossing (1988) . . . . Alexa Schubb
- 0:39—In wet white blouse, arguing in the water with her husband.

Smoke Screen (1988) . . . . Odessa Muldoon
- 0:31—Brief half of right breast sitting in bed with sheet pulled up on her.
- •• 1:16—Topless in bed on top of Gerald.
- ••• 1:17—Topless lying in bed under Gerald while he kisses her breasts.

The Return of the Musketeers (1989) . . . . Justine
The Bonfire of the Vanities (1990) . . . . Judy McCoy
Honeymoon Academy (1990) . . . . Chris
Star Trek VI: The Undiscovered Country (1991)
. . . . Lieutenant Valeris
Split Second (1992). . . . . Michelle
- •• 0:43—Topless in the shower.
- •• 0:45—Topless in the shower, when Rutger Hauer opens the curtains.

Made for Cable Movies:
Miracle in the Wilderness (1991; TNT) . . . . Dora
Miniseries:
Scruples (1980) . . . . Melanie
Made for TV Movies:
Sins of the Past (1984) . . . . Paula
TV:
Scruples (1980) . . . . Melanie Adams
Magazines:
Playboy (Nov 1987) . . . . Sex in Cinema 1987
- • 138—Left breast lying in bed with Rob Lowe.

Cayer, Kim

Films:
Screwballs (1983). . . . . Brunette Cheerleader
Loose Screws (1986) . . . . Pig Pen Girl
Graveyard Shift (1987). . . . . Suzy
- •• 0:06—In black bra, then brief left breast when vampire rips the bra off.
- • 0:53—Brief topless in junk yard with garter belt, black panties and stockings.

Psycho Girls (1987) . . . . n.a.

Cayton, Elizabeth

See: Kaitan, Elizabeth.

Celedonio, Maria

Films:
One Man Force (1989) . . . . Maria
- • 0:30—Brief topless, twice, hiding John Matuzak in her apartment. Long shot.

Backstreet Dreams (1990) . . . . Maria M.

Cellier, Caroline

Films:
Life Love Death (1969; French/Italian) . . . . n.a.
This Man Must Die (1970) . . . . Helene Lawson
Femmes de Persone (1986; French) . . . . Isabelle

Petit Con (1986; French). . . . . Annie Choupon
L'Annee Des Meduses (1987; French)
. . . . Claude, Chris' Mother
   •• 0:02—Topless taking off top at the beach.
   •• 0:56—Topless on boat at night with Romain.
   •• 1:06—Topless on the beach with Valerie Kaprisky.
   • 1:14—Left breast, lying on beach with Romain at
      night.

Chadwick, June

Films:
The Golden Lady (1979; British) . . . . Lucy
Forbidden World (1982) . . . . .Dr. Barbara Glaser
   •• 0:29—Topless in bed making love with Jesse Vint.
   •• 0:54—Topless taking a shower with Dawn Dunlap.
The Last Horror Film (1984) . . . . Reporter
This is Spinal Tap (1984) . . . . Jeanine Pettibone
Headhunters (1988) . . . . Denise Giuliani
Rising Storm (1989) . . . . Mila Hart
Backstab (1990) . . . . Mrs. Caroline Chambers
The Evil Below (1991) . . . . Sarah Livingston
   • 0:08—Very, very brief left breast, while on the floor
      with Max after he takes off her bra.
     0:39—In red, one piece swimsuit on boat.
   • 0:45—Very brief left breast, while on the floor with
      Max. Different angle from 0:08.
TV:
V: The Series (1984-85). . . . . .Lydia
Riptide (1986). . . . . Lt. Joanna Parisi
Going to Extremes (1992-). . . . . .Dr. Alice Davis

• Chambers, Marie

Films:
Street Asylum (1989) . . . . .Dr. Cane
Video Tapes:
Inside Out (1992) . . Terry's Female Half/My Better Half
   •• 1:20—Topless lying on couch with open robe.
   • 1:21—Brief left breast in open robe, while standing
      up.
   • 1:22—Brief right breast.
   ••• 1:24—Topless kissing Terry and rolling around on
      the couch and on the floor.

Chambers, Marilyn

Former adult film actress.
Films:
Rabid (1977; Canadian). . . . . Rose
   •• 0:14—Topless in bed.
   •• 1:04—Topless in closet selecting clothes.
   •• 1:16—Topless in white panties getting out of bed.
Angel of H.E.A.T. (1981) . . . . Angel Harmony
a.k.a. The Protectors, Book I
   •• 0:15—Full frontal nudity making love with an in-
      truder on the bed.
   • 0:17—Topless in a bathtub.
   •• 0:40—Topless in a hotel room with a short guy.
   • 0:52—Topless getting out of a wet suit.
   •• 1:01—Topless sitting on floor with some robots.
   • 1:29—Topless in bed with Mark.

Deadly Force (1983) . . . . .Actress in Video Tape
   • 0:25—Topless in adult video tape on projection TV.
My Therapist (1983) . . . . .Kelly Carson
   •• 0:01—Topless in sex therapy class.
   •• 0:07—Topless, then full frontal nudity undressing for
      Rip. Long scene.
   ••• 0:10—Topless undressing at home, then full frontal
      nudity making love on couch. Long scene. Nice.
      Then brief side view of right breast in shower.
   • 0:18—Topless on sofa with Mike.
   •• 0:21—Topless taking off and putting red blouse on
      at home.
   ••• 0:26—Nude in bedroom by herself masturbating on
      bed.
   ••• 0:32—Topless exercising on the floor, buns in bed
      with Mike, topless in bed getting covered with
      whipped cream.
   •• 0:41—Left breast and lower frontal nudity fighting
      with Don while he rips off her clothes.
   •• 1:08—Topless and brief buns in bed.
     1:12—In braless pink T-shirt at the beach.
Up 'n' Coming (1987) . . . . Cassie
(R-rated version reviewed, X-rated version available.)
   ••• 0:01—Nude, getting out of bed and taking a show-
      er.
   •• 0:08—Topless making love in bed with the record
      producer.
   • 0:30—Brief topless in bed with two guys.
   •• 0:47—Full frontal nudity getting suntan lotion
      rubbed on her by another woman.
   •• 0:55—Topless taking off her top at radio station.
Party Incorporated (1989). . . . . . . .Marilyn Sanders
a.k.a. Party Girls
   ••• 0:56—In lingerie, then topless in bedroom with
      Weston. Nice!
   • 1:11—Brief topless on the beach when Peter takes
      her swimsuit top off.
Breakfast in Bed (1990) . . . . .Marilyn Valentine
Private Screenings.
   •• 0:04—Full frontal nudity, getting out of bubble bath
      and drying herself off while talking to her manager.
   ••• 0:21—Topless, taking off swimsuit top and sunbath-
      ing. Nude, swimming underwater.
   •• 0:53—In bra, then topless making love.
     1:01—In black bra and panties, undressing in her
      room.
   •• 1:16—Full frontal nudity, getting out of bed, putting
      on robe, then getting back in with Jonathan.
The Marilyn Diaries (1990) . . . . Marilyn
Private Screenings.
   •• 0:02—Topless in bathroom with a guy during party.
   •• 0:26—In bra and panties in Istvan's studio, then top-
      less.
   ••• 0:27—Topless in panties when Istvan opens her
      blouse.
   • 0:45—Topless in trench coat, opening it up to give
      the Iranian secret documents.
   • 0:47—Topless when the Rebel Leader opens her
      trench coat.

- 0:48—Topless with Colonel South.
- •• 0:57—Topless opening her top for Hollywood producer.
- 1:10—In swimsuit, then topless with Roger.
- ••• 1:13—In black lingerie, then topless making love with Chet.
- 1:19—Left breast, in flashback with Roger.
- •• 1:25—In slip, then right breast, then topless with Chet.

Video Tapes:

Playboy Video Magazine, Volume 4 (1983)
. . . . Herself
- •• 0:48—Topless in scenes from miscellaneous films.

Magazines:

Playboy (Aug 1973) . . . . Porno Chic
- ••• 141—Full frontal nudity.

Playboy (Dec 1973). . . . . Sex Stars of 1973
- ••• 210—Full frontal nudity.

Playboy (Apr 1974) . . . . Sex, Soap and Success
- ••• 147-155—Nude.

Playboy (Dec 1974). . . . . Sex Stars of 1974
- ••• 208—Topless standing in bubble bath.

Playboy (Feb 1980) . . . . The Year in Sex
- • 159—Lower frontal nudity.

Playboy (Jul 1980) . . . . Grapevine
- •• 263—Topless with her body painted.

Playboy (Nov 1980) . . . . Sex in Cinema
- ••• 180—Left breast.

Playboy (Dec 1980). . . . . Sex Stars of 1980
- ••• 245—Full frontal nudity.

Playboy (Jan 1989) . . . . Women of the Seventies
- ••• 214—Topless.

Playboy (Nov 1989) . . . . Sex in Cinema 1989
- ••• 134—Topless still from *Party Incorporated*.

Chanel, Tally

a.k.a. Tally Brittany.

Films:

Alien Warrior (1985) .Barbara
- •• 0:46—In white lingerie, then topless and buns while undressing in room with the Police Captain.
- • 1:03—Brief topless and buns in flashback of 0:46 scene.

Bits and Pieces (1985). . . . . .Jennifer
- 0:58—In the woods with the killer, seen briefly in bra and panties before and after being killed.

Free Ride (1986) . . . . .Candy
- • 0:57—Brief topless in bedroom with Dan.

Sex Appeal (1986) . . . . Corinne
- • 1:22—Brief topless at the door of Tony's apartment when he opens the door while fantasizing about her.

The Nightstalker (1987) . . . . Brenda
- • 0:54—Brief frontal nudity lying dead in bed covered with paint. Long shot, hard to see anything.

Slammer Girls (1987). . . . . Candy Treat
- • 0:56—Buns, in G-string, doing a dance routine wearing feathery pasties for the Governor in the hospital.

Warrior Queen (1987) .Vespa
- ••• 0:09—Topless hanging on a rope, being auctioned.
- •• 0:20—Topless and buns with Chloe.
- •• 0:37—Nude, before attempted rape by Goliath.
- •• 0:58—Topless during rape by Goliath.

Hollywood Hot Tubs 2—Educating Crystal (1989)
. . . . Mindy Wright

Magazines:

Penthouse (May 1990) . . . . Dry as Dust

Playboy's Book of Lingerie (Jan 1992) . . . . . .Herself
- ••• 8—Topless.

Playboy's Book of Lingerie (Mar 1992). . . . . .Herself
- ••• 16—Topless.

Playboy's Book of Lingerie (May 1992) . . . . .Herself
- ••• 65—Topless.

Playboy's Book of Lingerie (Sep 1992) . . . . . .Herself
- •• 63—Left breast.

Chang, Lia

Films:

Frankenhooker (1990) . . . . .Crystal
- • 0:38—Buns, when Jeffrey draws a check mark on her.
- • 0:40—Brief buns, fighting with the other girls over the drugs.

A Kiss Before Dying (1991). . . . . Shoe Saleslady

Chaplin, Geraldine

Daughter of actor Charlie Chaplin.
Granddaughter of Eugene O'Neill.

Films:

Doctor Zhivago (1965) . . . . Tonya
Dr. Zhivago (1965). . . . . Tonya
The Three Musketeers (1973). . . . . Anne of Austria
Nashville (1975). . . . . Opal
Buffalo Bill and the Indians (1976) . . . . Annie Oakley
Roseland (1977). . . . . Marilyn
Welcome to L.A. (1977) . . . . Karen Hood
- •• 1:28—Full frontal nudity standing in Keith Carradine's living room.

Remember My Name (1978) . . . . Emily
- • 1:23—Very brief left breast, lying in bed, then right breast, with Anthony Perkins.

A Wedding (1978) . . . . Rita Billingsley
The Moderns (1988) . . . . .Nathalie de Ville
White Mischief (1988) . . . . Nina
The Return of the Musketeers (1989) . . . . . Queen Anne
The Children (1990). . . . . Joyce Wheater

Charbonneau, Patricia

Films:

Desert Hearts (1986) . . . . Cay Rivvers
- ••• 1:09—Brief topless making love in bed with Helen Shaver.

Manhunter (1986) . . . . Mrs. Sherman
Call Me (1988) . . . . Anna
- •• 1:18—Brief left breast making love in bed with a guy, then topless putting blouse on and getting out of bed.

Shakedown (1988) . . . . .Susan Cantrell
Brain Dead (1989). . . . . .Dana Martin
     0:43—Buns, on table with Bill Paxton. Briefly almost
     see side of left breast.
Robocop 2 (1990). . . . . .Uncredited Engineer
K2 (1991) . . . . Jacki Metcalfe
Made for Cable TV:
Tales From the Crypt: Strung Along (1992; HBO)
  . . . . Ellen
TV:
Wiseguy (1988-89) . . . . Carole Sternberg

Charlie
See: Spradling, Charlie.

Chase, Lynn
See: De Light, Venus.

Chen, Joan
Films:
Tai-Pan (1986). . . . . May May
     0:55—In sheer top sitting on bed talking to Bryan
     Brown.
     • 0:56—Brief left breast washing herself, hard to see
     anything.
     1:14—Sheer top again.
     1:30—Sheer top again.
The Last Emperor (1987). . . . . Wan Jung
The Nightstalker (1987) . . . . Mai Wong
The Blood of Heroes (1989) . . . . Kidda
   a.k.a. Salute of the Jugger
Turtle Beach (1992). . . . . .n.a.
Made for Cable Movies:
Dead Lock (1991; HBO) . . . . .Noelle
Made for TV Movies:
Steel Justice (1992) . . . . .Nicole
TV:
Twin Peaks (1990-91) . . . . .Jocelyn Packard

• Cheung, Daphne
Films:
Rich Girl (1991) . . . . Oriental Temptress
     • 1:14—Topless, taking off her jacket in back room try-
     ing to get Rick to do drugs.
Roots of Evil (1991) . . . . Tina
   (Unrated version reviewed.)
     ••• 0:09—Topless in alley with a customer.
A Time to Die (1991) . . . . .Sunshine

Chevalier, Catherine
Films:
Hellraiser II—Hellbound (1988). . . . . . . Tiffany's Mother
Riders of the Storm (1988) . . . . Rosita
Stormy Monday (1988). . . . . Cosmo's Secretary
Night Breed (1990) . . . . Rachel
     • 1:12—Topless in police jail, going through a door
     and killing a cop.

• Chiesa, Chana Jael
Video Tapes:
Inside Out (1992) . . . . My Secret Moments
     ••• 0:42—Topless, rubbing lotion on her breasts, then
     joined by a large cast of people during her fantasy as
     the camera pulls back.
     •• 0:44—Full frontal nudity, still in bed. Long shot.
Inside Out 4 (1992) . . . . .Actress/Motivation
   (Unrated version reviewed.)
     • 0:13—Lower frontal nudity, dropping her shorts to
     show Dick her haircut.
     ••• 0:14—Nude, out in the desert with Dick, shooting a
     scene.
     • 0:16—Topless, opening her blouse to show Dick her
     breasts, brief full frontal nudity, running to get into
     truck.
     •• 0:17—Brief full frontal nudity, out in the desert with
     Dick again.

Chiles, Lois
Films:
The Way We Were (1973). . . . . Carol Ann
Coma (1978) . . . . .Nancy Greenly
Moonraker (1979) . . . . .Dr. Holly Goodhead
Raw Courage (1983) . . . . Ruth
Sweet Liberty (1986) .Leslie
Broadcast News (1987) . . . . .Jennifer Mack
Creepshow 2 (1987) . . . . Annie Lansing
     •• 0:59—Brief topless getting out of boyfriend's bed,
     then getting dressed.
Until the End of the World (1991) . . . . .Elsa Farber
Diary of a Hitman (1992) . . . . Sheila
Made for TV Movies:
Obsessed (1992) . . . . Louise
TV:
Dallas (1982-84) . . . . Holly Harwood

Chin, Lonnie
Films:
Star 80 (1983) . . . . Playboy Mansion Guest
Video Tapes:
Playboy Video Magazine, Volume 1 (1982)
  . . . . Playmate
     •• 0:00—Full frontal nudity during introduction.
     ••• 0:15—Nude outside by pool.
     ••• 0:19—Nude posing in various clothes in clothes
     store.
     ••• 0:21—In bra and panties, then nude in garter belt
     and stockings in a house.
Playboy's Playmate Review 3 (1985) . . . . . Playmate
Magazines:
Playboy (Jan 1983). . . . . Playmate

Chong, Rae Dawn

Daughter of comedian/actor Tommy Chong.
Wife of actor C. Thomas Howell.
Films:
Quest For Fire (1981) . . . . Ika
    0:37—Topless and buns, running away from the bad
    tribe.
    0:40—Topless and buns, following the three guys.
    0:41—Brief topless behind rocks.
    • 0:43—Brief side view of left breast, healing Noah's
    wound.
    • 0:50—Right breast, while sleeping by the fire.
    0:53—Long shot, side view of left breast after mak-
    ing love.
    • 0:54—Topless shouting to the three guys.
    • 1:07—Topless standing with her tribe.
    • 1:10—Topless and buns, walking through camp at
    night.
    • 1:18—Topless in a field.
    • 1:20—Left breast, turning over to demonstrate the
    missionary position. Long shot.
    • 1:25—Buns and brief left breast running out of bear
    cave.
Beat Street (1984) . . . . Tracy
City Limits (1984) . . . . Yogi
The Corsican Brothers (1984) . . . . The Gypsy
Fear City (1984) . . . . Leila
  ••• 0:26—Topless and buns, dancing on stage.
  • 0:50—Brief topless in the hospital getting a shock to
    get her heart started.
American Flyers (1985) . . . . Sarah
The Color Purple (1985) . . . . Squeak
Commando (1985) . . . . Cindy
Running Out of Luck (1986) . . . . Slave Girl
  •• 0:42—Left breast, while hugging Mick Jagger, then
    again while lying in bed with him.
  •• 1:12—Left breast painting some kind of drug laced
    solution on herself.
  •• 1:14—Right breast, while in prison office offering
    her breast to the warden.
  • 1:21—Buns and left breast, in bed with Jagger dur-
    ing a flashback.
Soul Man (1986) . . . . Sarah
The Squeeze (1987) . . . . Rachel Dobs
Curiosity Kills (1990) . . . . Jane
Far Out Man (1990) . . . . Rae Dawn Chong
Tales From the Darkside, The Movie (1990)
. . . . .Carola
  • 1:09—Left breast in blue light, twice, with James Re-
    mar. Don't see her face.
Amazon (1991). . . . . Paola
The Borrower (1991). . . . . Diana Pierce
Common Bounds (1991) . . . . Ilene Curtis
Denial (1991) . . . . Julie
Made for Cable Movies:
Prison Stories, Women on the Inside (1990; HBO)
. . . . .Rhonda
  • 0:26—Very brief right breast several times in prison
    shower with Annabella Sciorra.

Magazines:
Playboy (Apr 1982) . . . . Quest For Fire

• Chong, Shelby

Films:
Cheech & Chong's Nice Dreams (1981). . . Body Builder
Far Out Man (1990). . . . . Tree
  • 0:11—Very brief side view of left breast, in gaping
    blouse when she leans over to light a joint.
Relentless 2: Dead On (1991) . . . . Waitress
The Spirit of '76 (1991) . . . . Waitress

• Christensen, Tonja

Video Tapes:
Playboy Video Calendar 1993 (1992). . . . December
Playboy's Playmate Review 1992 (1992)
. . . . Miss November
  ••• 0:02—Nude in hat and chair scenes in a house.
Magazines:
Playboy (Nov 1991) . . . . Playmate

Christian, Claudia

Films:
The Hidden (1987). . . . . Brenda Lee
Arena (1988) . . . . Quinn
Clean and Sober (1988) . . . . Iris
Never on Tuesday (1988) . . . . Tuesday
  (There are a lot of braless T-shirt shots of her throughout
  the film.)
  • 0:43—Brief side view of right breast in the shower
    with Eddie during his fantasy.
Mom (1989) . . . . Virginia
    0:03—Briefly in red bra, when Brion James rips her
    blouse open.
Mad About You (1990) . . . . .Casey
    0:56—On boat in a white, fairly transparent one
    piece swimsuit.
Maniac Cop 2 (1990). . . . . Susan Riley
Think Big (1990) . . . . Dr. Marsh
The Dark Backward (1991). . . . . Kitty
Made for Cable Movies:
Lies of the Twins (1991; USA). . . . . .Felice
Strays (1991; USA) . . . . Claire Lederer
Made for TV Movies:
Danielle Steel's "Kaleidoscope" (1990). . . . . . .Meagan
TV:
Berrengers (1985) . . . . Melody Hughes

Christie, Julie

Films:
Billy Liar (1963) . . . . Liz
Darling (1965) . . . . Diana Scott
Doctor Zhivago (1965) . . . . Lara
Fahrenheit 451 (1967). . . . . Linda/Clarisse
Petulia (1968; U.S./British) . . . . Petulia Danner
McCabe and Mrs. Miller (1971) . . . . .Mrs. Miller
Don't Look Now (1973) . . . . Laura Baxter
  • 0:27—Brief topless in bathroom with Donald Suth-
    erland.

•• 0:30—Topless making love with Sutherland in bed.
Shampoo (1975)........................ Jackie
Demon Seed (1977) .... Susan Harris
   • 0:25—Side view of left breast, getting out of bed.
   •• 0:30—Topless and buns getting out of the shower
     while the computer watches with its camera.
Heaven Can Wait (1978)............. Betty Logan
Heat and Dust (1982).....................Anne
Return of the Soldier (1983; British) .... Kitty
Power (1986) ....Ellen Freeman
Miss Mary (1987) .... Miss Mary Mulligan
Made for TV Movies:
Dadah is Death (1988) ....Barbara
Magazines:
Playboy (Nov 1974) .... Sex in Cinema 1974
  •• 147—Topless from *Don't Look Now.*

Cicciolina

See: Staller, Ilona.

Clark, Anna

Video Tapes:
Playboy Video Calendar 1988 (1987) .... Playmate
Wet and Wild (1989).....................Model
Magazines:
Playboy (Apr 1987) .... Playmate

Clark, Candy

Films:
Fat City (1972) .... Faye
American Graffiti (1973) .... Debbie
The Man Who Fell to Earth (1976; British)
.... Mary-Lou
  (Uncensored version reviewed.)
  •• 0:42—Topless in the bathtub, washing her hair and
    talking to David Bowie.
  •• 0:55—Topless sitting on bed and blowing out a can-
    dle.
  ••• 0:56—Topless in bed with Bowie.
  ••• 1:26—Full frontal nudity climbing into bed with
    Bowie after he reveals his true alien self.
    1:56—Nude with Bowie making love and shooting a
    gun.
Citizen's Band (1977) .... Electra/Pam
The Big Sleep (1978; British) ..... Camilla Sternwood
  ••• 0:18—Topless, sitting in a chair when Robert
    Mitchum comes in after a guy is murdered.
  • 0:30—Brief topless in a photograph that Mitchum is
    looking at.
    0:38—Topless in the photos again. Out of focus.
  •• 0:39—Topless sitting in chair during recollection of
    the murder.
  •• 1:03—Very brief full frontal nudity in bed, throwing
    open the sheets for Mitchum.
    1:05—Very, very brief buns, getting up out of bed.
When Ya Comin' Back Red Ryder (1979) .... Cheryl
  (Not available on video tape.)
Q (1982)................................. Joan
Blue Thunder (1983)....................... Kate

Hambone and Hillie (1984) .... Nancy
Cat's Eye (1985)...................... Sally Ann
At Close Range (1986) ....Mary Sue
The Blob (1988)..................... Fran Hewitt
Cool As Ice (1991) ....Grace
Magazines:
Playboy (Nov 1978) .... Sex in Cinema 1978
  • 181—Topless.

Clark, Dawn

Films:
The Happy Hooker Goes to Washington (1977)
.... Candy
  • 1:18—Topless, covered with spaghetti in a restau-
    rant.
The Hollywood Knights (1980) ...... Pom Pom Girl
  •• 0:01—Topless sunbathing outside with Fran
    Drescher and another Pom Pom Girl.
  • 0:11—In bra, then brief topless, changing clothes at
    night.
  • 0:20—Topless in B&W Polaroid photograph. Long
    shot.
Stripes (1981) ....Mud Wrestler

Clark, Marlene

Films:
The Landlord (1970) .... n.a.
Slaughter (1972) .... Kim Walker
  • 0:11—Very brief buns and right breast, getting
    thrown out of room by Jim Brown.
Night of the Cobra Woman (1974; U.S./Philippines)
.... Lena
Switchblade Sisters (1975).................... Muff

Clark, Sharon

a.k.a. Sharon Weber or Sharon Clark Weber.
Films:
Lifeguard (1975) ....Tina
  • 0:07—Brief side view of right breast undressing and
    getting into the shower.
  • 0:08—Buns and brief topless wrestling with Sam El-
    liott on the bed.
Lisa (1989).................... Porsche Passenger
Magazines:
Playboy (Aug 1970) ....Playmate
Playboy (Jan 1974)........ Twenty Years of Playmates
  • 110—Left breast.

Clark, Susan

Films:
Coogan's Bluff (1968) ....Julie
Colossus: 'The Forbin' Project (1969) .... Cleo
    1:12—After taking off her dress, she's seen through
    a wine glass, so it's very distorted. It looks like she's
    wearing a body suit.
Tell Them Willie Boy is Here (1969) .... Liz
    0:21—Very brief buns when Robert Redford turns
    her over in bed.
    0:57—In slip, after taking off dress for Redford.

Skin Game (1971) . . . . Ginger
Valdez is Coming (1971) . . . . Gay Erin
The Apple Dumpling Gang (1975)
    . . . . Magnolia Dusty Clydesdale
Night Moves (1975) . . . . Ellen
   • 1:09—Brief topless in bed with Gene Hackman.
French Quarter (1978) . . . . Bag Stealer/Sue
Deadly Companion (1979) . . . . Paula West
   • 0:19—Brief left breast, while consoling Michael Sar-
    razin in bed, then brief side view of left breast.
   • 0:20—Brief topless sitting up in bed.
The North Avenue Irregulars (1979) . . . . Anne
Promises in the Dark (1979) . . . . Fran Koenig
Nobody's Perfekt (1981) . . . . Carol
Porky's (1981; Canadian) . . . . Cherry Forever
Made for TV Movies:
Babe (1975) . . . . Babe Didrickson Zaharias
  (Emmy Award for Best Actress in a Special.)
TV:
Webster (1983-89)
    . . . . Katherine Calder Young Papadapolis
Magazines:
Playboy (Feb 1973) . . . . The Ziegfeld Girls
  ••• 75-79—Topless and buns in various poses.

Clarke, Caitlin

Films:
Dragonslayer (1981) . . . . Valerian
   0:27—Body double's very brief side of left breast
    from under water.
Penn & Teller Get Killed (1989) . . . . Carlotta
TV:
Once a Hero (1979) . . . . Emma Greely

• Clarke, Julie

Video Tapes:
Playboy Video Centerfold: Julie Clarke . . Playmate
Playboy Video Calendar 1992 (1991) . . . . . February
  ••• 0:05—Topless on stairs. Nude in warehouse, paint-
   ing on the floor and on herself.
  ••• 0:07—Nude, putting oil on herself.
Playboy Playmates in Paradise (1992) . . . Playmate
Playboy's Playmate Review 1992 (1992)
  . . . . Miss March
  ••• 0:10—Nude in indoor pool, then in art studio and
   then on horseback.
Wet and Wild IV (1992) . . . . Model
Magazines:
Playboy (Mar 1991) . . . . Playmate
  ••• 86-97—Nude.

Clarkson, Lana

Films:
Fast Times at Ridgemont High (1982) . . . . . . Mrs. Vargas
Deathstalker (1983) . . . . Kaira
  •• 0:26—Topless when her cape opens, while talking to
   Deathstalker and Oghris.
  ••• 0:29—Topless lying down by the fire when Deathstalker comes to make love with her.

  • 0:49—Brief topless with gaping cape, sword fighting with a guard.
Scarface (1983) . . . . Woman at the Babylon Club
Blind Date (1984) . . . . Rachel
  (Not the same 1987 *Blind Date* with Bruce Willis.)
  • 0:52—Brief topless rolling over in bed when Joseph
   Bottoms sneaks in. Dark, hard to see.
  1:11—In two piece swimsuit during a modeling assignment.
  1:18—In two piece swimsuit by pool.
Barbarian Queen (1985) . . . . Amethea
  •• 0:38—Brief topless during attempted rape.
  ••• 0:48—Topless being tortured with metal hand then
   raped by torturer.
Amazon Women on the Moon (1987) . . . . . . Alpha Beta
Barbarian Queen II: The Empress Strikes Back (1989)
  . . . . n.a.
The Haunting of Morella (1989) . . . . . Coel Deveroux
  ••• 0:17—Topless, taking a bath, then getting out and
   wrapping a towel around herself.
  ••• 1:00—Topless in white panties, standing under a
   waterfall.
Wizards of the Lost Kingdom, Part 2 (1991) . . . . n.a.
Magazines:
Playboy (Nov 1985) . . . . Sex in Cinema 1985
  •• 134—Topless, getting her breasts fondled in still
   from *Barbarian Queen.*

Clayburgh, Jill

Films:
The Wedding Party (1969) . . . . Josephine Fish
Portnoy's Complaint (1972) . . . . Naomi
The Thief Who Came to Dinner (1973) . . . . Jackie
The Terminal Man (1974) . . . . Angela Black
Silver Streak (1976) . . . . Hilly Burns
Semi-Tough (1977) . . . . Barbara Jane Bookman
An Unmarried Woman (1978) . . . . Erica
  0:05—Dancing around the apartment in white long
   sleeve T-shirt and white panties.
  •• 0:12—Brief topless getting dressed for bed, kind of
   dark and hard to see.
  •• 1:10—In bra and panties in guy's apartment, then
   brief topless lying on bed.
Luna (1979) . . . . Caterina Silveri
Starting Over (1979) . . . . Marilyn Holmberg
  • 0:45—Very brief upper half of breasts taking a shower while Burt Reynolds waits outside.
It's My Turn (1980) . . . . Kate Gunzinger
  • 1:10—Brief upper half of left breast in bed with
   Michael Douglas after making love.
First Monday in October (1981) . . . . Ruth Loomis
  1:29—Nude behind shower door, but you can't see
   anything. Only part of her left breast (seen from the
   back) when she gets out and puts on her robe.
I'm Dancing as Fast as I Can (1981) . . . . Barbara Gordon
Where Are the Children? (1986) . . . . . . Nancy Eldgridge
Shy People (1988) . . . . Diana
Whispers in the Dark (1992) . . . . n.a.

Made for TV Movies:
Hustling (1975). . . . . Wanda
Female Instinct (1985) .Mary
Reason for Living: The Jill Ireland Story (1991)
. . . . Jill Ireland
Trial: The Price of Passion (1992). . . . .Judge Louise Parker

• Clearbranch, Deborah

Films:
Caged Heat (1974) . . . . Debbie
a.k.a. Renegade Girls
Magazines:
Penthouse (Jun 1974). . . . . Georgia Girl
••• 82-87—Nude.

Clery, Corrine

Films:
Kleinhoff Hotel (1973) . . . . .n.a.
The Story of "O" (1975; French) . . . . O
•• 0:09—Topless in bedroom with two women.
•• 0:12—Topless being made love to.
•• 0:20—Frontal nudity making love with two men.
•• 0:29—Topless taking a bath while a man watches.
••• 0:42—Buns, on a sofa while her boyfriend lifts her
   dress up, then topless while another man plays with
   her, then nude except for white stockings.
•• 0:51—Brief topless chained by wrists and gagged.
••• 1:22—Nude making love with a young guy.
Covert Action (1978). . . . . .n.a.
The Switch (1978). Charlotte
a.k.a. The Con Artists
The Humanoid (1979; Italian). . . . . .n.a.
Moonraker (1979). . . . . Corinne Dufour
I Hate Blondes (1981) . . . . Angelica
Yor: The Hunter from the Future (1983) . . . . Ka-Laa
Dangerous Obsession (1990; Italian)
. . . . Carol Simpson
• 0:14—Right breast sticking out of lingerie while ly-
   ing in bed.
•• 0:36—Full frontal nudity lying in bed waiting for her
   husband, then with him, then getting out of bed.
Magazines:
Playboy (Sep 1987). . . . . .25 Years of James Bond
•• 131—Topless.

• Cleveland, Amanda

Films:
Blow Out (1981). . . . . .Coed Lover
• 0:02—Left breast in room while someone watches
   from the outside.
True Confessions (1981) . . . . .Lois

• Cleveland, Missy

Films:
Blow Out (1981). . . . . Shower Victim
•• 0:02—Topless in shower and on TV monitor while
   killer stalks outside.

Video Tapes:
Playboy Video Magazine, Volume 2 (1983)
. . . . .Herself/Playboy Playoffs
Magazines:
Playboy (Apr 1979) . . . . Playmate

Close, Glenn

Films:
World According to Garp (1982) . . . . Jenny Fields
The Big Chill (1983) . . . . .Sara
• 0:27—Topless sitting down in the shower crying.
The Natural (1984) . . . . Iris Gaines
The Stone Boy (1984) . . . . Ruth Hillerman
Jagged Edge (1985). . . . . .Teddy Barnes
0:46—Side view of left breast, making love in bed
   with Jeff Bridges.
1:38—Very brief side view of right breast running
   down the hall taking off her blouse. Back is toward
   camera. Blurry shot.
Maxie (1985). . . . . Jan/Maxie
Fatal Attraction (1987) . . . . Alex Forrest
•• 0:17—Left breast when she opens her top to let
   Michael Douglas kiss her. Then very brief buns, falling into bed with him.
• 0:20—Brief right breast in freight elevator with Douglas.
••• 0:32—Topless in bed talking to Douglas. Long
   scene, sheet keeps changing positions between
   cuts.
Dangerous Liaisons (1988). . . . . . .Marquise de Merteuil
Immediate Family (1989). . . . . Linda Spector
Hamlet (1990). . . . . Queen Gertrude
Meeting Venus (1990; British) . . . . Karin Anderson
Reversal of Fortune (1990). . . . . .Sunny von Bülow
Hook (1991) . . . . Gutless
Made for TV Movies:
Sarah Plain and Tall (1991). . . . . Sarah Wheaton

• Cochrane, Talie

Films:
The Centerfold Girls (1974) . . . . .Donna
I Spit on Your Corpse (1974) . . . . Hitchhiker
• 0:47—Brief right breast, then topless getting shot.
   More topless, dead, covered with blood.
Fugitive Girls (1975). . . . . n.a.

Cochrell, Elizabeth

a.k.a. Liza Cochrell.
Films:
The Big Bet (1985) . . . . Sister in Stag Film
••• 1:05—Topless and buns, undressing and getting
   into bathtub in a video tape that Chris is watching.
•• 1:08—Topless again on video tape, when Chris
   watches it on TV at home.
Free Ride (1986) . . . . Nude Girl #1
• 0:25—Brief buns taking a shower with another girl.
Sunset Strip (1986) . . . . Stripper

Cole, Debra

Films:
Crossing Delancey (1988) . . . . Waitress
The Hot Spot (1990) . . . . Irene Davey
- 1:26—Topless sunbathing next to Jennifer Connelly at side of lake. Long shot.
- • 1:27—Topless talking with Connelly some more.

Coleman, Renee

Films:
After School (1987) . . . . September Lane
- • 0:35—Topless and buns getting into bathtub. Almost lower frontal nudity.
Rocket Gibraltar (1988) . . . . Waitress
Who's Harry Crumb? (1989) . . . . Jennifer Downing

Collings, Jeannie

Films:
Happy Housewives . . . . .Mrs. Wain
- 0:16—Very, very brief right breast with the Newsagent's Daughter and Bob in the bathtub.
Confessions of a Window Cleaner (1974; British) . . . . Baby Doll
Carry on England (1976; British) . . . . . . Private Edwards
Emily (1976; British). . . . . Rosalind
- 1:05—Brief topless on the couch with Gerald while Richard watches.

Collins, Alana

a.k.a. Alana Hamilton or Alana Stewart.
Ex-wife of singer Rod Stewart.
Ex-wife of actor George Hamilton.
Films:
Evel Knievel (1972) . . . . Nurse
Night Call Nurses (1972) . . . . Janis
a.k.a. Young LA Nurses 2
- • 0:12—Topless in bed with Zach.
0:24—In white two piece swimsuit on boat.
- • 0:28—Topless and buns on bed with Kyle.
- 0:52—Brief right breast twice in shower with Kyle.
The Ravagers (1979) . . . . Miriam
Swing Shift (1984) . . . . .Frankie Parker
0:11—Buns in B&W photo that Christine Lahti shows to Fred Ward. Possible photo composite.
Where the Boys Are '84 (1984) . . . . .Maggie

Collins, Candace

Films:
Class (1983) . . . . .Buxom Girl
Smokey and the Bandit III (1983) . . . . .Maid
Magazines:
Playboy (Oct 1974) . . . . Bunnies of 1974
- 132—Lower frontal nudity.
Playboy (Dec 1979). . . . . Playmate
Playboy (Dec 1980). . . . . .Bunny Birthday
- • 156—Right breast and lower frontal nudity.

• Collins, Jo

Video Tapes:
Playboy Video Centerfold: Donna Edmondson (1987) . . . . .Playmate Update
- • • 0:21—Topless and buns in still photos.
Magazines:
Playboy (Dec 1964) . . . . Playmate
Playboy (Jan 1974). . . . . Twenty Years of Playmates
- • 107—Buns and side of left breast.

Collins, Joan

Films:
Decameron Nights (1953) . . . . .Maria
Stopover Tokyo (1957). .Tina
Subterfuge (1969) . . . . .Anne Langley
The Executioner (1970; British) . . . . .Sarah Booth
Quest for Love (1971) .Ottilie
Fear in the Night (1972; British) . . . . Molly Charmichael
a.k.a. Dynasty of Fear
Tales From the Crypt (1972). . . . . Joanne Clayton
Dark Places (1974; British) . . . . .Sarah
Oh, Alfie! (1975; British) . . . . Fay
a.k.a. Alfie Darling
0:28—In white bra and panties, running to answer the phone, then talking to Alfie.
- • • 1:00—Topless lying in bed after Alfie rolls off her.
Bawdy Adventures of Tom Jones (1976) . . . . . Black Bess
Empire of the Ants (1977) . . . . Marilyn Fryser
The Big Sleep (1978; British) . . . . .Agnes Lozelle
Fearless (1978). . . . . Bridgitte
- 0:01—In bra and panties, then brief right breast during opening credits.
- • 0:41—Topless after doing a strip tease routine on stage.
- 1:17—Undressing in front of Wally in white bra and panties, then right breast.
- 1:20—Brief right breast lying dead on couch.
The Stud (1978; British) . . . . Fontaine
- 0:10—Brief left breast making love with Tony in the elevator.
0:27—Brief buns in panties, stockings and garter belt in Tony's apartment.
0:58—Brief black bra and panties under fur coat in back of limousine with Tony.
- 1:03—Brief topless taking off dress to get in pool.
- 1:04—Nude in the pool with Tony.
The Bitch (1979; British) . . . . .Fontaine Khaled
0:01—In long slip getting out of bed and putting a bathrobe on.
- 0:03—Brief topless in the shower with a guy.
- • 0:24—Brief topless taking black corset off for the chauffeur in the bedroom, then buns getting out of bed and walking to the bathroom.
0:39—Making love in bed wearing a blue slip.
- 1:01—Left breast after making love in bed.
Sunburn (1979) . . . . Nera
Homework (1982) . . . . .Diane
Body double used for Joan's nude scene.

Miniseries:
Sins (1986) . . . . .n.a.
Dynasty: The Reunion (1991)
. . . . . . Alexis Morell Carrington Colby Dexter Rowan
Made for TV Movies:
Her Life as a Man (1984) . . . . Pam Dugan
The Cartier Affair (1985) . . . . .n.a.
Monte Carlo (1986) . . . . Katrina Petrovna
TV:
Dynasty (1981-89) . . . . Alexis Carrington Colby
Magazines:
Playboy (Nov 1978) . . . . Sex in Cinema 1978
• 185—Left breast and lower frontal nudity.
Playboy (Dec 1983) . . . . .n.a.
Playboy (Dec 1984) . . . . Sex Stars of 1984
••• 209—Topless in bed.
Playboy (Jan 1989) . . . . Women of the Eighties
•• 250—Buns and side view of right breast in B&W
photo.

Collins, Pamela

Films:
Sweet Sugar (1972) . . . . .Dolores
• 0:26—Brief topless when doctor tears her bra off.
••• 0:50—Topless in the shower with Phyllis Davis.
So Long, Blue Boy (1973) . . . . Cathy
Famous T & A (1982) .Dolores
(No longer available for purchase, check your video
store for rental.)
••• 1:05—Topless in scenes and outtakes from *Sweet
Sugar.*

Collins, Pauline

Films:
Secrets of a Windmill Girl (1966; British) . . . . . . Pat Lord
Shirley Valentine (1989; British) . . . . Shirley Valentine
(If you like older women, check this out.)
• 0:13—Brief left breast giving Joe a shampoo in the
bathtub.
•• 1:17—Topless jumping from the boat into the water
in slow motion. Very brief topless in the water.
•• 1:19—Buns, hugging Tom Conti, left breast several
times kissing him.
City of Joy (1992) . . . . .n.a.

Collins, Roberta

Films:
The Big Doll House (1971) . . . . Alcott
••• 0:33—Topless in shower. Seen through blurry window by prison worker, Fred. Blurry, but nice.
• 0:34—Brief left breast, while opening her blouse for
Fred.
Unholy Rollers (1972) .Jennifer
a.k.a. Leader of the Pack
The Roommates (1973) . . . . Beth
Caged Heat (1974) . . . . Belle
a.k.a. Renegade Girls
• 0:11—Very brief topless getting blouse ripped open
by Juanita.

••• 1:01—Topless while the prison doctor has her
drugged so he can take pictures of her.
Death Race 2000 (1975) . . . . Matilda the Hun
•• 0:27—Topless being interviewed and arguing with
Calamity Jane.
Train Ride to Hollywood (1975) . . . . .n.a.
Death Wish II (1982) . . . . .Woman at Party
Hardbodies (1984) . . . . Lana
School Spirit (1985) . . . . Helen Grimshaw
Hardbodies 2 (1986) . . . . Lana Logan
Vendetta (1986) . . . . .Miss Dice

Collins, Ruth Corrine

Films:
Blood Sisters (1986) . . . . .Prostitute
Sexpot (1986) . . . . Ivy Barrington
•• 0:09—Topless on table, taking her dress off for Phillip.
• 0:41—Buns, in Damon's arms.
•• 0:51—Left breast, while in shower talking to Boop-
sie.
Doom Asylum (1987) . . . . .Tina
•• 0:19—Topless pulling up her top while yelling at kids
below.
Firehouse (1987) . . . . Bubbles
Lurkers (1987) . . . . Jane (Model)
0:12—Undressing in white bra (on the right) with
another model.
•• 0:13—Topless, changing clothes with the other
model.
Prime Evil (1987) . . . . Cathy
••• 0:15—Topless making love with her boyfriend in
bed.
• 0:16—More topless sitting up and getting out of
bed.
••• 0:27—Topless, sitting up while the priest talks to her.
•• 1:13—Left breast, while removing her gown (she's
on the left) with Brett and Judy.
Wildest Dreams (1987) . . . . Stella
••• 0:22—Topless wearing panties in bedroom on bed
with Bobby.
• 1:10—Brief topless fighting on floor with two other
women.
Alexa (1988) . . . . Marshall
• 0:01—Topless a couple of times taking blue dress off
and putting it on again. Long shot.
New York's Finest (1988) . . . . Joy Sugarman
• 0:04—Brief topless with a bunch of hookers.
• 0:36—Topless with her two friends doing push ups
on the floor.
•• 1:02—Topless making love on top of a guy talking
about diamonds.
Cleo/Leo (1989) . . . . .Sally
••• 0:08—Topless getting dress pulled off by Leo.
Deadly Embrace (1989) . . . . Dede Magnolia
Galactic Gigolo (1989) . . . . .Dr. Ruth Pepper
a.k.a. Club Earth

Party Incorporated (1989) . . . . .Betty
a.k.a. Party Girls
- 0:07—Topless on desk with Dickie. Long shot.
- 1:08—Topless in bed with Weston when Marilyn Chambers comes in.

Death Collector (1990) . . . . Annie Northbride
Little Devils (1991). . . . . .n.a.
Hellroller (1992) . . . . .Eugene's Mother

Collinson, Madeleine
Identical twin sister of Mary Collinson.
Films:
Come Back Peter (1971; British) . . . . .n.a.
The Love Machine (1971) . . . . Sandy
- 1:22—Topless in shower with Robin and her sister when Dyan Cannon discovers them all together. Can't tell who is who.

Twins of Evil (1971) . . . . Freida Gelhorn
- 1:07—Right breast, then brief topless undoing dress, then full frontal nudity after turning into a vampire in bedroom.

Magazines:
Playboy (Oct 1970) . . . . Playmate
Playboy (Dec 1972). . . . . Sex Stars of 1972
- 211—Topless.

Playboy (Jan 1974) . . . . Twenty Years of Playmates
- 110—Topless on bed.

Playboy (Jan 1979) . . . . 25 Beautiful Years
- 161—Topless lying on bed.

Collinson, Mary
Identical twin sister of Madeleine Collinson.
Films:
Come Back Peter (1971; British) . . . . .n.a.
The Love Machine (1971) . . . . .Debbie
- 1:22—Topless in shower with Robin and her sister when Dyan Cannon discovers them all together. Can't tell who is who.

Twins of Evil (1971). . . . . Maria Gelhorn
Magazines:
Playboy (Oct 1970) . . . . Playmate
Playboy (Dec 1972). . . . . Sex Stars of 1972
- 211—Topless.

Playboy (Jan 1974) . . . . Twenty Years of Playmates
- 110—Topless on bed.

Playboy (Jan 1979) . . . . 25 Beautiful Years
- 161—Topless lying on bed.

Colpitts-Cameron, Cissie
a.k.a. Cisse Cameron.
Films:
Beyond the Valley of the Dolls (1970) . . . . .n.a.
Russ Meyer Film.
(Not available on video tape.)
Billy Jack (1971) . . . . Miss Eyelashes
The Happy Hooker Goes to Washington (1977)
. . . . Miss Goodbody
- 0:29—Very brief topless when her top pops open during the senate hearing.

Porky's II: The Next Day (1983; Canadian)
. . . . .Graveyard Gloria/Sandy Le Toi
0:26—Buns in G-string at carnival.
- 0:39—Topless and buns in G-string, stripping for Pee Wee at cemetery.
- 0:40—More topless, pretending to die.
- 0:42—Topless, being carried by Meat.

TV:
The Ted Knight Show (1978) . . . . Graziella

Condon, Iris
Films:
Party Plane (1988) . . . . Renee
- 0:29—Buns, in white lingerie during audition.
- 0:48—Topless plane doing a strip tease routine.
- 1:02—Topless on plane mud wrestling with Carol.
- 1:12—Left breast, covered with mud, holding the Mad Bomber.
- 1:17—Left breast, then topless in trunk with the Doctor.

Pucker Up and Bark Like a Dog (1989)
. . . . Stretch Woman
Video Tapes:
In Search of the Perfect 10 (1986)
. . . . Perfect Girl #6/Jackie
- 0:37—Topless (she's the blonde) playing Twister with Rebecca Lynn. Buns in G-string.

Congie, Terry
Films:
Malibu Hot Summer (1981) . . . . .Dit McCoy
a.k.a. Sizzle Beach
(*Sizzle Beach* is the re-released version with Kevin Costner featured on the cover. It is missing all the nude scenes during the opening credits before 0:06.)
- 0:02—Side view of right breast, while on floor during opening credits.
0:39—In bra, taking off her blouse in front of her drama class.
- 0:45—Topless in front of fireplace with Kevin Costner. Side view of right breast.

Shadows Run Black (1981) . . . . Lee Faulkner
- 0:22—Topless, going for a swim in pool at night.
- 0:23—Topless under water.

Connelly, Jennifer
Films:
Once Upon a Time in America (1984)
. . . . Young Deborah
(Long version reviewed.)
Creepers (1985; Italian) . . . . .Jennifer Corvino
Labyrinth (1986) . . . . .Sarah
Some Girls (1988) . . . . Gabriella
The Hot Spot (1990) . . . . .Gloria Harper
1:01—In black bra and panties walking out of lake with Don Johnson.
1:26—Buns, lying next to Irene next to lake. Long shot.
- 1:27—Topless, talking to Irene next to lake. Wow!

Career Opportunities (1991) . . . . Josie McClellan
The Rocketeer (1991) . . . . Jenny Blake

Conrad, Kimberley

Wife of *Playboy* magazine publisher Hugh Hefner.
Video Tapes:
Playboy Video Calendar 1989 (1988) . . . . . October
••• 0:38—Nude.
Playboy Video Calendar 1990 (1989) . . . .December
••• 1:03—Nude.
Playboy Video Centerfold: Kimberley Conrad
(1989). . . . . Playmate of the Year 1989
••• 0:00—Nude throughout.
Playboy's Playmates of the Year: The '80s (1989)
. . . . Playmate of the Year 1989
••• 0:44—Nude in still photos.
••• 0:49—Full frontal nudity in bathtub and in various
scenes around the house.
• 0:53—In lingerie.
Magazines:
Playboy (Jan 1988) . . . . Playmate
Playboy's Nudes (Oct 1990). . . . . Herself
••• 110—Full frontal nudity.

Contouri, Chantal

Films:
Alvin Rides Again (1974; Australian)
. . . . Boobs La Touche
• 1:15—Very brief lower frontal nudity, putting panties on in the car. Brief topless, putting red dress on.
The Day After Halloween (1978; Australian) . . Madeline
a.k.a. Snapshot

Cooke, Jennifer

Films:
Gimme an "F" (1981). . . . . Pam Bethlehem
1:10—Wearing United States flag pasties frolicking
with Dr. Spirit. Nice bouncing action.
1:38—Still of pasties scene during end credits.
Friday the 13th, Part VI: Jason Lives (1986) . . . . . Megan
Made for Cable TV:
The Hitchhiker: Man's Best Friend (1985; HBO)
. . . . .Elanor
(Available on *The Hitchhiker, Volume 4*.)
• 0:19—Brief side view topless getting undressed to
take a shower.
Miniseries:
A Year in the Life (1986) . . . . .n.a.
TV:
The Guiding Light (1981-83) . . . . Morgan Nelson
V: The Series (1984-85). . . . . .Elizabeth

•Cooke, Victoria

Video Tapes:
Playboy Video Magazine, Volume 2 (1983)
. . . . Herself/Playboy Playoffs
Magazines:
Playboy (Jan 1980) . . . . Playboy's Pajama Parties
••• 126—Full frontal nudity.

Playboy (Aug 1980) . . . . Playmate
•• 12—Full frontal nudity, posing as an artist's model.
••• 124-135—Nude.
Playboy (Dec 1980) . . . . .Sex Stars of 1980
• 243—Left breast.

Coolidge, Rita

Singer.
Films:
Pat Garrett and Billy the Kid (1973) . . . . .Maria
• 1:34—Brief right breast getting undressed to get
into bed with Kris Kristofferson.
Magazines:
Playboy (Nov 1973) . . . . Sex in Cinema 1973
• 151—Topless in photo from *Pat Garrett and Billy the
Kid*.

Cooper, Jeanne

Mother of actors Corbin and Collin Bernsen.
Films:
The Redhead from Wyoming (1952) . . . . Myra
The Man from the Alamo (1953) . . . . Kate Lamar
Let No Man Write My Epitaph (1960) . . . . .Fran
The Boston Strangler (1968) . . . . Cloe
There Was a Crooked Man (1970) . . . . . .Prostitute
• 0:18—Brief left breast trying to seduce the sheriff,
Henry Fonda, in a room.
Kansas City Bomber (1972) . . . . Vivien
The All-American Boy (1973) . . . . Nola Bealer
TV:
Bracken's World (1970) . . . . .Grace Douglas
The Young and the Restless (1973-)
. . . . Katherine Chancellor-Sterling

Copley, Teri

Films:
New Year's Evil (1981) . . . . Teenage Girl
• 0:48—Brief right breast in the back of the car with
her boyfriend at a drive-in movie. Breast is half sticking out of her white bra. Dark, hard to see anything.
Down the Drain (1989) . . . . Kathy Miller
0:04—Full frontal nudity making love on couch with
Andrew Stevens. Looks like a body double.
0:31—In two piece swimsuit, then body double
nude doing strip tease for Stevens. Notice body
double isn't wearing earrings.
0:33—Buns, (probably the body double) on top of
Stevens.
1:21—In black bra in motel room when bad guy
opens her blouse.
Masters of Menace (1990) . . . . Sunny
Transylvania Twist (1990). . . . . Marisa
Brain Donors (1992). . . . . Tina
Made for TV Movies:
I Married a Centerfold (1984) . . . . n.a.
In the Line of Duty: The F.B.I. Murders (1988) . . . .Vickie
TV:
We Got It Made (1983-84). . . . . .Mickey McKenzie
I Had Three Wives (1985). . . . . Samantha

Magazines:
Playboy (Nov 1990) . . . . Teri Copley
••• 90-99—Nude. Very nice!
Playboy (Dec 1990). . . . . Sex Stars of 1990
•• 173—Right breast, while leaning against wall.

Corri, Adrienne
Films:
Corridors of Blood (1957; British) . . . . Rachel
Three Men in a Boat (1958) . . . . Clara Willis
Doctor Zhivago (1965) . . . . Amelia
A Clockwork Orange (1971). . . . . Mrs. Alexander
•• 0:11—Breasts through cut-outs in her top, then full
frontal nudity getting raped by Malcolm McDowell
and his friends.
Revenge of the Pink Panther (1978) . . . Therese Douvier

Costa, Sara
Films:
Weekend Pass (1984) . . . . Tuesday Del Mundo
••• 0:07—Buns in G-string, then topless during strip
dance routine on stage.
Stripper (1985) . . . . Herself
••• 0:16—Topless doing strip dance routine.
••• 0:46—Topless and buns dancing on stage in a G-
string.
••• 1:12—Topless doing another strip routine.
Video Tapes:
Hot Bodies (1988) . . . . Herself
••• 0:00—Nude, dancing on stage. Long scene. Danc-
ing with a big boa snake.
••• 0:04—Topless and buns in G-string.
Magazines:
Playboy (Nov 1985) . . . . Sex in Cinema 1985
••• 130—Topless, doing dance routine in still from *Stripper.*

Courtney, Dori
Films:
Hollywood Hot Tubs 2—Educating Crystal (1989)
. . . . Hot Tub Girl
•• 1:00—Topless stuck in the spa and getting her hair
freed.
Tango & Cash (1989) . . . . Dressing Room Girl
• 1:06—Topless, sitting in chair looking in the mirror
in the background. Long shot.
Mob Boss (1990). . . . . Kathryn
••• 0:31—In black bra, talking with Eddie Deezen, then
topless. Nice close-up. Long scene.
Sorority Girls and the Creature from Hell (1990)
. . . . Belinda
•• 0:06—Topless, drying herself off after shower.
(Wearing panties.)
••• 0:08—More topless, still drying herself off.
• 0:12—Brief right breast, while in car with J.J.
••• 0:35—Topless in spa with J.J.
• 0:37—Buns, then left breast, while in spa during
Gerald's fantasy.

••• 0:41—Topless taking off her top by stream while J.J.
gets killed.
•• 0:43—Topless, running around at night getting
chased by the creature.
Millenium Countdown (1991) . . . . n.a.
Whore (1991). . . . . Topless woman on TV
a.k.a. If you're afraid to say it... Just see it
• 0:14—Brief topless on TV in old folks home in a
scene from *Mob Boss.*

• Courtney, Lorna
Films:
Ghoul School (1990) . . . . Mary
Affairs of the Heart (1992) . . . . .Jane
Private Screenings.
••• 1:04—Topless, making love in front of a fire in sleep-
ing bag with Dick.

Cox, Ashley
Films:
Drive-In (1976) . . . . .Mary-Louise
King of the Mountain (1981) . . . . .Elaine
Looker (1981) . . . . Candy
Night Shift (1982) . . . . .Jenny Lynn
Magazines:
Playboy (Dec 1977) . . . . Playmate

Cox, Courteney
Films:
Down Twisted (1987) .Farah
Masters of the Universe (1987). . . . . Julie Winston
Cocoon, The Return (1988) . . . . .Sara
Blue Desert (1990) . . . . Lisa Roberts
0:52—Silhouette of right breast, standing up with
Steve. Probably a body double. Very, very brief right
nipple between Steve's arms lying in bed. Dark, hard
to see.
•• 0:53—Left breast, lying in bed under Steve. A little
hard to see her face, but it sure looks like her to me!
1:14—Buns and part of left breast getting towel.
Looks like a body double.
Curiosity Kills (1990) . . . . Gwen
Mr. Destiny (1990). . . . . .Jewel Jagger
Shaking the Tree (1991). . . . . n.a.
Made for Cable TV:
Dream On: Come and Knock On Our Door...
(1992; HBO). .Alisha Littleton
Miniseries:
Till We Meet Again (1989) . . . . .Freddy
Made for TV Movies:
Roxanne: The Prize Pulitzer (1989). . . . Jacquie Kimberly
Battling for Baby (1992). . . . . .Katherine
TV:
Misfits of Science (1985-86). . . . . Gloria Dinallo
Family Ties (1987-89). . . . . Lauren Miller
Music Videos:
Dancing in the Dark/Bruce Springsteen
. . . . .Girl Who Goes Up on Stage

• Coyne, Ria

Films:

Corporate Affairs (1990). . . . . Mistress
- •• 0:10—Left breast several times in back of car with Arthur.

Naked Obsession (1990) . . . . .Cynthia
- •• 0:11—Topless on stage, dancing in black lingerie.
- • 0:13—Buns in G-string while dancing.
- •• 0:14—More topless and buns while dancing.

Magazines:

Playboy's Book of Lingerie (Jan 1992) . . . . . . Herself
- ••• 17—Full frontal nudity.

Playboy's Book of Lingerie (Mar 1992) . . . . . Herself
- ••• 8—Topless.

Playboy's Career Girls (Aug 1992) . . . . . . Funny Girls
- ••• 28—Topless.

Crampton, Barbara

Films:

Body Double (1984). . . . . .Carol Sculley
- •• 0:04—Brief right breast, while making love in bed with another man when her husband walks in.

Fraternity Vacation (1985) . . . . .Chrissie
- ••• 0:16—Topless and buns in bedroom with two guys taking off her swimsuit.

Re-Animator (1985). . . . . .Megan Halsey
(Unrated version reviewed.)
- •• 0:10—Brief buns putting panties on, then topless, putting bra on after making love with Dan.
- •• 1:09—Full frontal nudity, lying unconscious on table getting strapped down.
- • 1:10—Topless getting her breasts fondled by a headless body.
- • 1:19—Topless on the table.

Chopping Mall (1986) . . . . .Suzie
- •• 0:22—Brief topless taking off top in furniture store in front of her boyfriend on the couch.

From Beyond (1986) . . . . . .Dr. Katherine McMichaels
- •• 0:44—Brief topless after getting blouse torn off by the creature in the laboratory.
- 0:51—Buns getting on top of Jeffrey Combs in black leather outfit.

Kidnapped (1986) . . . . Bonnie
- 0:35—In white bra and panties in hotel room.
- ••• 0:37—Topless getting tormented by a bad guy in bed.
- •• 1:12—Topless opening her pajamas for David Naughton.
- •• 1:14—Topless in white panties getting dressed.

Puppet Master (1989). . . . . .Woman at Carnival
Trancers II (1991) . . . . .Sadie Brady
TV:
The Young and the Restless .Leanna Randolph Newman
Days of Our Lives (1983). . . . . .Trista Evans
Magazines:
Playboy (Dec 1986). .n.a.

• Craven, Mimi

Films:

Mikey (1992) . . . . n.a.
Made for Cable Movies:
Disaster in Time (1992; Showtime). . . . . Carolyn
a.k.a. Timescape
Made for Cable TV:

Dream On: The Thirty-Seven Year Itch (1991; HBO)
. . . . Monica
- ••• 0:22—Topless several times with Martin in his office.

Video Tapes:

Inside Out 4 (1992). . . . . Dolores/Put Asunder
(Unrated version reviewed.)
- • 0:18—Left breast in bed with her husband.
- ••• 0:22—Topless, lying in bed after making love with her husband.

• Crawford, Cindy

Supermodel and pin-up calendar girl.
Wife of actor Richard Gere.
Model for *Revlon* cosmetics and *Diet Pepsi*.
TV:
House of Style (1992-) . . . . Hostess
Video Tapes:
Cindy Crawford: Shape Your Body Workout (1992)
. . . . .Herself
Magazines:
Playboy (Jul 1988) . . . . .Skin Suits
- •• Topless B&W photos.

Playboy (Dec 1990) . . . . .Sex Stars of 1990
- • 176—Buns, while holding a sheet. B&W.

• Crespo, Teresa

Films:
Out of the Dark (1988) . . . . Debbie
Made for Cable Movies:
Nails (1992; Showtime). . . . . Elena Hernandez
- •• 0:44—Topless, taking off her top in room with Dennis Hopper.

• Cristiani, Tina

Films:
Badge 373 (1972) . . . . Mrs. Caputo
Magazines:
Playboy (Jun 1973). . . . . Next Month
- • 254—Full frontal nudity in B&W photo.

Playboy (Jul 1973) . . . . Tina of the Tanbark
- ••• 135-141—Full frontal nudity.

Crockett, Karlene

Films:
Charlie Chan & the Curse of the Dragon Queen (1981)
. . . . Brenda Lupowitz
Eyes of Fire (1983). . . . . Leah
- • 0:44—Brief topless sitting up in the water and scaring Mr. Dalton.
- • 1:16—Topless talking to Dalton who is trapped in a tree. Brief topless again when he pulls the creature out of the tree.

Massive Retaliation (1984) . . . . Marianne Briscoe
Return (1985) . . . . Diana
- 0:46—Topless sitting up and getting out of bed.
  Long shot.

Crosby, Cathy Lee

Films:
The Laughing Policeman (1974) . . . . Kay Butler
Coach (1978). . . . . Randy
- 0:31—Very brief side view of left breast when Micha-
  el Biehn opens the door while she's putting on her
  top.
  0:52—In wet white T-shirt at the beach and in her
  house with Biehn.
  1:11—Very, very brief topless in shower room with
  Biehn. Blurry, hard to see anything.
The Dark (1979) . . . . Zoe
TV:
That's Incredible (1980-84) . . . . Host

Crosby, Denise

Granddaughter of actor/singer Bing Crosby.
Films:
48 Hrs. (1982). . . . . Sally
  0:47—Very, very brief side view of half of left breast,
  while swinging baseball bat at Eddie Murphy.
- 1:24—Very brief side view of right breast when
  James Remar pushes her onto bed.
- 1:25—Very brief topless then very brief side view of
  right breast attacking Nick Nolte.
The Trail of the Pink Panther (1982) . . . . n.a.
Curse of the Pink Panther (1983). . . . . Bruno's Moll
The Man Who Loved Women (1983) . . . . Enid
Desert Hearts (1986). . . . . Pat
Eliminators (1986). . . . . Nora Hunter
  0:47—In wet white tank top inside an airplane cock-
  pit that has crashed in the water.
  0:50—Wet tank top getting out of the plane.
Arizona Heat (1988) . . . . Jill Andrews
- 1:13—Brief upper half of left breast in shower with
  Larry.
Miracle Mile (1989). . . . . Landa
Pet Sematary (1989) . . . . Rachel Creed
Skin Deep (1989) . . . . Angie Smith
Dolly Dearest (1992). . . . . n.a.
Made for Cable TV:
**Red Shoe Diaries: You Have the Right to Remain
  Silent** (1992; Showtime)
  . . . . Officer Lynn/Mona McCabe
  0:14—In black bra and panties, changing clothes in
  front of Nick.
- 0:22—Topless, taking off her bra and making love
  with Nick on barber's chair.
- 0:26—Brief buns, while sitting on Nick's lap in the
  chair.
TV:
Star Trek: The Next Generation (1987-88)
  . . . . Lt. Tasha Yar
Star Trek: The Next Generation (1991) . . . . Sela

Key West (1992-) . . . . n.a.
Magazines:
Playboy (Mar 1979) . . . . A Different Kind of Crosby
  ••• 99-103—Full frontal nudity.
Playboy (Feb 1980) . . . . The Year in Sex
  •• 160—Full frontal nudity.
Playboy (May 1988) . . . . Star Treat
  ••• 74-79—Nude, photos from the 1979 pictorial.

Crosby, Katja

Films:
It's Alive III: Island of the Alive (1988) . . . . . Girl in Court
A Return to Salem's Lot (1988) . . . . Cathy
  •• 0:36—Topless making love in bed with Joey.
- 0:48—Side view of right breast kissing Joey outside
  next to a stream.

Crosby, Lucinda

Films:
Blue Thunder (1983) . . . . Bel-Air Woman
The Naked Cage (1985). . . . . Rhonda
Stitches (1985). . . . . Nurse #5
Blue Movies (1988) . . . . Randy Moon
- 0:10—Topless in a spa, in a movie.
- •• 0:11—Topless, kneeling on a table, shooting a por-
  no movie.
- ••• 0:32—Topless auditioning for Buzz.
- 1:02—Topless on desk in a movie.
Pretty Woman (1990). . . . . Olsen Sister
Frankie & Johnny (1991) . . . . The Abused Neighbor

• Crow, Emilia

a.k.a. Emilia Lesniak.
Films:
Scarface (1983) . . . . Echevera
Fear City (1984). . . . . Bibi
- •• 0:16—Topless, dancing at the Metropole club.
- 1:00—Topless, dancing on the stage.
9 Deaths of the Ninja (1985) . . . . Jennifer Barnes
Hollywood Vice Squad (1986) . . . . Linda
Hitz (1992) . . . . Chelsea Walker
  a.k.a. Judgment
  ••• 0:27—Topless and very brief upper half of lower
  frontal nudity, making love in bed with Jimmy. Lit
  with red light.
Made for Cable Movies:
Disaster in Time (1992; Showtime) . . . . Reeve
  a.k.a. Timescape
- 0:18—Side view of left breast, sitting in front of vanity while Jeff Daniels watches. Long shot.

• Crowley, Jeananne

Films:
Educating Rita (1983; British). . . . . Julia
Reilly: Ace of Spies (1984) . . . . Margaret
  •• 0:52—Brief topless, opening her blouse for her in-
  valid husband.

Cruikshank, Laura

Films:
Ruthless People (1986) . . . . .n.a.
Buying Time (1987) . . . . .Jessica
•• 0:52—Topless several times making love with Ron on pool table.

Cser, Nancy

Films:
Joy (1983; French/Canadian). . . . . Unidentified
Perfect Timing (1984) . . . . Lacy
0:54—In white lingerie, taking off clothes for Harry and posing.
••• 0:56—Topless getting photographed by Harry.
• 0:58—Topless, making love with Harry.
• 1:01—Topless.
Separate Vacations (1985). . . . . Stewardess
Head Office (1986) . . . . Dantley's Secretary
Deceived (1991) . . . . Harvey's Girlfriend

Cummins, Juliette

Films:
Friday the 13th, Part V—A New Beginning (1985)
. . . . Robin
••• 1:01—Topless, wearing panties getting undressed and climbing into bed just before getting killed.
1:05—Very brief topless, covered with blood when Reggie discovers her dead.
Psycho III (1986). . . . . .Red
••• 0:39—Topless making love with Duke in his motel room, then getting thrown out.
Slumber Party Massacre II (1987) . . . . Sheila
•• 0:24—In black bra, then topless in living room during a party with her girlfriends.
Deadly Dreams (1988). . . . . Maggie Kallir
• 0:25—Topless on bed, taking off her blouse and kissing Alex.
••• 0:55—Topless and brief buns, making love with Jack in bed.
Magazines:
Playboy (Nov 1986) . . . . Sex in Cinema 1986
•• 129—Topless in a photo from *Psycho III*.

Curran, Lynette

Films:
Alvin Purple (1973; Australian). . . . . . First Sugar Girl
•• 0:02—Brief full frontal nudity when Alvin opens the door.
Heatwave (1983; Australian) . . . . Evonne
Bliss (1985; Australian) . . . . Bettina Joy
The Year My Voice Broke (1987; Australian). .Anne Olson

Currie, Cherie

Singer.
Identical twin sister of singer/actress Marie Currie Lukather.
Films:
Foxes (1980). . . . . Annie
Parasite (1982) . . . . Dana

Wavelength (1982) . . . . Iris Longacre
0:09—Brief side view of right breast and buns getting out of bed. Dark, don't really see anything.
The Rosebud Beach Hotel (1985) . . . . Cherie
1:13—Singing with her twin sister in braless pink T-shirt on the beach.
Rich Girl (1991) . . . . .Michelle

Currie, Sondra

Films:
Policewoman (1974) . . . . n.a.
Jessi's Girls (1976) . . . . Jessica
• 0:02—Nude in water cleaning up, then brief left breast getting dressed.
• 0:07—Topless getting raped by four guys. Fairly long scene.
• 0:37—Topless kissing Clay under a tree. Hard to see because of the shadows.
The Last Married Couple in America (1980)
. . . . Lainy
•• 1:32—Topless taking off her clothes in bedroom in front of Natalie Wood, George Segal and her husband.
The Concrete Jungle (1982) . . . . Katherine
Street Justice (1988). .Mandy
Illicit Behavior (1991). . . . . Yolanda
(Unrated version reviewed.)
Magazines:
Playboy (Nov 1980) . . . . Sex in Cinema 1980
• 174—Side view of right breast.

Curtin, Jane

Films:
How to Beat the High Cost of Living (1980)
. . . . .Elaine
1:28—In pink bra, distracting everybody in the mall so her friends can steal money.
• 1:29—Close up topless, taking off her bra. Probably a body double.
O.C. and Stiggs (1987) . . . . Elinore Schwab
Made for TV Movies:
Common Ground (1990). . . . . Alice McGoff
TV:
Saturday Night Live (1975-80)
. . . . .Not Ready For Primetime Player
Kate and Allie (1984-90) . . . . Allie Lowell
Working It Out (1990) . . . . Sarah Marshall

Curtis, Allegra

Daughter of actor Tony Curtis and his second wife, actress Christine Kaufmann.
Films:
Midnight Cop (1988; Italian) . . . . Monika Carstens
Guns (1990). . . . . Robyn
Magazines:
Playboy (Apr 1990) . . . . Brava, Allegra!
••• 92-97—Full frontal nudity.

Curtis, Jamie Lee

Daughter of actor Tony Curtis and actress Janet Leigh.
Wife of actor Christopher Guest.
Films:
Halloween (1978) . . . . Laurie
The Fog (1980) . . . . Elizabeth Solley
Prom Night (1980) . . . . Kim
Terror Train (1980; Canadian) . . . . Alena
Halloween II (1981). . . . . Laurie
Road Games (1981) . . . . Hitch/Pamela
Trading Places (1983) . . . . Ophelia
 ••• 1:00—Topless in black panties after taking red dress
   off in bathroom while Dan Aykroyd watches.
 ••• 1:09—Topless and black panties taking off halter top
   and pants getting into bed with a sick Aykroyd.
The Adventures of Buckaroo Banzai, Across the 8th
 Dimension (1984) . . . . Dr. Sandra Banzai
Grandview, U.S.A. (1984) . . . . Michelle "Mike" Cody
 ••• 1:00—Left breast, lying in bed with C. Thomas Howell.
Love Letters (1984) . . . . Anna Winter
 ••• 0:31—Topless in bathtub reading a letter, then topless in bed making love with James Keach.
 • 0:36—Brief topless in lifeguard station with Keach.
 ••• 0:44—Brief topless admiring a picture taken of her
   by Keach.
 ••• 0:46—Topless and buns in bedroom undressing
   with Keach.
 • 0:49—Topless in black and white Polaroid photographs that Keach is taking.
   1:02—In white slip in her house with Keach.
 • 1:07—Right breast, sticking out of slip, then right
   breast, while sleeping in bed with Keach.
Perfect (1985) . . . . Jessie Wilson
   0:14—No nudity, but doing aerobics in leotards.
   0:26—More aerobics in leotards.
   0:40—More aerobics, mentally making love with
   John Travolta while leading the class.
   1:19—More aerobics when photographer is shooting pictures.
   1:32—In red leotard after the article comes out in
   Rolling Stone.
Tall Tales and Legends: Annie Oakley (1985)
 . . . . Annie Oakley
A Man in Love (1987) . . . . Susan Elliot
Dominick and Eugene (1988) . . . . Jennifer Reston
A Fish Called Wanda (1988) . . . . Wanda
   0:21—In black bra and panties changing in the bed-
   room talking to Kevin Kline.
   0:35—In black bra sitting on bed getting undressed.
Blue Steel (1989). . . . . .Megan Turner
   1:27—Very, very brief buns twice when rolling out of
   bed, trying to get her gun. Dark.
My Girl (1991) . . . . Shelly DeVoto
Queens Logic (1991). Grace
Made for TV Movies:
Death of a Centerfold: The Dorothy Stratten Story
 (1981). . . . . .Dorothy Stratten
 Topless in European version.

She's in the Army Now (1981) . . . . n.a.
TV:
Operation Petticoat (1977-78) . . . . . . Lt. Barbara Duran
Anything but Love (1989-92). . . . . Hannah Miller
Magazines:
Playboy (Nov 1983) . . . . Sex in Cinema 1983
 ••• 151—Topless and right breast photo from *Trading
   Places.*

Cutter, Lise

Films:
Buy and Cell (1988) . . . . Ellen
Buy & Cell (1989) . . . . Dr. Ellen Scott
Havana (1990) . . . . Patty
 • 0:44—Most of side of left breast with Robert Red-
   ford. Very, very brief part of right breast while he
   turns her around. Very brief left breast when Redford
   puts a cold glass on her chest. Dark, hard to see.
Made for TV Movies:
Desperado: The Outlaw Wars (1989) . . . . Nora
TV:
Equal Justice (1991) . . . . .Andrea Kanin
Dangerous Curves (1992-) . . . . Gina

Cyr, Myriam

Films:
Gothic (1986; British) .Claire
 •• 0:53—Left breast, then topless lying in bed with
   Gabriel Byrne.
 • 0:55—Brief left breast lying in bed. Long shot.
 • 1:02—Topless sitting on pool table opening her top
   for Julian Sands. Special effect with eyes in her nip-
   ples.
 • 1:12—Buns and brief topless covered with mud.
Frankenstein Unbound (1990) . . . . . Information Officer

D'Abo, Maryam

Cousin of actress Olivia d'Abo.
Films:
Xtro (1982). . . . . .Analise
 ••• 0:25—Topless making love with her boyfriend on
   the floor in her bedroom.
 •• 0:56—Brief topless with her boyfriend again.
Until September (1984) . . . . .Nathalie
White Nights (1985) . . . . French Girl Friend
The Living Daylights (1987) . . . . Kara Milovy
Immortal Sins (1992) . . . . n.a.
Miniseries:
Master of the Game (1984) . . . . Dominique
Made for TV Movies:
Something Is Out There (1988) . . . . Ta'ra
Magazines:
Playboy (Sep 1987) . . . . D'Abo
Playboy (Dec 1987) . . . . .Sex Stars of 1987
 ••• 154—Right breast, sitting behind cello.
Playboy's Nudes (Oct 1990) . . . . .Herself
 •• 12—Topless, covered with gold paint.

D'Abo, Olivia

Cousin of actress Maryam d'Abo.
Films:
Bolero (1984) . . . . Paloma
- 0:38—Nude covered with bubbles taking a bath.
- 1:05—Brief topless in the steam room with Bo.
- 1:32—Topless in the steam room talking with Bo. Hard to see because it's so steamy.

Conan the Destroyer (1984) . . . . Princess Jehnna
Bullies (1985) . . . . Becky Cullen
- • 0:39—In wet white T-shirt swimming in river while Matt watches.

Dream to Believe (1985; Canadian) . . . . Robin Crew
  0:29—Working out in training room wearing a sexy cotton tank top.
Into the Fire (1988) . . . . Liette
a.k.a. Legend of Lone Wolf
  0:07—Very, very brief silhouette of left breast in bed with Wade.
- • 0:32—Topless on bed with Wade. A little bit dark and hard to see.
- • 1:10—Topless in the bathtub. (Note her panties when she gets up.)

The Spirit of '76 (1991) Chanel-6
TV:
The Wonder Years (1987-) . . . . Karen Arnold

D'Angelo, Beverly

Films:
Annie Hall (1977) . . . . Actress in Rob's TV Show
First Love (1977) . . . . Shelley
  0:05—Very, very brief half of left breast when her jacket opens up while talking to William Katt.
  0:11—In white bra and black panties in Katt's bedroom.
- • 1:10—Brief topless taking off her top in bedroom with Katt.
The Sentinel (1977) . . . . Sandra
  0:25—Masturbating in red leotard and tights on couch in front of Cristina Raines.
- • 0:33—Brief topless playing cymbals during Raines' nightmare (in B&W).
  1:24—Brief topless long shot with zombie make up, munching on a dead Chris Sarandon.
Hair (1979) . . . . Sheila
- • 0:59—In white bra and panties, then topless on rock near pond. Medium long shot.
- • • 1:01—Topless in panties getting out of the pond.
- • 1:38—Side view of right breast changing clothes in car with George.

Coal Miner's Daughter (1980) . . . . Patsy Cline
Honky Tonk Freeway (1981) . . . . Carmen
Paternity (1981) . . . . Maggie
Finders Keepers (1983) . . . . Standish Logan
National Lampoon's Vacation (1983) . Ellen Griswold
- • • 0:18—Brief topless taking a shower in the motel.
- • 1:19—Brief topless taking off shirt and jumping into the swimming pool.

Highpoint (1984; Canadian) . . . . Lise Hatcher

National Lampoon's European Vacation (1985)
. . . . Ellen Griswold
Big Trouble (1986) . . . . Blanche Ricky
Slow Burn (1986) . . . . Laine Fleischer
- 1:01—Topless making love with Eric Roberts. Don't see her face. Part of lower frontal nudity showing tattoo.

In the Mood (1987) . . . . Francine Glatt
Maid to Order (1987) . . . . Stella
Aria (1988; U.S./British) . . . . Gilda
High Spirits (1988) . . . . Sharon
Cold Front (1989; Canadian) . . . . . . Amanda O'Rourke
National Lampoon's Christmas Vacation (1989)
. . . . Ellen Griswold
Daddy's Dyin'... Who's Got the Will? (1990) . . . . Evalita
Pacific Heights (1990) . . . . Ann
- 0:01—Sort of topless in reflection on TV screen, then right breast, in bed with Michael Keaton.
  0:03—Very brief buns, turning over on bed when two guys burst in to the house.

Lonely Hearts (1991) . . . . n.a.
The Miracle (1991; British) . . . . Renee
The Pope Must Die (1991) . . . . Veronica Dante
a.k.a. The Pope Must Diet
Made for Cable TV:
Tales From the Crypt: Werewolf Concerto (1992; HBO)
. . . . Janice Baird
Made for TV Movies:
Trial: The Price of Passion (1992)
. . . . Johnnie Faye Boudreau
TV:
Captains and the Kings (1976) . . . . Miss Emmy

• D'Angelo, Mirella

Films:
Caligula (1980) . . . . Livia
  (X-rated, 147 minute version.)
- • 1:08—Buns and topless in kitchen with Malcolm McDowell. Full frontal nudity on table when he rapes her in front of her husband-to-be.
Magazines:
Penthouse (May 1980) . . . . Caligula
  83—Buns, after rape.
- • 84—Full frontal nudity.
Playboy (Jun 1980) . . . . Fellini's Feminist Fantasy
- • 132—Right breast and lower frontal nudity.

D'Arbanville, Patti

Ex-wife of actor Don Johnson.
Films:
Rancho Deluxe (1975) . . . . Betty Fargo
Big Wednesday (1978) . . . . Sally
The Fifth Floor (1978) . . . . Cathy Burke
The Main Event (1979) . . . . Donna
Time After Time (1979; British) . . . . Shirley
Hog Wild (1980; Canadian) . . . . Angie
Modern Problems (1981) . . . . Darcy
- 0:48—Very brief right breast in bed after Chevy Chase has telekinetic sex with her.

Bilitis (1982; French) . . . . Bilitis
••• 0:25—Topless copying Melissa undressing.
•• 0:27—Topless on tree.
••• 0:31—Full frontal nudity taking off swimsuit with Melissa.
0:36—Buns, cleaning herself in the bathroom.
•• 0:59—Topless and buns making love with Melissa.
The Boys Next Door (1985) . . . . Angie
Real Genius (1985) . . . . Sherry Nugil
Call Me (1988) . . . . Coni
Fresh Horses (1988) . . . . Jean
Made for TV Movies:
Crossing the Mob (1988) . . . . Lucy Conte
TV:
Wiseguy (1989-90) . . . . Amber Twine
Magazines:
Playboy (Aug 1974) . . . . Instant Warhol
• 83-85—Full frontal nudity in Polaroid photo collages.
Playboy (Nov 1974) . . . . Sex in Cinema 1974
•• 145—Topless on top of Jeff Bridges from *Rancho Deluxe.*
Playboy (May 1977) . . . . Our Lady D'Arbanville
••• Full frontal nudity in *Bilitis* photos taken by David Hamilton.
Playboy (Jun 1980) . . . . Grapevine
• 301—Topless under black fishnet top. B&W.

• D'Ortez, Cristobel

Films:
Outlaw of Gor (1987) . . . . Alicia
Edgar Allan Poe's "The Masque of the Red Death"
(1989). . . . . Dr. Karen
Wild Zone (1989) . . . . Mary
•• 1:19—Topless in the brush, getting molested by a bad guy.

Dahms, Gail

Films:
The Silent Partner (1978) . . . . Louise
• 0:31—Right breast in bathroom with another guy when Elliott Gould surprises them.
The Tomorrow Man (1979). . . . . n.a.

Daily, Elizabeth

a.k.a. E. G. Daily.
Films:
The Escape Artist (1982) . . . . Sandra
Funny Money (1982) . . . . Cass
One Dark Night (1983). . . . . Leslie
Valley Girl (1983) . . . . Loryn
•• 0:16—In bra through open jumpsuit, then brief topless on bed with Tommy.
Wacko (1983) . . . . Bambi
No Small Affair (1984). . . . . Susan
Streets of Fire (1984). . . . . Baby Doll
Fandango (1985) . . . . Judy
Pee Wee's Big Adventure (1985) . . . . Dottie
Bad Dreams (1988). . . . . Lana

Loverboy (1989) . . . . Linda
Dogfight (1991). . . . . Marcie
Dutch (1991) . . . . Halley
a.k.a. Driving Me Crazy
Magazines:
Playboy (Nov 1983) . . . . Sex in Cinema 1983
•• 146—Topless.

Dale, Cynthia

Films:
My Bloody Valentine (1981; Canadian) . . . . Patty
Heavenly Bodies (1985) . . . . Samantha Blair
• 0:30—Brief topless fantasizing about making love with Steve while doing aerobic exercises.
The Boy in Blue (1986; Canadian). . . . . Margaret
••• 1:15—Topless standing in a loft kissing Nicholas Cage.
Moonstruck (1987) . . . . Sheila
Made for Cable Movies:
The Liberators (1987; Disney) . . . . . . Elizabeth Giddings
Made for TV Movies:
Sadie and Son (1987). . . . . Paula Melvin
In the Eyes of a Stranger (1992). . . . . Nancy

Dale, Jennifer

Films:
Stone Cold Dead (1979; Canadian) . . . Claudia Grissom
Suzanne (1980; Canadian) . . . . Suzanne
•• 0:29—Topless when boyfriend lifts her sweatshirt up when she's sitting on couch doing homework.
•• 0:53—Topless with Nicky on the floor.
Your Ticket is No Longer Valid (1982) . . . . . . Laura
•• 0:27—In black panties, then topless when her husband fantasizes, then makes love with her.
1:23—Left breast in bed with Montoya, then sitting, waiting for Richard Harris.
Of Unknown Origin (1983; Canadian) . . . . . Lorrie Wells
Separate Vacations (1985). . . . . Sarah Moore
• 0:17—Brief right breast in bed with her husband after son accidentally comes into their bedroom.
0:20—In a bra and slip showing the baby sitter the house before leaving.
•• 1:14—Topless on the cabin floor with Jeff after having a fight with her husband.
• 1:19—Brief right breast, in bed with her husband.
Magazines:
Playboy (Nov 1980) . . . . Sex in Cinema 1980
•• 181—Right breast.

• *Dali, Tracy*

Films:
Click: Calendar Girl Killer (1989) . . . . June
Virgin High (1990) . . . . Christy
•• 0:04—Brief topless several times when her blouse and bra pop open while talking to her parents.

Sunset Heat (1991) . . . . Carl's Pool Girl
(Unrated version reviewed.)
- •• 1:08—Topless in pool with Dennis Hopper. Topless and buns, getting out of pool while wearing a G-string.

Made for Cable Movies:
Fatal Charm (1992; Showtime). . . . . Dream Girl
- •• 0:11—Topless in van with Christopher Atkins. Lots of diffusion.
- • 0:20—Brief topless in van during Amanda Peterson's fantasy.

Magazines:
Playboy's Book of Lingerie (Jan 1991) . . . . . . Herself
- ••• 72-73—Full frontal nudity.
- ••• 78—Full frontal nudity.

Playboy's Book of Lingerie (Mar 1991) . . . . . Herself
- •• 82—Right breast.

Playboy's Book of Lingerie (Sep 1991) . . . . . Herself
- ••• 25—Full frontal nudity.
- ••• 80—Full frontal nudity.

Playboy's Book of Lingerie (Nov 1991) . . . . . Herself
- ••• 96—Topless.

Playboy's Book of Lingerie (Mar 1992) . . . . . Herself
- • 16—Lower frontal nudity and partial left breast.
- ••• 32-33—Full frontal nudity.

Playboy's Book of Lingerie (May 1992) . . . . . Herself
- •• 9—Left breast.

Dalle, Béatrice

Films:
Betty Blue (1986; French). . . . . .Betty
- ••• 0:01—Topless making love in bed with Zorg. Long sequence.
- ••• 0:30—Nude on bed having sex with boyfriend.
- ••• 1:03—Nude trying to sleep in living room.
- ••• 1:21—Topless in white tap pants in hallway.
- ••• 1:29—Topless lying down with Zorg.
- ••• 1:39—Topless sitting on bathtub crying & talking.

On a Vole Charlie Spencer! (1987) . . . . Movie Star
Night on Earth (1992). . . . . The Blind Passenger
a.k.a. Une Nuit Sur Terre

Magazines:
Playboy (Nov 1987) . . . . Sex in Cinema 1987
- •• 141—Topless in blue light from *Betty Blue*.

Daly, Jeannie

See: Carol, Jean.

Daly, Tyne

Daughter of actor James Daly and actress Hope Newell. Sister of actor Tim Daly. Ex-wife of actor Georg Stanford Brown.
Films:
John and Mary (1969). Hilary
The Adultress (1973) . . . . Inez
- • 0:21—Brief side view of right breast in room with Carl. Brief out of focus topless in bed.
- •• 0:51—Topless outside with Hank.
- ••• 0:53—Topless on a horse with Hank.

The Enforcer (1976). . . . . Kate Moore
Telefon (1977). . . . . Dorothy Putterman
Zoot Suit (1981) . . . . Alice
The Aviator (1984). . . . . Evelyn Stiller
Movers and Shakers (1985) . . . . Nancy Derman
Made for TV Movies:
Intimate Strangers (1977) . . . . n.a.
Face of a Stranger (1991). . . . . Dollie Madison
The Last to Go (1991) . . . . n.a.
TV:
Cagney & Lacey (1982-88) . . . . Mary Beth Lacey
(Won four Emmy Awards.)

Danielson, Lynn

Films:
Mortuary Academy (1988). . . . . Valerie Levitt
Out of the Dark (1988). . . . . Kristi
- • 0:09—Brief topless getting out of bed. More topless outside getting photographed.
- •• 1:01—Topless in motel room making love with Kevin.
- • 1:06—Left breast, while getting out of bed.

Danner, Blythe

Films:
To Kill a Clown (1971) . . . . Lily Frischer
- • 1:10—Side view of left breast sitting on bed talking to Alan Alda. Hair covers breast, hard to see. Buns, getting up and running out of the house.

1776 (1972). . . . . Martha Jefferson
Hearts of the West (1975) . . . . Miss Trout
Futureworld (1976) . . . . Tracy Ballard
The Great Santini (1980) . . . . Lillian Meechum
Man, Woman and Child (1983) . . . . Sheila Beckwith
Brighton Beach Memoirs (1986) . . . . .Kate
Another Woman (1988). . . . . Lydia
Alice (1990) . . . . .Dorothy
Mr. & Mrs. Bridge (1990). . . . . .Grace
The Prince of Tides (1991) . . . . .Sallie Wingo
Made for Cable Movies:
Judgement (1990; HBO) . . . . Emmeline Guitry
Made for TV Movies:
Are You in the House Alone? (1978). . . . . Ann
Money, Power, Murder (1989) . . . . Jeannie
Cruel Doubt (1992) . . . . Bonnie Von Stein
TV:
Adam's Rib (1973) . . . . .Amanda Bonner

Danning, Sybil

a.k.a. Sybille Danninger.
Films:
Bluebeard (1972). . . . . The Prostitute
- • 1:08—Brief topless kissing Nathalie Delon showing her how to make love to her husband.
- • 1:09—Brief left breast, lying on the floor with Delon just before Richard Burton kills both of them.

Maiden Quest (1972) . . . . Kriemhild
a.k.a. The Long Swift Sword of Siegfried
Private Screenings.
- • 0:02—Topless in bath, surrounded by topless
  blonde servants.
- • 0:04—Topless in the bath again.
- ••• 0:10—Nude in tub surrounded by topless servant
  girls.
- ••• 0:12—Topless on bed, getting rubbed with ointment by the servant girls.
- •• 0:35—Topless while in bed with Siegfried.
- • 1:00—Topless in bed with Siegfried.
- ••• 1:19—Topless in bed with Siegfried.

Naughty Nymphs (1972; German) . . . . .Elizabeth
a.k.a. Passion Pill Swingers
a.k.a. Don't Tell Daddy
- ••• 0:21—Nude taking a bath while yelling at her two
  sisters.
- • 0:30—Topless and buns throwing Nicholas out of
  her bedroom.
- •• 0:38—Full frontal nudity running away from Burt.

Albino (1976) . . . . Sally
a.k.a. Night of the Askari
- • 0:19—Topless, then full frontal nudity getting raped
  by the Albino and his buddies.

The Loves of a French Pussycat (1976) . . . . . Andrea
- ••• 0:18—Topless dancing with her boss, then in bed.
- •• 0:24—Topless and buns in swimming pool.
- 0:40—In sheer white bra and panties doing things
  around the house. Long sequence.
- • 0:46—Topless in bathtub with a guy.
- • 1:03—Left breast sticking out of bra, then topless.

The Twist (1976) . . . . Jacques' Secretary
- •• 1:24—Brief topless sitting next to Bruce Dern during
  his daydream.

God's Gun (1977) . . . . Jenny
a.k.a. A Bullet from God
- • 1:09—Right breast popping out of dress with a guy
  in the barn during flashback.

Cat in the Cage (1978) . . . . .Susan Khan
- • 0:24—Brief topless getting slapped around by Ralph.
- • 0:25—Brief left breast several times smoking and
  talking to Ralph, brief left breast getting up.
- •• 0:30—Full frontal nudity getting out of the pool.
- • 0:52—Black bra and panties undressing and getting
  into bed with Ralph. Brief left breast and buns.
- 1:02—In white lingerie in bedroom.
- 1:10—In white slip looking out window.
- 1:15—In black slip.
- • 1:18—Very brief right breast several times, struggling with an attacker on the floor.

Kill Castro (1978) . . . . Veronica
a.k.a. Cuba Crossing
Separate Ways (1979) . . . . .Mary
Battle Beyond the Stars (1980) . . . . St. Exmin
The Day of the Cobra (1980) . . . . Brenda
- • 0:41—Buns and side view of right breast getting out
  of bed and putting robe on with Lou. Long shot.

How to Beat the High Cost of Living (1980) . . . Charlotte
The Man with Bogart's Face (1980) . . . . Cynthia
Nightkill (1981) . . . . Monika Childs
Daughter of Death (1982) . . . . .Susan
a.k.a. Julie Darling
- •• 0:36—Topless in bed with Anthony Franciosa.
- • 0:38—Brief right breast under Franciosa.

Famous T & A (1982) . . . . Hostess
(No longer available for purchase, check your video
store for rental.)
- • 0:00—Brief side view of buns and partial left breast,
  getting dressed.

S.A.S. San Salvador (1982) . . . . . .Countess Alexandra
- • 0:07—Brief left breast, while lying on the couch and
  kissing Malko.

Chained Heat (1983; U.S./German) . . . . Erika
- ••• 0:30—Topless in the shower with Linda Blair.

Hercules (1983) . . . . Arianna
Private Passions (1983) . . . . .Katherine
Howling II: Your Sister is a Werewolf (1984)
. . . . .Stirba
- • 0:35—Left breast, then topless with Mariana in bed-
  room about to have sex with a guy.
- • 1:20—Very brief topless during short clips during
  the end credits. Same shot repeated about 10 times.

Malibu Express (1984) . . . . .Countess Luciana
- • 0:13—Brief topless making love in bed with Cody.

They're Playing with Fire (1984) . . . . Diane Stevens
- 0:04—In two piece swimsuit on boat. Long scene.
- ••• 0:08—Topless and buns making love on top of Jay in
  bed on boat. Nice!
- •• 0:10—Topless and buns getting out of shower, then
  brief side view of right breast.
- 0:43—In black bra and slip, in boat with Jay.
- •• 0:47—In black bra and slip, at home with Michael,
  then panties, then topless and buns getting into
  shower.
- ••• 1:12—In white bra and panties in room with Jay
  then topless.

Jungle Warriors (1985) .Angel
- 0:53—Buns, getting a massage while lying face
  down.

Panther Squad (1986; French/Belgian) . . . . Ilona
Reform School Girls (1986) . . . . Warden Sutter
Young Lady Chatterley II (1986) . . . . Judith Grimmer
- ••• 1:02—Topless in the hut on the table with the Gardener.

Amazon Women on the Moon (1987) . . . . . Queen Lara
Phantom Empire (1987) . . . . The Alien Queen
Talking Walls (1987) . . . . Bathing Beauty
The Tomb (1987) . . . . .Jade
Warrior Queen (1987) . . . . Berenice
L.A. Bounty (1989) . . . . Ruger
Made for Cable TV:
The Hitchhiker: Face to Face (1984; HBO)
. . . . Gloria Loring
(Available on *The Hitchhiker, Volume 4.*)
- •• 0:10—In red bra and panties, then right breast mak-
  ing love with Robert Vaughn.

Magazines:
Playboy (Dec 1980) . . . . Sex Stars of 1980
•• 246—Right breast and buns.
Playboy (Aug 1983) . . . . .n.a.
Playboy (Nov 1983) . . . . Sex in Cinema 1983
•• 145—Topless.
Playboy (Dec 1983) . . . . Sex Stars of 1983
••• 210—Full frontal nudity.
Playboy (Dec 1984) . . . . Sex Stars of 1984
• 202—Half of right breast and lower frontal nudity.
Playboy (Dec 1986) . . . . Sex Stars of 86
Playboy's Nudes (Oct 1990) . . . . Herself
•• 20—Left breast and partial lower frontal nudity.

Danon, Leslie
Films:
Beach Balls (1988) . . . . Kathleen
• 1:06—In bra, then brief topless in car with Doug.
Marked for Death (1990) . . . . Girl #1
Illusions (1992) . . . . Young Laura

Dante, Crisstyn
Films:
Midnight Crossing (1988)
. . . . Body Double for Kim Cattrall
• 0:29—Brief left breast making love on small boat, body double for Kim Cattrall.
Phantom of the Mall: Eric's Revenge (1988)
. . . . Body Double for Ms. Whitman
•• 0:25—Topless in bed about five times with Peter.
State Park (1988; Canadian). . . . . Blond in Net
• 0:45—Very, very brief left breast putting swimsuit top back on after being rescued from net by the guy in the bear costume.
The Nightmare on Elm Street 5: The Dream Child (1989) . . . . Body Double for Alice
Last Call (1990) . . . . Hooker

Danziger, Maia
Films:
High Stakes (1989) . . . . Veronica
Last Exit to Brooklyn (1990). . . . . Mary Black
0:10—Out of focus buns and right breast taking off her slip.
• 0:12—Very brief topless making love with Harry. Topless after.

• Dare, Barbara
Adult film actress.
a.k.a. Stacey Nix.
Films:
Evil Toons (1991) . . . . Jan
••• 0:30—Topless, taking off robe and putting on red nightgown.
•• 1:06—Topless when her top is pulled down by Roxanne.

Video Tapes:
High Society Centerspread Video #10: Barbara Dare . . . . .Herself
•• 0:01—Topless undressing.
••• 0:03—Nude on bed with a guy video taping, then making love with her. Nice, long scene.
••• 0:08—Full frontal nudity during photo shoot and interview.
••• 0:13—Nude, on lounge chair, masturbating.
•• 0:18—Topless, sitting in chair during interview.

Dare, Debra
See: Dutch, Deborah.

Darnell, Vicki
Films:
Senior Week (1987) . . . . Everett's Dream Teacher
•• 0:03—Topless during classroom fantasy.
Alien Space Avenger (1988) . . . . .Bordello Lady
Brain Damage (1988). . . . . Blonde in Hell Club
Frankenhooker (1990) . . . . .Sugar
• 0:36—Brief middle part of each breast through slit bra during introduction to Jeffrey.
•• 0:37—Breasts, sticking out of black lingerie while getting legs measured.
• 0:38—Right breast, while sitting in chair.
• 0:39—Topless through slit lingerie three times while folding clothes.
0:40—Buns, fighting over drugs.
••• 0:41—Very brief right breast, sitting on bed (on the right) enjoying drugs. Topless dancing with the other girls.
Sorority Girls and the Creature from Hell (1990)
. . . . Dancer
0:17—Topless in bar in open blouse, dancing on stage. Lit with red light.
• 0:24—More topless dancing on stage.

Das, Alisha
Films:
The Slugger's Wife (1985) . . . . .Lola
Danger Zone II: Reaper's Revenge (1988). . . . . Francine
Nightwish (1988) . . . . Kim
(Unedited version reviewed.)
•• 1:09—Brief topless, then left breast in open dress caressing herself while lying on the ground.

• Datcher, Alex
Films:
Netherworld (1991). . . . . Mary Magdalene
Video Tapes:
Inside Out 3 (1992) . . . . .Annie/The Wet Dream
••• 1:24—Topless, taking off her blouse in front of the fish tank.
• 1:25—Topless, getting up when Dennis leaves.
• 1:26—Topless, getting into bathtub. Long shot.
• 1:28—Topless in bathtub.
• 1:29—Topless in bathtub with Greg Louganis.

Davidovich, Lolita

a.k.a. Lolita David.
Films:
Class (1983) . . . . 1st Girl (motel)
Recruits (1986; Canadian). . . . . Susan
• 0:19—Very brief topless when Steve bumps into her
in the shower room.
•• 0:54—Right breast, then topless making out with
Steve in car.
•• 0:56—Topless, twice, while driving around in car
with Steve, the Governor and his wife.
•• 0:58—Topless, getting out of the car.
The Big Town (1987) . . . . Black Lace Stripper
Blindside (1988; Canadian). . . . . Adele
•• 0:32—Topless dancing on stage.
0:39—Sort of buns bending over and pointing a gun
through her legs in front of mirror.
A New Life (1988). . . . . n.a.
Blaze (1989) . . . . Blaze Starr
0:09—In bra doing her first strip routine. Very brief
side views of left breast under hat.
0:15—Strip tease routine in front of Paul Newman.
At the end, she takes off bra to reveal pasties.
0:42—In black bra and panties with Newman.
•• 0:48—Topless on top of Newman, then side view of
left breast.
The Inner Circle (1991; Italian) . . . . Anastasia
The Object of Beauty (1991). . . . . Joan
Raising Cain (1992). . . . . n.a.
Made for Cable Movies:
Prison Stories, Women on the Inside (1990; HBO)
. . . . Lorretta
Keep the Change (1992; TNT) . . . . Ellen

Davidson, Eileen

Films:
Goin' All the Way (1981) . . . . BJ
••• 0:12—Topless in the girls' locker room shower.
Standing next to Monica.
••• 0:22—Exercising in her bedroom in braless pink T-
shirt, then topless talking on the phone to Monica.
House on Sorority Row (1983) . . . . Vicki
•• 0:16—Topless and buns in room making love with
her boyfriend.
0:19—In white bikini top by the pool.
Easy Wheels (1989). She Wolf
Eternity (1989) . . . . Dahlia/Valerie
0:33—In black bra and panties in dressing room.
Brief buns standing in bathtub during Jon Voight's
flashback.
• 0:52—Brief left breast, then topless, in bed with
Voight. Don't see face.
TV:
The Young and the Restless . . . . Ashley Abbott
Broken Badges (1990-91) . . . . Bullet

Davis, Carole

a.k.a. Carol Davis.
Singer.
Films:
Piranha II: The Spawning (1981; Dutch). . . . . n.a.
C.O.D. (1983) . . . . Contessa Bazzini
• 1:25—Brief topless in dressing room scene in black
panties, garter belt and stockings when she takes off
her robe.
1:29—In black top during fashion show.
The Princess Academy (1986; U.S./Yugoslavian/French)
. . . . Sonia
Mannequin (1987). . . . . Roxie
The Shrimp on the Barbie (1990). . . . . Domonique
0:58—Buns, in pool that is visible from inside restaurant. Don't see her face.
0:58—In black bra and panties, then topless doing
strip tease in front of Bruce. Very dark.
If Looks Could Kill (1991) . . . . Areola Canasta
a.k.a. Teen Agent
The Rapture (1991). . . . . Angie
• 0:20—Buns, on top of Vic in bed. Most of side of her
right breast.
• 0:21—Very brief right breast, then very brief topless
while turning around to talk.

Davis, Geena

Ex-wife of actor Jeff Goldblum.
Films:
Tootsie (1982) . . . . April
0:34—In white bra and panties in dressing room
with Dustin Hoffman.
0:44—In white bra and panties exercising in dress-
ing room while Hoffman reads his script.
Transylvania 6-5000 (1985) . . . . Odette
The Fly (1986) . . . . Veronica Quaife
0:40—Brief almost side view of left breast getting
out of bed.
The Accidental Tourist (1988). . . . . Muriel
(Academy Award for Best Supporting Actress.)
Beetlejuice (1988) . . . . Barbara
Earth Girls are Easy (1989) . . . . Valerie
0:11—In yellow two piece swimsuit during song and
dance number in beauty salon.
0:12—In frilly pink lingerie waiting at home for her
fiance to return.
0:22—In pink two piece swimsuit doing a lot of different things for a long time. This is probably the
greatest swimsuit scene in a PG movie!
Quick Change (1990). Phyllis
Thelma and Louise (1991) . . . . Thelma
Hero (1992). . . . . Gale Gayley
A Leauge of Their Own (1992). . . . . n.a.

Davis, Judy

Wife of actor Colin Friels.
Films:
High Rolling (1977; Australian). . . . . Lynn
My Brilliant Career (1979; Australian). . . . Syblla Melvyn

Winter of Our Dreams (1981) . . . . Lou
- • 0:19—Brief left breast sticking out of yellow robe in bed with Pete.
- • 0:26—Very brief side view of left breast taking off top to change. Long shot.
- •• 0:48—Topless taking off top and getting into bed with Bryan Brown, then brief right breast lying down with him.

The Final Option (1982; British) . . . . Frankie
Heatwave (1983; Australian) . . . . Kate
A Passage to India (1984; British) . . . . . . Adela Quested
Kangaroo (1986; Australian) . . . . Harriet Somers
High Tide (1987; Australian) Lilli
Alice (1990) . . . . Vicki
Barton Fink (1991) . . . . Audrey Taylor
Impromptu (1991) . . . . Sand
Naked Lunch (1991) . . . . Joan Frost/Joan Lee
Where Angels Fear to Tread (1992) . . . . Harriet
Made for TV Movies:
A Woman Called Golda (1982) . . . . .n.a.
One Against the Wind (1991) . . . . Mary Lindell

Davis, Phyllis
Films:
The Last of the Secret Agents? (1966) . . . . . Beautiful Girl
Live a Little, Love a Little (1968) . . . . 2nd Secretary
Beyond the Valley of the Dolls (1970) . . . . . . Susan Lake
Russ Meyer Film.
(Not available on video tape.)
Sweet Sugar (1972) . . . . Sugar
(With brown hair.)
- ••• 0:34—Topless in bed with a guard.
- ••• 0:50—Topless in the shower with Dolores.
- •• 0:57—Brief topless in the bathroom.

The Day of the Dolphin (1973) . . . . Secretary
Terminal Island (1973) . . . . Joy Lange
- ••• 0:39—Topless and buns in a pond, full frontal nudity getting out, then more topless putting blouse on while a guy watches.

Train Ride to Hollywood (1975). . . . . .n.a.
The Choirboys (1977) . . . . .Foxy/Gina
The Best of Sex and Violence (1981) . . . . . Sugar/Joy
- •• 0:56—Topless after bath and in bed in scenes from *Sweet Sugar.*
- ••• 0:59—Topless and buns walking out of lake in scene from *Terminal Island.*

Famous T & A (1982) . . . . Joy/Sugar
(No longer available for purchase, check your video store for rental.)
- ••• 0:02—Nude in lots of great out-takes from *Terminal Island.* Check this out if you are a Phyllis Davis fan!
- ••• 0:51—Topless in scenes from *Sweet Sugar.* Includes more out-takes.
- ••• 1:04—More out-takes from *Sweet Sugar.*

Guns (1990) . . . . Kathryn Hamilton
TV:
Love, American Style (1970-74) . . . . . . Repertory Player
Vega$ (1978-81). . . . . .Beatrice Travis

Davis-Voss, Sammi
No relation to the late entertainer Sammy Davis, Jr.
Films:
Hope and Glory (1987; British). . . . . Dawn Rohan
A Prayer for the Dying (1987) . . . . Anna
Consuming Passions (1988; U.S./British) . . . . . . .Felicity
The Lair of the White Worm (1988; British) . .Mary Trent
The Rainbow (1989) . . . . Winifred Inger
- ••• 0:21—Topless and buns with Amanda Donohoe undressing, running outside in the rain, jumping into the water, then talking by the fireplace.
- •• 0:30—Topless and buns posing for a painter.
- • 1:33—Brief right breast and buns getting out of bed.
- ••• 1:44—Nude running outside with Donohoe.

Horseplayer (1991) . . . . .Randi
Shadow of China (1991; U.S./Japanese) . . . . . .Katherine
Made for Cable Movies:
The Perfect Bride (1991) . . . . Stephanie
Made for TV Movies:
Pack of Lies (1987). . . . . .Julie
TV:
Homefront (1991-) . . . . Caroline Hailey

• Dax, Danielle
British alternative pop singer. Originally with the group the *Lemon Kittens.*
Films:
The Company of Wolves (1985) . . . . Wolfgirl
- • 1:26—Brief buns and topless running around outside. Her hair is in the way a lot.

Day, Alexandra
Films:
Erotic Images (1983). . . . . Logan's Girlfriend
- •• 0:37—Topless getting out of bed while Logan talks on the phone to Britt Ekland.

Boarding House (1984) . . . . Girl in Bathroom
Body Double (1984). . . . . .Girl in Bathroom #1
Young Lady Chatterley II (1986)
. . . . Jenny "Maid in Hut"
- ••• 0:06—Topless and buns in hut on the bed with the Gardener.
- ••• 0:28—Topless taking bath with Harlee McBride.

Video Tapes:
The Girls of Penthouse (1984)
. . . . Tattoo Woman & Use Me Woman
- ••• 0:34—Nude, getting tattooed by another woman, then making love with her.
- ••• 0:40—Nude, dancing and stripping off her clothes down to stockings and garter belt, then on bed. Quick cuts and strobe light make it hard to see.

Penthouse: On the Wild Side (1988) . . . . Honey Pot
- ••• 0:43—Topless, getting honey dribbled on her, then getting it licked off by her lover.

Day, Catlyn

Films:

Kandyland (1987)........................ Diva
- ••• 0:50—Topless wearing pasties doing strip routine.
- • 1:06—Brief topless talking on the telephone in dressing room.
- • 1:12—Brief topless during dance routine with the other girls.

Wilding, The Children of Violence (1990)
.... Officer Breedlove

De La Croix, Raven

Films:

Up! (1976).................... Margo Winchester
Russ Meyer film.
Topless.

The Happy Hooker Goes to Washington (1977)
.... Uncredited Ice Cream Girl
- • 0:31—Brief topless, while lying on table, getting her rear end covered with ice cream.

The Lost Empire (1983)........... White Star
- ••• 1:05—Topless with a snake after being drugged by the bad guy.
- •• 1:07—Topless lying on a table.

Screwballs (1983)............. Miss Anna Tomical
- ••• 1:08—Topless during strip routine in nightclub.

Video Tapes:

Best Chest in the West (1984)........... Herself
- ••• 0:34—Topless doing strip tease routine on stage.

Magazines:

Playboy (Nov 1976).......... Sex in Cinema 1976
- •• 153—Topless.

De Leeuw, Lisa

Adult film actress.

Films:

Up 'n' Coming (1987).......... Altheah Anderson
(R-rated version reviewed, X-rated version available.)
- • 0:33—Very brief topless by the pool when her robe opens.
- • 0:48—Brief topless walking around the house when her robe open.
- •• 0:49—Left breast talking with a guy, then topless walking into the bedroom.

De Light, Venus

a.k.a. Lynn Chase.

Films:

Stripper (1985)........................ Herself
- • 0:59—Brief topless, on stage, blowing fire.
- ••• 1:07—Topless and buns in black G-string, doing routine on stage, using fire.

Angel of Passion (1991)................. Carol
- •• 0:15—Topless taking a shower.
- ••• 0:19—Topless and buns in G-string dancing outside next to pool at a birthday party.
- ••• 0:23—Topless and buns in red lingerie in camper, then topless making love on top of Will.

Video Tapes:

In Search of the Perfect 10 (1986)... Perfect Girl #4
- ••• 0:18—Topless talking on the phone and buns in G-string seen through the Nude-Cam.
- ••• 0:21—In two piece swimsuit, then topless taking it off in the doorway.

The Stripper of the Year (1986).... Venus De Light
- ••• 0:37—Nude, doing strip routine that includes fire tricks.
- •• 0:53—Topless on stage with the other contestants.
- ••• 0:55—Topless as a finalist, then in dance-off.
  0:56—Topless as the winner.

Hot Bodies (1988)...................... Herself
- •• 0:22—Topless, dancing and taking off dress.
- ••• 0:24—Nude in large champagne glass prop.
- ••• 0:27—Nude dancing on stage.
- ••• 0:47—Topless and buns in G-string stripping in nurse uniform.
- ••• 0:49—Topless and buns on hospital gurney.
- ••• 0:52—Topless and buns dancing with a life-size dummy prop.

Starlets Exposed! Volume II (1991)........ Venus
- ••• 0:43—Buns in G-string, then topless dancing on stage with a life-size dummy and in a giant champagne glass.

De Liso, Debra

Films:

The Slumber Party Massacre (1982)......... Kim
- • 0:08—Very brief topless getting soap from Trish in the shower.
- •• 0:29—In beige bra and panties, then topless putting on a U.S.A. shirt while changing with the other girls.

Iced (1988)............................. Trina
- • 0:11—In a bra, then brief nude making love with Cory in hotel room.

Dr. Caligari (1989)................... Grace Butter

De Medeiros, Maria

Films:

1871 (1989; British).......................Maria

La Lectrice (1989; French)............. Silent Nurse
a.k.a. The Reader

Henry & June (1990)...................Anais Nin
- • 0:50—Brief right breast, popping out of dress top.
- •• 0:52—Topless lying in bed with Richard E. Grant.
- •• 1:13—Topless in bed with Fred Ward, buns getting out. Right breast standing by the window.
- ••• 1:31—Topless in bed with Brigitte Lahaie.
  1:37—Nude under sheer black patterned dress.
- •• 1:43—Close up of right breast as Ward plays with her.
- •• 2:01—Left breast, then topless after taking off her top in bed with Uma Thurman.

Meeting Venus (1990; British)............. Yvonne

Magazines:

Playboy (Nov 1991).......... Sex in Cinema 1991
- •• 145—Topless, lying in bed with Richard E. Grant. From Henry & June.

De Mornay, Rebecca

Films:

Risky Business (1983) . . . . Lana
- 0:28—Brief nude standing by the window with Tom Cruise.

Runaway Train (1985) . . . . Sara
The Slugger's Wife (1985) . . . . Debby Palmer
The Trip to Bountiful (1986) . . . . Thelma
And God Created Woman (1988) . . . . Robin
(Unrated version.)
- • 0:06—Brief Left breast and buns in gymnasium with Vincent Spano. Brief right breast making love.
- • 0:53—Brief buns and topless in the shower when Spano sees her.
- • 1:02—Brief left breast with Langella on the floor.
- ••• 1:12—Topless making love with Spano in a museum.

Feds (1988) . . . . Elizabeth De Witt
Dealers (1989) . . . . Anna Schuman
- 0:59—In black bra, making love with Daniel.

Backdraft (1991) . . . . Helen McCaffrey
The Hand That Rocks the Cradle (1992). . . . Peyton
- • 0:29—Upper half of right breast, breast feeding Claire's baby.
- 0:36—Partial right breast, breast feeding the baby again.
- 1:25—Briefly in wet nightgown in the kitchen with Michael.

Made for Cable Movies:
By Dawn's Early Light (1990; HBO) . . . . . Cindy Moreau
Made for TV Movies:
An Inconvenient Woman (1991) . . . . Flo March

De Moss, Darcy

Films:

Gimme an "F" (1981) . . . . One of the "Ducks"
Hardbodies (1984) . . . . Dede
- ••• 0:55—Topless in the back seat of the limousine with Rounder.

Friday the 13th, Part VI: Jason Lives (1986) . . . . . . Nikki
Reform School Girls (1986) . . . . Knox
Can't Buy Me Love (1987) . . . . Patty
0:46—In black bra and patterned panties in locker room.
Return to Horror High (1987) . . . . Sheri Haines
- • 0:21—Very brief left breast when her sweater gets lifted up while she's on some guy's back.

Night Life (1989) . . . . Roberta Woods
Coldfire (1990) . . . . Maria
- ••• 0:27—Partial right breast and buns, lying in bed with Nick. Left breast, then topless making love with him.
- •• 0:30—Topless in bathtub with Nick.

Living to Die (1990) . . . . Maggie Sams
0:11—Taking off clothes to white bra, panties, garter belt and stockings in hotel room with a customer.
- • 0:32—Buns, getting out of spa while Wings Hauser watches without her knowing.

0:33—Buns, in long shot when Hauser fantasizes about dancing with her.
- ••• 0:56—In black bra, then topless and buns making love with Hauser.
- • 1:20—Topless in mirror taking off black top for the bad guy.

Pale Blood (1990) . . . . Cherry
Vice Academy, Part 3 (1991) . . . Samantha (uncredited)

De Prume, Cathryn

Films:

Deadtime Stories (1985) . . . . Goldi-lox
- •• 1:08—Topless taking a shower, quick cuts.

Five Corners (1988) . . . . Brita
Bloodhounds of Broadway (1989) . . . . Showgirl
Navy SEALs (1990) . . . . Bartender

De Rossi, Barbara

Films:

Hearts and Armour (1983) . . . . Bradamante
- •• 1:05—Topless while sleeping with Ruggero.

La Cicala (The Cricket) (1983) . . . . Saveria
- •• 0:39—Nude swimming under waterfall with Clio Goldsmith.
- •• 0:43—Topless undressing in room with Goldsmith.
- • 0:57—Brief right breast changing into dress in room.
- • 1:05—In wet white lingerie in waterfall with a guy, then in a wet dress.
- 1:26—Very brief buns in bed with Anthony Franciosa.
- •• 1:28—Topless in bathroom with Franciosa.
- • 1:36—Brief right breast making love with trucker.

Made for Cable Movies:
Mussolini and I (1985; HBO) . . . . n.a.
Blood Ties (1986; Italian; Showtime) . . . . Luisa
- • 0:58—Brief topless on couch when bad guy rips her clothes off.

De Vasquez, Devin

Star Search Winner 1986—Spokesmodel.
Films:

Can't Buy Me Love (1987) . . . . Iris
House II: The Second Story (1987) . . . . The Virgin
Society (1989) . . . . Clarisa
- ••• 0:37—Topless, making love in bed with Billy.
- • 0:40—Left breast, while on sofa with Billy when her mother comes home.

Guns (1990) . . . . Cash
- • 1:12—Brief side of right breast and buns undressing for bath.

Video Tapes:
Playboy Video Magazine, Volume 8 . . . . . Playmate
Playmate Playoffs . . . . Playmate
Playboy Video Calendar 1988 (1987) . . . . . Playmate

Magazines:
Playboy (Oct 1981)
.........Girls of the Southeastern Conference, Part II
144—Topless. She was attending Louisiana State University.
Playboy (Jun 1985) .... Playmate
Playboy (Nov 1986) .... Revvin' Devin
••• 80-87—Nude.

Dean, Felicity

Films:
Crossed Swords (1978) .... Lady Jane
Success is the Best Revenge (1984; British) ....n.a.
Steaming (1985; British) .... Dawn
•• 1:12—Topless painting on herself.
The Whistle Blower (1987; British)... Cynthia Goodburn

Deane, Lezlie

Films:
976-EVIL (1988) ....Suzie
• 0:34—Brief right breast in open leather jacket, making love on top of Spike. Brief topless several times getting off him.
•• 0:37—Brief topless opening jacket after putting on underwear.
Girlfriend from Hell (1989) .... Diane
Freddy's Dead: The Final Nightmare (1991) ..... Tracy
Almost Pregnant (1992) .... Party Girl
(Unrated version reviewed.)
To Protect and Serve (1992)............. Harriet
• 0:47—Brief topless in front of fireplace with C. Thomas Howell. Hard to see because candles get in the way.
• 0:51—Brief topless, getting up off the floor.
• 1:18—Brief side view of left breast in mirror in bathroom. Long shot.

Deats, Danyi

Films:
The Allnighter (1987) .... Junkie
River's Edge (1987) .... Jamie
• 0:03—Topless, dead lying next to river with her killer. (All the shots of her topless in this film aren't exciting unless you like looking at dead bodies).
• 0:15—Close up topless, then full frontal nudity when Crispin Glover pokes her with a stick.
0:16—Full frontal nudity when the three boys leave.
0:22—Full frontal nudity when all the kids come to see her body. (She's starting to look very discolored).
0:24—Right breast when everybody leaves.
0:30—Right breast when they come to dump her body in the river.

DeBell, Kristine

Adult films:
Alice in Wonderland (1977) .... Alice
Films:
Meatballs (1979; Canadian) .................A.L.
The Big Brawl (1980) ....Nancy

Willie and Phil (1980) .... Rena
T.A.G.: The Assassination Game (1982) .... Nancy
Cheerleaders Wild Weekend (1985) ..... Debbie/Pierce
Club Life (1987)...........................Fern
Magazines:
Playboy (Nov 1976) .... Sex in Cinema 1976
• 152—Left breast.

• Del Sol, Laura

Films:
Carmen (1983; Spanish)..................Carmen
• 1:14—Left breast, while lying in bed with Antonio.
• 1:27—Brief partial left breast, standing up when Antonio catches her in wardrobe room with another dancer.
The Hit (1984) .... Maggie
The Stilts (Los Zancos) (1984; Spanish) .... Teresa

• Delaney, Cassandra

Ex-wife of Country music singer John Denver.
Films:
Fair Game (1985; Australian) .... Jessica
• 0:15—Buns and brief side of left breast, taking off her outfit and lying on bed.
• 0:16—Topless rolling over in bed.
0:19—Brief, out of focus buns, in Polaroid photograph taped to inside of the refrigerator.
• 0:32—Brief left breast, taking off outfit to take a shower.
•• 0:48—Brief topless when the bad guys cut her blouse open. Topless several times, while tied to front of truck.
• 0:49—Brief left breast while getting up off the ground.
0:50—Half of right breast, while sitting in the shower. Dark.
Rebel (1985; Australian) .... All-Girl Band Member
Hurricane Smith (1990) ....Julie
•• 0:45—Topless, while making love with Carl Weathers in bed.

Delaney, Kim

Films:
That Was Then... This Is Now (1985) .... Cathy Carlson
Campus Man (1987) .... Dayna Thomas
Hunter's Blood (1987) ....Melanie
The Drifter (1988)................... Julia Robbins
• 0:11—Brief topless making love with Miles O'Keeffe on motel floor.
•• 0:21—Topless in bed talking with Timothy Bottoms.
Hangfire (1990) .... Maria Slayton
Body Parts (1991) .... Karen Crushank
Made for TV Movies:
Cracked Up (1987)........................Jackie
Something Is Out There (1988) ....Mandy
The Broken Cord (1992) ....Suzanne
Jackie Collins' Lady Boss (1992) ......Lucky Santangelo
TV:
All My Children .... Jenny Gardner

Tour of Duty (1988-89) . . . . Alex Devilin
Fifth Corner (1992-) . . . . Erica Fontaine

Delon, Nathalie

Films:
When Eight Bells Toll (1971; British) . . . . Charlotte
Bluebeard (1972) . . . . Erika
- 1:03—Topless in bed, showing Richard Burton her breasts.
- 1:09—Brief right breast lying on the floor with Sybil Danning just before Richard Burton kills both of them.
The Godson (1972; Italian/French) . . . . . . Jan Lagrange
The Romantic Englishwoman (1975; British/French)
. . . . Miranda

Delora, Jennifer

Films:
Robot Holocaust (1986) . . . . Nyla
Sexpot (1986) . . . . Barbara
- ••• 0:28—In bra, then topless with her two sisters when their bras pop off. (She's in the middle.)
- 0:36—Topless on bed with Gorilla.
- 1:32—Topless during outtakes of 0:28 scene.
Deranged (1987) . . . . Maryann
- 1:09—Topless in bed with Frank. Long shot.
Young Nurses in Love (1987) . . . . Bunny
New York's Finest (1988) . . . . Loretta Michaels
- 0:02—Brief topless pretending to be a black hooker.
- 0:04—Brief topless with a bunch of hookers.
- 0:36—Topless with her two friends doing push ups on the floor.
Sensations (1988) . . . . Della Randall
- 0:11—Brief topless talking to Jenny to wake her up.
- 0:13—Brief topless a couple of times in open robe.
- •• 0:38—Topless making love with a guy on bed.
Bedroom Eyes II (1989) . . . . Gwendolyn
- •• 0:04—Undressing in hotel room with Vinnie. Topless, then making love.
Cleo/Leo (1989) . . . . Bernice
Club Fed (1990) . . . . Uncredited Girl at Pool
Frankenhooker (1990) . . . . Angel
- 0:36—Brief topless during introduction to Jeffrey.
- ••• 0:41—Topless dancing in room with the room with the other hookers. (Nice tattoos!)
Bad Girls Dormitory (1991) . . . . Lisa
Deadly Manor (1991) . . . . Amanda
Fright House (1991) . . . . Dr. Victoria Sedgewick
Phantasy (1991) . . . . Fantasy
Suburban Commando (1991) . . . . Hooker

• Delpy, Julie

Films:
Detective (1985; French/Swiss)
. . . . Wise Young Girl Groupie
Bad Blood (1987; French) . . . . Lise
The Passion of Beatrice (1988; French) . . . . Béatrice
- ••• 0:13—Full frontal nudity, wiping her crotch and burning her clothes.

- 0:58—Left breast, then topless getting out of bed.
- ••• 1:11—Side view of right breast, holding dress after getting raped by her father. Nude, running to the door and barricading it with furniture.
- •• 1:12—More nude, arranging furniture.
- 1:36—More of right breast, when her father puts soot on her face.
- •• 1:37—Brief left breast, then topless and brief buns standing with soot on her face. Long shot.
- ••• 1:44—Topless taking a bath. Subtitles get in the way a bit.
La Noche Oscura (1989; Spanish)
. . . . Anna de Jesus/Virgin Mary
Europa Europa (1991; German) . . . . Leni
Voyager (1992; German/French) . . . . Sabeth

Dempsey, Sandra

Films:
Video Vixens (1973) . . . . Actress
- •• 0:05—Full frontal nudity, lying down getting make up put on.
The Swinging Cheerleaders (1974) . . . 1st Girl at Tryout

Deneuve, Catherine

Films:
The Umbrellas of Cherbourg (1964) . . . Genevieve Emery
Repulsion (1965) . . . . Carol
The April Fool's (1969) . . . . Catherine Gunther
La Grande Bourgeoise (1974; Italian) . . . . . . Linda Murri
Hustle (1975) . . . . Nicole Britton
Lovers Like Us (1975) . . . . Nelly
a.k.a. The Savage
- 1:06—Brief left upper half of left breast in bed with Yves Montand. Dark.
- ••• 1:09—Topless sitting up in bed.
The Last Metro (1980) . . . . Marion
Je Vous Aime (1981) . . . . Alice
a.k.a. I Love You All
A Choice of Arms (1983; French) . . . . Nicole
The Hunger (1983) . . . . Miriam
- 0:08—Brief topless taking a shower with David Bowie. Probably a body double, you don't see her face.
Love Song (1985) . . . . Margaux
Scene of the Crime (1987; French) Lili
Magazines:
Playboy (Sep 1963) . . . . Europe's New Sex Sirens
Playboy (Oct 1965) . . . . France's Deneuve Wave
Playboy (Jan 1989) . . . . Women of the Sixties
- 159—Topless sitting by the window.

Denier, Lydie

Films:
The Nightstalker (1987) . . . . First Victim
- ••• 0:03—Topless making love with big guy.
Bulletproof (1988) . . . . Tracy
- •• 0:14—Topless in Gary Busey's bathtub.
- 0:20—Brief buns, putting on shirt after getting out of bed. Very, very brief side view of left breast.
Paramedics (1988) . . . . Liette

Red Blooded American Girl (1988) . Rebecca Murrin
••• 0:00—Topless in bed wearing panties, garter belt
    and stockings. Buns, rolling over. Long scene.
Blood Relations (1989) . . . . Marie
•• 0:07—Left breast making love with Thomas on stair-
    way.
  • 0:44—Brief left breast in bed with Thomas' father.
    Very brief cuts of her topless in B&W.
    0:47—Getting out of swimming pool in a one piece
    swimsuit.
••• 0:54—Full frontal nudity undressing for the Grand-
    father.
Satan's Princess (1989) . . . . Nicole St. James
  • 0:27—Full frontal nudity, getting out of pool.
••• 0:28—Full frontal nudity, next to bed and in bed
    with Karen.
••• 0:45—Topless and buns, making love in bed with
    Robert Forster.
Midnight Cabaret (1991) . . . . .Woman in White
Wild Orchid II: Two Shades of Blue (1992)
    . . . . Dominique
••• 0:28—Topless, undressing from lingerie while Blue
    and Elle watch.
Made for Cable TV:
  Red Shoe Diaries: Talk To Me (1992; Showtime)
    . . . . Elaine
  • 0:13—Brief left breast several times, making love in
    bed with Richard Tyson.
  •• 0:14—Topless and buns, taking off robe to shower
    with Rita.
TV:
  Tarzan (1991-) . . . . Jane

• Denise, Denise
Films:
  Lady Sings the Blues (1972) . . . . .n.a.
  Fox Style (1974) . . . . Cindy
    • 0:42—Brief topless rolling over on her stomach on
      river bank with A. J.
    1:21—Most of right breast, in bed with A. J.
  Doctor Death: Seeker of Souls (1975)
    . . . . Girl with Flat Tire

Derek, Bo
  Real name is Cathleen Collins.
  Wife of director John Derek.
Films:
  Fantasies (1974) . . . . Anastasia
    a.k.a. Once Upon a Love
    • 0:03—Left breast, in bathtub.
    •• 0:15—Topless taking off top, then right breast, in
      bathtub.
    • 0:43—Topless getting her dress top pulled down.
    • 0:59—Brief topless in the water. Very brief full frontal
      nudity walking back into the house.
    • 1:00—Buns and left breast several times outside the
      window.
    • 1:17—Upper left breast, in bathtub again.
  Orca, The Killer Whale (1977) . . . . Annie

10 (1979) . . . . Jennifer Hanley
    1:18—In yellow swimsuit running in slow motion to-
    wards Dudley Moore in his daydream.
  • 1:27—Brief buns and topless taking off towel and
    putting on robe when Moore visits her. Long shot,
    hard to see.
  • 1:34—Brief topless taking off dress trying to seduce
    Moore. Dark, hard to see.
  • 1:35—Topless, lying in bed. Dark, hard to see.
  •• 1:39—Topless, going to fix the skipping record.
    Long shot, hard to see.
A Change of Seasons (1980) . . . . . Lindsey Routledge
  •• 0:00—Topless in hot tub during the opening credits.
  • 0:25—Side view of left breast in the shower talking
    to Anthony Hopkins.
Tarzan, The Ape Man (1981) . . . . .Jane
••• 0:43—Nude taking a bath in the ocean, then in a
    wet white dress.
  • 1:35—Brief topless painted all white.
  • 1:45—Topless washing all the white paint off in the
    river with Tarzan.
  •• 1:47—Topless during the ending credits playing
    with Tarzan and the orangutan. (When I saw this
    film in a movie theater, the entire audience actually
    stayed to watch the credits!)
Bolero (1984) . . . . Ayre McGillvary
  • 0:04—Brief topless, stripping to panties, outside af-
    ter graduating from school.
••• 0:19—Topless making love with Arabian guy cov-
    ered with honey, messy.
••• 0:58—Topless making love in bed with Angel.
••• 1:38—Topless during fantasy love making session
    with Angel in fog.
Ghosts Can't Do It (1989) . . . . .Kate
••• 0:26—In one piece swimsuit on beach, then full
    frontal nudity taking it off. Brief buns covered with
    sand on her back. Long scene.
••• 0:32—Topless, sitting and washing herself. Very
    brief buns, jumping into tub.
  •• 0:48—Full frontal nudity taking a shower.
  • 0:49—Very, very brief topless and buns jumping into
    pool. Long shot. Full frontal nudity under water.
    0:52—Very, very brief partial topless pulling a guy
    into the pool.
    1:00—In wet dress, dancing sexily in the rain.
  •• 1:12—Topless behind mosquito net with her boy-
    friend.
Video Tapes:
  Playboy Video Magazine, Volume 1 (1982)
    . . . . .Herself
    • 0:02—Topless in still photos.
    •• 0:56—Topless in still photos.
    •• 0:57—Topless with brunette hair in scenes from *Fan-
      tasies.*
    •• 0:58—Topless in still photos.
Magazines:
  Playboy (Mar 1980) . . . . Bo
    ••• 146-157—Nude.

Playboy (Aug 1980). . . . . .Bo Is Back
••• 108-119—Nude in Japanese bath with a Japanese
woman.
Playboy (Nov 1980) . . . . Sex in Cinema 1980
• 173—Right breast and lower frontal nudity behind
shower door.
Playboy (Sep 1981). . . . . Tarzan
Playboy (Dec 1984). . . . . Sex Stars of 1984
••• 209—Topless lying in water.
Playboy (Jan 1989) . . . . Women of the Eighties
••• 255—Full frontal nudity.
Playboy (Nov 1989) . . . . Sex in Cinema 1989
••• 133—Topless in still from *Ghosts Can't Do It.*
Playboy's Nudes (Oct 1990). . . . . Herself
••• 16-17—Full frontal nudity.

Dern, Laura

Daughter of actor Bruce Dern and actress Diane Ladd.
Films:
Ladies and Gentlemen, The Fabulous Stains (1982)
. . . . .Jessica McNeil
(Not available on video tape.)
Teachers (1984) . . . . Diane
Mask (1985). . . . . Diana
Smooth Talk (1985) . . . . Connie
Blue Velvet (1986). . . . . Sandy Williams
Fat Man and Little Boy (1989). . . . . . Kathleen Robinson
Wild at Heart (1990) . . . . Lula
••• 0:07—Topless putting on black halter top.
•• 0:26—Left breast, then topless sitting on Nicholas
Cage's lap in bed.
•• 0:35—Topless wriggling around in bed with Cage.
• 0:41—Brief topless several times making love with
Cage. Hard to see because it keeps going overex-
posed. Great moaning, though.
Rambling Rose (1991) . . . . Rose
•• 0:23—Right breast several times, while lying on
bench with Robert Duvall while Lucas Haas peeks in.
Made for Cable Movies:
Afterburn (1992; HBO) . . . . Janet Harduvel

Derval, Lamya

Films:
The Lonely Guy (1983)
. . . . .One of "The Seven Deadly Sins"
Hellhole (1985). . . . . Jacuzzi Girl
••• 1:08—Topless (she's on the right) sniffing glue in
closet with another woman.
••• 1:12—Full frontal nudity in Jacuzzi room with Mary
Woronov.
Howling IV: The Original Nightmare (1988)
. . . . .Elanor
•• 0:32—Brief left breast, then topless making love
with Richard. Nice silhouette on the wall.

Desmond, Donna

Films:
Tender Loving Care (1974) . . . . .n.a.
The Black Gestapo (1975) . . . . White Whore

Fugitive Girls (1975). n.a.
The Naughty Stewardesses (1978) . . . . .Margie
•• 0:12—Topless leaning out of the shower.

Detmers, Maruschka

Films:
Devil in the Flesh (1986; French/Italian)
. . . . Giulia Dozza
• 0:20—Very brief side view of left breast and buns going past open door way to get a robe.
••• 0:27—Nude, talking to Andrea's dad in his office.
• 0:55—Topless putting a robe on. Dark.
•• 0:57—Topless and buns in bedroom with Andrea.
•• 1:09—Topless in hallway with Andrea.
1:19—Performing fellatio on Andrea. Dark, hard to
see.
••• 1:22—Full frontal nudity holding keys for Andrea to
see, brief buns.
1:42—Lower frontal nudity dancing in living room
in red robe.
Hanna's War (1988) . . . . Hanna Senesh
The Mambo Kings (1992). . . . . .Dolores Fuentes
•• 0:47—Topless several times, making love in bed
with Antonio Banderas.
Magazines:
Playboy (Nov 1986) . . . . Sex in Cinema 1986
••• 128—Topless in a photo from *Devil in the Flesh* with
Federico Pitzalis.

Devine, Loretta

Films:
Little Nikita (1988) . . . . Verna McLaughlin
• 1:03—Very brief left breast in bed after Sidney Poitier jumps out of bed when River Phoenix bursts into
their bedroom.
Sticky Fingers (1988) . . . . .Diane
Livin' Large (1991) . . . . .Nadine Biggs

Dey, Susan

Films:
Skyjacked (1972) . . . . Elly Brewster
First Love (1977) . . . . Caroline Hedges
••• 0:31—Topless making love in bed with William Katt.
Long scene.
• 0:51—Topless taking off her top in her bedroom
with Katt.
Looker (1981) . . . . Cindy
0:28—In white one piece swimsuit shooting a commercial at the beach.
• 0:36—Buns, then brief topless in computer imaging
device. Topless in computer monitor.
Echo Park (1986). . . . . Meg "May" Greer
• 1:17—Brief glimpse of right breast, while doing a
strip tease at a party.
The Trouble with Dick (1986). . . . . .Diane
Made for TV Movies:
The Gift of Life (1982) . . . . .Jolee Sutton
Sunset Limousine (1983) . . . . .Julie

TV:
The Partridge Family (1970-74)...... Laurie Partridge
Loves Me, Loves Me Not (1977)............. Jane
Emerald Point N.A.S. (1983-84) .. Celia Mallory Warren
L.A. Law (1986-92) .... Dep. D.A. Grace Van Owen
Love & War (1992-)...........Wallis "Wally" Porter
Magazines:
Playboy (Dec 1977)............. Sex Stars of 1977
  • 215—Left breast under sheer white gown in a photo
    from *First Love*.

di Lorenzo, Anneka

Real name is Marjorie Thoreson.
Films:
The Centerfold Girls (1974).................. Pam
Caligula (1980)...................... Messalina
  (X-rated, 147 minute version.)
  ••• 1:16—Nude, making love with Lori Wagner. Long
    scene.
Video Tapes:
Penthouse: On the Wild Side (1988)..... Messalina
  • 0:54—Nude with Lori Wagner during scenes from
    The Making of Caligula.
Magazines:
Penthouse (Sep 1973)..................... Pet
  ••• 73-85—Nude.
Penthouse (May 1980)................. Caligula
  ••• 74—Topless.
  ••• 86—Topless.
Penthouse (Jun 1980)............. Anneka and Lori
  ••• 142-153—Nude (she has darker hair) with Lori Wag-
    ner.

Di'Lazzaro, Dalila

Films:
Andy Warhol's Frankenstein
  (1974; Italian/German/French)............ The Girl
  •• 0:09—Topless lying on platform in the lab.
  • 0:37—Close up of left breast while the Count cuts
    her stitches. (Pretty bloody.)
  0:43—Topless, covered with blood, strapped to ta-
    ble
  • 0:49—Topless on table, all wired up.
  • 1:03—Right breast lying on table. Long shot.
  • 1:05—More right breast, long shot.
  •• 1:06—More topless on table, then standing in the
    lab.
  •• 1:20—Brief right breast when Otto pulls her top
    down.
  •• 1:23—Topless on table again, then walking around.
    (Scar on chest.) Lower frontal nudity when Otto
    pulls her bandage down, then more gross topless
    when he removes her guts.
The Last Romantic Lover (1978)...............n.a.
Creepers (1985; Italian).....................n.a.
Miss Right (1987; Italian) ....Art Student
Magazines:
Playboy (Aug 1974) .... Instant Warhol
  • 84-85—Topless in Polaroid photo collage.

Playboy (Nov 1974)........... Sex in Cinema 1974
  •• 146—Topless from *Andy Warhol's Frankenstein*.
Playboy (Jan 1990)......................n.a.
  ••• 104—Polaroid collage taken by Andy Worhol.

Dickinson, Angie

Films:
Rio Bravo (1959) ....Feathers
Ocean's Eleven (1960).............. Beatrice Ocean
Cast a Giant Shadow (1966) .... Emma Marcus
The Chase (1966)...................Ruby Calder
Point Blank (1967) .... Chris
  0:46—In white slip when John Vernon opens her
    dress.
  • 0:51—Topless in background putting dress on. Kind
    of a long shot.
Pretty Maids All in a Row (1971) ....Miss Smith
  • 1:04—Buns, in long shot, while lying on bed with
    Ponce.
Big Bad Mama (1974).......... Wilma McClatchie
  0:38—Buns, making love in bed with Tom Skerritt.
  ••• 0:48—Topless in bed with William Shatner.
  ••• 1:18—Topless and brief full frontal nudity putting a
    shawl and then a dress on.
Dressed to Kill (1980)................Kate Miller
  • 0:01—Brief side view behind shower door. Long
    shot, hard to see.
    0:02—Frontal nude scene in shower is a body dou-
    ble, Victoria Lynn Johnson.
    0:24—Brief buns getting out of bed after coming
    home from museum with a stranger.
Charlie Chan & the Curse of the Dragon Queen (1981)
  ....Dragon Queen
Death Hunt (1981)..................... Vanessa
Big Bad Mama II (1987) ....Wilma McClatchie
  • 0:48—Very brief full frontal nudity putting on her
    shawl scene from *Big Bad Mama* superimposed over
    a car chase scene.
  •• 0:52—Topless and brief buns (probably a body dou-
    ble) in bed with Robert Culp. You don't see her face
    with the body.
Made for Cable Movies:
Treacherous Crossing (1992; USA) .... Beverly
Miniseries:
Pearl (1978)......................... Midge
Hollywood Wives (1988) ....Sadie La Salle
Made for TV Movies:
Once Upon a Texas Train (1988) .... Maggie
TV:
Police Woman (1974-78)
  ....Sgt. Suzanne "Pepper" Anderson
Cassie and Company (1982) ....Cassie Holland
Magazines:
Playboy (Apr 1971) .... Vadim's "Pretty Maids"
  • 156—Buns, while lying in bed with John David Car-
    son.

Dickinson, Janice

Model.
Films:
Exposed (1983)........................Model
Magazines:
Playboy (Mar 1988)........ Going Wild with a Model
••• 70-77—Full frontal nudity.

Dietrich, Cindi

Films:
The Man Who Loved Women (1983)......... Darla
Out of Control (1984).................... Robin
• 0:29—Topless taking off her red top. Long shot.
St. Elmo's Fire (1985).......................Flirt
Death Spa (1987)........................ Linda

Digard, Uschi

a.k.a Uschi Digart or Ursula Digard.
Films:
The Beauties and the Beast...................Mary
Nude by lake.
Cherry, Harry & Raquel (1969)................ Soul
The Scavengers (1969).......................n.a.
Supervixens (1973)....................SuperSoul
Russ Meyer film.
Truck Stop Women (1974)...... Truck Stop Woman
•• 0:18—Topless getting arrested in the parking lot by
the police officer, then buns and topless getting
frisked in a room.
Fantasm (1976; Australian)...................n.a.
Kentucky Fried Movie (1977).... Woman in Shower
•• 0:09—Topless getting breasts massaged in the
shower, then squished breasts against the shower
door.
Superchick (1978)..................... Mayday
••• 0:42—Buns and topless getting whipped acting during the making of a film, then talking to three people.
Beneath the Valley of the Ultravixens (1979).. SuperSoul
The Best of Sex and Violence (1981)
.........................Truck Stop Woman
• 0:47—Topless getting chased by policeman in parking lot in scene from *Truck Stop Women*.
Famous T & A (1982)...........Truck Stop Woman
(No longer available for purchase, check your video
store for rental).
•• 0:44—Topless scenes from *Harry, Cherry & Raquel*
and *Truck Stop Women*.

• Dillard, Victoria

Films:
Coming to America (1988)...............Bather
•• 0:04—Topless, standing up in royal bathtub to an-
nounce "The royal penis is clean, Your Highness."
Internal Affairs (1990).......................Kee
Ricochet (1991).......................... Alice
Magazines:
Playboy (Nov 1988)......... Sex in Cinema 1988
•• 133—Topless in bathtub with Eddie Murphy.

Dillon, Melinda

Films:
Bound For Glory (1976)..............Mary Guthrie
Close Encounters of the Third Kind (1977)
.........................Jillian Guiler
Slap Shot (1977)......................Suzanne
••• 0:30—Right breast, lying in bed with Paul Newman,
then topless sitting up and talking. Nice, long scene.
F.I.S.T. (1978)..................... Anna Zerinkas
Absence of Malice (1981)................... Teresa
A Christmas Story (1983).............. Mrs. Parker
Songwriter (1984)................... Honey Carder
Harry and the Hendersons (1987)... Nancy Henderson
Spontaneous Combustion (1989).............. Nina
Staying Together (1989)......... Eileen McDermott
Captain America (1990)............... Mrs. Rogers
The Prince of Tides (1991)......... Savannah Wingo
Miniseries:
Space (1985)......................Rachel Mott
Made for TV Movies:
Shattered Spirits (1986)....................n.a.

• Ditmar, Marita

Films:
Auditions (1978)................... Frieda Volker
•• 1:05—Topless and partial buns with another woman
and a guy.
Fairytales (1979)................. S & M Dancer
• 0:38—Topless wearing masks with two other S&M
Dancers.

Dockery, Erika

a.k.a. Erika Dockray.
Films:
Basic Training (1984)................ Salesgirl 2
• 0:00—Brief topless standing behind the desk.
Hardbodies (1984)............... Hardbody in Car

• Doda, Carol

Films:
Head (1968)....................... Sally Silicone
Honky Tonk Nights (1978)......... Belle Barnette
••• 0:17—Topless changing blouses in bedroom with
Doris Ann.
• 0:28—Left breast several times while making out
with a guy.
••• 1:11—Topless in bedroom with Doris Ann during
flashback. (Different camera angle than 0:17.)
Video Tapes:
Playboy Video Magazine, Volume 3
.........................Queen of Burlesque

Dollarhide, April Dawn

Films:
Party Favors (1987)........................ n.a.
Caged Fury (1989)............... Rhonda Wallace
•• 0:41—Topless undressing to enter prison with other
topless women.

Dombasle, Arielle

Films:
Tess (1979; French/British) . . . . .Mercy Chant
The Story of "O" Continues (1981; French)
. . . . Nathalie
a.k.a. Les Fruits de la Passion
- 0:17—Brief left breast, lying on her stomach in bed with Klaus Kinski.
- 0:40—Full frontal nudity on bed, making love in front of O.
- 1:00—Very, very brief left breast, while grabbing her blouse out of Kinski's hands.
Le Beau Mariage (1982; French) . . . . .Clarisse
Pauline at the Beach (1983; French). . . . . . .Marion
- 0:24—Brief topless lying in bed with a guy when her cousin looks in the window.
- 0:43—Brief topless in house kissing Henri, while he takes her white dress off.
- 0:59—Topless walking down the stairs in a white bikini bottom while putting a white blouse on.
The Boss' Wife (1986) . . . . Mrs. Louise Roalvang
- 1:01—Brief topless getting a massage by the swimming pool.
- 1:07—Topless trying to seduce Daniel Stern at her place.
- 1:14—Brief topless in Stern's shower.
Twisted Obsession (1990) . . . . Marion Derain
Miniseries:
Lace II (1985) . . . . .Maxine
Magazines:
Playboy (Dec 1983). . . . . Sex Stars of 1983
- 209—Topless.

• Dommartin, Solveig

Films:
Wings of Desire (1987) . . . . Marion
a.k.a. Der Himmel Uber Berlin
- 0:34—Brief side of left breast, while putting robe on. (The film changes from B&W to color.)
Until the End of the World (1991)
. . . . .Claire Tourneur
- 0:34—Left breast, then topless, then full frontal nudity in bedroom with William Hurt and Winter.

• Doná, Linda

Films:
Worth Winning (1989) . . . . Lady at the Paddock
Final Embrace (1991) . . . . Jeri
Future Kick (1991) . . . . Tye
Ricochet (1991) . . . . Wanda
- 1:03—Topless, undoing her dress, then buns, getting on bed to make love with Denzel Washington while he's drugged.
- 1:16—Buns, on top of Washington during video playback.
Switch (1991) . . . . Gay Club Patron
Made for TV Movies:
In the Arms of a Killer (1992) . . . . Chrissy

Donnelly, Patrice

Films:
Personal Best (1982) . . . . Tory Skinner
- 0:16—Full frontal nudity after making love with Mariel Hemingway.
- 0:30—Full frontal nudity in steam room.
1:06—Topless in shower.
American Anthem (1987). . . . . .Danielle

Donohoe, Amanda

Films:
Castaway (1986) . . . . .Lucy Irvine
(Topless a lot, only the best are listed.)
- 0:32—Nude on beach after helicopter leaves.
- 0:48—Full frontal nudity lying on her back on the rocks at the beach.
- 0:51—Topless on rock when Reed takes a blue sheet off her, then catching a shark.
- 0:54—Nude yelling at Reed at the campsite, then walking around looking for him.
- 1:01—Topless getting seafood out of a tide pool.
- 1:03—Topless lying down at night talking with Reed in the moonlight.
- 1:18—Topless taking off bathing suit top after the visitors leave, then arguing with Reed.
- 1:22—Topless talking to Reed.
Foreign Body (1986; British) . . . . .Susan
0:37—Undressing in her bedroom down to lingerie. Very brief side view of right breast, then brief left breast putting blouse on.
- 0:40—Topless opening her blouse for Ram.
The Lair of the White Worm (1988; British)
. . . . Lady Sylvia Marsh
(Wears short black hair in this film.)
- 0:52—Nude, opening a tanning table and turning over.
- 0:57—Brief left breast licking the blood off a phallic-looking thing.
- 1:19—Brief topless jumping out to attack Angus, then walking around her underground lair (her body is painted for the rest of the film).
- 1:22—Topless walking up steps with a large phallic thing strapped to her body.
Dark Obsession (1989; British) . . . . Ginny
- 0:01—Topless getting felt by a pair of hands.
- 0:41—Left breast, topless, brief lower frontal nudity while making love with Gabriel Byrne.
- 0:47—In black bra and panties, then full frontal nudity getting into tub. Right breast while sitting in the tub.
Double Cross (1989) . . . . n.a.
The Rainbow (1989) . . . . Winifred Inger
- 0:21—Nude with Sammi Davis undressing, running outside in the rain, jumping into the water, then talking by the fireplace.
- 0:43—Full frontal nudity taking off nightgown and getting into bed with Davis, then right breast.
- 1:44—Nude running outside with Davis.
Paper Mask (1991; British) . . . . Christine Taylor

Made for Cable Movies:
Shame (1992; Lifetime) . . . . Diana Cadell
TV:
L.A. Law (1991-92) . . . . C. J. Lamb
Magazines:
Playboy (Nov 1987) . . . . Sex in Cinema 1987
•• 144-145—Full frontal nudity from *Castaway.*

• Doody, Alison

Films:
A Prayer for the Dying (1987) . . . . Siobhan
Taffin (1988; U.S./British) . . . . Charlotte
  • 0:14—Very, very brief side view of right breast when
    Pierce Brosnan rips her blouse open. Long shot, hard
    to see.
Indiana Jones and the Last Crusade (1989)
. . . . Dr. Elsa Schneider

• Dorado, Lorraine

Video Tapes:
Becky Bubbles (1987) . . . . Herself
  ••• 0:09—Brief right breast and buns in black and white
    swimsuit, then topless in pool.
  ••• 0:12—Topless while playing on pool float with Becky
    and Brandi.
  ••• 0:14—Topless getting in and out of pool, then rub-
    bing lotion on herself.
  ••• 0:18—Topless while playing on the grass in open
    swimsuit top.
Wild Bikinis (1987) . . . . Herself
  ••• 0:10—Topless in pool and buns in swimsuit from
    Becky Bubbles.
  •• 0:35—Topless playing with a ball on the grass with
    Jasaé.
L.A. Strippers (1992) . . . . Quisha Cori
  ••• 0:00—Topless dancing on stage during introduc-
    tion.
  ••• 0:05—In bra, then nude dancing on stage. Long
    scene.
  ••• 0:12—Topless, then nude dancing.

• Dorian, Antonia

Films:
Tough Cookies (1992) . . . . n.a.
Video Tapes:
Soft Bodies: Party Favors (1992) . . . . Herself
  ••• 0:03—In black bra and panties in bed, then topless
    and buns during photo session.
  ••• 0:08—Topless on hammock outside.
  ••• 0:11—In white lace dress in living room by piano.
    Topless and buns in G-string.
  ••• 0:18—Topless and buns outside by pool with Becky
    LeBeau.

• Dorman, Samantha

Video Tapes:
Playboy Playmates in Paradise (1992) . . . Playmate
Playboy Video Calendar 1993 (1992) . . . . . . August
Playboy's Erotic Fantasies (1992) . . . . Model

Playboy's Playmate Review 1992 (1992)
. . . . Miss September
  ••• 0:06—Nude on boat, then in laboratory and then in
    surreal artistic setting.
Sexy Lingerie IV (1992) . . . . Model
Wet and Wild IV (1992) . . . . Model
Magazines:
Playboy (Sep 1991) . . . . Playmate
  ••• 110-121—Nude.
Playboy's Book of Lingerie (Jul 1992) . . . . . . Herself
  ••• 24—Right breast and lower frontal nudity.
  ••• 79—Topless.
Playboy's Book of Lingerie (Sep 1992) . . . . . . Herself
  • 30—Lower frontal nudity.
  ••• 87—Topless.

• Dorsey, Fern

Films:
Love Crimes (1991) . . . . Colleen Dells
(Unrated version reviewed.)
  ••• 0:03—Topless, getting photographed by Patrick
    Bergin.
McBain (1991) . . . . Dr. Elliott

Doss, Terri Lynn

Films:
Lethal Weapon (1987) . . . . Girl in Shower #2
Die Hard (1988) . . . . Girl at Airport
Roadhouse (1989) . . . . Cody's Girlfriend
Video Tapes:
Swimwear Illustrated: On Location (1986)
. . . . Swimsuit Model
Playboy Video Calendar 1989 (1988) . . . . March
  ••• 0:09—Nude.
Sexy Lingerie (1988) . . . . Model
Glamour Through Your Lens—Outdoor Techniques
(1989) . . . . Herself
    0:07—Buns in blue swimsuit bottom in wet yellow
    top in the pool.
    0:47—In black bra, panties, garter belt and stock-
    ings standing outside. Most of her buns.
Sexy Lingerie II (1990) . . . . Model
Magazines:
Playboy (Jul 1988) . . . . Playmate
Playboy's Book of Lingerie (Jan 1991) . . . . . . Herself
  •• 86-87—Full frontal nudity.
Playboy's Book of Lingerie (Mar 1991) . . . . . Herself
  •• 98—Right breast and lower frontal nudity.
Playboy's Book of Lingerie (Mar 1992) . . . . . Herself
  ••• 90—Full frontal nudity.
Playboy's Book of Lingerie (May 1992) . . . . . Herself
  ••• 50—Full frontal nudity.
  ••• 92—Full frontal nudity.

Douglass, Robyn

Films:

Breaking Away (1979) . . . . Katherine

Partners (1982) . . . . Jill
- •• 1:00 — Brief topless taking off her top and getting into bed with Ryan O'Neal.

The Lonely Guy (1983) . . . . Danielle
- • 0:05 — Upper half of right breast in sheer nightgown in bed with Raoul while talking to Steve Martin. Great nightgown!
- 0:33 — In sheer beige negligee lying on couch talking to Martin on the phone.
- • 1:03 — Very, very brief peek at left nipple when she flashes it for Martin so he'll let her into his party.

Romantic Comedy (1983) . . . . Kate

Made for TV Movies:

Her Life as a Man (1984) . . . . Carly Perkins

TV:

Battlestar Galactica (1980) . . . . Jamie Hamilton

Houston Knights (1987-88) . . . . . . Lt. Joanne Beaumont

Magazines:

Playboy (Dec 1974) . . . . Cover Girl
- • Half of left breast.

Playboy (Jul 1975) . . . . A Long Look At Legs

Playboy (Jan 1980) . . . . The World of Playboy
- • 11 — Right breast and lower frontal nudity while wearing corset and white stockings. Small photo with lots of diffusion.

Down, Lesley-Anne

Films:

From Beyond the Grave (1973) . . . . . . Rosemary Seaton

The Pink Panther Strikes Again (1976) . . . . Olga

The Betsy (1978) . . . . Lady Bobby Ayres
- • 0:38 — Brief left breast with Tommy Lee Jones.
- • 0:57 — Very brief left breast in bed with Jones.

A Little Night Music (1978) . . . . Anne Egerman

The Great Train Robbery (1979) . . . . Miriam

Hanover Street (1979) . . . . Margaret Sallinger
- • 0:22 — In bra and slip, then brief topless in bedroom with Harrison Ford.

Rough Cut (1980; British) . . . . Gillian Bramley

Sphinx (1981) . . . . Erica Baron

Nomads (1986) . . . . Flax

Scenes from the Goldmine (1987) . . . . Herself

Miniseries:

North and South (1985) . . . . Madeline Fabray

North and South, Book II (1986) . . . . . . Madeline Fabray

TV:

Upstairs, Downstairs (1974-77) . . . . . . Georgina Worsley

Dallas (1990) . . . . Stephanie Rogers

Magazines:

Playboy (Dec 1979) . . . . Sex Stars of 1979
- •• 254 — Topless.

Playboy (May 1985) . . . . Grapevine
- 217 — B&W.

• Downes, Cathy

Films:

Winter of Our Dreams (1981) . . . . Gretel
- • 0:41 — Brief right breast putting top on while talking to Judy Davis.
- •• 1:04 — Topless sitting up in bed at night.
- • 1:11 — Topless sitting up in bed while Bryan Brown and Davis talk.

Monkey Grip (1983; Australian) . . . . Eve

• Downs, Brandi

Video Tapes:

Becky Bubbles (1987) . . . . Herself
- •• 0:11 — Topless in pool after Lorraine pushes her off the pool float.
- ••• 0:12 — Topless while playing on pool float with Lorraine and Becky.
- ••• 0:14 — Topless sunbathing on chair and putting her swimsuit back on.

Best Chest in the U.S. (1987) . . . . Charlene
- ••• 0:48 — Topless and buns, dancing in two piece swimsuit.
- ••• 0:54 — Topless on stage with the other finalists.
- ••• 0:57 — Topless winning.

The Perfect Body Contest (1987) . . . . Charlene
- • 0:18 — Buns, in two piece swimsuit, then topless.
- • 0:50 — Topless on stage with the other contestants.

Wild Bikinis (1987) . . . . Herself
- • 0:09 — Brief side of right breast, lying next to pool from *Becky Bubbles*.

Starlets Exposed! Volume II (1991) . . . . . . Charlene
(Same as *The Perfect Body Contest*.)
- ••• 0:21 — Buns in pink two piece swimsuit, then topless on stage doing strip routine.

Magazines:

Playboy's Book of Lingerie (Mar 1991) . . . . . . Herself
- ••• 44-45 — Topless and lower frontal nudity.
- •• 76 — Left breast and lower frontal nudity.

Playboy's Book of Lingerie (Jan 1992) . . . . . . Herself
- ••• 20 — Topless.
- ••• 80-81 — Topless and buns.

Playboy's Book of Lingerie (Mar 1992) . . . . . . Herself
- •• 99 — Left breast and lower frontal nudity.

Inside Sports (Apr 1992) . . . . Journey to St. John
- • 61 — Buns, while leaning over on a rock.

Playboy's Book of Lingerie (May 1992) . . . . . Herself
- ••• 30-31 — Topless and buns.

Playboy's Book of Lingerie (Jul 1992) . . . . Herself
- •• 28 — Left breast.

Playboy's Book of Lingerie (Sep 1992) . . . . . . Herself
- ••• 92 — Topless.

Drake, Gabrielle

Films:

The Man Outside (1968; British) . . . . B.E.A. Girl

There's a Girl in My Soup (1970)
. . . . Julia Halford-Smythe
- • 0:09 — In beige bra with Peter Sellers, brief left breast in bed with him. Don't see her face well, but it is her.

Connecting Rooms (1971; British). . . . . Jean
TV:
UFO (1970). . . . . .Lieutenant Gay Ellis

Drake, Marciee

Films:
Jackson County Jail (1976)
. . . . .Candy (David's Girlfriend)
  • 0:04—Brief topless wrapping towel around herself,
    in front of Howard Hessman. Long shot.
The Toolbox Murders (1978) . . . . Debbie
  •• 0:09—In wet blouse, then topless taking it off and
    putting a dry one on.

Drake, Michele

Films:
American Gigolo (1980) . . . . 1st Girl on Balcony
  • 0:03—Topless on the balcony while Richard Gere
    and Lauren Hutton talk.
The Hollywood Knights (1980) . . . . Cheerleader
  • 0:28—Brief lower nudity in raised cheerleader outfit
    doing cheers in front of school assembly.
History of the World, Part I (1981). . . . . . . Vestal Virgin
Magazines:
Playboy (May 1979) . . . . Playmate

Drescher, Fran

Films:
The Hollywood Knights (1980) . . . . Sally
Doctor Detroit (1983). . . . . Karen Blittstein
The Rosebud Beach Hotel (1985) . . . . Linda
The Big Picture (1989) . . . . Polo Habel
UHF (1989). . . . . Pamela Finklestein
Cadillac Man (1990). . . . . .Joy Munchack
  • 0:07—Very brief right breast several times while in
    bed with Robin Williams.
We're Talkin' Serious Money (1991) . . . . Valerie
Made for Cable TV:
Dream On: The Second Greatest Story Ever Told
  (1991; HBO) . . . . .Kathleen
TV:
Princesses (1991) . . . . Melissa

Drew, Linzi

Former Editor of the British edition of *Penthouse* maga-
zine.
Films:
An American Werewolf in London (1981)
. . . . Brenda Bristols
  • 1:26—Side view of left breast in porno movie while
    David Naughton talks to his friend, Jack.
  • 1:27—Brief topless in movie talking on the phone.
Emmanuelle in Soho (1981) . . . . .Showgirl
Topless on stage.
Salome's Last Dance (1987) . . . . .1st Slave
(Appears with 2 other slaves–can't tell who is who.)
  •• 0:08—Topless in black costume around a cage.
  •• 0:52—Topless during dance number.
Aria (1988; U.S./British). . . . . .Girl

  • 1:09—Topless on operating table after car accident.
    Hair is all covered with bandages.
  •• 1:10—Topless getting shocked to start her heart.
The Lair of the White Worm (1988; British) . . Maid/Nun

Driggs, Deborah

Films:
Total Exposure (1991) . . . . .Kathy
  ••• 0:08—Topless dancing in front of Jeff Conaway, then
    making love in bed with him. Long scene.
  • 0:22—Brief side view topless in B&W photos that
    Conaway looks at.
  • 0:24—Brief buns in black G-string and side of right
    breast changing clothes in locker room.
  •• 0:25—Topless and buns, trying to beat up Season
    Hubley.
Night Rhythms (1992) . . . . Cinnamon
(Unrated version reviewed.)
  ••• 1:15—Left breast, then topless and lower frontal nu-
    dity, making love with Martin Hewitt in bed.
  ••• 1:19—Topless, sitting on bed and talking to Hewitt.
Video Tapes:
Playboy Video Calendar 1991 (1990). . . . . .October
  ••• 0:40—Nude.
Playboy Video Centerfold: Deborah Driggs &
  Karen Foster (1990) . . . . Playmate
  ••• 0:02—Doing a strip tease, other dancing, some in
    bed. Nude.
Sexy Lingerie II (1990) . . . . Model
Wet and Wild II (1990). . . . . Model
Sexy Lingerie III (1991). . . . . Model
Wet and Wild III (1991) . . . . Model
Playboy Playmates in Paradise (1992). . . . Playmate
Sexy Lingerie IV (1992) . . . . Model
Magazines:
Playboy (Mar 1990) . . . . Playmate
Playboy's Book of Lingerie (Nov 1991) . . . . .Herself
  • 76—Buns.
Playboy's Book of Lingerie (Jan 1992) . . . . . .Herself
  • 12—Buns.
Playboy's Book of Lingerie (Mar 1992) . . . . .Herself
  ••• 22—Full frontal nudity.
  ••• 74—Full frontal nudity.
Playboy's Book of Lingerie (May 1992) . . . . .Herself
  •• 13—Right breast and lower frontal nudity.
Playboy's Book of Lingerie (Sep 1992) . . . . . .Herself
  ••• 10—Topless.

•Duce, Sharon

Films:
The Tamarind Seed (1974; British) . . . . . .Sandy Mitchell
Absolution (1978; British). . . . . .Louella
Outland (1981) . . . . .Prostitute
  • 0:30—Right breast, lying down in room with drug
    crazed guy.
  • 0:32—Topless going into medical scanning device.

Duffek, Patty

Films:
Hard Ticket to Hawaii (1987) . . . . Patticakes
•• 0:48—Topless talking to Michelle after swimming.
Picasso Trigger (1989) . . . . Patticakes
•• 1:04—Topless taking a Jacuzzi bath.
Savage Beach (1989) . . . . Patticakes
• 0:06—Topless in spa with Lisa London, Dona Speir
and Hope Marie Carlton.
•• 0:50—Topless changing clothes.
Video Tapes:
Playmate Playoffs . . . . Playmate
Magazines:
Playboy (May 1984) . . . . Playmate

Duffy, Julia

Films:
Battle Beyond the Stars (1980) . . . . Mol
Cutter's Way (1981) . . . . Young Girl
a.k.a. Cutter and Bone
Night Warning (1982) . . . . .Julie Linden
0:44—Upper half of left breast.
• 0:46—Brief topless when her boyfriend pulls the
sheets down.
•• 0:47—Brief topless when Susan Tyrrell opens the
bedroom door.
Wacko (1983) . . . . .Mary Graves
Miniseries:
Blue and the Gray (1982) . . . . .Mary Hale
Made for TV Movies:
Menu for Murder (1990) . . . . Susan Henshaw
_TV:_
Newhart (1983-90) . . . . .Stephanie Vanderkellen
Wizards and Warriors (1983) . . . . .Princess Ariel
Baby Talk (1991) . . . . .Maggie Campbell
Designing Women (1991-92) . . . . . . Allison Sugarbaker

Duke, Patty

a.k.a. Patty Duke Astin.
Ex-wife of actor John Astin.
Films:
4D Man (1959) . . . . .Marjorie Sullivan
The Miracle Worker (1962) . . . . Helen Keller
Valley of the Dolls (1967) . . . . Neely O'Hara
By Design (1982; Canadian) . . . . Helen
•• 0:49—Left breast, lying in bed.
•• 1:05—Brief left breast sitting on bed.
• 1:06—Brief left breast, then brief right breast lying in
bed with the photographer.
Something Special (1987) . . . . Mrs. Doris Niceman
Miniseries:
Captains and the Kings (1976)
. . . . Bernadette Hennessey Armagh
Made for TV Movies:
The Miracle Worker (1979) . . . . Anne Sullivan
Everybody's Baby: The Rescue of Jessica McClure (1989)
. . . . .n.a.
Always Remember I Love You (1990). . . . . Ruth Monroe
Absolute Strangers (1991) . . . . .Judge Ray

Grave Secrets: The Legacy of Hilltop Drive (1992)
. . . . Jean Williams
Last Wish (1992) . . . . Betty Rollin
_TV:_
The Patty Duke Show (1963-66) . . . Patty & Cathy Lane
It Takes Two (1982-83). . . . . Molly Quinn
Hail to the Chief (1985) . . . . . . President Julia Mansfield

Dumas, Sandrine

a.k.a. Sandra Dumas.
Films:
Twice a Woman (1979). . . . . .Sylvia
• 0:06—Topless, kneeling on the bed, then more brief
topless in bed with Bibi Andersson.
••• 0:47—Brief right breast, then topless in bed with
Andersson. Long scene.
• 1:15—Left breast, lying in bed with Anthony Perkins.
Long shot.
••• 1:23—Topless with Andersson.
Beyond Therapy (1987) . . . . Cindy
Aria (1988; U.S./British) . . . . n.a.
Valmont (1989) . . . . Martine
The Double Life of Veronique (1991; French) . Catherine

Dunaway, Faye

Films:
Bonnie and Clyde (1967) . . . . Bonnie Parker
The Thomas Crown Affair (1968) . . . . . . Vicky Anderson
The Arrangement (1969) . . . . Gwen
0:25—Brief buns in various scenes at the beach with
Kirk Douglas.
Little Big Man (1970) . . . . Mrs. Pendrake
The Three Musketeers (1973). . . . . Milady
Chinatown (1974) . . . . Evelyn
• 1:26—Very brief right breast, in bed talking to Jack
Nicholson.
• 1:28—Very brief right breast in bed talking to
Nicholson. Very brief flash of right breast under robe
when she gets up to leave the bedroom.
The Towering Inferno (1974) . . . . Susan Franklin
The Four Musketeers (1975). . . . . Milady
Three Days of the Condor (1975). . . . . . . .Kathy Hale
Network (1976) . . . . Diana Christensen
(Academy Award for Best Actress.)
• 1:10—Brief left breast twice, taking off clothes in
room with William Holden.
Voyage of the Damned (1976) . . . . .Denise Kreisler
Eyes of Laura Mars (1978) . . . . .Laura Mars
The Champ (1979) .Annie
The First Deadly Sin (1980) . . . . Barbara Delaney
Mommie Dearest (1981) . . . . .Joan Crawford
The Wicked Lady (1983; British). . . . . . . Barbara Skelton
Ordeal by Innocence (1984) . . . . .Rachel Argyle
Supergirl (1984; British) . . . . Selena
Barfly (1987) . . . . Wanda Wilcox
• 0:58—Brief upper half of breasts in bathtub talking
to Mickey Rourke.
Midnight Crossing (1988) . . . . Helen Barton
A Handmaid's Tale (1990) . . . . Serena Joy

The Two Jakes (1990) . . . . Evelyn Mulwray
Scorchers (1992). . . . . .n.a.
Miniseries:
Christopher Columbus (1985). . . . . .n.a.
TV:
Ladies of the Night (1986) . . . . Lil Hutton

Dunlap, Dawn

Films:
Laura (1979) . . . . Laura
  a.k.a. Shattered Innocence
- 0:20—Brief side view of left breast and buns talking to Maud Adams, then brief side view of right breast putting on robe.
- 0:23—Nude, dancing while being photographed.
- 1:15—Nude, letting Paul feel her so he can sculpt her, then making love with him.
  1:22—Buns, putting on panties talking to Maud Adams.
Forbidden World (1982) . . . . Tracy Baxter
- 0:27—Brief topless getting ready for bed.
- 0:37—Nude in steam bath.
- 0:54—Topless in shower with June Chadwick.
Night Shift (1982). . . . . Maxine
Heartbreaker (1983) . . . . Kim
- 0:49—Topless putting on dress in bedroom.
  0:51—Very, very brief right breast in open dress during rape attempt. Dark.
- 1:02—Left breast, lying on bed with her boyfriend. Long scene.
Barbarian Queen (1985) . . . . .Taramis
- 0:00—Topless, in the woods getting raped.

• Dunsheath, Lisa

Films:
The Prowler (1981) . . . . .Sherry
- 0:20—Very brief topless in the shower (overhead view).
- 0:21—More topless and buns in shower, then topless when Carl opens the door.
- 0:22—More topless from overhead.
- 0:23—Topless, getting killed by the prowler with a pitchfork.
- 1:23—Topless, dead in the bathtub when Pam discovers her.
Made for Cable TV:
The Hitchhiker: O. D. Feeling . . . . .n.a.

Dupree, Christine

a.k.a. Christine Dupré.
Films:
Armed and Dangerous (1986) . . . . . .Peep Show Girl
- 0:58—Very, very brief topless shots behind glass dancing in front of John Candy and Eugene Levy.
Magazines:
Penthouse (Sep 1985) . . . . Pet

Dusenberry, Ann

Films:
Jaws II (1978). . . . . Tina Wilcox
Heart Beat (1979) . . . . Stevie
- • 0:41—Full frontal nudity frolicking in bathtub with Nick Nolte.
Cutter's Way (1981). . . . . .Valerie Duran
  a.k.a. Cutter and Bone
Basic Training (1984) . . . . Melinda Griffin
- ••• 1:13—Topless in Russian guy's bedroom.
Lies (1984; British) . . . . .Robyn Wallace
- •• 0:10—Topless opening the shower curtain in front of her boyfriend.
- • 0:11—Right breast while kissing her boyfriend.
The Men's Club (1986) . . . . Page
- •• 1:05—Topless lying in bed after making love with Roy Scheider.
Play Nice (1992) . . . . Pam Crichmore
  (Unrated version reviewed.)
TV:
Little Women (1979) . . . . .Amy March Laurence
The Family Tree (1983) . . . . .Molly Nichols Tanner
Life with Lucy (1986-87) . . . . Margo McGibbon

• Dutch, Deborah

a.k.a. Debra Dare.
Films:
Bruce Lee Fights Back From the Grave (1981) . . Debbie
The Man Who Wasn't There (1983) . . . . . . Miss Dawson
Protocol (1984) .Safari Girl
Torchlight (1984). . . . . .Sydney's Girlfriend
The Haunting of Morella (1989). . . . . . . Serving Girl
- ••• 0:14—Topless and buns, taking off pink tap pants and getting into bath.
- • 0:15—Buns, lying dead on the floor, covered with blood.
Sorority Girls and the Creature from Hell (1990)
. . . . .Mary Anne
  0:08—Very brief, side of left breast changing clothes in background.
- • 0:32—Lower half of left breast, dancing in cabin.
976-EVIL II: The Astral Factor (1991)
. . . . Commerical Wife
Tower of Terror (1991). . . . . Jackie Webster
Death Dancers (1992). . . . . Shannon
Mind Twister (1992) . . . . .Sheila Harrison
Roadside Justice (1992) . . . . Mom
TV:
Capitol (1985) . . . . n.a.
The Young and the Restless (1987). . . . . n.a.
General Hospital (1988). . . . . n.a.
Video Tapes:
Scream Queen Hot Tub Party (1991)
. . . . Jackie Webster
- •• 0:19—Topless, taking off towel and getting into shower from *Tower of Terror.*

Duvall, Shelley

Producer.
Films:
Brewster McCloud (1970) . . . . Suzanne
McCabe and Mrs. Miller (1971) . . . . Ida Coyle
Thieves Like Us (1974) . . . . .Keechie
Nashville (1975) . . . . .L.A. Jane
Buffalo Bill and the Indians (1976) . . . . . . Mrs. Cleveland
Annie Hall (1977) . . . . Pam
Three Women (1977) . . . . Millie
Popeye (1980) . . . . Olive Oyl
The Shining (1980) . . . . Wendy Torrance
Time Bandits (1981; British) . . . . Pansy
Frankenweenie (1984) . . . . Susan Frankenstein
Roxanne (1987) . . . . .Dixie
Suburban Commando (1991) . . . . .Jenny Wilcox
Magazines:
Playboy (Dec 1975) . . . . Sex Stars of 75
••• 188—Topless photo.

Dziubinska, Anulka

a.k.a. Anulka.
Films:
Vampyres (1974; British) . . . . Miriam
• 0:00—Brief full frontal nudity in bed with Fran, kissing each other before getting shot.
• 0:43—Topless taking a shower with Fran.
••• 0:58—Topless and buns in bed with Fran, drinking
Ted's blood. Brief lower frontal nudity.
Lisztomania (1975; British) . . . . Lola Montez
•• 0:08—Topless sitting on Roger Daltrey's lap, kissing
him. Nice close up.
• 0:21—Topless, backstage with Daltrey after the concert.
• 0:39—Topless, wearing pasties, during Daltrey's
nightmare/song and dance number.
Magazines:
Playboy (May 1973) . . . . Playmate
••• 122-129—Full frontal nudity.

Easterbrook, Leslie

Films:
Just Tell Me What You Want (1980) . . . . . Hospital Nurse
Police Academy (1984) . . . . Callahan
Private Resort (1985) . . . . .Bobbie Sue
•• 0:14—Very brief buns taking off swimsuit, then top-
less under sheer white nightgown.
Police Academy III: Back in Training (1986) . . . . Callahan
Police Academy 4: Citizens on Patrol (1987) . . . Callahan
0:35—In wet T-shirt in swimming pool pretending
to be a drowning victim for the class.
Police Academy 5: Assignment Miami Beach (1988)
. . . . Callahan
Police Academy 6: City Under Siege (1989) . . . Callahan
Made for TV Movies:
The Taking of Flight 847: The Uli Derickson Story (1988)
. . . . Audrey
TV:
Laverne & Shirley (1980-83) . . . . Rhonda Lee

Easton, Jackie

a.k.a. Jacki Easton.
Films:
Hardbodies (1984) . . . . Girl in Dressing Room
•• 0:27—Topless taking off dress to try on swimsuit.
•• 0:40—Topless with other topless girls posing for
photographs taken by Rounder. She's wearing a
white skirt.
School Spirit (1985) . . . . .Hogette

Eastwood, Jayne

Films:
My Pleasure is My Business (1974) . . . . Isabella
• 1:16—Topless in bed trying to get His Excellency's
attention.
•• 1:28—Topless sitting up in bed with blonde guy.
One Man (1979; Canadian) . . . . Alicia Brady
Finders Keepers (1983) . . . . Anna-Marie Biddlecoff
Night Friend (1987; Canadian) . . . . . .Rita the Bag Lady
Candy Mountain (1988; Swiss/Canadian/French)
. . . . Lucille
Cold Comfort (1988) . . . . Mrs. Brocket
Hostile Takeover (1988; Canadian) . . . . . .Mrs. Talmage
a.k.a. Office Party
Made for TV Movies:
Anne of Green Gables (1985; Canadian)
. . . . Mrs. Hammond

Eccles, Aimée

Films:
Pretty Maids All in a Row (1971) . . . . Hilda
• 1:06—Partial buns while sitting on desk in Rock
Hudson's office. Her hair covers most of her right
breast.
Group Marriage (1972) . . . . Chris
0:15—Buns, getting into bed.
• 1:15—Brief side view of left breast and buns getting
into the shower.
Ulzana's Raid (1972) . . . . McIntosh's Indian Woman
Paradise Alley (1978) . . . . .Susan
The Concrete Jungle (1982) . . . . Spider
Lovelines (1984) . . . . Nisei
Magazines:
Playboy (Apr 1971) . . . . Vadim's "Pretty Maids"
•• 160—Topless under gold top.

Eden, Simone

Video Tapes:
Playboy Video Calendar 1990 (1989) . . . . . . .August
••• 0:40—Nude.
Wet and Wild (1989) . . . . Model
Playmates at Play (1990) . . . . Gotta Dance
Magazines:
Playboy (Feb 1989) . . . . Playmate
Playboy's Book of Lingerie (Jan 1991) . . . . . .Herself
• 26—Lower frontal nudity.
Playboy's Book of Lingerie (Mar 1991) . . . . . .Herself
•• 46-47—Right breast and lower frontal nudity.

Playboy's Book of Lingerie (Mar 1992) . . . . . Herself
• 30—Buns.
••• 31—Full frontal nudity.
Playboy's Book of Lingerie (May 1992) . . . . . Herself
• 103—Right breast.
Playboy's Career Girls (Aug 1992)
. . . . Baywatch Playmates
• 10—Left breast.
Playboy's Book of Lingerie (Sep 1992) . . . . . Herself
••• 50-51—Topless.

Edmondson, Donna

Video Tapes:
Playboy Video Calendar 1988 (1987) . . . . Playmate
Playboy Video Centerfold: Donna Edmondson
(1987). . . . . Playmate of the Year 1987
••• 0:00—Nude, behind shower door, in photo session,
on sofa in house, in empty house and in the rain.
Playboy Video Magazine, Volume 12 (1987)
. . . . Playmate
••• 0:08—Nude in clips from her Playmate video.
Playboy's Playmates of the Year: The '80s (1989)
. . . . Playmate of the Year 1987
••• 0:21—Modeling swimsuits and lingerie. Nude on
couch.
••• 0:22—In bra, garter belt and stockings, dancing in
strobe light. Lower frontal nudity. Nude seen
through open window.
••• 0:23—Nude, taking off her clothes in empty house.
Nude in bed.
•• 0:26—Topless, in the rain.
•• 0:52—Full frontal nudity in bed.
Wet and Wild (1989). . . . . .Model
Playmates at Play (1990) . . . . .Gotta Dance
Magazines:
Playboy (Nov 1986) . . . . Playmate
Playboy's Nudes (Oct 1990). . . . . Herself
••• 105—Full frontal nudity.

Edwards, Barbara

Films:
Malibu Express (1984). . . . . May
•• 0:10—Topless taking a shower with Kimberly
McArthur on the boat.
•• 1:05—Topless serving Cody coffee while he talks on
the telephone.
Terminal Entry (1986) . . . . Lady Electric
••• 0:05—Topless taking a shower and getting a towel
during video game scene.
Another Chance (1989) . . . . .Diana the Temptress
••• 0:38—Topless in trailer with Johnny.
Video Tapes:
Playboy Video Magazine, Volume 4 (1983)
. . . . Playmate
•• 0:20—Topless on sailboat.
••• 0:22—Nude, posing for centerfold photograph.
••• 0:24—Full frontal nudity on bed by herself.
••• 0:29—Nude, dancing in laser light show.
Playboy's Playmate Review 3 (1985) . . . . . Playmate

Playboy Video Calendar 1987 (1986). . . . . Playmate
Playboy's Fantasies (1987). . . . . Fashion
0:00—Full frontal nudity during modeling session.
Sexy Lingerie (1988). . . . . Model
Playboy's Playmates of the Year: The '80s (1989)
. . . . .Playmate of the Year 1984
••• 0:13—Nude in still photos.
••• 0:14—Full frontal nudity in centerfold photo session.
More in bed.
•• 0:52—Full frontal nudity in bed.
Wet and Wild (1989) . . . . Model
Playboy Video Centerfold: Kerri Kendall (1990)
. . . . Playmate
••• 0:37—Nude.
Playboy's Fantasies II (1990) . . . . . The Secret Garden
••• 0:07—Nude, walking around in garden while a guy
watches her.
Magazines:
Playboy (Sep 1983) . . . . Playmate
Playboy (Jun 1984). . . . . Playmate of the Year
Playboy's Nudes (Oct 1990) . . . . .Herself
••• 104—Full frontal nudity.
Playboy's Book of Lingerie (Jan 1991) . . . . . .Herself
••• 24-25—Full frontal nudity.
Playboy's Book of Lingerie (Mar 1991). . . . . .Herself
••• 40-41—Nude.
Playboy's Book of Lingerie (Sep 1991) . . . . . .Herself
••• 91—Full frontal nudity.
Playboy's Book of Lingerie (May 1992) . . . . .Herself
•• 108—Buns and side view of left breast.

Edwards, Ella

Films:
Sweet Sugar (1972). . . . . Simone
• 0:58—Topless in bed with Mojo.
Detroit 9000 (1973). . . . . .Helen
Mr. Ricco (1975) . . . . .Sally
Famous T & A (1982) . . . . Simone
(No longer available for purchase, check your video
store for rental.)
•• 1:07—Buns and topless in outtakes from *Sweet Sugar.*

Ege, Julie

Films:
On Her Majesty's Secret Sevice (1969; British)
. . . . Scandanavian Girl
Creatures the World Forgot (1971; British)
. . . . Nala, The Girl
0:56—Very brief topless several times (it looks like a
stunt double) fighting in cave with The Dumb Girl.
Hard to see.
• 1:32—Very, very brief half of right breast when fight-
ing a snake that is wrapped around her face.
The Mutations (1973; British) . . . . Hedi
a.k.a. Freakmaker
Topless in bathtub.

Eggar, Samantha

Films:

The Collector (1965) . . . . Miranda Grey
Doctor Dolittle (1967) . . . . .Emma
A Name for Evil (1973) . . . . .Joanna Blake
- 0:42—Very brief topless turning over in bed with
  Robert Culp. Dark, hard to see.

The Uncanny (1977; British) . . . . Edina
The Brood (1979; Canadian) . . . . Nola Carveth
Curtains (1983; Canadian) . . . . . . Samantha Sherwood
Round Numbers (1990) .n.a.

Made for Cable Movies:

A Ghost in Monte Carlo (1990) . . . . .n.a.

TV:

Anna and the King (1972) . . . . .Anna Owens

Egger, Jolanda

Video Tapes:

Playmates at Play (1990) . . Bareback, Making Waves

Magazines:

Playboy (Jun 1983) . . . . Playmate

• Eggert, Nicole

Films:

Clan of the Cave Bear (1985) . . . . Middle Ayla
Omega Syndrome (1986) . . . . Jessie Corbett
The Haunting of Morella (1989) . . . .Morella/Lenora
- 0:16—Topless taking a bath in blood. Don't see her
  face, probably a body double.
  0:47—Buns, on top of Guy in bed. Note the body
  double has different colored hair.
  0:48—Side view of right breast in bed with Guy.
  Body double again.

Kinjite (1989) . . . . .Dee Dee

TV:

T.J. Hooker (1982-87) .Chrissie
Charles in Charge (1987-90) . . . . Jamie Powell
Baywatch (1992-) . . . . Summer

Eichhorn, Lisa

Films:

The Europeans (1979; British) . . . . Gertrude Wentworth
Yanks (1979) . . . . Jean Moreton
- 1:48—Brief topless in bed when Richard Gere rolls
  off her.

Why Would I Lie? (1980) . . . . .Kay
Cutter's Way (1981) . . . . Maureen "Mo" Cutter
a.k.a. Cutter and Bone
- 1:07—Brief right breast, wearing bathrobe, lying on
  lounge chair while Jeff Bridges looks at her.

The Weather in the Streets (1983; British) . . . . Olivia
Wild Rose (1984) . . . . June Lorich
Opposing Force (1986) . . . . Lieutenant Casey
a.k.a. Hell Camp
- 0:17—Wet T-shirt after going through river.
- 0:33—Topless getting sprayed with water and dusted with white powder.
- 1:03—Topless after getting raped by Anthony Zerbe
  in his office, while another officer watches.

• 1:05—Topless and buns, getting dressed.

Grim Prairie Tales (1990) . . . . Maureen
Moon 44 (1990; West German) . . . . .Terry Morgan

Made for Cable Movies:

Devlin (1991; Showtime) . . . . Anita Brennan

Made for TV Movies:

A Woman Named Jackie (1991) . . . . Dr. Jordan

• Eilbacher, Lisa

Films:

An Officer and a Gentleman (1982) . . . . . . Casey Seeger
10 to Midnight (1983) . . . . .Laurie Kessler
Beverly Hills Cop (1984) . . . . Jenny Summers
Live Wire (1992) . . . . Terry O'Neill
- 1:01—Brief topless several times and partial buns, in
  bath tub and in bed with Pierce Brosnan.

Made for Cable Movies:

Blind Man's Bluff (1992; USA) . . . . n.a.

Miniseries:

Wheels (1978) . . . . .Jody Horton
The Winds of War (1983) . . . . .Madeline Henry

Made for TV Movies:

Ordeal of Patty Hearst (1979) . . . . .Patty Hearst
Manhunt: Search for the Night Stalker (1989) . . . . . Ann
Joshua's Heart (1990) . . . . Kit

TV:

The Texas Wheelers (1974-75) . . . . .Sally
The Hardy Boys Mysteries (1977) . . . . Callie Shaw
Ryan's Four (1983) . . . . Dr. Ingrid Sorenson
Me and Mom (1985) . . . . Kate Morgan

Eilber, Janet

Films:

Whose Life Is It, Anyway? (1981) . . . . Patty
- 0:30—Nude, ballet dancing during B&W dream sequence.
- 1:13—Very brief side of left breast when her back is
  turned while changing clothes.

Romantic Comedy (1983) . . . . Allison
Hard to Hold (1984) . . . . Diana Lawson

TV:

Two Marriages (1983-84) . . . . Nancy Armstrong
The Best Times (1985) . . . . .Joanne Braithwaite

Ekberg, Anita

Films:

Back from Eternity (1956) . . . . Rena
Hollywood or Bust (1956) . . . . .Herself
War and Peace (1956; U.S./Italian) . . . . .Helene
Paris Holiday (1957) . . . . .Zara
La Dolce Vita (1960; Italian) . . . . .Sylvia
Boccaccio 70 (1962; Italian) . . . . Anita
Four for Texas (1963) . . . . Elya Carlson
Woman Times Seven (1967) . . . . Claudie
Northeast of Seoul (1972) . . . . n.a.

Made for TV Movies:

S.H.E. (1979) . . . . n.a.

Magazines:

Playboy (Jan 1974) . . . . Twenty Years of Playboy
••• 199—Full frontal nudity in classic B&W photo.
Playboy (Jan 1989) . . . . .Women of the Fifties
•• 118—B&W photo sitting on the floor.
Playboy's Nudes (Oct 1990). . . . . Herself
••• 8—Full frontal nudity in B&W photo.

Ekland, Britt

Ex-wife of the late actor Peter Sellers.
Films:

After the Fox (1966) . . . . Gina Romantiea
The Bobo (1967). . . . . .Olimpia Segura
The Night They Raided Minsky's (1968)
. . . . Rachel Schpitendavel
Topless.
The Cannibals (1969) . . . . Antigone
Stiletto (1969). . . . . .Illeana
What the Peeper Saw (1972) . . . . Elise
0:38—Sort of side view of left breast in bed. Don't
really see anything.
The Wicker Man (1973; British) . . . . Willow
••• 0:58—Topless in bed knocking on the wall, then
more topless and buns getting up and walking
around the bedroom. Long scene.
The Man with the Golden Gun (1974; British)
. . . . .Mary Goodnight
The Ultimate Thrill (1974) . . . . Michele
Endless Night (1977) . . . . Greta
• 1:21—Brief topless several times with Michael.
Slavers (1977) . . . . .Anna
• 0:40—Topless undressing in front of Ron Ely.
Sex on the Run (1979; German/French/Italian)
. . . . .Countess Trivulsi
a.k.a. Some Like It Cool
a.k.a. Casanova and Co.
• 0:44—Left breast while making love in bed with
Tony Curtis (don't see her face).
The Monster Club (1981) . . . . .Lintom's Mother
Erotic Images (1983) . . . . .Julie Todd
• 0:16—Brief side view of left breast in bed with
Glenn.
••• 0:29—In bra, then topless in bed with Glenn.
0:33—In bra, in open robe looking at herself in the
mirror.
1:27—In black bra, talking to Sonny.
Love Scenes (1984). Annie
a.k.a. Ecstacy
Moon in Scorpio (1987) . . . . Linda
Beverly Hills Vamp (1989) . . . . Madam Cassandra
Scandal (1989) . . . . Mariella Novotny
(Unrated version reviewed.)
•• 0:31—Topless lying on table with John Hurt.
• 0:51—Right breast talking with Hurt and Christine.
The Children (1990) . . . . Zinnia Wrench
Cold Heat (1991) . . . . Jackie Mallon
Magazines:
Playboy (May 1989) . . . . .Scandal
• 87-88—Left and right breasts.

Eleniak, Erika

Films:

E.T. The Extraterrestrial (1982) . . . . Pretty Girl
The Blob (1988). . . . . .Vicki De Soto
Under Seige (1992) . . . . n.a.
Made for TV Movies:
Baywatch (1989) . . . . .Shauni
TV:
Charles in Charge (1988-89) . . . . Stephanie Curtis
Baywatch (1989-90). . . . . .Shauni McLain
Baywatch (1991-) . . . . .Shauni McLain
Video Tapes:
Playboy Video Centerfold: Fawna MacLaren
(1988) . . . . Playmate
••• 0:07—In studio, nude.
Playboy Video Calendar 1991 (1990). . . . . . . .May
••• 0:18—Nude.
Magazines:
Playboy (Jul 1989) . . . . Playmate
Playboy (Dec 1989) . . . . Holy Sex Stars of 1989!
••• 181—Topless, reclining.
Playboy (Aug 1990) . . . . Beauty on the Beach
••• 68-75—Nude.
Playboy's Nudes (Oct 1990) . . . . .Herself
••• 10—Full frontal nudity.
Playboy (Dec 1990) . . . . .Sex Stars of 1990
••• 173—Full frontal nudity, leaning back against wall.
Playboy (Dec 1991) . . . . .Sex Stars 1991
••• 182—Topless under sheer, wet, white swimsuit.
Playboy's Book of Lingerie (Mar 1992). . . . . .Herself
• 9—Lower frontal nudity.
Playboy's Book of Lingerie (May 1992) . . . . .Herself
••• 44-45—Topless.
Playboy's Book of Lingerie (Jul 1992) . . . . . .Herself
•• 66-67—Right breast and upper half of left breast.
Playboy's Career Girls (Aug 1992)
. . . . Baywatch Playmates
• 5—Lower frontal nudity.

Elian, Yona

Films:

The Jerusalem File (1972; U.S./Israel) . . . . Raschel
The Last Winter (1983; Israeli) . . . . .Maya
•• 0:48—Topless taking off her robe to get into pool.
0:49—Buns, lying on marble slab with Kathleen
Quinlan.

Elise, Esther

See: Alise, Esther.

Elvira

a.k.a. Cassandra Peterson.
Films:

The Working Girls (1973) . . . . .Katya
0:18—Dancing in a G-string on stage in a club.
••• 0:20—Topless, dancing on stage.
The Best of Sex and Violence (1981) . . . . .Katya
•• 0:40—Brief topless dancing on stage in scene from
Working Girls.

Famous T & A (1982) . . . . Katya
(No longer available for purchase, check your video
store for rental.)
••• 0:28—Topless scene from *Working Girls*.
Jekyll & Hyde... Together Again (1982)
. . . . Busty Nurse
• 0:56—Brief right breast, peeking out from smock in
operating room. (She's wearing a surgical mask.)
Stroker Ace (1983) . . . . .Woman with Lugs
Pee Wee's Big Adventure (1985) . . . . Biker Mama
Echo Park (1986). . . . . .Sheri
Allan Quartermain and the Lost City of Gold (1987)
. . . . Sorais
Elvira, Mistress of the Dark (1988). . . . . Elvira
0:31—Getting undressed into black lingerie in her
bedroom while being watched from outside the
window.
1:31—*Very* skillfully twirling two tassels on the tips of
her bra.
Ted & Venus (1991) . . . . .Lisa

Errickson, Krista
Films:
Little Darlings (1980) . . . . Cinder
The First Time (1981) . . . . Dana
a.k.a. Doin' It
Jekyll & Hyde... Together Again (1982). . . . . Ivy
0:31—In red bra and panties in bedroom with Mark
Blankfield.
Mortal Passions (1989) . . . . Emily
•• 0:08—Brief topless in bed with Darcy, while tied to
the bed. Topless getting untied and rolling over.
• 0:11—Very brief right breast, rolling back on top of
Darcy.
••• 0:40—Topless after dropping her sheet for Burke,
then making love with him.
•• 0:46—Topless getting into bed with her husband.
Killer Image (1991) . . . . Shelley
TV:
Hello, Larry (1979-80). . . . . .Diane Adler

Estores, Lourdes
Video Tapes:
Playmate Playoffs . . . . Playmate
Playboy's Playmate Review (1982) . . . . . . Playmate
••• 0:56—Nude at the beach, then under water, then
outside near river.
Magazines:
Playboy (Aug 1980) . . . . Girls of Hawaii
••• 159—Full frontal nudity.
Playboy (Jun 1982) . . . . Playmate

Evans, Linda
Films:
Beach Blanket Bingo (1965) . . . . .Sugar Kane
The Klansman (1974) . . . . Nancy Poteet
Mitchell (1975). . . . . Greta
The Avalanche Express (1979). . . . . Elsa Lang
Tom Horn (1980) . . . . .Glendoline Kimmel

Miniseries:
North and South, Book II (1986) . . . . Rose Sinclair
Dynasty: The Reunion (1991)
. . . . Krystle Jennings Carrington
Made for TV Movies:
The Last Frontier (1986). . . . . .Kate
TV:
Big Valley (1965-69). . . . . Audra Barkley
Hunter (1977) . . . . .Marty Shaw
Dynasty (1981-89). . . . . Krystle Jennings Carrington
Video Tapes:
Playboy Video Magazine, Volume 1 (1982)
. . . . .Herself
•• 0:58—Topless and side view of buns, in still photos
from *Playboy* layout.
Magazines:
Playboy (Jul 1971) . . . . Blooming Beauty
Playboy (Dec 1981) . . . . .Sex Stars of 1981
••• 241—Topless.
Playboy (Jan 1989). . . . . Women of the Seventies
••• 216—Topless sitting in water.

Evenson, Kim
Films:
The Big Bet (1985) . . . . Beth
•• 0:36—Right breast, sitting on couch with Chris.
•• 0:45—Brief topless, twice, taking off swimsuit top.
•• 0:54—Brief topless three times in elevator when
Chris pulls her sweater up.
•• 1:06—Nude when Chris fantasizes about her being
in the video tape that he's watching. Long shot.
••• 1:19—In white bra and panties, then nude while undressing for Chris.
Porky's Revenge (1985; Canadian) . . . . .Inga
•• 0:02—Right breast, while opening her graduation
gown during Pee Wee's dream.
•• 1:27—Topless showing Pee Wee that she doesn't
have any clothes under her graduation gown.
Kidnapped (1986) . . . . Debbie
• 0:25—Right breast in bed talking on the phone.
Long shot, hard to see.
0:30—In blue nightgown in room.
••• 1:28—Topless getting her arm prepared for a drug
injection. Long scene.
••• 1:30—Topless acting in a movie. Long shot, then
close up. Wearing a G-string.
Kandyland (1987) . . . . Joni
0:26—In purple bra and white panties practicing
dancing on stage.
••• 0:31—Topless doing first dance routine.
•• 0:45—Brief topless during another routine with bubbles floating around.
Video Tapes:
Playmate Playoffs. . . . . Playmate
Wet and Wild (1989) . . . . Model
Playboy Video Centerfold: Kerri Kendall (1990)
. . . . Playmate
••• 0:35—Nude.
Playmates at Play (1990) . . . . Flights of Fancy

Playboy (Sep 1984). . . . . Playmate
Playboy (Nov 1985) . . . . Sex in Cinema 1985
••• 128—Topless in graduation gown in still from *Porky's Revenge.*

• *Evridge, Melissa*

Video Tapes:
Playboy Video Calendar 1992 (1991) . . . . April
••• 0:13—Nude outside in garden.
••• 0:15—Nude in action-movie fantasy in the desert.
Magazines:
Playboy (Aug 1990). . . . . Playmate
Playboy's Book of Lingerie (Sep 1991) . . . . . Herself
••• 64-65—Full frontal nudity.
Playboy's Book of Lingerie (May 1992) . . . . . Herself
••• 39—Topless in sheer white panties.

Fabian, Ava

Films:
Dragnet (1987). . . . . .Baitmate
Terminal Exposure (1988) . . . . Bruce's Girl
To Die For (1988) . . . . Franny
Limit Up (1989) . . . . Sasha
Ski School (1990) . . . . .Victoria
••• 0:53—In white bra and panties, then topless making love with Johnny.
Welcome Home Roxy Carmichael (1990)
. . . . .Roxy Carmichael
• 0:10—Buns in water in swimming pool, then more while getting out.
Mobsters (1991) . . . . .Cute Girl
a.k.a. Mobsters—The Evil Empire
Video Tapes:
Playmate Playoffs . . . . Playmate
Playboy Video Magazine, Volume 12 (1987)
. . . . Playmate
••• 1:08—Nude, in bed, in still photos, in rainy scene, dancing like Kim Basinger in *9 1/2 Weeks.*
Sexy Lingerie (1988) . . . . .Model
Playboy Video Calendar 1990 (1989) . . . . .July
••• 0:34—Nude.
Wet and Wild (1989). . . . . .Model
Playmates at Play (1990) . . . . .Gotta Dance
Sexy Lingerie II (1990). . . . . .Model
Wet and Wild II (1990) . . . . .Model
Sexy Lingerie III (1991) . . . . .Model
Wet and Wild III (1991). . . . . .Model
Playboy Playmates in Paradise (1992) . . . Playmate
Magazines:
Playboy (Aug 1986). . . . . Playmate
Playboy's Book of Lingerie (Jan 1991) . . . . . . Herself
••• 60—Topless.
Playboy's Book of Lingerie (Mar 1991) . . . . . Herself
••• 33—Full frontal nudity.
Playboy's Book of Lingerie (Sep 1991) . . . . . Herself
•• 22—Left breast.
Playboy's Book of Lingerie (Nov 1991) . . . . . Herself
••• 78-81—Nude.

Playboy's Book of Lingerie (Mar 1992). . . . . .Herself
•• 11—Left breast and lower frontal nudity.
••• 77—Topless.
Playboy's Book of Lingerie (May 1992) . . . . .Herself
••• 91—Full frontal nudity.
••• 94-95—Topless.
• 98—Buns.
Playboy's Book of Lingerie (Jul 1992). . . . . . .Herself
••• 35—Full frontal nudity.
••• 61—Topless.

Fairchild, June

Films:
Pretty Maids All in a Row (1971)
. . . . .Sonya "Sonny" Swingle
• 1:10—Brief topless and lower frontal nudity, taking Polaroid photos of herself in Rock Hudson's office.
Drive, He Said (1972) . . . . .Sylvie
• 0:16—Buns and brief topless walking around in the dark while Gabriel shines a flashlight on her.
• 1:01—Topless, then brief nude getting dressed while Gabriel goes crazy and starts trashing a house.
Top of the Heap (1972) . . . . Balloon Thrower
Detroit 9000 (1973). Barbara
Your Three Minutes Are Up (1973). . . . . .Sandi
Thunderbolt and Lightfoot (1974). . . . . Gloria
• 0:20—Very brief right breast getting dressed in the bathroom after making love with Clint Eastwood.
The Student Body (1975) . . . . .Mitzi Mashall
• 0:15—Brief topless and buns, running and jumping into the pool during party. Brief long shot topless, while in the pool.
•• 0:21—Topless getting into bed.
Up in Smoke (1978). . . . . .Ajax Lady
Magazines:
Playboy (Apr 1971) . . . . Vadim's "Pretty Maids"
•• 160—Left breast.
Playboy (Nov 1974) . . . . Sex in Cinema 1974
••• 145—Full frontal nudity from *Thunderbolt and Lightfoot.*

Fairchild, Morgan

Films:
The Seduction (1982) . . . . .Jamie
• 0:02—Brief topless under water, swimming in pool.
• 0:05—Very brief left breast, getting out of the pool to answer the telephone.
0:13—In white bra changing clothes while listening to telephone answering machine.
0:50—In white lingerie in her bathroom while Andrew Stevens watches from inside the closet.
•• 0:51—Topless pinning her hair up for her bath, then brief left breast in bathtub covered with bubbles.
• 1:21—Topless getting into bed. Kind of dark, hard to see anything.
Terror in the Aisles (1984). . . . . .Jamie
•• 1:06—Topless in mirror in scene from *The Seduction.*
• 1:08—Brief left breast, getting out of pool from *The Seduction.*

Pee Wee's Big Adventure (1985) . . . . "Dottie"
Campus Man (1987). . . . . Katherine Van Buren
Deadly Illusion (1987). . . . . Jane Mallory/Sharon Burton
Midnight Cop (1988; Italian) . . . . Lisa
   0:23—In white panties with her dress pulled up in
   restroom with Alex.
Phantom of the Mall: Eric's Revenge (1988)
   . . . . Karen Wilton
Mob Boss (1990). . . . . Gina
Made for Cable Movies:
The Haunting of Sarah Hardy (1989; USA) . . . . n.a.
Miniseries:
79 Park Avenue (1977) . . . . n.a.
North and South (1985) . . . . Burdetta Halloran
North and South, Book II (1986). . . . . Burdetta Halloran
Made for TV Movies:
Initiation of Sarah (1978) . . . . n.a.
How to Murder a Millionaire (1990) . . . . Loretta
Menu for Murder (1990). . . . . Paula Preston
TV:
Search for Tomorrow (1971). . . . . n.a.
Dallas (1978) . . . . Jenna Wade
Flamingo Road (1981-82) . . . Constance Weldon Carlyle
Paper Dolls (1984) . . . . Racine
Falcon Crest (1985-86) . . . . Jordan Roberts
Video Tapes:
Playboy Video Magazine, Volume 5 (1983)
   . . . . The Seduction
   • 0:43—Brief topless in scenes from *The Seduction* in
   pool and bubble bath.
Morgan Fairchild Stress Management (1991) . . . Herself
Magazines:
Playboy (Oct 1980). . . . . Grapevine
   • 246—Left nipple peeking out of top. B&W.
Playboy (Apr 1982) . . . . Grapevine
   • 254—B&W photo, in bathtub. Upper half of right
   breast.

Faithfull, Marianne

Singer.
Former girlfriend of *Rolling Stones* singer Mick Jagger.
Films:
Girl on a Motorcycle (1968; French/British)
   . . . . Rebecca
   a.k.a. Naked Under Leather
   •• 0:05—Nude, getting out of bed and walking to the
   door.
   • 0:38—Brief side view of left breast putting nightgown on.
   • 1:23—Brief topless while lying down and talking
   with Alain Delon.
   • 1:30—Very brief right breast a couple of times making love with Delon.
Hamlet (1969; British). . . . . Ophelia
Madhouse Mansion (1974; British) . . . . Sophy
Assault on Agathon (1976) . . . . Helen Rochefort

Falana, Lola

Singer.
Films:
The Liberation of L. B. Jones (1970) . . . . Emma Jones
   0:19—Very brief topless walking by the doorway in
   the bathroom. Very long shot, don't really see any-
   thing.
The Klansman (1974). . . . . Loretta Sykes
Lady Cocoa (1974). . . . . Coco
   • 0:45—Left breast lying on bed, pulling up yellow
   towel. Long shot, hard to see.
   ••• 1:23—Topless on boat with a guy.
Mad About You (1990) . . . . Casey's Secretary
TV:
The New Bill Cosby Show (1972-73) . . . . Regular
Ben Vereen... Comin' At Ya (1975). . . . . Regular

Fallender, Deborah

Films:
Monty Python's Jabberwocky (1977)
   . . . . The Princess
   • 0:56—Buns and brief full frontal nudity in bath when
   Michael Palin accidentally enters the room.
   0:57—Topless under sheer white robe.
Best Defense (1984). . . . . Toni
Stitches (1985). . . . . Nurse #1

• Faria, Betty

Films:
Bye Bye Brazil (1980; Brazilian). . . . . Salomé
   •• 0:28—Topless, wearing red panties, backstage with
   Cigano.
   • 0:29—Left breast while sitting in a chair.
   •• 0:38—Topless backstage with Ciço.
   • 1:24—Buns, under a mosquito net with a customer.
The Story of Fausta (1988; Brazilian) . . . . Fausta
   • 1:10—Left breast, while leaning out of the shower to
   talk to Lourdes.

Farinelli, Patty

Video Tapes:
Playboy's Playmate Review (1982) . . . . Playmate
   ••• 0:11—Full frontal nudity during library photo shoot
   and then by swimming pool.
Magazines:
Playboy (Dec 1981) . . . . Playmate

• Farmer, Marva

Films:
Video Vixens (1973) . . . . Girl
   •• 0:59—Full frontal nudity in the swimming pool with
   three other women during commercial.
The Candy Tangerine Man (1975) . . . . n.a.

Faro, Caroline

Films:
Rendez-Vous (1986; French) . . . . Juliette
   • 0:22—Buns, walking up stairs, then full frontal nudity on second floor during play. Buns, while hugging Romeo and falling back into a net.
Sincerely Charlotte (1986; French)
. . . . Irene the Baby Sitter

Farrow, Mia

Sister of actress Tisa Farrow.
Daughter of actress Maureen O'Sullivan.
Ex-wife of actor/singer Frank Sinatra.
Films:
A Dandy in Aspic (1968) . . . . Caroline
Rosemary's Baby (1968) . . . . . Rosemary Woodhouse
   • 0:10—Brief left breast in room in new apartment on floor with John Cassavetes. Hard to see anything.
   • 0:43—Brief close up of her breasts while she's sitting on a boat during a nightmare.
  •• 0:44—Buns walking on boat, then breasts during impregnation scene with the devil.
Secret Ceremony (1968) . . . . Cenci
See No Evil (1971) . . . . Sarah
The Great Gatsby (1974) . . . . Daisy Buchanan
Avalanche (1978) . . . . Caroline Brace
Death on the Nile (1978; British)
. . . . Jacqueline de Bellefort
A Wedding (1978) . . . . Buffy Brenner
  ••• 1:10—Topless posing in front of a painting, while wearing a wedding veil.
Hurricane (1979) . . . . Charlotte Bruckner
   • 0:39—Brief left breast in open dress top while crawling under bushes at the beach.
High Heels (1980) . . . . Christine Du Pont
A Midsummer Night's Sex Comedy (1982) . . . . Ariel
Broadway Danny Rose (1984) . . . . Tina Vitale
Supergirl (1984; British) . . . . Alura
Zelig (1984) . . . . Dr. Fletcher
The Purple Rose of Cairo (1985) . . . . Cecelia
Hannah and Her Sisters (1986) . . . . Hannah
Radio Days (1987) . . . . Sally White
September (1987) . . . . n.a.
Crimes and Misdemeanors (1989) . . . . n.a.
New York Stories (1989) . . . . Lisa
Alice (1990) . . . . Alice
Husbands and Wives (1992) . . . . n.a.
Shadows and Fog (1992) . . . . n.a.
TV:
Peyton Place (1964-66) . . . Allison MacKenzie/Harrington

Farrow, Tisa

Sister of actress Mia Farrow.
Daughter of actress Maureen O'Sullivan.
Films:
Some Call It Loving (1972) . . . . Jennifer
  ••• 1:17—Topless in bed with Troy.
Fingers (1978) . . . . Carol
Winter Kills (1979) . . . . Nurse Two

Zombie (1980) . . . . Anne Bolles
Search and Destroy (1981) . . . . Kate
Magazines:
Playboy (Jul 1973) . . . . Tisa
  ••• 83-87—Topless.

Faulkner, Sally

Films:
Vampyres (1974; British) . . . . Harriet
   • 1:14—Side of left breast, partial buns, then right breast while making love with John in the trailer.
  •• 1:22—Full frontal nudity getting her clothes ripped off by Fran and Miriam in the wine cellar before being killed.
Alien Prey (1984; British) . . . . Josephine
   • 0:32—Very, very brief left breast taking off top.
   0:36—Buns, in bed with Glory Annen.
   0:37—Topless on her back in bed with Annen.

Favier, Sophie

Films:
Frank and I (1983) . . . . Maud
   • 0:16—Nude, undressing then topless lying in bed with Charles.
   • 0:40—Brief topless in bed with Charles.
Cheech and Chong's The Corsican Brothers (1984)
. . . . Lovely II

Fawcett, Farrah

Ex-wife of actor Lee Majors.
Films:
Myra Breckinridge (1970) . . . . n.a.
Logan's Run (1976) . . . . Holly
Sunburn (1979) . . . . Ellie
Saturn 3 (1980) . . . . Alex
  •• 0:17—Brief right breast taking off towel and running to Kirk Douglas after taking a shower.
The Cannonball Run (1981) . . . . Pamela
Extremities (1986) . . . . Marjorie
   • 0:37—Brief side view of right breast when Joe pulls down her top in the kitchen. Can't see her face, but reportedly her.
Double Exposure: The Story of Margaret Bourke-White (1989) . . . . Margaret Bourke-White
   0:39—Most of side of left breast, while sitting in bed giving Frederic Forrest a shave.
See You in the Morning (1989) . . . . Jo Livingston
Made for TV Movies:
The Burning Bed (1984) . . . . n.a.
The Red Light Sting (1984) . . . . n.a.
Between Two Women (1986) . . . . n.a.
Poor Little Rich Girl: The Barbara Hutton Story (1987)
. . . . Barbara Hutton
Small Sacrifices (1989) . . . . Diane Downs
Criminal Behavior (1992) . . . . Jessie Lee Stubbs
TV:
Harry-O (1974-76) . . . . Next door neighbor
Charlie's Angels (1976-77) . . . . Jill Munroe
Good Sports (1991) . . . . Gayle Roberts

Fenech, Edwige

Films:
Sex with a Smile (1976; Italian) . . . . Dream Girl
•• 0:03—Topless tied to bed with two holes cut in her
   red dress top.
   0:09—Buns, in jail cell in court when the guy pulls
   her panties down with his sword.
•• 0:13—Brief topless in bed with Dracula taking off
   her top and hugging him.
• 0:16—Topless in bathtub. Long shot.
Phantom of Death (1987; Italian) . . . . Helene

Fenn, Sherilyn

Films:
Out of Control (1984) . . . . .Katie
   0:19—In wet white T-shirt in pond with the other
   girls.
The Wild Life (1984) . . . . Penny Hallin
Just One of the Guys (1986) . . . . Sandy
Thrashin' (1986) . . . . Velvet
The Wraith (1986) . . . . .Keri
• 0:13—Very brief topless when Packard's gang catch-
   es her in bed with Jamie.
• 1:02—Brief topless during flashback when caught in
   bed by Packard's gang.
• 1:03—Very brief right breast, pulling her swimsuit
   top off in pond with Charlie Sheen.
Zombie High (1987) . . . . Suzi
Two Moon Junction (1988) . . . . April
(Blonde hair throughout the film.)
••• 0:07—Topless taking a shower in the country club
   shower room.
•• 0:27—Brief topless on the floor kissing Perry.
•• 0:42—Topless in gas station restroom changing
   camisole tops with Kristy McNichol.
• 0:54—Brief topless making love with Perry in a motel room.
••• 1:24—Nude at Two Moon Junction making love
   with Perry. Very hot!
• 1:40—Brief left breast and buns in the shower with
   Perry.
Crime Zone (1989) . . . . Helen
   0:16—In black lingerie and stockings in bedroom.
•• 0:23—Topless wearing black panties making love
   with Bone. Dark, long shot.
Meridian (1989) . . . . Catherine
a.k.a. Kiss of the Beast
a.k.a. Phantoms
•• 0:23—White bra and panties, getting clothes taken
   off by Lawrence. Then topless.
••• 0:28—Topless in bed with Oliver.
•• 0:51—Topless getting her blouse ripped open lying
   in bed.
   1:11—Briefly in white panties and bra putting red
   dress on.
True Blood (1989) . . . . Jennifer Scott
• 1:22—Very brief right breast in closet trying to stab
   Spider with a piece of mirror.

Backstreet Dreams (1990) . . . . Lucy
• 0:00—Right breast while sleeping in bed with Dean.
   Medium long shot.
Desire and Hell at Sunset Motel (1990) . . . . Bridey
Wild at Heart (1990) . . . . Girl in Accident
Diary of a Hitman (1992) . . . . Jain
Ruby (1992) . . . . .Candy Cane
Made for TV Movies:
Dillinger (1991) . . . . Billie Frechette
TV:
TV 101 (1988-89) . . . . n.a.
Twin Peaks (1990-91) . . . . Audrey Horne
Magazines:
Playboy (Dec 1990) . . . . Fenn-tastic!
••• 82-91—Topless photos, some are B&W.

Ferguson, Kate

Films:
Break of Day (1977; Australian) . . . . Jean
Spaced Out (1980; British) . . . . Skipper
• 1:07—Brief topless making love with Willy in bed. Lit
   with red light.
The Pirate Movie (1982; Australian) . . . . Edith

Ferrare, Ashley

Films:
Revenge of the Ninja (1983) . . . . Cathy
   0:33—In white lingerie sitting on couch with Dave.
• 0:48—Brief topless getting attacked by the Sumo
   Servant in the bedroom.
   1:13—In wet white tank top talking on the phone.
Cyclone (1986) . . . . Carla Hastings
   0:04—Working out at health club with Heather Thomas.

Ferrare, Cristina

Former model.
Ex-wife of ex-car maker John De Lorean.
Spokeswoman for *Ultra Slim-Fast*.
Films:
Mary, Mary, Bloody Mary (1975) . . . . Mary
•• 0:07—Brief topless making love with some guy on
   the couch just before she kills him.
••• 0:41—Topless when Greta helps pull down Ferrare's
   top to take a bath.
   1:12—Bun and brief silhouette of left breast getting
   out of bed and getting dressed.
Made for Cable TV:
Dream On: Nightmare on Bleecker Street (1992; HBO)
. . . . .Laura
TV:
Incredible Sunday (1988-89) . . . . Co-Host

Ferratti, Rebecca

Films:
Beverly Hills Cop II (1987) . . . . .Playboy Playmate
Cheerleader Camp (1987) . . . . Theresa Salazar
a.k.a. Bloody Pom Poms
Outlaw of Gor (1987) . . . . Talena

Silent Assassins (1988). . . . . Miss Amy
Gor (1989) . . . . .Talena
How I Got Into College (1989) . . . . Game Show Hostess
Small Kill (1991) . . . . Diana Conti
Video Tapes:
Playboy Video Calendar 1989 (1988) . . . . June
  ••• 0:21—Nude.
Wet and Wild (1989). . . . . .Model
Playmates at Play (1990) . . . . .Gotta Dance
Wet and Wild III (1991). . . . . .Model
Wet and Wild IV (1992) . . . . .Model
Magazines:
Playboy (Jun 1986) . . . . Playmate
Playboy's Book of Lingerie (Sep 1991) . . . . . Herself
  •• 24—Right breast.
Playboy's Book of Lingerie (May 1992) . . . . . Herself
  •• 61—Left breast.
  ••• 64—Topless.
Playboy's Book of Lingerie (Jul 1992) . . . . . . Herself
  ••• 34—Topless.

Ferréol, Andrea
Films:
Submission (1976; Italian) . . . . .Juliet
  •• 0:43—Topless in room with Franco Nero and Elaine.
Sex on the Run (1979; German/French/Italian) . Beatrice
  a.k.a. Some Like It Cool
  a.k.a. Casanova and Co.
La Nuit de Varennes (1983; French/Italian)
  . . . . Madame Adelaide Gagnon
Letters to an Unknown Lover (1985) . . . . Julia
A Zed and Two Noughts (1985; British) . . . Alba Bewick
The Sleazy Uncle (1991; Italian) . . . . .Teresa
Street of No Return (1991; U.S./French) . . . . . . .Rhoda
Stroke of Midnight (1991; U.S./French). . . . . . . Wanda

Ferris, Irena
Films:
Covergirl (1982; Canadian). . . . . .Kit Paget
  •• 0:19—Brief topless taking off robe and getting into
    bathtub with Dee.
  • 0:43—Very brief right breast sticking out of night-
    gown.
  • 0:46—Upper half of left breast during modeling ses-
    sion.
  • 0:47—Topless in mirror in dressing room.
  0:49—Brief topless getting attacked by Joel.
  • 0:53—Brief left breast, putting another blouse on.
  • 0:53—Brief left breast, putting on blouse.
TV:
Cover Up (1984-85) . . . . Billie

Feuer, Debra
Films:
Moment by Moment (1978). . . . . Stacie
The Hollywood Knights (1980) . . . . Cheetah

To Live and Die in L.A. (1985) . . . . Bianca Torres
  0:58—Side view of buns, lying on bed while watch-
    ing Willem Dafoe burn the counterfeit money. Long
    shot.
  • 1:47—Brief topless on video tape being played back
    on TV in empty house, hard to see anything.
Homeboy (1988) . . . . Ruby
Night Angel (1989) . . . . Kirstie
  • 0:46—Brief side of left breast. Dark.

Ficatier, Carol
Video Tapes:
Playboy Video Calendar 1987 (1986). . . . . Playmate
Playmates at Play (1990) . . . . Making Waves
Magazines:
Playboy (Dec 1985) . . . . Playmate
Playboy's Nudes (Oct 1990) . . . . Herself
  ••• 74—Full frontal nudity.
Playboy's Book of Lingerie (Sep 1991) . . . . . . Herself
  ••• 10—Topless.
  •• 92—Topless.
Playboy's Book of Lingerie (Mar 1992). . . . . .Herself
  •• 17—Buns and side of left breast in sheer black bod-
    ysuit.
Playboy's Book of Lingerie (Jul 1992) . . . . . . .Herself
  ••• 82—Topless.

Fiedler, Bea
Films:
Island of 1000 Delights. . . . . .Julia
  •• 0:25—Full frontal nudity washing herself in bathtub,
    then nude taking off her towel for Michael.
  •• 0:27—Topless lying on floor after making love, then
    buns walking to chair.
  •• 0:46—Full frontal nudity taking off her dress and
    kissing Howard.
  •• 0:50—Topless in white bikini bottoms coming out of
    the water to greet Howard.
  ••• 1:06—Topless sitting in the sand near the beach,
    then nude talking with Sylvia.
  ••• 1:17—Right breast (great close up) making love
    with Sylvia.
  ••• 1:18—Topless above Sylvia.
Popcorn and Ice Cream (1978; West German)
  . . . . .Policewoman
  ••• 0:47—Full frontal nudity getting dressed.
  ••• 1:13—Right breast, then topless in bed with a lover.
  ••• 1:14—Full frontal nudity in bed some more.
Private Popsicle (1982) . . . . Eva
  •• 0:04—In black bra with Bobby. Upper half of left
    breast, very brief side of right breast, then topless.
  ••• 0:06—Full frontal nudity with Bobby in bed.
  •• 0:07—More topless with Bobby.
  ••• 0:08—Topless on bed with Hughie.
  •• 0:09—More topless when her husband gets into
    bed.

Hot Chili (1985) . . . . The Music Teacher
  •• 0:08—Topless, while playing the cello and being fondled by Ricky.
    0:29—Buns, while playing the violin.
  •• 0:34—Nude during fight in restaurant with Chi Chi. Hard to see because of the flashing light.
  ••• 0:36—Topless lying on inflatable lounge in pool, playing a flute.
  ••• 0:43—Left breast, while playing a tuba.
  ••• 1:01—Topless and buns, while dancing in front of Mr. Lieberman.
  • 1:07—Buns, then right breast while dancing with Stanley.
Magazines:
Playboy (Nov 1985) . . . . Sex in Cinema 1985
  •• 129—Right breast and lower frontal nudity, lying on air matress in still from *Hot Chili*.

• *Field, Chelsea*
Films:
Commando (1985) . . . . Stewardess
Perfect (1985) . . . . Randy
Death Spa (1987) . . . . Darla
Masters of the Universe (1987) . . . . Teela
Prison (1987) . . . . Katherine Walker
Skin Deep (1989) . . . . Amy
Harley Davidson and The Marlboro Man (1991)
. . . . Virginia Slim
  • 0:40—Side of left breast, sitting up in bed. Very brief buns standing up. Don't see her face very well.
The Last Boy Scout (1991) . . . . Sarah Hollenbeck
Made for TV Movies:
An Inconvenient Woman (1991) . . . . Camilla Ebury
TV:
Bronx Zoo (1988) . . . . Chris Barnes
Nightingales (1989) . . . . Samantha "Sam" Sullivan
Capital News (1990) . . . . Cassy Swann

Field, Sally
Films:
Stay Hungry (1976) . . . . Mary Kay Farnsworth
  0:27—Buns, then very, very brief side view of left breast jumping back into bed. Very fast, everything is a blur, hard to see anything.
Heroes (1977) . . . . Carol
Smokey and the Bandit (1977) . . . . Carrie
The End (1978) . . . . Mary Ellen
Hooper (1978) . . . . Gwen
Beyond the Poseidon Adventure (1979)
. . . . Celeste Whitman
Norma Rae (1979) . . . . Norma Rae
  (Academy Award for Best Actress.)
  0:11—In white bra in motel room with George.
Absence of Malice (1981) . . . . Megan Carter
Back Roads (1981) . . . . Amy Post
Kiss Me Goodbye (1982) . . . . Kay Villano
Places in the Heart (1984) . . . . Edna Spalding
  (Academy Award for Best Actress.)
Murphy's Romance (1985) . . . . Emma Moriarity

Punchline (1988) . . . . Lilah Krytsick
Surrender (1988) . . . . Daisy Morgan
  0:06—In black slip getting up out of bed and washing up in the bathroom.
Steel Magnolias (1989) . . . . M'Lynn Eatenton
Not Without My Daughter (1991) . . . . Betty Mahmoody
Soapdish (1991) . . . . Celeste Talbert
Made for TV Movies:
Sybil (1976) . . . . Sybil
  (Emmy Award for Best Actress in a Drama Special.)
TV:
Gidget (1965-66) . . . . Francine "Gidget" Lawrence
The Flying Nun (1967-70) . . . . Sister Bertrille
Alias Smith and Jones (1971-73) . . . . . . Clementine Hale
Girl with Something Extra (1973-74) . . . . . . Sally Burton

• *Finzi, Lydia*
Films:
Alien Warrior (1985) . . . . Beverly
My Man Adam (1986) . . . . Sunbather
  • 0:32—Brief topless sunbathing by the swimming pool when Adam jumps into the pool and angers her.

Fiorentino, Linda
Films:
After Hours (1985) . . . . Kiki
  0:11—In black bra and skirt doing paper maché.
  •• 0:19—Topless taking off bra in doorway while Griffin Dunne watches.
Gotcha! (1985) . . . . Sasha
  •• 0:53—Brief topless getting searched at customs.
Visionquest (1985) . . . . Carla
The Moderns (1988) . . . . Rachel Stone
  • 0:40—Topless sitting in bathtub while John Lone shaves her armpits.
  • 0:41—Right breast while turning over onto stomach in bathtub.
  •• 1:18—Topless getting out of tub while covered with bubbles to kiss Keith Carradine.
Queens Logic (1991) . . . . Carla
Shout (1991) . . . . Molly
Made for Cable Movies:
The Neon Empire (1989) . . . . Lucy
Made for Cable TV:
Strangers: The Last Game (1992; HBO) . . . . . . Helen
  • 0:07—Left breast, three times, making love with James Remar when Etienne walks by. Dark.

• *Fischer, Vera*
Films:
I Love You (1982; Brazilian) . . . . Barbara Bergman
a.k.a. Eu Te Amo
  ••• 0:31—Left breast while in front of TV and in chair with Paulo.
  •• 0:46—Left breast sticking out of nightgown. Topless silhouette getting up. Full frontal nudity taking off nightgown.
  ••• 0:47—Nude in bed with Paulo.

••• 1:05—Topless on couch with Paulo.
• 1:09—Topless on TV while opening her dress.
Love Strange Love (1982; Brazilian). . . . . .Anna
•• 0:23—Brief topless and lower frontal nudity in bathtub. Topless and buns, getting out.
•• 0:38—Topless making love with Dr. Osmar.
• 0:39—Brief buns, while lying in bed.
•• 1:19—Topless in bed with Dr. Osmar when Hugo watches.
The Fifth Monkey (1990). . . . . Mrs. Watts

• Fisher, Frances
Films:
Can She Bake a Cherry Pie? (1983) . . . . .Louise
Tough Guys Don't Dance (1987). . . . . Jessica Pond
Lost Angels (1989) . . . . Judith Loftis
Patty Hearst (1989) . . . . Yolanda
Pink Cadillac (1989) . . . . .n.a.
Frame Up (1990). . . . . Jo Westlake
•• 0:52—Topless, lying back in bed with Wings Hauser.
•• 0:54—Left breast, while lying in bed with Hauser.
Welcome Home Roxy Carmichael (1990)
. . . . .Rochelle Bossetti
L.A. Story (1991). . . . . June
Unforgiven (1992) . . . . .n.a.
Made for Cable Movies:
Devlin (1991; Showtime) . . . . Maryellen

• FitzGerald, Helen
Films:
Nuns on the Run (1990; British) . . . . .Tracey
Close My Eyes (1991; British) . . . . Scottish Girl
•• 0:08—Nude, lying down, then getting up in room with Richard.
Magazines:
Playboy (Nov 1992) . . . . Sex in Cinema 1992
•• 146—Left breast and lower frontal nudity, lying on the floor with Clive Owen from *Close My Eyes*.

• Flaherty, Maureen
Films:
Shadowzone (1989) . . . . Jenna
•• 0:13—Topless lying under plastic cover.
• 0:18—Topless on table getting operated on.
•• 1:11—Topless again under plastic cover several times.
•• 1:17—Brief topless again, then full frontal nudity.
• 1:24—Topless alive under the plastic cover.
Rich Girl (1991). . . . . .Girl in Restroom #1

Flanagan, Fionnula
Films:
Ulysses (1967; U.S./British) . . . . Gerty MacDowell
Sinful Davey (1969; British). . . . . Penelope
Crossover (1980; Canadian) . . . . .Abadaba
a.k.a. Mr. Patman
• 0:27—Brief topless opening her robe and flashing James Coburn.

James Joyce's Women (1983). . . . . Molly Bloom
• 0:48—Brief topless getting out of bed.
••• 0:56—Topless getting back into bed.
••• 1:02—Full frontal nudity masturbating in bed talking to herself. Very long scene—9 minutes!
Reflections (1984; British). . . . . .Charlotte Lawless
Youngblood (1986) . . . . Miss McGill
P.K. and the Kid (1987) . . . . .Flo
Miniseries:
Rich Man, Poor Man (1976). . . . . Clothilde
Made for TV Movies:
Nightmare in Badham County (1976) . . . . .Dulce
(Nudity added for video tape.)
Mary White (1977). . . . . n.a.
Young Love, First Love (1979) . . . . .Audrey
The Ewok Adventure (1984). . . . . .Catarine
A Winner Never Quits (1986) . . . . Mrs. Wyshner
TV:
How the West was Won (1978-79)
. . . . .Aunt Molly Culhane

• Floria, Holly
Films:
Presumed Guilty (1990) . . . . .Mary Austin
• 1:02—Side view of left breast, very brief lower frontal nudity and buns, while making love with Jessie.
Bikini Island (1991) . . . . .Annie
Dark Rider (1991). Dani
Netherworld (1991). . . . . .Diane Palmer

Fluegel, Darlanne
Films:
Eyes of Laura Mars (1978) . . . . .Lulu
Battle Beyond the Stars (1980). . . . . Nanelia
The Last Fight (1983). . . . . .Sally
Once Upon a Time in America (1984) . . . . Eve
(Long version reviewed.)
To Live and Die in L.A. (1985) . . . . Ruth Lanier
•• 0:44—Brief topless and buns, in bed when William Petersen comes home.
1:29—In stockings on couch with Petersen.
• 1:50—Very brief topless on bed with Petersen in a flashback.
Running Scared (1986) . . . . Anna Costanzo
Tough Guys (1986) . . . . Skye Foster
• 0:47—Very brief side view of right breast, leaning over to kiss Kirk Douglas.
Border Heat (1988) . . . . .Peggy Martin
0:23—In black bra straddling Ryan in the bedroom.
Bulletproof (1988) . . . . Devon Shepard
Freeway (1988) . . . . Sarah "Sunny" Harper
• 0:27—In bra in bathroom taking a pill, then very, very brief right breast, getting into bed.
• 0:28—Brief left breast putting on robe and getting out of bed.
Lock Up (1989) . . . . Melissa
Project: Alien (1990). . . . . "Bird" McNamara
• 0:18—Buns, getting out of bed and putting on a kimono.

TV:
Crime Story (1986-89) . . . . .Julie Torello
Wiseguy (1989). . . . . Lacey
Hunter (1990-91) . . . . Joanne Malinski
Magazines:
Playboy (Aug 1978) . . . ."Eyes" Has It
•• 96—Left breast.
• 99—Topless in bed.

Fonda, Bridget

Daughter of actor Peter Fonda.
Granddaughter of actor Henry Fonda.
Films:
You Can't Hurry Love (1984). . . . . .Peggy
Aria (1988; U.S./British) . . . . Girl Lover
••• 0:59—Brief right breast, then buns and topless lying
down on bed in hotel room in Las Vegas.
•• 1:02—Topless in the bathtub with her boyfriend.
Scandal (1989) . . . . Mandy Rice-Davis
(Unrated version reviewed.)
• 0:20—Brief topless dressed as an Indian dancing
while Christine tries to upstage her.
0:54—In white lingerie, then lower frontal nudity in
sheer nightgown in room with a guy.
1:05—Brief buns walking back into bedroom. Long
shot.
Shag (1989) . . . . .Melaina Buller
Frankenstein Unbound (1990). . . . . .Mary
The Godfather, Part III (1990) . . . . Grace Hamilton
Out of the Rain (1990) . . . . .Jo
Strapless (1990) .Amy Hempel
Doc Hollywood (1991) . . . . Nancy Lee
Iron Maze (1991) . . . . .Chris
Single White Female (1992) . . . . Allie
Singles (1992). . . . . .Janet

Fonda, Jane

Daughter of actor Henry Fonda.
Sister of actor Peter Fonda.
Has done a lot of exercise video tapes.
Wife of Television Tychoon Ted Turner.
Films:
Period of Adjustment (1962) . . . . Isabel Haverstick
Joy House (1964) . . . . Melinda
Cat Ballou (1965) . . . . Cat Ballou
The Chase (1966) . . . . Anna Reeves
The Game is Over (1966) . . . . Renee Saccard
Barefoot in the Park (1967) . . . . Corrie Bratter
Barbarella (1968; French/Italian) . . . . Barbarella
•• 0:04—Topless getting out of space suit during open-
ing credits in zero gravity. Hard to see because the
frame is squeezed so the lettering will fit.
They Shoot Horses, Don't They? (1969) . . . . Gloria
Klute (1971) . . . . .Bree Daniel
(Academy Award for Best Actress.)
• 0:27—Side view of left and right breasts stripping in
the old man's office.
A Doll's House (1973; British) . . . . .Nora
Steelyard Blues (1973) . . . . Iris Caine

The Blue Bird (1976) . . . . .Night
Fun with Dick and Jane (1977). . . . . Jane Harper
Julia (1977) . . . . .Lillian Hellman
California Suite (1978) . . . . Hannah Warren
Comes a Horseman (1978). . . . . Ella
Coming Home (1978) . . . . Sally Hyde
(Academy Award for Best Actress.)
•• 1:26—Making love in bed with Jon Voight. Topless
only when her face is visible. Buns and brief left
breast when you don't see a face is a body double.
The China Syndrome (1979) . . . . Kimberly Wells
The Electric Horseman (1979) . . . . .Hallie
9 to 5 (1980) . . . . Judy Bernly
On Golden Pond (1981) . . . . . . .Chelsea Thayer Wayne
Rollover (1981) . . . . Lee Winters
Agnes of God (1985) . . . . Dr. Martha Livingston
The Morning After (1986) . . . . . . .Alex Sternbergen
• 1:08—Brief topless making love with Jeff Bridges.
Old Gringo (1989) . . . . .Harriet Winslow
• 1:24—Side of left breast, while undressing in front of
Jimmy Smits. Sort of brief right breast, while lying in
bed and hugging him.
Stanley and Iris (1990) . . . . .Iris King
Made for TV Movies:
The Dollmaker (1984) . . . . n.a.
(Emmy Award for Best Actress.)

• Fondren, Debra Jo

Video Tapes:
Playboy Playmates in Paradise (1992). . . . Playmate
Magazines:
Playboy (Sep 1977) . . . . Playmate
Playboy's Nudes (Oct 1990) . . . . .Herself
•• 100—Buns.
Playboy's Book of Lingerie (Sep 1992) . . . . . .Herself
••• 81—Full frontal nudity.

Fontaine, Alisha

Films:
The Gang that Couldn't Shoot Straight (1971)
. . . . .Jelly's Girl
The Gambler (1974) . . . . .Howie's Girl
French Quarter (1978)
. . . . Gertrude "Trudy" Dix/Christine Delaplane
• 0:12—Dancing on stage for the first time. Buns in G-
string. Topless in large black pasties.
• 0:47—Brief left breast several times, posing for Mr.
Beloq.
• 0:49—Left breast again.
•• 1:13—Topless during auction.
•• 1:18—Brief topless, then buns making love with
Tom, then topless again.
• 1:26—Brief topless getting her top pulled down during party.
• 1:31—Brief topless getting tied down during voodoo ceremony.
•• 1:32—More topless tied down during ceremony.

Ford, Anitra

Films:

The Big Bird Cage (1972) . . . . .Terry
- 0:15—Left breast and buns taking shower. Brief lower frontal nudity after putting shirt on when leaving.
  0:19—Brief lower frontal nudity turing around.
- 0:44—Brief left breast during gang rape.
  1:14—Brief left breast in gaping dress. Dark.

Invasion of the Bee Girls (1973) . . . Dr. Susan Harris
••• 0:47—Topless and buns undressing in front of a guy in front of a fire.

Stacey (1973) . . . . Tish
•• 0:13—Topless in bed making love with Frank.

Dead People (1974) . . . . Laura

The Longest Yard (1974) . . . . Melissa
  0:01—Topless under see-though red nightgown with Burt Reynolds.

Ford, Maria

Films:

Dance of the Damned (1988) . . . . .Teacher
- 0:11—Brief topless during dance routine in club wearing black panties, garter belt and stockings.

Stripped to Kill II (1988) . . . . .Shady
•• 0:21—Topless, dancing on table in front of the detective. Buns, walking away.
- 0:40—Brief upper half of left breast in the alley with the detective.
•• 0:52—Topless and buns during dance routine.

The Haunting of Morella (1989) . . . . Diane
••• 1:00—Topless taking off nightgown and swimming in pond, then walking to waterfall.

Naked Obsession (1990) . . . . Lynne Hauser
  0:16—Dancing on stage doing strip tease. Wearing bra, panties, garter belt and stockings.
••• 0:18—Buns in G-string.
••• 0:20—Topless and buns in G-string, dancing on stage in front of William Katt. Long scene.
••• 0:23—Nude, dancing with Katt's necktie.
•• 0:34—Nude, on stage at end of another dance routine.
•• 0:44—Topless in her apartment with Katt.
••• 0:45—Topless and buns on top of Katt in bed while he gently strangles her with his necktie for oxygen deprivation.
••• 0:47—Topless in bed after making love with Katt.

The Rain Killer (1990) . . . . .Satin
•• 0:29—Nude, dancing on stage in club. Backlit too much.
••• 0:37—Topless in bedroom with Jordan, taking off her clothes, getting tied to bed. Long scene.
- 0:41—Topless lying on her back on bed, dead.
- 0:48—Same scene from 0:41 when Rosewall looks at B&W police photo.

Body Chemistry 2: Voice of a Stranger (1991)
. . . . .Uncredited Victim
•• 0:37—Topless in bed during flashback. (This scene is from *Naked Obsession*.)

Future Kick (1991) . . . . Dancer

Ring of Fire (1991) . . . . .Julie
Mind Twister (1992). . . . . n.a.

Magazines:

Playboy (Nov 1988) . . . . Sex in Cinema 1988
••• 137—Full frontal nudity standing in front of a pole.

Foreman, Deborah

a.k.a. Debby Lynn Foreman.

Films:

I'm Dancing as Fast as I Can (1981) . . . . Cindy
Valley Girl (1983) . . . . .Julie
Real Genius (1985). . . . . .Susan

3:15—The Moment of Truth (1986)
. . . . Sherry Havilland
  0:26—Very brief blurry buns and side view of left breast jumping out of bed when her parents come home. Long shot, hard to see anything.

April Fool's Day (1986). . . . . Muffy/Buffy
Destroyer (1988) . . . . Susan Malone
Waxwork (1988) . . . . .Sarah
Friends, Lovers & Lunatics (1989). . . . . .Annie
Sundown: The Vampire in Retreat (1989). . . . . . . Sandy

Foreman, Michelle

Films:

Stripped to Kill (1987) . . . . .Angel
••• 0:02—Topless dancing on stage for Norman Fell.

Sunset Strip (1992). . . . . .Heather
•• 0:29—In black bra and G-string, practicing her dance routine in her living room.
  0:42—Brief back side of left breast, while in the shower.
  0:46—In black bra and G-string, practicing some more.
•• 1:24—Buns in G-string, while dancing during contest.
•• 1:28—Topless in the shower with Jeff Conaway. Don't see her face well, but it looks like her.
••• 1:30—Buns in G-string dancing on stage and topless (finally!) at the end.

Made for Cable Movies:

Fear (1991; Showtime) . . . . Gale the Stripper
- 0:50—Topless and buns dancing in bar. Hard to see because seen through the killer's eyes.

Forte, Valentina

Films:

Cut and Run (1985; Italian) . . . . Ana
••• 0:29—Brief left breast being made love to in bed. Then topless sitting up in bed and left side view and buns taking a shower.

Inferno in Diretta (1985; Italian). . . . . n.a.

•Fortea, Isabelle

Films:

Affairs of the Heart (1992) . . . . .Karen
Private Screenings.
••• 1:06—Topless making love in cabin with Tom.

Magazines:
Playboy's Book of Lingerie (Jul 1992) . . . . . . Herself
•• 46-47—Right breast and buns.
Playboy's Book of Lingerie (Sep 1992) . . . . . Herself
•• 107—Topless.

Fossey, Brigitte

Films:
Forbidden Games (1953; French) . . . . Paulette
Going Places (1974; French) . . . . Young Mother
••• 0:32—In bra, then topless in open blouse on the
train when she lets Pierrot suck the milk out of her
breasts.
Blue Country (1977; French) . . . . Louise
The Man Who Loved Women (1977; French)
. . . . Benevieve Bigey
Quintet (1979) . . . . Vivia
La Boum (1980; French) . . . . Francoise
Chanel Solitaire (1981) . . . . Adrienne
Enigma (1982) . . . . Karen
• 0:39—Brief topless after undressing in jail cell. Very
brief lower frontal nudity and buns, shielding herself
from the light.
•• 0:40—Topless getting interrogated.
Cinema Paradiso (1988; Italian/French) . . . . Elena

Foster, Jodie

Films:
Kansas City Bomber (1972) . . . . Rita
Napolean and Samantha (1972) . . . . Samantha
One Little Indian (1973) . . . . Martha
Tom Sawyer (1973) . . . . Becky Thatcher
Alice Doesn't Live Here Anymore (1975) . . . . Audrey
Bugsy Malone (1976) . . . . Tallulah
Echoes of Summer (1976) . . . . Deirdre Striden
Taxi Driver (1976) . . . . Iris Steensman
Candleshoe (1977) . . . . Casey
Freaky Friday (1977) . . . . Annabel Andrews
Carny (1980) . . . . Donna
Foxes (1980) . . . . Jeanie
O'Hara's Wife (1982) . . . . Barbara O'Hara
The Hotel New Hampshire (1984) . . . . Franny
Siesta (1987) . . . . Nancy
0:47—In a black slip combing Ellen Barkin's hair.
0:50—In a slip again in bedroom with Barkin.
The Accused (1988) . . . . Sarah Tobias
(Academy Award for Best Actress.)
• 1:27—Brief topless a few times during rape scene on
pinball machine by Dan and Bob.
Five Corners (1988) . . . . Linda
Backtrack (1989) . . . . Anne Benton
a.k.a. Catch Fire
• 0:50—Topless behind textured shower door.
••• 0:51—Topless, leaning out of the shower to get her
towel. Very, very brief side of left breast and buns,
while drying herself off in bedroom. Side of left
breast and buns, while putting on slip.
Silence of the Lambs (1990) . . . . Clarice Starling
(Academy Award for Best Actress.)

Little Man Tate (1991) . . . . Dede Tate
Shadows and Fog (1992) . . . . n.a.
Made for Cable Movies:
The Blood of Others (1984; HBO) . . . . n.a.
Made for TV Movies:
The Little Girl Who Lives Down the Lane
(1976; Canadian) . . . . n.a.
TV:
Bob & Carol & Ted & Alice (1973)
. . . . Elizabeth Henderson
Paper Moon (1974-75) . . . . Addie Pray

Foster, Karen

Video Tapes:
Playboy Video Calendar 1991 (1990) . . . . March
**Playboy Video Centerfold: Deborah Driggs &
Karen Foster** (1990) . . . . Playmate
••• 0:24—Baton twirling, outside on bed, other miscel-
laneous things. Nude.
Sexy Lingerie II (1990) . . . . Model
Wet and Wild II (1990) . . . . Model
Sexy Lingerie III (1991) . . . . Model
Wet and Wild III (1991) . . . . Model
Magazines:
Playboy (Oct 1989) . . . . Playmate
Playboy's Nudes (Oct 1990) . . . . Herself
••• 23—Full frontal nudity.
Playboy's Book of Lingerie (Jan 1991) . . . . . . Herself
••• 101—Topless.
Playboy's Book of Lingerie (Mar 1991) . . . . . . Herself
••• 71—Full frontal nudity.
••• 95—Topless.
Playboy's Book of Lingerie (Sep 1991) . . . . . . Herself
• 18—Partial lower frontal nudity.
Playboy's Book of Lingerie (Nov 1991) . . . . . Herself
••• 10-11—Topless and upper half of buns.
Playboy's Book of Lingerie (Jan 1992) . . . . . . Herself
••• 9—Topless and partial lower frontal nudity.
Playboy's Book of Lingerie (Mar 1992) . . . . . . Herself
•• 68—Full frontal nudity.
Playboy's Book of Lingerie (May 1992) . . . . . Herself
••• 20—Full frontal nudity.
Playboy's Book of Lingerie (Jul 1992) . . . . Herself
•• 31—Topless under necklace.
••• 76-77—Topless.
Playboy's Career Girls (Aug 1992)
. . . . Baywatch Playmates
•• 6—Right breast and partial lower frontal nudity.
Playboy's Book of Lingerie (Sep 1992) . . . . . . Herself
••• 90—Full frontal nudity.

Foster, Lisa Raines

a.k.a. Lisa Foster or Lisa Raines.
Films:
Fanny Hill (1981; British) . . . . Fanny Hill
•• 0:09—Nude, getting into bathtub, then drying herself off.
• 0:10—Full frontal nudity getting into bed.

••• 0:12—Full frontal nudity making love with Phoebe in bed.

••• 0:30—Nude, making love in bed with Charles.

•• 0:49—Topless, whipping her lover, Mr. H., in bed.

•• 0:53—Nude getting into bed with William while Hannah watches through the keyhole.

••• 1:26—Nude, getting out of bed, then running down the stairs to open the door for Charles.

Spring Fever (1983; Canadian) . . . . Lena

The Blade Master (1984). . . . . .n.a.

a.k.a. Ator, The Invincible

Made for Cable TV:

The Hitchhiker: Killer . . . . .Patty

• 0:02—Very brief topless standing in the bathtub just before getting shot.

• 0:23—Very brief topless again in Jenny Seagrove's flashback.

Magazines:

Playboy (Nov 1983) . . . . Sex in Cinema 1983

•• 145—Topless.

Foster, Meg

Films:

Thumb Tripping (1972). . . . . Shay

• 1:19—Very, very brief topless leaning back in field with Jack. Long shot.

• 1:20—Topless at night. Face is turned away from the camera.

Welcome to Arrow Beach (1973). . . . Robbin Stanley

a.k.a. Tender Flesh

0:12—Buns and brief side view of right breast getting undressed to skinny dip in the ocean. Don't see her face.

•• 0:40—Topless getting out of bed.

A Different Story (1979) . . . . Stella

(R-rated version reviewed.)

0:12—In white bra and panties exercising and changing clothes in her bedroom.

•• 0:53—Topless sitting on Perry King, rubbing cake all over each other on bed.

• 0:59—Brief buns and side view of right breast, while getting into bed with King.

Carny (1980) . . . . Greta

Ticket to Heaven (1981; Canadian) . . . . Ingrid

The Osterman Weekend (1983) . . . . .Ali Tanner

0:14—Very, very brief tip of right breast after getting nightgown out of closet.

The Emerald Forest (1985) . . . . Jean Markham

Masters of the Universe (1987) . . . . .Evil-Lyn

The Wind (1987). . . . . Sian Anderson

They Live (1988). . . . . .Holly

Leviathan (1989). Martin

Relentless (1989). . . . . Carol Dietz

Stepfather 2 (1989). . . . . Carol Grayland

Tripwire (1989) . . . . Julia

Backstab (1990) . . . . .Sara Rudnick

Blind Fury (1990) . . . . Lynn Devereaux

Jezebel's Kiss (1990) . . . . .Amanda Faberson

Diplomatic Immunity (1991). . . . . .Gerta Hermann

Future Kick (1991) . . . . Nancy Morgan

Relentless 2: Dead On (1991). . . . . Carol Dietz

Project: Shadowchaser (1992) . . . . .Sarah

Made for Cable TV:

The Hitchhiker: The Martyr (1989; USA). . . . . .n.a.

Made for TV Movies:

To Catch a Killer (1992; Canadian)

. . . . City Attorney Carlson

TV:

Sunshine (1975). . . . . Nora

Cagney & Lacey (1982) . . . . .Chris Cagney

• Fox, Marcia

Films:

Doctor in Trouble (1970; British) . . . . .Jean

Creatures the World Forgot (1971; British)

. . . . .The Dumb Girl

• 0:51—Right breast, then brief topless turning around by the pool.

• 0:58—Brief topless fighting with Julie Ege.

• 1:20—Very brief right breast when The Dark Boy gets his leg cut.

• Fox, Morgan

Video Tapes:

Playboy Video Calendar 1992 (1991). . . . December

••• 0:48—Nude in aqueduct shoot.

••• 0:49—Topless and buns in G-string while singing and dancing on stage.

Playboy Video Centerfold: Morgan Fox (1991)

. . . . Playmate

••• 0:02—Nude in aqueduct shoot.

••• 0:06—Nude in bedroom/factory fantasy.

• 0:15—Brief silhouette of topless and buns, several times while dancing.

••• 0:18—Nude, taking a bath.

••• 0:20—Topless and buns in still photos.

••• 0:22—Topless and buns in G-string, garter belt and stockings, dancing on stage.

Playboy's Erotic Fantasies (1992) . . . . Model

Sexy Lingerie IV (1992) . . . . Model

Wet and Wild IV (1992) . . . . Model

Magazines:

Playboy (Dec 1990) . . . . Playmate

Playboy's Book of Lingerie (Mar 1992). . . . . .Herself

• 50—Lower frontal nudity.

Playboy's Book of Lingerie (May 1992) . . . . .Herself

••• 16-17—Full frontal nudity.

Fox, Samantha

Adult film actress.

Not to be confused with the British singer with the same name.

a.k.a. Stacia Micula.

Adult Films:

Babylon Pink (1979). . . . . n.a.

Films:

C.O.D. (1983) . . . . Female Reporter

In Love (1983) . . . . n.a.

Simply Irresistible (1983) . . . . Arlene Brooks
(R-rated version. *Irresistible* is the X-rated version.)
- • 1:20—In see-through white nightgown, then brief peeks at right breast when nightgown gapes open.

Delivery Boys (1984) . . . . Woman in Tuxedo
Streetwalkin' (1985) . . . . Topless Dancer
- • 0:22—Topless, dancing on stage in nightclub (She's the one wearing a headband).
- • 0:27—More topless, dancing on stage.
- • 0:29—More topless, dancing on stage.
- • 0:56—Topless, giving Antonio Fargas a massage at the bar.

Sex Appeal (1986) . . . . Sheila
- ••• 1:14—In black lingerie, then topless and buns in black G-string with Rhonda. Long scene.

Slammer Girls (1987) . . . . Mosquito
- •• 0:17—Topless in the shower hassling Melody with Tank.

Warrior Queen (1987) . . . . Philomena/Augusta
- ••• 0:31—Nude, doing a dance with a snake during orgy scene.
- • 1:03—Brief right breast after unsuccessfully trying to seduce Marcus.

Fox, Samantha

Former British "Page 3 Girl."
Singer - "Touch Me."
Not to be confused with the adult film actress with the same name.
Magazines:
Penthouse (Jun 1987) . . . . n.a.
Playboy (Dec 1988) . . . . Sex Stars of 1988
- ••• 185—Topless.

Playboy (Feb 1989) . . . . The Year in Sex
- ••• 142—Topless.

Fox, Vivica

Films:
Born on the Fourth of July (1989) . . . . Hooker
- • 0:50—Brief right breast, while taking off bra on top of patient in hospital. Dark.

TV:
Generations (1990-) . . . . Maya Daniels
Out All Night (1992-) . . . . n.a.

• Frank, Diana

Films:
Not Since Casanova (1988) . . . . Gina
Monster High (1990) . . . . Candice Cain
Pale Blood (1990) . . . . Jenny
- •• 0:21—Topless lying on the bed with Michael when he bites her.
- • 0:36—Close up of left breast on TV monitor that Wings Hauser is editing with. Don't see face.
- • 0:42—Brief left breast on TV monitor several times while Hauser examines the bite marks.
- • 1:03—Very brief topless when Hauser pulls her dress top down to look at her bite mark.

Franklin, Diane

Films:
Amityville II: The Possession (1982)
. . . . .Patricia Montelli
- • 0:41—Half of right breast, while sitting on bed talking to her brother.

The Last American Virgin (1982) . . . . .Karen
- ••• 1:06—Topless in room above the bleachers with Jason.
- •• 1:17—Topless and almost lower frontal nudity taking off her panties in the clinic.

Better Off Dead (1985) . . . . .Monique Junet
Second Time Lucky (1986) . . . . Eve
- 0:07—In white bra and panties in frat house bedroom taking off her wet dress.
- •• 0:13—Topless a lot during first sequence in the Garden of Eden with Adam.
- ••• 0:28—Brief full frontal nudity running to Adam after trying an apple.
- • 0:41—Left breast, while taking top of dress down.
- ••• 1:01—Topless, opening her blouse in defiance, while standing in front of a firing squad.

Terrorvision (1986) . . . . Suzy Putterman
Bill and Ted's Excellent Adventure (1989)
. . . . Princess Joanna
How I Got Into College (1989) . . . . Sharon Browne
Made for TV Movies:
Deadly Lessons (1983) . . . . Stephanie

Franklin, Pamela

Films:
The Prime of Miss Jean Brodie (1969) . . . . . . Sandy
- •• 1:21—Topless posing as a model for Teddy's painting. Brief right breast, while kissing him. Long shot of buns, while getting dressed.

The Legend of Hell House (1973; British)
. . . . .Florence Tanner
- • 1:03—Topless silhouette taking off nightgown and getting into bed.

Food of the Gods (1976) . . . . .Lorna
The Witching (1983) . . . . Lori
a.k.a. Necromancy
(Originally filmed in 1971 as *Necromancy*, additional scenes were added and re-released in 1983.)
- •• 0:38—Topless lying in bed during nightmare.
- 0:46—Partial right breast, tied to a stake. Flames from fire are in the way.
- • 1:07—Brief topless putting on black robe.
- • 1:17—Brief topless in several quick cuts.

Frazier, Sheila

Films:
Superfly (1972) . . . . Georgia
- •• 0:40—Topless and buns, making love in the bathtub with Superfly.

Three the Hard Way (1974) . . . . Wendy Kane
California Suite (1978) . . . . Bettina Panama
Two of a Kind (1983) . . . . Reporter

Made for TV Movies:
The Lazarus Syndrome (1976)......... Gloria St. Clair

Frederick, Vicki
Films:
All That Jazz (1979)............... Menage Partner
...All the Marbles (1981)................... Iris
a.k.a. The California Dolls
- 1:03—Brief side view of left breast, while crying in the shower after fighting with Peter Falk.

Body Rock (1984)......................... Claire
A Chorus Line (1985)..................... Sheila
Stewardess School (1987)............ Miss Grummet
Chopper Chicks in Zombietown (1989) .... Jewel
Scissors (1990)......................Nancy Leahy
Made for Cable TV:
Dream On: Doing the Bossa Nova (1990; HBO)
.... Valerie

Freeman, Lindsay
Films:
Young Lady Chatterley (1977)
.... Sybil (light-duty maid)
- 1:35—Brief left breast, while on the floor, covered with cake.

Fairytales (1979)............................Jill
- •• 0:24—Nude on hill with Jack.

• Frost, Sadie
Films:
Hay, Hay, Hay (1983; British)..................n.a.
Empire State (1987; British)............. Tracy
Dark Obsession (1989; British)........... Rebecca
- 0:22—Very brief right breast in bed after she rolls off Jamie.
- ••• 0:33—Topless several times while making love with Jamie when Gabriel Byrne interrupts them.

Bram Stoker's Dracula (1992) ....n.a.

Gabrielle, Monique
Adult Films:
Bad Girls IV ....Sandy
(Credits have her listed as Luana Chass.)
- ••• 0:15—Left breast, then topless in bed masturbating while Ron Jeremy peeks from window.
- ••• 1:24—Nude, making love (non-explicitly) with Jerry Butler.

Films:
Night Shift (1982) .... Tessie
- 0:55—Brief topless on college guy's shoulders during party in the morgue.

Black Venus (1983)......................Ingrid
- ••• 0:03—Nude in Sailor Room at the bordello.
- ••• 1:01—Topless and buns, taking off clothes for Madame Lilli's customers.

Chained Heat (1983; U.S./German) .... Debbie
- ••• 0:08—Nude, stripping for the Warden in his office.
- ••• 0:09—Nude, getting into the spa with the Warden.

Bachelor Party (1984)................... Tracey
- •• 1:11—Full frontal nudity in the hotel bedroom with Tom Hanks as his bachelor party gift.

Hard to Hold (1984)..................... Wife #1
Hot Moves (1984) .... Babs
- 0:29—Nude on the nude beach.
- •• 1:07—Topless on and behind the sofa with Barry trying to get her top off.

Love Scenes (1984) .... Unnamed
a.k.a. Ecstacy
- ••• 1:11—Full frontal nudity making love with Rick on bed.

The Big Bet (1985) .... Fantasy Girl in Elevator
- ••• 0:51—In purple bra, then eventually nude in elevator with Chris.

The Rosebud Beach Hotel (1985) .... Lisa
- •• 0:22—Topless and buns undressing in hotel room with two other girls. She's on the right.
- •• 0:44—Topless taking off her red top in basement with two other girls and two guys.
- 0:56—In black see-through nightie in hotel room with Peter Scolari.

Emmanuelle 5 (1986) ....Emmanuelle
Screen Test (1986)..................... Roxanne
- •• 0:06—Topless taking off clothes in back room in front of a young boy.
- ••• 0:42—Nude, with Michelle Bauer, seducing a boy in his day dream.
- •• 1:20—Topless taking off her top for a guy.

Weekend Warriors (1986) .... Showgirl on plane
- •• 0:51—Brief topless taking off top with other showgirls.

Young Lady Chatterley II (1986)
.... Eunice "Maid in Woods"
- •• 0:15—Topless in the woods with the Gardener.
- ••• 0:43—Topless in bed with Virgil.

Amazon Women on the Moon (1987)
...........................Taryn Steele
- ••• 0:05—Nude during Penthouse Video sketch. Long sequence of her nude in unlikely places.

Deathstalker II (1987) .. Reena the Seer/Princess Evie
- 0:57—Brief topless getting dress torn off by guards.
- ••• 1:01—Topless making love with Deathstalker.
- 1:24—Topless, laughing during the blooper scenes during the end credits.

Up 'n' Coming (1987)................Boat Girl #1
(R-rated version reviewed, X-rated version available.)
- 0:39—Topless wearing white shorts on boat. Long shot.
- 0:40—More brief nude shots on the boat.

Not of This Earth (1988)..................... Agnes
The Return of the Swamp Thing (1988)
...........................Miss Poinsettia
Silk 2 (1989)................ Jenny "Silk" Sleighton
- ••• 0:27—Topless, then full frontal nudity taking a shower while killer stalks around outside.
- 0:28—Very, very brief blurry right breast in open robe when she's on the sofa during fight.

- 0:29—Brief topless doing a round house kick on the bad guy. Right breast several times during the fight.
- ••• 0:55—Topless taking off her blouse and making love on bed. Too much diffusion!

Transylvania Twist (1990) . . . . Patty (Patricia)

976-EVIL II: The Astral Factor (1991) . . . . . . .Miss Lawlor

Angel Eyes (1991). . . . . .n.a.

Body Chemistry 2: Voice of a Stranger (1991)
. . . . Brunette in Flashback
- 0:19—Very brief buns and left breast in bed:

Evil Toons (1991) . . . . Megan
0:21—In bra in open blouse when Roxanne tries to get her to do a strip tease.
- ••• 0:25—In bra, then topless undressing in front of mirror.

Tower of Terror (1991) . . . . .n.a.

Uncaged (1991) . . . . .Beautiful Hooker
a.k.a. Angel in Red

Made for Cable TV:

Dream On: 555-HELL (1990; HBO) . . . . . .Scuba Lady
- •• 0:07—Topless wearing a scuba mask and bikini bottom when she opens the door.

Video Tapes:

Red Hot Rock (1984) . . . . .Lab Girl
- ••• 0:06—Topless and brief buns dancing after throwing off lab coat during "Lovelite" by O'Bryan.

Penthouse Love Stories (1986)
. . . . .Monique and AC/DC Lover
- ••• 0:01—Nude in bedroom entertaining herself. A must for Monique fans!
- ••• 0:18—Nude making love with another woman.

Playboy's Fantasies (1987) . . . . Grand Theft
- ••• 0:25—Nude, in house after stealing jewelry.

Scream Queen Hot Tub Party (1991). . . . . . Herself
- •• 0:07—Topless, taking off blue outfit and putting on white teddy.
- 0:12—Buns, while walking up the stairs.
- ••• 0:21—Topless and buns making love with a guy from *Emmanuelle 5*.
- ••• 0:23—Topless taking off bra in front of mirror from *Sorority House Massacre 2*.
- ••• 0:25—Topless in black panties demonstrating the Dance of the Vampires.
- ••• 0:44—Topless taking off her swimsuit top and soaping up with the other girls.
- •• 0:46—Topless in still shot during the end credits.

Penthouse Satin & Lace: An Erotic History of Lingerie (1992). . . . . .Model
- ••• 0:06—Topless and buns with a blonde woman.
- ••• 0:33—Nude in blonde wig, with lover.
- ••• 0:47—Nude in bed with another blonde.

Magazines:

Playboy (Nov 1982) . . . . Sex in Cinema 1982
- •• 163—Topless still from *Night Shift*.

Penthouse (Dec 1982) . . . . Pet
- ••• 105-123—Nude.

Playboy (Jul 1989). . . . . B-Movie Bimbos
- ••• 131—Full frontal nudity sitting on a car/helicopter.

Gainsbourg, Charlotte

Films:

Kung Fu Master (1989; French) . . . . Lucy
a.k.a. Le Petit Amour

The Little Thief (1989; French). . . . . . .Janine Castang
a.k.a. La Petite Voleuse
- •• 0:41—Topless twice, taking off blouse in bedroom with Michel.

Galik, Denise

Films:

The Happy Hooker (1975) . . . . Cynthia

California Suite (1978) . . . . Bunny

Don't Answer the Phone (1979). . . . . Lisa

The Deadly Games (1980) . . . . Mary
- 1:13—Left breast, twice, making love on top of Roger in bed.

Humanoids from the Deep (1980) . . . . Linda Beale

Melvin and Howard (1980) . . . . Lucy

Partners (1982) . . . . Clara

Get Crazy (1983) . . . . n.a.

Eye of the Tiger (1986). . . . . Christie

Career Opportunities (1991) . . . . .Lorraine

Made for Cable TV:

The Hitchhiker: Dead Heat (1987; HBO) . . . . Arielle
- •• 0:20—Topless taking off blouse and standing up with Cal in the barn, then right breast lying down in the hay with him.

TV:

Knots Landing (1980-81) . . . . Linda Stiker

Flamingo Road (1981-82) . . . . Christie Kovacs

Gallardo, Silvana

Films:

Death Wish II (1982). . . . . Rosario
- 0:11—Buns, on bed getting raped by gang. Brief topless on bed and floor.
- 0:13—Nude, trying to get to the phone. Very brief full frontal nudity, lying on her back on the floor after getting hit.

Out of the Dark (1988) . . . . McDonald

Made for Cable Movies:

Prison Stories, Women on the Inside (1990; HBO)
. . . . .Mercedes

• Gallego, Gina

Films:

The Champ (1979) . . . . .Cuban Girl

Deadly Force (1983). . . . . .Maria

Lust in the Dust (1985) . . . . .Ninta

The Men's Club (1986) . . . . Felicia

My Demon Lover (1987) . . . . Sonia

Made for Cable Movies:

Keeper of the City (1991; Showtime). . . . . Elena
- 0:19—Brief half of left breast, getting out of bed and putting on black bra. Wearing black panties.

TV:

Flamingo Road (1981-82) . . . . Alicia Sanchez

Gamba, Veronica

Films:
A Night in Heaven (1983) . . . . Tammy
Video Tapes:
Playboy's Playmate Review 2 (1984) . . . . . Playmate
Magazines:
Playboy (Nov 1983) . . . . Playmate

Gannes, Gayle

Films:
The Prey (1980) . . . . Gail
  • 0:36—Brief topless putting T-shirt on before the
  creature attacks her.
Hot Moves (1984) . . . . Jamie
  • 1:09—Topless, taking off her white blouse and get-
  ting in bed with Joey.

Ganzel, Teresa

Films:
The Toy (1982) . . . . Fancy Bates
C.O.D. (1983). . . . . Lisa Foster
  • 0:46—Right breast hanging out of dress while danc-
  ing at disco with Zack.
  • 1:25—Brief side view of left breast taking off purple
  robe in dressing room scene. Then in white bra talk-
  ing to Albert.
  1:29—In white bra during fashion show.
Made for TV Movies:
Rest In Peace, Mrs. Columbo (1990) . . . . . .Dede Perkins
Backfield in Motion (1991) . . . . Joanne
TV:
Teachers Only (1983) . . . . Samantha "Sam" Keating
The Duck Factory (1984). . . . . Mrs. Shree Winkler

Garber, Terri

Films:
Toy Soldiers (1983) . . . . Amy
  • 0:18—Brief right breast taking off her tank top when
  the army guys force her. Her head is down.
Key Exchange (1985) . . . . Amy
Miniseries:
North and South (1985) . . . . .Ashton Main
North and South, Book II (1986). . . . . .Ashton Main
TV:
Mr. Smith (1983) . . . . Dr. Judy Tyson
Dynasty (1987-88) . . . . .Leslie Carrington

• Garner, Shay

Films:
Thumbelina (1970). . . . . .n.a.
Humongous (1982; Canadian) . . . . Ida Parsons
  • 0:05—Brief left breast and brief lower frontal nudity
  getting her clothes ripped off by a guy. Don't see her
  face.

Garr, Teri

Films:
Head (1968) . . . . Testy True
The Conversation (1974). Amy

Young Frankenstein (1974) . . . . .Inga
Won Ton Ton, The Dog Who Saved Hollywood (1976)
. . . . .Fluffy Peters
Close Encounters of the Third Kind (1977)
. . . . .Ronnie Neary
Oh God! (1977). . . . . Bobbie Landers
The Black Stallion (1979) . . . . Alec's Mother
Honky Tonk Freeway (1981). . . . . .Ericka
The Escape Artist (1982). . . . . Arlene
One from the Heart (1982) . . . . Frannie
  •• 0:09—Brief topless getting out of the shower.
     0:10—In a bra, getting dressed in bedroom.
  •• 0:40—Side view of right breast changing in. bed-
     room while Frederic Forrest watches.
  ••• 1:20—Brief topless in bed when standing up after
     Forrest drops in though the roof while she's in bed
     with Raul Julia.
Tootsie (1982) . . . . Sandy
The Black Stallion Returns (1983) . . . . Alec's Mother
Mr. Mom (1983) . . . . .Caroline
The Sting II (1983) . . . . Veronica
Firstborn (1984). . . . . .Wendy
After Hours (1985) . . . . .Julie
Miracles (1986) . . . . Jean Briggs
Full Moon in Blue Water (1988) . . . . Louise
  0:50—Walking around in Gene Hackman's bar in a
  bra while changing blouses and talking to him.
Let It Ride (1989). . . . . .Pam
Out Cold (1989) . . . . Sunny Cannald
Short Time (1990) . . . . Carolyn Simpson
Waiting for the Light (1991). . . . . n.a.
Made for Cable Movies:
To Catch a King (1984; HBO). . . . . n.a.
Made for Cable TV:
Dream On: And Bimbo Was His Name-O (1992; HBO)
. . . . .Sondra McCadden
Made for TV Movies:
Fresno (1986). . . . . .Talon Kensington
Pack of Lies (1987). . . . . n.a.
Deliver Them from Evil: The Taking of Alta View (1992)
. . . . Susan Woolley
TV:
The Sonny and Cher Comedy Hour (1973-74)
. . . . Regular
Girl with Something Extra (1973-74) . . . . .Amber
Burns and Schreiber Comedy Hour (1973). . . . . Regular
The Sonny Comedy Revue (1974) . . . . Regular
Good & Evil (1991) .Denise

Gastoni, Lisa

Films:
Female Friends (1958; British) . . . . .Marny Friend
Three Men in a Boat (1958) . . . . . . Primrose Porterhouse
Gidget Goes to Rome (1963) . . . . Anna Cellini
Submission (1976; Italian) . . . . .Elaine
  0:28—Lower frontal nudity on the floor behind the
  counter with Franco Nero.
  • 0:30—Left breast, while talking on the phone with
  her husband while Nero fondles her.

•• 0:32—Topless and buns, making love on bed with Nero. Slightly out of focus.

•• 0:33—Topless getting out of bed to talk to her daughter.

••• 0:43—Topless in room with Juliet and Nero. Long scene.

••• 0:45—More topless on the floor yelling at Nero.
0:54—Brief lower frontal nudity in slip, sitting on floor with Nero.

••• 0:57—Left breast, while wearing slip, walking in front of pharmacy. Then full frontal nudity while wearing only stockings. Long scene.

•• 1:00—Topless in pharmacy with Nero, singing and dancing.

•• 1:28—Topless when Nero cuts her slip open. Nice close up.

•• 1:29—Topless getting up out of bed.

Gauthier, Connie

Films:
18 Again! (1988) . . . . Artist's Model
   •• 0:29—Very brief topless, then buns taking her robe off during art class.
Magazines:
Penthouse (Jun 1987) . . . . Pet

Gavin, Erica

Films:
Vixen (1968) . . . . Vixen Palmer
Caged Heat (1974) . . . . Jacqueline Wilson
   a.k.a. Renegade Girls
   • 0:08—Buns, getting strip searched before entering prison.
   •• 0:25—Topless in shower scene.
   • 0:30—Brief side view of left breast in another shower scene.

Gavin, Mary

See: Samples, Candy.

Gaybis, Annie

Films:
Fairytales (1979). . . . . Snow White
   ••• 0:21—Nude in room with the seven little dwarfs singing and dancing.
10 Violent Women (1982). . . . . Vickie
Friday the 13th, Part III (1982) . . . . Cashier
The Lost Empire (1983). . . . . n.a.
The Witching (1983). . . . . Spirit
   a.k.a. Necromancy
   (Originally filmed in 1971 as *Necromancy*, additional scenes were added and re-released in 1983.)
Bachelor Party (1984) . . . . Arab Dressed Hooker
Hollywood Zap! (1986). . . . . Debbie
Bugsy (1991) . . . . Uncredited Mambo Dancer
Death Dancers (1992) . . . . n.a.
Distinguished Gentleman (1992). . . . . Maria
Twin Peaks: Fire Walk With Me (1992)
   . . . . Uncredited Dancer on Stage

Magazines:
Playboy (Mar 1992) . . . . Grapevine
   • 170—Topless through holes in her T-shirt. B&W.

Geeson, Judy

Films:
Berserk (1967; British) . . . . Angela Rivers
To Sir, with Love (1967; British) . . . . Pamela Dare
Hammerhead (1968) . . . . Sue Trenton
Here We Go Round the Mulberry Bush
   (1968; British) . . . . Mary Gloucester
   Nude, swimming.
The Executioner (1970; British) . . . . Polly Bendel
10 Rillington Place (1971; British). . . . . Beryl Evans
Fear in the Night (1972; British). . . . . Peggy Heller
   a.k.a. Dynasty of Fear
Brannigan (1975; British) . . . . Jennifer Thatcher
Carry on England (1976; British) . . . . . . Sgt. Tilly Willing
The Eagle Has Landed (1977; British) . . Pamela Verecker
Horror Planet (1980; British). . . . . Sandy
   a.k.a. Inseminoid
   •• 0:31—Brief topless on the operating table.
   • 0:37—Same scene during brief flashback.

Geffner, Deborah

Films:
All That Jazz (1979) . . . . Victoria
   • 0:17—Brief topless taking off her blouse and walking up the stairs while Roy Scheider watches. A little out of focus.
Star 80 (1983) . . . . Billie
Exterminator 2 (1984) . . . . Caroline
Magazines:
Playboy (Mar 1980) . . . . All That Fosse
   ••• 177—Topless sitting on couch.

Gemser, Laura

a.k.a. Moira Chen.
Films:
Emmanuelle, The Joys of a Woman (1975)
   . . . . Massage Woman
Black Emanuelle (1976) . . . . Emanuelle
   • 0:00—Brief topless daydreaming on airplane.
   • 0:19—Left breast in car kissing a guy at night.
   •• 0:27—Topless in shower with a guy.
   ••• 0:30—Full frontal nudity making love with a guy in bed.
   ••• 0:37—Topless taking pictures with Karin Schubert.
   •• 0:41—Full frontal nudity lying on bed dreaming about the day's events while masturbating, then full frontal nudity walking around.
   •• 0:49—Topless in studio with Johnny.
   ••• 0:52—Brief right breast making love on the side of the road. Full frontal nudity by the pool kissing Gloria.
   •• 1:00—Nude, taking a shower, then answering the phone.
   •• 1:04—Topless on boat after almost drowning.

- •• 1:08—Full frontal nudity dancing with African tribe, then making love with the leader.
- •• 1:14—Full frontal nudity taking off clothes by waterfall with Johnny.
- •• 1:23—Topless making love with the field hockey team on a train.

Emanuelle in Bangkok (1977) . . . . .Emanuelle
- •• 0:07—Topless making love with a guy.
- •• 0:12—Full frontal nudity changing in hotel room.
- ••• 0:17—Full frontal nudity getting a bath, then massaged by another woman.
- •• 0:35—Topless during orgy scene.
- •• 0:53—Topless in room with a woman, then taking a shower.
- •• 1:01—Topless in tent with a guy and woman.
- •• 1:08—Full frontal nudity dancing in a group of guys.
- •• 1:16—Full frontal nudity taking a bath with a woman.
- •• 1:18—Topless on bed making love with a guy.

Emanuelle in Egypt (1977) . . . . Laura

Emanuelle's Amazon Adventure (1977)
. . . . .Emanuelle
- • 0:17—Brief left breast in flashback sequence in bed with a man.
- • 0:21—Brief topless making love in bed.
- • 0:25—Brief topless in the water with a blonde woman.
- •• 1:10—Full frontal nudity painting her body.
- • 1:11—Brief topless in boat.
- • 1:13—Nude walking out of the water trying to save Isabelle.
- • 1:14—Brief topless getting into the boat with Isabelle.

Two Super Cops (1978; Italian) . . . . Susy Lee
Bushido Blade (1979; British/U.S.) . . . . Tomoe
- • 1:08—Brief right breast taking off her top in bedroom with Captain Hawk.

Emanuelle the Seductress (1979; Greek)
. . . . .Emanuelle
- • 0:01—Full frontal nudity lying in bed with Mario.
- • 0:02—Brief topless riding horse on the beach.
- •• 0:42—Topless making love then full frontal nudity getting dressed with Tommy.
- ••• 0:48—Topless undressing in bedroom, then in white panties, then nude talking to Alona.
- •• 0:54—Topless walking around in a skirt.
- •• 1:02—Topless outside taking a shower, then on lounge chair making love with Tommy.

The Best of Sex and Violence (1981) . . . . .Emanuelle
- • 0:23—Side of left breast while getting clothes taken off by a guy. Long shot. Scene from *Emanuelle Around the World*.

Ator, The Fighting Eagle (1982). . . . . Indun
Famous T & A (1982) . . . . .Emanuelle
(No longer available for purchase, check your video store for rental.)
- ••• 0:55—Topless scenes from *Emanuelle Around the World*.

Endgame (1983) . . . . Lilith
- • 1:10—Brief topless a couple of times getting blouse ripped open by a gross looking guy.

Caged Women (1984; French/Italian)
. . . . Emanuelle/Laura
a.k.a. Emanuelle in Hell

Metamorphosis (1989) . . . . .Prostitute
- • 0:37—Very brief topless several times in Peter's flashback.
- • 0:43—Very brief topless in flashback again.

Passionate Pleasures (1989) . . . . .Haunani
Quest for the Mighty Sword (1989) . . . . Grimilde
Top Model (1989; Italian) . . . . Dorothy/Eve
- • 0:44—Brief right breast and buns, frolicking with the cowboy.

Object of Desire (1991) . . . . . Uncredited Photographer
Private Screenings.
Magazines:
Playboy (May 1979) . . . . .Foreign Sex Stars
- •• 170-171—Nude.

• *Gentry, Jaki*

Video Tapes:
Hot Body International: #3 Lingerie Special
(1992) . . . . .Contestant
- •• 0:46—Buns, in G-string and bra.
- ••• 0:53—Topless, posing for photo shoot.

Hot Body International: #5 Miss Acapulco (1992)
. . . . .Contestant

George, Susan

Films:
The Looking Glass War (1970; British) . . . . .Susan
Die Screaming Marianne (1972). . . . . .Marianne
Straw Dogs (1972) . . . . .Amy
- •• 0:32—Topless taking off sweater, tossing it down to Dustin Hoffman, then looking out the door at the workers.
- ••• 1:00—Topless on couch getting raped by one of the construction workers.

Dirty Mary, Crazy Larry (1974) . . . . Mary
Mandingo (1975). . . . . Blanche
- • 1:36—Brief topless in bed with Ken Norton.

Out of Season (1975; British) . . . . .Joanna
Small Town in Texas (1976) . . . . Mary Lee
Tintorera (1977) . . . . Gabriella
- • 0:42—Very brief topless waking up Steve.

Enter the Ninja (1981) . . . . Mary-Ann Landers
Venom (1982; British) . . . . Louise
The Jigsaw Man (1984) . . . . Penny
House Where Evil Dwells (1985) . . . . .Laura
- ••• 0:21—Topless in bed making love with Edward Albert.
- •• 0:59—Topless making love again.

Lightning, The White Stallion (1986) . . . . Madame Rene
Made for TV Movies:
Jack the Ripper (1988) . . . . Catherine

Magazines:
Playboy (Nov 1972) . . . . Sex in Cinema 1972
•• 160—Topless on couch from *The Straw Dogs*.
Playboy (Dec 1972). . . . . Sex Stars of 1972
•• 208—Topless.

• Georges-Picot, Olga
Films:
Farewell, Friend (1968; French/Italian) . . Isabelle Manue
Connecting Rooms (1971; British). . . . . Claudia Fouchet
Day of the Jackal (1973) . . . . Denise
• 0:55—Brief topless and buns, getting out of bed to
use the phone.
Persecution (1974; British) . . . . Monique Kalfon
Love and Death (1975) . . . . Countess Alexandrovna
Goodbye Emmanuelle (1977) . . . . .n.a.

• Geraghty, Erin
Films:
Games Girls Play (1974; British). . . . . .Ducky
a.k.a. The Bunny Caper
• 1:11—In bra and panties, then topless running
around outside.
That'll Be the Day (1974; British). . . . . Joan

• Gerrish, Flo
Films:
Superchick (1978). . . . . Funky Jane
Don't Answer the Phone (1979) . . . Dr. Lindsay Gale
• 1:05—Very brief topless rolling over in bed with Mc-
Cabe. Brief topless when he pulls the covers down.
• 1:19—Side view of right breast, several times, while
taking off blouse and putting nightgown on.
Schizoid (1980). . . . . Pat
Hot Chili (1985) . . . . .Mrs. Baxter
The Naked Cage (1985) . . . . Mother
Over the Top (1987) . . . . Martha, the Waitress

Gershon, Gina
Films:
3:15—The Moment of Truth (1986)
. . . . One of the Cobrettes
Sweet Revenge (1987). . . . . K.C.
• 0:41—Brief topless in water under a waterfall with
Lee.
Cocktail (1988). . . . . Coral
• 0:31—Very, very brief right breast romping around
in bed with Tom Cruise.
Red Heat (1988) .Cat Manzetti
Voodoo Dawn (1989) . . . . Tina
City of Hope (1991) . . . . .Laurie
Out for Justice (1991) . . . . Patti Modono
Made for TV Movies:
Miss Rose White (1992). . . . . Angie

• Gertz, Jami
Films:
Endless Love (1981) .Patty
Alphabet City (1984). . . . . Sophia

Sixteen Candles (1984) .Robin
Mischief (1985) . . . . .Rosalie
Crossroads (1986) . . . . Frances
Quicksilver (1986) . . . . .Terri
Solarbabies (1986). . . . . Terra
Less than Zero (1987) .Blair
The Lost Boys (1987) . . . . Star
Listen to Me (1989) . . . . .Monica Tomanski
Renegades (1989) . . . . Barbara
Silence Like Glass (1989) . . . . Eva March
1:31—Very brief left breast on operating table, get-
ting defibrillated. Possible body double. The Doc-
tor's arm covers her face.
Don't Tell Her It's Me (1990) . . . . Emily Pear
Sibling Rivalry (1990). . . . . Jeanine
TV:
Sibs (1991-92) . . . . Lily

Gibb, Cynthia
Films:
Salvador (1986) .Cathy Moore
Youngblood (1986) . . . . .Jessie Chadwick
• 0:50—Brief topless and buns making love with Rob
Lowe in his room.
Jack's Back (1987) . . . . .Chris Moscari
1:00—Getting undressed in white camisole and
panties while someone watches her from outside.
1:30—Running around the house in a white slip try-
ing to get away from the killer.
Malone (1987). . . . . .Jo Barlow
Modern Girls (1987) . . . . Cece
Short Circuit 2 (1988) . . . . Sandy Banatoni
Death Warrant (1990) . . . . Amanda Beckett
0:52—In bra, undressing for prison guards.
Made for TV Movies:
The Karen Carpenter Story (1989) . . . . Karen Carpenter
When We Were Young (1989) . . . . Ellen
TV:
Search for Tomorrow (1981-83) . . . . . Suzi Wyatt Martin
Fame (1983-86). .Holly Laird

Giblin, Belinda
Films:
Jock Petersen (1974; Australian) . . . . . . Moira Winton
a.k.a. Petersen
•• 0:21—Left breast several times, under a cover with
Jock, then buns when cover is removed.
End Play (1975; Australian) . . . . .Margret Gifford
Demolition (1977) . . . . .n.a.
The Empty Beach (1985) . . . . Marion Singer

Gibson, Greta
Films:
Warlords (1988) . . . . .Harem Girl
•• 1:05—Topless in tent with the other harem girls.
Holding a snake.
•• 1:09—Topless again.

Beverly Hills Vamp (1989). . . . . . Screen Test Starlet
•• 0:53—Topless and brief buns in G-string lying on Mr. Pendleton's desk.

• *Gidley, Pamela*

Films:
Thrashin' (1986) . . . . Chrissy
The Blue Iguana (1988). . . . . Dakota
Cherry 2000 (1988) . . . . Cherry
Permanent Record (1988). . . . . Kim
Disturbed (1990) . . . . Sandy Ramirez
The Last of the Finest (1990). . . . . Haley
Liebestraum (1991) . . . . .Jane Kessler
(Unrated Director's cut reviewed.)
0:37—Caressing her right breast during dream. Don't see anything.
• 1:07—Buns, while taking a shower. Almost topless, but her arm gets in the way.

TV:
Angel Street (1992-). . . . . Dorothy Paretsky

Giftos, Elaine

Films:
Gas-s-s! (1970) . . . . Cilla
On a Clear Day You Can See Forever (1970) . . . . .Muriel
The Student Nurses (1970) . . . . Sharon
a.k.a. Young LA Nurses
• 1:14—Brief topless undressing and getting into bed with terminally ill boy. Dark, hard to see.
Everything You Wanted to Know About Sex, But Were Afraid to Ask (1972) . . . . Mrs. Ross
The Wrestler (1974) . . . . Debbie
Paternity (1981) . . . . .Woman in Bar
Angel (1983). . . . . .Patricia Allen
The Trouble with Dick (1986) . . . . Sheila

Gilbert, Pamela

Films:
Cyclone (1986) . . . . Uncredited Shower Girl
0:06—Buns and topless brunette in the showers. Long shot.
Evil Spawn (1987). . . . . .Elaine Talbot
••• 0:46—Nude taking off black lingerie and going swimming in pool. Hubba, hubba!
••• 0:49—Topless in the pool, then full frontal nudity getting out.
Demonwarp (1988) . . . . .Carrie Austin
••• 0:20—In bra, then topless in bed with Jack.
••• 0:22—Right breast, then topless lying in bed, making love with Jack.
•• 1:23—Topless, strapped to table.
• 1:24—Topless several more times on the table.
•• 1:25—Topless getting up and getting dressed.

Gilbert-Brinkman, Melissa

Sister of actress Sara Gilbert.
Wife of actor/writer Bo Brinkman.
Films:
Sylvester (1985). . . . . .Charlie
• 0:23—Very, very brief topless struggling with a guy in truck cab. Seen through a dirty windshield.
•• 0:24—Very brief left breast after Richard Farnsworth runs down the stairs to help her. Seen from the open door of the truck.
Ice House (1988) . . . . Kay
0:51—Making love with another guy while her real-life husband watches while he's tied up.
Made for TV Movies:
The Miracle Worker (1979). . . . . .Helen Keller
The Diary of Anne Frank (1980) . . . . Anne Frank
Donor (1990). . . . . n.a.
Joshua's Heart (1990). . . . . n.a.
TV:
Little House on the Prairie (1974-83)
. . . . Laura Ingalls Wilder
Stand by Your Man (1992). . . . . .Rochelle

Gildersleeve, Linda

Films:
Beach Bunnies (1977) . . . . n.a.
Cinderella (1977). . . . . Farm Girl (redhead)
••• 0:21—Topless and buns with her brunette sister in their house making love with the guy who is looking for Cinderella.
•• 1:24—Full frontal nudity with her sister again when the Prince goes around to try and find Cinderella.
The Happy Hooker Goes to Washington (1977)
. . . . .Honeymoon Wife
• 0:35—Brief topless in a diner during the filming of a commercial.

Gillingham, Kim

Films:
Valet Girls (1987) . . . . Madonna Wannabe
Captain America (1990). . . . . . . Bernice Stewart/Sharon
Corporate Affairs (1990) . . . . Ginny Malmquist
• 1:09—Topless, climbing out of cubicle.

• *Gilmore-Capps, Teresa*

Films:
The Arrogant (1987). . . . . Charlotte
• 0:23—Brief topless, making love in a barn.
The Marrying Man (1991) . . . . Bugsy's Blonde
a.k.a. Too Hot to Handle
Made for Cable Movies:
Fever (1991; HBO) . . . . Jeanine

• Giorgi, Eleonora

Films:
Diary of a Cloistered Nun (1973; Italian/German/French)
. . . . Carmela
Appassionata (1979; Italian) . . . . .Nicola
 • 0:14—Very brief left breast in open blouse with Emilio in his dentist office. Topless several times.
 •• 0:41—Full frontal nudity in bedroom when Emilio comes in. Dark.
 ••• 0:54—Nude in office with Emilio in stockings and garter belt.
 • 1:35—Brief right breast in bed with Emilio. Dark.
Beyond Obsession (1982) . . . . Nina
 •• 0:01—Topless, taking off her top and getting into the shower with Tom Berenger.
 • 0:59—Right breast in bed with Marcello Mastroianni, brief right breast after.
Nudo di Donna (1984; Italian) . . . . Laura
 a.k.a. Portrait of a Woman, Nude
 • 0:11—Very brief left breast, while taking off robe. Subtitles get in the way.
 • 0:12—Right breast, while in the shower, getting consoled.
 • 0:13—Brief upper half topless, getting into bed.
 • 0:14—Topless in bed.
 •• 0:36—Nude, mostly buns, sleeping in bed when Sandro pulls back the covers.
 • 1:12—Brief right breast, while in bed with Sandro.
 1:13—Right breast under sheer dress.
Il Volpone (1988; Italian). . . . . The Mayor

• Giosa, Susan

Films:
America 3000 (1986) . . . . Morha
The First Power (1990) . . . . Carmen
 0:12—In bra when the killer opens her blouse.
 • 0:22—Brief right breast, lying dead with a bloody pentagram cut into her stomach.
TV:
Reasonable Doubts (1992-) . . . . Diedre

Girling, Cindy

Films:
Left for Dead (1978) . . . . Pauline Corte
 •• 0:19—Nude, taking off shirt in bedroom.
Daughter of Death (1982) . . . . .Irene
 a.k.a. Julie Darling
 • 0:12—Topless in bathtub and getting out.
Hostile Takeover (1988; Canadian) . . . . . . Mrs. Gayford
 a.k.a. Office Party

• Giroux, Jackie

Films:
Cross and the Switchblade (1970). . . . . Rosa
Sweet Sugar (1972) . . . . Fara
 •• 0:33—Topless, skinny dipping in stream with Dolores.
Slaughter's Big Rip-Off (1975). . . . . .Mrs. Duncan
To Live and Die in L.A. (1985). . . . . Claudia Leith

• Givens, Robin

Ex-wife of boxer Mike Tyson.
Films:
A Rage in Harlem (1991) . . . . Imabelle
 ••• 0:32—Buns, while lying in bed with Forest Whitaker.
Boomerang (1992). . . . . Jacqueline
TV:
Head of the Class (1986-91) . . . . Darlene Merriman
Angel Street (1992-) . . . . Anita King

• Glaser, Lisa

Films:
Humanoids from the Deep (1980) . . . . .Becky
 (Brunette colored hair.)
 ••• 0:34—Full frontal nudity, undressing in tent with Billy and his ventriloquist dummy.
 • 0:35—Nude, running on the beach at night, trying to escape the humanoids.
Stripped to Kill II (1988) . . . . Victoria
 (Blonde colored hair.)
 •• 0:01—Topless and buns in G-string doing a strip dance routine during Shadey's nightmare.
Future Kick (1991) . . . . Uncredited Dancer
 • 0:36—Topless, dancing on stage in white outfit. (Taken from *Stripped to Kill II*.)

Glazowski, Liz

Films:
The Happy Hooker Goes Hollywood (1980) . . . . Liz
Magazines:
 Playboy (Jan 1980). . . . . Playboy's Pajama Parties
 •• 126—Right breast.
 Playboy (Apr 1980) . . . . Playmate
 ••• 140-151—Nude.

Glenn, Charisse

Films:
Bad Influence (1990) . . . . Stylish Eurasian Woman
 ••• 1:26—Topless and partial lower frontal nudity making love on Rob Lowe.
 • 1:28—Very brief left breast in bed with the blonde woman.
Magazines:
 Playboy (Nov 1990) . . . . Sex in Cinema 1990
 • 146—Left breast.

Go, Jade

Films:
Big Trouble in Little China (1986)
. . . . Chinese Girl in White Tiger
The Last Emperor (1987) . . . . Ar Mo
 • 0:10—Right breast in open top after breast feeding the young Pu Yi.
 • 0:20—Right breast in open top telling Pu Yi a story.
 • 0:29—Right breast in open top breast feeding an older Pu Yi. Long shot.

Goldsmith, Clio

Films:

Honey (1980; Italian) . . . . Annie
- •• 0:05—Nude kneeling in a room.
- •• 0:20—Nude getting into the bathtub.
- •• 0:42—Nude getting changed.
- ••• 0:44—Nude while hiding under the bed.
- •• 0:58—Nude getting disciplined, taking off clothes, then kneeling.

The Gift (1982; French) . . . . .Barbara
- •• 0:39—Brief topless several times in the bathroom, then right breast in bathtub.
- • 0:49—Topless lying in bed sleeping.
- 0:51—Very brief left breast turning over in bed.
- • 0:52—Brief right breast then buns, reaching for phone while lying in bed.
- 1:16—Very brief left breast getting out of bed. Dark, hard to see.

The Heat of Desire (1982; French) . . . . Carol
a.k.a. Plein Sud
- • 0:09—Topless and buns, getting out of bed in train to look out the window. Dark.
- • 0:12—Brief topless in bathroom mirror when Serge peeks in.
- •• 0:19—Full frontal nudity in the bathtub.
- •• 0:20—Nude, sitting on the floor with Serge's head in her lap.
- •• 0:21—Buns, lying face down on floor. Very brief topless. A little dark. Then topless sitting up and drinking out of bottle.
- • 0:22—Right breast, in gaping robe sitting on floor with Serge.
- • 0:24—Partial left breast consoling Serge in bed.
- • 0:25—Topless sitting on chair on balcony, then walking inside. Dark.
- • 0:56—Topless walking from bathroom and getting into bed. Dark.
- • 0:57—Brief right breast, while on couch with Guy Marchand.
- •• 0:58—Topless getting dressed while Serge is yelling.

La Cicala (The Cricket) (1983) . . . . Cicala
- •• 0:26—Nude when Wilma brings her in to get Anthony Franciosa excited again.
- •• 0:39—Nude swimming under waterfall with Barbara de Rossi.
- ••• 0:43—Full frontal nudity undressing in room with de Rossi.

Miss Right (1987; Italian) .n.a.

Golino, Valeria

Films:

Blind Date (1984) . . . . Girl in Bikini
(Not the same 1987 *Blind Date* with Bruce Willis.)
Detective School Dropouts (1986) . . . . Caterina
Big Top Pee Wee (1988) . . . . Gina Piccolapupula
Rain Man (1988) . . . . Suzanna
- • 0:35—Very brief left breast four times and very, very brief right breast once with open blouse fighting with Tom Cruise after getting out of the bathtub.

Torrents of Spring (1990) . . . . .Gemma
Hot Shots (1991) . . . . Ramada Thompson
The Indian Runner (1991) . . . . .Maria
Year of the Gun (1991). . . . . Lia Spinelli
- ••• 0:17—Topless, making love in bed with Andrew McCarthy.
- • 0:25—Half of buns and side of right breast, lying in bed with McCarthy.

Gonzalez, Cordelia

Films:

Homeboy (1988) . . . . Cuban Boxer's Wife
Born on the Fourth of July (1989) . . . . . Maria Elena
- ••• 1:43—Topless in black panties, then full frontal nudity in bed with Tom Cruise.

Goodfellow, Joan

Films:

Lolly-Madonna XXX (1973) . . . . Sister Gutshall
Buster and Billie (1974) . . . . Billie
- 0:33—Brief topless in truck with Jan-Michael Vincent. Dark, hard to see.
- • 1:06—Buns, then brief topless in the woods with Vincent.
- • 1:25—Brief left breast getting raped by jerks.

Sunburn (1979) . . . . .Joanna
A Flash of Green (1984) . . . . Mitchie

Gorcey, Elizabeth

Films:

Teen Wolf (1985) . . . . .Tina
The Trouble with Dick (1986) . . . . .Haley
- • 0:13—Very brief left breast in gaping T-shirt while she lies on bed, plays with a toy and laughs.
- 0:26—Lower half of buns under robe on sofa with Dick.
- 0:27—Half of right breast on top of Dick in bed.

Iced (1988) . . . . .Diane

• Gracen, Elizabeth

Real name is Elizabeth Ward.
Miss Arkansas and Miss America 1982.

Films:

Lisa (1989) . . . . Mary
Sundown: The Vampire in Retreat (1989) . . . . Alice
Lower Level (1990) . . . . Hillary
- • 0:11—Topless in back seat of BMW making love with Craig. Long shot.
- 0:12—Very, very brief partial left breast afterwards.
- • 0:13—Brief right breast and lower frontal nudity getting dressed. Then in black lingerie.
- 0:14—In wet black lingerie under fire sprinkler in parking garage.
- •• 0:23—In black lingerie, then brief topless changing in her office while Sam secretly watches.

Marked for Death (1990) . . . . Melissa
- 0:45—Very brief part of right breast in gaping blouse, while crawling on the floor.

Made for TV Movies:
  83 Hours 'til Dawn (1990). . . . . Maria
Magazines:
  Playboy (May 1992) . . . . There She Is...
  ••• 70–77—Nude.

• *Graham, Julie*

Films:
  Wonderland (1989; British) . . . . Hazel
  •• 1:11—Nude, taking off her clothes at the beach
      while talking to Eddie.
  Nuns on the Run (1990; British) . . . . . . .Casino Waitress
  The Big Man (1991; British) . . . . Melanie
  a.k.a. Crossing the Line
  •• 1:09—Topless when Liam Neeson undresses her and
      starts to make love with her.

Graham, Sherri

Films:
  Bad Girls from Mars (1990) . . . . Swimmer
  •• 0:22—Very brief topless diving into, then climbing
      out of pool.
  Haunting Fear (1990) . . . . Visconti's Girl
  • 0:45—Buns in swimming pool. (Breasts seen under
      water.)
  • 0:47—Topless, giving Visconti a massage while he
      talks on the phone.
  Mob Boss (1990). Bar Girl
  •• 0:46—Topless and buns, dancing on stage. Medium
      long shot.
  Naked Obsession (1990). . . . . Waitress
  Carnal Crimes (1991) . . . . Party Girl #1

Grant, Faye

Films:
  Internal Affairs (1990) . . . . Penny
  • 0:50—Right breast, while straddling Richard Gere
      while she talks on the telephone.
  Made for Cable TV:
  Tales From the Crypt: Spoiled (1991; HBO) . . . . . . .Janet
  Miniseries:
  V (1983) . . . . Dr. Julie Parrish
  V: The Final Battle (1984) . . . . Dr. Julie Parrish
  Made for TV Movies:
  Omen IV: The Awakening (1991) . . . . Karen York
  TV:
  Greatest American Hero (1981-83) . . . . . . Rhonda Blake
  V: The Series (1984-85). . . . . Dr. Julie Parrish

Grant, Lee

Mother of actress Dinah Manoff.
Films:
  In the Heat of the Night (1967). . . . . Mrs. Leslie Colbert
  Valley of the Dolls (1967) . . . . Miriam
  Marooned (1969) .Celia Pruett
  The Landlord (1970) . . . . .Mrs. Enders
  There Was a Crooked Man (1970). . . . . Mrs. Bullard
  Plaza Suite (1971) . . . . Norma Hubley
  Portnoy's Complaint (1972) . . . . .Sophie Portnoy

  Shampoo (1975) . . . . Felicia
  • 0:03—Brief topless in bed sitting up and putting bra
      on talking to Warren Beatty. Long shot, hard to see.
  Airport '77 (1977) . . . . Karen Wallace
  Damien, Omen II (1978) . . . . .Ann Thorn
  The Mafu Cage (1978). Ellen
    a.k.a. My Sister, My Love
  When Ya Comin' Back Red Ryder (1979)
    . . . . Clarisse Ethridge
    (Not available on video tape.)
  Little Miss Marker (1980) . . . . The Judge
  Charlie Chan & the Curse of the Dragon Queen (1981)
    . . . . Mrs. Lupowitz
  Visiting Hours (1982; Canadian). . . . . . . .Deborah Ballin
  Teachers (1984) . . . . Dr. Burke
  The Big Town (1987) . . . . Ferguson Edwards
  Defending Your Life (1991) . . . . Lena Foster
  Made for Cable Movies:
  Citizen Cohn (1992; HBO) . . . . Dora
  Miniseries:
  Backstairs at the White House (1979) . . . Grace Coolidge
  Made for TV Movies:
  The Neon Ceiling (1971) . . . . n.a.
  Something to Live For: The Alison Gertz Story (1992)
    . . . . n.a.
  TV:
  Peyton Place (1965-66) . . . . Stella Chernak
  Fay (1975-76) . . . . Fay Stewart

• *Gravatte, Marianne*

Video Tapes:
  Playboy Video Magazine, Volume 5 (1983)
    . . . . Playmate
  • 0:06—Full frontal nudity outside.
  ••• 0:09—Nude, posing at beach in a bed set.
  Playboy's Playmate Review 2 (1984) . . . . . Playmate
  Playboy's Playmates of the Year: The '80s (1989)
    .Playmate of the Year 1983
  ••• 0:32—Nude in still photos.
  ••• 0:33—Nude in bed at the beach during photo ses-
      sion.
  •• 0:51—Topless in bed scene.
  Playboy Video Centerfold: Reneé Tenison (1990)
    . . . . .Portrait of a Photographer: Richard Fegley
  ••• 0:32—Nude, in photo session at the beach.
  Magazines:
  Playboy (Oct 1982) . . . . Playmate
  Playboy's Nudes (Oct 1990) . . . . .Herself
  •• 54—Topless and buns.
  •• 108—Buns and partial left breast.

Gray, Andee

Films:
  Sno-Line (1984) . . . . Ruth Lyle
  9 1/2 Ninjas (1990) . . . . Lisa Thorne
  •• 1:02—Topless making love with Joe in the rain.
  • 1:19—Brief topless during flashback.
  Dead Men Don't Die (1991) . . . . Isadora

Gray, Julie

Films:
Gimme an "F" (1981) . . . . Falcon Marsha
Stryker (1983; Philippines) . . . . Laurenz
School Spirit (1985) . . . . Kendall
Dr. Alien (1989) . . . . Karla
  a.k.a. I Was a Teenage Sex Mutant
  ••• 0:44—In white bra, then topless in Janitor's room
    with Wesley.
Video Tapes:
Inside Out 3 (1992). . . . . Actress/The Branding

• Green, Marika

Films:
Pickpocket (1963; French). . . . . Jeanne
Singapore, Singapore (1969; French/Italian) . . . . Monica
Rider on the Rain (1970; French/Italian)
  . . . . Hostess at Tania's
Emmanuelle (1974) . . . . Bee
  (R-rated version reviewed.)
  • 0:46—Nude, undressing outside with Sylvia Kristel.
    Brief full frontal nudity, when leaving blanket.
  •• 0:47—Topless, getting dressed.
  • 0:50—Upper half of buns, while lying down, talking
    to Kristel.
Until September (1984) . . . . Banker

Greenberg, Sandy

Video Tapes:
Playmates at Play (1990) . . . . Easy Rider
Magazines:
Playboy (Jun 1987) . . . . Playmate

Grier, Pam

Cousin of actor/former football player Rosey Grier.
Films:
Beyond the Valley of the Dolls (1970)
  . . . . Black Party Goer
  Russ Meyer Film.
  (Not available on video tape.)
The Big Doll House (1971) . . . . Grear
  • 0:28—Very brief most of right breast rolling over in
    bed.
  •• 0:32—Topless getting her back washed by Collier.
    Arms in the way a little bit.
  • 0:44—Left breast covered with mud sticking out of
    her top after wrestling with Alcott.
The Big Bird Cage (1972) . . . . Blossom
Twilight People (1972) . . . . The Panther Woman
Coffy (1973) . . . . Coffy
  • 0:05—Upper half of right breast in bed with a guy.
    0:19—Buns, walking past the fireplace, seen
    through a fish tank.
  •• 0:25—Topless in open dress getting attacked by two
    masked burglars.
  ••• 0:38—Buns and topless undressing in bedroom.
    Wow!
  • 0:42—Brief right breast when breast pops out of
    dress while she's leaning over. Dark, hard to see.

0:49—In black bra and panties in open dress with a
  guy in the bedroom.
Naked Warriors (1973) . . . . Mamawi
  a.k.a. The Arena
  •• 0:08—Brief left breast, then lower frontal nudity and
    side view of right breast getting washed down in
    court yard.
  ••• 0:52—Topless getting oiled up for a battle. Wow!
Scream, Blacula, Scream (1973) . . . . Lisa Fortier
Foxy Brown (1974) . . . . Foxy Brown
  • 0:05—Topless, getting out of bed and taking off
    nightgown.
  • 0:40—Brief left breast, while getting dressed.
    1:04—Upper half of breasts, while tied to bed.
  ••• 1:05—Right breast, then topless rolling over in bed.
Bucktown (1975) . . . . Aretha
Friday Foster (1975) . . . . Friday Foster
  ••• 0:29—Topless, several times, while taking a shower
    while Carl Weathers stalks around in her apartment.
  ••• 1:12—Upper half of breast, while in bubble bath
    with Blake. Topless in bed with him.
Sheba, Baby (1975) . . . . Sheba Shayne
  • 0:26—Side view of left breast, while lying in bed
    with Brick.
Drum (1976). . . . . Regine
  • 0:58—Very brief topless getting undressed and into
    bed with Maxwell.
Greased Lightning (1977) . . . . Mary Jones
Fort Apache, The Bronx (1981) . . . . Charlotte
Something Wicked this Way Comes (1983)
  . . . . Dust Witch
Tough Enough (1983) . . . . Mura
On the Edge (1985) . . . . Cora
  (Unrated version reviewed.)
    0:18—In leotards, leading an aerobics dance class.
  •• 0:42—Topless in the mirror, then full frontal nudity
    making love with Bruce Dern standing up. Then
    brief left breast. A little dark.
Stand Alone (1985) . . . . Catherine
Vindicator (1986; Canadian) . . . . Hunter
  a.k.a. Frankenstein '88
The Allnighter (1987). . . . . Sgt. MacLeish
Above the Law (1988) . . . . Delores "Jacks" Jackson
Class of 1999 (1990) . . . . Ms. Connors
Bill and Ted's Bogus Journey (1991) . . . . . . Ms. Wardroe
Magazines:
Playboy (Nov 1972) . . . . Sex in Cinema 1972
  •• 162—Topless, sitting on Thalmus Rasulala.
Playboy (Nov 1973) . . . . Sex in Cinema 1973
  ••• 154—Nude scenes from *Coffy.*
Playboy (Dec 1973) . . . . Sex Stars of 1973
  •• 205—Half of left breast.

Griffeth, Simone

Films:

Death Race 2000 (1975) . . . . Annie Smith
- • 0:32—Side view of left breast, while holding David Carradine. Dark, hard to see.
- ••• 0:56—Topless and buns getting undressed and lying on bed with Carradine.

Hot Target (1985) . . . . Christine Webber
- •• 0:09—Topless taking off top for shower, then topless and brief frontal nudity taking shower.
- ••• 0:19—Topless in bed after making love with Steve Marachuck.
- •• 0:21—Buns, getting out of bed and walking to bathroom.
- •• 0:23—Topless in bed with Marachuck again.
- • 0:34—Topless in the woods with Marachuck while cricket match goes on.

The Patriot (1986) . . . . Sean
- •• 0:46—Brief topless lying in bed, making love with Ryder.

TV:

Ladies' Man (1980-81) . . . . Gretchen
Bret Maverick (1982). . . . . Jasmine DuBois
Amanda's (1983). . . . . Arlene Cartwright

Griffith, Melanie

Daughter of actress Tippi Hedren.
Wife of actor Don Johnson.
Sister of actress Tracy Griffith.

Films:

Smile (1974) . . . . Karen Love
0:07—Brief glimpse at panties, bending over to pick up dropped box.
- • 0:34—Very, very brief side view of right breast in dressing room, just before passing behind a rack of clothes.
- • 0:47—Very brief side view of right breast, then side view of left breast when Little Bob is outside taking pictures.
- • 0:48—Very brief topless as Polaroid photograph that Little Bob took develops.
- • 1:51—Topless in the same Polaroid in the policeman's sun visor.

Night Moves (1975) . . . . .Delly Grastner
- • 0:42—Brief topless changing tops outside while talking with Gene Hackman.
- • 0:46—Nude, saying "hi" from under water beneath a glass bottom boat.
- • 0:47—Brief side view of right breast getting out of the water.

The Drowning Pool (1976) . . . . Schuuler Devereaux

Joyride (1977). . . . . .Susie
- • 0:05—Topless in back of station wagon with Robert Carradine, hard to see anything.
- •• 0:59—Brief topless in spa with everybody.
- • 1:11—Brief topless in shower with Desi Arnaz, Jr.

One on One (1977) . . . . .Hitchhiker
Roar (1981). . . . . Melanie

Body Double (1984) . . . . .Holly Body
- •• 0:20—Topless in brunette wig dancing around in bedroom while Craig Wasson watches through a telescope.
- • 0:28—Topless in bedroom again while Wasson and the Indian welding on the satellite dish watch.
- •• 1:12—Topless and buns on TV that Wasson is watching.
- •• 1:13—Topless and buns on TV after Wasson buys the video tape.
- • 1:19—Brief buns in black leather outfit in bathroom during filming of movie.
- • 1:20—Brief buns again in the black leather outfit.

Fear City (1984). . . . . .Loretta
0:04—Buns, in blue G-string, dancing on stage.
- •• 0:07—Topless, dancing on stage.
- ••• 0:23—Topless dancing on stage wearing a red G-string.

Something Wild (1986) . . . . . . "Lulu"/Audrey Hankel
- ••• 0:16—Strips to topless in bed with Jeff Daniels.
- • 0:24—Buns and brief topless, while looking out the window.

Cherry 2000 (1988) . . . . E. Johnson
0:19—Topless in a shadow on the wall while changing clothes.

The Milagro Beanfield War (1988) . . . . . . Flossie Devine

Stormy Monday (1988) . . . . .Kate
0:03—Buns and side of right breast, behind shower door. Don't see anything because of the glass.
- • 1:11—Very brief left breast, while making love in bed with Brendan.

Working Girl (1989) . . . . Tess McGill
0:08—In bra, panties, garter belt and stockings in front of a mirror.
0:32—In black bra, garter belt and stockings trying on clothes.
0:43—In black bra, garter belt and stockings getting out of bed.
1:15—In white bra, taking off her blouse with Harrison Ford.
- • 1:18—Very, very brief right breast turning over in bed with Ford.
- • 1:20—Topless, vacuuming. Long shot seen from the other end of the hall.

The Bonfire of the Vanities (1990) . . . . . . Maria Ruskin
0:24—In bra, opening her jacket while on the couch with Tom Hanks.
0:47—In black bra and panties in apartment with Hanks.

In the Spirit (1990). . . . . .Lureen
Pacific Heights (1990) . . . . Patty Parker
Paradise (1991) . . . . Lily Reed

Shining Through (1992). . . . . .Linda Voss
- •• 0:22—Topless, making love in bed on top of Michael Douglas.

Stranger Among Us (1992) . . . . .Emily Eden

Made for Cable Movies:

Women & Men: Stories of Seduction (1990; HBO)
. . . . .Hadley

Made for TV Movies:
She's in the Army Now (1981) . . . . .n.a.
TV:
Once an Eagle (1976-77) . . . . Jinny Massengale
Carter Country (1978-79) . . . . Tracy Quinn
Magazines:
Playboy (Oct 1976) . . . . Fast Starter
   •• 100-103—Nude.
Playboy (Jan 1986) . . . . Double Take
   •• 94-103—Topless and buns in photos with Don
     Johnson in photos that were taken in 1976.

Griffith, Tracy

Sister of actress Melanie Griffith.
Films:
Fear City (1984) .Sandra Cook
The Good Mother (1988) . . . . .Babe
   • 0:06—Brief topless opening her blouse to show a
     young Anna what it's like being pregnant.
Fast Food (1989). . . . . .Samantha
Sleepaway Camp III: Teenage Wasteland (1989)
. . . . Marcia Holland
The First Power (1990) . . . . .Tess Seaton

• Groff, Nancy

Films:
Deranged (1987) . . . . .Teacher
Lurkers (1987) . . . . .Rita
   • 1:07—Partial right breast in bathroom with another
     woman while Cathy talks.

Grubel, Ilona

Films:
Jonathan (1973; German) . . . . Eleanore
Target (1985) . . . . .Carla
   • 1:12—Brief topless in bed with Matt Dillon.

Guerin, Florence

Films:
Black Venus (1983). .Louise
   •• 0:45—Nude talking, then making love with Venus in
     bed.
   ••• 1:16—Nude frolicking on the beach with Venus.
   ••• 1:18—Nude in bedroom getting out of wet clothes
     with Venus.
   • 1:21—Buns in bed with Jacques and Venus.
Bizarre (1986; Italian) .Laurie
   •• 0:03—Topless on bed with Guido. Lower frontal nu-
     dity while he molests her with a pistol.
   ••• 0:18—Nude after taking off her clothes in hotel
     room with a guy. Nice.
   ••• 0:30—Full frontal nudity making love with Edward
     in the water.
   • 0:34—Brief side of right breast, taking off robe in
     bathroom with Edward. (He's made himself up to
     look like a woman.)
   ••• 0:36—Topless in white panties making love with Ed-
     ward.

   •• 0:40—Topless and brief lower frontal nudity in Gui-
     do's office with him.
   ••• 0:45—Nude, playing outside with Edward, then
     making love with his toe.
   •• 0:47—Topless getting out of bed and putting a
     blouse on.
   •• 0:49—Topless with Edward when Guido comes in.
   • 1:11—Topless sitting in chair talking to Edward.
   • 1:20—Lower frontal nudity, putting the phone
     down there.
   • 1:28—Buns and lower frontal nudity on bed when
     Guido rips her clothes off and rapes her.

Guerra, Blanca

Films:
Falcon's Gold (1982) . . . . n.a.
   a.k.a. Robbers of the Sacred Mountain
Erendira (1983; Brazilian) . . . . Ulysses' Mother
Separate Vacations (1985). . . . . Alicia
   • 0:56—Topless on the bed with David Naughton
     when she turns out to be a hooker.
Walker (1988) . . . . .Yrena
Santa Sangre (1989; Italian/Spanish) . . . . Concha
   0:34—Half of buns, in sexy circus outfit.

Guerrero, Evelyn

Films:
Wild Wheels (1969) . . . . Sissy
Trackdown (1976) . . . . .Social Worker
The Toolbox Murders (1978) . . . . .Maria
Fairytales (1979) . . . . S & M Dancer
   •• 0:38—Topless wearing masks with two other blonde
     S&M Dancers.
   •• 0:56—Full frontal nudity dancing with the other
     S&M Dancers again.
Cheech & Chong's Next Movie (1980)
. . . . Welfare Office Worker
Cheech & Chong's Nice Dreams (1981) . . . . .Donna
   • 0:43—Brief left breast sticking out of her spandex
     outfit, sitting down at table in restaurant.
   0:56—In burgundy lingerie in her apartment with
     Cheech Marin.
Things are Tough all Over (1982). . . . . .Donna
TV:
Dallas (1989-90) . . . . Nancy
Magazines:
Playboy (Sep 1980) . . . . Lights, Camera, Chaos!
   ••• 103-107—Full frontal nudity.

Guerri, Ruth

Video Tapes:
Playboy's Playmate Review 2 (1984) . . . . . Playmate
Playmates at Play (1990) . . . . . Thrill Seeker, Bareback
Magazines:
Playboy (Jul 1983) . . . . Playmate
Playboy's Book of Lingerie (Sep 1991) . . . . . .Herself
   ••• 62—Topless.

Gunden, Scarlett

Films:

Island of 1000 Delights . . . . Francine
- ••• 0:02—Topless on beach dancing with Ching. Upper half of buns sitting down.
- 0:20—Dancing braless in sheer brown dress.
- •• 0:44—Full frontal nudity getting tortured by Ming.
- • 1:16—Topless on beach after Ching rescues her.

Melody in Love (1978) . . . . Angela
- ••• 0:17—Full frontal nudity taking off dress and dancing in front of statue.
- ••• 0:50—Nude with a guy on a boat.
- •• 0:53—Topless on another boat with Octavio.
- •• 0:59—Buns and topless in bed talking to Rachel.
- •• 1:12—Full frontal nudity getting a tan on boat with Rachel.
- • 1:14—Topless making love in bed with Rachel and Octavio.

Guthrie, Lynne

Films:

Night Call Nurses (1972) . . . . .Cynthia
a.k.a. Young LA Nurses 2
- • 0:00—Topless on hospital roof taking off robe and standing on edge just before jumping off.

The Working Girls (1973) . . . . Jill
- ••• 0:43—Topless, dancing on stage at club.
- •• 0:48—Topless in swimming pool with Nick.

Tears of Happiness (1974) . . . . Lisa

Gutteridge, Lucy

Films:

Top Secret (1984) . . . . .Hillary
The Trouble with Spies (1984) . . . . Mona Smith
Tusks (1990) . . . . Micah Hill
- •• 0:23—Topless in tub taking a bath.

Made for Cable TV:

The Hitchhiker: In the Name of Love (1987; HBO)
. . . . Jackie
- •• 0:08—Topless on bed talking to herself about Billy after unzipping and opening the top of her dress.
- • 0:16—Brief right breast, while pulling down her dress top in car with Greg Evigan.
- •• 0:17—Topless making love with Evigan in bed.
- 0:20—Topless in black and white photos that accidentally fall out of envelope.

Miniseries:

Little Gloria...Happy At Last! (1982) . . . . .n.a.
Till We Meet Again (1989). . . . . Eve

Made for TV Movies:

The Woman He Loved (1988) . . . . Thelma

• Haase, Heather

Films:

The 'burbs (1989). . . . . Ricky's Girlfriend
Gremlins 2: The New Batch (1990) . . . . Yogurt Jerk

Magazines:

Playboy (Jan 1991) . . . . .Grapevine
- • 226—Half of left breast in open blouse. B&W.

Hackett, Joan

Films:

The Group (1966) . . . . Dottie Renfrew
Will Penny (1968) . . . . Catherine Allen
Support Your Local Sheriff! (1969) . . . . . . .Prudy Perkins
The Terminal Man (1974). . . . . .Dr. Janet Ross
One Trick Pony (1980) . . . . .Lonnie Fox
- ••• 1:21—Nude getting out of bed and getting dressed while talking to Paul Simon.

Flicks (1981). . . . . .Capt. Grace
Only When I Laugh (1981). . . . . Toby
The Escape Artist (1982). . . . . Aunt Sybil

Made for TV Movies:

Paper Dolls (1982) . . . . n.a.

TV:

The Defenders (1961-62) . . . . Joan Miller
Another Day (1978) . . . . .Ginny Gardner

Haddon, Dayle

Films:

Paperback Hero (1973; Canadian) . . . . .Joanna
- 0:31—Lower half of buns, under T-shirt while standing behind a bar with Keir Dullea.

The World's Greatest Athlete (1973). . . . . .Jane
Sex with a Smile (1976; Italian) . . . . The Girl
- •• 0:23—Topless, covered with bubbles in the bathtub.
- • 0:43—Buns, taking off robe to take a shower, then brief topless with Marty Feldman.

Spermula (1976) . . . . .Spermula
The Last Romantic Lover (1978) . . . . n.a.
- 0:56—Topless.

The French Woman (1979) . . . . Elizabeth
a.k.a. Madame Claude
- • 0:15—Very, very brief topless in dressing room.
- •• 0:49—Topless on bed with Madame Claude.
- • 0:55—Topless kissing Pierre, then buns while lying on the floor.
- 1:10—In two piece swimsuit on sailboat.
- • 1:11—Left breast, then buns at the beach with Frederick.

North Dallas Forty (1979). . . . . .Charlotte
Cyborg (1989) .Pearl Prophet
Silence Like Glass (1989) . . . . Darlene Meyers

Made for Cable Movies:

Bedroom Eyes (1985; Canadian; HBO). . . . . Alixe
- 1:06—Getting undressed in tap pants and white camisole top while Harry watches in the mirror.

Made for Cable TV:

The Hitchhiker: Ghost Writer (1986; HBO)
. . . . .Debby Hunt
(Available on The Hitchhiker, Volume 3.)
- 0:05—In black slip kissing Barry Bostwick.
- • 0:14—Topless and buns, getting into hot tub with Willem DaFoe before trying to drown him.

Magazines:

Playboy (Apr 1973) . . . . Disney's Latest Hit
- ••• 147-153—Nude.

Playboy (Dec 1973) . . . . .Sex Stars of 1973
- ••• 209—Topless.

Hahn, Gisela

Producer.

Films:

They Call Me Trinity (1971; Italian) . . . . Sarah

Julia (1974; German) . . . . Miriam

•• 0:12—Topless tanning herself outside.

• 1:14—Brief topless sitting in the rain.

The Manhunters (1980; French/Spanish/German). . .n.a.

Hahn, Jessica

The woman in the TV evangelist Jim Bakker scandal.

Films:

Bikini Summer II (1992) .n.a.

Made for Cable TV:

Dream On: And Bimbo Was His Name-O (1992; HBO)

. . . . Reporter

Music Videos:

Wild Thing/Sam Kinison . . . . The Girl

Magazines:

Playboy (Nov 1987) . . . . . .Jessica, On Her Own Terms

••• 90-99—Topless.

Playboy (Dec 1987). . . . . Sex Stars of 1987

••• 157—Topless.

Playboy (Feb 1988) . . . . .The Year in Sex

••• 128—Topless wearing a hat.

Playboy (Sep 1988) . . . . .Jessica

••• 118-127— Nude.

Playboy (Dec 1988). . . . . Sex Stars of 1988

••• 188—Topless.

Playboy (Jan 1989) . . . . Women of the Eighties

••• 257—Full frontal nudity.

Playboy (Feb 1989) . . . . .The Year in Sex

137—Left breast.

Playboy's Nudes (Oct 1990). . . . . Herself

••• 48-49—Full frontal nudity.

• Haiduk, Stacy

Films:

Luther the Geek (1988). . . . . .Beth

(Hard to find video tape, but worth it when you find it!)

0:24—In bra and panties after undressing to take a shower.

••• 0:26—Topless with Rob in the shower. Wow!

••• 0:28—Topless taking off her robe in bed, then making love with Rob.

Steel and Lace (1990) . . . . Alison

Made for Cable Movies:

Sketch Artist (1992; Showtime). . . . . Claire

TV:

Superboy (1988-91) . . . . .Lana Lang

The Round Table (1992-) . . . . .Rhea McPherson

Hajek, Gwendolyn

Films:

Traxx (1988). . . . . Playmate

Magazines:

Playboy (Sep 1987) . . . . Playmate

Playboy's Book of Lingerie (Mar 1991) . . . . . Herself

••• 106-107—Full frontal nudity.

• Hall, Jerry

Former model.

Significant Other of singer/actor Mick Jagger.

Films:

Urban Cowboy (1980). . . . . n.a.

Willie and Phil (1980). . . . . .Karen

• 0:05—Brief topless getting dressed in bedroom with Phil.

Running Out of Luck (1986). . . . . .Herself

Batman (1989). . . . . .Alicia

Freejack (1992) . . . . Newswoman

• Hall, Leana

Films:

Witchcraft III: The Kiss of Death (1991) . . . . . Roxy

•• 1:08—Topless on bed with William making love when Charlotte gets trapped in the room.

Made for Cable Movies:

Red Shoe Diaries (1992; Showtime) . . . . Ingrid

Hallier, Lori

Films:

My Bloody Valentine (1981; Canadian) . . . . n.a.

Warning Sign (1985) . . . . Reporter

Higher Education (1987; Canadian) . . . Nicole Hubert

• 0:44—Right breast, twice, while making love with Andy in bed.

Blindside (1988; Canadian) . . . . .Julie

Made for TV Movies:

A Woman Scorned: The Betty Broderick Story (1992)

. . . . .Joan

Halligan, Erin

Films:

I'm Dancing as Fast as I Can (1981) . . . . .Denise

Joysticks (1983) . . . . Sandy

•• 1:08—Right breast, then topless in bed with Jefferson surrounded by candles.

• Halsey, Elizabeth

Films:

Cinderella (1977). . . . . .Farm Girl (brunette)

••• 0:21—Nude with her redhead sister in their house making love with the guy who is looking for Cinderella.

•• 1:24—Topless with her sister again when the Prince goes around to try and find Cinderella.

Cheerleaders Wild Weekend (1985). . . Susan/Pierce

••• 0:40—Topless in red panties, in contest.

••• 0:41—Topless with the other five girls during contest.

••• 0:43—Topless during getting measured with the other two girls.

Hamilton, Jane

a.k.a. Adult film actress Veronica Hart.

Films:

Deathmask (1983) . . . . .Victoria Howe

Delivery Boys (1984) . . . . Art Snob

R.S.V.P. (1984)............... Mrs. Ellen Edwards
Sex Appeal (1986) ....Monica
••• 0:58—Topless dancing on the bed with Tony in his apartment. Long scene.
Sexpot (1986)........................... Beth
••• 0:28—In bra, then topless with her two sisters when their bras pop off. (She's on the right.)
• 1:32—Topless during outtakes of 0:28 scene.
Deranged (1987) .... Joyce
• 0:29—Buns, getting undressed to take a shower. Side of left breast.
• 0:37—Side view of left breast, taking off towel and putting blouse on. Long shot.
• 1:01—Topless, changing blouses in her bedroom.
• 1:05—Topless in bedroom, taking off her blouse with Jamie Gillis.
• 1:07—Topless in bed when Jennifer wakes her up.
If Looks Could Kill (1987) ....Mary Beth
Slammer Girls (1987) .... Miss Crabapples
Student Affairs (1987) .... Veronica
•• 0:48—Topless changing in dressing room, showing herself off to a guy.
• 0:51—Brief topless in a school room during a movie.
•• 0:56—In black lingerie outfit, then topless in bedroom while she tape records everything.
Wildest Dreams (1987) .... Ruth Delaney
Wimps (1987)........................ Tracy
• 0:40—Lifting up her sweater and shaking her breasts in the back of the car with Francis. Too dark to see anything.
•• 0:44—Topless and buns taking off sweater in a restaurant.
Young Nurses In Love (1987) .... Franchesca
•• 1:05—Topless on top of a guy on a gurney.
New York's Finest (1988)....................Bunny
Sensations (1988) .... Tippy
Bedroom Eyes II (1989) ....JoBeth McKenna
• 0:50—Topless knifing Linda Blair, then fighting with Wings Hauser.
Bloodsucking Pharaohs from Pittsburgh (1989)... Grace
Cleo/Leo (1989) .... Cleo Clock
•• 0:13—Nude undressing in front of three guys.
• 0:21—Topless changing in dressing room.
••• 0:22—Topless changing in dressing room with the Store Clerk.
0:40—In bra and panties.
•• 1:07—Left breast and lower frontal nudity making love with Bob on bed.
Enrapture (1989)........................ Annie
Ruby (1992) .... Telephone Trixie

Hamilton, Linda

Has an identical twin sister.
Films:
T.A.G.: The Assassination Game (1982)... Susan Swayze
Children of the Corn (1984) .... Vicky Baxter
The Terminator (1984) .... Sarah Connor
•• 1:18—Brief topless about four times making love on top of Michael Biehn in motel room.

Black Moon Rising (1986) .... Nina
• 0:50—Brief left breast, while making love in bed with Tommy Lee Jones.
King Kong Lives! (1986)............. Amy Franklin
• 0:47—Very, very brief right breast getting out of sleeping bag after camping out near King Kong.
Mr. Destiny (1990)...................Ellen Burrows
Terminator 2: Judgement Day (1991).... Sarah Connor
Made for TV Movies:
Rape and Marriage: The Rideout Case (1980)...... n.a.
Secrets of a Mother and Daughter (1983) .... n.a.
Secret Weapons (1985) .... n.a.
Club Med (1986)..........................Kate
Go Toward the Light (1988)......... Claire Madison
TV:
Secrets of Midland Heights (1980-81) ......Lisa Rogers
King's Crossing (1982)............. Lauren Hollister
Beauty and the Beast (1987-90).... Catherine Chandler

Hamilton, Suzanna

Films:
Tess (1979; French/British)..................... Izz
Brimstone and Treacle (1982; British)
.... Patricia Bates
•• 0:47—Topless in bed when Sting opens her blouse and fondles her.
•• 1:18—Topless in bed when Sting fondles her again.
• 1:20—Brief lower frontal nudity writhing around on the bed after Denholm Elliott comes downstairs.
1984 (1984) .... Julia
•• 0:38—Full frontal nudity taking off her clothes in the woods with John Hurt.
••• 0:52—Nude in secret room standing and drinking and talking to Hurt. Long scene.
• 1:11—Side view of left breast kneeling down.
•• 1:12—Topless after picture falls off the view screen on the wall.
Out of Africa (1985)....................... Felicity
Wetherby (1985; British) .... Karen Creasy
0:42—In white lingerie top and bottom.
1:03—In white lingerie getting into bed and lying down.
1:06—In white lingerie, fighting with John.

• Hamilton, Wendy

Video Tapes:
Playboy Video Calendar 1993 (1992)......October
Playboy Video Centerfold: Pamela Anderson (1992) .... Playmate
••• 0:26—Nude throughout.
Playboy's Playmate Review 1992 (1992)
.... Miss December
••• 0:44—Nude in a house and then dancing next to a car.
Sexy Lingerie IV (1992) .... Model
Wet and Wild IV (1992) .... Model
Magazines:
Playboy (Dec 1991) .... Playmate
••• 130-141—Nude.

Playboy's Career Girls (Aug 1992)

.... Baywatch Playmates

••• 9—Topless.

Hammond, Barbara

Films:

Angel III: The Final Chapter (1988) . . . Video Girl #2
- 0:34—Topless (on the right) on video monitor during audition tape talking with her roommate.

Vampire at Midnight (1988) . . . . Kelly
- • 0:07—Topless and buns, getting out of the shower and drying herself off.
- 0:16—Left breast, dead, in Victor's car trunk. Blood on her.

Hannah, Daryl

Films:

The Final Terror (1981) . . . . Wendy
Blade Runner (1982) . . . . Pris
Summer Lovers (1982) . . . . .Cathy Featherstone
- 0:07—Very brief topless getting out of bed.
  0:17—In a two piece swimsuit.
  0:54—Buns, lying on rock with Valerie Quennessen watching Michael dive off a rock.
  0:56—In a swimsuit again.
- 1:03—Brief right breast sweeping the balcony.

The Pope of Greenwich Village (1984) . . . . Diane
Reckless (1984). . . . . Tracey Prescott
  0:48—In a white bra fighting in gymnasium with Johnny then in pool area in bra and panties.
- ••• 0:52—Topless in furnace room of school making love with Johnny. Lit with red light.

Splash (1984) . . . . Madison
- • 0:27—Brief right breast, swimming under water, entering the sunken ship.
- • 0:28—Buns, walking around the Statue of Liberty.
- • 1:26—Brief right, then left breast in tank when Eugene Levy looks at her.
- • 1:44—Brief right breast, under water when frogman grabs her from behind.

Clan of the Cave Bear (1985) . . . . Ayla
Legal Eagles (1986). . . . . Chelsea Deardon
Roxanne (1987) . . . . .Roxanne Kowalski
Wall Street (1987). . . . . Darian Taylor
High Spirits (1988) . . . . .Mary Plunkett
Steel Magnolias (1989) . . . . Annelle Dupuy Desoto
Crazy People (1990) . . . . Kathy
At Play in the Fields of the Lord (1991)

. . . . Andy Huben
  2:09—(0:39 into tape 2) Brief buns, swimming in water.
- ••• 2:10—(0:40 into tape 2) Buns, getting out and resting by tree. Long shot, then excellent closer shot. Very brief top of lower frontal nudity. (Skip tape 1 and fast forward to this!)
- •• 2:11—(0:41 into tape 2) Brief buns, running away after kissing Tom Berenger.

Memoirs of an Invisible Man (1992) . . . . . Alice Monroe

Made for TV Movies:
Paper Dolls (1982) . . . . Taryn Blake
Magazines:
Playboy (Nov 1992) . . . . Sex in Cinema 1992
••• 147—Topless while lying against a tree from *At Play in the Fields of the Lord*.

• Hansen, Tammy

Films:

In the Cold of the Night (1989) . . . . .Model 2
Another You (1991) . . . . .Hatcheck Girl
Boys N the Hood (1991) . . . . Rosa
Video Tapes:
Dream Babies (1989) .Herself
Magazines:
Playboy's Book of Lingerie (Jan 1991) . . . . . .Herself
••• 67—Topless.
Playboy's Book of Lingerie (Mar 1991). . . . .Herself
••• 19—Topless.
Playboy's Book of Lingerie (Jan 1992) . . . . . .Herself
••• 58—Topless.
Playboy's Book of Lingerie (Mar 1992). . . . .Herself
••• 47—Full frontal nudity.
Playboy's Book of Lingerie (Sep 1992) . . . . .Herself
•• 28—Right breast.

Harden, Marcia Gay

Films:

Miller's Crossing (1990) . . . . .Verna
Late for Dinner (1991) . . . . Joy Husband
Made for Cable Movies:
Fever (1991; HBO) . . . . .Lacy
- 0:18—Brief topless making love in bed with Sam Neill.
- •• 1:31—In bra in bed with bad guy, then topless when he opens her bra. Kind of dark.

Hargitay, Mariska

Daughter of the late actress Jayne Mansfield and Mickey Hargitay.
Films:
Jocks (1986). . . . . Nicole
Welcome to 18 (1986) . . . . .Joey
- 0:26—Buns, taking a shower when video camera is taping her.
  0:43—Watching herself on the videotape playback.
The Perfect Weapon (1991) . . . . Jennifer
TV:
Falcon Crest (1988) . . . . Carly Fixx
Tequila and Bonetti (1992). . . . . Garcia

• Harney, Corinna

Video Tapes:
Wet and Wild III (1991) . . . . Model
Playboy Video Calendar 1993 (1992). . . . . . . .June
Playboy Video Centerfold: Corrina Harney (1992)
. . . . .Playmate of the Year 1992

Playboy's Playmate Review 1992 (1992)
.... Miss August
••• 0:48—Nude posing in a house and then outside.
Sexy Lingerie IV (1992) ....Model
Wet and Wild IV (1992) ....Model
Magazines:
Playboy (Aug 1991) .... Playmate
Playboy (Jun 1992) ....Playmate of the Year
••• 126-135—Nude.
Playboy's Book of Lingerie (Sep 1992) ..... Herself
••• 13-15—Full frontal nudity.

Harper, Jessica
Films:
Phantom of the Paradise (1974) .... Phoenix
Love and Death (1975)................... Natasha
Inserts (1976) ....Cathy Cake
••• 1:15—Topless in garter belt and stockings, lying in bed for Richard Dreyfuss. Long scene.
Suspiria (1977; Italian) ....Susy Banyon
The Evictors (1979)...................... Ruth
Stardust Memories (1980)................Violinist
Pennies from Heaven (1981) .... Joan
• 0:43—Brief topless opening her nightgown for Steve Martin.
Shock Treatment (1981) .... Janet Majors
My Favorite Year (1982) .............K.C. Downing
The Imagemaker (1985) ....Cynthia
The Blue Iguana (1988)...................... Cora
Big Man on Campus (1991) .... Dr. Fisk
Made for Cable TV:
Tales From the Crypt: My Brother's Keeper
.... Marie Hilton
TV:
Aspen (1977) .... Kit Pepe
Studs Lonigan (1979) .... Loretta
Little Women (1979)...................Jo March

Harrell, Georgia
Films:
Incoming Freshman (1979).............. Student
The First Turn-On! (1983) .... Michelle Farmer
••• 1:17—Topless and brief buns in cave with everybody during orgy scene.
The Gig (1985) .... The Blonde

Harrington, Tabitha
Films:
Crossover (1980; Canadian) .... Montgomery
a.k.a. Mr. Patman
• 0:11—Brief right breast, then brief full frontal nudity lying in bed, then struggling with James Coburn in her room. Wearing white makeup on her face.
•• 0:29—Nude walking in to room to talk with Coburn, then topless and brief buns leaving.
Star 80 (1983)....................... Blonde

Harris, Gail
See: Thackray, Gail.

• Harris, Jo Ann
Films:
Mary Jane (1968)........................Jo Ann
The Gay Decievers (1969) ....Leslie Devlin
The Beguiled (1971) .... Carol
The Sporting Club (1971) .... Lu
The Deadly Games (1980) .... Keegan
• 0:48—Topless in the shower. Hard to see because of the pattern on the glass.
Miniseries:
Rich Man, Poor Man (1976)...........Gloria Bartley
TV:
Most Wanted (1976-77)........Officer Kate Manners
Detective School (1979).............. Teresa Cleary

Harris, Lee Anne
Identical twin sister of actress Lynette Harris.
a.k.a. Leigh Harris.
Films:
I, the Jury (1982)...................... 1st twin
••• 0:48—Topless on bed talking to Armand Assante.
• 0:52—Full frontal nudity on bed wearing red wig, talking to the maniac.
Sorceress (1982) .... Mira
••• 0:11—Topless (on the left) greeting the creature with her sister. Upper half of buns, getting dressed.
•• 0:29—Topless (she's the second one) undressing with her sister in front of Erlick and Baldar.
Magazines:
Playboy (Mar 1981) .... My Sister, My Self
••• 152-155—Topless and buns.
Playboy (Mar 1982) .... Aye, Barbara
• 152—Topless in small photos from *I, the Jury*.
Playboy's Nudes (Oct 1990) ....Herself
••• 36—Full frontal nudity.

Harris, Lynette
Identical twin sister of actress Leigh Harris.
Films:
I, the Jury (1982) .... 2nd twin
••• 0:48—Topless on bed talking to Armand Assante.
• 0:52—Full frontal nudity on bed wearing red wig, talking to the maniac.
Sorceress (1982) .... Mara
••• 0:11—Topless (on the right) greeting the creature with her sister.
••• 0:29—Topless (she's the first one) undressing with her sister in front of Erlick and Baldar.
Magazines:
Playboy (Mar 1981) .... My Sister, My Self
••• 152-155—Topless and buns.
Playboy (Mar 1982) .... Aye, Barbara
• 152—Topless in small photos from *I, the Jury*.
Playboy's Nudes (Oct 1990) ....Herself
••• 36—Full frontal nudity.

Harris, Moira

Films:

The Fanatasist (1986; Irish) . . . . Patricia Teeling
- 1:24—Brief topless and buns climbing onto couch for the weird photographer.
- 1:28—Brief right breast leaning over to kiss the photographer.
- 1:31—Very brief side view of left breast in bathtub.

One More Saturday Night (1986) . . . . .Peggy

Harris, Robyn

See: Thackray, Gail.

• Harrison, Cathryn

Films:

Images (1972; Irish) . . . . Susannah
The Pied Piper (1972; British)
. . . . Burgermeister's Daughter, Lisa
Black Moon (1975; French) . . . . Lily
The Dresser (1983) . . . . .Irene
Duet for One (1987) . . . . .Penny Smallwood
Empire State (1987; British) . . . . Marion
A Handful of Dust (1988) . . . . .Milly

Made for TV Movies:

Portrait of a Marriage (1992; British)
. . . . Violet Trefusis
- 0:48—Left breast when Vita admires her.

Harrison, Jenilee

Films:

Tank (1984) . . . . Sarah
Curse III: Bloody Sacrifice (1990)
. . . . Elizabeth Armstrong
••• 0:43—Topless sitting in bathtub. Almost side of right breast when wrapping a towel around herself.
Illicit Behavior (1991) . . . . .Charlene Lernoux
Prime Target (1991) . . . . Kathy Bloodstone
••• 0:12—Topless, lying back in bed with David Heavener. Short, but sweet!
- 0:13—Partial right breast, under Heavener's arm.

TV:

Three's Company (1980-82) . . . . Cindy Snow
Dallas (1984-86) . . . . .Jamie Ewing Barnes

Harrold, Kathryn

Films:

Nightwing (1979) . . . . Anne Dillon
The Hunter (1980) . . . . Dotty
Modern Romance (1981) . . . . Mary Harvard
- 0:46—Very brief topless taking off robe and getting into bed with Albert Brooks.
1:05—In pink lingerie opening her blouse to undo her skirt while talking to Brooks.
Pursuit of D.B. Cooper (1981) . . . . Hannah
The Sender (1982) . . . . .Gail Farmer
Yes, Giorgio (1982) . . . . .Pamela Taylor
Heartbreakers (1984) . . . . Cyd
0:02—In black bra and panties changing clothes in Peter Coyote's studio.

Into the Night (1985) . . . . Christie
Raw Deal (1986) . . . . Monique

Made for Cable Movies:

Best Legs in the 8th Grade (1984; HBO) . . . . n.a.
Dead Solid Perfect (1988; HBO) . . . . .Beverly T. Lee
Rainbow Drive (1990; Showtime) . . . . Christine
Deadly Desire (1991; USA) . . . . n.a.

Made for TV Movies:

Man Against the Mob (1988) . . . . Marilyn Butler

TV:

MacGruder & Loud (1985) . . . . . Jenny Loud McGruder
Bronx Zoo (1987-88) . . . . Sara Newhouse
Capital News (1990) . . . . Mary Ward
I'll Fly Away (1991-) . . . . .Christina LeKatzis

Harry, Deborah

Lead singer of the rock group *Blondie*.

Films:

Union City (1980) .Lillian
Videodrome (1983; Canadian) . . . . Nicki Brand
•• 0:16—Topless rolling over on the floor when James Woods is piercing her ear with a pin.
0:22—In black bra, sitting on couch with James Woods.
Forever Lulu (1987) .Lulu
Hairspray (1988) . . . . Velma
Satisfaction (1988) .Tina
Shown on TV as "Girls of Summer."
Tales From the Darkside, The Movie (1990) . . . . . . Betty

Made for Cable Movies:

Intimate Strangers (1991; Showtime) . . . . .Cory Wheeler

• Hart, Christina

Films:

Red Sky at Morning (1971) . . . . Velva Mae Cloyd
The Roommates (1973) . . . . Paula
Games Girls Play (1974; British) . . . . . . Bunny O'Hara
a.k.a. The Bunny Caper
- 0:00—Brief lower frontal nudity and buns when her dress blows up from the wind.
•• 0:01—Full frontal nudity in slow motion, jumping into bed. Then nude, twirling around in another room.
••• 0:18—Nude, undressing with the other girls, then walking around the house to the pool, then swimming nude.
- 1:01—Brief topless getting dressed.
Charley Varrick (1975) . . . . .Jana
Mean Dog Blues (1978) . . . . Gloria
The Check is in the Mail (1986) . . . . Janet

Hart, La Gena

Films:

Million Dollar Mystery (1987) . . . . Hope
Born to Race (1988) .Jenny

Made for Cable TV:

The Hitchhiker: The Last Scene . . . . Leda
(Available on *The Hitchhiker, Volume 2*.)
•• 0:01—Topless making love with a guy in bed.

Hart, Roxanne

Films:
The Bell Jar (1979) . . . . n.a.
The Verdict (1982) . . . . Sally Doneghy
Oh God, You Devill (1984) . . . . Wendy Shelton
Old Enough (1984). . . . . .Carla
The Tender Age (1984) . . . . Sara
    1:01—In bed in a camisole and tap pants talking to
    John Savage.
Highlander (1986) . . . . Brenda Wyatt
    • 1:30—Brief topless making love with Christopher
    Lambert. Dark, hard to see.
The Pulse (1988). . . . . .Ellen
Once Around (1990). . . . . Gail Bella
Made for Cable Movies:
The Last Innocent Man (1987; HBO) . . . . .n.a.
    ••• 1:06—Topless in bed making love, then sitting up
    and arguing with Ed Harris in his apartment.
Made for TV Movies:
Samaritan: The Mitch Snyder Story (1986) . . . . .n.a.

Hart, Veronica

See: Hamilton, Jane.

Hartman Black, Lisa

Wife of Country music singer Clint Black.
Films:
Deadly Blessing (1981) . . . . .Faith
    1:31—It looks like brief left breast after getting hit
    with a rock by Maren Jensen, but it's a special-effect
    appliance over her breasts because she's supposed
    to be a male in the film.
Where the Boys Are '84 (1984) . . . . .Jennie
Made for Cable Movies:
Bodily Harm (1989). . . . . Laura
Bare Essentials (1991) . . . . Sydney Wayne
Made for TV Movies:
Just Tell Me You Love Me (1978) . . . . .n.a.
Full Exposure: The Sex Tapes (1989) . . . . . Sarah Dutton
TV:
Tabitha (1977-78). . . . . Tabitha Stephens
Knots Landing (1982-83) . . . . Ciji Dunne
Knots Landing (1983-86) . . . . Cathy Geary
High Performance (1983) . . . . Kate Flannery
2000 Malibu Road (1992). . . . . Jade

Hassett, Marilyn

Films:
The Other Side of the Mountain (1975) . . . .Jill Kinmont
Two-Minute Warning (1976). . . . . Lucy
The Other Side of the Mountain, Part II (1978)
. . . . .Jill Kinmont
The Bell Jar (1979) . . . . Esther Greenwood
    • 0:10—In bra, then brief topless in bed with Buddy.
    Dark, hard to see.
    •• 1:09—Topless taking off her clothes and throwing
    them out the window while yelling.
Massive Retaliation (1984) . . . . Louis Fredericks
Messenger of Death (1988). . . . . .Josephine

Twenty Dollar Star (1991) . . . . n.a.
Made for Cable TV:
The Hitchhiker: Man of Her Dreams . . . . . . Jill McGinnis
Video Tapes:
Inside Out 3 (1992) . . . . Cindy/The Houseguest

Hawn, Goldie

Significant Other of actor Kurt Russell.
Films:
The One and Only, Genuine, Original Family Band
  (1967) . . . . .Giggly Girl
Cactus Flower (1969) . . . . Toni Simmons
There's a Girl in My Soup (1970) . . . . Marion
    • 0:37—Buns and very brief right side view of her
    body getting out of bed and walking to a closet to
    get a robe. Long shot.
Butterflies Are Free (1972) . . . . Jill
Dollars (1972) . . . . Dawn Divine
The Girl from Petrovka (1974) . . . . Oktyabrina
    1:30—Very, very brief topless in bed with Hal Hol-
    brook. Don't really see anything—it lasts for about
    one frame.
The Sugarland Express (1974) . . . . Lou Jean Poplin
Shampoo (1975) . . . . Jill
The Duchess and the Dirtwater Fox (1976)
. . . . Amanda Quaid
Foul Play (1978). . . . . Gloria Mundy
Lovers and Liars (1979) . . . . Anita
Private Benjamin (1980). . . . . Judy Benjamin
Seems Like Old Times (1980) . . . . Glenda
Best Friends (1982) . . . . Paula McCullen
    • 0:18—Very, very brief side view of right breast get-
    ting into the shower with Burt Reynolds.
    • 1:14—Upper half of left breast in the shower, twice.
Protocol (1984) . . . . Sunny
Swing Shift (1984) . . . . Kay Walsh
Wildcats (1986). . . . . .Molly
    • 0:30—Brief topless in bathtub.
Overboard (1987) . . . . Joanna Slayton/Annie
    0:07—Buns, wearing a revealing swimsuit that
    shows most of her derriere to Kurt Russell.
Bird on a Wire (1990). . . . . Marianne Graves
    • 0:31—Buns, in open dress climbing up ladder with
    Mel Gibson.
    • 1:18—Very brief top of right breast rolling over on
    top of Gibson in bed. Don't see her face.
Deceived (1991) . . . . .Adrienne Saunders
Criss Cross (1992) . . . . n.a.
Death Becomes Her (1992) . . . . .Helen Sharp
Housesitter (1992) . . . . n.a.
TV:
Good Morning, World (1967-68). . . . . . . Sandy Kramer
Rowan And Martin's Laugh-In (1968-70) . . . . . . Regular

Hay, Alexandra

Films:
Guess Who's Coming to Dinner? (1967) . . . . . .Car Hop
How Sweet It Is (1968). . . . . Gloria
Skidoo (1968) . . . . Darlene Banks

The Model Shop (1969) . . . . Gloria
1,000 Convicts and a Woman (1971; British)
. . . . Angela Thorne
The Love Machine (1971) . . . . .Tina St. Claire
  • 0:34—Brief topless in bed with Robin.
  • 0:38—Brief topless coming around the corner putting blue bathrobe on.
How to Seduce a Woman (1973) . . . . .Nell Brinkman
  • 1:05—Brief right breast in mirror taking off black dress.
  ••• 1:06—Topless posing for pictures. Long scene.
  • 1:47—Topless during flashback. Lots of diffusion.
How Come Nobody's on our Side? (1976) . . . . . Brigitte
One Man Jury (1978) . . . . Tessie
Magazines:
  Playboy (Feb 1974) . . . . Alexandra the Great
  ••• 81-87—Topless and side view of buns.
  Playboy (Nov 1974) . . . . Sex in Cinema 1974
  •• 151—Topless from *How to Seduce a Woman*.

Hayden, Jane
Films:
Confessions of a Pop Performer (1975; British) . . . . .n.a.
Emily (1976; British). . . . . Rachel
  •• 1:09—Topless in bed with Billy.

Hayden, Linda
Films:
Baby Love (1969) . . . . Luci
  0:32—Buns, standing in room when Nick sneaks in.
  0:34—Very brief right breast, white throwing doll at Robert.
  • 0:39—Topless in mirror taking a bath. Long shot. Brief left breast hidden by steam.
  • 0:52—Brief topless taking off her top to show Nick while sunbathing.
  1:25—Brief topless calling Robert from window. Long shot.
  1:27—Very brief topless sitting up while talking to Robert.
  • 1:28—Topless in open robe struggling with Robert.
Blood on Satan's Claw (1971; British). . . . . . . Angel
Confessions of a Window Cleaner (1974; British)
. . . . .Elizabeth
The House on Straw Hill (1976; British)
. . . . Linda Hindstatt
a.k.a. Exposé
  • 0:28—Topless getting undressed in her room.
  ••• 0:47—Topless, masturbating in bed.
  •• 1:06—Right breast, in bed with Fiona Richmond.
The Boys From Brazil (1978) . . . . .Nancy

• Hayes, Julia
Video Tapes:
  Soft Bodies: Party Favors (1992) . . . . Herself
  ••• 0:22—Buns in sheer nightie, while posing on bed, then topless during photo session.
  ••• 0:29—In bra and panties on couch, then topless and buns.

  ••• 0:35—Topless and buns, on floating bed in pool with Becky LeBeau.
Magazines:
  Penthouse (Oct 1991) . . . . Northern Exposure
  ••• 104-115—Nude.

• Hayland, Lysa
Films:
Novel Desires (1991) . . . . .Linda
Made for Cable TV:
  Dream On: Here Comes the Bribe (1992; HBO)
. . . . .Amanda
  •• 0:01—Topless on the floor, making love with Martin.

Haynes, Linda
Films:
The Drowning Pool (1976). . . . . .Gretchen
Rolling Thunder (1977) . . . . .Linda Forchet
Brubaker (1980) . . . . Carol
  • 1:03—Topless getting dressed with Huey in bedroom when Robert Redford comes in.
Human Experiments (1980) . . . . Rachel Foster

Hayward, Rachel
Films:
Breaking All the Rules (1985; Canadian). . . . .Angie
  ••• 0:16—Topless changing in the bathroom.
  • 0:43—Brief topless after being felt up on roller coaster.
Xtro 2, The Second Encounter (1991) . . . . . .Dr. Myers

Heasley, Marla
Films:
Born to Race (1988) . . . . Andrea Lombardo
  • 0:52—Buns, outside at night while kissing Joseph Bottoms.
The Marrying Man (1991) . . . . Sheila
a.k.a. Too Hot to Handle

Heatherton, Joey
Singer.
Films:
  Bluebeard (1972). . . . . Anne
  • 0:25—Topless under black see-through nightie while Richard Burton photographs her. Very brief right breast.
  ••• 1:46—Brief topless opening her dress top to taunt Richard Burton.
The Happy Hooker Goes to Washington (1977)
. . . . Xaviera Hollander
Cry Baby (1990). . . . . .Milton's Mother
TV:
Dean Martin Presents the Golddiggers (1968) . . Regular
Joey & Dad (1975). . . . . .Co-Host
Magazines:
  Playboy (Dec 1972) . . . . .Sex Stars of 1972
  •• 214—Topless.

• Helgenberger, Marg

Films:
After Midnight (1989). . . . . Alex
Always (1989). . . . . Rachel
Blind Vengeance (1990) . . . . Virginia Whitelaw
Crooked Hearts (1991) . . . . Jennetta
Made for Cable Movies:
Death Dreams (1991; Lifetime). . . . . . . .Crista Westfield
Made for Cable TV:
Tales From the Crypt: Deadline (1991). . . . . . . Vicki
   • 0:08—Brief side of right breast putting on halter top
    in Richard Jordan's apartment. Don't see her face,
    but it looks like her.
Made for TV Movies:
In Sickness and in Health (1992). . . . . .n.a.
TV:
Shell Game (1987) . . . . Natalie Thayer
China Beach (1988-91)
   . . . . Karen Charlene "K.C." Koloski

Helmcamp, Charlotte J.

a.k.a. Charlotte Kemp.
Films:
Posed for Murder (1988) . . . . Laura Shea
   • 0:00—Topless in photos during opening credits.
   ••• 0:22—Posing for photos in sheer green teddy, then
    topless in sailor's cap, then great topless shots wear-
    ing just a G-string.
   0:31—Very brief right breast in photo on desk.
   0:44—In black one piece swimsuit.
   ••• 0:52—Topless in bed making love with her boy-
    friend.
Frankenhooker (1990). . . . . .Honey
   •• 0:26—Topless yanking down her top outside of Jef-
    frey's car window.
Repossessed (1990). . . . . .Incredible Girl
Video Tapes:
Playboy Video Magazine, Volume 3 . . . . . Playmate
Playboy Video Magazine, Volume 5 (1983)
   . . . . Playmate
   • 0:05—Brief nude in bubble bath.
Playboy's Playmate Review 3 (1985). . . . . Playmate
Magazines:
Playboy (Dec 1982). . . . . Playmate

Hemingway, Margaux

Model.
Sister of actress Mariel Hemingway.
Granddaughter of writer Ernest Hemingway.
Films:
Lipstick (1976) . . . . Chris McCormick
   •• 0:10—Brief topless opening the shower door to an-
    swer the telephone.
   •• 0:19—Brief topless during rape attempt, including
    close-up of side view of left breast.
   0:24—Buns, lying on bed while rapist runs a knife up
    her leg and back while she's tied to the bed.
   •• 0:25—Brief topless getting out of bed.
Killer Fish (1979; Italian/Brazilian) . . . . .Gabrielle

They Call Me Bruce? (1982). . . . . Karmen
Over the Brooklyn Bridge (1983) . . . . Elizabeth
Inner Sanctum (1991). . . . . .Anna Rawlins
   • 0:09—Brief buns and tip of left breast in office with
    Joseph Bottoms.
   ••• 0:23—In bra with Bottoms, then topless, while in
    bed. (When you don't see her face, it's Michelle Bau-
    er doing the body double work.)
Magazines:
Playboy (May 1990). . . . . Papa's Girl
   ••• 126-135—Nude.
Playboy's Nudes (Oct 1990) . . . . Herself
   •• 34-35—Right breast.
Playboy (Dec 1990) . . . . .Sex Stars of 1990
   •• 175—Left breast, lying in bed.

Hemingway, Mariel

Younger sister of actress Margaux Hemingway.
Granddaughter of writer Ernest Hemingway.
Films:
Lipstick (1976) . . . . Kathy McCormick
Manhattan (1979) . . . . Tracy
Personal Best (1982). . . . . Chris Cahill
   (Before breast enlargement.)
   •• 0:16—Brief lower frontal nudity getting examined
    by Patrice Donnelly, then topless after making love
    with her.
   •• 0:30—Topless in the steam room talking with the
    other women.
Star 80 (1983) . . . . Dorothy Stratten
   (After breast enlargement.)
   •• 0:00—Topless in still photos during opening credits.
   • 0:02—Topless lying on bed in Paul's flashbacks.
   ••• 0:22—Topless during Polaroid photo session with
    Paul
   • 0:25—Topless during professional photography ses-
    sion. Long shot.
   • 0:36—Brief topless during photo session.
   • 0:57—Right breast, in centerfold photo on wall.
   • 1:04—Upper half of breasts, in bathtub.
   • 1:05—Brief topless in photo shoot flashback.
   • 1:17—Brief topless during layout flashbacks.
   • 1:20—Very brief topless in photos on the wall.
   •• 1:33—Topless undressing before getting killed by
    Paul. More brief topless layout flashbacks.
Creator (1985) . . . . .Meli
   0:38—Brief topless cooling herself off by pulling up
    T-shirt in front of a fan.
   • 1:10—Brief topless flashing David Ogden Stiers dur-
    ing football game to distract him.
The Mean Season (1985) . . . . Christine Connelly
   •• 0:15—Topless taking a shower.
Superman IV: The Quest for Peace (1987)
   . . . . Lacy Warfield
Suicide Club (1988) . . . . Sasha Michaels
Sunset (1988) . . . . Cheryl King
Delirious (1991) .Janet/Louise
Into the Badlands (1991) . . . . Alma
Falling From Grace (1992) . . . . n.a.

Made for Cable Movies:
Steal the Sky (1988; HBO)............. Helen Mason
Topless, but too dark to see anything.
Made for Cable TV:
Tales From the Crypt: Loved to Death (1991; HBO)
.................................Miranda Singer
  0:03—In black lingerie. Very brief buns.
•• 0:07—In bra, then side view of left breast several
  times in laundry room while Andrew McCarthy secretly watches.
  0:18—In red lingerie in bedroom with McCarthy.
  0:21—More buns in lingerie.
TV:
Civil Wars (1991-) .... Sydney Guilford
On the 9/30/92 episode, she had well-hyped "nude"
scene on network TV. You get to see very brief upper
half of buns between gaps in some plastic and side view
buns, while standing during photo shoot. Side view of
buns later when looking at B&W photos. Forget the
teasing and watch *Star 80.*
Magazines:
Playboy (Apr 1982) .... Personal Best
• 104-109—Topless in stills from the film, buns doing
  the splits.
Playboy (Jan 1984) .... Star 80
Playboy (Jan 1989) .... Women of the Eighties
••• 248—Topless.
Playboy's Nudes (Oct 1990).............. Herself
•• 35—Buns and left breast.

• Hempel, Anouska

Films:
Tiffany Jones .... Tiffany Jones
• 0:02—Brief topless walking in from the surf in wet
  white dress.
•• 0:13—Topless in bath. Buns also, getting out.
• 0:18—Brief left breast, taking off her top in front of
  bright light.
• 0:23—Topless, several times, changing clothes in
  her bedroom.
•• 0:24—Topless walking around her apartment in
  white panties.
• 0:31—Topless in bubble bath.
• 0:32—Brief left breast, wrapping an orange towel
  around herself.
••• 0:39—Lying on table in black and red bra, then topless. More right breast.
• 0:41—Side view topless, covered with sweat.
•• 0:55—Topless, partial lower frontal nudity, taking a
  shower.
• 1:26—Topless, running outside in a field when guys
  rip off her dress.
Sweet Suzy (1973) .... Lady Susan
TV:
UFO (1970)............... SHADO Radio Operator

• Hendrix, Lori Jo

Films:
Bikini Summer (1991) ....Smart Girl on Beach
Sunset Strip (1992) .... Tammy
•• 0:54—Topless, taking off her swimsuit top for Crystal's video camera.
••• 1:12—Topless and buns in G-string, doing strip routine on stage.
• 1:16—Topless in music video.
Magazines:
Playboy's Book of Lingerie (Jan 1992) ......Herself
••• 86-87—Topless and partial lower frontal nudity.
Playboy's Career Girls (Aug 1992)
.... Object of Beauty
••• 54-57—Nude.
Playboy's Book of Lingerie (Sep 1992) ......Herself
••• 43—Topless and top of lower frontal nudity.

Hendry, Gloria

Films:
Black Caesar (1973) ....Helen
Hell Up in Harlem (1973) .... Helen Bradley
Live and Let Die (1973; British) .... Rosie
Black Belt Jones (1974)................. Sidney
Savage Sisters (1974) .... Lynn Jackson
Bare Knuckles (1984) .... Barbara Darrow
Magazines:
Playboy (Jul 1973) .... Sainted Bond
••• 147-149—Topless and buns.
Playboy (Dec 1973) ....Sex Stars of 1973
••• 204—Full frontal nudity.

Henner, Marilu

Films:
Between the Lines (1977)..................Danielle
  0:27—Dancing on stage wearing pasties.
Bloodbrothers (1978)..................... Annette
Hammett (1982) .... Kit Conger/Sue Alabama
The Man Who Loved Women (1983)
.... Agnes Chapman
•• 0:18—Brief topless in bed with Burt Reynolds.
Cannonball Run II (1984)................. Betty
Johnny Dangerously (1984) Lil
Perfect (1985) .... Sally
  0:13—Working out on exercise machine.
Rustler's Rhapsody (1985) .... Miss Tracy
L.A. Story (1991) .... Trudi
Made for Cable Movies:
Love with a Perfect Stranger (1986; Showtime) .... n.a.
Chains of Gold (1991; Showtime) ....Jackie
Made for TV Movies:
Dream House (1981) .... Laura Griffith
TV:
Taxi (1978-83) .... Elaine Nardo
Evening Shade (1990-) ....Ava Evans Newton
Video Tapes:
Marilu Henner's Dancerobics (1992) ....Herself

Henry, Laura

Films:

Heavenly Bodies (1985) . . . . Debbie
- 0:46—Brief topless making love while her boyfriend, Jack, watches TV.

Separate Vacations (1985) . . . . Nancy

Hensley, Pamela

Films:

There Was a Crooked Man (1970) . . . . Edwina
- 0:12—Very brief left breast lying on pool table with a guy.

Making It (1971) . . . . Bar Girl
Doc Savage: The Man of Bronze (1975) . . . . Mona
Rollerball (1975) . . . . Mackie
Buck Rogers in the 25th Century (1979)
. . . . Princess Ardala
Double Exposure (1983) . . . . Sergeant Fontain

TV:

Marcus Welby, M.D. (1975-76) . . . . Janet Blake
Kingston: Confidential (1977) . . . . Beth Kelly
Buck Rogers (1979-80) . . . . Princess Ardala
240 Robert (1981) . . . . Deputy Sandy Harper
Matt Houston (1982-85) . . . . C. J. Parsons

Magazines:

Playboy (Sep 1980) . . . . Grapevine
- 252—Right breast in open blouse. B&W.

• Herd, Carla

Films:

Deathstalker III: The Warriors From Hell (1988)
. . . . Carlisa/Elizena
- 0:20—Side view of right breast, while making love in tent when guard looks in.
- 0:46—Topless taking a bath.

Wild Zone (1989) . . . . Nicole Laroche

Herred, Brandy

Films:

Some Call It Loving (1972) . . . . Cheerleader
- 1:12—Nude dancing in a club doing a strip tease dance in a cheerleader outfit.

The Arousers (1973) . . . . n.a.

Herrin, Kymberly

Films:

Ghostbusters (1984) . . . . Dream Ghost
Romancing the Stone (1984) . . . . Angelina
  0:00—In wet white blouse in Western setting as Kathleen Turner types her story.
Beverly Hills Cop II (1987) . . . . Playboy Playmate
Roadhouse (1989) . . . . Party Girl

Video Tapes:

Playmate Playoffs . . . . Playmate
Playboy Video Magazine, Volume 2 (1983)
. . . . Herself/Playboy Playoffs
- 0:33—Topless in tug-of-war game.

Playboy Video Magazine, Volume 5 (1983)
. . . . Playmate
- 0:05—Brief full frontal nudity next to car.

Magazines:

Playboy (Mar 1981) . . . . Playmate

Herring, Laura

Films:

Silent Night, Deadly Night III: Better Watch Out!
(1989) . . . . Jerri
- 0:48—Topless in bathtub with her boyfriend Chris.

The Forbidden Dance (1990) . . . . Nisa
Dead Women In Lingerie (1991) . . . . Marcia

Hershey, Barbara

a.k.a. Barbara Seagull.

Films:

Last Summer (1969) . . . . Sandy
- 0:19—Topless after taking off her swimsuit top on sailboat with Richard Thomas. Hair is in the way.
- 1:30—Very brief right breast, after taking off her top in the woods.

The Baby Maker (1970) . . . . Tish
- 0:14—Side view of left breast taking off dress and diving into the pool. Long shot and dark. Buns in water.
  0:23—Left breast (out of focus) under sheet in bed.

The Liberation of L. B. Jones (1970) . . . . . Nella Mundine
Boxcar Bertha (1972) . . . . Bertha Thompson
- 0:10—Topless making love with David Carradine in a railroad boxcar, then brief buns walking around when the train starts moving.
- 0:52—Nude, side view in house with David Carradine.
  0:54—Buns, putting on dress after hearing a gun shot.

Diamonds (1975) . . . . Sally
Flood! (1976) . . . . n.a.
The Stunt Man (1980) . . . . Nina
- 1:29—Buns and side view of left breast in bed in a movie within a movie while everybody is watching in a screening room.

Americana (1981) . . . . Girl
Take This Job and Shove It (1981) . . . . . . J. M. Halstead
The Entity (1983) . . . . Carla Moran
- 0:33—Topless and buns getting undressed before taking a bath. Don't see her face.
  0:59—"Topless" during special effect when The Entity fondles her breasts with invisible fingers while she sleeps.
- 1:32—"Topless" again getting raped by The Entity while Alex Rocco watches helplessly.

The Right Stuff (1983) . . . . Glennis Yeager
The Natural (1984) . . . . Harriet Bird
Hannah and Her Sisters (1986) . . . . Lee
Tin Men (1986) . . . . Nora
Beaches (1988) . . . . Hillary Whitney Essex

The Last Temptation of Christ (1988)
. . . . Mary Magdelene
- • 0:16—Brief buns behind curtain. Brief right breast making love, then brief topless.
  0:17—Buns, while sleeping.
- •• 0:20—Topless, tempting Jesus.
- • 2:12—Brief tip of left breast, lying on ground under Jesus.
- • 2:13—Left breast while caressing her pregnant belly.
Shy People (1988). . . . . Ruth
A World Apart (1988; British) . . . . Diana Roth
Tune in Tomorrow (1990) . . . . Aunt Julia
a.k.a. Aunt Julia and the Scriptwriter
Defenseless (1991) . . . . T. K. Katwuller
Made for Cable Movies:
Paris Trout (1991; Showtime) . . . . Hanna Trout
Made for TV Movies:
A Killing in a Small Town (1990) . . . . . . Candy Morrison
Stay the Night (1992) . . . . .Jimmie Sue Finger
TV:
The Monroes (1966-67) . . . . Kathy Monroe
From Here to Eternity (1980) . . . . Karen Holmes
Magazines:
Playboy (Aug 1972). . . . . Boxcar Bertha
- •• 82-85—Nude with David Carradine.
Playboy (Nov 1972) . . . . Sex in Cinema 1972
  161—Buns.
Playboy (Dec 1972). . . . . Sex Stars of 1972
- ••• 208—Topless.

Hetrick, Jennifer

a.k.a. Jenni Hetrick.
Films:
Squeeze Play (1979). . . . . Samantha
a.k.a. Jenni Hetrick.
- •• 0:00—Topless in bed after making love.
- • 0:26—Right breast, brief topless with Wes on the floor.
  0:37—In bra, in bedroom with Wes.
Made for TV Movies:
Absolute Strangers (1991). . . . . Nancy Klein
TV:
L.A. Law (1989-) . . . . Connie Hammond
UNSUB (1989) . . . . Ann Madison
Bodies of Evidence (1992-). . . . . Det. Haughton

Hey, Virginia

Films:
The Road Warrior (1981). . . . . Warrior Woman
Norman Loves Rose (1982; Australian) . . . . .n.a.
Castaway (1986). . . . . Janice
The Living Daylights (1987)
. . . . Rubavitch (Colonel Pushkin's girlfriend)
- • 1:10—Brief side view of left breast when James Bond uses her to distract bodyguard.

Obsession: A Taste For Fear (1987). . . . . .Diane
- • 0:04—Buns and very brief side view of right breast dropping towel to take a shower.
- •• 0:14—Brief right breast in bed when sheet falls down.
- • 0:38—Topless lying down, wearing a mask, while talking to a girl.
- ••• 1:03—Topless waking up in bed.
- ••• 1:17—Topless in hallway with Valerie.
- • 1:19—Brief lower frontal nudity and right breast in bed with Valerie, then buns in bed.
- ••• 1:20—Topless getting dressed, walking and running around the house when Valerie gets killed.
- • 1:26—Topless tied up in chair while Paul torments her.
Magazines:
Playboy (Sep 1982) . . . . Warrior Women
  162-163—Nude.

Heywood, Anne

Films:
Checkpoint (1957; British) . . . . .Gabriela
The Fox (1967) . . . . March
The Lady of Monza (1970; Italian) . . . . Virginia de Leyva
Trader Horn (1973) . . . . Nicole
The Shaming (1979) . . . . Evelyn Wyckoff
a.k.a. Good Luck, Miss Wyckoff
a.k.a. The Sin
- ••• 0:49—Right breast, then topless in open blouse after being raped by Rafe in her classroom.
  0:52—Topless on classroom floor, making love with Rafe.
What Waits Below (1986). . . . . Frida Shelley

• Hickey, Marilyn Faith

Films:
Incoming Freshman (1979)
. . . . .Sargeant Laverne Finterplay
- • 0:06—Topless and buns when Professor Bilbo fantasizes about her.
- • 0:56—Topless and buns during Bilbo's fantasy.
- • 1:18—Topless during end credits.
The Night the Lights Went Out in Georgia (1981)
. . . . Woman on Bus

• Hickland, Catherine

Ex-wife of actor David Hasselhoff.
Films:
The Last Married Couple in America (1980) . . . .Rebecca
Ghost Town (1988) . . . . .Kate
Witchery (1988). . . . . Linda Sullivan
Millions (1990). . . . . Connie
- • 0:36—Buns, getting out of bed to open safe. Don't see her face, probably a body double because the hair is too dark.
- • 1:20—Buns, walking away from John Stockwell. Very brief back side of right breast, when she bends over to pick up blouse. Don't see her face.

Hicks, Catherine

Films:

Death Valley (1982) . . . . Sally
Better Late Than Never (1983) . . . . Sable
Garbo Talks (1984) . . . . Jane
The Razor's Edge (1984) . . . . Isabel
  • 0:43—Brief upper half of left breast, in bed after seeing a cockroach.
Fever Pitch (1985) . . . . Flo
  • 0:11—Brief left breast, while sitting on bed in hotel room talking with Ryan O'Neal.
Peggy Sue Got Married (1986) . . . . Carol Heath
Star Trek IV: The Voyage Home (1986) . . . .Gillian Taylor
Like Father, Like Son (1987) . . . . Dr. Amy Larkin
Child's Play (1988) . . . . Karen Barclay
Souvenir (1988; British). . . . . Tina Boyer
Daddy's Little Girl (1989) . . . . .n.a.
Running Against Time (1990) . . . . .n.a.
Liebestraum (1991). . . . . Mary Parker
  (Unrated Director's cut reviewed.)
Made for Cable Movies:
Laguna Heat (1987; HBO) . . . . .Jane Algernon
  •• 0:50—Topless and buns, running around the beach with Harry Hamlin.
  •• 1:05—Brief topless in bed making love with Harry Hamlin, having her head hit the headboard.
TV:
The Bad News Bears (1979-80) . . . . . .Dr. Emily Rappant
Tucker's Witch (1982-83) . . . . .Amanda Tucker

Higgins, Clare

Films:

1919 (1984; British) . . . . .Young Sophie
Hellraiser (1987). . . . . Julia
  • 0:17—Very, very brief left breast and buns making love with Frank.
  1:10—In white bra in bedroom putting necklace on.
Hellraiser II—Hellbound (1988). . . . . Julia
  • 0:20—Very, very brief right breast, lying in bed with Frank. Scene from *Hellraiser.*
Wonderland (1989; British) . . . . Eve

Higginson, Jane

Films:

Danger Zone II: Reaper's Revenge (1988)
. . . . Donna
  •• 0:17—Topless unconscious on sofa while the bad guys take Polaroid photos of her.
  • 0:18—Brief topless in the photo that Wade looks at.
  • 0:22—Brief left breast adjusting her blouse outside. Long shot.
  • 0:34—Left breast in another Polaroid photograph.
  0:45—In black bra, panties and stockings posing on motorcycle for photograph.
Slaughterhouse (1988) . . . . Annie
Silent Night, Deadly Night 5: The Toy Maker (1991)
. . . . Sarah Quinn

Hill, Mariana

Films:

Paradise, Hawaiian Style (1966) . . . . Lani
Medium Cool (1969) . . . . Ruth
  • 0:18—Close-up of breast in bed with John.
  •• 0:36—Nude, running around the house frolicking with John.
El Condor (1971) . . . . Claudine
Thumb Tripping (1972) . . . . Lynn
  • 1:14—In black bra, then very, very brief left breast when Jack comes to cover her up.
  • 1:19—Topless frolicking in the water with Gary.
  1:20—In white swimsuit, dancing in bar.
High Plains Drifter (1973). . . . . .Callie Travers
Dead People (1974) . . . . .Arletty
The Godfather, Part II (1974) . . . . .Deanna Corleone
The Last Porno Flick (1974) . . . . n.a.
Schizoid (1980) . . . . .Julie
  0:58—Left breast, while making love in bed with Klaus Kinski. Dark, hard to see.
Blood Beach (1981) . . . . Catherine

Hilton, Robyn

Films:

Bloody Friday (1973) .Denise
  a.k.a. Single Girls
Video Vixens (1973) . . . . .Inga
  •• 1:18—Topless, opening her top in a room full of reporters.
Blazing Saddles (1974). n.a.
The Last Porno Flick (1974) . . . . n.a.
Malibu Express (1984) . . . . Maid Marian

Holcomb, Sarah

Films:

Animal House (1978) . . . . Clorette DePasto
  •• 0:56—Brief topless lying on bed after passing out in Tom Hulce's bed during toga party.
Walk Proud (1979) . . . . .Sarah Lassiter
Caddyshack (1980) . . . . Maggie O'Hooligan
Happy Birthday, Gemini (1980) . . . . Judith Hastings

Holden, Marjean

Films:

Stripped to Kill II (1988) . . . . Something Else
  •• 0:17—Topless during strip dance routine.
Silent Night, Deadly Night 4: Initiation (1990) . . . . .Jane
Stop! Or My Mom Will Shoot (1992) . . . . . . Stewardess

Hollander, Xaviera

Author of "The Happy Hooker."
Films:

My Pleasure Is My Business (1974) . . . . .Gabriele
  •• 0:14—Full frontal nudity in everybody's daydream.
  •• 0:39—Topless sitting up in bed and putting on a blouse.
  •• 0:40—Topless getting back into bed.
  ••• 0:59—Topless and buns taking off clothes to go swimming in the pool, swimming, then getting out.

•• 1:09—Topless, buns and very brief lower frontal nudity, underwater in indoor pool with Gus.
• 1:31—Buns and very brief side view of right breast, undressing at party.
Video Tapes:
Penthouse Love Stories (1986) . . . . Herself

Hollitt, Raye

Films:
Penitentiary III (1987) . . . . Female Boxer
Skin Deep (1989) . . . . Lonnie
(Check this out if you like muscular women.)
• 0:26—Brief side view topless and buns getting undressed and into bed with John Ritter.
Immortalizer (1990) . . . . Queenie
The Last Hour (1990) . . . . Adler
a.k.a. Concrete War

Holloman, Bridget

Films:
Slumber Party '57 (1976) . . . . Bonnie May
• 0:10—Topless with her five girl friends during swimming pool scene. Hard to tell who is who.
• 0:26—Left breast in truck with her cousin Cal.
Evils of the Night (1985) . . . . Heather

•Holmes, Jennifer

Films:
The Demon (1981; South African) . . . . .Mary
•• 0:22—Topless in dressing room.
• 1:18—Brief side of left breast, taking off robe to take a bath.
• 1:26—Topless, crawling around in the rafters. Dark.
••• 1:29—Topless climbing through a hole in the roof, then landing on the bed. More topless in the bathroom.
Raw Force (1981) . . . . Ann Davis
Made for TV Movies:
Hobson's Choice (1983) .n.a.
Sampson and Delilah (1984) . . . . .n.a.
TV:
Newhart (1982-83) . . . . Leslie Vanderkellen
Misfits of Science (1985-86) . . . . Jane Miller

Holvöe, Maria

Films:
Willow (1988) . . . . .Cherlindrea
The Last Warrior (1989) . . . . Katherine
•• 1:24—Right breast, after the Japanese warrior removes her dress.
Worth Winning (1989) . . . . Erin Cooper

•Hope, Amanda

Video Tapes:
Wet and Wild IV (1992) . . . . .Model
Magazines:
Playboy (Jul 1992) . . . . Playmate
••• 90-101—Nude.

•Hope, Erica

Films:
Bloody Birthday (1980) . . . . .Annie
• 0:04—Brief topless in cemetery, making out with Duke.
Graduation Day (1981) . . . . .Diane
• 1:02—Brief topless in open blouse running away from the killer.
TV:
The Young and the Restless (1978-79) . . . . . . Nikki Reed

•Hopkins, Kim

Films:
The Happy Hooker Goes Hollywood (1980)
. . . . Young Xaviera
The Hollywood Knights (1980) . . . . . . Pom Pom Girl
• 0:01—Topless, sunbathing outside with her two girlfriends.

•Hopkins, Rhonda Leigh

Films:
Summer School Teachers (1975) . . . . .Denise
• 0:45—Topless making love with a guy. Close up of a breast.
Tidal Wave (1975; U.S./Japanese) . . . . .Fran

•Horan, Barbra

Films:
My Favorite Year (1982) . . . . n.a.
The Malibu Bikini Shop (1985) . . . . Ronnie
• 0:33—In wet tank top during Alan's fantasy.
• 1:13—Most of side of left breast, while kissing Alan in the spa.
Delusion (1990) . . . . Carly

Horn, Linda

Films:
American Gigolo (1980) . . . . 2nd Girl on Balcony
• 0:03—Topless on the balcony while Richard Gere and Lauren Hutton talk.

•Horne, Suzi

Films:
Hot Moves (1984) . . . . Hooker #1
Jungle Warriors (1985) . . . . Pam Ross
• 0:51—Brief topless twice during jail scene. Wearing a white blouse, with a yellow shirt underneath. Brief buns. Don't see her face.

•Horrocks, Jane

Films:
The Dressmaker (1988; British) . . . . Rita
Getting It Right (1989) .Jenny
The Witches (1989) . . . . Miss Irvine
Memphis Belle (1990) . . . . Faith
Life is Sweet (1991; British) . . . . Nicola
• 0:50—Topless in bed with her boyfriend. Hard to see because she has chocolate all over her chest.

Howard, Barbara

Films:

Friday the 13th, Part IV—The Final Chapter
(1984) . . . . Sara
   0:52—In white bra and panties putting on a robe in
   the bedroom getting ready for her boyfriend.
   • 1:01—Buns, through shower door.
Racing with the Moon (1984) . . . . Gatsby Girl
Running Mates (1985) . . . . .n.a.
Lucky Stiff (1988) . . . . Frances
White Palace (1990) . . . . Sherri Klugman
Made for TV Movies:
Those Secrets (1992). Beth
TV:
Falcon Crest (1985-86) . . . . Robin Agretti

• Howell, Chéri

Films:

Bloody Friday (1973) . . . . Shannon
a.k.a. Single Girls
   • 1:01—Topless and buns after "accidentally" dropping her towel in front of Bud.
Soylent Green (1973) . . . . Furniture Girl

Howell, Margaret

Films:

Tightrope (1984) . . . . Judy Harper
   • 0:44—Brief left breast viewed from above in a room
   with Clint Eastwood.
Girls Just Want to Have Fun (1985) . . . . Mrs. Glenn

Hubley, Season

Ex-wife of actor Kurt Russell.
Films:

Hardcore (1979) . . . . Niki
   • 0:27—Topless acting in a porno movie.
   ••• 1:05—Full frontal nudity talking to George C. Scott
   in a booth. Panties mysteriously appear later on.
Vice Squad (1982). . . . . Princess
   0:34—In black bra in Ramrod's apartment.
   0:57—Buns, getting out of bed after making love
   with a John.
   1:25—In black bra, tied up by Ramrod.
Pretty Kill (1987). . . . . Heather Todd
Total Exposure (1991). . . . . Andi Robinson
   0:07—Buns, getting into hot tub. Probably a body
   double.
Stepfather III: Father's Day (1992) . . . . . . Jennifer Ashley
Made for Cable TV:
The Hitchhiker: Cabin Fever (1987; HBO) . . . . . Miranda
   0:12—In white bra, under cabin with Rick.
Made for TV Movies:
She Lives (1973) . . . . .n.a.
The Three Wishes of Billy Grier (1984). . . . . Phyllis
Shakedown on Sunset Strip (1988)
. . . . Officer Audre Davis
Child in the Night (1990) . . . . Valerie Winfield
Vestige of Honor (1990) . . . . Marilyn
Steel Justice (1992) . . . . Gina Morelli

TV:
All My Children . . . . Angelique Marrick
Kung Fu (1974-75). . . . . Margit McLean
Family (1976-77) . . . . Salina Magee

• Hughes, Ann Margaret

Films:

Transformations (1988) . . . . Myra
   • 0:42—Right breast, then topless under Rex Smith in
   bed.
   • 0:43—More topless, dead in bed.
Blue Tornado (1990) . . . . .n.a.

Hughes, Sharon

Films:

Chained Heat (1983; U.S./German). . . . . .Val
   •• 0:30—Brief topless in the shower with Linda Blair.
   •• 0:51—Buns, in lingerie, stripping for a guy.
   •• 1:04—Topless in the spa with the Warden.
The Man Who Loved Women (1983) . . . . Nurse
Hard to Hold (1984). . . . . .Wife
The Last Horror Film (1984) . . . . Stripper
American Justice (1986). . . . . Valerie
A Fine Mess (1986) . . . . Tina
Grotesque (1987). . . . . .n.a.

Hughes, Wendy

Films:

Jock Petersen (1974; Australian) . . . . Patricia Kent
a.k.a. Petersen
   ••• 0:12—Topless in her office with Tony.
   • 0:13—Topless making love with Tony on the floor.
   •• 0:44—Nude running around the beach with Tony.
   •• 0:50—Nude in bed making love with Tony.
   • 1:24—Full frontal nudity when Tony rapes her in her
   office.
Newsfront (1978; Australian) . . . . .Amy McKenzie
My Brilliant Career (1979; Australian). . . . . . Aunt Helen
Lonely Hearts (1983; Australian) . . . . Patricia
   • 1:05—Brief topless getting out of bed and putting a
   dress on. Dark, hard to see.
Careful, He Might Hear You (1984; Australian)
. . . . Vanessa
An Indecent Obsession (1985) . . . . . Honour Langtry
   0:32—Possibly Wendy topless, could be Sue because
   Luce is fantasizing about Wendy while making love
   with Sue. Dark, long shot, hard to see.
   •• 1:10—Left breast, making love in bed with Wilson.
My First Wife (1985). . . . . .Helen
   1:00—Brief topless and lower frontal nudity under
   water during husband's dream. Don't see her face.
   •• 1:08—In bra, then topless on the floor with her husband.
   •• 1:10—Topless in bed lying down, then fighting with
   her husband. A little dark.
Happy New Year (1987). . . . . Carolyn Benedict
Warm Nights on a Slow Moving Train (1987). . . The Girl
   1:23—Very, very brief silhouette of right breast getting back into bed after killing a man.

Echoes of Paradise (1989) . . . . Maria
Wild Orchid II: Two Shades of Blue (1992) . . . . Elle
Made for Cable Movies:
The Heist (1989; HBO) . . . . Susan
- 0:52—Very brief side view of right breast making love in bed with Pierce Brosnan.
Made for TV Movies:
Donor (1990) . . . . Dr. Farrell
A Woman Named Jackie (1991) . . . . . Janet Lee Bouvier

Hull, Dianne

Films:
The Arrangement (1969) . . . . Ellen
The Magic Garden of Stanley Sweetheart (1970)
. . . . Cathy
Hot Summer Week (1973; Canadian) . . . . n.a.
Man on a Swing (1974) . . . . Maggie Dawson
Aloha, Bobby and Rose (1975) . . . . Rose
The Fifth Floor (1978) . . . . Kelly McIntyre
- •• 0:29—Topless and buns in shower while Carl watches, then brief full frontal nudity running out of the shower.
- •• 1:09—Topless in whirlpool bath getting visited by Carl again, then raped.
You Better Watch Out (1980) . . . . Jackie Stadling
The New Adventures of Pippi Longstocking (1988)
. . . . Mrs. Settigren

Hunt, Marsha A.

Films:
The Sender (1982) . . . . Nurse Jo
Howling II: Your Sister Is a Werewolf (1984)
. . . . Mariana
- •• 0:33—Topless in bedroom with Sybil Danning and a guy.

Hunter, Heather

Adult film actress.
Films:
Frankenhooker (1990). . . . . Chartreuse
- 0:36—Brief topless during introduction to Jeffrey.
- 0:37—Brief topless bending over behind Sugar.
- ••• 0:41—Brief topless and buns, running in front of bed. A little blurry. Then topless and buns dancing with the other girls.
- 0:43—Topless dodging flying leg with Sugar.
- •• 0:44—Topless, crawling on the floor.

Hunter, Kaki

Films:
Roadie (1980) . . . . Lola Bouiliabase
Willie and Phil (1980) . . . . Patti Sutherland
Porky's (1981; Canadian) . . . . Wendy
- 1:02—Brief full frontal nudity, then brief topless in the shower scene.
Whose Life Is It, Anyway? (1981). . . . . .Mary Jo
Porky's II: The Next Day (1983; Canadian) . . . . . Wendy
Just the Way You Are (1984) . . . . .Lisa

Porky's Revenge (1985; Canadian) . . . . .Wendy
- 1:22—In white bra and panties taking off her clothes to jump off a bridge.

Hunter, Neith

Films:
Born in East L.A. (1987) . . . . .Marcie
Near Dark (1987). . . . . Lady in Car
Fright Night, Part 2 (1988). . . . . Young Admirer
Silent Night, Deadly Night 4: Initiation (1990)
. . . . Kim
- 0:03—Brief topless several times in bed with Hank.
- 0:47—Brief topless during occult ceremony when a worm comes out of her mouth.
- 1:05—Right breast, while lying on floor. Long shot. 1:06—Topless, covered with gunk, transforming into a worm.
- 1:07—Very brief side of right breast, while sitting up.
Silent Night, Deadly Night 5: The Toy Maker (1991)
. . . . Kim
Video Tapes:
Inside Out (1992) . . . . Angela/The Diaries
- 1:01—In black bra and panties, modeling lingerie for Richard and Elliott.
- 1:03—Buns, in swimsuit, while standing up.
- •• 1:04—Right breast, then brief topless in spa with Richard.
- ••• 1:06—Topless in bed, getting fondled by David.
- •• 1:08—Topless in the shower.
- •• 1:10—Right breast, while in bed with Richard.

Hunter, Rachel

Wife of singer Rod Stewart.
Sports Illustrated swimsuit model.
Video Tapes:
Sports Illustrated's 25th Anniversary Swimsuit Video (1989). . . . . .Herself
(The version shown on HBO left out two music video segments at the end. If you like buns, definitely watch the video tape!)
- 0:03—Right breast in see-through black swimsuit with white stars on it.
Sports Illustrated Super Shape-Up Program: Body Sculpting (1990) . . . . .Herself

Huntly, Leslie

Films:
The Naked Cage (1985). . . . . Peaches
Back to School (1986). . . . . Coed #1
- •• 0:14—Brief topless in the shower room when Rodney Dangerfield first arrives on campus.
Demon of Paradise (1987) . . . . .Gobby
- •• 0:51—Topless taking off her top on a boat, then swimming in the ocean.
Stewardess School (1987) . . . . Alison Hanover
- •• 0:46—Topless, doing a strip tease on a table at a party at her house.
Satan's Princess (1989). . . . . Karen Rhodes
- ••• 0:27—Topless sitting on bed and in bed with Nicole.

Huppert, Isabelle
Films:
Going Places (1974; French). . . . . .Jacqueline
- 1:53—Brief upper half of left breast making love with Jean-Claude.

The Lacemaker (1977; French) . . . . Beatrice
- 0:50—Briefly nude while getting into bed.
- 0:57—Topless under shawl, then nude while getting into bed.
- •• 0:58—Topless, lying in bed.
- 1:04—Nude, in her apartment.
- ••• 1:22—Nude, in her apartment with François.

Heaven's Gate (1980). . . . . Ella
- •• 1:10—Nude running around the house and in bed with Kris Kristofferson.
- ••• 1:18—Nude, taking a bath in the river and getting out.
- 2:24—Very brief left breast getting raped by three guys.

Loulou (1980; French). . . . . .Nelly
- 0:06—Very, very brief topless leaning over in bed.
- 0:18—Brief topless getting out of bed.
- 0:27—Brief topless turning over in bed.
- •• 0:36—Topless lying in bed talking on phone. Mostly right breast.
- 0:40—Lower frontal nudity and buns taking off panties and getting into bed.
- •• 0:59—Left breast in bed with André, then topless taking him to the bathroom.

Clean Slate (1981) . . . . .n.a.
La Truit (The Trout) (1982; French) . . . . . Frederique
Entre Nous (1983; French) . . . . .Helen Webber
a.k.a. Coup de Foudre
- 1:01—Brief topless in shower room talking about her breasts with Miou-Miou.

My Best Friend's Girl (1984; French)
. . . . Vivian Arthund
a.k.a. La Femme du Mon Ami
- 0:40—Brief left breast peeking out of bathrobe walking around in living room.
- 1:00—Buns, making love with Thierry Lhermitte while his friend watches.

Sincerely Charlotte (1986; French) . . . . Charlotte
- 0:20—Brief topless in bathtub. Long shot, out of focus.
- 1:07—Very brief left breast changing into red dress in the back seat of the car.
- •• 1:15—Topless in bed with Mathieu. Kind of dark.

The Bedroom Window (1987) . . . . Sylvia Wentworth
- •• 0:06—Briefly nude while looking out the window at attempted rape.

Story of Women (1988; French) . . . . .Marie Latour
Madame Bovary (1991; French) . . . . .Emma Bovary
Magazines:
Playboy (Dec 1980). . . . . .Grapevine
- ••• 388—Left breast. B&W.

Hurley, Elizabeth
Films:
Aria (1988; U.S./British) . . . . .Marietta
- 0:46—Brief topless, turning around while singing to a guy.
- 0:47—Buns while standing and hugging him.

Rowing with the Wind (1988) . . . . Clair Clairmont

Hushaw, Katherine
Video Tapes:
Playboy Video Calendar 1988 (1987). . . . . Playmate
Wet and Wild (1989) . . . . Model
Magazines:
Playboy (Oct 1986) . . . . Playmate

Hussey, Olivia
Films:
Romeo and Juliet (1968) . . . . Juliet
- 1:37—Very brief topless rolling over and getting out of bed with Romeo.

The Man with Bogart's Face (1980) . . . . .Elsa Borsht
Virus (1980; Japanese) . . . . Marit
Escape 2000 (1981). . . . . Chris
Undeclared War (1990) . . . . n.a.
Made for Cable Movies:
Psycho IV: The Beginning (1990; Showtime)
. . . . Norma Bates
- •• 0:49—Topless in motel room mirror while young Norman, watches through peephole.

Made for TV Movies:
Ivanhoe (1982) . . . . .Rebecca
Stephen King's "It" (1990). . . . . Audra

Huston, Anjelica
Daughter of actor/director John Huston.
Films:
Hamlet (1969; British) . . . . Court Lady
A Walk with Love and Death (1969). . . . . . Lady Claudia
The Last Tycoon (1976) . . . . Edna
Swashbuckler (1976) . . . . .Woman of Dark Visage
The Postman Always Rings Twice (1981) . . .Madge
- 1:30—Brief side view left breast sitting in trailer with Jack Nicholson.

Frances (1982). . . . . . .Hospital Sequence: Mental Patient
Ice Pirates (1984). . . . . Maida
This is Spinal Tap (1984) . . . . .Polly Deutsch
Prizzi's Honor (1985) . . . . Maerose Prizzi
The Dead (1987) . . . . Gretta Conroy
Gardens of Stone (1987) . . . . .Samantha Davis
Enemies, A Love Story (1989). . . . . Tamara
The Witches (1989) . . . . . . Grand High Witch/Eva Ernst
The Grifters (1990). . . . . Lilly Dillon
The Addams Family (1991) . . . . .Morticia Addams
Miniseries:
Lonesome Dove (1989) . . . . .Clara Allen

Hutchinson, Tracey E.

Films:
The Wild Life (1984) . . . . .Poker Girl #2
- 1:23—Brief topless in a room full of guys and girls playing strip poker when Lea Thompson looks in.

Into the Night (1985) . . . . .Federal Agent
Masterblaster (1986). . . . . .Lisa
- ••• 0:57—Topless taking a shower (wearing panties).

Amazon Women on the Moon (1987) . . . . . Floozie
1:18—Brief right breast, while hitting balloon while Carrie Fisher talks to a guy. This sketch is in B&W and appears after the first batch of credits.

Stone Cold (1991) . . . . Pool Playing Chick
- 0:25—Brief topless, playing pool with the guys.

Hutton, Lauren

Films:
Little Fauss and Big Halsy (1970) . . . . Rita Nebraska
The Gambler (1974) . . . . Billie
Gator (1976). . . . . Aggie Maybank
Viva Knievel (1977) . . . . Kate Morgan
Welcome to L.A. (1977). . . . . .Nora Bruce
- 0:56—Very brief, obscured glimpse of left breast under red light in photo darkroom.

A Wedding (1978) . . . . Florence Farmer
American Gigolo (1980) . . . . Michelle
- 0:37—Left breast, making love with Richard Gere in bed in his apartment.

Paternity (1981) .Jenny Lufton
Zorro, The Gay Blade (1981). . . . . Charlotte
Lassiter (1984) . . . . Kari Von Fursten
- 0:18—Brief topless over-the-shoulder shot making love with a guy on the bed just before killing him.

Once Bitten (1985) . . . . Countess
Malone (1987) . . . . .Jamie
Millions (1990) . . . . .Christina
Guilty as Charged (1992) . . . . .n.a.
Made for Cable Movies:
Fear (1991; Showtime) . . . . Jessica Moreau
TV:
The Rhinemann Exchange (1977) . . . Leslie Hawkewood
Paper Dolls (1984) . . . . .Colette Ferrier
Magazines:
Penthouse (Sep 1986)
. . . . The Secret Nudes of Lauren Hutton
- ••• 158-169—1962 B&W photos.

Hyde, Kimberly

Films:
The Last Picture Show (1971) . . Annie-Annie Martin
- •• 0:36—Full frontal nudity, getting out of pool to meet Randy Quaid and Cybill Shepherd.
- 0:37—Topless several times, sitting at edge of pool with Bobby.
- 0:38—More topless, sitting on edge of pool in background.

Video Vixens (1973) . . . . .Claudine
Candy Stripe Nurses (1974) . . . . April
Foxy Brown (1974) . . . . .Jennifer

Hyser, Joyce

Ex-girlfriend of singer Bruce Springsteen.
Films:
The Hollywood Knights (1980). . . . . Brenda Weintraub
They All Laughed (1981) .Sylvia
Staying Alive (1983). . . . . .Linda
Valley Girl (1983) . . . . Joyce
This is Spinal Tap (1984) . . . . Belinda
Just One of the Guys (1986). . . . . Terry Griffith
0:10—In two piece swimsuit by the pool with her boyfriend.
- •• 1:27—Brief topless opening her blouse to prove that she is really a girl.

Wedding Band (1989) . . . . Karla Thompson
TV:
L.A. Law (1988-89) . . . . .Alison Gottlieb

• Illiers, Isabelle

Films:
The Story of "O" Continues (1981; French) . . . . . .O
a.k.a. Les Fruits de la Passion
- ••• 0:06—Topless in chair, getting made up.
- •• 0:08—Topless and buns, walking up stairs.
- 0:10—Topless sitting in bed.
- •• 0:11—Topless sitting in bed putting up Klaus Kinski's picture on the wall.
- •• 0:12—Topless and buns getting out of bed and walking around the room.
- 0:13—Tip of right breast, while looking out the window.
- •• 0:18—Topless looking out the window.
- 0:24—Brief left breast, under her dress.
- 0:26—Tips of breasts, sticking out of dress top.
- •• 0:27—Topless and buns in chair, more in room with a customer.
- 0:35—Topless, sitting while looking at Kinski.
- •• 0:36—Brief left breast, then full frontal nudity lying on bed during fantasy.
0:40—Full frontal nudity, getting chained up by Kinski.
- •• 0:58—Full frontal nudity running in slow-motion during boy's fantasy.
- •• 1:02—Topless in room with the boy.
- •• 1:04—Topless making love with the boy.

Miranda (1985; Italian) . . . . n.a.
Luci lontane (1988; Italian) . . . . n.a.

Iman

Supermodel.
Wife of singer/actor David Bowie.
Films:
The Human Factor (1979) . . . . .Sarah
Exposed (1983) . . . . Model
Out of Africa (1985). . . . . Mariammo
No Way Out (1987) . . . . Nina Beka
Surrender (1988) . . . . Hedy
House Party 2 (1991) . . . . Sheila Landreaux
L.A. Story (1991) . . . . Cynthia
Star Trek VI: The Undiscovered Country (1991) . . Martia

Made for Cable Movies:
Lies of the Twins (1991; USA) . . . . Elle
Music Videos:
Remember the Time/Michael Jackson (1992) . . . Queen
Magazines:
Playboy (Jan 1986) . . . . .Beauty and the Beasts
••• 146-155—Topless.

• Imershein, Deirdre
Films:
Black Belt (1992) . . . . Shanna
••• 1:08—Topless in bed, making love with Don "The Dragon" Wilson.
Made for Cable TV:
Dream On: Martin Gets Lucky (1990; HBO)
. . . . Sheila
••• 0:06—Topless in bed making love with Martin. Nice sweaty shot.
TV:
Dallas (1991) . . . . .Jory

Inch, Jennifer
Films:
Frank and I (1983) . . . . Frank/Frances
0:10—Brief buns, getting pants pulled down for a spanking.
••• 0:22—Nude getting undressed and walking to the bed.
• 0:24—Brief nude when Charles pulls the sheets off her.
0:32—Brief buns, getting spanked by two older women.
••• 0:38—Full frontal nudity getting out of bed and walking to Charles at the piano.
•• 0:45—Full frontal nudity lying on her side by the fireplace. Dark, hard to see.
•• 1:09—Brief topless making love with Charles on the floor.
••• 1:11—Nude taking off her clothes and walking toward Charles at the piano.
Higher Education (1987; Canadian) . . . . . Gladys/Glitter
State Park (1988; Canadian). . . . . .Linnie
• 0:34—Brief right breast, undoing swimsuit top while sunbathing.
• 0:39—Brief topless, taking off swimsuit top while cutting Raymond's hair.
Physical Evidence (1989). . . . . Waitress
Made for Cable Movies:
Soft Touch (1987; Playboy). . . . . Tracy Anderson
(Shown on *The Playboy Channel* as *Birds in Paradise*.)
• 0:01—Full frontal nudity during the opening credits.
• 0:02—Topless with her two girlfriends during the opening credits.
••• 0:17—Topless exercising on the floor, walking around the room, the lying on bed. Long scene.
• 0:20—Full frontal nudity getting out of bed.
•• 0:23—Topless in bed.
••• 0:50—Topless sunbathing on boat with Carrie.

•• 1:01—Full frontal nudity, sitting on towel, watching Carrie.
• 1:02—Full frontal nudity, waving to a dolphin.
•• 1:04—Topless at night by campfire with Carrie.
••• 1:05—Brief left breast, then topless putting on skirt and walking around the island.
•• 1:13—Topless in hut with island guy.
• 1:19—Topless in stills during the end credits.
Soft Touch II (1987; Playboy) . . . . Tracy Anderson
(Shown on *The Playboy Channel* as *Birds in Paradise*.)
• 0:01—Topless during opening credits.
• 0:02—Topless with her two girlfriends during opening credits.
•• 0:14—Topless dancing in Harry's bar by herself.
• 0:27—Full frontal nudity on stage at Harry's after robbers tell her to strip.
• 0:29—Side of left breast tied to Neill on bed.
• 0:31—Topless tied up when Ashley and Carrie discover her.
•• 0:52—Full frontal nudity during strip poker game, then covered with whipped cream.
• 0:57—Full frontal nudity getting out of bed.
Made for TV Movies:
Anne of Green Gables (1985; Canadian) . . . . Ruby Gillis

• Ingalls, Joyce
Films:
The Man Who Would Not Die (1975) . . . . . Pat Reagan
Paradise Alley (1978) . . . . .Bunchie
Deadly Force (1983) . . . . .Eddie Cooper
•• 0:48—Topless, making out with Wings Hauser on hammock.

Ingersoll, Amy
Films:
Knightriders (1981) . . . . Linet
• 0:00—Very brief left breast, while lying down, then sitting up in woods next to Ed Harris.
Splash (1984). . . . . Reporter

Innes, Alexandra
Films:
Perfect Timing (1984) . . . . Salina
•• 1:06—Right breast and buns, posing for Harry.
Joshua Then and Now (1985; Canadian) . . . . . . .Joanna

• Irwin, Jennifer
Films:
The Gate (1988; Canadian) . . . . . Linda Lee, Lori's Sister
Bikini Summer (1991) . . . . Mindy
The Bikini Carwash Company (1992)
. . . . Awesome Beach Girl
(Unrated version reviewed.)
•• 0:00—Buns, on beach in a very small swimsuit.
••• 0:02—Brief right breast, turning over, then topless while yelling at Jack.
Made for TV Movies:
Anne of Green Gables (1985; Canadian) . . . . . . Student

Isaacs, Susan

Films:
Deadly Passion (1985) . . . . Trixie
•• 0:02—Topless sitting up in bed talking to Brent Huff.
She's Out of Control (1989) . . . . Receptionist
The War of the Roses (1989) . . . . . Auctioneer's Assistant
Delirious (1991) . . . . Marie

Jackson, Glenda

Films:
The Music Lovers (1971) . . . . Nina Milyukova
Full frontal nudity after stripping in railway carriage.
Sunday, Bloody Sunday (1971) . . . . Alex Greville
Women in Love (1971) . . . . Gudrun Brangwen
(Academy Award for Best Actress.)
••• 1:20—Topless taking off her blouse on the bed with
Oliver Reed watching her, then making love.
•• 1:49—Brief left breast making love with Reed in bed
again.
A Touch of Class (1972) . . . . Vicki Allessio
(Academy Award for Best Actress.)
The Nelson Affair (1973) . . . . Lady Emma Hamilton
The Triple Echo (1973; British) . . . . Alice
The Romantic Englishwoman (1975; British/French)
. . . . Elizabeth
• 0:30—Brief full frontal nudity outside, taking robe
off in front of Michael Caine.
• 0:31—Buns, walking back into the house.
• 1:08—Side view of right breast sitting at edge of
pool talking to Thomas.
• 1:45—Very, very brief topless in bed talking with Th-
omas.
The Incredible Sarah (1976) . . . . Sarah Bernhardt
Nasty Habits (1977) . . . . Alexandra
The Class of Miss MacMichael (1978)
. . . . Conor MacMichael
House Calls (1978) . . . . Ann Atkinson
Stevie (1978) . . . . Stevie Smith
Lost and Found (1979) . . . . Tricia
Hopscotch (1980) . . . . Isobel von Schmidt
Return of the Soldier (1983; British) . . . . Margaret
Turtle Diary (1986; British) . . . . Naerea Duncan
Beyond Therapy (1987) . . . . Charlotte
Salome's Last Dance (1987) . . . . . . Herodias/Lady Alice
The Rainbow (1989) . . . . Anna Brangwen
Magazines:
Playboy (Dec 1973). . . . . Sex Stars of 1973
• 206—Right breast under sheer blouse.
Playboy (Nov 1976) . . . . Sex in Cinema 1976
• 146—Topless sitting by the pool in a photo from *The
Romantic Englishwoman.*

• Jackson, Jennifer Lyn

Video Tapes:
Playboy Video Calendar 1990 (1989) . . . September
••• 0:46—Nude.
Magazines:
Playboy (Apr 1989) . . . . Playmate

Playboy's Book of Lingerie (Jan 1991) . . . . . . Herself
••• 85—Full frontal nudity.
Playboy's Book of Lingerie (Sep 1992) . . . . . . Herself
•• 47—Left breast and lower frontal nudity.

• Jackson, Kelly

Video Tapes:
Penthouse Passport to Paradise/Hawaii (1991)
. . . . Model
••• 0:17—Undressing outside by a spa. In lingerie, then
nude on a lounge chair and in the spa.
Magazines:
Penthouse (Oct 1990) . . . . Pet
••• 67-81—Nude.
Playboy's Book of Lingerie (Mar 1991) . . . . . . Herself
•• 79—Right breast and lower frontal nudity.
Playboy's Book of Lingerie (Sep 1991) . . . . . . Herself
••• 90—Topless.
Playboy's Book of Lingerie (Nov 1991) . . . . . Herself
• 21—Right breast.
Playboy's Book of Lingerie (Jan 1992) . . . . . . Herself
••• 75—Full frontal nudity.
•• 76-77—Left breast and buns.
Playboy's Book of Lingerie (Sep 1992) . . . . . . Herself
•• 17—Side of buns and right breast.
••• 22—Full frontal nudity.

Jackson, La Toya

Singer.
Member of the singing Jackson clan.
Magazines:
Playboy (Mar 1989) . . . . Don't Tell Michael
••• 122-133—Topless and buns.
Playboy (Dec 1989) . . . . Holy Sex Stars of 1989!
••• 185—Topless in bed.
Playboy's Nudes (Oct 1990) . . . . Herself
••• 37—Topless and buns.
Playboy (Nov 1991) . . . . Free at Last
•• 82-91—Topless and buns.
Playboy (Dec 1991) . . . . Sex Stars 1991
••• 186—Topless.
Playboy (Jan 1992) . . . . The Year in Sex
•• 149—Topless under fishnet lingerie.

• Jackson, Pamela

Films:
Roadhouse (1989) . . . . Strip Joint Girl
Angel of Passion (1991) . . . . Eileen
••• 1:13—Topless and upper half of buns while on bed
with Eric making love.

Jackson, Victoria

Films:
Double Exposure (1983) . . . . Racetrack Model #1
Baby Boom (1987) . . . . Eve, the Nanny
Casual Sex? (1988) . . . . Melissa
0:30—Brief buns lying down with Lea Thompson at
a nude beach.

0:33—Brief buns wrapping a towel around herself just before getting a massage. Long shot, hard to see.
1:06—Brief buns getting out of bed.
Family Business (1989) . . . . Christine
UHF (1989) . . . . Teri
I Love You to Death (1990) . . . . Lacey
TV:
Half Nelson (1985) . . . . Annie O'Hara
Saturday Night Live (1986-) . . . . Regular

• Jacob, Irène
Films:
Au Revoir, Les Enfants (1987; French) . . . . n.a.
The Double Life of Veronique (1991; French)
. . . . Veronika/Véronique
•• 0:04—Left breast, then topless lying in bed with her boyfriend.
0:22—In bra and panties in her bedroom.
••• 0:28—Brief lower frontal nudity, then topless while making love with her boyfriend.
• 0:41—Brief left breast, while sitting up in bed to answer the phone.

Jacobs, Emma
Films:
The Stud (1978; British) . . . . Alexandra
•• 0:44—In bra, then topless taking bra off in bedroom.
• 0:48—Close up of breasts making love with Tony in his dark apartment.
• 1:14—Topless in bed with Tony, yelling at him.
Lifeforce (1985). . . . . Crew Member

Jagger, Bianca
Ex-wife of singer Mick Jagger.
Films:
The American Success Company (1979) . . . Corinne
• 0:35—Topless under see-through black top while sitting on bed.
The Cannonball Run (1981) . . . . Sheik's Sister
C.H.U.D. II (1989). . . . . n.a.
Magazines:
Playboy (Dec 1980). . . . . Grapevine
• 389—Topless under sheer black top.

Jahan, Marine
Films:
Flashdance (1983)
. . . . Uncredited Dance Double for Jennifer Beals
Streets of Fire (1984). . . . . "Torchie's" Dancer
0:28—Buns in G-string dancing in club.
0:34—More dancing.
• 0:35—Very brief right breast under body stocking, then almost topless under stocking when taking off T-shirt.
Video Tapes:
Freedanse with Marine Jahan . . . . Herself

• James, Courtney
Films:
Galactic Gigolo (1989). . . . . Lisa
a.k.a. Club Earth
Breakfast in Bed (1990) . . . . Mitzi
Private Screenings.
••• 0:36—Topless, walking into the pool. Also seen from under water.
••• 0:37—Topless and bun in G-string, getting out of pool.
• 0:39—Topless on the beach with Mr. Stewart.

• James, Mikel
Films:
Hangup (1974) . . . . n.a.
I Spit on Your Corpse (1974) . . . . Laura
The Naughty Stewardesses (1978) . . . . Diane
•• 0:34—Topless in bed waiting for Ben then in bed with him.
Magazines:
Playboy (Nov 1973) . . . . Sex in Cinema 1973
•• 155—Full frontal nudity in photo from *Hangup* that is incorrectly identifying her as Marki Bey.

Janssen, Marlene
Films:
School Spirit (1985) . . . . Sleeping Princess
•• 0:16—Topless in shower room, shaving her legs.
•• 0:42—Topless and buns, sleeping when old guy goes invisible to peek at her.
Video Tapes:
Playboy Video Magazine, Volume 5 (1983)
. . . . Playmate
• 0:05—Brief topless with rose.
Playboy's Playmate Review 2 (1984) . . . . . Playmate
Playmates at Play (1990) . . . . Flights of Fancy
Magazines:
Playboy (Nov 1982) . . . . Playmate

Jasaé
Films:
Cave Girl (1985). . . . . Locker Room Student
•• 0:05—Topless with four other girls in the girls' locker room undressing, then running after Rex. She's sitting on a bench, wearing red and white panties.
Unexpected Encounters, Vol. 3 (1988). . . . Neighbor
••• 0:32—Doing strip tease in front of guitar playing neighbor. Buns in G-string and topless.
Roadhouse (1989) . . . . Strip Joint Girl
Bad Girls from Mars (1990) . . . . Terry
••• 0:03—Topless taking off her top.
•• 0:05—More topless going into dressing room.
Mob Boss (1990) . . . . Bar Girl
•• 0:46—Topless serving drinks to the guys at the table.
Carnal Crimes (1991) . . . . Christa
••• 0:19—Full frontal nudity in lingerie, making love with a guy while Linda Carol secretly watches.

Roots of Evil (1991) . . . . Subway Hooker
(Unrated version reviewed.)
••• 1:05—Topless taking off her top in subway stairwell,
then getting killed by the bad guy.
The Swindle (1991) . . . . Nina
••• 0:28—Nude, posing for Tom while he video tapes
her. Long scene.
••• 0:31—Nude, making love with Tom.
••• 0:36—Topless in back of limousine with Dude.
Video Tapes:
Candid Candid Camera, Volume 4 (1985) . . .Model
••• 0:03—Full frontal nudity, talking on the phone.
•• 0:18—Buns and lower frontal nudity, when her skirt
is blown upwards like Marilyn Monroe.
••• 0:31—Nude, trying to get people to sign a petition
against nudity on cable TV.
Becky Bubbles (1987) . . . . Herself
•• 0:16—Topless, taking off yellow swimsuit top and
getting pushed on swing, then pushing Brandi.
••• 0:17—Topless, playing with a ball on the grass with
Brandi.
••• 0:19—Topless, drinking wine and sitting on swing.
Wild Bikinis (1987) . . . . Herself
••• 0:32—Topless on swing, then pushing Brandi on
swing from *Becky Bubbles*.
••• 0:35—Topless playing with ball on the grass.
••• 0:37—Topless on swing, drinking wine.
• 0:55—Topless on swing, making a funny face.
Centerfold Screen Test, Take 3 (1988) . . . . . Herself
••• 0:42—Nude after undressing and posing on sofa.
Long scene.
Starlet Screen Test II (1991) . . . . .Jasae
••• 0:05—Nude on couch (same segment from *Center-
fold Screen Test, Take 3*.)
Magazines:
Playboy's Book of Lingerie (Sep 1991) . . . . . Herself
••• 75—Topless.
••• 105—Topless.
Playboy's Book of Lingerie (Nov 1991) . . . . . Herself
••• 12—Topless.
•• 37—Left breast.
Playboy (Jan 1992) . . . . .Grapevine
•• 208—Buns and side of right breast, wearing G-string
and boots. B&W.

• Jason, Chona
Films:
Summer Job (1989). . . . . .Beautiful Lady
Magazines:
Playboy's Book of Lingerie (Sep 1991) . . . . . Herself
•• 40-41—Left breast.

• Jean, Stevie
Video Tapes:
**Penthouse Satin & Lace: An Erotic History of
Lingerie** (1992) . . . . .Model
Magazines:
Penthouse (Jan 1992) . . . . Pet
••• 87-117—Nude.

Jemison, Anna
See: Monticelli, Anna-Maria.

• Jenkin, Devon
Films:
Slammer Girls (1987) . . . . Melody Campbell
0:08—In lingerie in her bedroom, then in jail.
• 0:12—Brief topless getting lingerie ripped off by the
prison matron.
• 0:16—Brief topless getting blouse ripped off by Tank
in the shower.
Twisted Nightmare (1987) . . . . n.a.
Music Videos:
Free Fallin'/Tom Petty. . . . . n.a.
Magazines:
Playboy (Jun 1992). Grapevine

Jennings, Claudia
Films:
The Love Machine (1971) . . . . Darlene
Group Marriage (1972) . . . . .Elaine
••• 1:02—Topless under mosquito net in bed with Phil.
Long scene.
Unholy Rollers (1972). . . . . .Karen
a.k.a. Leader of the Pack
40 Carats (1973) . . . . Gabriella
Bloody Friday (1973) . . . . Allison
a.k.a. Single Girls
• 0:40—Topless, taking off her dress to sunbathe on
rock at the beach. Long shot. Side view of right
breast, putting dress back on when George talks to
her.
•• 0:57—Topless, drying herself off after shower.
Gator Bait (1973) . . . . Desiree
• 0:06—Brief left and right breasts during boat chase
sequence.
Truck Stop Women (1974). . . . . Rose
• 0:27—Brief topless taking off blouse and getting
into bed.
0:48—Brief side view of right breast in mirror, getting dressed.
• 1:10—Brief topless wrapping and unwrapping a
towel around herself.
The Man Who Fell to Earth (1976; British)
. . . . Uncredited Girl by the Pool
(Uncensored version reviewed.)
• 1:42—Topless, standing by the pool and kissing
Bernie Casey.
The Great Texas Dynamite Chase (1977)
. . . . Candy Morgan
Moonshine County Express (1977). . . . . . Betty Hammer
Death Sport (1978) . . . . Deneer
Impulsion (1978) . . . . n.a.
Fast Company (1979; Canadian) . . . . Sammy
The Best of Sex and Violence (1981) . . . . Rose
•• 0:46—Topless taking off her blouse in scene from
Truck Stop Women.

Famous T & A (1982) . . . . Rose
(No longer available for purchase, check your video
store for rental.)
•• 0:26—Topless scenes from *Single Girls* and *Truck Stop
Women.*
Magazines:
Playboy (Nov 1969) . . . . Playmate
Playboy (Nov 1972) . . . . Sex in Cinema 1972
• 166—Topless lying down in a photo from *The Unho-
ly Rollers.*
Playboy (Dec 1972). . . . . Sex Stars of 1972
•• 211—Topless.
Playboy (Dec 1973). . . . . Sex Stars of 1973
••• 208—Full frontal nudity.
Playboy (Jan 1974) . . . . Twenty Years of Playmates
•• 110—Left breast.
Playboy (Dec 1974)
. . . . Claudia Observed & Sex Stars of 1974
••• 129-135—Nude.
••• 206—Topless in open blouse.
Playboy (Jan 1979) . . . . 25 Beautiful Years
••• 162—Topless.
Playboy (Sep 1979). . . . . Claudia Recaptured
••• 118-123—Topless.
Playboy (Jan 1989) . . . . Women of the Seventies
••• 217—Topless.

Jennings, Julia
Films:
Teachers (1984) . . . . The Blonde
•• 0:05—Brief left breast, while sitting up in bed with
Nick Nolte.
Dragnet (1987). Sylvia Wiss

Jenrette, Rita
Ex-wife of former U.S. Representative John Jenrette, who
was convicted in 1980 in the FBI's Abscam probe.
Now using her maiden name of Rita Carpenter.
Films:
Zombie Island Massacre (1984) . . . . Sandy
••• 0:01—Topless taking a shower while Joe sneaks up
on her. Topless in bed with Joe.
•• 0:10—Brief right breast with open blouse, in boat
with Joe. Left breast with him on the couch.
The Malibu Bikini Shop (1985) . . . . Aunt Ida
End of the Line (1987) . . . . Sharon
Made for Cable TV:
Dream On: And Bimbo Was His Name-O (1992; HBO)
. . . . Jennifer Klarik
Magazines:
Playboy (Apr 1981)
. . . . The Liberation of a Congressional Wife
••• 116-125—Full frontal nudity.
Playboy (May 1984) . . . . Hello, Young Lovers
•• 128-129—Right breast.

Jensen, Maren
Films:
Beyond the Reef (1981) . . . . .Diana
(Not available on video tape.)
Deadly Blessing (1981). . . . . Martha
•• 0:27—Topless and buns changing into a nightgown
while a creepy guy watches through the window.
0:52—Buns, getting into the bathtub. Kind of
steamy and hard to see.
• 0:56—Brief topless in bathtub with snake. (Notice
that she gets into the tub naked, but is wearing
black panties in the water).
TV:
Battlestar Galactica (1978-79) . . . . .Athena

Jillson, Joyce
Astrologer.
Films:
Slumber Party '57 (1976) . . . . Gladys
The Happy Hooker Goes to Washington (1977)
. . . . Herself
Superchick (1978) . . . . Tara B. True/Superchick
• 0:03—Brief upper half of right breast leaning back in
bathtub.
•• 0:06—Topless in bed throwing cards up.
• 0:16—Brief topless under net on boat with Johnny.
• 0:29—Brief right breast several times in airplane restroom with a Marine.
1:12—Buns, frolicking in the ocean with Johnny.
Don't see her face.
• 1:27—Close up of breasts (probably body double)
when sweater pops open.

•Jilot, Yolanda
Films:
Diving In (1990). . . . . Amanda Lansky
0:32—In red, one piece swimsuit, getting out of the
pool to talk to Wayne.
0:54—In blue, one piece swimsuit, getting out of
the pool.
• 0:55—Brief topless, in open blouse, getting dressed
while talking to Burt Young.
Waxwork II: Lost in Time (1991) . . . . . Lady of the Night
TV:
Reasonable Doubts (1992-) . . . . Marta

Johari, Azizi
Films:
Body and Soul (1981) . . . . Pussy Willow
••• 0:31—Topless sitting on bed with Leon Isaac
Kennedy, then left breast, while lying in bed.
Magazines:
Playboy (Jun 1975). . . . . Playmate

•John, Tylyn
a.k.a. Tylyn.
Video Tapes:
Playboy Video Calendar 1993 (1992). . . . November

Playboy Video Centerfold: Corrina Harney (1992)
.... Playmate
Magazines:
Playboy's Book of Lingerie (Jan 1991) ...... Herself
••• 96-97—Topless.
Playboy's Book of Lingerie (Mar 1991) ..... Herself
••• 57—Topless.
Playboy's Book of Lingerie (Sep 1991) ..... Herself
••• 47—Topless.
Playboy's Book of Lingerie (Nov 1991) ..... Herself
••• 59—Topless.
Playboy (Mar 1992)................... Playmate
••• 98-109—Nude.
Inside Sports (Apr 1992) .... Journey to St. John

Johns, Tracy Camilla
Films:
She's Gotta Have It (1987) .... Nola Darling
••• 0:05—Topless, making love in bed with Jamie.
•• 0:25—Brief left breast taking off leotard with Greer.
  More topless waiting for him to undress.
•• 0:27—Topless and buns in bed with Greer.
• 0:38—Topless, close up of breast, while making love
  with Spike Lee.
•• 0:41—Left breast, while lying in bed with Lee.
•• 1:05—Topless, twice, in bed masturbating.
Mo' Better Blues (1990) .... Club Patron
New Jack City (1991) .... Unigua
• 0:40—Buns, while dancing in red bra, panties, garter belt and stockings.
• 0:53—Buns and right breast in bed with Nino.
Magazines:
Playboy (Nov 1991) .... Sex in Cinema 1991
• 141—Buns, in scene from *New Jack City*.

Johnson, Anne-Marie
Films:
Hollywood Shuffle (1987) .... Lydia
I'm Gonna Git You Sucka (1988)............. Cherry
Robot Jox (1990) .... Athena
•• 0:35—Buns, walking to the showers after talking to
  Achilles and Tex.
The Five Heartbeats (1991) .... Sydney Todd
Strictly Business (1991) .... Diedre
True Identity (1991) .... Kristi
Miniseries:
Jackie Collins' Lucky/Chances (1990)............. n.a.
TV:
Double Trouble (1984-85)............. Aileen Lewis
In the Heat of the Night (1988)......... Althea Tibbs

Johnson, Deborah Nicholle
a.k.a. Debi Johnson.
Video Tapes:
Playmate Playoffs .... Playmate
Playmates at Play (1990) .... Hardbodies
Magazines:
Playboy (Oct 1984).................... Playmate

Playboy's Book of Lingerie (Jan 1991) ..... Herself
• 53—Buns.
Playboy's Book of Lingerie (Nov 1991) ..... Herself
•• 86—Full frontal nudity in sheer patterned black bodysuit.
Playboy's Book of Lingerie (Jan 1992) ...... Herself
••• 52—Topless.
••• 68—Topless.
Playboy's Book of Lingerie (Mar 1992)..... Herself
• 70-71—Right breast and lower frontal nudity.
Playboy's Book of Lingerie (Sep 1992) ...... Herself
••• 31—Topless.

Johnson, Jill
Films:
Party Favors (1987)...................... Trixie
•• 0:04—Topless in dressing room, taking off blue dress
  and putting on red swimsuit.
••• 0:35—Topless in doctors office taking off her
  clothes.
••• 1:03—Topless doing strip routine in cowgirl costume. More topless after.
• 1:16—Topless taking off swimsuit next to pool during final credits.
Wildest Dreams (1987)........... Rachel Richards
•• 0:51—Topless on bed underneath Bobby in a net.
• 1:10—Brief topless during fight with two other
  women.
Party Plane (1988) .... Laurie
••• 0:06—Topless and buns changing clothes and getting into spa with her two girlfriends. (She's wearing
  a black swimsuit bottom.)
••• 0:11—Topless getting out of spa.
•• 0:16—Topless in pool after being pushed in and her
  swimsuit top comes off.
•• 0:20—In bra and panties, then topless on plane doing a strip tease.
Taking Care of Business (1990)....... Tennis Court Girl

•Johnson, Kimberly
Video Tapes:
Hot Body International: #2 Miss Puerto Vallarta
(1990) ....Contestant
•• 0:43—Buns in two piece swimsuit.
Hot Body International: #4 Spring Break (1992)
................................Contestant
0:12—Dancing in one piece swimsuit on stage.
0:25—Wet T-shirt contest. Buns in G-string.
Magazines:
Playboy's Book of Lingerie (Sep 1991) ..... Herself
••• 23—Full frontal nudity.
Playboy's Book of Lingerie (Jan 1992) ...... Herself
••• 31—Full frontal nudity.
Playboy's Book of Lingerie (May 1992) ..... Herself
••• 40-41—Nude.
Playboy's Book of Lingerie (Jul 1992)....... Herself
• 88—Side view of left breast.
Playboy's Book of Lingerie (Sep 1992) ...... Herself
•• 82—Right breast.

•Johnson, Laura

Films:

Opening Night (1977) . . . . Nancy Stein

Fatal Instinct (1991) . . . . Catherine Merrims
(Unrated version reviewed.)

 • 0:45—Brief left breast in open robe, getting out of
 bed.

••• 0:47—Topless in bed talking with Michael Madsen,
 then making love.

••• 0:51—Topless in the bathtub when Bill comes in.
 Partial lower frontal nudity when standing up.

•• 0:52—Brief buns and topless getting dressed in bedroom.

 • 0:59—In wet T-shirt in pool. Brief buns, underwater,
 more when getting out.

Made for Cable TV:

Red Shoe Diaries: Double Dare (1992; Showtime)
. . . . Diane

 0:11—In white bra in her office.
 0:14—In black bra in her office.

••• 0:16—Topless, taking off her bra in her office.

•• 0:17—More topless, caressing herself.

 • 0:18—Topless in bed, making love with her husband, Sam.

•• 0:25—Topless in the shower.

Made for TV Movies:

Nick Knight (1989) . . . . Alyce

TV:

Falcon Crest (1983-86) . . . . .Terry Hartford Ranson
Heartbeat (1988-89) . . . . .Dr. Eve Autrey/Calvert

Johnson, Michelle

Films:

Blame It on Rio (1984) . . . . .Jennifer Lyons

•• 0:19—Topless on the beach greeting Michael Caine
 and Joseph Bologna with Demi Moore, then brief
 topless in the ocean.

 • 0:26—Topless taking her clothes off for Caine on the
 beach. Dark, hard to see.

•• 0:27—Topless seducing Caine. Dark, hard to see.

••• 0:56—Full frontal nudity taking off robe and sitting
 on bed to take a Polaroid picture of herself.

 • 0:57—Very brief topless in the Polaroid photo showing it to Caine.

 • 1:02—Brief topless taking off her top in front of
 Caine while her dad rests on the sofa.

Gung Ho (1985) . . . . Heather

Beaks The Movie (1987) . . . . .Vanessa

 • 0:26—Brief topless covered with bubbles after taking a bath. Don't see her face.

 • 0:31—Brief topless covered with bubbles after getting out of bathtub with Christopher Atkins. Don't
 see her face.

Slipping into Darkness (1987) . . . . Carlyle
The Jigsaw Murders (1988) . . . . .Kathy DaVonzo
 0:51—Posing in leotards in dance studio.
 1:07—Posing in lingerie on bed.
 1:20—In light blue dance outfit.
 1:27—Posing in blue swimsuit.

Waxwork (1988) . . . . China
Genuine Risk (1989) . . . . Girl
 0:27—In black bra in room with Henry.
 0:29—In bra in open top coming out of the bathroom.

 • 0:43—On bed in black bra and panties with Henry.
 Left breast peeking out of the top of her bra.

Driving Me Crazy (1991) . . . . .Ricki
Far and Away (1992) .Grace

Made for Cable TV:

Tales From the Crypt: Split Second (1991; HBO)
. . . . .Liz Kelly-Dixon

••• 0:15—Topless, offering her towel to Ted for him to
 dry her off.
 0:19—In bra and panties with Ted at night.

Made for TV Movies:

A Woman Scorned: The Betty Broderick Story (1992)
. . . . Linda

TV:

Werewolf (1987) . . . . n.a.

•Johnson, Penny

Films:

Swing Shift (1984) . . . . Genevieve

The Hills Have Eyes, Part II (1989) . . . . Sue

 • 0:49—Brief topless in bus, trying to get Foster's attention.

TV:

Paper Chase (1984-86) . . . . Vivian
Homeroom (1989). Virginia

Johnson, Sandy

Films:

Two-Minute Warning (1976) . . . . .Button's Wife
Gas Pump Girls (1978). . . . . n.a.

Halloween (1978) . . . . Judith Meyers
 0:06—Very brief topless covered with blood on floor
 after Michael stabs her to death.

H.O.T.S. (1979) . . . . Stephanie

•• 0:27—Topless on balcony in red bikini bottoms.

•• 1:34—Topless during football game during huddle
 with all the other girls.

Terror in the Aisles (1984) . . . . Judith Meyers

 • 0:15—Brief topless in scene from *Halloween*.

Magazines:

Playboy (Jun 1974). . . . . Playmate

••• 118-127—Full frontal nudity.

Johnson, Sunny

Films:

Animal House (1978) . . . . .Otter's Co-Ed
Dr. Heckyl and Mr. Hype (1980). . . . . Coral Careen
Where the Buffalo Roam (1980). . . . . n.a.
The Night the Lights Went Out in Georgia (1981)
. . . . .Wendy

Flashdance (1983). . . . . Jennie Szabo

 • 1:28—Topless on stage with other strippers.

Made for TV Movies:

The Red Light Sting (1984) . . . . n.a.

•Johnson, Terri

Films:

Video Vixens (1973). . . . . .Anita
•• 0:43—Full frontal nudity, talking with her mother in bedroom during commercial.
The Cocktail Hostess (1976) . . . . .n.a.

Johnson, Victoria Lynn

Films:

Dressed to Kill (1980)
. . . . Body Double for Angie Dickinson
•• 0:02—Frontal nudity in the shower body doubling for Angie Dickinson.
Terror in the Aisles (1984)
. . . . Body Double for Angie Dickinson
• 1:07—Topless in shower from Angie Dickinson's shower scene in *Dressed to Kill*.

Video Tapes:

The Girls of Penthouse (1984) . . . . Centerfold
••• 0:43—Nude during photo session with Bob Guccione.

Magazines:

Penthouse (Aug 1976) . . . . Pet
Penthouse (Nov 1977) . . . . Pet of the Year

•Johnston, Michelle

Films:

Dick Tracy (1990) . . . . Dancer
Opportunity Knocks (1990). . . . . Club Singer
California Casanova (1991) . . . . Laura
• 0:18—Brief topless under sheer black top in front of a guy.
Shout (1991). . . . . Loretta

Joi, Marilyn

Films:

The Happy Hooker Goes to Washington (1977)
. . . . Sheila
• 0:09—Left breast while on a couch.
• 0:47—Brief topless during car demonstration.
•• 1:14—Topless in military guy's office.
Kentucky Fried Movie (1977) . . . . Cleopatra
• 1:11—Topless in bed with Schwartz.
Ilsa, Harem Keeper of the Oil Sheiks (1978). . . . . . Velvet
Nurse Sherri (1978). . . . . .n.a.
C.O.D. (1983). . . . . Debbie Winter
•• 1:16—Topless during photo session.
• 1:25—Brief topless taking off robe wearing red garter belt during dressing room scene.
1:26—In red bra, while talking to Albert.
1:30—In red bra during fashion show.
Satan's Princess (1989) . . . . Hooker

•Jones, Amanda

Films:

Honky Tonk Nights (1978) . . . . .Honey
•• 0:41—Topless outside by car with Dan.
••• 0:42—Topless and buns, in the woods with Dan.
Winter Kills (1979) . . . . Beautiful Woman Seven

Jones, Charlene

Films:

Unholy Rollers (1972). Beverly
a.k.a. Leader of the Pack
The Woman Hunt (1975; U.S./Philippines). . . . . n.a.
Hard to Hold (1984). . . . . .Wife
Avenging Angel (1985) . . . . Hooker
Perfect (1985) . . . . Shotsy
• 0:17—Topless stripping on stage in a club. Buns in G-string.

Jones, Grace

Films:

Conan the Destroyer (1984). . . . . .Zula
Deadly Vengeance (1985) . . . . Slick's Girlfriend
(Although the copyright on the movie states 1985, it looks more like the 1970's.)
••• 0:06—Right breast, then topless in bed with Slick.
•• 0:13—Left breast, when Slick sits up in bed, then full frontal nudity after he gets up.
A View to a Kill (1985) . . . . May Day
Vamp (1986) . . . . .Katrina
0:23—Topless under wire bra, dancing on stage. Body is painted, so it's difficult to see.
Siesta (1987) . . . . Conchita
Straight to Hell (1987; British) . . . . Sonya

Magazines:

Playboy (Apr 1979) . . . . n.a.
Playboy (Jan 1985). . . . . n.a.
101—Small color photo.
Playboy (Jul 1985) . . . . Amazing Grace
• 82-87—Topless and buns in B&W photos of her and Dolph Lundgren.
Playboy (Nov 1992) . . . . Grapevine
• 190—Half of left breast in open blouse. B&W.

•Jones, Helen

Films:

Bliss (1985; Australian) . . . . .Honey Barbara
••• 0:58—Topless, lying on the floor with Harry. Brief part of lower frontal nudity. Long scene.
• 1:01—Brief topless on bed when Adrian runs to the bathroom.
1:24—Left breast while standing outside with arms outstretched.
• 1:39—Buns, while swimming. Long shot of buns while walking up rocks.
The Good Wife (1987; Australian) . . . . Rosie Gibbs
a.k.a. The Umbrella Woman

Made for TV Movies:

The Girl From Tomorrow (1990; Australian) . . . . n.a.

Jones, Josephine Jaqueline

a.k.a. J. J. Jones.
Former Miss Bahamas.
Films:
Black Venus (1983). Venus
- •• 0:05—Topless in Jungle Room.
- ••• 0:11—Nude, in bedroom, posing for Armand while he sketches.
- • 0:14—Topless and buns making love with Armand in bed.
- •• 0:17—Nude, posing for Armand while he models in clay, then on the bed, kissing him.
- • 0:21—Brief nude getting dressed.
- ••• 0:38—Nude, making love in bed with Karin Schubert.
- 0:45—Nude, talking and then making love in bed with Louise.
- •• 0:50—Topless when Pierre brings everybody in to see her.
- •• 0:57—Topless in silhouette while Armand fantasizes about his statue coming to life.
- ••• 1:04—Nude.
- ••• 1:07—Nude with the two diplomats on the bed.
- ••• 1:16—Nude frolicking on the beach with Louise.
- ••• 1:18—Topless in bedroom getting out of wet clothes with Louise.
- •• 1:21—Topless in bed with Jacques.
- •• 1:24—Full frontal nudity getting out of bed.
Love Circles Around the World (1984) . . . . . . Brigid
- •• 0:18—Topless, then nude running around her apartment chasing Jack.
- • 0:30—Topless, making love with Count Crispa in his hotel room.
Warrior Queen (1987) . . . . Chloe
- ••• 0:20—Topless making love with Vespa.

Jones, Marilyn

Films:
Support Your Local Sheriff! (1969). . . . . Bordello Girl
The Scenic Route (1978). . . . . Lena
Meteor (1979) . . . . Stunt
The Men's Club (1986). . . . . Allison
- •• 1:21—Topless wearing gold panties standing in bedroom talking to Harvey Keitel.
On the Block (1990) . . . . Libby
Made for TV Movies:
The Lakeside Killer (1979) . . . . Cindy Lee
TV:
Secrets of Midland Heights (1980-81) . . . . Holly Wheeler
King's Crossing (1982) . . . . Carey Hollister

Jones, Rachel

Films:
Dracula's Widow (1988) . . . . Jenny
- • 0:54—Brief left breast, then brief topless, twice, lying in the bathtub, getting stabbed by Sylvia Kristel.
Fresh Horses (1988) . . . . Bobo

Jones, Rebunkah

Films:
Frankenstein General Hospital (1988)
. . . . Elizabeth Rice
- •• 1:05—Topless in the office letting Mark Blankfield examine her back.
Hide and Go Shriek (1988). . . . . Bonnie Williams
- •• 0:27—Topless taking off her blouse. More topless sitting in bed.

•Jones, Sharon Lee

Films:
9 1/2 Ninjas (1990). . . . . Zelda
- • 0:52—Topless eating Chinese food in the shower with Joe.
Grand Canyon (1991) . . . . Studio Girl

•Jordan, Deanna

Video Tapes:
Hot Body International: #2 Miss Puerto Vallarta (1990)
. . . . Contestant
Hot Body International: #4 Spring Break (1992)
. . . . Contestant
- • 0:13—Dancing in two piece swimsuit on stage. Brief partial right breast.
- • 0:49—Brief topless several times when she rips her wet T-shirt open. Buns in G-string.

Jourdan, Catherine

Films:
Girl on a Motorcycle (1968; French/British) . . Catherine
a.k.a. Naked Under Leather
The Godson (1972; Italian/French). . . . . . .Hatcheck Girl
Aphrodite (1982; German/French) . . . . Valerie
- • 0:34—Brief upper half of breasts in bathtub.

•Jovovich, Milla

Model.
Daughter of Soviet actress Galina Jovovich.
Films:
Return to the Blue Lagoon (1991) Lilli
- • 0:49—Brief upper half topless in front of mirror.
- • 1:07—Very brief topless under water with Richard. Brief topless under waterfall with Richard.
- 1:09—Brief partial left breast on hilltop with Richard. Necklace gets in the way.
- • 1:20—Briefly in wet beige blouse, standing up in pond.
- • 1:26—Side view of right breast three times, washing make up off her face in the pond.
- •• 1:28—Side view of right breast again. Very brief left breast, while picking up her top off rock.
- 1:30—Side of left breast, lying on bed while held down.
Kuffs (1992). . . . . .Maya Carlton
- 0:00—Dancing, while wearing a braless blue tank top and white panties.
Made for Cable Movies:
Night Train to Kathmandu (1988; Disney) . . . . Lily

Joyner, Michelle

Films:

Grim Prairie Tales (1990) . . . . Jenny
- 0:35—Very brief right breast, then left breast while making love with Marc McClure. Kind of dark.

I Love You to Death (1990) . . . . Donna Joy

Made for TV Movies:

Baby of the Bride (1991) . . . . Judy
Bonnie and Clyde: The True Story (1992)
. . . . Blanche Barrow

TV:

Knots Landing . . . . Lynnette

Julian, Janet

a.k.a. Janet Louise Johnson.

Films:

Humongous (1982; Canadian) . . . . Sandy Ralston
Fear City (1984) . . . . Ruby
Choke Canyon (1986). . . . . Vanessa Pilgrim
King of New York (1990). . . . . Jennifer
- 0:26—Very brief left breast, standing in subway car kissing Christopher Walken. Don't see her face.

Heaven is a Playground (1991) . . . . Dalton Ellis

TV:

The Nancy Drew Mysteries (1978) . . . . Nancy Drew

Kafkaloff, Kim

a.k.a Adult film actress Sheri St. Clair or Sheri St. Cloud.

Films:

Sex Appeal (1986) . . . . Stephanie
- 0:29—Buns, in G-string in Tony's bachelor pad. Topless dancing and on bed.

Slammer Girls (1987). Ginny
- 0:23—Brief topless changing clothes under table in the prison cafeteria.

Kaitan, Elizabeth

a.k.a. Elizabeth Cayton.

Films:

Silent Night, Deadly Night, Part 2 (1986) . . . . . . Jennifer
0:58—Most of right breast, then buns, kissing Ricky.
Slavegirls from Beyond Infinity (1987). . . . . . Daria
(Wearing skimpy two piece loincloth outfit during most of the movie.)
- 0:38—Topless undressing and jumping into bed with Rik.

Assault of the Killer Bimbos (1988) . . . . Lulu
- 0:41—Brief topless during desert musical sequence, opening her blouse, then taking off her shorts, then putting on a light blue dress. Don't see her face.

Friday the 13th, Part VII: The New Blood (1988)
. . . . Robin
- 0:53—Brief left breast in bed making love with a guy.
- 0:55—Brief topless sitting up in bed after making love and the sheet falls down.
- 1:00—Brief topless again sitting up in bed and putting a shirt on over her head.

Necromancer (1988) . . . . Julie Johnson
- 0:41—Topless in the shower with Carl.
- 0:45—Very brief side view of right breast, taking off dress in front of Paul.
1:01—In red and black lingerie.

Nightwish (1988) . . . . Donna
(Unedited version reviewed.)
- 0:04—In wet T-shirt, then brief topless taking it off during experiment. Long shot.
- 1:10—Briefly in braless, see-through purple dress.

Twins (1988) . . . . Secretary
Dr. Alien (1989) . . . . Waitress
 a.k.a. I Was a Teenage Sex Mutant
Night Club (1989) . . . . Beth/Liza
- • 0:31—Left breast, while pulling down blouse and caressing herself.
- • 0:33—Left breast in pulled down blouse on stairwell with Nick.
- • • 0:36—Topless on warehouse floor with Nick.
- • • 0:46—Full frontal nudity, taking off her dress in front of Nick.
- • • 1:03—Topless, making love with another guy in front of Nick.

Under the Boardwalk (1989) . . . . Donna
Aftershock (1990) . . . . Sabina
Lockdown (1990). . . . . Monica Taylor
Roller Blade Warriors (1990). . . . . n.a.
The Girl I Want (1991) . . . . n.a.
Vice Academy, Part 3 (1991) . . . . Candy
- • • 0:12—Topless in back of van with her boyfriend.

Hellroller (1992). . . . . Lizzy

• Kalem, Toni

Films:

The Wanderers (1979) . . . . Despie Galasso
Private Benjamin (1980). n.a.
I'm Dancing as Fast as I Can (1981) . . . . Debbie
Paternity (1981) . . . . Diane Cassabello
Silent Rage (1982). . . . . Alison Halman
- • 0:22—Side view of left breast, then topless, while in bed with Chuck Norris.
- • 0:46—Right breast, while lying in bed with Norris.
1:01—Briefly in bra, undressing in bedroom to take a shower.

Two of a Kind (1983) . . . . Terri
Reckless (1984) . . . . Donna
Billy Galvin (1986) . . . . Nora
Sister Act (1992) . . . . Connie LaRocca

TV:

Another World . . . . Angie Perini
Arresting Behavior (1992-) . . . . Wendy

Kallianiotes, Helena

Films:

The Baby Maker (1970) . . . . Wanda
- 1:30—Brief topless when Barbara Hershey sees her in bed with Tad.

Five Easy Pieces (1970). . . . . Palm Apodaca
Kansas City Bomber (1972) . . . . Jackie Burdette

Shanks (1974). . . . . Mata Hari
The Drowning Pool (1976) . . . . Elaine Reaves
The Passover Plot (1976). . . . . Visionary Woman
Stay Hungry (1976). . . . . .Anita
Backtrack (1989). Grace Carelli
  a.k.a. Catch Fire

Kaminsky, Dana
Films:
Hot Resort (1984). Melanie
  •• 1:02—Topless taking off her white dress in a boat.
Irreconcilable Differences (1984)
  . . . . Woman in Dress Shop

Kane, Carol
Films:
Carnal Knowledge (1971). . . . . .Jennifer
Desperate Characters (1971). . . . . Young Girl
  (Not available on video tape.)
The Last Detail (1973). . . . . Young Whore
  • 1:02—Brief topless sitting on bed talking with Randy
    Quaid. Her hair is in the way, hard to see.
Dog Day Afternoon (1975). . . . . Jenny
Hester Street (1975) . . . . .Gitl
Annie Hall (1977) . . . . Allison
The World's Greatest Lover (1977) . . . . Annie
The Mafu Cage (1978) . . . . .Cissy
  a.k.a. My Sister, My Love
    0:08—Very brief tip of left breast in the bathtub.
When a Stranger Calls (1979) . . . . Jill Johnson
Norman Loves Rose (1982; Australian) . . . . .n.a.
Over the Brooklyn Bridge (1983). . . . . Cheryl
Racing with the Moon (1984) . . . . Annie
Transylvania 6-5000 (1985). . . . . Lupi
Jumpin' Jack Flash (1986) . . . . .Cynthia
Ishtar (1987). . . . . Carol
The Princess Bride (1987) . . . . Valerie
License to Drive (1988). . . . . Mom
Scrooged (1988). . . . . . . The Ghost of Christmas Present
Sticky Fingers (1988). Kitty
The Lemon Sisters (1990) . . . . Franki D'Angelo
My Blue Heaven (1990). . . . . Shaldeen
Ted & Venus (1991) . . . . . . Colette/Colette's Twin Sister
Made for Cable TV:
Tales From the Crypt: Judy, You're Not Yourself Today
  . . . . Judy
TV:
Taxi (1981-83) . . . . Simka Gravas
All Is Forgiven (1986) . . . . Nicolette Bingham
American Dreamer (1990). . . . . .Lillian Abernathy

• Kane, Kathleen
Films:
Shock 'Em Dead (1990) . . . . Pizza Girl 2
Angel of Passion (1991) . . . . Suzette
  •• 1:08—Topless posing for Marty in the house.

Kane, Sharon
Adult film actress.
Films:
Preppies (1984) . . . . Exotic Dancer
Slammer Girls (1987) . . . . Rita
  • 0:23—Brief topless changing clothes under table in
    the prison cafeteria.
  •• 1:01—Topless walking around an electric chair try-
    ing to distract a prison guard.
Video Tapes:
Inside Out 4 (1992) . . . . Video Mate
  (Unrated version reviewed.)
  •• 1:14—Topless on TV.
  ••• 1:16—Topless in Dave's living room.
  • 1:17—Nude, making love with Dave in fast speed.
  ••• 1:18—Topless and buns, on sofa with Dave.
  • 1:19—More topless in fast speed.
  ••• 1:20—Nude in Dave's living room.
  • 1:22—Nude on TV again.

Kaprisky, Valerie
Films:
Aphrodite (1982; German/French) . . . . Pauline
  ••• 0:12—Nude, washing herself off in front of a two-
    way mirror while a man on the other side watches.
Breathless (1983) . . . . Monica Poiccard
  0:23—Brief side view of left breast in her apartment.
    Long shot, hard to see anything.
  ••• 0:47—Topless in her apartment with Richard Gere
    kissing.
  •• 0:52—Brief full frontal nudity standing in the shower
    when Gere opens the door, afterwards, buns in bed.
  •• 0:53—Topless, holding up two dresses for Gere to
    pick from, then topless putting the black dress on.
  • 1:23—Topless behind a movie screen with Gere. Lit
    with red light.
L'Annee Des Meduses (1987; French). . . . . Chris
  •• 0:06—Topless pulling down swimsuit at the beach.
  ••• 0:24—Full frontal nudity while taking off dress with
    older man.
  ••• 0:42—Topless walking around the beach talking to
    everybody.
  ••• 0:46—Topless on the beach taking a shower.
  ••• 1:02—Topless on the beach with her mom.
  ••• 1:37—Nude dancing on the boat for Romain.
  •• 1:42—Topless walking from the beach to the bar.
  •• 1:43—Topless in swimming pool.
Magazines:
Playboy (Dec 1983) . . . . .Sex Stars of 1983
  •• 209—Topless.

Kapture, Mitzi
Films:
Private Road (1987) . . . . .Helen Milshaw
  0:50—Wearing a white bra during a strip-spin-the-
    bottle game.
  •• 1:29—Topless, making love in bed with Greg Evi-
    gan.
Angel III: The Final Chapter (1988). . . . . . Molly Stewart

Lethal Persuit (1989) . . . . Debra J.
- •• 0:32—Topless in motel shower, then getting out. (You can see the top of her swimsuit bottom.)
- 0:47—In wet tank top talking with Warren.

Liberty & Bash (1989) . . . . Sarah
- 0:45—Very briefly sitting up in bed in a semi-transparent yellow sheet.

TV:
Silk Stalkings (1991-) . . . . .Rita Lee Lance

• *Kârkkâinen, Kata*

Video Tapes:
Sexy Lingerie (1988) . . . . .Model
Magazines:
Playboy (Dec 1988) . . . . Playmate
Playboy's Nudes (Oct 1990) . . . . Herself
- ••• 78-79—Full frontal nudity.

Karlatos, Olga

Films:
Wifemistress (1977; Italian)
. . . . Miss Paula Pagano, M.D.
- •• 0:42—Topless undressing in room with Laura Antonelli. Right breast and part of left breast lying in bed with Marcello Mastroianni.
- • 0:46—Brief topless in bed with Mastroianni and Clara.

Zombie (1980) . . . . .Mrs. Menard
- • 0:40—Topless and buns taking a shower.

Once Upon a Time in America (1984)
. . . . Woman in the Puppet Theatre
(Long version reviewed.)
- •• 0:11—Right breast twice when bad guy pokes at her nipple with a gun.

Karman, Janice

Films:
Switchblade Sisters (1975) . . . . Bunnie
Slumber Party '57 (1976) . . . . .Hank
- •• 1:06—Topless, sitting watching Smitty and David make love in the stable.

Karr, Marcia

Films:
The Concrete Jungle (1982) . . . . .Marcy
Chained Heat (1983; U.S./German) . . . . Twinks
- ••• 0:30—Topless, getting soaped up by Edy Williams in the shower.
- • 0:37—Brief topless, taking off her top in bed with Edy Williams at night.
- •• 0:40—Topless in cell getting raped by the guard.

Savage Streets (1985) . . . . Stevie
Sex Appeal (1986) . . . . .Christina
- • 1:12—Brief left breast, then in bra and panties on bed with her boyfriend.

Killer Workout (1987) . . . . .Rhonda
a.k.a. Aerobi-Cide
- 1:03—Topless, opening her jacket to show the policeman her scars. Unappealing.

1:12—Topless in locker room, killing a guy. Covered with the special effects scars.
Night of the Kickfighters (1990) . . . . .Kedesha

Kasdorf, Lenore

Films:
Dark Horse (1984) . . . . Alice
Missing in Action (1984) . . . . .Ann
- • 0:41—Very brief topless when Chuck Norris sneaks back in room and jumps into bed with her.

L.A. Bounty (1989) . . . . Kelly Rhodes
Kid (1990) . . . . Alice
Made for Cable Movies:
Dinner At Eight (1989) . . . . Lucy
Made for TV Movies:
A Murderous Affair: The Carolyn Warmus Story (1992)
. . . . n.a.
TV:
The Guiding Light . . . . Rita Stapleton

• *Kastner, Daphna*

Films:
Julia Has Two Lovers (1990) . . . . .Julia
- • 0:11—Brief topless, changing blouses while talking on the telephone.
- • 0:25—Partial left breast, while in bubble bath.
- • 0:29—Right breast, while in bubble bath.
- • 0:30—Topless in mirror, getting out of bath tub.
- • 0:53—Left breast, while lying in bed with David Duchovny. Long shot.

Eating (1991) . . . . Jennifer

• *Kath, Camelia*

Ex-wife of actor Kiefer Sutherland.
Films:
Nevada Heat (1982) . . . . Voice #4
a.k.a. Stake Out
The Killing Time (1987) . . . . .Laura Winslow
- • 0:32—Very brief right breast, while making love with Beau Bridges. Hard to see anything. Dark, lit with red light.
- • 0:43—Brief topless lying in bed getting photographed with Beau Bridges to frame Kiefer Sutherland for a murder.

Katon, Rosanne

Films:
The Swinging Cheerleaders (1974) . . . . Lisa
- •• 0:25—Topless taking off her blouse in her teacher's office. Half of right breast while he talks on the phone.

Chesty Anderson, U.S. Navy (1975) . . . . Cocoa
Fox Fire (1976) . . . . n.a.
a.k.a. Fox Force
Coach (1978) . . . . Sue
- • 0:10—Very brief topless flashing her breasts along with three of her girlfriends for their four boyfriends.

Motel Hell (1980) . . . . Suzi

Body and Soul (1981) . . . . Melody
- 0:04—Left breast several times making love in re-stroom with Leon Isaac Kennedy.

Lunch Wagon (1981) . . . . Shannon
- 0:01—Brief topless getting dressed.
- 0:04—Brief side view of left breast changing tops in room in gas station with Pamela Bryant while a guy watches through key hole.
- 0:10—Topless changing again in gas station.

Zapped! (1982). . . . . Donna
Bachelor Party (1984) . . . . Bridal Shower Hooker
Harem (1985; French). . . . . Judy

Magazines:

Playboy (Sep 1978) . . . . Playmate
Playboy (Jan 1980) . . . . Playboy's Pajama Parties
- 125—Topless, standing in a tree.

Playboy (Nov 1980) . . . . The World of Playboy
- 12—Topless.

Playboy (Jul 1981) . . . . Body and Soulmates
- 148—Left breast.

Playboy (Jun 1991) . . . . Funny Girls
- 97—Full frontal nudity in lingerie.

Playboy's Career Girls (Aug 1992) . . . . . . Funny Girls
- 28—Full frontal nudity.

• *Kaye Lawrence, Wendy*

Video Tapes:

Playboy Video Centerfold: Morgan Fox (1991)
. . . . Playmate
- 0:27—Nude in different settings.
- 0:30—Nude in American-themed song and dance number.
- 0:31—Topless and buns in G-string at the beach.
- 0:33—Full frontal nudity in still photos.
- 0:34—Nude while dancing.

Wet and Wild III (1991). . . . . Model
Playboy Video Calendar 1993 (1992) . . . . July
Playboy's Playmate Review 1992 (1992) . . Miss July
- 0:36—Nude in patriotic scene and then in a surreal scene.

Sexy Lingerie IV (1992) . . . . Model
Wet and Wild IV (1992) . . . . Model

Magazines:

Playboy (Jul 1991). Playmate
- 88-110—Nude.

Playboy's Career Girls (Aug 1992)
. . . . Baywatch Playmates
- 8—Full frontal nudity.

Kaye, Caren

Films:

Checkmate (1973) . . . . Alex
The Lords of Flatbush (1974). . . . . Wedding Guest
Looking for Mr. Goodbar (1977) . . . . Rhoda
Kill Castro (1978) . . . . Tracy
a.k.a. Cuba Crossing
Some Kind of Hero (1982) . . . . Sheila

My Tutor (1983) . . . . Terry Green
- 0:25—Topless walking into swimming pool.
- 0:52—Topless in the pool with Matt Lattanzi.
- 0:55—Right breast, lying in bed making love with Lattanzi.

Satan's Princess (1989). Leah
Teen Witch (1989) . . . . Margaret

TV:

The Betty White Show (1977-78). . . . . Tracy Garrett
Blansky's Beauties (1977) . . . . Bambi Benton
Who's Watching the Kids? (1978). . . . . Stacy Turner
It's Your Move (1984-85) . . . . Eileen Burton
Empire (1984) . . . . Meredith

Kaye-Mason, Clarissa

Films:

Age of Consent (1969; Australian) . . . . Meg
- 0:05—Brief topless, crawling on the bed to watch TV.

Adam's Women (1972; Australian) . . . . Matron
The Good Wife (1987; Australian) . . . . Mrs. Jackson
a.k.a. The Umbrella Woman

Keaton, Camille

Films:

I Spit on Your Grave (1978) . . . . Jennifer
(Uncut, unrated version reviewed.)
- 0:05—Topless undressing to go skinny dipping in lake.
- 0:23—Left breast sticking out of bathing suit top, then topless after top is ripped off. Right breast several times.
- 0:25—Topless, getting raped by the jerks.
- 0:27—Buns and brief full frontal nudity, crawling away from the jerks.
- 0:29—Nude, walking through the woods.
- 0:32—Topless, getting raped again.
- 0:36—Topless and buns after rape.
- 0:38—Buns, walking to house.
- 0:40—Buns and lower frontal nudity in the house.
- 0:41—More topless and buns on the floor.
- 0:45—Nude, very dirty after all she's gone through.
- 0:51—Full frontal nudity while lying on the floor.
- 0:52—Side of left breast while in bathtub.
- 1:13—Full frontal nudity seducing Matthew before killing him.
- 1:23—Full frontal nudity in front of mirror, then getting into bathtub. Long scene.

Raw Force (1981). . . . . Girl in Toilet
- 0:28—Topless in bathroom with a guy.
- 0:29—Topless in bathroom again with the guy.
- 0:31—Topless in bathroom again when he rips her pants off.

The Concrete Jungle (1982). . . . . Rita
- 0:41—In black bra, then topless getting raped by Stone. Brief lower frontal nudity sitting up afterwards.

Keaton, Diane
Films:
Lovers and Other Strangers (1970) . . . . Joan
The Godfather (1972) . . . . Kay Adams
Play It Again, Sam (1972) . . . . Linda Christie
Sleeper (1973) . . . . Luna
The Godfather, Part II (1974) . . . . Kay Adams
Love and Death (1975) . . . . Sonja
Harry and Walter Go to New York (1976)
. . . . .Lissa Chestnut
I Will, I Will... For Now (1976) . . . . Katie Bingham
Annie Hall (1977) . . . . .Annie Hall
(Academy Award for Best Actress.)
Looking for Mr. Goodbar (1977) . . . . .Theresa
  •• 0:11—Right breast in bed making love with her
     teacher, Martin, then putting blouse on.
  • 0:31—Brief left breast over the shoulder when the
     Doctor playfully kisses her breast.
  •• 1:04—Brief topless smoking in bed in the morning,
     then more topless after Richard Gere leaves.
  ••• 1:17—Topless making love with Gere after doing a
     lot of cocaine.
  • 1:31—Brief topless in the bathtub when James
     brings her a glass of wine.
     2:00—Getting out of bed in a bra.
  •• 2:02—Topless during rape by Tom Berenger, before
     he kills her. Hard to see because of strobe lights.
Interiors (1978) . . . . Renata
Manhattan (1979) . . . . Mary Wilke
Reds (1981) . . . . Louise Bryant
Shoot the Moon (1982) . . . . .Faith Dunlap
The Little Drummer Girl (1984) . . . . Charlie
Mrs. Soffel (1984) . . . . Kate Soffel
Crimes of the Heart (1986) . . . . .Lenny Magrath
Baby Boom (1987) . . . . J.C. Wiatt
Radio Days (1987) . . . . .New Year's Singer
The Good Mother (1988) . . . . .Anna
The Godfather, Part III (1990) . . . . Kay Adams
The Lemon Sisters (1990) . . . . .Eloise Hamer
Father of the Bride (1991) . . . . Nina Banks
Made for Cable Movies:
Running Mates (1992; HBO) . . . . Aggie Snow

• Keisha
Adult film actress.
Video Tapes:
High Society Centerspread Video #11: Keisha
. . . . Herself
Penthouse Satin & Lace: An Erotic History of
  Lingerie (1992) . . . . .Model

Keller, Marthe
Films:
And Now My Love (1974; French)
. . . . Sarah/Her Mother/Her Grandmother
Marathon Man (1976) .Elsa
  •• 0:42—Topless lying on the floor after Dustin Hoff-
     man rolls off her.
Black Sunday (1977) . . . . .Dahlia

Bobby Deerfield (1977) . . . . .Lillian
The Formula (1980) . . . . Lisa
The Amateur (1982) . . . . Elisabeth
Wagner (1983; British) . . . . Mathilde Wesedonck
Red Kiss (1985; French) . . . . .Bronka
Femmes de Persone (1986; French) . . . . Cecile
Dark Eyes (1987; Italian/Russian) . . . . .Tina
Made for Cable Movies:
The Nightmare Years (1989) . . . . Tess
Young Catherine (1991) . . . . .Johanna

Kellerman, Sally
Films:
The Boston Strangler (1968) . . . . .Dianne Cluny
The April Fool's (1969) . . . . Phyllis Brubaker
Brewster McCloud (1970) . . . . Louise
  0:43—Brief back side of right breast giving a boy a
     bath.
  •• 1:07—Topless, playing in a fountain.
M*A*S*H (1970) . . . . Margaret "Hot Lips" Houlihan
  • 0:42—Very, very brief left breast opening her blouse
     for Frank in her tent.
  • 1:11—Very, very brief buns and side view of right
     breast during shower prank. Long shot, hard to see.
  • 1:54—Very brief topless in a slightly different angle
     of the shower prank during the credits.
Last of the Red Hot Lovers (1972) . . . . . . Elaine Navazio
Reflection of Fear (1973) . . . . Anne
Rafferty and the Gold Dust Twins (1975)
. . . . Mac Beachwood
The Big Bus (1976) . . . . Sybil Crane
Welcome to L.A. (1977) . . . . Ann Goode
A Little Romance (1979) . . . . Kay King
Foxes (1980) . . . . Mary
Serial (1980) . . . . Martha
  ••• 0:03—Topless sitting on the floor with a guy.
Fatal Attraction (1981; Canadian) . . . . .Michelle Keys
  a.k.a. Head On
  • 0:46—Brief topless in building making out with a
     guy. Dark, hard to see.
     1:19—Brief half of left breast, after struggling with a
     guy.
You Can't Hurry Love (1984) . . . . Kelly Bones
Moving Violations (1985) . . . . . Judge Nedra Henderson
Back to School (1986) . . . . .Diane
That's Life! (1986) . . . . Holly Parrish
Meatballs III (1987) . . . . Roxy Du Jour
Three for the Road (1987) . . . . Blanche
Made for Cable Movies:
Boris and Natasha (1992; Showtime) . . . .Natasha Fatale
Made for TV Movies:
Secret Weapons (1985) . . . . n.a.
TV:
Centennial (1978-79) . . . . Lise Bockweiss
Magazines:
Playboy (Dec 1980) . . . . .Sex Stars of 1980
  •• 243—Topless still from *Serial*.

Kelley, Sheila

Films:
Some Girls (1988) . . . . Irenka
  - 0:13—Topless and buns getting something at the end of the hall while Michael watches. Long shot, hard to see.
  - 1:01—Topless in window while Michael watches from outside. Long shot, hard to see.
  1:17—In black slip seducing Michael after funeral.
Breaking In (1989) . . . . Carrie
  0:51—In white body suit in bed with Casey Siemaszko.
Mortal Passions (1989) . . . . Adele
Staying Together (1989) . . . . Beth Harper
Where the Heart Is (1990) . . . . Sheryl
Pure Luck (1991) . . . . Valerie Highsmith
Soapdish (1991) . . . . Fran
Singles (1992) . . . . Debbie
Made for TV Movies:
The Fulfillment of Mary Gray (1989) . . . . Kate
TV:
L.A. Law (1990-) . . . . Gwen Taylor

Kelly, Paula

Films:
Sweet Charity (1969) . . . . Helene
The Andromeda Strain (1971) . . . . Nurse
Cool Breeze (1972) . . . . Mrs. Harris
Top of the Heap (1972) . . . . Singer
Trouble Man (1973) . . . . Cleo
Uptown Saturday Night (1974) . . . . Leggy Peggy
Drum (1976) . . . . Rachel
Jo Jo Dancer, Your Life Is Calling (1986) . . . . . . Satin Doll
  0:26—Doing a strip tease in the night club wearing gold pasties and a gold G-string.
Miniseries:
Chiefs (1983) . . . . Liz Watts
TV:
Night Court (1984) . . . . Liz Williams
Room For Two (1992-) . . . . Diahnn Boudreau
Magazines:
Playboy (Aug 1969) . . . . Sweet Paula
  Debut of pubic hair in *Playboy* magazine.
Playboy (Jul 1972) . . . . Too Much
  - 138—Topless.
  - 140-141—Topless.
Playboy (Nov 1972) . . . . Sex in Cinema 1972
  - 163—Topless in photo from *Top of the Heap.*
Playboy (Jan 1974) . . . . Twenty Years of Playboy
  - 208—Nude in strobe light photo.
Playboy (Jan 1979) . . . . 25 Beautiful Years
  - 160-161—Topless strobe photo from Aug 1969.
Playboy (Jan 1989) . . . . Women of the Sixties
  - 160-161—Topless strobe photo from Aug 1969.

Kelly, Sharon

a.k.a. Adult film actress Colleen Brennan.
Films:
The Beauties and the Beast . . . . n.a.
  Nude, being carried into a cave by the beast.
Innocent Sally (1973) . . . . Sally
  a.k.a. The Dirty Mind of Young Sally
  ••• 0:35—Topless, undressing in back of van. Long scene.
  ••• 0:37—Full frontal nudity, on pillow in back of van while caressing herself. Another long scene.
  ••• 0:39—More full frontal nudity in van.
  ••• 0:47—Right breast, then full frontal nudity, making love with Toby in van. Long scene.
  ••• 1:05—Topless, making love in bed with another guy. Long scene.
  ••• 1:10—Full frontal nudity, making more love. Long scene.
  •• 1:19—Topless, after making love.
  ••• 1:23—Full frontal nudity, while making love with a guy.
Supervixens (1973) . . . . SuperCherry
  Russ Meyer film.
Alice Goodbody (1974) . . . . n.a.
Delinquent School Girls (1974) . . . . Greta
  - 0:05—Left breast in mirror when she practices martial arts.
Gosh (1974) . . . . n.a.
Carnal Madness (1975) . . . . n.a.
Hustle (1975) . . . . Gloria Hollinger
  - 0:12—Brief topless several times getting rolled out of freezer, dead.
  - 1:03—In pasties, dancing behind curtain when Gloria's father imagines the dancer is Gloria.
  - 1:42—In black lingerie, brief buns and side views of breast in bed in film.
Shampoo (1975) . . . . Painted Lady
  - 1:17—Brief topless covered with tattoos all over her body during party. Lit with strobe light.
Slammer Girls (1987) . . . . Professor
  - 0:23—Brief topless changing clothes under table in the prison cafeteria.
  •• 0:34—Topless squishing breasts against the window during prison visiting hours.
  •• 0:36—Topless with an inflatable male doll.

• Kelsey, Tasmin

Films:
Who's Harry Crumb? (1989) . . . . Marie
Bingo (1991) . . . . Bunny
Common Bounds (1991) . . . . Ginger
  - 0:04—Topless in hotel room with the cop when Michael Ironside bursts into the room. Long shot. More out of focus topless shots in the mirror.

Kemp, Charlotte

See: Helmcamp, Charlotte J.

•Kemp, Elizabeth

Films:

He Knows You're Alone (1980). . . . . .Nancy
••• 1:12—Topless, taking off robe and taking a shower.
Sticky Fingers (1988). .Nancy
Eating (1991) . . . . .Nancy

Kendall, Kerri

Video Tapes:

Playboy Video Centerfold: Kerri Kendall (1990)
. . . . Playmate
••• 0:00—Nude throughout.
Wet and Wild II (1990) . . . . .Model
Playboy Video Calendar 1992 (1991) . . . . . .March
••• 0:09—Nude in photo studio.
••• 0:10—In bra, then nude in bedroom.
Sexy Lingerie III (1991) . . . . .Model
Wet and Wild III (1991). . . . . .Model

Magazines:

Playboy (Sep 1990). . . . . Playmate
Playboy's Book of Lingerie (May 1992). . . . . Herself
••• 34—Full frontal nudity.

Kennedy, Sheila

Films:

The First Turn-On! (1983) . . . . Dreamgirl
• 0:52—In red two piece swimsuit, then topless when
the top falls down during Danny's daydream.
• 0:59—Right breast, while in bed with Danny.
Spring Break (1983; Canadian) . . . . .Carla
•• 0:49—Topless during wet T-shirt contest.
Ellie (1984) . . . . .Ellie May
•• 0:29—Full frontal nudity posing for Billy while he
takes pictures of her just before he falls over a cliff.
0:38—In white bra and panties, in barn loft with
Frank.
0:58—In white bra and panties struggling to get
away from Edward Albert.
• 1:16—In bra and panties taking off dress with Art.
Topless taking off bra and throwing them on antlers.
Brief topless many times while frolicking around.

Magazines:

Penthouse (Dec 1981) . . . . Pet
Penthouse (Sep 1983) . . . . Pet of the Year Play-Off
•• 64-65—Nude.
Penthouse (Dec 1983) . . . . Pet of the Year
••• 115-130—Nude.
Penthouse (Oct 1987) . . . . Sheila Revisited

Kensit, Patsy

Was the lead singer in the British group *Eighth Wonder*.

Films:

The Great Gatsby (1974). . . . . .Daisy's Daughter
Oh, Alfie! (1975; British) . . . . .Penny
a.k.a. Alfie Darling
Hanover Street (1979). . . . . Sarah Sallinger

Absolute Beginners (1986; British) . . . . . . Crepe Suzette
Chicago Joe and the Showgirl (1989; British)
. . . . Joyce Cook
Lethal Weapon 2 (1989). . . . . .Rika Van Den Haas
•• 1:15—Right breast lying in bed with Mel Gibson.
•• 1:19—Topless in bed with Gibson.
Blue Tornado (1990) . . . . Christina
Bullseye! (1990) . . . . Sick Lady on Train
Timebomb (1990) . . . . Dr. Anna Nolmar
•• 1:15—Topless, mostly left breast, making love with
Michael Biehn in bed. Partial buns also.
The Skipper (1991) . . . . n.a.
Twenty-One (1991) . . . . Katie
••• 1:17—Topless in reflection in bathroom mirror un-
dressing, then dressing.
Blame It on the Bellboy (1992; British)
. . . . Caroline Wright

Made for TV Movies:

Silas Marner (1985; British) . . . . n.a.
Masterpiece Theatre: Adam Bede (1992)
. . . . Hetty Sorrel

Kenton, Linda

Films:

Hot Resort (1984) . . . . Mrs. Geraldine Miller
• 0:11—Very brief right breast, while in back of car
with a guy.
• 0:16—Right breast, while passed out in closet with a
bunch of guys.
• 0:24—Brief upper half of right breast, while on boat
with a guy.
• 0:46—Brief topless in Volkswagen.
• 0:51—Brief topless in bathtub with Bronson Pinchot.
• 1:24—Brief topless making love on a table while
covered with food.

Magazines:

Penthouse (May 1983) .Pet
••• 83-101—Nude.
Penthouse (Aug 1983). . . . . Penthouse Feedback
•• 190—Topless in small photo.
Playboy (Nov 1985) . . . . Sex in Cinema 1985
• 129—Left breast, covered with food in still from *Hot
Resort.*

Kernohan, Roxanne

Films:

Fatal Pulse (1987) . . . . .Ann
• 0:58—Brief topless in yellow outfit before getting
thrown out of the window.
Angel III: The Final Chapter (1988). . . . . . White Hooker
Critters 2: The Main Course (1988) . . . . Lee
•• 0:37—Brief topless after transforming from an alien
into a Playboy Playmate.
Not of This Earth (1988) . . . . Lead Hooker
••• 0:41—Topless in cellar with Paul just before getting
killed with two other hookers. Wearing a blue top.
Phoenix the Warrior (1988) . . . . .Meda
••• 0:15—Topless in waterfall (she's the white girl).

Tango & Cash (1989) . . . . .Dressing Room Girl
- 1:06—Brief topless in dressing room with three other girls. She's the second one in the middle.

Video Tapes:
Scream Queen Hot Tub Party (1991). . . . . . Herself
- •• 0:07—Topless, taking off black dress and putting on
sheer black robe.
- • 0:12—Buns, while walking up the stairs.
- •• 0:43—Topless, struggling with a monster in basement.
- ••• 0:44—Topless taking off her swimsuit top and soaping up with the other girls.
- •• 0:46—Topless in still shot during the end credits.

Magazines:
Playboy (Jul 1989). . . . . B-Movie Bimbos
- ••• 136—Topless straddling a car wearing an open
bathing suit.
Playboy's Book of Lingerie (Jan 1991). . . . . . Herself
- •• 44—Right breast.

Kerr, Deborah

Films:
The Gypsy Moths (1969) . . . . .Elizabeth Brandon
(Not available on video tape.)

Kerr, E. Katherine

Films:
Reuben, Reuben (1983). . . . . Lucille Haxby
- • 0:51—Brief left breast in bedroom, undressing in
front of Tom Conti.
Silkwood (1984) . . . . Gilda Schultz
Children of a Lesser God (1986) . . . . Mary Lee Ochs

Kerridge, Linda

Films:
Fade to Black (1980) . . . . .Marilyn
- • 0:44—Topless in the shower.
Strangers Kiss (1984). . . . . Shirley
Surf II (1984). . . . . Sparkle
Down Twisted (1987) . . . . .Soames
Alien from L.A. (1988). . . . . . . .Roeyis Freki/Auntie Pearl

Magazines:
Playboy (Nov 1980) . . . . Sex in Cinema 1980
Playboy (Dec 1980). . . . . Double Take
- ••• 218-227—Full frontal nudity.
Playboy's Nudes (Oct 1990). . . . . Herself
- ••• 6-7—Full frontal nudity.

Kersh, Kathy

Films:
Americanization of Emily (1964) . . . . .n.a.
Gemini Affair (1974) . . . . .Jessica
- 0:10—In white bra and black panties changing in
front of Marta Kristen.
- •• 0:11—Nude getting into bed with Kristen.
- • 0:12—Brief topless turning over onto her stomach in
bed.
- •• 0:17—Nude, standing up in bed and jumping off.
- ••• 0:57—Nude in bed with Kristen.

- •• 1:04—Left breast sitting up in bed after Kristen
leaves.

Kerwin, Maureen

Films:
The Destructors (1974; British). . . . . Lucianne
Laura (1979). . . . . Martine
a.k.a. Shattered Innocence
- • 0:03—Brief full frontal nudity getting out of bed and
putting white bathrobe on.
Reunion (1989; French/German)
. . . . .Lisa, Henry's Daughter

Kesner, Jillian

Films:
The Student Body (1975). . . . . Carrie Rafferty
- •• 0:29—Left breast, making out with Carter in the car.
Firecracker (1981) . . . . Susanne Carter
Raw Force (1981). . . . . .Cookie Winchell
Moon in Scorpio (1987) . . . . .Claire
- •• 0:39—Topless sitting on deck of boat with bathing
suit top down.
Beverly Hills Vamp (1989) . . . . Claudia
- 0:06—In white lingerie riding a guy like a horse.
- 0:33—In white slip with Brock.
- 0:42—Almost topless in bed with Brock. Too dark to
see anything.
- 1:09—In white nightgown attacking Russell in bed
with Debra Lamb and Michelle Bauer.
- 1:17—In white nightgown, getting killed as a vampire by Kyle.
Roots of Evil (1991). . . . . .Brenda
(Unrated version reviewed.)
- ••• 0:27—Topless, giving Alex Cord a back massage in
bed.
- • 0:30—Brief topless, getting up out of bed.

TV:
Co-ed Fever (1979) . . . . Melba

• Kestelman, Sara

Films:
Zardoz (1974; British). . . . . .May
- • 1:04—Left breast, in open blouse, under sheet with
Sean Connery.
- • 1:05—Very brief topless grabbing Connery from be-
hind during struggle.
Lisztomania (1975; British). . . . . Princess Carolyn
Break of Day (1977; Australian) . . . . Alice
Lady Jane (1987; British) . . . . Frances Grey

Kidder, Margot

Films:
Gaily Gaily (1969) . . . . Adeline
Quackser Fortune has a Cousin in the Bronx
(1970; Irish) . . . . .Zazel
- •• 1:03—Topless undressing on a chair, then brief
right, then breasts when Gene Wilder kisses her.
- • 1:05—Side view of left breast, then buns, getting
out of bed.

Sisters (1973) . . . . .Danielle Breton
- 0:11—Very brief left breast, undressing while walking down hallway. Long shot.
- 0:14—Topless opening her robe on couch for her new boyfriend. Shadows make it hard to see.

Gravey Train (1974) . . . . Margie

The Reincarnation of Peter Proud (1975)
. . . . Marcia Curtis
- 1:29—Brief topless sitting in bathtub masturbating while remembering getting raped by husband.

Superman (1978) . . . . Lois Lane

The Amityville Horror (1979) . . . . Kathleen Lutz
- 0:21—Brief right breast in reflection in mirror while doing dance streching exercises in the bedroom. Hard to see because of the pattern on the mirror tiles.
- 0:22—Cleavage in open blouse while talking to James Brolin.
- 0:23—Very brief partial right breast, on the floor, kissing Brolin.

Superman II (1980) . . . . Lois Lane

Willie and Phil (1980) . . . . Jeanette Sutherland
- 0:36—Brief topless in bed when Phil opens up her blouse. Long shot.
- 0:47—Brief topless playing in a lake with Willie and Phil.
- 1:36—Topless on the beach (mostly silhouette). Brief side of left breast.

Heartaches (1981; Canadian) . . . . .Rita Harris
Topless.

Some Kind of Hero (1982) . . . . Toni
0:52—In white corset making love with Richard Pryor on the floor.
0:56—In bra with robe standing outside the door talking to Pryor.

Trenchcoat (1983). . . . . Mickey Raymond

Little Treasure (1985) . . . . Margo
0:53—Stripping in bar, doesn't show anything.
1:13—Nude dancing by swimming pool. Long shot, don't see anything.

Miss Right (1987; Italian) . . . . .Juliet

Keeping Track (1988) . . . . Mickey Tremaine

Made for Cable Movies:
Glitter Dome (1985; HBO) . . . . Willie
1:04—Topless on balcony after making love with James Garner the night before. Long shot, hard to see anything.

Made for Cable TV:
The Hitchhiker: Night Shift (1985; HBO)
. . . . Jane Reynolds
(Available on *The Hitchhiker, Volume 2.*)
- 0:13—In a white corset, then brief left breast over the shoulder shot.

Tales From the Crypt: Curiosity Killed (1992; HBO)
. . . . .Cynthia

Made for TV Movies:
To Catch a Killer (1992; Canadian) . . . . .n.a.

TV:
Nichols (1971-72) . . . . Ruth
Shell Game (1987) . . . . Jennie Jerome
Magazines:
Playboy (Dec 1974) . . . . .Sex Stars of 1974
••• 211—Topless.
Playboy (Mar 1975) . . . . Margot
••• 86-93—Full frontal nudity.
Playboy (Nov 1980) . . . . Grapevine
- 302—Left breast under sheer blouse. B&W.
Playboy (Nov 1985) . . . . Sex in Cinema 1985
- 131—Buns, in G-string kneeling on stage in still from *Little Treasure.*

Kidman, Nicole
Wife of actor Tom Cruise.
Films:
Windrider . . . . n.a.
BMX Bandits (1984; Australian) . . . . .Judy
Dead Calm (1989) . . . . Rae Ingram
- 0:59—Brief buns and topless with the attacker.
Days of Thunder (1990) . . . . Dr. Claire Lewicki
Billy Bathgate (1991) . . . . .Drew Preston
•• 0:42—Briefly nude, throwing off towel in front of a vanity with three mirrors.
•• 0:52—Very brief full frontal nudity underwater. Brief full frontal nudity getting out of water and putting on dress.
Far and Away (1992) . . . . Shannon Christie
1:03—Back half of right breast, seen through sheer room divider when she changes clothes.
Made for Cable Movies:
Bangkok Hilton (1990) . . . . n.a.

Kiel, Sue
Films:
Red Heat (1987; U.S./German) . . . . Hedda
- 0:56—Brief topless in shower room scene (third girl behind Linda Blair). Long shot, hard to see.
Straight to Hell (1987; British) . . . . Leticia
Survivor (1987) .The Woman
••• 0:33—Right breast, then topless and buns making love with Survivor in hammock. Long scene.

Kiger, Susan Lynn
Adult Films:
Deadly Love (1974) . . . . n.a.
a.k.a. Hot Nasties
First Playboy Playmate to do an adult film *before* she became a Playmate.
Nude with snake and nude performing fellatio.
Films:
H.O.T.S. (1979) . . . . Honey Shayne
- 0:00—Topless in shower room with the other girls.
•• 0:33—Topless in pool making love with Doug.
- 1:33—Topless in football game.
Seven (1979) . . . . Jennie
Angels Brigade (1980) . . . . n.a.

The Happy Hooker Goes Hollywood (1980) . . . Susie
- 0:42—Topless, singing "Happy Birthday" to a guy tied up on the bed.
- ••• 0:43—Topless, wearing a red garter belt playing pool with K.C. Winkler.

The Return (1980). . . . . n.a.
Death Screams (1982). n.a.

Magazines:
Playboy (Jan 1977) . . . . Playmate
Playboy (Dec 1979). . . . . Sex Stars of 1979
- ••• 258—Full frontal nudity.

King, Tracey Ann

Films:
Hammer (1972) . . . . The Black Magic Woman
The Naughty Stewardesses (1978) . . . . Barbara
- •• 0:56—Topless dancing by the pool in front of everybody.

Cheerleaders Wild Weekend (1985) . . . LaSalle/Polk
- 0:00—Brief topless while tying her shoelace in locker room.
- 0:33—Brief topless in catfight with another girl in cabin.
- ••• 0:39—Topless, taking off her yellow blouse during contest.
- ••• 0:41—Topless with the other five girls during contest.
- 0:42—Topless, losing contest.

Kingsley, Danitza

Films:
You Can't Hurry Love (1984). . . . . Tracey
Amazons (1986) . . . . Tshingi
- ••• 0:30—Topless and buns quite a few times with Colungo out of and in bed.

Jack's Back (1987) . . . . Denise Johnson
South of Reno (1987) . . . . Louise
Verne Miller (1988) . . . . German Drink Girl

• Kingsley, Gretchen

Films:
Blood Sisters (1986). . . . . Ellen
- •• 0:32—Topless, changing clothes to go to sleep in bedroom.
- ••• 0:50—Topless in bed with Jim.

If Looks Could Kill (1987) . . . . Elizabeth
Wimps (1987). . . . . Debbie

Kinmont, Kathleen

Wife of actor Lorenzo Lamas.
Daughter of actress Abby Dalton.
Films:
Hardbodies (1984) . . . . Pretty Skater
Fraternity Vacation (1985) . . . . Marianne
- ••• 0:16—Topless and buns taking off her swimsuit in bedroom with two guys.

Winners Take All (1987). . . . . Party Girl #5
Halloween 4: The Return of Michael Meyers (1988)
. . . . Kelly

0:51—In bra and panties in front of the fireplace with Brady.
Phoenix the Warrior (1988) . . . . Phoenix
Bride of Re-Animator (1989). . . . . . Gloria/The Bride
- 0:58—Brief topless several times with her top pulled down to defibrillate her heart.
- 1:17—Topless under gauze. Her body has gruesome looking special effects appliances all over it.
- 1:22—More topless under gauze.
- 1:24—More topless. Pretty unappealing.
- 1:27—Brief buns, when turning around after ripping out her own heart.

Midnight (1989) . . . . Party
Rush Week (1989) . . . . Julie Ann McGuffin
- 0:07—Brief topless several times during modeling session. Buns in G-string getting dressed. Long shot.

SnakeEater II: The Drug Buster (1990)
. . . . Detective Lisa Forester
The Art of Dying (1991). . . . . Holly
- 0:28—Brief left breast, making love with Wings Hauser in the kitchen. Brief topless when he pours milk on her.
- •• 0:33—Topless in bathtub with Hauser. Intercut with Janet getting stabbed.

Night of the Warrior (1991) . . . . . . Katherine Pierce
0:29—Very brief upper half of right breast, leaning out of the shower to get a towel.
0:46—Very, very brief part of buns, lifting her leg up while kissing Lorenzo Lamas at the art gallery.
- 1:10—Brief right breast, while making love with Lamas on motorcycle.

Magazines:
Playboy (Nov 1991) . . . . Sex in Cinema 1991
- 144—Topless under sheer dress, but has the gruesome looking special effects on. From *Bride of Re-Animator.*

Kinnaman, Melanie

Films:
Friday the 13th, Part V—A New Beginning (1985)
. . . . Pam Roberts
1:08—In wet white blouse coming back into the house from the rain.
Thunder Alley (1985) . . . . Star
- 0:52—Brief topless under water in pool talking to a guy.
- 1:14—Topless and buns making love on bed and getting out.

Kinski, Nastassia

Daughter of the late actor Klaus Kinski.
Real last name is Nakzsynski.
Films:
To the Devil, a Daughter (1976)
. . . . Catherine Beddows
- ••• 1:24—Full frontal nudity, taking off her robe outside and walking towards Richard Widmark in slow motion.

Boarding School (1978; German) . . . Deborah Collins
a.k.a. Virgin Campus
a.k.a. Passion Flower Hotel
- 0:15—Brief topless in the shower with her room-mates. Hard to tell who is who.
- 1:11—Left breast, then topless in the shower (She's the second from the right) consoling Marie-Louise.
- 1:16—Topless under sheer nightie.
- ••• 1:32—Topless making love with Sinclair.

Stay As You Are (1978) . . . . .n.a.

For Your Love Only (1979; German) . . . . .Zena
- •• 0:04—Topless, twice, in the woods with her teacher, Victor, while Michael watches through the bushes.
- 0:15—Brief right breast, in the woods with Michael.
- •• 0:58—Partial left breast, sitting up in bed with Victor. Topless walking around and putting on robe.

Tess (1979; French/British) . . . . Tess Durbeyfield
- 0:47—Brief left breast, opening blouse in field to feed her baby.

Cat People (1982) . . . . Irena Gallier
- ••• 1:03—Nude at night, walking around outside chasing a rabbit.
- •• 1:35—Topless taking off blouse, walking up the stairs and getting into bed.
- 1:37—Brief right breast, lying in bed with John Heard.
- •• 1:38—Topless getting out of bed and walking to the bathroom.
- •• 1:40—Brief buns, getting back into bed. Topless in bed.
- •• 1:47—Full frontal nudity, walking around in the cabin at night.
- 1:49—Topless, tied to the bed by Heard.

One from the Heart (1982) . . . . Leila
- 1:13—Brief topless in open blouse when she leans forward after walking on a ball.

Exposed (1983) . . . . Elizabeth Carlson
- •• 0:54—Topless in bed with Rudolf Nureyev.

The Moon in the Gutter (1983; French/Italian) . . Loretta

Spring Symphony (1983) . . . . .Clara
0:29—Brief left breast, when it pops out of her corset when she tries on a dress.

The Hotel New Hampshire (1984). . . . . . . Susie the Bear

Paris, Texas (1984; French/German) . . . . Jane

Unfaithfully Yours (1984) . . . . Daniella Eastman
- 0:37—Topless and buns in the shower.

Harem (1985; French) . . . . Diane
- 0:14—Topless getting into swimming pool.
- •• 1:04—Topless in motel room with Ben Kingsley.

Maria's Lovers (1985) . . . . .Maria Bosic
0:59—In a black bra.
- 1:12—Brief right breast, while looking at herself in the mirror.

Revolution (1986) . . . . .Daisy McConnahay

Magdelena (1988) . . . . Magdalena

Torrents of Spring (1990) . . . . Maria

Magazines:

Playboy (Dec 1980) . . . . Sex Stars of 1980
- ••• 242—Topless.

Playboy (May 1983) .Exposed
- ••• 142-149—Topless.

Playboy (Nov 1985) . . . . Sex in Cinema 1985
- •• 132—Left breast in still from *Harem*.

Kirkland, Sally

Films:

Going Home (1971). . . . . Ann Graham
Cinderella Liberty (1973) . . . . .Fleet Chick
The Sting (1973) . . . . .Crystal
The Way We Were (1973). . . . . Pony Dunbar
Young Nurses (1973) . . . . .Patient

Big Bad Mama (1974). . . . . Barney's Woman
- •• 0:13—Topless and buns waiting for Barney then throwing shoe at Billy Jean.

Crazy Mama (1975). . . . . .Ella Mae
A Star is Born (1976) . . . . Photographer
Tracks (1977) . . . . Uncredited
Private Benjamin (1980). . . . . .Helga

Double Exposure (1983) . . . . Hooker
- •• 0:26—Topless in alley getting killed.

Fatal Games (1984) . . . . Diane Paine
Love Letters (1984) . . . . Hippie

Anna (1987) . . . . .Anna
- •• 0:28—Topless in the bathtub talking to Daniel.

Talking Walls (1987). . . . . Hooker

Cold Feet (1989) . . . . Maureen Linoleum
(In tight fitting spandex dresses throughout most of the film.)
- 0:56—In black bra and panties taking off her dress in bedroom with Keith Carradine. Brief right breast pulling bra down.
- 0:58—Brief side view of right breast sitting up in bed talking to Carradine.

High Stakes (1989) . . . . .Melanie "Bambi" Rose
- 0:01—In two piece costume, doing a strip tease routine on stage. Buns in G-string, then very, very brief topless flashing her breasts.
1:11—In black bra cutting her hair in front of a mirror.

Paint It Black (1989). . . . . Marion Easton
0:05—Most of left breast, while sitting in bed talking to Rick Rossovich.

Best of the Best (1990). . . . . n.a.
Bullseye! (1990) . . . . Willie
Revenge (1990) . . . . Rock Star

In the Heat of Passion (1991) . . . . . . .Dr. Lee Adams
(Unrated version reviewed.)
- ••• 0:21—In black bra, then topless making love with Charlie while her husband is downstairs.
- 0:23—Brief topless in the shower when her husband opens the shower curtain.
- •• 0:29—Topless with Charlie in stall in women's restroom.
- •• 0:42—Topless teasing Charlie from the bathroom.
- 0:45—Right breast, then topless in bed with Charlie.
- 1:11—Very brief buns, while on the couch with Charlie.

JFK (1991) . . . . .Rose Cheramie

Two Evil Eyes (1991) . . . . Eleonora
Primary Motive (1992) . . . . .n.a.
Made for TV Movies:
The Haunted (1991) . . . . .Janet

Kitaen, Tawny

Ex-wife of singer David Coverdale of the rock group
Whitesnake.
Films:
Bachelor Party (1984) . . . . Debbie Thompson
**The Perils of Gwendoline in the Land of the Yik
Yak** (1984; French). . . . . Gwendoline
••• 0:36—Topless in the rain in the forest, taking off her
top. More topless with Willard.
•• 0:52—Buns, while walking around with Willard in
costumes.
• 0:55—Buns, falling into jail cell, then in jail cell in
costume.
• 0:57—Buns, while rescuing Beth in torture chamber.
•• 1:01—Topless in S&M costume in front of mirrors.
• 1:04—Brief topless escaping from chains.
• 1:07—Buns, in costume while riding chariot and
next to wall.
• 1:09—Buns, while standing up.
•• 1:11—Buns, in costume during fight. Wearing green
ribbon.
•• 1:18—Topless making love with Willard.
Crystal Heart (1987) . . . . Alley Daniels
•• 0:46—Topless and buns, while "making love" with
Lee Curreri through the glass.
•• 0:50—Nude, crashing through glass shower door,
covered with blood during her nightmare.
• 1:14—Brief topless making love with Curreri in and
falling out of bed.
Happy Hour (1987). . . . . Misty Roberts
Instant Justice (1987) . . . . Virginia
Witchboard (1987) . . . . Linda
• 1:26—Nude, stuck in the shower and breaking the
glass doors to get out.
Made for Cable Movies:
The Glory Years (1987; HBO) . . . . .n.a.
TV:
Santa Barbara (1989-90) . . . . .Lisa
New WKRP in Cincinnati (1991-92). . . . .Mona Loveland
America's Funniest People (1992-) . . . . Co-Host
Video Tapes:
Whitesnake—Trilogy (1987) . . . . The Girl
• 0:10—(2 min., 17 sec. into "Here I Go Again.") Very
brief right breast, leaning out of car.
0:18—Most of her buns, while kissing David Cover-
dale in out-take from "Is This Love."

• Klarwein, Eleonore

Films:
Peppermint Soda (1979; French). . . . . Anne Weber
Stroke of Midnight (1991; U.S./French). . Second Model
Road to Ruin (1992). . . . . Girl Friend
•• 0:03—Topless and buns, getting out of bed and
walking into bathroom.

• Klein, Barbara Ann

Films:
Night Eyes (1990) . . . . Sleeping Woman
(Unrated version reviewed.)
• 0:02—Brief topless struggling with burglar/rapist.
Relentless 2: Dead On (1991). . . . . .Realtor
Straight Talk (1992) . . . . Stunts

Klenck, Margaret

Films:
Hard Choices (1986) . . . . .Laura
•• 1:10—Left breast, then topless making love with
Bobby. Nice close up shot.
• 1:11—Very brief half of left breast and lower frontal
nudity getting back into bed. Long shot.
Loose Cannons (1990) . . . . Eva Braun
TV:
One Life to Live . . . . .Edwina Lewis

• Knight, Shirley

Films:
The Couch (1962) . . . . n.a.
House of Women (1962) . . . . Erica
The Group (1966) . . . . Polly Andrews
Petulia (1968; U.S./British) . . . . .Polo
The Rain People (1969) . . . . .Natalie
• 0:15—Topless walking around in motel room and
getting into bed. Long shot.
• 1:36—Very brief buns, with sheet wrapped around
her, trying to get out of trailer.
Juggernaut (1974; British) . . . . .Barbara Banister
Beyond the Poseidon Adventure (1979)
. . . . Hannah Meredith
Endless Love (1981) . . . . Anne
The Sender (1982) . . . . .Jerolyn
Panther Squad (1986; French/Belgian). . . . . n.a.
Made for TV Movies:
Billionaire Boys Club (1987) . . . . n.a.

• Knudsen, Bitten

Films:
Hollywood Vice Squad (1986) . . . . Lucchesi's Girl Friend
Magazines:
Playboy's Nudes (Oct 1990) . . . . .Herself
• 50—Buns.

• Kober, Marta

Films:
Friday the 13th, Part II (1981) . . . . .Sandra
Baby, It's You (1983) . . . . Debra
Neon Maniacs (1985) . . . . .Lorraine
School Spirit (1985) . . . . Ursula
Rad (1986). . . . . .Becky
Vendetta (1986) . . . . .Sylvia
• 1:10—Very brief, dark, right breast in open blouse,
in her prison cell with the guard.

Video Tapes:
Inside Out (1992) . . . . The Girl/Doubletalk
••• 0:26—Topless in raised blouse, on top of Jack on
sofa.

• Kohnert, Mary

Films:
Valet Girls (1987) . . . . .n.a.
Beyond the Door III (1989; Yugoslavian) . . . . . Beverly
•• 0:03—Topless taking a shower.

Koizumi, Ariane

See: Ariane.

• Komorowska, Liliana

Films:
War and Love (1985) . . . . Esther
Astonished (1988). . . . . Sonia
Her Alibi (1989) . . . . Laura
Scanners III: The Takeover (1992) . . . .Helena Monet
•• 0:32—Topless in and out of spa, talking with her
dad.
• 0:35—Brief right breast, while sitting up.

Kong, Venice

Films:
Beverly Hills Cop II (1987). . . . . Playboy Playmate
Video Tapes:
Wet and Wild (1989). . . . . .Model
Playboy Video Centerfold: Kerri Kendall (1990)
. . . . Playmate
••• 0:41—Full frontal nudity.
Playmates at Play (1990) . . . . Making Waves
Magazines:
Playboy (Dec 1980). . . . . .Bunny Birthday
••• 156—Full frontal nudity.
Playboy (Sep 1985) . . . . Playmate

• Konop, Kelli

Films:
Bikini Summer (1991) . . . . Rene
Totally Exposed (1991) . . . . .Sue
• 0:18—Undressing to take a shower. Brief right
breast, bending over to take off panties. Brief side
view of left breast, while getting into the shower.
• 0:19—Sort of topless, while washing herself in the
shower. Her arms get in the way.
1:12—In white bra, making out with Bill.

Konopski, Sharry

Video Tapes:
Playboy Video Calendar 1989 (1988) . . . . .April
••• 0:13—Nude.
Wet and Wild (1989). . . . . .Model
Magazines:
Playboy (Aug 1987). . . . . Playmate

• Korn, Sandi

Video Tapes:
Penthouse Passport to Paradise/Hawaii (1991)
. . . . Model
•• 0:25—Topless, taking off her top and going down
into an underground cave.
••• 0:27—Nude, taking an outdoor shower to wash the
dirt off herself.
Magazines:
Penthouse (Mar 1991). . . . . .Pet
••• 67-81—Nude.
Penthouse (Jun 1992) . . . . Pet of the Year Playoff
••• 88-89—Nude.

• Korot, Alla

Films:
Night of the Cyclone (1990) . . . . Angelique
• 0:21—Right breast, then brief topless getting out of
the shower.
TV:
Another World (1991-) . . . . .Jenna Norris

Koscina, Sylva

Films:
Hercules (1959; Italian) . . . . Iole
Justine (1969; Italian/Spanish) . . . . n.a.
a.k.a. Maquis de Sade: Justine
The Secret War of Harry Frigg (1969)
. . . . Countess di Montefiore
The Slasher (1975) . . . . Barbara
•• 0:17—Left breast lying down getting a massage.
•• 1:18—Topless undressing and putting a robe on at
her lover's house. Left breast after getting stabbed.
Sex on the Run (1979; German/French/Italian)
. . . . .Jelsamina
a.k.a. Some Like It Cool
a.k.a. Casanova and Co.
••• 0:28—Topless and brief buns dropping her top for
Tony Curtis, then walking around with the "other"
Tony Curtis.
•• 1:20—Topless talking to her husband.

Kossack, Christine

Films:
Three Men and a Baby (1987) . . . . . . One of Jack's Girls
The Brain (1988) . . . . Vivian
•• 0:24—Topless on monitor, then topless in person
during Jim's fantasy.
•• 1:11—Topless again in the basement during Jim's
hallucination.

Kotero, Patty

See: Apollonia.

Kozak, Harley Jane

Films:
House on Sorority Row (1983) . . . . .Diane
Clean and Sober (1988). . . . . .Ralston Receptionist
Parenthood (1989). . . . . .Susan

When Harry Met Sally... (1989) . . . . Helen
Arachnophobia (1990) . . . . Molly Jennings
Side Out (1990). Kate Jacobs
  • 0:53—Brief left breast, then out of focus left breast,
    while in bed with Peter Horton.
All I Want for Christmas (1991) . . . . . Catherine O'Fallon
Necessary Roughness (1991). . . . . Suzanne Carter
The Taking of Beverly Hills (1991) . . . . Laura Sage
TV:
Santa Barbara . . . . Mary Duvall
Knightwatch (1988-89). . . . . .Barbara

Kozak, Heidi
Films:
Slumber Party Massacre II (1987) . . . . Sally
Friday the 13th, Part VII: The New Blood (1988)
. . . . Sandra
  • 0:36—Buns, while taking off clothes to go skinny
    dipping. Brief topless under water just before get-
    ting killed by Jason.
Society (1989). . . . . Shauna

Krige, Alice
Films:
Chariots of Fire (1981) . . . . Sybil Gordon
Ghost Story (1981). . . . . Alma/Eva
  • 0:41—Brief topless making love in bedroom with
    Craig Wasson.
  •• 0:44—Topless in bathtub with Wasson.
  •• 0:46—Topless sitting up in bed.
  ••• 0:49—Buns, then topless standing on balcony turn-
    ing and walking to bedroom talking to Wasson.
King David (1985) . . . . .Bathsheba
  •• 1:16—Full frontal nudity getting a bath outside at
    dusk while Richard Gere watches.
Barfly (1987). . . . . Tully
Haunted Summer (1988) . . . . Mary Godwin
See You in the Morning (1989) . . . . Beth Goodwin
Made for Cable Movies:
Baja Oklahoma (1988; HBO). . . . . Patsy Cline
Ladykiller (1992; USA). . . . . .May Packard
Made for Cable TV:
Iran: Days of Crisis (1991; TNT). . . . . .n.a.

• Krim, Viju
Films:
Bloodsucking Freaks (1982). . . . . Natasha
Twelfth Night (1988; Italian) . . . . Maria
  •• 1:09—Topless, dancing in tavern in open top.

Kriss, Katherine
Films:
American Flyers (1985) . . . . Vera
Hot Chili (1985) . . . . Allison Baxter
  ••• 0:56—Topless getting out of the pool and talking to
    Ricky.
  • 1:09—Buns and side view of left breast, while lying
    down and kissing Ricky.
Student Confidential (1987) . . . . .Elaine's Friend

Kristel, Sylvia
Films:
Emmanuelle (1974). . . . . .Emmanuelle
  (R-rated version reviewed.)
  • 0:00—Very brief left breast in robe, while sitting on
    bed.
  • 0:02—Topless in B&W photos.
  • 0:10—Topless and buns, making love in bed with
    her husband under a net.
  • 0:13—Brief topless taking off bikini top by swim-
    ming pool.
  ••• 0:14—Topless getting up from chair, then full frontal
    nudity while talking to Ariane.
  ••• 0:15—Nude, swimming under water. Nice.
  • 0:18—Partial left breast, while sleeping in bed.
  •• 0:24—Topless, making love with a stranger on an
    airplane.
  •• 0:31—Topless with Ariane in the squash court.
Julia (1974; German) . . . . .Julia
  0:23—Brief topless in the lake.
  •• 0:25—Topless on deck in the lake.
  •• 0:28—Brief topless changing clothes at night. Long
    shot.
  •• 0:34—Topless on boat with two boys.
  •• 0:42—Topless taking off her towel.
  • 1:12—Topless on tennis court with Patrick.
Emmanuelle, The Joys of a Woman (1975)
. . . . .Emmanuelle
  • 0:18—Topless making love with her husband in bed-
    room.
  •• 0:22—Topless, then full frontal nudity, undressing in
    bedroom, then making love with her husband.
  ••• 0:32—Topless with acupuncture needles stuck in
    her. More topless masturbating while fantasizing
    about Christopher.
  • 0:53—Right breast, while making love with polo
    player in locker room.
  ••• 0:58—Nude, getting massaged by another woman.
  ••• 1:14—Right breast in bedroom in open dress, then
    topless with Jean in bed. Flashback of her with three
    guys in a bordello.
Goodbye Emmanuelle (1977) . . . . .Emmanuelle
  •• 0:03—Full frontal nudity in bath and getting out.
  •• 0:04—Full frontal nudity taking off dress.
  ••• 0:06—Full frontal nudity in bed with Angelique.
  ••• 0:26—Topless with photographer in old house.
    0:42—Brief side view of right breast, in bed with
    Jean.
  ••• 1:03—Full frontal nudity on beach with movie direc-
    tor.
  •• 1:06—Full frontal nudity lying on beach sleeping.
  •• 1:28—Side view of left breast lying on beach with
    Gregory while dreaming.
Airport '79: The Concorde (1979) . . . . Isabelle
Tigers in Lipstick (1979) . . . . The Girl
  0:04—Topless in photograph on the sand.
  •• 0:09—Topless lying in bed with The Arab.
  •• 0:16—Lying in bed in red lingerie, then left breast
    for awhile.

Lady Chatterley's Lover (1981; French/British)
. . . . Constance Chatterley
•• 0:25—Nude in front of mirror.
• 0:59—Brief topless with the Gardener.
• 1:04—Brief topless.
••• 1:16—Nude in bedroom with the Gardener.
Private Lessons (1981). . . . . Mallow
• 0:20—Very brief topless sitting up next to the pool when the sprinklers go on.
•• 0:24—Topless and buns, stripping for Billy. Some shots might be a body double.
•• 0:51—Topless in bed when she "dies" with Howard Hessman.
• 1:28—Topless making love with Billy. Some shots might be a body double.
Private School (1983) . . . . Ms. Copuletta
0:57—In wet white dress after falling in the pool.
Emmanuelle IV (1984) . . . . Sylvia
•• 0:00—Topless in photos during opening credits.
The Big Bet (1985) . . . . Michelle
• 0:07—Left breast in open nightgown while Chris tries to fix her sink.
•• 0:20—Topless dressing while Chris watches through binoculars.
•• 0:28—Topless undressing while Chris watches through binoculars.
••• 0:40—Topless getting out of the shower and drying herself off.
• 1:00—Topless getting into bed while Chris watches through binoculars.
••• 1:13—Topless in bedroom with Chris, then making love.
Mata Hari (1985) . . . . Mata Hari
••• 0:11—Topless making love with a guy on a train.
•• 0:31—Topless standing by window after making love with the soldier.
• 0:35—Topless making love in empty house by the fireplace.
•• 0:52—Topless masturbating in bed wearing black stockings.
•• 1:02—Topless having a sword fight with another topless woman.
•• 1:03—Topless in bed smoking opium and making love with two women.
The Arrogant (1987) . . . . Julie
• 0:14—In wet blouse, in lake.
• 0:22—In wet blouse again, walking out of the lake.
• 0:44—Brief topless several times, in gaping dress.
Red Heat (1987; U.S./German) . . . . Sofia
0:23—In red lingerie.
•• 0:56—Topless in shower room scene.
• 1:01—Brief topless raping Linda Blair.
Dracula's Widow (1988) . . . . Vanessa
Hot Blood (1989; Spanish) . . . . Sylvia
• 0:44—Buns, getting molested by Dom Luis.
Video Tapes:
Playboy Video Magazine, Volume 2 (1983)
. . . . Herself
••• 0:16—Topless in various scenes from her films.

Magazines:
Playboy (Dec 1976) . . . . Sex Stars of 1976
•• 187—Topless drinking from champagne bottle.
Playboy (Dec 1977) . . . . Sex Stars of 1977
•• 214—Topless with Jeff Bridges.
Playboy (Nov 1980) . . . . Sex in Cinema 1980
• 172—Lower frontal nudity.
••• 182—Topless in still from *Private Lessons*.
Playboy (Dec 1980) . . . . Sex Stars of 1980
••• 245—Topless.
Playboy (Dec 1984) . . . . Sex Stars of 1984
• 205—Left breast, lying on chair.

Kristen, Marta
Films:
Terminal Island (1973) . . . . Lee Phillips
Gemini Affair (1974). . . . . Julie
••• 0:32—Topless wearing beige panties talking with Jessica in the bathroom.
• 0:56—Very, very brief left breast and lower frontal nudity standing next to bed with a guy. Very brief left breast in bed with him.
••• 0:59—Topless and buns making love in bed with Jessica. Wowzers!
Once (1974) . . . . Humanity
(Not available on video tape.)
Battle Beyond the Stars (1980) . . . . Lux
TV:
Lost in Space (1965-68) . . . . Judy Robinson

• Kudoh, Youki
Films:
The Crazy Family (1986; Japanese) . . . . Daughter
Typhoon Club (1986; Japanese) . . . . Rie
Mystery Train (1989) . . . . Mitzuko
•• 0:30—In black bra, in bed. Topless making love with Jun in bed.
0:37—In black bra, while packing suitcase.

Lahaie, Brigitte
Films:
Come Play with Me . . . . n.a.
Private Screenings.
Friendly Favors (1983) . . . . Greta
a.k.a. Six Swedes on a Pump
Private Screenings.
•• 0:02—Full frontal nudity riding a guy in bed. (She's wearing a necklace.)
••• 0:39—Full frontal nudity having fun on "exercise bike."
••• 0:46—Full frontal nudity taking off clothes and running outside with the other girls. Nice slow motion shots.
•• 0:53—Topless, making love with Kerstin.
••• 1:01—Full frontal nudity in room with the Italian.
••• 1:15—Full frontal nudity in room with guy from the band.

Joy: Chapter II (1985; French) . . . . Joy
a.k.a. Joy and Joan
- • 0:01—Left breast in coat during photo session.
- ••• 0:11—Nude, getting into bubble bath and out with Bruce.
- •• 0:20—Topless, lying in bed after party.
- •• 0:22—Topless, talking on the phone.
- ••• 0:27—Nude, getting a massage from Milaka. Nice.
- •• 0:32—Topless changing clothes.
- ••• 0:45—In bra, then topless changing clothes with Joanne.
- •• 0:47—Full frontal nudity, masturbating in bed. Medium long shot.
- ••• 0:54—Nude, making love with Joanne on train. Nice, long scene!
- • 1:03—Topless in the water with Joanne.
- •• 1:08—Topless, getting molested by a bunch of guys in the shower.
- • 1:10—Right breast, lying next to a pool.
- •• 1:17—Nude in bubble bath with Joanne and getting out.
- • 1:23—Buns, dancing with Joanne.
- ••• 1:27—Nude, making love with Joanne and Mark.

Henry & June (1990) . . . . .Harry's Whore
- •• 0:23—Brief buns and topless under sheer white dress going up stairs with Fred Ward.
- •• 1:22—Topless in sheer white dress again. Nude under dress walking up stairs.
- ••• 1:23—Topless and buns making love with another woman while Anais and Hugo watch.
- • 1:31—Topless in bed with Anais. Intercut with Uma Thurman, so hard to tell who is who.

Magazines:
Playboy (Nov 1985) . . . . .Grapevine

Laine, Karen

Films:
Pretty in Pink (1986) . . . . Girl at Prom
Made for Cable Movies:
Baja Oklahoma (1988; HBO) . . . . Girl at Drive-In
- • 0:04—Left breast, in truck with a jerk guy. Dark, hard to see anything.

Lamarr, Hedy

First instance of celebrity nudity in film.
Films:
Ecstasy (1932) . . . . The Wife
- • 0:25—Brief topless starting to run after a horse in a field.
- • 0:26—Long shot running through the woods, side view naked, then brief topless hiding behind a tree.

Algiers (1938) . . . . Gaby
Ziegfield Girl (1941) . . . . Sandra Kolter
Dishonored Lady (1947) . . . . Madeleine Damien
Samson and Delilah (1949) . . . . Delilah
Instant Karma (1990) . . . . .Movie Goddess

Lamb, Debra

Films:
Stripped to Kill (1987) . . . . Amateur Dancer
B.O.R.N. (1988) . . . . Sue
Deathrow Game Show (1988) . . . . . . Shanna Shallow
- ••• 0:23—Topless dancing in white G-string and garter belt during the show.

Stripped to Kill II (1988) . . . . Mantra
- •• 0:04—Topless during strip dance routine.
- ••• 0:42—Topless in black lingerie during strip dance routine.

W. B., Blue and the Bean (1988) . . . . Motel Clerk
a.k.a. Bail Out
- • 0:42—Full frontal nudity opening door in motel to talk to David Hasselhoff.

Warlords (1988) . . . . .Harem Girl
- ••• 0:14—Topless, getting her blouse ripped off by a bad guy, then kidnapped.
- ••• 0:17—Topless in harem pants while shackled to another girl.

Beverly Hills Vamp (1989) . . . . Jessica
- 0:33—In black slip, with Russell.
- ••• 0:36—Topless and buns in red G-string posing for Russell while he photographs her.
- ••• 0:41—More topless posing on bed.
- 1:09—In white nightgown attacking Russell in bed with Michelle Bauer and Jillian Kesner.
- 1:19—In white nightgown, getting killed as a vampire by Kyle.

Out Cold (1989) . . . . .Panetti's Dancer
- • 1:04—Brief topless dancing in G-string on stage. Don't see her face.

Satan's Princess (1989) . . . . .Fire Eater/Dancer
- •• 0:23—Topless in G-string doing a fire dance in club.
- • 0:25—Topless, doing more dancing. Long shot.

Invisible Maniac (1990) . . . . Betty
- • 0:21—Buns and very brief side view of right breast in the shower with the other girls.
- ••• 0:43—In bra, then topless and buns standing on the left in the locker room with the other girls.
- • 0:44—Buns and brief topless in the shower with the other girls.
- •• 0:56—In bra, then topless getting killed by Dr. Smith.
- • 0:58—Brief topless, dead, discovered by April and Joan.

Mob Boss (1990) . . . . .Janise
Evil Spirits (1991) . . . . Dancer
Point Break (1991) . . . Uncredited Flame Blower at Party
Made for Cable TV:
Dream On: And Your Little Dog, Too (1991; HBO)
. . . . Snake Lady
Video Tapes:
Best Buns on the Beach (1987) . . . . .Buns Model
- 0:03—In bra and mini skirt, holding model buns.
- ••• 0:04—Buns, in G-string, bending over during "Ideal Buns" demonstration.

Trashy Ladies Wrestling (1987) . . . . .n.a.
- •• 0:48—In black and silver S&M costume. Buns in G-string.
  0:49—In black bra, G-string, stockings and boots, while fire eating.

Magazines:
Playboy (Jul 1991) . . . . .Grapevine
- ••• 174—In boots, lying on the floor. B&W.

Landon, Laurene

Girlfriend of Christian Brando (Marlon Brando's son).
Films:
...All the Marbles (1981) . . . . Molly
a.k.a. The California Dolls
I, the Jury (1982) . . . . Velda
Hundra (1983) . . . . .Hundra
- • 0:29—Very brief topless, several times, riding her horse in the surf. Partial buns. Blurry.
Yellow Hair and the Fortress of Gold (1984)
. . . . Yellow Hair
America 3000 (1986) . . . . .Vena
Armed Response (1986) . . . . .Deborah
It's Alive III: Island of the Alive (1988) . . . . Sally
Maniac Cop (1988) .Theresa
Wicked Stepmother (1989) . . . . .Vanilla
Maniac Cop 2 (1990) . . . . Teresa Mallory

Landry, Karen

Films:
The Personals (1982) .Adrienne
Patti Rocks (1988) . . . . Patti
- 0:48—Buns, walking from bathroom to bedroom and shutting the door. Long shot.
- • 0:48—Very brief right breast in shower with Billy.
- •• 1:04—Topless in bed with Eddie while Billy is out in the living room.
Ambition (1991) . . . . Woman in Bookstore

Landry, Tamara

Films:
R.S.V.P. (1984) . . . . .Vicky
- •• 0:43—Topless sitting in van taking top off.
- •• 0:48—Topless making love in the van with two guys.
Tango & Cash (1989) . . . . Girl in Bar
Delusion (1990) . . . . Arabella
Mob Boss (1990) . . . . .n.a.

Lands, Wendy

Films:
One Night Only (1984; Canadian) . . . . Jane
- •• 0:36—Topless taking a bath while Jamie watches through keyhole.
- •• 0:38—Brief left breast in open robe.
- • 1:15—Brief topless in bed with policeman.
Busted Up (1986) . . . . Drayton's Date

Lane, Diane

Wife of actor Christopher Lambert.
Films:
A Little Romance (1979) . . . . .Lauren
Touched by Love (1980) . . . . .Karen
Ladies and Gentlemen, The Fabulous Stains
(1982) . . . . Corinne Burns
(Not available on video tape.)
Six Pack (1982) . . . . Breezy
The Outsiders (1983) . . . . Cherry Valance
Rumble Fish (1983) . . . . Patty
The Cotton Club (1984) . . . . Vera Cicero
Streets of Fire (1984) . . . . .Ellen Aim
The Big Town (1987) . . . . Lorry Dane
  0:51—Doing a strip routine in the club wearing a G-string and pasties while Matt Dillon watches.
- ••• 1:17—Topless making love on bed with Dillon in ho-tel room.
  1:27—Brief left breast wearing pasties walking into dressing room while Dillon plays craps.
Lady Beware (1987) . . . . Katya Yarno
  0:10—Walking around in her apartment in a red silk teddy getting ready for bed.
  0:14—Lying down in white semi-transparent paja-mas after fantasizing.
  0:24—In black bra in apartment.
- ••• 0:46—Topless in her apartment and in bed making love with Mack.
- •• 0:52—Brief topless during Jack's flashback when he is in the store.
- •• 0:59—Brief side view topless in bed with Mack again during another of Jack's flashbacks.
- • 1:02—Very brief topless in bed with Mack.
  1:06—Brief topless lying in bed behind thin curtain in another of Jack's flashbacks.
Priceless Beauty (1989; Italian) . . . . .China/Anna
- •• 0:34—Topless in bed with Christopher Lambert.
- • 0:35—Brief left breast, then side of right breast on top of Lambert.
Vital Signs (1989) . . . . .Gina Wyler
- ••• 1:11—In white bra, then topless making love with Michael in the basement.
Made for Cable Movies:
Descending Angel (1990; HBO) . . . . .Irina Stroia
- • 0:01—Brief right breast, while making love with Eric Roberts on train during opening credits.
- •• 0:44—In white camisole top with Roberts, then top-less lying in bed with him.
Miniseries:
Lonesome Dove (1989) . . . . .Lorena Wood

Lane, Krista

See: Lynn, Rebecca.

Lane, Nikki

Films:
Death of a Soldier (1985) . . . . Stripper in bar
- •• 0:49—Nude, dancing on stage.
The Big Hurt (1987) . . . . n.a.

Lange, Jessica

Films:

King Kong (1976) . . . . Dwan
    1:20—Almost topless when King Kong is playing
    with her in his hand. Hand covers nipple of left
    breast.
All That Jazz (1979) . . . . Angelique
How to Beat the High Cost of Living (1980) . . . . . Louise
The Postman Always Rings Twice (1981)
. . . . Cora Papadakis
    0:17—Making love with Jack Nicholson on the kitch-
    en table. No nudity, but still exciting.
    0:18—Pubic hair peeking out of right side of her
    panties when Nicholson grabs her crotch.
    • 1:03—Very, very brief topless, then very, very brief
    right breast twice, when Nicholson rips her dress
    down to simulate a car accident.
    1:26—Brief lower frontal nudity when Nicholson
    starts crawling up over her in bed.
Frances (1982) . . . . Frances Farmer
    • 0:41—Very brief upper half of left breast, while lying
    on bed and throwing a newspaper.
    • 0:50—Brief full frontal nudity covered with bubbles
    standing up in bathtub and wrapping a towel
    around herself. Long shot, hard to see.
    • 1:01—Brief buns and right breast running into the
    bathroom when the police bust in. Very, very brief
    full frontal nudity, then buns closing the bathroom
    door. Reportedly her, even though you don't see her
    face clearly.
Tootsie (1982) . . . . Julie Nichols
(Academy Award for Best Supporting Actress.)
Country (1984) . . . . Jewell Ivy
Sweet Dreams (1985) . . . . Patsy Kline
Crimes of the Heart (1986) . . . . Meg Magrath
Everybody's All-American (1988) . . . . Babs
    0:32—Brief breasts under sheer nightgown in bed-
    room with Dennis Quaid.
    • 0:54—Buns and very, very brief side view of left
    breast by the campfire by the lake with Timothy
    Hutton at night. Might be a body double.
Far North (1988) . . . . Kate
Men Don't Leave (1989) . . . . Beth Macauley
Cape Fear (1991) . . . . Leigh Bowden
Made for Cable Movies:
Cat on a Hot Tin Roof (1985; HBO) . . . . n.a.
Made for TV Movies:
O Pioneers! (1992) . . . . Adult Alexandra Bergson

Langencamp, Heather

Films:

Nickel Mountain (1985) . . . . Callie
    ••• 0:24—Topless in bed lying with Willard.
    • 0:29—Side view of left breast and brief topless fall-
    ing on bed with Willard.
    0:29—In white panties, peeking out the window.
A Nightmare on Elm Street (1985) . . . Nancy Thompson
A Nightmare on Elm Street 3: The Dream Warriors
(1987) . . . . Nancy Thompson

TV:
Just the Ten of Us (1989-90) . . . . Marie

Langenfeld, Sarah

Films:

Blood Link (1983) . . . . Christine
    •• 1:01—Topless in bed taking off her top in bed with
    Craig.
    • 1:04—Topless in bed with Keith.
The Act (1984) . . . . Leslie

Langlois, Lisa

Films:

Blood Relatives (1978; French/Canadian) . . . . Muriel
Happy Birthday to Me (1980) . . . . Amelia
Class of 1984 (1982) . . . . Patsy
Deadly Eyes (1982; Canadian) . . . . Trudy
The Man Who Wasn't There (1983) . . . Cindy Worth
    •• 0:58—Nude running away from two policemen af-
    ter turning visible.
    ••• 1:08—Topless in white panties dancing in her apart-
    ment with an invisible Steve Guttenberg.
    1:47—Very, very brief upper half of left breast, while
    throwing bouquet at wedding.
The Nest (1987) . . . . Elizabeth Johnson
Transformations (1988) . . . . Miranda
Mind Field (1990) . . . . Sarah Paradis

Langrick, Margaret

Films:

My American Cousin (1985; Canadian) . . . . Sandy
Harry and the Hendersons (1987) . . . . Sarah Henderson
Cold Comfort (1988) . . . . Dolores
    •• 0:16—In tank top and panties, then topless undress-
    ing in front of Stephen.
    • 0:19—Very brief side of left breast and buns getting
    robe.
    •• 0:41—Doing strip tease in front of her dad and
    Stephen. In black bra and panties, then topless.
    • 0:42—Very brief topless jumping into bed.
Martha, Ruth & Edie (1988; Canadian) . . . . Young Edie
Thunderground (1989) . . . . Casey
American Boyfriends (1990) . . . . Sandy Wilcox
TV:
Camp Wilder (1992-) . . . . Beth

Lankford, Kim

Films:

Malibu Beach (1978) . . . . Dina
    0:32—Buns, running into the ocean.
    • 0:34—Brief right breast getting out of the ocean.
    • 1:16—Right breast on beach at night with boy-
    friend.
    • 1:19—Brief topless at top of the stairs.
    •• 1:20—Brief topless when her parent's come home.
    • 1:21—Topless in bed with her boyfriend.
The Octagon (1980) . . . . Nancy
Cameron's Closet (1989) . . . . Dory Lansing

Made for Cable TV:
The Hitchhiker: A Time for Rifles (1985; HBO)
. . . . Rae Bridgeman
••• 0:03—Topless on the pool table while making love
with a guy.
Dream On: Premarital Ex (1990; HBO) . . . . Hannah
TV:
The Waverly Wonders (1978) . . . . Connie Rafkin
Knots Landing (1979-83) . . . . Ginger Ward

Large, Bonnie
Films:
The Happy Hooker Goes to Washington (1977)
. . . . Carolyn (Model)
• 0:06—Topless during photo shoot.
Magazines:
Playboy (Mar 1973). . . . . Playmate
••• 106-113—Nude.

•Larsen, Annabelle
Films:
Hard Rock Zombies (1985) . . . . Groupie
Alligator Eyes (1990) . . . . Pauline
•• 0:42—Nude, getting up from bed and walking
around.

Lasseter, Vicki
Video Tapes:
Playboy's Playmate Review (1982) . . . . . . Playmate
••• 0:43—Full frontal nudity in office, then in the
woods.
Magazines:
Playboy (Feb 1981) . . . . Playmate

Laure, Carole
Films:
Get Out Your Handkerchiefs (1978) . . . . . . Solange
•• 0:21—Topless sitting in bed listening to her boyfriend talk.
•• 0:31—Topless sitting in bed knitting.
• 0:41—Upper half of left breast in bed.
•• 0:47—Left breast, while sitting in bed and the three
guys talk.
• 1:08—Brief right breast when the little boy peeks at
her while she sleeps.
1:10—Lower frontal nudity while he looks at her
some more.
••• 1:17—Full frontal nudity taking off nightgown while
sitting on bed for the little boy.
Victory (1981). . . . . Renee
Naked Massacre (1983) . . . . Amy
Heartbreakers (1984) . . . . Liliane
• 0:56—Brief topless making love in car with Nick
Mancuso. Dark, hard to see.
• 1:25—In sheer black dress, then brief right breast
making love in art gallery with Peter Coyote.
The Surrogate (1984; Canadian) . . . . Anouk Vanderlin
• 0:48—Very brief topless when Frank rips her blouse
open in his apartment.

Sweet Country (1985). Eva
•• 0:31—Topless changing in apartment while Randy
Quaid watches.
• 0:43—Nude in auditorium with other women prisoners.
••• 1:13—Nude in bed with Quaid.
Magazines:
Playboy (Nov 1979) . . . . Sex in Cinema 1979
•• 181—Topless.

Laurin, Marie
Films:
The Lonely Guy (1983)
. . . . One of "The Seven Deadly Sins"
Creature (1985) . . . . Susan Delambre
•• 0:41—Topless and brief buns with blood on her
shoulders, getting Jon to take his helmet off.
Talking Walls (1987). Jeanne
Made for Cable TV:
The Hitchhiker: Petty Thieves . . . . Pearl
•• 0:09—Topless making love with Steve Railsback on
the couch.
•• 0:15—Topless playing with a doll in the bathtub,
then buns, standing up and wrapping herself with a
towel.
0:18—In black bra, then topless undressing in front
of John Colicos.
Magazines:
Playboy (Jun 1992). . . . . Grapevine
• 179—Topless under sheer blouse with dots on it.
B&W.

Law, Barbara
Films:
The Surrogate (1984; Canadian) . . . . . Maggie Simpson
Made for Cable Movies:
Bedroom Eyes (1985; Canadian; HBO) . . . . Jobeth
• 0:02—Topless taking off clothes while Harry watches
through the window.
•• 0:07—Topless and buns, kissing a woman.
• 0:14—Topless during Harry's flashback when he
talks to the psychiatrist.
•• 0:23—Topless and buns dancing in bedroom.
•• 0:57—Topless with Mary, kissing on floor.
1:17—In beige bra, panties, garter belt and stockings in bed with Harry.
• 1:23—Brief topless on top of Harry.

•Lawrence, Mitte
Films:
Funny Girl (1968). . . . . Emma
The New Centurions (1972). . . . . Gloria
Night Call Nurses (1972) . . . . Sandra
a.k.a. Young LA Nurses 2
•• 0:49—Topless in bed with a guy.

Lawrence, Suzanne Remey

Films:

Delivery Boys (1984) . . . . Nurse
0:34—In bra and panties after doing a strip tease with another nurse while dancing in front of a boy who is lying on an operating table.

R.S.V.P. (1984) . . . . Stripper
•• 0:56—Topless dancing in a radio station in front of a D.J.

• Layng, Lissa

Films:

Whose Life Is It, Anyway? (1981) . . . . Nurse
Night of the Comet (1984) . . . . Davenport
Say Yes (1986) . . . . Annie
•• 1:06—Topless, getting her dress ripped off.
• 1:07—More topless, putting on jacket in restroom.

• Lazar, Ava

Films:

Death Wish II (1982) . . . . Girl in TV Soap Opera
Fast Times at Ridgemont High (1982) . . . . Playmate
Night Shift (1982) . . . . Sharon
Diamond Run (1988; Indonesian) . . . . Samantha
a.k.a. Java Burn
•• 0:07—Brief topless, several times, making love in bed with Nicky. Hard to see her face.

TV:

Santa Barbara . . . . Santana Andrade

Le Brock, Kelly

Spokeswoman for Pantene cosmetics.
Wife of actor/martial arts expert Steven Seagal.
Films:

The Woman in Red (1984) . . . . Charlotte
0:02—Wearing the red dress, dancing over the air vent in the car garage while Gene Wilder watches.
• 1:13—Brief right breast, getting into bed. Too far to see anything.
1:15—Brief lower frontal nudity getting out of bed when her husband comes home. Very brief left breast, but it's blurry and hard to see.
Weird Science (1985) . . . . Lisa
0:12—In blue underwear and white top baring her midriff for the two boys when she is first created.
1:29—In blue leotard and grey tube top gym clothes to teach boy's gym class.
Hard to Kill (1990) . . . . Andy Stewart

• Leardini, Christina

Video Tapes:

Playboy Video Calendar 1992 (1991) . . . . . . August
••• 0:32—Nude trying on various outfits.
••• 0:33—Nude in old building.
Sexy Lingerie III (1991) . . . . Model
Playboy Playmates in Paradise (1992) . . . Playmate

Playboy's Playmate Review 1992 (1992)
. . . . Miss April
••• 0:32—Nude in a car, then in a bed, then inside an old building.
Sexy Lingerie IV (1992) . . . . Model

Magazines:

Playboy (Apr 1991) . . . . Playmate
••• 102-113—Nude.
Playboy's Book of Lingerie (Jul 1992) . . . . Herself
••• 12-13—Topless.
Playboy's Book of Lingerie (Sep 1992) . . . . . . Herself
•• 72—Left breast.

• Leary, Laura Jane

Films:

The Best of Sex and Violence (1981) . . . . Girl Victim
• 0:00—Getting clothes ripped off, then in bra and panties, then topless.
Famous T & A (1982) . . . . Motorcycle Rider
(No longer available for purchase, check your video store for rental.)
• 0:29—Lower nudity, riding a motorcycle with only a jacket on.

LeBeau, Becky

Films:

Joysticks (1983) . . . . Liza
Hollywood Hot Tubs (1984) . . . . Veronica
•• 0:49—Topless changing in the locker room with other girl soccer players while Jeff watches.
• 0:54—Topless in hot tub with the other girls and Shawn.
School Spirit (1985) . . . . Hogette
• 1:07—Topless sliding down water slide at dance, wearing black and white swimsuit bottoms.
Back to School (1986) . . . . . . Bubbles, the Hot Tub Girl
Takin' It All Off (1987) . . . . Becky
•• 0:16—Topless and brief full frontal nudity getting introduced to Allison.
••• 0:23—In black bra and panties, then nude doing a strip routine outside.
• 0:35—Brief full frontal nudity pushing Elliot into the pool.
• 0:36—Brief topless in studio with Allison again.
• 0:36—Brief left breast in dance studio with Allison.
•• 1:23—Nude, dancing with all the other women on stage.
The Underachievers (1987) . . . . Ginger Bronsky
••• 0:40—Topless in swimming pool playing with an inflatable alligator after her exercise class has left.
Not of This Earth (1988) . . . . Happy Birthday Girl
••• 0:47—Topless doing a Happy Birthday strippergram for the old guy.
Nudity Required (1989) . . . . Melanie
•• 0:35—Topless, taking off pink swimsuit.
•• 0:36—Brief topless (third girl) standing in line.
• 0:37—Topless, standing behind Scammer.
• 0:39—Very brief topless.

•• 0:41—Topless while sitting next to Scammer by the pool.

Ninja Academy (1990) . . . . Nudist
  •• 0:26—Nude, carrying plate, then going to swing at nudist colony. Then playing volleyball (she's the first one to hit the ball).

Transylvania Twist (1990) . . . . .Rita

The Malibu Beach Vampires (1991) . . . The Census Taker

Sins of Desire (1992) . . . . .n.a.

Music Videos:

California Girls/David Lee Roth
  . . . . Girl Squeezing Suntan Lotion Bottle

Video Tapes:

Centerfold Screen Test (1985) . . . . Herself
  0:14—In wet white T-shirt, auditioning in pool.

Best Chest in the West II (1986) . . . . Herself
  ••• 0:46—Dancing in red two piece swimsuit. Buns, then topless.
  •• 0:55—Buns and topless after winning semi-finals.

Becky Bubbles (1987) . . . . Herself
  ••• 0:00—Topless, waking up and getting out of bed.
  ••• 0:01—Topless, going outside for a swim in white panties. Long scene.
  ••• 0:06—Topless, rubbing lotion on herself.
  ••• 0:08—Topless outside on chair and in pool with her friends.
  ••• 0:12—Topless while playing on pool float with Lorraine and Brandi.
  ••• 0:22—Topless drying her hair outside with hairdryer.
  ••• 0:24—Topless putting on makeup and fingernail polish.
  •• 0:25—Buns and topless taking off swimsuit then getting dressed.

Trashy Ladies Wrestling (1987) . . . . Round Girl

Soft Bodies (1988) . . . . Herself
  ••• 0:01—In two piece swimsuit, then topless in swimming pool.
  •• 0:08—On bed during photo session in various lingerie, then topless and buns in G-string.
  ••• 0:16—In bra and panties, then topless on bed.

Soft Bodies Invitational (1990) . . . . Herself
  0:00—Buns, under short skirt playing tennis with Nina Alexander.
  ••• 0:15—Topless posing with Alexander in photo session.
  •• 0:24—In two piece swimsuit, then topless arguing with Alexander about who has better breasts.
  ••• 0:38—In red bra and panties outside on brides, then topless.
  ••• 0:44—Topless and buns in G-string in spa.

Soft Bodies: Curves Ahead (1991) . . . . Herself
  0:00—Buns in G-string, playing Frisbee with Kylie Rose.
  ••• 0:32—Topless in pool with Tamara. Buns and partial lower frontal nudity. Long scene.
  ••• 0:36—Topless posing for photographs in various outfits.

••• 0:41—On balcony in two piece swimsuit, then topless and buns taking an outdoor shower. Long scene.
  ••• 0:45—Topless and buns in G-string, posing on bed for photo session in various lingerie. Long scene.
  ••• 0:51—In two piece swimsuit outside at night in spa. Topless and buns in G-string. Long scene.

Soft Bodies: Party Favors (1992) . . . . Herself
  0:18—In swimsuit by pool with Antonia.
  ••• 0:35—Topless and buns, on floating bed in pool with Julia Hayes.
  ••• 0:39—Topless and buns posing in bed in various lingerie outfits.
  ••• 0:46—Topless and buns on couch.
  ••• 0:52—On balcony taking off dress, then in white lingerie, then topless and buns.

Magazines:

Playboy (Feb 1989) . . . . Grapevine
  • 166—Left breast sticking out from under T-shirt in B&W photo.

Playboy (Jul 1989) . . . . B-Movie Bimbos
  ••• 139—Full frontal nudity, wearing pink stockings and a garter belt, standing in a car filled with bubbles.

Lee, Adriane

Films:

Breeders (1986) . . . . .Alec
  •• 0:49—Topless, undressing while talking on the phone.
  • 1:07—Brief topless, covered with goop, in the alien nest.
  • 1:08—Brief topless in nest behind Frances Raines.
  • 1:09—Brief topless behind Raines again.
  • 1:11—Topless, lying back in the goop, then long shot topless.

Mutant Hunt (1987) . . . . .Amber Dawn

Necropolis (1987) . . . . .Cult Member

Slammer Girls (1987) . . . . Dead Convict

Lee, Cynthia

Films:

New York Nights (1981) . . . . .The Porn Star
  •• 1:15—Topless in the steam room talking to the prostitute.
  ••• 1:26—Topless in office with the financier and making love on his desk.

Hot Resort (1984) . . . . Alice
  • 1:08—Topless in the bathtub.

Hired to Kill (1990) . . . . .Armwrestler

• Lee, Hyapatia

Adult film actress.

Films:

Hellroller (1992) . . . . Dancer
  ••• 0:43—Topless, dancing in room by herself.
  ••• 0:45—Topless and buns, while taking a shower.

Lee, Joie

Sister of actor/director Spike Lee.
Films:
She's Gotta Have It (1987) . . . . Clorinda Bradford
School Daze (1988). Lizzie Life
Do the Right Thing (1989) . . . . Jade
Mo' Better Blues (1990) . . . . Indigo Downes
•• 1:06—Right breast while in bed with Bleek.
• 1:08—Very, very brief right breast while pounding
the bed and yelling at Bleek.
A Kiss Before Dying (1991) . . . . Cathy

Lee, Kaaren

Films:
The Right Stuff (1983). . . . . Young Widow
Roadhouse 66 (1984). . . . . Jesse Duran
•• 1:00—Topless, taking off her top to go skinny dip-
ping with Willem Dafoe. Dark.
St. Elmo's Fire (1985) . . . . Welfare Woman
Remote Control (1987) . . . . Patricia

• Lee, Kelli

Films:
Slash Dance (1989). . . . . Dancer
Sorority Girls and the Creature from Hell (1990)
. . . . Nude Double for Dori Courtney
• 0:23—Topless in bedroom with J.J.
• 0:36—Topless getting playfully strangled by Skip in
the spa. Buns, getting out.

Lee, Luann

Films:
Beverly Hills Cop II (1987) . . . . Playboy Playmate
Terminal Exposure (1988) . . . . Bruce's Girl
Video Tapes:
Playboy Video Centerfold: Luann Lee . . . Playmate
Playboy Video Calendar 1988 (1987) . . . . Playmate
Wet and Wild (1989). . . . . Model
Magazines:
Playboy (Jan 1987) . . . . Playmate
Playboy's Book of Lingerie (Jul 1992) . . . . . . Herself
• 73—Left breast.
•• 106—Left breast and lower frontal nudity.

• Lee, Margaret

Films:
Casanova '70 (1965; Italian) . . . . Dolly Greenwater
Secret Agent Super Dragon
(1966; French/Italian/German) . . . . Cynthia Fulton
Dorian Gray (1970; Italian/British/German)
. . . . Gwendolyn Wotten
Venus in Furs (1970) . . . . Olga
Original version.
• 0:53—Buns, lying on floor with Maria.
• 0:54—Buns, while walking and holding candelabra.
The Rogue (1976). . . . . n.a.

Lee, Pat

Films:
Porky's (1981; Canadian) . . . . Stripper
• 0:33—Brief topless dancing on stage at Porky's
showing her breasts to Pee Wee.
Starman (1984) . . . . Bracero Wife
And God Created Woman (1988). . . . . .Inmate
(Unrated version.)
Young Guns (1988) . . . . Janey

Lee, Robin

a.k.a. Robbie Lee.
Films:
Big Bad Mama (1974) . . . . Polly McClatchie
• 0:09—Brief left breast in open dress in car when
cops try to pull her car over.
0:22—In see-through slip on stage with her sister
and a stripper.
• 0:32—Brief topless running around the bedroom
chasing her sister.
Switchblade Sisters (1975) . . . . .Lace
• 0:48—Topless sitting up in bed to talk to Dominic.
Dark.

Lee, Tamara

Former adult film actress.
Video Tapes:
Soft Bodies: Curves Ahead (1991) . . . . .Herself
••• 0:23—In lingerie on chair, then topless during photo
session. Brief lower frontal nudity under sheer lingerie. Long scene.
••• 0:31—In chair by pool. Topless and partial lower
frontal nudity.

Lee-Hsu, Diana

Films:
License to Kill (1989) . . . . Loti
Video Tapes:
Playboy Video Calendar 1989 (1988). . . . . February
••• 0:05—Nude.
Playmates at Play (1990) . . . . Gotta Dance
Wet and Wild III (1991) . . . . Model
Playboy Video Playmate Six-Pack 1992 (1992)
. . . . Playmate
Magazines:
Playboy (May 1988). . . . . Playmate
Playboy (Aug 1989) . . . . License to Thrill
••• 126-131—Nude.
Playboy's Nudes (Oct 1990) . . . . .Herself
••• 13—Full frontal nudity.

Légerè, Phoebe

Singer.
Films:
Mondo New York (1987) . . . . Singer
0:01—On stage, singing "Marilyn Monroe." Buns
and most of lower frontal nudity while writhing on
stage in a mini-skirt.

The Toxic Avenger: Part II (1988) . . . . Claire
- 0:31—Brief right breast, while caressing herself while making out with the Toxic Avenger.

The Toxic Avenger III: The Last Temptation of Toxie (1989) . . . . Claire

King of New York (1990). . . . . .Bordello Woman

Magazines:

Playboy (Jun 1988) . . . . .Mondo Phoebe
- • 70-77—Nude.

Playboy (Nov 1988) . . . . Sex in Cinema 1988
- 138—Left breast, while lying on bed, getting a hug from the Toxic Avenger.

Playboy (Dec 1988). . . . . Sex Stars of 1988
- 184—Right breast, popping out of top.

Leigh, Barbara

Films:

The Student Nurses (1970) . . . . Priscilla
a.k.a. Young LA Nurses
- • 0:43—Topless on the beach with Les. Long scene.

The Christian Licorice Store (1971) . . . . .Starlet

Pretty Maids All in a Row (1971). . . . . Jean McDrew
- 0:30—Brief partial side view of right breast when she leans over chess board on bed to touch Rock Hudson.

Junior Bonner (1972) . . . . Charmagne

Terminal Island (1973) . . . . .Bunny Campbell
- • 0:22—Topless and buns undressing in room while Bobbie watches from the bed.

Boss (1974). . . . . Miss Pruitt
a.k.a. Boss Nigger

Seven (1979) . . . . Alexa

Mistress of the Apes (1981) . . . . .n.a.

Famous T & A (1982) . . . . .Bunny Campbell
(No longer available for purchase, check your video store for rental.)
- • 0:45—Topless scene from *Terminal Island*. Includes additional takes that weren't used.

Miniseries:

The Search for the Nile (1972) . . .Isabel Arundel Burton

Magazines:

Playboy (Apr 1971) . . . . .Vadim's "Pretty Maids"
- • 158—Topless in wet T-shirt.

Playboy (May 1973) .Indian
- • 149-155—Topless.

Playboy (Jan 1977) . . . . Natural Leigh
- • 85-91—B&W photos. Full frontal nudity.

Leigh, Carrie

Former girlfriend of *Playboy* publisher Hugh Hefner.

Films:

A Fine Mess (1986) . . . . Second Extra

Beverly Hills Cop II (1987). . . . . Herself

Blood Relations (1989) . . . . Thomas' Girlfriend

Magazines:

Playboy (Jul 1986). . . . . Carrie Leigh
- • 114-125—Nude.

Playboy (Aug 1988). . . . . . . The Great Palimony Caper
- • 64—Left breast and lower frontal nudity, B&W.

Playboy (Dec 1988) . . . . .Sex Stars of 1988
- • 188—Full frontal nudity.

Playboy (Feb 1989) . . . . The Year in Sex
- • 143—Topless in B&W photo.

Leigh, Jennifer Jason

Daughter of the late actor Vic Morrow.

Films:

Eyes of a Stranger (1981). . . . . Tracy
- 1:15—Very brief topless lying in bed getting attacked by rapist.
- • 1:19—Left breast, while cleaning herself in bathroom.

Fast Times at Ridgemont High (1982)
. . . . Stacy Hamilton
- 0:18—Left breast, while making out with Ron in a dugout.
- • 1:00—Topless in poolside dressing room.

Wrong is Right (1982) . . . . .Young Girl

Easy Money (1983) . . . . Allison Capuletti

Grandview, U.S.A. (1984). . . . . Candy Webster

Flesh + Blood (1985). Agnes
- 0:45—Brief right breast, while being held down.
- • 1:05—Full frontal nudity getting into the bath with Rutger Hauer and making love.
- • 1:16—Full frontal nudity getting out of bed with Hauer and walking to the window.
- • 1:35—Nude throwing clothes into the fire.

The Hitcher (1986). . . . . Nash

The Men's Club (1986) . . . . .Teensy

Sister Sister (1987) . . . . Lucy Bonnard
- • 0:01—Topless making love during a dream.
  0:52—In lingerie talking with Eric Stoltz.
- • 0:53—Left breast, while making love with Stoltz in her bedroom.
- 0:58—Topless in bathtub surrounded by candles.

Under Cover (1987). . . . . .Tanille Lareoux

Heart of Midnight (1988) . . . . Carol
- 0:27—Very brief side view of right breast, while reaching for soap in the shower.

The Big Picture (1989) . . . . Lydia Johnson

Last Exit to Brooklyn (1990) . . . . .Tralata
- • 1:28—Topless, opening her blouse in bar after getting drunk.
- 1:33—Topless getting drug out of car, placed on mattress, then basically raped by a long line of guys. Long, painful-to-watch scene.
- 1:35—Topless lying on mattress when Spook comes to save her.

Miami Blues (1990). . . . . .Susie Waggoner
  0:07—Very brief upper half of right breast, while changing clothes behind Alec Baldwin.
- • 0:10—Topless in panties, taking off red dress and getting into bed.
  0:24—Very, very brief half of right breast while taking a bath. Long shot.
- 0:33—Topless making love with Baldwin in the kitchen.

Backdraft (1991) . . . . .Jennifer Vaitkus
- • 1:16—Very, very brief left breast on back of fire truck with William Baldwin. (Right after someone knocks open a door with an axe.)

Crooked Hearts (1991) . . . . Harriet
- •• 1:10—In black bra, then topless in bathtub with Tom.

Rush (1991). . . . . .Kristen Cates
- • 1:09—Brief buns, when Jason Patric takes off her pajama bottoms and forces himself on her.

Single White Female (1992) . . . . Hedy Carlson

Made for Cable Movies:

Buried Alive (1990; USA) . . . . Joanna

Made for TV Movies:

Girls of the White Orchid (1983) . . . . .n.a.

The Killing of Randy Webster (1985) . . . . .n.a.

Magazines:

Playboy (Nov 1985) . . . . Sex in Cinema 1985
- ••• 135—Topless in scenes from *Flesh + Blood.*

• *Leigh, Melissa*

Films:

Affairs of the Heart (1992). . . . . .Jealous Woman
Private Screenings.
- ••• 0:38—Buns, then topless with the Jealous Man.

Magazines:

Penthouse (May 1987) . . . . Pet

• *Leigh-Hunt, Barbara*

Films:

Frenzy (1972; British). . . . . .Brenda Blaney
- • 0:31—Left breast, while sitting in chair with the necktie killer. Don't see her face.

Henry VIII and His Six Wives (1972; British)
. . . . Catherine Parr

The Nelson Affair (1973) . . . . Catherine Matcham

Oh Heavenly Dog! (1980). . . . . Margaret

Wagner (1983; British) . . . . Queen Mother

Paper Mask (1991; British) . . . . Celia Mumford

Leighton, Roberta

Films:

Barracuda (1978) . . . . .n.a.

Stripes (1981) . . . . .Anita
- • 0:07—Topless, wearing blue panties, while putting her shirt on and talking to Bill Murray.

Covergirl (1982; Canadian). . . . . .Dee Anderson
0:16—Almost topless, while making love dressed like a nun.

TV:

The Young and the Restless (1978-86)
. . . . Dr. Casey Reed

Days of Our Lives (1991-). . . . . Ginger

Lemmons, Kasi

Films:

School Daze (1988) . . . . Perry

Vampire's Kiss (1989) . . . . .Jackie
- •• 0:05—In black bra and panties, then topless in living room with Nicholas Cage.

Silence of the Lambs (1990). . . . . .Ardelia Mapp

The Five Heartbeats (1991) . . . . .Cookie

Candyman (1992) . . . . .Bernadette

Made for Cable Movies:

The Court-Martial of Jackie Robinson (1990) . . . . Rachel

Afterburn (1992; HBO). . . . . Carol

Made for TV Movies:

The Lakeside Killer (1979) . . . . .Hostage

TV:

Under Cover (1991). . . . . Alex Robbins

• *Lennox, Lisa*

Video Tapes:

Hot Body International: #1 Miss Cancun (1990)
. . . . .Contestant

Hot Body International: #2 Miss Puerto Vallarta (1990)
. . . . .Contestant

Hot Body International: #4 Spring Break (1992)
. . . . .Contestant
- 0:11—Dancing in one piece swimsuit on stage.
- • 0:48—Brief left breast during wet T-shirt contest. Buns in G-string.

Lenska, Rula

Films:

Confessions of a Pop Performer (1975; British). . . . . n.a.

Oh, Alfie! (1975; British) . . . . Louise
a.k.a. Alfie Darling
- •• 0:12—Topless, then left breast in bed after making love with Alfie.

Undercovers Hero (1975). . . . . Grenier Girl

The Deadly Females (1976) . . . . Luisa

Lentini, Susan

Films:

Action Jackson (1988) . . . . VW Driver

Roadhouse (1989) . . . . .Bandstand Babe

Ricochet (1991) . . . . Reporter

Made for Cable TV:

Dream On: Sex and the Single Parent (1990; HBO)
. . . . .Ms. Susan Brodsky
- 0:04—In white bra and panties in front of class while Jeremy fantasizes about her.
- •• 0:10—Brief topless, twice, talking to Martin while he fantasizes about her.

Tales From the Crypt: Dead Right (1990; HBO)
. . . . Leanne

(Available on *Tales From the Crypt, Volume 3.*)

Lenz, Kay

Ex-wife of actor/singer David Cassidy.
Films:
Breezy (1974) . . . . Breezy
Topless and nude.
White Line Fever (1975) . . . . Jerri Hummer
The Great Scout and Cathouse Thursday (1976)
. . . . Thursday
Moving Violation (1979) . . . . Cam Johnson
The Passage (1979; British). . . . . Leah Bergson
Topless.
Fast Walking (1981). Moke
 • 0:26—Brief topless closing the door after pulling
 James Woods into the room.
 0:42—Caressing herself under her dress while in
 prison visiting room, talking to George.
 ••• 1:27—Right breast in store. Topless getting hosed
 down and dried off outside by James Woods.
 • 1:32—Brief left breast, making love with Woods.
House (1986) . . . . Sandy Sinclair
Death Wish 4: The Crackdown (1987). . . Karen Sheldon
Stripped to Kill (1987) . . . . Cody Sheehan
 •• 0:23—Topless dancing on stage.
 ••• 0:47—Topless dancing in white lingerie.
Fear (1988). . . . . Sharon Haden
Headhunters (1988) . . . . Katherine Hall
Physical Evidence (1989). . . . . Deborah Quinn
Streets (1989) . . . . Sergeant
Falling From Grace (1992). . . . . n.a.
Made for Cable Movies:
Hitler's Daughter (1990) . . . . n.a.
Miniseries:
Rich Man, Poor Man (1976) . . . . Kate Jordache
Made for TV Movies:
Initiation of Sarah (1978) . . . . n.a.
Sanctuary of Fear (1979). . . . . n.a.
TV:
Rich Man, Poor Man—Book II (1976-77)
. . . . Kate Jordache
Reasonable Doubts (1992-) . . . . Maggie Zombro
Magazines:
Playboy (Nov 1982) . . . . Sex in Cinema 1982
 ••• 161—Topless photo from *Fast Walking*.

Leo, Melissa

Films:
Always (1984). . . . . Peggy
Streetwalkin' (1985) . . . . Cookie
 • 0:05—Brief topless taking off red blouse in front of
 mirror.
 •• 0:15—Topless, stripping and taking off her top for a
 customer.
 • 0:18—Brief right breast, having sex with her pimp
 on the floor.
 • 0:44—Topless, taking off her top and sitting on bed
 with a customer (long shot seen in mirror).
 0:53—Buns, in body suit, in hotel room with customer.
A Time of Destiny (1988) . . . . Josie

TV:
Young Riders (1989-90) . . . . Emma Shannon

• Leong, Page

Films:
White Phantom (1987) . . . . Mai Lin
The Wizard of Speed & Time (1988) . . . . Dancer
Ghostbusters II (1989) . . . . Spengler's Assistant
Another 48 Hrs. (1990) . . . . Angel Lee
 • 1:00—Brief topless getting out of bed with Willie.

• Leprince, Catherine

Films:
Bilitis (1982; French) . . . . Helene
 •• 0:13—Topless taking off dress and getting into bed
 with Bilitis.
Escalier C (1985; French) . . . . Florence
Vive Les Femmes (1985). . . . . n.a.
Paulette (1986; French) . . . . Joseph, Female

Lesniak, Emilia

see: Crow, Emilia.

Levin, Rachel

Films:
Gaby, A True Story (1987) . . . . Gaby
 • 0:56—Right breast, then topless on the floor making
 love with another handicapped boy, Fernando.
White Palace (1990). Rachel

Lewis, Charlotte

Films:
The Golden Child (1986) . . . . Kee Nang
Pirates (1986; French) . . . . Dolores
Dial Help (1988) . . . . Jenny Cooper
 1:06—Black panties and bare back dressing in black
 corset top and stockings. Yowza!
 •• 1:09—Brief right breast while rolling around in the
 bathtub.
Tripwire (1989) . . . . Trudy
Made for Cable Movies:
Bare Essentials (1991). . . . . Tarita
 0:55—Upper half of buns, in G-string swimsuit,
 while talking to Mark Linn-Baker.
 0:59—Buns in swimsuit, while giving Linn-Baker a
 massage. Topless, but her long hair gets in the way.
 1:31—Very brief side view of buns in swimsuit, walking from the ocean onto the beach.
Sketch Artist (1992; Showtime) . . . . Leese
 ••• 0:02—Topless making love on sofa. Buns in G-string,
 side of right breast, while changing CD. (Does this
 woman have the most awesome waist-to-chest ratio
 or what?)

Lewis, Fiona

Films:
The Fearless Vampire Killers (1967). . . . . Maid
Dr. Phibes Rises Again (1972). . . . . Diana

Lisztomania (1975; British)........Countess Marie
•• 0:00—Topless in bed getting breasts kissed by Roger
   Daltrey to the beat of a metronome.
• 0:01—Brief topless swinging a chandelier to Daltrey.
•• 0:03—Brief topless and buns while running from
   chair (long shot). Brief topless when catching a candle on the bed.
•• 0:04—Brief left breast when her dress top is cut
   down. Left breast, sitting inside a piano with Daltrey.
Drum (1976)................. Augusta Chauvet
••• 0:57—Topless taking a bath, getting out, then having Pam Grier dry her off.
Tintorera (1977)...................... Patricia
   0:20—Side view of left breast in silhouette. Long
   shot, hard to see. Nude swimming under water just
   before getting eaten by a shark. Don't see her face.
The Fury (1978) .... Dr. Susan Charles
Dead Kids (1981) .... Gwen Parkinson
   a.k.a. Strange Behavior
Strange Invaders (1983) ....Waitress/Avon Lady
Innerspace (1987).............Dr. Margaret Canker
Magazines:
Playboy (Dec 1976)............. Sex Stars of 1976
••• 186—Full frontal nudity.

Lightstone, Marilyn
Films:
Lies My Father Told Me (1975; Canadian)
.... Annie Herman
In Praise of Older Women (1978; Canadian) ... Klari
• 0:45—Left breast, twice, while on floor with Tom Be-
   renger before being discovered by Karen Black.
Spasms (1983; Canadian) ....Dr. Rothman
The Surrogate (1984; Canadian) .... Dr. Harriet Forman
Made for Cable Movies:
Disaster in Time (1992; Showtime) .....Madame Iovine
   a.k.a. Timescape
Made for TV Movies:
Anne of Green Gables (1985; Canadian) ....Miss Stacey

Lindeland, Liv
Films:
Picasso Trigger (1989)...................... Inga
Guns (1990) ....Ace
Magazines:
Playboy (Jan 1971) .... Playmate
Playboy (Dec 1972)............... Sex Stars of 1972
Playboy (Jan 1974) .... Twenty Years of Playmates
••• 110—Topless and buns, while in bed.
Playboy's Nudes (Oct 1990)............. Herself
••• 29—Full frontal nudity.

Lindemulder, Janine
Films:
Spring Fever USA (1988) .... Heather Lipton
   a.k.a. Lauderdale
•• 0:14—Taking off her stockings, then brief topless
   undressing for bath, then taking a bath.

Caged Fury (1989)........................Lulu
   0:14—Dancing in bar in black bra and G-string.
• 0:16—Brief topless dancing in front of Erik Estrada.
Video Tapes:
Penthouse Passport to Paradise/Hawaii (1991)
.... Model
••• 0:37—Stripping out of a dress and lingerie, then
   nude dancing during her fantasy.
**Penthouse Satin & Lace: An Erotic History of
   Lingerie** (1992) .... Model
Magazines:
Penthouse (Dec 1987).....................Pet
Penthouse (Sep 1990)...........Tony and Janine
•• 82-91—Nude with a guy.
Penthouse (Mar 1991)................. Robo-Pet
••• 42-51—Nude, partially covered with silver paint.

Linden, Jennie
Films:
Nightmare (1963; British) .... Janet
Dr. Who and the Daleks (1965; British)....... Barbara
A Severed Head (1971; British)........Georgie Hands
   0:02—Buns, rolling over on the floor with Ian Holm.
Women in Love (1971)........... Ursula Bragwen
• 0:38—Brief topless skinny dipping in the river with
   Glenda Jackson.
• 1:11—Brief topless in a field with Alan Bates. Scene
   is shown sideways.
Hedda (1975; British)................Mrs. Elvsted
Old Dracula (1975; British)..................Angela
A Deadly Game (1979; British)............... Edith

Lindley, Gisele
Films:
Forbidden Zone (1980)..............The Princess
••• 0:21—Topless in jail cell.
••• 0:39—Topless turning a table around.
•• 0:45—Topless bending over, making love with a
   frog.
•• 0:51—Topless in a cave.
•• 0:53—More topless scenes.
•• 1:06—Even more topless scenes.
S.O.B. (1981)........................... n.a.

• Linssen, Saskia
Video Tapes:
Playboy's Playmate Review 1992 (1992)
.... Miss June
••• 0:27—Nude doing futuristic dance and then taking
   a bath.
Magazines:
Playboy (Jun 1991)................... Playmate
••• 112-125—Nude.
Playboy's Book of Lingerie (Jul 1992) .... Herself
••• 96—Topless.
• 98-99—Topless under fishnet body stocking.
Playboy's Book of Lingerie (Sep 1992) ......Herself
••• 94-95—Full frontal nudity.

Little, Michele
Films:
Out of the Blue (1982) . . . . .n.a.
Radioactive Dreams (1984) . . . . Rusty Mars
My Demon Lover (1987). . . . . Denny
Out of Bounds (1987) . . . . Crystal
Sweet Revenge (1987) . . . . Lee
   • 0:41—Brief topless in water under a waterfall with
     K.C.
Appointment with Fear (1988) . . . . Carol
Blood Clan (1990). Katy Bane
Mystery Date (1991) . . . . Stella

• Liu, Carolyn
Films:
Do or Die (1991) . . . . Silk
   ••• 0:14—Topless, getting up off massage table and
     putting robe on.
   •• 1:04—Topless in bed with Pat Morita.
Video Tapes:
Sexy Lingerie III (1991) . . . . .Model
**Penthouse Satin & Lace: An Erotic History of
   Lingerie** (1992) . . . . .Model
Magazines:
Playboy (Mar 1992). . . . . Society Darlings
   ••• 130-131—Full frontal nudity.

Lizer, Kari
Films:
Smokey Bites the Dust (1981) . . . . Cindy
Private School (1983) . . . . .Rita
   • 0:30—Very brief left breast popping out of cheer-
     leader's outfit along with the Coach.
Gotcha! (1985) . . . . Muffy
Made for TV Movies:
Double Edge (1992) . . . . Sister Theresa
TV:
Sunday Dinner (1991). . . . . Diana

Lloyd, Emily
Films:
Wish You Were Here (1987) . . . . Lynda
   • 0:43—Buns, while singing in the alley and lifting up
     her skirt to moon an older neighbor woman.
Chicago Joe and the Showgirl (1989; British)
. . . . Betty Jones
Cookie (1989). . . . . Carmella "Cookie" Voltecki
In Country (1989). . . . . Samantha Hughes
Scorchers (1992). . . . . .n.a.

Lloyd, Sue
Films:
Happy Housewives .The Blonde
Revenge of the Pink Panther (1978)
. . . . Claude Russo/Claudine Russo
The Stud (1978; British) . . . . .Vanessa
   • 1:04—Topless in the swimming pool with Joan Col-
     lins and Tony.

The Bitch (1979; British) . . . . Vanessa Grant
   • 1:12—Side view of left breast and topless in the
     swimming pool.
Rough Cut (1980; British) . . . . n.a.

Locke, Sondra
Films:
The Heart is a Lonely Hunter (1968) . . . . Mick Kelley
Willard (1971) . . . . .Joan
Suzanne (1973) . . . . .Suzanne
   a.k.a. The Second Coming of Suzanne
   (*Suzanne* has nudity in it, *The Second Coming of Suzanne*
   has the nudity cut out.)
   •• 0:27—Topless sitting, looking at a guy. Brief left
     breast several times lying down.
   ••• 0:29—Topless lying down.
The Outlaw Josey Wales (1976). . . . . .Laura Lee
   •• 1:20—Briefly nude in rape scene.
Death Game, The Seducers (1977) . . . . Jackson
   a.k.a. Mrs. Manning's Weekend
   0:16—Buns and brief right breast in spa with Col-
     leen Camp trying to get George in with them.
   • 0:48—Brief topless running around the room trying
     to keep George away from the telephone.
The Gauntlet (1977) . . . . Gus Mally
   •• 1:10—Brief right breast, then topless getting raped
     by two biker guys in a box car while Clint Eastwood
     is tied up.
Every Which Way But Loose (1978)
. . . . Lynn Halsey Taylor
Any Which Way You Can (1980) . . . . .Lynne
Bronco Billy (1980) . . . . .Antoinette
Sudden Impact (1983). . . . . Jennifer Spencer
Ratboy (1986) .Nikki Morrison

Lockhart, Anne
Daughter of actress June Lockhart.
Films:
Joyride (1977) . . . . Cindy
   •• 0:59—Brief topless in the spa with everybody.
   ••• 1:00—Topless, standing in the kitchen kissing Desi
     Arnaz Jr.
The Young Warriors (1983; U.S./Canadian) . . . . Lucy
   •• 0:42—Topless and buns making love with Kevin on
     the bed. Looks like a body double.
Troll (1986) . . . . Young Eunice St. Clair
Dark Tower (1987). . . . . .Elaine
Big Bad John (1989). . . . . .Lady Police Officer
Made for TV Movies:
Just Tell Me You Love Me (1978) . . . . n.a.
TV:
Battlestar Galactica (1979). . . . . Sheeba

Locklin, Loryn
Films:
Catch Me... If You Can (1989) . . . . Melissa
    0:18—In blue one-piece swimsuit by the pool.
    1:32—In bra trying to get policeman's attention.
    Very, very brief side of right breast turing around.
    Looks like she's wearing flesh-colored pasties.
Taking Care of Business (1990) . . . . Jewel
  • 0:42—Buns and very brief side view, twice, seen
    through door, changing by the pool. Then in black
    two piece swimsuit.
Made for TV Movies:
Shoot First: A Cop's Vengeance (1991) . . . . Lea

Lombardi, Leigh
Films:
The Wild Life (1984) . . . . Stewardess
Murphy's Law (1986) . . . . Stewardess
A Tiger's Tale (1988) . . . . Marcia
Moontrap (1989) . . . . .Mera
  •• 1:08—Topless with Walter Koenig in moon tent.

Lomez, Céline
Films:
The Far Shore (1976) . . . . Eulalia Turner
Plague (1978; Canadian). . . . . .n.a.
  a.k.a. The Gemini Strain
The Silent Partner (1978) . . . . Elaine
  • 1:05—Side view of left breast, then topless, then
    buns with Elliott Gould.
The Kiss (1988) . . . . Aunt Irene

London, Lisa
Films:
H.O.T.S. (1979) . . . . Jennie O'Hara
  • 1:22—Topless changing clothes by the closet while
    a crook watches her.
  • 1:33—Topless playing football.
The Happy Hooker Goes Hollywood (1980) . . . . . Laurie
Sudden Impact (1983). . . . . .Young Hooker
  •• 1:04—Topless in bathroom, walking to Nick in the
    bed.
The Naked Cage (1985). . . . . .Abbey
  •• 0:22—Topless in S&M costume with Angel Tomp-
    kins.
  •• 0:38—Left breast making out in bed with Angel
    Tompkins.
Private Resort (1985). . . . . Alice
    0:51—In beige bra and panties several times with
    Ben and Jack while she's drunk.
Savage Beach (1989) . . . . Rocky
  • 0:06—Topless in spa with Patty Duffek, Dona Speir
    and Hope Marie Carlton.
  •• 0:50—Topless changing clothes.
Guns (1990) . . . . Rocky
Made for Cable Movies:
Prey of the Chameleon (1992; Showtime). . . . . . . Alice

Made for Cable TV:
Dream On: The Charlotte Letter (1991; HBO)
  . . . . Candy Striper #2
  • 0:06—Topless several times, acting in adult film that
    Martin is watching on TV. (She's first to take her out-
    fit off.)
Video Tapes:
Inside Out 2 (1992) . . . . .June/The Right Number
(Unrated version reviewed.)
  •• 1:25—Topless, lying on the floor having phone sex
    and in bed.
  •• 1:28—More topless talking on the phone.

• Long, Nia
Films:
Edgar Allan Poe's "Buried Alive" (1989) . . . . . . .Fingers
Boys N the Hood (1991) . . . . Brandi
    1:16—In bra, lying in bed with Tre.
  • 1:17—Left breast, while in bed with Tre. Don't see
    her face, but it is her.
TV:
The Guiding Light . . . . Kat Speakes

Long, Shannon
Video Tapes:
Playboy Video Calendar 1990 (1989). . . . November
  ••• 0:57—Nude.
Magazines:
Playboy (Oct 1988) . . . . Playmate

Long, Shelley
Films:
A Small Circle of Friends (1980) . . . . Alice
Caveman (1981) . . . . Tala
Night Shift (1982) . . . . Belinda Keaton
    0:20—In black teddy and robe talking to Henry Win-
    kler in the hallway.
    0:37—In panties, socks and tank top cooking break-
    fast in Winkler's kitchen.
The Money Pit (1986) . . . . Anna Crowley
Hello Again! (1987). . . . . Lucy Chadman
  • 0:58—Brief buns, in hospital gown, walking down
    hallway.
Outrageous Fortune (1987) . . . . Lauren Ames
Troop Beverly Hills (1989) . . . . Phyllis Nefler
Don't Tell Her It's Me (1990) . . . . .Lizzie Potts
TV:
Cheers (1982-87). . . . . Diane Chambers

Lopez, Maria Isabel
a.k.a. Isabel Lopez.
Films:
Joy: Chapter II (1985; French) . . . . Milaka
  a.k.a. Joy and Joan
  •• 0:10—Topless, showing Joy her breasts at Bruce's re-
    quest.
  ••• 0:27—Topless, taking off her robe and massaging
    Joy.

Silip (1985; Philippines)................... Tonya
a.k.a. Daughters of Eve
Mission Manila (1989)................... Jessie
• 0:22—Brief right breast several times in bed while
Harry threatens her with knife.
Dune Warriors (1990) .... Miranda
•• 0:25—Topless in underground lake with Val.
••• 0:43—Topless making love with a guy in bed.

Lords, Traci

Infamous under age adult film actress. Unfortunately, all
of the adult films she was in before she was 18 years old
are now illegal. The only legal adult film she did is *Traci,
I Love You*.
Real name is Nora Louise Kuzma.
Films:
Not of This Earth (1988) .... Nadine
•• 0:25—Buns and side view of left breast drying her-
self off with a towel while talking to Jeremy.
0:27—In blue swimsuit by swimming pool.
•• 0:42—Topless in bed making love with Harry.
0:46—Walking around the house in white lingerie.
Fast Food (1989)......................Dixie Love
1:10—In black bra in storage room with Auggie.
Cry Baby (1990) .... Wanda
Shock 'Em Dead (1990) .... Lindsay Roberts
Raw Nerve (1991)................... Gina Clayton
A Time to Die (1991) .... Jackie
Video Tapes:
Red Hot Rock (1984) ....Miss Georgia
•• 0:41—Topless several times in open-front swimsuit
during beauty pageant during "Gimme Gimme
Good Lovin'" by Helix.
•• 0:42—Topless on stage wearing black outfit with
mask, smashing a large avocado during the same
song.
Warm Up with Traci Lords (1989) .... Herself
Magazines:
Penthouse (Sep 1984) .... Pet
••• 97-115—Nude.

Loren, Sophia

Films:
Two Nights with Cleopatra (1954; Italian)
.... Cleopatra/Nisca
(It seems that her nude scenes have been cut for the vid-
eo tape version.)
Boy on a Dolphin (1957) .... Phaedra
Wet blouse.
Era Lui, Si, Si (1957)........................n.a.
The Pride and the Passion (1957) .... Juana
Desire Under the Elms (1958) .... Anna Cabot
Houseboat (1958)................Cinzia Zaccardi
A Breath of Scandal (1960) .... Princess Olympia
Heller in Pink Tights (1960)..........Angela Rossini
Two Women (1960; Italian)................. Cesira
(Academy Award for Best Actress.)
El Cid (1961)........................Chimene
Boccaccio 70 (1962; Italian) ....Zoe

The Fall of the Roman Empire (1964) .... Lucilla
Yesterday, Today and Tomorrow (1964; Italian)
.... Adelina
Arabesque (1966) .... Yasmin Azir
Man of La Mancha (1972) .... Dulcinea/Aldonza
Angela (1977; Canadian) ....Angela
The Cassandra Crossing (1977; British) .... Jennifer
A Special Day (1977) .... Antonietta
Brass Target (1978) .... Mara
Firepower (1979) .... Adele Tasca
Magazines:
Playboy (Feb 1980) .... The Year in Sex
• 157—Sort of topless under sheer black dress.
Penthouse (May 1982)...................Titillation
• 132—In wet dress. B&W.
Playboy (Jan 1989)........... Women of the Fifties
• 120—B&W photo from *Era Lui, Si, Si*.

• Loring, Jeana

Films:
The Malibu Bikini Shop (1985) ....Margie Hill
•• 0:43—Topless, dancing on stage during bikini contest (Contestant #4).
Magazines:
Playboy (Nov 1985)........... Sex in Cinema 1985
••• 128—Topless in scene from *The Malibu Bikini Shop*.

Loring, Lisa

Wife of adult film actor Jerry Butler.
Films:
Iced (1988) ....Jeanette
• 0:46—Brief left breast in bathtub.
• 0:53—Buns and brief right breast in bathtub with
Alex.
•• 1:05—Brief lower frontal nudity and buns, while getting into hot tub. Topless in hot tub just before getting electrocuted.
•• 1:13—Full frontal nudity lying dead in the hot tub.
• 1:18—Brief full frontal nudity lying dead in the hot
tub again.
Death Feud (1989)....................... Roxey
0:06—Dancing in club with feathery pasties. Later,
wearing the same thing under a sheer negligee.
0:41—Dancing again with the same pasties.
1:20—Dancing with red tassel pasties.
TV:
As the World Turns .... Cricket Montgomery
The Addams Family (1964-66)
.... Wednesday Thursday Addams

Lorraine, Nita

Films:
Happy Housewives................... Jenny Elgin
• 0:31—Brief side view of left breast and buns in barn
chasing after Bob.
• 0:32—Brief topless in open dress talking to policeman.
The Viking Queen (1967; British) .....Nubian Girl-Slave
All Neat in Black Stockings (1969) .... Jolasta

Louise, Helli

Films:
Happy Housewives . . . . Newsagent's Daughter
•• 0:16—Topless with Mrs. Wain and Bob in the bathtub.
Confessions of a Pop Performer (1975; British) . . . . .n.a.

• Louise, Jeanine

Made for Cable Movies:
Soft Touch (1987; Playboy). . . . . Carrie Crawford
(Shown on *The Playboy Channel* as *Birds in Paradise*.)
• 0:00—Topless during opening credits.
• 0:02—Topless with her two girlfriends during the opening credits.
• 0:03—Brief topless getting out of the shower.
• 0:17—Topless seen in mirror, while taking a shower.
•• 0:19—Full frontal nudity during pillow fight on bed.
•• 0:23—Topless in bed with the other two girls.
• 0:27—Topless in T-shirt, leaning over to wash car.
• 0:32—Topless with Neill in open dress.
••• 0:35—Dancing on stage in red lingerie, then topless and buns in G-string.
•• 0:41—Full frontal nudity walking in water with a guy.
••• 0:50—Topless sunbathing on the boat with Tracy.
• 1:01—Nude, swinging into water. Long shot.
• 1:02—Buns, waving to a dolphin.
• 1:04—Topless at night by campfire with Tracy.
• 1:05—Brief left breast, while sleeping.
• 1:06—Topless when Tracy wakes her up.
• 1:19—Topless in stills during the end credits.
Soft Touch II (1987; Playboy) . . . . Carrie Crawford
(Shown on *The Playboy Channel* as *Birds in Paradise*.)
• 0:00—Topless during opening credits.
• 0:02—Topless with her two girlfriends during opening credits.
•• 0:24—Topless in bed feeling herself.
•• 0:41—Full frontal nudity undressing and putting swimsuit on.
• 0:51—Topless with her diving instructor.

Love, Lucretia

Films:
Battle of the Amazons (1973; Italian/Spanish) . . . Eraglia
Naked Warriors (1973) . . . . Deidre
a.k.a. The Arena
• 0:07—Brief topless getting clothes torn off by guards.
•• 0:08—Brief nude getting washed down in court yard.
1:08—Brief buns, while bent over riding a horse.
The Tormented (1978; Italian). . . . . .n.a.
Dr. Heckyl and Mr. Hype (1980) . . . . Debra Kate

Love, Patti

Films:
Butley (1974; British) . . . . Female Student
That'll Be the Day (1974; British) . . . . . . Sandra's Friend
Terror (1979; British) . . . . n.a.
The Long Good Friday (1980; British). . . . . Carol
Steaming (1985; British) . . . . .Josie
• 0:08—Frontal nudity, getting undressed.
• 0:45—Brief topless.
• 1:30—Topless, jumping around in the pool.

Love, Suzanna

Films:
Cocaine Cowboys (1979). . . . . Lucy
1:02—Undressing to see-through bra and panties with Herman.
Brainwaves (1983) . . . . Kaylie Bedford
Devonsville Terror (1983) . . . . .Jessica Scanlon
•• 0:30—Topless as an aparition getting Mr. Gibbs attention.
• 0:36—Brief topless during flashback to 0:30 scene.
• 0:43—Brief right breast during Ralph's past-life recollection.
Olivia (1983) . . . . .Olivia
a.k.a. A Taste of Sin
•• 0:34—Buns and topless making love in bed with Mike.
•• 0:58—Topless and buns making love with Mike in the shower.
• 1:08—Very brief full frontal nudity getting into bed with Richard. Dark, long shot.
•• 1:09—Buns, lying in bed. Dark. Full frontal nudity getting out of bed and going to the bathroom.

Lovelace, Linda

Adult Films:
Deep Throat (1972) . . . . n.a.
Nude, etc.
Films:
Linda Lovelace for President (1975) . . . . n.a.
Magazines:
Playboy (Mar 1973) . . . . Next Month
• 222—Left breast in B&W photo.
Playboy (Apr 1973) . . . . .Say "Ah!"
••• 95-101—Topless.
Playboy (Aug 1973) . . . . Porno Chic
• 132—Partial buns.
• 141—Partial lower frontal nudity.
Playboy (Dec 1973) . . . . .Sex Stars of 1973
• 200—Partial left breast.
Playboy (Nov 1974) . . . . Sex in Cinema 1974
•• 145—Topless from *Deep Throat II*.
Playboy (Dec 1974) . . . . .Sex Stars of 1974
•• 208—Full frontal nudity in sheer dress.
Playboy (Feb 1980) . . . . The Year in Sex
•• 156—Topless.
Playboy (Jan 1989). . . . . Women of the Seventies
•• 214—Topless.

• *Loving, Candy*

Video Tapes:

Playboy Video Magazine, Volume 2 (1983)
. . . . Playmate
••• 0:14—Full frontal nudity posing for her centerfold photograph.

Playboy Video Centerfold: Kimberley Conrad (1989) . . . . Playboy Update
••• 0:42—Nude in old still photos.

Magazines:

Playboy (Jan 1979) . . . . Playmate
Playboy (Apr 1980) . . . . . . Playboy's Playmate Reunion
•• 130—Left breast and lower frontal nudity.
Playboy's Nudes (Oct 1990) . . . . Herself
••• 30—Full frontal nudity.

Lowell, Carey

Films:

Club Paradise (1986) . . . . Fashion Model
Dangerously Close (1986) . . . . Julie
Down Twisted (1987) . . . . Maxine
Me & Him (1988; West German) . . . . . . Janet Anderson
• 0:37—Very brief upper half of right breast sticking out of nightgown after turning over in bed with Griffin Dunne.
License to Kill (1989) . . . . Pam Bouvier
The Guardian (1990) . . . . Kate
•• 0:37—Right breast twice, in bed with Phil.
Road to Ruin (1992) . . . . Jessie Taylor
• 0:25—Lower half of buns, while sitting in bed with Peter Weller.
0:26—Very, very brief buns, when Weller pulls her onto the bed.

Lowry, Lynn

Films:

Sugar Cookies (1973) . . . . .Alta/Julie
••• 0:03—Brief topless falling out of hammock, then topless on couch with Max, then nude. Long scene. (Brunette wig as Alta.)
0:13—Brief right breast in B & W photo.
• 0:14—Left breast on autopsy table.
•• 0:20—Topless in movie.
•• 0:52—Topless taking off clothes for Mary Woronov. Topless on bed. (Blonde as Julie.)
••• 1:00—Topless and buns with Woronov in bedroom, nude while wrestling with her.
• 1:04—Topless with Woronov in bathtub.
••• 1:06—Nude in bed with Woronov. Long scene.
•• 1:11—Right breast outside displaying herself to Max.
• 1:16—Right breast, then topless making love with Woronov.
••• 1:20—Nude with Woronov and Max. Long scene.
They Came From Within (1975; Canadian) . . . . Forsythe
Fighting Mad (1976) . . . . Lorene
Cat People (1982) . . . . .Ruthie

• *Lund, Deanna*

Films:

Dr. Goldfoot and the Bikini Machine (1965) . . . . . Robot
Johnny Tiger (1966) . . . . Louise
Sting of Death (1966) . . . . Jessica
Tony Rome (1967) . . . . Georgia McKay
Hardly Working (1981) . . . . Millie
Stick (1985) . . . . .Diane
Elves (1989) . . . . Kirsten's Mother
1:05—Buns and side of right breast getting into bathtub. Body double is Janet Fikany.
1:07—Topless, getting electrocuted in bathtub. (Body double again.)
Transylvania Twist (1990) . . . . Teacher
Roots of Evil (1991) . . . . Marissa
(Unrated version reviewed.)
• 0:19—Most of left breast, then brief right breast, while making love in bed with Johnny.
•• 0:20—More right breast, while making love.
•• 0:21—Still more right breast.
••• 1:33—Right breast, then topless while lying in bed with Brinke Stevens.

TV:

Land of the Giants (1968-70) . . . . .Valerie Scott

• *Lumley, Joanna*

Films:

Games That Lovers Play (1970) . . . . Fanny
Private Screenings.
•• 0:17—Nude, getting out of bed and putting on robe.
• 0:50—Right breast, while in bed with Jonathan.
•• 1:18—Topless sitting in bed, talking on the phone.
•• 1:29—Brief topless several times in bed with Constance and a guy. Topless after and during the end credits.
Shirley Valentine (1989; British) . . . . .Marjorie

TV:

The New Avengers (1976) . . . . .Purdy

• 0:16—In black bra in Malcolm McDowell's hotel room, then brief topless when bra pops open after crawling down the stairs.

Magazines:

Playboy (Nov 1973) . . . . Sex in Cinema 1973
• 152—Left breast in photo from *Sugar Cookies.*

Lunghi, Cherie

Films:

Excalibur (1981; British) . . . . .Guenevere
• 1:25—Brief topless in the forest kissing Lancelot.
King David (1985) . . . . .Michal
•• 0:28—Topless lying in bed with Richard Gere. (Her hair is in the way a little bit.)
Letters to an Unknown Lover (1985) . . . . .Helene
0:40—In white slip in her bedroom.
Parker (1985; British) . . . . n.a.
The Mission (1986; British) . . . . Carlotta
To Kill a Priest (1988) . . . . Halina

Miniseries:
Master of the Game (1984). . . Margaret Van der Merwe
TV:
Covington Cross (1992-) . . . . Lady Elizabeth

Lussier, Sheila
Films:
Bits and Pieces (1985) . . . . Tanya
•• 0:07—In bra, tied down by Arthur, then brief topless as he cuts her bra off before he kills her. Brief right breast several times with blood on her.
My Chauffeur (1986) . . . . Party Girl
• 1:23—Brief topless taking off her blue blouse in the back of the limousine.

• Lutra, Mara
Films:
Fantasm (1976; Australian) . . . . .n.a.
Auditions (1978) . . . . Jenny Marino
•• 0:58—Nude during her audition.
•• 1:07—Topless and buns during orgy scene.

Luu, Thuy Ann
Films:
Diva (1982; French) . . . . Alba
• 0:13—Topless in B&W photos when record store clerk asks to see her portfolio.
• 0:15—More of the B&W photos on the wall.
1:27—Very brief upper half of left breast taking off top, seen through window. Long shot.
Off Limits (1988) . . . . .Lanh
•• 0:48—Topless dancing on stage in a nightclub.

Lynch, Kelly
Films:
Portfolio (1983) . . . . Elite Model
Light of Day (1987) . . . . Elaine
Cocktail (1988) . . . . Kerry Coughlin
0:45—Buns, wearing a two piece swimsuit at the beach.
1:01—Buns, in string bikini swimsuit on boat with Tom Cruise and Bryan Brown.
Drugstore Cowboy (1989) . . . . .Dianne Hughes
0:17—In black bra and pants in living room with Matt Dillon.
Roadhouse (1989) . . . . Doc
•• 1:04—Topless and buns getting out of bed with a sheet wrapped around her.
Warm Summer Rain (1989) . . . . Kate
• 0:03—Brief topless and side view of buns in B&W lying on floor during suicide attempt. Quick cuts topless getting shocked to start her heart.
•• 0:23—Full frontal nudity when Guy gets off her in bed.
•• 0:24—Side view of right breast in bed, then topless.
••• 0:58—Buns then topless, getting washed by Guy on the table.

••• 1:07—Brief buns making love. Quick cuts full frontal nudity spinning around. Side view of left breast with Guy.
••• 1:09—Nude picking up belongings and running out of burning house with Guy.
Desperate Hours (1990) . . . . Nancy Breyers
• 0:10—Brief topless, walking on sidewalk with Mickey Rourke when her breasts pop out of her suit.
• 1:19—Brief topless, getting wired with a hidden microphone in bathroom.
Curly Sue (1991) . . . . Grey Ellison
Made for Cable TV:
The Hitchhiker: The Joker (1987; HBO)
. . . . .Theresa/Melissa
0:11—Very, very brief left breast, while in storage room with Alan getting tied up by Timothy Bottoms.
Magazines:
Playboy (Nov 1989) . . . . Sex in Cinema 1989
• 137—Upper half of left breast from *Roadhouse*.

Lynley, Carol
Films:
The Light in the Forest (1958) . . . . Shenandoe Hastings
The Poseidon Adventure (1972) . . . . Nonny Parry
Son of Blob (1972) . . . . n.a.
The Four Deuces (1975) . . . . .Wendy
Flood! (1976) . . . . n.a.
The Cat and The Canary (1978; British) . . Anabelle West
Vigilante (1983) . . . . D.A. Fletcher
Dark Tower (1987) . . . . Tilly
Blackout (1989) . . . . .Esther Boyle
•• 1:01—Brief topless leaning against the wall while someone touches her left breast.
Howling VI—The Freaks (1990) . . . . Miss Eddington
Spirits (1991) . . . . Sister Jillian
TV:
The Immortal (1970-71) . . . . .Sylvia

Lynn, Amber
Adult film actress.
Films:
52 Pick-Up (1986) . . . . Party Goer
• 0:23—Topless opening her blouse while being video taped at party.
• 0:24—Topless and buns on TV. B&W.
• 0:26—Left breast, then topless being video taped with another woman.

Lynn, Rebecca
a.k.a. Adult film actress Cameron or Krista Lane.
Films:
Free Ride (1986) . . . . Nude Girl #2
• 0:25—Brief buns taking a shower with another girl.
Sensations (1988) . . . . Jenny Hunter
• 0:11—Topless, sleeping on couch.
•• 0:23—Topless talking on the telephone.
•• 1:09—Topless making love in bed with Brian.
Thrilled to Death (1988) . . . . Elaine Jackson
• 0:01—Topless twice when Baxter opens her blouse.

•• 0:31—Topless in locker room talking to Nan.
Video Tapes:
High Society Centerspread Video #1: Krista Lane
. . . . Krista Lane
In Search of the Perfect 10 (1986)
. . . . Perfect Girl #7/Ellen
••• 0:37—Topless (she's the redhead) playing Twister
with Iris Condon. Buns in G-string.

• Lyon, Lisa
Bodybuilder.
Films:
Vamp (1986). . . . . Cimmaron
Magazines:
Playboy (Oct 1980). . . . . Body Beautiful
••• 103-107—Topless and buns.

• Lyon, Wendy
Films:
Hello Mary Lou: Prom Night II (1987)
. . . . Vicki Carpenter
0:58—Very, very brief left breast, while turning
around after getting sucked into the blackboard.
••• 1:04—Nude in shower with Monica. Nude a lot
walking around shower room.
••• 1:06—Full frontal nudity, walking in locker room,
stalking Monica.
Made for TV Movies:
Anne of Green Gables (1985; Canadian)
. . . . Prissy Andrews

Lyons, Susan
Films:
The Good Wife (1987; Australian) . . . . . .Mrs. Fielding
a.k.a. The Umbrella Woman
• 1:22—Very brief topless coming in from the balcony.
...Almost (1990; Australian) . . . . Caroline

MacDonald, Wendy
Films:
Dark Side of the Moon (1989) . . . . Alex
• 0:54—In bra, then brief topless having it torn off.
Don't see her face.
Living to Die (1990) . . . . .Rookie Policewoman
Naked Obsession (1990) . . . . Saundra Carlyle
••• 0:28—In black bra, panties and stockings on the din-
ing table during William Katt's fantasy, then topless.
Sinners! (1990) . . . . Fran
Blood Money (1991). . . . . Susan
a.k.a. The Killers Edge
Legal Tender (1991). . . . . Verna Wheeler
0:22—Brief buns in lingerie in Morton Downey Jr.'s
office. Don't see her face.
•• 1:20—Long shot of buns and side of left breast taking off robe in front of Downey. Topless on bed with
him.
Magazines:
Playboy (Oct 1990). . . . . .Grapevine
• 183—Buns in stocking/garter belt. B&W.

MacGraw, Ali
Ex-wife of the late actor Steve McQueen.
Films:
Goodbye, Columbus (1969) . . . . .Brenda
• 0:50—Very brief side view of left breast, taking off
dress before running and jumping into a swimming
pool. Brief right breast jumping into pool.
• 1:11—Very brief side view of right breast in bed with
Richard Benjamin. Brief buns, getting out of bed and
walking to the bathroom.
Love Story (1970) . . . . Jenny Cavilleri
The Getaway (1972) . . . . Carol McCoy
0:16—In wet white blouse after jumping in pond
with Steve McQueen.
• 0:19—Very brief left breast lying back in bed kissing
McQueen.
Convoy (1978). . . . . Melissa
Players (1979) . . . . Nicole
Just Tell Me What You Want (1980). . .Bones Burton
•• 0:16—Topless getting dressed in her bedroom.
•• 1:26—Brief topless in bathroom getting ready to
take a shower.
Made for TV Movies:
Survive the Savage Sea (1992) . . . . Claire Carpenter
TV:
Dynasty (1985) . . . . Lady Ashley Mitchell
Magazines:
Playboy (May 1980). . . . . Grapevine

• Machart, Maria
Films:
Blood Sisters (1986) .Marnie
•• 0:45—In bra, then brief topless putting on night-
gown and caressing herself.
Slammer Girls (1987) . . . . Hooker
•• 0:06—Topless, getting fondled by a cop.

• Mack, Kerry
Films:
Fair Game (1982; Australian) . . . . .Joanne
Savage Attraction (1983; Australian)
. . . . Christine Maresch
••• 0:10—Topless, getting out of shower and putting on
robe.
• 0:11—Topless behind shower door, making love
with Walter.
•• 0:17—Topless sitting at the end of the bed.
•• 0:59—Topless undressing in bedroom, then in bathtub with Walter.
••• 1:04—Topless getting her blouse unbuttoned, then
topless in bed with Walter.
1:19—On boat, in semi-sheer white blouse.

MacKenzie, Jan
Films:
Gator Bait II—Cajun Justice (1988) . . . . . Angelique
0:13—Most of right breast while kissing her husband.
0:29—Most of right breast while in bed.

•• 0:34—Buns and side view of left breast, taking a bath outside. Brief topless a couple of times while the bad guys watch.
• 0:41—Brief side view of left breast taking off towel in front of the bad guys.
1:05—Brief buns occasionally when her blouse flaps up during boat chase.

The American Angels, Baptism of Blood (1989) . . . . Luscious Lisa
0:07—Buns in G-string on stage in club. More buns getting lathered up for wrestling match.
• 0:11—Topless and buns when a customer takes her top off. She's covered with shaving cream.
•• 0:12—Topless taking a shower when Diamond Dave looks in to talk to her.
• 0:56—Right breast, while in wrestling ring with Dave.
Magazines:
Playboy (Dec 1989) . . . . Lethal Women
• 151—Buns and not quite side view of right breast.

Mackenzie, Patch

Films:
Goodbye, Norma Jean (1975) . . . . Ruth Latimer
Serial (1980) . . . . Stella
• 0:59—Brief topless in mirror in swinger's club with Martin Mull.
Graduation Day (1981) . . . . Anne Ramstead
Fighting Back (1982) . . . . Lilly Morelli
It's Alive III: Island of the Alive (1988) . . . . Robbins

MacLaine, Shirley

Films:
The Trouble with Harry (1955) . . . . Jennifer Rogers
Around the World in 80 Days (1956) . . . . Princess Houda
Hot Spell (1958) . . . . Virginia Duval
Some Came Running (1958) . . . . Ginny Moorhead
The Apartment (1960) . . . . Fran Kubelik
Can-Can (1960) . . . . Simone Pistache
All In a Night's Work (1961) . . . . Katie Robbins
Irma La Douce (1963) . . . . Irma La Douce
Gambit (1966) . . . . Nicole
Woman Times Seven (1967) . . . . Paulette
Sweet Charity (1969) . . . . Charity Hope Valentine
Two Mules for Sister Sara (1970) . . . . Sara
Desperate Characters (1971) . . . . Sophie
(Not available on video tape.)
Topless in bed with Kenneth Mars.
The Turning Point (1977) . . . . DeeDee
Being There (1979) . . . . Eve Rand
A Change of Seasons (1980) . . . . Karen Evans
Loving Couples (1980) . . . . Evelyn
Terms of Endearment (1983) . . . . . Aurora Greenway
(Academy Award for Best Actress.)
1:00—Very, very brief right breast wrestling with Jack Nicholson in the ocean when she finally frees his hand from her breast. One frame. Hard to see, but for the sake of thoroughness. . . .
Cannonball Run II (1984) . . . . Veronica

Madame Sousatzka (1988) . . . . Madame Sousatzka
Steel Magnolias (1989) . . . . Ouiser Boudreaux
Postcards from the Edge (1990) . . . . Doris Mann
Defending Your Life (1991) . . . . Shirley MacLaine
Waiting for the Light (1991) . . . . n.a.
Video Tapes:
Shirley MacLaine's Inner Workout (1989) . . . . Herself
Magazines:
Playboy (Nov 1972) . . . . Sex in Cinema 1972
• 159—Topless lying in bed with Kenneth Mars. Small photo, hard to tell it's her.

MacLaren, Fawna

Films:
Dragonfight (1990) . . . . Dark Servant
Video Tapes:
Playboy Video Centerfold: Fawna MacLaren
(1988) . . . . 35th Anniversary Playmate
••• 0:11—In front of brick wall. In studio, in bed. Nude.
Playboy Video Calendar 1990 (1989) . . . . . . January
••• 0:01—Nude.
Playmates at Play (1990) . . . . Gotta Dance
Sexy Lingerie II (1990) . . . . Model
Magazines:
Playboy (Jan 1989) . . . . Playmate
Playboy's Nudes (Oct 1990) . . . . Herself
••• 31—Full frontal nudity.
Playboy's Book of Lingerie (Jan 1991) . . . . . . Herself
• 71—Lower frontal nudity.
••• 108—Full frontal nudity.
Playboy's Book of Lingerie (May 1992) . . . . . Herself
•• 48—Half of right breast and lower frontal nudity.

Macpherson, Elle

Sports Illustrated magazine swimsuit model. Cover girl in 1986, 1987 and 1988.
Spokesmodel for *Biotherm* cosmetics.
Films:
Alice (1990) . . . . Model
Video Tapes:
Sports Illustrated's 25th Anniversary Swimsuit Video (1989) . . . . Herself
(The version shown on HBO left out two music video segments at the end. If you like buns, definitely watch the video tape!)
0:22—In wet yellow tank top and orange bikini bottoms at the beach.
• 0:23—Very, very brief lower topless readjusting the yellow tank top.
Sports Illustrated Super Shape-Up Program: Stretch and Strengthen (1990) . . . . Herself
Magazines:
GQ (Jan 1991) . . . . A Man and an Elle of a Woman
• 118-127—Wearing a blue fishnet top, a wet white swimsuit and just a swimsuit bottom (hair gets in the way a bit).
Playboy (Dec 1991) . . . . Sex Stars 1991
• 185—Almost topless. Arm and hands cover most of her breasts.

Madigan, Amy

Wife of actor Ed Harris.
Films:

Love Child (1982) . . . . Terry Jean Moore
- 0:08—Brief side view of right breast and buns taking a shower in jail while the guards watch.
- • 0:53—Brief topless and buns, making love with Beau Bridges in a room at the women's prison.

Love Letters (1984) . . . . Wendy
Places in the Heart (1984) . . . . Viola Kelsey
Streets of Fire (1984) . . . . McCoy
Alamo Bay (1985). . . . . Glory
- •• 0:28—Topless lying in motel bed with Ed Harris.
- •• 0:30—Topless sitting up in the bed.
- 0:40—Walking in parking lot in a wet T-shirt.

Twice in a Lifetime (1985) . . . . Sunny Sobel
Nowhere to Hide (1987) . . . . Barbara Cutter
- • 1:04—Brief side view of right breast taking off towel to get dressed in cabin. Long shot, hard to see.

The Prince of Pennsylvania (1988)

. . . . Carla Headlee
- • 0:37—Left breast and buns, while getting out of bed with Keanu Reeves and putting on a robe.

Field of Dreams (1989) . . . . Annie
Uncle Buck (1989). . . . . Chanice Kobolowski
Miniseries:

The Day After (1983) . . . . Alison
Made for TV Movies:

Roe vs. Wade (1989) . . . . Sarah Weddington
Lucky Day (1991) . . . . Kari Campbell

Madison

see: Stone, Madison.

Madonna

Full name is Madonna Louise Cicconi.
Singer.
Ex-wife of actor Sean Penn.
Nude in her book, *Sex* (1992).
Films:

A Certain Sacrifice (1981). . . . . Bruna
(Very grainy film, done before she got famous.)
- ••• 0:22—Topless during weird rape/love scene with one guy and two girls.
- • 0:40—Brief right breast in open top lying on floor after getting attacked by guy in back of restaurant.
- • 0:57—Brief topless during love making scene, then getting smeared with blood.

Desperately Seeking Susan (1985). . . . . Susan
- 0:09—Briefly in black bra taking off her blouse in bus station restroom.
- 1:16—In black bra getting out of pool and lying down on lounge chair.

Visionquest (1985) . . . . Nightclub Singer
Shanghai Surprise (1986) . . . . Gloria Tatlock
Who's That Girl? (1987) . . . . Nikki Finn
Bloodhounds of Broadway (1989)

. . . . Hortense Hathaway

Dick Tracy (1990). . . . . Breathless Mahoney
- 0:20—Topless under sheer black gown, talking to Warren Beatty.

Truth or Dare (1991) . . . . Herself
- ••• 0:44—Brief topless changing clothes backstage. B&W.
- 1:16—Wearing a bra, in a store, trying on earrings. B&W.
- 1:35—Very brief half of left breast, while wearing robe and jumping up. B&W.
- 1:43—Sort of topless in bed with her dancers. Her hands cover her breasts. B&W.

Body of Evidence (1992) . . . . n.a.
A Leauge of Their Own (1992). . . . . n.a.
Shadows and Fog (1992) . . . . n.a.
Video Tapes:

Penthouse: On the Wild Side (1988) . . . . . Madonna
- ••• 0:14—Full frontal nudity in B&W and color still photographs.

Madonna: The Immaculate Collection (1990)

. . . . Herself
- • 0:18—(2 min., 10 sec. into "Papa Don't Preach.") Very, very brief left breast in black strapless outfit when she throws her head back. (After the daughter character she plays walks up the subway stairs.)
- 0:18—(1 min., 36 sec. into "Papa Don't Preach.") Very, very brief upper half of right breast after first head throwback in black strapless outfit. Long shot.
- 0:50—(1 min., 6 sec. into "Vogue.") Wearing sheer black blouse. (Also at 1:18 and 1:33).

Magazines:

Penthouse (Sep 1985) . . . . Pictorial
- • 150-161—B&W photos, need to shave her armpits!
Playboy (Sep 1985) . . . . Pictorial
- • 119-131—B&W photos, need to shave her armpits!
Playboy (Dec 1986) . . . . Sex Stars of 86
Playboy (Jan 1989) . . . . Women of the Eighties
- •• 247—Topless B&W photo.
Vanity Fair (Apr 1990) . . . . White Heat
- •• 144—Left breast in B&W photo taken by Helmut Newton. She's standing on a table, opening her vest.
Playboy's Nudes (Oct 1990) . . . . Herself
- ••• 39—Full frontal nudity B&W.
Playboy (Dec 1990) . . . . Sex Stars of 1990
- •• 171—In sheer top from "Vogue" music video.
Vanity Fair (Apr 1991) . . . . The Misfit
- •• 167—Topless under sheer sheet. Other Marilyn Monroe-like photographs.
Penthouse (Sep 1991)

. . . . Truth or Bare, Madonna: The Lost Nudes
- ••• 179-183—B&W photos taken by Jere Threndgill in spring of 1979.
Playboy (Jul 1992) . . . . Blond Exhibition
- ••• 82-85—Full frontal nudity at the beach for her book.
Vanity Fair (Oct 1992) . . . . n.a.

Madsen, Virginia

Sister of actor Michael Madsen.

Films:

Class (1983). . . . . Lisa
  •• 0:20—Brief left breast when Andrew McCarthy acci-
     dentally rips her blouse open at the girl's school.
Dune (1984). .Princess Irulan
Electric Dreams (1984) . . . . Madeline
Creator (1985) . . . . .Barbara
    0:53—Walking on beach in a blue one piece swim-
    suit with Vincent Spano.
  ••• 0:58—Nude in shower with Spano.
Modern Girls (1987) . . . . Kelly
Slam Dance (1987) . . . . Yolanda Caldwell
Zombie High (1987) . . . . Andrea
Hot to Trot (1988). . . . . .Allison Rowe
Heart of Dixie (1989) . . . . .Delia
The Hot Spot (1990) . . . . Dolly Harshaw
  • 0:41—Side view of left breast while sitting on bed
    talking to Don Johnson.
  • 0:47—Tip of right breast when Johnson kisses it.
  •• 1:16—Buns, undressing for a swim-outside at night.
    Topless hanging on rope.
  • 1:18—Buns, getting out of water with Johnson.
    Long shot.
  • 1:21—Left breast when robe gapes open while sit-
    ting up.
    1:23—Brief lower frontal nudity and buns in open
    robe after jumping off tower at night.
    1:24—Topless at bottom of hill with Johnson. Long
    shot.
    1:45—Nude, very, very briefly running out of house.
    Very blurry, could be anybody.
Highlander 2: The Quickening (1991). . . .Louise Marcus
Love Kills (1991) . . . . .Rebecca Bishop
Candyman (1992). . . . . .Helen Lyle
Made for Cable Movies:
Mussolini and I (1985; HBO). . . . . .Claretta Petacci
Fire With Fire (1986; Showtime) . . . . .Lisa
Long Gone (1987; HBO) . . . . Dixie Lee Boxx
    0:05—Buns, sleeping on bed face down in bedroom
    with William L. Petersen and a young kid.
Gotham (1988; Showtime) . . . . .Rachel Carlyle
a.k.a. The Dead Can't Lie
  • 0:50—Brief topless in the shower when Tommy Lee
    Jones comes over to her apartment, then topless ly-
    ing on the floor.
  •• 1:12—Topless, dead, in the freezer when Jones
    comes back to her apartment, then brief topless on
    the bed.
  • 1:18—Topless in the bathtub under water.
Third Degree Burn (1989; HBO) . . . . Anne Scholes
Ironclads (1991) . . . . Betty Stuart
Made for Cable TV:
The Hitchhiker: Perfect Order (1987; HBO)
. . . . .Christina
    0:11—In black lingerie being photographed by the
    photographer in his studio.

  •• 0:14—Brief topless changing clothes while Simon
    watches her on video monitor.
    0:16—Topless getting into water in Simon's studio.
    Her body is covered with white makeup.
Made for TV Movies:
A Murderous Affair: The Carolyn Warmus Story (1992)
. . . . Carolyn Warmus

Magnuson, Ann

Films:

Vortex (1982). . . . . .Pamela Fleming
The Hunger (1983) . . . . . . .Young Woman from Disco
  • 0:05—Brief topless in kitchen with David Bowie just
    before he kills her.
Perfect Strangers (1984). . . . . Maida
Desperately Seeking Susan (1985) . . . . . .Cigarette Girl
Making Mr. Right (1987) . . . . .Frankie Stone
Mondo New York (1987) . . . . Poetry Reader
A Night in the Life of Jimmy Reardon (1987)
. . . . Joyce Fickett
    1:01—Right leg in stocking and garter belt kissing
    River Phoenix in the library of her house.
Tequila Sunrise (1988) . . . . Shaleen
Checking Out (1989) . . . . Connie Hagen
Heavy Petting (1989) . . . Herself/Television Spokesmodel
Love at Large (1990) . . . . Doris
TV:
Anything but Love (1989-92) . . . . . . Catherine Hughes
Magazines:
Playboy (Apr 1992) . . . . Grapevine
  • 174—Topless under fishnet blouse with ribbons tied
    near the nipple area. B&W.

Mahalia

See: Maria, Mahalia.

• Maillé, Maïté

Films:

A Nos Amours (1984; French) . . . . Martine
The Passion of Beatrice (1988; French)
. . . . .La Noiraude
  • 1:24—Brief left breast, showing Béatrice how she
    was abused.
Henry & June (1990) . . . . Frail Prostitute
  • 1:22—In black see-through dress.
  ••• 1:23—Topless making love with Brigitte Lahaie in
    front of Anais and Hugo.

Malin, Kym

Films:

Joysticks (1983) . . . . .Lola
  • 0:03—Topless with Alva showing a nerd their breasts
    by pulling their blouses open.
  ••• 0:18—Topless during strip-video game with Jeffer-
    son, then in bed with him.
  • 0:57—Topless during fantasy sequence, lit with red
    lights, hard to see anything.
  • 1:02—Brief topless in slide show in courtroom.
Mike's Murder (1984) . . . . .Beautiful Girl #1

Weird Science (1985) . . . . Girl Playing Piano
- 0:55—Brief topless several times as her clothes get torn off by the strong wind and she gets sucked up and out of the chimney.

Die Hard (1988) . . . . Hostage
Picasso Trigger (1989) . . . . Kym
- •• 1:04—Topless taking a shower.

Roadhouse (1989) . . . . Party Girl
Guns (1990) . . . . Kym
- 0:27—Oil wrestling with Hugs.
- ••• 0:28—Showering (in back) while talking to Hugs (in front).

Video Tapes:
Playboy's Playmate Review (1982) . . . . . . Playmate
- ••• 0:37—Nude in bar, then on empty stage.

Playboy Video Magazine, Volume 2 (1983)
. . . . Herself/Playboy Playoffs

Magazines:
Playboy (May 1982) . . . . Playmate
Playboy (Nov 1983) . . . . Sex in Cinema 1983
- 147—Right breast in photo from *Joysticks.*

Mandel, Suzy

Adult Films:
Blonde Ambition (1980; British) . . . . Sugar Kane
Nude in hard core sex scenes.
Films:
Confessions of a Driving Instructor (1976; British) . . .n.a.
Playbirds (1978; British) . . . . Lena
- •• 0:12—Nude stripping in Playbird office.

Mani, Karen

Films:
Alley Cat (1982) . . . . Billie
- 0:01—Brief topless in panties taking night gown off during opening credits.
- 0:17—In two piece swimsuit sitting by the pool.
- ••• 0:38—Brief side view of right breast and buns getting into the shower. Full frontal nudity in the shower.
- ••• 0:48—Topless in women's prison shower room scene. Long scene.

Avenging Angel (1985) . . . . Janie Soon Lee
- ••• 0:06—Nude taking a shower, right breast in mirror drying herself off, then in bra getting dressed.

Manion, Cindy

Films:
Blow Out (1981) . . . . Dancing Coed
Preppies (1984) . . . . Jo
- 0:11—Brief topless changing into waitress costumes with her two friends.
- 0:44—Topless during party with the three preppie guys.

The Toxic Avenger (1985) . . . . Julie
- 0:14—In two piece swimsuit in locker room with Melvin.
- ••• 0:15—Topless, after untying her swimsuit top in front of Melvin.

Mansfield, Jayne

Films:
Pete Kelly's Blues (1955) . . . . Cigarette Girl
Underwater! (1955) . . . . n.a.
The Girl Can't Help It (1957) . . . . Jerri Jordan
Promises, Promises (1963) . . . . Sandy Brooks
- 0:02—Bubble bath scene.
- ••• 0:04—Topless drying herself off with a towel. Same shot also at 0:48.
- ••• 0:06—Topless in bed. Same shot also at 0:08, 0:39 and 0:40.
- ••• 0:59—Buns, kneeling next to bathtub, right breast in bathtub, then topless drying herself off.

A Guide for the Married Man (1967)
. . . . Technical Advisor
The Wild, Wild World of Jayne Mansfield (1968)
. . . . Herself
Topless.
TV:
Down You Go (1956) . . . . Regular Panelist
Video Tapes:
Hollywood Scandals and Tragedies (1988)
. . . . Herself
- 1:11—Topless in color still photographs from *Playboy* pictorial.

Playboy Video Centerfold: Dutch Twins (1989)
. . . . Herself
- ••• 0:39—Topless in color and B&W shots from *Promises, Promises.*

Magazines:
Playboy (Feb 1955) . . . . Playmate
Playboy (Jan 1974) . . . . Twenty Years of Playmates
- 103—Buns, while lying on cushion.

Playboy (Jan 1979) . . . . 25 Beautiful Years
- •• 154—Topless lying on a pink bed.

Playboy's Nudes (Oct 1990) . . . . Herself

Marceau, Sophie

Films:
La Boum (1980; French) Vic
L'Amour Braque (1985; French) . . . . n.a.
Police (1985; French) . . . . Noria
- 0:10—Brief left breast in window during police strip search.
- 1:36—Right and left breasts several times, while in bed with Gérard Depardieu

Magazines:
Playboy (Nov 1985) . . . . Sex in Cinema 1985
- •• 132-133—Topless, lying in bed in still from *L'Amour Braque.*

Margolin, Janet

Films:
David and Lisa (1962) . . . . Lisa
Bus Riley's Back in Town (1965) . . . . Judy
Take the Money and Run (1969) . . . . Louise
The Last Embrace (1979) . . . . Ellie "Eva" Fabian
- 1:10—Brief topless in bathtub with Bernie, before strangling him.

  •• 1:14—Right breast, while reaching for the phone in bed with Roy Scheider.
  • 1:20—Left breast in photo that Scheider is looking at with a magnifying glass (it's supposed to be her grandmother).
  1:22—Almost topless in the shower talking to Scheider.
Distant Thunder (1988). . . . . .Barbara Lambert
Ghostbusters II (1989). . . . . The Prosecutor
TV:
Lanigan's Rabbi (1977) . . . . Miriam Small

Margot, Sandra

a.k.a. Adult film actress Tiffany Million.
Gorgeous Ladies of Wrestling (GLOW) wrestler from 1987-90.
Films:
Caged Fury (1989) . . . . .Crazy Daisy
  1:13—Buns in G-string and bra dancing for some men.
  •• 1:15—Topless taking off bra.
Demon Wind (1990) . . . . .Beautiful Demon
  •• 0:50—Topless trying to tempt Stacy and Chuck out of the cabin.
The Sleeping Car (1990) . . . . 19-Year Old Girl
  •• 0:00—Brief topless shots taking off clothes then making love with a guy. Left breast while making love.
Prime Target (1991) . . . . .Girl in Shower
  ••• 0:52—Side view of left breast and buns, taking a shower.
  • 0:53—Buns, in hotel room after getting out of the shower.
Spirits (1991) . . . . Nun Demon
Made for Cable TV:
Tales From the Crypt: Dead Right (1990; HBO)
. . . . Stripper #2
(Available on *Tales From the Crypt, Volume 3.*)
  0:07—Dancing on stage wearing pasties. Long shot.
  • 0:13—Dancing on stage wearing pasties.

•Maria, Mahalia

Video Tapes:
Penthouse Satin & Lace: An Erotic History of Lingerie (1992) . . . . .Model
Magazines:
Penthouse (Jan 1991) . . . . Pet
  ••• 87-117—Nude.
Penthouse (Jun 1992) . . . . .Pet of the Year Playoff
  ••• 86-87—Nude.

Marie, Jeanne

Films:
If Looks Could Kill (1987) . . . . Jeannie Burns
  •• 0:06—Topless taking off her robe and kissing George.
Prime Evil (1987) . . . . Judy
  1:13—Topless removing her gown (she's on the right) with Cathy and Brett.

Student Affairs (1987) . . . . Robin Ready
  • 0:35—Brief topless wearing black panties in bed trying to seduce a guy.
  ••• 0:41—Topless making love with another guy, while banging her back against the wall.
  • 0:44—Very brief topless in VW with a nerd.
  • 1:09—Very brief topless falling out of a trailer home filled with water.
Wildest Dreams (1987). . . . . Isabelle
  •• 0:35—Topless in panties in bedroom with Bobby.
Wimps (1987) . . . . Janice
  •• 0:20—Topless in bed taking off top with Charles.
Young Nurses in Love (1987). . . . . . Nurse Ellis Smith
  • 0:31—Brief side view of left breast in mirror with Dr. Riley.
  •• 1:09—Topless in panties, getting into bed with Dr. Riley.

Marino, Bonnie

Video Tapes:
Playboy Video Calendar 1991 (1990). . . . . . . .June
  ••• 0:22—Nude.
Magazines:
Playboy (Jun 1990). . . . . Playmate
Playboy's Book of Lingerie (Mar 1992). . . . . .Herself
  ••• 74-75—Full frontal nudity.
Playboy's Book of Lingerie (Jul 1992) . . . . . . .Herself
  ••• 49—Full frontal nudity.
Playboy's Book of Lingerie (Sep 1992) . . . . . .Herself
  ••• 54-55—Full frontal nudity.

Markov, Margaret

Films:
Pretty Maids All in a Row (1971) . . . . Polly
The Hot Box (1972). . . . . .Lynn Forrest
  • 0:12—Topless when bad guy cuts her swimsuit top open.
  •• 0:16—Topless in stream consoling Bunny.
  • 0:21—Topless in the furthest hammock from camera. Long shot.
  ••• 0:45—Topless bathing in stream with the other girls.
Black Mama, White Mama (1973; U.S./Philippines)
. . . . Karen Brent
Naked Warriors (1973). . . . . Bodicia
a.k.a. The Arena
  • 0:07—Brief topless getting clothes torn off by guards.
  • 0:13—Topless getting her dress ripped off, then raped during party.
  • 0:19—Brief left breast, on floor making love, then right breast and buns.
  0:45—In sheer white dress consoling Septimus, then walking around.
  • 0:52—Brief topless sitting down, listening to Cornelia.
Magazines:
Playboy (Apr 1971) . . . . Vadim's "Pretty Maids"
  ••• 161—Right side view nude.

• Maroney, Kelli

Films:
Fast Times at Ridgemont High (1982) . . . . Cindy
Night of the Comet (1984) . . . . Samantha
The Zero Boys (1985) . . . . Jamie
Chopping Mall (1986) . . . . Alison
Big Bad Mama II (1987) . . . . Willie McClatchie
Not of This Earth (1988) . . . . .Nurse Mary Oxford
Transylvania Twist (1990) . . . . .Script Supervisor
Miniseries:
Celebrity (1984) . . . . .n.a.
TV:
Ryan's Hope (1983) . . . . .n.a.
Video Tapes:
Scream Queen Hot Tub Party (1991) . . . . . . Herself
  •• 0:07—Topless taking off flower print blouse and put-
    ting on pink teddy.
  • 0:12—Buns, while walking up the stairs.
  ••• 0:30—Topless and buns after stripping out of cheer-
    leader outfit, rubbing lotion on herself and demon-
    strating the proper Scream Queen way to pump
    iron.
  ••• 0:44—Topless taking off her swimsuit top and soap-
    ing up with the other girls.
  •• 0:46—Topless in still shot during the end credits.

Marsillach, Blanca

Films:
Flesh + Blood (1985) .Clara
  •• 0:11—Full frontal nudity on bed having convulsions
    after getting hit on the head with a sword.
Collector's Item (1988) . . . . .Jacqueline
a.k.a. The Trap
  •• 0:52—In white bra cleaning up Tony Musante in
    bed, then topless.
    1:04—Lower frontal nudity while watching Musante
    and Laura Antonelli making love in bed.
  • 1:18—Topless getting dressed. A little dark.
  •• 1:22—Topless changing clothes in bedroom while
    Antonelli talks to her.
Dangerous Obsession (1990; Italian). . . . . . . .Jessica
  • 0:02—Left breast, getting fondled by Johnny in re-
    cording studio. Lower frontal nudity when he pulls
    down her panties.
  •• 0:05—Topless opening her blouse while Johnny
    plays his saxophone.
  • 0:17—Lower frontal nudity on the stairs with
    Johnny, then brief topless.
  • 0:29—Brief topless in video tape on T.V.
  •• 0:40—Topless changing blouses.
  ••• 0:56—Full frontal nudity masturbating while looking
    at pictures of Johnny. Buns, then more full frontal
    nudity getting video taped.
  ••• 0:58—Topless in bed with a gun. Nude walking
    around the house. Long scene.
  • 1:05—Brief topless on beach taking off sweater and
    burying a dog.
  • 1:06—Brief full frontal nudity during video taping
    session.

  •• 1:07—Topless cleaning up Dr. Simpson.
  ••• 1:13—Topless taking chains off Dr. Simpson, then ly-
    ing in bed. Full frontal nudity making love with him.

Marsillach, Cristina

Films:
Every Time We Say Goodbye (1986). . . . . . . .Sarah
    1:00—In white slip in her bedroom.
    1:03—In white slip again.
  •• 1:09—Right breast, then brief topless lying in bed
    with Tom Hanks.
Collector's Item (1988). . . . . Young Marie
a.k.a. The Trap
  •• 0:12—Right breast in elevator with Tony Musante.
  •• 0:36—Topless in open blouse, then full frontal nudi-
    ty in hut with Musante.
Terror at the Opera (1989; Italian) . . . . Betty
  • 0:23—Brief left breast during nightmare. Brief top-
    less, sitting up in bed and screaming.

Martin, Danielle

a.k.a. Adult film actress Danielle.
Adult Films:
The Blond Next Door . . . . n.a.
Films:
My Therapist (1983) . . . . Francine
  •• 0:29—In bra, garter belt, stockings and panties,
    then topless in room with Rip.
Video Tapes:
The Girls of Penthouse (1984)
    . . . . Bad to the Bone Woman
  ••• 0:07—Nude, taking off her leather outfit.
Magazines:
Penthouse (Feb 1983) . . . . Million Dollar Baby
  ••• 107-121—Nude.

Martin, Pamela Sue

Films:
Buster and Billie (1974) . . . . n.a.
The Lady in Red (1979) . . . . Polly Franklin
  • 0:07—Right breast, while in bedroom with a guy
    clutching her clothes.
  ••• 0:20—Topless in jail with a group of women prison-
    ers waiting to be examined by a nurse.
Flicks (1981). . . . . Liz
Torchlight (1984) . . . . Lillian Gregory
Made for TV Movies:
Human Feelings (1978) . . . . n.a.
TV:
The Nancy Drew Mysteries (1977-78) . . . . Nancy Drew
The Hardy Boys Mysteries (1977-78) . . . . . Nancy Drew
Dynasty (1981-84) . . . . .Fallon Carrington Colby
Magazines:
Playboy (Jul 1978) . . . . Nancy Drew Grows Up
  •• 87-91—Sort of topless.

• *Martin, Sandy*

Films:
Scalpel (1976)............................Sandy
48 Hrs. (1982).....................Policewoman
Real Genius (1985) ....Mrs. Meredith
Extremities (1986)...............Officer Sudow
Vendetta (1986).....................Kay Butler
 • 0:34—Brief left breast, while making love with her
   boyfriend. Don't see her face.
Barfly (1987)............................Janice
Defenseless (1991) ....Judge

Mason, Marsha

Ex-wife of playwright Neil Simon.
Films:
Blume in Love (1973)....................Arlene
 • 0:22—Side view of right breast, then brief topless lying in bed with George Segal.
 • 0:35—Very brief right breast reaching over the bed.
 •• 0:54—Brief topless twice, reaching over to get a pillow while talking to Segal.
Cinderella Liberty (1973) ....Maggie Paul
   0:09—Brief panties shot leaning over pool table
   when James Caan watches.
 •• 0:17—Side view of left breast in room with Caan.
   Brief right breast sitting down on bed.
 ••• 0:38—Topless sitting up in bed, yelling at Caan.
 • 0:54—Very brief left breast turning over in bed and
   sitting up.
Audrey Rose (1977)...............Janice Templeton
The Goodbye Girl (1977) ....Paula McFadden
The Cheap Detective (1978).........Georgia Merkle
Chapter Two (1979) ....Jennie MacLaine
Promises in the Dark (1979) ......Dr. Alexandra Kenda
Only When I Laugh (1981) ....Georgia
Max Dugan Returns (1983)..................Nora
Heartbreak Ridge (1986)...................Aggie
Drop Dead Fred (1991).....................Polly
Made for Cable Movies:
Dinner At Eight (1989) ....Millicent Jordan
The Image (1990; HBO) ....Jean Cromwell
 • 0:08—Two brief side views of left breast standing in
   bathroom after Albert Finney gets out of the shower.
TV:
Sibs (1991-92) ....Nora Rucio

Massey, Anna

Films:
Peeping Tom (1960; British) ....Helen Stephens
Frenzy (1972; British)...............Babs Milligan
 •• 0:45—Topless getting out of bed and then buns,
   walking to the bathroom. Most probably a body
   double.
Sweet William (1980; British) ....Edna
Five Days One Summer (1982) ....Jennifer Pierce
Foreign Body (1986; British) ....Miss Furze
Mountains of the Moon (1989).........Mrs. Arundell
The Tall Guy (1990) ....Mary

Mastrantonio, Mary Elizabeth

Wife of film director Pat O'Connor.
Films:
Scarface (1983) ....Gina
 • 2:36—(0:39 into tape 2) Very, very brief left breast
   when she gets shot and her nightgown opens up
   when she gets hit.
The Color of Money (1986) ....Carmen
 • 0:41—Brief topless in bathroom mirror drying herself off while Paul Newman talks to Tom Cruise.
   Long shot, hard to see.
Slam Dance (1987) ....Helen Drood
The January Man (1988).........Bernadette Flynn
 • 0:40—Topless in bed with Kevin Kline. Side view of
   left breast squished against Kline.
 ••• 0:42—Topless after Kline gets out of bed. Brief shot,
   but very nice!
The Abyss (1989)................Lindsey Brigman
 • 1:41—Topless during C.P.R. scene.
Class Action (1991) ....Margaret Ward
Robin Hood: Prince of Thieves (1991) ....Marian
Consenting Adults (1992) ....Priscilla Parker
White Sands (1992) ....Lane Bodine
 • 1:11—Brief left breast in shower with Willem Dafoe.
   You see her face, so this shot is really her.
Made for Cable Movies:
Mussolini and I (1985; HBO) .... Edda Mussolini Ciano

• *Mastrogiacomo, Gina*

Films:
Alien Space Avenger (1988) ....Ginny
 ••• 0:19—Topless in bed, making love with Matt. Top-
   less and buns, getting out and getting dressed.
GoodFellas (1990) ....Janice Rossi
Jungle Fever (1991) ....Louise
The Naked Gun 2 1/2: The Smell of Fear (1991)
 ...."Is this some kind of bust?"

Mathias, Darian

Films:
My Chauffeur (1986) ....Dolly
Blue Movies (1988) ....Kathy
 • 0:37—Very brief topless twice acting for the first
   time in a porno film.
   0:39—Topless from above during screening of movie. Hard to see.

Mathis, Samantha

Daughter of actress Bibi Besch.
Films:
Pump Up the Volume (1990).........Nora Diniro
 •• 1:13—Topless taking off sweater on patio with
   Christian Slater.
This is My Life (1992)..................Erica Ingels
Made for TV Movies:
83 Hours 'til Dawn (1990) ....Julie Burdock
Extreme Close-Up (1990).....................n.a.
To My Daughter (1990)......................n.a.

TV:
Knightwatch (1988-89) . . . . Jake
Aaron's Way (1988) . . . . Roseanne Miller

Matlin, Marlee

Films:
Children of a Lesser God (1986) . . . . Sarah
(Academy Award for Best Actress.)
    0:44—Brief buns under water in swimming pool.
    Don't see her face.
    0:47—Part of left breast hugging William Hurt seen
    from under water.
Walker (1988) . . . . Ellen Martin
Made for TV Movies:
Bridge to Silence (1988) .n.a.
TV:
Reasonable Doubts (1991-) . . . . Tess Kaufman

Matthews, Lisa

Video Tapes:
Playboy Video Calendar 1991 (1990) . . . September
Sexy Lingerie II (1990) . . . . .Model
Playboy Video Calendar 1992 (1991) . . . . July
  • 0:27—Nude in fashion show fantasy.
  ••• 0:28—Nude in mansion doing various things.
Playboy Video Centerfold: Lisa Matthews (1991)
  . . . . Playmate of the Year 1991
  ••• 0:00—Nude in front of curtains, then in bed, then in
  medical segment, then at the beach and finally in a
  fantasy modeling session.
Magazines:
Playboy (Apr 1990) . . . . Playmate
Playboy (Jun 1991) . . . . Playmate of the Year
  ••• 144-155—Nude.
Playboy's Book of Lingerie (Jul 1992) . . . . . . Herself
  •• 62—Left breast and lower frontal nudity.
  ••• 107—Topless.
Playboy's Book of Lingerie (Sep 1992) . . . . . Herself
  ••• 74-75—Topless.

Mattson, Robin

Films:
Namu, The Killer Whale (1966) . . . . Lisa Rand
Bonnie's Kids (1973) . . . . .Myra
  • 0:05—Brief side view of right breast, changing in
  bedroom while two men watch from outside.
  ••• 0:07—Topless washing herself in the bathroom.
Candy Stripe Nurses (1974) . . . . Dianne
  •• 0:22—Nude in gym with the basketball player.
  ••• 0:40—Nude in bed with the basketball player.
Return to Macon County (1975) . . . . Junell
Wolf Lake (1978) . . . . Linda
a.k.a. Survive the Night at Wolf Lake
  • 0:54—Brief full frontal nudity during rape in cabin.
  Dark.
  • 0:55—Brief topless afterwards.
Take Two (1988) . . . . Susan Bentley
  0:21—Exercising in yellow outfit while Frank Stallone plays music.

  •• 0:25—Brief topless taking a shower.
  0:26—Showing Grant Goodeve her new two piece
  swimsuit.
  ••• 0:29—Topless in bed with Goodeve.
  ••• 0:45—Right breast in shower, then topless getting
  into bed.
  • 0:47—Brief topless getting out of bed and putting
  an overcoat on.
  0:51—One piece swimsuit by the swimming pool.
  1:12—In two piece swimsuit at the beach.
  ••• 1:28—Topless taking a shower after shooting Goodeve in bed.
Made for TV Movies:
Are You in the House Alone? (1978)
  . . . . Allison Bremmer
False Witness (1989) . . . . .Jody
TV:
The Guiding Light (1976-77) . . . . Hope Bauer
General Hospital (1980-83) . . . . .Heather Grant Webber
Ryan's Hope (1984) . . . . Delia Reid
Santa Barbara (1985-) . . . . Gina Capwell Timmons

Maur-Thorp, Sarah

Films:
Edge of Sanity (1988) . . . . .Susannah
  • 0:00—Left breast pulling down top to show the little
  boy in the barn.
  •• 0:09—Topless talking to the two doctors after they
  examine her back.
  •• 0:50—Topless in red room with Anthony Perkins and
  Johnny.
  • 0:56—Very brief topless in nun outfit.
  • 1:10—Brief topless in Perkins' hallucination at Flora's
  whorehouse.
Ten Little Indians (1989) . . . . .Vera Claythorne
River of Death (1990) . . . . Anna

• Maura, Carmen

Films:
Matador (1986; Spanish) . . . . .Julie
Women on the Verge of a Nervous Breakdown
  (1988; Spanish) . . . . Pepa Marcos
Ay, Carmela! (1991; Spanish) . . . . .Carmela
  •• 0:42—Showing her left breast to the Lieutenant to
  explain why she had a Republican flag. Subtitles get
  in the way.
  •• 1:38—Topless taking off flag on stage during play.
  Subtitles get in the way again.
High Heels (1991; Spanish) . . . . Tina

May, Mathilda

a.k.a. Mathilda May Haim.
Daughter of French playwright Victor Haim.
Films:
Dream One (1984; British/French) . . . . Alice
Letters to an Unknown Lover (1985) . . . . Agnes
  • 0:43—Upper half of breasts in bathtub when Gervais
  opens the door.

••• 0:58—Buns and topless taking off her robe in Gervais' room.
Lifeforce (1985) . . . . Space Girl
• 0:08—Full frontal nudity in glass case upside down.
• 0:13—Topless, lying down in space shuttle. Blue light.
••• 0:16—Topless sitting up in lab to suck the life out of military guard. Brief full frontal nudity.
• 0:17—Topless again in the lab.
• 0:19—Topless walking around, then buns.
••• 0:20—Topless walking down the stairs. Brief nude fighting with the guards.
•• 0:44—Topless with Steve Railsback in red light during his nightmare.
• 1:10—Brief topless in space shuttle with Railsback.
Naked Tango (1990) . . . . Alba/Stephanie

Mayne, Belinda
Films:
Krull (1983). . . . . Vella
Don't Open 'Till Christmas (1984; British) . . . . Kate
Lassiter (1984) . . . . Helen Boardman
••• 0:06—In bra then topless letting Tom Selleck undress her while her husband is in the other room.
Fatal Beauty (1987). . . . . Traci

Mayo-Chandler, Karen
Films:
Beverly Hills Cop (1984) . . . . Maitland Receptionist
Explorers (1986) . . . . Starkiller's Girl Friend
Hamburger—The Motion Picture (1986)
. . . . Dr. Victoria Gotbottom
• 0:03—Brief topless in her office trying to help, then seduce Russell.
Out of the Dark (1988) . . . . Barbara
• 0:16—Brief topless pulling red dress down wearing black stocking in Kevin's studio.
••• 0:17—Topless and buns posing during photo shoot.
Stripped to Kill II (1988) . . . . Cassandra
0:06—Black bra and panties in dressing room.
•• 0:18—Topless taking off her top for a customer.
Take Two (1988). . . . . Dorothy
•• 1:17—Brief topless on bed when her gold dress is pulled down a bit.
Death Feud (1989). . . . . .Anne
0:26—In lingerie with a customer.
•• 0:36—In white lingerie, then topless several times outside taking off robe.
976-EVIL II: The Astral Factor (1991) . . . . Laurie
(With blonde hair.)
•• 0:00—Topless in shower room, then putting on wet T-shirt.
0:01—Running around the school hallways wearing white panties and wet, white T-shirt.
Magazines:
Playboy (Dec 1989). . . . . The Joker Was Wild
••• 94-103—Nude.
Playboy's Nudes (Oct 1990). . . . . Herself
••• 21—Full frontal nudity.

Mayor, Cari
Films:
Spring Fever USA (1988) . . . . Girl on Campus
a.k.a. Lauderdale
Summer Job (1989). Donna
• 0:10—Brief topless twice, taking off her top before and after Herman comes into the room.

Mayron, Melanie
Films:
Harry and Tonto (1974) . . . . Ginger
(She's a lot heavier in this film than she is now.)
• 0:57—Very brief topless in motel room with Art Carney taking off her towel and putting on blouse. Long shot, hard to see.
Car Wash (1976) . . . . Marsha
Gable and Lombard (1976) . . . . Dixie
The Great Smokey Roadblock (1976) . . . . .Lulu
You Light Up My Life (1977) . . . . Annie Gerrara
Girlfriends (1978) . . . . Susan Weinblatt
(She's still a bit overweight.)
• 0:14—Buns, very brief lower frontal nudity and brief left breast getting dressed in bathroom.
Heartbeeps (1981). . . . . .Susan
Missing (1982). . . . . Terry Simon
The Boss' Wife (1986) . . . . Janet Keefer
Sticky Fingers (1988) . . . . Lolly
Checking Out (1989) . . . . Jenny Macklin
My Blue Heaven (1990) . . . . Crystal
Made for TV Movies:
Hustling (1975) . . . . Dee Dee
Playing for Time (1980) . . . . n.a.
(Lost a lot of weight.)
0:11—Brief side view of left breast getting her hair cut. She's behind Vanessa Redgrave. You can't really see anything.
TV:
thirtysomething (1987-91). . . . . Melissa Steadman

•Mays, Melinda
Video Tapes:
Playboy Video Magazine, Volume 5 (1983)
. . . . Playmate
• 0:05—Brief topless in hay.
Playboy's Playmate Review 3 (1985) . . . . . Playmate
Magazines:
Playboy (Feb 1983) . . . . Playmate

McArthur, Kimberly
Films:
Young Doctors in Love (1982). . . . . Jyll Omato
•• 0:58—Topless in front of Dabney Coleman after taking off her Santa Claus outfit in his study.
Easy Money (1983) . . . . Ginger Jones
•• 0:47—Topless sunbathing in the backyard when seen by Rodney Dangerfield.
Malibu Express (1984) . . . . .Faye
•• 0:10—Topless taking a shower on the boat with Barbara Edwards.

Slumber Party Massacre II (1987) . . . . Amy
TV:
Santa Barbara (1988-90) . . . . Kelly
Video Tapes:
Playmate Playoffs . . . . Playmate
Playboy's Playmate Review (1982) . . . . . . Playmate
••• 0:19—Nude in sauna, then taking a shower, then in
    front of fireplace.
Playboy Video Magazine, Volume 2 (1983)
    . . . . Herself/Playboy Playoffs
Playboy Video Magazine, Volume 5 (1983)
    . . . . Playmate
    • 0:06—Brief topless in front of fire.
Magazines:
Playboy (Jan 1982) . . . . Playmate
Playboy's Career Girls (Aug 1992)
    . . . . Baywatch Playmates
    ••• 10—Full frontal nudity.

McBride, Harlee

Films:
Young Lady Chatterley (1977) . . . Cynthia Chatterley
    •• 0:19—Nude masturbating in front of mirror.
    • 0:28—Brief topless with young boy.
    ••• 0:41—Nude in bathtub while maid washes her.
    ••• 0:52—Nude in back of car with the hitchhiker while
        the chauffeur is driving.
    ••• 1:03—Nude in the garden with the sprinklers on
        making love with the Gardener.
    ••• 1:31—Topless and buns in bed with the gardener.
House Calls (1978) . . . . n.a.
Young Lady Chatterley II (1986)
    . . . . Cynthia Chatterley
    •• 0:20—Topless getting a massage with Elanor.
    •• 0:22—Full frontal nudity during flashback to the first
        time she made love with Robert.
    ••• 0:28—Topless taking a bath with Jenny.
    ••• 0:35—Topless in library seducing Virgil.
    ••• 0:50—Topless in back of the car with the Count.
    ••• 0:58—Topless in the garden with Robert.
Magazines:
Playboy (Dec 1977) . . . . Sex Stars of 1977
    ••• 217—Full frontal nudity lying on bed.

• McBride, Michelle

Films:
Edgar Allan Poe's "The Masque of the Red Death"
    (1989) . . . . Rebecca
Subspecies (1990) . . . . Lillian
    • 0:34—Left breast, while sleeping in bed when the
        vampire comes to get her.
Made for Cable Movies:
Prey of the Chameleon (1992; Showtime) . . . . Leslie

McBroom, Dirga

Films:
Flashdance (1983) . . . . Heels

The Rosebud Beach Hotel (1985) . . . . Bellhop
    • 0:49—Buns, then topless, standing with the other
        bell hops, outfitted with military attire. (She's the
        one at the far end, furthest from the camera.)
Vendetta (1986) . . . . Willow

• McCartney, Kimberly

Video Tapes:
Hot Body International: #2 Miss Puerto Vallarta
    (1990) . . . . Contestant
    •• 0:48—Buns in one piece swimsuit. Practically topless
        wearing pasties.
    0:56—4th runner up.
Hot Body International: #4 Spring Break (1992)
    . . . . Contestant

McClellan, Michelle

See: Bauer, Michelle.

McClure, Tané

a.k.a. Tané.
Films:
Crawlspace (1986) . . . . Sophie Fisher
    • 0:00—Nipples, sticking out of holes that she cuts in
        her red bra. Brief topless in bed making love with
        Hank. Dark.
Commando Squad (1987) . . . . Sunny
Death Spa (1987) . . . . Vicky
    •• 1:10—Topless in sauna with Tom.
    • 1:19—Brief topless during the fire.
Video Tapes:
Inside Out 2 (1992)
    . . . . Melanie Moss/Mis-Apprehended
    (Unrated version reviewed.)
    •• 0:09—Topless, taking off her blouse outside for Tim.

• McComas, Lorissa

Films:
Can It Be Love (1992) . . . . Montana
    ••• 0:55—Topless and buns, changing into lingerie be-
        hind two way mirror while David watches.
Magazines:
Playboy's Book of Lingerie (Sep 1991) . . . . . . Herself
    ••• 3-7—Topless and buns.
Playboy's Book of Lingerie (Nov 1991) . . . . . Herself
    •• 101—Topless.
Playboy's Book of Lingerie (Jan 1992) . . . . . . Herself
    •• 49—Right breast.
    • 83—Left breast.
Playboy's Book of Lingerie (Mar 1992) . . . . . Herself
    ••• 58-59—Topless and buns.
Playboy's Book of Lingerie (May 1992) . . . . . Herself
    ••• 18—Topless.
Playboy's Book of Lingerie (Jul 1992) . . . . . . Herself
    ••• 21—Topless.
Playboy's Book of Lingerie (Sep 1992) . . . . . Herself
    • 59—Side of left breast.

• McConnell, Denise
Video Tapes:
Playboy Video Magazine, Volume 2 (1983)
. . . . Herself/Playboy Playoffs
Magazines:
Playboy (Mar 1979). . . . . Playmate

McCormick, Maureen
Films:
Take Down (1978) . . . . Brooke Cooper
Skatetown, U.S.A. (1979) . . . . Susan
The Idolmaker (1980) . . . . Ellen Fields
Texas Lightning (1980) . . . . Fay
　1:04—Very brief upper half of right breast popping
　out of slip while struggling on bed with two jerks.
　Long shot, hard to see.
Return to Horror High (1987) . . . . Officer Tyler
Made for TV Movies:
A Very Brady Christmas (1988) . . . . Marcia Brady
TV:
The Brady Bunch (1969-74) . . . . Marcia Brady

McCullough, Julie
Films:
Big Bad Mama II (1987). . . . . .Polly McClatchie
　•• 0:12—Topless with Danielle Brisebois playing in a
　pond underneath a waterfall.
　•• 0:36—In lingerie, then topless sitting on Jordan who
　is tied up in bed.
The Blob (1988) . . . . .Susie
Round Trip to Heaven (1992) . . . . .Lucille
TV:
Growing Pains (1989-90) . . . . Julie
Video Tapes:
Playboy Video Calendar 1987 (1986) . . . . Playmate
Playboy Video Calendar 1988 (1987) . . . . Playmate
Playboy Video Centerfold: Peggy McIntagart
　(1989). . . . . Playmate
　••• 0:35—Nude in still photos and videos.
Magazines:
Playboy (Feb 1986) . . . . Playmate
Playboy (Oct 1989) . . . . Julie McCullough
　••• 74-79—Nude.
Playboy (Dec 1989). . . . . .Holy Sex Stars of 1989!
　•• 181—Left breast, while sitting in a chair.
Playboy's Nudes (Oct 1990). . . . . Herself
　••• 11—Full frontal nudity.

McCurry, Natalie
Films:
Dead-End Drive-In (1986; Australian). . . . . . . Carmen
　•• 0:19—Topless in red car with Ned Manning.
Made for TV Movies:
Danger Down Under (1988) . . . . . Katherine Dillingham

McDaniel, Donna
Films:
Angel (1983) . . . . .Crystal
　• 0:19—Brief topless, dead in bed when the killer pulls
　the covers down.
Hollywood Hot Tubs (1984) . . . . Leslie Maynard

McDermott, Colleen
Films:
Paradise Motel (1985) . . . . Debbie
　•• 0:24—Topless in motel room with Mic, when Sam
　lets them use a room.
Demonwarp (1988). . . . . Cindy
　•• 0:23—Topless and buns drying herself off after tak-
　ing a shower.
　• 0:24—Very brief lower frontal nudity, under her tow-
　el, trying to run up the stairs.

McDonough, Mary
Films:
Mortuary (1981) . . . . .Christie Parson
　(All scenes with nudity are probably a body double.)
　0:45—Buns and very brief topless making love with
　her boyfriend on the floor. Long shot, hard to see.
　1:06—Full frontal nudity on table in the morgue,
　dead.
Mom (1989) . . . . Alice
TV:
The Waltons (1972-81) . . . . Erin Walton

• McEachin, Bianca
Films:
Coming to America (1988)
　. . . . . .Uncredited Miss Black Awareness
　• 0:37—Buns, wearing pink sequined, two piece
　swimsuit on stage during Black Awareness meeting.
Video Tapes:
Dream Babies (1989) . . . . .Herself
　••• 0:06—Dancing in red two-piece swimsuit, then top-
　less and buns in G-string. Nice!
　•• 0:40—Topless, introducing her segment.
　••• 0:41—More topless, dancing in red two-piece swim-
　suit.
Hot Body International: #1 Miss Cancun (1990)
　. . . . . .Contestant

McEnroe, Annie
Films:
The Hand (1981) .Stella Roche
　•• 0:51—Topless undressing for Michael Caine.
Warlords of the 21st Century (1982) . . . . .Carlie
　a.k.a. Battletruck
The Survivors (1983) . . . . Doreen
Howling II: Your Sister is a Werewolf (1984) . . . . . .Jenny
Purple Hearts (1984) . . . . Hallaway
　•• 1:23—Brief topless coming out of the bathroom sur-
　prising Ken Wahl and Cheryl Ladd.
True Stories (1986). . . . . .Kay Culver
Wall Street (1987) . . . . .Muffie Livingston

Beetlejuice (1988) . . . . Jane Butterfield
Cop (1988) . . . . Amy Cranfield
The Doors (1991) . . . . Secretary
Magazines:
Playboy (Nov 1981) . . . . Sex in Cinema 1981
•• 172—Topless.

McGavin, Graem

Films:
Angel (1983) . . . . Lana
•• 0:31—Topless standing in hotel bathroom talking to her John.
My Tutor (1983) . . . . Sylvia
••• 0:21—In white bra, then topless in back seat of a car in a parking lot with Matt Lattanzi.
Weekend Pass (1984) . . . . Tawny Ryatt

McGillis, Kelly

Films:
Reuben, Reuben (1983) . . . . Geneva Spofford
Witness (1985) . . . . Rachel
••• 1:18—Topless taking off her top to take a bath while Harrison Ford watches.
Top Gun (1986) . . . . Charlie
Made in Heaven (1987) . . . Annie Packert/Ally Chandler
Unsettled Land (1987) . . . . Anda
The Accused (1988) . . . . Kathryn Murphy
Cat Chaser (1988) . . . . Mary De Boya
••• 0:23—Topless on the floor with Peter Weller. Long scene.
••• 1:04—Full frontal nudity taking off her slip and getting raped by her husband's pistol. Kind of dark.
•• 1:06—Brief buns, getting pushed around the house. Right breast while signing a paper.
The House on Carroll Street (1988) . . . . Emily
• 0:39—Brief topless reclining into the water in the bathtub.
Winter People (1989) . . . . Collie Wright
The Babe (1992) . . . . n.a.
Made for TV Movies:
Code of Honor (1984) . . . . n.a.
Original title: *Sweet Revenge*.

McGovern, Elizabeth

Films:
Ordinary People (1980) . . . . Jeanine
Ragtime (1981) . . . . Evelyn Nesbit
••• 0:52—Topless in living room sitting on couch and arguing with a lawyer. Very long scene.
Lovesick (1983) . . . . Chloe Allen
Once Upon a Time in America (1984) . . . . . Deborah
(Long version reviewed.)
• 2:33—(0:32 into tape 2) Brief glimpses of left breast when Robert De Niro tries to rape her in the back seat of a car.
Racing with the Moon (1984) . . . . . . Caddie Winger
• 0:45—Upper half of breast in pond with Sean Penn.

The Bedroom Window (1987) . . . . Denise
1:25—Topless silhouette on shower curtain when Steve Guttenberg peeks in the bathroom.
She's Having a Baby (1988) . . . . Kristy
Johnny Handsome (1989) . . . . Donna McCarty
•• 0:47—Right breast, while in bed with Mickey Rourke.
A Handmaid's Tale (1990) . . . . Moira
A Shock to the System (1990) . . . . Stella Anderson
Tune in Tomorrow (1990) . . . . Elena Quince
a.k.a. Aunt Julia and the Scriptwriter
Made for Cable Movies:
Women & Men: Stories of Seduction (1990; HBO)
. . . . Vicki
0:18—In white lingerie in train car with Beau Bridges.
••• 0:22—Topless when Bridges takes her top off when she lies back in bed.

McGregor, Angela Punch

Films:
The Island (1980) . . . . Beth
•• 0:45—Topless taking off poncho to make love with Michael Caine in hut after rubbing stuff on him.
0:50—Braless under poncho walking towards Caine.
We of the Never Never (1983) . . . . Jeannie
A Test of Love (1984; Australian) . . . . . Jessica Hathaway

McIntaggart, Peggy

Video Tapes:
Playboy Video Centerfold: Peggy McIntagart (1989) . . . . Playmate
••• 0:00—Nude throughout.
Playboy Video Calendar 1991 (1990) . . . . . February
••• 0:05—Nude.
Playmates at Play (1990) . . . . Gotta Dance
Rock Video Girls 2 (1992) . . . . Herself
Magazines:
Playboy (Jan 1990) . . . . Playmate
Playboy's Book of Lingerie (Sep 1991) . . . . . Herself
••• 28-29—Full frontal nudity.
Playboy's Book of Lingerie (Jan 1992) . . . . . . Herself
•• 72—Right breast.
Playboy's Book of Lingerie (Mar 1992) . . . . . Herself
••• 68—Topless.
Playboy's Book of Lingerie (May 1992) . . . . . Herself
••• 14—Full frontal nudity.
Playboy's Career Girls (Aug 1992)
. . . . Baywatch Playmates
••• 6—Full frontal nudity.

McIntosh, Valerie

Films:
Gimme an "F" (1981) . . . . One of the "Vikings"
Weekend Pass (1984) . . . . Etta
The Naked Cage (1985) . . . . Ruby
••• 0:24—Topless and buns in infirmary, then getting attacked by Smiley. Brief lower frontal nudity.
• 0:28—Topless, hanging by rope dead.

Quicksilver (1986). . . . . Hooker
The Mambo Kings (1992) . . . . .Tracy Blair
  •• 1:10—Topless, getting her bathing suit after Armand Assante discovers her with Antonio Banderas.

McIssac, Marianne

Films:
In Praise of Older Women (1978; Canadian)
. . . . Julika
  •• 0:23—Topless and buns, getting into bed with Tom Berenger.
TV:
The Baxters (1980-81). . . . . Allison Baxter

• McIver, Susan

Films:
I Spit on Your Corpse (1974) . . . . Donna
  ••• 0:24—Topless undressing for a guy. More topless and buns making love in bed with him, then getting out of bed.
Shampoo (1975). . . . . Customer
Smokey and the Bandit (1977) . . . . Hot Pants
Thunder Alley (1985) . . . . .Redhead

• McKamy, Kim

Films:
Evil Laugh (1986) . . . . Connie
Creepozoids (1987). . . . . Kate
Dreamaniac (1987). . . . . Pat
Angel III: The Final Chapter (1988) . . . . . . Video Girl #1
Fatal Instinct (1991) . . . . . . Frank Stegner's Girlfriend
(Unrated version reviewed.)
  •• 0:01—Topless, opening her towel in front of Frank at night before he gets shot.

• McKee, Lonette

Films:
Sparkle (1976) . . . . Sister
Which Way Is Up? (1977) . . . . .Vanetta
Cuba (1979). . . . . .Therese
The Cotton Club (1984) . . . . Lila Rose Oliver
Brewster's Millions (1985). . . . . Angela Drake
Round Midnight (1986; U.S./French) . . . . Darcey Leigh
Gardens of Stone (1987). . . . . Betty Rae
Jungle Fever (1991) . . . . Drew
  •• 0:04—Left breast while making love with Wesley Snipes in bed.
  • 2:03—Brief left breast in bed with Snipes again.

McNeil, Kate

a.k.a. Kathryn McNeil.
Films:
Beach House (1981) . . . . Cindy
House on Sorority Row (1983) . . . . Katherine
Monkey Shines: An Experiment in Fear (1988)
. . . . Melanie Parker
  • 1:07—Brief upper half of right breast, while making love with Allan. Dark, hard to see anything.

Miniseries:
North and South, Book II (1986) . . . . . . Augusta Barclay
TV:
As the World Turns . . . . Karen Haines-Stenbeck
WIOU (1990-91) . . . . Taylor Young

McNichol, Kristy

Films:
The End (1978) . . . . .Julie Lawson
Little Darlings (1980) . . . . .Angel
The Night the Lights Went Out in Georgia (1981)
. . . . Amanda Child
Only When I Laugh (1981). . . . . Polly
The Pirate Movie (1982; Australian) . . . . Mabel
White Dog (1982) . . . . .Julie Sawyer
Brief topless when blouse gapes open.
Just the Way You Are (1984) . . . . .Susan
  • 0:50—Very brief left breast showing her friend that she's not too hot because there is nothing under her white coat. Medium long shot.
You Can't Hurry Love (1984) . . . . Rhonda
Dream Lover (1986) . . . . Kathy Gardner
  • 0:17—Very, very brief right breast getting out of bed, then walking around in a white top and underwear.
  0:21—Walking around in the white top again. Same scene used in flashbacks at 0:34, 0:46 and 0:54.
Two Moon Junction (1988) . . . . .Patti Jean
  •• 0:42—Topless in gas station restroom changing camisole tops with Sherilyn Fenn.
The Forgotten One (1989). . . . . .Barbara Stupple
  0:06—Jogging in braless pink top, then talking to Terry O'Quinn.
  1:33—In pink top, lying in bed.
Made for TV Movies:
Like Mom, Like Me (1978) . . . . n.a.
My Old Man (1979). . . . . n.a.
Women of Valor (1986) . . . . n.a.
Baby of the Bride (1991) . . . . Mary
TV:
Apple's Way (1974-75). . . . . Patricia Apple
Family (1976-80) . . . . Letitia "Buddy" Lawrence
Empty Nest (1989-) . . . . Barbara Weston

McQuade, Kris

Films:
Alvin Purple (1973; Australian) . . . . Samantha
  ••• 0:21—Topless and buns, while painting Alvin's body.
Alvin Rides Again (1974; Australian) . . . . .Mandy
  ••• 0:48—Full frontal nudity, taking off red dress and getting into bed with Alvin. More topless lying in bed. Long scene.
Lonely Hearts (1983; Australian). . . . . Rosemarie
The Coca-Cola Kid (1985; Australian). . . . . Juliana

• McTeer, Janet

Films:
Half Moon Street (1986) . . . . Van Arkady's Ambassador
a.k.a. Escort Girl

Made for TV Movies:
Portrait of a Marriage (1992; British)
.... Vita Sackville-West
- • 0:47—Brief right breast, while lying in bed with Violet.
- •• 2:28—(0:04 into Part 3) Left breast and buns, getting out of bed. Brief topless and buns, putting robe
  on.

McVeigh, Rose
a.k.a. Rosemary McVeigh.
Films:
A Night in Heaven (1983)................... Alison
Porky's Revenge (1985; Canadian) .... Miss Webster
- ••• 0:39—In black bra, panties, garter belt and stockings then topless in her apartment with Mr. Dobish
  while Pee Wee and his friends secretly watch.

• McWhirter, Jillian
Films:
After Midnight (1989)..................... Allison
Nowhere to Run (1989) ....Cynthia
Dune Warriors (1990) .... Val
- • 0:25—Brief right breast with Miranda in under-
  ground lake. (Her hair is in the way of her left
  breast.)

Medak, Karen
Films:
A Girl to Kill For (1989)....................Sue
- ••• 0:17—Topless showering at the beach after surfing
  with Chuck.
  0:38—In bra lying on desk in office with Chuck.
- •• 1:08—Topless in spa when Chuck takes her shirt off.
  Then miscellaneous shots making love.
The Marrying Man (1991)...................Sherry
a.k.a. Too Hot to Handle
Switch (1991) .... Saleswoman

Mejias, Isabelle
Films:
Daughter of Death (1982)................... Julie
a.k.a. Julie Darling
Bay Boy (1985; Canadian)........... Mary McNeil
- •• 1:28—Brief topless in her bedroom with Kiefer Suth-
  erland, then brief topless in bed with him.
Higher Education (1987; Canadian) .....Carrie Hanson
Meatballs III (1987)..................... Wendy
Fall From Innocence (1988)......... Marsa Cummins
State Park (1988; Canadian) ....Marsha
Scanners 2: The New Order (1991)..... Alice Leonardo
Made for TV Movies:
Special People (1984) .... Julie
Magazines:
Playboy (Nov 1985) .... Sex in Cinema 1985
- •• 133—Right breast in still from *The Bay Boy*.

Melato, Mariangela
Films:
Love and Anarchy (1974; Italian) .... Salome
The Nada Gang (1974; French/Italian)......... Cash
The Seduction of Mimi (1974; Italian) .... n.a.
Swept Away (1975; Italian) ....Raffaela Lenzetti
*a.k.a. Swept Away...by an unusual destiny in the blue sea
of august*
- •• 1:10—Topless on the sand when Giancarlo Giannini
  catches her and makes love with her.
Moses (1976; British/Italian)........... Princess Bithia
Flash Gordon (1980) ....Kala
So Fine (1981) .... Lira
Summer Night (1987; Italian) .... Signora Bolk
- •• 0:26—Topless behind gauze net over bed making
  love with a German guy.
- •• 1:02—Topless on the bed making love with the prisoner.
- •• 1:09—Topless again.
- ••• 1:13—Buns, walking out of the ocean, then topless
  with wet hair.

• Melini, Angela
Video Tapes:
Playboy Video Calendar 1993 (1992)..... February
Wet and Wild IV (1992).................. Model
Magazines:
Playboy (Jun 1992)................... Playmate
- ••• 98-109—Nude.

Mell, Marisa
Films:
5 Sinners (1961)........................... Liliane
French Dressing (1964) .... Francoise Fayol
Casanova '70 (1965; Italian)............... Thelma
City of Fear (1965; British) .... Ilona
Masquerade (1965) ....Sophie
Objective 500 Million (1966)................... Yo
Secret Agent Super Dragon
  (1966; French/Italian/German)........ Charity Farrell
Anyone Can Play (1968; Italian) ....Paola
Danger: Diabolik (1968)................... Eva Kant
Mahogany (1975) .... Carlotta Gavin
Sex on the Run (1979; German/French/Italian)
....Francesca
a.k.a. Some Like It Cool
a.k.a. Casanova and Co.
- • 0:52—Very, very brief left breast, while getting out
  of bed with Tony Curtis.
  1:12—Braless in white nightgown.
Quest for the Mighty Sword (1989).........Nephele
Magazines:
Playboy (Mar 1977) .... Comeback for Casanova
- •• 89—Topless in water.

Meneghel, Xuxa

See: Xuxa.

• Menuez, Stephanie

Films:
Clean and Sober (1988) . . . . Ticket Agent
Gremlins 2: The New Batch (1990) . . . Clamp's Secretary
The Rapture (1991) . . . . Diane
••• 0:06—Topless in furniture store with Mimi Rogers, Vic and Randy.
Magazines:
Playboy (Nov 1991) . . . . Sex in Cinema 1991
••• 142—Topless in a scene from *The Rapture.*

Menzies, Heather

Wife of actor Robert Urich.
Films:
The Sound of Music (1965) . . . . .Louisa
Hawaii (1966) . . . . Mercy Bromley
How Sweet It Is (1968) . . . . .Tour Girl
Hail, Hero! (1969) . . . . Molly Adams
Outside In (1972) . . . . .Chris
Sssssssss (1973) . . . . Kristine Stoner
a.k.a. Ssssnake
Piranha (1978) . . . . Maggie McKeown
Endangered Species (1982) . . . . Susan
TV:
Logan's Run (1977-78) . . . . .Jessica
Magazines:
Playboy (Aug 1973) . . . . Tender Trapp
••• 81-85—Nude.

• Meredith, Lee

Films:
The Producers (1968) . . . . .Ulla
Hello Down There (1969) . . . . Dr. Wells
Welcome to the Club (1971) . . . . Betsie Wholecloth
The Stoolie (1972) . . . . .n.a.
Hail (1973) . . . . Mrs. Maloney
Sunshine Boys (1975) . . . . Nurse in Sketch
Magazines:
Playboy (Sep 1973) . . . . A Star is Made
••• 105-111—Nude in different settings.

Meredith, Penny

Films:
Happy Housewives . . . . Margaretta
• 0:02—Brief right breast, while talking on the telephone while Bob makes love with her.
•• 0:19—Topless standing up in bathtub talking to Bob.
• 0:34—In sheer black lingerie.
• 1:05—Brief topless pulling her top down when interrupted by the policeman at the window.
The Flesh & Blood Show (1974; British) . . . . .n.a.

• Meyer, Bess

Films:
One More Saturday Night (1986) . . . . .Tobi
• 1:02—Brief topless in bed with Tom Davis.
In the Mood (1987) . . . . Teenage Girl (Slapper)
She's Out of Control (1989) . . . . Cheryl
The Inner Circle (1991; Italian) . . . . Katya—Age 16
TV:
Parenthood (1990) . . . . .Julie
Room For Two (1992-) . . . . .Naomi Dillon

• Michael, Joy

Films:
Homework (1982)
. . . . Diane, Age 16/Body Double for Joan Collins
•• 0:39—In bra, then topless in car making out with her boyfriend.
•• 1:18—Topless, taking off her bra and making love with Tommy. (Supposed to be Joan Collins.)
Fear City (1984) . . . . Metropole Dancer
Johnny Dangerously (1984) . . . . Chorus Girl

• Michaels, Julie

Films:
Roadhouse (1989) . . . . .Denise
••• 1:18—Topless dancing on stage in club in front of Patrick Swayze.
Point Break (1991) . . . . Freight Train
• 0:53—Brief topless in the shower.
• 0:54—Nude, beating up Keanu Reeves in the bathroom during shootout. Full frontal nudity while stabbing an FBI agent.

Michaels, Lorraine

Films:
Star 80 (1983) . . . . Paul's Party Guest
Malibu Express (1984) . . . . .Liza Chamberlin
••• 0:23—Topless in the shower making love with Shane, while getting photographed by a camera.
B.O.R.N. (1988) . . . . Dr. Black
Magazines:
Playboy (Apr 1981) . . . . Playmate

• Michaels, Michele

Films:
The Slumber Party Massacre (1982) . . . . Trish
•• 0:01—Topless in white panties while getting dressed.
•• 0:08—Buns, then brief topless passing the soap to Kim.
•• 0:29—Topless in white panties putting shirt on while two boys watch from outside.
Video Tapes:
Scream Queen Hot Tub Party (1991) . . . . Trish
•• 0:14—Topless and buns in shower scene from *Slumber Party Massacre.*

• Michaels, Roxanna

Films:

The Newlydeads (1988) . . . . .n.a.

Caged Fury (1989) . . . . .Katherine "Kat" Collins

Video Tapes:

Inside Out 3 (1992) . . . . Laila/The Perfect Woman

••• 0:38—Topless and buns in G-string, changing out of her wet clothes, while Joe watches.

• 0:43—Brief topless, taking off clothes on talk show on TV.

Magazines:

Playboy's Book of Lingerie (Sep 1991) . . . . . Herself

• 55—Buns.

•• 72—Right breast and lower frontal nudity.

Playboy's Book of Lingerie (Nov 1991) . . . . . Herself

••• 18—Topless.

Playboy's Book of Lingerie (Jul 1992) . . . . Herself

Michaelsen, Helle

Video Tapes:

Playboy Video Calendar 1991 (1990) . . . . April

••• 0:14—Nude.

Magazines:

Playboy (Aug 1988). . . . . Playmate

Playboy's Nudes (Oct 1990). . . . . Herself

••• 76—Full frontal nudity.

Michan, Cherie

Films:

Wrong is Right (1982). Erika

Fever Pitch (1985). . . . . Rose O'Sharon

Made for Cable TV:

Dream On: The Name of the Game is Five-Card Stud (1991; HBO) . . . . Alison

••• 0:16—In black bra, then topless, literally losing her shirt during poker game.

0:17—Very brief nipple seen through her folded arms.

Michelle, Ann

Films:

Haunted (1974) . . . . .n.a.

House of Whipcord (1974; British) . . . . Julia

Young Lady Chatterley (1977). . . . . . Gwen (roommate)

French Quarter (1978)

. . . . . . "Coke Eye" Laura/Policewoman in French Hotel

• 0:42—Right breast, when Josie wakes her up.

••• 0:43—Topless in bed, caressing Josie's breasts.

•• 0:58—Topless during voodoo ceremony. Close ups of breasts with snake.

• 1:19—Brief topless, sitting in bed.

••• 1:20—More topless sitting in bed, talking to a customer. Long scene.

Michelle, Shelley

Films:

My Stepmother Is An Alien (1988)

. . . . Body Double for Kim Basinger

0:12—Pulling stocking on her leg in zero gravity.

In the Cold of the Night (1989) . . . . .Model 3

Overexposed (1990)

. . . . Body Double for Catherine Oxenberg

•• 0:54—Left breast several times, buns when taking off panties, lower frontal nudity while in bed with Hank. Wearing a wig with wavy hair.

Pretty Woman (1990). . . . Body Double for Julia Roberts (Body double for Julia Roberts only at the *begining* of the film when she is getting dressed.)

0:04—In black panties and bra, waking up and getting dressed.

Bikini Summer (1991). Jazz

•• 0:33—Topless and buns in the shower while Max peeks through hole.

•• 0:49—Topless and buns, trying on swimsuits, then having a water fight with Cheryl.

Final Analysis (1992) . . . . Body Double for Kim Basinger

Sunset Strip (1992) . . . . Veronica

Made for Cable Movies:

Nails (1992; Showtime). . . . . Stunt Player

•• 0:16—Topless and buns, several times body double for Anne Archer during love scene with Dennis Hopper.

Magazines:

Playboy (Dec 1991) . . . . .Sex Stars 1991

••• 187—Side view of right breast and partial lower frontal nudity.

Playboy (Apr 1992) . . . . Double Vision

••• 72-77—Nude.

Playboy's Career Girls (Aug 1992) . . . .Double Visions

••• 30-35—Nude.

Micula, Stacia

See: Fox, Samantha.

Mierisch, Susan

Films:

Cave Girl (1985). . . . . Locker Room Student

•• 0:05—Topless with four other girls in the girls' locker room undressing, then running after Rex. She's blonde, wearing red panties and a necklace.

Neon Maniacs (1985) . . . . Young Lover

• 0:07—Very brief upper half of right breast while kissing her boyfriend at night.

Miles, Sarah

Films:

The Servant (1963) . . . . .Vera

Those Magnificent Men in their Flying Machines (1965) Patricia Rawnsley

Blow-Up (1966; British/Italian) . . . . Patricia

Ryan's Daughter (1970) . . . . Rosy Ryan

Lady Caroline Lamb (1973) . . . . .Lady Caroline Lamb

The Man Who Loved Cat Dancing (1973)

. . . . Catherine Crocker

Topless.

The Sailor Who Fell From Grace with the Sea
(1976)........................ Anne Osborne
- 0:18—Topless sitting at the vanity getting dressed while her son watches through peephole.
- 0:23—Topless, fantasizing about her husband.
- 0:42—Nude, making love with Kris Kristofferson.
- 1:15—Brief right breast, in bed with Kristofferson.

The Big Sleep (1978; British)..... Charlotte Sternwood
Venom (1982; British)............ Dr. Marion Stowe
Ordeal by Innocence (1984)......... Mary Durrant
Steaming (1985; British).................. Sarah
- 0:23—Topless getting into pool with Vanessa Redgrave.
- 0:49—Topless getting undressed.
- 1:31—Nude lying down next to pool.

Hope and Glory (1987; British)......... Grace Rohan
Queenie (1987)........................ Lady Sybil
White Mischief (1988)...................... Alice
Made for Cable Movies:
A Ghost in Monte Carlo (1990)................ n.a.
Magazines:
Playboy (Jul 1976)
.... Kris and Sarah & The Soul of Sarah
••• 122-129—Nude.
Playboy (Dec 1976)............. Sex Stars of 1976
••• 181—Full frontal nudity standing on bed with Kris Kristofferson.
Playboy (Jan 1989)........ Women of the Seventies
•• 213—Topless in bed with Kris Kristofferson.

• *Miles, Sherry*
Films:
Making It (1971)...................... Debbie
The Velvet Vampire (1971).......... Susan Ritter
- 0:08—Brief topless in bed with Lee.
••• 0:18—Topless sitting up in bed, then making love with Lee.
- 0:21—Topless in bed in desert during dream scene.
••• 0:22—Topless sitting up in bed and turning on the light.
- 0:42—Topless in bed during desert dream scene, long shot.
- 0:55—Topless in bed during desert dream scene.
••• 0:56—Topless in bed in desert scene, closer shot with Diane.
- 1:19—Brief topless in desert scene during flashback.

Your Three Minutes Are Up (1973).......... Debbie
The Harrad Summer (1974).................. Dee
a.k.a. Student Union
The Long Dark Night (1977).................. Lois
a.k.a. The Pack
TV:
Hee Haw (1971-72)..................... Regular

Miles, Sylvia
Films:
Midnight Cowboy (1969)................. Cass
- 0:20—Brief buns, running into bedroom and jumping onto bed with Jon Voight. More when changing

the TV channel with the remote control. Most of her right breast in bed under Voight.
The Sentinel (1977)..................... Gerde
- 0:33—Brief left breast, three times, standing behind Beverly D'Angelo. Right breast, ripping dress of Christina Raines. B&W dream.
1:23—Brief topless, three times, with D'Angelo made up to look like zombies, munching on a dead Chris Sarandon.
1:27—Very brief right breast during big zombie scene.
- 1:28—Brief topless when the zombies start dying.

The Funhouse (1981)................ Madame Zena
Wall Street (1987)...................... Realtor
Crossing Delancey (1988)...... Hannah Mandelbaum
Spike of Bensonhurst (1988)........ Congresswoman
She-Devil (1989)...................... Mrs. Fisher

Milford, Penelope
Films:
Man on a Swing (1974)............. Evelyn Moore
Coming Home (1978)............. Viola Munson
- 1:19—Doing strip tease in room with Jane Fonda and two guys. Sort of right breast peeking out between her arms when she changes her mind.

The Last Word (1979)............. Denise Travis
Endless Love (1981)..................... Ingrid
Take This Job and Shove It (1981)...... Lenore Meade
Blood Link (1983).................. Julie Warren
•• 0:22—Topless in bed with Craig. Very brief left breast grabbing pillow.
•• 1:24—In black bra in greenhouse with Keith, then topless, then brief right breast.
••• 1:35—Topless in bedroom with Keith.

The Golden Seal (1983)................ Tania Lee
Heathers (1989)................. Pauline Fleming
Made for Cable TV:
The Hitchhiker: Man at the Window (1985; HBO)
.... Diane Hampton
•• 0:09—Topless in white panties making love with her husband on the couch.
Made for TV Movies:
The Burning Bed (1984)...................... n.a.

Milhench, Ann
Films:
Blood Debts (1983)....................... Lisa
Sloane (1984)................... Janice Thursby
•• 0:02—Topless and buns getting out of shower and being held by kidnappers.

Miller, Ginger
Video Tapes:
Wild Bikinis (1987)...................... Herself
- 0:23—Buns in white two piece swimsuit, while rubbing oil on herself.
0:26—Buns on pool float with Beckie Mullen.
Boxing Babes (1991)..................... Herself

Made for Man: Intimate Fantasy (1992)
.... Darling Nikki
- 0:03—Buns in G-string, doing strip routine out of black outfit.
- 0:11—Buns, during gelatin wrestling with Baby Driver.
  0:19—Stripping to two piece swimsuit.
- 0:37—Stipping down to two piece silver swimsuit.
- 0:47—Wrestling with Sugar Ray Rene in lettuce.
- 0:55—Brief left breast, popping out of swimsuit top.

Magazines:
Penthouse (Sep 1986) .... Pet

Miller, Marjorie
See: Blondi.

Miller, Sherrie
Films:
Goin' All the Way (1981) .... Candy
  0:47—Brief right breast getting out of bubble bath.
•• 0:49—Topless with Artie during his fantasy.
Separate Vacations (1985).................. Sandy

Millian, Andra
Films:
Stacy's Knights (1983)..................... Stacy
Nightfall (1988) .... Anna
- 0:12—Very brief topless making love with David Birney.
- 0:41—Very brief topless making love in front of a fire.
  0:58—Same scene in a flashback while the guy is talking to another woman.

TV:
Paper Chase (1984-86) .... Laura

Million, Tiffany
See: Margot, Sandra.

•Mills, Brooke
Films:
The Big Doll House (1971) .... Harrad
- 0:28—Side of right breast, while lying in bed before rolling over.
Legacy of Blood (1973).................. Leslie Dean
The Student Teachers (1973) .... n.a.
Walking Tall, Part II (1975) .... Ruby Ann
Two-Minute Warning (1976)........ Tyler's Girlfriend
Freaky Friday (1977) .... Mrs. Gibbons

Mills, Donna
Films:
The World's Oldest Living Bridesmaid .... n.a.
Play Misty for Me (1971)................. Tobie
- 1:10—Brief side view of right breast hugging Clint Eastwood in a pond near a waterfall. Long shot, hard to see.
Murph the Surf (1975) .... Ginny Eaton
Fire! (1977)............................... n.a.

Miniseries:
False Arrest (1991) .... Joyce Lukezic
Made for TV Movies:
Bunco (1977)............................. n.a.
Doctor's Private Lives (1978) .... n.a.
TV:
The Good Life (1971-72) .... Jane Miller
Knots Landing (1980-89)
.... Abby Ewing Sumner Cunningham
Magazines:
Playboy (Nov 1989) .... Oh! Donna
- 82-87—Buns in photos taken around 1966.

Mills, Hayley
Daughter of actor Sir John Mills.
Sister of actress Juliet Mills.
Films:
Tiger Bay (1959; British)..................... Gillie
Pollyanna (1960) .... Pollyanna
Whistle Down the Wind (1961; British)
.... Kathy Bostock
In Search of the Castaways (1962) .... Mary grant
The Chalk Garden (1964)................... Laurel
The Moon-Spinners (1964) .... Nikky Ferris
The Parent Trap (1964)
.... Sharon McKendirck/Susan Evers
That Darn Cat (1965)................. Patti Randall
The Trouble with Angels (1966) .... Mary Clancy
Deadly Strangers (1974; British)............ Belle
  1:02—Buns in bathtub when her uncle watches her.
  1:05—In black bra, garter belt and panties while Steven fantasizes as he sees her through a keyhole.
••• 1:13—In white bra and panties while Steven watches through keyhole, then topless taking off bra and reading a newspaper.
  1:15—In white bra, getting dressed.
Endless Night (1977) .... Ellie
Appointment with Death (1988) .... Miss Quinton
Miniseries:
The Flame Trees of Thika (1982)............... Tilly
Made for TV Movies:
The Parent Trap II (1986) .... n.a.

Mills, Juliet
Daughter of actor Sir John Mills.
Sister of actress Hayley Mills.
Films:
The Rare Breed (1966) .... Hilary Price
Avanti! (1973) .... Pamela Piggott
(Not available on video tape. Shown on *The Arts and Entertainment Channel* periodically. Scenes are listed as 0:00 since I can't time correctly with the commercials.)
  0:00—Buns, climbing out of the water onto a rock.
- 0:00—Side view of right breast lying on rock talking to Jack Lemmon.
••• 0:00—Brief topless waving to fishermen on a passing boat.
  0:00—Brief buns putting something up in the closet in Jack Lemmon's hotel room.

Beyond the Door (1975; Italian/U.S.) . . . . .Jessica
Waxwork II: Lost in Time (1991) . . . The Defense Lawyer
Miniseries:
Till We Meet Again (1989). . . . . Vivianne
Made for TV Movies:
Columbo: No Time To Die (1992). . . . . . . Elaine Hacker
TV:
Nanny and the Professor (1970-71) . . . .Phoebe Figalilly
Magazines:
Playboy (Nov 1973) . . . . Sex in Cinema 1973
••• 153—Topless in photo from *Avanti*.

Mimieux, Yvette

Films:
The Time Machine (1960). . . . . Weena
Where the Boys Are (1960) . . . . Melanie
Diamond Head (1962) . . . . Sloan Howland
The Four Horsemen of the Apocalypse (1962)
. . . . Chi-Chi Desnoyers
Three in the Attic (1968). . . . . .Tobey Clinton
Jackson County Jail (1976) . . . . Dinah Hunter
• 0:39—Topless in jail cell getting raped by police-
man.
The Black Hole (1979). . . . . Dr. Kate McGraw
Made for TV Movies:
Perry Mason: The Case of the Desperate Deception
(1990). . . . . Danielle Altmann
TV:
The Most Deadly Game (1970-71) . . . . . .Vanessa Smith
Berrengers (1985). . . . . .Shane Bradley

Minnick, Dani

Films:
Lena's Holiday (1990) . . . . Julie Eden
The Sleeping Car (1990). . . . . Joanne
Made for Cable TV:
Tales From the Crypt: The Man Who was Death
(1989; HBO) . . . . Cynthia Baldwin
• 0:17—Very brief side view of right breast in shower.

Miou-Miou

Films:
Going Places (1974; French). . . . . .Marie-Ange
••• 0:14—Topless sitting in bed, filing her nails. Full
frontal nudity standing up and getting dressed.
•• 0:48—Topless in bed with Pierrot and Jean-Claude.
• 0:51—Left breast under Pierrot.
••• 0:52—Buns in bed when Jean-Claude rolls off her.
Full frontal nudity sitting up with the two guys in
bed.
•• 1:21—Brief topless opening the door. Topless and
panties walking in after the two guys.
• 1:27—Partial left breast taking off dress and walking
into house.
1:28—Very brief topless closing the shutters.
•• 1:31—Full frontal nudity in open dress running after
the two guys. Long shot. Full frontal nudity putting
her wet dress on.
• 1:41—Topless in back of car. Dark.

The Genius (1976; Italian/German/French) . . . . . . Lucy
Jonah—Who Will be 25 in the Year 2000
(1976; Swiss) . . . . .Marie
Memories of a French Whore (1979) . . . . n.a.
My Other Husband (1981; French) . . . . n.a.
Entre Nous (1983; French). . . . . Madeleine
a.k.a. Coup de Foudre
Dog Day (1984; French) . . . . Jessica
La Lectrice (1989; French) . . . . Constance/Marie
a.k.a. The Reader
1:06—Making love with a guy while reading to him
in bed.
• 1:18—Full frontal nudity lying in bed. Close-up pan
shot from lower frontal nudity, then left breast, then
right breast.
• 1:20—Very brief right breast, then lower frontal nudity getting dressed.
Magazines:
Playboy (Nov 1990) . . . . Sex in Cinema 1990
•• 144—Topless in still from *Going Places*.

Miracle, Irene

Films:
Midnight Express (1978; British) . . . . .Susan
•• 1:39—Topless in prison visiting booth showing her
breasts to Brad Davis so he can masturbate.
Inferno (1980; Italian) . . . . Rose Elliot
In the Shadow of Kilimanjaro (1985)
. . . . Lee Ringtree
• 0:18—Brief topless in bed with Timothy Bottoms.
Kind of hard to see anything because it's dark.
The Last Days of Philip Banter (1987)
. . . . .Elizabeth Banter
Puppet Master (1989) . . . . Dana Hadley
Watchers II (1990) . . . . Sarah Ferguson
0:28—In pink leotard, going into aerobics studio.
••• 0:40—Side view in black bra, then topless a few
times in the bathtub.
Made for TV Movies:
Shattered Dreams (1990). . . . . .Elaine
Magazines:
Playboy (Nov 1978) . . . . Sex in Cinema 1978
•• 183—Topless still from *Midnight Express*.

Mirren, Helen

Films:
A Midsummer Night's Dream (1968) . . . . Hermia
Age of Consent (1969; Australian) . . . . Cora
• 0:48—Topless several times in the mirror. Brief lower
frontal nudity, kneeling on the floor.
•• 0:55—Brief topless and buns quite a few time, snorkeling under water.
••• 1:20—Topless and half of buns, posing in the water
for James Mason. Then getting out.
Savage Messiah (1972; British) . . . . Gosh Smith-Boyle
0:40 & 1:13.
O Lucky Man! (1973; British) . . . . Patricia Burgess

Caligula (1980) . . . . .Caesonia
(X-rated, 147 minute version.)
    1:02—Side view of buns with Malcolm McDowell
    • 1:13—Brief topless several times getting out of bed
    to run after McDowell. Dark.
    1:15—Very brief left breast taking off her dress to dry
    McDowell off.
The Fiendish Plot of Dr. Fu Manchu (1980) . . .Alice Rage
Hussy (1980; British) . . . . Beaty
  •• 0:22—Left breast, then side of right breast, while ly-
    ing in bed with John Shea.
  ••• 0:29—Nude, making love in bed with Shea.
  •• 0:31—Full frontal nudity in bathtub.
The Long Good Friday (1980; British) . . . . .Victoria
Excalibur (1981; British) . . . . Morgana
  • 1:31—Side view of left breast under a fishnet outfit
    climbing into bed.
2010 (1984) . . . . .Tanya Kirbuk
Cal (1984; Irish) . . . . Marcella
    1:18—In a white bra and slip.
  •• 1:20—Brief frontal nudity taking off clothes and get-
    ting into bed with Cal in his cottage, then right
    breast making love.
White Knights (1985) . . . . Galina Ivanova
The Mosquito Coast (1986) . . . . .Mother
Pascall's Island (1988; British) . . . . Lydia Neuman
  • 1:00—Left breast, lying in bed with Charles Dance.
    Long shot.
Red King, White Knight (1989) . . . . .Anna
When the Whales Came (1989) . . . . . .Clemmie Jenkins
The Cook, The Thief, His Wife & Her Lover (1990)
. . . . .Georgina Spica
    0:22—In black bra in restroom performing fellatio
    on Michael.
  •• 0:32—In lingerie undressing, then lower frontal nu-
    dity, buns and left breast in kitchen with Michael.
  • 0:42—Buns and right breast, while making love with
    Michael again.
  •• 0:57—Topless sitting and talking with Michael.
    1:01—Buns, kneeling on table.
  • 1:05—Brief topless, while leaning back on table with
    Michael.
    1:07—Lower frontal nudity opening her coat for
    Michael.
  • 1:11—Buns and topless in kitchen.
  ••• 1:14—Buns, getting into meat truck. Full frontal nu-
    dity in truck and walking around with Michael.
The Comfort of Strangers (1991) . . . . Caroline
Where Angels Fear to Tread (1992) . . . . . . .Lilia Herriton
Made for TV Movies:
Mystery! Cause Célèbre (1991) . . . .Alma Rattenbury
  •• 0:27—Topless in bed when Bowman pulls down the
    sheets in bed.
  • 0:28—Brief topless and buns putting slip on.
Mystery! Prime Suspect (1992)
. . . . Detective Chief Inspector Jane Tennison
Magazines:
Playboy (Nov 1990) . . . . Sex in Cinema 1990
  • 147—Topless and buns.

Misch Owens, Laura
Films:
  French Quarter (1978) . . . ."Ice Box" Josie/Girl on Bus
    • 0:41—Topless under sheer white nightgown.
    ••• 0:43—Full frontal nudity taking off nightgown,
      wearing garter belt. Getting into bed with Laura.
Magazines:
  Playboy (Oct 1974) . . . . Bunnies of 1974
    ••• 137—Full frontal nudity.
  Playboy (Feb 1975) . . . . Playmate

• *Moase, Robyn*
Films:
  Journey Among Women (1977; Australian) . . . . . Moira
  Midnight Dancer (1987; Australian) . . . . .Brenda
  a.k.a. Belinda
    • 0:43—Brief topless putting her black top on.

• *Moen, Jackie*
Films:
  Shock 'Em Dead (1990) . . . . Groupie 4
    •• 1:05—Topless, taking off her top to tempt Martin.
  Wilding, The Children of Violence (1990)
  . . . . .Car Rape Victim
    • 0:23—Very brief right breast in back of car with her
      boyfriend when the gang of kids terrorizes them.
  Class of Nuke 'Em High Part II: Subhumanoid Meltdown
  (1991) . . . . Diane/Bald Subhumanoid
  Switch (1991) . . . . Girl at City Grille

Moffat, Kitty
a.k.a. Katherine Moffat.
Films:
  The Beast Within (1982) . . . . .Amanda Platt
    •• 1:32—Topless, getting her dress torn off by the
      beast while she is unconscious. Don't see her face,
      could be a body double.
Made for TV Movies:
  The Prince of Bel Air (1986) . . . . n.a.
TV:
  Boone (1983-84) . . . . .Susannah Sawyer

• *Moffett, Michelle*
Films:
  Hollywood Boulevard II (1989) . . . . .Mary Randolf
  Hired to Kill (1990) . . . . Ana
    • 0:46—Left breast in dress, then topless when Oliver
      Reed lowers her top.
    •• 0:47—More topless in open dress top.
    •• 1:04—Very, very brief tip of right breast, lying on ta-
      ble when Brian Thompson rips her blouse open.
      More topless, lying on the table. Dark.
Made for Cable TV:
  The Hitchhiker: Best Shot (1987; HBO) . . . . . .Lorri Ann

Molina, Angela

Films:

That Obscure Object of Desire
(1977; French/Spanish) . . . . .Conchita
- 0:53—Brief topless in bathroom.
- 1:20—Nude dancing in front of a group of tourists.
- 1:29—Brief topless behind a gate taunting Fernando Rey.

The Sabina (1979; Spanish/Swedish). . . . . .Pepa
The Eyes, The Mouth (1983; Italian/French) . . . . .Vanda
Demons in the Garden (1984; Spanish). . . . . . . Angela
Camorra (1986; Italian). . . . . .Annunziata
Streets of Gold (1986). . . . . Elena

Moncure, Lisa

Films:

Moving (1988) . . . . Nina Franklin
Lisa (1989) . . . . Sarah
Corporate Affairs (1990). . . . . Carolyn Bean
- 1:07—Very, very brief left breast, while kicking Douglas out of cubicle.

Monroe, Marilyn

Films:

Love Happy (1949) . . . . Grunion's Client
All About Eve (1950). . . . . Miss Casswell
Gentlemen Prefer Blondes (1953) . . . . Lorelei
How to Marry a Millionaire (1953) . . . . Pola
There's no Business like Show Business (1954). . . . .Vicky
Bus Stop (1956) . . . . Cherie
The Prince and the Showgirl (1957) . . . . . . Elsie Marina
The Seven Year Itch (1957) . . . . The Girl
Some Like it Hot (1959) . . . . Sugar Kane Kowa
The Misfits (1961). . . . . .Roslyn Taber
    0:33—Almost left breast twice stretching and sitting up in bed.
    0:39—In two piece swimsuit running out of the lake.
Video Tapes:
Playboy Video Magazine, Volume 12 (1987)
. . . . .A Loving Tribute to Marilyn Monroe
- 1:02—Buns and left breast in still photos by swimming pool from unreleased last film.
- 1:03—Topless in B&W reference photos for artist Earl Moran. Taken around 1946-50.
Magazines:
Playboy (Dec 1953). . . . . Sweetheart of the Month
Premiere issue of *Playboy* magazine.
Playboy (Jan 1974) . . . . Twenty Years of Playmates
- 102—Topless in centerfold photo.
Playboy (Jan 1979) . . . . 25 Beautiful Years
- 152—Topless in pose from premiere issue.
Playboy (Jan 1987) . . . . .Marilyn Remembered
Playboy (Jan 1989) . . . . .Women of the Fifties
- 114—Topless in pose from premiere issue.
Playboy's Nudes (Oct 1990). . . . . Herself
- 3—Topless
Entertainment Weekly (Jun 26, 1992) . . . . . . Herself
- 16—Topless behind sheer fabric. Large red "X" drawn by Monroe over the photo.

Montgomery, Julie

Films:

Girls Night Out (1984). n.a.
a.k.a. Scared to Death
Revenge of the Nerds (1984). . . . . Betty
- 0:49—Frontal nudity getting ready for a shower.
- 1:10—Topless in the pie pan.
Up the Creek (1984) . . . . Lisa
The Kindred (1987) . . . . Cindy Russell
South of Reno (1987) . . . . .Susan
- 1:22—Brief topless kissing Martin. Dark, hard to see.
    1:25—In motel room wearing black top and panties, then pink spandex top with the panties.
Stewardess School (1987) . . . . .Pimmie Polk
Made for TV Movies:
Earth-Star Voyager (1988) . . . . Dr. Sally Arthur
Revenge of the Nerds III: The Next Generation (1992)
. . . . Betty Skolnick
TV:
One Life to Live . . . . n.a.

Monticelli, Anna-Maria

a.k.a. Anna Jemison.
Films:

Smash Palace (1981; New Zealand) . . . . .Jacqui Shaw
    0:21—Silhouette of right breast changing while sitting on the edge of the bed.
- 0:39—Topless in bed after arguing, then making up with Bruno Lawrence.
Heatwave (1983; Australian) . . . . Victoria
My First Wife (1985). Hillary
Nomads (1986) . . . . Niki
- 0:57—Left breast, making love in bed with Pierce Brosnan. Dark, hard to see anything.

• Moody, Lynne

Films:

The Evil (1977). . . . . Felecia
Miniseries:
Roots (1977) . . . . Irene
Roots: The Next Generation (1979) . . . . . . Irene Harvey
Made for TV Movies:
Nightmare in Badham County (1976)
. . . . Diane Emery
(Nudity added for video tape.)
- 0:16—Brief topless close-up of her breasts when Chuck Connors rips her T-shirt off in jail cell. (Don't see her face.)
The Atlanta Child Murders (1985) . . . . n.a.
TV:
That's My Mama (1974-75) . . . . Tracy Curtis Taylor
Soap (1979-81) . . . . .Polly Dawson
E/R (1984-85) . . . . Nurse Julie Williams
Knots Landing (1988-90) . . . . .Patricia Williams

• Moore, Brooke

Films:
Nudity Required (1989) . . . . Bikini Girl
Magazines:
Playboy's Book of Lingerie (Mar 1991) . . . . . Herself
•• 70—Partial right breast and lower frontal nudity.
•• 72—Partial right breast and lower frontal nudity.

• Moore, Candy

Films:
Tomboy and the Champ (1961) . . . . Tommy Joe
The Night of the Grizzly (1966). . . . . Meg
Lunch Wagon (1981) . . . . Diedra
•• 0:53—Topless under sheer robe, then topless on
couch with Arnie.
TV:
The Lucy Show (1962-65). . . . . Chris Carmichael
The Donna Reed Show (1963-65). . . . . .n.a.

Moore, Christine

Films:
Lurkers (1987) . . . . Cathy
••• 0:19—Topless in bed, making love with her boyfriend.
• 0:42—Brief topless in bubble bath during hallucination scene with her mother.
Prime Evil (1987). . . . . .Alexandra Parkman
0:09—In white bra in locker room.
Alexa (1988) . . . . Alexa
0:04—In red slip in bedroom.
0:06—In black bra, on bed with Tommy.
0:11—In black lingerie talking on phone in bed.
•• 0:24—Topless lying in bed with Anthony while reminiscing.
•• 1:08—Topless in bed with Anthony again.
Thrilled to Death (1988) . . . . Nan Christie
0:31—In bra in women's locker room.
••• 0:38—Topless in office with Mr. Dance just before
killing him.

Moore, Demi

Wife of actor Bruce Willis.
Films:
Parasite (1982) .Patricia Welles
Blame It on Rio (1984) . . . . Nicole Hollis
• 0:19—Very brief right breast turning around to greet
Michael Caine and Joseph Bologna.
No Small Affair (1984). . . . . Laura
• 1:34—Very, very brief side view of left breast in bed
with Jon Cryer.
St. Elmo's Fire (1985) . . . . Jules
About Last Night... (1986) . . . . Debbie
0:32—In white bra getting dressed.
• 0:34—Brief upper half of right breast in the bathtub
with Rob Lowe.
0:35—In white bra getting dressed.
• 0:50—Side view of right breast, then very brief topless.

••• 0:51—Buns and topless in bed with Lowe, arching
her back, then lying in bed when he rolls off her.
•• 0:52—Topless and buns in kitchen with Lowe.
One Crazy Summer (1986) . . . . .Cassandra
Wisdom (1986) . . . . .Karen
The Seventh Sign (1988) . . . . .Abby Quinn
• 1:03—Brief topless, taking off bathrobe to take a
bath. Her pregnant belly is not real—it's a full body
prosthetic.
We're No Angels (1989) . . . . .Molly
• 0:18—One long shot, then two brief side views of
left breast when Robert De Niro watches from out-
side. Reflections in the window make it hard to see.
Ghost (1990) . . . . Molly Jensen
The Butcher's Wife (1991) . . . . .Marina
Mortal Thoughts (1991). . . . . .Cynthia Kellogg
Nothing But Trouble (1991). . . . . Diane Lightson
Made for Cable TV:
Tales From the Crypt: Dead Right (1990; HBO)
. . . . .Cathy Fitch-Marno
(Available on *Tales From the Crypt, Volume 3.*)
TV:
General Hospital (1982-83) . . . . Jackie Templeton
Magazines:
Vanity Fair (Aug 1992) . . . . . . Demi's Body Language
••• 112-119—Topless with painted body on the cover.
Topless in B&W photo. Topless with painted body.

Moore, Glenda

Video Tapes:
Nudes in Limbo (1983) . . . . Model
Hot Bodies (1988) .Herself
••• 0:37—Topless, dancing with a sword. Sort of buns,
under skirt.
••• 0:40—Dancing without the sword. Buns in G-string.
••• 0:44—Topless and buns dancing with sword again.

Moore, Jeanie

Films:
Vampire at Midnight (1988) . . . . .Amalia
•• 0:32—Topless getting up to run an errand.
Wild Man (1988) .Lady at Pool
Dream Trap (1989) .Blondee
After Dark, My Sweet (1990) . . . . Nanny
The Final Alliance (1990) . . . . Carrie
• 1:03—Brief topless getting into bed with David Has-
selhoff, then brief right breast twice in bed with him.
A little dark.
We're Talkin' Serious Money (1991) . . . . Amelia

• Moore, Jessica

Films:
Eleven Days, Eleven Nights (1988; Italian)
. . . . Sarah Asproon
• 0:03—Topless opening her raincoat on boat for
Michael, then making love.
• 0:11—Buns, taking off robe in front of Michael.
•• 0:16—Right breast, on T.V., then side of breast.

•• 0:29—Topless with Michael, changing clothes with him in restroom.

••• 0:33—Topless in motel room with Michael, then making love.

• 0:44—Brief topless and buns when leaving Michael all tied up.

•• 0:51—Topless and buns in recording studio with Michael.

• 1:17—Topless in flashbacks.

••• 1:19—Nude, making love with Michael on bed.

Top Model (1989; Italian) . . . . . . Sarah Asproon/Gloria

••• 0:03—Nude, posing for photographer customer in his loft with mannequins, then talking on the phone.

• 0:08—Topless in dressing room, when seen by Cliff.

•• 0:23—Buns and brief side of right breast, undressing in front of a customer.

•• 0:24—Topless, rubbing oil on him.

•• 0:30—Full frontal nudity, in her bedroom when Peter blackmails her.

••• 0:35—Nude in photographer customer's loft again.

• 0:40—Brief buns, turning over in bed.

•• 0:43—Topless on couch, making love (disinterestedly) with cowboy.

• 0:56—Buns and partial right breast, while getting dressed.

••• 1:00—Topless making love with Cliff on sofa, then sleeping afterward.

•• 1:04—Nude, undressing and walking down hallway.

••• 1:08—Nude, in hotel room, making love with Cliff.

••• 1:19—Buns, with Cliff in stairwell. Topless and buns in bathroom with him.

Moore, Melissa

Films:

Caged Fury (1989) . . . . Gloria

Scream Dream (1989) . . . . .Jamie Summers

••• 0:39—Topless in black panties in room with Derrick. Then straddling him.

•• 0:58—Topless in dressing room pulling her top down during transformation into monster.

Invisible Maniac (1990) . . . . .Bunny

• 0:21—Buns in shower with the other girls.

••• 0:43—In bra, then topless sitting with yellow towel in locker room with the other girls.

• 0:44—Topless in shower with the other girls.

••• 1:09—In bra, then topless making out in Principal's Office with Chet. Long scene.

Repossessed (1990) . . . . Bimbo Student

•• 0:05—Topless pulling her top down in classroom in front of Leslie Nielsen.

Sorority House Massacre 2 (1990) . . . . .Jessica

••• 0:22—Topless, talking to Kimberly, then taking a shower.

0:50—In wet lingerie.

• 0:53—Buns, while going up the stairs.

Vampire Cop (1990) . . . . Melanie Roberts

••• 0:46—Topless in bed with the Vampire Cop.

•• 0:51—Right breast, sitting in bed talking with Hans.

• 1:21—Right breast, in bed on the phone during end credits.

Vice Academy, Part 2 (1990) . . . . .Glaze

Into the Sun (1991) . . . . Female Sergeant

The Killing Zone (1991) . . . . Tracy

Poker Night (1991) . . . . n.a.

Soul Mates (1991) . . . . n.a.

Tower of Terror (1991) . . . . n.a.

Consenting Adults (1992) . . . . n.a.

The Other Woman (1992) . . . . .Elysse

(Unrated version reviewed.)

•• 0:58—Topless, taking off her blouse while taking pictures during photo shoot.

Video Tapes:

Scream Queen Hot Tub Party (1991) . . . . . . .Jessica

• 0:00—Topless during opening credits.

••• 0:17—Topless opening her towel, then in the shower from *Sorority House Massacre 2.*

Sexy Lingerie IV (1992) . . . . Model

Magazines:

Playboy (Jul 1991) . . . . .The Height Report

••• 140-141—Full frontal nudity on bed.

Moore, Terry

Ex-wife of the late billionaire Howard Hughes.

Films:

Mighty Joe Young (1949) . . . . .Jill Young

Come Back, Little Sheba (1952) . . . . . Marie Buckholder

Daddy Long Legs (1955) . . . . .Linda

Double Exposure (1983) . . . . Married Woman

Hellhole (1985) . . . . Sidnee Hammond

Beverly Hills Brats (1989) . . . . Veronica

TV:

Empire (1962-63) . . . . .Constance Garret

Magazines:

Playboy (Aug 1984) . . . . The Merriest Widow

••• 130-139—Topless and buns. 55 years old.

Playboy (Dec 1984) . . . . .Sex Stars of 1984

••• 208—Topless.

Playboy (Jan 1989) . . . . .Women of the Eighties

••• 254—Topless.

Moran, Sharon

Films:

If Looks Could Kill (1987) . . . . Madonna Maid

•• 0:17—Full frontal nudity after Laura leaves the apartment.

Young Nurses in Love (1987) . . . . .Bambi/Bibi

• Morante, Laura

Films:

The Tragedy of a Ridiculous Man (1981; Italian)

. . . . .Laura

••• 1:30—Topless taking off her sweater in front of Primo because she's "uneasy."

Blow to the Heart (1985; Italian) . . . . n.a.

Distant Lights (1987; Italian) . . . . .Renata

Man On Fire (1987; Italian/French) . . Julia, David's Wife

Luci lontane (1988; Italian) . . . . n.a.

More, Camilla

Identical twin sister of actress Carey More.
Films:
Friday the 13th, Part IV—The Final Chapter
(1984). . . . . Tina
- 0:26—Very brief topless in the lake jumping up with her twin sister to show they are skinny dipping.
- 0:48—Left breast, in bed with Crispin Glover.

Dark Side of the Moon (1989). . . . . Lesli
The Serpent of Death (1989) . . . . Rene
- • 0:15—Brief topless in bed with Jeff Fahey.
- • 1:22—Brief left breast while in bed, then topless and buns, getting out of bed (in mirror).

More, Carey

Identical twin sister of actress Camilla More.
Films:
Friday the 13th, Part IV—The Final Chapter
(1984). . . . . Terri
- 0:26—Very brief topless in the lake jumping up with her twin sister to show they are skinny dipping.

Once Bitten (1985) . . . . Moll Flanders Vampire
TV:
Days of Our Lives (1987). . . . . Grace Forrester

Morgan, Alexandra

Films:
The First Nudie Musical (1979) . . . . Mary La Rue
- 0:54—Topless, singing and dancing during dancing dildo routine.
- ••• 1:04—Full frontal nudity in bed trying to do a take.
  1:07—Topless in bed with a guy with a continuous erection.
- •• 1:17—Topless in bed in another scene.

The Deadly Games (1980). . . . . Linda
- • 0:03—In bra, standing in doorway at night, then topless. Dark.
- • 0:04—Very brief left breast and lots of cleavage in open blouse talking on the phone.
  0:05—Most of right breast, standing up.

The Happy Hooker Goes Hollywood (1980) . . . . . . Max
Erotic Images (1983) . . . . Emily Stewart
- •• 0:57—In black lingerie, then topless on the living room floor with Glenn.
- • 1:05—Topless in bed, making love with Glenn.
- ••• 1:12—Topless in the kitchen with Glenn.
- •• 1:21—Right breast, on couch with Glenn.

Spellbinder (1988) . . . . Pamela

• Morgan, Brittany

Adult film actress.
Video Tapes:
High Society Centerspread Video #5: Brittany Morgan . . . . Herself
Magazines:
Penthouse (Mar 1987) . . . . Pet

Morgan, Cindy

Films:
Up Yours . . . . .Elaine
Caddyshack (1980) . . . . .Lacey Underall
- 0:50—Very, very brief side view of left breast sliding into the swimming pool. Very blurry.
- •• 0:58—Topless in bed with Danny three times.

Tron (1982) . . . . Lora/Yori
TV:
Bring 'Em Back Alive (1982-83) . . . . Gloria Marlowe
Falcon Crest (1987-88). . . . . .Gabrielle Short

Morgan, Debbi

Films:
Mandingo (1975). . . . . .Dite
- 0:17—Topless in bed talking to Perry King.

Miniseries:
Roots: The Next Generation (1979)
. . . . Elizabeth Harvey
Made for TV Movies:
The Jesse Owens Story (1984) . . . . n.a.
TV:
All My Children . . . . Angie Hubbard
Behind the Screen (1981-82) . . . . Lynette Porter
Generations (1990-) . . . . Chantal Marshall

Morgan, Shelly Taylor

Films:
The Sword and the Sorcerer (1982) . . . . Bar-Bra
- 0:54—Brief topless when Lee Horsley crashes through the window and almost lands on her.

My Tutor (1983). . . . . Louisa
Scarface (1983) . . . . Woman at the Babylon Club
Malibu Express (1984) . . . . .Anita Chamberlain
- • 0:22—Topless doing exercises on the floor.
- •• 0:26—Topless making love with Shane in bed while being video taped. Then right breast while standing by door.

Made for Cable TV:
Tales From the Crypt: The Ventriloquist's Dummy
(1990; HBO). . . . . .Sally
TV:
General Hospital . . . . Lorena Sharpe

Moritz, Louisa

Films:
Death Race 2000 (1975). . . . . Myra
- 0:28—Topless and buns getting a massage and talking to David Carradine.

One Flew Over the Cuckoo's Nest (1975). . . . . Rose
The Happy Hooker Goes to Washington (1977)
. . . . Natalie Naussbaum
- 0:39—Brief topless and buns, lying down on top of Larry Storch in tennis court.

Loose Shoes (1977) .Margie
Up in Smoke (1978). . . . . Officer Gloria
Lunch Wagon (1981) . . . . Sunshine
- 0:37—Topless in spa taking off her swimsuit top.

True Confessions (1981). . . . . .Whore

The Last American Virgin (1982). . . . . Carmela
••• 0:42—Topless and buns in her bedroom with Rick.
Chained Heat (1983; U.S./German) . . . . Bubbles
Hot Chili (1985) . . . . Chi Chi
    0:06—Brief buns turning around in white apron af-
    ter talking with the boys.
    •• 0:34—Nude during fight in restaurant with the Mu-
    sic Teacher. Hard to see because of the flashing light.
Jungle Warriors (1985) . . . . Laura McCashin
Magazines:
Playboy (Apr 1974)
    . . . . Foreplay (A Comedy in Three Acts)
••• 112—Topless with Jerry Orbach while hanging onto
rope.

Moro, Alicia

Films:
Velvet Dreams. . . . . .n.a.
The Exterminators of the Year 3000 (1985; Italian)
. . . . Trash
Slugs (1988; Spanish) . . . . Maureen Watson
Hot Blood (1989; Spanish) . . . . Alicia
• 0:00—Buns and lower frontal nudity in stable with
  Ricardo. Long shot.
• 0:06—In bra and panties with Julio, then buns and
  topless. Looks like a body double because hair
  doesn't match.

• Morrell, Carla

Twin sister of Carmen Morrell.
Films:
Basket Case 3: The Progeny (1991). . . . . . . Twin #1
•• 0:41—Topless in bed with her twin sister and Duane's brother.
• 1:29—Brief breast, lying in bed with her twin sister
  and Duane's brother after the end credits.
Made for Cable TV:
Sessions: Episode 2 (1991; HBO). . . . . Twin #2
Magazines:
Playboy's Book of Lingerie (Sep 1991) . . . . . Herself
••• 25—Topless.
••• 54—Full frontal nudity with her sister.
Playboy's Book of Lingerie (Nov 1991) . . . . . Herself
••• 28—Topless with her sister.

• Morrell, Carmen

Twin sister of Carla Morrell.
Films:
Basket Case 3: The Progeny (1991). . . . . . . Twin #2
•• 0:41—Topless in bed with her twin sister and Du-
  ane's brother.
• 1:29—Brief breast, lying in bed with her twin sister
  and Duane's brother after the end credits.
Made for Cable TV:
Sessions: Episode 2 (1991; HBO). . . . . Twin #1
Magazines:
Playboy's Book of Lingerie (Sep 1991) . . . . . Herself
••• 54—Full frontal nudity with her sister.

Playboy's Book of Lingerie (Nov 1991) . . . . . Herself
••• 28—Topless with her sister.

Morris, Anita

Films:
The Happy Hooker (1975) . . . . . Linda Jo/Mary Smith
• 0:59—Topless lying on table while a customer puts
  ice cream all over her.
• 1:24—Topless covered with whipped cream getting
  it sprayed off with champagne by another customer.
So Fine (1981) . . . . So Fine Dancer
The Hotel New Hampshire (1984) . . . . Ronda Ray
Maria's Lovers (1985). . . . . Mrs. Wynic
Absolute Beginners (1986; British) . . . . Dido Lament
Blue City (1986). . . . . Molvina Kerch
Ruthless People (1986). . . . . Carol
18 Again! (1988) . . . . Madeline
Aria (1988; U.S./British) . . . . Phoebe
Bloodhounds of Broadway (1989) . . . . . Missouri Martin
Made for Cable TV:
Tales From the Crypt: Spoiled (1991; HBO) . . . . Fuschia
TV:
Berrengers (1985) . . . . Babs Berrenger

Morris, Kim

Video Tapes:
Playboy Video Calendar 1988 (1987). . . . . Playmate
Wet and Wild (1989) . . . . Model
Magazines:
Playboy (Mar 1986) . . . . Playmate

• Morrow, Deirdre

Films:
Carnal Crimes (1991) . . . . Leggy Girl
• 1:22—Buns, in G-string, leaning over to talk to Renny and Stanley.
Mirror Images (1991) . . . . Slave Girl
••• 0:58—Buns in G-string, then topless with masked
  guy.
••• 1:00—Topless on bed with masked guy and Julie
  Strain.

• Morrow, Sue

Made for Cable Movies:
Soft Touch (1987; Playboy) . . . . Ashley Keyes
(Shown on *The Playboy Channel* as *Birds in Paradise*.)
• 0:01—Topless during opening credits.
• 0:02—Topless with her two girlfriends during the
  opening credits.
•• 0:19—Topless taking off her T-shirt in bed. More
  topless sleeping, then waking up.
• 0:20—Topless getting out of bed.
•• 0:22—Topless making love with a guy.
• 0:23—Topless in bed.
•• 0:53—Topless on bed with Ensign Landers.
••• 0:59—Topless and buns in play pool with Landers.
• 1:19—Topless in stills during end credits.

Soft Touch II (1987; Playboy) . . . . Ashley Keyes
(Shown on *The Playboy Channel* as *Birds in Paradise*.)
- 0:01—Topless during opening credits.
- 0:02—Topless with her two girlfriends during the opening credits.
- •• 0:26—Topless sitting and sunbathing on boat.
- 0:50—Brief topless in the water.
- 0:52—Topless during strip poker game, then covered with whipped cream.
- •• 0:56—Full frontal nudity getting out of bed.

• Mucciante, Christie
Films:
Fatal Pulse (1987). . . . . Karen
- •• 0:52—Topless, getting dressed for bed.
Tango & Cash (1989) . . . . .Dressing Room Girl
- 1:06—Brief topless in dressing room. (She's the first topless blonde.)

Mulford, Nancy
Films:
Any Man's Death (1989) . . . . Tara
Act of Piracy (1990). . . . . Laura Warner
- 0:11—Very brief left breast under Gary Busey in bed. Dark, hard to see.
- 0:12—In white lingerie, walking around on the boat shooting everybody.
- 0:34—Brief, upper half of left breast, in bed with Ray Sharkey.
- 0:35—In white nightgown.

• Mullen, Beckie
Films:
Affairs of the Heart (1992). . . . . Pool Girl
Private Screenings.
- ••• 0:52—Topless, after taking off her bikini top, then diving into pool.
- •• 0:53—Topless, lying on towel on diving board, then turning over.
Made for Cable Movies:
Cast a Deadly Spell (1991; HBO). . . . . .Drop Dead Babe
Made for Cable TV:
Sessions: Episode 2 (1991; HBO). . . . . Vicki
Video Tapes:
The Perfect Body Contest (1987) . . . . .Beckie
Wild Bikinis (1987) . . . . Herself
Bikini Blitz (1990) . . . . .Model
Rock Video Girls (1991). . . . . Herself
Magazines:
Playboy's Book of Lingerie (Jan 1991) . . . . . . Herself
- 15—Buns.
Playboy's Book of Lingerie (May 1992) . . . . . Herself
- •• 18—Right breast.
Playboy's Book of Lingerie (Jul 1992) . . . . . . Herself
- ••• 20—Topless.

Mullen, Patty
Films:
Doom Asylum (1987). . . . . Judy LaRue/Kiki LaRue
In red two piece swimsuit a lot.
Frankenhooker (1990) . . . . Elizabeth
- •• 1:01—Topless and buns in garter belt and stockings, in room with a customer.
Magazines:
Penthouse (Aug 1986). .Pet
Penthouse (Jan 1988) . . . . Pet of the Year

Müller, Lillian
a.k.a. Liliane Mueller or Yulis Ruvaal.
Films:
Sex on the Run (1979; German/French/Italian)
. . . . .Angela
a.k.a. Some Like It Cool
a.k.a. Casanova and Co.
- ••• 0:15—Second woman (blonde) to take off her clothes with the other two women, nude. Long scene.
Best Defense (1984). . . . . French Singer
Magazines:
Playboy (Aug 1975) . . . . Playmate
Playboy (Nov 1977) . . . . Sex in Cinema 77
- •• 166—Topless.
Playboy's Nudes (Oct 1990) . . . . Herself
- •• 101—Right breast and lower frontal nudity.

Munro, Caroline
Films:
Captain Kronos, Vampire Hunter (1972; British)
. . . . Carla
- 0:24—"Nude" scene in the barn with Kronos. Dark, strategically placed shadows hide everything.
- 0:51—In barn again, but now she has strategically placed hair hiding everything.
The Golden Voyage of Sinbad (1974; British)
. . . . .Margiana
- 0:51—Very brief right nipple, sticking out of top when Sinbad carries her from the boat to the shore. Long shot.
The Spy Who Loved Me (1977; British) . . . . . . .Naomi
Starcrash (1979; Italian) . . . . Stella Star
The Last Horror Film (1984) . . . . Jana Bates
Slaughter High (1986) . . . . Carol
- 0:19—Walking around her house in lingerie and a robe.

Murakoshi, Suzen
Films:
Wall Street (1987). . . . . Girl in Bed
- 0:13—Brief full frontal nudity getting out of bed and walking past the camera in Charlie Sheen's bedroom (slightly out of focus).
Quick Change (1990). . . . . .Hostage

• *Murgia, Antonella*

Films:
Reborn (1978). . . . . Maria
   • 0:35—Topless in bed with Michael Moriarty.
   •• 0:37—More topless in bed with Moriarty.
   ••• 0:38—Nude, getting out of bed.
   ••• 0:39—Nude, walking around in bedroom.
Anguish (1987; Spanish). . . . . Ticket Girl

• *Murray, Beverley*

Films:
Cathy's Curse (1976; Canadian). . . . . Vivian
   • 1:13—Very, very brief left breast, while jumping
      around in bathtub, brushing leaches off her body.
The Last Straw (1987; Canadian). . . . . Nurse Thompson

• *Muscarella, Lynn*

Hostess of Manhattan Cable TV "Voyeurvision" live call-in
tele-fantasy show.
Made for Cable TV:
Real Sex 4 (1992; HBO) . . . . Voyeurvision
   • 0:33—Buns, in lingerie doing her phone-in sex cable
      TV show.
Magazines:
Playboy (Jun 1992) . . . . Video Vamp
   ••• 78-83—Topless and buns.

Muti, Ornella

Films:
Appassionata (1979; Italian) . . . . Virginia
   • 0:32—Brief topless in bathroom when her father rips
      open her T-shirt while looking for hickies.
   0:57—Partial left breast, leaning over to tempt her
      father.
   1:07—In white bra, changing clothes during party.
   1:21—In white bra, in bathroom, giving herself hick-
      ies.
   1:25—In white bra in bed, showing her father her
      pubic hair.
   • 1:35—Buns, getting out of bed with her father. Brief
      side of left breast when leaving the room.
Summer Affair (1979). Lisa
   • 0:44—Topless silhouette in cave by the water.
   • 1:00—Brief topless getting chased around in the
      grass and by the beach.
Flash Gordon (1980). . . . . Princess Aura
Love and Money (1980) . . . . Catherine Stockheinz
   0:31—In bra and panties in bedroom with Ray Shar-
      key getting dressed.
Famous T & A (1982). Lisa
   (No longer available for purchase, check your video
   store for rental.)
   •• 0:07—Topless in scenes from *Summer Affair*. Nude
      underwater and running around the beach.
Tales of Ordinary Madness (1983). . . . . Cass

Swann in Love (1984; French/German)
   . . . . Odette de Crêcy
   a.k.a. Un Amour de Swann
   •• 1:15—Brief left breast, making love with Jeremy
      Irons.
   ••• 1:28—Topless sitting on bed talking to Irons.
Oscar (1991) . . . . Sofia Provolone
Once Upon A Crime (1992) . . . . n.a.
Made for Cable TV:
The Hitchhiker: True Believer . . . . n.a.
   (Available on *The Hitchhiker, Volume 3*.)
Magazines:
Playboy (Dec 1980) . . . . Sex Stars of 1980
   •• 245—Right breast.

• *Myers, Cynthia*

Films:
Beyond the Valley of the Dolls (1970)
   . . . . Casey Anderson
   Russ Meyer Film.
   (Not available on video tape.)
Molly and Lawless John (1972). . . . . Dolly
Magazines:
Playboy (Dec 1968) . . . . Playmate
Playboy (Jan 1974). . . . . Twenty Years of Playmates
   ••• 109—Topless while kneeling on bed.
Playboy (Dec 1980) . . . . Bunny Birthday
   ••• 152—Topless.

• *Nail, Joanne*

Films:
Switchblade Sisters (1975) . . . . Maggie
   • 0:21—Very, very brief right breast in ripped blouse
      when she tries to rip Dominic's shirt off.
The Gumball Rally (1976). . . . . Jane
The Visitor (1980; Italian/U.S.) . . . . Barbara Collins

Nankervis, Debbie

Films:
Alvin Purple (1973; Australian) . . . . Girl in Blue Movie
   •• 1:04—Nude, running after Alvin in bedroom during
      showing of movie.
Libido (1973; Australian) . . . . First Girl
Alvin Rides Again (1974; Australian)
   . . . . Woman Cricketer

• *Nann, Erika*

Films:
Death Feud (1989). Hooker
Millenium Countdown (1991) . . . . n.a.
Mind Twister (1992) . . . . n.a.
Night Rhythms (1992) . . . . Alex
   (Unrated version reviewed.)
   ••• 1:00—Buns in G-string and bra, then topless, un-
      dressing in front of Martin Hewitt and making love
      with him.

• Nanty, Isabelle
Films:
Red Kiss (1985; French) . . . . Jeanine
On a Vole Charlie Spencer! (1987) . . . . Suzette
The Passion of Beatrice (1988; French)
. . . . La Nourrice
  •• 1:53—Right breast, offering her breast milk to Arnaud.
Tatie Danielle (1991; French). . . . . Sandrine

Naples, Toni
Films:
Doctor Detroit (1983) . . . . Dream Girl
Chopping Mall (1986) . . . . Bathing Beauty
Deathstalker II (1987) . . . . Sultana
  • 0:55—Brief topless in strobe lights making love with
the bad guy. Hard to see because of blinking lights.
Might be a body double, don't see her face.
Transylvania Twist (1990) . . . . Maxine

Napoli, Susan
a.k.a. Stephanie Ryan.
Susan Napoli is her real name.
Films:
Wildest Dreams (1987) . . . . Punk #4
  • 0:21—Brief left breast, leaning backwards on couch
with her boyfriend.
Party Incorporated (1989). . . . . .n.a.
a.k.a. Party Girls
Frankenhooker (1990). . . . . Anise
  • 0:42—Brief left breast on bed with Amber, taking off
her top. Brief topless after Angel explodes.
  • 0:43—Topless, kneeling on bed screaming before
exploding.
Street Hunter (1990) . . . . Eddie's Girl
  •• 0:40—Topless in bed with Eddie (she's on the left,
wearing white panties).
Magazines:
Penthouse (Feb 1986) . . . . Pet

Nassar, Deborah Ann
Films:
Stripped to Kill (1987) . . . . Dazzle
  ••• 0:07—Topless wearing a G-string dancing on stage
with a motorcycle prop.
Dance of the Damned (1988) . . . . La Donna
  • 0:07—Brief topless during dance routine in club.

Natividad, Francesca "Kitten"
Vital statistics: 5' 3" tall, 116 pounds, 44-25-35.
Adult Films:
Bad Girls IV . . . . .n.a.
  •• 0:26—Topless in back of pizza truck.
Bodacious Ta-Tas . . . . .n.a.
Titillation (1982) . . . . .n.a.
Topless.
Films:
Up! (1976) . . . . Greek Chorus
Russ Meyer film.

Beneath the Valley of the Ultravixens (1979)
. . . . Lavonia & Lola Langusta
The Lady in Red (1979) . . . . . . .Uncredited Partygoer
  • 0:39—Brief topless outside during party.
An Evening with Kitten (1983) . . . . Herself
  •• 0:02—Topless busting out of her blouse.
  •• 0:09—Topless in miniature city scene.
  • 0:11—Brief topless on stage.
  • 0:20—Left breast, in bed with a vampire.
  ••• 0:21—Topless and buns in G-string during dance in
large champagne glass prop. Long scene.
  ••• 0:24—Topless on beach in mermaid costume with
little shell pasties.
  ••• 0:25—Topless in the glass again.
  •• 0:28—Topless in and out of glass.
  •• 0:29—Brief topless during end credits.
My Tutor (1983) . . . . Anna Maria
  ••• 0:10—Topless in room with Matt Lattanzi, then lying
in bed.
Doin' Time (1984) . . . . .Tassle
Takin' It Off (1984) . . . . .Betty Bigones
  •• 0:01—Topless dancing on stage.
  ••• 0:04—Topless and buns dancing on stage.
  •• 0:29—Topless in the Doctor's office.
  •• 0:32—Nude dancing in the Psychiatrists' office.
  ••• 0:39—Nude in bed with a guy during fantasy sequence playing with vegetables and fruits.
  •• 0:49—Topless in bed covered with popcorn.
  • 0:51—Nude doing a dance routine in the library.
  ••• 1:09—Nude splashing around in a clear plastic bathtub on stage.
  •• 1:20—Nude at a fat farm dancing.
  •• 1:24—Nude running in the woods in slow motion.
The Wild Life (1984) . . . . Stripper #2
  ••• 0:50—Topless doing strip routine in a bar just before
a fight breaks out.
Night Patrol (1985). . . . . Hippie Woman
  •• 1:01—Topless in kitchen with Pat Paulsen, the other
police officer and her hippie boyfriend.
Takin' It All Off (1987) . . . . .Betty Bigones
  ••• 0:12—Nude, washing herself in the shower.
  •• 0:39—Nude, on stage in a giant glass, then topless
backstage in her dressing room.
  •• 0:42—Topless in flashbacks from *Takin' It Off.*
  0:46—Topless in group in the studio.
  ••• 0:53—Nude, dancing on the deck outside. Some
nice slow motion shots.
  •• 1:16—Topless on stage in club.
  ••• 1:23—Nude, dancing with all the other women on
stage.
The Tomb (1987) . . . . Stripper
  ••• 0:19—Topless and buns in G-string dancing on
stage.
  • 0:21—Brief topless again.
Another 48 Hrs. (1990) . . . . Girl in Movie
  • 1:04—Brief topless on movie screen when two motorcycles crash through it.
Buford's Beach Bunnies (1991). . . . . n.a.

The Girl I Want (1991) .n.a.
Video Tapes:
The Stripper of the Year (1986). . . . . Kitten
• • • 0:51—Nude, stripping out of black outfit.
• • 0:53—Topless on stage with the other contestants.
Inside Out 2 (1992) . . Busty Dusty/Profiles in Cleavage
(Unrated version reviewed.)
• • 0:56—Bouncing her breasts while wearing pasties.
• 1:02—Dancing in disco wearing pasties. B&W.
• 1:03—Brief topless with pasties.
Magazines:
Playboy (Oct 1980) . . . . The World of Playboy
• 11—Topless in small photo.
Playboy (Nov 1982) . . . . Sex in Cinema 1982
• • • 160—Topless.
Playboy (Nov 1990) . . . . Sex in Cinema 1990
• • 138—Topless in still from *Another 48 Hrs.*

• *Neal, Billie*
Films:
Down by Law (1986) . . . . Bobbie
• • 0:11—Topless lying in bed, talking to Jack. Medium
long shot. Long scene.
• • • 0:12—Side view of right breast, partial lower frontal
nudity, lying in bed.
• • 0:13—More topless, medium long shot again, lying
in bed.
• • 0:14—Right breast when Jack covers her up with
sheet.
The January Man (1988) . . . . Gwen
Born on the Fourth of July (1989) . . . Nurse Washington
Internal Affairs (1990) . . . . Dorian's Wife
Jacob's Ladder (1990) .Della
A Kiss Before Dying (1991) . . . . Nurse
Mortal Thoughts (1991) . . . . Linda Nealon

Neal, Christy
Films:
Coming Together (1978). . . . . Vicky Hughes
a.k.a. A Matter of Love
0:12—In bra and panties, in bedroom with Frank.
• 0:30—Brief right breast in shower with Angie.
• 0:37—Topless and buns making love standing up in
front of sliding glass door with Frank. Quick cuts.
• 0:49—Brief topless again during flashbacks.
• 0:57—Topless with Angie and Richard.
• 1:05—Topless on beach with Angie. Long shot.
Take Down (1978) . . . . Suzette Smith

Negoda, Natalya
Films:
Little Vera (1988; U.S.S.R.) . . . . Vera
0:15—Very brief topless and buns getting dressed.
Dark, hard to see.
• • • 0:50—Topless making love with Sergei.
• • 1:05—Topless taking off her dress in the kitchen.

Back in the U.S.S.R. (1992) . . . . Lena
• • 0:46—Side view of left breast, making love with
Sloan in the bathtub. Brief right breast when Dimitri
comes into the bathroom.
Made for Cable Movies:
The Comrades of Summer (1992; HBO). . . . . . . .Tanya
Magazines:
Playboy (May 1989). . . . . That Glasnost Girl
• • • 140-149—Topless.
Playboy (Nov 1989) . . . . Sex in Cinema 1989
• • 131—Topless in out-of-focus still from *Little Vera.*
Playboy (Dec 1989) . . . . Holy Sex Stars of 1989!
• • • 184—Topless.
Playboy (Dec 1991) . . . . Sex Stars 1991
• • • 183—Left breast.

Neidhardt, Elke
Films:
Alvin Purple (1973; Australian)
. . . . Woman in Blue Movie
• • 1:07—In red bra, then full frontal nudity in bedroom
with Alvin during showing of film.
Libido (1973; Australian) . . . . Penelope
Inside Looking Out (1977; Australian) . . . . . . .Marianne

Nelligan, Kate
Films:
The Romantic Englishwoman (1975; British/French)
. . . . .Isabel
Dracula (1979). . . . . Lucy
Crossover (1980; Canadian). . . . . Peabody
a.k.a. Mr. Patman
Eye of the Needle (1981) . . . . Lucy
• • 0:52—Brief left breast, while drying herself off in the
bathroom when Donald Sutherland accidentally
sees her.
1:15—Top half of buns, making love in bed with
Sutherland.
• 1:26—Topless making love in bed with Sutherland
after he killed her husband. Dark, hard to see.
Without a Trace (1983) . . . . Susan Selky
Eleni (1985) . . . . Eleni
Frankie & Johnny (1991) . . . . Cora
0:34—Upper half of buns, in bed on top of Al Paci-
no. Don't see her face.
The Prince of Tides (1991) . . . . Lila Wingo
Shadows and Fog (1992) . . . . n.a.
Made for Cable Movies:
Control (1987; HBO) . . . . n.a.
The Diamond Fleece (1992; USA). . . . . Holly
Made for TV Movies:
Therese Raquin (1981) . . . . n.a.
Kojak: The Price of Justice (1987) . . . . Kitty

Nero, Toni
Films:
Silent Night, Deadly Night (1984) . . . . Pamela
• 0:30—Brief right breast twice just before Billy gets
stabbed during fantasy scene.

• 0:42—Topless in stock room when Andy attacks her.
• 0:44—Topless in stock room struggling with Billy, then getting killed by him.

Silent Night, Deadly Night, Part 2 (1986)
.... Pamela
•• 0:22—Topless in back of toy store in flashback from *Silent Night, Deadly Night*.
Commando Squad (1987) .... Putita

Newmar, Julie

Films:
Mackenna's Gold (1969) .... Hesh-ke
1:09—Brief topless and buns under water. Long shots, hard to see anything. Not clear because of all the dirty water. Brief buns, getting out of the pond.
Love Scenes (1984)...................... Belinda
a.k.a. Ecstacy
Streetwalkin' (1985) .... Queen Bee
Deep Space (1988)................... Lady Elaine
Ghosts Can't Do It (1989) .... Angel
Nudity Required (1989)................... Irina
• 0:57—Side of left breast and side view of buns behind textured shower door with Buddy.
TV:
Batman (1966-67)................. The Catwoman

Nicholas, Angela

Films:
Psychos in Love (1987) .... Diane
Wildest Dreams (1987) .... Claudia
•• 1:01—Topless typing on computer doing Bobby's book keeping.
Alien Space Avenger (1988) .... Doris
• 0:56—Brief topless making whoopee with Jaimie Gillis.
••• 0:57—More topless making love on top of Gillis while killing him.
Galactic Gigolo (1989) .... Peggy Sue Peggy
a.k.a. Club Earth
Affairs of the Heart (1992)............. Dreamgirl
Private Screenings.
•• 0:14—In bra, then left breast while in bed with the Geek.
Magazines:
Penthouse (Aug 1985) .... Pet

• Nichols, Kelly

Adult film actress.
Films:
The Toolbox Murders (1978)................ Victim
Deathmask (1983) .... n.a.
In Love (1983) .... n.a.
Delivery Boys (1984)................... Elizabeth
• 0:44—Top half of right breast, while eating rolls with a young boy.
Sno-Line (1984) .... Ellen

• Nickson-Soul, Julia

Films:
The Chinatown Murders: Man Against the Mob (1989)
.... Kei Lee
1:15—Topless, taking off her dress in bedroom in front of George Peppard. Very dark. It looks like she's wearing pasties when she gets into bed.
1:18—Very brief topless getting out of bed. It looks like she's wearing the pastie things again.
K2 (1991) .... Cindy
• 0:26—Briefly nude, getting up out of bed and putting robe on.

• Nicolodi, Daria

Films:
Deep Red (1976; Italian) .... Gianna
Beyond the Door II (1977; Italian) .... Dora
• 0:30—Buns, in the shower.
• 0:47—Brief left breast in gaping nightgown, sitting up in bed.
Inferno (1980; Italian) .... Countess Elise
Macaroni (1985; Italian)............. Laura Di Falco
Terror at the Opera (1989; Italian) .... Mira

Nielsen, Brigitte

Ex-wife of actor Sylvester Stallone.
Films:
Red Sonja (1985) .... Red Sonja
• 0:01—Half of right nipple through torn outfit, while sitting up.
Rocky IV (1985) .... Ludmilla
Cobra (1986)......................... Ingrid
Beverly Hills Cop II (1987) .... Karla Fry
Bye Bye Baby (1989; Italian) .... Lisa
• 0:20—Brief side view of right breast, while lying on a guy in bed. Nice buns shot also.
Domino (1989)........................ Domino
• 0:05—Right breast, lying down next to swimming pool, topless getting out.
••• 1:04—Right breast, caressing herself in a white lingerie body suit, wearing a black wig.
976-EVIL II: The Astral Factor (1991) .... Agnes
Made for TV Movies:
Murder by Moonlight (1989)................. n.a.
Magazines:
Playboy (Aug 1986) .... Brigitte
•• 70-77—Topless.
Playboy (Dec 1987) .... Gitte the Great
••• 80-93—Nice.
Playboy (Feb 1988) .... The Year in Sex
••• 129—Topless at the beach.
Playboy (Dec 1988) .... Sex Stars of 1988
• 187—Buns and side view of right breast.
Playboy (Jan 1989).......... Women of the Eighties
•• 251—Topless.

Niemi, Lisa

Wife of actor Patrick Swayze.

Films:

Slam Dance (1987) . . . . Ms. Schell
••• 0:54—Nude in Tom Hulce's apartment.
• 1:00—Topless, dead, lying on the floor in Hulce's apartment.
She's Having a Baby (1988). . . . . .Model
Steel Dawn (1988) . . . . Kasha

TV:

Super Force (1990) . . . . Carla Frost

Nirvana, Yana

Films:

Cinderella (1977) . . . . Drucella
• 0:02—Topless taking off clothes with her sister Maribella to let Cinderella wash.
• 0:06—Brief topless sitting up in bed with Maribella.
Brewster's Millions (1985) . . . . .Louise
Club Life (1987) . . . . Butchette
He's My Girl (1987). . . . . Olga
Another 48 Hrs. (1990). . . . . CHP Officer

TV:

The Last Precinct (1986) . . . . Sgt. Martha Haggerty

Nix, Stacey

See: Dare, Barbara.

Noel, Monique

Video Tapes:

Wet and Wild (1989) .Model

Magazines:

Playboy (May 1989) . . . . Playmate
Playboy's Book of Lingerie (Jan 1991) . . . . . . Herself
••• 95—Full frontal nudity.
Playboy's Book of Lingerie (Mar 1991) . . . . . Herself
•• 35—Full frontal nudity.
Playboy's Book of Lingerie (Mar 1992) . . . . . Herself
••• 37—Full frontal nudity.
Playboy's Book of Lingerie (Jul 1992) . . . . . . Herself
•• 82—Side of left breast and buns.
Playboy's Book of Lingerie (Sep 1992) . . . . . Herself
•• 73—Left breast and partial lower frontal nudity.

North, Noelle

Films:

Report to the Commissioner (1975) . . . . Samantha
Slumber Party '57 (1976) . . . . Angie
•• 0:37—Buns, then topless in bed with a party guest of her parents.
Sweater Girls (1978) . . . . .n.a.
Jekyll & Hyde... Together Again (1982). . . . . . . Student

North, Sheree

Films:

Lawman (1971). . . . . .Laura Shelby
(Not available on video tape.)

Norton-Taylor, Judy

TV:

The Waltons (1972-81) . . . . . Mary Ellen Walton Willard

Video Tapes:

Playboy Video Magazine, Volume 10 (1986)
. . . . .Herself
••• 0:45—Nude in still photos.

Magazines:

Playboy (Aug 1985) . . . . The Punch in Judy
••• 77-81—Frontal nudity.
Playboy's Nudes (Oct 1990) . . . . .Herself
•• 20—Side view of right breast.

Novak, Lenka

Films:

Kentucky Fried Movie (1977) . . . . . Linda Chambers
• 0:09—Topless sitting on a couch with two other girls.
Coach (1978) . . . . Marilyn
• 0:10—Very brief topless flashing her breasts along with her girlfriends for their boyfriends.
Vampire Hookers (1979) . . . . Suzy
0:22—In sheer green dress getting into coffin.
0:33—In sheer green dress again.
0:45—In sheer green dress again.
•• 0:51—Topless in bed during the orgy with the guy and the other two Vampire Hookers.

Video Tapes:

Terror on Tape (1985) . . . . Suzy
0:00—Topless scene from *Vampire Hookers*.

Nychols, Darcy

Adult film actress.

Films:

Mugsy's Girls (1985) . . . . .Madame Antoinette
Slammer Girls (1987) . . . . Tank
• 0:17—Topless ripping blouse open while hassling Melody.

Nygren, Mia

Films:

Emmanuelle IV (1984) . . . . .Emmanuelle IV
0:13—Buns, lying on table after plastic surgery.
••• 0:15—Full frontal nudity walking around looking at her new self in the mirror.
• 0:20—Brief topless a couple of times making love on top of a guy getting coached by Sylvia Kristel in dream-like sequence.
•• 0:22—Full frontal nudity taking off blouse in front of Dona.
0:25—Almost making love with a guy in bar.
••• 0:30—Nude undressing in front of Maria.
•• 0:39—Full frontal nudity taking her dress off and getting covered with a white sheet.
••• 0:40—Full frontal nudity lying down and then putting dress back on.
•• 0:45—Full frontal nudity during levitation trick.
0:49—Right bra cup reclining on bed.
• 0:52—Brief topless in stable.

••• 0:54—Topless taking off black dress in chair. Brief lower frontal nudity.

0:57—Brief lower frontal nudity putting on white panties.

• 1:00—Brief topless when Susanna takes her dress off.

• 1:03—Brief right breast making love on ground with a boy.

••• 1:07—Topless walking on beach.

• 1:09—Topless with Dona. Dark.

Plaza Real (1988)..............................n.a.

Magazines:

Playboy (Dec 1984)...............Sex Stars of 1984

• 204—Right breast.

O'Brien, Maureen

Films:

She'll be Wearing Pink Pyjamas (1985; British)

.... Joan

• 0:46—Brief topless making love in bed with Tom. Dark.

Zina (1985; British).........................n.a.

O'Connell, Natalie

Films:

Breeders (1986) .... Donna

• 0:02—Very brief left breast, getting her blouse ripped by creature.

•• 0:44—Topless, sitting up in hospital bed, then buns, walking down the hall.

••• 0:47—More topless and buns, walking around outside.

• 1:10—Brief topless, standing up in the alien nest.

I Was a Teenage T.V. Terrorist (1987)

.... Woman on Audition Line

O'Connell, Taaffe

Films:

Galaxy of Terror (1981)................ Damelia

•• 0:42—Topless getting raped by a giant alien slug. Nice and slimy.

0:46—Buns, covered with slime being discovered by her crew mates.

Caged Fury (1984) ....Honey

•• 0:17—Topless on bed with a guard. Mostly left breast.

0:40—Very, very brief tip of left breast peeking out between arms in shower.

• 1:06—Very brief topless getting blouse ripped open by a guard in the train.

Hot Chili (1985) .... Brigitte

••• 0:21—Topless lying on the bed. Shot with lots of diffusion.

• 0:30—Brief topless playing the drums.

• 1:11—Brief topless in bed making love with Ernie, next to her drunk husband.

Not of This Earth (1988) .... Damelia

• 0:04—Brief topless and buns from *Galaxy of Terror* during the opening credits.

TV:

Blansky's Beauties (1977) ....Hillary S. Prentiss

O'Connor, Glynnis

Films:

Ode to Billy Joe (1976)........... Bobby Lee Hartley

California Dreaming (1978).............. Corky

•• 0:11—Topless pulling her top over her head when T.T. is using the bathroom.

1:12—In white bra, in bed with T.T.

••• 1:14—Topless in bed with T.T.

Those Lips, Those Eyes (1980)............Ramona

• 0:37—Left breast in car with Tom Hulce. Dark, hard to see.

•• 1:12—Topless and buns on bed with Tom Hulce. Dark.

Night Crossing (1981) .... Petra Wetzel

Melanie (1982)......................Melanie

• 0:08—Very brief right breast, while turning over in bed next to Don Johnson.

•• 0:09—Topless, while sitting up and putting on a T-shirt, then getting out of bed.

Made for TV Movies:

The Boy in the Plastic Bubble (1976) .... Gina

Why Me? (1984) ....n.a.

TV:

Sons and Daughters (1974) ....Anita Cramer

O'Grady, Lani

Films:

Massacre at Central High (1976) ....Jane

••• 1:09—Topless walking out of a tent and getting back into it with Rainbeaux Smith and Robert Carradine.

TV:

The Headmaster (1970-71) ....Judy

Eight is Enough (1977-81) ....Mary Bradford

O'Neal, Tatum

Wife of tennis player John McEnroe.

Daughter of actor Ryan O'Neal and actress Joanna Moore.

Films:

Paper Moon (1973) .... Addie Loggins

The Bad News Bears (1976) ....Manda Whurlizer

International Velvet (1978)............. Sarah Brown

Circle of Two (1980) ....Sarah Norton

•• 0:56—Topless standing behind a chair in Richard Burton's studio talking to him.

Little Darlings (1980) .... Ferris

• 0:35—Very, very brief half of left nipple, sticking out of swimsuit top when she comes up for air after falling into the pool to get Armand Assante's attention.

Certain Fury (1985) .... Scarlet

Magazines:

Playboy (Nov 1982) .... Sex in Cinema 1982

•• 165—Topless photo from *Circle of Two*.

• O'Neill, Maggie

Films:
Gorillas in the Mist (1988). . . . . Kim
Under Suspicion (1992). . . . . Hazel
- 0:02—Topless and lower frontal nudity in shower with Liam Neeson.
- 0:03—Very brief right breast, while ducking to avoid shotgun blast.

O'Neill, Remy

Films:
Angel of H.E.A.T. (1981) . . . . Andrea Shockley
a.k.a. The Protectors, Book I
- • 0:43—Topless, wearing a blue swimsuit, wrestling in the mud with Mary Woronov.
Erotic Images (1983) . . . . Vickie Coleman
- • • 0:04—Topless sitting in chaise lounge talking to Britt Ekland about sex survey. Long scene.
- • 0:06—Topless in bed with Marvin. Brief lower frontal nudity.
- • • 0:07—Brief left breast in spa with TV repairman, then brief topless.
Hollywood Hot Tubs (1984) . . . . Pam Landers
- • 1:00—Brief right breast in hot tub with Jeff.
Return to Horror High (1987) . . . . Esther Molvania
To Die For (1988) . . . . Jane
Hollywood Hot Tubs 2—Educating Crystal (1989)
. . . . Pam Landers
0:57—Swinging tassels on the tips of her belly dancing top.
The Forbidden Dance (1990) . . . . Robin
To Die For 2 (1991). . . . . Jane

O'Reilly, Erin

Films:
How Sweet It Is (1968) . . . . Tour Girl
Little Fauss and Big Halsy (1970). . . . . . . Sylvene McFall
T. R. Baskin (1971) . . . . Kathy
Blume in Love (1973). . . . . Cindy
- 0:40—Topless and buns, getting out of bed with George Segal.
Busting (1974) . . . . Doris

O'Reilly, Kathryn

Films:
Jack's Back (1987). . . . . Hooker
Puppet Master (1989) . . . . Carissa Stamford
- 0:41—Left breast in bathtub, covered with bubbles.
- 0:43—Brief left breast getting out of tub. Nipple covered with bubbles.
0:50—Riding on Frank in bed. Don't see anything, but still exciting. Very brief buns under sheer nightgown when she gets off Frank.
1:11—Right breast under sheer black nightgown, dead sitting at the table. Blood on her face.

O'Shea, Missy

Films:
Blow Out (1981) . . . . Dancing Coed
0:00—Dancing in sheer nightgown while a campus guard watches from outside the window.
New York Nights (1981) . . . . The Model
0:30—In white bra in restroom making love with the photographer.
- • 0:37—in black bra, panties, garter belt and stockings then topless taking off bra and getting into bed.
- • 0:40—Topless on floor when the photographer throws her on the floor and rips her bra off.
- • • 0:41—Full frontal nudity putting bathrobe on.
- • 0:44—Topless standing in front of a mirror with short black hair and a moustache getting dressed to look like a guy.

O'Toole, Annette

Films:
Smile (1974) . . . . Doria Houston
0:34—In white bra and panties in dressing room.
1:06—In white bra and slip talking to Joan Prather in bedroom.
One on One (1977) . . . . Janet Hays
King of the Gypsies (1978). . . . . Sharon
Foolin' Around (1980) . . . . Susan
48 Hrs. (1982) . . . . Elaine
Cat People (1982) . . . . Alice Perrin
- • • 1:30—In a bra, then topless undressing in locker room.
- 1:31—Some topless shots of her in the pool. Distorted because of the water.
- 1:33—Brief right breast, after getting out of the pool.
Superman III (1983) . . . . Lana Lang
Cross My Heart (1987) . . . . Kathy
0:44—In pink bra standing in bedroom with Martin Short.
- • 0:46—Left breast, in bed with Short.
- • 0:48—Topless in bed when Short heads under the covers.
- • 0:49—Brief topless again getting her purse.
- 1:05—Brief topless and buns, dressing after Short finds out about her daughter.
Love at Large (1990) . . . . Mrs. King
Made for Cable Movies:
Best Legs in the 8th Grade (1984; HBO). . . . . n.a.
Miniseries:
The Kennedys of Massachusetts (1990)
. . . . Rose Fitzgerald
Made for TV Movies:
Love for Rent (1979) . . . . n.a.
Stand by Your Man (1981). . . . . n.a.
The Dreamer of Oz (1990). . . . . Maud
Stephen King's "It" (1990) . . . . Beverly Marsh
Magazines:
Playboy (Nov 1982) . . . . Sex in Cinema 1982
166—Buns, in a photo from *48 Hours*, but scene is not on video tape.

Obregon, Ana

Films:
Bolero (1984) . . . . Catalina Terry
• 1:32—Brief topless making love with Robert.
Killing Machine (1986) . . . . .Liza

Ohana, Claudia

Films:
Erendira (1983; Brazilian) . . . . Erendira
• 0:14—Topless getting fondled by a guy against her will.
•• 0:26—Topless lying in bed sweating and crying after having to have sex with an army of men.
••• 1:04—Topless lying in bed sleeping.
1:08—Brief topless getting out of bed. Long shot, hard to see.
•• 1:24—Topless and buns on bed with Ulysses.
Priceless Beauty (1989; Italian) . . . . .Lisa
Magazines:
Playboy (Oct 1984) . . . . The Girls from Brazil
•• 88-89—Nude.
Playboy (Dec 1984) . . . . Sex Stars of 1984
•• 205—Left breast, leaning on table.

Olin, Lena

Films:
Fanny and Alexander (1983; Swedish/French/German)
. . . . .n.a.
After the Rehearsal (1984; Swedish) . . . . Anna Egerman
The Unbearable Lightness of Being (1988)
. . . . Sabina
•• 0:03—Topless in bed with Tomas looking at themselves in a mirror.
0:17—In black bra and panties looking at herself in a mirror on the floor.
1:21—In black bra, panties, garter belt and stockings.
•• 1:29—Topless and buns while Tereza photographs her. Long shots, hard to see.
• 1:43—Very brief left breast, in bed with Tomas.
2:32—Brief topless in B&W photo found in a drawer by Tomas.
Enemies, A Love Story (1989) . . . . Masha
•• 0:16—In white bra, then brief topless several times in bed with Ron Silver. Topless again after making love and starting to make love again.
Havana (1990) . . . . Bobby Duran

• Oliver, Anne Marie

Films:
Spring Fever USA (1988) . . . . Rita Durango
a.k.a. Lauderdale
•• 1:02—Topless during wet T-shirt contest.
Summer Job (1989) . . . . Kathy's Friend #2

Oliver, Leslie

Films:
The Student Teachers (1973) . . . . .n.a.

Thunderbolt and Lightfoot (1974) . . . . . . Teenager
•• 1:16—Brief topless in bed when robbers break in and George Kennedy watches her.

Oliver, Pita

Films:
Deadly Companion (1979) . . . . .Lorraine
• 0:14—Very brief left breast, then very brief topless sitting up in bed during Michael Sarrazin's daydream. Dark.
1:32—Brief full frontal nudity, dead on bed when Susan Clark comes into the bedroom.
Prom Night (1980) . . . . Vicki
•• 0:35—Brief buns, mooning Mr. Sykes outside of tennis court.

• Olivia, Lorraine

Video Tapes:
Playboy Video Calendar 1992 (1991) . . . . .May
••• 0:18—Full frontal nudity in the desert.
••• 0:19—Nude in Egyptian bed fantasy.
Playboy Video Centerfold: Lisa Matthews (1991)
. . . . Playmate
••• 0:28—Nude in the desert, then washing an old car, then on an airplane, then in Egyptian style bedroom.
Magazines:
Playboy (Nov 1990) . . . . Playmate
Playboy's Book of Lingerie (Nov 1991) . . . . .Herself
•• 105—Side of left breast and partial lower frontal nudity.
Playboy's Book of Lingerie (Mar 1992) . . . . . Herself
•• 24-25—Topless and buns.
Playboy's Book of Lingerie (May 1992) . . . . Herself
••• 28—Full frontal nudity.
Playboy's Book of Lingerie (Jul 1992) . . . . . . Herself
••• 9—Full frontal nudity.
••• 70-71—Nude.
Playboy's Book of Lingerie (Sep 1992) . . . . . Herself
•• 29—Topless in wet bodysuit.

Ono, Yoko

Wife of the late singer John Lennon.
Films:
Imagine: John Lennon (1988) . . . . .Herself
• 0:43—Nude in B&W photos from John Lennon's White Album.
0:57—Brief full frontal nudity from album cover again during an interview.
1:27—Almost topless in bed with Lennon.

Otis, Carré

Model.
Wife of actor Mickey Rourke.
Films:
Wild Orchid (1990) . . . . .Emily Reed
•• 0:51—Left breast in mirror looking at herself while getting dressed.

••• 1:01—Topless when a guy takes off her dress while Mickey Rourke watches.

••• 1:02—Right breast, then topless on the floor with Jerome.

• 1:31—Brief topless in flashback with Jerome.

• 1:42—Topless opening her blouse for Rourke.

••• 1:44—Nude making love with Rourke. Nice and sweaty.

Magazines:

Playboy (Jun 1990) . . . . Wild Orchid

••• 83-87—Nude in photos from *Wild Orchid*.

Playboy (Nov 1990) . . . . Sex in Cinema 1990

•• 146—Topless in still from *Wild Orchid*.

Owens, Susie

Films:

They Bite (1991) . . . . Kate

• 1:01—Right breast, while lying on the beach after getting attacked.

••• 1:02—Topless and buns, while in bed on top of a guy before killing him.

Video Tapes:

Playboy Video Calendar 1989 (1988) . . . . . . August

••• 0:29—Nude.

Wet and Wild (1989) .Model

Playmates at Play (1990) . . . . .Gotta Dance

Magazines:

Playboy (Mar 1988) . . . . Playmate

Playboy's Book of Lingerie (Jan 1991) . . . . . . Herself

•• 20—Topless.

Pacula, Joanna

Films:

Gorky Park (1983) . . . . Irina

•• 1:20—Brief topless in bed making love with William Hurt.

Not Quite Paradise (1986; British) . . . . .Gila

a.k.a. Not Quite Jerusalem

• 1:04—Left breast, lying in bed with Sam Robards.

Death Before Dishonor (1987) . . . . Elli

The Kiss (1988) . . . . Felice

•• 0:49—Side view topless making love with a guy. Intercut with Meredith Salenger seeing a model of a body spurt blood.

• 0:57—Topless covered with body paint doing a ceremony in a hotel room.

•• 1:24—Brief right breast, while making love with a guy on bed while Salenger is asleep in the other room.

Sweet Lies (1989) . . . . Joëlle

Marked for Death (1990) . . . . Leslie

Husbands and Lovers (1991; Italian) . . . . Helena

(Unrated version reviewed.)

••• 0:03—Topless, making love on top of Julian Sands in bed. Left breast, while lying in bed after.

••• 0:10—Nude, walking around and getting into bed with Sands.

••• 0:18—Topless in bathroom, brushing her teeth, then getting dressed.

• 0:32—Buns and topless, getting into the shower with Sands.

• 0:35—Brief topless getting into bed.

•• 0:37—Topless in white panties, putting on stockings.

•• 0:59—Buns, getting spanked by Paolo.

••• 1:17—Buns, then topless making love in bed with Sands. Nude getting out of bed.

• 1:19—Brief topless, putting on stockings, then white bra and panties.

• 1:21—Buns, in greenhouse with Paolo when he beats her.

Made for Cable Movies:

36 Hours (1989) . . . . n.a.

Breaking Point (1989) . . . . Nurse

TV:

E.A.R.T.H. Force (1990) . . . . Diana Randall

• Paes, Dira

Films:

The Emerald Forest (1985) . . . . .Kachiri

•• 0:24—Brief buns while running from waterfall and diving into the pond.

• 0:33—Topless in water talking to Tomme.

• 0:56—Left breast in courtyard when Tomme proposes marriage to her.

• 0:57—Left breast in forest with Tomme. Long shot.

•• 1:01—Topless by the river.

•• 1:04—Topless and buns during wedding ceremony.

•• 1:16—Topless with the other tribe women after being captured by the fierce people.

• 1:18—Topless with the other girls being herded into the building.

•• 1:38—Topless in forest taking off clothes.

• 1:40—Buns, returning to the forest.

• 1:48—Topless in the river.

Magazines:

Playboy (Nov 1985) . . . . Sex in Cinema 1985

••• 127—Topless with Charley Boorman.

Pai, Sue Francis

a.k.a. Suzie Pai.

Films:

Sharky's Machine (1981) . . . . .Siakwan

Big Trouble in Little China (1986) . . . . Miao Yin

Jakarta (1988) . . . . .Esha

• 1:01—Brief right breast, while making love in the courtyard with Falco.

1:13—Brief side of right breast while kissing Falco.

•• 1:13—Side view of right breast, then brief topless twice, making love under a mosquito net with Falco. Hard to see her face clearly.

Magazines:

Penthouse (Jan 1981) . . . . .Pet

Penthouse (Jan 1983) . . . . Penthouse Feedback

•• 44—Buns in small photo.

Paige, Kym

Films:
Beverly Hills Cop II (1987) . . . . Playboy Playmate
Mortuary Academy (1988) . . . . Nurse
Video Tapes:
Playboy Video Calendar 1988 (1987) . . . . Playmate
Playboy Video Magazine, Volume 12 (1987)
. . . . Music Video
••• 0:55—Full frontal nudity.
Playmates at Play (1990) . . . . .Hoops
Magazines:
Playboy (May 1987) . . . . Playmate

Paine, Bonnie

Films:
Ninja Academy (1990) . . . . Nudist
• 0:26—Brief buns and topless playing volleyball.
(She's the second blonde on the far side of the net
who misses the ball.)
Repo Jake (1990) . . . . R.V. Girl
•• 0:28—Topless (mostly left breast) while in R.V. with
her boyfriend.
• 0:29—More topless, making love with him.
Twisted Justice (1990) . . . . Hooker
•• 0:11—Topless in black panties and stockings, getting photographed.

Paine, Heidi

Films:
Wildest Dreams (1987) . . . . .Dancee
• 0:23—Topless in the arms of a gladiator in Bobby's
bedroom.
New York's Finest (1988). . . . . .Carley Pointer
• 0:04—Brief topless with a bunch of hookers.
• 0:36—Topless with her two friends doing push ups
on the floor.
Nudity Required (1989) . . . . Jane
Roadhouse (1989). . . . . Party Girl
Skin Deep (1989) . . . . Tina
• 0:01—Brief side view topless sitting on John Ritter's
lap while Denise Crosby watches.
Alien Seed (1991) . . . . .n.a.
Demon Sword (1991) . . . . Malina
a.k.a. Wizards of the Demon Sword
Video Tapes:
In Search of the Perfect 10 (1986)
. . . . Perfect Girl #8
••• 0:45—Brief topless pulling down her top outside of
car.

Pallenberg, Anita

Films:
A Degree of Murder (1967). . . . . Marie
Barbarella (1968; French/Italian) . . . . . The Black Queen
Candy (1968) . . . . Nurse Bullock
Performance (1970). . . . . .Pherber
• 0:44—Side view of left breast, while in bed with
Mick Jagger.

••• 0:47—Topless and buns, while in bathtub with Lucy
and Jagger.
• 0:50—Buns, injecting herself with drugs.
•• 1:20—Right breast, while lying on the floor. Then
topless and buns, in bed with Chas.

Pallett, Lori Deann

Films:
Summer's Games (1987). . . . . Torch Carrier
• 0:00—Half topless running in short T-shirt carrying
torch.
•• 0:04—Topless opening her swimsuit top after contest. (2nd place winner.)
Screwball Hotel (1988). . . . . Candy
••• 0:26—Topless in the shower while Herbie is accidentally in there with her.
Video Tapes:
How to Fill a Wild Wet T-shirt (1986)
. . . . Lori from Dallas
••• 0:16—Topless dancing on stage, then being interviewed backstage with two other topless girls.
•• 0:28—Topless during quiz time.
••• 0:43—Topless dancing during semi-finals.
••• 0:45—Topless dancing during finals.
••• 0:46—Topless dancing as the winner.
• 0:48—Topless during final credits "report card."
Daydreams (1988). . . . . Lori
••• 0:01—Topless cleaning sail boat. Long scene.
••• 0:03—Topless on sail boat during daydream.
• 0:09—Brief topless, sitting up on lounge chair when
beer is spilled on her back.
•• 0:10—Topless sitting on bar during beer daydream.
••• 0:13—Topless in kitchen after spilling whipped
cream on herself.
••• 0:14—Topless and buns, getting into bathtub.
••• 0:16—Nude, in bathtub during daydream.
••• 0:20—Topless in open tuxedo jacket during dance
number.
••• 0:21—More topless during end credits.
The Best of the Mermaids (1992)
. . . . The Snakecharmer
••• 1:05—Topless while scuba diving, posing on boat
and at the beach. Buns in swimsuit.
Hot Body International: #3 Lingerie Special (1992)
. . . . .Contestant
•• 0:21—Buns in G-string and black top.
0:54—5th runner up.
Hot Body International: #5 Miss Acapulco (1992)
. . . . .Contestant
•• 0:26—Buns, while dancing in two piece swimsuit.
0:53—4th place winner.
Mermaids of the Aztec Empire (1992)
. . . . Carla Monroe
•• 0:01—Topless scuba diving under water during the
opening credits.
••• 0:04—Topless in swimsuit bottom, posing for photographer outside by pool.
•• 0:06—Topless outside by pool and under water.
••• 0:13—Topless on boat.

••• 0:15—Topless and buns in swimsuit bottom while scuba diving under water.

•• 0:19—Full frontal nudity during disco fantasy.

••• 0:23—Topless and buns at the beach. Long scene.

••• 0:33—Topless snorkeling under water.

••• 0:37—Topless and buns at the beach again.

••• 0:41—Topless scuba diving.

••• 0:45—Topless in spa by herself, then with a girl-friend.

••• 0:49—Topless and buns in swimsuit bottom, un-dressing at the beach during the end credits.

Magazines:
Penthouse (Jun 1989) . . . . .n.a.

Palme, Beatrice
Films:
Foxtrap (1986; U.S./Italian). . . . . Marianna
  •• 0:41—Brief breasts and buns in bed with Fred Williamson, then more breasts making love.
Cinema Paradiso (1988; Italian/French). . . . . .n.a.
The Sleazy Uncle (1991; Italian) . . . . .Singer

Palmer, Gretchen
One of the three *Diet Pepsi* Uh-huh! Girls (1992-).
Films:
The Malibu Bikini Shop (1985) . . . . .Woman
Crossroads (1986). . . . . Beautiful Girl/Dancer
Red Heat (1988) . . . . Hooker
  • 1:20—Topless and buns in hotel during shoot out.
Chopper Chicks in Zombietown (1989) . . . . Rusty
When Harry Met Sally... (1989) . . . . Stewardess

• Palmer, Jacqueline
Films:
Party Plane (1988) . . . . .Suzie
  ••• 0:06—Topless and buns changing clothes and getting into spa with her two girlfriends. (She's the dark haired one.)
  ••• 0:11—Topless again, getting out of spa.
  ••• 0:23—In bra, then topless doing strip tease routine on plane.
  •• 0:35—Topless doing another routine on the plane.
Sensations (1988) . . . . Tess
Roadhouse (1989). Party Girl
Repo Jake (1990) . . . . Porn Gal
  ••• 0:47—Topless and buns, while on bed, acting in a movie.
Legal Tender (1991). . . . . Mal's Girl
  • 0:24—Topless in bubble bath with blonde girl and Morton Downey Jr.
  •• 0:31—Topless outside by the swimming pool.
Millenium Countdown (1991). . . . . .n.a.

Paluzzi, Luciana
Films:
Muscle Beach Party (1964) . . . . Julie
Thunderball (1965; British) . . . . .Fiona Volpe
99 Women (1969). . . . . .n.a.
Black Gunn (1972) . . . . Toni

Manhunt (1973) . . . . Eva
  a.k.a. The Italian Connection.
The Klansman (1974). . . . . Trixie
The Sensuous Nurse (1975; Italian) . . . . n.a.
  •• 0:20—Topless in room, ripping off her clothes and reluctantly making love with Benito.

Papanicolas, Tanya
Films:
Vamp (1986) . . . . .Waitress
Blood Diner (1987) . . . . Sheetar & Bitsy
  • 0:15—Brief topless as photographer during topless aerobics photo shoot.
  • 0:24—Topless, dead on operating table, then dead, standing up.

• Paré, Marisa
Ex-wife of actor Michael Paré.
TV:
American Gladiators (1989-) . . . . Gladiator Lace
Magazines:
Playboy (Oct 1990) . . . . .Gladiator Marisa Paré
  ••• 78: Nude.
Playboy's Career Girls (Aug 1992)
. . . . Power and Glory
  ••• 20-25—Nude.

• Parent, Monique
Films:
Secret Games (1991). . . . . .Robin
(Unrated version reviewed.)
  • 0:33—Right breast, buns and crotch, while in bed with Julianne.
Video Tapes:
Playboy's Erotic Fantasies (1992) . . . . Model

• Parillaud, Anne
Films:
Patricia (1984). . . . . Patricia Cook
Private Screenings.
  •• 0:25—Topless, opening her jumpsuit top to get attention while trying to hitchhike.
  •• 0:30—Topless in white panties, running around at a seminary, trying to get away from a group of guys.
  •• 0:31—Topless in confessional booth.
  • 0:32—Running around some more.
  •• 0:37—Nude making love with Priscilla on bed.
  0:46—Sort of briefly topless running around in skimpy costume.
  ••• 0:49—Dancing in two piece swimsuit, then topless.
  •• 0:50—Topless while lying on her stomach.
  • 0:52—Brief topless running into the ocean.
  • 0:53—Brief topless under water.
  • 0:55—More brief topless shots under the water.
  •• 0:56—Nude, getting out of the ocean and lying down on the beach.
  •• 1:09—Topless taking off her dress and playing bull-fight with Harry.

•• 1:10—Nude, dancing in her room. Hard to see because the curtains get in the way.

• 1:24—Brief buns while making love with Harry.

• 1:26—Brief topless while making love with Harry.

••• 1:27—Full frontal nudity making love on top of Harry in bed.

Juillet en Septembre (1988; French) . . . . Marie

La Femme Nikita (1991; French/Italian) . . . . . . Nikita
a.k.a. Nikita

• 0:59—Very brief right nipple, peeking out of her top when she sits up in bed.

Innocent Blood (1992) . . . . .n.a.

• *Parker, Mary-Louise*

Films:

Longtime Companion (1990) . . . . .Lisa

Fried Green Tomatoes (1991) . . . . Ruth
a.k.a. Fried Green Tomatoes at the Whistle Stop Café

Grand Canyon (1991) . . . . Dee

• 1:00—Topless, pulling sheet down, while lying in bed during dream sequence.

• *Parkhurst, Heather*

Video Tapes:

Hot Body International: #1 Miss Cancun (1990)
. . . . Contestant

•• 0:26—Buns, in two piece swimsuit.

•• 0:52—Winnner. Buns, in two piece swimsuit during photo session after the contest.

Inside Out 2 (1992)
. . . . .Woman/I've Got a Crush on You
(Unrated version reviewed.)

•• 0:14—Brief buns, in swimsuit, suntanning. Topless, trying to prevent guy from jumping.

• 0:15—More topless and buns shots when she's flattened during the rest of the segment.

Magazines:

Playboy (Jan 1992) . . . . .The Swedish Bikini Team Hilgar Oblief.

••• 78-85—Full frontal nudity with swimmask. Topless while reading magazine on boat. Buns, while holding up surfboard (2nd from the left). Topless holding white telephone. Full frontal nudity, lying down on parachute. Topless drinking beer from mug. Topless holding sleeping bag with her left hand.

Parkins, Barbara

Films:

Valley of the Dolls (1967) . . . . Anne Welles

• 0:28—Very brief silhouette of a breast, taking off nightgown and getting into bed.

The Mephisto Waltz (1971) . . . . .Roxanne

• 1:26—Left breast, while kissing Alan Alda during witchcraft sequence.

Asylum (1972; British). . . . . Bonnie

Christina (1974) . . . . .Christina

Shout at the Devil (1976; British) . . . . Rosa

Bear Island (1980; British/Canadian) . . . . . .Judith Ruben

Made for Cable Movies:

To Catch a King (1984; HBO). . . . . n.a.

TV:

Peyton Place (1964-69)
. . . . .Betty Anderson/Harrington/Cord

Captains and the Kings (1976). . . . . .Martinique

Magazines:

Playboy (Dec 1977) . . . . .Sex Stars of 1977

• 215—Left breast standing looking out the window.

• *Parkinson, Dian*

TV:

The Price is Right (1975-) . . . . Hostess

Magazines:

Playboy (Dec 1991)
. . . . Dian Parkinson, Come On Down!

••• 94-101—Topless and buns.

Parton, Julia

a.k.a. Adult film actress Nina Alexander.
Cousin of singer/actress Dolly Parton.

Films:

Erotic Images (1983). . . . . Marvin's Nurse

• 0:08—Brief topless in office with Marvin. Dark, hard to see.

The Rosebud Beach Hotel (1985) . . . . Bellhop

•• 0:49—Buns, then topless, standing in line. Second from the camera.

Vice Academy, Part 3 (1991) . . . . Melanie/Malathion

•• 0:44—Topless, opening her blouse after seeing all the money.

Video Tapes:

Love Skills: A Guide to the Pleasures of Sex (1984)
. . . . Model

••• 0:49—Nude in bed with Barbara Peckinpaugh while a guy watches.

Penthouse Love Stories (1986) . . . Loveboat Woman

••• 0:51—In white bra and panties in bed. Nude masturbating while the other girls watch. Nice, long, sweaty scene.

Penthouse: On the Wild Side (1988)
. . . . Punk or Bust Customer

••• 0:34—Nude while wearing black leather outfit, making love with Michelle Bauer.

High Society Centerspread Video #15: Julia Parton
(1990) . . . . .Herself

••• 0:01—Topless and buns taking off her clothes.

••• 0:04—Full frontal nudity in bathtub making love with a girl friend. Nice, long scene.

••• 0:09—Nude, doing a strip tease dance.

••• 0:17—Nude, relaxing on the floor and masturbating.

••• 0:18—Nude on bed, making love with the maid during fantasy.

Soft Bodies Invitational (1990) . . . . . Nina Alexander

0:00—Buns, under short skirt, playing tennis with Becky LeBeau.

••• 0:03—In lingerie during photo session, then topless and buns in G-string. Long scene.

••• 0:15—Topless posing with LeBeau.
••• 0:18—Outside in dress, then undressing to two piece swimsuit, then topless. Long scene.
0:24—In two piece swimsuit, then topless arguing with LeBeau about who has better breasts.
••• 0:28—In two piece swimsuit, then topless by the pool.

Pascal, Olivia
Films:
Bloody Moon . . . . Angela
Island of 1000 Delights . . . . .Peggy
•• 0:16—Topless, tied up while being tortured by two guys. Upper half lower frontal nudity.
•• 0:23—Full frontal nudity lying in bed, then buns running out the door. Full frontal nudity running up stairs, nude hiding in bedroom.
0:33—In braless black dress.
••• 0:57—Nude, taking off her clothes in shower with Michael.
• 1:26—Brief topless running on the beach with Michael.
Vanessa (1977) . . . . .Vanessa
••• 0:08—Nude undressing, taking a bath and getting washed by Jackie. Long scene.
••• 0:16—Buns, then full frontal nudity getting a massage.
• 0:26—Topless getting fitted for new clothes.
• 0:47—Full frontal nudity when Adrian rips her clothes off.
••• 0:56—Full frontal nudity on beach with Jackie.
••• 1:05—Nude making love with Jackie in bed. Nice close up of left breast.
•• 1:19—Full frontal nudity lying on the table.
•• 1:27—Topless in white panties, garter belt and stockings shackled up by Kenneth.
Popcorn and Ice Cream (1978; West German)
. . . . Vivi
• 0:26—Full frontal nudity (she's on the right), covered with soap, taking a shower with Bea.
The Joy of Flying (1979) . . . . Maria
•• 0:39—Topless wearing panties, in bedroom with George, then nude.
•• 0:46—Nude with George in bathroom.
Sex on the Run (1979; German/French/Italian)
. . . . Convent Girl
a.k.a. Some Like It Cool
a.k.a. Casanova and Co.
••• 0:15—First woman (brunette) to take off her clothes with the other two women, full frontal nudity. Long scene.
C.O.D. (1983). . . . . Holly Fox
1:30—In white top during fashion show.

• Pasco, Isabelle
Films:
Ave Maria (1984; French) . . . . .Ursula
Hors La Loi (1985; French) . . . . .n.a.

Prospero's Books (1991; Dutch/French/Italian)
. . . . .Miranda
Magazines:
Playboy (Dec 1991) . . . . Isabelle
••• 156-162—Nude in mostly two-tone photos.

Paul, Alexandra
Films:
American Nightmare (1981; Canadian)
. . . . .Isabelle Blake/Tanya Kelly
••• 0:02—Left breast while smoking in bed. Topless before getting killed. Long scene.
Christine (1983). . . . . .Leigh
Just the Way You Are (1984). . . . . .Bobbie
American Flyers (1985) . . . . .Becky
• 0:50—Very brief right breast, then very brief half of left breast changing tops with David Grant. Brief side view of right breast. Dark.
•• 1:13—Brief topless in white panties getting into bed with David Grant.
8 Million Ways to Die (1986). . . . . Sunny
•• 0:24—Full frontal nudity, standing in bathroom while Jeff Bridges watches.
Dragnet (1987) . . . . Connie Swail
Harlequin Romance: Out of the Shadows (1988)
. . . . Jan Lindsey
Millions (1990). . . . . .Julia
0:19—In black stockings and body suit, changing clothes.
••• 0:44—Topless while making love in bed with Billy Zane.
• 0:59—Topless in bed with Zane.
Kuffs (1992). . . . . Uncredited Police Chief's Wife
Made for Cable Movies:
Prey of the Chameleon (1992; Showtime) . . . . . . Carrie
Made for Cable TV:
The Hitchhiker: Minuteman . . . . .Julie
•• 0:04—Brief left breast in car with husband, then brief topless flashing the couple on the motorcycle.
Made for TV Movies:
Paper Dolls (1982) . . . . Laurie
Perry Mason: The Case of the Lethal Lesson (1988)
. . . . .Amy
The Laker Girls (1990) . . . . Heidi/Jenny
TV:
Baywatch (1992-) . . . . .Lt. Stephanie Holden

Paul, Nancy
Films:
Sheena (1984) . . . . Betsy Ames
Gulag (1985) . . . . .Susan
•• 0:42—Buns, then topless taking a shower while David Keith daydreams while he's on a train.
V. I. Warshawski (1991) . . . . .Paige

Paul, Sue
Films:
All That Jazz (1979) . . . . Stacy
- 1:18—Brief right breast in bed with Roy Scheider at the hospital.

Magazines:
Playboy (Mar 1980). . . . . All That Fosse
- 176—Right breast, while kneeling on her hands and knees.

Pavis, Bobbi
Films:
The Malibu Bikini Shop (1985). . . . . . . Stunning Girl
- •• 0:19—Topless trying on bikini behind two-way glass.

Mortuary Academy (1988) . . . . Sexy Dancer

Payne, Julie
Films:
The Lonely Guy (1983) . . . . .Rental Agent
Private School (1983) . . . . Coach Whelan
- 0:30—Very, very brief left breast popping out of cheerleader's outfit along with Rita.

Fraternity Vacation (1985). . . . . Naomi Tvedt
Jumpin' Jack Flash (1986)
. . . . .Receptionist at Elizabeth Arden
Just Between Friends (1986) . . . . Karen
Misery (1990) . . . . Reporter #1

Peabody, Dixie Lee
Films:
Bury Me an Angel (1972) . . . . Dag
- 0:11—Very brief silhouette of left breast, while getting into bed.
- 0:13—Very brief right breast, while getting back into bed.
- ••• 0:41—Nude, skinny dipping in river and getting out.
- 1:16—Topless making love in bed with Dan Haggerty. Lit with red light.

Night Call Nurses (1972) . . . . Robin
a.k.a. Young LA Nurses 2
- •• 0:35—Topless taking off clothes in encounter group.
- 0:39—Brief topless in Barbara's flashback.

Peake, Teri Lynn
a.k.a. Terri Lenée Peake.
Films:
Murphy's Law (1986) .n.a.
Boys Night Out (1987). . . . . .Maid
- ••• 0:25—Buns in G-string, then topless doing a strip routine. Long scene.

Summer's Games (1987). . . . . Penthouse Girl
Wet Water T's (1987) . . . . Herself
- ••• 0:13—Topless and buns, dancing on stage in white G-string, in a contest.
- 0:36—Topless again during judging.
- •• 0:39—Topless during semi-finals.
- ••• 0:40—Topless dancing with the other women.

- ••• 0:43—Topless dancing during finals.
- •• 0:46—Topless during final judging.

Video Tapes:
The Girls of Malibu (1986). . . . . Lenee
- ••• 0:51—Nude outside and in a hot tub.

In Search of the Perfect 10 (1986)
. . . . Perfect Girl #9
- ••• 0:47—Buns and topless taking a shower.

The Stripper of the Year (1986) . . . . Lenee
- ••• 0:47—Nude, stripping out of red sequined dress.
- ••• 0:53—Topless on stage with the other contestants.
- •• 0:54—Topless as a finalist.
- ••• 0:55—Topless as a finalist, then in dance-off.

Night of the Living Babes (1987) . . . . Vesuvia
- ••• 0:25—Topless and buns in G-string, dancing in front of Chuck and Buck. Long scene.

Starlets Exposed! Volume II (1991) . . . . Lenee
(Same as *The Girls of Malibu*.)
- ••• 0:52—Nude outside and in a hot tub.

Magazines:
Penthouse (Oct 1987) .Pet

Pearce, Adrienne
Films:
Lethal Woman (1988) .Trudy
Out on Bail (1988) . . . . Maggie
Purgatory (1988). Janine
- •• 0:51—Brief topless in shower scene with Kirsten.

American Ninja 3: Blood Hunt (1989)
. . . . Minister's Secretary

Pearce, Jacqueline
Films:
How to Get Ahead in Advertising (1988) . . . . Maud
White Mischief (1988) . . . . Idina
- •• 0:07—Topless standing up in the bathtub while several men watch.

TV:
Blake's 7 . . . . .Servalan

• Pease, Patsy
Films:
He Knows You're Alone (1980) . . . . .Joyce
- 0:42—Very, very brief left breast in open blouse when she turns around to turn off the lights.

Space Raiders (1983) . . . . .Amanda

Peckinpaugh, Barbara
a.k.a. Adult film actress Susanna Britton.
Films:
Shadows Run Black (1981) . . . . Sandy
- ••• 0:57—Full frontal nudity, undressing in bedroom.
- •• 0:58—Buns and very, very brief topless getting into the shower.
- ••• 0:59—Full frontal nudity, drying herself off. Nude, walking around the house. Long scene.
- •• 1:01—Nude, in the bathroom, trying to avoid the killer.

Homework (1982) . . . . . .Uncredited Magazine Model
••• 0:01—Brief topless in magazine layout. In lingerie,
then topless in Tommy's photo session fantasy.
Erotic Images (1983) . . . . Cheerleader
• 0:07—Topless dancing in an office with another
cheerleader.
The Witching (1983) . . . . .Jennie
a.k.a. Necromancy
(Originally filmed in 1971 as *Necromancy*, additional
scenes were added and re-released in 1983.)
••• 0:02—Topless and buns in open gown during occult
ceremony. Brief full frontal nudity holding a doll up.
Basic Training (1984). . . . . .Salesgirl 1
• 0:00—Topless on desk with another salesgirl.
Body Double (1984) . . . Girl #2 (Holly Does Hollywood)
Roller Blade (1986) . . . . Bod Sister
•• 0:33—Topless during ceremony. Cut on her throat is
unappealing.
••• 0:35—Full frontal nudity after dip in hot tub with the
other two Bod Sisters. (She's the first to leave.)
•• 0:40—Nude, on skates with the other two Bod Sisters. (She's in the middle.)
Video Tapes:
Nudes in Limbo (1983). . . . . .Model
Best Chest in the West (1984) . . . . Chrissy
••• 0:28—In two piece swimsuit, then topless and buns.
Love Skills: A Guide to the Pleasures of Sex (1984)
. . . . .Model
•• 0:02—Topless, falling back into bed.
••• 0:09—Nude outside in field, making love with her
lover.
••• 0:36—Nude, making love in bed with her lover.
••• 0:49—Nude in bed with Julie Parton while a guy
watches.
Penthouse Love Stories (1986). . Therapist's Assistant
••• 0:45—Nude, making love in Therapist's office, with
the patient.

Pedriana, Lesa
Video Tapes:
Playmates at Play (1990)
. . . . Thrill Seeker, Flights of Fancy
Magazines:
Playboy (Apr 1984) . . . . Playmate

• Peluso, Felicia
Films:
Enrapture (1989). . . . . Ingenue
Magazines:
Playboy's Book of Lingerie (Jan 1992) . . . . . . Herself
••• 45—Topless.
•• 67—Buns and right breast.

Peña, Elizabeth
Films:
Times Square (1980). . . . . Disco Hostess
Crossover Dreams (1985) . . . . Liz
Down and Out in Beverly Hills (1986) . . . . Carmen
*batteries not included (1987) . . . . Marisa

La Bamba (1987) . . . . Rosie Morales
• 0:06—Brief side view of right breast taking a shower
outside when two young boys watch her from a water tower. Long shot, hard to see.
Blue Steel (1989) . . . . Tracy Perez
Jacob's Ladder (1990) .Jezzie
• 0:14—Side view of right breast taking off robe and
getting into shower with Tim Robbins.
••• 0:16—Topless several times opening dress and putting pants on. Then in black bra.
•• 0:31—Very, very brief topless in bed with Robbins,
then left breast a lot. Dark.
Made for TV Movies:
Shannon's Deal (1989). . . . . Lucy
Fugitive Among Us (1992) . . . . Flo Martin
TV:
Tough Cookies (1986) . . . . .Officer Connie Rivera
I Married Dora (1987-88) . . . . Dora
Shannon's Deal (1991). Lucy

Pendlebury, Anne
Films:
Alvin Purple (1973; Australian) . . . . . Woman with Pin
•• 0:48—Right breast and lower frontal nudity, while
lying in bed, talking with Alvin.
Jock Petersen (1974; Australian) . . . . Peggy
a.k.a. Petersen

Penhaligon, Susan
Films:
Soldier of Orange (1977; Dutch) . . . . .Susan
• 1:34—Brief topless kissing her boyfriend when Rutger Hauer sees them through the window. Medium
long shot.
••• 1:36—Topless in bed with her boyfriend and Hauer.
The Uncanny (1977; British). . . . . Janet

• Perez, Rosie
Dancer/Choreographer.
Films:
Do the Right Thing (1989). . . . . .Tina
•• 1:22—Topless when Spike Lee rubs ice all over her.
Don't see her face.
Night on Earth (1992) . . . . .Angela
a.k.a. Une Nuit Sur Terre
White Men Can't Jump (1992) . . . . Gloria Clemente
•• 0:36—Topless in shower and making love in bed
with Woody Harrelson.
• 0:39—Brief right breast, while sitting up in bed.
• 0:40—Very brief side of right breast, three times,
while getting out of bed quickly.

Perkins, Elizabeth
Films:
About Last Night... (1986). . . . . .Joan
From the Hip (1987) .Jo Ann
Big (1988) . . . . .Susan
Sweet Hearts Dance (1988) . . . . Adie Nims
Avalon (1990) . . . . Ann

Love at Large (1990) . . . . Stella Wynkowski
The Doctor (1991) . . . . June Ellis
he said, she said (1991) . . . . Lorie Bryer
   • 1:15—Brief topless getting into the shower with
    Kevin Bacon.

Perle, Rebecca

Films:
Bachelor Party (1984) . . . . Screaming Woman
Tightrope (1984) .Becky Jacklin
Savage Streets (1985) . . . . .Cindy Clark
   0:24—In bra and panties, fighting with Brenda in
    the locker room.
  •• 0:53—Brief topless in biology class getting her top
    torn off by Linda Blair.
Stitches (1985) . . . . .Bambi Belinka
 ••• 0:33—Topless during female medical student's class
    where they examine each other.
   • 1:00—Brief topless on bed with Parker Stevenson
    when discovered by Nancy.
Heartbreak Ridge (1986) . . . . Student in Shower
   • 1:48—Very brief topless getting out of shower when
    the Marines rescue the students.
Not of This Earth (1988) . . . . Alien Girl
   0:53—In black swimsuit wearing sunglasses.

Perrine, Valerie

Films:
Slaughterhouse Five (1972) . . . . . Montana Wildhack
   • 0:39—Topless in *Playboy* magazine as a Playmate.
   • 0:43—Topless getting into the bathtub.
 ••• 1:27—Topless in a dome with Michael Sacks.
The Last American Hero (1973) . . . . Marge
a.k.a. Hard Driver
Lenny (1974) . . . . .Honey Bruce
   0:04—Doing a strip tease on stage down to pasties
    and buns in a G-string. No nudity, but still nice.
 ••• 0:14—Topless in bed when Dustin Hoffman pulls the
    sheet off her then makes love.
  •• 0:17—Topless sitting on the floor in a room full of
    flowers when Hoffman comes in.
   0:24—Left breast wearing pastie doing dance in
    flashback.
   • 0:43—Right breast with Kathryn Witt.
Mr. Billion (1977) . . . . Rosi Jones
Superman (1978) . . . . Eve
The Electric Horseman (1979) . . . . Charlotta Steele
The Magician of Lublin (1979) . . . . Zeftel
Can't Stop the Music (1980) . . . . . . .Samantha Simpson
Agency (1981; Canadian) . . . . Brenda Wilcox
The Border (1982) . . . . .Marcy
Water (1986; British) . . . . Pamela
Maid to Order (1987) . . . . .Georgette Starkey
Bright Angel (1990) . . . . .Alleen
TV:
Leo and Liz in Beverly Hills (1986) . . . . Liz Green
Magazines:
Playboy (May 1972) . . . . Valerie
 ••• 103-107—Nice.

Playboy (Dec 1972) . . . . .Sex Stars of 1972
 •• 210—Topless.
Playboy (Nov 1973) . . . . Sex in Cinema 1973
 •• 151—Topless in bed.
Playboy (Dec 1973) . . . . .Sex Stars of 1973
  • 208—Half of right breast.
Playboy (Dec 1974) . . . . .Sex Stars of 1974
 •• 211—Left breast.
Playboy (Dec 1977) . . . . .Sex Stars of 1977
  • 211—Left breast.
Playboy (Aug 1981) . . . . Viva Valerie!
 •• 152-159—Topless.
Playboy (Nov 1981) . . . . Sex in Cinema 1981
 •• 165—Topless.
Playboy (Jan 1989) . . . . .Women of the Eighties
 •• 251—Topless.

• Persaud, Jenna

Films:
The Other Woman (1992) . . . . Traci Collins
(Unrated version reviewed.)
  •• 0:21—Topless under sheer black top in her apart-
    ment with her boyfriend.
 ••• 0:22—Topless taking off her top and getting milk
    poured on her.
 ••• 0:23—Topless and buns, making love in kitchen
    while Jessica secretly watches.
  •• 0:31—Topless posing with Sheila at the the beach
    for Elysse.
 ••• 0:32—Full frontal nudity at the beach some more.
   • 0:33—Topless and buns, running in the surf. Long
    shot.
  •• 0:40—Topless with the milk and at the beach during
    Jessica's flashbacks.
 ••• 0:53—Nude, taking a shower, drying herself off and
    putting on robe.
 ••• 0:57—Topless posing with Carl during photo shoot.
  •• 0:59—More topless during photo shoot.
 ••• 1:09—Topless and buns, on the floor making love
    with Jessica. Interesting camera angles.
    1:23—Topless on floor with Jessica during video
    playback on TV.
Magazines:
Penthouse (Apr 1987) . . . . .Pet

Persson, Carina

Video Tapes:
Playboy's Playmate Review 2 (1984) . . . . . Playmate
Playmates at Play (1990)
   . . . . .Thrill Seeker, Free Wheeling
Magazines:
Playboy (Aug 1983) . . . . Playmate

Pescia, Lisa

Films:
Tough Guys (1986) . . . . Customer #1
Body Chemistry (1990) . . . . .Claire
 ••• 0:18—Topless making love with Marc Singer stand-
    ing up, then at foot of bed.

0:35—In purple bra in van with Singer.
0:55—Buns, standing in hallway. Long shot.
Body Chemistry 2: Voice of a Stranger (1991)
. . . . Claire Archer
- • 0:42—Brief buns and side of left breast, making love on stairs with Dan.
- ••• 0:52—Topless and buns, in bathtub, standing up, sitting back down while talking with Dan.
- • 1:07—Buns, in leather outfit in radio control booth with Morton Downey Jr.
- • 1:18—Very brief buns and left breast on the stairs in flashback.

Peters, Lorraine

Films:
More Deadly than the Male (1961). . . . . Rita
The Wicker Man (1973; British). . . . . . . Girl on Grave
- • 0:22—Side view of right breast sitting on grave, crying. Dark, long shot, hard to see.
The Innocent (1985; British) . . . . .n.a.

Peterson, Cassandra

See: Elvira.

• Peterson, Julie

Video Tapes:
Playboy Video Calendar 1988 (1987) . . . . Playmate
Sensual Pleasures of Oriental Massage (1990)
. . . . .n.a.

Magazines:
Playboy (Feb 1987) . . . . Playmate

Pettet, Joanna

Films:
The Group (1966). Kay Strong
Casino Royale (1967; British). . . . . Mata Bond
The Night of the Generals (1967; British/French)
. . . . .Ulrike von Seidlitz-Gaber
Robbery (1967; British) . . . . Kate Clifton
Blue (1968) . . . . Joanne Morton
The Best House in London (1969; British)
. . . . Josephine Pacefoot
Welcome to Arrow Beach (1973). . . . . Grace Henry
a.k.a. Tender Flesh
The Evil (1977) . . . . Caroline
Double Exposure (1983) . . . . Mindy Jordache
•• 0:55—Topless, making love in bed with Adrian.
Sweet Country (1985). . . . . Monica
Miniseries:
Captains and the Kings (1976) . . . .Katherine Hennessey
TV:
Knots Landing (1983) . . . . Janet Baines

Pettijohn, Angelique

a.k.a. Heaven St. John.
Adult Films:
Body Talk (1982) . . . . .Cassie
Topless and more!

Titillation (1982) . . . . Brenda Weeks
Topless and more!
Films:
Clambake (1967). . . . . Gloria
Childish Things (1969). . . . . Angelique
The Curious Female (1969) . . . . .Susan
Heaven with a Gun (1969). . . . . Emily
The Mad Doctor of Blood Island (1969; Philippines/U.S.)
. . . . .Sheila Willard
Tell Me That You Love Me, Junie Moon (1970)
. . . . Melissa
The G.I. Executioner (1971). . . . . .Bonnie
- •• 0:16—Doing a strip routine on stage. Buns in G-string, very brief side view of right breast, then topless at end.
- •• 0:40—Topless, lying asleep in bed.
- ••• 0:58—Topless and buns, undressing in front of Dave, getting into bed, fighting an attacker and getting shot. Long scene.
- • 1:14—Topless, lying shot in rope net.
The Lost Empire (1983) . . . . .Whiplash
0:29—In a sexy, black leather outfit fighting in prison with Heather.
Bio-Hazard (1984). . . . . Lisa Martyn
- •• 0:30—Partial left breast on couch with Mitchell. In beige bra and panties talking on telephone, breast almost falling out of bra.
- ••• 1:15—Left breast, on couch with Mitchell, in outtake scene during the end credits.
- • 1:16—Upper half of left breast on couch again during a different take.
Repo Man (1984). . . . . Repo Wife No. 2
Takin' It Off (1984). . . . . Anita Little
The Wizard of Speed & Time (1988) . . . . . . .Dora Belair
TV:
Star Trek: The Gamesters of Triskelion . . . . Shahna

• Petty, Lori

Films:
Cadillac Man (1990) . . . . Lila
Point Break (1991) . . . . Tyler
- • 1:14—Very brief buns, running out of Keanu Reeves' bedroom.
TV:
The Thorns (1988). . . . . .Cricket
Booker (1990) . . . . Suzanne Dunne

• Petty, Rhonda

a.k.a. Adult film actress Rhonda Jo Petty.
Films:
Auditions (1978) . . . . Patty Rhodes
- •• 0:26—Topless during audition.
- •• 0:30—Topless, standing next to Larry and full frontal nudity straddling him on the table.

Pfeiffer, Michelle

Sister of actress DeDee Pfeiffer.
Ex-wife of actor Peter Horton.
Films:
Falling in Love Again (1980) . . . . Sue Wellington
The Hollywood Knights (1980) . . . . Suzi Q.
Charlie Chan & the Curse of the Dragon Queen (1981)
. . . . Cordella Farrington III
Grease 2 (1982) . . . . Stephanie Zinone
Scarface (1983). . . . . Elvira
Into the Night (1985) . . . . Diana
  • 0:27—Buns and very brief side nudity in her broth-
    er's apartment getting dressed. Long shot, hard to
    see.
Ladyhawke (1985) . . . . Isabeau
Sweet Liberty (1986). . . . . Faith Healey
Amazon Women on the Moon (1987)
. . . . Brenda Landers
The Witches of Eastwick (1987). . . . . . Sukie Ridgemont
Dangerous Liaisons (1988) . . . . Madame de Tourvel
Married to the Mob (1988). . . . . Angela de Marco
Tequila Sunrise (1988). . . . . Jo Ann
    1:14—Upside down reflection in water getting on
    top of Mel Gibson. Can't tell it's her. Only see silhou-
    ette. Probably wearing a body suit. Brief buns, hold-
    ing onto Gibson when he pulls a sheet over their
    heads. Blurry.
The Fabulous Baker Boys (1989) . . . . Susie Diamond
The Russia House (1990). . . . . Katya
Frankie & Johnny (1991). . . . . Frankie
    1:06—Most of the top half of her breasts, while lying
    in bed with Al Pacino.
Batman Returns (1992) . . . . Selina Kyle/Catwoman
Made for TV Movies:
Natica Jacks . . . . Natica Jackson
The Children Nobody Wanted (1980). . . . . Jennifer
TV:
Delta House (1979). . . . . Bombshell

Pflanzer, Krista

Films:
Cheerleader Camp (1987). . . . . Suzy
  a.k.a. Bloody Pom Poms
  •• 0:11—Topless several times sunbathing on the
    rocks.
  • 0:14—Brief topless in flashback.
  • 0:17—Topless on TV in Timmy's video tape of sun-
    bathing on the rocks.
Magazines:
Penthouse (Jul 1986) . . . . Pet
Penthouse (Jun 1991). . . . . Krista Revisited
  ••• 40-45—Nude.

• Phillips, Samantha

Films:
Phantasm II (1988) . . . . Alchemy
  •• 1:00—Topless making love in bed with Lance.
Dollman (1990) . . . . Tina

Video Tapes:
Rock Video Girls (1991) . . . . Herself
  •• 0:47—Brief topless and buns quite a few times,
    while wearing a G-string.

Picard, Nicole

Films:
Deadtime Stories (1985)
. . . . Rachel (Red Riding Hood)
  • 0:48—Very brief right breast in shack with boy-
    friend.
Dangerous Love (1988) . . . . Jane
A Time to Die (1991) . . . . Patti

• Pick, Amelie

Films:
Souvenir (1988; British) . . . . Janni
Reunion (1989; French/German) . . . . Young Lover
  • 0:47—Brief topless, twice, while making out in the
    woods with her boyfriend while two boys watch.

• Pickett, Blake

Former hostess on the Nashville Network game show *Top Card.*
Films:
Hauntedween (1991) . . . . n.a.
They Bite (1991) . . . . Model
    0:00—Posing for photographer in two piece swim-
    suit.
  ••• 0:03—Left breast, then topless and buns, taking off
    swimsuit for the photographer. More topless in the
    water, struggling with the monster.
Traces of Blood (1991) . . . . n.a.
Vampire Trailer Park (1991) . . . . Jana Wisher
Can It Be Love (1992) . . . . Dyanne

Pickett, Cindy

Films:
Night Games (1980) . . . . Valerie St. John
  •• 0:05—Brief topless getting scared by her husband in
    the shower.
  • 0:45—Buns and topless by and in the swimming
    pool with Joanna Cassidy.
    0:46—Topless in sheer blue dress during fantasy se-
    quence with Cassidy.
  •• 0:48—Brief full frontal nudity getting out of the
    pool, then topless lying down with Cassidy.
    1:03—Dancing at night in a see through night-
    gown.
  ••• 1:14—Full frontal nudity standing up in bathtub,
    then topless during fantasy with a guy in gold.
  •• 1:18—Topless getting out of pool at night.
  ••• 1:24—Topless sitting up in bed and stretching.
Ferris Bueller's Day Off (1986) . . . . Katie Bueller
The Men's Club (1986) . . . . Hannah
Hot to Trot (1988) . . . . Victoria Peyton
Deepstar Six (1989) . . . . Diane Norris
Crooked Hearts (1991). . . . . Jill

Made for TV Movies:
Into the Homeland (1987) . . . . .n.a.
Plymouth (1991). . . . . Addy
TV:
The Guiding Light (1976-80) . . . . . . Jackie Scott Marler
Call to Glory (1984-85). . . . . Vanessa Sarnac
St. Elsewhere (1986-88) . . . . .Dr. Carol Novino
Magazines:
Playboy (Nov 1979) . . . . Sex in Cinema 1979
• 175—Topless, small photo, hard to see.
Playboy (Dec 1980). . . . . Sex Stars of 1980
•• 244—Topless and partial lower frontal nudity.

• Pigg, Alexandra

Films:
Letter to Brezhnev (1986; British). . . . . Elaine
•• 0:57—Brief topless in bed with a guy.
Chicago Joe and the Showgirl (1989; British) . . . . Violet
Bullseye! (1990) . . . . Car Hire Girl

Pisier, Marie-France

Films:
Love at Twenty (1963; French/Italian/Japan) . . . . Colette
Trans-Europ-Express (1968; French) . . . . Eva
Stolen Kisses (1969; French) . . . . .Colette Tazzi
Cousin, Cousine (1975; French) . . . . .Karine
Other Side of Midnight (1977) . . . . Noëlle Page
• 0:10—Very brief topless in bed with Lanchon.
0:28—Buns, in bed with John Beck. Medium long shot.
0:45—In white bra, in dressing room talking to Henri.
0:50—Topless in bathtub, giving herself an abortion with a coat hanger. Painful to watch!
•• 1:11—Topless wearing white slip in room getting dressed in front of Henri.
••• 1:17—Full frontal nudity in front of fireplace with Armand, rubbing herself with oil, then making love with ice cubes. Very nice!
• 1:35—Full frontal nudity taking off dress for Constantin in his room.
The Bronte Sisters (1979; French) . . . . Charlotte
French Postcards (1979) . . . . Madame Tessier
•• 0:16—In white bra, then topless in dressing room while a guy watches without her knowing.
Love on the Run (1979). . . . . Colette
Chanel Solitaire (1981) . . . . Gabrielle Chanel
Miss Right (1987; Italian) . . . . .Bebe
•• 0:07—Topless in open top dress when the reporter discovers her in a dressing room behind a curtain.
Miniseries:
Scruples (1980). . . . . .Valentine O'Neill

Pitt, Ingrid

Films:
Where Eagles Dare (1969). . . . . .Heidi
The House That Dripped Blood (1970) . . . . .Carla

Vampire Lovers (1970; British) . . . . Marcilla/Carmilla
•• 0:32—Topless and buns in the bathtub and reflection in the mirror talking to Emma.
The Wicker Man (1973; British) . . . . Librarian
•• 1:11—Brief topless in bathtub seen by Edward Woodward.
Transmutations (1986). . . . . Pepperdine
Hanna's War (1988) . . . . Margit

Plato, Dana

Films:
Return to Boggy Creek (1977) . . . . n.a.
TV:
Diff'rent Strokes (1978-84). . . . . . .Kimberly Drummond
Magazines:
Playboy (Jun 1989). . . . . Diff'rent Dana
• 78-83—Lower nudity and wearing a pink see-through bra.

Player Jarreau, Susan

a.k.a. Susie Player.
Films:
Invasion of the Bee Girls (1973) . . . . Girl
Malibu Beach (1978). . . . . .Sally
• 0:28—Side view of left breast with boyfriend at night on the beach. Long shot.
0:32—Buns, running into the ocean with her two male friends.
0:33—Brief side view of left breast in water. Long shot.
• 0:34—Brief topless in the ocean, then topless by the fire getting dressed.

• Plimpton, Shelley

Films:
Alice's Restaurant (1969). . . . . Reenie
•• 0:21—Topless, taking off her blouse while sitting on bed and talking to Arlo Guthrie.
Putney Swope (1969). . . . . Face-Off Girl

Podewell, Cathy

Films:
Night of the Demons (1987) . . . . .Judy
(Unrated version reviewed.)
• 0:06—Brief buns, while changing clothes and talking on the phone.
0:07—In white bra taking off her sweater.
Beverly Hills Brats (1989) . . . . Tiffany
Made for TV Movies:
Earth Angel (1991). . . . . .Angela
TV:
Dallas (1988-91) . . . . Cally Harper Ewing

• Poole, Tonya

Video Tapes:
Playboy's Erotic Fantasies (1992) . . . . Model
Magazines:
Playboy's Book of Lingerie (Sep 1991) . . . . . . Herself
••• 9—Full frontal nudity.

Playboy's Book of Lingerie (Nov 1991) . . . . . Herself
- • 19—Left breast.
- •• 107—Buns and side of right breast.

Playboy's Book of Lingerie (Mar 1992) . . . . . Herself
- ••• 29—Topless.

Playboy's Book of Lingerie (May 1992) . . . . . Herself
- • 38—Lower frontal nudity.

Playboy's Book of Lingerie (Jul 1992) . . . . . . Herself
- •• 105—Right breast.

Poremba, Jean

a.k.a. Adult film actress Candie Evans.
Films:

You Can't Hurry Love (1984) . . . . . . .Model in Back
- • 0:05—Topless posing in the backyard getting photographed.
- •• 0:48—Nude in backyard again getting photographed.

Takin' It All Off (1987) . . . . Allison
- 0:36—In pink bra and G-string.
- ••• 0:49—In white lingerie, then topless, then nude dancing.
- ••• 0:58—Topless, dancing outside when she hears the music.
- ••• 0:59—Nude dancing in a park.
- •• 1:01—Nude dancing in a laundromat.
- ••• 1:03—Nude dancing in a restaurant.
- ••• 1:07—Nude in shower with Adam.
- •• 1:13—Topless dancing for the music in a studio.
- ••• 1:23—Nude dancing with all the other women on stage.

Potter, Madeleine

Films:
The Bostonians (1984) . . . . Verena Tarrant
Suicide Club (1988) . . . . .Nancy
Bloodhounds of Broadway (1989). . . . . . . .Widow Mary
Slaves of New York (1989) . . . . Daria
- • 1:14—Topless making love with Stash on chair. Mostly see left breast. Dark.

Two Evil Eyes (1991) . . . . .Annabelle

Potts, Annie

Films:
Corvette Summer (1978) . . . . .Vanessa
- • 0:51—Silhouette of right breast in van with Mark Hamill. Out of focus topless washing herself in the van while talking to him. Don't really see anything.

King of the Gypsies (1978) . . . . .Persa
Heartaches (1981; Canadian) . . . . .Bonnie Howard
Crimes of Passion (1984). . . . . .Amy Grady
(Unrated version reviewed.)
Ghostbusters (1984) . . . . .Janine Melnitz
Jumpin' Jack Flash (1986) . . . . Liz Carlson
Pretty in Pink (1986) . . . . Iona
Pass the Ammo (1988) . . . . Darla Potter
Ghostbusters II (1989). . . . . .Janine Melnitz

Who's Harry Crumb? (1989) . . . . .Helen Downing
- 0:55—In sheer black bra lying in bed with Jeffrey Jones.
- 1:00—More in the same bra in photograph that Jones is looking at.

Texasville (1990) . . . . Karla Jackson
- 1:29—In white bra, getting dressed in bedroom while talking to Jeff Bridges.

TV:
Goodtime Girls (1980) . . . . .Edith Bedelmeyer
Designing Women (1986-) . . . . Mary Jo Shively

Pouget, Ely

Films:
Endless Descent (1989) . . . . .Ana Rivera
Cool Blue (1990) . . . . Christiane
- •• 0:18—Side view of right breast, then topless with Woody Harrelson.

Curly Sue (1991) . . . . Dinah Tompkins
TV:
Dark Shadows (1991). . . . . Maggie Evans

Power, Deborah

Films:
Emmanuelle IV (1984) . . . . .Dona
- • 1:09—Buns, while lying down and getting a massage from Mia Nygren.

Glamour (1985; French). n.a.

Power, Taryn

Daughter of actor Tyrone Power.
Films:
Sinbad and the Eye of the Tiger (1977; U.S./British)
. . . . Dione
- 1:16—Very brief buns, skinny dipping in pond with Jane Seymour. Long shot, but still pretty amazing for a G-rated film.
- 1:18—Very brief partial side view of right breast, running away from the troglodyte.

Tracks (1977) . . . . Stephanie
- • 0:32—Brief side view of right breast changing in her room on the train. Don't see her face.
- • 1:15—Brief left breast making love with Dennis Hopper in a field.

Eating (1991). . . . . .Anita
Made for TV Movies:
The Count of Monte Cristo (1975). . . . . n.a.

Powers, Beverly

Films:
Kissin' Cousins (1964) .Trudy
More Dead than Alive (1968). . . . . .Sheree
Angel in My Pocket (1969). . . . . Charlene de Gaulle
J. W. Coop (1971) . . . . Dora Mae
Invasion of the Bee Girls (1973) . . . . Harriet Williams
- • 1:14—In white bra and panties, then right breast and buns, taking off her clothes for her husband.

Powers, Stefanie

Films:
Crescendo (1972; British) . . . . Susan
(Not available on video tape.)

Prather, Joan

Films:
Bloody Friday (1973) . . . . Lola
a.k.a. Single Girls
•• 1:06—Topless, acting out her fantasy with Blue just
before getting killed. Dark.
Big Bad Mama (1974) . . . . Jane Kingston
•• 1:15—Topless and buns in the bathroom with Tom
Skerritt.
Smile (1974) . . . . Robin
• 0:47—Brief buns in dressing room, while taking off
pants while Little Bob is outside taking pictures.
(She's wearing a pink ribbon in her hair.)
The Devil's Rain (1975; U.S./Mexican). . . . . Julie Preston
Rabbit Test (1978). . . . . .Segoynia
The Best of Sex and Violence (1981). . . . . . . Herself
•• 0:38—Topless getting her breasts squeezed by an
attacker. Dark.
Famous T & A (1982) . . . . Herself
(No longer available for purchase, check your video
store for rental.)
•• 0:49—Brief topless in scene from *Bloody Friday.*
Made for TV Movies:
The Deerslayer (1978). .n.a.
TV:
Executive Suite (1976-77) . . . . .Glory Dalessio
Eight is Enough (1979-81) . . . . Janet Bradford

• Prati, Pamela

Films:
Monsignor (1982) . . . . 1st Roman Girl
• 1:22—Brief topless (on the left, wearing necklaces)
next to a guy sitting in a chair, with another Roman
girl on the right.
Hercules II (1985) . . . . Aracne
Man Spricht Deutsh (1988; West German) . . . . .Violetta
Transformations (1988) . . . . .Woman Succubus
••• 0:05—Topless and buns making love on top of Rex
Smith in bed. She starts transforming into a creature.
• 0:21—Brief topless again during Smith's flashback.
• 0:24—Brief topless again, while transforming.
• 0:26—Brief topless again, while transforming.

Prentiss, Paula

Films:
Where the Boys Are (1960) . . . . Tuggle Carpenter
Man's Favorite Sport? (1964) . . . . Abigail Page
The World of Henry Orient (1964). . . . . Stella
In Harm's Way (1965) . . . . .Bev
What's New, Pussycat? (1965; U.S./French). . . . . . . Liz

Catch-22 (1970). . . . . Nurse Duckett
• 0:22—Full frontal nudity in water throwing her dress
to Alan Arkin who is swimming in the water during
his dream. Long shot, over exposed, hard to see.
Move (1970). . . . . Dolly Jaffe
Last of the Red Hot Lovers (1972) . . . . . . Bobbi Michele
The Parallax View (1974) . . . . Lee Carter
The Stepford Wives (1975). . . . . Bobby
The Black Marble (1980) . . . . . Sgt. Natalie Zimmerman
Buddy Buddy (1981) . . . . Celia Clooney
Saturday the 14th (1981). . . . . Mary
TV:
He & She (1967-68). . . . . Paula Hollister

Preston, Kelly

a.k.a. Kelly Palzis.
Wife of actor John Travolta.
Films:
10 to Midnight (1983) . . . . Doreen
Christine (1983) . . . . .Roseanne
Metalstorm: The Destruction of Jared-Syn (1983)
. . . . Dhyana
Mischief (1985) . . . . Marilyn McCauley
••• 0:56—In a bra, then topless and brief buns, while
making love with Doug McKeon in her bedroom.
Secret Admirer (1985) . . . . Deborah Anne Fimple
•• 0:53—Brief topless in car with C. Thomas Howell.
• 1:17—Very brief topless in and out of bed.
52 Pick-Up (1986) . . . . Cini
• 0:09—Brief buns in video tape made by blackmail-
ers.
• 0:36—Topless, tied to chair on video tape made by
blackmailers.
0:39—Very brief topless covered with blood after
being shot.
SpaceCamp (1986) . . . . Tish
Amazon Women on the Moon (1987) . . . . .Violet
Love at Stake (1988) . . . . .Sara Lee
Spellbinder (1988) . . . . Miranda Reed
••• 0:19—Topless in bed making love with Timothy
Daly.
1:26—Dancing around in a sheer white gown with
nothing underneath during cult ceremony at the
beach.
A Tiger's Tale (1988). . . . . Shirley
•• 0:03—Topless in the car, letting C. Thomas Howell
open her blouse and look at her breasts.
Twins (1988) . . . . Marnie Mason
The Experts (1989). .Bonnie
Run (1990). . . . . Karen Landers
Only You (1992) . . . . Amanda Hughes
Made for Cable Movies:
The Perfect Bride (1991) . . . . .Laura
Made for Cable TV:
Tales From the Crypt: The Switch (1990; HBO) . . .Linda
(Available on *Tales From the Crypt, Volume 3.*)
TV:
For Love and Honor (1983) . . . . Mary Lee

• *Price, Karen*

Films:
Swamp Thing (1981) . . . . Messenger
The Running Man (1987) . . . . Amber (Stunts)
Magazines:
Playboy (Jan 1981) . . . . Playmate

Primeaux, Suzanne

Films:
Stripper (1985) . . . . Herself
•• 0:03—Topless dancing on stage, kneeling on her left
knee. Very brief buns in G-string.
Traxx (1988) . . . . Hooker #1
•• 0:37—Topless, dancing on stage while wearing a
mask.

Principal, Victoria

Films:
The Life and Times of Judge Roy Bean (1972)
. . . . .Marie Elena
The Naked Ape (1972). . . . . Cathy
(Not available on video tape.)
Topless.
Earthquake (1974) . . . . Rosa
I Will, I Will... For Now (1976) . . . . .Jackie Martin
Vigilante Force (1976). . . . . Linda
Miniseries:
The Burden of Proof (1992). . . . . Margy Allison
Made for TV Movies:
Naked Lie (1989) . . . . .Joanne Dawson
Don't Touch My Daughter (1991). . . . . .n.a.
Seduction: Three Tales from "The Inner Sanctum"
(1992). . . . . .Sylvia/Lisa/Joan
TV:
Dallas (1978-89) . . . . Pamela Barnes Ewing
Magazines:
Playboy (Dec 1972). . . . . Sex Stars of 1972
••• 210—Left breast.
Playboy (Aug 1973). . . . . Next Month
• 218—Topless in B&W photo.
Playboy (Sep 1973). . . . . The Naked Ape & "Ape" Girl
••• 161-167—Topless and buns.
Playboy (Dec 1973). . . . . Sex Stars of 1973
•• 210—Right breast.
Playboy (Dec 1976). . . . . Sex Stars of 1976
••• 183—Topless and in black panties lying down.
Playboy (Dec 1980). . . . . Sex Stars of 1980
••• 240—Side view of left breast.

Prophet, Melissa

Films:
Players (1979). . . . . Ann
Van Nuys Blvd. (1979) . . . . Cameille
Looker (1981) . . . . Commercial Script Girl
Time Walker (1982). . . . . Jennie
• 0:27—Brief topless putting bra on while a guy
watches from outside the window.
1:17—Very, very brief right breast in shower when
the mummy comes to get the crystal.

Fatal Games (1984) . . . . Nancy Wilson
• 0:14—Buns and side view of left breast in shower
with other girls. Long shot. (She's wearing a
white towel on her head.)
Invasion U.S.A. (1985) . . . . .McGuirre
Action Jackson (1988) . . . . Newscaster
GoodFellas (1990) . . . . .Angie
Magazines:
Playboy (May 1987). . . . . Diary of a Hollywood Starlet
••• 86-93—Full frontal nudity.
Playboy's Nudes (Oct 1990) . . . . .Herself
• 15—Full frontal nudity.

Props, Renée

a.k.a. Babette Props.
Films:
Weird Science (1985). . . . . .One of The Weenies
Free Ride (1986) . . . . .Kathy
• 0:13—Brief topless in the shower while Dan watch-
es.
TV:
As the World Turns . . . . Ellie Snyder

Purl, Linda

Films:
Crazy Mama (1975). . . . . Cheryl
0:05—In pink, two piece swimsuit at the beach.
• 0:52—Very brief buns, then brief topless when
Snake and Donny Most keep opening the door after
she has taken a shower. Long shot, hard to see.
The High Country (1980; Canadian). . . . . Kathy
• 1:03—Brief buns, while taking a shower in the wa-
terfall.
Visiting Hours (1982; Canadian). . . . . . . Sheila Munroe
Viper (1988). . . . . Laura Macalla
Web of Deceit (1991). n.a.
Made for Cable Movies:
Body Language (1992; USA) . . . . .Norma
Made for TV Movies:
Pleasures (1986). . . . . n.a.
Danielle Steel's "Secrets" (1992) . . . . Jane Adams
TV:
Happy Days (1974-75). . . . . Gloria
Happy Days (1982-83). . . . . Ashley Pfister
Matlock (1986-89). . . . . Charlene Matlock
Under Cover (1991) . . . . Kate Del'Amico

Quennessen, Valerie

Films:
French Postcards (1979). . . . . .Toni
Like a Turtle on Its Back (1981; French) . . . . . .Nietzsche
Conan the Barbarian (1982). . . . . .The Princess
Summer Lovers (1982) . . . . Lina
• 0:12—Topless on balcony.
••• 0:19—Nude on the beach with Michael.
• 0:23—Brief topless in a cave with Michael.
•• 0:30—Topless lying on the floor with Michael.
0:54—Buns, lying on a rock with Daryl Hannah
watching Michael dive off a rock.

• 1:03—Left breast in bed.
•• 1:05—Topless dancing on the balcony.
1:09—Topless on the beach.

Quick, Diana

Films:
The Big Sleep (1978; British) . . . . Mona Grant
1919 (1984; British) . . . . .Anna
Ordeal by Innocence (1984) . . . . .Gwenda Vaughn
The Misadventures of Mr. Wilt (1990) . . . . Sally
Miniseries:
Brideshead Revisited (1981; British) . . . . . . Julia Flyte
0:18—(Part 10 on TV or Book 5 on video tape.) Several quick peeks at partial right breast in mirror, while lying under Jeremy Irons in bed.
•• 0:19—Left breast, while lying on top of Jeremy Irons after making love with him.

Quigley, Linnea

Adult Films:
Sweethearts (1986) . . . . .Cupid's Corner Hostess
(Appears fully clothed, only as a hostess to introduce the explicit segments.)
Films:
Auditions (1978) . . . . Sally Webster
••• 0:06—Topless and buns, undressing and dancing during her audition.
••• 0:26—Full frontal nudity, acting with two guys.
Don't Go Near the Park (1979) . . . . . Bondi's Mother
0:08—Full frontal nudity, behind shower door.
• 0:09—Brief left breast, while wrapping a towel around herself.
••• 0:19—Left breast, while lying in bed with Mark.
Fairytales (1979) . . . . Dream Girl
•• 1:07—Topless waking up after being kissed by The Prince.
Nightstalker (1979) . . . . .n.a.
Stone Cold Dead (1979; Canadian) . . . . .n.a.
Summer Camp (1979) . . . . .n.a.
Cheech & Chong's Nice Dreams (1981)
. . . . .Blondie Group #2
Graduation Day (1981) . . . . .Dolores
•• 0:36—Topless by the piano in classroom with Mr. Roberts unbuttoning her blouse.
The Young Warriors (1983; U.S./Canadian) . . Ginger
• 0:05—Nude in and getting out of bed in bedroom.
The Black Room (1984). . . . . .Milly
Fatal Games (1984). . . . . Athelete
Silent Night, Deadly Night (1984) . . . . Denise
••• 0:52—Topless on pool table with Tommy, then putting on shorts and walking around the house. More topless, impaled on antlers.
The Return of the Living Dead (1985) . . . . . . Trash
••• 0:05—Topless and buns, strip tease and dancing in cemetery. (Lower frontal nudity is covered with some kind of make-up appliance).
• 1:08—Topless, walking out of the cemetery to eat someone.

Savage Streets (1985). . . . . Heather
• 0:28—Topless getting raped by the jerks.
Silent Night, Deadly Night, Part 2 (1986)
. . . . .Denise
••• 0:26—Topless on pool table and getting dressed flashback from *Silent Night, Deadly Night.*
Creepozoids (1987) . . . . Blanca
•• 0:15—Topless taking off her top to take a shower.
•• 0:16—Right breast, while standing in shower with Butch.
• 0:24—Right breast several times while sleeping in bed with Butch.
Night of the Demons (1987) . . . . .Suzanne
(Unrated version reviewed.)
•• 0:52—Topless twice, opening her dress top while acting weird. Pushes a tube of lipstick into her left breast. (Don't try this at home kids!)
0:56—Lower frontal nudity, lifting her skirt up for Jay.
Nightmare Sisters (1987) . . . . Melody
••• 0:39—Topless standing in panties with Mickey and Marci after transforming from nerds to sexy women.
••• 0:40—Topless in the kitchen with Mickey and Marci.
••• 0:44—Topless in the bathtub with Mickey and Marci. Excellent, long scene.
••• 0:46—Topless in the bathtub. Nice close up.
••• 0:48—Still more topless in the bathtub.
••• 0:55—Topless dancing and singing in front of Kevin. Long scene.
••• 0:57—Topless on the couch with Bud.
Treasure of the Moon Goddess (1987) . . . . . Lu De Belle
American Rampage (1988). . . . . n.a.
Hollywood Chainsaw Hookers (1988) . . . Samantha
•• 0:32—Topless, dancing on stage.
• 1:02—Topless, (but her body is painted) dancing in a ceremony.
A Nightmare on Elm Street 4: The Dream Master (1988) . . . . Soul from Freddy's Chest
• 1:23—Brief topless twice, trying to get out of Freddy's body. Don't see her face clearly.
Sorority Babes in the Slimeball Bowl-O-Rama (1988)
. . . . Spider
Vice Academy (1988) .Didi
••• 0:45—Topless making love with Chuck while he's handcuffed.
Assault of the Party Nerds (1989) . . . . Bambi
••• 0:25—Topless straddling Cliff in bed.
Deadly Embrace (1989) . . . . Michelle Arno
•• 0:15—In white lingerie, then topless and buns during Chris' fantasy.
•• 0:34—Topless and buns caressing herself.
•• 0:43—Topless again.
0:46—Brief topless.
•• 0:50—Topless and buns undressing.
••• 0:58—Topless in bed on top of Chris, then making love.
• 1:02—Topless and buns on top of Chris while Charlotte watches on T.V.
1:11—Topless in Chris' fantasy.

- 1:12—Topless and buns in playback of video tape.

Dr. Alien (1989) . . . . Rocker Chick #2

a.k.a. I Was a Teenage Sex Mutant

••• 0:21—Topless in white outfit during dream sequence with two other rocker chicks.

Murder Weapon (1989). . . . . Dawn

- 0:08—Buns and very brief side of left breast walking into shower. Long shot.
- •• 0:40—Topless taking off her top in car.
- •• 0:48—Topless and buns taking off her top in bedroom.
- ••• 0:50—Topless in bed on top of a guy. Excellent long scene. Brief buns, getting out of bed.

Robot Ninja (1989) . . . . Miss Barbeau

Witchtrap (1989) . . . . Ginger Kowowski

- ••• 0:34—Nude taking off robe and getting into the shower.
- • 0:36—Topless just before getting killed when the shower head goes into her neck.

Vice Academy, Part 2 (1990) . . . . Didi

- •• 1:04—Buns in G-string, then topless dancing with Ginger Lynn Allen on stage at club.

Virgin High (1990) . . . . Kathleen

- •• 0:24—Topless, nonchalantly making love on top of Derrick.
- •• 0:55—Brief topless several times on top of Derrick, then topless.
- • 1:21—Topless in photo during party.

Blood Church (1991) . . . . .n.a.

Freddy's Dead: The Final Nightmare (1991)

. . . . Soul from Freddy's Chest

- • 1:25—Brief topless, struggling in Freddy's stomach during the end credits special-effects review.

The Guyver (1991) . . . . Scream Queen

A Psycho in Texas (1991). . . . . .n.a.

Sex Bomb (1991) . . . . .n.a.

Video Tapes:

Nudes in Limbo (1983) . . . . .Model

Playboy Video Magazine, Volume 4 (1983)

. . . . Flashdancer

- • 0:15—Full frontal nudity.
- •• 0:16—Nude, fighting with Brinke Stevens in the shower.

Linnea Quigley's Horror Workout (1990)

. . . . Herself

- ••• 0:00—Topless and buns, taking a shower and drying herself off. Nice.
- ••• 0:09—Topless in scene from *Assault of the Party Nerds*, making love on top of a guy in bed.
- • 0:19—Topless in still photo from *Return of the Living Dead*.
- •• 0:34—Topless, singing and dancing in living room, in scene from *Nightmare Sisters*.
- • 0:54—Topless, screaming.
- • 0:57—Topless in still photos during end credits.

Scream Queen Hot Tub Party (1991). . . . . Samantha

- • 0:01—Topless during opening credits.
- •• 0:36—Topless with painted body, doing double chainsaw dance from *Hollywood Chainsaw Hookers*.

Magazines:

Playboy (Jan 1985) . . . . The Girls of Rock 'n' Roll

Playboy (Nov 1985) . . . . Sex in Cinema 1985

- •• 134—Side view of right breast and buns, in still from *The Return of the Living Dead.*

Playboy (Nov 1988) . . . . Sex in Cinema 1988

- •• 137—Topless with tattoos across her breasts holding a chainsaw.

Playboy (Jul 1989) . . . . B-Movie Bimbos

- ••• 134—Full frontal nudity leaning on a car wearing stockings and an orange garter belt.

Quinlan, Kathleen

Films:

Lifeguard (1975) . . . . .Wendy

I Never Promised You a Rose Garden (1977)

. . . . Deborah

- • 0:27—Topless changing in a mental hospital room with the orderly.
- • 0:52—Brief topless riding a horse in a hallucination sequence. Blurry, hard to see. Then close up of left breast (could be anyone's).

The Promise (1979) . . . . Nancy/Marie

The Runner Stumbles (1979) . . . . .Sister Rita

Hanky Panky (1982) . . . . Janet Dunn

Independence Day (1983) . . . . Mary Ann Taylor

The Last Winter (1983; Israeli) . . . . Joyce

- •• 0:48—Brief side view of left breast taking off her robe and diving into pool Very brief buns.

0:49—Buns, lying on marble slab, talking with Maya.

0:50—Very brief right breast sitting up. Long shot, hard to see.

Twilight Zone—The Movie (1983) . . . . .Helen

Warning Sign (1985) . . . . Joanie Morse

Man Outside (1987). . . . . .Grace Freemont

Wild Thing (1987) . . . . .Jane

Clara's Heart (1988) . . . . .Leona Hart

Sunset (1988) . . . . Nancy Shoemaker

The Doors (1991) . . . . Patricia Kennealy

- ••• 1:00—Brief left breast, while in bed with Val Kilmer, topless (while wearing glasses) out of bed.
- • 1:02—Left breast, while crawling on the floor.
- ••• 1:03—Nude, dancing around her apartment with Kilmer.

Made for Cable Movies:

Blackout (1985; HBO) . . . . Chris

0:26—Brief side view of left breast while making love in bed. Dark, hard to see.

Bodily Harm (1989) . . . . Dr. Virginia Betters

Trapped (1989) . . . . n.a.

Strays (1991; USA) . . . . Lindsay Jarrett

•Quinn, Patricia

Films:

The Rocky Horror Picture Show (1975; British)

. . . . Magenta

Shock Treatment (1981). . . . . Nation McKinley

Monty Python's the Meaning of Life (1983; British)
. . . . .n.a.

Miniseries:

I, Claudius—Episode 4, What Shall We Do About Claudius? (1976; British) . . . . Livilla
(Available on video tape in *I, Claudius—Volume 2.*)
- 1:28—(0:39 into episode 4) Brief right breast, while climbing back onto bed after framing Postumus for rape.

I, Claudius—Episode 7, Queen of Heaven (1976; British) . . . . Livilla
(Available on video tape in *I, Claudius—Volume 4.*)
- 0:20—Very brief tip of right breast under arm of Patrick Stewart in bed.

Rabett, Catherine

Films:
The Living Daylights (1987) . . . . .n.a.
Maurice (1987; British) . . . . Pippa Durham
Frankenstein Unbound (1990) . . . . .Elizabeth
1:10—Very brief left breast, while lying dead after getting shot by Frankenstein. Unappealing looking because of all the gruesome makeup.

Rae, Taija

Adult film actress.
Films:
Delivery Boys (1984) . . . . Nurse
0:34—In bra and panties after doing a strip tease with another nurse while dancing in front of a boy who is lying on an operating table.
Sex Appeal (1986) . . . . .Rhonda
•• 1:14—In black lingerie, then topless in black push-up teddy with Sheila.

Raines, Cristina

a.k.a. Tina Herazo.
Films:
Hex (1973) . . . . .Oriole
Stacey (1973) . . . . Pamela
Nashville (1975) . . . . .Mary
Russian Roulette (1975) . . . . Bogna Kirchoff
The Duellists (1977; British) . . . . Adele
The Sentinel (1977) . . . . Alison Parker
- 0:18—Briefly in sheer beige bra, putting her blouse on.
- 0:33—Very, very brief left breast immediately after Sylvia Miles rips her dress off. B&W dream sequence.
Touched by Love (1980) . . . . Amy
North Shore (1987) . . . . Rick's Mother
TV:
Centennial (1978-79) . . . . Lucinda
Flamingo Road (1981-82) . . . . Lane Ballou

Raines, Frances

Films:
The Mutilator (1983) . . . . .n.a.
Topless by the pool.

Breeders (1986) . . . . .Karinsa Marshall
••• 0:12—Nude stretching and exercising in photo studio.
- 0:16—Brief full frontal nudity, getting attacked by the creature.
••• 0:53—Topless and buns, taking off her blouse and walking down the hall and into the basement. Long scene.
- 1:07—Very brief right breast in the alien nest with the other women.
- 1:10—Brief topless standing up.

Raines, Lisa

See: Foster, Lisa Raines.

Rains, Gianna

Films:
Firehouse (1987) . . . . Barrett Hopkins
••• 0:33—Topless taking a shower, then drying herself just before the fire alarm goes off.
•• 0:56—Topless making love with the reporter on the roof of a building.
Homeboy (1988) . . . . Phyllis

Rampling, Charlotte

Films:
Rotten to the Core (1965; British) . . . . .Sara
Georgy Girl (1966; British) . . . . Meredith
The Long Duel (1967; British) . . . . Jane Stafford
The Damned (1969; German) . . . . . Elizabeth Thallman
Three (1969; British) . . . . Marty
Asylum (1972; British) . . . . Barbara
Corky (1972) . . . . .Corky's Wife
Henry VIII and His Six Wives (1972; British)
. . . . Anne Boleyn
'Tis a Pity She's a Whore (1972; Italian)
. . . . Annabella
Topless.
Caravan to Vaccares (1974; British/French) . . . . . Lila
Brief buns standing at window, then brief full frontal nudity getting back into bed.
The Night Porter (1974; Italian/U.S.) . . . . Lucia
•• 0:11—Side nudity being filmed with a movie camera in the concentration camp line.
- 0:13—Nude running around a room while a Nazi taunts her by shooting his gun near her.
••• 1:12—Topless doing a song and dance number wearing pants, suspenders and a Nazi hat. Long scene.
Zardoz (1974; British) . . . . .Consuella
0:29—Topless under yellow net blouse.
- 1:05—Very brief left breast, when Sean Connery grabs her during struggle.
- 1:26—Wearing yellow blouse, trying to kill Connery.
- 1:44—Very brief right breast feeding her baby in time lapse scene at the end of the film.
Farewell, My Lovely (1975; British) . . . . Velma
Foxtrot (1976; Mexican/Swiss) . . . . .Julia
Orca, The Killer Whale (1977) . . . . Rachel Bedford

The Purple Taxi (1977; French/Italian/Irish)
. . . . Sharon
Stardust Memories (1980). . . . . .Dorrie
The Verdict (1982) . . . . Laura
Angel Heart (1987) . . . . Margaret Krusemark
(Original Unedited Version reviewed.)
- 1:10—Brief left breast, lying dead on the floor, covered with blood.
- 1:46—Very brief left breast during flashback of the dead-on-the-floor-covered-with-blood scene.

Mascara (1987; French/Belgian) . . . . .Gaby Hart
- 1:03—Brief topless putting on sweater when Michael Sarrazin watches through binoculars.
- 1:18—Right breast, while making love with Chris.

D.O.A. (1988) . . . . .Mrs. Fitzwaring
Magazines:
Playboy (Nov 1972) . . . . Sex in Cinema 1972
- 167—Topless lying down in bed in a photo from *'Tis a Pity She's a Whore.*

Playboy (Mar 1974). Zardoz
- •• 144-145—Buns and side view of left breast and partial lower frontal nudity.

Playboy (Nov 1974) . . . . Sex in Cinema 1974
- ••• 148—Topless from *The Night Porter.*

Playboy (Dec 1974). . . . . Sex Stars of 1974
- ••• 209—Full frontal nudity.

Playboy (Dec 1977). . . . . Sex Stars of 1977
- •• 215—Right breast and half of lower frontal nudity standing against fireplace.

Randall, Anne

Films:
The Split (1968) . . . . Negli's Girl
The Model Shop (1969) . . . . 2nd Model
Hell's Bloody Devils (1970) . . . . Amanda
The Christian Licorice Store (1971) . . . . Texas Girl
A Time for Dying (1971) . . . . Nellie Winters
Get to Know Your Rabbit (1972) . . . . Stewardess
Stacey (1973) . . . . Stacey Hansen
- ••• 0:01—Topless taking off her driving jump suit.
- ••• 0:12—Topless changing clothes.
- ••• 0:39—Topless in bed with Bob.

Westworld (1973) .Servant Girl
TV:
Hee Haw (1972-73) .Regular
Magazines:
Playboy (May 1967) . . . . Playmate
Playboy (Dec 1973) . . . . Sex Stars of 1973
- •• 208—Left breast.

Randolph, Windsor Taylor

a.k.a. Ty Randolph.
a.k.a. Adult film actress Lisa Berenger.
Films:
Body Double (1984). .Mindy
- ••• 1:50—Topless in the shower during filming of movie with Craig Wasson made up as a vampire.

Amazons (1986) . . . . .Dyala
- •• 0:22—Topless skinny dipping then getting dressed with Tashi.
- •• 0:24—Brief topless getting her top opened by bad guys then fighting them.

Penitentiary III (1987). . . . . .Sugar
Caged Fury (1989). . . . . .Warden Sybil Thorn
- •• 0:55—Topless and buns undressing for bath, then in the bathtub.

Deadly Embrace (1989) . . . . Charlotte Morland
- 0:19—In yellow one piece swimsuit by the pool with Chris.
- 0:27—In wet, white T-shirt in the kitchen with Chris.
- •• 0:28—Topless taking off her top. Mostly side view of left breast.
- 0:29—More left breast, while in bed with Chris.
- ••• 0:30—Topless, making love in bed with Chris.
- 1:10—Brief right breast, on T.V. when she replays video tape for Linnea Quigley.

Hollywood Boulevard II (1989)
. . . . Amazon Warrior from Brooklyn
Nudity Required (1989) . . . . .Brenda

Rattray, Heather

Films:
Across the Great Divide (1976). . . . . Holly
The Further Adventures of the Wilderness Family
(1978) . . . . Jenny Robinson
The Sea Gypsies (1978) . . . . .Courtney
Mountain Family Robinson (1979) . . . . .Jenny
Basket Case 2 (1989) .Susan
- 1:20—Brief right breast twice, when white blouse gapes open in bedroom with Duane. Special effect scar on her stomach makes it a little unappealing looking.

Basket Case 3: The Progeny (1991) . . . . .Susan
TV:
As the World Turns (1990-) . . . . Lily Walsh

• Rau, Andrea

Films:
Daughters of Darkness
(1971; Belgian/French/German/Italian) . . . . n.a.
Beyond Erotica (1979) .Lola
- 0:26—Topless, undressing in her bedroom.
- •• 0:30—Nude, undressing, then lying in bed, then trying on bunny costume.
- 0:47—Left breast, while lying on the floor.
- 0:56—Brief buns, running around in her cell.
- 0:57—Brief nude, behind wall with holes in it.
- 0:59—Left breast, seen though hole in the wall.
- •• 1:10—Topless in her bedroom.
- 1:23—Left breast, in flashback to 0:47 scene.

Ray, Ola

Films:
Body and Soul (1981) . . . . Hooker #1
- 0:54—Brief topless sitting on top of Leon Isaac Kennedy in bed with two other hookers.

48 Hrs. (1982). . . . . .Vroman's Dancers
Night Shift (1982). . . . . Dawn
10 to Midnight (1983). .Ola
   • 1:30—Very brief buns and very brief left breast, tak-
     ing off robe and getting into the shower.
   •• 1:31—Topless in the shower.
   •• 1:32—More topless in the shower.
   • 1:39—Very brief topless, dead, covered with blood
     in the shower.
Fear City (1984) .Honey Powers
Beverly Hills Cop II (1987). . . . . Playboy Playmate
The Nightstalker (1987) . . . . Sable Fox
Music Videos:
Thriller/Michael Jackson (1983). . . . . His Girlfriend
Magazines:
Playboy (Jun 1980) . . . . Playmate
   ••• 144-155—Topless and buns.
Playboy (Jul 1981). . . . . .Body and Soulmates
   • 148—Right breast.
Playboy (Dec 1984). . . . . Sex Stars of 1984
   ••• 206—Topless.

Raymond, Candy
Films:
Alvin Rides Again (1974; Australian) . . . . Girl in Office
   • 0:05—Lower frontal nudity and buns, in office with
     Alvin.
Don's Party (1976; Australian). . . . . Kerry
Monkey Grip (1983; Australian) . . . . Lillian

Reams, Cynthia
Films:
10 to Midnight (1983). . . . . Hooker
   ••• 1:25—Topless in hotel room with killer when he tries
     to elude Charles Bronson.
   • 1:26—Brief right breast, lying in bed, covered with
     sheet.
Radioactive Dreams (1984) . . . . .Buster Heavy

Redgrave, Lynn
Daughter of actor Sir Michael Redgrave.
Sister of actress Vanessa Redgrave.
Spokeswoman for *Weight Watchers* products.
Films:
Georgy Girl (1966; British) . . . . .Georgy
The Virgin Soldiers (1969). . . . . .Phillipa Raskin
The Happy Hooker (1975). . . . . Xaviera Hollander
   (Before Weight Watchers.)
   0:43—In black bra and panties doing a strip tease
     routine in a board room while Tom Poston watches.
Morgan Stewart's Coming Home (1987)
   . . . . Nancy Stewart
Getting It Right (1989) . . . . Joan
   •• 0:46—Brief right breast, then brief topless on couch
     seducing Gavin. More right breast shot when wres-
     tling with him.
Midnight (1989). . . . . Midnight
Made for TV Movies:
What Ever Happened to Baby Jane? (1991). Jane Hudson

TV:
Centennial (1978-79)
   . . . . Charlotte Buckland Lloyd Seccombe
House Calls (1979-81) . . . . Ann Anderson
Teachers Only (1982-83) . . . . Diana Swanson
Chicken Soup (1989) . . . . Maddie
Magazines:
Playboy (Nov 1989) . . . . Sex in Cinema 1989
   • 131—Right breast lying in sofa in a still from *Getting
     It Right.*

Redgrave, Vanessa
Daughter of actor Sir Michael Redgrave.
Sister of actress Lynn Redgrave.
Films:
Blow-Up (1966; British/Italian) . . . . .Jane
Camelot (1967) . . . . .Guenevere
Isadora (1968; British) . . . . Isadora Duncan
   0:47—Brief glimpses of topless and buns dancing
     around in her boyfriend's house at night. Hard to see
     anything.
   • 2:19—Very brief topless dancing on stage after com-
     ing back from Russia.
The Sea Gull (1968) . . . . Nina
Murder on the Orient Express (1974; British) . . . . . Mary
Out of Season (1975; British) . . . . .Ann
The Seven-Per-Cent Solution (1976) . . . . Lola Deveraux
Julia (1977) . . . . .Julia
Agatha (1979) . . . . Agatha Christie
Yanks (1979) . . . . .Helen
   • 1:25—Brief side of left breast and buns, taking off
     robe and getting into bed.
Bear Island (1980; British/Canadian) . . . . Hedi Lindquist
Wagner (1983; British). . . . . Cosima
The Bostonians (1984) . . . . Olive Chancellor
Steaming (1985; British) . . . . Nancy
   • 1:32—Buns and brief side view of right breast get-
     ting into pool.
Wetherby (1985; British) . . . . Jean Travers
Prick Up Your Ears (1987; British) . . . . Peggy Ramsay
Consuming Passions (1988; U.S./British) . . . .Mrs. Garza
   0:40—Almost side view of left breast making love
     with a guy on her bed.
The Ballad of the Sad Cafe (1991) . . . . Miss Amelia
Howards End (1992) . . . . .Ruth Wilcox
Made for Cable Movies:
Young Catherine (1991). . . . . .Empress
Made for TV Movies:
Playing for Time (1980) . . . . Fania Fenelon
   0:11—Very brief buns, while sitting down to get her
     hair cut.
A Man for All Seasons (1988) . . . . Lady Alice
What Ever Happened to Baby Jane? (1991)
   . . . . Blanche Hudson

Redman, Amanda
Films:
Richard's Things (1980) . . . . .Josie
   •• 0:51—Topless, lying in bed talking to Liv Ullman.

Give My Regards to Broad Street (1984; British)
.... Office Receptionist
For Queen and Country (1989; British) .... Stacey

• *Reed, Pamela*
Films:
The Long Riders (1980) .... Belle Starr
  • 0:18—Buns, while standing up in bathtub to hug
    David Carradine. (Don't see her face.)
Melvin and Howard (1980) .... Bonnie Dummar
Eyewitness (1981) .... Linda
Young Doctors in Love (1982) .... Norine Sprockett
The Right Stuff (1983) .... Trudy Cooper
Clan of the Cave Bear (1985) .... Iza
The Best of Times (1986) .... Gigi Hightower
Rachel River (1989) .... Mary Graving
Cadillac Man (1990) .... Tina
Chattahoochee (1990) .... Earlene
Kindergarten Cop (1990) .... Phoebe
Passed Away (1992) .... n.a.
Made for TV Movies:
Woman with a Past (1992) .... n.a.
TV:
The Andros Targets (1977) .... Sandi Farrell
Grand (1990) .... Janice Pasetti

Reed, Penelope
Films:
Amazons (1986) .... Tashi
  •• 0:22—Topless and buns undressing to go skinny
    dipping. More topless getting dressed.
  • 0:24—Brief topless getting top opened by bad guys.
Hollywood Boulevard II (1989)
.... Amazon Warrior with Crystal
Far Out Man (1990) .... Stewardess
Hired to Kill (1990) .... Katrina

Reed, Tracy
Films:
...All the Marbles (1981) .... Diane
  a.k.a. The California Dolls
Running Scared (1986) .... Maryann
  • 0:18—Brief buns.
  • 1:30—Very brief topless in bed with Gregory Hines.
Made for TV Movies:
Death of a Centerfold: The Dorothy Stratten Story
  (1981) .... Mindy
TV:
Love, American Style (1969-70) ...... Repertory Player
Barefoot in the Park (1970-71) .... Corie Bratter
Love, American Style (1972-74) ...... Repertory Player
Knots Landing (1990-) .... Charlotte Anderson

• *Reeves, Saskia*
Films:
Antonia & Jane (1991; British) .... Antonia McGill
Close My Eyes (1991; British) .... Natalie Gillespie
  •• 0:29—Very brief right breast, twice, then topless
    twice in room with Richard.

••• 0:31—Full frontal nudity, getting up and getting
  dressed.
••• 0:45—In white bra, then topless standing, then lying on the floor with Richard.
•• 0:46—Buns, while lying in bed with Richard. Nude,
  getting out of bed and putting on robe.
• 0:56—Right breast, while lying in bed.

• *Regan, Linda*
Films:
The Adventures of a Private Eye (1974; British)
.... Clarissa
  • 0:34—Full frontal nudity in boat with Scott.
  • 0:36—Very brief side view of left breast, getting up
    and diving off boat.
Confessions of a Pop Performer (1975; British) ..... n.a.
Carry on England (1976; British) .... Pvt. Taylor
Fiona (1978; British) .... Secretary

Regan, Mary
Films:
Heart of the Stag (1983; New Zealand)
.... Cathy Jackson
  • 0:03—Brief right breast twice, very brief lower fron-
    tal nudity in bed with her father.
  •• 1:06—Topless in bed, ripping her blouse open while
    yelling at her father.
Midnight Dancer (1987; Australian) .... Crystal
  a.k.a. Belinda
  •• 0:29—Topless in dressing room, undressing and
    rubbing makeup on herself.
  •• 0:56—In bra, then topless in panties, changing
    clothes and getting into bed.
The Year My Voice Broke (1987; Australian)
.... Miss McColl
Out of the Body (1988; Australian) ...... Marry Mason
Fever (1989; Australian) .... Leanne Welles

Regard, Suzanne M.
Films:
48 Hrs. (1982) .... Cowgirl Dancer
  0:39—Dancer in red-neck bar wearing silver star
  pasties.
Malibu Express (1984) .... Sexy Sally
  • 0:50—Brief topless talking on the telephone.
  •• 1:06—Topless talking on the telephone.

Reidy, Gabrielle
Films:
Educating Rita (1983; British) .... Barbara
The Fanatasist (1986; Irish) .... Kathy O'Malley
  • 0:03—Topless getting attacked in a room.

Relph, Emma
Films:
Eureka (1983; British) .... Mary (blue dress)
  • 1:17—Brief topless during African voodoo ceremo-
    ny.
The Witches (1989) .... Millie

Renet, Sinitta

Films:

Shock Treatment (1981) . . . . n.a.

Foreign Body (1986; British) . . . . . . Lovely Indian Girl
- 0:06—Buns, then topless in bedroom.

Reyes, Pia

Video Tapes:

Sexy Lingerie (1988) . . . . .Model

Playboy Video Calendar 1990 (1989) . . . . June
- ••• 0:28—Nude.

Sensual Pleasures of Oriental Massage (1990)
. . . . .n.a.

Magazines:

Playboy (Nov 1988) . . . . Playmate

Playboy's Nudes (Oct 1990) . . . . Herself
- •• 52—Right breast and lower frontal nudity.

Playboy's Book of Lingerie (Jan 1991) . . . . . . Herself
- ••• 42-43—Topless.

Playboy's Book of Lingerie (Mar 1991) . . . . . Herself
- ••• 52—Topless.

Playboy's Book of Lingerie (Nov 1991) . . . . . Herself
- ••• 43—Topless.

Rialson, Candice

Films:

Candy Stripe Nurses (1974) . . . . Sandy
- •• 0:05—Topless in hospital linen closet with a guy.
- •• 0:08—Topless smoking and writing in bathtub.
- • 0:14—Topless in hospital bed.

Pets (1974) . . . . Bonnie
- •• 0:26—Topless dancing in field while Dan is watching her while he's tied up.
- ••• 0:33—Topless making love on top of Dan while he's still tied up.
- 0:35—Running through woods in braless orange top.
- •• 0:40—Topless getting into bath at Geraldine's house.
- • 0:45—Topless posing for Geraldine.
- 0:54—In black and red lingerie outfit getting ready for bed.
- ••• 1:02—Topless taking off lingerie in bed with Ron, then making love with him.
- 1:34—Almost topless, getting whipped by Vincent.

The Eiger Sanction (1975) . . . . Art Student

Summer School Teachers (1975) . . . . Conklin T.
- • 0:14—Breasts and buns when Mr. Lacy fantasizes about what she looks like. Don't see her face, but it looks like her.
- ••• 0:38—Topless outside with other teacher, kissing on the ground.

Hollywood Boulevard (1976) . . . . Candy Wednesday
- •• 0:29—Topless getting her blouse ripped off by actors during a film.
- ••• 0:32—Topless sunbathing with Bobbi and Jill.
- •• 0:45—Brief topless in the films she's watching at the drive-in. Same as 0:29.

Chatterbox (1977) . . . . Penny
- •• 0:01—Left breast, in bed with Ted, then topless getting out of bed.
- 0:10—In white bra wrestling on couch with another woman.
- ••• 0:15—Side view of right breast then topless during demonstration on stage.
- ••• 0:26—Topless in bed talking on phone.
- 0:32—In open dress letting her "chatterbox" sing during talk show. Something covers pubic area.
- •• 0:35—Topless during photo shoot.
- •• 0:38—Topless again for more photos while opening a red coat.
- •• 0:43—Topless in bed with Ted.
- ••• 0:55—Topless taking off white dress, walking up the stairs and opening the door.
- •• 1:09—Topless opening her raincoat for Ted.

Moonshine County Express (1977) . . . . Mayella

Stunts (1977) . . . . Judy Blake

Winter Kills (1979) . . . . Second Blonde Girl

Richarde, Tessa

Films:

The Beach Girls (1982) . . . . Doreen

Cat People (1982) . . . . Billie
- •• 1:00—Topless in bed with Malcolm McDowell trying to get him excited.

The Last American Virgin (1982) . . . . .Brenda
- •• 0:15—Brief topless walking into the living room when Gary's parents come home.

Young Doctors in Love (1982) . . . . Rocco's Wife

Richards, Kim

Films:

Escape to Witch Mountain (1975) . . . . .Tia

Assault on Precinct 13 (1976) . . . . .Kathy

No Deposit, No Return (1976) . . . . Tracy

Special Delivery (1976) . . . . .Juliette

The Car (1977) . . . . Lynn Marie

Return from Witch Mountain (1978) . . . . .Tia

Meatballs, Part II (1984) . . . . Cheryl

Tuff Turf (1984) . . . . Frankie Croyden
- 1:07—In black lingerie getting dressed.
- • 1:29—Brief topless supposedly of a body double (Fiona Morris) in bedroom with James Spader but I have heard from a very reliable source that it really was her.

Escape (1988) . . . . Brooke Howser

TV:

Nanny and the Professor (1970-71) . . . Prudence Everett

Here We Go Again (1973) . . . . .Jan

James at 15 (1977-78) . . . . Sandy Hunter

Hello, Larry (1979-80) . . . . .Ruthie Adler

Richardson, Joely

Daughter of actress Vanessa Redgrave and director Tony Richardson.

Sister of actress Natasha Richardson.

Films:

The Hotel New Hampshire (1984). . . . . Waitress

Wetherby (1985; British). . . . . Young Jean Travers
 •• 1:10—Topless in room with Jim when he takes off her coat.

Drowning by Numbers (1988; British)
 . . . . .Cisse Colpitts 3
 • 0:28—Topless, taking off swimsuit and drying herself off. Long shot.
 ••• 0:43—Topless and buns, making love on couch with Bellamy.
 • 1:23—Topless under water in pool with Bellamy.
 •• 1:24—Topless getting out of pool.
 ••• 1:25—Topless standing up and putting swimsuit back on.
 •• 1:37—Left breast, while in car with Madgett.

King Ralph (1991). . . . . Princess Anna

Shining Through (1992) . . . . . . .Margrete von Eberstien

Magazines:

Playboy (Nov 1991) . . . . Sex in Cinema 1991
 •• 146—Topless on sofa. From *Drowning by Numbers*.

• Richardson, Miranda

Films:

Dance with a Stranger (1985; British) . . . . .Ruth Ellis
 0:08—Very brief upper half of left breast, twice, while in bed making love with David.
 0:18—Very brief tip of left breast getting into bed with David. Dark.
 • 0:20—Very, very brief side view of left breast, putting robe on in bed.

The Innocent (1985; British) . . . . .n.a.

Underworld (1985; British) . . . . Oriel

The Death of the Heart (1986; British). . . . . Daphne

Transmutations (1986) . . . . Oriel

Empire of the Sun (1987) . . . . Mrs. Victor

Twisted Obsession (1990) . . . . .Marilyn

Enchanted April (1991; British) . . . . Rose

Made for TV Movies:

Mystery! Die Kinder (1991) . . . . .Sidonie Reiger

Richardson, Natasha

Daughter of actress Vanessa Redgrave and director Tony Richardson.

Sister of actress Joely Richardson.

Films:

Gothic (1986; British) . . . . .Mary

A Month in the Country (1988; British). . . . .Alice Keach

Fat Man and Little Boy (1989). . . . . Jean Tatlock

Patty Hearst (1989) . . . . .Patricia Hearst
 •• 0:13—Topless, blindfolded in the bathtub while talking to a woman member of the S.L.A.

A Handmaid's Tale (1990). . . . . Kate
 •• 0:30—Topless twice at the window getting some fresh air.

 • 0:59—Topless making love with Aidan Quinn.
 ••• 1:00—Topless after Quinn rolls off her.

The Comfort of Strangers (1991) . . . . Mary
 ••• 0:45—Topless sleeping in bed. Long shot. Then closer topless after waking up. Long scene.
 •• 1:05—Topless making love with Colin. Lit with blue light.
 •• 1:06—Right breast, lying in bed with Colin. Lit with blue light.

The Favour, the Watch and the Very Big Fish (1991; French/British). . . . . Sybil
a.k.a. Rue Saint-Sulpice

The Favor, The Watch and the Very Big Fish (1992)
 . . . . n.a.

Richardson, Rickey

Films:

Bloody Trail (1972) . . . . .Miriam
 1:01—Peek at left breast in torn blouse.
 • 1:05—Right breast while sleeping, dark, hard to see.

The Hot Box (1972). . . . . Ellie St. George
 •• 0:16—Topless cleaning herself off in stream and getting out.
 • 0:21—Topless sleeping in hammocks. (She's the second one from the front.)
 • 0:26—Topless getting accosted by the People's Army guys.
 ••• 0:43—Full frontal nudity making love with Flavio.
 ••• 0:45—Topless in stream bathing with the other three girls.
 • 1:01—Topless taking off top in front of soldiers.

Richmond, Fiona

Films:

The House on Straw Hill (1976; British). . . . .Suzanne
a.k.a. Exposé
 ••• 0:05—Buns and topless undressing and getting into bed and making love with Udo Kier.
 •• 0:56—In black bra, then topless undressing in front of Kier.
 ••• 1:00—Topless in bedroom, then making love with Kier.
 1:03—Brief buns, lying on Linda's bed.
 1:05—Buns, lying on Linda's bed.
 •• 1:06—Right breast, in bed with Linda.
 •• 1:07—Topless in bed with Linda.
 • 1:09—Buns and side of left breast getting up from bed.
 • 1:11—Full frontal nudity, getting stabbed in the bathroom. Covered with blood.

Fiona (1978; British) . . . . Fiona Richmond
 •• 0:23—Topless on boat with a blonde woman rubbing oil on her.
 •• 0:27—In a bra, then frontal nudity stripping in a guy's office for an audition.
 •• 0:35—Topless, then frontal nudity lying down during photo session.
 • 0:51—Topless walking around her apartment in boots.

•• 1:00—Topless with old guy ripping each other's
clothes off.
•• 1:08—Frontal nudity taking off clothes for a shower.
History of the World, Part I (1981)............ Queen

Richmond, Laura

Video Tapes:
Sexy Lingerie (1988) ....Model
Playboy Video Calendar 1990 (1989) ..... February
••• 0:07—Nude.
Playboy Video Centerfold: Kerri Kendall (1990)
.... Playmate
••• 0:39—Nude.
Playboy Video Playmate Six-Pack 1992 (1992)
.... Playmate
Magazines:
Playboy (Sep 1988)................... Playmate
Playboy's Book of Lingerie (Jan 1991)...... Herself
• 79—Left breast.

Richter, Debi

Miss California 1975.
Films:
Hometown, U.S.A. (1979)...................Dolly
Swap Meet (1979) .... Susan
Gorp (1980) ....Barbara
Hot Moves (1984)........................Heidi
0:06—Brief left bun, pulling pink swimsuit bottom
aside for the boys at the beach.
• 0:29—Topless on nude beach.
••• 1:09—Topless, taking off her red dress in bed with
Michael.
Square Dance (1987) .... Gwen
Winners Take All (1987)............. Cindy Wickes
0:25—In bra, in bed with motorcycle racer.
Promised Land (1988).................. Pammie
The Banker (1989) .... Melanie
Cyborg (1989)....................Nady Simmons
0:28—Buns, after taking off clothes and running into
the ocean.
• 0:30—Brief left breast by the fire showing herself to
Jean-Claude Van Damme.
TV:
Aspen (1977) .... Angela Morelli
All Is Forgiven (1986) ....Sherry Levy

Richters, Christine

Video Tapes:
Playmates at Play (1990) .... Free Wheeling
Magazines:
Playboy (May 1986) .... Playmate

Richwine, Maria

Films:
The Buddy Holly Story (1978)....... Maria Elena Holly
Hamburger—The Motion Picture (1986)
.................................Conchita
•• 0:49—Topless trying to seduce Russell in a room.
Ministry of Vengeance (1989) .... Fatima

• Riley, Colleen

Films:
Deadly Blessing (1981).................... Melissa
The Hills Have Eyes, Part II (1989) ....Jane
• 0:55—Very brief left breast, twice, while taking a
shower outside when Foster talks to her.

• Ringstrom, Erica

Films:
Last Dance (1992) .... Heather
•• 0:48—Buns in G-string, dancing on stage during
DTV contest.
Magazines:
Playboy's Book of Lingerie (Nov 1991) .....Herself
••• 65—Full frontal nudity.
Playboy's Book of Lingerie (Jan 1992) ......Herself
•• 24—Right breast and lower frontal nudity.
Playboy's Book of Lingerie (May 1992) .....Herself
•• 69—Left breast and lower frontal nudity.

Rio, Nicole

Films:
The Zero Boys (1985)...................... Sue
Sorority House Massacre (1987) .... Tracy
•• 0:20—In a sheer bra changing clothes with two other girls in a bedroom.
•• 0:49—Topless in a tepee with her boyfriend, Craig,
just before getting killed.
The Visitants (1987) .... n.a.
Terminal Exposure (1988) .... Hostage Girl

Rixon, Cheryl

Films:
Swap Meet (1979)........................Annie
Used Cars (1980) .... Margaret
•• 0:29—Topless after getting her dress torn off during
a used car commercial.
Magazines:
Penthouse (Dec 1977)....................Pet
Penthouse (Nov 1979)............. Pet of the Year
Penthouse (Jul 1980) .... Used Cars
••• 64-71—Nude.

Roberts, Julia

Films:
Blood Red (1988)..................Maria Collogero
Mystic Pizza (1988) .... Daisy Araujo
Satisfaction (1988) ....Daryle Shane
Shown on TV as "Girls of Summer."
Steel Magnolias (1989) ..... Shelby Eatenton Latcherio
Flatliners (1990)................... Rachel Mannus
Pretty Woman (1990)................Vivian Ward
(Shelley Michelle, the body double for Julia Roberts, only
did the *opening* scenes when Roberts is supposed to be
getting dressed in her sexy outfit—*not* for the nude
scene at 1:30.)
• 1:30—Very, very brief tip of left breast, then right
breast, then left breast seen through head board, in
bed with Gere. It's her—look especially at the verti-

cal vein that pops out in the middle of her forehead whenever her blood pressure goes up.

Dying Young (1991) . . . . Hilary O'Neil
Hook (1991) . . . . Tinkerbell
Sleeping with the Enemy (1991) . . . . . Sara/Laura Burney
Made for Cable Movies:
Baja Oklahoma (1988; HBO) . . . . Candy

Roberts, Luanne

Films:
The Dark Side of Tomorrow (1970) . . . . . Producer's Wife
Weekend with the Babysitter (1970) . . . . . Mona Carlton
Welcome Home, Soldier Boys (1972) . . . . Charlene
Thunderbolt and Lightfoot (1974)
. . . . Suburban Housewife
• 0:57—Brief full frontal nudity standing behind a sliding glass door tempting Jeff Bridges.

Roberts, Mariwin

Films:
Cinderella (1977) . . . . Trapper's Daughter
••• 0:11—Frontal nudity getting a bath outside by her blonde sister. Long scene.
Jailbait Babysitter (1978) . . . . Trisha
•• 0:08—Topless and buns, taking off her dress and getting into van with Cal.
•• 0:18—Topless and buns in shower with Marion while Mike and Cal help them.
Fairytales (1979) . . . . Elevator Operator
• 0:20—Brief full frontal nudity in the elevator.
•• 0:23—Topless again, closer shot.
Magazines:
Penthouse (Apr 1978) . . . . Pet

Roberts, Tanya

Films:
Forced Entry (1975) . . . . Nancy Ulman
0:57—In white bra and panties walking around the house.
The Yum-Yum Girls (1976) . . . . April
California Dreaming (1978) . . . . Stephanie
Fingers (1978) . . . . Julie
Racquet (1979) . . . . Bambi
The Tourist Trap (1979) . . . . Becky
The Beastmaster (1982) . . . . Kiri
••• 0:35—Topless in a pond while Marc Singer watches, then topless getting out of the water when his pet ferrets steal her towel.
Hearts and Armour (1983) . . . . Angelica
Sheena (1984) . . . . Sheena
•• 0:18—Topless and buns taking a shower under a waterfall. Full frontal nudity (long shot), diving into the water.
••• 0:54—Nude taking a bath in a pond while Ted Wass watches.
A View to a Kill (1985) . . . . Stacey Sutton
Purgatory (1988) . . . . Carly Arnold
• 0:29—Nude, getting into the shower.
• 0:42—Very brief topless in bed with the Warden.

0:43—In white lingerie in whorehouse.
•• 0:57—Left breast, then brief topless in bed talking to Tommy.
Night Eyes (1990) . . . . Nikki
(Unrated version reviewed.)
0:18—In white one piece swimsuit by the pool.
• 0:20—Side view of left breast, while getting dressed while sitting on bed.
0:25—In white lingerie, making love in bed with Michael.
0:30—Repeat of last scene on TV when Andrew Stevens brings the video tape home to watch.
0:55—Making love with Stevens. Don't see anything, but still steamy. Bubble covered left breast in tub with Stevens.
••• 1:09—Topless giving Stevens a massage, then making love. Nice! Buns and left breast, while in the shower making love.
• 1:27—Buns, making love with Stevens in a chair.
Twisted Justice (1990) . . . . Secretary
Inner Sanctum (1991) . . . . Lynn Foster
• 0:35—Right breast, several times, while looking out the window.
••• 0:40—Buns in lingerie on sofa with Joseph Bottoms, then topless while making love.
••• 0:57—In black lingerie under trench coat, stripping for Bret Clark. Buns, then topless making love.
Legal Tender (1991) . . . . Rikki Rennick
• 0:41—Buns and topless making love with Robert Davi. Don't see her face.
Second Nature (1991) . . . . n.a.
Almost Pregnant (1992) . . . . Linda Alderson
(Unrated version reviewed.)
••• 0:04—Topless and buns, in bed with a guy. Long scene.
• 0:10—Brief right breast, while under Conaway in bed.
• 0:18—Brief left breast, while in bed with another guy during Conaway's dream.
0:40—Very brief side view of buns, in lingerie, walking down stairs.
• 1:08—Buns, lying in bed while Gordon writes.
••• 1:11—Topless and buns in bed.
••• 1:12—Nude with Conaway.
Sins of Desire (1992) . . . . n.a.
TV:
Charlie's Angels (1980-81) . . . . Julie Rogers
Magazines:
Playboy (Dec 1980) . . . . Sex Stars of 1980
• 240—In sheer blue swimsuit.
Playboy (Oct 1982) . . . . n.a.
••• Nice.
Playboy (Nov 1982) . . . . Sex in Cinema 1982
••• 161—Topless from *The Beastmaster*.
Playboy (Jan 1989) . . . . Women of the Eighties
•• 251—Topless.
Playboy (Nov 1991) . . . . Sex in Cinema 1991
• 144—Side view of left breast, straddling Andrew Stevens. From *Night Eyes*.

Roberts, Teal

Films:

Fatal Games (1984) . . . . .Lynn Fox
••• 0:08—Topless on bed and floor when Frank takes
   her clothes off, more topless in shower.
•• 0:21—Topless in sauna with Sue.

Hardbodies (1984) .Kristi Kelly
•• 0:03—Topless in bed after making love with Scotty,
   then putting her sweater on.
••• 0:47—Topless standing in front of closet mirrors
   talking about breasts with Kimberly.
••• 0:56—Topless making love with Scotty on the
   beach.
•• 1:22—Topless on fancy car bed with Scotty.

Beverly Hills Cop II (1987). . . . . Stripper
•• 0:45—Topless and buns, wearing G-string at the
   385 North Club.

The Last Boy Scout (1991) . . . . Dancer
Night of the Warrior (1991) . . . . Still Model

Video Tapes:

The Perfect Body Contest (1987) . . . . Judge

Robertson, Kimmy

Films:

The Last American Virgin (1982) . . . . Rose
Bad Manners (1989) . . . . Sarah Fitzpatrick
•• 0:38—Topless and buns taking off robe and getting
   into the shower when Mouse takes a picture of her.
   1:16—In white bra when Piper rips her blouse open
   while she's tied up on the piano.
   1:18—Briefly on piano again.
Honey, I Shrunk the Kids (1989) . . . . . . .Gloria Forrester
Trust Me (1989) . . . . .Party Gal
Don't Tell Mom the Babysitter's Dead (1991) . . . . Cathy

Made for Cable TV:

Tales From the Crypt: Top Billing (1991) . . . . .Lisa

TV:

Twin Peaks (1990-91) . . . . Lucy

• Robey

First name is Louise.
Singer.

Films:

The Money Pit (1986). . . . . .Female Vocalist
Raw Deal (1986). . . . . Lamanski's Girl
Play Nice (1992) . . . . Jill/Rapunzel
(Unrated version reviewed.)
• 0:28—Side view of right breast, while sitting on top
   of a victim in bed. Don't see her face.
••• 0:35—Topless, making love in bed with Jack. Nice,
   long scene.
•• 0:46—Topless, making love on the floor with Jack.
••• 1:09—Topless in bed on top of Jack, then getting
   out of bed and getting dressed.

TV:

Friday the 13th: The Series (1987-90) . . . . . Micki Foster

Rochelle, Amy

See: Weiss, Amy-Rochelle.

• Rogers, Mimi

Ex-wife of Tom Cruise.

Films:

Gung Ho (1985) . . . . .Audrey
Someone to Watch Over Me (1987). . . . . Claire Gregory
Street Smart (1987) . . . . Alison Parker
Hider in the House (1989) . . . . Julie Dreyer
The Mighty Quinn (1989) . . . . .Hadley
The Palermo Connection (1989; Italian) . . . . Carrie
Desperate Hours (1990). . . . . Nora Cornell
The Doors (1991). . . . . Magazine Photographer
The Rapture (1991). . . . . .Sharon
• 0:08—Most of her left breast, while lying in bed with
   Randy
•• 0:36—Very brief side view of right breast, dropping
   nightgown and walking into closet.
White Sands (1992) . . . . .Uncredited Molly Dolezal

Made for Cable Movies:

The Fourth Story (1990; Showtime)
. . . . Valerie McCoughlin
Dead Lock (1991; HBO). . . . . Tracy Riggs
Ladykiller (1992; USA) . . . . .Michael Madison

Made for Cable TV:

Dream On: The Second Greatest Story Ever Told
   (1991; HBO). . . . . Julia Montana
   0:18—In black lingerie on bed with Martin.
Dream On: And Bimbo Was His Name-O (1992; HBO)
. . . . Julia Montana
Tales From the Crypt: Beauty Rest (1992; HBO)
. . . . .Helen
   0:25—In bra and panties, lying in a chair before getting "made up" after winning beauty contest.

TV:

The Rousters (1983-84) . . . . .Ellen Slade
Paper Dolls (1984) . . . . Blair Harper-Fenton

• Rohm, Maria

Films:

City of Fear (1965; British) . . . . Maid
Justine (1969; Italian/Spanish) . . . . n.a.
   a.k.a. Maquis de Sade: Justine
Dorian Gray (1970; Italian/British/German) . . . . . . Alice
Venus in Furs (1970) . . . . Wanda Reed
Original version.
• 0:05—Topless on beach, dead, after getting
   dragged from the ocean.
• 0:08—Topless in stockings and panties, getting
   whipped by Olga.
•• 0:10—Topless before getting stabbed by Klaus Kinski.
• 0:11—More topless on beach, dead.
• 0:17—Brief topless.
• 0:21—Right breast several times, making love in bed
   with a guy.
••• 0:22—Topless, lying in bed with the guy afterwards.
• 0:23—Brief topless on beach again.

- 0:32—Topless, dead on the beach with two cuts.
- 0:43—Topless on couch when Olga opens her blouse.
- • 0:45—Topless in bed.
- 0:52—Topless posing for Olga.
- 0:54—Topless, dead.
- • 0:56—Topless walking down stairs, wearing panties.
- 0:59—Topless in bed again.
- 1:02—Brief side view of right breast, hugging Jimmy.
- 1:05—Left breast while acting as a slave girl.
- 1:06—Brief topless seen through sheer curtain.
  1:09—Very brief right breast, dead.
- • 1:10—Left breast, with Klaus Kinski.
  1:12—Buns, lying on couch.

Black Beauty (1971; British/German) . . . . Anne
Count Dracula (1971; Spanish/Italian). . . . . n.a.
Treasure Island (1972; British/Spanish) . . . Mrs. Hawkins
Ten Little Indians (1975) . . . . Elsa

Rohmer, Patrice
Films:
The Harrad Summer (1974) . . . . Marcia
a.k.a. Student Union
- 0:33—Brief topless, starting to take off her blouse in motel room with Harry.

Hustle (1975) . . . . Linda (Dancer)
- 1:03—In pasties, dancing on stage behind beaded curtain. Buns in G-string.

Jackson County Jail (1976) . . . . Cassie Anne
Revenge of the Cheerleaders (1976). . . . . . . Sesame
- 0:28—Brief topless and buns in the boys shower room.

Small Town in Texas (1976). . . . . Trudy

Rojo, Helena
Films:
Aguirre, The Wrath of God (1972; West German)
. . . . Inez
Mary, Mary, Bloody Mary (1975) . . . . Greta
- 0:42—Buns and brief topless getting into bathtub with Cristina Ferrare.

Foxtrot (1976; Mexican/Swiss) . . . . Alexandra

• Roman, Candice
Films:
The Big Bird Cage (1972) . . . . Carla
- 0:16—Buns, while in the shower.

Unholy Rollers (1972) . . . . Donna
a.k.a. Leader of the Pack

Romanelli, Carla
Films:
Steppenwolf (1974). Maria
- ••• 0:59—Topless sitting on bed with John Huston. Long scene.

The Sensuous Nurse (1975; Italian) . . . . Tosca
- •• 0:06—Topless, then nude standing in the winery, then running around.

- •• 0:41—Nude, in basement, playing army, then making love with bearded guy.

The Lonely Lady (1983) . . . . Carla Maria Peroni
- •• 1:10—Brief topless taking off her top to make love with Pia Zadora while a guy watches.

A Very Moral Night (1985; Hungarian). . . . . n.a.

Rome, Sydne
Films:
Diary of Forbidden Dreams (1973; Italian)
. . . . The Girl
- ••• 0:06—Brief topless taking off torn T-shirt in a room, then topless sitting on edge of bed.
- ••• 0:09—Nude getting out of shower, drying herself off and getting dressed.
- 0:20—Brief side view of right breast, while talking to Marcello Mastroianni in her room.
- •• 0:22—Brief topless putting shirt on.
- •• 1:28—Topless outside on stairs fighting for her shirt.
- 1:30—Brief buns and topless climbing onto truck.

Sex with a Smile (1976; Italian)
. . . ."A Dog's Day" segment
The Twist (1976) . . . . Nathalie
Just a Gigolo (1979; German). . . . . Cilly
Looping (1981) . . . . n.a.
Magazines:
Playboy (Nov 1980) . . . . Sex in Cinema 1980
- ••• 178—Topless.

Rose, Gabrielle
Films:
The Journey of Natty Gann (1985) . . . . . Exercise Matron
Family Viewing (1987; Canadian). . . . . Sandra
- 0:27—Brief left breast, lying down with Stan. Seen on TV that Van watches.
- 0:29—Same 0:27 scene again.

The Stepfather (1987) . . . . Dorothy
Speaking Parts (1989; Canadian) . . . . Clara
- •• 0:41—Right breast, on TV monitor, masturbating with Lance. Then topless getting dressed.

Made for Cable Movies:
Devlin (1991; Showtime) . . . . Sister Anne Elizabeth

Rose, Jamie
Films:
Just Before Dawn (1980) . . . . Megan
  0:33—Topless in pond. Long shot.
- 0:34—Brief topless in pond, closer shot.
- •• 0:36—Brief upper half of left breast, then brief topless several times splashing in the water.
- 0:37—Topless getting out of the water.

Heartbreakers (1984) . . . . Libby
- ••• 0:09—Topless in bed talking with Nick Mancuso and Peter Coyote.

Tightrope (1984) . . . . Melanie Silber
  0:07—Buns, lying face down on bed, dead.
Rebel Love (1985) . . . . Columbine Cromwell
Chopper Chicks in Zombietown (1989) . . . . Dede

Playroom (1989). . . . . .Marcy
   a.k.a. Schizo
Crack Down (1990). . . . . .Constance Bigelow
Made for TV Movies:
Voices Within: The Lives of Truddi Chase (1990)
  . . . . Truddi's Mother
Death Hits the Jackpot (1991). . . . . .Nancy Brower
TV:
Falcon Crest (1981-83) . . . . Victoria Gioberti Hogan
Lady Blue (1985-86) . . . . .Detective Katy Mahoney
St. Elsewhere (1986-88) . . . . Dr. Susan Birch

• *Rose, Kristine*

Films:
Total Exposure (1991). .Rita
Night Rhythms (1992). . . . . .Marilyn
  (Unrated version reviewed.)
  ••• 0:17—Taking off her blouse at bar with Martin He-
    witt, then nude, making love on the bar with him.
Round Trip to Heaven (1992) . . . . Tina
Video Tapes:
Playboy's Erotic Fantasies (1992) . . . . .Model
Magazines:
Playboy's Book of Lingerie (Jan 1991) . . . . . . Herself
  ••• 12—Topless.
  ••• 46—Full frontal nudity.
  • 90—Right breast.
Playboy's Book of Lingerie (Mar 1991) . . . . . Herself
  ••• 3-7—Topless and buns.
  ••• 96—Full frontal nudity.
Playboy (Aug 1991) . . . . .California Dreamin'
  •• 135—Left breast and lower frontal nudity.
Playboy's Book of Lingerie (Nov 1991) . . . . . Herself
  ••• 90-91—Topless.
Playboy's Book of Lingerie (Jan 1992) . . . . . . Herself
  ••• 28-29—Topless.
  • 74—Right breast.
Playboy's Book of Lingerie (Sep 1992) . . . . . Herself
  •• 24-25—Left breast.
  ••• 67—Topless.

Rose, Laurie

Films:
The Hot Box (1972) . . . . .Sue
  •• 0:16—Topless cleaning herself off in stream and get-
    ting out.
  •• 0:21—Topless sleeping in hammocks. (She's the first
    one from the front.)
  • 0:26—Topless getting accosted by the People's
    Army guys.
  ••• 0:45—Topless in stream bathing with the other
    three girls.
  • 0:58—Full frontal nudity getting raped by Major
    Dubay.
The Roommates (1973). . . . . Brea
The Working Girls (1973) . . . . Denise
Policewoman (1974). . . . . .n.a.
The Woman Hunt (1975; U.S./Philippines) . . . . .n.a.
The Wizard of Speed & Time (1988) . . . . . . .Bellydancer

Rose, Sherrie

Films:
After School (1987) . . . . First Tribe Member
Spring Fever USA (1988) . . . . Vinyl Vixen #1
  a.k.a. Lauderdale
American Tiger (1989; Italian) . . . . Mary Jo
Summer Job (1989). . . . . .Kathy Shields
  0:25—In bed wearing white bra and panties talking
    to Bruce. Long scene.
  0:52—Buns, walking around in swimsuit and jacket.
  •• 0:53—Topless taking off swimsuit top kneeling by
    the phone, then brief buns standing up.
  1:15—In yellow two piece swimsuit walking on the
    beach.
  •• 1:24—Brief topless taking off her yellow top on the
    beach talking to Bruce.
A Climate for Killing (1990) . . . . Rita Paris
  •• 1:30—Topless in bed while Wayne recollects his
    crime to John Beck.
King of the Kickboxers (1990) . . . . .Molly
  • 1:05—Very brief buns in G-string and partial side of
    left breast, while getting into tub with Jake.
Body Waves (1991) .Suzanne
Deadly Bet (1992) . . . . Doris
Made for Cable TV:
Dream On: Terms of Employment (1992; HBO)
  . . . . n.a.
  Topless with Martin in his office.
Tales From the Crypt: On a Dead Man's Chest
  (1992; HBO). . . . . Danny's Girlfriend
  ••• 0:06—Topless, then full frontal nudity, under Danny
    in bed.
  ••• 0:06—Topless, opening her blouse to show Danny
    her new snake tattoo.
  ••• 0:08—Left breast, then topless, getting dressed.
  • 0:18—Brief buns in G-string, showing Danny her
    tattoo scar.
Video Tapes:
Wet and Wild II (1990). . . . . Model
Inside Out (1992) . . . . Bethany/The Leda
  • 0:35—Right breast, while making love with the oth-
    er criminal. Dark.
  • 0:40—Upper half of right breast while making love
    with him again after he's connected to the comput-
    er.
Inside Out 2 (1992). . . . . .Marina/The Freak
  (Unrated version reviewed.)
  • 0:29—Topless, getting her clothes and mask taken
    off in front of other masked people. B&W.
  •• 0:35—Topless in bed with alien guy. B&W.
Magazines:
Playboy (Apr 1989) . . . . The Girls of Spring Break
  ••• 74—Topless lying down, wearing a bikini bottom.
Playboy's Book of Lingerie (Jan 1991) . . . . . .Herself
  •• 16—Left breast.
Playboy's Book of Lingerie (Mar 1991). . . . . .Herself
  •• 64-65—Left breast.
Playboy's Book of Lingerie (Sep 1991) . . . . . .Herself
  •• 56—Left breast and buns.

Ross, Annie

Films:
Straight on Till Morning (1974) . . . . .Liza
Oh, Alfie! (1975; British) . . . . Claire
   a.k.a. Alfie Darling
   •• 1:34—Topless on top of Alfie in open black dress
      while he's lying injured in bed.
Yanks (1979) . . . . .Red Cross Lady
Superman III (1983) . . . . Vera Webster
Witchery (1988) . . . . Rose Brooks
Basket Case 2 (1989) . . . . .Granny Ruth
Basket Case 3: The Progeny (1991) . . . . . . .Granny Ruth

Ross, Katharine

Wife of actor Sam Elliott.
Films:
The Graduate (1967) . . . . Elaine Robinson
Butch Cassidy and the Sundance Kid (1969)
  . . . . Etta Place
Tell Them Willie Boy is Here (1969) . . . . Lola
   0:22—Very, very brief breast, while sitting up with
      Robert Blake. Topless getting up when guy with rifle
      disturbs her and Blake. Buns, getting dressed. Long
      shot, dark, hard to see.
They Only Kill Their Masters (1972) . . . . Kate
   (Not available on video tape.)
The Betsy (1978) . . . . Sally Hardeman
The Legacy (1979; British) . . . . .Maggie Walsh
The Final Countdown (1980) . . . . Laurel Scott
Wrong is Right (1982) . . . . .Sally Blake
A Climate for Killing (1990) . . . . Grace Hines
The Shadow Riders (1991) . . . . Kate Connery
Made for TV Movies:
Secrets of a Mother and Daughter (1983) . . . . .n.a.

Ross, Ruthy

Films:
The Centerfold Girls (1974) . . . . Glory
   ••• 0:49—Topless and buns posing for photographer
      outside with Charly.
Magazines:
Playboy (Jun 1973) . . . . Playmate
   •• 120-129—Topless.
Playboy (Oct 1973) . . . . Bunnies of 1973
   ••• 137—Left breast and lower frontal nudity.

Ross, Shana

Video Tapes:
Penthouse Love Stories (1986) . . . . AC/DC Lover
   ••• 0:17—Full frontal nudity in bedroom with Monique
      Gabrielle.
Magazines:
Penthouse (Aug 1983) . . . . Pet
   ••• 83-101—Nude.

Rossellini, Isabella

Daughter of actress Ingrid Bergman.
Spokesmodel for Lancôme cosmetics.
Films:
A Matter of Time (1976; Italian/U.S.) . . . . Sister Pia
White Nights (1985) . . . . Darya Greenwood
Blue Velvet (1986) . . . . .Dorothy
   • 1:08—Brief topless in apartment.
   • 1:40—Nude, standing on porch, bruised.
Siesta (1987) . . . . .Marie
Tough Guys Don't Dance (1987) . . . . Madeleine
Cousins (1989) . . . . .Maria Hardy
Wild at Heart (1990) . . . . .Perdita
Death Becomes Her (1992) . . . . n.a.
Made for Cable Movies:
Lies of the Twins (1991; USA) . . . . Rachel Marks
   0:33—In bra, on bed with Aidan Quinn.
   0:44—Very brief lower half of buns, while putting
      blouse on.

• Rossini, Bianca

Films:
Moon Over Parador (1988) . . . . Tilde
Mobsters (1991) . . . . Rosalie Luciano
   a.k.a. Mobsters—The Evil Empire
Video Tapes:
Inside Out 3 (1992) . . . . .Ollala/The Branding
   ••• 0:23—Topless, making love in bed with Mike.

• Roth, Andrea

Films:
Princess in Exile (1991; Canadian) . . . Marlene Lancaster
Seedpeople (1992) . . . . .Heidi Tucker
Made for Cable Movies:
Psychic (1992; USA) . . . . April Morris
   • 1:01—Brief buns, partially covered with leaves, lying
      dead in park.

Routledge, Alison

Films:
The Quiet Earth (1985; New Zealand) . . . . . . .Joanne
   0:49—Brief buns, after making breakfast for Zac.
   •• 1:24—Topless in guard tower making love with Api.
Bridge to Nowhere (1986; New Zealand) . . . . Lise

Rowan, Gay

Films:
The Girl in Blue (1973; Canadian) . . . . .Bonnie
   a.k.a. U-turn
   • 0:06—Left breast, in bed with Scott.
   • 0:31—Brief topless in bathtub.
   • 0:48—Right breast, while in shower talking to Scott.
      Brief topless (long shot) on balcony throwing water
      down at him.
   • 1:21—Brief right breast and buns getting out of bed
      and running out of the room.
Sudden Fury (1975) . . . . Janet
S.O.B. (1981) . . . . n.a.
Second Thoughts (1983) . . . . .Annie

Rowe, Misty

Films:

The Hitchhikers (1971) . . . . .Maggie
- 0:00—Brief side view of left breast getting dressed.
- 0:17—Very brief topless getting dress ripped open, then raped in van.
- 0:48—Brief right breast while getting dressed.
- 1:09—Left breast, making love with Benson.
- 1:10—Brief topless taking a bath in tub.
- 1:13—Very brief right breast in car with another victim.

Goodbye, Norma Jean (1975) . . . . .Norma Jean Baker
- 0:02—In white bra putting makeup on.
- •• 0:08—In white bra and panties, then topless.
- 0:14—Brief topless in bed getting raped.
- 0:31—Very, very brief silhouette of right breast, in bed with Rob.
- ••• 0:59—Topless during shooting of stag film, then in B&W when some people watch the film.
- 1:14—In white bra and panties undressing.

Loose Shoes (1977). . . . . .Louise
The Man with Bogart's Face (1980). . . . . Duchess
National Lampoon's Class Reunion (1982)
. . . . .Cindy Shears
- 0:37—Very brief topless running around school stage in Hawaiian hula dance outfit.

Double Exposure (1983) . . . . .Bambi
Meatballs, Part II (1984) . . . . Fanny
Made for TV Movies:
When Things Were Rotten (1975) . . . . . . .Maid Marion
TV:
Hee Haw (1972-91) .Regular
Happy Days (1974-75) . . . . Wendy
When Things Were Rotten (1975) . . . . . . .Maid Marion
Hee Haw Honeys (1978-79) . . . . Misty Honey
Joe's World (1979-80). . . . . .Judy Wilson
Magazines:
Playboy (Nov 1976) . . . . Misty
••• 104-107—Nude.
Playboy (Dec 1980). . . . . Sex Stars of 1980
•• 246—Topless.

• Rowland, Leesa

Films:

The Book of Love (1991). . . . . .Honeymoon
0:56—Stripping in tent at carnival, wearing pasties.
Class of Nuke 'Em High Part II: Subhumanoid Meltdown (1991) . . . . .Victoria
- •• 0:24—Topless in room with Roger. Special effect mouth in her stomach.
- 0:25—Most of side of left breast, making love on top of Roger.

Royce, Roselyn

Films:

Cheech & Chong's Nice Dreams (1981)
. . . . Beach Girl #3
- 0:29—Brief topless on the beach with two other girls. Long shot, unsteady, hard to see.

Malibu Hot Summer (1981). . . . . .Cheryl Rielly
a.k.a. Sizzle Beach
(*Sizzle Beach* is the re-released version with Kevin Costner featured on the cover. It is missing all the nude scenes during the opening credits before 0:06.)
- •• 0:15—On exercise bike, then topless getting into bed.
- ••• 0:16—Topless sitting up in bed, buns going to closet to get dressed to go jogging.
- 0:26—In pink two piece swimsuit running to answer the phone.
- •• 0:52—Topless on boat with Brent.

Off the Wall (1982). . . . . .Buxom Blonde
- 0:35—Left breast, while kissing an inmate in visiting room while the guards watch.
- •• 0:51—Left breast again, while kissing inmate through bars while the guards watch.

• Rubanoff, Annie

Films:

Breathing Fire (1990). . . . . April
Video Tapes:
Inside Out 4 (1992) . . . . .Ms. Morely/Save the Wetlands
(Unrated version reviewed.)
- •• 0:32—Left breast, while playing with herself while being interviewed.
- 0:33—Partial buns, while bending over to pick up photo off the floor.

Rubens, Mary Beth

Films:

Prom Night (1980) . . . . Kelly
- 0:59—Very brief right breast making out with Drew in the locker room.
- 1:02—Brief upper half of breasts, standing up to put dress on. Dark.

Firebird 2015 AD (1981) . . . . n.a.
Perfect Timing (1984) . . . . .Judy
- 0:04—In a bra, then topless in bedroom with Joe.
- •• 0:05—Nude, walking to kitchen, then talking with Harry.
- 0:08—Left breast seen through the camera's view finder.
- 0:10—Nude, getting dressed in bedroom.
- 0:49—In red bra and panties.
- •• 0:50—Nude, in bed with Joe.
- ••• 1:00—Nude, discovering Joe's hidden video camera, then going downstairs.

TV:
E.N.G. (1989-90) . . . . Bobby

• Rubin, Jennifer

Films:

A Nightmare on Elm Street 3: The Dream Warriors
(1987) . . . . .Taryn
1969 (1988). . . . . .Wife
Bad Dreams (1988) . . . . Cynthia
Permanent Record (1988) . . . . .Lauren

Delusion (1990) . . . . Patti
- 0:34—Brief buns, pulling her panties down to moon the guys before entering the lake.
   0:37—Walking out of the lake in red bra and panties. More in red bra while playing with her lizard.
   0:46—Very briefly in wet bra, coming up for air from the water. Slow motion.
- ••• 1:07—Topless in motel bathroom, drying her hair. More topless in the motel room with George.
- 1:12—Right breast, in open blouse, while sitting on the bed, talking with George.

Too Much Sun (1990). .Gracia
The Doors (1991) . . . . Edie
A Woman, Her Man And Her Futon (1992) . . . . .n.a.

Made for Cable Movies:
The Fear Inside (1992; Showtime) . . . . . . Jane Caswell
- 0:26—Topless with Peter. Hard to see because of the strobe light effect.
- 0:53—Buns and partial left breast visible under water while skinny dipping in pool.
   0:55—Full frontal nudity under water. Hard to see because of the distortion.

Made for Cable TV:
Tales From the Crypt: Beauty Rest (1992; HBO)
. . . . Druscilla

Ruiz, Mia M.

Films:
Witchcraft II: The Temptress (1989) . . . . . Michelle
- 0:27—Brief topless several times making love with a guy on the floor during William's hallucination.

Demon Wind (1990). .Reana
Wild at Heart (1990) . Mr. Reindeer's Resident Valet #1
- •• 0:32—Topless standing next to Mr. Reindeer on the right, holding a tray. Long scene.

Black Belt (1992) . . . . Hooker
- ••• 0:04—Topless sitting on bed.
   0:16—Topless, dead on bed, covered with blood.

• Runyon, Jennifer

Films:
To All a Goodnight (1980). . . . . .n.a.
Ghostbusters (1984) . . . . .Female Student
Up the Creek (1984) . . . . .Heather Merriweather
The Falcon and the Snowman (1985) . . . . .Carole
Flight of the Spruce Goose (1986). . . . . .Terry
18 Again! (1988). . . . . Robin
A Man Called Serge (1990) . . . . Fifi
Killing Streets (1991). . . . . Sandra Ross
- 1:00—In white lingerie then brief topless taking off lingerie in bed with Michael Paré. Hard to see.

Miniseries:
Space (1985) . . . . Marcia Grant
Made for TV Movies:
A Very Brady Christmas (1988) . . . . Cindy Brady
TV:
Charles in Charge (1984-85). . . . . . . .Gwendolyn Pierce

• Russell, Andaluz

Films:
The Assassin (1989) . . . . Amanda Portales
- 0:21—Brief topless while changing clothes in room with the other assassins.

Pure Luck (1991) . . . . Reception Manager

Russell, Betsy

Films:
Private School (1983) . . . . Jordan Leigh-Jensen
(Blonde hair.)
   0:02—Taking a shower behind a frosted door.
- 0:04—Very, very brief right breast and buns when Bubba takes her towel off through window.
- ••• 0:19—Topless riding a horse after Kathleen Wilhoite steals her blouse.
   0:35—In jogging outfit stripping down to black bra and panties, brief upper half of buns.
   1:15—In white bra and panties, in room with Bubba.
   1:24—Upper half of buns flashing with the rest of the girls during graduation ceremony.

Out of Control (1984). . . . . Chrissie
(Brunette hair.)
   0:19—In white corset and panties in the pond.
- •• 0:29—Topless taking off her top while playing Strip Spin the Bottle.
   0:30—Buns, taking off her panties.

Avenging Angel (1985) . . . . Angel/Molly Stewart
Tomboy (1985) . . . . Tomasina "Tommy" Boyd
- •• 0:44—In wet T-shirt, then brief topless after landing in the water with her motorcycle.
- •• 0:59—Topless making love with the race car driver in an exercise room.

Cheerleader Camp (1987) . . . . Alison Wentworth
   a.k.a. Bloody Pom Poms
Made for TV Movies:
Roxanne: The Prize Pulitzer (1989). . . . . . . Liza Pulitzer

Russell, Karen

Films:
Vice Academy (1988) . . . . Shawnee
- •• 0:09—Topless exposing herself to Duane to disarm him.
- •• 1:13—Topless pulling her top down to distract a bad guy.

Dr. Alien (1989) . . . . Coed #2
   a.k.a. I Was a Teenage Sex Mutant
- ••• 0:53—Topless taking off her top (she's on the right) in the women's locker room before another coed takes her's off in front of Wesley.

Easy Wheels (1989) . . . . Candy
Hell High (1989) . . . . Teen Girl
- •• 0:04—Topless in shack with Teen Boy while little girl watches through a hole in the wall.

Murder Weapon (1989) . . . . .Amy
- ••• 0:05—Topless in bed with a guy after taking off her swimsuit top, then making love on top of him. Long scene.
- 0:34—Brief topless in shower.

Dick Tracy (1990) . . . . Dancer
Havana (1990) . . . . Dancer #2
Mob Boss (1990). . . . . .Mary
Shock 'Em Dead (1990) . . . . Michelle
•• 0:16—In lingerie, then topless twice with Martin.
Wilding, The Children of Violence (1990)
. . . . Cathy
•• 0:20—Topless in bedroom when Wings Hauser pulls
her lingerie down.
Mobsters (1991) . . . . Showgirl
a.k.a. Mobsters—The Evil Empire

Russell, Theresa
Wife of director Nicholas Roeg.
Films:
Straight Time (1978) . . . . Jenny Mercer
••• 1:00—Left breast, while in bed with Dustin Hoffman. Don't see her face.
Bad Timing: A Sensual Obsession (1980)
. . . . .Milena Flaherty
0:14—Buns and topless under short, sheer blouse.
0:17—Almost brief right breast in bed during Art
Garfunkel's flashback. Very brief left breast kneeling
on bed with him.
• 0:31—Full frontal nudity in bed with Garfunkel. Intercut with tracheotomy footage. Kind of gross.
•• 0:32—Right breast, while sitting in bed talking to
Garfunkel.
• 0:41—Brief topless several times on operating table.
• 0:55—Full frontal nudity making love on stairwell
with Garfunkel. Quick cuts.
• 0:56—Brief topless twice after stairwell episode
while throwing a fit.
•• 1:45—In bra, then topless passed out on bed while
Garfunkel cuts her clothes off. Brief full frontal nudity.
•• 1:48—More topless cuts while Garfunkel makes love
to her while she's unconscious from an overdose of
drugs.
Eureka (1983; British) . . . . Tracy
0:38—In lingerie talking to Rutger Hauer.
• 0:40—Right breast, lying in bed with Hauer.
• 1:04—Very brief left breast in bed with Hauer, then
brief lower frontal nudity and brief buns when Gene
Hackman bursts into the room.
•• 1:09—Topless on a boat with Hauer.
• 1:41—Left breast peeking out from under black top
while lying in bed.
••• 1:59—Full frontal nudity kicking off sheets in the
bed.
The Razor's Edge (1984) . . . . Sophie
Insignificance (1985). . . . . Actress
Black Widow (1987) . . . . Catherine
• 0:28—Briefly nude, making love in cabin.
•• 1:18—Nude in pool with Paul.
Aria (1988; U.S./British). . . . . King Zog
Track 29 (1988; British) . . . . Linda Henry
Impulse (1989) . . . . Lottie
•• 0:37—Left breast, making love with Stan in bed.

Physical Evidence (1989) . . . . Jenny Hudson
Cold Heaven (1990). . . . . Marie Davenport
• 0:09—Very brief upper half of right breast, when it
pops out of her swimsuit top when struggling to get
Mark Harmon onto boat.
• 0:18—Side of left breast while washing herself at the
sink.
• 1:14—Brief topless several times, making love in bed
with James Russo.
Whore (1991). . . . . Liz
a.k.a. If you're afraid to say it... Just see it
•• 0:13—Topless and buns in G-string outfit, taking off
her coat.
••• 0:25—In black bra, doing sit ups. Topless making
love in spa with Blake.
• 1:18—Brief buns, in open skirt in back of car with a
customer.
Kafka (1992; U.S./French) . . . . .Gabriela
Magazines:
Playboy (Nov 1980) . . . . Sex in Cinema 1980
• 181—Topless.
Playboy (Nov 1983) . . . . Sex in Cinema 1983
• 145—Topless.

Ruval, Yulis
See: Müller, Lillian.

Ryan, Meg
Wife of actor Dennis Quaid.
Films:
Rich and Famous (1981) . . . . .Debbie at 18 years
Armed and Dangerous (1986) . . . . . Maggie Cavanaugh
Top Gun (1986) . . . . Carole
Innerspace (1987) . . . . Lydia
D.O.A. (1988) . . . . Sydney Fuller
The Presidio (1988) . . . . Donna
Promised Land (1988) . . . . Beverly
• 0:22—Very brief side view of left breast in bed with
Kiefer Sutherland.
When Harry Met Sally... (1989) . . . . Sally Albright
Joe vs. the Volcano (1990) . . . . . DeDe/Angelica/Patricia
The Doors (1991). . . . . Pamela Courson
•• 1:06—Right breast, while lying in bed with Val Kilm-
er.
Prelude to a Kiss (1992) . . . . Rita
TV:
One of the Boys (1982) . . . . Jane
Wildside (1985) . . . . Cally Oaks

• Ryan, Rachel
Adult film actress.
a.k.a. Serina Robinson and Penny Morgan.
Wife of actor Richard Mulligan.
Films:
Clean and Sober (1988)
. . . . Uncredited Dead Girlfriend
• 0:02—Buns, lying dead in Michael Keaton's bed.
Don't see her face, but it's her.

Video Tapes:
Secrets of Making Love... To the Same Person Forever (1991). . . . . .Blonde Girl/Boat
••• 0:04—Topless in boat and on river bank with her lover.
•• 0:47—Topless in boat again.
Inside Out (1992) . . . . .Love the One You're With
•• 1:13—Left breast, in bed with a guy.
•• 1:14—Right breast and buns, climbing on top of him in bed.
•• 1:15—Topless and buns, making love on top of him. More topless after making love.

Ryan, Stephanie
See: Napoli, Susan.

Sachs, Adrianne
Films:
Cat Chaser (1988). . . . . .Anita De Boya
Two to Tango (1988) . . . . Cecilia Lorca
•• 0:29—Side of left breast and buns in bedroom with Lucky Lara. More left breast while Dan Stroud watches through camera.
•• 0:59—Topless and buns in bed with Dan Stroud.
In the Cold of the Night (1989) . . . . Kimberly Shawn
••• 0:52—Buns and topless in shower, then making love with Scott. Long, erotic scene.
• 0:59—Brief topless in outdoor spa.
•• 1:06—Topless making love on Scott's lap in bed.
Best of the Best (1990) . . . . Kelly
Magazines:
Playboy (Oct 1992). . . . . .Grapevine

Sägebrecht, Marianne
Films:
Sugarbaby (1985; German). . . . . Sugarbaby
The Bagdad Café (1988) . . . . Jasmin
(Check this out if you like full-figured women.)
•• 1:09—Right breast slowly lowering her top, posing while Jack Palance paints.
•• 1:12—More topless posing for Palance.
Moon Over Parador (1988). . . . . Magor
The War of the Roses (1989) . . . . Susan
Rosalie Goes Shopping (1990) . . . . .Rosalie Greenspace
Magazines:
Playboy (Nov 1988) . . . . Sex in Cinema 1988
• 136—Topless from *Bagdad Café*.

Sahagun, Elena
Films:
Caged Fury (1989) . . . . .Tracy Collins
0:54—In bra when Buck holds her hostage.
•• 1:01—Left breast while taking a shower.
Corporate Affairs (1990) . . . . Stacy
Marked for Death (1990) . . . . Carmen
• 0:06—Topless in room, shooting Steven Seagal's partner.

Naked Obsession (1990). . . . . .Becky
1:07—Dancing on stage in white outfit (She's got a mask over her face).
••• 1:10—In white bra, panties, garter belt and stockings while wearing the mask. Topless and buns in G-string.
Sunset Heat (1991) . . . . Brandon's Model
(Unrated version reviewed.)
Uncaged (1991). . . . . .Joey
a.k.a. Angel in Red
Magazines:
Playboy (Nov 1991) . . . . Sex in Cinema 1991
••• 143—Topless, wearing white mask, in scene from *Naked Obsession*. (Incorrectly identified as Maria Ford.)

• Sal, Jeanne
Films:
Corporate Affairs (1990) . . . . Sandy
• 0:38—Left breast in open dress while sneaking around the office with Buster.
Dead Women In Lingerie (1991) . . . . .Bing

Salem, Pamela
Films:
The Bitch (1979; British) . . . . Lynn
•• 0:46—Topless in bed making love with a guy after playing at a casino.
After Darkness (1985). . . . . Elizabeth Huninger
Salome (1986) . . . . Herodias

• Salt, Jennifer
Films:
Midnight Cowboy (1969). . . . . .Annie
• 0:31—Very brief buns, while running away from some bad guys in flashback.
• 0:42—Brief left breast on bed with Voight in flashback.
• 0:49—Very brief topless in car in B&W flashback. More brief topless and buns in car and running on porch.
The Wedding Party (1969) . . . . Phoebe
Brewster McCloud (1970) . . . . .Hope
Play It Again, Sam (1972). . . . . .Sharon
Sisters (1973). . . . . Grace Collier
It's My Turn (1980) . . . . Maisie
TV:
Soap (1977-81) . . . . Eunice Tate
The Marshall Chronicles (1990) . . . . Cynthia Brightman

Samples, Candy
Adult film actress.
a.k.a. Mary Gavin.
Films:
Fantasm (1976; Australian). . . . . n.a.
Up! (1976). .The Headsperson
Russ Meyer film.
Superchick (1978) . . . . Lady on Boat
••• 0:08—Topless in bed with Johnny on boat.

Beneath the Valley of the Ultravixens (1979)
. . . . The Very Big Blonde
Video Tapes:
Best Chest in the West (1984) . . . . Herself
••• 0:54—Topless dancing on stripping and dancing on stage with Pat McCormick.

Sanda, Dominique

Films:
First Love (1970; German/Swiss). . . . . Sinaida
The Conformist (1971; Italian/French)
. . . . .Anna Quadri
The Garden of the Finzi-Continis
(1971; Italian/German) . . . . Micol
0:24—In braless wet white T-shirt after getting caught in a rainstorm.
• 1:12—Topless sitting on a bed after turning a light on so the guy standing outside can see her.
Without Apparent Motive (1972; French)
. . . . Sandra Forest
Impossible Object (1973; French) . . . . Nathalie
a.k.a. Story of a Love Story
The Makintosh Man (1973; British) . . . . .n.a.
Conversation Piece (1974; Italian/French) . . . . . .Mother
Steppenwolf (1974). . . . . .Hermine
1:40—Brief lower frontal nudity, sleeping with a guy.
• 1:41—Very brief left breast, waking up and rolling over to hug John Huston.
1900 (1976; Italian) .Ada
•• 2:12—(0:05 into tape 2.) Full frontal nudity under thin fabric dancing with Robert De Niro for photographer.
Damnation Alley (1977) . . . . Janice
The Inheritance (1978; Italian) . . . . .Irene
•• 0:18—Full frontal nudity getting undressed and lying on the bed with her new husband.
••• 0:37—Full frontal nudity lying in bed with her lover.
• 1:19—Very brief right breast, while undoing top for Anthony Quinn.
••• 1:22—Left breast, lying in bed. Full frontal nudity jumping out of bed after realizing that Quinn is dead.
Cabo Blanco (1982) . . . . Marie Claire Allesandri
Beyond Good and Evil (1984; Italian/German/French)
. . . . .Lou-Andreas-Salome
Made for TV Movies:
Voyage of Terror: The Achillie Largo Affair . . . . .n.a.
Magazines:
Playboy (Mar 1972). . . . . .Magnifique Dominique
••• 87-89—Nice.
Playboy (Nov 1972) . . . . Sex in Cinema 1972
• 159—Topless.
Playboy (Dec 1972). . . . . Sex Stars of 1972
•• 207—Left breast.
Playboy (Jan 1973) . . . . .Impossible Object
• 192—Right breast in open dress top.
Playboy (Nov 1973) . . . . Sex in Cinema 1973
• 158—Partial left breast.

Playboy (Dec 1973) . . . . .Sex Stars of 1973
••• 211—Left breast.
Playboy (Nov 1978) . . . . Sex in Cinema 1978
• 184—Right breast.

Sandlund, Debra

Films:
Tough Guys Don't Dance (1987) . . . . . . Patty Lareine
•• 1:24—Topless ripping her blouse off to kiss the policeman after they have killed and buried another woman.
• 1:24—Very brief left breast, twice, in bed with Ryan O'Neal. Long shot.
Murder by Numbers (1990) . . . . .Leslie
TV:
Full House (1990). . . . . Cindy

Sandrelli, Stefania

Films:
Seduced and Abandoned (1964; Italian)
. . . . Agnese Ascalone
The Conformist (1971; Italian/French) . . . . .Giulia
1900 (1976; Italian) . . . . .Anita Foschi
The Key (1983; Italian) . . . . Teresa
(Nude a lot. Only the best are listed.)
••• 0:31—Nude when Nino examines her while she's passed out. Long scene.
•• 0:42—Full frontal nudity in bathtub while Nino peeks in over the door.
•• 1:04—In lingerie, then topless and buns, undressing sexily in front of Nino.
•• 1:16—Left breast, sticking out of nightgown so Nino can suck on it.
••• 1:19—Topless and buns making love in bed with Laszlo.
•• 1:21—Topless and buns getting up and cleaning herself.
•• 1:28—Topless sitting in bed talking to Nino.
••• 1:30—Nude, getting on top of Nino in bed.
The Sleazy Uncle (1991; Italian) . . . . Isabella

Sands, Peggy

a.k.a. Peggie Sanders.
Films:
Into the Night (1985) . . . . Shameless Woman
• 0:43—Topless putting dress on after coming out of men's restroom stall after a man leaves the stall first.
Beverly Hills Cop II (1987) . . . . Stripper
• 0:48—Very brief topless, dancing at the 385 North Club.
Phoenix the Warrior (1988) . . . . Keela
Far Out Man (1990). Misty
••• 0:50—Topless and buns in black G-string, undressing and getting into bathtub with Tommy Chong.
Lady Avenger (1991). . . . . Maggie
(In braless tank top for most of the film.)
••• 0:18—Topless in bed with Kevin.
Millenium Countdown (1991) . . . . n.a.

Sara, Mia

Films:
Ferris Bueller's Day Off (1986) . . . . Slone Peterson
Legend (1986) Lili
Apprentice to Murder (1987). . . . . Alice
- 0:29—Left side view topless making love with Chad Lowe.

Queenie (1987). . . . . Queenie Kelly/Dawn Avalon
Shadows in the Storm (1988) . . . . Melanie
0:51—Standing in bathtub all covered with bubbles talking to Ned Beatty.
Any Man's Death (1989) . . . . Gerlind
- 0:50—Brief right nipple when John Savage undoes her top. Don't see her face.

A Climate for Killing (1990). . . . . Elise Shipp
Miniseries:
Till We Meet Again (1989). . . . . .Delphine

Sarandon, Susan

Significant Other of actor Tim Robbins.
Ex-wife of actor Chris Sarandon.
Films:
Joe (1970) . . . . Melissa Compton
- 0:02—Topless and very brief lower frontal nudity taking off clothes and getting into bathtub with Frank.

Lady Liberty (1972; Italian/French) . . . . Sally
The Front Page (1974) .Peggy
The Great Waldo Pepper (1975) . . . . .Mary Beth
The Rocky Horror Picture Show (1975; British)
. . . . Janet Weiss
The Great Smokey Roadblock (1976) . . . . Ginny
Other Side of Midnight (1977)
. . . . Catherine Douglas
- 1:10—Topless in bedroom with John Beck. Long shot, then right breast while lying in bed.
2:18—In wet white nightgown running around outside during a storm.
King of the Gypsies (1978) . . . . Rose
- 0:49—Brief right breast during fight with Judd Hirsch.
Pretty Baby (1978). . . . . Hattie
0:12—Feeding a baby with her left breast, while sitting by the window in the kitchen.
- 0:24—Brief side view, taking a bath.
••• 0:39—Topless on the couch when Keith Carradine photographs her.
Something Short of Paradise (1979) . . . .Madeleine Ross
Loving Couples (1980) . . . . Stephanie
Atlantic City (1981; French/Canadian). . . . . Sally
•• 0:50—Left breast cleaning herself with lemon juice while Burt Lancaster watches through window.
The Tempest (1982). . . . . Aretha
0:58—In braless white tank top washing clothes with Molly Ringwald in the ocean.
1:53—In wet white T-shirt on balcony during rainstorm with Jason Robards and Raul Julia.

1:55—In wet white T-shirt on the beach.
- 1:57—Brief right, then left breasts in open T-shirt saving someone in the water.
The Hunger (1983) . . . . Sarah Roberts
••• 0:59—In a wine stained white T-shirt, then topless during love scene with Catherine Deneuve.
The Buddy System (1984) . . . . Emily
Compromising Positions (1985) . . . . Judith Singer
The Witches of Eastwick (1987) . . . . .Jane Spofford
Bull Durham (1988) . . . . .Annie Savoy
1:39—Brief right breast peeking out from under her dress after crawling on the kitchen floor to get a match.
The January Man (1988) . . . . Christine Starkey
Sweet Hearts Dance (1988) . . . . Sandra Boon
1:23—Almost a left breast in bathroom mirror changing clothes.
1:25—Very, very brief left breast under white bathrobe arguing with Don Johnson in the bathroom.
White Palace (1990) . . . . Nora Baker
••• 0:28—Topless on top of James Spader. Great shots of right breast.
- 0:38—Topless on bed with Spader.
Thelma and Louise (1991) . . . . Louise
Light Sleeper (1992). . . . . .Ann
Made for Cable Movies:
Mussolini and I (1985; HBO) . . . . n.a.
Made for TV Movies:
Women of Valor (1986) . . . . n.a.

• Sassoon, Catya

Films:
Tuff Turf (1984) . . . . Feather
Dance with Death (1991). . . . . Jodie
••• 0:29—Topless and buns in G-string, while dancing on stage.
••• 0:37—Topless and buns, dancing on stage. Her body is painted gold.
••• 0:38—More topless and buns.
Secret Games (1991). . . . . Sandra
(Unrated version reviewed.)
••• 0:21—Topless during modeling session with the other girls. (She's the only brunette.)
••• 0:26—Topless, making love in bed with Emil.
•• 0:34—Topless in yellow bikini bottoms, sunbathing with the other girls.
••• 0:40—Topless, getting out of the swimming pool and lying on lounge chair.
Video Tapes:
Inside Out 4 (1992) . . . . Pauline/Natalie Would
(Unrated version reviewed.)
0:07—Doing a strip routine in bra and panties in hotel room for Ted.
••• 0:08—Topless in bed with Ted, then getting out and getting dressed.

• Saunders, Loni

Adult film actress.

Films:

Up 'n' Coming (1987) . . . . Dixanne
(R-rated version reviewed, X-rated version available.)
- 0:19—Topless kissing a guy on the bus.

Magazines:

Penthouse (Apr 1980) . . . . Orient Exposed
••• 76-85—Nude.

Saunders, Pamela

Video Tapes:

Playboy Video Calendar 1987 (1986) . . . . Playmate
Playboy Video Magazine, Volume 11 (1986)
. . . . Playmate
••• 0:52—Nude, undressing after party, in still photos
and at the beach.
Playmates at Play (1990) . . . . Bareback

Magazines:

Playboy (Nov 1985) . . . . Playmate
Playboy's Book of Lingerie (Jan 1991) . . . . . . Herself
•• 36—Topless.

Saura, Marina

Films:

Flesh + Blood (1985) . . . . Polly
- 0:59—Brief left breast during feast in the castle.
- 1:09—Topless on balcony of the castle with everybody during the day.
Crystal Heart (1987) . . . . Justine
The Monk (1990; British/Spanish) . . . . Jacinta

Savoy, Theresa Ann

Films:

La Bambina (1976; Italian) . . . . n.a.
Caligula (1980) . . . . Druscilla
(X-rated, 147 minute version.)
•• 0:01—Nude, running around in the forest with Malcolm McDowell.
- 0:05—Buns, rolling in bed with McDowell. Very brief
topless getting out of bed.
- 0:26—Left breast several times in bed.
- 0:46—Brief right breast in bed with McDowell
again.
- 1:15—Left breast with McDowell and Helen Mirren.
- 1:22—Very brief left breast getting up in open dress.
•• 1:45—Full frontal nudity, then buns when dead and
McDowell tries to revive her.

Video Tapes:

Penthouse: On the Wild Side (1988) . . . . . . Druscilla
- 0:51—Topless in scenes from *Caligula*.

Magazines:

Penthouse (May 1980) . . . . Caligula
•• 81—Topless, carried by Malcolm McDowell.

• Saxton, Lisa

Films:

Night Eyes 2 (1991) . . . . Car Rental Girl
••• 0:05—Topless and buns, making love in bed with
Jesse.
- 0:09—Buns, on TV when video tape is played back.
Ring of Fire (1991) . . . . Linda
- 0:17—Brief buns, in G-string swimsuit, getting into
spa with Brad.

Made for Cable TV:

Dream On: The Second Greatest Story Ever Told
(1991; HBO) . . . . Coed #2
•• 0:08—(She's the brunette one.) Topless taking off
her purple sweater in bedroom set with Coed #1
(redhead). More topless opening the closet door
and falling back onto the bed.
- 0:34—Brief topless (on the right) with swamp creature and Coed #1 (on the left) during Martin's daydream.

Video Tapes:

Bikini Blitz (1990) . . . . Model
Intimate Workout For Lovers (1992)
. . . . Intimate Harmony
••• 0:39—Nude, in dance studio and in the showers. Excellent!

Magazines:

Playboy (Oct 1991) . . . . Grapevine
Playboy's Book of Lingerie (Jan 1992) . . . . . . Herself
••• 65—Topless.
Playboy's Book of Lingerie (Mar 1992) . . . . . . Herself
••• 66—Topless and buns.
•• 86—Topless.
Playboy's Book of Lingerie (May 1992) . . . . . Herself
••• 12—Topless.

Scacchi, Greta

Films:

Heat and Dust (1982) . . . . Olivia Rivers
•• 1:25—Buns, lying in bed under a mosquito net with
Douglas, then topless rolling over.
Burke and Wills (1985; Australian) . . . . . . Julia Matthews
The Coca-Cola Kid (1985; Australian) . . . . Terri
••• 0:49—Nude taking a shower with her daughter.
•• 1:20—Brief topless wearing a Santa Claus outfit
while in bed with Eric Roberts.
The Ebony Tower (1985) . . . . Mouse
- 0:38—Topless having a picnic.
- 0:43—Brief nude walking into the lake.
Good Morning, Babylon (1987; Italian/French)
. . . . Edna
•• 1:05—Topless in the woods making love with Vin-
cent Spano.
A Man in Love (1987) . . . . Jane Steiner
••• 0:31—Topless with Peter Coyote.
•• 1:04—Buns and left breast in bed with Coyote.
1:10—Brief side view topless, putting black dress on.
- 1:24—Brief topless in bed.

White Mischief (1988) . . . . Diana Broughton
- •• 0:16—Topless taking a bath while an old man watches through a peephole in the wall.
- •• 0:24—Brief topless in bedroom with her husband.
- •• 0:29—Brief topless taking off bathing suit top in the ocean in front of Charles Dance.
- •• 0:30—Topless lying in bed talking to Dance.

Presumed Innocent (1990) . . . . . . .Carolyn Polhemus
- • 0:46—Left breast, while making love on desk with Harrison Ford.
- • 0:53—Buns, lying in bed on top of Ford.

Fires Within (1991) . . . . Isabel
- • 0:18—Upper half of buns, very brief topless in bed.
- 0:19—In bra, changing clothes.
- • 0:38—Very brief topless in bed.

Shattered (1991) . . . . .Judith Merrick
- •• 0:14—Topless, turning over in bed.
- • 0:16—Topless in a strip of B&W photos that Tom Berenger looks at.
- • 0:36—Topless in B&W photos in Bob Hoskins' office. Brief topless in flashback.
- •• 1:24—Topless during love-making flashback.

The Player (1992) . . . . .n.a.
Turtle Beach (1992). . . . . .n.a.

Magazines:
Playboy (Nov 1988) . . . . Sex in Cinema 1988
- •• 141—Topless in bathtub in a photo from *White Mischief.*

Scarabelli, Michele

Films:
Covergirl (1982; Canadian). . . . . .Snow Queen
Perfect Timing (1984) . . . . Charlotte
- •• 1:11—Brief buns, then topless in bed with Harry.
- • 1:18—Topless in bed with Harry during the music video.

SnakeEater II: The Drug Buster (1990) . . . . Dr. Pierce
Made for Cable Movies:
Age-Old Friends (1989; HBO) . . . . Nurse Wilson
Made for Cable TV:
The Hitchhiker: Face to Face (1984; HBO)
. . . . .Dr. Ensman
(Available on *The Hitchhiker, Volume 4.*)
- ••• 0:07—Topless in Robert Vaughn's office.

Made for TV Movies:
Age-Old Friends (1992). . . . . Nurse Wilson
TV:
Airwolf (1987-88) . . . . .n.a.
Alien Nation (1989-91) . . . . Susan Francisco
True Colors (1992) . . . . .n.a.

• Schick, Stephanie

Films:
Do or Die (1991). . . . . Atlanta Lee
- ••• 1:09—Topless making love with Shane outside at night.
- • 1:15—Brief topless in background, getting dressed. Out of focus.

Magazines:
Playboy (Nov 1991) . . . . Sex in Cinema 1991
- ••• 140—Left breast, standing in front of a guy.

• Schmidtmer, Christiane

Films:
The Big Doll House (1971) . . . . Miss Dietrich
The Specialist (1975) . . . . Nude Model
- ••• 0:12—Topless, posing for artist, then buns when she gets up to leave.

Schneider, Maria

Films:
Last Tango In Paris (1972) . . . . .Jeanne
(X-rated, letterbox version.)
- • 0:15—Lower frontal nudity and very brief buns, rolling on the floor.
- • 0:44—Topless in jeans, walking around the apartment.
- •• 0:53—Left breast, while lying down, then walking to Marlon Brando, then topless.
- ••• 0:55—Topless, kneeling while talking to Brando.
- • 0:56—Side of left breast.
- • 0:57—Topless, rolling off the bed, onto the floor.
- •• 1:01—Right breast, in bathroom. Topless in mirror.
- • 1:03—Brief topless in bathroom with Brando while she puts on makeup.
- ••• 1:04—Nude, in bathroom with Brando, then sitting on counter.
- • 1:27—Brief lower frontal nudity, pulling up her dress in elevator.
- • 1:30—Topless in bathtub with Brando.
- ••• 1:32—Nude, standing up in bathtub while Brando washes her. More topless, getting out. Long scene.

La Baby Sitter (1975; French/Italian/German)
. . . . Michele
The Passenger (1975; Italian) . . . . Girl
Memories of a French Whore (1979) . . . . n.a.
A Woman Called Eva (1979) . . . . n.a.
Mamma Dracula (1980; Belgian/French)
. . . . Nancy Hawaii

Magazines:
Playboy (Feb 1973) . . . . .Two to "Tango" & Maria
- ••• 131-137—Nude.

Playboy (Nov 1973) . . . . Sex in Cinema 1973
- •• 159—Right breast and lower frontal nudity from *Last Tango in Paris.* Out of focus.

Playboy (Dec 1973) . . . . .Sex Stars of 1973
- •• 211—Half of right breast.

Schneider, Romy

Films:
Vengeance... One by One . . . . n.a.
- 0:02—In black slip getting dressed.
- • 0:28—Very brief left breast when a soldier rips her bra open during struggle.
- 1:14—In black lingerie in her husband's flashback.

Boccaccio 70 (1962; Italian). . . . . . . "The Job" Segment
- 1:18—In white slip talking on the phone.

What's New, Pussycat? (1965; U.S./French)
. . . . Carole Werner
Dirty Hands (1975; French) . . . . Julie
  • 0:01—Buns and right breast getting a tan, lying on
    the grass after a man's kite lands on her.
  •• 0:09—Side view of right breast, while lying in bed
    with a man, then topless.
  • 1:04—Topless lying on floor, then brief topless sit-
    ting up and looking at something on the table.
Bloodline (1979) . . . . Helene Martin
Magazines:
Playboy (Dec 1976) . . . . Sex Stars of 1976
  •• 186—Topless lying down, hard to recognize it's her.

Schoelen, Jill
Films:
D.C. Cab (1983) . . . . Claudette
Hot Moves (1984) . . . . Julie Ann
That Was Then... This Is Now (1985). . . Angela Shepard
Thunder Alley (1985) . . . . Beth
The Stepfather (1987) . . . . Stephanie Maine
  •• 1:16—Buns and brief side of right breast, while get-
    ting into the shower. Topless in the shower.
Curse II: The Bite (1988) . . . . Lisa Snipes
Cutting Class (1988) . . . . Paula Carson
    0:58—Side view of left breast, while taking off robe.
    Long shot. Almost topless turing around.
  • 1:00—Very, very brief topless in mirror when Gary
    helps put her robe on. (Out of focus.)
Phantom of the Opera (1989) . . . . Christine
Popcorn (1991) . . . . Maggie
Rich Girl (1991) . . . . Courtney
Made for TV Movies:
Shattered Spirits (1986) . . . . Allison

• Schofield, Annabel
Films:
Blood Tide (1982) . . . . Vicki
Dragonard (1988) . . . . Honore
  • 0:26—Brief side view of left breast, brief topless lying
    down, then left breast again in stable with Abdee.
TV:
Dallas (1988) . . . . Laurel Ellis

Schubert, Karin
Films:
Bluebeard (1972) . . . . Greta
  • 1:43—Brief topless, spinning around, unwrapping
    herself from a red towel for Richard Burton.
Till Marriage Do Us Part (1974; Italian) . . . . Evelyn
Black Emanuelle (1976) . . . . Anne Danielli
  • 0:06—Brief topless adjusting a guy's tie.
  ••• 0:14—Topless making love in gas station with the
    gas station attendant.
  ••• 0:37—Nude, running in the jungle while Laura
    Gemser takes pictures of her.
  • 0:40—Topless, kissing Gemser.
  • 0:44—Right breast, making love with Johnny in bed.

Black Venus (1983) . . . . Marie
  •• 0:38—Nude in bed with Venus, making love.
Panther Squad (1986; French/Belgian) . . . . Barbara

Schygulla, Hanna
Films:
The Bitter Tears of Petra von Kant (1972; German)
. . . . Karin Thimm
The Marriage of Maria Braun (1979; German)
. . . . Maria Braun
Berlin Alexanderplatz (1983; West German) . . . . n.a.
La Nuit de Varennes (1983; French/Italian)
. . . . Countess Sophie de la Borde
A Love in Germany (1984; French/German)
. . . . Pauline Kropp
The Delta Force (1986) . . . . Ingrid
Forever Lulu (1987) . . . . Elaine
  • 1:03—Brief topless in and getting out of bubble
    bath.
Dead Again (1991) . . . . Inge

• Sciorra, Annabella
Films:
True Love (1989) . . . . Donna
Cadillac Man (1990) . . . . Donna
Reversal of Fortune (1990) . . . . Sarah
The Hard Way (1991) . . . . Susan
Jungle Fever (1991) . . . . Angie Tucci
    0:32—In black bra
The Hand That Rocks the Cradle (1992)
. . . . Claire Bartel
  • 0:08—Brief side of right breast in open gown, while
    lying on Dr. Mott's examination table.
    0:38—Partial right breast, trying to breast feed her
    baby.
Whispers in the Dark (1992) . . . . n.a.
Made for Cable Movies:
Prison Stories, Women on the Inside (1990; HBO)
. . . . Nicole

Scoggins, Tracy
Films:
Toy Soldiers (1983) . . . . Monique
In Dangerous Company (1988) . . . . Evelyn
    0:12—In a white bra, lying on bed making love with
    a guy.
    0:42—Very, very brief half of left breast in bed with
    Blake. Then, very, very brief left breast getting out of
    bed. Blurry, hard to see.
    0:58—Brief upper half of left breast taking a bath.
    Long shot, hard to see.
The Gumshoe Kid (1990) . . . . Rita Benson
    0:33—In two piece white swimsuit. Nice bun shot
    while Jay Underwood hides in the closet.
  ••• 1:10—Side view of left breast in the shower with Un-
    derwood. Excellent slow motion topless shot while
    turning around. Brief side view of right breast in bed
    afterwards.
One Last Run (1990) . . . . Cindy

The Raven Red Kiss-Off (1990) . . . . .Vala Vuvalle
Timebomb (1990). . . . . Ms. Blue
Watchers II (1990). . . . . .Barbara White
Play Murder For Me (1991). . . . . .n.a.
Ultimate Desires (1991) . . . . Samantha Stewart
    0:44—In white bra and panties, dancing sexily in her
    house, while two guys watch from outside.
    0:53—Getting dressed in white bra and panties.
    Don't see her face.
    • 0:59—Very brief buns and side of left breast taking
    off her dress and walking out of the room.
    1:07—In black bra, panties, garter belt and stock-
    ings with Marc Singer.
    ••• 1:10—Topless, several times, in bed with Singer.
TV:
Renegades (1983). . . . . Tracy
Hawaiian Heat (1984). . . . . Irene Gorley
The Colbys (1985-87). . . . . .Monica Colby
Dynasty (1989). . . . . .Monica Colby
Video Tapes:
Tracy Scoggins' Tough Stuff Workout . . . . Herself

Scott, Susie
Films:
Student Confidential (1987). . . . . Susan Bishop
    • 0:02—Lying in bed covered with a gold sheet. Sort
    of right breast through her hair.
    •• 1:26—Full frontal nudity standing in front of Greg.
Video Tapes:
Playboy Video Magazine, Volume 5 (1983)
    . . . . Playmate
    • 0:05—Brief topless stroking her hair.
Playboy's Playmate Review 3 (1985). . . . . Playmate
Playmates at Play (1990) . . . . Making Waves
Magazines:
Playboy (May 1983) . . . . Playmate
Playboy's Nudes (Oct 1990). . . . . Herself
    •• 54—Full frontal nudity.
Playboy's Book of Lingerie (Mar 1991) . . . . . Herself
    •• 18—Left breast.

Seagrove, Jenny
Films:
Nate and Hayes (1983). . . . . Sophia
Appointment with Death (1988). . . . . . . Dr. Sarah King
Harlequin Romance: Magic Moments (1989)
    . . . . Melanie James
Bullseye! (1990) . . . . Health Club Receptionist
The Guardian (1990) . . . . Camilla
    ••• 0:21—Side view of left breast, while in bathtub with
    the baby. Right breast, then topless.
    0:23—Buns, drying herself off. Long shot.
    •• 0:38—Topless, mostly left breast on top of Phil.
    Don't see her face, probably a body double.
    0:46—Buns, skinny dipping. Long shot.
    •• 0:47—Topless healing her wound by a tree. Side
    view of right breast.
    • 1:18—Very brief topless under sheer gown in forest
    just before getting hit by a Jeep.

    1:24—Very briefly topless scaring Carey Lowell.
    Body is painted all over.
Made for Cable TV:
The Hitchhiker: Killer . . . . Meg
Miniseries:
A Woman of Substance (1984). . . . . . Young Emma Hart
Made for TV Movies:
In Like Flynn (1985). . . . . n.a.
Sherlock Holmes and the Incident at Victoria Falls (1991)
    . . . . Lillie Langtry

• Sedgwick, Kyra
Wife of actor Kevin Bacon.
Films:
War and Love (1985) . . . . Halina
Tai-Pan (1986) . . . . Tess
Kansas (1988) . . . . Prostitute Drifter
Born on the Fourth of July (1989). . . . . .Donna
Mr. & Mrs. Bridge (1990). . . . . Ruth Bridge
Pyrates (1991) . . . . .Sam
    ••• 0:19—In sheer lingerie on top of Kevin Bacon in bed,
    then topless.
    0:21—Partial buns, bouncing in bed with Bacon.
    • 0:22—Brief buns, lying on top of Bacon.
    • 0:26—Topless under water in hot tub with Bacon.
Singles (1992) . . . . .Linda
Made for Cable Movies:
Women & Men 2: Three Short Stories (1991; HBO)
    . . . . .Arlene Megaffin
Made for TV Movies:
Miss Rose White (1992) . . . . . . Rose White/Reyzel Weiss

• Seigner, Emmanuelle
Wife of director Roman Polanski.
Films:
Detective (1985; French/Swiss) . . . . Grace Kelly
Frantic (1988) . . . . .Michelle
    • 1:02—Brief side view of right breast, while changing
    blouses in bedroom.
Magazines:
Playboy (Nov 1992) . . . . Sex in Cinema 1992
    ••• 144—Topless with Peter Coyote from *Bitter Moon.*

Senit, Laurie
Films:
Body and Soul (1981) . . . . Hooker #3
    • 0:54—Brief topless lying next to Leon Isaac Kennedy
    in bed with two other hookers.
Doctor Detroit (1983) . . . . .Dream Girl
The Witching (1983) . . . . .Witches Coven
a.k.a. Necromancy
(Originally filmed in 1971 as *Necromancy*, additional
scenes were added and re-released in 1983.)
R.S.V.P. (1984) . . . . Sherry Worth
    •• 1:00—Topless in the shower with Harry Reems.
    •• 1:06—Topless again.

Sennet, Susan

Films:
Big Bad Mama (1974) . . . . .Billy Jean
  • 0:49—Topless and buns with Tom Skerritt.
  •• 0:51—Topless and buns in bed with Skerritt.
Tidal Wave (1975; U.S./Japanese) . . . . .n.a.
TV:
Ozzie's Girls (1973) . . . . Susie Hamilton

• Serena

Adult film actress.
Films:
Fantasm (1976; Australian) .n.a.
Honky Tonk Nights (1978) . . . . Dolly Pop
  • 0:04—Topless in open blouse, getting restrained after getting in a fight with a guy who tries to molest her.
  ••• 0:10—Topless in bed with Bobby, then putting on a robe.
  ••• 0:38—Topless standing in doorway, then in kitchen with Bill.

Serna, Assumpta

Films:
Lola (1986) . . . . Silvia
Matador (1986; Spanish) . . . . Maria Cardinal
  • 0:03—Topless taking off wrap and making love with a guy just before she kills him.
  ••• 1:38—Topless on floor with Diego. Long shot, hard to see. Topless in front of the fire.
  • 1:41—Brief topless making love with Diego.
  • 1:43—Topless lying on floor dead.
Wild Orchid (1990) . . . . Hanna
  ••• 0:39—Topless at the beach and in the limousine. Very erotic.
Revolver (1992). . . . . .Countess Angela Rosetta
TV:
Falcon Crest (1989). . . . . Anna Cellini
Magazines:
Playboy (Jun 1990) . . . . Wild Orchid
  •• 84—Topless in photos from *Wild Orchid*.

Severance, Joan

Films:
No Holds Barred (1989) . . . . Samantha Moore
See No Evil, Hear No Evil (1989). . . . . .Eve
  •• 1:08—Topless in and leaning out of the shower while Gene Wilder tries to get her bag.
Worth Winning (1989) . . . . Lizbette
Bird on a Wire (1990) . . . . Rachel Varnay
Write to Kill (1990) . . . . .Belle Washburn
  0:59—Wearing purple bra in house with Scott Valentine.
  ••• 1:01—Topless, making love in bed with Valentine.
  • 1:04—Very brief, blurry topless when Valentine tosses her a blouse.

Illicit Behavior (1991). . . . . .Melissa Yarnell
(Unrated version reviewed.)
(The nude scenes where you don't see faces are body doubles.)
  • 0:12—Buns, while making love standing up in the kitchen with Jack Scalia. Don't see face.
  ••• 0:13—Topless on table making love with Scalia. Don't see her face.
  •• 0:54—Right breast and buns, while taking off stockings, panties and bra in bathtub. Don't see face.
  •• 1:10—Topless and buns in car with Davi. (Sometimes you see her face with her breasts, sometimes not.)
  •• 1:16—Right breast, while lying in bed and talking to Davi.
Second Nature (1991) . . . . n.a.
Almost Pregnant (1992) . . . . .Maureen Mallory
(Unrated version reviewed.)
  ••• 0:58—In belly dancer outfit in bedroom with Jeff Conaway, then topless.
  •• 1:06—In black leather outfit, then topless and buns in G-string. Her hair gets in the way a lot.
  •• 1:09—Brief topless and buns in various sexual positions in bed with Conaway.
Made for Cable Movies:
Another Pair of Aces (1991) . . . . Susan Davis
(Video tape has nude scenes not shown on cable TV.)
  •• 1:00—Brief topless several times, making love with Kris Kristofferson in bed.
Made for Cable TV:
Red Shoe Diaries: Safe Sex (1992; Showtime)
  . . . . .The Woman
  • 0:11—Topless, standing up, then lying on the floor. Medium long shot.
  ••• 0:12—Topless, lying on the floor, then making love with Steven Bauer.
  • 0:13—Brief topless, gathering her clothes.
  •• 0:16—Nude, in front of mirror when Bauer takes her dress off.
  ••• 0:17—More nude in bed and in front of mirror.
  • 0:19—Topless during flashback.
Tales From the Crypt: The New Arrival (1992; HBO)
  . . . . Rona
TV:
Wiseguy (1988) . . . . Susan Profitt
Magazines:
Playboy (Jan 1990). . . . . Texas Twister
  ••• 84-95—Nude.
Playboy's Nudes (Oct 1990) . . . . Herself
  ••• 14—Full frontal nudity.
Playboy (Nov 1992) . . . . .Director's Choice
  ••• 90-97—Nude. Awesome!

• Severeid, Suzanne

Films:
Don't Answer the Phone (1979) . . . . Hooker
  • 0:43—Very brief right breast in open blouse after the killer strangles her.
Howling IV: The Original Nightmare (1988) . . . . . Janice

Seymour, Jane

Her eyes are different colors—left is green and right is brown.

Films:

Young Winston (1972; British) . . . . Pamela Plowden
Live and Let Die (1973; British) . . . . Solitaire
Sinbad and the Eye of the Tiger (1977; U.S./British)
. . . . Farah
     1:16—Very brief buns, skinny dipping in pond with
     Taryn Power. Long shot, but still pretty amazing for
     a G-rated film.
     1:17—Very brief partial right breast (arm covers
     most of it) screaming when scared by the troglo-
     dyte.
Oh Heavenly Dog! (1980) . . . . .Jackie Howard
Somewhere in Time (1980) . . . . Elise McKenna
Lassiter (1984) . . . . Sara
   • 0:10—Buns and brief side view of right breast lying
     on stomach on bed with Tom Selleck.
Head Office (1986) . . . . Jane
The Tunnel (1987) . . . . Maria
   • 0:29—Very brief left breast, while in bed with Peter
     Weller when the sheet is pulled down.
   •• 0:44—Brief right beast, while getting dressed,
     throwing off her robe.
Matters of the Heart (1990) . . . . .n.a.
Made for Cable Movies:
Jamaica Inn (1982) . . . . .Mary Yellan
     1:47—(0:14 into volume 2) Braless under a wet
     white dress changing clothes in a stagecoach.
Miniseries:
Captains and the Kings (1976) . . . . . .Chisholm Armagh
Seventh Avenue (1977) . . . . Eva Meyers
East of Eden (1981) . . . . Cathy/Kate Ames
War and Remembrance (1988) . . . . Natalie Jastrow
Made for TV Movies:
The Story of David (1976) . . . . .Bathsheba
Battlestar Gallactica (1978) . . . . Serina
The Dallas Cowboy Cheerleaders (1979) . . . . .n.a.
The Sun Also Rises (1984) . . . . Lady Brett
Jack the Ripper (1988) .Emma
The Richest Man in the World: The Story of Aristotle
     Onassis (1988) . . . . Maria Callas
The Woman He Loved (1988) . . . . Wallis Simpson
Magazines:
Playboy (Dec 1973) . . . . Sex Stars of 1973
   • 204—Wet dress.

Seymour, Stephanie

Sports Illustrated swimsuit model.

Video Tapes:

Sports Illustrated's 25th Anniversary Swimsuit Video
     (1989). . . . . Herself
     (The version shown on HBO left out two music video
     segments at the end. If you like buns, definitely watch
     the video tape!)
Magazines:
Playboy (Mar 1991) . . . . Stephanie
   ••• 112-123—Topless and buns.

• Seyrig, Delphine

Films:

Day of the Jackal (1973) . . . . Colette
   • 1:25—Side view of right breast while lying in bed
     with the Jackal. Dark.
   • 1:40—Very brief side view of left breast, when she
     rolls on her back. Brief side view of left breast after
     the Jackal kills her.
Golden Eighties (1987; French/Belgian) . . . . .Jeanne

• Shaffer, Stacey

Films:

The Naked Cage (1985) . . . . .Amy
   ••• 1:03—Nude in shower room getting hassled by the
     other girls.
Blood Screams (1986; U.S./Mexican) . . . . .Karen

• Shannon, Moriah

Films:

Alley Cat (1982) . . . . .Sam
D.C. Cab (1983) . . . . Venus Club Passenger
   •• 0:16—In bra, then topless, undressing in back seat
     of cab.
   •• 0:17—Topless when Albert tries to get his fare.
   • 0:18—Topless, then buns when Gary Busey takes her
     money. Buns and very brief lower frontal nudity run-
     ning out of the club after him.

Shapiro, Hilary

See: Shepard, Hilary.

Sharkey, Rebecca

See: Wood-Sharkey, Rebecca.

Sharpe, Cornelia

Films:

Kansas City Bomber (1972) . . . . Tammy O'Brien
Serpico (1973) . . . . Leslie
   •• 0:41—Topless in bathtub with Al Pacino.
Busting (1974) . . . . .Jackie
Open Season (1974; U.S./Spanish) . . . . Nancy
The Reincarnation of Peter Proud (1975)
. . . . Nora Hayes
   •• 0:03—Topless in bed with Michael Sarrazin, then
     buns when getting out of bed.
The Next Man (1976) . . . . .Nicole Scott
   a.k.a. Double Hit
Venom (1982; British) . . . . .Ruth Hopkins
Made for TV Movies:
S.H.E. (1979) . . . . n.a.
Magazines:
Playboy (Nov 1974) . . . . Sex in Cinema 1974
   •• 145—Topless in tub from *Serpico.*

Shattuck, Shari

Wife of actor Ronn Moss.

Films:

Tainted . . . . Cathy
   •• 0:09—Buns, while lying on top of Frank.

••• 0:27—Topless in bubble bath, getting up, drying herself off, then putting on white bra while wearing panties.

0:28—In white bra and panties, masturbating on chair.

0:30—Briefly in white bra and panties, getting attacked by rapist.

••• 0:49—Topless taking a shower.

• 0:51—Brief side view of left breast in the shower again.

Portfolio (1983). . . . . Elite Model

The Naked Cage (1985). . . . . Michelle

•• 0:42—Buns and topless in shower, then getting slashed by Rita during a dream.

•• 1:00—Left breast getting attacked by Smiley in jail cell, then fighting back.

1:28—In panties, during fight with Rita.

Death Spa (1987) . . . . Catherine

Hot Child in the City (1987) . . . . Abby

Arena (1988). . . . . Jade

1:06—Upper half of buns sitting up in bed. Brief half of right breast, getting up while wearing robe.

The Uninvited (1988) . . . . Suzanne

The Spring (1989) . . . . .Dyanne

• 0:00—Nude, several times, swimming under the water. Shot from under water.

• 0:50—Topless and buns, swimming under water.

•• 0:51—Topless, getting out of the water.

•• 0:59—Brief topless, turning over in bed with Dack Rambo.

• 1:05—Standing up in wet lingerie, then swimming under water.

Lower Level (1990) . . . . Dawn Simms

Mad About You (1990) . . . . Renee

Immortal Sins (1992) . . . . .n.a.

Made for TV Movies:

The Laker Girls (1990). Libby

Shaver, Helen

Films:

Shoot (1976; Canadian) . . . . .Paula Lissitzen

The Supreme Kid (1976; Canadian) . . . . Girl

Outrageous! (1977; Canadian) . . . . Jo

High-Ballin' (1978) . . . . Pickup

In Praise of Older Women (1978; Canadian)

. . . . Ann MacDonald

••• 1:40—Blue bra and panties, then topless with Tom Berenger.

••• 1:42—Nude lying in bed with Berenger, then getting out and getting dressed.

Starship Invasions (1978; Canadian) . . . . .Betty

The Amityville Horror (1979). . . . . .Carolyn

Gas (1981; Canadian) .Rhonda

Harry Tracy (1982; Canadian) . . . . Catherine

The Osterman Weekend (1983) . . .Virginia Tremayne

•• 0:24—Topless in an open blouse yelling at her husband in the bedroom.

• 0:41—Topless in the swimming pool when everyone watches on the TV.

Best Defense (1984). . . . . .Claire Lewis

The Color of Money (1986) . . . . .Janelle

Desert Hearts (1986) . . . . Vivian Bell

• 1:05—Brief topless in bed in hotel room.

••• 1:09—Topless making love in bed with Patricia Charboneau.

The Men's Club (1986) . . . . Sahra (uncredited)

The Believers (1987) . . . . .Jessica Halliday

• 0:38—Brief glimpse of right breast while lying in bed with Martin Sheen.

1:17—Buns, getting out of bed.

Innocent Victim (1988) . . . . Benet Archdale

• 1:05—Very brief side of left breast on top of a guy in bed.

Made for Cable Movies:

The Park is Mine (1985; HBO) . . . . Valery Weaver

• 0:46—Very brief topless undressing then very, very brief left breast, while catching clothes from Tommy Lee Jones.

Made for TV Movies:

Mothers, Daughters and Lovers (1989) . . . . n.a.

Rest In Peace, Mrs. Columbo (1990) . . . . .Vivian Dimitri

TV:

United States (1980) . . . . .Libby Chapin

Jessica Novak (1981) . . . . .Jessica Novak

WIOU (1990-91) . . . . Kelby Robinson

Magazines:

Playboy (Oct 1978) . . . . . . Observing "Older Women"

•• 193-194—Topless and buns.

Playboy (Nov 1978) . . . . Sex in Cinema 1978

•• 185—Full frontal nudity on bed.

Shaw, Fiona

Films:

Mountains of the Moon (1989). . . . . .Isabel

•• 0:33—Topless and very brief lower frontal nudity letting Patrick Bergin wax the hair off her legs.

•• 1:43—Topless in bed after Bergin returns from Africa.

My Left Foot (1989; British) . . . . .Dr. Eileen Cole

Three Men and a Little Lady (1990) . . . . Miss Lomax

Shaw, Linda

Adult film actress.

Films:

Body Double (1984) . . . . Linda Shaw

• 1:11—Left breast on monitor while Craig Wasson watches TV.

Shaw, Tina

Films:

The Secrets of Love—Three Rakish Tales (1986)

. . . . The Weaver's Wife

••• 0:10—Topless in bed with Luke.

••• 0:17—Topless in the barn.

Salome's Last Dance (1987) . . . . .2nd Slave

(Appears with 2 other slaves–can't tell who is who.)

•• 0:08—Topless in black costume around a cage.

•• 0:52—Topless during dance number.

The Lair of the White Worm (1988; British)
. . . . .Maid/Nun
Taffin (1988; U.S./British) . . . . Lola the Stripper
  •• 1:04—Topless doing routine in a club.
Split Second (1992) . . . . Nightclub Stripper
  •• 0:07—Topless, dancing in club in black S&M outfit, wearing a mask over her head.

Shayne, Linda
Films:
Humanoids from the Deep (1980). . . . . Miss Salmon
  • 1:06—Topless after getting bathing suit ripped off by a humanoid.
The Lost Empire (1983). . . . . Cindy Blake
Screwballs (1983). . . . . Bootsie Goodhead
  ••• 0:43—Right breast, while in back of van at drive-in theater, then topless.
Big Bad Mama II (1987) . . . . Bank Teller
Out of Bounds (1987). . . . . Chris Cage
Daddy's Boys (1988) . . . . Nanette

Shé, Elizabeth
Films:
Howling V (1989). . . . . Mary Lou Summers
  • 0:33—Buns and side view of right breast getting into pool with Donovan.
  • 0:36—Very brief full frontal nudity climbing out of pool with Donovan.
Howling VI—The Freaks (1990) . . . Mary Lou Summers

Shea, Katt
a.k.a. Kathleen M. Shea or Katt Shea Ruben.
Actress turned Director.
Films:
The Cannonball Run (1981) . . . . Starting Girl
My Tutor (1983) . . . . Mud Wrestler
  • 0:48—Brief topless when a guy rips her dress off.
Scarface (1983). . . . . Woman at the Babylon Club
Cannonball Run II (1984) . . . . n.a.
Hollywood Hot Tubs (1984) . . . . .Dee-Dee
  • 0:21—Topless with her boyfriend while Shawn is working on the hot tub.
Preppies (1984) . . . . .Margot
  ••• 0:20—Topless teasing Richard through the glass door of her house.
  0:54—In bra and panties with Trini, practicing sexual positions on the bed.
  • 1:07—Brief topless after taking off bra in bed.
R.S.V.P. (1984). . . . . .Rhonda Rivers
  • 0:31—Side view of left breast, making love in bed with Jonathan.
Barbarian Queen (1985) . . . . Estrild
  • 0:31—Brief topless getting top torn off by guards.
The Destroyers (1985). . . . . Audrey
Psycho III (1986) . . . . .Patsy

Shear, Rhonda
Films:
Basic Training (1984) . . . . Debbie
  •• 0:07—Topless making love with Mark.
  0:15—In bra, making love on Mark's desk.
Doin' Time (1984) . . . . Adrianne
Spaceballs (1987). . . . . Woman in Diner
Made for Cable TV:
Up All Night. . . . . Host
Magazines:
Playboy (Jun 1991). . . . . Funny Girls
  ••• 92—Full frontal nudity.
Playboy's Career Girls (Aug 1992) . . . . . . Funny Girls
  ••• 26—Full frontal nudity.

Sheedy, Ally
Films:
Bad Boys (1983). . . . . .J. C. Walenski
  • 0:12—Very, very brief left breast, while kneeling on floor next to bed when Sean Penn leaves. A little blurry and a long shot.
Wargames (1983) . . . . Jennifer
The Breakfast Club (1985) . . . . .Allison Reynolds
St. Elmo's Fire (1985) . . . . Leslie
Blue City (1986). . . . . Annie Rayford
  0:44—Very very brief left breast, while lying on bed reaching her arm around Judd Nelson while kissing him. Dark and blurry.
Short Circuit (1986) . . . . Stephanie Speck
Maid to Order (1987) . . . . Jessie Montgomery
  0:40—Buns, taking off dress and diving into the pool. Long shot and dark. Don't see her face.
  0:42—Buns, walking with a towel around her hair. Another long shot and you don't see her face.
Heart of Dixie (1989) . . . . Maggie
Betsy's Wedding (1990) . . . . Connie Hopper
Only the Lonely (1991) . . . . .Theresa Luna
Made for Cable Movies:
The Lost Capone (1990). . . . . Kathleen
Fear (1991; Showtime). . . . . Cayce Bridges

Sheen, Jacqueline
Video Tapes:
Playboy Video Calendar 1991 (1990). . . . December
  ••• 0:49—Nude.
Playboy Video Centerfold: Tawnni Cable (1990)
. . . . Playmate
  ••• 0:14—Nude in Hawaii with Tawnni Cable and Pamela Stein.
Wet and Wild III (1991) . . . . Model
Playboy Playmates in Paradise (1992). . . . Playmate
Magazines:
Playboy (Jul 1990) . . . . Playmate
Playboy's Book of Lingerie (Sep 1991) . . . . . .Herself
  ••• 82-83—Nude.
Playboy's Book of Lingerie (Nov 1991) . . . . .Herself
  ••• 89—Full frontal nudity.
Playboy's Book of Lingerie (Mar 1992). . . . . .Herself
  • 34—Lower frontal nudity.

Playboy's Book of Lingerie (May 1992) . . . . . Herself
• 76—Lower frontal nudity and sheer bra.
••• 100-101—Nude.
Playboy's Book of Lingerie (Jul 1992) . . . . . . Herself
••• 16-17—Full frontal nudity.

• *Shelton, Deborah*

Miss USA in the 1970-71 Miss Universe Pageant.
Films:
Blood Tide (1982) . . . . Madeline
   0:29—Braless in wet white dress in the ocean.
   1:15—Braless in wet white dress sacrificing herself
   while lying on a rock.
Body Double (1984) . . . . Gloria
Hunk (1987) . . . . O'Brien
Perfect Victims (1988) . . . . Liz Winters
   0:55—Very brief, upper half of breasts, lying back in
   bubble bath.
Blind Vision (1990) . . . . Leanne Dunaway
••• 0:25—Topless, making love with her boyfriend on
   the floor.
TV:
The Yellow Rose (1983-84) . . . . Juliette Hollister
Dallas (1984-87) . . . . Mandy Winger
Magazines:
Playboy (Mar 1974) . . . . Cover Model

Shepard, Hilary

a.k.a. Hilary Shapiro.
Films:
Soup for One (1982) . . . . n.a.
Radioactive Dreams (1984) . . . . Biker Leader
Weekend Pass (1984) . . . . Cindy Hazard
•• 1:05—In red bra, then topless taking off bra.
• 1:07—Buns and topless getting into bathtub.
Private Resort (1985) . . . . Shirley
••• 0:36—Topless, then buns, taking off her dress in
   front of Ben.
Tough Guys (1986) . . . . Sandy
Hunk (1987) . . . . Alexis Cash
Lucky Stiff (1988) . . . . Cissy
Peace Maker (1990) . . . . Dori Caisson
• 1:08—Brief upper half of buns, taking off shirt and
   getting into shower. Brief side view of upper half of
   left breast, twice while making love with Townsend.
Made for Cable TV:
Dream On: The First Episode (1990; HBO) . . . . . Date 2

Shepard, Jewel

Films:
Raw Force (1981) . . . . Drunk Sexpot
• 0:31—Topless in black swimsuit, when a guy adjusts
   her straps and it falls open.
The Junkman (1982) . . . . Credit Girl
Zapped! (1982) . . . . Uncredited Girl in Car
• 0:39—Brief topless after red and white top pops off
   when Scott Baio uses his Telekinesis on her.
My Tutor (1983) . . . . Girl in Phone Booth

• 0:40—Brief left breast in car when Matt Lattanzi fan-
   tasizes about making love with her.
Christina (1984) . . . . Christina
Hollywood Hot Tubs (1984) . . . . Crystal Landers
(Not topless, but bouncing around a lot in short, braless
T-shirts.)
The Return of the Living Dead (1985) . . . . Casey
Party Camp (1987) . . . . Dyanne Stein
••• 0:57—In white bra and panties, then topless playing
   strip poker with the boys.
Scenes from the Goldmine (1987) . . . . Dana
The Underachievers (1987) . . . . Sci-Fi Teacher
• 0:27—Topless ripping off her Star Trek uniform
   when someone enters her classroom. Dark, hard to
   see.
Going Undercover (1988; British) . . . . Peaches
Hollywood Hot Tubs 2—Educating Crystal (1989)
. . . . Crystal Landers
   0:38—In white slip during Gary's fantasy.
• 1:12—Brief left breast, while lying down, kissing
   Gary.
Roots of Evil (1991) . . . . Wanda
(Unrated version reviewed.)
• 1:31—Brief right breast, a couple of times, when it
   pops out of her blouse while she's in police station.

Shepherd, Cybill

Films:
The Last Picture Show (1971) . . . . Jacy Farrow
•• 0:37—Undressing on diving board. Very brief left
   breast falling onto diving board. Brief topless tossing
   bra aside.
• 0:38—Brief left breast jumping into the water.
••• 1:05—Topless and buns in motel room with Jeff
   Bridges.
The Heartbreak Kid (1972) . . . . Kelly Corcoran
Daisy Miller (1974) . . . . Annie P. "Daisy" Miller
Special Delivery (1976) . . . . Mary Jane
Taxi Driver (1976) . . . . Betsy
The Lady Vanishes (1979; British) . . . . . . Amanda Kelly
The Return (1980) . . . . Daughter
Chances Are (1989) . . . . Corrine Jeffries
   1:11—In white bra and tap pants getting dressed.
   1:22—In bra with Robert Downey Jr. and Ryan
   O'Neal in living room.
Alice (1990) . . . . Nancy Brill
Texasville (1990) . . . . Jacy Farrow
Once Upon A Crime (1992) . . . . n.a.
Made for Cable Movies:
Memphis (1991; TNT) . . . . n.a.
Which Way Home (1991) . . . . Karen Parsons
Made for TV Movies:
Moonlighting (1985) . . . . Maddie Hayes
Stormy Weathers (1992) . . . Samantha "Sam" Weathers
TV:
The Yellow Rose (1983-84) . . . . Colleen Champion
Moonlighting (1985-89) . . . . Maddie Hayes

Magazines:
Playboy (Nov 1972) . . . . Sex in Cinema 1972
  • 170—B&W topless.
Playboy (Dec 1972). . . . . Sex Stars of 1972
  •• 208—B&W topless.

Sheppard, Delia

Films:
Witchcraft II: The Temptress (1989) . . . . . . .Dolores
  •• 1:20—Brief topless several times with William.
Haunting Fear (1990) . . . . .Lisa
  ••• 0:13—Topless on desk, making love with Terry.
  ••• 1:10—Full frontal nudity, making love in bed with
    Terry. Long scene.
Rocky V (1990) . . . . Karen
The Adventures of Ford Fairlane (1991) . . . . . . Pussycat
Mirror Images (1991) . . . . Kaitlin/Shauna
  •• 0:07—Right breast, while undressing in front of van-
    ity mirror.
  •• 0:08—More topless. Topless as Shauna in bed.
    0:12—Buns, while dancing on stage with a band,
    wearing a sexy outfit.
  ••• 0:14—Topless in bed with Georgio.
  ••• 0:27—Topless and buns in G-string, making love
    with Joey. Long scene.
  ••• 0:33—Buns in black bra and panties, walking
    around her sister's apartment. Long scene.
  •• 0:39—Right breast, while with a guy with a mask.
  ••• 0:41—Nude, taking a shower. Great!
  ••• 0:43—Topless in bedroom after her shower.
  •• 0:48—Left breast, while making love in bed with
    Julie Strain.
  ••• 1:29—Topless in bed in lingerie with the policeman.
Roots of Evil (1991) . . . . .Monica
  (Unrated version reviewed.)
  ••• 0:04—Topless and buns in G-string, dancing on
    stage.
  • 0:07—Topless and buns, while on stage when
    wounded guy disturbs her act.
  ••• 0:38—Buns in outfit, then topless dancing on stage.
  ••• 0:41—More buns and topless in bed, making love
    with Johnny. Long scene.
Secret Games (1991) . . . . Celeste
  (Unrated version reviewed.)
  • 0:38—Topless under sheer black body suit.
    0:45—Buns, under sheer robe.
  •• 0:48—Topless with her lover, while watching
    Julianne and Eric on TV.
Sex Bomb (1991) . . . . .n.a.
Night Rhythms (1992). . . . . Bridget
  (Unrated version reviewed.)
  ••• 1:25—Full frontal nudity, making love with Kit in
    bed. Long scene.
Magazines:
Penthouse (Apr 1988). . . . . Pet
Playboy (Nov 1990) . . . . Sex in Cinema 1990
  •• 143—Right breast, in still from *Witchcraft, Part II*.
Playboy (Dec 1990). . . . . Sex Stars of 1990
  •• 177—Buns.

Sheridan, Nicollette

Ex-wife of actor Harry Hamlin.
Films:
The Sure Thing (1985) . . . . The Sure Thing
Made for Cable Movies:
Deceptions (1990; Showtime) . . . . . Adrienne Erickson
  • 0:35—Very, very brief silhouette of breasts, while
    hugging Harry Hamlin when the camera tilts down
    from her head to her buns.
Miniseries:
Jackie Collins' Lucky/Chances (1990)
  . . . . .Lucky Santangelo
TV:
Paper Dolls (1984) . . . . Taryn Blake
Knots Landing (1986-) . . . . .Paige Matheson

Sherman, Geraldine

Films:
Interlude (1968; British) . . . . .Natalie
Poor Cow (1968) . . . . Trixie
Take a Girl Like You (1970). . . . . Anna
There's a Girl in My Soup (1970) . . . . .Caroline
  •• 0:43—Topless in bed, then getting out after Goldie
    Hawn splashes water on her.
Get Carter (1971) . . . . Girl in Cafe
Cry of the Penguins (1972) . . . . Penny

Sherwood, Robin

Films:
Loose Shoes (1977) . . . . Biker Chic #2
The Tourist Trap (1979) . . . . .Eileen
Hero at Large (1980) . . . . n.a.
Serial (1980) . . . . Woman
Blow Out (1981) . . . . Screamer
Death Wish II (1982). . . . . Carol Kersey
  • 0:15—Topless after getting raped by gang member
    in their hideout.
The Love Butcher (1982) . . . . Sheila

Shields, Brooke

Films:
Alice, Sweet Alice (1977) . . . . .Karen
King of the Gypsies (1978). . . . . Tita
Pretty Baby (1978) .Violet
  (She was only 11–12 years old at this time so there isn't
  really a whole lot to see here!)
  • 0:57—Topless and buns taking a bath.
  • 1:26—Topless posing on couch for Keith Carradine.
  • 1:28—Buns, getting thrown out of the room, then
    trying to get back in.
Tilt (1978) . . . . .Tilt
Just You and Me, Kid (1979) . . . . .Kate
  • 0:07—Brief buns, running down stairs after her tow-
    el gets caught in fence.
Wanda Nevada (1979) . . . . Wanda Nevada
Blue Lagoon (1980) . . . . Emmeline
  (Nudity is a body double, Kathy Trout.)
    0:27—Nude swimming underwater after growing
    up from little children.

0:43—More underwater swimming.
1:00—Topless body double lying on a rock.
1:09—Right breast of body double in hammock.
1:24—Body double breast feeding the baby.
Endless Love (1981) . . . . Jade
    0:37—Body double, side view of right breast in bed with David.
    1:08—Body double very brief left breast, in bed with another guy during David's dream.
Sahara (1984) . . . . Dale
    0:51—In a wet T-shirt taking a shower under a water fall.
Brenda Starr (1986). . . . . Brenda Starr
    (Finally released in 1992.)
Speed Zone (1989) . . . . Stewardess
Backstreet Dreams (1990) . . . . Stephanie "Stevie" Bloom

Shirley, Aleisa

Films:
Sweet Sixteen (1982) . . . . Melissa Morgan
    • 0:16—Side view of body, nude, taking a shower.
    • 1:11—Topless undressing to go skinny dipping with Hank. Dark, hard to see.
    • 1:13—Topless, getting out of the water.
Made for Cable TV:
The Hitchhiker: Shattered Vows . . . . Pamela
    • 0:08—Topless and buns in bathroom with Jeff.
    0:12—In bedroom wearing white lingerie.
    •• 0:18—In bed wearing black bra, panties, garter belt and stockings, then topless.
Video Tapes:
Rock Video Girls (1991) . . . . Herself

Shoop, Pamela Susan

Films:
Empire of the Ants (1977) . . . . Coreen Bradford
One Man Jury (1978) . . . . Wendy
Halloween II (1981) . . . . Karen
    ••• 0:48—Topless getting into the whirlpool bath with Budd in the hospital.
Made for TV Movies:
The Dallas Cowboy Cheerleaders (1979) . . . . .n.a.

Shower, Kathy

Films:
Velvet Dreams . . . . Laura
    •• 0:15—Left breast, while making love with Paul in the dressing room.
    • 0:35—Brief buns, while getting a massage.
    •• 0:42—Topless, tied to a tree during her writing fantasy.
Double Exposure (1983) . . . . Mudwrestler #1
Commando Squad (1987) . . . . .Kat Withers
The Further Adventures of Tennessee Buck (1987)
. . . . Barbara Manchester
    0:22—In white lingerie in her hut getting dressed.
    ••• 0:57—Topless getting rubbed with oil by the cannibal women. Nice close up shots.
    •• 1:02—Topless in a hut with the Chief of the tribe.

Frankenstein General Hospital (1988)
. . . . Dr. Alice Singleton
    0:35—In white lingerie outfit pacing around in her office.
    • 1:15—Brief topless running out of her office after the monster, putting her lab coat on.
Out on Bail (1988). . . . . Sally Anne
    • 1:01—Brief topless in shower with Robert Ginty.
Bedroom Eyes II (1989) . . . . Carolyn Ross
    •• 0:22—Topless in the artist's studio fighting with her lover while Wings Hauser watches through the window.
Robo C.H.I.C. (1990) . . . . Robo C.H.I.C.
TV:
Santa Barbara (1987-90) . . . . n.a.
Video Tapes:
Playboy Video Magazine, Volume 9 . . . . . Playmate
Playboy Video Calendar 1987 (1986) . . . . . Playmate
Playboy's Playmates of the Year: The '80s (1989)
. . . . Playmate of the Year 1986
    ••• 0:17—Full frontal nudity outside by spa.
    ••• 0:19—Topless in still photos. Full frontal nudity, posing in bed.
Magazines:
Playboy (May 1985) . . . . Playmate
Playboy (Dec 1986) . . . . .Sex Stars of 86
Playboy (May 1988) . . . . Kathy Goes Hollywood
    ••• 130-137—Nude.
Playboy (Jan 1989) . . . . .Women of the Eighties
    ••• 254—Full frontal nudity.
Playboy's Nudes (Oct 1990) . . . . Herself
    ••• 109—Full frontal nudity.

Shue, Elisabeth

Films:
The Karate Kid (1984) . . . . Ali
Link (1986). . . . . .Jane Chase
    • 0:50—Brief right breast and buns, side view of a body double, standing in bathroom getting ready to take a bath while Link watches.
Adventures in Babysitting (1987) . . . . Chris Parker
Cocktail (1988) . . . . Jordan Mooney
    0:52—Side view of left breast while standing up in waterfall with Tom Cruise when she takes off her swimsuit top.
Back to the Future, Part II (1989) . . . . Jennifer
Back to the Future, Part III (1990). . . . . Jennifer
The Marrying Man (1991) . . . . Adele Horner
    a.k.a. Too Hot to Handle
Soapdish (1991). . . . . Lori Craven
Made for TV Movies:
Call to Glory (1984) . . . . Jackie Sarnac
TV:
Call to Glory (1984-85) . . . . Jackie Sarnac

Shugart, Reneé

Films:
Screwball Hotel (1988). . . . . Blue Bell

Spring Fever USA (1988). . . . . Beach Beauty
a.k.a. Lauderdale
Summer Job (1989) . . . . Karen
- 0:15—In lingerie reading a magazine.
- 0:42—Topless taking off her top. Long shot, dark.
- 0:45—In white lingerie, standing on stairs, then very brief left breast flashing.

Siani, Sabrina
Films:
Ator, The Fighting Eagle (1982). . . . . .Roon
  0:44—Topless bathing in stream. This is such a long shot, you can't see anything, much less tell it's her.
2020 Texas Gladiators (1983; Italian) . . . . . . .Maida
- 0:07—Left breast, in open white dress after gang rape.
- 0:34—Topless during rape.
The Throne of Fire (1983; Italian) . . . . Princess Belkaren

• Sidney, Ann
Films:
Sebastian (1968; British) . . . . Naomi
Performance (1970). . . . . Dana
- 0:01—Very brief topless and buns.
- 0:24—Brief topless with Chas in flashbacks.
The Treasure of the Amazon (1985; Mexican)
. . . . .Barbara

• Siemaszko, Nina
Sister of actor Casey Siemaszko.
Films:
One More Saturday Night (1986) . . . . . . Karen Lundahl
License to Drive (1988). . . . . .n.a.
Tucker: The Man and His Dream (1988)
. . . . Marilyn Lee Tucker
Lost Angels (1989) . . . . Merilee
- 0:38—Brief topless and buns, running through courtyard. Long shot, don't really see anything.
- 0:45—Buns, sitting at table outside, undressing and rubbing feces (yuck!) on herself.
Wild Orchid II: Two Shades of Blue (1992)
. . . . Blue
- 0:27—Topless and buns, getting undressed in front of Wendy Hughes.
- 0:43—Topless and buns in steam room with a customer.
- 0:58—Topless in panties, garter belt and stockings while undressing for Josh.
- 1:06—Topless while humiliating J. J. in front of everyone at a party.

Silver, Cindy
Films:
Gimme an "F" (1981) . . . . One of the "Ducks"
Hardbodies (1984) . . . . .Kimberly
- 0:07—Brief topless on beach when a dog steals her bikini top.
- 0:47—Topless standing in front of closet mirrors talking about breasts with Kristi.

Simmons, Allene
Films:
Porky's (1981; Canadian) . . . . .Jackie
- 1:02—Topless in the shower scene.
Time Walker (1982) . . . . Nurse
R.S.V.P. (1984) . . . . Patty De Fois Gras
- • 0:13—Topless taking off red top behind the bar with the bartender.
- • 0:38—Topless in bed with Mr. Edwards, then buns running to hide in the closet.
- • 0:41—Frontal nudity in room with Mr. Anderson.
- • • 0:51—Topless talking to Toby in the hallway trying to get help for the Governor.
The Malibu Bikini Shop (1985). . . . . Milinda Riley
Young Lady Chatterley II (1986)
. . . . Marta "Maid in Bed"

Simms Wiegers, Ona
a.k.a. Adult film actress Ona Zee.
Films:
Enrapture (1989). . . . . Chase Webb
- • 0:13—In red bra, panties, garter belt and stockings. Buns in G-string, then topless undressing when she doesn't know Keith is watching.
- • 0:17—Topless when Keith fantasizes about her while he's making love with Martha.
- • 0:21—Topless in back of limousine with a lucky guy.
- • • 1:08—Full frontal nudity making love on top of Keith in bed.
The Art of Dying (1991) . . . . Frances Warner

• Simonsen, Renee
Films:
Nothing Underneath (1985; Italian). . . . . Barbara
a.k.a. Sotto Il Vestito Niente
- 0:51—Brief side view of left breast, changing backstage during fashion show.
Via Montenapoleone (1987; Italian) . . . . Elena

• Simpson, Suzi
Video Tapes:
Playboy Video Calendar 1993 (1992). . . .September
Magazines:
Playboy (Jan 1992). Playmate
- • • 116-127—Nude.
Playboy's Career Girls (Aug 1992)
. . . . Baywatch Playmates
- • • 7—Topless.

• Sinclair, Annette
Films:
Thief of Hearts (1984) . . . . College Girl #1
(Special Home Video Version reviewed.)
Weekend Pass (1984). Maxine
Hide and Go Shriek (1988). . . . . Kim Downs
- 0:51—Brief topless and buns, undressing and getting into bed. Long shot.
- • 0:57—Topless, getting up and out of bed, then getting dressed.

- 1:02—Topless and buns, tied up on top of freight elevator.
- 1:05—Topless on top of elevator.
- 1:17—Topless on top of elevator fighting with the killer. Lit with red light.

Listen to Me (1989) . . . . .Fountain Girl
Instant Karma (1990) . . . . Amy

Singer, Lori

Sister of actor Marc Singer.
Films:
Footloose (1984). . . . . Ariel
The Falcon and the Snowman (1985) . . . . Lana
The Man With One Red Shoe (1985). . . . . Maddy
Trouble in Mind (1986) . . . . Georgia
- 1:01—Very brief left breast, in bed with Kris Kristofferson.

Summer Heat (1987) . . . . .Roxy
•• 0:36—Topless in bed with Jack. Kind of dark and hard to see.
Made in U.S.A. (1988) . . . . Annie
- 0:26—Brief left breast and very brief lower frontal nudity in the back of a convertible with Dar at night.
0:44—In white, braless tank top talking to a used car salesman.

Warlock (1990) . . . . .Kassandra
Made for TV Movies:
Storm and Sorrow (1990) . . . . Molly Higgins
TV:
Fame (1982-83) . . . . Julie Miller

Sirtis, Marina

Films:
The Wicked Lady (1983; British) . . . . . . Jackson's Girl
••• 1:06—Full frontal nudity in and getting out of bed when Faye Dunaway discovers her in bed with Alan Bates.
••• 1:20—Topless getting whipped by Dunaway during their fight during Bates' hanging.
Blind Date (1984). Hooker
(Not the same 1987 *Blind Date* with Bruce Willis.)
••• 0:21—Topless walking to and lying in bed just before taxi driver kills her.
Death Wish III (1985) . . . . Maria
- 0:42—Topless getting blouse ripped open next to a car by the bad guys.
- 0:43—More topless on mattress at the bad guy's hangout.

Waxwork II: Lost in Time (1991) . . . . Gloria
TV:
Star Trek: The Next Generation (1987-)
. . . . Counselor Deanna Troi

Sissons, Kimber

Films:
You Can't Hurry Love (1984). . . . . Brenda
0:48—Partial side of right breast in open shirt, bending over to pick up her bra off the coffee table.

Master of Dragonard Hill (1987) . . . . . . Jane Abdee
•• 0:08—Topless making love in bed with Richard.
Phantom of the Mall: Eric's Revenge (1988) . . . . . . Suzie
0:14—Briefly in bra, in dressing room on B&W security monitor.
The Adventures of Ford Fairlane (1991) . . . . . . .Pussycat
Made for Cable TV:
Dream On: The Charlotte Letter (1991; HBO)
. . . . Candy Striper #3
•• 0:06—Topless several times, getting examined by a doctor while acting in adult film that Martin is watching on TV. (She's the blonde one.)
TV:
Sea Hunt (1987-88) . . . . n.a.

Skinner, Anita

Films:
Girlfriends (1978). . . . . Anne Munroe
Sole Survivor (1982) . . . . .Denise Watson
- 0:29—Very, very brief right breast in bed with Dr. Richardson. Brief side view of right breast when he jumps out of bed.
1:13—In bra, zipping up pants.

Skinner, Rainee

Films:
Rebel (1985; Australian) . . . . Prostitute in bed
- 0:37—Brief topless sitting up in bed.
Kiss the Night (1988; Australian) . . . . n.a.
Pandemonium (1988) . . . . n.a.

• Skriver, Ina

Films:
Emily (1976; British) . . . . Augustine
••• 0:43—Topless getting into the shower with Koo Stark to give her a massage.
Victor/Victoria (1982). . . . . Simone Kallisto

Skye, Ione

a.k.a. Ione Skye Leitch.
Daughter of '60s singer Donovan Leitch.
Wife of Beastie Boy Adam Horovitz.
Films:
A Night in the Life of Jimmy Reardon (1987)
. . . . Denise Hunter
River's Edge (1987) . . . . Clarissa
Stranded (1987). . . . . Deirdre Clark
The Rachel Papers (1989; British). . . . . Rachel
•• 0:58—Topless getting undressed and into bed with Charles. Long shot, then topless in bed.
••• 1:03—Brief topless in three scenes. From above in bathtub, in bed and in bathtub again.
•• 1:04—Left breast, making love sitting up with Charles.
- 1:06—Brief topless sitting up in bathtub.
- 1:08—Brief topless long shot getting dressed in Charles' room.
- 1:28—Brief topless kissing Charles in bed during his flashback.

Say Anything (1989) . . . . Diane Court
Mindwalk (1991) . . . . Kit
Gas Food Lodging (1992) . . . . .Trudi
Wayne's World (1992). . . . . Elyse
Made for Cable TV:
Nightmare Classics: Carmilla (1989; HBO) . . . . . . Marie
TV:
Covington Cross (1992-) . . . . Eleanor

Slater, Helen
Films:
Supergirl (1984; British) . . . . .Linda Lee/Supergirl
The Legend of Billie Jean (1985) . . . . Billie Jean
    0:06—Brief wet T-shirt getting out of pond.
Ruthless People (1986) . . . . Sandy Kessler
The Secret of My Success (1987). . . . . Christy
Happy Together (1988) . . . . . . Alexandra "Alex" Page
  •• 0:17—Brief right breast changing clothes while talk-
    ing to Patrick Dempsey. Unfortunately, she has a
    goofy expression on her face.
    0:57—In red lingerie tempting Dempsey. Later,
    panties under panty hose when Dempsey pulls her
    dress up while she's on roller skates.
    1:07—Very brief panties under panty hose again
    straddling Dempsey in the hallway.
    1:14—Panties under white stockings while changing
    in the closet.
Sticky Fingers (1988). . . . . .Hattie
City Slickers (1991) . . . . Bonnie Rayburn
Made for Cable TV:
Dream On: Theory of Relativity (1992; HBO). . . . . Sarah
TV:
Capital News (1990) . . . . Anne McKenna

Slater, Suzanne
a.k.a. Suzee Slater.
Films:
Savage Streets (1985) . . . . Uncredited
  •• 0:09—Topless being held by jerks when they yank
    her tube top down.
Chopping Mall (1986). . . . . Leslie
  •• 0:28—Brief topless in bed showing breasts to Mike.
    0:31—Walking around the mall in panties and a
    blouse.
Real Men (1987) . . . . Woman in Bed
  • 0:07—Brief left breast, in bed with James Belushi.
Take Two (1988) . . . . Sherrie
  •• 0:11—Topless in office talking with Grant Goodeve,
    wearing panties, garter belt and stockings.
  • 1:00—Topless undressing to get into hot tub wear-
    ing black underwear bottom.
The Big Picture (1989) . . . . Stewardess
Cartel (1990). . . . . .Nancy
    0:28—In red two piece swimsuit modeling on mo-
    torcycle.
    0:35—Brief bra and panties on bed during struggle.
  • 0:36—Topless during brutal rape/murder scene.
Mind Twister (1992) .n.a.

Magazines:
Playboy (Jul 1989) . . . . B-Movie Bimbos
  •• 137—Full frontal nudity lying on a car wearing a gir-
    dle and stockings.

• Sloan, Tiffany
Video Tapes:
Playboy Video Centerfold: Tiffany Sloan (1992)
  . . . . Playmate
Magazines:
Playboy (Oct 1992) . . . . Playmate
  ••• 102-113—Nude.

• Small, Marya
Films:
Sleeper (1973) . . . . Dr. Nero
One Flew Over the Cuckoo's Nest (1975). . . . Candy
  • 1:00—Very brief side view of left breast, bending
    over to pick up her clothes on boat.
The Wild Party (1975) . . . . Bertha
The Great Smokey Roadblock (1976) . . . . Alice
The World's Greatest Lover (1977) . . . . n.a.
Thank God It's Friday (1978) . . . . .Jackie
Fade to Black (1980) . . . . Doreen
National Lampoon's Class Reunion (1982) . . . Iris Augen
Zapped! (1982) . . . . Mrs. Springboro

Smith Bouchér, Savannah
Films:
Five Days from Home (1978) . . . . Georgie Haskin
North Dallas Forty (1979) . . . . .Joanne
  • 0:27—Very brief topless in bed tossing around with
    Nick Nolte.
The Long Riders (1980) . . . . Zee
Meet the Applegates (1989). . . . . Dottie
Eating (1991). . . . . .Eloise

• Smith, Amanda
Films:
Dancing In the Dark (1986; Canadian). . . . . . .Neighbor
Fall From Innocence (1988) . . . . .Janis Cummins
  • 0:05—Brief right breast while lying in bed when Bob
    gets out.
  • 0:48—Left breast, in open nightie top, while walking
    down hallway.
    0:52—Very brief side view of right breast standing
    up from the bed.
The Freshman (1990). . . . . Mall Patron

Smith, Cheryl
a.k.a. Rainbeaux Smith.
Films:
Video Vixens (1973) . . . . .Twinkle Twat Girl
  ••• 0:24—Full frontal nudity doing a commercial, sitting
    next to pool.
Caged Heat (1974) . . . . .Lauelle
a.k.a. Renegade Girls
  • 0:04—Brief left breast, dreaming in her jail cell that
    a guy is caressing her through the bars.

•• 0:25—Topless in the shower scene.
•• 0:50—Brief nude in the solitary cell.
The Swinging Cheerleaders (1974) . . . . Andrea
•• 0:12—Topless taking off her bra and putting sheer blouse on.
• 0:17—Left breast, several times, sitting in bed with Ross.
Farewell, My Lovely (1975; British) . . . . .Doris
• 0:56—Frontal nudity in bedroom in a bordello with another guy before getting beaten by the madam.
Drum (1976) . . . . Sophie Maxwell
•• 0:54—Topless in the stable trying to get Yaphet Kotto to make love with her.
Massacre at Central High (1976) . . . . .Mary
• 0:27—Brief topless in a classroom getting attacked by some guys.
••• 1:09—Nude walking around on a mountain side with Robert Carradine and Lani O'Grady.
Revenge of the Cheerleaders (1976) . . . . . . Heather
• 0:00—Brief topless changing tops in back of car. (Blonde on the far right.)
0:28—Buns, in shower room scene.
0:36—Full frontal nudity, but covered with bubbles.
Slumber Party '57 (1976) . . . . .Sherry
Cinderella (1977) . . . . Cinderella
•• 0:03—Topless dancing and singing.
••• 0:30—Frontal nudity getting "washed" by her sisters for the Royal Ball.
•• 0:34—Topless in the forest during a dream.
••• 0:41—Topless taking a bath. Frontal nudity drying herself off.
• 1:16—Brief topless with the Prince.
• 1:30—Brief left breast after making love with the Prince to prove it was her.
• 1:34—Brief side view of left breast making love in the Prince's carriage.
Laserblast (1978). . . . . Kathy
Up in Smoke (1978) . . . . Laughing Lady
The Best of Sex and Violence (1981) . . . . . Cinderella
• 0:14—Topless taking a bath in scene from *Cinderella*.
Parasite (1982) . . . . Captive Girl
•• 0:08—Topless tied by wrists in kitchen.
•• 0:12—Topless knocking gun out of guy's hands standing behind fence.

Smith, Crystal
Films:
Hot Dog... The Movie (1984) . . . . .Motel Clerk
•• 0:10—Nude getting out of spa and going to the front desk to sign people in.
Magazines:
Playboy (Sep 1971) . . . . Playmate

Smith, Donna
Video Tapes:
Playmate Playoffs . . . . Playmate
Playboy Video Calendar 1987 (1986) . . . . Playmate
Playmates at Play (1990) . . . . .Hoops

Magazines:
Playboy (Mar 1985) . . . . Playmate
Playboy's Book of Lingerie (Jan 1992) . . . . . .Herself
•• 77—Buns and tip of left breast.

Smith, Julie Kristen
Films:
Pretty Smart (1986) . . . . Samantha Falconwright
•• 0:20—Nude in her room when Daphne sees her.
•• 0:26—Topless in bed talking to Jennifer.
•• 0:40—Topless in bed.
•• 0:52—Topless sitting in lounge by the pool.
• 0:57—Brief left breast, while brushing teeth.
• 1:10—Brief right breast, while making love with boyfriend in bed.
• 1:13—More brief right breast.
••• 1:14—Nude, sitting on pillow on top of her boyfriend in bed.
Angel III: The Final Chapter (1988) . . . . Darlene
••• 0:40—Topless during caveman shoot with a brunette girl.
••• 0:44—Topless again dancing in caveman shoot.

Smith, Laurie
Films:
Paradise Motel (1985) . . . . .Honeymoon Wife
•• 0:02—Left breast, then topless in Honeymoon Suite with her new husband, then making love in bed.
Video Tapes:
Nudes in Limbo (1983) . . . . Model

Smith, Linda
Films:
Hardcore (1979) . . . . .Hope (Mistress Victoria)
The Beastmaster (1982) . . . . Kiri's Friend
• 0:35—Topless in a pond with Tanya Roberts.

Smith, Madeline
Films:
Vampire Lovers (1970; British) . . . . Emma
•• 0:32—Topless trying on a dress in the bedroom after Carmilla has taken a bath.
• 0:49—Topless in bed, getting her top pulled down by Carmilla.
Live and Let Die (1973; British) . . . . .Miss Caruso
Bawdy Adventures of Tom Jones (1976) . . . . . . .Sophia
TV:
Doctor in the House (1970-73) . . . . Nurse

Smith, Maggie
Films:
The Prime of Miss Jean Brodie (1969) . . . . . . Jean Brodie
(Academy Award for Best Actress.)
California Suite (1978) . . . . .Diana Barrie
• 1:05—Very brief side of left breast, putting nightgown on over her head.
Clash of the Titans (1981) . . . . Thetis
Quartet (1981; British/French) . . . . Lois
Lily in Love (1985) . . . . Lily Wynn

A Private Function (1985) . . . . Joyce Chilvers
A Room with a View (1986; British) . . . Charlotte Bartlett
The Lonely Passion of Judith Hearne (1988)
. . . . Judith Hearne
Hook (1991) . . . . Granny Wendy
Sister Act (1992) . . . . Mother Superior

Smith, Martha
Films:
Animal House (1978) . . . . Babs Jansen
Blood Link (1983). . . . . .Hedwig
- •• 0:41—Topless, wearing black panties while in bed with Keith.
- • 0:50—Topless getting slapped around by Keith.
- ••• 0:51—Topless sitting up in bed when Craig and Keith meet each other for the first time.
- • 1:13—Topless, wearing red panties, in bed with Keith.

TV:
Scarecrow and Mrs. King (1983-88)
. . . . Francine Desmond
Magazines:
Playboy (Jul 1973) . . . . Playmate
- ••• 106-113—Full frontal nudity.

Smith, Rainbeaux
See: Smith, Cheryl.

• Smith, Vickie
Video Tapes:
Playboy Video Calendar 1993 (1992) . . . . . . January
Magazines:
Playboy (May 1992) . . . . Playmate
- ••• 90-101—Nude.

• Smith, Yeardley
Films:
Heaven Help Us (1985) . . . . .Cathleen
The Legend of Billie Jean (1985) . . . . Putter
Maximum Overdrive (1986) . . . . Lonnie
Ginger Ale Afternoon (1989) . . . . Bonnie Cleator
- • 0:53—Brief upper half of left breast, taking off top in trailer with Hank.
Listen to Me (1989) . . . . Cootz
City Slickers (1991) . . . . .Nancy
TV:
The Simpsons (1989-) . . . . Voice of Lisa Simpson
Herman's Head (1991-) . . . . Louise Fitzer

Snodgress, Carrie
Films:
Diary of a Mad Housewife (1970) . . . . . . Tina Balser
- ••• 0:01—Topless taking off nightgown and getting dressed, putting on white bra while Richard Benjamin talks to her.
- 0:36—Buns and brief side view of left breast, while kissing Frank Langella.
- • 0:41—Very brief topless lying on floor when Langella pulls the blanket up.

- • 0:54—Topless lying in bed with Langella.
- 1:03—In white bra and panties getting dressed in Langella's apartment.
- 1:10—In white bra and panties in Langella's apartment again.
- ••• 1:21—Topless in the shower with Langella, then drying herself off.
The Fury (1978) . . . . Hester
Homework (1982) . . . . Dr. Delingua
Trick or Treats (1982) . . . . .Joan
A Night in Heaven (1983) . . . . Mrs. Johnson
Pale Rider (1985) . . . . Sarah Wheeler
Murphy's Law (1986) . . . . Joan Freeman
Across the Tracks (1990) . . . . Rosemary Maloney
Made for TV Movies:
Woman with a Past (1992) . . . . .Florence

Snyder, Susan Marie
Films:
Sleepaway Camp II: Unhappy Campers (1988)
. . . . Mare
- • 0:08—Brief topless lifting up her T-shirt.
- • 0:24—Brief topless flashing in boy's cabin.
- • 0:33—Topless in Polaroid photograph that Angela confiscates from the boys.
TV:
Santa Barbara . . . . Laken Capwell
As the World Turns . . . . Julie Wendall

Snyder, Suzanne
Films:
The Oasis (1984) . . . . Jennifer
Remo Williams: The Adventure Begins (1985)
. . . . .Nurse/Soap Opera
Weird Science (1985) . . . . Deb
Night of the Creeps (1986) . . . . Lisa
Pretty Kill (1987) . . . . .Franci/Stella/Paul
Killer Klowns from Outer Space (1988). . . . . . . Debbie
The Night Before (1988) . . . . Lisa
Retribution (1988) . . . . .Angel
- 0:50—Very, very brief blurry left breast getting up in bed with George after his nightmare.
The Return of the Living Dead II (1988) . . . . . . .Brenda
Femme Fatale (1990) . . . . .Andrea
- ••• 0:08—Topless, nonchalantly taking off her top and posing for Billy Zane's painting. (She sometimes has a bag over her head.)
- •• 0:46—Topless posing again with the bag on and off her head.

• Soares, Alana
Films:
Beverly Hills Cop II (1987) . . . . .Playboy Playmate
Video Tapes:
Playboy Video Magazine, Volume 5 (1983)
. . . . Playmate
- • 0:06—Brief topless on chair.
Magazines:
Playboy (Mar 1983) . . . . Playmate

Playboy's Nudes (Oct 1990) . . . . Herself
••• 72—Topless.
Playboy's Book of Lingerie (Jan 1991) . . . . . . Herself
•• 18-19—Right breast and lower frontal nudity.
Playboy's Book of Lingerie (Mar 1992) . . . . . Herself
••• 64—Topless.

Socas, Maria

Films:
The Warrior and the Sorceress (1984) . . . . Naja
(Topless in every scene she's in.)
••• 0:15—Topless wearing robe and bikini bottoms in room with Zeg. Sort of brief buns, leaving the room.
•• 0:22—Topless standing by a wagon at night.
•• 0:27—Topless in room with David Carradine. Dark. Most of buns when leaving the room.
•• 0:31—Topless and buns climbing down wall.
• 0:34—Brief topless, then left breast with rope around her neck at the well.
• 0:44—Topless when Carradine rescues her.
• 0:47—Topless walking around outside.
• 0:57—More topless outside.
• 1:00—Topless watching a guy pound a sword.
• 1:05—Topless under a tent after Carradine uses the sword. Long shot.
• 1:09—Topless during big fight scene.
• 1:14—Topless next to well. Long shot.
Soldier's Revenge (1986) . . . . Baetriz
Deathstalker II (1987) . . . . .Amazon Queen
0:50—In see-through nightgown after telling Deathstalker she is going to marry him.
Hollywood Boulevard II (1989) . . . . . . .Amazon Queen

• Søeberg, Camilla

Films:
Twist & Shout (1986; Danish) . . . . .Anna
Manifesto (1988) . . . . Svetlana
••• 0:15—Nude, in bathtub and bedroom with Emile. Long scene.
• 0:19—Brief left breast when Emile cuts off her hair.
•• 1:04—Left breast, several times when Emile is in her room. More left breast cleaning up after Emile accidentally dies.
• 1:15—Brief side of left breast, while making love with Eric Stoltz. Dark. Buns, getting out of bed.
•• 1:16—Topless and buns unrolling Emile in the rug.
•• 1:23—Topless sitting in bed with puppies.

Solari, Suzanne

Films:
Roller Blade (1986) . . . . Sister Sharon Cross
0:04—Buns, in G-string, lying in bed.
• 1:21—Brief upper half of right breast, taking off suit. Buns in G-string.
Hell Comes to Frogtown (1987) . . . . Runaway Girl
Class of Nuke 'Em High Part II: Subhumanoid Meltdown (1991) . . . . Toxie Squirrel Gang Member

Soles, P.J.

P.J. stands for Pamela Jane.
Ex-wife of actor Dennis Quaid.
Films:
Carrie (1976) . . . . .Norma
Halloween (1978) . . . . Lynda
• 1:04—Brief right breast, sitting up in bed after making love in bed with Bob.
• 1:07—Brief topless getting strangled by Michael in the bedroom.
Breaking Away (1979) . . . . Suzy
Old Boyfriends (1979) . . . . Sandy
Rock 'n' Roll High School (1979) . . . . Riff Randell
Private Benjamin (1980) . . . . Private Wanda Winter
Stripes (1981) . . . . Stella
Terror in the Aisles (1984) . . . . Lynda
• 0:24—Brief topless in scene from *Halloween*.
Sweet Dreams (1985). . . . . .Wanda
B.O.R.N. (1988) . . . . Liz
Alienator (1990) . . . . .Tara
Magazines:
Playboy (Nov 1981) . . . . Sex in Cinema 1981
•• 166—Topless.

Somers, Kristi

Films:
Rumble Fish (1983) . . . . n.a.
Hardbodies (1984) . . . . .Michelle
•• 0:53—Nude, dancing on the beach while Ashley plays the guitar and sings.
Girls Just Want to Have Fun (1985). . . . . .Rikki
Mugsy's Girls (1985) . . . . Laurie
• 0:15—Brief topless several times while mud wrestling.
•• 0:29—Topless and buns in bathtub on bus.
• 0:34—Brief topless holding up sign to get truck driver to stop.
Savage Streets (1985) . . . . Valerie
0:24—In bra and panties in the locker room.
Tomboy (1985) . . . . Seville Ritz
•• 0:14—Topless taking a shower while talking to Betsy Russell.
• 0:53—Brief topless stripping at a party.
Hell Comes to Frogtown (1987) . . . . .Arabella
Return to Horror High (1987). . . . . .Ginny McCall

Somers, Suzanne

Films:
American Graffiti (1973). . . . . . The Blonde in the T-bird
Magnum Force (1973) . . . . Uncredited Pool Girl
•• 0:26—In blue swimsuit getting into a swimming pool, brief topless a couple of times before getting shot, brief topless floating dead.
Yesterday's Hero (1979; British) . . . . Cloudy Martin
Nothing Personal (1980; Canadian) . . . . .Abigail
1:07—In wet T-shirt sitting with her feet in a pond talking with Donald Sutherland.
Miniseries:
Hollywood Wives (1988) . . . . Gina Germaine

Made for TV Movies:
Keeping Secrets (1991) . . . . Suzanne Somers
TV:
Three's Company (1977-81) . . . . Chrissy Snow
She's the Sheriff (1987-89) . . . . . . Sheriff Hildy Granger
Step by Step (1991-) . . . . Carol Foster
Magazines:
Playboy (Feb 1980) . . . Suzanne Somers' Playmate Test
••• 136-145—Old photos taken before she was famous. Nude.
Playboy (Dec 1984) . . . . Suzanne Take Two
••• 120-129—New photos. Topless and buns.

Sommer, Elke

Films:
Sweet Ecstasy (1962) . . . . Elke
Nude.
A Shot in the Dark (1964) . . . . Maria Gambrelli
Boy, Did I Get a Wrong Number (1966) . . . . Didi
The Corrupt Ones (1966) . . . . Lily
The Oscar (1966) . . . . Kay Bergdahl
The House of Exorcism (1975) . . . . n.a.
Topless.
Ten Little Indians (1975) . . . . Vera
Left for Dead (1978) . . . . Magdalene Krushcen
•• 0:38—Left breast, while posing for photographer.
• 0:39—Very brief left breast in B&W photo.
0:58—Buns and topless when police officers lift her up to put plastic under her. Covered with blood, can't see her face.
• 1:09—Very brief left breast in B&W photo.
The Prisoner of Zenda (1979) . . . . The Countess
Lily in Love (1985) . . . . Alicia Brown
Magazines:
Playboy (Sep 1970) . . . . n.a.
Playboy (Jan 1974) . . . . Twenty Years of Playboy
•• 209—Topless getting into pool.
Playboy (Jan 1979) . . . . 25 Beautiful Years
•• 159—Topless getting into a pool.
Playboy (Jan 1989) . . . . Women of the Seventies
•• 217—Topless getting into pool.

Sommerfield, Diane

Films:
Love in a Taxi (1980) .Carine
Back Roads (1981) . . . . Liz
The Nightstalker (1987) . . . . Lonnie Roberts
• 0:35—Side view of right breast lying dead in morgue.

Sorenson, Heidi

Films:
History of the World, Part I (1981) . . . . Vestal Virgin
Fright Night (1985) . . . . Hooker
Spies Like Us (1985) . . . . Fitz-Hume's Supervisor
Roxanne (1987) . . . . Trudy
For the Boys (1991) . . . . Showgirl

Video Tapes:
Playboy Video Magazine, Volume 5 (1983)
. . . . Playmate
• 0:06—Brief topless in library.
Magazines:
Playboy (Jul 1981) . . . . Playmate

Soutendijk, Reneé

Films:
Spetters (1980; Dutch) . . . . Fientje
•• 1:12—Topless making love in trailer with Jeff.
The Girl with the Red Hair (1983; Dutch) . . . . . . .Hannie
The Cold Room (1984) Lili
The Fourth Man (1984; Dutch) . . . . Christine
••• 0:27—Full frontal nudity removing robe, brief buns in bed, side view left breast, then topless in bed with Gerard.
• 0:32—Brief left breast in bed with Gerard after he hallucinates and she cuts his penis off.
••• 0:53—Left breast, then right breast in red dress when Gerard opens her dress.
• 1:11—Topless making love with Herman while Gerard watches through keyhole.
Grave Secrets (1990) . . . . Iris Norwood
Eve of Destruction (1991)
. . . . Dr. Eve Simmons/Eve VIII
0:17—Left breast, while on table as a robot, with half her skin removed. Possibly a special-effect body.
• 0:22—Brief topless in bathroom (as a robot), fixing her wound. Topless sitting on bed, butting a large bandage over the wound.
Made for Cable Movies:
Murderers Among Us: The Simon Wiesenthal Story (1989; HBO) . . . . .Cyla
Keeper of the City (1991; Showtime)
. . . . Vickie Benedetto
Made for Cable TV:
The Hitchhiker: Murderous Feelings
. . . . Sara Kendal
••• 0:04—In bra, then topless with stockings and a garter belt on couch with a guy.
• 0:18—Right breast when mysterious attacker surprises her from behind.

Spacek, Sissy

Films:
Prime Cut (1972) . . . . Poppy
• 0:25—Brief side view of left breast lying in hay, then buns when Gene Hackman lifts her up to show to Lee Marvin.
••• 0:30—Topless sitting in bed, then getting up to try on a dress while Marvin watches.
0:32—Close up of breasts though sheer black dress in a restaurant.
Badlands (1973) . . . . Holly
Ginger in the Morning (1973) . . . . .Ginger
Carrie (1976) . . . . Carrie White
•• 0:02—Nude, taking a shower, then having her first menstrual period in the girls' locker room.

- 1:25—Brief topless taking a bath to wash all the pig blood off her after the dance.

Three Women (1977) . . . . Pinky Rose

Welcome to L.A. (1977) . . . . Linda Murray
- 0:51—Brief topless after bringing presents into Keith Carradine's bedroom.

Heart Beat (1979) . . . . Carolyn Cassady

Coal Miner's Daughter (1980) . . . . Loretta Lynn
(Academy Award for Best Actress.)

Raggedy Man (1981) . . . . Nita
0:43—Side view of left breast washing herself off while two guys peep from outside window. Long shot, don't really see anything.

Missing (1982) . . . . Beth Horman

The River (1984) . . . . Mae Garvey

Marie (1986). . . . . Marie Ragghianti

'night Mother (1986) . . . . Jessie Cates

Violets Are Blue (1986) . . . . Gussie Sawyer

The Long Walk Home (1990) . . . . . . Miriam Thompson

JFK (1991) . . . . Liz Garrison

Hard Promises (1992) . . . . n.a.

Made for Cable Movies:

A Private Matter (1992; HBO) . . . . Sherri Finkbine

• *Spangler, Donna*

Films:

Guns (1990) . . . . Hugs Huggins
0:27—Oil wrestling with Kym.
0:28—Showering (in front) while talking to Kym (in back).

Roots of Evil (1991) . . . . Scarlett
(Unrated version reviewed.)
- 0:04—Topless, getting attacked by the crazy guy, then killed.
- 0:07—Brief topless, dead, covered with blood when Alex Cord discovers her.

Video Tapes:

Sexy Lingerie II (1990) . . . . Model

Wet and Wild II (1990) . . . . Model

Sexy Lingerie III (1991) . . . . Model

Magazines:

Playboy (Dec 1989) . . . . Lethal Women
- 153—Full frontal nudity.

Playboy's Book of Lingerie (Mar 1991) . . . . . Herself
- 22—Right breast.
- 101—Topless.

Playboy's Career Girls (Aug 1992) . . . Lethal Women
- 104—Full frontal nudity.

Speir, Dona

Films:

Doin' Time (1984) . . . . Card Holder

Dragnet (1987) . . . . Baitmate

Hard Ticket to Hawaii (1987) . . . . Donna
- 0:01—Topless on boat kissing her boyfriend, Rowdy.
- 0:23—Topless in the spa with Hope Marie Carlton looking at diamonds they found.

- 1:04—Topless and buns with Rowdy after watching a video tape.
- 1:33—Topless during the end credits.

Mortuary Academy (1988) . . . . Nurse

Click: Calendar Girl Killer (1989) . . . . Nancy
0:00—Posing in yellow two piece swimsuit during photo session.
0:06—In wet, white dress after being pushed into the spa.
- 0:11—Brief glimpses of breasts during photo session. Buns and topless under sheer fabric.
- 0:12—Brief buns, dropping the piece of fabric.
0:28—Posing in yellow two piece swimsuit during photo session.

Picasso Trigger (1989) . . . . Donna
0:17—In white lingerie on boat with Hope Marie Carlton.
- 0:49—Topless and buns standing, then making love in bed.

Savage Beach (1989) . . . . Dona
0:06—Almost topless in spa with the three other women.
- 0:32—Topless changing clothes in airplane with Hope Marie Carlton.
- 0:48—Nude, going for a swim on the beach with Carlton.

Guns (1990) . . . . Donna Hamilton
- 1:00—Topless and buns in black G-string getting dressed in locker room. Then in black lingerie.

Do or Die (1991) . . . . Donna Hamilton
- 0:06—Brief topless taking off towel and getting into spa.
- 0:32—Topless, mostly right breast, changing clothes in back of airplane.
- 1:21—Topless and buns, in swimming pool with Erik Estrada.

Video Tapes:

Playmate Playoffs . . . . Playmate

Playboy Video Calendar 1987 (1986) . . . . . Playmate

Playboy Video Centerfold: Teri Weigel (1986)
. . . . Playmate

Glamour Through Your Lens—Outdoor Techniques
(1989) . . . . Herself
0:22—Posing by Corvette in white shorts and red top.
0:35—In white two piece swimsuit on lounge chair by the pool.

Wet and Wild (1989) . . . . Model

Sexy Lingerie III (1991) . . . . Model

Magazines:

Playboy (Mar 1984) . . . . Playmate

Playboy's Nudes (Oct 1990) . . . . Herself
- 24—Full frontal nudity.

Playboy's Book of Lingerie (Mar 1991) . . . . . . Herself
- 54—Topless under sheer black gown.

Spelvin, Georgina

Adult flim actress.
Films:
I Spit on Your Corpse (1974) . . . . Sandra
- 0:38—Flashing her left breast to get three guys to stop their car.
••• 0:39—Topless, fighting with the three guys.
- 0:47—Brief right breast in gaping blouse.
••• 0:53—Topless outside, de-virginizing the backwoods kid.
•• 1:08—Topless, close-up view, showing her breasts to him.
- 1:10—Buns, in lowered pants and left breast in open blouse.

Honky Tonk Nights (1978) . . . . Georgia
- 0:06—Topless, lying with her head in a guy's lap.

Police Academy III: Back in Training (1986) . .The Hooker
Magazines:
Playboy (Nov 1973) . . . . Sex in Cinema 1973
••• 157—Topless with a snake in photo from *Behind the Green Door.*
Playboy (Dec 1973). . . . . Sex Stars of 1973
- 210—Partial right breast and lower frontal nudity.

• Sportolaro, Tina

Films:
Sincerely Charlotte (1986; French) . . . . .n.a.
Frantic (1988) . . . . TWA Clerk
The Passion of Beatrice (1988; French)
. . . . Mère de François Enfant
- 0:06—Brief topless when the young François discovers her in bed with another man and kills him.

Paris By Night (1989; British) . . . . Violet

Spradling, Charlie

a.k.a. Charlie.
Films:
The Blob (1988) . . . . .Co-ed
Unexpected Encounters, Vol. 3 (1988)
. . . . Woman in House
••• 0:50—In lingerie, then topless on sofa with the gardener.
Meridian (1989) . . . . Gina
a.k.a. Kiss of the Beast
a.k.a. Phantoms
•• 0:22—Topless getting her blouse torn off by Lawrence while lying on the table.
••• 0:28—Topless standing next to fireplace, then topless on the couch. Hot!
Twice Dead (1989) . . . . Tina
•• 1:11—Topless taking off jacket next to bed.
••• 1:14—Topless making love with her boyfriend in bed.
- 1:18—Brief topless dead in bed.
Mirror Mirror (1990) . . . . Charleen Kane
- 1:05—Very, very brief side of left breast, after taking of swimsuit in locker room.

- 1:06—Buns, taking a shower. Brief topless a couple of times when the hot water pipes break.
1:09—Buns, lying on the floor, dead, covered with blisters.
Puppet Master II (1990). . . . . .Wanda
•• 1:04—Topless getting out of bed and adjusting her panties.
Ski School (1990). . . . . .Paulette
Wild at Heart (1990) . . . . Irma
•• 0:40—Brief topless in bed during flashback.
The Doors (1991). . . . . .CBS Girl Backstage
Bad Channels (1992) . . . . .Cookie
TV:
Twin Peaks (1990-91). . . . . Swabbie

• Springsteen, Pamela

Sister of singer Bruce Springsteen.
Films:
Reckless (1984) . . . . .Karen Sybern
My Science Project (1985) . . . Hall Monitor/Ellie's Friend
Dixie Lanes (1987). .Judy
•• 1:00—Topless, turning around in pond, while talking to Everett at night.
Modern Girls (1987) . . . . .Tanya
Scenes from the Goldmine (1987) . . . . Stephanie
Sleepaway Camp II: Unhappy Campers (1988)
. . . . .Angela
Fast Food (1989) . . . . Mary Beth Bensen
Sleepaway Camp III: Teenage Wasteland (1989)
. . . . Angela Baker
The Gumshoe Kid (1990). . . . . Mona Krause

Sprinkle, Annie

Adult film actress.
Films:
Mondo New York (1987) . . . . .Model/Performer
- 0:17—Nude, painted body with other models during "Rapping & Rocking" segment.
Wimps (1987) . . . . Head Stripper
•• 1:12—Topless on stage with two other strippers, teasing Francis.
Young Nurses in Love (1987). . . . . .Twin Falls
•• 0:23—Topless getting measured by Dr. Spencer.
Shadows in the City (1991) . . . . Ex-Girlfriend
Made for Cable TV:
Real Sex 2 (1991; HBO) . . . . .Herself
Real Sex 4 (1992; HBO)
. . . . Annie Sprinkle's One Woman Show
•• 0:00—Brief topless during opening credits.
•• 0:01—Topless several times during her show.
••• 0:09—Topless with vibrator during a ceremonial sex routine in her show.

• Squire, Janie

Films:
Piranha (1978). . . . . Barbara
•• 0:02—Topless taking off her top to go swimming with her boyfriend.

Cheerleaders Wild Weekend (1985)
. . . . Donna/Darwell
- ••• 0:39—Topless and brief buns, taking off her white blouse during contest.
- ••• 0:41—Topless with the other five girls during contest.
- ••• 0:43—Topless during getting measured with the other two girls.

• St. Croix, Dominique
Films:
Recruits (1986; Canadian). . . . . .n.a.
Magazines:
Penthouse (Apr 1986). Pet

St. George, Cathy
Films:
Star 80 (1983). . . . . Playboy Mansion Guest
Beverly Hills Brats (1989). . . . . Sally
    0:22—In sheer purple bra, while talking on the phone.
Video Tapes:
Playboy's Playmate Review 2 (1984). . . . . Playmate
Wet and Wild (1989). . . . . .Model
Magazines:
Playboy (Aug 1982) . . . . Playmate
Playboy's Book of Lingerie (Nov 1991) . . . . . Herself
- • 82—Right breast.
Playboy's Book of Lingerie (Mar 1992) . . . . . Herself
- •• 60—Right breast.
Playboy's Book of Lingerie (May 1992) . . . . . Herself
- • 71—Partial lower frontal nudity.
Playboy's Book of Lingerie (Sep 1992) . . . . . Herself
- •• 8—Left breast.
- • 37—Lower frontal nudity.
- ••• 89—Topless.

St. Jon, Ashley
Films:
Takin' It Off (1984) . . . . Sin
- ••• 0:20—Topless and buns doing two dance routines on stage.
- •• 0:53—Nude, stripping and dancing in the library.
Weekend Pass (1984) . . . . Xylene B-12
- •• 0:13—Topless dancing on stage.
The Wild Life (1984) . . . . Stripper #1
- ••• 0:47—Topless and brief buns doing strip tease routine in front of Christopher Penn and his friends.
Sorority Girls and the Creature from Hell (1990)
. . . . Bar Patron
Video Tapes:
Centerfold Screen Test (1985) . . . . Herself
- ••• 0:32—Topless and buns in G-string, taking off her fur coat while auditioning in a car.
The Stripper of the Year (1986) . . . . Judge

• St. Pierre, Monique
Films:
Motel Hell (1980) . . . . Debbie

Magazines:
Playboy (Nov 1978) . . . . Playmate
Playboy (Dec 1980) . . . . .The World of Playboy
- ••• 18—Full frontal nudity.
Playboy's Nudes (Oct 1990) . . . . Herself
- ••• 101—Full frontal nudity.

• Stakis, Anastassia
Films:
Nevada Heat (1982) . . . . Wooly
a.k.a. Stake Out
- • 0:13—Topless in the shower room scene.
Siesta (1987) . . . . .Desdra

Staley, Lora
Films:
American Nightmare (1981; Canadian)
. . . . Louise Harmon
- •• 0:44—Topless and buns in G-string dancing on stage.
- ••• 0:54—Topless making love in bed with Eric.
- • 0:59—Brief right breast, then topless auditioning in TV studio.
Thief (1981) . . . . Paula
Deadly Weapon (1989) . . . . Leslie

Staller, Ilona
a.k.a. Italian adult film actress Cicciolina.
Was a member of the Italian Parliament from 1987-92.
Films:
Inhibition (1984; Italian) . . . . Anna
- ••• 0:08—Nude taking a shower with Carol.
- • 0:43—Brief full frontal nudity getting out of swimming pool.
- ••• 0:55—Topless making love in the water with Robert.
- ••• 1:00—Full frontal nudity getting disciplined by Carol.
Made for Cable TV:
Real Sex 3 (1992; HBO) . . . . Ciccolina
- •• 0:00—Topless several times during the opening credits.
- • 0:16—Topless several times.
- • 0:17—Brief lower frontal nudity and buns. More topless in clips.
- ••• 0:20—More topless clips.
- • 0:24—More topless shots.
Magazines:
Playboy (Feb 1988) . . . . The Year in Sex
- ••• 134—Full frontal nudity.
Playboy (Feb 1991) . . . . The Year in Sex
- • Left breast, making the "victory" sign with her hand.

• Starbuck, Cheryl
Films:
Angel III: The Final Chapter (1988). . . . . . . Video Girl #3
Mortuary Academy (1988). . . . . .Linda Hollyhead
- • 1:08—Topless, dead, in morgue when Paul Bartel tries to make love with her.
Shy People (1988) . . . . Stewardess

• Stark, Kimberleigh
Films:
Crime Lords (1990). . . . . .Lieutenant Sylvestri
Night of the Cyclone (1990). . . . . .Venna
- 0:01—Brief left breast while posing for the painter.
- 0:40—Topless on the boat, fighting with the businessman. Topless on the floor, dead.

Stark, Koo
Former girlfriend of Prince Andrew of England in 1982, before he met and married "Fergie."
Special Stills Photographer in the film *Aria*.
Films:
Justine. . . . . Justine
- • 0:09—Topless getting fondled by a nun.
- • 0:16—Topless getting attacked by a nun.
- 0:57—Topless in open dress getting attacked by old guy.
- • • 1:00—Topless getting bathed, then lower frontal nudity.
- 1:28—Right breast and buns taking off clothes, then brief full frontal nudity getting dressed again.
- 1:32—Topless getting thrown in to the water.

The Rocky Horror Picture Show (1975; British)
. . . . Bridesmaid
Emily (1976; British). Emily
- • 0:08—Topless, lying in bed caressing herself while fantasizing about James.
- • • 0:30—Topless in studio posing for Augustine, then kissing her.
- • • 0:42—Buns and topless taking a shower after posing for Augustine.
- • 0:56—Left breast, under a tree with James.
- 1:16—Topless in the woods seducing Rupert.

Cruel Passion (1978). . . . . .n.a.
Electric Dreams (1984). . . . . Girl in Soap Opera

Stavin, Mary
Films:
Octopussy (1983; British). . . . . Octopussy Girl
A View to a Kill (1985). . . . . Kimberley Jones
House (1986). . . . . Tanya
Open House (1987). . . . . Katie Thatcher
Howling V (1989). . . . . .Anna
- • 1:09—Topless three times drying herself off while Richard watches in the mirror. Possible body double.

TV:
Twin Peaks (1990-91). . . . . Heba

Steenburgen, Mary
Ex-wife of actor Malcolm McDowell.
Films:
Goin' South (1978). . . . . .Julia Tate
Time After Time (1979; British). . . . . Amy Robbins
Melvin and Howard (1980). . . . . .Lynda Dummar
- • 0:31—Topless and buns, ripping off barmaid outfit and walking out the door.

Ragtime (1981). . . . . Mother
A Midsummer Night's Sex Comedy (1982). . . . . Adrian

Cross Creek (1983). . . . . Marjorie Kinnan Rawlings
Romantic Comedy (1983). . . . . Phoebe
Dead of Winter (1987)
. . . . Julie Rose/Katie McGovern/Evelyn
End of the Line (1987). . . . . Rose Pickett
Miss Firecracker (1989). . . . . Elain
Parenthood (1989). . . . . Karen Buckman
Back to the Future, Part III (1990). . . . . . .Clara Clayton
The Butcher's Wife (1991). . . . . Stella
Made for TV Movies:
One Magic Christmas (1985; U.S./Canadian)
. . . . Ginny Grainger
The Attic—The Hiding of Anne Frank (1988)
. . . . Miep Gies

Stefanelli, Simonetta
Films:
The Godfather (1972). . . . . .Apollonia
- • • 1:50—Topless in bedroom on honeymoon night.
Three Brothers (1982; Italian). . . . . Young Donato's Wife
Magazines:
Playboy (Nov 1972). . . . . Sex in Cinema 1972
- 161—Left breast, grainy photo from *The Godfather*.
Playboy (Mar 1974). . . . . . The Don's Daughter-In-Law
- • • 97-99—Topless.

Stein, Pamela J.
Video Tapes:
Playboy Video Calendar 1989 (1988)
. . . . .September
- • • 0:33—Nude.
Playboy Video Centerfold: Tawnni Cable (1990)
. . . . Playmate
- • • 0:14—Nude in Hawaii with Tawnni Cable and Jacqueline Sheen.
Playboy Playmates in Paradise (1992). . . . Playmate
Magazines:
Playboy (Nov 1987). . . . . Playmate
Playboy's Nudes (Oct 1990). . . . . .Herself
- • • 73—Full frontal nudity.
Playboy's Book of Lingerie (Jan 1991). . . . . .Herself
- 10—Parital right breast and lower frontal nudity.
Playboy's Book of Lingerie (Mar 1991). . . . . .Herself
- • • 61—Left breast and lower frontal nudity.
Playboy's Book of Lingerie (Nov 1991). . . . .Herself
- • • 13—Full frontal nudity.
Playboy's Book of Lingerie (Mar 1992). . . . . .Herself
- • • 27—Topless.
- • • 49—Full frontal nudity.
Playboy's Book of Lingerie (May 1992). . . . .Herself
- • • 32—Topless.
- • • 38—Buns.
- • • 93—Topless and buns.

Stensgaard, Yutte

Real name is Jytte Stensgaard.

Films:

Lust for a Vampire (1970; British) . . . . Mircalla
- ••• 0:19—Topless, three times, getting a massage from another school girl.
  0:22—Very, very brief full frontal nudity while diving into the water. Long shot, don't see anything.
- •• 0:53—Topless outside with Lestrange. Left breast when lying down.
- • 0:58—Topless during Lestrange's dream.

Scream and Scream Again (1970; British) . . . . Erika
The Buttercup Chain (1971; British) . . . . n.a.

• Stephen, Karen

Films:

Pick-Up Summer (1979; Canadian) . . . . Donna
- • 0:25—Very brief lower half of breast, pulling her T-shirt up to distract someone.
  0:34—Very, very brief topless when the boys spray her and she jumps up.

Happy Birthday to Me (1980) . . . . Miss Calhoun
Hog Wild (1980; Canadian). . . . . Brenda

Stephenson, Pamela

Films:

Stand Up Virgin Soldiers (1976) . . . . Nurse
Topless and brief buns after removing clothes and getting into bed.
History of the World, Part I (1981)
. . . . Mademoiselle Rimbaud
  1:17—In lingerie, under blouse, when she flashes herself in front of Harvey Korman.
  1:18—In lingerie again, flashing herself for Mel Brooks.
The Secret Policeman's Other Ball (1982; British)
. . . . n.a.
Finders Keepers (1983) . . . . Georgiana Latimer
Scandalous (1983) . . . . Fiona Maxwell Sayle
Superman III (1983) . . . . Lorelei Ambrosia
Bloodbath at the House of Death (1985; British)
. . . . Barbara Coyle
- • 0:50—Very brief topless getting clothes ripped off by an unseen being.

TV:
Saturday Night Live (1984-85) . . . . Regular

Stern, Ellen

Films:

The Duchess and the Dirtwater Fox (1976) . . . . . . .Bride
Jessi's Girls (1976) . . . . .Kana
- ••• 1:10—Left breast, then topless in bed with a guy.

Stevens, Brinke

Ex-wife of *The Rocketeer* comic book creator David Stevens.

Films:

The Slumber Party Massacre (1982) . . . . .Linda
- •• 0:07—Buns, then topless taking a shower during girls locker room scene.

Sole Survivor (1982) . . . . Jennifer
- •• 0:45—In bra playing cards, then topless.

The Man Who Wasn't There (1983) . . . . . .Nymphet
- • 0:45—Buns and brief topless in the girls' shower, when she gets shampoo from an invisible Steve Guttenberg.

Private School (1983) . . . . . . .Uncredited School Girl
- •• 0:42—Brief topless and buns in shower room scene. She's the brunette wearing a pony tail who passes in front of the chalkboard.

The Witching (1983) . . . . Black Sabbath Member
a.k.a. Necromancy
(Originally filmed in 1971 as *Necromancy*, additional scenes were added and re-released in 1983.)

Body Double (1984) . . . . .Girl in Bathroom #3
- • 1:12—Topless sitting in chair in adult film preview that Craig Wasson watches on TV.

Emmanuelle IV (1984) . . . . . . .Uncredited Dream Girl
- ••• 0:19—Topless, getting coached by Sylvia Kristel during dream-like sequence on how to get a guy aroused.

Fatal Games (1984) . . . . .Uncredited Shower Girl
- • 0:14—Brief, out of focus side of left breast and upper half of buns, taking a shower in the background while two girls talk. (She's wearing a light blue towel around her hair.)

Psycho III (1986) . . . . . Body Double for Diana Scarwid
- •• 0:30—Brief topless and buns getting ready to take a shower, body doubling for Diana Scarwid.

Nightmare Sisters (1987). . . . . .Marci
- ••• 0:39—Topless standing in panties with Melody and Mickey after transforming from nerds to sexy women.
- ••• 0:40—Topless in the kitchen with Melody and Mickey.
- ••• 0:44—Nude in the bathtub with Melody and Mickey. Excellent, long scene.
- ••• 0:47—Topless in the bathtub. Nice close up.
- ••• 0:48—Still more buns and topless in the bathtub.

Slavegirls from Beyond Infinity (1987) . . . . . . Shala
  0:29—Chained up wearing black lingerie.
- • 0:31—Brief side view of left breast on table. Nice pan from her feet to her head while she's lying face down.

Grandmother's House (1988). . . . . Woman
The Jigsaw Murders (1988) . . . . Stripper #1
- • 0:28—Very, very brief topless posing for photographer in white bra and panties when camera passes between her and the other stripper.

Phantom of the Mall: Eric's Revenge (1988)
. . . . .Girl in Dressing Room
• 0:14—Topless in dressing room and on B&W monitor several times (second room from the left).

Sorority Babes in the Slimeball Bowl-O-Rama (1988). . . . . Taffy
0:07—In panties getting spanked with Michelle Bauer.
••• 0:12—Nude showering off whipped cream in bathtub while talking to a topless Michelle Bauer. Excellent long scene!

Warlords (1988) . . . . Dow's Wife
Murder Weapon (1989). . . . . . . .Girl in Shower on TV
• 1:00—Brief left breast on TV that the guys are watching. Scene from *Nightmare Sisters.*

Bad Girls from Mars (1990) . . . . .Myra
• 0:11—Brief side of left breast, then topless getting massaged on diving board.

Haunting Fear (1990) . . . . .Victoria
••• 0:10—Full frontal nudity, taking a bath and getting out.
•• 0:22—Topless changing into nightgown in bedroom.
••• 0:32—Topless on Coroner's table.

Mob Boss (1990). . . . . Sara
Transylvania Twist (1990) . . . . Betty Lou
Roots of Evil (1991) .Candy
(Unrated version reviewed.)
•• 1:33—Right breast, then topless while sitting on bed talking to Deanna Lund.

Shadows in the City (1991). . . . . Fortune Teller
Spirits (1991) . . . . .Amy Goldwyn
Video Tapes:

Playboy Video Magazine, Volume 1 (1982)
. . . . Marie/Ribald Classic
• 0:01—Full frontal nudity.
• 0:46—Topless on the bed with Jean-Pierre.
••• 0:47—Topless in bathtub. Full frontal nudity in front of fire.
•• 0:49—Topless outside in the garden.

More Candid Candid Camera (1983)
. . . . Horseriding Student
••• 0:00—Buns and lower frontal nudity, learning how to ride a horse "bareback" style.

Playboy Video Magazine, Volume 4 (1983)
. . . . .Flashdancer/Dream Lover
• 0:15—Very brief lower frontal nuidty and buns in orange lingerie.
••• 0:16—Nude, fighting over blue towel with Linnea Quigley in the shower.
••• 0:43—Nude in a sheet covered chair during fantasy sequence. Best for Brinke fans!

Playboy Video Magazine, Volume 5 (1983)
. . . . Candid Camera Girl
•• 0:18—Lost of buns shots, during prank learning how to ride a horse "bare back."

The Girls of Penthouse (1984) . . . . .Ghost Town Woman

Red Hot Rock (1984). . . . . Miss Utah
• 0:41—Brief topless several times in open-front swimsuit during beauty pageant during "Gimme Gimme Good Lovin'" by Helix.

Scream Queen Hot Tub Party (1991) . . . . . . .Herself
•• 0:07—Topless, taking off white outfit and putting on black teddy.
• 0:12—Buns, while walking up the stairs.
•• 0:14—Buns and topless in shower scene from *Slumber Party Massacre.*
••• 0:19—Topless and buns, demonstrating the proper Scream Queen way to take a shower.
••• 0:44—Topless taking off her swimsuit top and soaping up with the other girls.
•• 0:46—Topless in still shot during the end credits.

Brinke Stevens Private Collection Volume 1 (1992) . . . . .Herself
•• 0:16—Topless in *Flashdancers* segment from *Playboy* video magazine.
•• 0:19—Nude in still photo sequence in shower with Linnea Quigley.
• 0:22—Brief topless lying on slab from *Bad Girls from Beyond Infinity.*
• 0:30—Topless scenes from *Nightmare Sisters.*
••• 0:41—Topless, in scenes from that were cut from the U.S. version of *Bad Girls From Mars.*
• 0:43—Buns, in G-string outfit posing for photo session.
Magazines:

Penthouse (Jul 1982) . . . . .Marlene & Brinke
•• 50-67—Left breast and buns.

Stevens, Connie

Films:
Scorchy (1971) . . . . Jackie Parker
•• 0:23—Open blouse, revealing left bra cup while talking on the telephone. Brief topless swimming in the water after taking off bathing suit top.
•• 0:52—Side view left breast, taking a shower.
••• 0:56—Brief right breast making love in bed with Greg Evigan. Topless getting tied to the bed by the thieves. Kind of a long shot and a little dark and hard to see.
• 1:00—Brief topless getting covered with a sheet by the good guy.

Grease 2 (1982) . . . . Miss Mason
Back to the Beach (1987). . . . . Connie
Tapeheads (1988) . . . . .June Tager
Miniseries:
Scruples (1980) . . . . .Maggie McGregor
Made for TV Movies:
The Littlest Angel (1969) . . . . n.a.
Playmates (1972). . . . . n.a.
Love's Savage Fury (1979) . . . . n.a.
TV:
Hawaiian Eye (1959-63). . . . . Cricket Blake
Wendy and Me (1964-65) . . . . .Wendy Conway

Stevens, Stella

Mother of actor Andrew Stevens.
Films:
Li'l Abner (1959). . . . . Appasionata von Climax
Girls! Girls! Girls! (1962) . . . . Robin Gantner
The Nutty Professor (1963) . . . . Stella Purdy
The Ballad of Cable Hogue (1970). . . . . .Hildy
    1:12—Buns changing into nightgown in bedroom.
   • 1:14—Brief top half of breasts in outdoor tub, then
    buns running into cabin when stagecoach arrives.
The Poseidon Adventure (1972) . . . . .Linda Rogo
Slaughter (1972) . . . . Ann
  •• 0:47—Left breast, several times in bed with Jim
    Brown.
  • 0:55—Left breast, making love in bed with Brown
    again. Dark.
  • 0:57—Brief right breast, in bed afterwards. Close up
    shot.
  ••• 1:14—Buns and topless taking a shower and getting
    out. This is her best nude scene.
Arnold (1973) . . . . Karen
The Manitou (1977) . . . . Amelia Crusoe
Chained Heat (1983; U.S./German) . . . . Taylor
The Longshot (1986) .Nicki
Down the Drain (1989). . . . . Sophia
    0:45—In black lingerie yelling at Dino in the bath-
    room.
Mom (1989). . . . . Beverly Hills
Last Call (1990). . . . . .Betty
    0:52—Very brief left nipple popping out of black lin-
    gerie top while making love with Jason on a pool ta-
    ble.
The Terror Within II (1992) . . . . Kara
Made for TV Movies:
Man Against the Mob (1988) . . . . Joey Day
TV:
Santa Barbara . . . . Phyllis Blake
Ben Casey (1965) . . . . Jane Hancock
Flamingo Road (1981-82) . . . . .Lute-Mae Sanders
Magazines:
Playboy (Jan 1960) . . . . Playmate
Playboy (Dec 1973). . . . . Sex Stars of 1973
  •• 210—Topless behind plants.
Playboy (Jan 1974) . . . . Twenty Years of Playboy
  • 201-202—Buns, posing with a cross-eyed funny
    face.
Playboy (Jan 1989) . . . . Women of the Sixties
    161—Half of left breast behind pink material.

Stevenson, Judy

Films:
Alvin Rides Again (1974; Australian) . . . . . .Housewife
  •• 0:01—Full frontal nudity, dropping her towel while
    Alvin washes her window.
Cathy's Child (1979; Australian) Lil

• Stevenson, Juliet

Films:
Drowning by Numbers (1988; British)
  . . . . Cisse Colpitts 2
  • 0:57—Lower frontal nudity and left breast, while try-
    ing to entice Hardy. Long shot.
Truly, Madly, Deeply (1991) . . . . Nina
    0:46—Very, very brief, blurry tip of left breast, when
    Alan Rickman pushes her out of the bedroom.
Made for TV Movies:
Masterpiece Theatre: A Doll's House (1992) . . . . . . Nora

Stewart, Alexandra

Films:
Goodbye Emmanuelle (1977) . . . . .Dorothee
The Uncanny (1977; British). . . . . Mrs. Blake
In Praise of Older Women (1978; Canadian)
  . . . . Paula
  •• 1:21—Topless in bed with Tom Berenger.
  •• 1:23—Nude, in and out of bed with Berenger.
The Last Chase (1980) . . . . .Eudora
Agency (1981; Canadian). . . . . Mimi
Chanel Solitaire (1981). . . . . n.a.
Under the Cherry Moon (1986) . . . . .Mrs. Sharon
Frantic (1988) . . . . .Edie
Made for Cable TV:
The Hitchhiker: Shattered Vows . . . .Jackie Winslow
  • 0:04—In white bra and panties, then side view top-
    less making love in bed with Jeff.
Magazines:
Playboy (Oct 1978) . . . . . . Observing "Older Women"
  •• 193-195—Nude.

• Stewart, Catherine Mary

Films:
Nighthawks (1981) .Salesgirl
The Beach Girls (1982). . . . . Surfer Girl
The Last Starfighter (1984). . . . . .Maggie Gordon
Night of the Comet (1984) . . . . .Regina
Mischief (1985) . . . . Bunny
Dudes (1987). . . . . Jessie, Gas Station Owner
Nightflyers (1987) .Miranda
Scenes from the Goldmine (1987) . . . . . .Debi D'Angelo
World Gone Wild (1988) . . . . .Angie
Weekend at Bernie's (1989) . . . . Gwen Saunders
  a.k.a. Hot and Cold
Cafe Romeo (1991) . . . . .Lia
Made for Cable Movies:
Psychic (1992; USA) . . . . Laurel
  • 0:45—Very brief right breast, twice, at the end of
    love making scene with Zach Galligan.
TV:
Hearts are Wild (1991) . . . . Kyle Hubbard

Stewart, Liz

Video Tapes:
Playmate Playoffs . . . . Playmate

Playboy Video Magazine, Volume 10 (1986)
. . . . The Goldner Girls
•• 0:17—Topless during modeling session for photographer David Goldner.
Wet and Wild (1989) . . . . Model
Magazines:
Playboy (Jul 1984) . . . . Playmate

Steyn, Jennifer

Films:
Curse III: Bloody Sacrifice (1990) . . . . Cindy
• 0:35—Side of left breast, kissing Roger while at the beach inside a tent. Upper half of left breast when blade tears through tent.
0:40—Topless, covered with blood when Geoff looks in the tent.
Night of the Cyclone (1990) . . . . Celeste

Stone, Dee Wallace

See: Wallace Stone, Dee.

• Stone, Madison

a.k.a. Adult film actress Madison.
Films:
Naked Obsession (1990) . . . . Jezebel
•• 0:35—In black leather outfit. Buns in G-string and topless.
•• 0:37—More topless and buns.
• 0:38—More.
•• 0:39—Brief full frontal nudity.
Evil Toons (1991) . . . . Roxanne
••• 0:20—Buns in G-string, then topless doing a strip routine in front of her girlfriends.
••• 0:33—Topless, taking off blouse and putting on bra and panties. Buns in sheer panties.
•• 0:36—Topless on the floor, getting attacked by the monster.
••• 0:38—Topless walking around, covered with blood, talking with Megan.
•• 0:41—Topless putting blouse on.
• 0:42—Topless on couch with Biff.
• 0:55—Left breast in open blouse, seducing Burt.
• 0:59—Brief topless several times, dead, when the other girls discover her.

Stone, Sharon

Films:
Stardust Memories (1980) . . . . . Blonde on Passing Train
Deadly Blessing (1981) . . . . Lana
Irreconcilable Differences (1984)
. . . . Blake Chandler
•• 0:56—Topless lowering her blouse in front of Ryan O'Neal during film test.
King Solomon's Mines (1985) . . . . Jessica
Allan Quartermain and the Lost City of Gold (1987)
. . . . Jesse Huston

Cold Steel (1987) . . . . Kathy Conners
• 0:33—Brief left breast making love in bed with Brad Davis. Dark, hard to see. Brief topless turning over after making love.
Police Academy 4: Citizens on Patrol (1987)
. . . . Claire Matson
Above the Law (1988) . . . . Sara Toscani
Action Jackson (1988) . . . . Patrice Dellaplane
•• 0:34—Topless in a steam room. Hard to see because of all the steam.
• 0:56—Brief right breast, dead, on the bed when police view her body.
Blood and Sand (1989; Spanish) . . . . Doña Sol
0:57—Very brief upper half of right breast, making love on table with Juan.
•• 0:58—Left breast, making love in bed with Juan. Don't see her face well.
••• 1:04—Topless quite a few times, making love with Juan in the woods.
Scissors (1990) . . . . Angela Anderson
0:04—Upper half of left breast sitting up after attack in elevator.
•• 0:12—Topless changing clothes.
0:36—In bra with Steve Railsback. Brief upper half of left breast. Dark.
Total Recall (1990) . . . . Lori
• 0:04—Brief right breast in gaping lingerie when leaning over Arnold Schwarzenegger in bed.
he said, she said (1991) . . . . Linda
Year of the Gun (1991) . . . . Alison King
• 1:00—Brief left breast, standing against the door, with Andrew McCarthy. Long shot.
• 1:01—Side of left breast, making love on bed.
Basic Instinct (1992) . . . . Catherine Tramell
Diary of a Hitman (1992) . . . . Kiki
Miniseries:
War and Remembrance (1988) . . . . Janice Henry
TV:
Bay City Blues (1983) . . . . Cathy St. Marie
Magazines:
Playboy (Jul 1990) . . . . Dishing with Sharon
••• 118-127—Topless in B&W photos.

Stoner, Sherri

Story editor for Steven Spielberg.
She was Disney's animator's model for Ariel in *The Little Mermaid* and Belle in *Beauty and the Beast*.
Films:
Impulse (1984) . . . . Young Girl
Lovelines (1984) . . . . Suzy
Reform School Girls (1986) . . . . Lisa
• 1:03—Very brief topless and buns, lying on stomach in the restroom, getting branded by bad girls.

Stowe, Madeleine

Wife of actor Brian Benben.

Films:

Stakeout (1987) . . . . Maira McGuire
   0:43—Buns and brief side view of right breast getting a towel after taking a shower while Richard Dreyfuss watches her.

Tropical Snow (1989). . . . . Marina
   • 0:05—Very brief side view of left breast putting red dress on.
   • 0:11—Buns, lying in bed. Very brief right breast sitting up. (I wish they could have panned the camera to the right!)
   •• 0:24—Topless in mirror putting red dress on.
   0:32—Buns, lying on top of Tavo in bed.
   • 0:54—Brief topless making love in the water with Tavo. Then buns, lying on the beach (long shot.)
   1:22—Long shot side view of right breast in water with Tavo.

Worth Winning (1989) . . . . .Veronica Briskow
Closet Land (1990) . . . . The Author
Revenge (1990). . . . . Miryea
   0:44—Side view of buns when Kevin Costner pulls up her dress to make love with her.
   0:52—In white slip talking to Costner in bedroom.
   • 1:00—Buns, making love with Costner in jeep. Very brief topless coming out of the water.
   • 1:07—Very brief topless when Costner is getting beat up.

The Two Jakes (1990) . . . . Lillian Bodine
   0:23—Very brief buns, when Jack Nicholson lifts her slip up in bed.

The Last of the Mohicans (1992). . . . . .n.a.
Unlawful Entry (1992). . . . . Karen Carr

TV:

The Gangster Chronicles (1981) . . . . .Ruth Lasker

Strain, Julie

Films:

Carnal Crimes (1991). . . . . Ingrid
   ••• 0:55—Topless and partial buns, wearing black garter belt and stockings, making love with Renny in restroom. Long scene.

Double Impact (1991). . . . . Student
   • 0:09—Brief buns, lying on floor in pink leotard in exercise class.

Mirror Images (1991) . . . . Gina
   •• 0:48—Buns and right breast, making love in bed with Kaitlin.
   •• 0:49—Buns in black bra and panties.
   • 0:57—Buns in black body suit.
   ••• 0:58—Topless lying on bed, watching the slave girl and guy with the mask make love.

Out for Justice (1991) . . . . .Roxanne Ford
   • 0:53—Brief side view of right breast in Polaroid photograph that Steven Seagal looks at.
   • 1:06—Brief side view of right breast in Polaroid again.

   • 1:11—Brief right breast, twice, dead in bed when discovered by Seagal.
   • 1:12—Briefly in Polaroid again.

Sunset Heat (1991)
   . . . . Carl's Breakfast Girl/Party Statuette
(Unrated version reviewed.)
   •• 0:51—Topless, covered with silver paint, made up to look like a statue at the party.

Kuffs (1992). . . . . .Kane's Girl
Night Rhythms (1992) . . . . .Linda
(Unrated version reviewed.)
   ••• 0:03—In white bra, then left breast, while talking on the phone and playing with herself.

Witchcraft IV: Virgin Heart (1992). . . . . Belladonna
   • 0:25—Buns, while dancing on stage in a red bra and red G-string.
   ••• 0:27—Topless, dancing on stage.
   •• 0:46—Topless on the floor with Santara.
   • 0:49—Brief topless in open dress on couch with Will.
   • 1:15—Topless, lying on couch in her dressing room while Will tries to talk to her.

Video Tapes:

Penthouse Centerfold—Julie Strain (1991) . . . .Pet
Sexy Lingerie III (1991). . . . . Model
Penthouse Satin & Lace: An Erotic History of Lingerie (1992) . . . . Model
   ••• 0:01—Nude with blonde woman.
   ••• 0:09—Nude with blonde woman in elevator.
   ••• 0:29—Nude outside.
   ••• 0:46—Full frontal nudity with three guys.
   ••• 0:49—Full frontal nudity with two blonde women.

Sexy Lingerie IV (1992) . . . . Model

Magazines:

Playboy (May 1991). . . . . Grapevine
   •• 183—Left breast.

Penthouse (Jun 1991) . . . . .Pet
   ••• 71-85—Nude.

Playboy (Jul 1991) . . . . The Height Report
   ••• 134-135—Full frontal nudity.

Penthouse (Feb 1992) . . . . .Julie
   ••• 39-47—Nude in B&W photos.

Penthouse (Jun 1992) . . . . Pet of the Year Playoff
   ••• 92-93—Nude.

Strasberg, Susan

Daughter of acting teacher Lee Strasberg.

Films:

The Trip (1967) . . . . Sally Groves
The Brotherhood (1968) . . . . Emma Ginetta
Psych-Out (1968). . . . . .Jennie Davis
Psycho Sisters (1974) .Brenda
The Manitou (1977). . . . . Karen Tandy
   1:33—Topless, fighting the creature in bed. Really bad special effects. Too dark to see anything.

Rollercoaster (1977). . . . . .Fran
In Praise of Older Women (1978; Canadian)
   . . . . .Bobbie
   •• 1:03—Left breast, while making love in bed with Tom Berenger.

••• 1:04—Topless in bed after Berenger rolls off her.
Bloody Birthday (1980) . . . . .Miss Davis
Sweet Sixteen (1982) . . . . .Joanne Morgan
The Delta Force (1986) . . . . Debra Levine
The Runnin' Kind (1988). . . . . Carol Curtis
TV:
The Marriage (1954). . . . . .Emily Marriott
Toma (1973-74) . . . . Patty Toma

Stratten, Dorothy

Films:
Americathon (1979) . . . . .n.a.
Autumn Born (1979) . . . . Tara
0:03—In dressing room in beige bra, panties, garter belt and stockings changing clothes. Long, close-up lingering shots.
0:16—Unconscious in beige lingerie, then conscious, walking around the room.
0:21—In bra and panties getting her rear end whipped while tied to the bed.
•• 0:26—Left breast taking bath, then right breast getting up, then topless dressing.
• 0:30—Side view of left breast, then topless climbing back into bed.
0:35—In beige bra and panties in the shower with her captor.
0:43—Quick cuts of various scenes.
••• 0:46—In white bra and panties, side view of left breast and buns, then topless in bathtub. Long scene.
• 0:50—Side view of left breast and buns getting undressed. Nice buns shot. Right breast lying down in chair.
• 1:03—Brief topless shots during flashbacks.
Skatetown, U.S.A. (1979) .n.a.
Galaxina (1980) . . . . Galaxina
They All Laughed (1981). . . . . Dolores Martin
Video Tapes:
Dorothy Stratten, The Untold Story . . . . . . Herself
Playboy Video Magazine, Volume 4 (1983)
. . . . Playmate
• 1:09—Brief topless in black lingerie during photo shoot.
•• 1:13—Topless and buns in bubble bath.
•• 1:19—Topless posing in dance studio.
• 1:22—More brief topless shots from photo shoot.
Playboy's Playmates of the Year: The '80s (1989)
. . . . Playmate of the Year 1980
••• 0:27—Topless and buns in various settings during photo session.
•• 0:32—Brief topless holding flowers in a field.
•• 0:51—Topless in field.
Magazines:
Playboy (Aug 1979). . . . . Playmate
Playboy (Dec 1979). . . . . Sex Stars of 1979
••• 258—Topless.
Playboy (Jun 1980) . . . . Playmate of the Year
••• 168-179—Nude.

Playboy (Oct 1980) . . . . Girls of Canada
••• 151—Full frontal nudity.
Playboy (Dec 1980) . . . . .Sex Stars of 1980
•• 247—Left breast.
Playboy (Jan 1989). . . . . .Women of the Eighties
219—Full frontal nudity.
Playboy's Nudes (Oct 1990) . . . . Herself
••• 102—Full frontal nudity.

Streep, Meryl

Films:
Julia (1977) . . . . Anne Marie
The Deer Hunter (1978). . . . . .Linda
Kramer vs. Kramer (1979) . . . . .Joanna Kramer
Manhattan (1979) . . . . Jill
The Seduction of Joe Tynan (1979) . . . . . Karen Traynor
The French Lieutenant's Woman (1981) . . . . Sarah/Anna
Sophie's Choice (1982) . . . . .Sophie
(Academy Award for Best Actress.)
Still of the Night (1982). . . . . Brooke Reynolds
0:22—Side view of right breast and buns taking off robe for the massage guy. Long shot, don't see her face.
Falling In Love (1984) . . . . Molly Gilmore
Silkwood (1984) . . . . Karen Silkwood
• 0:24—Very brief glimpse of upper half of left breast when she flashes it in nuclear reactor office.
Out of Africa (1985). . . . . Karen Blixen
Plenty (1985). . . . . .Susan
Heartburn (1986). . . . . .Rachel
Ironweed (1987) . . . . .Helen
A Cry in the Dark (1988) . . . . Lindy Chamberlain
1:44—Brief side view of right breast in jail being examined by two female guards. Don't see her face, probably a body double.
She-Devil (1989) . . . . Mary Fisher
Postcards from the Edge (1990). . . . . Suzanne Vale
Defending Your Life (1991) . . . . .Julia
Death Becomes Her (1992) . . . . Madeline Ashton
Miniseries:
Holocaust (1978) . . . . .Inga Helms Weiss

• Strickland, Connie

Films:
The Roommates (1973) . . . . Alice
Act of Vengeance (1974) . . . . Teresa
The Centerfold Girls (1974). . . . . Patsy
•• 1:07—Topless in bathroom washing her halter top just before getting killed.

Stromeir, Tara

a.k.a. Tara Strohmeier.
Films:
Truck Turner (1974) . . . . Turnpike
Hollywood Boulevard (1976). . . . . Jill McBain
•• 0:00—Topless getting out of van and standing with film crew.
• 0:31—Silhouette of breasts, making love with P.G.
••• 0:32—Topless sunbathing with Bobbi and Candy.

••• 0:33—Topless acting for film on hammock. Long
scene.
Kentucky Fried Movie (1977) . . . . Girl
•• 1:16—In bra, then topless making love on couch
with her boyfriend while people on the TV news
watch them.
Malibu Beach (1978) . . . . Glorianna
• 0:08—Topless kissing her boyfriend at the beach
when someone steals her towel.
Made for TV Movies:
The Lakeside Killer (1979) . . . . Janie

Strong, Brenda
Films:
Weekend Warriors (1986) . . . . Danny El Dubois
• 0:44—Topless, lit from the side, standing in the dark.
Spaceballs (1987) . . . . Nurse
Stepfather III: Father's Day (1992)
. . . . Crime Search Reporter
TV:
Twin Peaks (1990-91) . . . . Jones

Struthers, Sally
Films:
Five Easy Pieces (1970) . . . . Betty
0:15—In a bra sitting on a couch in the living room
with Jack Nicholson and another man and a woman.
•• 0:34—Brief topless a couple of times making love
with Nicholson. Lots of great moaning, but hard to
see anything.
The Getaway (1972) . . . . Fran Clinton
1:15—In black bra getting out of bed and leaning
over injured bad guy to get something.
Made for TV Movies:
Hey, I'm Alive (1975). . . . . n.a.
Intimate Strangers (1977) . . . . n.a.
In the Best Interest of the Children (1992)
. . . . Patty Pepper
TV:
The Tim Conway Comedy Hour (1970). . . . . Regular
The Summer Smother's Show (1970) . . . . Regular
All In the Family (1971-78) . . . . Gloria Bunker Stivic
Gloria (1982-83) . . . . Gloria Bunker Stivic
9 to 5 (1986-88) . . . . Marsha Shrimpton

Stuart, Cassie
Films:
Ordeal by Innocence (1984) . . . . Maureen Clegg
•• 1:14—Topless in bed talking to Donald Sutherland.
Slayground (1984; British). . . . . Fran
Stealing Heaven (1988; British/Yugoslavian)
. . . . Petronilla

Stubbs, Imogen
Films:
Deadline (1988) . . . . Lady Romy-Burton
0:42—Doing handstands in a bikini top.

• 0:44—Brief left breast, while getting out of bed with
John Hurt. Full frontal nudity turning toward bed,
brief topless getting back into bed.
A Summer Story (1988) . . . . Megan David
•• 0:36—Left breast several times, then right breast
while making love with Frank in barn.
0:41—Very, very brief buns, frolicking in pond at
night with Frank.
1:03—Very brief silhouette of left breast during
Frank's flashback sequence.
Erik the Viking (1989; British). . . . . Aud
True Colors (1991) . . . . Diana Stiles
Made for Cable Movies:
Fellow Traveller (1989; HBO) . . . . Sarah Aitchison
• 0:54—Topless in bed with Asa. Very, very brief right
breast when he rolls off her.

• Styler, Trudie
Wife of singer/actor Sting.
Films:
Fair Game (1988; Italian) . . . . Eva
0:14—Very, very brief blurry top of right breast in
gaping blouse, while standing up after changing
clothes.
• 0:37—Brief buns, kneeling in bathtub. Very brief
buns in the mirror several times putting on robe and
getting out of the bathtub.

Sukowa, Barbara
Films:
Berlin Alexanderplatz (1983; West German) . . . . n.a.
The Sicilian (1987) . . . . . . Camila Duchess of Crotone
(Director's uncut version reviewed.)
•• 0:05—Buns and brief topless taking a bath, three
times.
• 0:07—Brief right breast reading Time magazine. Full
frontal nudity in the mirror standing up in the tub.
• 0:08—Brief right breast standing at the window
watching Christopher Lambert steal a horse.
••• 1:01—In bra, then topless in bedroom with Lambert. More topless, then nude. Long scene.
Voyager (1992; German/French) . . . . Hannah
Miniseries:
Space (1985) . . . . Liesl Kolff

Sullivan, Sheila
Films:
Hickey and Boggs (1972) . . . . Edith Boggs
A Name for Evil (1973) . . . . Luanna Baxter
• 0:51—Full frontal nudity dancing in the bar with everybody.
• 0:54—Topless while Robert Culp makes love with
her.
• 0:56—Topless getting dressed.
• 1:17—Nude, skinny dipping with Culp.
Magazines:
Playboy (Mar 1973) . . . . "Evil" Doings
• 147—Partial topless.
• 149—Right breast while kissing Robert Culp.

Sutton, Lori

Films:

History of the World, Part I (1981). . . . . Vestal Virgin

Looker (1981) . . . . Reston Girl

Fast Times at Ridgemont High (1982) . . . . Playmate

Malibu Express (1984) . . . . Beverly

••• 0:54—Topless and buns, making love in bed with
Cody.

Up the Creek (1984) . . . . .Cute Girl

• 0:40—Brief topless pulling up her T-shirt to get the
crowd excited while cheerleading the crowd.

Night Patrol (1985) . . . . .Edith Hutton

••• 0:47—In white bra, panties, garter belt and stockings, then topless three times taking off bra in bedroom with the Police officer.

Swanson, Brenda

Films:

Dangerous Love (1988). . . . . Felicity

Skin Deep (1989) . . . . Emily

Steel and Lace (1990) . . . . Miss Fairweather

•• 0:58—Topless in lunchroom, opening her blouse in
front of one of the bad guys on the table.

Video Tapes:

Inside Out 2 (1992)

. . . . . Mrs. Jenkins/There's This Traveling Salesman, See
(Unrated version reviewed.)

0:42—In braless, wet tank top, in barn.

•• 0:43—Topless, taking off her top in barn.

Swanson, Jackie

Films:

Lethal Weapon (1987). . . . . Amanda Huntsacker

•• 0:01—Brief topless standing on balcony rail getting
ready to jump.

It's Alive III: Island of the Alive (1988) . . . . Tenant

Perfect Victims (1988) . . . . Carrie Marks

•• 0:13—In bra, then left breast, while changing
clothes by closet.

• 0:23—Brief left breast, while lying on sofa when
Brandon opens her robe while she's drugged out.
Brief right breast and lower frontal nudity when he
rips off her panties.

0:25—Right breast several more times, while lying
on sofa while Brandon torments her.

••• 1:15—Left breast and buns, seen through clear
shower door. Nice shot for bun lovers!

• 1:16—Brief buns in the shower, seen from above.

TV:

Cheers (1989-). Kelly Gaines

• Swift, Sally

Films:

Auditions (1978) . . . . .Melinda Sale

••• 0:21—Full frontal nudity, undressing and masturbating during her audition.

•• 0:30—Topless and buns, whipping Harry.

Hell Squad (1986). . . . . Ann

Sykes, Brenda

Films:

The Baby Maker (1970) . . . . .Francis

Getting Straight (1970) . . . . Luan

The Liberation of L. B. Jones (1970) . . . . Jelly

Honky (1971) . . . . Sheila Smith

••• 0:42—Topless with her boyfriend, making love on
the floor.

• 1:22—Brief topless several times getting raped by
two guys.

Pretty Maids All in a Row (1971) . . . . . . .Pamela Wilcox

Skin Game (1971) . . . . .Naomi

Black Gunn (1972) . . . . Judith

• 0:45—Brief side view of right breast, while getting
out of bed with Jim Brown.

Cleopatra Jones (1973) . . . . .Tiffany

Mandingo (1975). . . . . Ellen

• 0:58—Topless in bed with Perry King.

Drum (1976). . . . . Calinda

• 0:19—Topless standing next to bed with Ken
Norton.

TV:

Ozzie's Girls (1973) . . . . . . Brenda (Jennifer) MacKenzie

Executive Suite (1976-77) . . . . .Summer Johnson

Magazines:

Playboy (Oct 1972) . . . . .Brown, Black and White

• 88—Almost topless.

Playboy (Nov 1972) . . . . Sex in Cinema 1972

• 162—Left breast, in a photo from Black Gunn.

• Tabrizi, Tera

Films:

Cool As Ice (1991) . . . . Club Dancer

White Sands (1992)

. . . . . . .Body Double for Mary Elizabeth Mastrontonio

•• 1:10—Left breast and upper half of buns in the
shower undressing in the shower with Willem Dafoe.
Don't see face, so it's probably Tera.

Made for Cable Movies:

Red Shoe Diaries (1992; Showtime) . . . . . . Alex's Friend

Magazines:

Playboy's Book of Lingerie (Jan 1991) . . . . . .Herself

•• 14—Side of right breast and buns.

Playboy's Book of Lingerie (Mar 1991). . . . . .Herself

•• 62—Buns and side of right breast.

Playboy's Book of Lingerie (Sep 1991) . . . . . .Herself

••• 48—Topless.

• 76-77—Right breast.

Playboy's Book of Lingerie (Nov 1991) . . . . .Herself

••• 104—Right breast.

•• 106-107—Buns and side of right breast.

Playboy's Book of Lingerie (Jan 1992) . . . . . .Herself

••• 3-7—Topless and buns.

Playboy's Book of Lingerie (Mar 1992). . . . . .Herself

• 96-97—Topless.

Playboy's Career Girls (Aug 1992) . . . . Double Visions

••• 38-39—Topless and buns.

Playboy's Book of Lingerie (Sep 1992) . . . . .Herself

Taggart, Sharon
Films:
The Last Picture Show (1971) . . . . . Charlene Duggs
•• 0:11—In bra, then topless making out in truck with
Timothy Bottoms.
The Harrad Experiment (1973) . . . . .Barbara

Tallman, Patricia
Films:
Knightriders (1981) . . . . Julie
• 0:46—Brief topless in the bushes in moonlight talk-
ing to her boyfriend while a truck driver watches.
Monkey Shines: An Experiment in Fear (1988)
. . . . Party Guest and Stunts
After Midnight (1989). . . . . Stunt Player
Roadhouse (1989). . . . . Bandstand Babe
Night of the Living Dead (1990) . . . . .Barbara

Tamerlis, Zoe
a.k.a. Zoë Tamerlaine.
Films:
Ms. 45 (1980). . . . . .Thana
Special Effects (1984) . . . . Amelia/Elaine
0:01—Side view of right breast, wearing pasties during photo session.
• 0:16—Brief topless sitting by pool with Eric Bogozian.
•• 0:19—Topless getting into bed and in bed with
Bogozian.
• 0:22—Topless, dead in spa while Bogozian washes
her off.
0:44—Brief topless in moviola that Bogozian watches.
•• 1:12—Topless making love on bed with Keefe.
• 1:17—Topless getting into bed during filming of
movie. Brief topless during Bogozian's flashbacks.
1:20—More left breast shots on moviola getting
strangled.
••• 1:33—Topless with Bogozian when he takes her
dress off.
• 1:35—Topless sitting on bed kissing Bogozian. More
topless and more flashbacks.
• 1:40—Brief topless during struggle. Dark.
Heavy Petting (1989) . . . . .Herself/Writer, Actress

Tané
See: McClure, Tané.

• Tate, Laura
Films:
Dead Space (1990) . . . . Marissa Salinger
•• 0:33—Topless in bed with Marc Singer during her
dream.
Subspecies (1990). Michelle

Tate, Sharon
Late wife of director Roman Polanski.
Victim of the Manson Family murders on August 9, 1969.
Films:
The Fearless Vampire Killers (1967) . . . Sarah Shagal
• 0:24—Very, very brief topless struggling in bathtub
with vampire. Hard to see.
Valley of the Dolls (1967) . . . . Jennifer North
• 1:21—In bra, acting in a movie. Very, very brief left
breast in bed with a guy (curtain gets in the way).
• 1:23—Very brief side view of right breast, while sit-
ting up in bed.
Ciao Frederico! (1971) . . . . n.a.
TV:
Petticoat Junction (1963) . . . . Billie Jo Bradley
The Beverly Hillbillies (1963-65) . . . . Janet Trego
Magazines:
Playboy (Mar 1967) . . . . .The Tate Gallery
70-73—Topless and buns, in photographs taken by
Roman Polanski on the set of The Fearless Vampire
Killers.
Playboy (Jan 1989) . . . . .Women of the Sixties
• 160—Side view of right breast, taking a bubble
bath.

Taylor, Elizabeth
Ex-wife (twice) of actor Richard Burton.
Films:
Cleopatra (1963) . . . . .Cleopatra
• 0:28—Half of buns, lying face down, getting a mas-
sage.
2:02—(0:08 into tape 2) Taking a bath—You can't
see anything.
X, Y and Zee (1972). . . . . Zee
1:11—Brief right breast, in bloody bathtub water,
trying to commit suicide. Probably a body double—
Don't see her face.
Psychotic (1975; Italian). . . . . n.a.
a.k.a. Driver's Seat
0:03—In sheer beige bra in changing room.
0:34—In sheer white slip walking around.

Taylor, Kimberly
Films:
Bedroom Eyes II (1989) . . . . .Michelle
Cleo/Leo (1989). . . . . .Store Clerk
••• 0:22—Topless in white panties, changing in dressing
room with Jane Hamilton. Very nice!
Party Incorporated (1989). . . . . Felicia
a.k.a. Party Girls
•• 0:26—Topless shaking her breasts trying an outfit
on.
••• 0:39—Topless and buns in G-string in the bar with
the guys.
Frankenhooker (1990) . . . . .Amber
• 0:36—Brief left breast in green top during introduction to Jeffrey.
•• 0:37—Brief topless during exam by Jeffrey. Then
topless getting breasts measured with calipers.

- 0:41—Brief right breast, twice, enjoying drugs.
- •• 0:42—Topless, getting off bed and onto another bed with Anise.
- 0:43—Topless kneeling in bed screaming before exploding.

Magazines:

Penthouse (Dec 1988) . . . . Pet

• Taylor, Lili

Films:

Born on the Fourth of July (1989) . . . . .Jamie Wilson
Say Anything (1989) . . . . Corey
Bright Angel (1990). . . . . Lucy
- 0:26—Brief top of breasts under water, taking a bath in a pond.
- •• 0:27—Topless, walking out of the pond.
Dogfight (1991) . . . . Rose

• Taylor, Lisa

Films:

Eyes of Laura Mars (1978) . . . . Michele
- 0:59—Very brief right breast, while on table just before getting killed.
Where the Buffalo Roam (1980) . . . . .Ruthie
Windy City (1984). . . . . .Sherry

• Taylor, Marianne

Films:

Vendetta (1986) . . . . .Star
Bloodmatch (1991) . . . . Max Manduke
- 0:13—Topless and buns, making love in bed on top of Caldwell.

• Taylor, Vida

Films:

God Told Me To (1976). . . . . . . .Mrs. Mulling as a Child
Clash of the Titans (1981) . . . . .Danae
- 0:11—Right breast while breast feeding her baby. Buns, walking on beach.

Taylor-Young, Leigh

Films:

I Love You, Alice B. Toklas (1968) . . . . .Nancy
The Big Bounce (1969) . . . . Nancy Barker
(Not available on video tape.)
The Adventurers (1970) . . . . Amparo
The Buttercup Chain (1971; British) . . . . Manny
The Gang that Couldn't Shoot Straight (1971)
. . . . Angela Palumbo
The Horsemen (1971). . . . . Zereh
Soylent Green (1973) . . . . Shirl
Can't Stop the Music (1980) . . . . .Claudia Walters
Looker (1981) . . . . Jennifer Long
Jagged Edge (1985) . . . . Virginia Howell
Secret Admirer (1985). . . . . Elizabeth Fimple
Honeymoon Academy (1990) . . . . .Mrs. Doris Kent

TV:

The Devlin Connection (1982) . . . . .Lauren Dane
Dallas (1987-88) . . . . Kimberly Cryder

Tenison, Reneé

Films:

Shout (1991) . . . . Girl in Bar

Video Tapes:

Playboy Video Calendar 1991 (1990). . . . . . .August
••• 0:31—Nude.
Playboy Video Centerfold: Reneé Tenison (1990)
. . . . .Playmate of the Year 1990
••• 0:00—Nude throughout.
Wet and Wild III (1991) . . . . Model

Magazines:

Playboy (Nov 1989) . . . . Playmate
Playboy's Nudes (Oct 1990) . . . . .Herself
•• 106-107—Left breast and lower frontal nudity.
Playboy's Book of Lingerie (Mar 1991). . . . . .Herself
•• 23—Left breast and buns.
Playboy's Book of Lingerie (Sep 1991) . . . . . .Herself
••• 16-17—Full frontal nudity.
•• 60—Right breast and lower frontal nudity.
Playboy's Book of Lingerie (Nov 1991) . . . . .Herself
•• 20—Left breast and lower frontal nudity.
Playboy's Book of Lingerie (Jan 1992) . . . . . .Herself
• 70-71—Right breast.
Playboy's Book of Lingerie (Mar 1992). . . . . .Herself
••• 56—Full frontal nudity.
Playboy's Book of Lingerie (May 1992) . . . . .Herself
•• 46-47—Buns and side of right breast.
Playboy's Career Girls (Aug 1992)
. . . . Baywatch Playmates
••• 12—Full frontal nudity.
Playboy's Book of Lingerie (Sep 1992) . . . . . .Herself
•• 108-109—Left breast and buns.

Tennant, Victoria

Wife of comedian/actor Steve Martin.

Films:

The Ragman's Daughter (1974; British)
. . . . Doris Randall
Horror Planet (1980; British). . . . . Barbara
a.k.a. Inseminoid
All of Me (1984). . . . . Terry Hoskins
The Holcroft Covenant (1985) . . . . . . .Helden Tennyson
Flowers in the Attic (1987). . . . . Mother
Best Seller (1988). . . . . .Roberta Gillian
Whispers (1989) . . . . Hilary Thomas
- 0:43—Buns and side of right breast getting into bathtub. Long shot, looks like a body double (the ponytail in her hair changes position).
- 0:44—Buns and brief topless running down the stairs. Looks like the same body double.
A Handmaid's Tale (1990) . . . . .Aunt Lydia
L.A. Story (1991) . . . . .Sara

Terashita, Jill

Films:

The Big Bet (1985). . . . . Koko
Terminal Entry (1986) . . . . Gwen

Night of the Demons (1987) . . . . Frannie
(Unrated version reviewed.)
•• 0:57—Topless making love with her boyfriend in a
coffin.
Sleepaway Camp III: Teenage Wasteland (1989)
. . . . Arab
•• 0:16—Topless putting sweatshirt on.
Why Me? (1990). . . . . Hostess
Magazines:
Playboy's Book of Lingerie (Jan 1991) . . . . . . Herself
•• 23—Buns and partial left breast.
Playboy's Book of Lingerie (Nov 1991) . . . . . Herself
• 38—Right breast.
Playboy's Book of Lingerie (Mar 1992) . . . . . Herself
••• 72—Topless.
Playboy's Book of Lingerie (May 1992) . . . . . Herself
•• 104-105—Left breast and side view of buns.
Playboy's Book of Lingerie (Jul 1992) . . . . . . Herself
••• 95—Topless.
Playboy's Book of Lingerie (Sep 1992) . . . . . Herself
••• 47—Full frontal nudity.

Texter, Gilda

Films:
Angels Hard as They Come (1971) . . . . Astrid
• 0:26—Brief topless several times when bad guys try
to rape her. Dark.
Vanishing Point (1971) . . . . Nude Rider
• 1:17—Topless riding motorcycle.
••• 1:19—Topless riding motorcycle and walking
around without wearing any clothes. Long scene.

Thackray, Gail

a.k.a. Robyn Harris and Gail Harris.
Films:
Party Favors (1987) . . . . Nicole
• 0:04—Topless in dressing room with the other three
girls changing into blue swimsuit.
• 0:11—Brief left breast in the swimsuit during dance
practice.
• 0:12—Topless during dance practice.
• 0:17—More topless during dance practice.
•• 0:42—Topless doing strip routine at anniversary party. Great buns in G-string shots.
••• 1:01—Topless and buns in G-string after stripping
from cheerleader outfit. Lots of bouncing breast
shots. Mingling with the men afterwards.
• 1:16—Nude by the swimming pool during the final
credits.
Takin' It All Off (1987) . . . . Hannah
Death Feud (1989) . . . . Harry's Girl Friend
•• 1:12—Topless on bed with Harry.
1:16—In black lingerie on boat with Harry.
The Haunting of Morella (1989) . . . . Ilsa
•• 0:38—Topless in bed with Niles. Buns also when getting out and getting dressed.
Nudity Required (1989). . . . . .Midge
•• 0:36—Topless, asking Buddy a question. Brief topless (tenth girl) standing in line.

••• 0:37—Topless doing her song and tap dance audition.
• 0:44—Topless while playing in pool.
Sorority House Massacre 2 (1990) . . . . Linda
•• 0:25—In bra and panties, then topless while changing clothes.
0:50—In wet lingerie.
Tower of Terror (1991). n.a.
Video Tapes:
The Girls of Malibu (1986). . . . . Gail
••• 0:28—In two piece swimsuit. Nude taking a shower
and drying herself off.
In Search of the Perfect 10 (1986)
. . . . Perfect Girl #5
••• 0:31—Topless and buns trying on all sorts of lingerie
in dressing room.
Starlet Screen Test (1986) . . . . .Susan
••• 0:31—In robe, on red sofa, then in bra and panties,
then nude.
The Stripper of the Year (1986) . . . . Billy Jean
••• 0:32—Nude, stripping from red overalls and a hat.
•• 0:53—Topless on stage with the other contestants.
Trashy Ladies Wrestling (1987) . . . . .Fifi
•• 0:02—Buns in G-string, black bra, garter belt and
stockings. Topless getting oil dribbled on her.
Starlets Exposed! Volume II (1991) . . . . Gail
(Same as *The Girls of Malibu*.)
••• 0:07—Nude, taking off robe, taking a shower, then
drying herself off.

Theel, Lynn

Films:
Fyre (1979) . . . . n.a.
Humanoids from the Deep (1980) . . . . Peggy Larsen
• 0:22—Very, very brief half of right breast, when fight
in parking lot startles her and her boyfriend in back
of truck.
• 0:30—Brief topless getting raped on the beach by a
humanoid.
• 0:51—Brief topless, dead, lying on the beach all covered with seaweed.
Without Warning (1980) . . . . Beth
Hollywood Boulevard II (1989). . . . . Ann Gregory

Thelen, Jodi

Films:
Four Friends (1981). Georgia
•• 0:17—Left breast in open blouse three times with
her three male friends.
0:58—In pink bra taking off her blouse.
The Black Stallion Returns (1983). . . . . Tabari
Twilight Time (1983) . . . . Lena
Made for TV Movies:
Follow Your Heart (1990) . . . . Cecile

Theodore, Sondra
Video Tapes:
Wet and Wild (1989) . . . . .Model
Magazines:
Playboy (Jul 1977) . . . . Playmate
Playboy (Apr 1980) . . . . . . Playboy's Playmate Reunion
• 130—Buns.

• Thom, Cristy
Video Tapes:
Playboy Video Calendar 1992 (1991) . . . September
••• 0:35—Full frontal nudity walking and posing around the house.
••• 0:37—Nude in room of mirrors.
••• 0:38—Nude in bathtub.
Playboy's Playmate Review 1992 (1992)
. . . . Miss February
••• 0:22—Nude on motorcycle, then with a snake and then in a house.
Wet and Wild IV (1992) . . . . .Model
Magazines:
Playboy (Feb 1991) . . . . Playmate
••• Nude.
Playboy's Book of Lingerie (Jul 1992) . . . . . . Herself
•• 26-27—Right breast and lower frontal nudity.
••• 41—Topless.
••• 52-53—Topless.
•• 64—Left breast and lower frontal nudity.
Playboy's Book of Lingerie (Sep 1992) . . . . . Herself
••• 44-45—Topless.
•• 62—Right breast.

Thomas, Betty
Films:
Jackson County Jail (1976) . . . . Waitress
Tunnelvision (1976) . . . . .n.a.
Loose Shoes (1977) . . . . Biker Chick #1
• 0:02—Brief right breast dancing on the table during the *Skateboarders from Hell* sketch.
Used Cars (1980) . . . . .Bunny
0:37—Dancing on top of a car next to Kurt Russell wearing pasties to attract customers (wearing a brunette wig).
Homework (1982) . . . . Reddog's Secretary
Troop Beverly Hills (1989) . . . . Velda Plendor
TV:
Hill Street Blues (1981-87) . . . . Lucy Bates

Thomas, Heather
Films:
Zapped! (1982) .Jane Mitchell
0:20—Brief open sweater, wearing a bra when Scott Baio uses telekinesis to open it.
1:28—Body double, very, very brief topless in photo that Willie Aames gives to Robby.
1:29—Body double brief topless when Baio drops her dress during the dance.
Cyclone (1986) .Teri Marshall
Deathstone (1986) . . . . .n.a.

Red Blooded American Girl (1988) . . . . . Paula Bukowsky
1:19—Lower half of right breast when Andrew Stevens is on top of her. Very, very brief silhouette of right breast. Probably a body double.
TV:
Co-ed Fever (1979) . . . . .Sandi
The Fall Guy (1981-86) . . . . Jodi Banks
The Ultimate Challenge (1991) . . . . Co-Host

• Thomas, Heidi
Films:
Crack House (1989) . . . . .Annie
• 1:09—Brief left breast and buns in a G string, on table getting raped by a gang.
• 1:14—Topless in bathtub, dead.
Ricochet (1991) . . . . Reporter
Made for Cable TV:
Tales From the Crypt: Split Personality
(1992; HBO) . . . . .Prostitute
•• 0:06—Topless, lying in bed with Joe Pesci.

• Thompson, Brooke
Video Tapes:
Hot Body International: #1 Miss Cancun (1990)
. . . . .Contestant
•• 0:40—Buns, in one piece swimsuit.
Hot Body International: #2 Miss Puerto Vallarta
(1990) . . . . .Contestant
••• 0:26—Buns in red one piece swimsuit. Brief left breast a couple of times when it accidentally falls out.
0:56—3rd runner up.
Hot Body International: #4 Spring Break (1992)
. . . . .Contestant
0:10—Dancing in one piece swimsuit on stage.
0:38—Wet T-shirt contest. Buns in G-string.

Thompson, Cynthia Ann
Films:
Cave Girl (1985) . . . . Eba
•• 1:04—Topless making love with Rex.
Tomboy (1985) . . . . .Amanda
• 0:23—Brief right breast getting out of car in auto repair shop.
•• 1:02—Topless delivering drinks to two guys in the swimming pool.
Not of This Earth (1988) . . . . . Third Hooker (black dress)

Thompson, Emma
Wife of actor/director Kenneth Branagh.
Films:
Henry V (1989) . . . . Princess Katherine
The Tall Guy (1990) . . . . .Kate
••• 0:33—Very brief right breast, brief buns, then topless during funny love making scene with Jeff Goldblum.
Dead Again (1991) . . . . Margaret Strauss/Jane Doe
Impromptu (1991) . . . . Duchess d'Antan
Howards End (1992) . . . . Margaret Schlegel

Thompson, Lea

Films:
All The Right Moves (1983) . . . . .Lisa
••• 1:00—Topless and brief buns and lower frontal nudity, getting undressed and into bed with Tom Cruise in his bedroom.
Jaws 3 (1983) . . . . .Kelly Ann Bukowski
Red Dawn (1984) . . . . Erica
The Wild Life (1984) . . . . .Anita
    0:38—In bra and panties putting body stocking on.
Back to the Future (1985) . . . . . . .Lorraine Baines-McFly
Howard the Duck (1986) . . . . .Beverly Switzler
SpaceCamp (1986) . . . . Kathryn
Some Kind of Wonderful (1987) . . . . . . .Amanda Jones
Casual Sex? (1988) . . . . Stacy
    0:27—Buns, lying down at nude beach with Victoria Jackson.
    0:30—Buns at the beach. Pan shot from her feet to her head.
Going Undercover (1988; British)
. . . . Marigold De La Hunt
The Wizard of Loneliness (1988) . . . . Sybil
Back to the Future, Part II (1989)
. . . . .Lorraine Baines-McFly
Back to the Future, Part III (1990)
. . . . .Maggie McFly/Lorraine McFly
Article 99 (1992). . . . . .n.a.
Made for Cable TV:
Tales From the Crypt: Only Sin Deep (1989; HBO)
. . . . Sylvia

Thompson, Victoria

Films:
The Harrad Experiment (1973) . . . . . . .Beth Hillyer
    0:08—Buns, in the bathroom while talking to Harry.
• 0:10—Brief topless getting into bed.
•• 0:21—Topless in nude encounter group.
• 0:41—Topless getting into the swimming pool with Don Johnson and Laurie Walters.
    0:49—Buns, getting dressed after making love with Johnson.
The Harrad Summer (1974) . . . . .Beth Hillyer
a.k.a. Student Union
•• 0:57—Buns and brief topless running down hallway and jumping into bed, pretending to be asleep.
    1:03—Buns, lying on inflatable lounge in the pool.
    1:04—Buns, lying face down on lounge chair.
Famous T & A (1982) . . . . .Beth Hillyer
(No longer available for purchase, check your video store for rental.)
• 1:07—Brief topless and bun scene from *The Harrad Experiment.*
• 1:12—Brief nude, getting up from the floor with Don Johnson.

• Thomson, Kim

Films:
The Lords of Discipline (1983). . . . . .n.a.
Party Party (1983; British) . . . . .n.a.

Stealing Heaven (1988; British/Yugoslavian)
. . . . Heloise
• 0:42—Side of left breast kneeling on floor with steam. Long shot.
•• 0:43—Closer view of left breast.
••• 0:47—Topless and very brief lower frontal nudity lying in bed with Abelard. More left breast afterwards.
• 1:07—Nude, left side view on top of Abelard in bed. Long shot.

Thorne, Dyanne

Films:
Ilsa, She Wolf of the S.S. (1974) . . . . .Ilsa
•• 0:00—Buns, then topless making love in bed.
••• 0:01—Topless taking a shower.
••• 0:29—Buns and topless in bed with Wolfe.
•• 0:32—Right breast several times in bed with Wolfe.
••• 0:48—In white bra, then topless undressing for Wolfe.
•• 0:50—Right breast, while lying in bed.
    1:18—In black bra, panties, garter belt and stockings, tied to the bed.
Ilsa, Harem Keeper of the Oil Sheiks (1978)
. . . . .Ilsa
Ilsa, The Wicked Warden (1980). . . . . .Ilsa
a.k.a. Ilsa—Absolute Power
a.k.a. Greta, The Mad Butcher.
Ilsa—Absolute Power is about 4 minutes shorter.
Hellhole (1985) . . . . Chrysta
Real Men (1987) . . . . .Dad

• Thornton, Ann

Films:
Eureka (1983; British) . . . . Jane (red dress)
• 1:17—Brief topless during African voodoo ceremony.
Hope and Glory (1987; British). . . . . . .Honeymoon Wife

Thornton, Sigrid

Films:
The Day After Halloween (1978; Australian)
. . . . .Angela
a.k.a. Snapshot
• 0:04—Very brief topless in ad photos on wall.
•• 0:19—Topless during modeling session at the beach.
••• 0:21—More topless at the beach.
•• 0:37—Topless in magazine ad several times.
• 0:43—Brief right breast in magazine ad.
• 0:46—Topless in ad again.
• 1:18—Entering room covered with the ad.
    1:20—In beige bra in room with weirdo guy.
The Man from Snowy River (1982; Australian) . . . Jessica
Slate, Wyn & Me (1987; Australian) . . . . . . Blanche/Max
The Lighthorsemen (1988; Australian) . . . . Anne
Return to Snowy River (1988) . . . . Jessica
TV:
Paradise (1989-90). . . . . .Amelia Lawson
Guns of Paradise (1991). . . . . .Amelia Lawson

Thulin, Ingrid
Films:
Brink of Life (1957; Swedish) . . . . Cecila
Wild Strawberries (1957; Swedish) . . . . . Marianne Borg
The Magician (1959). . . . . Manda Aman
The Four Horsemen of the Apocalypse (1962)
. . . . Marguerite Laurier
The Winter Light (1963; Swedish) . . . . . Marta Lundberg
Hour of the Wolf (1968; Swedish) . . . . . .Veronica Vogler
The Damned (1969; German)
. . . . .Sophie Von Essenbeck
•• 1:23—Topless in bed with Frederick. Long scene for
a 1969 film.
• 2:03—Left breast in bed with Martin (her son in the
film).
Cries and Whispers (1972; Swedish) . . . . .Karin
a.k.a. Viskingar Och Rop
•• 0:57—Topless and buns, undressing and getting
ready for bed. Something covers lower frontal nudity.
Moses (1976; British/Italian) . . . . Miriam
After the Rehearsal (1984; Swedish) . . . . .Rakel

Thurman, Uma
Films:
Kiss Daddy Goodnight (1987) . . . . Laura
Dangerous Liaisons (1988) . . . . . . Cécile de Volanges
••• 0:59—Topless taking off her nightgown in her bed-
room with John Malkovich.
Johnny Be Good (1988) . . . . Georgia Elkans
The Adventures of Baron Munchausen (1989)
. . . . .Venus/Rose
1:14—Brief upper half of right breast when the fly-
ing ladies wrap her with the flowing cloth.
Henry & June (1990). . . . . June Miller
Where the Heart Is (1990) . . . . Daphne McBain
• 0:08—Topless during art film, but her entire body is
artfully painted to match the background paintings.
The second segment.
0:40—More topless with body painted posing for
her sister. Long shot.
1:16—In slide of painting taken at 0:40.
1:43—Same painting from 0:40 during the end
credits.
Final Analysis (1992) . . . . .Diana Baylor
Made for TV Movies:
Robin Hood (1991) . . . . .Maid Marian
Magazines:
Playboy (Dec 1990). . . . . Sex Stars of 1990
• 179—Left breast, while kneeling. B&W.

• Tia
Video Tapes:
The Best of the Mermaids (1992) . . . Sand and Lace
••• 1:12—Topless and buns in G-string on boat, at the
beach and while scuba diving.
Mermaids of the Aztec Empire (1992)
. . . . Mona Brock
•• 0:01—Topless during opening credits.

••• 0:02—Topless and buns in G-string at the beach
during opening credits.
•• 0:06—Topless outside with Lori Pallett by pool and
under water.
• 0:10—In bra and panties, then topless in jewelry
store fantasy.
• 0:11—Buns, in swimsuit, by the pool.
• 0:13—Brief buns, while turning over in the spa.
••• 0:14—Topless and buns in G-string bottom on boat.
••• 0:23—Topless and buns at the beach. Long scene.
••• 0:31—Topless and buns in G-string while snorkeling
under water.
••• 0:37—Topless and buns at the beach again.
••• 0:49—Topless and buns in swimsuit bottoms undressing at the beach during the end credits.

Ticotin, Rachel
Films:
Fort Apache, The Bronx (1981). . . . . Isabelle
• 1:25—Brief upper half of breasts in bathtub while
Paul Newman pours bubble bath in.
Critical Condition (1987) . . . . Rachel
Total Recall (1990) . . . . .Melina
FX 2 (1991) . . . . Kim Brandon
One Good Cop (1991). . . . . .Grace
Made for Cable Movies:
Prison Stories, Women on the Inside (1990; HBO)
. . . . Iris
0:07—Brief buns, squatting while getting strip
searched in jail. Don't see her face.
Keep the Change (1992; TNT) . . . . .Astrid
Made for TV Movies:
Spies, Lies & Naked Thighs (1988) . . . . .Sonia
TV:
For Love and Honor (1983) . . . . Cpl. Grace Pavlik
Ohara (1987-88) . . . . Teresa Storm

Tilly, Meg
Sister of actress Jennifer Tilly.
Films:
Fame (1980) . . . . Principal Dancer
Tex (1982). . . . . Jamie Collins
The Big Chill (1983). Chloé
One Dark Night (1983) . . . . .Julie
Psycho II (1983). . . . . Mary
0:35—Buns and very brief topless of body double,
getting out of the shower while Anthony Perkins
watches through a peep hole.
Impulse (1984) . . . . .Jenny
0:58—In wet red swimsuit in photograph, then top-
less in B&W photograph (don't see her face) when
Tim Matheson looks at photos.
Agnes of God (1985) . . . . .Sister Agnes
Off Beat (1986) . . . . Rachel Wareham
Masquerade (1988) . . . . Olivia Lawrence
0:55—In pink nightgown in bedroom.
The Girl in a Swing (1989; U.S./British)
. . . . Karin Foster
•• 0:44—In white bra, then topless and buns.

•• 0:50—Nude, swimming under water.
••• 1:14—Topless sitting on swing, then making love.
1:18—In white bra, sitting in front of a mirror.
••• 1:44—Topless at the beach.
Valmont (1989). . . . . Tourvel
The Two Jakes (1990) . . . . .Kitty Berman
Leaving Normal (1992). . . . . Marianne
Made for Cable TV:
Nightmare Classics: Carmilla (1989; HBO) . . . . Carmilla
Made for TV Movies:
In the Best Interest of the Child (1990)
. . . . Jennifer Colton

Tippo, Patti
Films:
10 to Midnight (1983). . . . . Party Girl
•• 0:52—Topless, making love with a guy in the laundry room at a party.
Omega Syndrome (1986) . . . . Sally
Sid and Nancy (1986; British)
. . . . .Tanned and Sultry Blonde
Brain Dead (1989). . . . . Resident
TV:
Sledge Hammer! (1987-88). . . . . .Officer Daley

Tolan, Kathleen
Films:
Death Wish (1974). . . . . Carol Toby
• 0:09—Brief topless and buns getting raped by three punks.
The Line (1982) . . . . .n.a.
The Rosary Murders (1987). . . . . Sister Ann Vania

Tolo, Marilu
Films:
The Oldest Profession (1967) . . . . "Anticipation"
1:23—Brief side view of left breast walking to the bathroom. Shown as a negative image, so it's hard to see.
Confessions of a Police Captain (1971)
. . . . .Serena Li Puma
Bluebeard (1972) . . . . Brigitt
• 1:25—Topless in sheer blue blouse arguing with Richard Burton.
•• 1:27—Topless getting whipped by Burton.
Beyond Fear (1975). . . . . .Nicole
The Greek Tycoon (1978) . . . . Sophia Matalas
Magazines:
Playboy (Nov 1978) . . . . Sex in Cinema 1978
• 184—Upper half of left breast.

Tomasina, Jeana
Films:
History of the World, Part I (1981). . . . . . . Vestal Virgin
Looker (1981). . . . . Suzy
The Beach Girls (1982) . . . . .Ducky
•• 0:12—Topless and buns, lying on the beach with Ginger, while a guy looks through a telescope.
••• 0:54—Topless on a sailboat with a guy.

• 0:55—Brief topless on the beach after being "saved" after falling off the boat.
•• 1:12—Topless in sauna with Ginger and an older guy.
10 to Midnight (1983). . . . . .Karen
0:26—In white body suit, changing in bedroom while the killer watches from inside the closet.
Double Exposure (1983). . . . . Renee
• 0:20—Very brief glimpse of left breast under water in swimming pool.
Up the Creek (1984) . . . . .Molly
Video Tapes:
Playboy Video Magazine, Volume 2 (1983)
. . . . .Herself/Playboy Playoffs
Playboy Video Magazine, Volume 5 (1983)
. . . . Playmate
• 0:06—Brief topless on piano.
• 0:12—Topless, then full frontal nudity posing on piano.
Playboy Video Centerfold: Reneé Tenison (1990)
. . . . .Portrait of a Photographer: Richard Fegley
•• 0:34—Full frontal nudity, posing on piano for centerfold photo.
Magazines:
Playboy (Nov 1980) . . . . Playmate
••• 144-155—Nude.

Tompkins, Angel
Films:
Hang Your Hat on the Wind (1969) . . . . . . Fran Harper
I Love My Wife (1970) . . . . Helene Donnelly
Prime Cut (1972). . . . . Clarabelle
• 1:03—Very brief left breast sitting up in bed to talk to Lee Marvin.
1:04—Very brief back side view of left breast jumping out of bed.
The Don is Dead (1973). . . . . Ruby
How to Seduce a Woman (1973) . . . . Pamela
1:28—In bra and panties for a long time getting a massage in bedroom.
The Teacher (1974) . . . . .Diane Marshall
••• 0:09—Topless on a boat taking off her swimsuit.
••• 0:12—More topless on the boat getting a suntan.
••• 0:36—Topless taking off her top in bedroom, then buns and topless taking a shower.
• 0:41—Brief right breast lying back on bed.
•• 0:43—Brief topless opening her bathrobe for Jay North.
•• 0:47—Side view of right breast lying on bed, then right breast from above.
•• 0:52—Topless in boat after making love.
Walking Tall, Part II (1975) . . . . .Marganne Stilson
The Farmer (1977). . . . . Betty
The Bees (1978). . . . . Sandra Miller
One Man Jury (1978). . . . . Kitty
Alligator (1980) . . . . .News Reporter
The Naked Cage (1985) . . . . Diane Wallace
•• 0:22—In lingerie, then topless with Abbey.
• 0:38—Brief right breast, in bed with Abbey.

Dangerously Close (1986) . . . . Mrs. Waters
Murphy's Law (1986) . . . . Jan
- 0:19—Topless doing a strip routine on stage while
  Charles Bronson watches.
- 0:27—Brief topless doing another routine.

Amazon Women on the Moon (1987) . . . . . . First Lady
1:00—In white nightgown, then black bra, panties,
  garter belt and stockings.
A Tiger's Tale (1988) . . . . La Vonne
Crack House (1989) . . . . Mother
Relentless (1989) . . . . Carmen

Made for Cable TV:
The Hitchhiker: Homebodies . . . . Janet O'Mell

TV:
Search (1972-73) . . . . Gloria Harding

Magazines:
Playboy (Feb 1972) . . . . Angel
••• 87-91—Lots of photos of her in a river.
Playboy (Jun 1972) . . . . Prime Cut
••• 123—Topless.
Playboy (Dec 1972) . . . . Sex Stars of 1972
••• 210—Full frontal nudity.
Playboy (Dec 1973) . . . . Sex Stars of 1973
••• 209—Full frontal nudity.
Playboy (Dec 1974) . . . . Sex Stars of 1974
••• 211—Right breast and lower frontal nudity in waterfall.

Toothman, Lisa

Films:
Hard Rock Zombies (1985) . . . . Elsa
- 0:01—Buns, undressing to go skinny dipping. Top-
  less long shot.
••• 0:32—Buns, while getting into the shower. Topless
  and buns in the shower behind clear plastic curtain.
Witchcraft III: The Kiss of Death (1991)
. . . . Charlotte
•• 1:02—Buns and topless in shower with Louis while
  William has a bad dream.
•• 1:12—Left breast, while on bed with Louis, against
  her will.

Torek, Denise

Films:
New York's Finest (1988) . . . . Hooker #2
Sensations (1988) . . . . Phone Girl #2
- 0:23—Topless talking on the phone sex line.

• Toscano, Gabriela

Films:
South (1988; Argentinian/French) . . . . Blondi
Satanic Attraction (1991; Italian) . . . . Fernanda
- 0:43—Partial left breast, making love with Lionel.
  Brief side view of left breast, eating fruit afterwards.

Tough, Kelly

Video Tapes:
Playboy's Playmate Review (1982) . . . . . . Playmate
••• 0:27—Nude, camping, then in bedroom setting.

Playmates at Play (1990) . . . . Making Waves
Magazines:
Playboy (Oct 1981) . . . . Playmate

Townsend, K.C.

Films:
Husbands (1970) . . . . Barmaid
All That Jazz (1979) . . . . Stripper
- 0:21—Topless backstage getting Joey excited before
  he goes on stage. Lit by red light.
Below the Belt (1980) . . . . Thalia

• Tranelli, Deborah

Films:
Naked Vengeance (1985) . . . . Carla Harris
0:18—In black bra and panties in bedroom while a
  guy peek in from the window.
- 0:25—In black bra, then topless during gang rape.
••• 0:43—Buns and topless walking into the water to seduce a guy before killing him.

TV:
Dallas (1989-90) . . . . Phyllis

Travis, Nancy

Films:
Three Men and a Baby (1987) . . . . Sylvia
Married to the Mob (1988) . . . . Karen Lutnig
- 0:15—Buns and brief side view of right breast, with
  Tony in hotel room. Brief topless in the bathtub.
Air America (1990) . . . . Corinne Landreaux
Internal Affairs (1990) . . . . Kathleen Avila
- 0:38—Side view of left breast when Raymond opens
  the shower door to talk to her.
Loose Cannons (1990) . . . . Riva
Three Men and a Little Lady (1990) . . . . Sylvia

Travis, Stacey

Films:
Deadly Dreams (1988) . . . . Librarian
Phantasm II (1988) . . . . Jeri
Dr. Hackenstein (1989) . . . . Melanie Victor
Hardware (1990) . . . . Jill
- 0:21—Almost topless in shower. Brief left breast in
  bed with Moses. Lit with blue light.
0:38—Brief topless in bedroom seen by a guy
  through telescope. Infrared-looking effect.
The Super (1991) . . . . Heather

Treas, Terri

Films:
The Nest (1987) . . . . Dr. Morgan Hubbard
Deathstalker III: The Warriors From Hell (1988)
. . . . Camlearde
The Terror Within (1988) . . . . Linda
The Fabulous Baker Boys (1989) . . . . Girl in Bed
- 0:00—Brief upper half of right breast when sheet
  falls down when she leans over in bed.
Frankenstein Unbound (1990) . . . . Computer Voice

House IV (1991) . . . . Kelly Cobb
   0:45—Very, very brief side view of right breast (wearing pastie) getting into the shower.
   0:46—Topless, when the shower water becomes blood. Probably a body double because you don't see her face.
   1:08—In bra, in her bedroom after waking up in the morning.
TV:
Seven Brides for Seven Brothers (1982-83)
   . . . . Hannah McFadden
Alien Nation (1989-91) . . . . Cathy Frankel

• Trentini, Peggy

Films:
Young Doctors in Love (1982) . . . . .Christmas Elf
  •• 0:55—Brief topless greeting visitors to the party.
  • 0:57—Topless again sitting on couch.
Up the Creek (1984) . . . . Co-Ed
Magazines:
Playboy (Jan 1992) . . . . .The Swedish Bikini Team
Ulla Swensen.
  ••• 78-85—Topless while stretching swimsuit top with her hands. Topless standing on pool ladder. Buns while holding surfboard (2nd from the right). Topless holding her arms up. Right breast while inside phone booth holding black phone. Topless standing and holding her left arm up. Topless, while feeding raccoon. Topless, lying on sleeping bag with her left arm on her stomach.

Trickey, Paula

Films:
Maniac Cop 2 (1990) . . . . Cheryl
  •• 0:41—In orange two piece swimsuit on stage, then topless and buns in G-string.
Carnal Crimes (1991) .Jasmine
Made for Cable TV:
Dream On: Futile Attraction (1991; HBO). . . . Janice
  •• 0:02—Topless sitting in bed with Martin.
Sessions: Episode 3 (1991; HBO) . . . . . . Fantasy Woman

• Trigger, Sarah

Films:
Kid (1990). . . . . Kate
  0:36—Almost topless in gaping T-shirt while washing a horse.
Bill and Ted's Bogus Journey (1991) . . . . Joanna
Grand Canyon (1991). . . . . .Vanessa
Paradise (1991). . . . . .Darlene
  • 0:14—Brief topless ironing her clothes in open window while Willard and Billie watch from their tree house. Long shot after. Hard to see her face.
Made for Cable Movies:
Fellow Traveller (1989; HBO) . . . . Gloria
  •• 0:02—Topless, sitting up in bed, stretching, then getting out.

• Tripoldi, Idy

Films:
Auditions (1978) .Bonnie Tirol
  ••• 1:01—Full frontal nudity, taking off sweater.
  •• 1:07—Topless and buns during orgy scene.
Fairytales (1979) .Naked Girl
  ••• 0:06—Nude, dancing in bedroom and getting in and out of bed with The Prince.
Famous T & A (1982) . . . . .Bonnie Tirol
(No longer available for purchase, check your video store for rental.)
  ••• 0:35—Full frontal nude scene from *Auditions*.

• Tripplehorn, Jeanne

Films:
Basic Instinct (1992). . . . . .Beth Gardner
Made for TV Movies:
The Perfect Tribute (1991) . . . . .Julia

Tristan, Dorothy

Films:
Klute (1971). . . . . .Arlyn Page
Scarecrow (1973). . . . . .Coley
Man on a Swing (1974) . . . . Janet
Swashbuckler (1976) . . . . Alice
California Dreaming (1978). . . . . Fay
  0:05—In braless white top, jogging on the beach with Glynnis O'Connor.
  • 0:20—Brief topless changing clothes while a group of boys peek through a hole in the wall.

Truchon, Isabelle

Films:
Backstab (1990). . . . . Jennifer
  •• 0:08—In bra, then topless in back seat of car with James Brolin.
  • 0:16—Buns, black panties and stockings while on the floor with Brolin. Brief right breast.
  • 0:18—Brief buns in front of fireplace. Side view of right breast. Buns, while walking into the other room.
Jesus of Montreal (1990; French/Canadian)
  . . . . Richard's Girlfriend
If Looks Could Kill (1991) . . . . 1st Class Stewardess
  a.k.a. Teen Agent

Turner, Janine

Films:
Young Doctors in Love (1982) . . . . Cameo
Tai-Pan (1986) . . . . Shevaun
Monkey Shines: An Experiment in Fear (1988)
  . . . . .Linda Aikman
  0:01—Side view of buns, lying in bed when Jason Beghe wakes up. Don't really see anything.
Steel Magnolias (1989) . . . . Nancy Beth Marmillion
TV:
Behind the Screen (1981). . . . . .Janie-Claire Willow
General Hospital (1982-83) . . . . Laura Templeton
Northern Exposure (1990-) . . . . .Maggie O'Connell

Turner, Kathleen
Films:

Body Heat (1981) . . . . Maddy Walker
- 0:22—Brief side view of left breast in bed with William Hurt.
- • 0:24—Topless in a shack with Hurt.
  0:32—Buns, getting dressed. Long shot, hard to see.
- 0:54—Brief left breast in bathtub. Long shot, hard to see.

The Man with Two Brains (1983)
. . . . Dolores Benedict
- 0:08—Right breast when Steve Martin is operating on her in the operating room.
  0:22—In sheer lingerie in bedroom with Steve Martin, teasing him and driving him crazy.
- 0:36—Buns, in hotel room with a guy about to squeeze her buns when Steve Martin walks in.

Crimes of Passion (1984) . . Joanna Crane/China Blue
(Unrated version reviewed.)
- ••• 0:45—Topless, wearing black panties and stockings, in bed with Bobby. Shadows of them making love on the wall.
- 1:00—Right breast in back of a limousine with a rich couple.
  1:22—In blue bra and panties.
- 1:27—Right breast in bed with Bobby.

Romancing the Stone (1984) . . . . Joan Wilder
The Jewel of the Nile (1985) . . . . Joan Wilder
Prizzi's Honor (1985) . . . . Irene Walker
- 0:30—Very brief left breast making love with Jack Nicholson on bed.

Peggy Sue Got Married (1986) . . . . Peggy Sue
Julia and Julia (1987; Italian) . . . . Julia
(This movie was shot using a high-definition video system and then transferred to film.)
- ••• 0:32—Topless making love in bed with her husband.
- ••• 1:08—Topless, then right breast making love in bed with Sting.

The Accidental Tourist (1988) . . . . Sarah
Switching Channels (1988) . . . . Christy
The War of the Roses (1989) . . . . Barbara Rose
  0:06—In braless white blouse walking around on the sidewalk with Michael Douglas.
- 0:12—Brief left breast, while in bed with Michael Douglas.

V. I. Warshawski (1991) Vic
  0:21—Briefly in lingerie, changing clothes in back of cab.

Made for Cable Movies:
A Breed Apart (1984; HBO) . . . . Stella Clayton
- •• 1:12—Topless in bed with Rutger Hauer, then left breast.

• Tuscany
a.k.a. Heather Tuscany.
Films:
Angel of Passion (1991) . . . . Ellen
- ••• 0:36—Buns and topless making love with a guy on a boat.

Video Tapes:
Bikini Blitz (1990) . . . . Model
  0:09—Very brief partial back side view of left breast, pulling up bikini top.
Magazines:
Playboy (Sep 1992) . . . . Grapevine
- 163—Lower half of left breast.

Tweed, Shannon
Sister of model/actress Tracy Tweed.
Films:
Of Unknown Origin (1983; Canadian)
. . . . Meg Hughes
- 0:00—Brief side view of right breast taking a shower.

Hot Dog... The Movie (1984) . . . . Sylvia Fonda
- ••• 0:42—Topless getting undressed, then making love in bed and in hot tub with Harkin.

The Surrogate (1984; Canadian) . . . . Lee Wake
- ••• 0:03—Topless taking a Jacuzzi bath.
- 0:42—Brief topless changing in bedroom, then in bra getting dressed. Long shot.
- ••• 1:02—Topless in sauna talking with Frank. Long scene.

Meatballs III (1987) . . . . The Love Goddess
Steele Justice (1987). . . . . Angela
Cannibal Women in the Avocado Jungle of Death (1988)
. . . . Dr. Margot Hunt
Lethal Woman (1988). . . . . Tory
- ••• 1:01—Topless at the beach with Derek. Brief buns in white bikini bottom.

In the Cold of the Night (1989) . . . . Lena
- 0:02—Right breast while making love with Scott.

Night Visitor (1989) . . . . Lisa Grace
Last Call (1990) . . . . Cindy/Audrey
- 0:12—In black body stocking, dancing on stage. Topless and buns in G-string underneath.
- •• 0:29—Right breast, on the floor with William Katt.
- •• 0:39—Brief buns, rotating in chair with Katt. Topless leaning against column.
- 0:40—Topless on stair railing.
- 1:01—Left breast, while leaning against column and kissing Katt.
- 1:02—Left breast in bed with Katt.
- ••• 1:05—Topless making love on roof with Katt.

The Last Hour (1990) . . . . Susan
a.k.a. Concrete War
- 0:05—Topless in bed, making love with Eric.
- 0:07—Brief buns and side of left breast, in the shower.

Twisted Justice (1990) . . . . Hinkle
Firing Line (1991). . . . . Sandra Spencer
Night Eyes 2 (1991) . . . . Marilyn Mejenes
- ••• 0:49—Buns and topless making love with Andrew Stevens in bed.
- ••• 1:06—Topless, making love with Stevens (nice use of raspberries).

Sensual Response (1992). Eve
(Unrated version reviewed.)
••• 0:25—Topless in studio with Edge, while he checks
     her out.
••• 0:29—Topless, making love with him. Long scene.
••• 0:31—Full frontal nudity, lying in bed, then sitting
     up.
••• 0:43—Topless, while making love in her house with
     Edge.
•• 0:51—Topless in pool at night with Edge.
•• 0:52—Nude, getting up out of bed and putting robe
     on.
•• 0:55—Topless in study with Edge.
••• 1:07—Topless and buns, while taking a shower.
     Nude, getting out and drying herself off.
Made for Cable TV:
Hitchhiker: Videodate . . . . .n.a.
(Available on *The Hitchhiker, Volume 4.*)
The Hitchhiker: Doctor's Orders (1987; HBO)
. . . . Dr. Rita de Roy
     0:15—In black bra, panties, garter belt and stock-
     ings.
TV:
Falcon Crest (1982-83) . . . . Diana Hunter
Fly By Night (1991). . . . . Sally "Slick" Monroe
Video Tapes:
Playboy Video Magazine, Volume 1 (1982)
. . . . Playmate of the Year
•• 0:02—Full frontal nudity, posing by bath tub for
     photo session.
••• 1:13—Nude, posing in bed.
••• 1:15—Full frontal nudity in photo session.
••• 1:21—Full frontal nudity in front of piano, in bath
     tub and in bed.
Playboy's Playmate Review (1982) . . . . . . Playmate
••• 0:47—Nude in bed, then in photo shoot by a table,
     then by a piano, then in bathtub.
Playboy Video Magazine, Volume 5 (1983)
. . . . Playmate
• 0:05—Brief topless in bath tub.
••• 0:13—Full frontal nudity in bedroom set.
Playboy's Playmates of the Year: The '80s (1989)
. . . . Playmate of the Year 1982
••• 0:36—Full frontal nudity in photo session in a house.
••• 0:37—Nude in still photos. Nude posing by piano,
     in bathtub, in bed.
•• 0:51—Full frontal nudity standing by bed.
Playboy Video Centerfold: Reneé Tenison (1990)
. . . . Portrait of a Photographer: Richard Fegley
••• 0:36—Full frontal nudity, posing by bed for center-
     fold photo.
Magazines:
Playboy (Nov 1981) . . . . Playmate
Playboy (Nov 1983) . . . . Sex in Cinema 1983
•• 146—Topless.
Playboy (Jan 1989) . . . . Women of the Eighties
• 249—Full frontal nudity, lying in bed. B&W photo.
Playboy's Nudes (Oct 1990). . . . . Herself
••• 108—Topless.

Playboy (May 1991) . . . . Boss Tweeds
••• 144-153—Nude, with her sister, Tracy Tweed.
Playboy (Dec 1991) . . . . .Sex Stars 1991
••• 184—Topless.
Playboy's Career Girls (Aug 1992)
. . . . Baywatch Playmates
••• 11—Topless.

• *Tweed, Tracy*
Sister of *Playboy* Playmate/actress Shannon Tweed.
Films:
Sunset Heat (1991) . . . . Lena
(Unrated version reviewed.)
••• 0:19—Topless making love with Michael Paré. Nice,
     long scene.
••• 0:22—Topless and buns, making love with Paré on
     stairs, sofa and the floor.
••• 0:24—Topless, lying on the floor when the bad guys
     come in. Brief partial right breast, standing up and
     covering herself with a jacket.
Live Wire (1992). . . . . Rolls Royce Girl
Night Rhythms (1992) . . . . .Honey
(Unrated version reviewed.)
••• 0:28—Topless making love with Martin Hewitt in ra-
     dio station. Nice, long scene.
••• 0:31—Nude, getting up after changing positions.
•• 0:33—Topless, lying dead on the floor.
Magazines:
Playboy (May 1991) . . . . Boss Tweeds
••• 144-153—Nude, with her sister, Shannon Tweed.
Playboy (Jul 1991) . . . . The Height Report
•• 132-133—Buns, in chair.

Twomey, Anne
Films:
Refuge (1981) . . . . n.a.
The Imagemaker (1985). . . . . Molly Grainger
     0:11—Very, very brief topless reading newspaper in
     bedroom (wearing flesh colored tape over her nip-
     ples). Then in white bra and panties talking to a guy
     in bed.
     1:04—In bra and skirt undressing in front of Michael
     Nouri.
Deadly Friend (1986) . . . . .Jeannie Conway
Last Rites (1988) . . . . Zena Pace
Made for TV Movies:
Bump in the Night (1991) . . . . .Sarah

Tylyn
See: John, Tylyn.

Tyrrell, Susan
Likes to show only one breast in nude scenes!
Films:
The Steagle (1971) . . . . Louise
• 0:48—Brief left breast twice, lying on bed with Rich-
     ard Benjamin.
Fat City (1972). . . . . Oma

The Killer Inside Me (1975) . . . . Joyce Lakeland
•• 1:27—Very brief left breast, then very brief topless
(both breasts!) in bed with Stacy Keach during flashback scene.
Andy Warhol's Bad (1977; Italian) . . . . Mary Aiken
I Never Promised You a Rose Garden (1977) . . . . Lee
Islands in the Stream (1977) Lil
Loose Shoes (1977). Boobies
Forbidden Zone (1980) . . . . Queen Doris
•• 0:19—Left breast sticking out of dress, sitting on big
dice with Herve Villechaize.
•• 1:02—Left breast sticking out of dress after fighting
with the Ex-Queen.
Fast Walking (1981) . . . . Evie
Night Warning (1982) . . . . Cheryl Roberts
• 0:17—Left breast, sticking out of dress just before
she stabs the TV repairman.
Angel (1983). . . . . Selly Mosler
Avenging Angel (1985). . . . . Selly Mosler
Flesh + Blood (1985) . . . . Celine
• 1:35—Right breast sticking out of her dress when
everybody throws their clothes into the fire.
The Offspring (1986) . . . . Beth Chandler
The Underachievers (1987) . . . . Mrs. Grant
Big Top Pee Wee (1988) . . . . Midge Montana
Far From Home (1989) . . . . Agnes Reed
• 0:29—Very, very brief right breast in bathtub getting
electrocuted.
Cry Baby (1990) . . . . Ramona
Rockula (1990) . . . . Chuck the Bartender
Made for Cable TV:
The Hitchhiker: In the Name of Love (1987; HBO)
. . . . Doris
Made for TV Movies:
Sidney Sheldon's Windmill of the Gods (1988)
. . . . Neusa
TV:
Open All Night (1981-82) . . . . Gretchen Feester

Tyson, Cathy
Films:
Mona Lisa (1987) . . . . Simone
Business as Usual (1988; British) . . . . n.a.
The Serpent and the Rainbow (1988)
. . . . Dr. Marielle Duchamp
• 0:41—Brief topless making love with Dennis. Proba-
bly a body double, don't see her face.

Udenio, Fabiana
Films:
Boarding School (1978; German) . . . . Gina
a.k.a. Virgin Campus
a.k.a. Passion Flower Hotel
Hardbodies 2 (1986). . . . . Cleo/Princess
Summer School (1987) . . . . Anna-Maria
Bride of Re-Animator (1989) . . . . Francesca Danelli
0:45—Most of her left breast in bed with Dan. His
hand covers it most of the time.

Robocop 2 (1990) . . . . Sunblock Woman
Diplomatic Immunity (1991). . . . . Teresa
•• 1:06—Topless in panties, on the floor with her hands
tied behind her back when Klaus rips her blouse
open to photograph her.
TV:
One Life to Live (1985-86) . . . . Gulietta

Udy, Claudia
Films:
American Nightmare (1981; Canadian) . . . . . . Andrea
••• 0:08—Buns, then topless dancing on stage.
• 0:22—Buns getting into bathtub. Topless during
struggle with killer.
Joy (1983; French/Canadian) . . . . Joy
•• 0:11—Nude, undressing, getting into bath then into
and out of bed.
••• 0:14—Nude in bed with Marc.
••• 0:31—In swimsuits, posing for photos, then full
frontal nudity.
•• 0:54—Topless sitting with Bruce at encounter
group.
• 1:04—Buns and topless getting into bathtub.
Out of Control (1984). Tina
0:19—In leopard skin pattern bra and panties.
• 0:28—In leopard bra and panties playing Strip Spin
the Bottle, then very brief topless taking off her top.
Long shot.
• 0:47—Brief left breast getting raped by bad guy on
the boat.
• 0:54—Brief left breast, then right breast making love
with Cowboy.
Savage Dawn (1984) . . . . n.a.
Night Force (1986) . . . . Christy Hanson
•• 0:07—Topless making love in the stable with Steve
during her engagement party.
••• 0:10—Nude, fantasizing in the shower.
The Pink Chiquitas (1986; Canadian) . . . . Helen
Master of Dragonard Hill (1987) . . . . Arabella
••• 0:11—Nude, undressing to seduce Calabar. More
topless and buns while kissing him.
•• 0:14—Silhouette topless while making love with
Calabar, then topless.
• 0:58—Brief buns and side of right breast during flash
back. Brief right breast when she gets out of bed.
Dragonard (1988) . . . . Arabella
•• 1:11—Topless dressed as Cleopatra dancing a rou-
tine in front of a bunch of guys.
Edge of Sanity (1988). . . . . Liza
Any Man's Death (1989) . . . . Laura
Thieves of Fortune (1989) . . . . Marissa

Udy, Helene
Films:
Pick-Up Summer (1979; Canadian) . . . . Suzy
0:34—Very, very brief topless when the boys spray
her and she jumps up.
My Bloody Valentine (1981; Canadian) . . . . Sylvia

One Night Only (1984; Canadian) . . . . Suzanne
  • 0:50—Buns and right breast in bed talking with a
    guy.
  • 1:12—Over the shoulder, brief left breast on top of
    a guy in bed.
Nightflyers (1987). . . . . .Lilly
Pin (1988) . . . . Marcia Bateman
••• 1:03—Topless in bedroom with Leon.
Made for TV Movies:
The Hollywood Detective (1989). . . . . . Lois Wednesday
TV:
As the World Turns (1983). . . . . .Frannie Hughes

Vaccaro, Brenda

Films:
Midnight Cowboy (1969) . . . . Shirley
  • 1:30—Very, very brief out of focus left breast in open
    fur coat, lying down with Jon Voight.
  • 1:31—Very brief left bresat when falling back onto
    bed with Voight.
  •• 1:32—Brief right breast, while rollling in bed with
    Voight.
I Love My Wife (1970). . . . . Jody Burrows
Once is Not Enough (1975) . . . . Linda
Airport '77 (1977). . . . . Eve Clayton
House by the Lake (1977; Canadian). . . . . Diane
  Topless.
The First Deadly Sin (1980). . . . . Monica Gilbert
Chanel Solitaire (1981) .n.a.
Zorro, The Gay Blade (1981). . . . . Florinda
Supergirl (1984; British) . . . . Bianca
Water (1986; British). . . . . Bianca
Heart of Midnight (1988) . . . . .Betty
Edgar Allan Poe's "The Masque of the Red Death"
  (1989). . . . . Elaina
Ten Little Indians (1989) . . . . Marion Marshall
Made for Cable Movies:
Red Shoe Diaries (1992; Showtime) . . . . Martha
Made for TV Movies:
Paper Dolls (1982) . . . . .Julia Blake
TV:
Sara (1976). . . . . .Sara Yarnell
Dear Detective (1979)
. . . . .Detective Sergeant Kate Hudson
Paper Dolls (1984) . . . . .Julia Blake

Vaccaro, Tracy

Films:
The Man Who Loved Women (1983) . . . . Legs
Magazines:
Playboy (Oct 1983). . . . . Playmate

Valen, Nancy

Films:
The Heavenly Kid (1985). . . . . Melissa
Porky's Revenge (1985; Canadian) . . . . Ginger
The Big Picture (1989) . . . . .Young Sharon

Listen to Me (1989). . . . . Mia
  • 0:06—Very, very brief left breast in bed with Garson
    when Kirk Cameron first meets him.
Loverboy (1989) . . . . Jenny Gordon
Final Embrace (1991) . . . . Candy Vale/Laurel Parrish
Made for TV Movies:
Perry Mason: The Case of the Fatal Framing (1992)
. . . . Mala Sikorski
TV:
Hull High (1990) . . . . .Donna Breedlove

• Valez, Karen

Wife of actor Lee Majors.
Video Tapes:
Playboy Video Magazine, Volume 7 (1985)
. . . . Playmate
••• 1:01—Topless and buns on lounge chair, rubbing oil
    on herself.
••• 1:04—Nude, undressing outside in gazebo and on
    porch.
••• 1:09—Full frontal nudity undressing in living room.
Playboy's Playmates of the Year: The '80s (1989)
. . . . .Playmate of the Year 1985
••• 0:39—Topless and buns, in lounge chair, rubbing oil
    on herself.
••• 0:42—Nude, in a gazebo.
•• 0:52—Right breast in open dress.
Wet and Wild (1989) . . . . Model
Magazines:
Playboy (Dec 1984) . . . . Playmate
Playboy's Nudes (Oct 1990) . . . . .Herself
••• 97—Full frontal nudity.

van Breeschooten, Karin

Identical twin sister of Miryam van Breeschooten.
Video Tapes:
Playboy Video Calendar 1990 (1989). . . . . .October
••• 0:51—Nude.
Playboy Video Centerfold: Dutch Twins (1989)
. . . . Playmate
••• 0:00—Nude throughout.
Magazines:
Playboy (Sep 1989) . . . . Playmate
Playboy's Nudes (Oct 1990) . . . . .Herself
••• 75—Full frontal nudity.

van Breeschooten, Miryam

Identical twin sister of Karin van Breeschooten.
Video Tapes:
Playboy Video Calendar 1990 (1989). . . . . .October
••• 0:51—Nude.
Playboy Video Centerfold: Dutch Twins (1989)
. . . . Playmate
••• 0:00—Nude throughout.
Magazines:
Playboy (Sep 1989) . . . . Playmate
Playboy's Nudes (Oct 1990) . . . . .Herself
••• 75—Full frontal nudity.

Van De Ven, Monique
Films:
Turkish Delight (1974; Dutch) . . . . .Olga
- •• 0:24—Topless when Rutger Hauer opens her blouse, then nude on the bed.
- •• 0:27—Topless, waking up in bed.
- ••• 0:33—Topless on bed with Hauer, then nude getting up to fix flowers.
- 0:42—Buns, with Hauer at the beach.
- •• 0:46—Topless modeling for Hauer, then brief nude running around outside.
- •• 0:54—Topless in bed with open blouse with flowers.
- • 1:04—In wet T-shirt in the rain with Hauer, then brief topless coming down the stairs.

Katie's Passion (1978; Dutch) . . . . Katy
- 0:38—Brief buns when guy rips her panties off.
- •• 0:45—Topless in hospital when a group of doctors examine her.
- 0:50—Left breast a couple of times talking to a doctor. Brief buns sitting down.
- 1:12—Buns, getting into bed.
- ••• 1:18—Nude burning all her old clothes and getting into bathtub.

The Assault (1986; Dutch)
. . . . Truus Coster/Saskia de Graaff
Amsterdamned (1988; Dutch) . . . . Laura
Lily Was Here (1989) . . . . Midwife
Paint It Black (1989) . . . . Kyla Leif

Van Doren, Mamie
Films:
Running Wild (1955) . . . . .Irma Bean
High School Confidential (1958) . . . . .Gwen Dulaine
Teacher's Pet (1958) . . . . Peggy De Fore
Sex Kittens Go to College (1960) . . . .Dr. Mathilda West
Three Nuts in Search of a Bolt (1964) . . . . Saxie Symbol
Free Ride (1986) . . . . Debbie Stockwell
Magazines:
Playboy (Jan 1989) . . . . Women of the Sixties
- • 156—Topless under sheer yellow dress in photo from 1964.

Van Kamp, Merete
Films:
The Osterman Weekend (1983) . . . . . Zuna Brickman
- •• 0:01—Topless and brief buns in bed on a TV monitor, then topless getting injected by two intruders.
- • 0:35—Brief topless on video again while Rutger Hauer watches in the kitchen on TV.
- • 1:30—Topless again on video during TV show.

You Can't Hurry Love (1984) . . . . .Monique
Lethal Woman (1988) . . . . .Diana/Christine
- • 1:23—Very brief side view of left breast, reaching for towel after bath. Hard to see.

Miniseries:
Princess Daisy (1983) . . . . Daisy
TV:
Dallas (1985-86) . . . . Grace

Van Patten, Joyce
Films:
Making It (1971) . . . . Betty Fuller
Housewife (1972) . . . . .Bernadette
- • 0:46—Topless and buns on pool table getting attacked by Yaphet Kotto. Probably a body double, don't see her face.
- 1:04—Most of left breast getting on top of Kotto. In side view, you can see black tape over her nipple.
- • 1:05—Brief side of right breast under Kotto's arm several times after she falls on the floor with him.

The Falcon and the Snowman (1985) . . . . . .Mrs. Boyce
St. Elmo's Fire (1985) . . . . .Mrs. Beamish
Billy Galvin (1986) . . . . .Mae
Blind Date (1987) . . . . Nadia's Mother
Monkey Shines: An Experiment in Fear (1988)
. . . . .Dorothy Mann
Trust Me (1989) .Nettie Brown
TV:
The Good Guys (1968-70) . . . . .Claudia Gramus

• Van Tilborgh, Guusje
Films:
A Zed and Two Noughts (1985; British)
. . . . Caterina Bolnes
- • 0:42—Brief lower frontal nudity when Oliver lifts her skirt up in restroom to check to see what kind of panties she's wearing.
- • 0:51—Lower frontal nudity, then very brief topless while posing for photo by Van Meegeren.

Zjoek (1987; Dutch) . . . . Olga

Van Vooren, Monique
Films:
Tarzan and the She-Devil (1953) . . . . Lyra
Gigi (1958) . . . . Showgirl
Ash Wednesday (1973) . . . . German Woman
Sugar Cookies (1973) .Helene
Andy Warhol's Frankenstein
(1974; Italian/German/French) . . . . .Katherine
- •• 0:47—Topless in bed with Nicholas. Brief lower frontal nudity twice when he rolls on top of her.
- • 1:21—Left breast letting Sascha, the creature, caress her breast
- • 1:26—Topless, dead, when her breasts pop out of her blouse.

Wall Street (1987) . . . . n.a.

Vander Woude, Teresa
Films:
Killer Workout (1987) .Jaimy
a.k.a. Aerobi-Cide
- •• 0:43—Topless in locker room with Tommy during his nightmare.

Night Visitor (1989) . . . . Kelly Fremont

• *Vandernoot, Alexandra*
Films:
Mascara (1987; French/Belgian) . . . . Euridice
Made for Cable TV:
Strangers: Windows (1992; HBO). . . . . . The Woman
- •• 0:10—Topless, making love with her lover while Timothy Hutton watches from across the street.
- • 0:12—Right breast, while in bed struggling with her lover.
- • 0:13—Right breast, while tied to bed when Hutton comes to rescue her.
- • 0:14—Brief topless while sitting on toilet.

TV:
Highlander: The Series (1992-) . . . . .n.a.

Vanity
Singer.
a.k.a. D. D. Winters.
Real name is Denise Matthews.
Sister of model Patricia Matthews.
Films:
Tanya's Island (1980; Canadian) . . . . Tanya
0:04—Very brief topless and buns covered with paint during B&W segment.
- ••• 0:07—Nude caressing herself and dancing during the opening credits.
- •• 0:09—Nude making love on the beach.
0:11—Brief right breast, while talking to Lobo.
- •• 0:19—Brief topless on the beach with Lobo, then more topless while yelling at him.
- • 0:28—Mostly topless in flimsy halter top exploring a cave.
- • 0:33—Full frontal nudity undressing in tent.
- • 0:35—Left breast sleeping. Dark, hard to see.
0:37—Buns while sleeping.
- • 0:40—Topless superimposed over another scene.
0:48—Brief buns swimming in the ocean.
- •• 0:51—Full frontal nudity walking out of the ocean and getting dressed.
- • 0:53—Brief topless in open blouse.
- •• 1:08—Topless in middle of compound when Lobo rapes her in front of Blue.
- • 1:16—Full frontal nudity running through the jungle in slow motion. Brief buns.
Terror Train (1980; Canadian) . . . . Merry
The Best of Sex and Violence (1981). . . . . . . Tanya
- • 0:24—Buns and topless in various scenes from *Tanya's Island.*
Famous T & A (1982) . . . . Tanya
(No longer available for purchase, check your video store for rental.)
- • 1:02—Topless scenes from *Tanya's Island.*
The Last Dragon (1985) . . . . Laura
52 Pick-Up (1986). Doreen
- ••• 0:47—Topless, stripping in room while Roy Scheider takes Polaroid pictures.
- • 0:52—Topless under sheer purple nightgown. Partial buns in G-string underneath also.

Never Too Young to Die (1986) . . . . . . Donja Deering
- • 1:04—Wearing a bikini swimsuit, putting on suntan lotion. Brief topless in quick cuts making love with John in a cabin bedroom.
Deadly Illusion (1987) . . . . .Rina
Action Jackson (1988) . . . . Sydney Ash
- •• 0:29—Topless in bed with Craig T. Nelson.
Neon City (1991). . . . . Reno
Made for Cable Movies:
Memories of Murder (1990; Lifetime). . . . . Carmen
Made for Cable TV:
Tales From the Crypt: Dead Wait (1991)
. . . . .Catarine
- • 0:15—Brief topless and buns several times in and out of bed with James Remar.
Magazines:
Playboy (Jan 1985) . . . . The Girls of Rock 'n' Roll
Playboy (May 1985). . . . . n.a.
Playboy (Sep 1986) . . . . Playboy Gallery
129—Photo taken Jan 1981
Playboy (Apr 1988) . . . . Vanity
- ••• 68-79—Nude.
Playboy (Dec 1988) . . . . .Sex Stars of 1988
- ••• 185—Topless.
Playboy (Jan 1989). . . . . .Women of the Eighties
- •• 256—Right breast.
Playboy (Oct 1989) . . . . Grapevine
- • 175—Upper half topless in B&W photo.
Playboy's Nudes (Oct 1990) . . . . .Herself
- ••• 25—Topless.

Vargas, Valentina
Films:
The Name of the Rose (1986) . . . . The Girl
- ••• 0:46—Topless and buns making love with Christian Slater in the monastery kitchen.
The Big Blue (1988) . . . . Bonita
Street of No Return (1991; U.S./French). . . . . Celia

Vasquez, Roberta
Films:
Easy Wheels (1989) . . . . Tondalco
Picasso Trigger (1989) . . . . Pantera
Street Asylum (1989) . . . . Kristen
Guns (1990) . . . . Nicole Justin
- •• 0:50—Right breast while making love on motorcycle with her boyfriend.
The Rookie (1990) . . . . .Heather Torres
Do or Die (1991) . . . . Nicole Justin
0:06—Sort of topless under water in spa.
- •• 0:56—Topless, making love with Bruce, outside.
Video Tapes:
Playmate Playoffs . . . . Playmate
Playboy Video Calendar 1987 (1986). . . . . Playmate
Wet and Wild (1989) . . . . Model
Playmates at Play (1990) . . . . Hardbodies
Magazines:
Playboy (Nov 1984) . . . . Playmate

Vaughn, Linda Rhys

Video Tapes:
Playboy's Playmate Review (1982) . . . . . . Playmate
••• 1:06—Nude on horseback, then next to stream.
Playmates at Play (1990) . . . . .Bareback
Magazines:
Playboy (Apr 1982) . . . . Playmate

Vega, Isela

Films:
Bring Me the Head of Alfredo Garcia (1974)
. . . . Elita
• 0:25—Brief right breast a couple of times, then brief
topless in bed with Warren Oaks.
••• 0:44—Topless when Kris Kristofferson rips her top
off. Long scene.
•• 0:52—Topless sitting in shower with wet hair.
•• 1:49—Still from shower scene during credits.
Drum (1976) . . . . Marianna
• 0:04—Topless in bed with the maid, Rachel.
•• 0:22—Brief topless standing next to the bed with
Maxwell.
Barbarosa (1982) . . . . Josephina
Magazines:
Playboy (Jul 1974). . . . . .Viva Vega!
••• 80-83—Full frontal nudity.
Playboy (Nov 1974) . . . . Sex in Cinema 1974
••• 147—Topless from *Bring Me the Head of Alfredo Gar-
cia.*
Playboy (Nov 1976) . . . . Sex in Cinema 1976
•• 155—Topless.

Venora, Diane

Films:
Wolfen (1981). Rebecca Neff
The Cotton Club (1984) . . . . .Gloria Swanson
Terminal Choice (1985; Canadian) . . . . .Anna
0:44—In lingerie, talking to Frank.
• 0:48—Brief left breast, making love in bed with
Frank. Don't see her face.
F/X (1986) . . . . Ellen
0:37—Walking around her apartment in a white slip.
Bird (1988) . . . . Chan Richardson Parker

Venus, Brenda

Films:
Foxy Brown (1974) . . . . Arabella
The Eiger Sanction (1975) . . . . George
• 0:50—Very brief topless opening her blouse to get
Clint Eastwood to climb up a hill.
• 1:06—Topless taking off her clothes in Eastwood's
room, just before she tries to kill him. Dark, hard to
see.
Swashbuckler (1976). . . . . .Bath Attendant
48 Hrs. (1982). . . . . Hooker
Magazines:
Playboy (Jul 1986). . . . . .Henry's Venus
•• 72-79—B&W photos. Full frontal nudity with lots of
diffusion.

Verkaik, Petra

Films:
Pyrates (1991) . . . . Basia
Video Tapes:
Playboy Video Calendar 1991 (1990)
. . . . November
••• 0:45—Nude.
Sexy Lingerie II (1990) . . . . Model
Wet and Wild II (1990). . . . . Model
Sexy Lingerie III (1991). . . . . Model
Wet and Wild III (1991) . . . . Model
Playboy Playmates in Paradise (1992). . . . Playmate
Magazines:
Playboy (Dec 1989) . . . . Playmate
Playboy's Book of Lingerie (Jan 1991) . . . . . .Herself
••• 29-31—Full frontal nudity.
Playboy's Book of Lingerie (Mar 1991). . . . . .Herself
• 22—Left breast.
•• 100—Right breast.
Playboy's Book of Lingerie (Mar 1992) . . . . . .Herself
••• 26—Full frontal nudity.
••• 57—Full frontal nudity.
Playboy's Book of Lingerie (May 1992) . . . . .Herself
•• 26-27—Right breast and partial lower frontal nudity.
•• 51—Right breast.
Playboy's Book of Lingerie (Jul 1992) . . . . . . .Herself
• 84—Lower frontal nudity.

Vernon, Kate

Daughter of actor John Vernon.
Films:
Chained Heat (1983; U.S./German) . . . . Cellmate
Alphabet City (1984) . . . . Angie
Roadhouse 66 (1984) . . . . Melissa Duran
• 1:03—Brief topless in back of car with Judge Rein-
hold. Dark.
Pretty in Pink (1986) . . . . Benny
The Last Days of Philip Banter (1987). . . . . Brent
Hostile Takeover (1988; Canadian). . . . . .Sally
a.k.a. Office Party
• 0:35—Very brief, left breast undressing in office with
John Warner. Dark.
•• 0:39—Right breast, turning over in her sleep, then
playing with the chain.
Made for TV Movies:
Daughters of Privilege (1990). . . . . .Diana
TV:
Falcon Crest (1984-85). . . . . Lorraine Prescott
Who's the Boss? (1990) . . . . Kathleen Sawyer

Veronica, Christina

a.k.a. Christina Veronique.
Films:
Sexpot (1986) . . . . Betty
••• 0:28—In bra, then topless with her two sisters when
their bras pop off. (She's on the left.)
•• 0:46—Topless taking off her top in boat with Gorilla.
• 0:54—Topless lying on the grass with Gorilla.
• 1:28—Topless during outtakes of 0:28 scene.

Thrilled to Death (1988) . . . . Satin
- •• 0:33—Topless talking to Cliff during porno film shoot.

Girlfriend from Hell (1989) . . . . Dancer
- ••• 1:17—Topless dancing on stage in club.

Party Incorporated (1989) . . . . Christina
a.k.a. Party Girls
- ••• 0:52—Buns and topless dancing in front of everybody at party.

Roadhouse (1989). . . . . Strip Joint Girl

A Woman Obsessed (1989). . . . . Crystal the Maid

Corporate Affairs (1990) . . . . Tanning Woman
- 0:47—Side of right breast, getting tanned.

They Bite (1991). . . . . Tammy
- ••• 0:20—Topless in bed during porno movie shoot.
- ••• 0:55—Topless, sunbathing on the beach while a guy rubs suntan lotion on her.
- • 1:03—Topless on the beach during playback of film.
- •• 1:08—Topless on boat, getting attacked by monster.
- • 1:09—Topless in water, struggling with the monster.
- • 1:10—Brief topless on beach during playback of film.

Verrell, Cec

Films:

Runaway (1984) . . . . Hooker
- •• 0:44—Topless in hotel bathroom while Tom Selleck sneaks into her room.

Hollywood Vice Squad (1986). . . . . Judy

Silk (1986) . . . . Jenny Sleighton

Hell Comes to Frogtown (1987). . . . . Centinella
- •• 0:19—Topless taking off her blouse and getting into sleeping bag with Roddy Piper. Brief topless again after he throws her off him.

Transformations (1988). . . . . Antonia

TV:

Supercarrier (1988)
- . . . . Lt. Cmdr. Ruth "Beebee" Rutkowski

Video Tapes:

Inside Out (1992) . . . . The Psychiatrist/Shrink Wrap
- ••• 0:18—In red bra, then topless making love with the guy she picked up in the bar.

Inside Out 3 (1992). . . . . Susan/Tango

Veruschka

Ballet dancer.

Films:

Blow-Up (1966; British/Italian) . . . . Veruschka

The Bride (1985). . . . . Countess

Magazines:

Playboy (Jan 1974) . . . . Painted Lady
- ••• 122-129—Full frontal nudity in various artfully painted body poses.

Playboy (Jan 1989) . . . . Women of the Seventies
- •• 214—Topless wearing body paint.

Playboy's Nudes (Oct 1990). . . . . Herself
- •• 55—Full frontal nudity with a painted body.

Vetri, Victoria

a.k.a. *Playboy* Playmate Angela Dorian.

Films:

Group Marriage (1972) . . . . Jan
- ••• 0:28—Buns and topless getting into bed with Dennis, Sander and Chris. More topless sitting in bed. Long scene.
- • 1:19—Brief side view of right breast in lifeguard booth.

Invasion of the Bee Girls (1973) . . . . Julie Zorn
- • 0:30—Brief topless getting molested by jerks.
- ••• 1:19—Topless in the bee transformer, then brief buns getting rescued.

Made for TV Movies:

Night Chase (1970) . . . . n.a.

Magazines:

Playboy (Sep 1967) . . . . Playmate
Used alternate name of Angela Dorian for the centerfold. Playmate of the Year 1968.

Playboy (Nov 1972). . . . . Sex in Cinema 1972
- • 166—Topless in a photo from *Group Marriage*. Small photo, hard to see anything.

Playboy (Jan 1974). . . . . Twenty Years of Playmates
- •• 108—Left breast while wearing shawl.

Vickers, Vicki

a.k.a. Adult film actress Raven.

Films:

Angel Eyes (1991) . . . . n.a.

Video Tapes:

The Girls of Penthouse (1984) . . . . The Locket
- ••• 0:17—Topless, then nude, making love.

Penthouse Love Stories (1986)
- . . . . Snapshot and Loveboat Woman
- ••• 0:37—Nude, taking pictures of herself.
- •• 0:51—Topless on hammock watching Julie Parton.
- •• 0:55—Left breast, twice while lying on hammock.

Vogel, Darlene

Films:

Back to the Future, Part II (1989) . . . . Spike

Ski School (1990). . . . . Lori
- • 1:03—Topless in bed with Johnny.

Vold, Ingrid

Films:

Side Roads (1988) . . . . Bonnie Velasco
- • 0:29—Brief topless in motel room, getting undressed and carried into bed by Joe.
- 0:30—In white lingerie, talking with Joe. Long scene.
- 0:56—In white bra and panties, changing clothes.
- • 1:45—Brief topless in mirror, getting out of bed.

Communion (1989). . . . Uncredited Magician's Assistant

Angel of Passion (1991) . . . . Vanessa
- • 1:01—Brief topless posing on the couch for the photographer.

Von Palleske, Heidi

Films:
Dead Ringers (1988) . . . . Cary
- 0:45—Brief left breast sticking out of bathrobe, while talking to Jeremy Irons in the bathroom.

Blind Fear (1989; Canadian) . . . . Marla
Renegades (1989) . . . . Hooker in Bar
White Light (1990) . . . . Debra Halifax
Deceived (1991) . . . . Mrs. Peabody

Voorhees, Deborah

a.k.a. Debisue Voorhees.
Films:
Avenging Angel (1985) . . . . Roxie
Friday the 13th, Part V—A New Beginning (1985)
. . . . Tina
- ••• 0:41—Topless after making love with Eddie, then lying down and relaxing just before getting killed.
- • 0:43—Buns and brief left breast when Eddie turns her over and discovers her dead.

Appointment with Fear (1988) . . . . Ruth
- • 0:21—Very, very brief side view of left breast taking off bra to go swimming, then very brief topless getting out of the pool.

Vorgan, Gigi

Films:
Hardcore (1979) . . . . Teenage Girl
- • 0:32—Topless on sofa in Peter Boyle's apartment.

Caveman (1981) . . . . Folg's Daughter
Children of a Lesser God (1986) . . . . Announcer
Rain Man (1988) . . . . Voice-Over Actress
Red Heat (1988) . . . . Audrey
Vital Signs (1989) . . . . Nell
TV:
Knots Landing (1984) . . . . Carol

• Wagner, Lindsay

Films:
Two People (1973) . . . . Deidre McCluskey
(Not available on video tape.)

Wagner, Lori

Films:
Caligula (1980) . . . . Agrippina
(X-rated, 147 minute version.)
- ••• 1:16—Nude, making love with Anneka Di Lorenzo. Long scene.

UHF (1989) . . . . Mud Wrestler
Video Tapes:
Penthouse: On the Wild Side (1988) . . . . Lover
- • 0:54—Nude with Anneka de Lorenzo during scenes from The Making of Caligula.

Magazines:
Penthouse (May 1980) . . . . The Making of Caligula
- • 142—Lower frontal nudity and left breast.

Penthouse (Jun 1980) . . . . Anneka and Lori
- ••• 142-153—Nude (she has lighter hair) with Anneka di Lorenzo.

Penthouse (Feb 1991) . . . . Lori–Caligula Revisited
- •• Nude in recent photos and Caligula photos.

Wahl, Corinne

See: Alphen, Corrine.

• Walden, Lynette

Films:
Split Image (1982) . . . . Sexy Girl
Mobsters (1991) . . . . Cute Debutante
a.k.a. Mobsters—The Evil Empire
- •• 0:32—Topless when Richard Grieco undoes her dress.

Walker, Arnetia

Films:
The Wizard of Speed & Time (1988)
. . . . Tina Dreem/Running Girl
Scenes from the Class Struggle in Beverly Hills
(1989) . . . . To-Bel
- • 0:37—Topless making love with Frank on the sofa.
- •• 1:10—Topless in bed waking up with Howard.
- ••• 1:23—Topless making love on top of Ed Begley, Jr. on the floor.

Love Crimes (1991) . . . . Maria Johnson
(Unrated version reviewed.)
Made for Cable Movies:
Cast a Deadly Spell (1991; HBO) . . . . Hipolite Kropolkin
TV:
Nurses (1991-) . . . . Annie

• Walker, Christina

Films:
The Banker (1989) . . . . Girl
- • 0:18—Topless on bed with Jeff Conaway

The Malibu Beach Vampires (1991)
. . . . Vice President Vampire Affairs

Walker, Kathryn

Films:
Midnight Dancer (1987; Australian) . . . . Kathy
a.k.a. Belinda
Dangerous Game (1988; Australian) . . . . Kathryn
- • 1:19—Very, very brief topless when her black top is pulled up while struggling with Murphy.

• Walker, Tracy

Films:
Invisible Maniac (1990) . . . . Telescope Gal
- •• 0:01—Nude, taking off clothes during opening credits. Nice dancing.

Video Tapes:
Bikini Blitz (1990) . . . . Model

Wallace Stone, Dee

a.k.a. Dee Wallace.
Wife of actor Christopher Stone.
Films:
The Hills Have Eyes (1977) . . . . Lynne Wood

10 (1979) . . . . Mary Lewis
The Howling (1981) . . . . Karen White
E.T. The Extraterrestrial (1982) . . . . .Mary
Cujo (1983) . . . . Donna
    0:33—Brief left thigh and left bun, getting felt up by
    Christopher Stone in the kitchen.
Secret Admirer (1985). . . . . .Connie Ryan
Critters (1986) . . . . .Helen Brown
Shadow Play (1986). . . . . .Morgan Hanna
  • 1:06—Brief topless making love with Ron Kuhlman.
    Kind of dark and hard to see.
The Christmas Visitor (1987). . . . . .Elizabeth
Club Life (1987) . . . . .Tilly Francesca
I'm Dangerous Tonight (1990) . . . . Wanda
Alligator II: The Mutation (1991). . . . . Christine Hodges
Popcorn (1991). . . . . Suzanne
Made for TV Movies:
Sins of Innocence (1986). . . . . Vicki McGary
Addicted to his Love (1988) . . . . . . Betty Ann Brennan
Stranger on My Land (1988). . . . . Annie
TV:
Together We Stand (1986) . . . . .Lori Randall

Walter, Jessica

Films:
Lilith (1964) . . . . Laura
Grand Prix (1966). . . . . Pat
The Group (1966). . . . . Libby MacAusland
Play Misty for Me (1971). . . . . .Evelyn
  • 0:13—Very brief right breast in bed with Clint East-
    wood. Lit with blue light. Hard to see anything.
The Flamingo Kid (1984). . . . . .Phyllis Brody
Miniseries:
Wheels (1978). . . . . .Ursula
Bare Essence (1983) . . . . .Ava Marshall
TV:
For the People (1965) . . . . Phyllis Koster
Amy Prentiss (1974-75). . . . . .Amy Prentiss
All That Glitters (1977) . . . . .Joan Hamlyn
The Round Table (1992-) . . . . .n.a.

Walters, Julie

Films:
Educating Rita (1983; British) . . . . .Rita
She'll be Wearing Pink Pyjamas (1985; British)
. . . . Fran
  ••• 0:07—Full frontal nudity taking a shower with the
    other women. Long scene.
  •• 0:58—Nude, undressing and going skinny dipping
    in mountain lake, then getting out. Nice bun shot
    walking into the lake.
Personal Services (1987). . . . . Cynthia Payne
  • 0:21—Very brief side view of left breast, while reach-
    ing to turn off radio in the bathtub. Her face is cov-
    ered with cream.
Prick Up Your Ears (1987; British) . . . . Elise Orton
Buster (1988) . . . . .June
Stepping Out (1991). Vera

Walters, Laurie

Films:
The Harrad Experiment (1973). . . . . . . Sheila Grove
  • 0:29—Topless in white panties with Don Johnson.
  • 0:40—Nude taking off blue dress and getting into
    the swimming pool with Johnson.
The Harrad Summer (1974). . . . . Sheila Grove
a.k.a. Student Union
    0:02—Topless undressing in bathroom. Long shot,
    out of focus.
  •• 1:04—Topless lying on lounge chair, then buns and
    more topless getting up and pushing Harry into the
    pool.
Famous T & A (1982) . . . . Sheila Grove
(No longer available for purchase, check your video
store for rental.)
  • 1:08—Topless scene from *The Harrad Experiment.*
  •• 1:11—Nude pool scene from *The Harrad Experiment.*
Made for TV Movies:
Eight is Enough: A Family Reunion (1987)
. . . . Joannie Bradford
TV:
Eight is Enough (1977-81) . . . . Joannie Bradford

Waltrip, Kim

Films:
Pretty Smart (1986) . . . . . . .Sara Gentry (the teacher)
  •• 0:53—Topless sunbathing with her students.
Nights in White Satin (1987) . . . . Stevie Hughes
    0:37—In white wig, bra, panties, garter belt and
    stocking during photo session.
    0:39—Brief side view of left breast in black slip dur-
    ing photo session.
  • 0:53—Topless in bathtub with Walker. Out of focus,
    hard to see.

Ward, Pamela

Films:
Hellhole (1985) . . . . .Tina
School Spirit (1985) . . . . .Girl in Sorority Room
  ••• 0:15—Buns, then topless in her room while Billy is
    invisible.
  ••• 0:16—More topless and buns with other women in
    shower room.
The Women's Club (1987) . . . . . . Fashion Show Woman
Video Tapes:
Battling Beauties (1983). . . . . Foxy Boxer/Valley Girl

Ward, Rachel

Wife of actor Bryan Brown.
Films:
Night School (1980) . . . . Elanor
  • 0:24—In sheer white bra and panties, taking off
    clothes to take a shower. Topless taking off bra. Hard
    to see because she's behind a shower curtain.
    0:28—Buns, when her boyfriend rubs red paint all
    over her in the shower.
The Final Terror (1981). . . . . .Margaret
Sharky's Machine (1981) . . . . .Dominoe

Dead Men Don't Wear Plaid (1982) . . . . . . Juliet Forrest
Against All Odds (1984) . . . . Jessie Wyler
    0:49—Very brief buns lying down with Jeff Bridges.
    0:50—Wet white dress in water. Long shot, don't see
    anything.
    1:01—The sweaty temple scene. Erotic, but you
    don't really see anything.
The Good Wife (1987; Australian) . . . . Marge Hills
    a.k.a. The Umbrella Woman
Hotel Colonial (1988) . . . . Irene Costa
How to Get Ahead in Advertising (1988). . . . . Julia
After Dark, My Sweet (1990) . . . . Fay Anderson
    • 1:22—Very, very brief half of right breast under Jas-
    on Patric in bed when he moves slightly.
Christopher Columbus: The Discovery (1992) . . . . . .n.a.
Made for Cable Movies:
Fortress (1985; HBO) . . . . Sally Jones
    • 0:38—Swimming in a sheer bra underwater.
Black Magic (1992; Showtime) . . . . Lillian Blatman
Miniseries:
The Thorn Birds (1983) . . . . Meggie Cleary
Made for TV Movies:
And the Sea Will Tell (1991) . . . . Jennifer Jenkins
Magazines:
Playboy (Mar 1984). . . . . Roving Eye
    ••• 203—Topless in photos that weren't used in *Night
    School.*

Warner, Julie
Films:
Flatliners (1990) . . . . One of Joe's Women
Doc Hollywood (1991). . . . . Lou
    • 0:15—Silhouette of left breast in water while Micha-
    el J. Fox sleeps.
    ••• 0:16—Topless several times, skinny dipping in lake,
    then getting out while Fox watches.

Warren, Jennifer
Films:
Night Moves (1975) . . . . Paula
    •• 0:56—Topless in bed with Gene Hackman.
    • 0:57—Right breast after making love in bed with
    Hackman.
Another Man, Another Chance (1977; U.S./French)
    . . . . .Mary
Slap Shot (1977). . . . . Francine Dunlop
Ice Castles (1979) . . . . Deborah Macland
TV:
Paper Dolls (1984) . . . . .Dinah Caswell

• Warren, Sandra
Films:
Curtains (1983; Canadian) . . . . Tara Demillo
    • 0:58—Side view of left breast practicing a scene in
    the play with Summers.
Terminal Choice (1985; Canadian) . . . . . . Nurse Tipton

Wasa, Maxine
Films:
L.A. Bounty (1989) . . . . Model
    • 0:07—Right breast while posing for Wings Hauser
    while he paints. Left breast, getting up. Long shot.
    • 0:26—Left breast while posing on couch for Hauser.
    •• 0:38—Topless lying on couch again.
Savage Beach (1989). . . . . Sexy Beauty
    ••• 0:08—Side view of left breast, in pool with Shane,
    then topless getting out of pool.
    ••• 0:10—Topless while Shane talks on the phone.
Made for Cable TV:
Dream On: The First Episode (1990; HBO)
    . . . . Andrea Kelly
Video Tapes:
Wet and Wild (1989) . . . . Model
Magazines:
Playboy (Nov 1989) . . . . Sex in Cinema 1989
    •• 134—Side view of left breast from *Savage Beach.*

Watkins, Michelle
Films:
Terms of Endearment (1983) . . . . Woman
The Outing (1987). Faylene
    •• 0:12—Topless taking off her top, standing by the
    edge of the swimming pool, then running topless
    through the house with panties on.

Watson, Alberta
Films:
In Praise of Older Women (1978; Canadian)
    . . . . Mitzi
    •• 0:51—Topless sitting in chair talking with Tom Be-
    renger, then more topless lying in bed. Long scene.
Power Play (1978; Canadian) . . . . Donna
    0:21—Brief topless lying on table getting shocked
    through her nipples.
Stone Cold Dead (1979; Canadian) . . . . Olivia Page
The Soldier (1982) . . . . Susan Goodman
The Keep (1983) . . . . Eva Cuza
    • 0:59—Very brief topless making love with Scott
    Glenn, then brief lower frontal nudity.
Best Revenge (1984) . . . . n.a.
White of the Eye (1988). . . . . Ann Mason
The Hitman (1991) . . . . Christine De Vera
Made for TV Movies:
Women of Valor (1986) . . . . .Helen

Way, Renee
Films:
The Newlydeads (1988). . . . . n.a.
Party Plane (1988) . . . . Andy
    ••• 0:01—Topless taking off her blouse to fix the plane.
    ••• 0:06—Topless sitting on edge of spa.
    ••• 0:11—Topless again, getting out of spa.
    • 0:12—Brief topless dropping her towel while talking
    to Tim.

Wayne, April

Former model for Ujena Swimwear (*Swimwear Illustrated* magazine).

Films:

Moon in Scorpio (1987)................... Isabel
- 0:32—Brief right breast in bed with a guy.
- 0:35—Brief topless putting bathing suit on in a bathroom on a boat when a guy opens the door.

Party Camp (1987) .... Nurse Brenda

Video Tapes:

Swimwear Illustrated: On Location (1986)
.... Swimsuit Model

Wayne, Carol

Films:

The Party (1968).................... June Warren
Scavenger Hunt (1979)..................... Nurse
Savannah Smiles (1983) .... Doreen
Heartbreakers (1984) .... Candy
    0:22—In black wig and bra posing for Peter Coyote in his studio.
  ••• 0:41—In white bra and panties, then brief topless in the mirror stripping in front of Coyote and Nick Mancuso. Then brief topless lying in bed with Coyote.
Surf II (1984)..................... Mrs. O'Finlay

TV:

The Tonight Show .... Regular

Magazines:

Playboy (Feb 1984)......... 101 Nights with Johnny
  ••• 56-61—Full frontal nudity.

Weatherly, Shawn

Miss South Carolina 1980.
Miss U.S.A. 1980.
Miss Universe 1980.

Films:

Cannonball Run II (1984) .... Dean's Girl
Police Academy III: Back in Training (1986)
.... Cadet Adams
Party Line (1988) .... Asst. D.A. Stacy Sloane
Shadowzone (1989) .... Dr. Kidwell
Thieves of Fortune (1989)................... Peter
- 1:09—Brief topless several times, taking a shower (while wearing beard and moustache disguise).
  ••• 1:21—Topless in white panties distracting tribe so she can get away.
Amityville 1992: It's About Time (1992) .... n.a.

TV:

Shaping Up (1984) .... Melissa McDonald
Baywatch (1988-90) .... Jil Riley

Weaver, Jacki

Films:

Alvin Purple (1973; Australian)..... Second Sugar Girl
  •• 0:33—Brief full frontal nudity, lying in bean bag chair.

Jock Petersen (1974; Australian) ...... Susie Petersen
  a.k.a. Petersen
  ••• 0:01—Full frontal nudity lying in bed with Jock.
Picnic at Hanging Rock (1975) .... Minnie
The Removalists (1975) .... Marilyn Carter
Caddie (1976) .... Josie
Squizzy Taylor (1984)...................... Dolly

Weaver, Sigourney

Films:

Annie Hall (1977)........ Alvy's Date Outside Theatre
Alien (1979)............................ Ripley
Eyewitness (1981) .... Tony Sokolow
Deal of the Century (1983) .... Mrs. De Voto
The Year of Living Dangerously (1983; Australian)
.... Jill Bryant
Ghostbusters (1984) .... Dana Barrett
Aliens (1986)........................... Ripley
Half Moon Street (1986) .... Lauren Slaughter
  a.k.a. Escort Girl
- 0:05—Brief topless in the bathtub.
  •• 0:11—Brief topless in the bathtub again.
- 0:18—Brief buns and side view of right breast putting on makeup in front of the mirror. Wearing a black garter belt and stockings.
  ••• 0:39—Topless riding exercise bike while being photographed, then brief topless getting out of the shower.
    0:46—Very, very brief topless wearing a sheer black blouse with no bra during daydream sequence.
- 0:50—Brief topless in bed with Michael Caine, then left breast.
    1:16—In braless, wet, white blouse in bathroom after knocking a guy out.
One Woman or Two (1986; French)........ Jessica
  a.k.a. Une Femme Ou Deux
    1:30—In braless white blouse.
  •• 1:31—Very brief side view of left breast in bed with Gerard Depardieu.
Gorillas in the Mist (1988) .... Dian Fossey
Ghostbusters II (1989) .... Dana Barrett
Working Girl (1989).............. Katherine Parker
    1:22—In white lingerie, sitting in bed, then talking to Harrison Ford.
1492 (1992)...................... Queen Isabella

Magazines:

Playboy (Oct 1992) .... Grapevine

Webb, Chloe

Films:

Sid and Nancy (1986; British) .... Nancy
- 0:21—Left breast, under Sid's arm in bed with him. Covered up, hard to see.
  •• 0:44—Topless in bed after making love, then arguing with Sid.

The Belly of an Architect (1987; British/Italian)
. . . . .Louisa Kracklite
- •• 0:01 — Very brief right breast, making love on train with Brian Dennehy. Brief side view of right breast sitting up and putting camisole top on.
- • 0:56 — Brief buns in room with Lambert Wilson.
- • 1:07 — Brief buns, lying in bed with Wilson.
  1:27 — Topless B&W photos of a pregnant woman. Supposedly her, but probably not.
Twins (1988). . . . . .Linda Mason
Heart Condition (1990). . . . . Crystal Gerrity
  0:00 — In black lingerie, photographing the Senator with Peisha.
  1:00 — In black lingerie in bedroom with Bob Hoskins.
Queens Logic (1991). . . . . .Patricia
Made for TV Movies:
Lucky Day (1991) . . . . .Allison Campbell
TV:
Thicke of the Night (1983) . . . . .Regular
China Beach (1988) . . . . .Laurette Barber

Weber, Sharon Clark
See: Clark, Sharon.

Weigel, Teri
The first *Playboy* Playmate to star in adult films *after* she became a Playmate.
Adult Films:
The Barlow Affairs (1991) . . . . .n.a.
Lingerie Busters (1991). . . . . .n.a.
Starr (1991). . . . . .n.a.
Wicked (1991) . . . . .n.a.
  and many more...
Films:
Cheerleader Camp (1987). . . . . Pam Bently
  a.k.a. Bloody Pom Poms
- •• 0:12 — Topless taking off her swimsuit top while sunbathing.
Glitch (1988). . . . . .Lydia
  0:41 — In pink bathing suit talking to blonde guy.
- • 0:54 — Very brief side view of right breast in bathtub with dark haired guy.
Return of the Killer Tomatoes (1988). . . Matt's Playmate
The Banker (1989) . . . . .Jaynie
- ••• 0:02 — Taking off dress, then in lingerie, then topless making love with Osbourne in bed. More topless after.
Far From Home (1989) . . . . Woman in Trailer
- •• 0:16 — Topless making love when Drew Barrymore peeks in window.
Night Visitor (1989). . . . . .Victim in Cellar
- • 0:50 — Brief out of focus topless changing tops in the cellar.
- • 0:55 — Right breast, during ceremony. Very brief topless just before being stabbed.
Savage Beach (1989) . . . . .Anjelica
- ••• 0:33 — Topless taking off black teddy and getting into bed to make love.

- •• 0:47 — Topless making love in the back seat of car.
Marked for Death (1990). . . . . .Sexy Girl #2
- • 0:39 — Brief topless on bed with Jimmy when Steven Seagal bursts into the room. (She's the brunette.)
Predator 2 (1990) . . . . Columbian Girl
- • 0:22 — Brief topless making love on bed. More topless several times being held on the floor, brief full frontal nudity getting up when the Predator starts his attack.
Video Tapes:
Playboy Video Centerfold: Teri Weigel (1986)
. . . . Playmate
- ••• 0:00 — Nude, in shower, taking a bath, in bedroom.
- ••• 0:15 — Nude outside in spa, and modeling lingerie with Dona Speir and Hope Marie Carlton.
- ••• 0:18 — Nude in bed taking of black lingerie outfit.
Playboy Video Calendar 1988 (1987). . . . . Playmate
Playboy's Fantasies (1987). . . . . The Mannequin
- ••• 0:21 — Nude, after coming to life from being a mannequin.
Wet and Wild (1989) . . . . Model
Playboy's Fantasies II (1990) . . . . .Grand Illusions
- ••• 0:31 — Nude outside in the woods during a surveyor's fantasy.
Sexy Lingerie II (1990) . . . . Model
Wet and Wild II (1990). . . . . Model
**Secrets of Making Love... To the Same Person
Forever** (1991) . . . . Mirror, Spa & Bed
- ••• 0:33 — Topless and buns in front of mirror, in spa and tied up in bed.
- • 0:48 — Topless and lower frontal nudity in spa and in bed.
Sexy Lingerie III (1991). . . . . Model
Inside Out 3 (1992). . . . . .Woman/The Portal
- •• 0:27 — Brief topless, standing up in the water.
Magazines:
Playboy (Apr 1986) . . . . Playmate
Playboy's Book of Lingerie (Mar 1991). . . . . .Herself
- • 14 — Lower frontal nudity in hot pink lingerie.
- ••• 30 — Topless.
Penthouse (May 1992) . . . . .Shooting Star
- ••• 110-121 — Nude.

• Weiss, Amy-Rochelle
Films:
Round Trip to Heaven (1992) . . . . Yvette
- ••• 0:19 — In black bra and G-string in bedroom with Corey Feldman, then topless and buns on top of him in bed.
Music Videos:
What Comes Naturally/Sheena Easton
. . . . Body Double for Sheena
Video Tapes:
Sexy Lingerie III (1991). . . . . Model
Intimate Workout For Lovers (1992) Water Workout
- ••• 0:21 — Nude, outside by swimming pool and in pool.

Playboy's Erotic Fantasies (1992) . . . . .Model
Magazines:
Playboy's Book of Lingerie (Nov 1991) . . . . . Herself
••• 52—Topless.
Playboy's Book of Lingerie (Jan 1992) . . . . . . Herself
••• 66—Topless.
Playboy's Book of Lingerie (Mar 1992) . . . . . Herself
••• 100-101—Buns and topless.
Playboy's Book of Lingerie (May 1992) . . . . . Herself
••• 70—Full frontal nudity.
Playboy (Jul 1992) . . . . .Grapevine
••• 170—Topless in swimming pool. B&W.

Weiss, Roberta

Films:
Autumn Born (1979) . . . . Melissa
    0:07—Buns, wearing panties and bending over desk
    to get whipped.
Cross Country (1983; Canadian) . . . . .Alma Jean
    •• 0:59—Topless on bed with two other people.
The Dead Zone (1983) . . . . .Alma Frechette
    • 0:49—Briefly in beige bra, then brief topless when
    the killer rips her blouse open during Christopher
    Walken's vision.
Abducted (1986; Canadian) . . . . Renee
Made for Cable TV:
The Hitchhiker: And If We Dream (1987; HBO)
. . . . Rosanne Lucas
(Available on *The Hitchhiker, Volume 3*.)
    •• 0:11—Topless and buns in barn making love with
    Stephen Collins.
    •• 0:17—Topless in dream classroom with Collins.
    • 0:23—Brief topless in bed after second dream with
    Collins.

Welch, Lisa

Films:
Revenge of the Nerds (1984) . . . . Suzy
Magazines:
Playboy (Sep 1980) . . . . Playmate
    ••• 118-129—Full frontal nudity.

Welch, Tahnee

Daughter of actress Raquel Welch.
Films:
Cocoon (1985) . . . . Kitty
    1:01—Buns walking into swimming pool.
Lethal Obsession (1987) . . . . Daniela Santini
    a.k.a. The Joker
    0:14—Buns, putting on robe after talking to John on
    the phone.
    • 0:15—Half of left breast, taking off coat to hug John
    in the kitchen.
    0:16—Sort of left breast, in bed with John. Too dark
    to see anything.
    1:16—Buns, getting an injection.
Cocoon, The Return (1988) . . . . Kitty
TV:
Falcon Crest (1987-89) . . . . .Shannon

Weller, Mary Louise

Films:
The Evil (1977) . . . . .Laurie Belden
Animal House (1978) . . . . Mandy Pepperidge
    ••• 0:38—In white bra, then topless in bedroom while
    John Belushi watches on a ladder through the win-
    dow.
The Bell Jar (1979) . . . . Doreen
Blood Tide (1982) . . . . Sherry
Forced Vengeance (1982) . . . . .Claire Bonner
    • 1:04—Brief topless, struggling with the bad guy.
    • 1:08—Very brief right breast then left breast, while
    lying dead on the floor.
Q (1982) . . . . Mrs. Pauley

Welles, Gwen

Films:
A Safe Place (1971) . . . . Bari
Hit (1973) . . . . Sherry Nielson
California Split (1974) . . . . Susan Peters
Nashville (1975) . . . . Sueleen Gay
    •• 2:09—In bra singing to a room full of men, then top-
    less doing a strip tease, buns walking up the steps
    and out of the room.
Between the Lines (1977) . . . . .Laura
    •• 0:32—Buns and topless drying off with a towel in
    front of a mirror.
Desert Hearts (1986) . . . . Gwen
The Men's Club (1986) . . . . Redhead
Sticky Fingers (1988) . . . . .Marcie
Eating (1991) . . . . .Sophie
Magazines:
Playboy (Nov 1972) . . . . . . Variation of a Vadim Theme
    ••• 111-115—Full frontal nudity.
Playboy (May 1975) . . . . .The Splendor of Gwen
    ••• 96-99—Full frontal nudity.

Welles, Terri

Films:
Looker (1981) . . . . Lisa
    • 0:02—Brief topless getting photographed for opera-
    tion. In black bra and panties in her apartment a lot.
Video Tapes:
Playboy's Playmates of the Year: The '80s (1989)
. . . . .Playmate of the Year 1981
    ••• 0:08—Nude in still photos.
    ••• 0:10—Nude at the beach.
    ••• 0:11—Nude in still photos.
    •• 0:51—Topless coming out of the water.
Magazines:
Playboy (Dec 1980) . . . . Playmate
    ••• 184-197—Nude.
Playboy (Jun 1981) . . . . Playmate of the Year
Playboy's Nudes (Oct 1990) . . . . .Herself
    • 103—Side view of left breast.

• *Wells, Aarika*

Films:

Sharky's Machine (1981) . . . . Tiffany
- 0:52—Brief side view topless in Rachel Ward's apartment.

Walking the Edge (1985) . . . . Julia

TV:

Supertrain (1979) . . . . Gilda

Wells, Jennifer

a.k.a. Jennifer Welles.

Films:

Sugar Cookies (1973) . . . . Max's Secretary
- 0:28—Topless in red panties in Max's office while he talks on the phone, then lower frontal nudity.
- 0:56—Full frontal nudity getting dressed.

The Groove Tube (1974) . . . . The Geritan Girl
- 0:21—Dancing nude around her husband, Chevy Chase.

Wells, Victoria

Films:

Cheech & Chong's Nice Dreams (1981)
. . . . Beach Girl #1
- 0:29—Brief topless on the beach with two other girls. Long shot, unsteady, hard to see.

Losin' It (1982) . . . . .n.a.

• *Wendel, Lara*

Films:

Desire, The Interior Life (1980; Italian/German)
. . . . Desideria

Identification of a Woman (1983; Italian) . . . . .n.a.

Ghosthouse (1989; Italian) . . . . Martha

Husbands and Lovers (1991; Italian). . . . . Louisa
(Unrated version reviewed.)
- 0:47—In bra and panties with Julian Sands, then topless making love with him.

Magazines:

Playboy (Nov 1992) . . . . Sex in Cinema 1992
- 144—Left breast with Julian Sands from *Husbands and Lovers.*

• *Werchan, Bonnie*

Films:

Auditions (1978) . . . . Tracy Matthews
- 0:02—Topless, then full frontal nudity, undressing for her audition.
- 0:31—Nude, undressing herself and Van.
- 0:33—Buns and side of right breast, making love with Van.
- 1:07—Topless and buns during orgy scene.

Summer Camp (1979) .n.a.

• *Wharton, Ann*

Films:

Cheerleaders Wild Weekend (1985). . . .Lisa/Darwell
- 0:06—Topless in back of school bus, flashing a guy in pickup truck, then pressing her breasts against the window.
- 0:37—Topless, opening her white blouse during contest.
- 0:39—Topless and brief buns, in white skirt during contest.

Magazines:

Playboy (Nov 1985) . . . . Sex in Cinema 1985
- 129—Topless in back of bus from *Cheerleaders Wild Weekend.*

Whitaker, Christina

Films:

The Naked Cage (1985) . . . . Rita
- 0:08—Topless in bed with Willy.
- 0:55—Brief topless in gaping sweatshirt during fight with Sheila.
  1:28—Panties during fight with Shari Shattuck.
  1:29—Sort of left breast in gaping dress.

Assault of the Killer Bimbos (1988) . . . . Peaches

Stormquest (1988) . . . . n.a.

Vampire at Midnight (1988) . . . . Ingrid

Whitcraft, Elizabeth

Films:

Birdy (1985) . . . . .Rosanne

Angel Heart (1987) . . . . Connie
(Original Unedited Version reviewed.)
(Blonde hair.)
- 0:33—Topless in bed talking with Mickey Rourke while taking off her clothes.

Working Girl (1989) . . . . Doreen DiMucci
(Brunette hair.)
- 0:29—Topless on bed on Alec Baldwin when Melanie Griffith opens the door and discovers them.

GoodFellas (1990) . . . . Tommy's Girlfriend at Copa

Video Tapes:

Inside Out 2 (1992)
. . . . .Sarah/Some Guys Have All the Luck
(Unrated version reviewed.)
- 1:10—Topless taking off her top in bed. More topless in bed. Brief partial buns.

White, Sheila

Films:

Here We Go Round the Mulberry Bush (1968; British)
. . . . .Paula

Oliver! (1968; British). .Bet

Confessions of a Window Cleaner (1974; British)
. . . . Rosie

Confessions of a Pop Performer (1975; British). . . . Rosie

Oh, Alfie! (1975; British). . . . . .Norma
a.k.a. Alfie Darling

Miniseries:

I, Claudius—Episode 12, A God in Colchester
(1976; British) . . . . Lady Messalina
(Available on video tape in *I, Claudius—Volume 6*.)
- •• 0:00—Left breast, in bed with Mnester.
- • 0:02—Buns, getting out of bed and putting on a
  sheer dress.
- • 0:18—Right breast, in bed with Silius.
- ••• 0:29—Topless in bed with Silius.

White, Vanna

Films:

Gypsy Angels . . . . Micki
(Unreleased film.)
Graduation Day (1981) . . . . .Doris
Looker (1981) . . . . Reston Girl
Made for TV Movies:
The Goddess of Love (1988) . . . . Venus
TV:
Wheel of Fortune (1982-) . . . . .Hostess
Video Tapes:
Vanna White—Get Slim, Stay Slim . . . . Herself
Magazines:
Penthouse (Feb 1983) . . . . . Ad for Paradise Company
- •• 165—In lingerie in four small photos.

Playboy (May 1987) .Vanna
- ••• 134-143—In sheer lingerie from catalog she did before *Wheel of Fortune*.

Playboy (Dec 1987) . . . . Sex Stars of 1987
- ••• 150—In sheer black lingerie.

Playboy (Dec 1988) . . . . Sex Stars of 1988
- •• 183—Right breast under lingerie.

Whitfield, Lynn

Films:

Doctor Detroit (1983) . . . . Thelma Cleland
Silverado (1985) . . . . Ray
The Slugger's Wife (1985) . . . . Tina Alvarado
Dead Aim (1987) . . . . Sheila Freeman
Jaws: The Revenge (1987) . . . . .Louisa
Made for Cable Movies:
The Josephine Baker Story (1991; HBO)
. . . . Josephine Baker
- • 0:00—Topless dancing during opening credits. Slow
  motion.
- •• 0:13—Topless taking off her dress top for the French
  painter.
- ••• 0:14—Topless in the mirror and dancing with the
  painter after making love. Nice. Dancer doing splits
  looks like a body double.
- 0:16—Brief buns, in wet dress, getting out of swimming pool.
- ••• 0:31—Topless on stage doing the Banana Dance.
- ••• 0:33—Topless some more, doing the Banana Dance.
- • 2:02—Brief topless dancing during flashback.
Miniseries:
Women of Brewster Place (1989) . . . . .Ciel

Made for TV Movies:
Triumph of the Heart: The Ricky Bell Story (1991)
. . . . Natala
TV:
Heartbeat (1988-89) . . . . .Dr. Cory Banks
Equal Justice (1991) . . . . Maggie Mayfield
Magazines:
Playboy (Apr 1991) . . . . Grapevine
- ••• 170—Topless in B&W photo from *The Josephine Bak-
  er Story*.

Playboy (Jan 1992) . . . . The Year in Sex
- ••• 148—Topless from *The Josephine Baker Story*.

Whitlow, Jill

Films:

Porky's (1981; Canadian) . . . . Mindy
Mask (1985) . . . . .Annie Marie
Weird Science (1985) . . . . .Perfume Salesgirl
Night of the Creeps (1986) . . . . Cynthia Cronenberg
- 0:31—In bra and panties taking off sweater.
- • 0:33—Brief topless putting nightgown on over her
  head in her bedroom.
Thunder Run (1986) . . . . Kim
Twice Dead (1989) . . . . .Robin/Myrna
- 0:27—In white slip, getting ready for bed, then
  walking around the house.

Whitman, Kari

Films:

Masterblaster (1986) . . . . Jennifer
Beverly Hills Cop II (1987) . . . . .Playboy Model
Phantom of the Mall: Eric's Revenge (1988)
. . . . Melody Austin
Men at Work (1990) . . . . .Judy
Video Tapes:
Rock Video Girls (1991) . . . . Small Town Girl
- • 0:31—Topless under sheer white nightie.

• Whitting, Robyn

Films:

Innocent Sally (1973) . . . . n.a.
a.k.a. The Dirty Mind of Young Sally
Video Vixens (1973) . . . . Patient and Virginia
- •• 0:40—Topless, then nude on couch in psychiatrist's
  office. In B&W.
- •• 0:52—Full frontal nudity acting in bed with Rex for
  a film. In B&W.

Whitton, Margaret

Films:

Love Child (1982) . . . . .Jacki Steinberg
9 1/2 Weeks (1986) . . . . Molly
The Best of Times (1986) . . . . Darla
Ironweed (1987) . . . . .Katrina
- •• 1:19—Full frontal nudity leaving the house and
  walking down steps while young Francis brushes a
  horse.

The Secret of My Success (1987) . . . . . .Vera Prescott
- 0:31—Very brief topless taking off swimsuit top in swimming pool with Michael J. Fox.

Little Monsters (1989). . . . . Holly Stevenson
Major League (1989). . . . . Rachel Phelps
Made for TV Movies:
The Summer My Father Grew Up (1991) . . . . . . Naomi
TV:
Hometown (1985) . . . . Barbara Donnelly
Fine Romance (1989) .Louisa
Good & Evil (1991). . . . . Genny

Widdoes, Kathleen
Films:
The Group (1966). . . . . .Helena Davidson
Petulia (1968; U.S./British) . . . . .Wilma
The Sea Gull (1968) . . . . Masha
The Mephisto Waltz (1971). . . . . Maggie West
Savages (1972). . . . . Leslie
The End of August (1974) . . . . Adele
I'm Dancing as Fast as I Can (1981) . . . . . . Dr. Rawlings
Without a Trace (1983) . . . . Ms. Hauser
TV:
As the World Turns . . . . Emma Snyder
Magazines:
Playboy (Mar 1972). . . . . Savages
- 142—Topless.
- 145—Topless.

Wiesmeier, Lynda
Films:
Joysticks (1983). . . . . .Candy
Private School (1983) . . . . School Girl
- ••• 0:42—Nude in shower room scene. First blonde in shower on the left.

Malibu Express (1984). . . . . .June Khnockers
- •• 0:04—Topless in locker room taking jumpsuit off.
- • 1:16—Topless leaning out of racing car window while a helicopter chases her and Cody.

Preppies (1984) . . . . Trini
0:54—In bra and panties, practicing sexual positions on beds with Margot.
- ••• 1:06—Topless on bed with Mark.

R.S.V.P. (1984). . . . . .Jennifer Edwards
- •• 0:11—Topless diving into the pool while Toby fantasizes about her being nude.
- • 0:19—Topless in kitchen when Toby fantasizes about her again.
- ••• 1:21—Nude getting out of the pool and kissing Toby, when she really is nude.

Wheels of Fire (1984) . . . . .Harley
a.k.a. Desert Warrior
Avenging Angel (1985) . . . . Debbie
Real Genius (1985) . . . . .Chris' Girl at Party
Evil Town (1987) . . . . Dianne
- ••• 0:09—Topless on top of Tony outside while camping.
- •• 0:11—Right breast while making out with boyfriend outside. Topless getting up.

- • 0:13—Topless in open blouse running from bad guy. Nice bouncing action.
- •• 0:15—Topless getting captured by bad guys.
- •• 0:17—Topless getting out of car and brought into the house.
- •• 0:23—Topless tied up in chair.

Video Tapes:
Playboy's Playmate Review (1982). . . . . . . Playmate
- ••• 1:17—Nude undressing and taking a shower. Wow! Then in ballet studio.

Playboy Video Magazine, Volume 2 (1983)
. . . . Playmate
- ••• 1:12—In bra, stockings and garter belt. Undressing then full frontal nudity taking a shower.
- ••• 1:18—Nude, working out in dance studio.

Playboy Video Magazine, Volume 5 (1983)
. . . . Playmate
- • 0:06—Brief topless in shower.

Red Hot Rock (1984). . . . . Girl in Shower
- • 0:01—Brief upper half of buns, then topless taking off bra while a guy peeks into the locker room during "Girls" by Dwight Tilley.
- • 0:02—Brief full frontal nudity in the shower. (On the left.)

Wet and Wild (1989) . . . . Model
Playmates at Play (1990) . . . . Hardbodies
Magazines:
Playboy (Jul 1982) . . . . Playmate

• Wilcox, Mary
Films:
Lepke (1975; U.S./Israeli) . . . . Marion
Magazines:
Playboy (Oct 1974) . . . . Lepke's Lady
- ••• 85-91—Nude.

• Wild, Kelley
Video Tapes:
The Best of the Mermaids (1992) . . . . . .Heartstrings
- ••• 0:35—Nude, while playing harp.

Hot Body International: #3 Lingerie Special
(1992) . . . . .Contestant
- ••• 0:22—Buns in purple and black bra and G-string.
- ••• 0:55—1st place winner. Topless, getting out of bed. Buns, in G-string. Topless in bathtub.
- ••• 0:57—Buns and topless, getting a massage.

Hot Body International: #5 Miss Acapulco (1992)
. . . . .Contestant
- •• 0:01—Brief topless saying "Hi Mom!"
- ••• 0:39—Topless, taking off her bikini top.
- ••• 0:40—Buns, dancing in green two piece swimsuit.

Magazines:
Penthouse (May 1988) . . . . .Pet

Wild, Sándra

Films:
Body Waves (1991) . . . . .Anita
••• 0:39—Topless under sheer white robe, then topless
  with Larry on chair.
••• 1:12—Topless in bedroom with Larry.
Made for Cable TV:
Sessions: Episode 2 (1991; HBO) . . . . Amber
Video Tapes:
Wet and Wild (1989) . . . . .Model
Sexy Lingerie II (1990) . . . . .Model
Inside Out 4 (1992) . . . . Blonde Woman/The Thief
  (Unrated version reviewed.)
••• 0:44—Topless, sitting up in bed and getting out.
Rock Video Girls 2 (1992) . . . . Herself
  0:00—Brief partial right breast, by water pump dur-
  ing opening credits.
  0:16—In sheer black blouse in B&W photo session.
  0:19—In braless white tank top in music video.
••• 0:21—Topless taking off her tank top by water
  pump in music video.
Magazines:
Playboy (Aug 1991) . . . . .California Dreamin'
•• 136—Side view of right breast, bending over.
Playboy's Book of Lingerie (Sep 1991) . . . . . Herself
••• 11—Topless.
Playboy's Book of Lingerie (Nov 1991) . . . . . Herself
••• 40—Topless.
Playboy's Book of Lingerie (Jan 1992) . . . . . . Herself
••• 32—Topless.
Playboy's Book of Lingerie (Sep 1992) . . . . . Herself
•• 16—Right breast.

Wildman, Valerie

Films:
Splash (1984) .Wedding Guest
The Falcon and the Snowman (1985)
. . . . U.S. Embassy Official
A Fine Mess (1986) . . . . Anchorwoman
Inner Sanctum (1991) . . . . Jennifer Reed
  0:05—Wearing transparent light blue nightgown,
  getting out of bed, into wheelchair.
•• 0:11—Right breast, while sitting on bed with Joseph
  Bottoms.
Neon City (1991) . . . . Sandy

Wildsmith, Dawn

Ex-wife of director Fred Olen Ray.
Films:
Armed Response (1986) . . . . Thug
Cyclone (1986) . . . . Henna
Star Slammer—The Escape (1986) . . . . Muffin
Surf Nazis Must Die (1986) . . . . .Eva
• 0:25—Topless being fondled at the beach wearing a
  wet suit by Adolf. Mostly right breast.
Commando Squad (1987) . . . . Consuela
Evil Spawn (1987) . . . . Evelyn Avery
a.k.a. Donna Shock in this film.

Phantom Empire (1987) . . . . Eddy Colchilde
The Tomb (1987) . . . . Anna Conda
••• 0:54—Topless taking off robe in room with Michelle
  Bauer, then getting pushed onto a bed full of snakes.
B.O.R.N. (1988) . . . . Singer
Deep Space (1988) . . . . Janice
Hollywood Chainsaw Hookers (1988) . . . . Lori
It's Alive III: Island of the Alive (1988)
. . . . Uncredited Dancer in Club
Warlords (1988) . . . . Danny
Beverly Hills Vamp (1989) . . . . Sherry Santa Monica
Alienator (1990) . . . . .Caroline
Demon Sword (1991) . . . . Selena
a.k.a. Wizards of the Demon Sword

• Wilkening, Catherine

Films:
Contrainte Par Corps (1988; French) . . . . .Lola
Deux Minutes de Soleil en Plus (1988; French) . . . . .Aina
Jesus of Montreal (1990; French/Canadian)
. . . . Mireille Fontaine
• 1:08—Brief topless starting to take off her sweatshirt
  during an audition.

Wilkes, Donna

Films:
Schizoid (1980) .Allison Foles
  0:12—Topless taking off her bra in bathroom while
  Klaus Kinski watches. Buns, getting into the shower.
  Out of focus shots.
•• 0:13—Side view topless getting into the shower.
Angel (1983) . . . . .Angel/Molly
Grotesque (1987) . . . . .Kathy
TV:
Hello, Larry (1979) . . . . Diane Adler

Wilkinson, June

Films:
The Immoral Mr. Teas (1959) . . . . Uncredited torso
  Russ Meyer film.
Sno-Line (1984) . . . . .Audrey
Talking Walls (1987) .Blonde
• 0:13—Brief left breast, in car room, getting green
  towel yanked off.
  0:14—Very, very brief left breast in car room again.
  Dark.
•• 1:08—Brief topless, getting green towel taken off.
Keaton's Cop (1990) . . . . Archie "Big Mama" Gish
Magazines:
Playboy (Jan 1974) . . . . Twenty Years of Playboy
• 200—Right breast, in bed, in small photo.
Playboy (May 1980) . . . . .The World of Playboy
• 13—Parital right breast and half of buns.
Playboy (Jan 1989) . . . . Women of the Fifties
••• 116—Topless, wearing a gold bikini bottom.

Williams, Barbara

Films:

Thief of Hearts (1984) . . . . Mickey Davis
(Special Home Video Version reviewed.)
- 0:46—Right breast in bathtub when her husband comes in and tries to read her diary.
- ••• 0:53—Topless making love with Steven Bauer in his condo.

Jo Jo Dancer, Your Life Is Calling (1986). . . . . Dawn
Tiger Warsaw (1988) . . . . Karen
Watchers (1988) . . . . .Nora
City of Hope (1991) . . . . Angela
Made for Cable Movies:
Keeper of the City (1991; Showtime) . . . . Grace
Made for TV Movies:
Quiet Killer (1992) . . . . .Charlene

• Williams, Carol Ann

Films:

1941 (1979) . . . . .USO Girl
Butch and Sundance: The Early Days (1979) . . . . . . .Lilly
The Hollywood Knights (1980) . . . . Jane
- 0:51—Very brief topless, opening her blouse to distract Dudley. Don't see her face.

• Williams, Cynda

Films:

Mo' Better Blues (1990) . . . . .Clarke Betancourt
- •• 0:24—Topless, then left breast after kissing Bleek.
- ••• 1:07—Topless on bed when Bleek accidentally calls her "Indigo."
- •• 1:28—Left breast while making love in bed with Wesley Snipes.

One False Move (1992). . . . . Fantasia

Williams, Edy

Films:

The Secret Life of an American Wife (1968)
. . . . .Susie Steinberg
0:32—In blonde wig wearing black bra and panties getting into bed.
1:15—In black bra and panties again coming out of bedroom into the hallway.

Beyond the Valley of the Dolls (1970) . . . .Ashley St. Ives
Russ Meyer Film.
(Not available on video tape.)

The Seven Minutes (1971) . . . . .Faye Osborn
Dr. Minx (1975) . . . . .n.a.
Topless.
The Best of Sex and Violence (1981). . . . . . . Herself
- •• 0:46—Topless in various scenes from *Dr. Minx.*
Famous T & A (1982) . . . . Herself
(No longer available for purchase, check your video store for rental.)
- •• 0:39—Topless and bun scenes from *Dr. Minx.*
Chained Heat (1983; U.S./German) . . . . Paula
- •• 0:30—Full frontal nudity in the shower, soaping up Twinks.
- •• 0:36—Topless at night in bed with Twinks.

Hollywood Hot Tubs (1984). . . . . Desiree
- ••• 0:26—Topless, trying to seduce Shawn while he works on a hot tub.
- 1:26—In black lingerie outfit in the hallway.
- • 1:30—Partial topless with breasts sticking out of her bra while she sits by hot tub with Jeff.
- •• 1:32—Topless in hot tub room with Shawn.
- • 1:38—Topless again in the hot tub lobby.
Hellhole (1985) . . . . .Vera
- ••• 0:22—Topless on bed posing for Silk.
- ••• 0:24—Topless in white panties in shower, then fighting with another woman.
- ••• 1:03—Topless in mud bath with another woman. Long scene.
Mankillers (1987). . . . . Sergeant Roberts
Rented Lips (1988) . . . . .Heather Darling
- • 0:22—Topless in bed, getting fondled by Robert Downey, Jr. during porno movie shoot.
Bad Manners (1989) . . . . .Mrs. Slatt
Dr. Alien (1989) .Buckmeister
a.k.a. I Was a Teenage Sex Mutant
- ••• 0:54—Topless taking off her top in the women's locker room in front of Wesley.
Nudity Required (1989) . . . . Isabella
- ••• 1:05—Topless with whip, while acting in movie.
- •• 1:07—More topless in movie.
- •• 1:09—More right breast.
- •• 1:13—Topless during screening of the movie.
Bad Girls from Mars (1990) . . . . Emanuelle
- •• 0:17—Topless several times changing in back of convertible car.
- ••• 0:23—Topless changing out of wet dress in bathroom.
- ••• 0:30—Topless taking off blouse to get into spa.
- • 0:32—Topless in back of Porsche and getting out.
- ••• 0:35—Topless in store, signing autograph for robber.
- • 0:46—Buns in G-string, then topless taking off her top again.
- ••• 0:58—Topless in T.J.'s office. More topless when wrestling with Martine.
- • 1:05—Topless tied up.
- • 1:07—Topless again.
- •• 1:17—Topless taking off her outfit during outtakes.
Magazines:
Playboy (Feb 1973) . . . . Next Month
- 210—Left breast in B&W photo.
Playboy (Mar 1973) . . . . .All About Edy
- ••• 135-141—Nude.
Playboy (Jan 1978). . . . . The Year in Sex
- •• 201—Nude in swimming pool.
Playboy (Nov 1989) . . . . Sex in Cinema 1989
- ••• 134—Topless still from *Bad Girls From Mars.*

Williams, JoBeth

Films:

Kramer vs. Kramer (1979) . . . . .Phyllis Bernard
- • 0:45—Buns and brief topless in the hallway meeting Dustin Hoffman's son.

The Dogs of War (1980; British) . . . . Jessie
Stir Crazy (1980). . . . . Meredith
Endangered Species (1982). . . . . Harriet Purdue
Poltergeist (1982) . . . . Diane Freeling
The Big Chill (1983) . . . . Karen
American Dreamer (1984). . . . . Cathy Palmer
Teachers (1984) . . . . Lisa
   • 1:39—Brief topless taking off clothes and running
     down school hallway yelling at Nick Nolte.
Desert Bloom (1986). . . . . Lily
Poltergeist II: The Other Side (1986) . . . . Diane Freeling
Memories of Me (1988) . . . . Lisa McConnell
Welcome Home (1989). . . . . Sarah
Dutch (1991) . . . . Natalie
   a.k.a. Driving Me Crazy
Switch (1991) . . . . Margo Brofman
Stop! Or My Mom Will Shoot (1992) . . . . Gwen Harper
Miniseries:
The Day After (1983) . . . . Nancy
Made for TV Movies:
Adam (1983) . . . . n.a.
Baby M (1988) . . . . Mary Beth Whitehead
My Name is Bill W. (1989). . . . . Lois Wilson
Child in the Night (1990) . . . . Dr. Jackie Hollis
TV:
Somerset (1975). . . . . Carrie Wheeler
The Guiding Light (1977-81) . . . . Brandy Shelooe

Williams, Vanessa

Dethroned Miss America 1984.
Singer.
Not the same Vanessa Williams in *New Jack City*.
Films:
Under the Gun (1989) . . . . Samantha Richards
Another You (1991) . . . . Gloria
Harley Davidson and The Marlboro Man (1991)
. . . . Lulu Daniels
Made for TV Movies:
Full Exposure: The Sex Tapes (1989) . . . . Valentine
Magazines:
Penthouse (Sep 1984)
. . . . Here She Comes, Miss America
••• 66-75—B&W nude photos.
Penthouse (Nov 1984) . . . . Tom Chaipel interview
••• 85-89—More B&W nude photos.

Williams, Wendy O.

Lead singer of *The Plasmatics*.
Adult Films:
Candy Goes to Hollywood (1979). . . . . n.a.
Films:
Reform School Girls (1986). . . . . Charlie
   •• 0:26—Topless talking to two girls in the shower.
Pucker Up and Bark Like a Dog (1989) . . . . Butch
Magazines:
Playboy (Aug 1980) . . . . Grapevine
   • 263—Right breast with tape over the nipple.
Playboy (Oct 1986). . . . . Oh, Wendy O.!
   •• 70-75—Topless.

Wilsey, Shannon

a.k.a. Adult film actress Savannah.
Films:
Invisible Maniac (1990) . . . . Vicky
   • 0:21—Buns and very, very brief side of left breast in
     the shower with the other girls.
   • 0:33—Right breast covered with bubbles.
   ••• 0:43—In bra, then topless and lots of buns in locker
     room with the other girls.
   •• 0:44—Buns and left breast in the shower with the
     other girls.
   ••• 1:04—Undressing in locker room in white bra and
     panties, then topless. More topless taking a shower
     and getting electrocuted.
Sorority House Massacre 2 (1990) . . . . Satana
   •• 0:43—Topless and buns in G-string, dancing in club.
Legal Tender (1991) . . . . Mal's Girl
   •• 0:24—Topless in bubble bath with brunette girl and
     Morton Downey Jr.
   •• 0:31—Topless and buns in G-string bringing phone
     to Downey.

Wilson, Ajita

Films:
Love Lust and Ecstasy . . . . Sara
   •• 0:02—Nude taking a shower and getting into bed
     with an old guy.
   •• 0:04—Nude making love with a young guy.
   •• 0:17—Topless in bathtub, then making love on bed.
   •• 0:22—Topless making love in a swimming pool, in a
     river, by a tree.
   •• 0:26—Nude getting undressed and taking a shower.
   •• 0:35—Full frontal nudity changing clothes.
   ••• 0:54—Full frontal nudity making love in bed.
The Joy of Flying (1979) . . . . Madame Gaballi
   •• 1:20—Full frontal nudity undressing for George.
   •• 1:23—Topless, making love on top of George.
   • 1:25—Left breast, while in bed with George.
Catherine Cherie (1982). . . . . Dancer/Miss Ajita
   • 0:23—Topless and buns dancing in club. Covered
     with paint. Long shot.
   0:24—Brief buns, greeting Carlo after the show.
   •• 0:43—Full frontal nudity in room with Carlo.
A Man for Sale (1982) . . . . Dancer/Model
   • 0:02—Topless several times posing for photogra-
     pher with another model.
   • 0:26—Topless and buns, dancing in an erotic ballet
     show.
Savage Island (1985) . . . . Marie
Twelfth Night (1988; Italian). . . . . Antonia
   •• 0:50—Buns, taking off her dress and walking into
     stream with a guy.
   • 0:51—Very brief topless, making love with him in
     the stream.
   •• 1:11—Right breast, hanging out of black dress,
     dancing in tavern.

Wilson, Alisa

Films:
The Terror on Alcatraz (1986) . . . . Clarissa
- 1:14—Brief topless opening her blouse to distract Frank, so she can get away from him.

Loverboy (1989) . . . . Nurse Darlene

Wilson, Cheryl-Ann

Films:
Terminal Choice (1985; Canadian) . . . . Nurse Fields
Cellar Dweller (1987) . . . . Lisa
- - 0:59—Brief right breast, then topless taking a shower.

TV:
Days of Our Lives . . . . n.a.

Wilson, Sheree J.

Films:
Fraternity Vacation (1985) . . . . Ashley Taylor
0:43—In white leotard at aerobics class.
- 0:47—Topless and buns of her body double in the bedroom (Roberta Whitewood) when the guys photograph her with a telephoto lens.
1:01—In white leotard exercising in living room with Leigh McCloskey.

Crimewave (1986) . . . . Nancy
Miniseries:
Kane and Able . . . . n.a.
TV:
Our Family Honor (1985-86) . . . . Rita Danzig
Dallas (1987-91) . . . . April

Winchester, Maude

Films:
Birdy (1985) . . . . Doris Robinson
- - 1:32—Topless in car letting Mathew Modine feel her.

Brain Dead (1989) . . . . Crazy Anna
The Spirit of '76 (1991) . . . . Cyndi the Waitress

Windsor, Romy

Films:
Thief of Hearts (1984) . . . . Nicole
(Special Home Video Version reviewed.)
- - - 0:12—Full frontal nudity with Steven Bauer getting dressed.

Up the Creek (1984) . . . . Corky
Howling IV: The Original Nightmare (1988) . . . . . Marie
Big Bad John (1989) . . . . Marie Mitchelle
Edgar Allan Poe's "The House of Usher" (1990)
. . . . Molly

Winger, Debra

Ex-wife of actor Timothy Hutton.
Films:
Slumber Party '57 (1976) . . . . Debbie
- 0:10—Topless with her five girl friends during swimming pool scene. Hard to tell who is who.

- - - 0:53—Topless three times, lying down, making out with Bud.

Thank God It's Friday (1978) . . . . Jennifer
French Postcards (1979) . . . . Melanie
Urban Cowboy (1980) . . . . Sissy
Cannery Row (1982) . . . . Suzy
An Officer and a Gentleman (1982)
. . . . Paula Pokrifki
- - - 1:05—Brief side view of right breast, then topless making love with Richard Gere in a motel.

Terms of Endearment (1983)
. . . . Emma Greenway Horton
Mike's Murder (1984) . . . . Betty
- 0:26—Brief left breast in bathtub.

Legal Eagles (1986) . . . . Laura Kelly
Black Widow (1987) . . . . Alexandra
Made in Heaven (1987) . . . . Emmett
Betrayed (1988) . . . . Katie Phillips/Cathy Weaver
Everybody Wins (1990) . . . . Angela Crispini
0:50—Side view of left breast, lying on Nick Nolte in bed. Long shot.
The Sheltering Sky (1990) . . . . Kit Moresby
0:13—Upper half of lower frontal nudity in open robe when John Malkovich caresses her stomach.
0:24—Buns, getting out of bed.
- 0:41—Very brief topless grabbing sheets and getting out of bed with Tunner.
1:58—Lower frontal nudity and sort of buns, getting undressed with Belqassim.

TV:
Wonder Woman (1976-77) . . . . . . Drusilla/Wonder Girl

Winkler, K.C.

Films:
H.O.T.S. (1979) . . . . Cynthia
- 0:27—Topless in blue bikini bottom on balcony.
- - 0:31—Topless in van making love, then arguing with John.

The Happy Hooker Goes Hollywood (1980)
. . . . Amber
- - 0:41—Topless in cowboy outfit on bed with a guy.
- - - 0:43—Topless, wearing a blue garter belt playing pool with Susan Kiger.

Night Shift (1982) . . . . Cheryl
They Call Me Bruce? (1982) . . . . n.a.
Armed and Dangerous (1986) . . . . Vicki
TV:
High Rollers . . . . Hostess
Magazines:
Playboy (Jan 1979) . . . . The Great Playmate Hunt
- - - 190—Full frontal nudity.
Playboy (Oct 1985) . . . . Grapevine
- 241—In swimsuit, showing left breast. B&W.
Playboy (Mar 1986) . . . . Grapevine
- 176—In wet swimsuit. B&W.
Playboy (Sep 1989) . . . . Body by Winkler
- - - 82-87—Nude.
Playboy's Nudes (Oct 1990) . . . . Herself
- - - 42-43—Full frontal nudity.

Winningham, Mare

Films:

One Trick Pony (1980) . . . . McDeena Dandridge
•• 0:14—Topless in the bathtub with Paul Simon, smoking a cigarette. Long scene.
Threshold (1983; Canadian) . . . . Carol Severance
• 0:56—Brief full frontal nudity, lying on operating table, then side view of left breast getting prepped for surgery.
St. Elmo's Fire (1985) . . . . Wendy
Nobody's Fool (1986) . . . . Pat
Made in Heaven (1987) . . . . Brenda Carlucci
Shy People (1988) . . . . Candy
Miracle Mile (1989) . . . . Julie Peters
Turner & Hooch (1989) . . . . Emily Carson
Hard Promises (1992) . . . . n.a.

Miniseries:

The Thorn Birds (1983) . . . . Justine O'Neill

Made for TV Movies:

Helen Keller: The Miracle Continues (1984) . . . . n.a.
Who is Julia? (1986) . . . . Mary Frances
A Winner Never Quits (1986) . . . . Annie
Crossing to Freedom (1990) . . . . Nicole Rougeron
Love & Lies (1990) . . . . Kim Paris
She Stood Alone (1991) . . . . Prudence Crandall
Intruders (1992) . . . . Mary Wilkes
Those Secrets (1992) . . . . Faye

Magazines:

Playboy (Nov 1981) . . . . Sex in Cinema 1981
•• 170—Topless in bathtub from *One Trick Pony*.

Winters, D.D.

See: Vanity.

• Witherspoon, Reese

Films:

The Man in the Moon (1991) . . . . Dani Trant
• 0:09—Brief buns, running to go skinny dipping. Don't see her face. Long shot of back side of left breast while running on pier.
0:12—Brief buns, climbing up ladder. Tree branches get in the way. Don't see her face again.

Made for Cable Movies:

Wildflower (1991; Lifetime) . . . . Ellie Perkins

Witt, Kathryn

Films:

Lenny (1974) . . . . Girl
• 0:43—Right breast with Valerie Perrine while Dustin Hoffman watches.
Looker (1981) . . . . Tina Cassidy
0:17—In beige lingerie undressing in her room.
Star 80 (1983) . . . . Robin
Cocaine Wars (1986) . . . . Janet
• 0:36—Brief topless and buns making love in bed with John Schneider.
Demon of Paradise (1987) . . . . Annie

TV:

Flying High (1978-79) . . . . Pam Bellagio

• Witter, Cherie

Video Tapes:

Playboy Video Calendar 1987 (1986) . . . . . Playmate

Magazines:

Playboy (Feb 1985) . . . . Playmate

Witter, Karen

Films:

Dangerously Close (1986) . . . . Betsy
The Perfect Match (1987) . . . . Tammy
Hero and the Terror (1988) . . . . Ginger
Mortuary Academy (1988) . . . . Christie Doll
Out of the Dark (1988) . . . . Jo Ann
Paramedics (1988) . . . . Danger Girl
0:03—In white bra and panties in bedroom with a heart attack victim while the paramedics try to save him.
0:07—In wet blouse after getting in a car crash with a guy in the fountain.
Silent Assassins (1988) . . . . Sushi Bar Girl
The Vineyard (1988) . . . . n.a.
Another Chance (1989) . . . . Nancy Burton
• 0:44—Brief side view of right breast and buns getting out of bed.
0:45—In two piece swimsuit.
Edgar Allan Poe's "Buried Alive" (1989) . . . . Janet
Midnight (1989) . . . . Missy Angel
• 0:32—In bed with Mickey. Nice squished breasts against him, but only a very brief side view of left breast.
0:48—In two piece swimsuit, going into the pool.
0:58—In nightgown, walking around with lots of makeup on her face.
Popcorn (1991) . . . . Joy

TV:

One Life to Live (1990-) . . . . Tina Lord Roberts

Video Tapes:

Playboy's Playmate Review (1982) . . . . Playmate
••• 0:00—Nude deep sea fishing, then sunbathing on sailboat.
Playmates at Play (1990) . . . . Making Waves

Magazines:

Playboy (Mar 1982) . . . . Playmate
Playboy (Dec 1991) . . . . Sex Stars 1991
••• 182—Buns and side of left breast.

Wolf, Rita

Films:

My Beautiful Laundrette (1985; British) . . . . . . Tania
•• 0:15—Topless holding blouse up, showing off her breasts outside window to Omar.
Slipstream (1990) . . . . Maya

Wood, Cyndi

Films:

Apocalypse Now (1979) . . . . Playmate of the Year
Van Nuys Blvd. (1979) . . . . Moon

Video Tapes:

Playboy Video Centerfold: Teri Weigel (1986)
. . . . Playmate Update
••• 0:25—Nude in still photos.

Magazines:

Playboy (Feb 1973) . . . . Playmate
••• 100-107—Full frontal nudity.

Playboy (Jun 1974) . . . . Playmate of the Year
••• 146-155—Nude.

Playboy (Apr 1980) . . . . . . Playboy's Playmate Reunion
• 126—Small topless centerfold photo.

Wood, Jane

Films:

The Ragman's Daughter (1974; British)
. . . . Older Tony's Wife

Lassiter (1984) . . . . Mary Becker

She'll be Wearing Pink Pyjamas (1985; British)
. . . . Jude
• 0:07—Nude, shaving her legs in the women's shower room.

Blood Red Roses (1986; Scottish) . . . . n.a.

Wood, Janet

Films:

Angels Hard as They Come (1971) . . . . Vicki
•• 1:09—Topless taking off her top, dancing with Clean Sheila at the biker's party.
•• 1:16—Topless outside when the General rips her blouse open.

Terror House (1972) . . . . Pamela

The Centerfold Girls (1974) . . . . Linda
•• 0:14—Topless putting on robe and getting out of bed.

Slumber Party '57 (1976) . . . . Smitty
• 0:10—Topless with her five girl friends during swimming pool scene. Hard to tell who is who.
•• 1:06—Left breast, then topless in stable with David while his sister watches.

Wood, Lana

Sister of the late actress Natalie Wood.

Films:

The Searchers (1956) . . . . Debbie as a Child

Diamonds are Forever (1971) . . . . Plenty O'Toole

A Place Called Today (1972) . . . . . . Carolyn Scheider
••• 0:40—Side view of left breast, then topless lying down talking to Ron.

Demon Rage (1981) . . . . n.a.
a.k.a. Dark Eyes
Topless in bed.

Made for TV Movies:

Nightmare in Badham County (1976) . . . . n.a.
(Nudity added for video tape.)

TV:

The Long Hot Summer (1965-66) . . . . Eula Harker

Peyton Place (1966-67) . . . . Sandy Webber

Capitol (1983) . . . . Fran Bruke

Magazines:

Playboy (Apr 1971) . . . . . .The Well-Versed Lana Wood
••• 100-103—Topless.

Playboy (Nov 1972) . . . . Sex in Cinema 1972
159—Hard to see anything.

Playboy (Sep 1987) . . . . 25 Years of James Bond
••• 128—Topless.

Wood, Laurie

Video Tapes:

Playboy Video Calendar 1990 (1989) . . . . April
••• 0:18—Nude.

Magazines:

Playboy (Mar 1989) . . . . Playmate

Playboy's Book of Lingerie (Mar 1992) . . . . . .Herself
•• 88-89—Buns and right breast.

Playboy's Book of Lingerie (May 1992) . . . . .Herself
• 52—Left breast.

Playboy's Book of Lingerie (Sep 1992) . . . . . .Herself
•• 96—Buns and right breast.

Wood-Sharkey, Rebecca

a.k.a. Rebecca Sharkey.

Films:

Friday the 13th, Part V—A New Beginning (1985)
. . . . Lana
• 0:33—Brief topless opening her dress while changing to go out with Billy.

Mask (1985) . . . . .Angel

Barbarian Queen II: The Empress Strikes Back (1989) n.a.

The Forgotten One (1989) . . . . .Barmaid

Switch (1991) . . . . Gay Club Patron

Woodell, Pat

Films:

The Big Doll House (1971) . . . . .Bodine
• 0:27—Brief topless hung by wrists and whipped by a guard. Hair covers most of her breasts.

The Roommates (1973) . . . . Heather

The Woman Hunt (1975; U.S./Philippines) . . . . n.a.

TV:

Petticoat Junction (1963-65) . . . . Bobby Jo Bradley

• Woods, Barbara Alyn

Films:

Circuitry Man (1990) . . . . Yoyo

Delusion (1990) . . . . .Julie

Dance with Death (1991) . . . . Kelly
••• 0:16—In black bra, panties and stockings, doing strip tease on stage. Topless and buns in G-string.
•• 0:24—Topless, dancing in red bra and panties.
••• 0:46—Topless and buns in G-string, dancing on stage.
• 0:47—Brief side view of left breast, while changing back stage. Buns seen in mirror.
••• 0:59—Topless and buns, doing strip tease routine in Marilyn Monroe outfit.
••• 1:01—Topless, making love in bed with Maxwell Caulfield.

We're Talkin' Serious Money (1991)
. . . . Baggage Claim Agent
The Terror Within II (1992) . . . . Sharon
Video Tapes:
Inside Out (1992) . . . . Terri/Brush Strokes
••• 0:07—Topless and buns in G-string, undressing for Jack.
••• 0:08—Close-up of breasts as Jack paints on her with his paintbrush.
••• 0:09—Full frontal nudity, getting paint poured all over her body.
• 0:11—Brief topless, while holding onto chair while making love.

Woods, Connie

Films:
The Forbidden Dance (1990) . . . . Trish
Made for Cable TV:
Dream On: Futile Attraction (1991; HBO)
. . . . Darlene
•• 0:03—Topless dressed as a cheerleader on top of Martin in bed.
Video Tapes:
Night of the Living Babes (1987). . . . . Lulu
• 0:46—Topless and buns in lingerie, in a cell with Buck.
••• 0:48—More topless in cell with Buck.
• 0:50—Topless getting rescued with Michelle Bauer.

• Woods, Jerii

Films:
Switchblade Sisters (1975) . . . . Toby
Revenge of the Cheerleaders (1976). . . . . Gail
• 0:00—Topless changing in front left seat of car.
  0:05—Lower frontal nudity taking off cheerleader skirt in girl's restroom and putting on panties.
• 0:26—Brief right breast, while sitting in bleachers with the other cheerleaders.
••• 0:28—Nude in boy's shower room scene.
•• 0:37—Topless sitting up in sleeping bag.
• 0:44—Brief topless in front seat of car with David Hasselhoff.
••• 0:53—Nude with Leslie and hiker guy while frolicking in the woods.
•• 0:55—Nude some more making out with the hiker guy with Leslie.
••• 0:57—Nude walking down road with Leslie when stopped by a policeman.
••• 1:23—Topless during Hawaiian party.

Woronov, Mary

Films:
Sugar Cookies (1973). . . . . Camila
••• 0:10—Topless in bathtub, then wearing white panties exercising topless on the floor. Long scene.
• 1:04—Topless with Julie in the bathtub.

• 1:07—Brief topless, then left breast, making love with Julie.
• 1:17—Brief right breast when Lynn Lowry yanks her dress up.
Silent Night, Bloody Night (1974) . . . . Diane
Death Race 2000 (1975). . . . . Calamity Jane
• 0:27—Brief topless arguing with Matilda the Hun.
Hollywood Boulevard (1976) . . . . Mary McQueen
Jackson County Jail (1976) . . . . Pearl
Mr. Billion (1977). . . . . Actress
The Lady in Red (1979) . . . . Woman Bankrobber
Rock 'n' Roll High School (1979) . . . . Evelyn Togar
Angel of H.E.A.T. (1981). . . . . Samantha Vitesse
a.k.a. The Protectors, Book I
••• 0:11—Frontal nudity changing clothes on a boat dock after getting out of the lake.
•• 0:43—Topless wrestling in the mud after wearing white bathing suit.
Heartbeeps (1981) . . . . Party House Owner
Eating Raoul (1982) . . . . Mary Bland
••• 0:46—Topless on the couch struggling with Ed Begley, Jr. More topless while Raoul counts money on her stomach. Long scene.
• 0:53—Buns and side view of right breast in hospital room with Raoul. A little dark.
Get Crazy (1983) . . . . n.a.
Night of the Comet (1984) . . . . Carol
Hellhole (1985) . . . . Dr. Fletcher
Chopping Mall (1986) . . . . Mary Bland
Nomads (1986) . . . . Dancing Mary
Mortuary Academy (1988). . . . . Mary Purcell
Let It Ride (1989). Quinella
Scenes from the Class Struggle in Beverly Hills
(1989) . . . . Lizabeth
••• 1:06—In black lingerie, then topless in bedroom, then in bed with Juan.
Club Fed (1990). . . . . Jezebel
Dick Tracy (1990). . . . . Welfare Person
Rock 'n' Roll High School Forever (1990)
. . . . Doctor Vadar
Warlock (1990) . . . . Channeller
Watchers II (1990) . . . . Dr. Glatman
Made for TV Movies:
A Bunny's Tale (1985) . . . . Miss Renfroe

Wren, Clare

Films:
Season of Fear (1989). . . . . Sarah Drummond
0:23—Topless in bed with Mick. Long shot, hard to see.
0:25—Brief silhouette, behind shower door.
• 0:42—Side view of left breast, on top of Mick. Very, very brief left breast, turning over when they hear a noise outside.
Steel and Lace (1990) . . . . Gally
TV:
Young Riders (1990-92) . . . . Rachel Dunn

Wright, Amy

Films:
The Deer Hunter (1978) . . . . Bridesmaid
Girlfriends (1978). . . . . .Ceil
- 0:42—Brief topless getting out of bed to talk to Melanie Mayron.

The Amityville Horror (1979). . . . . Jackie
Breaking Away (1979). . . . . .Nancy
Wise Blood (1979; U.S./German). . . . . Sabbath Lilly
Heartland (1980) . . . . .Clara
Inside Moves (1980) . . . . Ann
Stardust Memories (1980). . . . . Shelley
The Accidental Tourist (1988) . . . . Rose Leary
Crossing Delancey (1988) . . . . Ricki
Deceived (1991) . . . . Evelyn Wade
Love Hurts (1991) . . . . Karen Weaver

Made for TV Movies:
Settle the Score (1989) . . . . Becky

Wright, Jenny

Films:
Pink Floyd The Wall (1982). . . . . . .American Groupie
- 0:41—Topless backstage in back of a truck doing a strip tease dance in front of some people.

World According to Garp (1982). . . . . Curbie
- 0:33—Brief topless behind the bushes with Robin Williams giving him "something to write about."

The Wild Life (1984) . . . . Eileen
- 0:22—In bra and panties, then topless changing in her bedroom while Christopher Penn watches from the window.

St. Elmo's Fire (1985) . . . . Felicia
Near Dark (1987) . . . . Mae
Out of Bounds (1987) . . . . Dizz
The Chocolate War (1988) . . . . .Lisa
Valentino Returns (1988). . . . . .Sylvia Fuller
I, Madman (1989). .Virginia
A Shock to the System (1990) . . . . . . Melanie O'Connor
Young Guns II (1990) . . . . Jane Greathouse
- 1:07—Buns, taking off her clothes, getting on a horse and riding away. Hair covers breasts.
- 1:38—Buns, walking down stairs during epilogue.

Queens Logic (1991). . . . . .Asha
The Lawnmower Man (1992) . . . . Marnie Burke
- 1:04—Brief right breast, while in bed with Jeff Fahey.

TV:
Capital News (1990) . . . . Doreen Duncan

Wright, Robin

Films:
Hollywood Vice Squad (1986). . . . . .Lori
The Princess Bride (1987) . . . . Buttercup
State of Grace (1990) . . . . Kathleen
- 0:38—Topless making love standing up with Sean Penn in the hall. Dark.

1:01—In bra on bed with Penn, than walking around while talking to him.
- 1:58—Brief side of right breast taking off towel and putting on blouse.

Denial (1991) . . . . .Sarah
- 0:37—Side view of buns, while lying on top of Jason Patric.

The Playboys (1992) . . . . Tara Maguire

TV:
Santa Barbara . . . . .Kelly Capwell

Wright, Sylvia

Films:
Bloody Birthday (1980) .n.a.
Terror on Tour (1980). Carol
Malibu Hot Summer (1981). . . . . Actress at Party
a.k.a. Sizzle Beach
(*Sizzle Beach* is the re-released version with Kevin Costner featured on the cover. It is missing all the nude scenes during the opening credits before 0:06.)
- 0:01—Nude, standing up during opening credits.
- 1:07—Topless fixing her hair in front of mirror, then full frontal nudity talking to Howard.
- 1:09—Topless on top of Howard.

• Wyhl, Jennifer

Made for Cable Movies:
Soft Touch (1987; Playboy) . . . . Nancy
(Shown on *The Playboy Channel* as *Birds in Paradise*.)
- 0:00—Topless during opening credits.

Soft Touch II (1987; Playboy) . . . . Nancy
(Shown on *The Playboy Channel* as *Birds in Paradise*.)
- 0:01—Topless during opening credits.
- 0:05—Topless in bed with Neill.
- 0:18—Topless undressing for robbers. Brief full frontal nudity.
- 0:57—Topless in bed with Neill.
- 1:01—Full frontal nudity in bed with Neill.

Wyss, Amanda

Films:
Fast Times at Ridgemont High (1982) . . . . Lisa
Better Off Dead (1985) . . . . Beth Truss
A Nightmare on Elm Street (1985). . . . . .Tina Gray
Silverado (1985). . . . . Phoebe
Deadly Innocents (1988) . . . . Andy/Angela
- 0:12—Topless, taking off T-shirt and putting on lingerie.
- 1:29—Right breast, twice, with Andrew Stevens.

Powwow Highway (1988; U.S./British). . . Rabbit Layton
To Die For (1988). .Celia Kett
Black Magic Woman (1990) . . . . .Diane Abbott
To Die For 2 (1991) . . . . Celia

• Xuxa

Full name is Xuxa Meneghel.
Brailian children's television show host.
Films:
Love Strange Love (1982; Brazilian) . . . . Tamara
- 0:26—Topless standing on table, getting measured for outfit.
- 0:29—Topless again when Hugo watches. Long scene.

•• 0:58—Right breast when she lets Hugo caress it. (Film is reversed since mole above her right breast appears over the left.)

• 1:00—More right breast.

•• 1:09—Topless, stripping out of bear costume during party.

••• 1:13—Topless several times undressing in room. Long scene.

•• 1:27—Side view of left breast in bed with Hugo.

• *Yarnall, Celeste*

Films:

The Nutty Professor (1963) . . . . College Student

Bob & Carol & Ted & Alice (1969) . . . . Susan

The Velvet Vampire (1971) . . . . .Diane Le Fanu

• 0:32—Brief topless, zipping up her blouse after trying to seduce Lee.

•• 0:42—Topless in desert scene when Lee pulls her blouse down.

••• 0:45—Topless on the floor, making love with Lee.

•• 0:55—Topless in desert scene with Lee.

• 0:57—Side view of buns, lying on top of someone in a coffin.

•• 1:02—Topless in bed with Lee.

The Mechanic (1972) . . . . The Mark's Girl

Scorpio (1973) . . . . Helen Thomas

Fatal Beauty (1987). . . . . Laura

Funny About Love (1990) . . . . Delta Gamma

Ambition (1991). . . . . Beverly Hills Shopper

Driving Me Crazy (1991). . . . . Volvo Boss

Yates, Cassie

Films:

The Evil (1977) . . . . .Mary

Rolling Thunder (1977). . . . . .Candy

Convoy (1978). . . . . Violet

• 0:21—Very brief left breast, while in truck sleeper with Kris Kristofferson.

F.I.S.T. (1978) . . . . Molly

FM (1978). . . . . .Laura Coe

The Osterman Weekend (1983). . . . . Betty Cardone

•• 0:48—Topless getting into bed with Chris Sarandon while Rutger Hauer watches on TV.

• 0:51—Right breast, making love with Sarandon.

Unfaithfully Yours (1984). . . . . Carla Robbins

Made for TV Movies:

Of Mice and Men (1981) . . . . .n.a.

St. Helens (1981) . . . . .n.a.

Listen To Your Heart (1983). . . . . .n.a.

TV:

Rich Man, Poor Man—Book II (1976-77)

. . . . Annie Adams

Nobody's Perfect (1980) . . . Detective Jennifer Dempsey

Detective in the House (1985). . . . . .Diane Wyman

Dynasty (1987) . . . . Sarah Curtis

• *Yazel, Carrie Jean*

Video Tapes:

Playboy Video Calendar 1992 (1991). . . . . .June

••• 0:22—Topless and buns in kitchen shoot. More when pouring honey on her body.

••• 0:25—Nude, dancing in bar fantasy.

Sexy Lingerie III (1991). . . . . Model

Playboy's Playmate Review 1992 (1992)

. . . . .Miss May

••• 0:14—Nude outside with piano, then outside in doorway and then in a house.

Magazines:

Playboy (May 1991). . . . . Playmate

••• 110-121—Nude.

Playboy's Book of Lingerie (Jul 1992). . . . . . .Herself

••• 34—Full frontal nudity.

••• 42-43—Topless.

Playboy's Book of Lingerie (Sep 1992). . . . . .Herself

•• 57—Buns and left breast.

• *York, Brittany*

Films:

I Posed for Playboy (1991). . . . . .Herself

a.k.a. Posing: Inspired by Three Real Stories

(Shown on network TV without the nudity.)

(Nude scenes added for video tape.)

••• 0:20—Right breast, then topless on motorcycle during photo shoot.

••• 0:22—In T-shirt, then topless during second photo shoot.

Video Tapes:

Playboy Video Calendar 1992 (1991)

. . . . November

••• 0:43—Topless in lingerie. Nude in studio shoot.

••• 0:45—In black body stocking and nude in oriental style shoot.

Wet and Wild III (1991) . . . . Model

Sexy Lingerie IV (1992) . . . . Model

Wet and Wild IV (1992) . . . . Model

Magazines:

Playboy (Oct 1990) . . . . Playmate

••• 102—Nude.

Playboy's Book of Lingerie (Nov 1991) . . . . .Herself

• 9—Lower frontal nudity.

Playboy's Book of Lingerie (Mar 1992). . . . . .Herself

••• 55—Full frontal nudity.

Playboy's Book of Lingerie (Sep 1992). . . . . .Herself

•• 17—Left breast and lower frontal nudity.

•• 100—Left breast and buns.

• *York, Linda*

Films:

Chain Gang Women (1972). . . . . .n.a.

Video Vixens (1973) . . . . Dial-A-Snatch Girl

•• 0:34—Nude on a turntable during a commercial, getting felt by four blindfolded guys.

York, Susannah
Films:
Tunes of Glory (1960) . . . . Morag Sinclair
Tom Jones (1963) . . . . Sophie
A Man for All Seasons (1966) . . . . Margaret More
The Killing of Sister George (1968)
. . . . Alice McNaught
    0:19—Topless under sheer blue nightgown.
    0:59—In black bra and panties.
    1:45—In black bra and panties getting undressed.
 •• 2:07—(0:09 into tape 2) Topless lying in bed with
    another woman.
Images (1972; Irish). . . . . Cathryn
 • 0:59—Brief lower frontal nudity, then right breast ly-
    ing on the bed.
    1:38—Brief buns in the shower.
X, Y and Zee (1972) . . . . Stella
That Lucky Touch (1975). . . . . Julia Richardson
The Adventures of Eliza Fraser (1976; Australian)
. . . . Elisa Fraser
 • 1:10—Brief topless twice during ceremony. Paint on
    her face while running from hut.
The Silent Partner (1978) . . . . Julie
 • 0:38—Very brief right breast pulling her dress back
    up with Elliott Gould.
Superman (1978) . . . . Lara
The Shout (1979) . . . . Rachel Fielding
 •• 0:53—Brief topless changing from a bathrobe to a
    blouse in bedroom.
 • 1:02—Brief nude in upstairs room getting ready to
    make love with Alan Bates.
    1:05—Brief buns, standing at end of hallway.
    1:09—In white slip inside and outside house.
    1:11—Topless in bathtub with John Hurt.
 • 1:18—Brief topless getting up from bed with Bates.
    Long shot, hard to see anything.
The Awakening (1980) . . . . Jane Turner
Falling in Love Again (1980) . . . . Sue Lewis
Pretty Kill (1987). . . . . Toni
A Summer Story (1988) . . . . Mrs. Narracrombe
Illusions (1992) . . . . Dr. Sinclair

• Young, Gabriela
Video Tapes:
Intimate Workout For Lovers (1992)
. . . . Romantic Relaxation
 ••• 0:01—Nude, in bedroom, in bathtub and in bed.
Magazines:
Playboy's Book of Lingerie (Jan 1992) . . . . . . Herself
 •• 31—Buns and side of right breast.

Young, Karen
Films:
Handgun (1983; British) . . . . Kathleen Sullivan
a.k.a. Deep in the Heart
Brief buns and topless when rapist forces her to remove
her clothes.

Almost You (1984) . . . . Lisa Willoughby
    1:00—Partial left breast while kissing Griffin Dunne
    in bed.
Birdy (1985). . . . . Hannah Rourke
9 1/2 Weeks (1986) . . . . Sue
Heat (1987) . . . . Holly
Jaws: The Revenge (1987) . . . . Carla Brody
Torch Song Trilogy (1988) . . . . Laurel
Criminal Law (1989) . . . . Ellen Falkner
 • 1:21—Very brief buns, then brief topless in bed with
    Ben.
Night Game (1989) . . . . Roxy
    0:02—In white slip with Roy Scheider.
 • 0:06—Right breast, while in bed with Scheider after
    he answers the phone.
Made for TV Movies:
The Summer My Father Grew Up (1991) . . . . Chandelle

Young, Robbin
Films:
For Your Eyes Only (1981) . . . . Flower Shop Girl
Night Shift (1982) . . . . Nancy
Magazines:
Playboy (Jun 1981) . . . . For Your Eyes Only
 ••• 126-127—Topless (won a contest to appear in the
    film and in *Playboy* magazine).
Playboy (Dec 1981) . . . . Sex Stars of 1981
 ••• 244—Frontal nudity.

Young, Sean
Films:
Jane Austen in Manhattan (1980). . . . . Ariadne
Stripes (1981) . . . . Louise Cooper
Blade Runner (1982) . . . . Rachael
Young Doctors in Love (1982) . . . . . Dr. Stephanie Brody
    0:48—In white panties and camisole top in the sur-
    gery room with Michael McKean.
Dune (1984) . . . . Chani
    On the back of the laser disc cover, there is a small photo
    of her in a sheer black blouse lying down with Kyle Ma-
    cLachlan.
Baby... Secret of the Lost Legend (1985)
. . . . Susan Matthew-Loomis
No Way Out (1987) . . . . Susan Atwell
    0:11—In black stockings, garter belt & corset in love
    scene in back of limousine with Kevin Costner.
 ••• 0:13—Side view of left breast, then brief right
    breast, going into Nina's apartment with Costner.
    0:21—In bed in pink lingerie and a robe talking on
    telephone when Costner is in Manila.
    0:31—In corset and stockings with garter belt in
    bathroom talking to Costner.
Wall Street (1987) . . . . Kate Gekko
The Boost (1989) . . . . Linda Brown
 • 0:16—Very, very brief topless jumping into the
    swimming pool with James Woods. Very, very brief
    side view of right breast and buns, twice, getting out
    of the pool, sitting on edge, then getting pulled
    back in by James Woods.

•• 0:17—Left breast, while in pool talking to Woods. Right breast visible under water.

0:48—Brief topless under water in spa with Woods.

Cousins (1989) . . . . Tish Kozinski
    1:28—In black bra, in hotel room with William Petersen.

Fire Birds (1990). . . . . .Billie Lee Guthrie
a.k.a. Wings of the Apache
    • 0:52—Very, very brief right breast twice in bed with Nicholas Cage.

A Kiss Before Dying (1991). . . Ellen/Dorothy Carlsson
    •• 0:31—Brief topless making love in bed with Matt Dillon. Kind of dark.
    • 0:35—Brief side view or right breast in shower with Dillon. Don't see her face.
    1:11—Very brief partial left breast in gaping pajama top when she leans over to turn off the light.

Love Crimes (1991) . . . . Dana Greenway
(Unrated version reviewed.)
    •• 0:20—Almost left breast, getting out of bathtub. Buns and partial lower frontal nudity, getting dressed.
    •• 0:55—Topless in open blouse, yelling at Patrick Bergin.
    • 0:57—Brief right breast, on bed in open blouse.
    ••• 0:59—Nude in bathtub.
    ••• 1:01—Topless, making love with Bergin. Lit with red light.
    ••• 1:03—Full frontal nudity, getting covered with a towel.
    • 1:08—Full frontal nudity, in Polaroid that Maria looks at.
    • 1:11—More full frontal nudity in Polaroid.
    1:21—Partial right breast, while taking a shower.
    • 1:23—Brief topless in the shower.
    1:25—Very brief right breast in gaping robe.
    1:27—Full frontal nudity in burning Polaroid.

Once Upon A Crime (1992) . . . . .n.a.
Made for Cable Movies:
Sketch Artist (1992; Showtime). . . . . Rayanne
    0:51—In black bra in bed with Jeff Fahey.
    •• 0:52—Right breast, several times while making love in bed with Fahey.

Zabou

Films:
The Perils of Gwendoline in the Land of the Yik Yak (1984; French). . . . . Beth
    •• 0:36—Topless in the rain in the forest, taking off her blouse.
    •• 0:57—Topless in torture chamber getting rescued by Tawny Kitaen.
    •• 1:04—Topless after Kitaen escapes.
    • 1:11—Buns, in costume during fight.

One Woman or Two (1986; French) . . . . . Constance
a.k.a. Une Femme Ou Deux
    •• 0:28—Brief topless pulling up her blouse for Gerard Depardieu.

C'est La Vie (1990; French) . . . . Bella

Zadora, Pia

Singer.
Films:
Santa Claus Conquers the Martians (1964). . . . . .Girmar
Butterfly (1982). . . . . Kady
    0:15—Silhouette changing while Stacey Keach watches.
    •• 0:33—Topless and buns getting into the bath.
    ••• 0:35—Topless in bathtub when Stacey Keach is giving her a bath.

Nevada Heat (1982) . . . . .Bobbi
a.k.a. Stake Out
    • 0:14—Very brief partial right breast and brief buns, in the showers.
    • 0:47—Side of left breast, while in bubble bath with Desi Arnaz, Jr.

The Lonely Lady (1983) . . . . JeniLee Randall
    • 0:12—Brief topless getting raped by Joe, after getting out of the pool.
    •• 0:22—Brief topless, then left breast, while making love with Walter.
    •• 0:28—Side view topless lying in bed with Walter.
    •• 0:44—Buns and side view of left breast taking a shower.
    • 0:46—Very brief right breast, in bed with George.
    •• 1:05—Left breast, then brief topless making love with Vinnie.

Voyage of the Rock Aliens (1985). . . . . DeeDee
a.k.a. When the Rains Begin to Fall
Hairspray (1988) . . . . The Beatnik Chick
Magazines:
Penthouse (Oct 1983) . . . . .Pia
Playboy (Nov 1983) . . . . Sex in Cinema 1983
    •• 144—Frontal nudity.

• Zambelli, Zaira

Films:
Bye Bye Brazil (1980; Brazilian). . . . . Dasdô
    •• 1:11—Buns, then topless outside by a boat with Cigano.
Fulaninha (1986; Brazilian). . . . . Sulamita

Zane, Lisa

Wife of actor Billy Zane.
Maiden name is Lisa Collins.
Films:
Gross Anatomy (1989) . . . . Luann
Pucker Up and Bark Like a Dog (1989)
    . . . . .Taylor Phillips
    •• 0:52—Topless in shower with Max. Left breast, while in bed.
Bad Influence (1990) . . . . .Claire
    • 0:39—Brief topless on video tape seen on TV at party.
Femme Fatale (1990). . . . . Cynthia
Freddy's Dead: The Final Nightmare (1991)
    . . . . .Maggie Burroughs

Zann, Lenore

Films:

Happy Birthday to Me (1980) . . . . .Maggie
American Nightmare (1981; Canadian) . . . . Tina
••• 0:25—Topless and buns dancing on stage.
•• 1:05—Topless and buns dancing on stage again.
Visiting Hours (1982; Canadian) . . . . .Lisa
0:39—In panties with Michael Ironside.
One Night Only (1984; Canadian) . . . . .Anne
•• 0:20—Topless getting dressed in bedroom with
Jamie.
• 1:04—Right breast in bedroom with Jamie.
••• 1:19—Topless and buns making love with Jamie.
Def-Con 4 (1985) . . . . J. J.
Return (1985) . . . . Susan
Pretty Kill (1987) . . . . Carrie

Made for TV Movies:

Love and Hate (1989) . . . . .Lynne
Tom Alone (1989) . . . . Lily Manse

Magazines:

Playboy (Jan 1992) . . . . .The Year in Sex
•• 145—Topless in bed in photo from a stage play in
Chicago.

• Zhivago, Stacia

Films:

Sorority House Massacre 2 (1990) . . . . . . .Kimberly
••• 0:21—Nude, taking a shower.
0:50—In wet lingerie.
• 0:53—Buns, while going up the stairs.
0:55—Brief buns, while going up the stairs.
• 1:00—Brief topless, sitting up in bathtub filled with
bloody water to strangle Linda.

Video Tapes:

Scream Queen Hot Tub Party (1991) . . . . . .Kimberly
••• 0:16—Nude, in shower scene from *Sorority House
Massacre 2.*

Zinszer, Pamela

Films:

The Happy Hooker Goes to Washington (1977)
. . . . Linda
• 1:19—Brief topless in raincoat flashing in front of
congressional panel.

Video Tapes:

Playboy Video Magazine, Volume 2 (1983)
. . . . Herself/Playboy Playoffs

Magazines:

Playboy (Mar 1974) . . . . Playmate
••• 102-111—Nude.
Playboy (Jul 1980) . . . . The World of Playboy
••• 12—Topless.

Zucker, Miriam

Films:

Prime Evil (1987) . . . . Nancy Deans
•• 0:03—Topless several times, during sacrificial ceremony.
Senior Week (1987) . . . . Princeton Dream Girl

•• 0:42—Topless during dream.
Wildest Dreams (1987) . . . . Customer
Alien Space Avenger (1988) . . . . .Bordello Reporter
New York's Finest (1988) . . . . Mrs. Rush
Sensations (1988) . . . . Cookie Woman
• 0:06—Topless on couch making love with a guy
while Jenny and Brian watch.
A Woman Obsessed (1989) . . . . Betsy

Zuniga, Daphne

Films:

The Initiation (1984) . . . . Kelly Terry
The Sure Thing (1985) . . . . .Alison Bradbury
Visionquest (1985) . . . . .Margie Epstein
Modern Girls (1987) . . . . Margo
Spaceballs (1987) . . . . Princess Vespa
Last Rites (1988) . . . . .Angela
• 0:04—Very brief topless running into the bathroom
to escape from being shot. Covered with blood,
don't see her face. Very brief right breast reaching
for a bathrobe. Don't really see anything.
0:40—Buns, behind a shower door.
0:50—Buns, getting out of bed and standing in front
of Tom Berenger.
The Fly II (1989) . . . . Beth
Gross Anatomy (1989) . . . . .Laurie Rorbach
Staying Together (1989) . . . . Beverly Young
•• 0:56—Buns, lying in bed with Kit. Nice, long buns
scene.

Made for Cable Movies:

Prey of the Chameleon (1992; Showtime)
. . . . Patricia/Elizabeth Burrows
0:08—Buns, of dead body, lying on ground. Don't
see face.

TV:

Melrose Place (1992-) . . . . n.a.

Actors

Aames, Willie

Films:
Scavenger Hunt (1979) . . . . Kenny Stevens
Paradise (1981). . . . . David
   0:42—Buns, while walking into the ocean with a fishing net. Dark, hard to see anything.
  •• 1:12—Nude swimming with Phoebe Cates under water.
Zapped! (1982). . . . . Peyton
Made for TV Movies:
An Eight is Enough Wedding (1989) . . . . Tommy
TV:
Swiss Family Robinson (1975-76) . . . . . . Fred Robinson
We'll Get By (1975). . . . . Kenny Platt
Eight is Enough (1977-81) . . . . .Tommy Bradford
We're Movin' (1982). . . . . Host
Charles in Charge (1984-85). . . . . Buddy Lembeck
Charles in Charge (1987-90). . . . . Buddy Lembeck

Abele, Jim

Films:
Student Affairs (1987) . . . . .Andrew Armstrong
  • 1:07—Buns, when his friends play a practical joke on him in the shower.
Wimps (1987) .Charles Conrad

Abraham, Ken

Films:
Creepozoids (1987) . . . . Butch
  •• 0:16—Side view of buns, while standing in shower with Linnea Quigley.
Vice Academy (1988) . . . . Dwayne
Deadly Embrace (1989) . . . . .Chris Thompson
  •• 0:17—Buns, while taking a shower.
  • 1:01—Brief buns, while making love on top of Linnea Quigley.
Ministry of Vengeance (1989) . . . . Sparky

• Addabbo, Anthony

Video Tapes:
Inside Out 4 (1992) . . . . Kenner/Put Asunder
(Unrated version reviewed.)
  ••• 0:22—Buns, while lying in bed with Dolores.
  •• 0:25—Buns, while lying in bed on top of Dolores.

• Adell, Steve

Films:
Almost Pregnant (1992) . . . . Muscle Man
(Unrated version reviewed.)
  • 0:04—Buns, while making love in bed with Tanya Roberts.
  •• 0:20—Buns, while on top of Roberts during Jeff Conaway's dream.

Agterberg, Toon

Films:
Spetters (1980; Dutch) . . . . .Hans
  ••• 0:35—Frontal nudity, measuring and comparing his manlihood with his friends in the auto shop.

  • 1:21—Buns, getting gang raped by gay guy he has been stealing money from.
Kafka (1992; U.S./French) . . . . Youthful Anarchist

Albert, Edward

Son of actor Eddie Albert.
Films:
Butterflies Are Free (1972) . . . . .Don
Forty Carats (1973) . . . . .Peter Latham
The Domino Principle (1977). . . . . Ross Pine
The Purple Taxi (1977; French/Italian/Irish) . . . . . . .Jerry
The Greek Tycoon (1978). . . . . Nico Tomasis
Galaxy of Terror (1981) . . . . Cabren
Ellie (1984). . . . . .Tom
House Where Evil Dwells (1985) . . . . Ted
  • 1:00—Very brief, upper half of buns, while making love with Susan George on the floor.
Getting Even (1986). . . . . .Taggar
The Underachievers (1987) . . . . Danny Warren
The Rescue (1988) . . . . Commander Merrill
Wild Zone (1989). . . . . .Colonel Lavera
Made for Cable Movies:
Body Language (1992; USA) . . . . Charles
Made for Cable TV:
The Hitchhiker: Man at the Window (1985; HBO)
  . . . . .Arthur Brown
Miniseries:
The Last Convertible (1979). . . . . .Ron Dalrymple
TV:
The Yellow Rose (1983-84). . . . . Quisto Champion
Falcon Crest (1986-89). . . . . Jeff Wainwright

Alden, John

Films:
The Young Warriors (1983; U.S./Canadian). . . . Jorge
  • 0:16—Dropping his pants in a room during pledge at fraternity.
Making the Grade (1984). . . . . Egbert Williamson

Alin, Jeff

Films:
Coming Together (1978) . . . . Frank Hughes
a.k.a. A Matter of Love
  • 1:05—Buns, while putting pants on with Richard.

Altamura, John

Films:
Young Nurses in Love (1987) . . . . n.a.
New York's Finest (1988) . . . . .Brian Morrison
The Toxic Avenger: Part II (1988) . . . . Toxic Avenger
The Toxic Avenger III: The Last Temptation of Toxie (1989) . . . . Toxic Avenger
The Marilyn Diaries (1990) . . . . .Frankie
Private Screenings.
  • 0:13—Buns, while in hall after Marilyn Chambers takes his sheet away.
Affairs of the Heart (1992) . . . . Jock #1
Private Screenings.

Amer, Nicholas

Miniseries:

I, Claudius—Episode 12, A God in Colchester
(1976; British) . . . . Mnester
(Available on video tape in *I, Claudius—Volume 6*.)
- • 0:04—Brief buns, while in bed with Lady Messalina.

Anderson, Marc

Films:

Coming Together (1978) . . . . Richard Duncan
a.k.a. A Matter of Love
- •• 0:13—Buns, while kneeling and kissing Angie, then
more buns making love.
- • 0:58—Buns, while making love with Vicky.
- • 1:05—Buns, while putting pants on with Frank.

Andrews, Anthony

Films:

Under the Volcano (1984) . . . . Hugh Firmin
The Second Victory (1986) . . . . Major Hanlon
Hanna's War (1988) . . . . . Squadron Leader McCormick
The Lighthorsemen (1988; Australian)
. . . . Major Meinertzhagen

Miniseries:

Brideshead Revisited (1981; British)
. . . . Sebastian Flyte
- •• 0:17—(Part 3 on TV or Book 2 on video tape.) Buns,
while standing on roof with Jeremy Irons after talking with Cordelia.

Made for TV Movies:

The Scarlet Pimpernel (1982) . . . . n.a.
Bluegrass (1988) . . . . Fitzgerald

Anglade, Jean-Hughes

Films:

Betty Blue (1986; French) . . . . Zorg
- ••• 0:09—Frontal nudity.
- •• 1:03—Nude trying to sleep in living room.
- •• 1:39—Frontal nudity walking to the bathroom.
- •• 1:45—Frontal nudity talking on the telephone.
La Femme Nikita (1991; French/Italian) . . . . Marco
a.k.a. Nikita

Anthony, Corwyn

Films:

Student Confidential (1987) . . . . Greg
- • 1:26—Buns, while getting into bed with Susan.

Antin, Steve

Films:

The Last American Virgin (1982) . . . . Rick
Sweet Sixteen (1982) . . . . Hank Burke
The Goonies (1985) . . . . Troy
Penitentiary III (1987) . . . . Roscoe
The Accused (1988) . . . . Bob Joiner
- • 1:29—Buns, while raping Jodi Foster on the pinball
machine.
Without You I'm Nothing (1990) . . . . Steve Antin

• Ardi, Richard

Films:

Bikini Island (1991) . . . . Tasha's Girlfriend
Video Tapes:

Intimate Workout For Lovers (1992)
. . . . Morning Stretch
- ••• 0:29—Nude, in bed and on the patio.

Arkin, Alan

Films:

The Russians are Coming, The Russians are Coming
(1966) . . . . Rozanov
Wait Until Dark (1967) . . . . Boat
Woman Times Seven (1967) . . . . Fred
The Heart is a Lonely Hunter (1968) . . . . . . John Singer
Catch-22 (1970) . . . . Captain Yossarian
- • 0:52—Buns, while standing wearing only his hat,
talking to Dreedle. Don't see his face.
Last of the Red Hot Lovers (1972) . . . Barneau Cashman
Freebie and the Bean (1974) . . . . Bean
Hearts of the West (1975) . . . . Kessler
Rafferty and the Gold Dust Twins (1975) . . . . . . Rafferty
The Seven-Per-Cent Solution (1976) . . . Sigmund Freud
The In-Laws (1979) . . . . Sheldon Kornpett
Simon (1980) . . . . Simon Mendelssohn
Chu Chu and the Philly Flash (1981) . . . . Flash
Improper Channels (1981; Canadian) . . . . Jeffrey
Bad Medicine (1985) . . . . Dr. Madera
Joshua Then and Now (1985; Canadian)
. . . . Reuben Shapiro
Big Trouble (1986) . . . . Leonard Hoffman
Coupe de Ville (1990) . . . . Fred Libner
Edward Scissorhands (1990) . . . . Bill
Havana (1990) . . . . Joe Volpi
The Rocketeer (1991) . . . . Peevy
Glengarry Glen Ross (1992) . . . . n.a.

Ashby, Linden

Films:

Night Angel (1989) . . . . Craig
- • 1:22—Buns, while kneeling down to pick up picture.
Don't see his face.
Into the Sun (1991) . . . . n.a.
Video Tapes:

Inside Out 3 (1992) . . . . Jed/Tango

• Astin, Sean

Son of actress Patty Duke and actor John Astin.
Films:

The Goonies (1985) . . . . Mikey
Like Father, Like Son (1987) . . . . Trigger
White Water Summer (1987) . . . . . . Alan Block/Narrator
Staying Together (1989) . . . . Duncan McDermott
The War of the Roses (1989) . . . . Josh, Age 17
Memphis Belle (1990) . . . . Richard "Rascal" Moore
Toy Soldiers (1991) . . . . Billy Tepper
- • 1:08—Brief buns, while taking off his wet clothes af-
ter coming in through the window.
The Willies (1991) . . . . Michael

Atkins, Christopher
Films:
Blue Lagoon (1980) . . . . .Richard
- •• 0:27—Nude swimming underwater after growing up from little children.
- • 0:29—Buns, while underwater.
- •• 1:03—Nude swimming under water.
- • 1:05—Buns, while kissing Brooke Shields.
- •• 1:09—Very brief frontal nudity in water slide with Shields.

The Pirate Movie (1982; Australian). . . . . Frederic
A Night in Heaven (1983) . . . . Rick
- • 1:03—Very brief frontal nudity when he pulls down his pants in hotel room with Leslie Ann Warren.
- • 1:15—Brief buns while on boat with Leslie Ann Warren's angry husband.

Beaks The Movie (1987) .Peter
Mortuary Academy (1988) . . . . Sam Grimm
Listen to Me (1989) . . . . Bruce Arlington
Made for Cable Movies:
Fatal Charm (1992; Showtime) . . . . Adam Brenner
TV:
Dallas (1983-84) . . . . .Peter Richards
Rock 'n' Roll Summer Action (1985) . . . . Host
Magazines:
Playboy (Nov 1980) . . . . Sex in Cinema 1980
- ••• 183—Frontal nudity.

Babb, Roger
Films:
Working Girls (1987) . . . . Paul
- • 1:18—Frontal nudity with Molly.

Bacon, Kevin
Husband of actress Kyra Sedgwick.
Films:
Animal House (1978) . . . . Chip Diller
Friday the 13th (1980) . . . . Jack
- • 0:39—Close up of buns when Marci squeezes them.

Only When I Laugh (1981) . . . . Don
Diner (1982) . . . . Fenwick
Forty Deuce (1982) . . . . .Rickey
Footloose (1984) . . . . .Ren
Enormous Changes at the Last Minute (1985)
. . . . Dennis
Quicksilver (1986) . . . . Jack Casey
End of the Line (1987) . . . . Everett
Planes, Trains and Automobiles (1987) . . . . . .Taxi Racer
White Water Summer (1987) Vic
She's Having a Baby (1988) . . . . . Jefferson "Jake" Briggs
The Big Picture (1989) . . . . Nick Chapman
Criminal Law (1989) . . . . Martin Thiel
Tremors (1989) . . . . Valentine McKee
Flatliners (1990) . . . . David Labraccio
he said, she said (1991) . . . . Dan Hanson
JFK (1991) . . . . Willie O'Keefe
Pyrates (1991) . . . . Ari
- • 0:06—Brief side view of buns several times while making love with Kyra Sedgwick. Long shot.

- •• 0:22—Buns in jock strap, while horsing around in bed with Sedgwick.

Queens Logic (1991) .Dennis
TV:
The Guiding Light . . . . Tim Werner

Baggetta, Vincent
Films:
Two-Minute Warning (1976) . . . . Ted Shelley
The Man Who Wasn't There (1983) . . . . Riley
- • 0:23—Buns, while lying on the floor after fighting with the other guys.

TV:
Chicago Story (1982) . . . . Lou Pellegrino

Bahner, Blake
Films:
Sensations (1988) . . . . Brian Ingles
- •• 0:10—Very, very brief lower frontal nudity pushing the covers off the bed, then buns, while getting out of bed.

Caged Fury (1989) .Buck Lewis
Lethal Persuit (1989) . . . . Warren
Demon Sword (1991) . . . . Thane
a.k.a. Wizards of the Demon Sword

Baio, Scott
Films:
Bugsy Malone (1976) . . . . Bugsy Malone
Skatetown, U.S.A. (1979) . . . . Richie
Foxes (1980) . . . . Brad
Zapped! (1982) . . . . Barney
I Love N.Y. (1987) . . . . Mario Colone
- • 1:19—Brief, upper half of buns, while getting out of bed. Dark, hard to see.

Made for TV Movies:
Happy Days Reunion (1992) . . Charles "Chachi" Arcola
TV:
Happy Days (1977-84) . . . . Charles "Chachi" Arcola
Blansky's Beauties (1977) . . . . Anthony DeLuca
Who's Watching the Kids? (1978)
. . . . Frankie "The Fox" Vitola
Joanie Loves Chachi (1982-83)
. . . . Charles "Chachi" Arcola
Charles in Charge (1984-85) . . . . Charles
Charles in Charge (1987-90) . . . . Charles
Baby Talk (1991-92) .James

• Baker, Henry Judd
Films:
Neighbors (1981) . . . . Policeman
After Hours (1985) . . . . Jett
The Money Pit (1986) . . . . .Oscar
Clean and Sober (1988) . . . . Xavier
- •• 0:15—Buns, when going crazy in drug rehabilitation room.

The Mighty Quinn (1989) . . . . Nicotine
The Super (1991) . . . . First Man on Stoop

Baker, Scott

Films:
Delivery Boys (1984) . . . . Snooty Man
Cleo/Leo (1989) . . . . Leo Blockman
• 0:09—Very brief buns after getting his butt kicked.
The Butcher's Wife (1991) . . . . Fire Eater

Baldwin, William

Brother of actors Alec, Steven and Daniel Baldwin.
Films:
Flatliners (1990) . . . . Joe Hurley
Backdraft (1991) . . . . Brian McCaffrey
•• 0:33—Brief buns (on the left) in the shower room
with Jason Gedrick.

Ball, Rod

Films:
Porky's (1981; Canadian) . . . . Steve
• 0:18—Brief frontal nudity sitting on bench in the
cabin.
• 0:21—Very brief frontal nudity, following Meat out
the front door of the cabin, then buns, while in front
of the house.
Porky's II: The Next Day (1983; Canadian) . . . . . . Steve
Rhinestone (1984). . . . . Heckler
Cape Fear (1991) . . . . Prisoner

Banderas, Antonio

Films:
Matador (1986; Spanish) . . . . Angel
Women on the Verge of a Nervous Breakdown
(1988; Spanish). . . . . Carlos
Tie Me Up! Tie Me Down! (1990; Spanish) . . . . . Ricky
• 1:17—Buns in mirror on ceiling, while making love
with Victoria Abril. Long shot.
Truth or Dare (1991). Himself
The Mambo Kings (1992) . . . . Nestor Castillo
• 0:48—Buns, while in bed on top of Maruschka Detmers.
• 1:10—Upper half of buns, sitting on side of bed,
while putting his pants on.

Barbareschi, Luca

Films:
Bye Bye Baby (1989; Italian) . . . . Paulo
• 0:20—Brief buns, while on top of Brigitte Nielsen in
bed.

•Barber, Paul

Films:
The Long Good Friday (1980; British) . . . . Erroll
• 0:42—Brief buns, getting cut on his rear end during
interrogation.

Barro, Cesare

Films:
My Father's Wife (1976; Italian) . . . . Claudio
• 0:52—Buns, while bringing Patricia champagne.
Inhibition (1984; Italian) . . . . n.a.

Bates, Alan

Films:
Whistle Down the Wind (1961; British)
. . . . Arthur Blakey, The Man
Zorba the Greek (1963) . . . . Basil
Georgy Girl (1966; British) . . . . Jos
King of Hearts (1966; French/Italian)
. . . . Private Charles Plumpick
Women in Love (1971) . . . . Rupert
• 0:25—Buns and brief frontal nudity walking around
the woods rubbing himself with everything.
• 0:50—Buns, while making love with Ursula after a
boy and girl drown in the river.
••• 0:54—Nude fighting with Oliver Reed in a room in
front of a fireplace. Long scene.
Impossible Object (1973; French) . . . . Harry
An Unmarried Woman (1978) . . . . Saul
The Rose (1979) . . . . Rudge
The Shout (1979). . . . . Charles Crossly
Quartet (1981; British/French) . . . . H.J. Heidler
Return of the Soldier (1983; British) . . . . Chris
The Wicked Lady (1983; British). . . . . Jerry Jackson
Duet for One (1987) . . . . David Cornwallis
A Prayer for the Dying (1987) . . . . Jack Meehan
We Think the World of You (1988; British) . . . . . Frank
Club Extinction (1990). . . . . Dr. Marsfeldt
a.k.a. Doctor M
Hamlet (1990) . . . . King Claudius
Mr. Frost (1990; French/British) . . . . Inspector Detweiler
Made for TV Movies:
Pack of Lies (1987). Stewart

•Bauer, Steven

Films:
Scarface (1983) . . . . Manny Ray
Thief of Hearts (1984) . . . . Scott Muller
(Special Home Video Version reviewed.)
•• 0:53—Brief side view of buns, carrying Barbara Wil-
liams into bed.
Running Scared (1986) . . . . Frank
The Beast (1988) . . . . Taj
Wildfire (1988). . . . . Frank
Gleaming the Cube (1989) . . . . Al Lucero
A Climate for Killing (1990) . . . . Paul McGraw
Raising Cain (1992) . . . . n.a.
Made for Cable TV:
Red Shoe Diaries: Safe Sex (1992; Showtime)
. . . . The Man/Michael
• 0:12—Buns, taking off his pants and making love
with Joan Severance on the floor. Don't see his face
very well, but it's him.
Miniseries:
False Arrest (1991) . . . . Det. Dan Ryan
TV:
Wiseguy (1990) . . . . Michael Santana
Magazines:
Playgirl (Nov 1987) . . . . Raw Footage
35—Buns and blurred frontal nudity in stills from
Thief of Hearts.

Bean, Sean
Films:
How to Get Ahead in Advertising (1988). . . . Carry Frisk
Stormy Monday (1988) . . . . Brendan
•• 0:37—Buns, putting on his underwear while Melanie Griffith watches.
The Field (1991) . . . . .n.a.

Beatty, Warren
Brother of actress/author Shirley MacLaine.
Husband of actress Annette Bening.
Films:
Splendor in the Grass (1961). . . . . Bud Stamper
Lilith (1964) . . . . Vincent Bruce
Bonnie and Clyde (1967) . . . . Clyde
McCabe and Mrs. Miller (1971) . . . . John McCabe
Dollars (1972). . . . . .Joe Collins
The Parallax View (1974). . . . . Joe
The Fortune (1975) . . . . Nicky
Shampoo (1975). . . . . George
• 0:42—Upper half of buns with pants a little bit down in the bathroom with Julie Christie.
• 1:24—Buns, while making love with Christie when Goldie Hawn discovers them. Long shot, hard to see.
Heaven Can Wait (1978). . . . . Joe Pendleton
Reds (1981) . . . . .John Reed
Ishtar (1987). . . . . Lyle Rogers
Dick Tracy (1990) . . . . .Dick Tracy
Bugsy (1991) . . . . Benjamin "Bugsy" Siegel
Truth or Dare (1991). . . . . .Himself
TV:
The Many Loves of Dobie Gillis (1959-60)
. . . . Milton Armitage

•Beckley, Tony
Films:
Get Carter (1971) . . . . .Peter
Revenge of the Pink Panther (1978) . . . . Guy Algo
When a Stranger Calls (1979) . . . . . . .Curt Duncan
• 1:07—Side view of buns, while kneeling in restroom.

Beghe, Jason
Films:
Compromising Positions (1985) . . . . Cupcake
Monkey Shines: An Experiment in Fear (1988)
. . . . .Allan Mann
• 0:01—Side view of buns while on the floor, stretching to go running.
The Chinatown Murders: Man Against the Mob (1989)
. . . . .Sammy
Made for Cable Movies:
Bodily Harm (1989). . . . . John

Begley, Ed, Jr.
Films:
Blue Collar (1978). . . . . .Bobby Joe
Hardcore (1979) . . . . Soldier
Private Lessons (1981). . . . . .Jack Travis

Cat People (1982) . . . . Joe Creigh
Eating Raoul (1982) . . . . Hippie
Young Doctors in Love (1982) . . . Young Simon's Father
Get Crazy (1983) . . . . Colin
Protocol (1984) . . . . .Hassler
Streets of Fire (1984) . . . . Ben Gunn
Transylvania 6-5000 (1985) . . . . Gil Turner
Amazon Women on the Moon (1987) . . . . . . Griffin
• 0:54—Buns, while walking around as the Son of the Invisible Man. This section is in B&W.
The Accidental Tourist (1988). . . . . Charles
Meet the Applegates (1989) . . . . Dick Applegate
• 0:46—Buns, while runnning around nuclear power plant after his pile of clothes are taken away by the janitor.
Scenes from the Class Struggle in Beverly Hills (1989)
. . . . Peter
Made for Cable Movies:
Running Mates (1992; HBO) . . . . Chapman
Made for TV Movies:
A Shining Season (1979) . . . . n.a.
Spies, Lies & Naked Thighs (1988). . . . . n.a.
In the Best Interest of the Child (1990). . Howard Feldon
Chance of a Lifetime (1991). . . . . Darrel
In the Line of Duty: Siege at Marion (1992)
. . . . Fred House
TV:
Roll Out (1973-74). . . . . Lt. Robert W. Chapman
St. Elsewhere (1982-88). . . . . Dr. Victor Erlich
Parenthood (1990). . . . . Gil Buckman

Belle, Ekkhardt
Films:
Julia (1974; German) .Patrick
• 1:01—Very brief buns, while in bed with Terry.

Beltran, Robert
Films:
Zoot Suit (1981) . . . . Lowrider
Eating Raoul (1982) . . . . .Raoul
Lone Wolf McQuade (1983). . . . . Kayo
Night of the Comet (1984) . . . . Hector
Gaby, A True Story (1987) . . . . Luis
Scenes from the Class Struggle in Beverly Hills
(1989) . . . . .Juan
• 1:34—Brief buns, when his shorts are pulled down by Frank.
Crack Down (1990) . . . . .Juan Delgado
Bugsy (1991) . . . . .Alejandro
Kiss Me a Killer (1991) . . . . Tony
To Die Standing (1991) . . . . n.a.
Made for TV Movies:
The Chase (1991). . . . . Mike Silva
Stormy Weathers (1992) . . . . Gio

Benben, Brian

Husband of actress Madeleine Stowe.
Films:
Clean and Sober (1988) . . . . Martin Laux
I Come in Peace (1990). . . . . .Laurence Smith
Made for Cable TV:
Dream On: Doing the Bossa Nova (1990; HBO)
. . . . Martin Tupper
  • 0:07—Brief lower half of buns while making love on
     photocopier with Vicki Frederick.
Dream On: Sex and the Single Parent (1990; HBO)
. . . . Martin Tupper
  •• 0:11—Brief buns when Ms. Brodsky fantasizes about
     him when he walks out the classroom door.
Dream On: And Bimbo Was His Name-O
(1992; HBO) . . . . Martin Tupper
  • 0:07—Buns, four times, on top of Teri Garr in bed.
     Don't see his face, but it's him.
Dream On: Come and Knock On Our Door...
(1992; HBO) . . . . Martin Tupper
  •• 0:16—Buns, while getting out of bed in hotel room
     with Eddie.
TV:
The Gangster Chronicles (1981) . . . . Michael Lasker
Kay O'Brien (1986) . . . . Dr. Mark Doyle

Beneyton, Yves

Films:
The Lacemaker (1977; French) . . . . François
  • 0:57—Buns, while walking to bed. Dark.

Benjamin, Richard

Actor turned director.
Husband of actress Paula Prentiss.
Films:
Goodbye, Columbus (1969) . . . . Neil
  • 1:11—Brief buns, while walking into the bathroom.
     Very, very brief frontal nudity. Blurry, hard to see
     anything.
Catch-22 (1970) . . . . Major Danby
Diary of a Mad Housewife (1970) . . . . . .Jonathan Balser
The Marriage of a Young Stockbroker (1971)
. . . . William Alren
The Steagle (1971) . . . . .Harold Weiss
Portnoy's Complaint (1972) . . . . Alexander Portnoy
The Last of Sheila (1973). . . . . Tom
Westworld (1973) . . . . Peter Martin
Sunshine Boys (1975) . . . . Ben Clark
House Calls (1978) . . . . Dr. Norman Solomon
Love at First Bite (1979) . . . . . .Dr. Jeff Rosenberg
Scavenger Hunt (1979). . . . . Stuart
First Family (1980) . . . . Press Secretary Bunthorne
How to Beat the High Cost of Living (1980) . . . . . Albert
The Last Married Couple in America (1980)
. . . . Marv Cooper
Saturday the 14th (1981) . . . . John
TV:
He & She (1967-68) . . . . Dick Hollister
Quark (1978) . . . . .Adam Quark

Benson, Robby

Films:
Lucky Lady (1973) . . . . Billy Webber
Ode to Billy Joe (1976). . . . . Billy Joe McAllister
One on One (1977) . . . . Henry Steele
The Chosen (1978; Italian/British) . . . . Danny Saunders
The End (1978) . . . . The Priest
Ice Castles (1979). . . . . Nick Peterson
Walk Proud (1979). Emilio
Tribute (1980; Canadian) . . . . .Jud Templeton
Running Brave (1983; Canadian) . . . . Billy Mills
Harry and Son (1984) . . . . Howard
Modern Love (1990). . . . . .Greg Frank
  •• 0:35—Brief buns while running out of room after
     finding out he's going to be a father.
     0:36—Long shot of buns, while standing on roof of
     house yelling the good news to the world.
TV:
Tough Cookies (1986) . . . . Det. Cliff Brady

Berenger, Tom

Films:
Looking for Mr. Goodbar (1977) . . . . Gary
The Sentinel (1977) . . . . Man at End
In Praise of Older Women (1978; Canadian)
. . . . .Andras Vayda
  • 0:32—Buns, while in bed with Karen Black (seen in
     mirror). Long shot.
  •• 1:04—Buns, while rolling off Susan Strasberg. Kind
     of dark.
  •• 1:07—Very brief lower frontal nudity three times,
     standing up and picking up Strasberg.
  • 1:20—Very brief frontal nudity turning over in bed
     waiting for Alexandra Stewart.
  • 1:23—Very, very brief blurry frontal nudity turning
     over in bed after getting mad at Alexandra Stewart.
  ••• 1:42—Buns, while undressing with Helen Shaver.
     Very brief balls.
Butch and Sundance: The Early Days (1979)
. . . . Butch Cassidy
The Dogs of War (1980; British) . . . . .Drew
Beyond Obsession (1982) . . . . Matthew
The Big Chill (1983). . . . . .Sam
Eddie and the Cruisers (1983) . . . . Frank
Fear City (1984). Matt Rossi
Rustler's Rhapsody (1985) . . . . Rex O'Herlihan
Platoon (1986). . . . . Barnes
Someone to Watch Over Me (1987). . . . . . Mike Keagan
Betrayed (1988). . . . . .Gary Simmons
Last Rites (1988) . . . . Michael
Shoot to Kill (1988) . . . . .Jonathan Knox
Born on the Fourth of July (1989)
. . . . Recruiting Sergeant
Major League (1989) . . . . .Jake Taylor
Love at Large (1990) . . . . Harry Dobbs
At Play in the Fields of the Lord (1991)
. . . . .Lewis Moon
  •• 0:45—Buns, while taking off his clothes after para-
     chuting into the jungle.

••• 0:46—Nude, arriving at the Niaruna village.
• 0:47—Very brief buns and frontal nudity.
• 0:50—Buns, while entering hut.
••• 0:52—Brief frontal nudity while standing up, then buns, while walking.
•• 0:54—Buns, while wearing G-string.
••• 0:55—More buns, wearing G-string, while walking in the forest.
•• 0:56—More buns, with Pindi.
• 1:31—(0:01 into tape 2) Buns, in G-string.
••• 2:14—(0:44 into tape 2) Buns, in G-string, with Pindi.
• 2:47—(1:17 into tape 2) Buns, outside in G-string.
•• 2:50—(1:20 into tape 2) Buns, in G-string when the white men in the helicopter fire bomb the village.
The Field (1991) . . . . .n.a.
Shattered (1991). Dan Merrick
Made for Cable TV:
Dream On: The Second Greatest Story Ever Told (1991; HBO) . . . . Nick Spencer
TV:
One Life to Live . . . . .Tim Siegel
Magazines:
Playboy (Nov 1992) . . . . Sex in Cinema 1992
•• 147—Frontal nudity from *At Play in the Fields of the Lord.*

Berger, Helmut
Films:
The Damned (1969; German). . . Martin Von Essenbeck
• 2:03—Buns, while walking up to his mother and ripping her dress off. Dark, don't see his face.
Dorian Gray (1970; Italian/British/German)
. . . . Dorian Gray
The Garden of the Finzi-Continis (1971; Italian/German)
. . . . Alberto
Ash Wednesday (1973) .Erich
Ludwig (1973; Italian). . . . . .Ludwig
Conversation Piece (1974; Italian/French) . . . . . . Konrad
The Romantic Englishwoman (1975; British/French)
. . . . Thomas
• 1:08—Upper half of buns, while sitting at edge of pool talking to Glenda Jackson.
Code Name: Emerald (1985). . . . . Ernst Ritter
The Godfather, Part III (1990) . . . . . . .Frederick Keinszig
TV:
Dynasty (1983-84) . . . . .Peter de Vilbis

• Bergin, Patrick
Films:
The Courier (1988; British) . . . . Christy
Mountains of the Moon (1989). . . . . Richard Burton
Love Crimes (1991) . . . . David Hanover
(Unrated version reviewed.)
• 1:02—Buns, during love scene with Sean Young. Lit with red light, don't see his face.
Sleeping with the Enemy (1991) . . . . Martin Bruney

Berling, Peter
Films:
Aguirre, The Wrath of God (1972; West German)
. . . . Don Fernando de Guzman
Julia (1974; German) . . . . Alex Lovener
• 0:12—Brief buns, while playing the piano outside on the dock.
The Marriage of Maria Braun (1979; German)
. . . . Bronski
Fitzcarraldo (1982). . . . . Opera Manager

• Bernard, Erick
Films:
The Passion of Beatrice (1988; French) . . . . . L'amant
• 0:06—Brief buns, in bed with François' mother when discovered by François.
Cyrano De Bergerac (1990; French) . . . . Cadet

Bernsen, Collin
Son of actress Jeanne Cooper.
Brother of actor Corbin Bernsen.
Films:
Dangerous Love (1988) . . . . .Brooks
Hangfire (1990) . . . . .RTO
Mr. Destiny (1990). . . . . Tom Robertson
Puppet Master II (1990) . . . . Michael
•• 1:10—Buns, while putting out fire on the bed.
Double Trouble (1991). . . . . Whitney Regan
Made for Cable Movies:
Sketch Artist (1992; Showtime) . . . . Phillipe
Video Tapes:
Inside Out 3 (1992) . . . . Dennis/The Wet Dream

Bernsen, Corbin
Son of actress Jeanne Cooper.
Brother of actor Collin Bernsen.
Husband of actress Amanda Pays.
Films:
Three the Hard Way (1974) . . . . Boy
S.O.B. (1981). . . . . n.a.
Hello Again! (1987) . . . . Jason Chadman
Bert Rigby, You're a Fool (1989) . . . . Jim Shirley
Disorganized Crime (1989) . . . . Frank Salazar
Major League (1989). . . . . Roger Dorn
• 0:58—Brief buns, while running in locker room to cover himself with a towel when Rachel comes in to talk to the team.
Shattered (1991) . . . . Jeb Scott
Made for Cable Movies:
Dead on the Money (1991) . . . . n.a.
Miniseries:
Grass Roots (1992). . . . . Will Lee
Made for TV Movies:
Line of Fire: The Morris Dees Story (1991)
. . . . Morris Dees
TV:
L.A. Law (1986-) . . . . Arnie Becker

Biehn, Michael

Films:
Coach (1978). . . . . Jack
  • 1:11—Upper half of buns, while in shower with
    Cathy Lee Crosby.
Hogwild (1980; Canadian) .Tim
The Fan (1981) . . . . Douglas Breen
The Lords of Discipline (1983). . . . . .Alexander
The Terminator (1984) . . . . .Kyle Reese
  • 0:06—Side view of buns after arriving from the fu-
    ture. Brief buns running down the alley. A little dark.
Aliens (1986). Corporal Hicks
In a Shallow Grave (1988). . . . . Garnet Montrose
The Seventh Sign (1988). . . . . Russell Quinn
The Abyss (1989) . . . . Lieutenant Coffey
Navy SEALS (1990) . . . . Curran
Timebomb (1990). . . . . Eddy Kay
K2 (1991). . . . . Taylor Brooks
  • 0:43—Brief buns, while standing up in pool outside.
Made for Cable Movies:
A Taste For Killing (1992; USA) . . . . .Bo Landry

Blake, Robert

Films:
PT 109 (1963). . . . . "Bucky" Harris
This Property is Condemned (1966) . . . . Sidney
In Cold Blood (1967) . . . . .Perry Smith
Tell Them Willie Boy is Here (1969) . . . . Willie
  0:22—Sort of buns when Katherine Ross lies down
    with him. Very, very brief lower frontal nudity seen
    through spread legs (one frame). More buns. Long
    shot, hard to see.
Electra Glide in Blue (1973). . . . . John Wintergreen
Busting (1974) . . . . Farrell
Coast to Coast (1980). . . . . Charlie Callahan
Made for TV Movies:
Of Mice and Men (1981) . . . . .n.a.
TV:
Baretta (1975-78) . . . . Detective Tony Baretta
Hell Town (1985) . . . . Father Noah Rivers

• Blodgett, Michael

Films:
The Catalina Caper (1967) . . . . .Bob Draper
There Was a Crooked Man (1970). . . . . . Coy Cavendish
The Velvet Vampire (1971) . . . . Lee Ritter
  •• 0:21—Buns, getting up out of bed during desert
    dream scene.
  ••• 0:42—Buns, in desert dream scene.
  •• 0:46—Buns, while on floor with Diane.
The Carey Treatment (1972) . . . . .Roger Hudson
The Ultimate Thrill (1974) . . . . Tom

Blundell, Graeme

Films:
Alvin Purple (1973; Australian). . . . . Alvin Purple
  •• 0:21—Brief nude, while painting Samantha's body.
  •• 0:22—Buns and brief frontal nudity in bedroom with
    the Kinky Lady.

• 0:25—Brief buns with Mrs. Warren—who turns out
  to be a man.
• 0:26—Very brief frontal nudity running out of room,
  then buns going down the stairs.
••• 0:33—Nude, undressing and taking a shower. Shot
  at fast speed.
•• 1:04—Nude, running away from the girl during
  showing of movie.
• 1:21—Buns, while getting chased by a group of
  women down the street.
Alvin Rides Again (1974; Australian) . . . .Alvin Purple
• 0:06—Buns, while running out of the office after he's
  awakened. Blurry.
Don's Party (1976; Australian) . . . . Simon
Pacific Banana (1980). .n.a.
The Year My Voice Broke (1987; Australian)
. . . . Nils Olson

• Bluteau, Lothaire

Films:
Jesus of Montreal (1990; French/Canadian)
. . . . .Daniel Coulombe
  • 0:43—Buns, getting whipped while tied to a tree
    during a play. Long shot.
  • 0:44—Buns, during crucifixion during play.
  • 1:13—Upper half of frontal nudity when police ar-
    rest him during play.
  • 1:36—Very brief frontal nudity when the cross he's
    on falls over.
Black Robe (1991; Canadian/Australian)
. . . . Father Laforgue
  • 0:29—Brief buns, while making love with Annuka in
    the woods at night.
  •• 1:04—Buns, while standing in Iroquois hut.
Magazines:
Playboy (Nov 1990) . . . . Sex in Cinema 1990
  •• 141—Full frontal nudity from *Jesus of Montreal*.

Bogosian, Eric

Films:
Special Effects (1984) .Neville
  • 0:21—Buns, while fighting with Zoe Tamerlis in bed.
    Medium long shot.
Talk Radio (1988) . . . . Barry Champlain
Sex, Drugs, Rock & Roll (1991) . . . . Himself

• Bolano, Tony

Films:
Cat Chaser (1988) . . . . Corky
  •• 1:16—Nude, undressing in bathroom with Andres,
    before getting shot by Charles Durning.

Bonanno, Louis

Films:
Sex Appeal (1986) . . . . Tony
Slammer Girls (1987) .Cubby
Student Affairs (1987) . . . . Louie Balducci
Wimps (1987) . . . . .Francis
  • 1:13—Buns, while running into a restaurant kitchen.

Cool As Ice (1991) . . . . .Sugar Shack Singer
Video Tapes:
Night of the Living Babes (1987). . . . . .Buck

Bond, Steve

Films:
Massacre at Central High (1976). . . . . Craig
H.O.T.S. (1979) . . . . .John
  • 0:32—Buns, while trapped in van with K. C. Winkler.
The Prey (1980) . . . . .Joel
Magdelena (1988) . . . . .Joseph Mohr
To Die For (1988) . . . . Tom
Picasso Trigger (1989). .n.a.
To Die For 2 (1991). . . . . Tom
TV:
Santa Barbara . . . . Mack Blake
General Hospital (1983-86). . . . . .Jimmy Lee Holt

Bondy, Christopher

Made for Cable Movies:
Deadly Survallance (1991; Showtime). . . . . . . Nickels
  • 0:31—Buns, while dropping his towel to run after
  Michael.

Boorman, Charley

Son of British director John Boorman.
Films:
Dream One (1984; British/French) . . . . Cunegond
The Emerald Forest (1985) . . . . .Tommy
  • 0:23—Brief buns, while running through camp.
  • 0:24—Brief buns, while running from waterfall and
  diving into pond.
  • 0:30—Buns, during ceremony.
  • 0:45—Buns, while running away from the Fierce
  People with his dad.
  • 1:02—Buns while running on the rocks, then bun in
  hut.
  •• 1:31—Buns while climbing up the building.
  • 1:35—Buns while running down the hall to save
  Kachiri.
Hope and Glory (1987; British) . . . . .Luftwaffe Pilot

Boretski, Paul

Films:
Spacehunter: Adventures in the Forbidden Zone (1983)
Jarrett
Perfect Timing (1984) . . . . Joe
  •• 0:11—Brief frontal nudity and buns, while rolling
  over on the bed.
  • 0:29—Frontal nudity on the roof in the snow with
  Bonnie.
  • 0:35—Buns, while on bed getting slapped on the
  behind.
  • 0:50—Buns, while in bed with Judy.
  •• 1:03—Brief frontal nudity on TV with Judy while he
  and Bonnie watch.

Bottoms, Joseph

Brother of actors Sam and Timothy Bottoms.
Films:
The Dove (1974; British) . . . . .Robin Lee Graham
Crime and Passion (1976) . . . . Larry
High Rolling (1977; Australian). . . . . .Texas
The Black Hole (1979) . . . . . . .Lieutenant Charles Pizer
Cloud Dancer (1980) . . . . .Tom Loomis
Surfacing (1980) . . . . .Joe
  • 0:23—Buns, while in bed with Kathleen Beller.
King of the Mountain (1981) . . . . Buddy
Blind Date (1984). . . . . Jonathon Ratcliffe
  (Not the same 1987 *Blind Date* with Bruce Willis.)
Born to Race (1988) . . . . .Al Pagura
  • 0:55—Brief buns, while taking off bathrobe on deck
  and jumping into the lake.
Inner Sanctum (1991). . . . . .Baxter Reed
  • 0:10—Lower half of buns, while in office with Mar-
  gaux Hemingway.
  ••• 0:43—Buns, while on sofa with Tanya Roberts.
Made for Cable Movies:
Treacherous Crossing (1992; USA) . . . . n.a.
Miniseries:
Holocaust (1978) . . . . Rudi Weiss
Made for TV Movies:
Gunsmoke: To the Last Man (1992) . . . Tommy Graham

Bottoms, Sam

Brother of actors Joseph and Timothy Bottoms.
Films:
The Last Picture Show (1971) . . . . .Billy
  • 0:41—Brief buns, after falling out of car with Jimmy
  Sue.
Class of '44 (1973). Marty
The Outlaw Josey Wales (1976) . . . . .Jamie
Apocalypse Now (1979). . . . . .Lance
Bronco Billy (1980) . . . . .Leonard
Prime Risk (1985). . . . . Bill Yeoman
Dolly Dearest (1992) . . . . n.a.

Bottoms, Timothy

Brother of actors Joseph and Sam Bottoms.
Films:
Johnny Got His Gun (1971) . . . . .Joe Bonham
The Last Picture Show (1971). . . . . Sonny Crawford
The Paper Chase (1973). . . . . .Hart
The White Dawn (1974). . . . . .Daggett
Small Town in Texas (1976) . . . . Poke
Rollercoaster (1977) . . . . Young Man
The Other Side of the Mountain, Part II (1978)
. . . . John Boothe
Hurricane (1979) . . . . .Jack Sanford
The High Country (1980; Canadian). . . . . .Jim
  • 1:19—Buns, while walking into the pond with Linda
  Purl.
  • 1:24—Buns, while pulling underwear on after get-
  ting out of sleeping bag.
Tin Man (1983) . . . . n.a.
Hambone and Hillie (1984) . . . . Michael

In the Shadow of Kilimanjaro (1985)
. . . . Jack Ringtree
- •• 0:18—Buns, three times, while in bedroom with
  Irene Miracle.
- • 0:21—Brief buns, in mirror, while putting towel
  around himself.

Invaders from Mars (1986) . . . . George Gardner
What Waits Below (1986) . . . . Maj. Stevens
The Drifter (1988). . . . . .Arthur
Istanbul (1990) . . . . Frank
Texasville (1990) . . . . Sonny Crawford
Made for Cable TV:
The Hitchhiker: The Joker (1987; HBO) . . . . .Peter
Miniseries:
East of Eden (1981). . . . . .Adam Trask

Bowen, Michael
Films:
Forbidden World (1982) . . . . Jimmy Swift
Valley Girl (1983) . . . . .Tommy
Night of the Comet (1984). . . . . .Larry
The Wild Life (1984) . . . . Vince
The Check is in the Mail (1986). . . . . .Gary Jackson
Echo Park (1986). . . . . August
Iron Eagle (1986) . . . . Knotcher
Mortal Passions (1989) . . . . Burke
- • 0:42—Brief buns, while on top of Adele.

Kid (1990). . . . . Harlan
The Taking of Beverly Hills (1991)
. . . . L.A. Cop at Roadblock
Made for TV Movies:
Bonnie and Clyde: The True Story (1992)
. . . . Buck Barrow

Bowie, David
Singer.
Husband of model/actress Iman.
Films:
The Man Who Fell to Earth (1976; British)
. . . . Thomas Jerome Newton
(Uncensored version reviewed.)
    0:58—Brief buns, while turning over in bed with
    Candy Clark.
    1:56—Frontal nudity and brief buns in bed with
    Clark. Don't see his face.
Just a Gigolo (1979; German) . . . . Paul
The Hunger (1983) . . . . John
Merry Christmas, Mr. Lawrence (1983; Japanese/British)
. . . . Celliers
Yellowbeard (1983). . . . . .Henson
Into the Night (1985) . . . . Colin Morris
Absolute Beginners (1986; British). . . . . Vendice Partners
Labyrinth (1986). . . . . Jareth
The Last Temptation of Christ (1988) . . . . Pontius Pilate
Made for Cable TV:
Dream On: The Second Greatest Story Ever Told
(1991; HBO) . . . . .Sir Roland Moorecock

Boyle, Lance
Films:
Maiden Quest (1972) . . . . Siegfried
a.k.a. The Long Swift Sword of Siegfried
Private Screenings.
- •• 0:24—Buns, during orgy scene.

Boyle, Peter
Films:
Medium Cool (1969) . . . . Gun Clinic Manager
Diary of a Mad Housewife (1970)
. . . . Man in Group Therapy Session
Joe (1970) . . . . .Joe Curran
T. R. Baskin (1971) . . . . Jack Mitchell
The Candidate (1972) . . . . .Lucas
Kid Blue (1973) . . . . .Preacher Bob
Steelyard Blues (1973) . . . . Eagle Throneberry
Young Frankenstein (1974) . . . . .Monster
Swashbuckler (1976) . . . . .Lord Durant
Taxi Driver (1976) . . . . .Wizard
F.I.S.T. (1978). . . . . Max Graham
Beyond the Poseidon Adventure (1979)
. . . . Frank Massetti
Hardcore (1979) . . . . .Andy Mast
North Dallas Forty (1979). . . . . Emmett
Where the Buffalo Roam (1980) . . . . Lazlo
Outland (1981) . . . . .Sheppard
Hammett (1982) . . . . .Jimmy Ryan
Yellowbeard (1983) . . . . Moon
Johnny Dangerously (1984) . . . . Dundee
The Dream Team (1989). . . . . Jack
- •• 0:05—Buns, while getting up out of chair.

Kickboxer 2: The Road Back (1990) . . . . . .Justin Maciah
Men of Respect (1990). . . . . Duffy
Honeymoon in Vegas (1992) . . . . n.a.
Made for Cable Movies:
The Tragedy of Flight 103: The Inside Story (1990; HBO)
. . . . .Fred Ford
Miniseries:
From Here to Eternity (1979) . . . . Fatso Judson
TV:
Joe Bash (1986) . . . . Officer Joe Bash

• Bradshaw, Billy
Films:
Opportunity Knocks (1990) . . . . .David
The Other Woman (1992) . . . . Scott
(Unrated version reviewed.)
- • 0:52—Half of buns, making love with Sally in the of-
  fice screening room.

Branagh, Kenneth
Director.
Husband of actress Emma Thompson.
Films:
High Season (1988; British) . . . . Rich Lamb
- • 0:56—Buns, while putting a wrap around Jacqueline
  Bisset after they fool around in the water.

A Month in the Country (1988; British) . . . . Moon

Henry V (1989) . . . . King Henry V
Dead Again (1991) . . . . . . .Roman Strauss/Mike Church

Brando, Marlon

Films:
A Streetcar Named Desire (1951) . . . . . Stanley Kowalski
On the Waterfront (1954) . . . . Terry Malloy
   (Academy Award for Best Actor.)
The Nightcomers (1971; British) . . . . .Peter Quint
   0:30—Looks like you can see something between his
   legs, but most of his midsection is hidden by bed
   post.
The Godfather (1972) . . . . Don Vito Corleone
   (Academy Award for Best Actor.)
Last Tango In Paris (1972) . . . . Paul
   (X-rated, letterbox version.)
   • 1:59—Brief buns, while pulling his pants down to
   moon a woman at a dance.
The Missouri Breaks (1976) . . . . Lee Clayton
A Dry White Season (1989) . . . . Ian McKenzie
The Freshman (1990) . . . . Carmine Sabatini
Christopher Columbus: The Discovery (1992)
   . . . . Torquemada

• Brandon, Cory

Films:
Auditions (1978) . . . . Van Scott
   •• 0:32—Frontal nudity when Tracy undresses him.

• Brandon, David

Films:
The Naked Sun. . . . . Lucas
   • 0:58—Buns, while kneeling in bed, undressing Gina.
   ••• 1:00—Buns, while making love on top of Gina in
   bed.
   • 1:15—Buns, while making love with Gina.
The Boys From Brazil (1978) . . . . Schmidt
She (1983) . . . . .Pretty Boy
Good Morning, Babylon (1987; Italian/French) . . . Grass
High-Frequency (1988; Italian) . . . . .Spy

Brannan, Gavin

Films:
Private Passions (1983) . . . . .Mark
   • 1:19—Buns, while lying in bed on top of Sybil Danning.

Bridges, Jeff

Son of actor Lloyd Bridges.
Brother of actor Beau Bridges.
Films:
The Last Picture Show (1971) . . . . Duane Jackson
Fat City (1972) . . . . .Ernie
The Last American Hero (1973). . . . . . . Elroy Jackson, Jr.
   a.k.a. Hard Driver
Thunderbolt and Lightfoot (1974) . . . . Lightfoot
Hearts of the West (1975) . . . . Lewis Tater
Rancho Deluxe (1975) . . . . .Jack McKee
King Kong (1976) . . . . .Jack Prescott

Stay Hungry (1976) . . . . Craig Blake
The American Success Company (1979). . . . . . . .Harry
Winter Kills (1979) . . . . Nick Kegan
   •• 0:50—Buns, while getting dressed after making love
   with Belinda Bauer.
Heaven's Gate (1980). John
Cutter's Way (1981) . . . . .Richard Bone
   a.k.a. Cutter and Bone
Kiss Me Goodbye (1982) . . . . .Rupert Baines
Tron (1982) . . . . .Flynn/Clu
Against All Odds (1984) . . . . Terry Brogan
Starman (1984) . . . . Scott/Starman
   • 0:11—Brief buns, while standing up after growing
   from DNA to a man.
Jagged Edge (1985) . . . . Jack Forester
8 Million Ways to Die (1986) . . . . Matthew Scudder
The Morning After (1986) . . . . .Turner
Nadine (1987) . . . . .Vernon Hightower
Tucker: The Man and His Dream (1988)
   . . . . .Preston Tucker
The Fabulous Baker Boys (1989). . . . . Jack Baker
See You in the Morning (1989) . . . . Larry
Texasville (1990) . . . . .Duane Jackson
The Fisher King (1991). Jack

Brockette, Gary

Films:
The Last Picture Show (1971) . . . . .Bobby Sheen
   • 0:36—Upper frontal nudity and buns, while getting
   out of pool and greeting Randy Quaid and Cybill
   Shepherd. More buns, getting back into the pool.
Ice Pirates (1984) . . . . .Percy the Robot
The Philadelphia Experiment (1984)
   . . . . Adjutant/Andrews
Mac and Me (1988) . . . . .Doctor

Brosnan, Pierce

Husband of the late actress Cassandra Harris.
Films:
The Long Good Friday (1980; British). . . . .First Irishman
Nomads (1986) . . . . Pommier
   • 0:56—Buns, while taking his pants off by the win-
   dow. Kind of dark, hard to see.
The Fourth Protocol (1987; British) . . . . Petrofsky
The Deceivers (1988) . . . . William Savage
Taffin (1988; U.S./British) . . . . Mark Taffin
Mister Johnson (1991) . . . . .Harry Rudbeck
The Lawnmower Man (1992). . . . . . . .Lawrence Angelo
Live Wire (1992) . . . . Danny O'Neill
   •• 1:02—Brief buns in bed with Lisa Eilbacher.
Made for Cable Movies:
The Heist (1989; HBO). . . . . Bobby Skinner
Miniseries:
James Clavell's Noble House (1988) . . . . .Dunross
TV:
Remington Steele (1982-87) . . . . Remington Steele

Brown, Bryan

Husband of actress Rachel Ward.
Films:
Breaker Morant (1979; Australian)
. . . . Lt. Peter Handcock
Cathy's Child (1979; Australian) . . . . Nicko
Winter of Our Dreams (1981) . . . . .Reb
• 0:48—Brief buns while falling into bed with Judy
Davis.
The Empty Beach (1985). . . . . Cliff Hardy
Parker (1985; British). . . . . .n.a.
Rebel (1985; Australian) . . . . .Tiger Kelly
F/X (1986) . . . . Rollie Tyler
Tai-Pan (1986) . . . . Dirk Struan/"Tai-Pan"
The Good Wife (1987; Australian) . . . . Sonny Hills
a.k.a. The Umbrella Woman
Cocktail (1988) . . . . .Doug Coughlin
Gorillas in the Mist (1988). . . . . .Bob Campbell
Prisoners of the Sun (1990; Australian)
. . . . Captain Cooper
FX 2 (1991). . . . . Rollie Tyler
Sweet Talker (1991; Australian) . . . . Harry Reynolds
Blame It on the Bellboy (1992; British)
. . . . Charlton Black
Made for Cable Movies:
Dead In the Water (1991) . . . . .Charlie Deegan
Devlin (1991; Showtime) . . . . Frank Devlin
Miniseries:
The Thorn Birds (1983) .n.a.

Brown, Clancy

Films:
Bad Boys (1983) . . . . Viking Lofgren
The Adventures of Buckaroo Banzai, Across the 8th
Dimension (1984) . . . . Rawhide
The Bride (1985). . . . . Viktor
Thunder Alley (1985) . . . . Weasel
Highlander (1986) . . . . Kuragan
Extreme Prejudice (1987) . . . . .Sgt. Larry McRose
Shoot to Kill (1988). Steve
Blue Steel (1989) . . . . Nick Mann
• 1:27—Upper half of buns, while lying on the bath-
room floor. Don't see his face, so it could be any-
body.
Season of Fear (1989) . . . . Ward St. Clair
Ambition (1991). . . . . Albert
Made for Cable Movies:
Cast a Deadly Spell (1991; HBO). . . . . Harry Borden
Made for TV Movies:
Love, Lies and Murder (1991) . . . . .David Brown

Brown, Dwier

Films:
House (1986) . . . . Lieutenant
Field of Dreams (1989) . . . . .John Kinsella
The Guardian (1990). .Phil
0:37—Soft of buns, while in bed with Carey Lowell.
Don't see his face.

• Brown, Max M.

Films:
Wolfen (1981) . . . . .Christopher Van der Veer
• 0:21—Brief frontal nudity, lying dead as a corpse on
the coroner's table. Don't see his face.

Brown, Murray

Films:
Vampyres (1974; British) . . . . Ted
•• 0:22—Buns, while making love in bed with Fran.
• 0:56—Buns, while falling into bed.

• Brown, Timothy

Films:
Black Gunn (1972). . . . . Larry
Sweet Sugar (1972). . . . . Mojo
Girls Are For Loving (1973) . . . . n.a.
Nashville (1975). . . . . .Tommy Brown
Famous T & A (1982) . . . . Mojo
(No longer available for purchase, check your video
store for rental.)
• 1:05—Buns in outtake from *Sweet Sugar.*
Losin' It (1982). . . . . n.a.
TV:
M*A*S*H (1972) . . . . Spearchucker Jones

Brown, Woody

Films:
The Accused (1988). Danny
• 1:28—Buns, while raping Jodi Foster on the pinball
machine.
Off Limits (1988) . . . . Co-Pilot
The Rain Killer (1990). . . . . Jordan Rosewall
••• 0:39—Buns, while getting into bed, kneeling next to
bed, then getting into bed with Satin. Long scene.
Alligator II: The Mutation (1991) . . . . Rich Harmon
TV:
Flamingo Road (1981-82) . . . . Skipper Weldon
The Facts of Life (1983-84). . . . . Cliff

Bullington, Perry

Films:
Chatterbox (1977) . . . . Ted
• 0:02—Buns, while stumbling around the room.

Bumiller, William

Films:
Last Resort (1985) . . . . Etienne
Guns (1990). . . . . .Lucas
Overexposed (1990) . . . . Hank
• 0:54—Brief buns, while taking off his pants to get
into bed with Catherine Oxenberg.
Do or Die (1991) . . . . .Lucas
Video Tapes:
Inside Out (1992). . . . . Jack/Brush Strokes

•Burns, Stephen W.

Films:

Spiker . . . . Sonny Flestow
• 0:03—Buns in room.
Herbie Goes Bananas (1980) . . . . Pete

Burton, Jeff

Films:

Planet of the Apes (1968) . . . . Dodge
• 0:26—Very brief buns while taking off clothes to go
skinny dipping. (Guy on the right.)
Sweet Charity (1969) . . . . .Policeman

Butcher, Glenn

Films:

Young Einstein (1989; Australian)
. . . . Ernest Rutherford
• 0:56—Buns, while standing in front of sink when
Marie comes to rescue Einstein. (He's the one on the
left.)

•Butler, Jerry

Adult film actor.
Real name is Paul Siederman.
Husband of actress Lisa Loring.
Adult Films:
Bad Girls IV . . . . .n.a.
Films:
Deranged (1987) . . . . Frank

Byrd, Tom

Films:

Twilight Zone—The Movie (1983) . . . . .G.I.
Out Cold (1989) . . . . Mr. Holstrom
• 0:10—Brief frontal nudity getting out of bed with
Teri Garr when her husband comes home.
Young Guns II (1990) . . . . .Pit Inmate
TV:
Boone (1983-84). . . . . .Boone Sawyer

Byrne, Gabriel

Husband of actress Ellen Barkin.
Films:
Excalibur (1981; British) . . . . Uther
The Keep (1983) . . . . .Kaempffer
Wagner (1983; British) . . . . Karl Ritter
Defense of the Realm (1986; British) . . . . . . Nick Mullen
Gothic (1986; British) . . . . Byron
Hello Again! (1987). . . . . .Kevin Scanlon
Julia and Julia (1987; Italian) . . . . Paolo
(This movie was shot using a high-definition video sys-
tem and then transferred to film.)
Lionheart (1987). . . . . The Black Prince
Siesta (1987) . . . . .Augustine
• 1:28—Brief buns and frontal nudity, while getting
out of bed. Long shot, hard to see.
A Soldier's Tale (1988; New Zealand) . . . . Saul
Dark Obsession (1989; British) . . . . Hugo
Miller's Crossing (1990) . . . . Tom Reagan

Shipwrecked (1990; Norwegian) . . . . . . Lt. John Merrick
A Soldier's Tale (1991) . . . . n.a.
Cool World (1992). . . . . .Jack Deebs
Made for Cable Movies:
Mussolini and I (1985; HBO) . . . . .Vittorio Mussolini
Miniseries:
Christopher Columbus (1985) . . . . n.a.

Cadman, Josh

Films:

Goin' All the Way (1981) . . . . .Bronk
• 1:05—Buns, while in the shower talking to Boom
Boom.
Pennies from Heaven (1981) . . . . n.a.
Angel (1983) . . . . Spike

Cage, Nicholas

Real name is Nicholas Coppola.
Nephew of director Francis Coppola.
Films:
Rumble Fish (1983) . . . . Smokey
Valley Girl (1983) . . . . Randy
The Cotton Club (1984). . . . . .Vincent Dwyer
Racing with the Moon (1984) . . . . .Nicky
Birdy (1985). . . . . Al Columbato
The Boy in Blue (1986; Canadian) . . . . .Ned Hanlan
Peggy Sue Got Married (1986). . . . . Charlie Bodell
Moonstruck (1987) . . . . Ronny Cammareri
Raising Arizona (1987). . . . . H.I. McDonnough
Vampire's Kiss (1989) . . . . .Peter Loew
Fire Birds (1990). . . . . .Jake Preston
a.k.a. Wings of the Apache
Wild at Heart (1990) . . . . .Sailor
Zandalee (1991) . . . . Johnny Collins
•• 0:30—Buns, while making love in bed with Zanda-
lee.
Honeymoon in Vegas (1992) . . . . n.a.

Calderon, Paul

Films:

Band of the Hand (1986) . . . . Tito
The Chair (1988) . . . . Pizza
Sticky Fingers (1988) . . . . Speed
Sea of Love (1989). . . . . .Serafino
King of New York (1990) . . . . .Joey Dalesio
Q & A (1990) . . . . .Roger Montalvo
• 1:50—Brief buns, while on floor of boat, getting
strangled by Nick Nolte.

•Calfa, Don

Films:

1941 (1979). . . . . .Telephone Operator
Chopper Chicks in Zombietown (1989)
. . . . Ralph Willum
• 0:41—Brief buns, while trapped in walk-in locker
with zombie Lucile. Don't see his face.
Weekend at Bernie's (1989) . . . . Paulie
a.k.a. Hot and Cold
Bugsy (1991) . . . . .Louie Dragna

TV:
Park Place (1981) . . . . Howard "Howie" Beech
Legmen (1984) . . . . Oscar Armismendi

Cali, Joseph
Films:
Saturday Night Fever (1977) . . . . Joey
Voices (1979) . . . . Pinky
The Competition (1980) . . . . Jerry Di Salvo
The Lonely Lady (1983) . . . . Vincent Dacosta
   • 1:05—Buns, while near pool table and walking
     around the house with Pia Zadora.
TV:
Flatbush (1979) . . . . Presto Prestopopolos
Today's F.B.I. (1981-82) . . . . .Nick Frazier

Callow, Simon
Director.
Films:
Amadeus (1984) . . . . Emanuel Schikaneder
The Good Father (1986) . . . . Mark Varner
A Room with a View (1986; British)
 . . . . .The Reverend Mr. Beebe
   • 1:04—Frontal nudity taking off clothes and jumping
     into pond.
   ••• 1:05—Nude running around with Freddy and
     George in the woods. Lots of frontal nudity.
Maurice (1987; British) . . . . Mr. Ducie
Manifesto (1988) . . . . Police Chief Hunt
Mr. & Mrs. Bridge (1990) . . . . Dr. Sauer
Postcards from the Edge (1990) . . . . Simon Asquith

• Calvin, John
Films:
California Dreaming (1978) . . . . Rick
Norma Rae (1979) . . . . Ellis Harper
Foolin' Around (1980) . . . . .Whitley
Making Love (1982) . . . . David
Swordkill (1984) . . . . Dr. Alan Richards
Back to the Beach (1987) . . . . Troy
Primary Target (1990) . . . . Cromwell
Critters 3 (1991) . . . . Clifford
Almost Pregnant (1992) . . . . Gordon Mallory
  (Unrated version reviewed.)
   •• 1:11—Buns, while on top of Tanya Roberts in bed.
TV:
The Paul Lynde Show (1972-73) . . . . . .Howie Dickerson
From Here to Eternity (1980) . . . . . . Lt. Kenneth Barrett
Tales of the Gold Monkey (1982-83)
 . . . . Rev. Willie Tenboom

• Campanaro, Philip
Films:
Sex Appeal (1986) . . . . Ralph
Slammer Girls (1987) . . . . Gary
   • 0:48—Buns, while dancing in G-string in front of the
     girls in their prision cell.
   • 0:49—More buns in G-string, while wrestling with
     Melody.

Campbell, Nicholas
Films:
Certain Fury (1985) . . . . Sniffer
   •• 0:38—Buns, while getting undressed to rape Irene
     Cara.
The Big Slice (1991) . . . . .Nick Papadopoulis
Naked Lunch (1991) . . . . Hank

Carradine, David
Son of actor John Carradine.
Brother of actors Keith and Robert Carradine.
Films:
Macho Callahan (1970) . . . . . Colonel David Mountford
Boxcar Bertha (1972) . . . . Big Bill Shelly
   • 0:54—Buns, while putting pants on after hearing a
     gun shot.
Mean Streets (1973) . . . . Drunk
Death Race 2000 (1975) . . . . Frankenstein
Bound For Glory (1976) . . . . Woody Guthrie
Cannonball (1976; U.S./Hong Kong)
 . . . . "Cannonball" Buckman
Gray Lady Down (1977) . . . . Captain Gates
The Serpent's Egg (1977) . . . . Abel Rosenberg
Thunder and Lightning (1977) . . . . .Harley Thomas
Death Sport (1978) . . . . Kaz Oshay
Circle of Iron (1979) . . . . Chang-Sha
Cloud Dancer (1980) . . . . .Brad Randolph
The Long Riders (1980) . . . . .Cole Younger
Americana (1981) . . . . Soldier
Q (1982) . . . . Detective Shepard
Lone Wolf McQuade (1983) . . . . .Rawley
On the Line (1984; Spanish) . . . . Bryant
   • 0:11—Buns, while lying on a table, getting a mas-
     sage by three women.
The Warrior and the Sorceress (1984) . . . . .Kain
Armed Response (1986) . . . . Jim Roth
P.O.W.: The Escape (1986) . . . . Colonel Cooper
Warlords (1988) . . . . Dow
Crime Zone (1989) . . . . Jason
Sundown: The Vampire in Retreat (1989) . . . . . Mardulak
Tropical Snow (1989) . . . . .Oskar
Bird on a Wire (1990) . . . . Eugene
Dune Warriors (1990) . . . . Michael
Double Trouble (1991) . . . . .Mr. C
Evil Toons (1991) . . . . Gideon Fisk
Martial Law (1991) . . . . .Dalton Rhodes
Waxwork II: Lost in Time (1991) . . . . The Beggar
Night Rhythms (1992) . . . . Vincent
  (Unrated version reviewed.)
Made for Cable Movies:
Deadly Survailance (1991; Showtime) . . . . . . Lieutenant
Miniseries:
North and South (1985) . . . . .Justin LaMotte
North and South, Book II (1986) . . . . . . .Justin LaMotte
Made for TV Movies:
A Winner Never Quits (1986) . . . . .Pete Gray
TV:
Shane (1966) . . . . Shane
Kung Fu (1972-75) . . . . .Kwai Chang Caine

Carradine, Keith

Son of actor John Carradine.
Brother of actors David and Robert Carradine.
Films:

McCabe and Mrs. Miller (1971) . . . . Cowboy
Hex (1973) . . . . Whizzer
Thieves Like Us (1974) . . . . Bowie
Nashville (1975) . . . . Tom Frank
  • 0:47—Buns, while sitting on floor after getting out
     of bed.
Lumiere (1976; French). . . . . David Foster
The Duellists (1977; British). . . . . D'Hubert
Welcome to L.A. (1977) . . . . Carroll Barber
Pretty Baby (1978) . . . . Bellocq
An Almost Perfect Affair (1979) . . . . Hal
Old Boyfriends (1979). . . . . Wayne
The Long Riders (1980). . . . . Jim Younger
Southern Comfort (1981) . . . . Spencer
Choose Me (1984) . . . . Mickey
Maria's Lovers (1985) . . . . Clarence Butts
The Inquiry (1986) . . . . .Titus Valerius
Trouble in Mind (1986). . . . . Coop
Backfire (1987) . . . . Clinton James
The Moderns (1988) . . . . Nick Hart
  •• 1:17—Buns, while walking into bathroom with Lin-
     da Fiorentino.
Cold Feet (1989). . . . . Monte
Daddy's Dyin'... Who's Got the Will? (1990) . . . . Clarence
The Ballad of the Sad Cafe (1991). . . . . . . Marvin Macy
Street of No Return (1991; U.S./French) . . . . . . Michael
Criss Cross (1992). . . . . .n.a.
Made for Cable Movies:
Judgement (1990; HBO). . . . . Perre Guitry
Payoff (1991; Showtime). . . . . .Peter "Mac" MacAlister
  • 0:01—Sort of buns, while in shower, seen from
     above, looking down.
Miniseries:
Chiefs (1983) . . . . .Foxy Funderburke

Carrier, Gene

Video Tapes:
The Girls of Penthouse (1984)
  . . . . Ghost Town Cowboy
  ••• 0:31—Frontal nudity with Jody Swafford. Buns,
     while carrying her to couch and making love.

• Carson, John David

Films:
Pretty Maids All in a Row (1971). . . . . Ponce
  • 1:04—Very brief buns, sticking out from under sheet
     when he uses it to cover Angie Dickinson in bed.
The Day of the Dolphin (1973) . . . . .Larry
Stay Hungry (1976). . . . . .Halsey
Empire of the Ants (1977) . . . . .Joe Morrison
The Fifth Floor (1978) . . . . Ronnie Denton
Pretty Woman (1990) . . . . .Mark
TV:
Falcon Crest (1987-88) . . . . Jay Spence

Case, Robert

Films:
Hot Blood (1989; Spanish). . . . . Ricardo
  •• 1:20—Buns, with Alicia in stable.

Casey, Bernie

Former football player.
Films:
Black Gunn (1972). .Seth
Boxcar Bertha (1972). . . . . .Von Morton
Cleopatra Jones (1973) . . . . Reuben
The Man Who Fell to Earth (1976; British)
  . . . . Peters
  (Uncensored version reviewed.)
  • 1:42—Buns, while getting out of swimming pool
     during a black and white dream sequence.
Sharky's Machine (1981) . . . . Arch
Never Say Never Again (1983). . . . . .Felix Leiter
Revenge of the Nerds (1984) . . . . U. N. Jefferson
Spies Like Us (1985) . . . . Colonel Rhombus
Backfire (1987). . . . . Clinton James
Steele Justice (1987). . . . . .Reese
I'm Gonna Git You Sucka (1988) . . . . .John Slade
Bill and Ted's Excellent Adventure (1989). . . . . Mr. Ryan
Another 48 Hrs. (1990) . . . . .Kirkland Smith
Made for Cable Movies:
Chains of Gold (1991; Showtime) . . . . Sgt. Palco
Made for TV Movies:
Brian's Song (1971) . . . . n.a.
Love is Not Enough (1978) . . . . n.a.
Ring of Passion (1978) . . . . Joe Louis
TV:
Harris and Company (1979). . . . . Mike Harris
Bay City Blues (1983). . . . . Ozzie Peoples

Casey, Lawrence

Films:
The Student Nurses (1970) . . . . Dr. Jim Casper
  a.k.a. Young LA Nurses
  •• 0:52—Buns, while walking to Karen Carlson to talk.
The Great Waldo Pepper (1975). . . . . German Star
Borderline (1980). . . . . Andy Davis
TV:
The Rat Patrol (1966-68) . . . . . . Private Mark Hitchcock

• Cassidy, Rick

Films:
Auditions (1978) . . . . .Charlie White
  ••• 0:04—Nude, undressing for his audition.
  •• 0:29—Buns, during sex scene with a woman.
  • 1:07—Buns in bed during orgy scene.
  •• 1:13—Nude on kneeling on bed.
Video Tapes:
Love Skills: A Guide to the Pleasures of Sex (1984)
  . . . . Model

Castillo, Eduardo
Films:
Gnaw: Food of the Gods II (1988; Canadian)
....Carlos
- • 0:46—Buns, while walking through bushes to take a leak. More buns, while running away from the giant rats.

• Caulfield, Maxwell
Films:
Grease 2 (1982) ....Michael Carrington
Electric Dreams (1984) .... Bill
The Supernaturals (1987) .... Lt. Ray Ellis
Sundown: The Vampire in Retreat (1989) ......Shane
Project: Alien (1990) .... George Abbott
Dance with Death (1991) ....Shaughnessy
- • 1:01—Brief side view of buns, while making love in bed with Kelly.
Waxwork II: Lost in Time (1991) .... Mickey
TV:
The Colbys (1985-87) .... Miles Colby

Cazenove, Christopher
Films:
There's a Girl in My Soup (1970)............. Nigel
East of Elephant Rock (1976; British)............n.a.
Eye of the Needle (1981) ....David
Heat and Dust (1982) .... Douglas Rivers
- •• 1:25—Buns while lying in bed with Greta Scacchi under a mosquito net.
Until September (1984) .... Philip
Mata Hari (1985) .... Captain Karl Von Byerling
Souvenir (1988; British)................William Root
Three Men and a Little Lady (1990) ....Edward
Made for TV Movies:
To Be The Best (1992).............Jonathan Ainsley
TV:
Dynasty (1986-87) ....Ben Carrington

Ceinos, José Antonio
Films:
Black Venus (1983).................... Armand
- • 0:14—Buns, while making love with Venus in bed.
Patricia (1984) ....n.a.
Private Screenings.

• Chan, Jackie
Films:
The Big Brawl (1980) .... Jerry
The Cannonball Run (1981) ...... Subaru Driver No. 1
Cannonball Run II (1984) .... Jackie
The Fearless Hyena, Part II (1984; Chinese)
.... Chan Lung
- • 0:06—Brief buns, jumping up in the water while trying to catch a fish. Don't see his face clearly.
The Protector (1985; Hong Kong/U.S.) ..... Billy Wong

Chapman, Graham
Films:
Monty Python and the Holy Grail (1974; British)
.... King Arthur
Monty Python's Life of Brian (1979; British)
.... Brian Called Brian
- ••• 1:03—Buns before opening window, frontal nudity after opening window and being surprised by his flock of followers, buns while putting clothes on. Funniest frontal nude scene.
The Secret Policeman's Other Ball (1982; British)
....n.a.
Monty Python's the Meaning of Life (1983; British)
....n.a.
Yellowbeard (1983) ....Yellowbeard
The Secret Policeman's Private Parts (1984) .... n.a.
TV:
Monty Python's Flying Circus (British) .... Regular
The Big Show (1980) .... Regular

• Charles, Emile
Films:
Wonderland (1989; British) ....Eddie
- ••• 1:27—Nude, taking off his clothes and swimming under water with the dolphins. Long scene.

• Charles, Timothy
Films:
Uncaged (1991)...................... Evan
a.k.a. Angel in Red
- • 0:42—Brief buns, while on the floor with Micki.

• Clark, Brett
Films:
Night Shift (1982) ....Nick "The Dick"
Alien Warrior (1985) .... Buddy
- •• 0:03—Buns, while walking naked after getting transported to Earth.
Last Resort (1985) ....Manuello
Young Lady Chatterley II (1986)
.... Thomas "Gardener"
- •• 0:15—Brief buns, while pulling up his pants after getting caught with Monique Gabrielle in the woods by Adam West.
- • 0:16—Very brief buns, when Monique pulls his pants down again.
Eye of the Eagle (1987; Philippines)
........................Sgt. Rick Stratton
Inner Sanctum (1991) ....Neil Semple

Clay, Nicholas
Films:
Excalibur (1981; British)..................Lancelot
- •• 1:13—Buns, while fighting with himself in a suit of armor.
- • 1:31—Brief buns, while running into the woods after waking up. Long shot, hard to see.

Lady Chatterley's Lover (1981; French/British)
. . . . .Oliver Mellors (The Gardener)
••• 0:21—Nude, washing himself while Sylvia Kristel
    watches from the trees.
Evil Under the Sun (1982) . . . . Patrick Redfern
Lionheart (1987) . . . . Charles de Montfort
Made for TV Movies:
Poor Little Rich Girl: The Barbara Hutton Story (1987)
. . . . Prince Alexis Mdivani
Video Tapes:
Playboy Video Magazine, Volume 2 (1983)
. . . . Gardener
  • 0:18—Buns, in scene from *Lady Chatterley's Lover.*

• Cleese, John
Films:
Interlude (1968; British) . . . . .TV Publicist
Monty Python and the Holy Grail (1974; British)
. . . . Black Knight
Monty Python's Life of Brian (1979; British)
. . . . Third Wise Man
Time Bandits (1981; British) . . . . Robin Hood
Monty Python's the Meaning of Life (1983; British)
. . . . .n.a.
Yellowbeard (1983) . . . . Blind Pew
Silverado (1985) . . . . Sheriff Langston
Clockwise (1986; British) . . . . Brian Stimpson
A Fish Called Wanda (1988) . . . . .Archie
  • 1:13—Very brief upper half of buns, in house when
    he's surprised by the returning family. Looks like
    very, very brief frontal nudity when he stands up af-
    ter pulling his underwear down.
The Big Picture (1989) . . . . Bartender
Erik the Viking (1989; British) . . . . Halfdan the Black
Bullseye! (1990) . . . . . Man Who Looks Like John Cleese
TV:
Monty Python's Flying Circus (British) . . . . .Regular

Clementi, Pierre
Films:
The Conformist (1971; Italian/French)
. . . . Nino Seminara
Steppenwolf (1974) . . . . Pablo
  • 1:40—Very brief frontal nudity, sleeping on floor
    with Dominique Sanda.
Quartet (1981; British/French) . . . . .Theo
Exposed (1983) Vic

Coates, Kim
Films:
The Boy in Blue (1986; Canadian) . . . McCoy Man No. 2
Red Blooded American Girl (1988) . . . . Dennis
  • 0:01—Buns, while giving Rebecca a glass in bed.
  • 0:30—Very brief buns, while getting into bathtub.
Cold Front (1989; Canadian) . . . . Mantha
The Last Boy Scout (1991) . . . . .Chet

Cochran, Ian
Films:
Bolero (1984) .Robert Stewart
  • 1:26—Buns, while making love with Catalina.

• Coe, George
Films:
The Stepford Wives (1975) . . . . Claude Axhelm
French Postcards (1979) . . . . Mr. Weber
Kramer vs. Kramer (1979) . . . . Jim O'Connor
The First Deadly Sin (1980) . . . . Dr. Bernardi
Bustin' Loose (1981) . . . . .Dr. Wilson T. Renfrew
The Amateur (1982) . . . . Rutledge
The Entity (1983) . . . . Dr. Weber
Remo Williams: The Adventure Begins (1985)
. . . . .Gen. Scott Watson
Head Office (1986) . . . . Senator Issel
Blind Date (1987) . . . . .Harry Gruen
Best Seller (1988) . . . . Graham
Cousins (1989) . . . . Uncle Phil
  •• 0:08—Buns, while mooning everybody during wed-
    ding reception.
  • 0:34—Buns again, during video playback.
The End of Innocence (1989) . . . . .Dad
TV:
Goodnight, Beantown (1983) . . . . Dick Novak
Max Headroom (1987) . . . . .Ben Cheviot

Coleman, Dabney
Films:
This Property is Condemned (1966) . . . . Salesman
I Love My Wife (1970) . . . . Frank Donnelly
Cinderella Liberty (1973) . . . . Executive Officer
The Dove (1974; British) . . . . Charles Huntley
The Towering Inferno (1974) . . . . . . .Assistant Fire Chief
Bite the Bullet (1975) . . . . .Jack Parker
The Other Side of the Mountain (1975)
. . . . Dave McCoy
Midway (1976) . . . . Captain Murray Arnold
Rolling Thunder (1977) . . . . .Maxwell
Viva Knievel (1977) . . . . Ralph Thompson
How to Beat the High Cost of Living (1980)
. . . . Jack Heintzel
Melvin and Howard (1980) . . . . Judge Keith Hayes
Nothing Personal (1980; Canadian) . . . . .Tom Dickerson
Modern Problems (1981) . . . . Mark
  ••• 1:09—Buns, while taking off towel in front of Patti
    D'Arbanville.
On Golden Pond (1981) . . . . .Bill Ray
Tootsie (1982) . . . . Ron
Young Doctors in Love (1982) . . . . Dr. Joseph Prang
Wargames (1983) . . . . McKittrick
Cloak and Dagger (1984) . . . . . . Jack Flack/Hal Osborne
Meet the Applegates (1989) . . . . Aunt Bea
Short Time (1990) . . . . .Burt Simpson
Where the Heart Is (1990) . . . . Stewart McBain
Made for Cable TV:
Never Forget (1991; TNT) . . . . .William Cox

Made for TV Movies:
Baby M (1988) . . . . Skoloff
TV:
That Girl (1966-67) . . . . Dr. Leon Bessemer
Mary Hartman, Mary Hartman (1975-78)
. . . . Merle Jeeter
Apple Pie (1978) . . . . Fast Eddie Murtaugh
Buffalo Bill (1983-84) . . . . Bill Bittinger
The Slap Maxwell Story (1987-88) . . . . . . Slap Maxwell
Drexell's Class (1991-92) . . . . .Otis Drexell

Coleman, Warren

Films:
Young Einstein (1989; Australian) . . .Lunatic Professor
 • 0:55—Buns while in Lunatic Asylum, taking a shower.
 • 0:56—More buns while standing in front of sink when Marie comes to rescue Einstein. (He's the one on the right.)
 • 0:58—Brief buns while crowding into the shower stall with the other Asylum people.

Conaway, Jeff

Films:
The Eagle Has Landed (1977; British) . . . . .n.a.
I Never Promised You a Rose Garden (1977)
. . . . Lactamaeon
Grease (1978) . . . . Kenickie
Covergirl (1982; Canadian) . . . . T. C. Sloane
 •• 0:43—Very brief lower frontal nudity getting out of bed.
The Patriot (1986) . . . . Mitchell
The Sleeping Car (1990) . . . . Bud Sorenson
Mirror Images (1991) . . . . Jeffrey
A Time to Die (1991) . . . . Frank
Total Exposure (1991) . . . . Peter Keynes
Almost Pregnant (1992) . . . . Charlie Alderson
 (Unrated version reviewed.)
 ••• 0:10—Buns, while making love on top of Tanya Roberts in bed.
 •• 1:12—Buns in bed in alternate scenes with Roberts and Joan Severance.
Sunset Strip (1992) . . . . Tony
TV:
Taxi (1978-83) . . . . Bobby Wheeler
Wizards and Warriors (1983) . . . . . Prince Erik Greystone
Berrengers (1985) . . . . John Higgins

Conlon, Tim

Films:
Prom Night III (1989) . . . . Alex
 • 0:15—Brief buns and very brief balls when the flag he's wearing falls off.

Cooper, Terence

Films:
Casino Royale (1967; British) . . . . Cooper

Heart of the Stag (1983; New Zealand)
. . . . Robert Jackson
 • 0:03—Buns, while making love in bed on top of his daughter. Don't see his face.
The Shrimp on the Barbie (1990) . . . . Ian Hobart

• Cooper, Trevor

Films:
Moonlighting (1982; British) . . . . Hire Shop Man
The Whistle Blower (1987; British) . . . . Inspector Bourne
Drowning by Numbers (1988; British) . . . . Hardy
 •• 0:12—Full frontal nudity, lying in bed sleeping.

Corbo, Robert

Films:
Last Rites (1988) . . . . Gino
 • 0:03—Buns and frontal nudity in a room with Daphne Zuniga just before getting caught by another woman and shot.

Corri, Nick

Films:
Gotcha! (1985) . . . . Manolo
A Nightmare on Elm Street (1985) . . . . Rod Lane
Lawless Land (1988) . . . . n.a.
Slaves of New York (1989) . . . . Marley Mantello
Tropical Snow (1989) . . . . Tavo
 •• 0:11—Buns while in bed with Madeleine Stowe.
 •• 0:44—Buns, while standing naked in police station.
Predator 2 (1990) . . . . Detective
In the Heat of Passion (1991) . . . . .Charlie
 (Unrated version reviewed.)

• Costello, Anthony

Films:
Blue (1968) . . . . Jess Parker
Will Penny (1968) . . . . Bigfoot
The Molly Maguires (1970) . . . . Frank McAndrew
Doctor's Wives (1971) . . . . #31 Mike Traynor
 • 0:52—Brief buns, while getting tape recorder and running back to bed.

Costner, Kevin

Films:
Chasing Dreams (1981) . . . . n.a.
Malibu Hot Summer (1981) . . . . John Logan
 a.k.a. Sizzle Beach
 (*Sizzle Beach* is the re-released version with Kevin Costner featured on the cover. It is missing all the nude scenes during the opening credits before 0:06.)
Shadows Run Black (1981) . . . . .Jimmy Scott
Night Shift (1982) . . . . Frat Boy #1
Stacy's Knights (1983) . . . . Will
Table for Five (1983) . . . . Newlywed
Testament (1983) . . . . Phil Pitkin
American Flyers (1985) . . . . Marcus
 • 0:53—Brief, upper half of buns, while riding bicycles when his pants get yanked down by David.
Fandango (1985) . . . . Gardner Barnes

Silverado (1985) . . . . Jake
No Way Out (1987) . . . . Lt. Cmdr. Tom Farrell
The Untouchables (1987) . . . . Eliot Ness
Bull Durham (1988) . . . . .Crash Davis
Field of Dreams (1989) . . . . .Ray Kinsella
The Gunrunner (1989) . . . . Ted Beaubien
Dances with Wolves (1990) . . . . Lt. John Dunbar
    •• 0:37—Brief buns, while washing his clothes in the
    pond.
    ••• 0:40—Buns, while standing by himself after scaring
    away Kicking Bird.
Revenge (1990). . . . . Cochran
    •• 1:14—Brief buns while getting out of bed and wrap-
    ping a sheet around himself.
JFK (1991). . . . . Jim Garrison
Robin Hood: Prince of Thieves (1991) . Robin of Locksley
    1:14—Body double's buns, while bathing under wa-
    terfall when Marian sees him. Hard to see because of
    the falling water. Body double was used because the
    water was so cold.

Cramer, Grant
Films:
New Year's Evil (1981). . . . . .Derek Sullivan
Hardbodies (1984) . . . . .Scotty
    • 0:03—Brief buns, while getting out of bed after
    making love with Kristi.
Killer Klowns from Outer Space (1988) . . . . .Mike
Beverly Hills Brats (1989). . . . . .Officer #1
Hangfire (1990) . . . . Snake
Made for TV Movies:
An Inconvenient Woman (1991) . . . . .Lonny

Crawford, Johnny
Films:
The Restless Ones (1965) . . . . David Winton
Village of the Giants (1965). . . . . Horsey
El Dorado (1967) . . . . Luke MacDonald
The Naked Ape (1972). Lee
    (Not available on video tape.)
    Frontal nudity.
The Great Texas Dynamite Chase (1977). . . . . Slim
Tilt (1978). . . . . Mickey
TV:
The Rifleman (1958-63) . . . . Mark McCain
Magazines:
Playboy (Sep 1973). . . . . .The Naked Ape
    ••• 159-161—Nude.
Playboy (Dec 1973). . . . . Sex Stars of 1973
    ••• 211—Frontal nudity.

Crew, Carl
Films:
Blood Diner (1987). . . . . George Tutman
    • 1:02—Buns, while mooning Sheeba through the
    passenger window of a van.
The Underachievers (1987) . . . . Thug 2

Cruise, Tom
Husband of actress Nicole Kidman.
Ex-husband of actress Mimi Rogers.
Films:
Endless Love (1981). . . . . Billy
Taps (1981) . . . . David Shawn
Losin' It (1982). . . . . .Woody
All The Right Moves (1983) . . . . Stef
    •• 1:00—Very brief frontal nudity getting undressed in
    his bedroom with Lea Thompson.
The Outsiders (1983) . . . . Steve Randle
Risky Business (1983) . . . . Joel
The Color of Money (1986) . . . . Vincent
Legend (1986). . . . . Jack
Top Gun (1986) . . . . Maverick
Cocktail (1988) . . . . .Brian Hanagan
Rain Man (1988) . . . . .Charlie Babbitt
Born on the Fourth of July (1989) . . . . . . Ron Kovic
    • 0:47—Very brief buns, sort of, while in bed at hospi-
    tal when his rear end is sticking through the bottom
    of a bed.
Days of Thunder (1990). . . . . Cole Trickle
Far and Away (1992) . . . . .Joseph Donelly
    1:02—Upper half of buns, bending over to fix his
    bedding while Nicole Kidman peeks through hole in
    room divider.

Culp, Robert
Films:
PT 109 (1963) . . . . .Ens. "Barney" Ross
Bob & Carol & Ted & Alice (1969). . . . . Bob
Hickey and Boggs (1972). . . . . .Frank Boggs
A Name for Evil (1973) . . . . .John Blake
    •• 0:52—Frontal nudity running through the woods
    with a woman.
    • 1:07—Buns, while going skinny dipping. Lots of bun
    shots underwater.
The Great Scout and Cathouse Thursday (1976)
    . . . . .Jack Colby
Goldengirl (1979) . . . . Esselton
Turk 182 (1985) . . . . Mayor Tyler
Big Bad Mama II (1987) . . . . Daryl Pearson
Pucker Up and Bark Like a Dog (1989) . . . . .Gregor
Silent Night, Deadly Night III: Better Watch Out! (1989)
    Lt. Connely
Timebomb (1990) . . . . .Mr. Phillips
Made for TV Movies:
Voyage of Terror: The Achillie Largo Affair General Davies
Her Life as a Man (1984) . . . . Dave Fleming
Columbo Goes to College (1990). . . . . . . Jordan Rowe
TV:
I Spy (1965-68) . . . . Kelly Robinson
Greatest American Hero (1981-83). . . . . . . Bill Maxwell
Magazines:
Playboy (Mar 1973) . . . . "Evil" Doings
    • 148—Side view nude.

Cvetkovic, Svetozar

Films:

Montenegro (1981; British/Swedish) . . . . Montenegro
••• 1:07—Frontal nudity taking a shower while Susan Anspach watches.
Manifesto (1988) . . . . Rudi

Dacus, Don

Films:

Hair (1979) . . . . Woof
• 0:57—Buns, while taking off clothes and diving into pond with Treat Williams and Hud.

Dafoe, Willem

Films:

Roadhouse 66 (1984). . . . . Johnny Harte
•• 1:02—Buns, standing up while kissing Jesse.
Streets of Fire (1984). Raven
To Live and Die in L.A. (1985) . . . . Eric Masters
0:58—Side view of buns, while kneeling on floor, burning counterfeit money.
0:59—Lower half of buns, while making love in bed with Debra Feuer in bed. Seen on TV.
• 1:06—Buns, while sitting on bench in locker room, changing clothes.
The Last Temptation of Christ (1988)
. . . . Jesus Christ
• 1:56—Buns, getting beaten and whipped.
• 1:57—Buns, while getting crown of thorns placed on his head.
2:02—Side view of buns, while hanging on cross.
Mississippi Burning (1988) . . . . Alan Ward
Off Limits (1988). . . . . Bud McGriff
Born on the Fourth of July (1989) . . . . Charlie
Triumph of the Spirit (1989) . . . . Salamo Arouch
Cry Baby (1990) . . . . Hateful Guard
Wild at Heart (1990) . . . . Bobby Peru
Flight of the Intruder (1991) . . . . Cole
Body of Evidence (1992). n.a.
Light Sleeper (1992) . . . . John LeTour
White Sands (1992) . . . . Ray Dolezal

Daltrey, Roger

Singer with *The Who* and on his own.
Films:

Lisztomania (1975; British). . . . . Franz Liszt
• 0:01—Brief buns while standing on bed tying a sheet to make some pants. Dark, don't see his face.
Tommy (1975; British) . . . . Tommy
The Kids are Alright (1979; British) . . . . n.a.
The Legacy (1979; British). . . . . Clive
McVicar (1980; British) . . . . Tom McVicar
If Looks Could Kill (1991) . . . . Blade
a.k.a. Teen Agent

Damian, Leo

Films:

The Last Temptation of Christ (1988)
. . . . Person in Crowd

Ghosts Can't Do It (1989) . . . . Fasto
• 1:31—Brief, lower buns while sliding down stack of hay. Long shot.

• Danare, Malcolm

Films:

Christine (1983). . . . . Moochie
Flashdance (1983) . . . . Cecil
The Lords of Discipline (1983) . . . . Poteete
Heaven Help Us (1985) . . . . Caesar
• 0:36—Buns, while walking to the pool after all the other guys jump in. Long shot.
National Lampoon's European Vacation (1985)
. . . . The Froegers' Son
The Curse (1987). . . . . Cyrus
Popcorn (1991) . . . . Bud

Daniels, Jeff

Films:

Ragtime (1981) . . . . O'Donnell
Terms of Endearment (1983) . . . . Flap Horton
The Purple Rose of Cairo (1985)
. . . . Tom Baxter/Gil Shepherd
Heartburn (1986). . . . . Richard
Marie (1986) . . . . Eddie Sisk
Something Wild (1986) . . . . Charles Driggs
•• 0:16—Buns, while lying in bed after making love with Melanie Griffith.
The House on Carroll Street (1988) . . . . Cochran
Sweet Hearts Dance (1988) . . . . Sam Manners
Checking Out (1989). . . . . Ray Macklin
Arachnophobia (1990). . . . . Dr. Ross Jennings
Welcome Home Roxy Carmichael (1990)
. . . . Denton Webb
The Butcher's Wife (1991) . . . . Alex
Love Hurts (1991) . . . . Paul Weaver
••• 1:24—Buns, several times in motel room with Judith Ivey.
Made for Cable Movies:
Disaster in Time (1992; Showtime). . . . . . . Ben Wilson
a.k.a. Timescape

Daughton, James

Films:

Animal House (1978) . . . . Greg Marmalard
Malibu Beach (1978). . . . . Bobby
• 0:32—Buns, while running into the ocean with his friends.
The Beach Girls (1982) . . . . Scott
• 0:33—Buns and very brief frontal nudity while taking off clothes and running into the ocean.
Blind Date (1984). . . . . David
(Not the same 1987 *Blind Date* with Bruce Willis.)
House of the Rising Sun (1987) . . . . n.a.
Mortuary Academy (1988). . . . . Yuppie at Car Lot
Girlfriend from Hell (1989). . . . . David

Daveau, Alan

Films:
Screwballs (1983) . . . . Howie Bates
 • 1:00—Buns, after losing at strip bowling.

Davies, Stephen

Films:
Inserts (1976) . . . . Rex
 •• 0:31—Buns and balls, while on bed with Veronica
 Cartwright, making a porno movie for Richard Drey-
 fuss.
Heart Beat (1979) . . . . Bob Bendix
The Long Good Friday (1980; British) . . . . Tony
The Razor's Edge (1984) . . . . Malcolm
The Nest (1987) . . . . Homer
Corporate Affairs (1990) . . . . Ukranian #2
The Berlin Conspiracy (1991) . . . . Klaus Heinlein
Made for Cable Movies:
Philip Marlowe, Private Eye: Finger Man (1983; HBO)
 . . . . n.a.

Davis, Brad

Films:
Midnight Express (1978; British) . . . . Billy Hayes
 • 0:12—Buns, while standing naked in front of guards
 after getting caught trying to smuggle drugs.
A Small Circle of Friends (1980) . . . . . . Leo DaVinci
 •• 1:22—Brief buns, while dropping his pants with sev-
 eral other guys for Army draft inspection.
Chariots of Fire (1981) . . . . Jackson Scholz
Querelle (1982) . . . . Querella
Cold Steel (1987) . . . . Johnny Modine
Hangfire (1990) . . . . Sheriff Ike Slayton
Rosalie Goes Shopping (1990) . . . . Liebling Ray
Made for Cable Movies:
Blood Ties (1986; Italian; Showtime) . . . . n.a.
Miniseries:
Roots (1977) . . . . Ol' George Johnson
Chiefs (1983) . . . . Chief Sonny Butts
Made for TV Movies:
A Rumor of War (1980) . . . . n.a.

• Davis, Gene

Films:
Night Games (1980) . . . . Timothy
10 to Midnight (1983) . . . . Warren Stacy
 •• 0:08—Nude, running after girl in the woods.
 •• 0:28—Buns, in Betty's bedroom, while attempting
 to get her diary.
 •• 1:31—Buns, lots of times, while attacking the girls in
 their apartment.
 •• 1:36—Buns and very brief frontal nudity leaving the
 apartment at the top of the stairs.
 •• 1:37—Nude, running after Lisa Eilbacher in the
 street.
Messenger of Death (1988) . . . . Junior Assassin

Davis, Mac

Singer.
Films:
North Dallas Forty (1979) . . . . Maxwell
 • 0:53—Brief buns while getting a can of Coke in the
 locker room.
Cheaper to Keep Her (1980) . . . . Bill Dekkar
The Sting II (1983) . . . . Hooker
Blackmail (1991) . . . . Norm
TV:
The Mac Davis Show (1974-76) . . . . Host

Day-Lewis, Daniel

Films:
Gandhi (1982) . . . . Colin
The Bounty (1984) . . . . Fryer
My Beautiful Laundrette (1985; British) . . . . Johnny
A Room with a View (1986; British) . . . . Cecil Vyse
Stars and Bars (1988) . . . . Henderson Bores
 •• 1:21—Brief buns, while trying to open the window.
 Very, very brief frontal nudity when he throws the
 statue out the window. Blurry and dark. More buns,
 climbing out the window and into a trash dumpster.
The Unbearable Lightness of Being (1988) . . . . . Thomas
My Left Foot (1989; British) . . . . Christy Brown
 (Academy Award for Best Actor.)
The Last of the Mohicans (1992) . . . . n.a.

De La Brosse, Simon

Films:
Pauline at the Beach (1983; French) . . . . Sylvain
The Little Thief (1989; French) . . . . Raoul
 a.k.a. La Petite Voleuse
 • 1:07—Very brief buns and frontal nudity while
 jumping into bed (seen in mirror).
Strike it Rich (1990) . . . . Philippe

De Lint, Derek

Films:
Soldier of Orange (1977; Dutch) . . . . Alex
Mata Hari (1985) . . . . Handsome Traveler
The Assault (1986; Dutch) . . . . Anton Steenwijk
Mascara (1987; French/Belgian) . . . . Chris Brine
Stealing Heaven (1988; British/Yugoslavian)
 . . . . Abelard
 ••• 0:47—Brief frontal nudity taking off his shirt. Then
 buns, while in bed making love with Kim Thomson.
 1:07—Brief side view of buns under Kim. Long shot.
The Unbearable Lightness of Being (1988) . . . . . . Franz
Made for Cable Movies:
The Endless Game (1990; Showtime) . . . . Abramov

• de Meijo, Carlo

Films:
Twelfth Night (1988; Italian) . . . . Orsino
 • 0:00—Buns, while standing up after bath. Out of focus.
 • 0:49—Half of buns, while sitting on rock, talking to
 Viola.

De Niro, Robert

Films:

The Wedding Party (1969) . . . . Cecil
Bloody Mama (1970) . . . . Lloyd Barker
Bang the Drum Slowly (1973) . . . . Bruce Pearson
Mean Streets (1973) . . . . Johnny Boy
The Godfather, Part II (1974) . . . . Vito Corleone
1900 (1976; Italian) . . . . Alfredo Berlinghieri
- • 1:59—Very brief buns while making love with Domi-
  nique Sanda in the hay. Don't see his face.
The Last Tycoon (1976) . . . . Monroe Stahr
Taxi Driver (1976) . . . . Travis Bickle
New York, New York (1977) . . . . Jimmy Doyle
The Deer Hunter (1978) . . . . Michael
- •• 0:50—Nude, running in street, then more nude by
  basketball court. Brief frontal nudity getting covered
  by Christopher Walken's jacket. Long shot.
Raging Bull (1980) . . . . Jake La Motta
  (Academy Award for Best Actor.)
True Confessions (1981) . . . . Des Spellacy
King of Comedy (1983) . . . . Rupert Pupkin
Falling In Love (1984) . . . . Frank Raftis
Once Upon a Time in America (1984) . . . . Noodles
  (Long version reviewed.)
Brazil (1985; British) . . . . Tuttle
The Mission (1986; British) . . . . Mendoza
Angel Heart (1987) . . . . Louis Cyphre
  (Original Unedited Version reviewed.)
The Untouchables (1987) . . . . Al Capone
Midnight Run (1988) . . . . Jack Walsh
Jackknife (1989) . . . . Joseph "Megs" Megessey
We're No Angels (1989) . . . . Ned
GoodFellas (1990) . . . . James Conway
Stanley and Iris (1990) . . . . Stanley Everett Cox
Awakenings (1991) . . . . Leonard Lowe
Backdraft (1991) . . . . Donald Rimgale
Cape Fear (1991) . . . . Max Cady
Guilty by Suspicion (1991) . . . . David Merrill
Mistress (1992) . . . . n.a.

• Deacon, Brian

Films:

The Triple Echo (1973; British) . . . . Barton
Vampyres (1974; British) . . . . John
Jesus (1979) . . . . Jesus
Nelly's Version (1983; British) . . . . David
A Zed and Two Noughts (1985; British)
. . . . Oswald Deuce
- • 1:12—Buns (he's on the right), getting into bed with
  Alba and Oliver.
- •• 1:25—Nude (on the right), walking to chair and sitting down while Oliver does the same.
- ••• 1:27—Frontal nudity, standing up.
- ••• 1:50—Nude, injecting himself and lying down to
  time lapse photograph himself decay with Oliver.

• Deacon, Eric

Films:

A Zed and Two Noughts (1985; British)
. . . . Oliver Deuce
- •• 0:24—Buns in bed, then nude while throwing Venus
  out, then her clothes.
- ••• 0:30—Frontal nudity, sitting on bathroom floor.
- • 1:12—Buns (he's on the left), getting into bed with
  Alba and Oswald.
- • 1:25—Nude (on the left), walking to chair and sitting down while Oswald does the same.
- ••• 1:27—Frontal nudity, standing up.
- ••• 1:50—Nude, injecting himself and lying down to
  time lapse photograph himself decay with Oswald.

Dempsey, Patrick

Films:

Heaven Help Us (1985) . . . . Corbet
Can't Buy Me Love (1987) . . . . Ronald Miller
In the Mood (1987) . . . . . Ellsworth "Sonny" Wisecarver
Meatballs III (1987) . . . . Rudy
- •• 0:19—Buns, while in the shower when first being
  visited by Sally Kellerman.
Happy Together (1988) . . . Christopher "Chris" Wooden
Some Girls (1988) . . . . Michael
- • 0:34—Brief frontal nudity, then buns while running
  all around the house chasing Jennifer Connelly.
Loverboy (1989) . . . . Randy Bodek
Coupe de Ville (1990) . . . . Bobby Libner
Run (1990) . . . . Charlie Farrow
Mobsters (1991) . . . . Meyer Lansky
  a.k.a. Mobsters—The Evil Empire

TV:

Fast Times (1986) . . . . Mike Damone

• Dennehy, Brian

Films:

Semi-Tough (1977) . . . . T.J. Lambert
F.I.S.T. (1978) . . . . Frank Vasko
Foul Play (1978) . . . . Fergie
10 (1979) . . . . Bartender
Little Miss Marker (1980) . . . . Herbie
First Blood (1982) . . . . Teasle
Split Image (1982) . . . . Kevin
Finders Keepers (1983) . . . . Mayor Fizzoli
Gorky Park (1983) . . . . William Kirwill
Never Cry Wolf (1983) . . . . Rosie
The River Rat (1984) . . . . Doc
Cocoon (1985) . . . . Walter
Silverado (1985) . . . . Cobb
Twice in a Lifetime (1985) . . . . Nick
The Check is in the Mail (1986) . . . . Richard Jackson
F/X (1986) . . . . Leo McCarthy
Legal Eagles (1986) . . . . Cavanaugh
The Belly of an Architect (1987; British/Italian)
. . . . Stourley Kraclite
- ••• 0:12—Buns, while taking off underwear and getting
  into bed with Chloe Webb. Kind of a long shot.
Best Seller (1988) . . . . Det. Lt. Dennis Meechum

Miles From Home (1988) . . . . Frank Roberts, Sr.
The Last of the Finest (1990). . . . . Frank Daly
Presumed Innocent (1990) . . . . Raymond Horgan
FX 2 (1991). . . . . .Leo McCarthy
Gladiator (1992) . . . . .Horn
Made for Cable Movies:
The Diamond Fleece (1992; USA)
. . . . Lieutenant Merritt Outlaw
Made for TV Movies:
A Killing in a Small Town (1990) . . . . .Ed Reivers
To Catch a Killer (1992; Canadian) . . . John Wayne Gacy
TV:
Big Shamus, Little Shamus (1979). . . . . . . Arnie Sutter
Star of the Family (1982). . . . . .Buddy Krebs

Denney, David
Films:
Under Cover (1987) . . . . .Hassie Pearl
  • 0:43—Brief buns while walking around boy's locker
    room wearing his jock strap.
Rush Week (1989). . . . . Greg Ochs

Depardieu, Gérard
Films:
Going Places (1974; French). . . . . Jean-Claude
  • 0:42—Upper half of buns and pubic hair, while talk-
    ing to Pierrot.
  •• 0:49—Buns while in bed, then more buns making
    love to Miou-Miou. Nice up and down action.
  • 0:50—Brief buns while switching places with Pierrot.
  • 0:51—Brief frontal nudity getting out of bed. Dark,
    hard to see. Subtitles get in the way.
1900 (1976; Italian) . . . . Olmo Dalco
  • 1:36—Brief frontal nudity sitting at table with Robert
    De Niro. Again when walking into the bedroom.
  ••• 1:40—Nude getting out of bed after the girl has a
    seizure.
Get Out Your Handkerchiefs (1978). . . . . Raoul
The Last Metro (1980) . . . . .Bernard Granger
Loulou (1980; French) . . . . Loulou
  • 0:07—Brief buns, while getting out of bed after it
    breaks. Dark.
  •• 0:36—Buns, while lying in bed with Isabelle Hup-
    pert.
The Moon in the Gutter (1983; French/Italian)
. . . . Gerard
Return of Martin Guerre (1983; French) . .Martin Guerre
Police (1985; French) . . . . .Mangin
Jean de Florette (1986; French). . . . . .Jean Cadoret
Camille Claudel (1989; French). . . . . Auguste Rodin
Cyrano De Bergerac (1990; French)
. . . . Cyrano De Bergerac
Green Card (1990) . . . . Georges
Too Beautiful for You (1990; French). . . . . Bernard
Uranus (1991; French) . . . . Leopold
1492 (1992). . . . . Christopher Columbus

Depp, Johnny
Films:
A Nightmare on Elm Street (1985). . . . . .Glen Lantz
Private Resort (1985) . . . . .Jack
  •• 0:12—Buns, while in hotel room with Leslie Easter-
    brook.
Platoon (1986). . . . . Lerner
Cry Baby (1990). .Cry-Baby
Edward Scissorhands (1990). . . . . . Edward Scissorhands
Freddy's Dead: The Final Nightmare (1991)
. . . . .Glen Lantz
TV:
21 Jump Street (1987-90) . . . . Tommy Hanson

Dern, Bruce
Father of actress Laura Dern.
Ex-husband of actress Diane Ladd.
Films:
Marnie (1964) . . . . .Sailor
Hush...Hush, Sweet Charlotte (1965) . . . . John Mayhew
The Wild Angels (1966) . . . . Loser (Joey Kerns)
Rebel Rousers (1967) .J. J.
The St. Valentine's Day Massacre (1967) . . . . .John May
The Trip (1967) .John, Guru
Waterhole 3 (1967) . . . . Deputy
Support Your Local Sheriff! (1969) . . . . Joe Danby
Bloody Mama (1970). . . . . Kevin Kirkman
Silent Running (1971) . . . . Lowell
The Cowboys (1972) . . . . Long Hair
King of Marvin Gardens (1972) . . . . Jason Staebler
Thumb Tripping (1972) . . . . n.a.
The Great Gatsby (1974) . . . . Tom Buchanan
The Laughing Policeman (1974) . . . . Leo Larsen
Smile (1974) . . . . Big Bob
The Twist (1976) . . . . William
  •• 0:45—Buns, while taking off his clothes and walking
    onto stage during a play. Long shot.
Black Sunday (1977) . . . . .Lander
Coming Home (1978) . . . . Captain Bob Hyde
  •• 2:03—Buns, while taking off his clothes at the beach
    and running into the ocean.
The Driver (1978). . . . . The Detective
Tattoo (1981). . . . . Karl Kinski
  •• 1:36—Buns, while making love with Maud Adams
    before she kills him.
Harry Tracy (1982; Canadian). . . . . Harry Tracy
That Championship Season (1982) . . .George Sitkoswki
On the Edge (1985). . . . . .Wes
  (Unrated version reviewed.)
  • 0:52—Brief buns, seen from below while floating in
    a pond.
The Big Town (1987) . . . . Mr. Edwards
1969 (1988). . . . . Cliff
World Gone Wild (1988) . . . . .Ethan
The 'burbs (1989) . . . . Mark Rumsfield
After Dark, My Sweet (1990) . . . . Uncle Bud
Into the Badlands (1991) . . . . Barston

Made for Cable Movies:
The Court-Martial of Jackie Robinson (1990)
. . . . Ed Higgins
Miniseries:
Space (1985) . . . . Stanley Mott
Made for TV Movies:
Toughlove (1985) . . . . n.a.
TV:
Stoney Burke (1962-63) . . . . E. J. Stocker

Desarthe, Gerard

Films:
A Love in Germany (1984; French/German)
. . . . Karl Wyler
• 0:28—Buns, while lying in bed with Maria.
Uranus (1991; French) . . . . Maxine Loin

Dewaere, Patrick

Films:
Going Places (1974; French). . . . . Pierrot
• 0:42—Upper half of buns while starting to leave the
room. Surgical tape on his buns.
•• 0:48—Buns while in bed with Marie-Ange.
• 0:50—Brief buns, while switching places with Jean-
Claude.
1:41—Sort of buns, while making love in back seat
of car. Dark.
• 1:42—Buns, while getting out of car and pulling up
his pants.
Catherine & Co. (1975; French) . . . . Francois
Beau Pere (1981; French) . . . . .Remi
The Heat of Desire (1982; French) . . . . . . Serge Laine
a.k.a. Plein Sud
• 0:17—Buns, while getting out of bed and going into
Carol's "house" that she has made out of sheets.
0:20—Pubic hair, while lying on his back.
• 0:21—Side view of buns, while on the floor with
Carol.
0:57—Brief side view of buns, while getting out of
bed and putting on pants.
• 1:02—Buns, while getting into bed with Carol. Very,
very brief frontal nudity hidden by subtitles.
• 1:14—Buns, while taking off pants and getting into
bed.

Dewee, Patrick

Films:
Master of Dragonard Hill (1987). . . . . .Calabar
•• 0:14—Buns, while getting out of bed after being discovered in bed with Claudia Udy by her father.

Diehl, John

Films:
Stripes (1981) . . . . Cruiser
Angel (1983) . . . . Crystal
• 0:35—Buns, while washing blood off himself. Dark,
hard to see. Long scene.
D.C. Cab (1983) .Kidnapper
Joysticks (1983) . . . . .Arnie

National Lampoon's Vacation (1983)
. . . . Assistant Mechanic
City Limits (1984) . . . . .Whitey
A Climate for Killing (1990) . . . . Wayne Paris
Kickboxer 2: The Road Back (1990) . . . . Morrison
Whore (1991) . . . . Derelict
a.k.a. If you're afraid to say it... Just see it
TV:
Miami Vice (1984-89) . . . . Detective Larry Zito

Dimone, Jerry

Films:
Tomboy (1985) . . . . .Randy Star
•• 0:59—Buns, while making love with Betsy Russell in
the exercise room.

• Dolan, Michael

Films:
Hamburger Hill (1987) . . . . .Murphy
Light of Day (1987) . . . . Gene Bodine
Biloxi Blues (1988) . . . . James J. Hennessey
Necessary Roughness (1991)
. . . . Eric "Samurai" Hanson
• 1:09—Buns, while taking a shower, kind of hard to
see. (He's the guy in the middle.)

Dorison, Zag

Films:
Deadly Innocents (1988) . . . . .Crazy Norm
• 0:04—Buns, while standing on top of van and
mooning the paramedics.

Douglas, Kirk

Father of actor Michael Douglas.
Films:
Out of the Past (1947) . . . . Whit Sterling
Champion (1949) . . . . Midge Kelly
A Letter to Three Wives (1949) . . . . .George Phipps
The Glass Menagerie (1950). . . . . Jim O'Connor
Along the Great Divide (1951) . . . . Len Merrick
The Big Carnival (1951) . . . . Charles Tatum
Detective Story (1951) . . . . Jim McLeod
The Big Sky (1952). . . . . Deakins
20,000 Leagues Under the Sea (1954) . . . . . . Ned Land
Man without a Star (1955) . . . . .Dempsey Rae
Ulysses (1955; Italian) . . . . .Ulysses
Gunfight at the O.K. Corral (1957)
. . . . John H. "Doc" Holliday
Paths of Glory (1957). . . . . .Colonel Dax
The Vikings (1958) . . . . Einar
Last Train from Gun Hill (1959) . . . . Matt Morgan
Spartacus (1960) .Spartacus
Seven Days in May (1964)
. . . . .Colonel Martin "Jiggs" Casey
In Harm's Way (1965) . . . . Paul Eddington
Cast a Giant Shadow (1966) . . . Colonel Mickey Marcus
The Way West (1967). . . . . Senator William J. Tadlock
The Brotherhood (1968) . . . . .Frank Ginetta
The Arrangement (1969) . . . . Eddie and Evangelos

There Was a Crooked Man (1970)
. . . . Paris Pitman, Jr.
- 0:11—Brief upper half of buns, while leaving bedroom wearing only his gun belt.
- •• 1:09—Brief buns and balls, while jumping into a barrel to take a bath in prison.

A Gunfight (1971). . . . . Will Tenneray
Once is Not Enough (1975) . . . . Mike Wayne
The Chosen (1978; Italian/British). . . . . Caine
The Fury (1978) . . . . Peter Sandza
Holocaust 2000 (1978) . . . . Robert Caine
- •• 0:52—Buns, during nightmare sequence. Long shots, hard to tell it's him.

The Villain (1979) . . . . Cactus Jack
The Final Countdown (1980)
. . . . Captain Matthew Yelland
Saturn 3 (1980) . . . . Adam
- 0:57—Brief buns while fighting with Harvey Keitel, more brief buns sitting down in bed with Farrah Fawcett.

The Man from Snowy River (1982; Australian)
. . . . Spur/Harrison
Eddie Macon's Run (1983) . . . . Marazack
Tough Guys (1986). . . . . Archie Long
- 1:36—Buns, while standing on moving train, mooning Charles Durning.

Oscar (1991). Snap's Father
Made for Cable Movies:
Draw! (1984; HBO). . . . . Harry H. Holland
Made for TV Movies:
The Secret (1992) . . . . Mike Dunmore

Douglas, Michael
Son of actor Kirk Douglas.
Films:
Napolean and Samantha (1972) . . . . Danny
Coma (1978) . . . . Dr. Mark Bellows
The China Syndrome (1979). . . . . Richard Adams
Running (1979). . . . . Michael Andropolis
It's My Turn (1980) . . . . Ben Lewin
The Star Chamber (1983) . . . . Steven Hardin
Romancing the Stone (1984) . . . . Jack Colton
A Chorus Line (1985) . . . . Zack
The Jewel of the Nile (1985) . . . . Jack Colton
Fatal Attraction (1987) . . . . Dan Gallagher
- •• 0:16—Brief buns, while pulling his pants down to make love with Glenn Close on the kitchen sink.
- 0:17—Very brief buns while falling into bed with Close.
- 0:22—Brief buns, while taking a shower.

Wall Street (1987). . . . . Gordon Gekko
(Academy Award for Best Actor.)
Black Rain (1989) . . . . Nick Conklin
The War of the Roses (1989) . . . . Oliver Rose
1:36—Almost buns, while cleaning himself in the bidet.
Basic Instinct (1992) . . . . Nick Curran
Shining Through (1992) . . . . Ed Leland

TV:
The Streets of San Francisco (1972-76)
. . . . Inspector Steve Keller

• Dourif, Brad
Films:
One Flew Over the Cuckoo's Nest (1975). . . . . . Billy
- •• 1:50—Buns in hallway, putting on his pants after getting caught with Candy.

Eyes of Laura Mars (1978) . . . . Tommy Ludlow
Wise Blood (1979; U.S./German) . . . . Hazel Motes
Ragtime (1981) . . . . Younger Brother
Dune (1984) . . . . Piter De Vries
Blue Velvet (1986) . . . . Raymond
Impure Thoughts (1986) . . . . Kevin Harrington
Fatal Beauty (1987) . . . . Leo Nova
Child's Play (1988) . . . . Charles Lee Ray
Mississippi Burning (1988) . . . . Deputy Dell
Spontaneous Combustion (1989). . . . . David
The Exorcist III (1990) . . . . James Venamon
Grim Prairie Tales (1990) . . . . Farley
Hidden Agenda (1990; British) . . . . Paul
Stephen King's Graveyard Shift (1990)
. . . . Tucker Cleveland
Body Parts (1991) . . . . Reno Lacey
Common Bounds (1991) . . . . Johnny
Horseplayer (1991) . . . . Bud Cowan
Jungle Fever (1991) . . . . Leslie
Made for TV Movies:
Desperado: The Outlaw Wars (1989) . . . . . . Camillus Fly
TV:
Studs Lonigan (1979). . . . . Danny O'Neill

Downey, Robert, Jr.
Films:
Baby, It's You (1983) . . . . Stewart
Firstborn (1984). . . . . Lee
Tuff Turf (1984) . . . . Jimmy Parker
Weird Science (1985). Ian
Back to School (1986) . . . . Derek
Less than Zero (1987) . . . . Julian
1:22—Very brief blurry buns in bedroom with another guy when Andrew McCarthy discovers them.
The Pick-Up Artist (1987) . . . . Jack Jericho
1969 (1988). . . . . Ralph
Johnny Be Good (1988) . . . . Leo Wiggins
Rented Lips (1988) . . . . Wolf Dangler
- 0:01—Buns, while wearing fishnet shorts in S&M outfit during porno movie shoot.
- 0:22—Buns, while through shorts again during playback of the film.

Chances Are (1989) . . . . Alex Finch
Air America (1990). . . . . Billy Covington
Too Much Sun (1990) . . . . Reed Richmond
Soapdish (1991). . . . . David Barnes
TV:
Saturday Night Live (1985-86) . . . . Regular

• Dubac, Bob

Stand-up comedian.
Films:
Stitches (1985) . . . . Al Rosenberg
- 0:03—Very brief buns, while walking around in classroom. Made up to look like a bald corpse. 0:04—Brief buns, while chasing people down hallway. Don't see face. (He's in the middle, holding a beer can.)

• Duchovny, David

Films:
New Year's Day (1989) . . . . Billy
Julia Has Two Lovers (1990) . . . . Daniel
- 0:42—Frontal nudity, standing outside during Julia's fantasy. Hard to see because vertical blinds get in the way. Upper half of buns, while in bed with her (in B&W).
- 0:54—Brief side view of buns, getting out of bed and putting underwear on. Long shot.
Don't Tell Mom the Babysitter's Dead (1991) . . . . Bruce
The Rapture (1991) . . . . Randy
- ••• 0:24—Buns and brief frontal nudity getting out of bed in Mimi Roger's bedroom.
. . . . Officer Tippit
Ruby (1992) . . . . Officer Tippit
Made for Cable Movies:
Red Shoe Diaries (1992; Showtime) . . . . Jake
Made for Cable TV:
Red Shoe Diaries: Safe Sex (1992; Showtime) . . . . . Jake
Made for TV Movies:
Baby Snatcher (1992) . . . . David

Dukes, David

Films:
The Strawberry Statement (1970) . . . . Guard
The Wild Party (1975) . . . . James Morrison
A Little Romance (1979) . . . . George De Marco
The First Deadly Sin (1980) . . . . Daniel Blank
Without a Trace (1983) . . . . Graham Selky
The Men's Club (1986) . . . . Phillip
See You in the Morning (1989) . . . . Peter
A Handmaid's Tale (1990) . . . . Doctor
The Rutanga Tapes (1991) . . . . Bo Petersen
Made for Cable Movies:
Cat on a Hot Tin Roof (1985; HBO) . . . . n.a.
The Josephine Baker Story (1991; HBO) . . . . Jo Bouillon
Made for Cable TV:
The Hitchhiker: Remembering Melody
(1984; HBO) . . . . Ted
- 0:05—Buns, while taking a shower.
Miniseries:
Beacon Hill (1975) . . . . Robert Lassiter
79 Park Avenue (1977) . . . . Mike Koshko
The Winds of War (1983) . . . . Leslie Slote
Space (1985) . . . . Leopold Strabismus
Made for TV Movies:
She Woke Up (1992) . . . . Sloan
TV:
Sisters (1991-) . . . . Wade

• Dunn, Matthew Cary

Films:
The Bikini Carwash Company (1992)
. . . . Donovan Drake
(Unrated version reviewed.)
••• 0:44—Buns, while making love with Amy.

Dye, Cameron

Films:
Valley Girl (1983) . . . . Fred
Body Rock (1984) . . . . E-Z
Heated Vengeance (1984) . . . . Bandit
The Joy of Sex (1984) . . . . Alan Holt
The Last Starfighter (1984) . . . . Andy
Fraternity Vacation (1985) . . . . Joe Gillespie
Scenes from the Goldmine (1987) . . . . . . Niles Dresden
Stranded (1987) . . . . Lt. Scott
Out of the Dark (1988) . . . . Kevin Silver/Bobo
- 0:32—Brief buns when Kristi yanks his underwear down while he is throwing a basketball. Don't see his face.
Men at Work (1990) . . . . Lurinski

Earhar, Kirt

Films:
Summer Job (1989) . . . . Tom
- 0:30—Buns in black G-string bikini when his swim trunks get ripped off.
- 0:43—Buns in G-string underwear getting out of bed and going to the bathroom.

Eastwood, Clint

Former Mayor of Carmel, California (1986-88).
Films:
For a Few Dollars More (1965; Italian/German)
. . . . The Man With No Name
A Fistful of Dollars (1967; Italian)
. . . . The Man With No Name
The Good, The Bad, and The Ugly
(1967; Italian/Spanish) . . . . Joe
Coogan's Bluff (1968) . . . . Coogan
Hang 'em High (1968) . . . . Jed Cooper
Where Eagles Dare (1969) . . . Lieutenant Morris Schaffer
Kelly's Heroes (1970) . . . . Kelly
Two Mules for Sister Sara (1970) . . . . Hogan
The Beguiled (1971) . . . . John McBurney
Dirty Harry (1971) . . . . Harry Callahan
Play Misty for Me (1971) . . . . Dave Garland
Joe Kidd (1972) . . . . Joe Kidd
High Plains Drifter (1973) . . . . The Stranger
Magnum Force (1973) . . . . Harry Callahan
Thunderbolt and Lightfoot (1974)
. . . . John "Thunderbolt" Doherty
The Eiger Sanction (1975) . . . . Jonathan Hemlock
The Enforcer (1976) . . . . Harry Callahan
The Outlaw Josey Wales (1976) . . . . Josey Wales
The Gauntlet (1977) . . . . Ben Shockley
Every Which Way But Loose (1978) . . . . . . Philo Beddoe

Escape from Alcatraz (1979) . . . . Frank Morris
   0:07—Buns, while walking down jail hallway with
   two guards, don't see his face, so probably a body
   double.
Any Which Way You Can (1980) . . . . Philo Beddoe
Bronco Billy (1980) . . . . Bronco Billy
Firefox (1982) . . . . Mitchell Gant
Honkytonk Man (1982). . . . . Red Stovall
Sudden Impact (1983) . . . . Harry Callahan
City Heat (1984) . . . . .Lieutenant Speer
Tightrope (1984) . . . . Wes Block
   • 0:33—Buns, while on the bed on top of Becky. Slow
    pan, red light, covered with sweat.
Pale Rider (1985). . . . . Preacher
Heartbreak Ridge (1986). . . . . .Highway
The Dead Pool (1988). . . . . Harry Callahan
Pink Cadillac (1989) . . . . Tommy Nowak
The Rookie (1990). . . . . Nick Pulovski
White Hunter Black Heart (1990). . . . . John Wilson
Unforgiven (1992) . . . . .William Munny
TV:
Rawhide (1959-66) . . . . Rowdy Yates

Edwards, Anthony

Films:
Fast Times at Ridgemont High (1982) . . . . . . Stoner Bud
Revenge of the Nerds (1984) . . . . Gilbert
Gotcha! (1985). . . . . Jonathan Moore
The Sure Thing (1985) . . . . Lance
Top Gun (1986) . . . . .Lt. Nick Bradshaw
Summer Heat (1987) . . . . Aaron Walston
How I Got Into College (1989) . . . . Kip Hammet
Downtown (1990) . . . . .Alex Kearney
   • 0:19—Buns, while outside after getting his police
    uniform ripped off.
Made for Cable Movies:
Hometown Boy Makes Good (1990; HBO)
  . . . . .Boyd Geary
TV:
It Takes Two (1982-83) . . . . Andy Quinn

Eek-A-Mouse

Films:
New Jack City (1991) . . . . Fat Smitty
   • 0:15—Buns, when Nino holds a gun to his head and
    makes him walk nude outside.

Elwes, Cary

Films:
Another Country (1984; British) . . . . .Harcourt
Oxford Blues (1984) . . . . Lionel
The Bride (1985). . . . . Josef
Lady Jane (1987; British) . . . . Guilford Dudley
   • 1:19—Brief buns, while getting out of bed.
The Princess Bride (1987) . . . . Westley the Farmboy
Glory (1989). Cabot Forbes
Days of Thunder (1990) . . . . Russ Wheeler
Hot Shots (1991) . . . . Kent Gregory

Estevez, Emilio

Son of actor Martin Sheen.
Brother of actor Charlie Sheen.
Films:
Tex (1982) . . . . Johnny Collins
Nightmares (1983) . . . . .J. J.
The Outsiders (1983) . . . . Two-Bit Matthews
Repo Man (1984). . . . . Otto
The Breakfast Club (1985) . . . . .Andrew Clark
St. Elmo's Fire (1985) . . . . Kirbo
That Was Then... This Is Now (1985) . . . . Mark Jennings
Maximum Overdrive (1986). . . . . Bill Robinson
Wisdom (1986) . . . . .John Wisdom
Stakeout (1987) . . . . Bill Reimers
Young Guns (1988) . . William H. Bonney (Billy the Kid)
   • 1:19—Brief buns while standing up in the bathtub.
Men at Work (1990). . . . . James St. James
Young Guns II (1990)
  . . . . William H. Bonney (Billy the Kid)
   •• 1:00—Buns, while getting up out of bed, putting his
    pants on.
Freejack (1992) . . . . Alex Furlong

Eubanks, Corey Michael

Films:
Payback (1991) . . . . Clinton
   • 0:49—Brief buns, while putting his pants on after
    jerks tip his trailer over.

• Evans, Brian

Films:
The Book of Love (1991) . . . . .Schank
   • 0:21—Buns, while tied up to cot with candle stuck
    in his rear end by the bad guys.

Everett, Rupert

Films:
Dance with a Stranger (1985; British). . . . .David Blakely
Duet for One (1987) . . . . Constantine Kassanis
Hearts of Fire (1987) . . . . .James Colt
The Right Hand Man (1987) . . . . Harry Ironminster
The Comfort of Strangers (1991). . . . . Colin
   •• 0:47—Buns, while walking around the room, look-
    ing for his clothes.
   • 1:05—Buns, while making love with Natasha Rich-
    ardson on bed. Lit with blue light.

Fahey, Jeff

Films:
Silverado (1985). . . . . Tyree
Psycho III (1986) . . . . Duane
Backfire (1987) . . . . Donnie
   • 0:22—Brief, partial buns while taking a shower, then
    very brief, out of focus frontal nudity in shower
    when blood starts to gush out of the shower head.
Split Decisions (1988) . . . . .Ray McGuinn
Impulse (1989) . . . . .Stan
The Serpent of Death (1989) . . . . Jake Bonner
True Blood (1989) . . . . Raymond Trueblood

Curiosity Kills (1990) .Matthew
The Last of the Finest (1990) . . . . Rick Rodrigues
White Hunter Black Heart (1990) . . . . Pete Verrill
Body Parts (1991) . . . . .Bill Crushank
Iron Maze (1991) . . . . .Barry
The Lawnmower Man (1992) . . . . Jobe Smith
Made for Cable Movies:
Sketch Artist (1992; Showtime) . . . . Jack
  • 0:52—Brief upper half of buns in bed on top of Sean
  Young.
Made for Cable TV:
Iran: Days of Crisis (1991; TNT) . . . . .n.a.
Made for TV Movies:
Parker Kane (1990) . . . . Parker Kane

• *Fairbanks Fogg, Kirk*
Films:
Alien Space Avenger (1988) . . . . .Matt
  • 0:22—Buns, while walking out of apartment after
  Ginny.

Falconeti, Sonny
Films:
Angel of Passion (1991) .Will
  • 0:22—Buns frolicking in the surf with Carol while
  wearing a G-string.

Falk, Peter
Films:
Penelope (1966) . . . . .Lieutenant Bixbee
Anzio (1968; Italian) . . . . .Corporal Rabinoff
Husbands (1970) . . . . .Archie
Woman Under the Influence (1974) . . . . Nick Longhetti
Murder by Death (1976) . . . . Sam Diamond
The Brink's Job (1978) . . . . Tony Pino
The Cheap Detective (1978) . . . . Lou Peckinpaugh
The In-Laws (1979) . . . . Vince Ricardo
...All the Marbles (1981) . . . . Harry
  a.k.a. The California Dolls
Big Trouble (1986) . . . . Steve Rickey
Wings of Desire (1987) . . . . .Himself
  a.k.a. Der Himmel Uber Berlin
Cookie (1989) . . . . .Dominick "Dino" Capisco
In the Spirit (1990) . . . . Roger Flan
  •• 0:17—Buns, three times while standing up, a little
  embarrassed, talking to Crystal.
Tune in Tomorrow (1990) . . . . Pedro Carmichael
  a.k.a. Aunt Julia and the Scriptwriter
Made for TV Movies:
Death Hits the Jackpot (1991) . . . . Columbo
Columbo: No Time To Die (1992) . . . . Columbo
TV:
The Untouchables (1959-63) . . . . Nate Selko
Columbo (1971-77) . . . . Lieutenant Columbo

Farmer, Gary
Films:
Police Academy (1984) . . . . Sidewalk Store Owner
Powwow Highway (1988; U.S./British)
  . . . . .Philbert Bono
  •• 1:00—Buns, while in bedroom getting out of bed to
  wake up Buddy.
Renegades (1989) . . . . George
Made for TV Movies:
Plymouth (1991) . . . . Todd

Ferris, Larry
Video Tapes:
Penthouse Love Stories (1986) . . . . . . Ecstacize Man
  •• 0:32—Frontal nudity and buns, with a woman in the
  shower.

Field, Todd
a.k.a. William Field.
Films:
Radio Days (1987) . . . . .Crooner
The End of Innocence (1989) . . . . n.a.
Eye of the Eagle II: Inside the Enemy (1989)
  . . . . Anthony Glenn
Fat Man and Little Boy (1989) . . . . Robert Wilson
Gross Anatomy (1989) . . . . .David Schreiner
Back to Back (1990) . . . . Todd Brand
  •• 0:33—Buns, while walking to and jumping into
  swimming pool.
Full Fathom Five (1990) . . . . Johnson
Queens Logic (1991) . . . . n.a.
TV:
Take Five (1987) . . . . Kevin Davis

Finney, Albert
Films:
Wolfen (1981) . . . . Dewey Wilson
Under the Volcano (1984) . . . . Geoffrey Firmin
  ••• 0:49—Buns and brief frontal nudity in bathroom
  with Jacqueline Bisset and Anthony Andrews when
  they try to give him a shower.
  •• 0:52—Buns and very brief frontal nudity, putting on
  his underwear.
Orphans (1987) . . . . .Harold
Miller's Crossing (1990) . . . . Leo
The Playboys (1992) . . . . Hegarty
Made for Cable Movies:
The Endless Game (1990; Showtime) . . . . . Alec Hillsden

Firth, Peter
Films:
Equus (1977) . . . . Alan Strang
  • 1:19—Frontal nudity standing in a field with a horse.
  ••• 2:00—Nude in loft above the horses in orange light
  with Jenny Agutter. Long scene.
Joseph Andrews (1977; British/French) . .Joseph Andrews
Tess (1979; French/British) . . . . Angel Clare

When Ya Comin' Back Red Ryder (1979)
. . . . Stephen Ryder
(Not available on video tape.)
Lifeforce (1985). . . . . Caine
Letter to Brezhnev (1986; British) . . . . .Peter
Innocent Victim (1988) . . . . .Terence
The Hunt for Red October (1990) . . . . .Ivan Putin

Fitzpatrick, Bob

Films:
Deranged (1987) . . . . .Valet
If Looks Could Kill (1987) . . . . Doorman
  ••• 0:18—Buns, while undressing and getting into bed
    with the maid.

Fletcher, Dexter

Films:
Bugsy Malone (1976) . . . . .Baby Face
The Elephant Man (1980) . . . . .Bytes' Boy
The Long Good Friday (1980; British) . . . . Kid
The Bounty (1984) . . . . .Ellison
Revolution (1986) . . . . Ned Dobb
Lionheart (1987) . . . . Michael
The Rachel Papers (1989; British) . . .Charles Highway
  • 0:58—Very brief buns, while jumping into bed with
    Ione Skye.
Twisted Obsession (1990) . . . . .Malcolm Greene

Flower, George "Buck"

Films:
Innocent Sally (1973). . . . . .Toby
a.k.a. The Dirty Mind of Young Sally
  • 0:50—Brief frontal nudity, changing places with Sal-
    ly.
  ••• 0:53—Buns, while making love on top of Sally in
    back of van.
Video Vixens (1973). . . . . .Rex Boorski
  •• 0:52—Frontal nudity taking off his pants, then buns
    in bed with actress during filming of a movie. In
    B&W.
Delinquent School Girls (1974) . . . . .Earl
Cheerleader Camp (1987). . . . . .Pop
a.k.a. Bloody Pom Poms
Code Name Zebra (1987). . . . . .Bundy
Party Favors (1987) . . . . .Pop
Mac and Me (1988) . . . . Security Guard
Sorority Babes in the Slimeball Bowl-O-Rama (1988)
. . . . .Janitor
They Live (1988). . . . . .Drifter
Back to the Future, Part II (1989). . . . . Bum
Relentless (1989). . . . . .n.a.
Sundown: The Vampire in Retreat (1989) . . . . . . Bailey
Dragonfight (1990). . . . . Jericho
Masters of Menace (1990) . . . . Sheriff Hayward C. Julip
Puppet Master II (1990) . . . . .Matthew
976-EVIL II: The Astral Factor (1991) . . . . Turrell
Mirror Images (1991) . . . . .Wolfman
Waxwork II: Lost in Time (1991) . . . . .Stepfather

Video Tapes:
Inside Out 2 (1992)
. . . . Farmer/There's This Traveling Salesman, See
(Unrated version reviewed.)

Forster, Robert

Films:
Justine (1969; Italian/Spanish) . . . . Narouz
Medium Cool (1969). John
  •• 0:36—Nude, running around the house frolicking
    with Ruth.
The Don is Dead (1973). . . . . .Frank
Avalanche (1978). . . . . .Nick Thorne
The Black Hole (1979) . . . . .Capt. Dan Holland
Vigilante (1983) . . . . .Eddie
Hollywood Harry (1985). . . . . Harry Petry
The Delta Force (1986) . . . . Abdul
The Banker (1989) . . . . .Dan
Satan's Princess (1989). . . . . Lou Cherney
Committed (1990). . . . . .Desmond
29th Street (1991) . . . . Sergeant Tartaglia
Diplomatic Immunity (1991) . . . . .Stonebridge
TV:
Banyon (1972-73) . . . . .Miles C. Banyon
Nakia (1974) . . . . Deputy Nakia Parker
Once a Hero (1979). . . . . .Gumshoe

• Fox, Edward

Films:
The Long Duel (1967; British) . . . . Hardwicke
Day of the Jackal (1973). . . . . The Jackal
  • 1:40—Brief buns, twice, while in bedroom after kill-
    ing Colette. Dark.
A Doll's House (1973; British) . . . . Krogstad
A Bridge Too Far (1977; British) . . . . . .Lt. Gen. Horrocks
The Duellists (1977; British) . . . . Col. Raynard
Soldier of Orange (1977; Dutch) . . . . Col. Rafelli
The Big Sleep (1978; British) . . . . .Joe Brody
The Cat and The Canary (1978; British) . . . . . Hendricks
Force Ten from Navarone (1978) . . . . .Miller
Nighthawks (1981) . . . . .A.T.A.C. Man
Gandhi (1982) . . . . Gen. Dyer
Never Say Never Again (1983) . . . . M
The Bounty (1984) . . . . .Captain Greetham
The Shooting Party (1985; British)
. . . . Lord Gilbert Hartup
Wild Geese II (1985; British) . . . . Alex Faulkne

Fox, James

Films:
The Chase (1966). . . . . Jason "Jake" Rogers
Thoroughly Modern Millie (1967) . . . . Jimmy Smith
Isadora (1968; British) . . . . Gordon Craig
Performance (1970) . . . . Chas
  • 0:00—Very brief frontal nudity and buns while mak-
    ing love with a woman. Don't see his face.
  • 0:02—Buns, while getting up next to his girlfriend.
  • 0:24—Brief buns, while getting roughed up by bad
    guys.

Greystoke: The Legend of Tarzan, Lord of the Apes
  (1984)..............................Lord Eskar
A Passage to India (1984; British) ..... Richard Fielding
Absolute Beginners (1986; British).... Henley of Mayfair
The Whistle Blower (1987; British).............. Lord
The Mighty Quinn (1989)....................Elgin

• *Frank, Billy*

Films:
Grotesque (1987)...........................n.a.
Nudity Required (1989)..................Buddy
•• 0:32—Buns, while walking around bathtub and talking to Scammer, then jumping into tub.
• 0:57—Side view of buns, behind textured shower
  door with Julie Newmar.
Lady Avenger (1991).......................Arnie

Frey, Sam

Films:
Nea (A Young Emmanuelle) (1978; French)........n.a.
The Little Drummer Girl (1984).............. Khalil
Black Widow (1987) .... Paul
•• 1:18—Buns, while walking into swimming pool.
Miniseries:
War and Remembrance (1988) ....Rabinovitz

Friels, Colin

Husband of actress Judy Davis.
Films:
Monkey Grip (1983; Australian) .... Javo
Kangaroo (1986; Australian)........Richard Somers
•• 1:08—Buns, while running into the ocean.
• 1:09—Frontal nudity walking towards Judy Davis.
  Long shot, hard to see anything.
Malcolm (1986; Australian)................Malcolm
High Tide (1987; Australian) ....Mick
Warm Nights on a Slow Moving Train (1987)
  ....The Man
Ground Zero (1988; Australian) ...... Harvey Denton
Darkman (1990)................... Louis Strack, Jr.
Class Action (1991)............... Michael Grazier

• *Frye, Brittain*

Films:
Hide and Go Shriek (1988) .... Randy Flint
• 0:51—Brief buns, while undressing and getting into
  bed. Long shot.
• 0:52—Brief buns, while putting on his pants after
  getting out of bed.
• 0:58—Very brief buns, while pulling up his pants.
  Dark.
Slumber Party Massacre 3 (1990) ....Ken

• *Gains, Tyler*

Films:
Novel Desires (1991) .... Brian/Eric
• 0:18—Buns, as Eric, making love with the Model on
  picnic table.

Gallagher, Peter

Films:
The Idolmaker (1980) ....Cesare
Summer Lovers (1982) .... Michael Pappas
• 0:22—Buns, while running into the water after Vale-
  rie Quennessen.
• 0:54—Frontal nudity getting ready to dive off a rock
  while Daryl Hannah and Quennessen watch. Long
  shot, hard to see anything.
Dreamchild (1986; British)............... Jack Dolan
sex, lies and videotape (1989) .... John
Late for Dinner (1991) ....Bob Freeman
The Player (1992)........................n.a.
Made for TV Movies:
Skag (1980) .... John Skagska

Ganios, Tony

Films:
The Wanderers (1979) .... Peppy
Back Roads (1981)....................... Bartini
Continental Divide (1981) .... Possum
Porky's (1981; Canadian) .... Meat
•• 0:21—Brief buns, while running out of the cabin
  during practical joke.
Porky's Revenge (1985; Canadian) .... Meat
•• 0:16—Buns, while getting out of swimming pool
  (the fifth guy getting out). More buns running
  around.
Die Hard 2 (1990) ....Baker
The Taking of Beverly Hills (1991) .... EPA Man

Garcia, Andres

Films:
Tintorera (1977) ....Miguel
• 0:41—Very brief frontal nudity in boat kitchen with
  Susan George and Steve.
•• 0:42—Nude, picking up George and throwing her
  overboard.

Garfunkel, Art

Films:
Catch-22 (1970) .... Captain Nately
Carnal Knowledge (1971) .... Sandy
Bad Timing: A Sensual Obsession (1980)
  .... Alex Linden
• 0:55—Buns, while making love with Theresa Russell
  on stairwell. Don't see his face.
• 0:57—Buns (Sort of see his balls through his legs),
  while on top of Russell when visited by Harvey Keitel.
1:48—Side view of buns while in bed with an unconscious Russell.

Garrison, Bob

Films:
Hollywood Hot Tubs 2—Educating Crystal (1989)
  .... Billy "Derrick" Dare
• 0:53—Buns, while running up to hot dog stand.

• Gaylord, Mitch

Gymnast.

Films:

American Anthem (1987) . . . . Steve Tevere

American Tiger (1989; Italian) . . . . .Scott

a.k.a. American Rickshaw

> • 0:17—Buns, while on boat with Joanna. Long shot, don't see his face.

Gedrick, Jason

Films:

Massive Retaliation (1984) . . . . Eric Briscoe

The Heavenly Kid (1985) . . . . Lenny

> •• 0:31—Brief buns, while in clothing store when Bobby magically dresses him in better looking clothes.

Iron Eagle (1986) . . . . Doug

Born on the Fourth of July (1989) . . . . .Martinez

Rooftops (1989) . . . . .T

Backdraft (1991) . . . . Tim Krizminski

> •• 0:33—Brief buns (on the right) in the shower room with William Baldwin.

Queens Logic (1991). . . . . .n.a.

TV:

Class of '96 (1992-) . . . . .n.a.

Gere, Richard

Husband of model Cindy Crawford.

Films:

Report to the Commissioner (1975) . . . . Billy

Looking for Mr. Goodbar (1977) . . . . .Tony

> •• 1:00—Buns, while on Diane Keaton's floor doing push-ups, then running around in his jock strap.

Days of Heaven (1978) . . . . Bill

Yanks (1979) . . . . .Matt

American Gigolo (1980) . . . . Julian

> •• 0:39—Buns and frontal nudity. Long shot, so it's hard to see anything.

An Officer and a Gentleman (1982) . . . . Zack Mayo

Beyond the Limit (1983) . . . . Dr. Eduardo Plarr

> • 0:21—Buns.

Breathless (1983) . . . . Jesse

> •• 0:11—Frontal nudity dancing and singing in the shower. Hard to see because of the steam.

> •• 0:52—Buns, while taking his pants off to get into the shower with Valerie Kaprisky, then more buns in bed. Very brief frontal nudity. Dark, hard to see.

> •• 0:53—Very, very brief top of frontal nudity popping up when Kaprisky gets out of bed.

The Cotton Club (1984) . . . . Dixie Dwyer

King David (1985). . . . . David

No Mercy (1986) . . . . Eddie Jilletie

Power (1986) .Pete St. John

Miles From Home (1988) . . . . Frank Roberts

Internal Affairs (1990) . . . . Dennis Peck

Pretty Woman (1990) . . . . Edward Lewis

Final Analysis (1992) . . . . Dr. Isaac Barr

> ••• 0:21—Buns while, making love on top of Kim Basinger in bed.

• Getty, Balthazar

Films:

Lord of the Flies (1990) .Ralph

Young Guns II (1990). . . . . .Tom O'Folliard

My Heroes Have Always Been Cowboys (1991)

. . . . .Jud Meadows

The Pope Must Die (1991) . . . . .Joe Don Dante

a.k.a. The Pope Must Diet

> • 0:46—Buns, making love with Luccia in his motor home.

• Ghadban, Alle

Films:

Prom Night IV: Deliver Us From Evil (1991) . . . .Jeff

> • 0:37—Buns, mooning out the limousine window.

> • 0:59—Buns, standing up while carrying Laura. Don't see his face.

• Giamatti, Marcus

Films:

Necessary Roughness (1991) . . . . Sargie

> • 1:09—Buns, while taking a shower. (He's the tall guy on the left.)

Gibson, Mel

Films:

Mad Max (1979) . . . . .Max

Tim (1979). . . . . .Tim Melville

Gallipoli (1981) . . . . Frank Dunne

> •• 1:18—Buns, while running into the water. (He's the guy on the left.)

The Road Warrior (1981) . . . . .Max

The Year of Living Dangerously (1983; Australian)

. . . . Guy Hamilton

The Bounty (1984). . . . . .Fletcher Christian

Mrs. Soffel (1984) . . . . Ed Biddle

The River (1984) . . . . .Tom Garvey

Mad Max Beyond Thunderdome (1985) . . . . .Max

Lethal Weapon (1987) . . . . Martin Riggs

> ••• 0:06—Buns, while getting out of bed and walking to the refrigerator.

Tequila Sunrise (1988) . . . . .McKussie

Lethal Weapon 2 (1989). . . . . Martin Riggs

Air America (1990). . . . . Gene Ryack

Bird on a Wire (1990). . . . . Rick Jarmin

> •• 1:01—Brief close-up of buns when Rachel operates on his gunshot wound. Don't see his face, but it is him.

Hamlet (1990) . . . . Hamlet

Lethal Weapon 3 (1992). . . . . Martin Riggs

• Gillis, Jamie

Adult film actor.

Adult Films:

Blonde Ambition (1980; British) . . . . The Director

Films:

Deranged (1987) . . . . Eugene

> • 1:06—Buns, while getting into bed with Jane Hamilton.

If Looks Could Kill (1987) . . . . Jack Devonoff
Young Nurses in Love (1987) . . . . .Dr. Spencer
Alien Space Avenger (1988) . . . . Businessman
Enrapture (1989). . . . . James

Glenn, Scott

Films:
The Baby Maker (1970). . . . . .Tad
   • 1:30—Buns while in bed with Charlotte.
Angels Hard as They Come (1971) . . . . .Long John
Hex (1973) . . . . Jimbang
Nashville (1975) . . . . Glenn Kelly
Fighting Mad (1976). Charlie
Apocalypse Now (1979) . . . . Civilian
More American Graffiti (1979) . . . . Newt
Urban Cowboy (1980) . . . . Wes
The Challenge (1982). Rich
Personal Best (1982) . . . . Terry Tingloff
The Keep (1983). . . . . Glaeken Trismegestus
The Right Stuff (1983). . . . . Alan Shepard
Silverado (1985) . . . . Emmett
Wild Geese II (1985; British) . . . . John Haddad
Off Limits (1988). . . . . Colonel Dexter Armstrong
Verne Miller (1988). . . . . Verne Miller
Miss Firecracker (1989) . . . . Mac Sam
The Hunt for Red October (1990) . . . . Bart Mancuso
Silence of the Lambs (1990) . . . . Jack Crawford
Backdraft (1991). . . . . .John Adcox
My Heroes Have Always Been Cowboys (1991)
. . . . H.D. Dalton
Made for Cable Movies:
Women & Men 2: Three Short Stories (1991; HBO)
. . . . Henry

• Goddard, Trevor

Video Tapes:
Inside Out (1992) . . . . . . The Other Criminal/The Leda
   • 0:37—Buns, walking down the hallway and stand-
     ing by Sherrie Rose's bed.

Goldan, Wolf

Films:
Melody in Love (1978). . . . . .Octavio
   • 1:14—Buns, while making love in bed with Rachel
     and Angela.

Goldblum, Jeff

Ex-husband of actress Geena Davis.
Films:
California Split (1974). . . . . Lloyd Harris
Death Wish (1974) . . . . Freak 1
   • 0:10—Brief buns, while standing with pants down in
     living room raping Carol with his two punk friends.
Nashville (1975) . . . . Tricycle Man
Special Delivery (1976) . . . . Snake
St. Ives (1976). . . . . Hood
Annie Hall (1977) . . . . .Party Guest
Between the Lines (1977) . . . . Max
The Sentinel (1977). . . . . Jack

Invasion of the Body Snatchers (1978) . . . . . Jack Bellicec
Remember My Name (1978) . . . . .Mr. Nadd
Thank God It's Friday (1978) . . . . Tony
The Big Chill (1983). . . . . Michael
The Right Stuff (1983) . . . . Recruiter
Threshold (1983; Canadian). . . . . .Aldo Gehring
The Adventures of Buckaroo Banzai, Across the 8th
   Dimension (1984) . . . . New Jersey
Into the Night (1985). . . . . .Ed Okin
Silverado (1985). . . . . .Slick
Transylvania 6-5000 (1985) . . . . Jack Harrison
The Fly (1986) . . . . Seth Brundle
Beyond Therapy (1987) . . . . .Bruce
Vibes (1988). . . . . Nick Deezy
Earth Girls are Easy (1989) . . . . .Mac
Mr. Frost (1990; French/British) . . . . Mr. Frost
The Tall Guy (1990) . . . . .Dexter King
   0:34—Brief right cheek of buns, while rolling around
     on the floor with Kate. Don't see his face.
Twisted Obsession (1990) . . . . Daniel Gillis
The Favour, the Watch and the Very Big Fish
   (1991; French/British). . . . . Pianist
   a.k.a. Rue Saint-Sulpice
Deep Cover (1992) . . . . David Jason
The Favor, The Watch and the Very Big Fish (1992) . n.a.
TV:
Tenspeed and Brown Shoe (1980)
. . . . Lionel "Brown Shoe" Whitney

Gonzales, Joe

Films:
Brain Damage (1988) . . . . .Guy in Shower
   • 0:54—Buns, while taking a shower.

Goodeve, Grant

Films:
License to Drive (1988) . . . . Mr. Nice Guy
Take Two (1988) . . . . Barry Griffith/Frank Bentley
   • 0:31—Buns, while in bed with Robin Mattson.
   ••• 0:46—Buns, while getting into bed with Mattson
     again.
Made for TV Movies:
An Eight is Enough Wedding (1989). . . . . .David
TV:
Eight is Enough (1977-81) . . . . David Bradford
Dynasty (1983) .Chris Deegan
Northern Exposure (1990-) . . . . Rick

• Gooding, Cuba, Jr.

Films:
Coming to America (1988) . . . . . .Boy Getting Haircut
Boys N the Hood (1991) . . . . Tre Styles
   • 0:42—Buns, in bed with Tisha. Don't see his face,
     but it is him.
Gladiator (1992) . . . . Lincoln

Goodman, Caleb

Films:

Up Yours . . . . .Virgil
- 0:50—Buns, while dancing on roof of building with Mary Lou.

Graham, Gary

Films:

The Hollywood Knights (1980) . . . . .Jimmy Shine
The Arrogant (1987) .Giovanni
The Last Warrior (1989) . . . . .Gibb
- 0:07—Brief buns, while taking off his towel when he sees a ship.

Robot Jox (1990) . . . . .Achilles
- 0:32—Very brief buns, getting dressed in his room while talking to Athena.

Made for TV Movies:

In the Best Interest of the Children (1992)
. . . . .John Birney

TV:

Alien Nation (1989-91) . . . . .Det. Matthew Sikes

Grant, David

Films:

The End of August (1974) . . . . Robert
French Postcards (1979) . . . . Alex
Happy Birthday, Gemini (1980). . . . . . . .Randy Hastings
American Flyers (1985) . . . . David
- 0:05—Brief buns and very, very brief frontal nudity taking off shorts and walking to bathroom.

Bat 21 (1988) . . . . .Ross Carver
Strictly Business (1991) . . . . David

Grant, Richard E.

Films:

Withnail and I (1987; British). . . . . Withnail
How to Get Ahead in Advertising (1988)
. . . . Bagley
- 0:19—Brief buns, while wearing apron in kitchen all covered with food. Brief buns again talking with Rachel Ward at top of stairs.

Mountains of the Moon (1989). . . . . .Oliphant
Henry & June (1990). . . . . Hugo
Warlock (1990) . . . . .Redferne
Hudson Hawk (1991) . . . . Darwin Mayflower
L.A. Story (1991). . . . . Roland
The Player (1992) . . . . .n.a.

Graves, Rupert

Films:

A Room with a View (1986; British)
. . . . Freddy Honeychurch
- 1:05—Nude running around with Mr. Beebe and George in the woods. Lots of frontal nudity.

Maurice (1987; British) . . . . Alec Scudder
A Handful of Dust (1988) . . . . John Beaver
The Children (1990) . . . . Gerald Ormerod
Where Angels Fear to Tread (1992) . . . . Phillip

Greene, Daniel

Films:

Stitches (1985). . . . . .Ted Fletcher
- 0:45—Brief buns, twice, while pulling his pants down in front of visiting medical students.

Weekend Warriors (1986). . . . . Phil McCracken
American Tiger (1989; Italian) . . . . .Francis
a.k.a. American Rickshaw
Skeleton Coast (1989) . . . . .Rick Weston

Greenquist, Brad

Films:

The Bedroom Window (1987). . . . . .Henderson
- 0:35—Buns, turning off the light while Steve Guttenberg spies on him.

The Chair (1988) .Mushmouth

Greenwood, Bruce

Films:

Bear Island (1980; British/Canadian) . . . . . . .Technician
The Malibu Bikini Shop (1985). . . . . Todd
Another Chance (1989) . . . . n.a.
Wild Orchid (1990) . . . . Jermone McFarland
- • 1:02—Buns, while in room with Carré Otis.

Made for Cable TV:

The Hitchhiker: Shattered Vows . . . . .Jeff

TV:

Legmen (1984) . . . . Jack Gage
St. Elsewhere (1986-88). . . . . .Dr. Seth Griffin
Knots Landing (1991-) . . . . Pierce Lawton

Gregory, Andre

Films:

My Dinner with Andre (1981) . . . . Andre
Author! Author! (1982) . . . . .J.J.
Protocol (1984) . . . . Nawaf Al Kabeer
The Mosquito Coast (1986) . . . . Mr. Spellgood
Street Smart (1987) . . . . Ted Avery
The Last Temptation of Christ (1988)
. . . . .John the Baptist
Some Girls (1988) . . . . .Mr. D'Arc
- 1:24—Buns, while standing in the study looking at a book. Very brief frontal nudity when he turns around to sit at his desk.

The Bonfire of the Vanities (1990) . . . . . .Aubrey Buffing

Guest, Christopher

Husband of actress Jamie Lee Curtis.

Films:

The Hospital (1971) .Resident
The Hot Rock (1972) . . . . Policeman
Death Wish (1974). . . . . .Patrolman Reilly
The Fortune (1975) . . . . Boy Lover
Girlfriends (1978) . . . . Eric
- 1:04—Buns, while running after Melanie Mayron in her apartment, then hugging her.

The Last Word (1979) . . . . Roger
The Long Riders (1980) . . . . .Charlie Ford
Heartbeeps (1981) . . . . Calvin

This is Spinal Tap (1984) . . . . Nigel Tufnel
Little Shop of Horrors (1986). . . . . 1st Customer
Beyond Therapy (1987) . . . . Bob
Sticky Fingers (1988). Sam
TV:
Saturday Night Live (1984-85) . . . . Regular

Gunner, Robert
Films:
Planet of the Apes (1968). . . . . Landon
  • 0:26—Very brief buns while taking off clothes to go
    skinny dipping. (Guy on the left.)

Guttenberg, Steve
Films:
The Chicken Chronicles (1977) . . . . David Kessler
The Boys From Brazil (1978) . . . . Barry Kohler
Can't Stop the Music (1980) . . . . Jack Morell
Diner (1982). . . . . Eddie
The Man Who Wasn't There (1983) . . . Sam Cooper
  ••• 0:54—Buns, while dropping his pants in office with
    three other men.
  • 1:46—Brief buns, while kissing Cindy during their
    wedding ceremony.
Police Academy (1984) . . . . Carey Mahoney
Bad Medicine (1985). . . . . Jeff Marx
Cocoon (1985) . . . . Jack Bonner
Police Academy II: Their First Assignment (1985)
. . . . Carey Mahoney
Police Academy III: Back in Training (1986)
. . . . Carey Mahoney
Short Circuit (1986) . . . . Newton Crosby
Amazon Women on the Moon (1987). . . . . . Jerry Stone
The Bedroom Window (1987) . . . . Terry Lambert
  •• 0:05—Buns, while getting out of bed and walking to
    the bathroom.
Police Academy 4: Citizens on Patrol (1987)
. . . . Carey Mahoney
Three Men and a Baby (1987). . . . . Michael
Cocoon, The Return (1988). . . . . Jack Bonner
High Spirits (1988) . . . . Jack
Surrender (1988) . . . . Marty
Don't Tell Her It's Me (1990) . . . . Gus Kubicek
Three Men and a Little Lady (1990) . . . . Michael
Miniseries:
The Day After (1983) . . . . Stephen
TV:
Billy (1979) . . . . Billy Fisher
No Soap, Radio (1982) . . . . Roger

Haggerty, Dan
Films:
The Tender Warrior (1971) . . . . Cal
Bury Me an Angel (1972) . . . . .Ken
  • 1:17—Brief buns, while making love with Dag in
    bed. Lit with red light. Kind of a long shot, don't see
    his face very well.
Hex (1973) . . . . Brother Billy
The Life and Times of Grizzly Adams (1974)

. . . . James Capen Adams
King of the Mountain (1981) . . . . Rick
Abducted (1986; Canadian). . . . . .Joe
Elves (1989) . . . . Mike McGavin
Inheritor (1990) . . . . Dr. Berquist
Repo Jake (1990) . . . . Jake
The Chilling (1991) . . . . n.a.
Soldier's Fortune (1991). . . . . n.a.
Spirit of the Eagle (1991) . . . . Big Eli McDonaugh
TV:
The Life and Times of Grizzly Adams (1977-78)
. . . . James "Grizzly" Adams
Video Tapes:
Best Chest in the U.S. (1987) . . . . .Judge

Hall, Michael Keyes
Films:
Blackout (1989). . . . . Alan Boyle
  • 1:19—Buns and balls viewed from the rear while
    stabbing Richard in bed.

Hamilton, Neil
Films:
The Tall Guy (1990). . . . . Naked George
  •• 0:04—Buns, while walking around apartment talk-
    ing to Jeff Goldblum. Brief frontal nudity (out of fo-
    cus).
  • 0:06—More buns, when getting introduced to
    Goldblum.
  • 1:22—Brief buns, during end credits.

Hamlin, Harry
Ex-husband of actress Nicollette Sheridan.
Films:
Movie Movie (1978) . . . . Joey Popchik
Clash of the Titans (1981) . . . . Perseus
King of the Mountain (1981) . . . . Steve
Making Love (1982). Bart
Blue Skies Again (1983) . . . . Sandy
Target: Favorite Son (1988) . . . . n.a.
Made for Cable Movies:
Laguna Heat (1987; HBO). . . . . .Tom Shephard
  • 0:50—Buns, while walking into the ocean with
    Catherine Hicks.
Dinner At Eight (1989). . . . . Larry Renault
Deceptions (1990; Showtime) . . . . Nick Gentry
Made for Cable TV:
The Hitchhiker: The Curse . . . . .Jerry
  (Available on The Hitchhiker, Volume 1.)
Miniseries:
Master of the Game (1984) . . . . Tony Blackwell
Space (1985) . . . . John Pope
Made for TV Movies:
Deadly Intentions...Again? (1991) . . . . . Charles Raynor
Deliver Them from Evil: The Taking of Alta View (1992)
. . . . Richard Worthington
TV:
Studs Lonigan (1979). . . . . Studs Lonigan
L.A. Law (1986-91) . . . . Michael Kuzak

Haney, Daryl

Films:

Daddy's Boys (1988)...................Jimmy
- 0:17—Buns, while getting undressed in room with Christie.

The Unborn (1991)....................Policeman
Uncaged (1991) ....John in Nova
a.k.a. Angel in Red

• Harmon, Mark

Films:

Comes a Horseman (1978) ....Billy Joe Meynert
Beyond the Poseidon Adventure (1979)

............................Larry Simpson
Let's Get Harry (1986)...............Harry Burke, Jr.
Summer School (1987)...............Freddy Shoop
Worth Winning (1989) ....Taylor Worth
Cold Heaven (1990) ....Alex Davenport

Made for Cable Movies:

The Fourth Story (1990; Showtime)

.........................David Shepard
- ••• 0:53—Buns, while getting out of bed with Mimi Rogers. More buns, while walking outside and around the house.

TV:

Sam (1978)....................Officer Mike Breen
Centennial (1978-79) ....John McIntosh
240 Robert (1979-80) .....Deputy Dwayne Thibideaux
Flamingo Road (1981-82)..........Fielding Carlyle
St. Elsewhere (1983-86) ....Dr. Robert Caldwell
Moonlighting (1987) ....Sam Crawford
Reasonable Doubts (1991-) ....Dicky Cobb

• Harrelson, Woody

Films:

Wildcats (1986)......................Krushinski
Doc Hollywood (1991) ....Hank
Ted & Venus (1991) ....Homeless Vietnam Veteran
White Men Can't Jump (1992).........Billy Hoyle
- 0:21—Very, very brief half of buns, while getting into shower.
- 0:37—Very, very brief half of buns, while getting out of bed.

TV:

Cheers (1985-)....................Woody Boyd

Harris, Ed

Husband of actress Amy Madigan.

Films:

Borderline (1980) ....Hotchkiss
Knightriders (1981)...................Billy Davis
- 0:01—Buns, while kneeling in the woods. Long shot, hard to see.
- 1:51—Upper half of buns, while standing in a pond doing something with a stick.

Creepshow (1982) ....Hank
The Right Stuff (1983)..................John Glenn
Under Fire (1983) ....Gates
A Flash of Green (1984) ....Jimmy Wing

Places in the Heart (1984) ....Wayne Lomax
Swing Shift (1984) ....Jack Walsh
- 0:03—Very brief frontal nudity when he sits down in chair wearing a towel around his waist.

Alamo Bay (1985) ....Shang
Code Name: Emerald (1985)..............Gus Lang
Sweet Dreams (1985)..................Charlie Dick
To Kill a Priest (1988) ....Stefan
Walker (1988) ....William Walker
The Abyss (1989)..............Virgil "Bud" Brigman
Jackknife (1989).........................Dave
State of Grace (1990)....................Frankie
Glengarry Glen Ross (1992) ....n.a.

Made for Cable Movies:

The Last Innocent Man (1987; HBO) ....n.a.
Paris Trout (1991; Showtime)........Harry Seagraves
Running Mates (1992; HBO) ....Hugh Hathaway

Harris, Jim

Films:

Squeeze Play (1979) ....Wes
- •• 0:39—Buns, tied up in a room while people walking by look in through open door.

Waitress! (1982).........................Jerry
American Ninja 4: The Annihilation (1991)........n.a.

Harris, Richard

Films:

The Bible (1966) ....Cain
Hawaii (1966) ....Rafer Hoxworth
Camelot (1967) ....King Arthur
Cromwell (1970; British) ....Cromwell
A Man Called Horse (1970) ....Lord John Morgan
The Molly Maguires (1970)

....................James McParlan/McKenna
99 and 44/100% Dead (1974)..........Harry Crown
Juggernaut (1974; British) ....Fallon
Return of a Man Called Horse (1976) .....John Morgan
Robin and Marian (1976)...........King Richard
The Cassandra Crossing (1977; British) ...Chamberlain
Orca, The Killer Whale (1977) ....Captain Nolan
The Wild Geese (1978; British).........Rafer Janders
The Last Word (1979) ....Danny Travis
Tarzan, The Ape Man (1981) ....Parker
Your Ticket Is No Longer Valid (1982) ....Jason
- 1:19—Buns, while taking off robe and sitting on the floor.

Triumphs of a Man Called Horse (1983; U.S./Mexican)
.........................Man Called Horse
Highpoint (1984; Canadian) ....Louis Kinney
Martin's Day (1985; Canadian).........Martin Steckert
Wetherby (1985; British) ....Sir Thomas
The Field (1991)....................Bull McCabe
Unforgiven (1992) ....n.a.

• Harrison, Gregory

Films:
North Shore (1987). Chandler
Body Chemistry 2: Voice of a Stranger (1991)
. . . . Dan
••• 0:45—Buns on stairs when Brenda finds him in the
morning.
Made for Cable Movies:
Bare Essentials (1991) . . . . Bill
Duplicates (1992; USA) . . . . Bob Boxletter
TV:
Logan's Run (1977-78) . . . . Logan
Centennial (1978-79) . . . . Levi Zandt
Trapper John, M.D. (1979-86)
. . . . Dr. George "Gonzo" Alonzo Gates
Falcon Crest (1989-90) . . . . Michael Sharpe
True Detectives (1990-91) . . . . Host
The Family Man (1990-91) . . . . Jack Taylor

Hartman, Billy

Films:
Slaughter High (1986). . . . . Frank
• 1:00—Brief buns while in bed with Stella.

Hasselhoff, David

Husband of actress Pamela Bach.
Ex-husband of actress Catherine Hickland.
Films:
Revenge of the Cheerleaders (1976). . . . . Boner
• 0:28—Buns in shower room scene.
••• 0:30—Frontal nudity in shower room scene while
soaping Gail.
Starcrash (1979; Italian) . . . . Simon
W. B., Blue and the Bean (1988) . . . . White Bread
a.k.a. Bail Out
Witchery (1988) . . . . Gary
The Final Alliance (1990). . . . . Will Colton
Made for TV Movies:
The Cartier Affair (1985) . . . . .n.a.
Knight Rider 2000 (1991) . . . . Michael Knight
TV:
The Young and the Restless . . . . Snapper
Knight Rider (1982-86) . . . . Michael Knight
Baywatch (1989-90) . . . . Mitch Bucannon
Baywatch (1991-). . . . . Mitch Bucannon

• Hatch, Richard

Films:
Best Friends (1975) . . . . Jesse
Charlie Chan & the Curse of the Dragon Queen (1981)
Lee Chan, Jr.
Heated Vengeance (1984). . . . . Hoffman
••• 0:38—Buns, while making love in bed with Michelle
during his dream.
•• 0:40—Buns, while getting up out of bed and walk-
ing to bathroom.
Party Line (1988) . . . . Lt. Dan Bridges
Ghettoblaster (1989). . . . . Travis

Delta Force Commando 2 (1991). . . . . Brett Haskell
Made for TV Movies:
Battlestar Gallactica (1978) . . . . .Captain Apollo
TV:
All My Children . . . . Phil
The Streets of San Francisco (1976-77)
. . . . .Inspector Dan Robbins
Mary Hartman, Mary Hartman (1977-78)
. . . . Harmon Farinella
Battlestar Galactica (1978-79) . . . . .Captain Apollo

Hauer, Rutger

Films:
Surrogate Romance . . . . n.a.
Turkish Delight (1974; Dutch) . . . . Erik
••• 0:01—Brief nude walking around his apartment talking to a woman he has just picked up.
• 0:04—Buns, while in bed (covered with a sheet),
then very brief frontal nudity throwing another girl
out.
•• 0:36—Frontal nudity getting up to answer the door
with flowers.
•• 1:12—Frontal nudity lying in bed depressed.
•• 1:16—Buns, while making love with Olga in bed.
Soldier of Orange (1977; Dutch) . . . . Erik Lanshoff
Katie's Passion (1978; Dutch) . . . . Dandy
• 1:12—Buns seen through torn pants while he is
kneeling on the floor.
•• 1:15—Brief frontal nudity getting out of bed.
Spetters (1980; Dutch). . . . . Witkamp
Chanel Solitaire (1981). . . . . Etienne De Balsan
Nighthawks (1981) . . . . Wulfgar
Blade Runner (1982) . . . . Roy Batty
Eureka (1983; British) . . . . Claude Maillot Van Horn
The Osterman Weekend (1983) . . . . .John Tanner
Flesh + Blood (1985) . . . . .Martin
• 1:35—Buns, while in a jock strap running up stairs
after everybody throws their clothes into the fire.
Ladyhawke (1985) . . . . .Etienne of Navarre
The Hitcher (1986). . . . . .John Ryder
Wanted: Dead or Alive (1987) . . . . Nick Randall
The Blood of Heroes (1989) . . . . Sallow
a.k.a. Salute of the Jugger
Bloodhounds of Broadway (1989) . . . . .The Brain
Blind Fury (1990) . . . . Nick Parker
Split Second (1992) . . . . .Stone
Made for Cable Movies:
A Breed Apart (1984; HBO) . . . . Jim Malden
Dead Lock (1991; HBO). . . . . .Frank Warren
Magazines:
Playboy (Nov 1974) . . . . Sex in Cinema 1974
•• 151—Buns from *Turkish Delight.*

Hauser, Wings

Films:
Homework (1982) . . . . Reddog
Vice Squad (1982) . . . . Ramrod

Deadly Force (1983) . . . . Stoney Cooper
- •• 0:44—Very brief buns, leaping out of bathtub when gunman starts shooting. More buns, while lying on the floor.
- •• 0:49—Buns, while in hammock, lying on top of Joyce Ingalls.

A Soldier's Story (1984) . . . . .Lt. Byrd
3:15—The Moment of Truth (1986) . . . . . Mr. Havilland
Jo Jo Dancer, Your Life Is Calling (1986) . . . . Cliff
No Safe Haven (1987) . . . . .Clete Harris
Tough Guys Don't Dance (1987) . . . . Regency
The Wind (1987) . . . . .Phil
The Carpenter (1988) . . . . .Ed
Dead Man Walking (1988) . . . . John Luger
Bedroom Eyes II (1989) . . . . Harry Ross
L.A. Bounty (1989) . . . . Cavanaugh
Street Asylum (1989) . . . . Sgt. Arliss Ryder
Beastmaster 2: Through the Portal of Time (1990)
. . . . .Arklon
Coldfire (1990) . . . . Lars
Frame Up (1990) . . . . Ralph Baker
Living to Die (1990) . . . . Nick Carpenter
Pale Blood (1990) . . . . Van Vandameer
The Art of Dying (1991) . . . . Jack
- •• 0:28—Buns, while standing in kitchen making love with Kathleen Kinmont.

Blood Money (1991) . . . . John
a.k.a. The Killers Edge
Mind, Body & Soul (1992) . . . . .n.a.
TV:
Lightning Force (1991-)
. . . . Lieutenant Colonel "Trane" Coltrane

Hayes, Alan
Films:
Friday the 13th, Part IV—The Final Chapter
(1984) . . . . Paul
- • 0:26—Brief buns, while swinging on a rope and jumping into the lake.

Neon Maniacs (1985) . . . . Steven

Heard, John
Films:
Between the Lines (1977) . . . . Harry
- •• 1:17—Buns, while putting his pants on.

First Love (1977) . . . . David
Chilly Scenes of Winter (1979) . . . . .Charles
Heart Beat (1979) . . . . .Jack Kerouac
Cutter's Way (1981) . . . . .Alex Cutter
a.k.a. Cutter and Bone
Cat People (1982) . . . . .Oliver Yates
- • 1:37—Very brief side view of buns, while taking off his pants and sitting on bed next to Kinski.
- •• 1:50—Buns, while making love with Nastassia Kinski in bed in a cabin.

C.H.U.D. (1984) . . . . .George Cooper
After Hours (1985) . . . . Bartender
Heaven Help Us (1985) . . . . Brother Timothy
The Trip to Bountiful (1986) . . . . .Ludie Watts

Beaches (1988) . . . . John Pierce
Big (1988) . . . . .Paul
The Milagro Beanfield War (1988) . . . . . . Charlie Bloom
The End of Innocence (1989) . . . . .Dean
Home Alone (1990) . . . . Peter
Deceived (1991) . . . . Jack Saunders
Mindwalk (1991) . . . . Thomas Harriman
Rambling Rose (1991) . . . . Willcox Hillyer
Gladiator (1992) . . . . n.a.
Made for TV Movies:
Necessity (1988) . . . . .Charlie
Cross of Fire (1989) . . . . Steve Stephenson

Hearne, Michael
Films:
Young Lady Chatterley (1977) . . . . Hitchhiker
- ••• 0:52—Buns, several times in back of car with Harlee McBride.
- • 0:54—Brief buns when he's let out of the car.

Hehn, Sascha
Films:
Naughty Nymphs (1972; German) . . . . n.a.
a.k.a. Passion Pill Swingers
a.k.a. Don't Tell Daddy
Melody in Love (1978) . . . . Alain
- •• 1:08—Buns while outside with Melody. Very brief erect penis under covers.
- • 1:16—Buns, twice while making love with Melody near an erupting volcano.

Patricia (1984) . . . . Harry Miller
Private Screenings.
- • 0:41—Lower half of buns, while scratching his butt in the hallway.

• Hennessy, Michael
Films:
Extremities (1986) . . . . Pizza Man
Transformations (1988) . . . . Stephens
- • 1:07—Brief, partial buns, while pulling his pants down.

Herrier, Mark
Films:
Tank (1984) . . . . Elliot
Porky's Revenge (1985; Canadian) . . . . Billy
- •• 0:16—Buns, while getting out of swimming pool (the second guy getting out). More buns running around.

Real Men (1987) . . . . .Bradshaw

Hershberger, Gary
Films:
Paradise Motel (1985) .Sam
- •• 0:33—Buns, while running away from the Coach's house.

Heston, Charlton

Films:

The Ten Commandments (1956) . . . . .Moses
Ben-Hur (1959). Judah Ben-Hur
　(Academy Award for Best Actor.)
El Cid (1961). . . . . .Rodrigo Diaz de Bivar/El Cid
Planet of the Apes (1968). . . . . .George Taylor
　• 0:26—Buns, seen through a waterfall and while
　　walking on rocks. Long shots.
　• 1:04—Buns while standing in middle of the room
　　when the apes tear his loin cloth off.
The Omega Man (1971) . . . . Neville
Soylent Green (1973) . . . . Detective Thorn
The Three Musketeers (1973) . . . . . . .Cardinal Richelieu
Airport 1975 (1974) . . . . .Alan Murdock
Earthquake (1974) . . . . .Graff
Midway (1976). . . . . Captain Matt Garth
Gray Lady Down (1977) . . . . Capt. Paul Blanchard
Almost an Angel (1990) . . . . .Moses

TV:

The Colbys (1985-87). . . . . Jason Colby

Hewitt, Martin

Films:

Endless Love (1981) . . . . David
　• 0:22—Buns when seen in front of fireplace in living
　　room with Brooke Shields. Long shot.
　• 0:27—Very brief buns in bedroom when Shields
　　closes the door. Another long shot.
　•• 0:28—Buns, while jumping into bed with Shields.
　• 0:38—Buns, while lying on top of Shields in bed.
Yellowbeard (1983). . . . . Dan
Out of Control (1984). . . . . .Keith
Alien Predators (1986). . . . . Michael
Killer Party (1986). . . . . Blake
Crime Lords (1990) . . . . .Peter Russo
　•• 0:50—Buns, while getting back into bed with two
　　Chinese girls.
Carnal Crimes (1991). . . . . .Renny
　•• 0:29—Buns, while making love with Linda Carol and
　　Mia.
Secret Games (1991) .Eric
　(Unrated version reviewed.)
　• 0:38—Brief side view of buns, while in bed with
　　Julianne.
　　0:48—Almost buns, on top of Julianne in bed. (Her
　　foot gets in the way.)
Night Rhythms (1992). . . . . Nick West
　(Unrated version reviewed.)
　•• 0:29—Buns, while making love with Tracy Tweed.
　••• 0:31—Buns, while making love with Tweed.
　• 0:33—Partial buns, while getting up off the floor.
　••• 1:18—Buns, while making love on top of Deborah
　　Driggs in bed.

TV:

The Family Tree (1983) . . . . Sam Benjamin

Hewlett, David

Films:

The Dark Side (1987). . . . . .Chuckie
Pin (1988) . . . . Leon
Where the Heart Is (1990). . . . . Jimmy
　• 0:56—Buns, while walking around the hall in an an-
　　gel costume.
Scanners 2: The New Order (1991) . . . . . .David Kellum

• Hill, Bernard

Films:

The Bounty (1984). . . . . .Cole
The Chain (1985; British). . . . . .Nick
No Surrender (1986; British) . . . . Bernard
Drowning by Numbers (1988; British) . . . . . Madgett
　•• 0:35—Buns, getting out of bed to throw papers out
　　the window.
Mountains of the Moon (1989) . . .Dr. David Livingstone
Shirley Valentine (1989; British) . . . . .Joe Bradshaw

Hindley, Tommy

Films:

Silent Night, Deadly Night 4: Initiation (1990)
　. . . . . Hank
　• 0:03—Brief buns, while carrying Kim onto bed.

• Hines, Gregory

Films:

History of the World, Part I (1981) . . . . Josephus
Wolfen (1981) . . . . .Whittington
　• 1:24—Buns, twice when he moons Albert Finney,
　　who is looking through a green-tinted night vision
　　scope.
Deal of the Century (1983) . . . . Ray Kasternak
White Nights (1985) . . . . Raymond Greenwood
Running Scared (1986) . . . . Ray Hughes
Tap (1989). . . . . Max Washington
Eve of Destruction (1991) . . . . Jim McQuade
A Rage in Harlem (1991) . . . . Goldy

Hinton, Darby

Films:

Son of Flubber (1963) . . . . .Second Hobgoblin
Without Warning (1980) . . . . Randy
Firecracker (1981) . . . . .Chuck Donner
Malibu Express (1984) . . . . .Cody Abilene
　• 0:08—Brief buns, while taking a shower on his boat.

TV:

Daniel Boone (1964-70). . . . . .Israel Boone

Hoffman, Dustin

Films:

The Graduate (1967) . . . . Ben Braddock
John and Mary (1969) . . . . John
Midnight Cowboy (1969) . . . . Ratso
Little Big Man (1970). . . . . .Jack Crabb
Straw Dogs (1972). .David
Papillon (1973) . . . . Louis Dega
Lenny (1974). . . . . .Lenny Bruce

All the President's Men (1976) . . . . Carl Bernstein
Marathon Man (1976) . . . . Babe
•• 1:09—Buns, getting out of the bathtub and putting some pajamas on while someone lurks outside the bathroom.
Straight Time (1978) . . . . Max Dembo
0:38—Very, very brief tip of penis in jail shower scene after getting sprayed by guard. Don't really see anything.
Agatha (1979) . . . . Wally Stanton
Kramer vs. Kramer (1979) . . . . Ted Kramer
(Academy Award for Best Actor.)
Tootsie (1982) . . . . Michael
Ishtar (1987) . . . . Chuck Clarke
Rain Man (1988) . . . . Raymond Babbitt
(Academy Award for Best Actor.)
Family Business (1989) . . . . Vito
Dick Tracy (1990) . . . . Mumbles
Billy Bathgate (1991) . . . . Dutch Schultz
Hook (1991) . . . . Captain Hook
Hero (1992) . . . . Bernie LaPlante

Hoffman, Thom
Films:
The Fourth Man (1984; Dutch) . . . . Herman
• 1:00—Frontal nudity on cross when Gerard pulls his red trunks down. Long shot.
•• 1:10—Nude in bathroom when Gerard comes in.
••• 1:11—Buns making love on bed with Christine while Gerard watches through keyhole.

•Hofschneider, Marco
Films:
Europa Europa (1991; German)
. . . . Young Salomon Perel
••• 0:03—Buns, while taking off underwear to take a bath.
• 0:05—Very, very brief frontal nudity, getting into tub.
••• 0:06—Nude, getting out of the bathtub and running to hide in a barrel.
•• 0:45—Nude, running around in barn, trying to get away from his fellow German officer.
• 1:19—Brief, discolored frontal nudity, after he tries to "create" a foreskin.

Holbrook, Hal
Husband of actress Dixie Carter.
Films:
Wild in the Streets (1968) . . . . Senator John Fergus
The People Next Door (1970) . . . . David Hoffman
Magnum Force (1973) . . . . Lieutenant Briggs
The Girl from Petrovka (1974) . . . . Joe
• 0:40—Brief buns, while getting out of bed, putting on a robe and talking to Goldie Hawn.
Midway (1976) . . . . Commander Joseph Rochefort
The Fog (1980) . . . . Malone
The Kidnapping of the President (1980; Canadian)
. . . . President Adam Scott

Creepshow (1982) . . . . Henry Northrup
The Star Chamber (1983) . . . . Benjamin Caulfield
Wall Street (1987) . . . . Lou Mannheim
The Unholy (1988) . . . . Archbishop Mosley
Miniseries:
Blue and the Gray (1982) . . . President Abraham Lincoln
North and South, Book II (1986) . . . . . Abraham Lincoln
Made for TV Movies:
A Killing in a Small Town (1990) . . . . Dr. Beardsley
TV:
The Senator (1970-71) . . . . Senator Hayes Stowe
Evening Shade (1990-) . . . . Evan Evans

•Holmes, T. C.
Video Tapes:
Intimate Workout For Lovers (1992)
. . . . Intimate Harmony
••• 0:39—Nude, in dance studio and in the showers.

Hooten, Peter
Films:
Fantasies (1974) . . . . Damir
a.k.a. Once Upon a Love
• 1:06—Buns, while dropping his towel in front of Bo Derek. Long shot, don't see his face.
• 1:18—Buns again. Same shot from 1:06.
The Student Body (1975) . . . . Carter Blalock
Orca, The Killer Whale (1977) . . . . Paul
The Soldier (1982) . . . . n.a.

•Hoppe, Nicholas
Films:
Night Club (1989) . . . . Nick
• 0:27—Brief buns, while making love on roof with stripper. Long shot.
••• 0:37—Frontal nudity, getting up off the floor.
••• 0:47—Buns, while making love with Elizabeth Kaitan.

Hopper, Dennis
Films:
Rebel Without a Cause (1955) . . . . Goon
Giant (1956) . . . . Jordan Benedict III
The Trip (1967) . . . . Max
Easy Rider (1969) . . . . Billy
Mad Dog Morgan (1976) . . . . Daniel Morgan
The American Friend (1977) . . . . Ripley
Tracks (1977) . . . . Sgt. Jack Falen
•• 0:58—Frontal nudity running through the train. Long scene.
Reborn (1978) . . . . Rev. Tom Harley
King of the Mountain (1981) . . . . Cal
The Osterman Weekend (1983) . . . . . Richard Tremayne
Rumble Fish (1983) . . . . Father
My Science Project (1985) . . . . Bob Roberts
Blue Velvet (1986) . . . . Frank Booth
Hoosiers (1986) . . . . Shooter
Running Out of Luck (1986) . . . . Video Director

The Texas Chainsaw Massacre 2 (1986)
.... Lieutenant "Lefty" Enright
Black Widow (1987) .... Ben
River's Edge (1987) .... Feck
Straight to Hell (1987; British)............ I.G. Farben
Blood Red (1988) .... William Bradford Berrigan
Riders of the Storm (1988) .... Captain
Backtrack (1989)........................... Milo
a.k.a. Catch Fire
Chattahoochee (1990)............. Walker Benson
- 0:32—Brief buns, while leaving the shower room after talking to Gary Oldman.
Flashback (1990). .... Huey Walker
Eye of the Storm (1991) .... Marvin
The Indian Runner (1991).................. Caesar
Sunset Heat (1991) .... Carl Madson
(Unrated version reviewed.)
Made for Cable Movies:
Doublecrossed (1991; HBO) .... Barry Seal
Paris Trout (1991; Showtime) .... Paris Trout
Nails (1992; Showtime) .... Harry "Nails" Niles
- ••• 0:39—Buns, while getting out of the bathtub and running outside after the guy who shot at him.
- • 0:40—Very, very brief frontal nudity, dropping towel to drape on his shoulder.
Magazines:
Playboy (Dec 1976). .... The Year in Sex 1976
- •• 141—Frontal nudity running through train.

• Horenstein, Jay
Films:
American Taboo (1984).................. Paul
- •• 0:33—Frontal nudity, getting out of shower and drying himself off. Foggy.
- • 1:11—Buns, while on top of Lisa in bed.
- • 1:28—Buns, while making love with Lisa during flashback.

• Houston, Robert
Films:
The Hills Have Eyes (1977) .... Bobby Carter
Cheerleaders Wild Weekend (1985) .... Billy
- • 0:45—Brief buns, getting caught watching Frankie give Jeanne a bath.
The Hills Have Eyes, Part II (1989) ....Bobby

Howard, Adam Coleman
Films:
Quiet Cool (1986)...................Joshua Greer
Slaves of New York (1989) .... Stash
- • 1:15—Buns, while putting on his pants and silhouette of penis. Dark, hard to see.
No Secrets (1991)...................... Manny

Howard, Alan
Films:
Americanization of Emily (1964) .... Port Ensign
Little Big Man (1970) .... Adolescent Jack Crabb
Oxford Blues (1984) .... Simon

The Cook, The Thief, His Wife & Her Lover (1990)
.... Michael
- •• 0:32—Buns, while then brief frontal nudity with Helen Mirren.
- • 0:42—Buns, while on top of Mirren.
- • 1:11—Buns, with Mirren in kitchen.
- ••• 1:14—Buns, while getting into meat truck. Frontal nudity getting hosed off and walking around with Mirren.

Howell, C. Thomas
Husband of actress Rae Dawn Chong.
Films:
The Outsiders (1983) .... Ponyboy Curtis
Grandview, U.S.A. (1984)............... Tim Pearson
Red Dawn (1984)....................... Robert
Tank (1984) .... Billy
Secret Admirer (1985) .... Michael Ryan
The Hitcher (1986)................... Jim Halsey
Soul Man (1986) .... Mark Watson
A Tiger's Tale (1988).............. Bubber Drumm
- • 0:38—Upper half of buns getting undressed in bedroom while Ann-Margret changes in the bathroom.
The Return of the Musketeers (1989) .... Raoul
Curiosity Kills (1990) .... Cat Thomas
Far Out Man (1990)............ C. Thomas Howell
Kid (1990) ....Kid
Side Out (1990)................... Monroe Clark
To Protect and Serve (1992) .... Egan
- ••• 0:07—Buns, while getting out of bed to get dressed. Don't see his face.
Made for TV Movies:
Into the Homeland (1987) .... n.a.
TV:
Two Marriages (1983-84)............ Scott Morgan

Howes, Dougie
Films:
Salome's Last Dance (1987)........ Phoney Salome
- • 1:05—Very brief frontal nudity at the end of a dance routine when you think he's a female Salome.

Howman, Karl
Films:
The House on Straw Hill (1976; British)
.... Small Youth
a.k.a. Exposé
- •• 0:36—Buns, raping Linda Hayden in a field, while his friend holds a gun.

Huff, Brent
Films:
Coach (1978)........................... Keith
The Perils of Gwendoline in the Land of the Yik Yak (1984; French) .... Willard
- • 0:51—Brief buns, in G-string while wearing costume.
- •• 0:52—Buns, in G-string, walking around with Tawny Kitaen in costumes.

•• 0:54—More buns, after the women realize he's a man.
••• 0:56—Buns, in jail while wearing only the G-string.
Deadly Passion (1985). . . . . .Sam Black
Stormquest (1988) . . . . Zar

Hughes, Brendan
Films:
Return to Horror High (1987) . . . . .Steven Blake
Stranded (1987) . . . . Prince
To Die For (1988) . . . . Vlad Tepish
• 1:13—Buns, while making love with Kate.
Sundown: The Vampire in Retreat (1989) . . . . James
Howling VI—The Freaks (1990) . . . . Ian

Hurt, John
Films:
10 Rillington Place (1971; British)
. . . . Timothy John Evans
The Ghoul (1975; British) . . . . Tom
East of Elephant Rock (1976; British) . . . . .n.a.
The Disappearance (1977) . . . . .n.a.
Midnight Express (1978; British) . . . . Max
Alien (1979) . . . . .Kane
The Shout (1979) . . . . Anthony Fielding
The Elephant Man (1980) . . . . .John Merrick
Heaven's Gate (1980) . . . . Irvine
History of the World, Part I (1981). . . . . .Jesus
Night Crossing (1981) . . . . .Peter Strelzyks
Partners (1982) . . . . Kerwin
The Osterman Weekend (1983). . . . .Lawrence Fassett
• 0:01—Buns, while getting out of bed and walking to the shower.
1984 (1984). . . . . Winston Smith
• 1:11—Buns, while walking from the bed to the window next to Suzanna Hamilton.
Champions (1984) . . . . .Bob Champion
The Hit (1984) . . . . Braddock
Jake Speed (1986). . . . . Sid
From the Hip (1987) . . . . .Douglas Benoit
Aria (1988; U.S./British). . . . . The Actor
Deadline (1988) . . . . Granville Jones
White Mischief (1988). . . . . Colville
Scandal (1989) . . . . .Stephen Ward
(Unrated version reviewed.)
Frankenstein Unbound (1990). . . . . .Buchanan
The Field (1991) . . . . .n.a.
King Ralph (1991) . . . . Graves

Hurt, William
Films:
Altered States (1980) . . . . Eddie Jessup
0:46—Brief pubic hair twice when Charles Haid and Bob Balaban help him out of isolation tank.
• 0:54—Very brief buns, while standing in the shower when he starts transforming. More buns standing near door and walking to bed.
Body Heat (1981) . . . . .Ned Racine
Eyewitness (1981) . . . . Daryll Deever

The Big Chill (1983). .Nick
Gorky Park (1983) . . . . .Arkady Renko
Kiss of the Spider Woman (1985; U.S./Brazilian)
. . . . Luis Molina
(Academy Award for Best Actor.)
Children of a Lesser God (1986). . . . . .James Leeds
Broadcast News (1987). . . . . Tom Grunik
•• 0:59—Brief buns when getting up from bed after making love with Jennifer. Shadow of semi-erect penis on the wall when she notices it.
The Accidental Tourist (1988). . . . . .Macon
A Time of Destiny (1988) . . . . Martin
Alice (1990) . . . . .Doug
I Love You to Death (1990) . . . . Harlan
The Doctor (1991). . . . . Dr. Jack McKee
Until the End of the World (1991)
. . . . Sam Farber/Trevor McPhee

• Hurwitz, Stan
Films:
Necromancer (1988). . . . . Paul DuShane
• 0:46—Brief buns, when Julie pulls his underwear down. Don't see his face.

Hutton, Timothy
Ex-husband of actress Debra Winger.
Films:
Daniel (1983). . . . . Daniel Isaacson
Made in Heaven (1987) . . . . Mike Shea/Elmo Barnett
•• 0:08—Buns, while standing in a room when he first gets to heaven.
Everybody's All-American (1988) . . . . Donnie
A Time of Destiny (1988) . . . . Jack McKenna
Q & A (1990) . . . . Al Rielly
Torrents of Spring (1990) . . . . .Dimitri Sanin
Made for Cable TV:
Strangers: Windows (1992; HBO) . . . . .Tom

Ipalé, Aharon
Films:
Too Hot To Handle (1975) . . . . .Dominco de la Torres
• 0:39—Buns, while in bed with Cheri Caffaro. Dark, hard to see.
The Final Option (1982; British) . . . . Malek
One Man Out (1988). . . . . .The General
Made for TV Movies:
The Great Pretender (1991) . . . . Bratso

Irons, Jeremy
Films:
Nijinsky (1980; British). . . . . .Mikhail Fokine
The French Lieutenant's Woman (1981)
. . . . .Charles/Mike
Moonlighting (1982; British) . . . . .Nowak
Betrayal (1983; British). . . . . .Jerry
Swann in Love (1984; French/German)
. . . . .Charles Swann
a.k.a. Un Amour de Swann
The Mission (1986; British). . . . . Gabriel

Reversal of Fortune (1990) . . . . Claus von Bülow
(Academy Award for Best Actor.)
Kafka (1992; U.S./French) . . . . Kafka
Miniseries:
Brideshead Revisited (1981; British)
. . . . Charles Ryder
•• 0:17—(Part 3 on TV or Book 2 on video tape.) Buns,
while standing on roof with Anthony Andrews after
talking with Cordelia.

Jagger, Mick

Singer with *The Rolling Stones.*
Significant Other of model/actress Jerry Hall.
Films:
Performance (1970) . . . . Turner
0:48—Side view of buns, while getting out of bath-
tub.
Burden of Dreams (1982) . . . . n.a.
Running Out of Luck (1986) . . . . Himself
• 0:42—Brief buns in mirror in room with Rae Dawn
Chong lying in bed. Another buns long shot in bed
on top of Chong.
Freejack (1992) . . . . Vacendak

Janssen, David

Films:
To Hell and Back (1955) . . . . Lieutenant Lee
The Green Berets (1968) . . . . George Beckworth
The Shoes of a Fisherman (1968) . . . . George Faber
Marooned (1969) . . . . Ted Dougherty
Macho Callahan (1970). . . . . . Diego "Macho" Callahan
Once is Not Enough (1975) . . . . Tom Colt
• 1:22—Buns, while taking off clothes and walking to
the bathroom.
Two-Minute Warning (1976). . . . . Steve
Golden Rendezvous (1977) . . . . Charles Conway
Inchon (1981) . . . . David Feld
TV:
Richard Diamond, Private Detective (1957-60)
. . . . Richard Diamond
The Fugitive (1963-67) . . . . Dr. Richard Kimble
O'Hara, U.S. Treasury (1971-72) . . . . Jim O'Hara
Harry-O (1974-76) . . . . Harry Orwell
Centennial (1978-79) . . . . Paul Garrett

Jenkins, John

Films:
Patti Rocks (1988) . . . . Eddie
• 1:07—Buns, while making love with Patti in bed.

Jeremy, Ron

Adult film actor.
Films:
52 Pick-Up (1986). . . . . Party Goer
They Bite (1991) . . . . Darryl

Jeter, Michael

Films:
Hair (1979). . . . . Woodrow Sheldon
• 1:06—Buns while in front of Army guys.
Ragtime (1981) . . . . n.a.
Soup for One (1982) . . . . n.a.
The Money Pit (1986) . . . . Arnie
Dead Bang (1989) . . . . Dr. Krantz
Tango & Cash (1989). . . . . Skinner
The Fisher King (1991) . . . . . . Homeless Cabaret Singer

• Jodorowsky, Axel

Films:
Santa Sangre (1989; Italian/Spanish). . . . . Fenix
•• 0:00—Buns, in room in an asylum.

Johnson, Don

Husband of actress Melanie Griffith.
Films:
The Magic Garden of Stanley Sweetheart (1970)
. . . . Stanley Sweetheart
Zachariah (1971) . . . . Matthew
The Harrad Experiment (1973) . . . . Stanley Cole
•• 0:18—Brief frontal nudity after getting out of the
shower while Laurie Walters watches.
Return to Macon County (1975) . . . . Harley McKay
A Boy and His Dog (1976) Vic
Melanie (1982) . . . . Carl
Miami Vice (1984) . . . . Sonny Crockett
Cease Fire (1985). . . . . Tim Murphy
Sweet Hearts Dance (1988) . . . . Wiley Boon
Dead Bang (1989) . . . . Detective Jerry Beck
The Hot Spot (1990) . . . . Harry Madox
•• 0:41—Brief buns, while pulling up his underwear,
talking to Virginia Madsen.
• 1:17—Buns, while undressing to go swimming with
Madsen.
• 1:18—Buns, while getting out of the water. Long
shot.
Harley Davidson and The Marlboro Man (1991)
. . . . Robert Lee Anderson, Marlboro Man
Paradise (1991) . . . . Ben Reed
Made for TV Movies:
Beulah Land (1980) . . . . n.a.
The Revenge of the Stepford Wives (1980). . . . . . . n.a.
TV:
From Here to Eternity (1980) . . . . Jefferson Davis Prewitt
Miami Vice (1984-89) . . . . Sonny Crockett

Johnson, Joseph Alan

Films:
The Slumber Party Massacre (1982) . . . . Neil
Berserker (1988). . . . . n.a.
Iced (1988) . . . . Alex
• 0:46—Brief buns while in bathtub reminiscing about
making love with a girl.

Jones, Griff Rhys

Films:
The Misadventures of Mr. Wilt (1990)
.... Henry Wilt
- 0:34—Sort of buns, while naked and tied to inflatable doll.
- 0:36—More buns, while up on balcony. Long shot.

Jones, Sam

Films:
10 (1979) .... David Hanley
Flash Gordon (1980)................. Flash Gordon
My Chauffeur (1986) .... Battle
••• 0:42—Buns, while running around the park naked.
Jane and the Lost City (1987; British) .... "Jungle" Jack
Silent Assassins (1988)................. Sam Kettle
One Man Force (1989) .... Pete
Under the Gun (1989) .... Braxton
- 0:41—Brief buns, while taking a shower at Vanessa Williams place. Don't see his face.
Driving Force (1990)...................... Steve
Night Rhythms (1992) .... Jackson
(Unrated version reviewed.)
The Other Woman (1992)............. Mike Florian
(Unrated version reviewed.)
TV:
Code Red (1981-82) .... Chris Rorchek
Highwayman (1987-88) .... Highwayman
Magazines:
Playgirl (Jun 1975) .... Man of the Month
Frontal nudity.
Playgirl (Jun 1988) .... Where Are They Now?
38—Frontal nudity.

Jones, Tommy Lee

Films:
Jackson County Jail (1976) ....Coley Blake
Rolling Thunder (1977).............Johnny Vohden
The Betsy (1978)................... Angelo Perino
Eyes of Laura Mars (1978).............. John Neville
Coal Miner's Daughter (1980)
.... Doolittle "Mooney" Lynn
Back Roads (1981) .... Elmore Pratt
The Executioner's Song (1982)....... Gary Gillmore
(European Version reviewed.)
•• 0:48—Buns, while walking to kitchen after hitting Rosanna Arquette.
Nate and Hayes (1983) .... Captain Bully Hayes
The River Rat (1984) .... Billy
Black Moon Rising (1986) .... Quint
The Big Town (1987) .... George Cole
Stormy Monday (1988)................... Cosmo
Fire Birds (1990) .... Brad Little
a.k.a. Wings of the Apache
JFK (1991)......................... Clay Shaw
Under Seige (1992)......................... n.a.
Made for Cable Movies:
Cat on a Hot Tin Roof (1985; HBO)...........n.a.
The Park is Mine (1985; HBO).............. Mitch

Gotham (1988; Showtime).......... Eddie Mallard
a.k.a. The Dead Can't Lie
- 0:50—Buns, while walking over to Virginia Madsen. Dark, hard to see anything.
Miniseries:
Lonesome Dove (1989) .... Woodrow F. Call
TV:
One Life to Live .... Dr. Mark Toland

Jones, Tyronne Granderson

Films:
Angel III: The Final Chapter (1988) ......L.A. Pimp
•• 0:32—Buns, while standing in alley after Angel pushes him out of the car.
Twins (1988) ....Mover #2
Harlem Nights (1989) .... Crapshooter

Julia, Raul

Films:
Panic in Needle Park (1971) .... Marco
The Gumball Rally (1976)................. Franco
Eyes of Laura Mars (1978) ....Michael Reisler
The Escape Artist (1982)..............Stu Quinones
One from the Heart (1982) .... Ray
- 1:20—Very brief buns while getting out of bed with Teri Garr when Frederic Forrest crashes through the ceiling.
The Tempest (1982)....................Kalibanos
Compromising Positions (1985)........ David Suarez
Kiss of the Spider Woman (1985; U.S./Brazilian)
.... Valentin
The Morning After (1986) ....Joaquin Manero
Moon Over Parador (1988) ...... Roberto Strausmann
Tequila Sunrise (1988) .... Escalante
Trading Hearts (1988)..................... Vinnie
Frankenstein Unbound (1990) ..... Victor Frankenstein
Presumed Innocent (1990)............. Sandy Stern
The Rookie (1990) .... Strom
The Addams Family (1991) ....Gomez Addams

Juliano, Al

Films:
True Love (1989) ....Male Stripper
- 0:43—Buns while in G-string dancing on stage in a club.

• Junior, Fábio

Films:
Bye Bye Brazil (1980; Brazilian)..............Ciço
•• 0:38—Buns, while backstage with Salomé.

Kantor, Richard

Films:
Baby, It's You (1983) ....Curtis
Out of Control (1984)................... Gary
- 0:29—Buns, while pulling his underwear down during a game of strip spin the bottle.
TV:
Finder of Lost Loves (1984-85) .... Brian Fletcher

Katt, William

Films:
Carrie (1976) . . . . Tommy Ross
First Love (1977) . . . . Elgin Smith
Big Wednesday (1978) . . . . Jack
Baby... Secret of the Lost Legend (1985)
. . . . George Loomis
House (1986) . . . . Roger Cobb
White Ghost (1988) . . . . .Steve Shepard
Last Call (1990). . . . . .Paul Avery
  • • • 0:29—Buns, while on floor with Shannon Tweed.
  • 0:41—Brief buns, while getting up from bed and
    putting his pants on.
  • 1:02—Brief buns, while in bed with Tweed.
Naked Obsession (1990) . . . . Franklyn Carlyle
  • 0:46—Very, very brief buns, while turning over in
    bed with Maria Ford. Long shot.
House IV (1991) . . . . Roger Cobb
TV:
Greatest American Hero (1981-83) . . . . . . Ralph Hanley

• Katzur, Iftach

Films:
Private Popsicle (1982) . . . . Benji
  • • 1:26—Buns, while walking around after Rena steals
    his clothes.
The Ambassador (1984) .n.a.

Kay, Norman

Films:
Lonely Hearts (1983; Australian) . . . . .Peter
  • 1:03—Buns, while getting out of bed. Very brief
    frontal nudity.
Man of Flowers (1984; Australian). . . . . .Charles Bremer

Keitel, Harvey

Films:
Who's That Knocking at My Door? (1968). . . . . J.R.
  • 0:42—Buns, several times, while in bed and stand-
    ing up. Quick cuts.
Mean Streets (1973) . . . . Charlie
Alice Doesn't Live Here Anymore (1975) . . . . .Ben
Buffalo Bill and the Indians (1976). . . . . .Ed
Mother, Jugs & Speed (1976) . . . . Speed
Taxi Driver (1976) . . . . Sport
The Duellists (1977; British). . . . . Feraud
Welcome to L.A. (1977) . . . . Ken Hood
Blue Collar (1978). . . . . Jerry
Eagle's Wing (1978; British). . . . . Henry
Fingers (1978). . . . . .Jimmy Angelelli
Bad Timing: A Sensual Obsession (1980)
. . . . .Inspector Netusil
Death Watch (1980) .Roddy
Saturn 3 (1980). . . . . Benson
The Border (1982). . . . . Cal
Exposed (1983). . . . . Rivas
La Nuit de Varennes (1983; French/Italian)
. . . . Thomas Paine
Dream One (1984; British/French) . . . . . . .Mr. Legend

Falling In Love (1984) . . . . .Ed Lasky
Camorra (1986; Italian) . . . . Frankie Acquasanta
The Inquiry (1986). . . . . .Pontius Pilate
The Men's Club (1986) . . . . Sully
  • 1:22—Buns, while getting up off the bed to talk to
    Allison.
Off Beat (1986) . . . . Bank Robber
Wise Guys (1986). . . . . .Bobby Dilea
The Pick-Up Artist (1987) . . . . .Alonzo
Blindside (1988; Canadian) . . . . .Gruber
The January Man (1988) . . . . .Frank Starkey
The Last Temptation of Christ (1988) . . . . Judas
GoodFellas (1990) . . . . J. R.
The Two Jakes (1990). . . . . Jake Berman
Bugsy (1991) . . . . Mickey Cohen
Mortal Thoughts (1991). . . . . Detective John Woods
Thelma and Louise (1991) . . . . Hal
Two Evil Eyes (1991) .Usher
Sister Act (1992) . . . . Vince LaRocca

Keith, David

Films:
The Rose (1979). . . . . Mal
Brubaker (1980). . . . . .Larry Lee Bullen
The Great Santini (1980) . . . . .Red Pettus
Back Roads (1981) . . . . Mason
Take This Job and Shove It (1981) . . . . Harry Meade
An Officer and a Gentleman (1982) . . . . .Sid Worley
Independence Day (1983) . . . . .Jack Parker
The Lords of Discipline (1983) . . . . Will
Firestarter (1984) . . . . Andrew McGee
Gulag (1985) . . . . Mickey Almon
  • • 1:26—Buns, while standing outside with Malcolm
    McDowell in the snow being hassled by guards.
Heartbreak Hotel (1988) . . . . Elvis Presley
White of the Eye (1988). . . . . .Paul White
Made for TV Movies:
Friendly Fire (1978) . . . . n.a.
TV:
Co-ed Fever (1979) . . . . Tuck
Flesh and Blood (1991) . . . . Arlo Weed

Keller, Todd

Video Tapes:
Nudes in Limbo (1983) . . . . Model
Penthouse Love Stories (1986) . . Service Station Man
  • • 0:11—Brief frontal nudity in bedroom with a wom-
    an.
Penthouse: On the Wild Side (1988)
. . . . Bytes & Pieces
  • • • 0:09—Nude, making love with a female technician
    in the computer lab.

Kerwin, Brian

Films:
Hometown, U.S.A. (1979) . . . . T.J. Swackhammer
Murphy's Romance (1985) . . . . .Bobbie Jack Moriarity
  • • 0:55—Brief buns while walking into the bathroom.
Nickel Mountain (1985) . . . . George

King Kong Lives! (1986) . . . . Hank Mitchell
Torch Song Trilogy (1988) . . . . .Ed
Code Name: Chaos (1990) . . . . .n.a.
Hard Promises (1992) . . . . .n.a.
Made for Cable TV:
Tales From the Crypt: Judy, You're Not Yourself Today
. . . . Donald
Miniseries:
Blue and the Gray (1982) . . . . .Malachi Hale
Made for TV Movies:
Bluegrass (1988) . . . . .Dancy
Switched at Birth (1991) . . . . Bob Mays
TV:
Lobo (1979-81) . . . . Deputy Birdwell Hawkins
The Chisholms (1979) . . . . Gideon Chisholm

Kime, Jeffrey
Films:
Quartet (1981; British/French) . . . . James
•• 0:49—Nude, posing with two women for the por-
nographer.
Joy (1983; French/Canadian) . . . . .Helmut
The State of Things (1983) . . . . .Mark

King, Perry
Films:
Slaughterhouse Five (1972) . . . . Robert Pigrim
The Lords of Flatbush (1974) . . . . Chico
Mandingo (1975) . . . . Hammond
•• 0:17—Frontal nudity walking to bed to make love
with Dite.
The Wild Party (1975) . . . . .Dale Sword
Lipstick (1976) . . . . Steve Edison
Andy Warhol's Bad (1977; Italian) . . . . L-T
The Choirboys (1977) . . . . .Slate
A Different Story (1979) . . . . .Albert
(R-rated version reviewed.)
• 1:33—Buns, through shower door, then brief buns
while getting out of the shower to talk to Meg Fos-
ter.
Search and Destroy (1981) . . . . Kip Moore
Class of 1984 (1982) . . . . .Andy
Switch (1991) . . . . .Steve Brooks
Miniseries:
Captains and the Kings (1976) . . . . Rory Armagh
Aspen (1977) . . . . Lee Bishop
The Last Convertible (1979) . . . . Russ Currier
Made for TV Movies:
Love's Savage Fury (1979) . . . . .n.a.
Shakedown on Sunset Strip (1988) . . . . .n.a.
Roxanne: The Prize Pulitzer (1989)
. . . . Herbert "Peter" Pulitzer
Danielle Steel's "Kaleidoscope" (1990)
. . . . John Chapman
TV:
The Quest (1982) . . . . .Dan Underwood
Riptide (1984-86) . . . . Cody Allen

Kingsley, Ben
Films:
Gandhi (1982) . . . . Mahatma Gandhi
(Academy Award for Best Actor.)
Betrayal (1983; British) . . . . .Robert
Harem (1985; French) . . . . Selim
Turtle Diary (1986; British) . . . . .William Snow
Maurice (1987; British) . . . . Lasker Jones
Pascali's Island (1988; British) . . . . Basil Pascali
Without a Clue (1988) . . . . .Dr. Watson
The Children (1990) . . . . .Martin Boyne
The Fifth Monkey (1990) . . . . Kunda
1:04—Brief buns, while standing under waterfall.
Don't see his face and water is in the way.
Slipstream (1990) . . . . Avatar
Bugsy (1991) .Meyer Lansky
Sneakers (1992) . . . . .Cosmo
Made for Cable Movies:
**Murderers Among Us: The Simon Wiesenthal
Story** (1989; HBO) . . . . Simon Wiesenthal
•• 0:27—Buns and brief frontal nudity standing in and
leaving a line in a concentration camp.

• Kinski, Klaus
Father of actress Nastassia Kinski.
Real last name is Nakzsynski.
Films:
Doctor Zhivago (1965) . . . . .Kostoyed
For a Few Dollars More (1965; Italian/German)
. . . . Hunchback
Justine (1969; Italian/Spanish) . . . . . . Marquis de Sade
a.k.a. Maquis de Sade: Justine
Venus in Furs (1970) . . . . Ahmed
Original version.
Count Dracula (1971; Spanish/Italian) . . . . . . .Renfield
Aguirre, The Wrath of God (1972; West German)
. . . . Don Lope de Aguirre
Web of the Spider (1972; Italian/French)
. . . . Edgar Allan Poe
Lifespan (1975; U.S./British) . . . . Industrialist
Nosferatu, The Vampire (1979; French/German)
. . . . .Count Dracula
Love and Money (1980) . . . . Frederick Stockheinz
Schizoid (1980) . . . . Dr. Peter Fales
The Story of "O" Continues (1981; French)
. . . . Sir Stephen
a.k.a. Les Fruits de la Passion
• 0:40—Very, very brief part of buns while making
love on bed with Arielle Dombasle.
Android (1982) . . . . Dr. Daniel
Fitzcarraldo (1982)
. . . . Brian Sweeney Fitzgerald/Fitzcarraldo
The Soldier (1982) . . . . Dracha
The Little Drummer Girl (1984) . . . . .Kurtz
Creature (1985) . . . . Hans Rudy Hofner
Crawlspace (1986) . . . . Dr. Karl Gunther

Kirby, Bruno

a.k.a. B. Kirby, Jr.
Films:
Cinderella Liberty (1973)................... Alcott
The Harrad Experiment (1973) ......Harry Schacht
- 0:41—Brief frontal nudity, getting into the swimming pool with Beth, Don Johnson and Laurie Walters.

The Godfather, Part II (1974) .... Young Clemenza
Between the Lines (1977) .... David
Borderline (1980) .... Jimmy Fante
Where the Buffalo Roam (1980) .... Marty Lewis
Modern Romance (1981) .... Jay
This is Spinal Tap (1984) .... Tommy Pischedda
Birdy (1985) .... Renaldi
Tin Men (1986)............................n.a.
Good Morning, Vietnam (1987) ...... Lt. Steven Hauk
Bert Rigby, You're a Fool (1989) .... Kyle DeForest
We're No Angels (1989) .... Deputy
When Harry Met Sally... (1989) .... Jess
City Slickers (1991).................... Ed Furillo
TV:
The Super (1972) .... Anthony Girelli

Kirby, Michael

Films:
My Pleasure is My Business (1974) ....Gus
- 0:41—Brief buns while making love with Xaviera Hollander.

Bugsy Malone (1976) .... Angelo
In Praise of Older Women (1978; Canadian) ....n.a.
The Silent Partner (1978) ....Packard
Meatballs (1979; Canadian) ....Eddy
Crossover (1980; Canadian) .... Dr. Turley
a.k.a. Mr. Patman
Agency (1981; Canadian) .... Peters

Kleemann, Gunter

Films:
I Spit on Your Grave (1978) ....Andy
(Uncut, unrated version reviewed.)
- 0:33—Buns, while raping Jennifer.

Kline, Kevin

Husband of actress Phoebe Cates.
Films:
Sophie's Choice (1982) ....Nathan Landau
The Big Chill (1983) .... Harold
The Pirates of Penzance (1983) .... Pirate King
Silverado (1985) ....Paden
Violets Are Blue (1986)........... Henry Squires
- 1:02—Brief buns, while standing up and putting on his shorts, on island with Sissy Spacek.

Cry Freedom (1987; British) .... Donald Woods
A Fish Called Wanda (1988) .... Otto
The January Man (1988) .... Nick Starkey
I Love You to Death (1990)................ Joey
- 0:10—Buns, while wearing an apron walking from the bedroom in Victoria Jackson's apartment.

Grand Canyon (1991) .... Mack
Soapdish (1991)................. Jeffrey Anderson
Consenting Adults (1992) .... Richard Parker

Knight, Wyatt

Films:
Porky's (1981; Canadian) .... Tommy Turner
Porky's Revenge (1985; Canadian) .... Tommy Turner
- •• 0:16—Buns, while getting out of swimming pool (the first guy getting out). More buns running around.
- 0:54—Buns, getting his underwear pulled down while trying to escape from a motel room from Balbricker.

• Knoph, Gregory

Films:
Ilsa, She Wolf of the S.S. (1974) ....Wolfe
- 0:31—Buns, while in bed with Ilsa.
- 0:32—More buns, while in bed with Ilsa.
- ••• 0:46—Buns, while in bed with the two blonde female guards.

• Koenig, Tommy

Films:
Stitches (1985)..................... Barfer Bogan
- 0:03—Brief buns, while getting off gurney. Made up to look like a bald corpse. Something is covering his frontal nudity. Brief buns, while walking in classroom.
- 0:04—Brief buns, while chasing people down hallway. Don't see face. (He's in front.)

Kologie, Ron

Films:
Iced (1988) .... Carl
- 0:39—Buns, while in bathroom snorting cocaine.

Kotto, Yaphet

Films:
The Liberation of L. B. Jones (1970)
.... Sonny Boy Mosby
Man and Boy (1971) .... Nate Hodges
Across 110th Street (1972)............Det. Lt. Pople
Housewife (1972)........................ Bone
Live and Let Die (1973; British) .... Kananga
Truck Turner (1974) .... Blue
Friday Foster (1975) .... Colt Hawkins
Report to the Commissioner (1975)
.................Richard "Crunch" Blackstone
Shark's Treasure (1975) .... Ben
Drum (1976)......................... Blaise
- 1:02—Buns, while getting hung upside down in barn and spanked along with Ken Norton.

Blue Collar (1978) .... Smokey
Alien (1979)........................... Parker
Brubaker (1980).................. Dickie Coombes
Fighting Back (1982) .... Ivanhoe Washington
The Star Chamber (1983).......... Det. Harry Lowes

Warning Sign (1985) . . . . .Major Connolly
Eye of the Tiger (1986) . . . . .J. B. Deveraux
Pretty Kill (1987) . . . . Harris
The Running Man (1987) . . . . Laughlin
The Jigsaw Murders (1988) . . . . .Dr. Fillmore
Midnight Run (1988) . . . . Alonzo Mosely
Ministry of Vengeance (1989) . . . . Mr. Whiteside
Tripwire (1989) . . . . Lee Pitt
Hangfire (1990) . . . . Police Lieutenant
Freddy's Dead: The Final Nightmare (1991) . . . . . . Doc
Made for Cable Movies:
The Park is Mine (1985; HBO) . . . . Eubanks
Made for TV Movies:
Raid on Entebbe (1977) . . . . .n.a.
For Love and Honor (1983)
. . . . Platoon Sgt. James "China" Bell

• Kove, Martin
Films:
Savages (1972) . . . . .Archie
Death Race 2000 (1975) . . . . Nero the Hero
The Four Deuces (1975) .n.a.
White Line Fever (1975) . . . . Clem
The Wild Party (1975) . . . . Editor
Mr. Billion (1977) . . . . Texas Gambler
Seven (1979) . . . . Skip
Blood Tide (1982) . . . . Neil
The Karate Kid (1984) .Kreese
Rambo: First Blood, Part II (1985) . . . . Ericson
The Karate Kid, Part II (1986) . . . . .Kreese
Steele Justice (1987) . . . . John Steele
White Light (1990) . . . . Sean Craig
    1:23—Upper half of buns, while on the floor with
    Rachel.
    • 1:24—Very brief buns, while getting out of bed.
Project: Shadowchaser (1992) . . . . Dasilva
TV:
We've Got Each Other (1977-78) . . . . Ken Redford
Code R (1977) . . . . George Baker
Cagney & Lacey (1982-88) . . . . .Det. Victor Isbecki
Hard Time on Planet Earth (1989) . . . . Jesse

Krabbé, Jeroen
Films:
Soldier of Orange (1977; Dutch) . . . . .Gus
Spetters (1980; Dutch) . . . . Henkhof
The Fourth Man (1984; Dutch) . . . . Gerard
   ••• 0:03—Frontal nudity getting out of bed and walking
     down the stairs.
   •• 0:26—Frontal nudity drying himself off and getting
     into bed.
   • 0:33—Buns, while getting out of bed.
A World Apart (1988; British) . . . . .Gus
The Punisher (1989) . . . . Gianni Franco
The Prince of Tides (1991) . . . . Herbert Woodruff
Kafka (1992; U.S./French) . . . . Bizzlebek
Miniseries:
Dynasty: The Reunion (1991) . . . . Jeremy Van Dorn

Kristofferson, Kris
Films:
Blume in Love (1973) . . . . Elmo
Pat Garrett and Billy the Kid (1973)
. . . . Billy the Kid
   • 0:37—Buns, while getting into bed with a girl after
     Harry Dean Stanton gets out. Long shot, hard to see.
Bring Me the Head of Alfredo Garcia (1974) . . . . . Paco
Alice Doesn't Live Here Anymore (1975) . . . . . . .David
The Sailor Who Fell From Grace with the Sea (1976)
. . . . Jim Cameron
A Star is Born (1976) .Johnny
Vigilante Force (1976) . . . . .Aaron Arnold
Semi-Tough (1977) . . . . Shake Tiller
Convoy (1978) . . . . Rubber Duck
Heaven's Gate (1980) . . . . Averill
Rollover (1981) . . . . .Hub Smith
Flashpoint (1984) . . . . Logan
Songwriter (1984) . . . . .Blackie Buck
Trouble in Mind (1986) . . . . .Hawk
Big Top Pee Wee (1988) . . . . Mace Montana
Welcome Home (1989) .Jake
Millenium (1990) .Bill Smith
Night of the Cyclone (1990) . . . . .Stan
Made for Cable Movies:
The Tracker (1988; HBO) . . . . .Noble Adams
Another Pair of Aces (1991) . . . . Capt. Elvin Metcalf
   (Video tape includes nude scenes not shown on cable
   TV.)
Miracle in the Wilderness (1991; TNT) . . . Jericho Adams
Magazines:
Playboy (Nov 1973) . . . . Sex in Cinema 1973
   • 151—Side view of buns in photo from *Pat Garrett*
    and Billy the Kid.
Playboy (Jul 1976) . . . . Kris and Sarah
   •• 126—Buns, while in bed with Sarah Miles.

Kuhlman, Ron
Films:
To Be or Not To Be (1983) . . . . Polish Flyer
Splash (1984) . . . . Man with Date
Omega Syndrome (1986) . . . . n.a.
Shadow Play (1986) . . . . .John Crown
   • 1:06—Buns, while standing and holding Dee Wal-
    lace in his arms.
Made for TV Movies:
The Brady Brides (1981) . . . . Phillip Covington III

Lackey, Skip
Films:
Once Bitten (1985) . . . . .Russ
   • 1:11—Brief buns while in the school showers trying
    to see if Mark got bitten by a vampire.

Lafayette, John

Films:

The Shaming (1979) . . . . Rafe
a.k.a. Good Luck, Miss Wyckoff
a.k.a. The Sin
•• 0:43—Very brief frontal nudity, taking off his jumpsuit in classroom with Anne Heywood.
• 0:52—Buns, while making love on top of Heywood
in classroom.
Deadly Weapon (1989) . . . . Sgt. Conroy
Switch (1991) . . . . Sgt. Phillips
White Sands (1992) . . . . Demott

Lambert, Christopher

Husband of actress Diane Lane.
Films:

Greystoke: The Legend of Tarzan, Lord of the Apes
(1984) . . . . John Clayton/Tarzan
Subway (1985; French) . . . . Fred
Highlander (1986) . . . . Conner MacLeod
• 1:30—Buns while making love with Roxanne Hart.
The Sicilian (1987) . . . . Salvatore Giullano
(Director's uncut version reviewed.)
•• 1:02—Buns, when the Duchess yanks his underwear
down. Don't see his face, but probably him.
To Kill a Priest (1988) . . . . Father Alek
Priceless Beauty (1989; Italian) . . . . Monroe
Why Me? (1990). Gus Cardinale
Highlander 2: The Quickening (1991) . . . . MacLeod

Lamden, Derek

Films:

Baby Love (1969) . . . . Nick
• 1:29—Brief buns while in shower when Luci opens
the door.

Landrum, Bill

Films:

The Doors (1991)
. . . . Choreographer/Body Double for Val Kilmer
•• 1:04—Buns, while making love in bed with Kathleen
Quinlan.

Lang, Perry

Films:

Teen Lust (1978). . . . . Terry
a.k.a. Girls Next Door
• 0:01—Buns in jock strap getting his pants pulled
down while he does pull ups.
1941 (1979) . . . . Dennis
Alligator (1980). . . . . Kelly
The Big Red One (1980) . . . . Kaiser
The Hearse (1980). . . . . Paul
Body and Soul (1981) . . . . Charles Golphin
O'Hara's Wife (1982) . . . . Rob O'Hara
T.A.G.: The Assassination Game (1982) . . . . Frank

Spring Break (1983; Canadian) . . . . Adam
• 0:27—Brief buns while opening his towel in the
shower, mooning his three friends.
Sahara (1984) . . . . Andy
Jocks (1986) . . . . Jeff
Mortuary Academy (1988) . . . . Max Grimm
Jacob's Ladder (1990) . . . . Jacob's Assailant
Relentless 2: Dead On (1991) . . . . Ralph Bashi
TV:
Bay City Blues (1983) . . . . Frenchy Nuckles

• Larson, Eric

Films:

Demon Wind (1990) . . . . Cory
•• 0:10—Buns, while standing outside at gas station.
Don't see his face.

Lattanzi, Matt

Husband of singer/actress Olivia Newton-John.
Films:

Rich and Famous (1981) . . . . The Boy, Jim
••• 1:10—Buns, while making love with Jacqueline Bis-
set.
Grease 2 (1982) . . . . n.a.
My Tutor (1983). . . . . Bobby Chrystal
That's Life! (1986) . . . . Larry Bartlet
Roxanne (1987) . . . . Trent
Catch Me... If You Can (1989) . . . . Dylan
Diving In (1990). . . . . Jerome Colter

• Lauer, Andrew

Films:

Blame It on the Night (1984) . . . . Boy in Audience
Born on the Fourth of July (1989) . . . . Vet
The Doors (1991). . . . . UCLA Student
Necessary Roughness (1991) . . . . Charlie Banks
• 1:09—Buns, while taking a shower. (He's the bru-
nette guy on the far right.)
TV:
Grand (1990) . . . . Officer Wayne Kasmurski

Laughlin, John

Films:

An Officer and a Gentleman (1982) . . . . Troy
Crimes of Passion (1984) . . . . Bobby Grady
(Unrated version reviewed.)
• 0:50—Buns, while getting dressed after having sex
with Kathleen Turner. (Viewed through peep hole by
Anthony Perkins.)
Footloose (1984) . . . . Woody
Space Rage (1987) . . . . Walker
Midnight Crossing (1988) . . . . Jeffrey Schubb
The Hills Have Eyes, Part II (1989) . . . . Hulk
Made for Cable Movies:
Memphis (1991; TNT) . . . . n.a.
TV:
The White Shadow (1980-81) . . . . Paddy Falahey

Lawrence, Bruno

Films:

Smash Palace (1981; New Zealand) . . . . Al Shaw
••• 0:39—Buns while in bed after arguing, then making up with Jacqui.
Treasure of the Yankee Zephyr (1981) . . . . Barker
Warlords of the 21st Century (1982) . . . . Willie
a.k.a. Battletruck
Heart of the Stag (1983; New Zealand) . . . . . Peter Daley
Utu (1984; New Zealand) . . . . Williamson
An Indecent Obsession (1985) . . . . Matt Sawyer
The Quiet Earth (1985; New Zealand) . . . Zac Hobson
•• 0:02—Brief frontal nudity lying on the bed.
•• 0:04—Brief nude getting back into bed.
• 0:33—Very brief frontal nudity jumping out of the ocean. Blurry, hard to see anything.
•• 1:01—Frontal nudity during flashback lying in bed.
Rikky & Pete (1988; Australian) . . . . Sonny

Layne, Scott

Films:

Vice Academy, Part 2 (1990) . . . . Petrolino
• 0:49—Buns, twice, while in men's locker room when Linnea Quigley and Ginger Lynn Allen come in.

•Le Fever, Chuck

Films:

The Naked Gun 2 1/2: The Smell of Fear (1991)
. . . . Mr. Griffith's Stunt Butt
• 1:07—Side view of buns when Leslie Nielsen yanks Dr. Meinheimer's pants down.

•Le Gros, James

Films:

Solarbabies (1986) . . . . Metron
Fatal Beauty (1987). . . . . Zack Jaeger
Blood & Concrete: A Love Story (1991) . . . . Lance
Point Break (1991). Roach
• 0:07—Brief buns, twice, while mooning the bank security camera. Wearing Richard Nixon mask. Could be anybody.
• 0:11—Buns, on B&W monitor in the FBI office.
• 0:59—Buns, mooning his friends while riding surfboard. Can't see his face clearly.
The Rapture (1991). . . . . Tommy

Lee, Mark

Films:

Gallipoli (1981). . . . . Archy Hamilton
•• 1:18—Buns, while running into the water with Mel Gibson. (Mark is the guy on the right.)
Emma's War (1986). . . . . John Davidson

Legein, Marc

Films:

The Secrets of Love—Three Rakish Tales (1986)
. . . . Luke
• 0:18—Buns, while in the hay with the Weaver's wife.
• 0:24—More buns.

Leguizamo, John

Stand-up comedian.
Films:

Casualties of War (1989) . . . . .Diaz
• 0:53—Buns, while pulling his pants down to rape Oahn.
Die Hard 2 (1990) . . . . .Burke
Revenge (1990) . . . . Ignacio
Street Hunter (1990) .Angel
Hangin' With The Homeboys (1991) . . . . .Johnny
Out for Justice (1991). . . . . Boy in Alley
Regarding Henry (1991). . . . . Gunman
Whispers in the Dark (1992). . . . . n.a.

Leina, Jonathan

Films:

Police (1985; French) . . . . Simon
•• 0:11—Upper half of buns and brief frontal nudity in police station. Typewriter gets in the way.

Leinert, Mike

Films:

Easy Wheels (1989). . . . . Meatball
• 0:52—Brief buns, while putting his pants on.

Lemmon, Jack

Films:

It Should Happen to You (1954). . . . . . . .Pete Sheppard
Mister Roberts (1955) . . . . . Ens. Frank Thurlowe Pulver
Fire Down Below (1957) . . . . Tony
Bell, Book and Candle (1959). . . . . Nicky Holroyd
Some Like it Hot (1959) . . . . .Jerry/Daphne
The Apartment (1960) . . . . .C. C. Baxter
The Wackiest Ship in the Army (1961)
. . . . Lt. Rip Crandall
Days of Wine and Roses (1962) . . . . .Joe
Irma La Douce (1963) . . . . .Nestor
Good Neighbor Sam (1964). . . . . Sam Bissel
The Great Race (1965). . . . . Professor Fate
The Fortune Cookie (1966) . . . . .Harry Hinkle
Luv (1967). . . . . Harry Berlin
The Odd Couple (1968). . . . . Felix Ungar
The April Fool's (1969) . . . . .Howard Brubaker
The Out of Towners (1970) . . . . George Kellerman
Avanti! (1973) . . . . .Wendell Armbruster
(Not available on video tape. Shown on *The Arts and Entertainment Channel* periodically. Scenes are listed as 0:00 since I can't time correctly with the commercials.)
• 0:00—Buns, while standing up in bathtub talking to Juliet Mills.
Save the Tiger (1973). . . . . Harry Stoner
The Front Page (1974). . . . . Hildy Johnson
The Prisoner of Second Avenue (1975). . . . . Mel
Airport '77 (1977) . . . . .Don Gallagher
The China Syndrome (1979) . . . . Jack Godell
Tribute (1980; Canadian) . . . . Scottie Templeton
Buddy Buddy (1981) . . . . .Victor Clooney
Missing (1982). Ed Horman
Mass Appeal (1984) . . . . Father Farley

Macaroni (1985; Italian) . . . . Robert Traven
That's Life! (1986) . . . . Harvey Fairchild
JFK (1991) . . . . Jack Martin
Glengarry Glen Ross (1992) . . . . .n.a.
Made for Cable Movies:
For Richer, For Poorer (1992; HBO) . . . . Aronn Katourian
TV:
That Wonderful Guy (1949-50) . . . . Harold
Toni Twin Time (1950) . . . . Host
Ad Libbers (1951) . . . . .Regular
Heaven for Betsy (1952) . . . . Pete Bell

Lennon, John
Late singer with *The Beatles* and on his own.
Films:
A Hard Day's Night (1964; British) . . . . John
Help! (1965; British) . . . . John
How I Won the War (1967) . . . . Gripweed
Imagine: John Lennon (1988) . . . . Himself
• 0:43—Nude in B&W photos from his White Album.
0:57—Brief frontal nudity of album cover again dur-
ing interview.

Lester, Jeff
Films:
In the Cold of the Night (1989) . . . . Scott Bruin
• 0:05—Very brief buns, whhile rolling over to stran-
gle Shannon Tweed.
TV:
Once a Hero (1979) . . . . Captain Justice/Brad Steele
Walking Tall (1981) . . . . Deputy Grady Spooner

Levine, Mark
Films:
Spring Fever USA (1988) . . . . Duke Dork
a.k.a. Lauderdale
• 1:17—Buns, twice, while in boat hallway with his
skinny brother after being tricked.

• Levisetti, Emile
Films:
Sensual Response (1992) . . . . Edge
(Unrated version reviewed.)
••• 0:31—Buns, while standing and looking out the
window, then sitting on the bed.
••• 0:43—Buns, while making love with Shannon
Tweed.

• Levitt, Steve
Films:
Those Lips, Those Eyes (1980) . . . . .Westervelt
Private School (1983) . . . . Bellboy
Last Resort (1985) . . . . Pierre
Hunk (1987) . . . . Bradley Brinkman
Blue Movies (1988) . . . . Buzz
•• 0:46—Buns, while walking around naked when Ran-
dy and Kathy make him and Cliff take their clothes
off.
The Experts (1989) . . . . .n.a.

Levy, Eugene
Films:
Going Beserk (1983) . . . . .Sal di Pasquale
National Lampoon's Vacation (1983) . . . . .Car Salesman
Splash (1984) . . . . Walter Kornbluth
Armed and Dangerous (1986) . . . . Norman Kane
• 1:02—Cheeks of his buns through the back of leath-
er pants while dressed in drag with John Candy to
escape from the bad cops.
Club Paradise (1986) . . . . Barry Steinberg
Father of the Bride (1991) . . . . n.a.
TV:
Second City TV Comedy (1977-81) . . . .Earl Camembert
SCTV Network 90 (1981-83) . . . . Regular

Lhermitte, Thierry
Films:
Next Year if All Goes Well (1983; French) . . . . . .Maxime
My Best Friend's Girl (1984; French) . . . . . Pascal Saulnier
a.k.a. La Femme du Mon Ami
My New Partner (1984; French) . . . . .Francois
Until September (1984) . . . . .Xavier de la Pérouse
•• 0:43—Buns, after making love with Karen Allen.
0:53—Almost frontal nudity getting out of bathtub.

Liebman, Ron
Films:
Where's Poppa? (1970) . . . . Sidney Hocheiser
• 0:45—Buns while running across the street, then in
front of door in hall, then brief buns leaving George
Segal's apartment.
The Hot Rock (1972) . . . . Murch
Slaughterhouse Five (1972) . . . . .Paul Lazzaro
Your Three Minutes Are Up (1973) . . . . Mike
Won Ton Ton, The Dog Who Saved Hollywood (1976)
. . . . .Rudy Montague
Norma Rae (1979) . . . . Reuben
Zorro, The Gay Blade (1981) . . . . Esteban
Romantic Comedy (1983) . . . . Leo
Phar Lap (1984; Australian) . . . . Dave Davis
TV:
Kaz (1978-79) . . . . Martin "Kaz" Kazinsky

Lindon, Vincent
Films:
Half Moon Street (1986) . . . . Sonny
a.k.a. Escort Girl
• 1:04—Buns, while getting out of bed with Sigourney Weaver.

Lipton, Robert
Films:
Blue (1968) . . . . Antonio
Bullitt (1968) . . . . First Aide
Tell Them Willie Boy is Here (1969) . . . . Newcombe
God's Gun (1977) . . . . n.a.
a.k.a. A Bullet from God
Death Spa (1987) . . . . .Tom

Lethal Woman (1988) . . . . Major Derek Johnson
- 1:02—Very brief frontal nudity in the ocean with Shannon Tweed, when the water goes down.
- 1:05—Brief buns while in the water on the beach with Tweed.

TV:
The Survivors (1969-70) . . . . Tom

Lithgow, John
Films:
Obsession (1976) . . . . Robert La Salle
The Big Fix (1978). . . . . Sam Sebastian
All That Jazz (1979). . . . . Lucas Sergeant
Rich Kids (1979) . . . . Paul Philips
Blow Out (1981). . . . . Burke
World According to Garp (1982). . . . . .Roberta
Terms of Endearment (1983). . . . . Sam Burns
Twilight Zone—The Movie (1983) . . Airplane Passenger
2010 (1984) . . . . Walter Curnow
The Adventures of Buckaroo Banzai, Across the 8th Dimension (1984) . . . . Dr. Emilio Lizardo/John Whorfin
Footloose (1984). . . . . .Reverend Moore
Santa Claus (1985) . . . . .Bozo
Harry and the Hendersons (1987) . . . George Henderson
The Manhattan Project (1987) . . . . . . John Mathewson
Distant Thunder (1988). . . . . .Mark Lambert
Out Cold (1989) . . . . .Dave Geary
Memphis Belle (1990). . . . . Colonel Bruce Derringer
At Play in the Fields of the Lord (1991) . . . .Leslie Huben
Ricochet (1991) . . . . Earl Talbot Blake
Raising Cain (1992). . . . . .n.a.
Made for Cable Movies:
Glitter Dome (1985; HBO) . . . . .n.a.
Traveling Man (1989; HBO). . . . . Ben Cluett
- 0:48—Brief buns, while trying to get the VCR away from Mona in her living room.
Miniseries:
The Day After (1983) . . . . .n.a.
Made for TV Movies:
The Boys (1991) . . . . Artie Margulies

Lloyd, Christopher
Films:
One Flew Over the Cuckoo's Nest (1975) . . . . Taber
Goin' South (1978) . . . . Towfield
The Lady in Red (1979) . . . . Frognose
Schizoid (1980). . . . . Gilbert
Mr. Mom (1983). . . . . .Larry
To Be or Not To Be (1983). . . . . Capt. Schultz
The Adventures of Buckaroo Banzai, Across the 8th Dimension (1984) . . . . .John Bigboote
Star Trek III: The Search for Spock (1984) . . . . . . Kruge
Back to the Future (1985) . . . . Dr. Emmett Brown
Clue (1985). Professor Plum
Miracles (1986). . . . . Harry
Walk Like a Man (1987). . . . . Reggie
Eight Men Out (1988). . . . . Bill Burns

Track 29 (1988; British) . . . . Henry Henry
- 0:34—Very brief side view of his buns, while lying in the hospital getting spanked by Sandra Bernhard.
Who Framed Roger Rabbit (1988) . . . . Judge Doom
Back to the Future, Part II (1989) . . . .Dr. Emmett Brown
The Dream Team (1989) . . . . Henry
Back to the Future, Part III (1990). . . .Dr. Emmett Brown
Why Me? (1990) . . . . .Bruno Daley
The Addams Family (1991) . . . . .Uncle Fester
Suburban Commando (1991) . . . . Charlie Wilcox
TV:
Taxi (1979-83) . . . . "Reverend Jim" Ignatowski

• Louden, Jay
Films:
Opposing Force (1986) . . . . Stevenson
a.k.a. Hell Camp
- 0:31—Buns, while getting yanked out of the line by Becker.
- 0:32—Buns, while getting sprayed with water and dusted with white powder. He's the first guy through.

• Louganis, Greg
Olympic diving champion.
Films:
Dirty Laundry (1987) . . . . Larry
Video Tapes:
Inside Out 3 (1992). . . . . .Max/The Wet Dream
- •• 1:28—Buns, in G-string, while walking around after turning into a human being from a fish. Unfortunately, he's wearing some goofy looking fish make-up.
- •• 1:30—Buns, in G-string, while getting out of the bathtub.

Lowe, Rob
Films:
Class (1983). . . . . .Skip
The Outsiders (1983) . . . . .Sodapop
The Hotel New Hampshire (1984) . . . . John
Oxford Blues (1984). . . . . Nick Di Angelo
St. Elmo's Fire (1985) .Billy
About Last Night... (1986). . . . . Danny
- •• 0:52—Buns and almost frontal nudity when he opens the refrigerator with Demi Moore.
Youngblood (1986) . . . . Dean Youngblood
- ••• 0:16—Buns, standing in hallway in jockstrap and walking around while Cindy Gibb watches.
Square Dance (1987) .Rory
a.k.a. Home is Where the Heart Is
Illegally Yours (1988) . . . . Richard Dice
Masquerade (1988). . . . . Tim Whalen
- ••• 0:04—Buns, while getting up from bed with Kim Cattrall.
- •• 0:30—Buns, while making love with Meg Tilly in bed.
Bad Influence (1990) . . . . .Alex
- ••• 1:27—Buns, while going into the bathroom.

The Dark Backward (1991) . . . . Dirk Delta
Stroke of Midnight (1991; U.S./French). . . . . . Salvitore
Wayne's World (1992). . . . . Benjamin Oliver
TV:
A New Kind of Family (1979-80) . . . . Tony Flanagan
Video Tapes:
Rob Lowe's Home Video (1989) . . . . Himself
Nude. A little bit hard to tell it's him (it's a copy of a copy
of a copy...) Rob's video tape of his sexual tryst with
two teenage girls can be purchased from *Midnight Blue*.
The address is located at the end of this book.

Lundgren, Dolph
Films:
A View to a Kill (1985). . . . . Venz
Masters of the Universe (1987) . . . . He-Man
The Punisher (1989) . . . . Frank Castle
  • 0:06—Upper half of buns, while kneeling in his un-
  derground hideout. Don't see his face.
  • 1:23—Same shot at 00:06 used again.
Red Scorpion (1989). . . . . .Lt. Nikolai
Cover Up (1990). . . . . Mike Anderson
I Come in Peace (1990). . . . . .Jack Caine
Showdown in Little Tokyo (1991)
. . . . Detective Kenner
  ••• 0:53—Buns, while getting out of bed to check on
  noise outside.
Universal Soldier (1992) . . . . .n.a.

Luther, Michael
Films:
Malibu Beach (1978) . . . . Paul
  • 0:32—Buns, while running into the ocean with his
  friends.

• Lutze, Rick
Films:
Auditions (1978) . . . . Ron Wilson
  • 1:00—Nude during audition.

Lynch, John
Films:
Cal (1984; Irish) . . . . Cal
  • 1:20—Buns, while getting into bed with Helen Mir-
  ren.

• Lyon, Steve
Films:
Campus Man (1987). . . . . Brett Wilson
  •• 0:25—Brief buns, while putting on swim trunks for
  photo session.
Valet Girls (1987) . . . . Ike

Maccanti, Roberto
Films:
1900 (1976; Italian) . . . . Olmo as a Child
  • 0:53—Frontal nudity undressing and showing the
  young Alfredo his penis.

MacGowran, Jack
Films:
Age of Consent (1969; Australian) . . . . Nat Kelly
  • 1:01—Brief buns, while running into the ocean
  when Miss Marley sees him.
  •• 1:02—Buns, running away from her to the cabin
  while holding a dog to cover up his private parts.

MacLachlan, Kyle
Films:
Dune (1984) . . . . Paul Atreides/Maudib
Blue Velvet (1986). Jeffrey
  •• 0:41—Buns and very brief frontal nudity while run-
  ning to closet in Isabella Rossellini's apartment.
The Hidden (1987). . . . . Lloyd Gallagher
Don't Tell Her It's Me (1990) . . . . Trout
The Doors (1991). . . . . Ray Manzarek
Twin Peaks: Fire Walk With Me (1992) . . . . Dale Cooper
TV:
Twin Peaks (1990-91). . . . . Dale Cooper

Madsen, Michael
Brother of actress Virginia Madsen.
Films:
Wargames (1983) . . . . Steve
The Natural (1984) . . . . Bump Bailey
Racing with the Moon (1984) . . . . Frank
The End of Innocence (1989). . . . . .n.a.
Kill Me Again (1989) . . . . Vince
The Doors (1991). . . . . Tom Baker
Fatal Instinct (1991) . . . . Cliff Burden
  (Unrated version reviewed.)
  • 0:43—Half of buns, while lying in bed.
  •• 0:48—Upper half of buns, while making love in bed
  with Laura Johnson.
Thelma and Louise (1991) . . . . Jimmy
Straight Talk (1992) . . . . Steve
Made for Cable TV:
The Hitchhiker: Man at the Window (1985; HBO)
. . . . .John Hampton
  •• 0:09—Buns, while making love with his wife on the
  couch.
Made for TV Movies:
Baby Snatcher (1992). . . . . Cal Hudson
TV:
Our Family Honor (1985-86) . . . . .Augie Danzig

• Mahinda, Edwin
Films:
The Kitchen Toto (1987; British). . . . . .Mwangi
  • 0:24—Nude, getting a bath outside.

Maiden, Tony
Films:
Spaced Out (1980; British). . . . . Willy
  • 0:38—Buns, while getting examined by Cosia.

Malkovich, John

Ex-husband of actress Glenne Headly.
Films:
The Killing Fields (1984) . . . . Al
Places in the Heart (1984) . . . . .Mr. Will
Eleni (1985) . . . . Nick
The Glass Menagerie (1987) . . . . Tom
Making Mr. Right (1987) . . . . Dr. Jeff Peters/Ulysses
Miles From Home (1988) . . . . .Barry Maxwell
The Sheltering Sky (1990) . . . . Port
  ••• 0:32—Frontal nudity and half of buns, while getting
     out of bed and opening door.
The Object of Beauty (1991) . . . . Jake
Queens Logic (1991) . . . . Eliot
Shadows and Fog (1992) .n.a.

•Malone, Joseph

Video Tapes:
Inside Out (1992) . . . . Terry/My Better Half
  •• 1:25—Buns, while lying on the floor. Brief partial
     frontal nudity. Long shot.

March, John

Films:
Moon 44 (1990; West German) . . . . . .Moose Haggerty
  • 0:43—Brief buns while in shower room. (Sort of see
     frontal nudity through grating in shower divider.)

Marchand, Guy

Films:
Cousin, Cousine (1975; French) . . . . Pascal
Loulou (1980; French) .André
  •• 0:59—Buns, while getting out of bed with Isabelle
     Huppert.
The Heat of Desire (1982; French) . . . . Max
  a.k.a. Plein Sud
Entre Nous (1983; French) . . . . Michel
  a.k.a. Coup de Foudre
May Wine (1990; French) . . . . Dr. Paul Charmant

•Margold, William

Films:
Fantasm (1976; Australian) . . . . .n.a.
Auditions (1978) . . . . Larry Krantz
  •• 0:23—Frontal nudity during his audition.
  •• 0:26—Frontal nudity during audition with Linnea
     Quigley and Harry.
  •• 0:30—Frontal nudity, tied up on table.

Margotta, Michael

Films:
The Strawberry Statement (1970) . . . . Swatch
Drive, He Said (1972) . . . . Gabriel
  •• 1:21—Running nude across the grass and up some
     stairs, then trashing a biology room at the university.
Times Square (1980) . . . . Jo Jo
Can She Bake a Cherry Pie? (1983) . . . . .Larry
Made for TV Movies:
She Lives (1973) . . . . Al

Marin, Richard "Cheech"

Films:
Up in Smoke (1978) . . . . Pedro De Pacas
Cheech & Chong's Next Movie (1980) . . . . Himself
Cheech & Chong's Nice Dreams (1981) . . . . Himself
  • 0:57—Brief buns when climbing over railing to es-
     cape Donna's husband, Animal.
Things are Tough all Over (1982) . . . . . . Mr. Slyman
  • 0:21—Buns while in the laundromat dryer.
Still Smokin' (1983) . . . . Himself
Yellowbeard (1983) . . . . El Segundo
The Corsican Brothers (1984) . . . . Corsican Brother
After Hours (1985) . . . . .Neil
Echo Park (1986) . . . . .Sid
Born in East L.A. (1987) . . . . .Rudy Robles
Rude Awakening (1989) . . . . Zeus
Far Out Man (1990) . . . . Cheech Marin
The Shrimp on the Barbie (1990) . . . . Carlos Muñoz
TV:
The Golden Palace (1992-) . . . . n.a.

Marinaro, Ed

Films:
Fingers (1978) . . . . Gino
Dead Aim (1987) . . . . Malcolm "Mace" Douglas
  • 0:52—Buns, while in bed making love with Amber.
     Dark, hard to see.
Queens Logic (1991) . . . . Jack
Made for TV Movies:
Policewoman Centerfold (1983) . . . . .Nick
Menu for Murder (1990) . . . . Det. Russo
TV:
Laverne & Shirley (1980-81) . . . . Sonny St. Jacques
Hill Street Blues (1981-87) . . . . Officer Joe Coffey
Sisters (1991-) . . . . Mitch Margolis

Markle, Stephen

Films:
Ticket to Heaven (1981; Canadian) . . . . Karl
Perfect Timing (1984) . . . . .Harry
  • 0:58—Buns, while making love with Lacy.

Marotte, Carl

Films:
Pick-Up Summer (1979; Canadian) . . . . .Steve
  • 0:18—Side view of buns, while hanging a B.A. out
     passenger window at Rod.
Gas (1981; Canadian) . . . . Bobby
My Bloody Valentine (1981; Canadian) . . . . Dave

•Marshall, Bryan

Films:
The Viking Queen (1967; British) . . . . Dominic
I Started Counting (1970; British) . . . . George
The Tamarind Seed (1974; British) . . . .George MacLeod
The Spy Who Loved Me (1977; British)
  . . . . Commander Talbot, H.M.S. Ranger
The Long Good Friday (1980; British) . . . . .Harris

Bliss (1985; Australian). . . . . .Adrian Clunes
- 1:01—Very brief buns, while running to the bathroom.

The Punisher (1989) . . . . .Dino Moretti

Marshall, David Anthony

Films:
Across the Tracks (1990) . . . . Louie
Another 48 Hrs. (1990) . . . . .Willie Hickok
- 0:57—Buns, while putting pants on after getting out of bed.

Martin, Ray

Films:
Young Lady Chatterley (1977)
. . . . .Ronnie (stable boy)
- • 1:35—Frontal nudity, covered with cake during cake orgy.

Martinez, Nacho

Films:
Matador (1986; Spanish) . . . . .Diego Montes
- • • 0:29—Buns, while making love with Eva in bed.

High Heels (1991; Spanish). . . . . Juan

Masterson, Sean

Made for Cable TV:
**Dream On: The Name of the Game is Five-Card
Stud** (1991; HBO) .Carter
- 0:17—Brief buns, after losing his clothes during poker game.
- • 0:18—Buns again getting up from the table.

•Mateo, Steve

Films:
Vice Academy, Part 3 (1991)
. . . . Professor Dirk Kaufinger
- • 0:47—Buns, when Ginger Lynn Allen and Elizabeth Kaitan come into his lab.

Mathers, James

Films:
Aria (1988; U.S./British) . . . . Boy Lover
- • 1:00—Brief dark outline of frontal nudity in hotel room, then buns while making love with Bridget Fonda.
- 1:02—Frontal nudity under water in the bathtub with her.

Matheson, Tim

Films:
Magnum Force (1973) . . . . Sweet
Almost Summer (1978). . . . . Kevin Hawkins
Animal House (1978). . . . . .Eric "Otter" Stratton
- 0:08—Buns, changing clothes in his bedroom while talking to Boone.

1941 (1979) . . . . Birkhead
A Little Sex (1982). . . . . Michael Donovan
To Be or Not To Be (1983). . . . . .Lieutenant Sobinski

The House of God (1984). . . . . .Dr. Basch
(Not available on video tape.)
Impulse (1984). . . . . Stuart
- 0:17—Buns, when getting out of bed with Meg Tilly.

Up the Creek (1984) . . . . Bob McGraw
Fletch (1985). .Alan Stanwyk
Speed Zone (1989) . . . . Jack
Drop Dead Fred (1991) . . . . Charles
Made for Cable Movies:
Buried Alive (1990; USA) . . . . Clint
Made for TV Movies:
The Quest (1976). . . . . Quentin Beaudine
Listen To Your Heart (1983) . . . . n.a.
Joshua's Heart (1990). n.a.
Stephen King's "Sometimes They Come Back" (1991)
. . . . .Jim Norman
TV:
Window on Main Street (1961-62). . . . . . . Roddy Miller
The Virginian (1969-70). . . . . Jim Horn
Bonanza (1972-73) . . . . .Griff King
Tucker's Witch (1982-83) . . . . Rick Tucker
Just in Time (1988). . . . . Harry Stadlin
Charlie Hoover (1991-) . . . . .Charlie Hoover

•Mathews, Stephen Kean

Films:
Young Lady Chatterley II (1986)
. . . . Robert Downing
- 0:59—Buns, while making love with Cynthia Chatterley outside on the grass.

•Matshikiza, John

Films:
Dust (1985; French/Belgian) . . . . .Hendrik
- 0:38—Buns, while on top of a girl, trying to rape her.

Cry Freedom (1987; British). . . . . .Mapetla

•Mauro, Jospeh E.

Films:
Affairs of the Heart (1992) . . . . .Jealous Man
Private Screenings.
- 0:38—Buns in G-string, walking into room with the Jealous Woman.

Maury, Derrel

Films:
Massacre at Central High (1976) . . . . .David
- 0:32—Buns, while romping around in the ocean with Kimberly Beck. Dark, long shot. Hard to see anything.

TV:
Apple Pie (1978) . . . . Junior Hollyhock
Joanie Loves Chachi (1982-83). . . . . Mario

Mazmanian, Marius

Films:
Video Vixens (1973) . . . . Psychiatrist
- • 0:42—Buns and balls from behind, while frolicking on couch with his patient. In B&W.

McCarthy, Andrew

Films:

Class (1983) . . . . Jonathan
Heaven Help Us (1985) . . . . Michael Dunn
• 0:35—Upper half of buns, while standing by the pool next to Caesar when he blows his nose.
St. Elmo's Fire (1985) . . . . Kevin
Pretty in Pink (1986) . . . . Blane McDonough
Less than Zero (1987) . . . . Clay
• 0:03—Very brief buns when getting out of bed to answer the phone.
Mannequin (1987) . . . . Jonathan Switcher
Fresh Horses (1988) . . . . Matt Larkin
Kansas (1988) . . . . Wade Corey
Weekend at Bernie's (1989) . . . . Larry Wilson
a.k.a. Hot and Cold
Club Extinction (1990) . . . . The Assassin
a.k.a. Doctor M
Year of the Gun (1991) . . . . David Raybourne
Only You (1992) . . . . Clifford Godfrey
Made for Cable TV:
Tales From the Crypt: Loved to Death (1991; HBO)
. . . . Edward Foster

McCleery, Gary

Films:

Hard Choices (1986) . . . . Bobby
•• 1:11—Buns, while making love on top of Laura.
The Chair (1988) . . . . Rick Donner

McDonald, Joshua

Films:

Eleven Days, Eleven Nights (1988; Italian)
. . . . Michael
• 0:33—Buns, when Sarah removes his underwear.

McDowell, Malcolm

Ex-husband of actress Mary Steenburgen.
Films:

If... (1969) . . . . Mick Travers
Long Ago Tomorrow (1970) . . . . Bruce Pritchard
A Clockwork Orange (1971) . . . . Alex
• 0:27—Very brief nude having sex with two women in his bedroom. Shot at fast speed.
0:52—Upper half of frontal nudity getting admitted to jail.
O Lucky Man! (1973; British) . . . . Mick Travis
Voyage of the Damned (1976) . . . . Max Gunter
Time After Time (1979; British) . . . . Herbert G. Wells
Caligula (1980) . . . . Caligula
(X-rated, 147 minute version.)
• 0:05—Buns, while rolling around in bed with Drusilla.
• 0:36—Brief buns, while taking ring off of Peter O'Toole.
• 0:46—Very brief buns while running to bed.
0:51—Buns, while putting Drusilla down in bed.
• 1:14—Nude walking around outside in the rain. Dark, long shot.

2:23—Very brief buns while under his white robe.
Cat People (1982) . . . . Paul Gollier
• 1:06—Side view of buns, while lying on the bathroom floor. Partial lower frontal nudity when he gets up.
Blue Thunder (1983) . . . . Cochrane
Get Crazy (1983) . . . . Reggie
Gulag (1985) . . . . Englishman
•• 1:26—Buns, while standing outside with David Keith in the snow being hassled by guards.
The Caller (1989) . . . . n.a.
Class of 1999 (1990) . . . . Dr. Miles Langford
Disturbed (1990) . . . . Dr. Derek Russell
Jezebel's Kiss (1990) . . . . Benjamin J. Faberson
•• 1:12—Buns, while making love with Jezebel.
Moon 44 (1990; West German) . . . . Major Lee
Made for Cable TV:
Tales From the Crypt: The Reluctant Vampire (1991)
. . . . Longtooth
Video Tapes:
Penthouse: On the Wild Side (1988) . . . . . . Caligula
••• 0:50—Nude, in rainstorm seen from above during *The Making of Caligula*. Kind of a long shot.

McGann, Paul

Films:

Withnail and I (1987; British) . . . . Marwood
Innocent Victim (1988) . . . . Barry
The Rainbow (1989) . . . . Anton Skrebensky
•• 1:30—Buns, while opening a bottle of wine in room with Sammi Davis.
• 1:44—Very brief frontal nudity and buns when running up a hill with Amanda Donohoe.
The Monk (1990; British/Spanish) . . . . . . Father Lorenzo
Paper Mask (1991; British) . . . . Matthew Harris

McGill, Bruce

Films:

Animal House (1978) . . . . D-Day
The Hand (1981) . . . . Brian Ferguson
Tough Enough (1983) . . . . Tony Fallon
Silkwood (1984) . . . . Mace Hurley
Club Paradise (1986) . . . . Dave the Fireman
No Mercy (1986) . . . . Lt. Hall
Wildcats (1986) . . . . Dan Darwill
Out Cold (1989) . . . . Ernie Cannald
•• 0:12—Frontal nudity, while opening the shower door, talking to Teri Garr. Brief buns, when putting on underwear.
The Last Boy Scout (1991) . . . . Mike Matthews
My Cousin Vinny (1992) . . . . Sheriff Farley
Play Nice (1992) . . . . Captain Foxx
(Unrated version reviewed.)
Made for TV Movies:
Shoot First: A Cop's Vengeance (1991) . . . . Shifton
TV:
Delta House (1979) . . . . D-Day

McKenna, Travis

Films:
Cheerleader Camp (1987) . . . . Timmy Moser
  a.k.a. Bloody Pom Poms
    0:05—Buns, while hanging a B.A. out the van window. He's a very heavy guy.
Real Men (1987) . . . . Oaf
Dead Women In Lingerie (1991) . . . . Billy

McKeon, Doug

Films:
Turnaround . . . . Ben
Uncle Joe Shannon (1978) . . . . Robbie
Night Crossing (1981) . . . . Frank Strelzyks
On Golden Pond (1981) . . . . Billy Ray
Mischief (1985). . . . . Jonathan
  • 0:56—Brief buns, while putting on his underwear after making love with Kelly Preston.
TV:
Centennial (1978-79) . . . . Philip Wendell
Big Shamus, Little Shamus (1979) . . . . Max Sutter

McNichol, Peter

Films:
Dragonslayer (1981) . . . . Galen
  • 0:27—Very brief buns while diving into pond. Sort of frontal nudity swimming under water. Hard to see because the water is so murky.
American Blue Note (1991) . . . . Jack Solow

Meadows, Stephen

Films:
Night Eyes (1990) . . . . Michael Vincent
  (Unrated version reviewed.)
  • 0:27—Buns and balls in bed with Tanya Roberts while Andrew Stevens watches on monitor.
V. I. Warshawski (1991) . . . . Boom-Boom

• Mednick, Michael

Video Tapes:
Intimate Workout For Lovers (1992)
    . . . . Water Workout
  ••• 0:21—Nude, outside and in swimming pool.

• Meek, Jeffrey

Films:
Winter People (1989) . . . . Cole Campbell
Heart Condition (1990). . . . . Graham
Night of the Cyclone (1990). . . . . Adam
  • 1:07—Brief buns, while putting on his pants, when he's interrupted in bed with Angelique. Long shot.
TV:
The Exile (1991) . . . . John Stone/Phillips
Raven (1992-) . . . . Raven

• Melymick, Mark

Made for Cable Movies:
Devlin (1991; Showtime). . . . . Jack Brennan
  • 0:08—Buns, lying on bed while tied up.

Metrano, Art

Films:
Cheaper to Keep Her (1980) . . . . Tony Turino
History of the World, Part I (1981) . . . Leonardo da Vinci
Police Academy II: Their First Assignment (1985)
    . . . . Lt. Mauser
  • 0:39—Buns, while in the locker room after the guys put epoxy resin in his shampoo.
Police Academy III: Back in Training (1986)
    . . . . Commandant Mauser

• Meyer, Michael

Films:
Mirror Images (1991) . . . . Georgio
  •• 0:15—Buns, while getting out of bed with Shauna.

• Milian, Tomas

Films:
Cat Chaser (1988) . . . . Andres De Boya
  •• 1:16—Full frontal nudity, undressing in bathroom with Corky, before getting shot by Charles Durning.

• Mills, Thomas

Films:
Luther the Geek (1988) . . . . Rob
  • 0:27—Very brief buns when Stacey Haiduk gooses him.

Mitchell, Mark

Films:
The Outing (1987). . . . . Mike Daley
  • 1:08—Buns when his friend gets killed, then very brief frontal nudity sitting up.

• Mitchell, Scott

Films:
Thou Shalt Not Kill...Except (1987) . . . . Philo Crazy
Video Tapes:
Inside Out (1992) . . . . Love the One You're With
  •• 1:14—Very brief frontal nudity when the girl climbs on top of him.

Modine, Matthew

Films:
Baby, It's You (1983) . . . . Steve
Private School (1983). . . . . Jim
Streamers (1983) . . . . Billy
The Hotel New Hampshire (1984) . . . . Chip Dove
Mrs. Soffel (1984) . . . . Jack Biddle
Birdy (1985). . . . . Birdy
  • 1:25—Buns, while squatting on the end of his bed, thinking he's a bird.
  • 1:29—Buns, while sitting on the bed. Longer shot.
  •• 1:33—Buns, while walking around naked in his bedroom.
  • 1:42—Buns, after waking up when Nicholas Cage comes into his bedroom.

Visionquest (1985) . . . . Louden Swain
- 1:29—Very brief buns while taking off underwear to get weighed for wrestling match.

Full Metal Jacket (1987) . . . . Private Joker
Orphans (1987) . . . . Treat
Married to the Mob (1988) . . . . Mike Downey
Gross Anatomy (1989) . . . . Joe Slovac
Memphis Belle (1990) . . . . Dennis Dearborn
Pacific Heights (1990) . . . . Drake Goodman
Wind (1992) . . . . Will Parker

Moir, Richard
Films:

In Search of Anna (1978; Australian) . . . . Tony
Chain Reactions (1980; Australian)
. . . . Junior Constable Pillott
Heatwave (1983; Australian) . . . . Steven
An Indecent Obsession (1985) . . . . Luce Daggett
- 0:31—Buns when at the beach with his pals. Don't see his face.

Monahan, Dan
Films:

Only When I Laugh (1981) . . . . Jason
Porky's (1981; Canadian) . . . . Pee Wee
- 0:22—Buns, while running down the road at night. Long shot.

Porky's II: The Next Day (1983; Canadian)
. . . . Pee Wee
- 0:39—Buns while at cemetery with Graveyard Gloria, then upper half of lower frontal nudity when he's holding her.
- 0:40—Upper half of lower frontal nudity when he drops Gloria.
- 0:42—Nude, trying to hide Steve.
- ••• 0:44—Nude when guys with shotguns shoot at him.

Up the Creek (1984) . . . . Max
Porky's Revenge (1985; Canadian) . . . . Pee Wee
- •• 0:02—Buns, when his graduation gown gets accidentally torn off during a dream.
- •• 0:16—Buns, while getting out of swimming pool (the fourth guy getting out). More buns while running around.
- •• 1:27—Buns, while getting his graduation gown town off.

From the Hip (1987) . . . . Larry
The Prince of Pennsylvania (1988). . . Tommy Rutherford

• Montana, Michael
Films:

Affairs of the Heart (1992) . . . . Richard
Private Screenings.
- •• 1:13—Buns, with Amy Lynn Baxter during smoky dream scene.

Montgomery, Chad
Films:

Nightmare at Shadow Woods (1983). . . . . . . Gregg
a.k.a. Blood Rage
- 0:52—Brief buns, while making love with Andrea on diving board just before getting killed.

Moore, Dudley
Films:

The Wrong Box (1966; British) . . . . John Finsbury
30 is a Dangerous Age, Cynthia (1968; British)
. . . . Rupert Street
Bedazzled (1968; British) . . . . Stanley Moon
Foul Play (1978). . . . . Stanley Tibbets
10 (1979) . . . . George Webber
- 0:47—Buns, while at neighbor's party just before Julie Andrews sees him through a telescope.

Wholly Moses (1980) . . . . Harvey/Herschel
Arthur (1981). . . . . Arthur Bach
Six Weeks (1982) . . . . Patrick Dalton
Lovesick (1983) . . . . Saul Benjamin
Romantic Comedy (1983) . . . . Jason
Best Defense (1984). . . . . Wylie Cooper
Micki & Maude (1984). . . . . Rob Salinger
Unfaithfully Yours (1984) . . . . Claude Eastman
Santa Claus (1985). Patch
Like Father, Like Son (1987) . . . . . . Dr. Jack Hammond
Arthur 2 On the Rocks (1988) . . . . Arthur Bach
Crazy People (1990). . . . . Emory
Blame It on the Bellboy (1992; British) . . . Melvyn Orton

Moore, Kenny
Films:

Personal Best (1982). . . . . Denny Stiles
- •• 1:31—Nude, getting out of bed and walking to the bathroom.

Moore, Michael J.
Films:

Border Heat (1988). . . . . J. C. Ryan
- 0:14—Buns, while taking off his clothes and getting into spa with Darlanne Fluegel.

• Moore, Stephen
Films:

The Last Shot You Hear (1969; British)
. . . . Peter's Colleague
Rough Cut (1980; British) . . . . n.a.
Laughter House (1984; British). . . . . Howard
Clockwise (1986; British) . . . . Mr. Jolly
The Doctor (1991) . . . . Dominic
Under Suspicion (1992) . . . . Roscoe
- 1:01—Very, very brief frontal nudity when Frank pulls the sheet down after catching Roscoe in bed with a young boy.

Moreno, Jaime
Films:
Amor Ciego (1980; Mexican) . . . . Daniel
- ••• 0:51—Frontal nudity standing up from bed, then buns when Apollonia hugs him.
- • 0:53—Buns, while making love in bed with Apollonia.

• Moriarity, Daniel
Films:
The Other Woman (1992) . . . . Carl
(Unrated version reviewed.)
- • 0:59—Buns, during photo shoot.
- ••• 1:15—Buns, while in the shower with Jessica.

• Moriarty, Michael
Films:
Hickey and Boggs (1972) . . . . Ballard
Bang the Drum Slowly (1973) . . . . Henry Wiggen
The Last Detail (1973) . . . . Marine Duty Officer
Report to the Commissioner (1975)
. . . . Beauregard "Bo" Lockley
Reborn (1978) . . . . Mark
- • 0:38—Brief buns, while rolling off Maria in bed.
Who'll Stop the Rain? (1978) . . . . John
Q (1982) . . . . Jimmy Quinn
Odd Birds (1985) . . . . Brother T.S. Murphy
Pale Rider (1985) . . . . Hull Barret
The Stuff (1985) . . . . David "Moe" Rutherford
Troll (1986) . . . . Harry Potter Sr.
Dark Tower (1987) . . . . Dennis Randall
The Hanoi Hilton (1987) . . . . Lt. Cmdr. Williamson
It's Alive III: Island of the Alive (1988) . . . . . . Steve Jarvis
A Return to Salem's Lot (1988) . . . . Joey
Full Fathom Five (1990) . . . . Mackenzie
TV:
Law & Order (1990-) . . . . Assistant D.A. Ben Stone

• Morrissey, David
Films:
Drowning by Numbers (1988; British) . . . . . Bellamy
- • 0:43—Buns, while on couch with Joely Richardson.
- •• 1:24—Nude, getting drowned in the swimming pool.
Made for TV Movies:
Mystery! Cause Célèbre (1991)
. . . . George Percy Bowman

Morrow, Rob
Films:
Private Resort (1985) . . . . Ben
- • 0:36—Brief buns while standing with Hillary Shapiro worshiping Baba Rama.
- •• 0:39—Buns while getting caught naked by Mrs. Rawlins, then more buns, while running through the halls.
TV:
Northern Exposure (1990-) . . . . Joel Fleischman

• Mortensen, Viggo
Films:
Witness (1985) . . . . Moses Hochleitner
Prison (1987) . . . . Connie Burke
Salvation! (1987) . . . . Jerome Stample
Fresh Horses (1988) . . . . Green
Leatherface: The Texas Chainsaw Massacre III (1990)
. . . . Tex
The Reflecting Skin (1990; British) . . . . . Cameron Dove
Young Guns II (1990) . . . . John W. Poe
The Indian Runner (1991) . . . . Frank
- ••• 1:01—Brief frontal nudity in mirror, then in real life in room.

Moses, Mark
Films:
Someone to Watch Over Me (1987) . . . . . Win Hockings
Born on the Fourth of July (1989) . . . . Optomistic Doctor
Dead Men Don't Die (1991) . . . . Jordan
The Doors (1991) . . . . Jac Holzman
Made for Cable Movies:
The Tracker (1988; HBO) . . . . Tom Adams
- •• 0:35—Buns, while getting out of the river after washing himself, then getting hassled by bandits.
TV:
Grand (1990) . . . . Richard Peyton

Moss, Robert
Films:
Spring Fever USA (1988) . . . . Dick Dork
a.k.a. Lauderdale
- • 1:17—Buns, twice, while in boat hallway with his heavy brother after being tricked.

Mulcahy, Jack
Films:
Porky's (1981; Canadian) . . . . Frank Bell
- • 0:21—Very brief frontal nudity, getting up from bench. Then buns while in front of the cabin.
Porky's II: The Next Day (1983; Canadian) . . . . Frank Bell

Mulkey, Chris
Films:
Loose Ends (1975) . . . . Billy Regis
The Long Riders (1980) . . . . Vernon Biggs
48 Hrs. (1982) . . . . Cop
First Blood (1982) . . . . Ward
Timerider (1983) . . . . Daniels
Heartbreak Hotel (1988) . . . . Steve Ayres
Patti Rocks (1988) . . . . Billy
- •• 0:24—Nude in restroom with Eddie, undressing and putting on underwear.
Denial (1991) . . . . Chad

Nassi, Joe
Films:
Sorority House Massacre (1987) . . . . Craig
- • 0:50—Buns, while running away from the killer that has just killed his girlfriend Tracy in a tepee.

Naughton, David
Films:
Separate Ways (1979) . . . . Jerry Lansing
Midnight Madness (1980) . . . . Adam
An American Werewolf in London (1981)
. . . . David Kessler
- 0:24—Very brief buns while running naked through the woods.
- 0:58—Buns, during his transformation into a werewolf.
- • 1:09—Brief frontal nudity and buns after waking up in wolf cage at the zoo. Long shot, hard to see anything. More buns, while running around the zoo.

Hot Dog... The Movie (1984) . . . . Dan
Not for Publication (1984) . . . . .Barry
Terror in the Aisles (1984) . . . . David Kessler
- 0:17—Brief buns during transformation into a werewolf from *An American Werewolf in London*.

Separate Vacations (1985) . . . . Richard Moore
The Boy in Blue (1986; Canadian) . . . . Bill
Kidnapped (1986) . . . . Vince McCarthy
Overexposed (1990) . . . . Phillip
The Sleeping Car (1990) . . . . Jason McCree
Steel and Lace (1990) . . . . Dunn
Made for TV Movies:
The Goddess of Love (1988) . . . . Ted
TV:
Makin' It (1979) . . . . Billy Manucci
At Ease (1983) . . . . .P.F.C. Tony Baker
My Sister Sam (1986-89) . . . . Jack

Nazario, Al
Films:
Incoming Freshman (1979) . . . . Mooner
- 0:44—Buns, while mooning Professor Bilbo during his daydream.
- 0:56—Buns again during Bilbo's daydream.
- 1:19—Buns, during end credits.

Neeson, Liam
Films:
Excalibur (1981; British) . . . . .Gawain
Krull (1983) . . . . .Kegan
The Bounty (1984) . . . . .Churchill
The Innocent (1985; British) . . . . .n.a.
The Mission (1986; British) . . . . Fielding
Duet for One (1987) . . . . Totter
- 1:07—Buns, while behind shower door, getting out of shower. Very, very brief buns, falling into bed when robe flies up. Long shot.

Next of Kin (1989) . . . . Briar
Darkman (1990) . . . . Peyton Westlake/Darkman
The Big Man (1991; British) . . . . Danny Scoular
a.k.a. Crossing the Line
Shining Through (1992) . . . . .Franz-Otto Dietrich
Under Suspicion (1992) . . . . .Tony
- 0:02—Buns, making love in bathroom with Hazel in bathroom while standing up. (Don't see his face.)

- 0:03—Brief nude, running outside at night to get away from the husband. Long shot.
- 0:04—Very brief frontal nudity, helping Frank over the fence.

Neidorf, David
Films:
Bull Durham (1988) . . . . Bobby
Born on the Fourth of July (1989) . . . . .Patient
Made for Cable Movies:
Rainbow Drive (1990; Showtime) . . . . Bernie Maxwell
- 1:16—Buns, while in shower room when Peter Weller is interrogating him.

• Neill, Sam
Films:
Sleeping Dogs (1977; New Zealand) . . . . Smith
Just Out of Reach (1979; Australian) . . . . Mike
My Brilliant Career (1979; Australian) . . . Harry Beecham
The Final Conflict (1981) . . . . .Damien Thorn
Possession (1981; French/German) . . . . Marc
Enigma (1982) . . . . Dimitri Vasilkov
Reilly: Ace of Spies (1984) . . . . Sidney Reilly
- • • 0:21—Buns, while getting out of bed and putting on his pants during an earthquake.

For Love Alone (1986; Australian) . . . . James Quick
The Good Wife (1987; Australian) . . . . . .Neville Gifford
a.k.a. The Umbrella Woman
A Cry in the Dark (1988) . . . . . . .Michael Chamberlain
Dead Calm (1989) . . . . John Ingram
The Hunt for Red October (1990)
. . . . .Capt. Vasily Borodin
Until the End of the World (1991) . . . Eugene Fitzpatrick
Memoirs of an Invisible Man (1992) . . . . . .David Jenkins
Made for TV Movies:
One Against the Wind (1991) . . . . . Capt. James Leggatt

Nelson, Bob
Films:
Sorceress (1982) . . . . Erlick
- 0:43—Brief buns, just before being put to death.
- • 0:45—Buns, while getting massaged.

The Falcon and the Snowman (1985) . . . . . . .FBI Agent
Miracles (1986) . . . . Sargeant Levit

Nero, Franco
Films:
Submission (1976; Italian) . . . . .Armond
- 0:32—Brief side view of buns when making love with Lisa on the bed.

The Day of the Cobra (1980) . . . . n.a.
Die Hard 2 (1990) . . . . Esperanza

Nicholson, Jack
Films:
The Little Shop of Horrors (1960) . . . . Wilbur Force
Studs Lonigan (1960) . . . . .Weary Reilly
The Raven (1963) . . . . Rexford Bedlo
The Terror (1963) . . . . Lt. Andre Duvalier

Ride in the Whirlwind (1965) . . . . Wes
Rebel Rousers (1967). . . . . Bunny
Easy Rider (1969) . . . . George Hanson
Five Easy Pieces (1970). . . . . Robert Dupea
On a Clear Day You Can See Forever (1970)
. . . . Tad Pringle
Carnal Knowledge (1971). . . . . Jonathan
A Safe Place (1971). . . . . Mitch
King of Marvin Gardens (1972). . . . . David Staebler
The Last Detail (1973). . . . . Buddusky
Chinatown (1974) . . . . J.J.
- 1:28—Very brief buns, while putting pants on and
getting out of bed after making love with Faye Dun-
away.
One Flew Over the Cuckoo's Nest (1975)
. . . . R. P. McMurphy
(Academy Award for Best Actor.)
The Passenger (1975; Italian) . . . . David Locke
Tommy (1975; British) . . . . Specialist
The Last Tycoon (1976). . . . . Brimmer
The Missouri Breaks (1976). . . . . Tom Logan
The Shooting (1976). . . . . Billy Spear
Goin' South (1978). . . . . Henry Moon
The Shining (1980). . . . . Jack Torrance
The Postman Always Rings Twice (1981)
. . . . Frank Chambers
- 1:25—Buns, while lying across the bed.
Reds (1981) . . . . Eugene O'Neill
The Border (1982). . . . . Charlie
Terms of Endearment (1983). . . . . Garrett Breedlove
Prizzi's Honor (1985). . . . . Charley Partanna
2:05—Buns, sort of. Viewed from above while he
takes a shower. Hard to see anything.
Heartburn (1986) . . . . Mark
Ironweed (1987). . . . . Francis Phelan
The Witches of Eastwick (1987). . . . . . . Daryl Van Horne
Batman (1989) . . . . Jack Napier/The Joker
The Two Jakes (1990) . . . . Jake Gittes
Man Trouble (1992) . . . . Harry Bliss

Nock, Thomas

Films:
Alpine Fire (1985; Swiss) . . . . Bob
- 0:08—Brief buns, while outside taking a bath.

Nolan, Tom

Films:
Fast Times at Ridgemont High (1982) . . . . Dennis Taylor
Up the Creek (1984). Whitney
School Spirit (1985). . . . . Billy Batson
- 0:17—Buns in open hospital smock. More buns
while running up stairs.
- 1:29—Brief buns, in hospital gown, while leaving
Judy's room.
TV:
Jessie (1984) . . . . Officer Hubbell

Nolte, Nick

Films:
Return to Macon County (1975) . . . . Bo Hollinger
The Deep (1977) . . . . David Sanders
Who'll Stop the Rain? (1978). . . . . Ray
Heart Beat (1979) . . . . Neal Cassady
North Dallas Forty (1979) . . . . Phillip Elliott
- 0:49—Brief buns, while pulling down underwear to
get into whirlpool bath in locker room.
48 Hrs. (1982) . . . . Jack Cates
Cannery Row (1982) . . . . Doc
Under Fire (1983). . . . . Russel Price
Teachers (1984) . . . . Alex
Down and Out in Beverly Hills (1986)
. . . . Jerry Baskin
- 0:28—Buns, while changing out of wet clothes on
patio.
- 1:37—Brief buns, while changing out of Santa Claus
outfit.
Weeds (1987). . . . . Lee Umstetter
•• 0:51—Buns, while getting out of bed and putting
his pants on.
New York Stories (1989). . . . . Lionel Dobie
Three Fugitives (1989) . . . . Daniel Lucas
Another 48 Hrs. (1990) . . . . Jack Cates
Everybody Wins (1990) . . . . Tom O'Toole
Q & A (1990). Mike Brennan
Cape Fear (1991). . . . . Sam Bowden
The Prince of Tides (1991) . . . . Tom Wingo
Miniseries:
Rich Man, Poor Man (1976). . . . . Tom Jordache

Norton, Ken

Former boxer.
Films:
Mandingo (1975). . . . . Mede
•• 1:36—Buns, while standing in bed with Susan
George. More buns when making love with her.
Drum (1976). . . . . Drum
- 1:02—Buns, while getting hung upside down in
barn and spanked along with Yaphet Kotto.
Mugsy's Girls (1985) . . . . Branscombe
TV:
The Gong Show (1976-80) . . . . Panelist

Nouri, Michael

Films:
Flashdance (1983) . . . . Nick Hurley
The Imagemaker (1985). . . . . Roger Blackwell
Thieves of Fortune (1989) . . . . Juan Luis
- 0:57—Buns, while taking a shower outside. Long
shot.
Captain America (1990). . . . . Lt. Colonel Louis
Project: Alien (1990) . . . . Jeff Milker
Total Exposure (1991) . . . . Dave Murphy
Made for Cable Movies:
Psychic (1992; USA). . . . . Professor Steering
Miniseries:
Beacon Hill (1975) . . . . Giorgia Bellonci

The Last Convertible (1979) . . . . . Jean R.G.R. des Barres
Made for TV Movies:
Shattered Dreams (1990) . . . . .n.a.
In the Arms of a Killer (1992) . . . . Brian Venible
TV:
The Gangster Chronicles (1981)
. . . . .Charles "Lucky" Luciano
Bay City Blues (1983) . . . . Joe Rohner
Downtown (1986-87) . . . . .Detective John Forney
Love & War (1992-) . . . . .n.a.

• Noy, Zachi
Films:
Popcorn and Ice Cream (1978; West German)
. . . . Johnny
Enter the Ninja (1981) . . . . The Hook
Private Popsicle (1982) . . . . Hughie
• 0:09—Buns while in bed with Eva.
The Ambassador (1984) . . . . .n.a.

Nureyev, Rudolf
Ballet dancer.
Films:
Valentino (1977; British) . . . . Rudolph Valentino
Exposed (1983). .Daniel Jelline
••• 0:54—Buns, while in bed with Nastassia Kinski.

O'Brien, Myles
Films:
Evil Laugh (1986) . . . . .Mark
0:30—Sort of buns and brief lower frontal nudity
rolling over on top of Tina in bed. Very, very brief
frontal nudity when she takes the sheet away from
him.

• O'Hara, Adore
Films:
Auditions (1978) . . . . Adore O'Hara
•• 0:47—Nude, while singing opera.
The Hard Way (1991) . . . . .Dead Entertainer

O'Keeffe, Miles
Films:
Tarzan, The Ape Man (1981) . . . . Tarzan
• 0:45—Sort of buns, under loin cloth in the surf. Lots
of other semi-bun shots in the loin cloth throughout
the rest of the film.
1:09—Buns, while in loin cloth at side of lake with Bo
Derek.
• 1:48—Buns, while in loin cloth wrestling with oran-
gutan during end credits.
Ator, The Fighting Eagle (1982). . . . . Ator
S.A.S. San Salvador (1982) . . . . .Prince Malko
The Blade Master (1984). . . . . .n.a.
a.k.a. Ator, The Invincible
Sword of the Valiant (1984; British). . . . . .Gawain
Campus Man (1987). . . . . .Cactus Jack
Iron Warrior (1987) . . . . Ator

The Drifter (1988). . . . . .Trey
• 0:11—Brief upper half of buns while on the motel
floor with Kim Delaney.
Waxwork (1988) . . . . .Count Dracula
Liberty & Bash (1989) . . . . .Liberty
Cartel (1990) . . . . Chuck Taylor
Relentless 2: Dead On (1991) . . . . .Gregor
••• 0:17—Buns, while putting ice cubes into bathtub,
then getting in.

O'Neal, Ryan
Father of actress Tatum O'Neal.
Films:
Love Story (1970) . . . . Oliver Barret IV
What's Up Doc? (1972) . . . . Professor Howard Bannister
Paper Moon (1973) . . . . Moses Pray
The Thief Who Came to Dinner (1973) . . . . . . .Webster
Barry Lyndon (1975; British). . . . . .Barry Lyndon
The Driver (1978). The Driver
Oliver's Story (1978) . . . . Oliver Barret IV
The Main Event (1979). . . . Eddie "Kid Natural" Scanlon
Green Ice (1981; British) . . . . .Wiley
So Fine (1981) . . . . Bobby
Partners (1982) . . . . Benson
•• 0:48—Buns, while wearing Indian outfit for photo
session with Robyn Douglass. Don't see his face.
Irreconcilable Differences (1984) . . . . . . .Albert Brodsky
Fever Pitch (1985) . . . . Taggart
Tough Guys Don't Dance (1987) . . . . Tim Madden
Chances Are (1989) . . . . .Philip Train
TV:
Empire (1962-63). . . . . .Tal Garret
Peyton Place (1964-69) . . . . Rodney Harrington
Good Sports (1991) . . . . Bobby Tannen

O'Quinn, Terry
Films:
Heaven's Gate (1980). . . . . Captain Minardi
Without a Trace (1983) . . . . Parent
Mrs. Soffel (1984) . . . . Buck McGovern
Places in the Heart (1984) . . . . Buddy Kelsey
Mischief (1985) . . . . .Claude Harbrough
Stephen King's "Silver Bullet" (1985)
. . . . Sheriff Joe Haller
SpaceCamp (1986) . . . . .Launch Director
Black Widow (1987). .Bruce
The Stepfather (1987) . . . . Jerry Blake
••• 0:02—Buns, while getting undressed, frontal nudity
in mirror as he gets into the shower.
Pin (1988) . . . . Dr. Linden
Young Guns (1988) . . . . .Alex McSween
The Forgotten One (1989) . . . . Bob Anderson
• 1:11—Brief buns while turning over in bed with Eve-
lyn.
Stepfather 2 (1989) . . . . The Stepfather
Blind Fury (1990) . . . . Frank Devereaux
Company Business (1990) . . . . Colonel Grissom
Prisoners of the Sun (1990; Australian) . . . Major Beckett
The Rocketeer (1991) . . . . .Howard Hughes

The Cutting Edge (1992) . . . . .n.a.
Made for TV Movies:
Danielle Steel's "Kaleidoscope" (1990) . . . . Henry
Perry Mason: The Case of the Desperate Deception
(1990). . . . . Curt Mitchell
The Last to Go (1991). . . . . .Daniel
Shoot First: A Cop's Vengeance (1991) . . . Sgt. Nicholas
Deliver Them from Evil: The Taking of Alta View (1992)
. . . . Sgt. Don Bell

O'Reilly, Cyril

Films:
Porky's (1981; Canadian) .Tim
• 0:21—Very, very brief frontal nudity, getting up from
bench. Then buns, while in front of the cabin.
Porky's II: The Next Day (1983; Canadian) . . . . .Tim
Purple Hearts (1984). . . . . Zuma
Dance of the Damned (1988) . . . . Vampire
Across the Tracks (1990) . . . . .Coach Ryder
Navy SEALS (1990) . . . . Rexer

• O'Ross, Ed

Films:
The Cotton Club (1984) . . . . Monk
The Pope of Greenwich Village (1984)
. . . . Bartender at Sal's
Seven Minutes in Heaven (1986). . . . . .Mall Security
Full Metal Jacket (1987) . . . . Walter J. Schinoski
The Hidden (1987) . . . . Cliff Willis
Lethal Weapon (1987). . . . . Mendez
Action Jackson (1988). . . . . Stringer
Red Heat (1988) . . . . Viktor Rostavili
Verne Miller (1988). . . . . .Ralph Capone
Another 48 Hrs. (1990) . . . . Frank Cruise
Dick Tracy (1990) . . . . .Itchy
Play Nice (1992) . . . . .Jack "Mouth" Penucci
(Unrated version reviewed.)
• 0:35—Buns, while making love in bed with Jill.
•• 0:46—Buns, while making love with Jill on the floor.

O, George

Films:
Summer Job (1989) . . . . Herman
• 0:17—Buns, while getting his underwear torn off by
five angry women, then running back to his room.
Popcorn (1991). 1st Hood
Made for Cable Movies:
Chains of Gold (1991; Showtime). . . . . Corner Man

Occhipinti, Andrea

Films:
Bolero (1984) . . . . .Angel the Bullfighter
•• 0:57—Buns, while lying in bed with Bo Derek, then
making love with her.
• 1:39—Side view of buns, during fantasy love making
session with Bo in fog.
Conquest (1984; Italian) . . . . .Ilias
A Blade in the Dark (1986; Italian). . . . . Bruno

Olandt, Ken

Films:
April Fool's Day (1986). Rob
Summer School (1987) . . . . Larry
•• 0:48—Brief buns while wearing a red G-string in a
male stripper club.
Made for TV Movies:
The Laker Girls (1990) . . . . Rick
TV:
Supercarrier (1988) . . . . Lt. Jack "Sierra" DiPalma
SuperForce (1990-) . . . . Zack Stone

Oldman, Gary

Films:
Sid and Nancy (1986; British). . . . . Sid Vicious
Prick Up Your Ears (1987; British) . . . . .Joe Orton
Track 29 (1988; British) . . . . Martin
• 1:24—Buns, while holding onto Christopher Lloyd
and stabbing him.
We Think the World of You (1988; British)
. . . . .Johnny Burney
Criminal Law (1989) . . . . Ben Chase
• 1:21—Very, very brief blurry frontal nudity in bed
with Ellen.
Chattahoochee (1990) . . . . Emmett Foley
• 1:17—Brief buns, standing while guards search his
clothes. Very, very brief frontal nudity turning
around to get a high-pressure enema. Long shot,
don't really see anything.
State of Grace (1990). . . . . .Jackie
JFK (1991) . . . . Lee Harvey Oswald
Rosencrantz and Guildenstern are Dead (1991)
. . . . .Rosencrantz
Bram Stoker's Dracula (1992). . . . . n.a.

Oliviero, Silvio

Films:
Graveyard Shift (1987). . . . . Stephen Tsepes
• 0:09—Buns, while climbing into his coffin.
Nightstick (1987). . . . . Ismael
The Understudy: Graveyard Shift II (1988) . . . . . . Baisez

• Olmos, Edward James

Films:
Wolfen (1981) . . . . Eddie Holt
• 1:04—Buns, while lapping water, then nude, run-
ning around the beach. Dark.
•• 1:05—Very brief frontal nudity, leaping off pier in
front of Albert Finney.
• 1:12—Very brief frontal nudity, running under pier
during Finney's vision.
Zoot Suit (1981) .El Pachoco
Blade Runner (1982) . . . . .Gaff
Saving Grace (1986) . . . . .Ciolino
Triumph of the Spirit (1989). . . . . Gypsy
Talent for the Game (1991) . . . . Virgil Sweet
American Me (1992) . . . . Santana
TV:
Miami Vice (1984-89) . . . . Lt. Martin Castillo

Ontkean, Michael

Films:

The Peace Killers (1971) . . . . Jeff
Hot Summer Week (1973; Canadian) . . . . .n.a.
Slap Shot (1977) . . . . Ned Braden
•• 1:56—Brief buns while wearing a jock strap, while
skating off the hockey rink and carrying a trophy.
Voices (1979) . . . . .Drew Rothman
Willie and Phil (1980) . . . . Willie
•• 1:36—Buns, while taking off his swimsuit at the
beach and jumping around.
•• 1:45—Buns, while getting into the hot tub. (He's on
the left.)
Making Love (1982) . . . . Zack
The Witching (1983) . . . . Frank Brandon
a.k.a. Necromancy
(Originally filmed in 1971 as *Necromancy*, additional
scenes were added and re-released in 1983.)
Just the Way You Are (1984) . . . . .Peter
The Allnighter (1987) . . . . .Mickey Leroi
Maid to Order (1987) . . . . Nick McGuire
Clara's Heart (1988) . . . . Bill Hart
Street Justice (1988) . . . . Curt Flynn
Cold Front (1989; Canadian) . . . . Derek McKenzie
Postcards from the Edge (1990) . . . . Robert Murch
Made for Cable Movies:
The Blood of Others (1984; HBO) . . . . .n.a.
Made for TV Movies:
In a Child's Name (1991) . . . . Kenneth
TV:
The Rookies (1972-74) . . . . .Officer Willie Gillis
Twin Peaks (1990-91) . . . . Harry S. Truman

• Osbon, Harry

Films:

Auditions (1978) . . . . Harry Boran
••• 0:26—Nude during audition with Linnea Quigley
and Larry.
•• 0:30—Frontal nudity, getting whipped while standing up, chained at the wrists.

• Otto, Barry

Films:

Bliss (1985; Australian) . . . . Henry Joy
••• 0:48—Buns, while peddling on exercise bike.
•• 0:58—Buns, while lying on the floor with Honey.

• Owen, Clive

Films:

Close My Eyes (1991; British) . . . . .Richard
•• 0:09—Brief frontal nudity, then buns, while getting
up from the floor and talking on the telephone.
0:29—Side view of buns, while lying on floor with
Natalie.
••• 0:30—Buns, while getting up and walking around.
•• 0:32—Very brief frontal nudity, rolling over. Out of
focus buns, lying on his stomach.
•• 0:46—Buns, while lying in bed with Natalie.

•• 0:56—Buns, while getting out of bed and walking to
the window.
Magazines:
Playboy (Nov 1992) . . . . Sex in Cinema 1992
•• 146—Buns, while on the floor with Helen Fitzgerald
from *Close My Eyes*.

Pace, Richard

Films:

I Spit on Your Grave (1978) . . . . Matthew
(Uncut, unrated version reviewed.)
• 0:42—Buns, while undressing in the house to rape
Jennifer.
1:15—Silhouette of penis while getting hung (by
the neck) by Jennifer.

Packer, David

Films:

You Can't Hurry Love (1984) . . . . .Eddie
• 0:59—Buns, in store taking his pants off while peo-
ple watch him from the sidewalk.
The Runnin' Kind (1988) . . . . .Joey Curtis
Trust Me (1989) . . . . Sam Brown
Crazy People (1990) . . . . Mark Olander
Miniseries:
V: The Final Battle (1984) . . . . Daniel Bernstein
TV:
The Best Times (1985) . . . . .Niel "Trout" Troutman
What's Alan Watching? (1989) . . . . .Jeff

• Palese, Joe

Films:

Fear City (1984) . . . . Tony
Freeway (1988) . . . . Gomez
Sinners! (1990) . . . . .Al
• 0:00—Brief buns, while on top of a woman. Don't
see his face.
Blood Money (1991) . . . . Burt
a.k.a. The Killers Edge

Pankow, John

Films:

The Hunger (1983) . . . . 1st Phone Booth Youth
To Live and Die in L.A. (1985) . . . . John Vukovich
•• 1:06—Buns, while changing in the locker room.
*batteries not included (1987) . . . . .Kovacs
The Secret of My Success (1987) . . . . Fred Melrose
Monkey Shines: An Experiment in Fear (1988)
. . . . Geoffrey Fisher
Talk Radio (1988) . . . . Dietz
Mortal Thoughts (1991) . . . . Arthur Kellogg
Year of the Gun (1991) . . . . .Italo Bianchi

• Paré, Michael

Films:

Eddie and the Cruisers (1983) . . . . .Eddie
The Philadelphia Experiment (1984) . . . . . David Herdeg
Streets of Fire (1984) . . . . .Tom Cody
Instant Justice (1987) . . . . Scott Youngblood

Space Rage (1987) . . . . Grange
The Women's Club (1987). . . . . Patrick
   1:05—Brief buns, during nightmare. Hard to see be-
   cause of fog.
   • 1:06—Buns, while standing in hallway during night-
   mare. Long shot.
Eddie and the Cruisers II: Eddie Lives (1989)
   . . . . Eddie Wilson/Joe West
Dragonfight (1990). Moorpark
The Last Hour (1990) . . . . Jeff
   a.k.a. Concrete War
Moon 44 (1990; West German) . . . . Felix Stone
The Closer (1991) . . . . Larry Freed
Into the Sun (1991). . . . . Captain Paul Watkins
Killing Streets (1991). . . . . Chris/Craig Brandt
Sunset Heat (1991) . . . . Eric Wright
   (Unrated version reviewed.)
   • 0:00—Buns, while standing and looking out the
   window.
   ••• 0:22—Buns, while standing on stairs with Tracy
   Tweed, then making love with her on the floor.
   • 0:24—Buns, while standing up and walking up the
   stairs.
Blink of an Eye (1992) . . . . Sam Browning
TV:
Greatest American Hero (1981-83) . . . . . . Tony Villicana
Houston Knights (1987-88). . . . . Sgt. Joey La Fiamma

Parker, Jameson

Films:
The Bell Jar (1979) . . . . Buddy
   • 0:09—Frontal nudity silhouette standing in bed-
   room with Marilyn Hassett, then buns. Dark, hard to
   see.
A Small Circle of Friends (1980) . . . . Nick Baxter
White Dog (1982). . . . . Roland Gray
American Justice (1986) . . . . Dave Buchanon
Prince of Darkness (1987) . . . . Brian
Made for TV Movies:
Who is Julia? (1986) . . . . Don North
TV:
Simon & Simon (1981-89)
   . . . . Andrew Jackson (A.J.) Simon

Pasdar, Adrian

Films:
Solarbabies (1986) . . . . Darstar
Streets of Gold (1986). . . . . Timmy Boyle
Near Dark (1987) . . . . Caleb
Made in U.S.A. (1988) . . . . Dar
   • 0:12—Buns, while walking to sit down at the laun-
   dromat when he washes all his clothes with Christo-
   pher Penn.
Vital Signs (1989) . . . . Michael Chatham
   1:11—Upper half of buns, with his pants partially
   down in basement with Diane Lane.
Torn Apart (1990). . . . . Ben Arnon
Made for Cable Movies:
The Lost Capone (1990) . . . . Jimmy

• Patinkin, Mandy

Films:
French Postcards (1979). . . . . Sayyid
The Last Embrace (1979) . . . . Commuter
Night of the Juggler (1980) . . . . Cabbie
Ragtime (1981) . . . . Tateh
Daniel (1983). . . . . Paul Isaacson
Yentl (1983) . . . . Avigdor
   •• 0:49—Buns, after taking off his clothes to go skinny
   dipping.
   • 0:51—Brief buns while sitting down next to Barbra
   Streisand, the brief buns, while standing up.
   • 0:52—Buns, while walking around and sitting down.
   Long shot.
Maxie (1985). . . . . Nick
The Princess Bride (1987). . . . . Inigo Montoya
Alien Nation (1988) . . . . Sam Francisco
The House on Carroll Street (1988) . . . . Ray Salwen
Dick Tracy (1990). . . . . 88 Keys
The Doctor (1991). . . . . Murray
Impromptu (1991). . . . . Alfred DeMusset
True Colors (1991) . . . . John Palmeri

Patric, Jason

Son of actor/author Jason Miller.
Grandson of actor/comedian Jackie Gleason.
Films:
Solarbabies (1986). . . . . Jason
The Lost Boys (1987) . . . . Michael
After Dark, My Sweet (1990)
   . . . . Kevin "Collie" Collins
   •• 1:19—Buns, while taking off pants and getting into
   bed with Rachel Ward. More brief buns on top of
   her.
Frankenstein Unbound (1990) . . . . Lord Byron
Denial (1991). . . . . Michael
Rush (1991) . . . . Jim Raynor
Made for TV Movies:
Toughlove (1985) . . . . n.a.

Patrick, Randal

Films:
Livin' Large (1991) . . . . Jimmy
Made for Cable Movies:
By Dawn's Early Light (1990; HBO) . . . . O'Toole
   • 0:14—Brief buns while in shower room getting
   dressed during red alert.

Patterson, Jimmy

Films:
The Young Warriors (1983; U.S./Canadian)
   . . . . "Ice Test" Monty
   • 0:14—Buns, while dropping pants and sitting on a
   block of ice during pledge at fraternity.

Paxton, Bill

Films:
Mortuary (1981) . . . . Paul Andrews
Stripes (1981) . . . . n.a.

Impulse (1984) . . . . Eddie
Streets of Fire (1984) . . . . Clyde
The Terminator (1984) . . . . Punk Leader
Commando (1985) . . . . Intercept Officer
Weird Science (1985) . . . . Chet
 •• 0:30—Buns, while taking off towel to give to his
   younger brother in the kitchen.
Aliens (1986) . . . . Private Hudson
Near Dark (1987) . . . . Severen
Pass the Ammo (1988) . . . . Jesse
Brain Dead (1989) . . . . Jim Reston
Next of Kin (1989) . . . . Gerald Gates
Back to Back (1990) . . . . Bo Brand
The Last of the Finest (1990) . . . . . Howard "Hojo" Jones
Navy SEALS (1990) . . . . Dane
Predator 2 (1990) . . . . Jerry
Slipstream (1990) . . . . Matt Owens
The Dark Backward (1991) . . . . Gus
 •• 0:44—Buns, while taking off his jumpsuit and diving
   into bed with his three fat girlfriends.
One False Move (1992) . . . . Hurricane
Made for TV Movies:
Deadly Lessons (1983) . . . . n.a.

Peck, Brian
Films:
The Last American Virgin (1982) . . . . Victor
 • 0:20—Buns, during penis measurement in boy's
   locker room. Don't see his face.

Penn, Christopher
Brother of actor Sean Penn.
Films:
All The Right Moves (1983) . . . . Brian
Rumble Fish (1983) . . . . B.J.
Footloose (1984) . . . . Willard
The Wild Life (1984) . . . . Tom Drake
Pale Rider (1985) . . . . Josh LaHood
At Close Range (1986) . . . . Tommy Whitewood
Made in U.S.A. (1988) . . . . Tuck
 • 0:12—Buns, while walking to sit down at the laun-
   dromat when he washes all his clothes with Adrian
   Pasdar.
Future Kick (1991) . . . . Bang
Mobsters (1991) . . . . Tommy Reina
a.k.a. Mobsters—The Evil Empire

Penn, Sean
Ex-husband of singer/actress Madonna.
Brother of actor Christopher Penn.
Films:
Taps (1981) . . . . Alex Dwyer
Fast Times at Ridgemont High (1982) . . . . . . Jeff Spicoli
Bad Boys (1983) . . . . Mick O'Brien
 • 0:10—Brief buns while getting up off the floor with
   Ally Sheedy.
 •• 0:46—Buns while taking a shower.
Crackers (1984) . . . . Dillard
Racing with the Moon (1984) . . . Henry "Hopper" Nash

The Falcon and the Snowman (1985) . . . . . Daulton Lee
At Close Range (1986) . . . . Brad Whitewood, Jr.
Shanghai Surprise (1986) . . . . Glendon Wasey
Colors (1988) . . . . Danny McGavin
Judgment in Berlin (1988) . . . . Gunther X
Casualties of War (1989) . . . . Sergeant Meserve
We're No Angels (1989) . . . . Jim
State of Grace (1990) . . . . Terry

Pepe, Paul
Films:
Saturday Night Fever (1977) . . . . Double J.
 (R-rated version reviewed.)
 • 0:22—Buns, while making love in back seat of car
   with a girl.

• Pereio, Paulo Cesar
Films:
I Love You (1982; Brazilian) . . . . Paulo
 a.k.a. Eu Te Amo
 • 0:35—Brief side view of buns and frontal nudity,
   while kneeling on the floor with Sonia Braga.
 • 0:38—Buns, in mirror, while walking in hallway.
 •• 0:59—Buns and part of frontal nudity covered with
   paint with Braga.
 • 1:36—Side view of buns, while making love on top
   of Braga.
 • 1:37—Brief buns while lying on floor with Braga. Lit
   with neon lights.

Peter, Jens
Films:
Wild Orchid (1990) . . . . Voleyball Player
 ••• 1:29—Buns, while in room with Jacqueline Bisset
   and Carré Otis.

Petersen, William L.
Films:
Thief (1981) . . . . Katz & Jammer Bartender
To Live and Die in L.A. (1985) . . . . . . Richard Chance
 • 0:44—Brief frontal nudity, but hard to see anything
   because it's dark.
Manhunter (1986) . . . . Will Graham
Cousins (1989) . . . . Tom Hardy
Young Guns II (1990) . . . . Pat Garrett
Hard Promises (1992) . . . . n.a.
Made for Cable Movies:
Long Gone (1987; HBO) . . . . Cecil "Stud" Cantrell
Keep the Change (1992; TNT) . . . . Joe Starling

Phelps, Matthew
Films:
Dreamaniac (1987) . . . . Foster
Nightmare Sisters (1987) . . . . J.J.
 •• 0:53—Buns, while taking off his pants and getting
   into bed with Michelle Bauer.

Pitzalis, Fredrico

Films:

Devil in the Flesh (1986; French/Italian) . . . . . Andrea
  • 0:57—Brief buns while in bed with Maruschka Detmers.
  • 1:19—Frontal nudity when Detmers performs fellatio on him. Dark, hard to see.

Placido, Donato

Films:

Caligula (1980) . . . . Proculus
  (X-rated, 147 minute version.)
  • 1:11—Frontal nudity taking his robe off for Malcolm McDowell. Buns, while getting raped by McDowell's fist.

Magazines:

Playboy (Nov 1980) . . . . Sex in Cinema 1980
  • 180—Buns in still from *Caligula*.

• Popper, Alan

Films:

Kandyland (1987) . . . . Heckler
Small Kill (1991) . . . . Thomas Stanzak
  • 0:21—Buns, while crazily running around outside in a jockstrap.

Prescott, Robert

Films:

Bachelor Party (1984) . . . . Richard Chance
  • 1:18—Buns, after being hung out the window tied up with sheets by Tom Hanks and his friends.
The Joy of Sex (1984) . . . . Tom Pittman
Real Genius (1985) . . . . Kent

Price, Alan

Films:

O Lucky Man! (1973; British) . . . . n.a.
Oh, Alfie! (1975; British) . . . . Alfie Elkins
  a.k.a. Alfie Darling
  •• 0:14—Buns washing himself off in the kitchen while talking to Louise's husband.

• Price, Marc

Films:

The Zoo Gang (1985) . . . . Val
Trick or Treat (1986) . . . . .Eddie Weinbauer
  •• 0:04—Buns, while lying on the floor and also kneeling at boys' locker room door when the bullies leave him outside where the girls can see him.
  • 0:12—Brief buns, in Polaroid photo of the previous incident.
The Rescue (1988) . . . . .Max Rothman

TV:

Family Ties (1982-89) . . . . . . Irwin "Skippy" Handelman
Condo (1983) . . . . Billy Kirkridge

• Pringle, Bryan

Films:

Damn the Defiant! (1962; British) . . . . . . Sgt. Kneebone

Cromwell (1970; British) . . . . Trooper Hawkins
Monty Python's Jabberwocky (1977)
  . . . . Second Gate Guard
Brazil (1985; British). . . . . Spiro
Haunted Honeymoon (1986) . . . . Pfister
Drowning by Numbers (1988; British) . . . . Jake
  • 0:04—Buns, while undressing with Nancy.
  • 0:06—Nude, in the tub, drunk.
Getting It Right (1989) . . . . .Mr. Lamb
Three Men and a Little Lady (1990) . . . . Old Englishman

• Prochnow, Jürgen

Films:

Das Boot (1982; German) . . . . .The Captain
The Keep (1983) . . . . Woorman
Dune (1984) . . . . .Duke Leto Atreides
Killing Cars (1986) . . . . .Ralph Korda
  • 0:48—Buns, while getting up from bed to look at cigarette lighter. Slightly out of focus. Don't see his face well.
Beverly Hills Cop II (1987) . . . . Maxwell Dent
A Dry White Season (1989) . . . . .Capt. Stolz
The Fourth War (1990). . . . . Col. N.A. Valachev
Hurricane Smith (1990) . . . . Charlie Dowd
The Man Inside (1990). . . . . Gunter Wallraff

Pryor, Richard

Comedian.

Films:

Lady Sings the Blues (1972) . . . . .Piano Man
Some Call It Loving (1972). . . . . .Jeff
Uptown Saturday Night (1974) . Sharpe Eye Washington
Car Wash (1976) . . . . Daddy Rich
Silver Streak (1976) . . . . Grover Muldoon
Greased Lightning (1977) . . . . Wendell Scott
Which Way Is Up? (1977)
  . . . . .Leroy Jones/Rufus Jones/Rev. Thomas
Blue Collar (1978) . . . . Zeke
The Wiz (1978) . . . . The Wiz
Richard Pryor—Live in Concert (1979). . . . . . . Himself
Stir Crazy (1980) . . . . Harry Monroe
Wholly Moses (1980) . . . . .Pharaoh
Bustin' Loose (1981) . . . . Joe Braxton
Some Kind of Hero (1982) . . . . Eddie Keller
The Toy (1982) . . . . Jack Brown
Richard Pryor—Here and Now (1983) . . . . Himself
Superman III (1983) . . . . Gus Gorman
Brewster's Millions (1985) . . . . . .Montgomery Brewster
Richard Pryor—Live and Smokin' (1985) . . . . . . Himself
Jo Jo Dancer, Your Life Is Calling (1986)
  . . . . Jo Jo Dancer/Alter Ego
  •• 0:06—Buns, while walking naked out of the hospital waiting for the limousine.
Moving (1988). . . . . Arlo Pear
Harlem Nights (1989) . . . . Sugar Ray
See No Evil, Hear No Evil (1989) . . . . Wally
Another You (1991) . . . . Eddie Dash

TV:

The Richard Pryor Show (1977) . . . . Host

Pucci, Robert
Films:
The Last Hour (1990) . . . . Eric
a.k.a. Concrete War
- 0:05—Brief buns, while making love in bed with Shannon Tweed.

Purcell, James
Films:
S.O.B. (1981) . . . . .n.a.
Where Are the Children? (1986) . . . . Robin Legler
Bad Dreams (1988). . . . . Paramedic
Playroom (1989). . . . . Paul
a.k.a. Schizo
- •• 0:25—Buns, while making love with Jamie Rose on a chair.
White Light (1990) . . . . Bill Dockerty
The Hitman (1991) . . . . Sal

Quaid, Dennis
Brother of actor Randy Quaid.
Husband of actress Meg Ryan.
Films:
9/30/55 (1977). . . . . Frank
Our Winning Season (1978) . . . . Paul Morelli
Seniors (1978). . . . . Alan
Breaking Away (1979). . . . . Mike
Gorp (1980) . . . . Mad Grossman
The Long Riders (1980). . . . . Ed Miller
All Night Long (1981). . . . . Freddie Dupler
Caveman (1981). . . . . Lar
The Night the Lights Went Out in Georgia (1981)
. . . . .Travis Child
Jaws 3 (1983) . . . . .Mike Brody
The Right Stuff (1983). . . . . Gordon Cooper
Tough Enough (1983). . . . . .Art Long
Dreamscape (1984). . . . . Alex Gardner
Enemy Mine (1985) . . . . Davidge
The Big Easy (1987) . . . . .Remy McSwain
- 0:24—Brief buns when Ellen Barkin pulls his underwear down in bed.
- ••• 0:51—Buns, while putting underwear on after getting out of bed.
Innerspace (1987) . . . . .Tuck Pendleton
- •• 0:08—Buns, while standing naked in the street as taxi drives off with his towel. Kind of a long shot.
Suspect (1987) . . . . Eddie Sanger
D.O.A. (1988) . . . . Dexter Cornell
Everybody's All-American (1988). . . . . Gavin
Great Balls of Fire (1989). . . . . Jerry Lee Lewis
Come See the Paradise (1990) . . . . .Jack McGurn
Postcards from the Edge (1990) . . . . .Jack Falkner
- 1:03—Side view of buns, while leaning out of the shower, talking to Meryl Streep.
Made for TV Movies:
Are You in the House Alone? (1978) . . . . .Phil
Bill (1981). . . . . .n.a.

Quaid, Randy
Brother of actor Dennis Quaid.
Films:
The Last Picture Show (1971) . . . . Lester Marlow
- 0:38—Very brief frontal nudity jumping into pool after Cybill Shepherd jumps in.
The Last Detail (1973) . . . . .Meadows
Lolly-Madonna XXX (1973) . . . . .Finch Feather
Paper Moon (1973) . . . . .Leroy
Bound For Glory (1976). . . . . Luther Johnson
The Missouri Breaks (1976) . . . . .Little Tod
The Choirboys (1977) . . . . Proust
Midnight Express (1978; British) . . . . Jimmy Booth
Foxes (1980) . . . . .Jay
The Long Riders (1980) . . . . .Clell Miller
Heartbeeps (1981) .Charlie
National Lampoon's Vacation (1983) . . . . . Cousin Eddie
The Wild Life (1984). . . . . .Charlie
The Wraith (1986) . . . . Sheriff Loomis
Bloodhounds of Broadway (1989) . . . . Feet Samuels
National Lampoon's Christmas Vacation (1989)
. . . . Cousin Eddie
Out Cold (1989) . . . . Lester Atlas
Days of Thunder (1990). . . . . Tim Daland
Quick Change (1990). . . . . .Loomis
TV:
Saturday Night Live (1985-86) . . . . Regular
Davis Rules (1990-92) . . . . Dwight

Quill, Tom
Films:
Staying Together (1989) . . . . .Brian McDermott
- 0:03—Brief buns while getting out of bed with Stockard Channing. Hard to see because of the reflections in the window.

Quinn, Aidan
Films:
Reckless (1984) . . . . .Johnny Rourke
- 1:03—Very brief frontal nudity and buns while running into Daryl Hannah's brother's room when her parents come home early.
- 1:12—Side view nude, taking a shower.
Desperately Seeking Susan (1985) . . . . Dez
The Mission (1986; British). . . . . .Felipe
Stakeout (1987) . . . . .Richard "Stick" Montgomery
Crusoe (1989) . . . . .Crusoe
Avalon (1990) . . . . Jules Krichinsky
A Handmaid's Tale (1990) . . . . .Nick
The Lemon Sisters (1990). . . . . .Frankie McGuinness
At Play in the Fields of the Lord (1991)
. . . . Martin Quarrier
The Playboys (1992) .Tom
Made for Cable Movies:
Lies of the Twins (1991; USA)
. . . . Jonathan & James McEwan
A Private Matter (1992; HBO). . . . . Bob Finkbine

• Race, Hugo

Films:
Dogs In Space (1987; Australian) . . . . Pierre
In Too Deep (1990; Australian) . . . . .Mark
- 0:39—Buns, while talking with Wendy when JoJo watches. Long shot.
- 0:41—Buns, while in bedroom talking with Wendy.
- 0:59—Brief buns, while walking past sliding glass door.
- •• 1:00—Nude, outside with Wendy, spraying her with a garden hose.
- •• 1:27—Buns, while getting up from the bed.

Railsback, Steve

Films:
The Visitors (1972) . . . . .Mike Nickerson
Angela (1977; Canadian) . . . . Jean
The Deadly Games (1980). . . . . Billy
The Stunt Man (1980). . . . . Cameron
Escape 2000 (1981) . . . . Paul
The Golden Seal (1983) . . . . .Jim Lee
Torchlight (1984) . . . . .Jake Gregory
Lifeforce (1985) . . . . Carlsen
- 1:26—Buns, while standing with Mathilda May after he stabs her with the sword. Surrounded by special effects.
Armed and Dangerous (1986). . . . . .The Cowboy
The Blue Monkey (1987). . . . . .Detective Jim Bishop
Scenes from the Goldmine (1987). . . . . Harry Spiros
The Wind (1987). . . . . Kesner
The Assassin (1989). . . . . Hank Wright
Scissors (1990) . . . . .Alex Morgan/Cole Morgan
Alligator II: The Mutation (1991). . . . . Vincent Brown
Made for TV Movies:
Helter Skelter (1976). . . . . Charles Manson
Good Cops, Bad Cops (1990) . . . . Jimmy Donnelly

• Rajot, Pierre-Loup

Films:
A Nos Amours (1984; French) . . . . Bernard
- 0:56—Brief buns, while walking around in the background. Long shot. Out of focus.
- 0:58—Partial frontal nudity, lying in bed talking to Sandrine Bonnaire.
Baton Rouge (1985; French) . . . . . . .Abadenour Colbert
Garcon! (1985; French). . . . . Maurice

• Rally, Steve

Films:
Overkill (1987) . . . . Mickey Delano
TV:
The Young and the Restless . . . . .n.a.
Santa Barbara . . . . .n.a.
Magazines:
Playgirl (Sep 1984) . . . . Man of the Month
Playgirl (Jan 1985) . . . . Man of the Year
Playgirl (Jun 1988) . . . . The Return of Steve Rally
28-35—Nude.

Rano, Corey

Films:
Predator 2 (1990) . . . . Ramon Vega
- 0:23—Buns, while hanging upside down several times.
- 0:26—Nude, hanging upside down, dead.

Ratray, Peter

Films:
Young Lady Chatterley (1977)
. . . . .Paul (young gardener)
- 0:37—Very brief buns, while pulling his pants up after getting caught with Janette.
- 1:03—Buns, while making love with Harlee McBride in the rain.
- •• 1:32—Buns, while in bed with McBride.

Reckert, Winston

Films:
Your Ticket is No Longer Valid (1982)
. . . . Antonio Montoya
- 1:24—Buns, while in bed with Jennifer Dale.

Reed, Mathew

Films:
Perfect (1985) . . . . Roger
- 1:01—Buns, while dancing in a jock strap at Chippendale's.

Reed, Oliver

Films:
The Curse of the Werewolf (1961) . . . . Leon
Oliver! (1968; British). . . . . .Bill Sikes
Women in Love (1971) . . . . Gerald Crich
- ••• 0:54—Nude, fighting with Alan Bates in a room in front of a fireplace. Long scene.
The Three Musketeers (1973). . . . . Althos
The Triple Echo (1973; British) . . . . Sergeant
Blood in the Streets (1974; French/Italian)
. . . . .Vito Cipriani
The Four Musketeers (1975). . . . . .Athos
Ten Little Indians (1975). . . . . .Hugh
Tommy (1975; British) . . . . Frank Hobbs
Burnt Offerings (1976). . . . . Ben
The Great Scout and Cathouse Thursday (1976)
. . . . Joe Knox
The Big Sleep (1978; British) . . . . Eddie Mars
The Class of Miss MacMichael (1978)
. . . . Terence Sutton
The Prince and the Pauper (1978) . . . . . . Miles Hendon
a.k.a. Crossed Swords
The Brood (1979; Canadian) . . . . Dr. Raglan
Dr. Heckyl and Mr. Hype (1980). . . Dr. Heckyl/Mr. Hype
Condorman (1981) .Krokov
Venom (1982; British) . . . . Dave
Spasms (1983; Canadian) . . . . Suzanne Kincaid
The Sting II (1983). . . . . Doyle Lonnegan
Black Arrow (1984) . . . . Sir Daniel Brackley

Castaway (1986). . . . . Gerald Kingsland
•• 1:46—Nude, doing things around the hut during
the storm.
Master of Dragonard Hill (1987) . . . . . . .Captain Shanks
Dragonard (1988). . . . . .Captain Shanks
The Return of the Musketeers (1989) . . . . Athos
Skeleton Coast (1989). . . . . Captain Simpson
Edgar Allan Poe's "The House of Usher" (1990)
. . . . Roderick Usher
Hired to Kill (1990) . . . . .Bartos
The Pit and the Pendulum (1991) . . . . .The Cardinal
Miniseries:
Christopher Columbus (1985). . . . . .n.a.
Made for TV Movies:
The Lady and the Highwayman (1989)
. . . . Sir Philip Gage

• Reems, Harry

Former adult film actor.
Is now married and selling real estate.
Adult Films:
Deep Throat (1972) . . . . .n.a.
Films:
R.S.V.P. (1984). . . . . Grant Garrison
Made for TV Movies:
Dream House (1981). .Phil
Magazines:
Playboy (Aug 1973). . . . . Porno Chic
••• 141—Full frontal nudity, standing outside.

• Reeves, Keanu

Films:
Flying (1986; Canadian) . . . . .Tommy
Youngblood (1986). . . . . Hoover
River's Edge (1987) . . . . .Matt
Bill and Ted's Excellent Adventure (1989)
. . . . Ted "Theodore" Logan
Parenthood (1989) . . . . .Tod
I Love You to Death (1990) . . . . Marlon James
Tune in Tomorrow (1990) . . . . .Martin Loader
a.k.a. Aunt Julia and the Scriptwriter
Bill and Ted's Bogus Journey (1991)
. . . . Ted "Theodore" Logan
My Own Private Idaho (1991) . . . . Scott Favor
• 1:17—Very brief side view of buns, in quick cuts,
standing with Carmilla.
Point Break (1991). . . . . .Johnny Utah
• 1:14—Very brief buns, while standing up to run after
Tyler.

Regehr, Duncan

Films:
The Monster Squad (1987) . . . . Count Dracula
The Banker (1989) . . . . .Osbourne
• 0:03—Buns, while getting out of bed with Teri Wei-
gel. Don't see his face.
Gore Vidal's Billy the Kid (1989) . . . . Pat Garrett
TV:
Wizards and Warriors (1983) . . . . . Prince Dirk Blackpool

Reinhold, Judge

Films:
Stripes (1981) . . . . Elmo
Fast Times at Ridgemont High (1982) . . . Brad Hamilton
The Lords of Discipline (1983) . . . . Macabbee
Beverly Hills Cop (1984). . . . . .Detective Billy Rosewood
Gremlins (1984). . . . . .Gerald
Roadhouse 66 (1984). . . . . Beckman Hallsgood, Jr.
Head Office (1986) . . . . Jack Issel
Off Beat (1986) . . . . Joe Gower
Ruthless People (1986). . . . . Ken Kessler
Beverly Hills Cop II (1987) . . . .Detective Billy Rosewood
Vice Versa (1988) . . . . Marshall
Rosalie Goes Shopping (1990) . . . . .Priest
A Soldier's Tale (1991) .n.a.
Zandalee (1991) . . . . Thierry Martin
••• 0:21—Buns while in bed with Zandalee.
• 0:23—Upper half of buns, while standing by the
window.
Made for Cable Movies:
Black Magic (1992; Showtime). . . . . Alex Gage

• Reiser, Robert

Films:
The Harrad Summer (1974). . . . . Stanley
a.k.a. Student Union
• 0:57—Buns, while getting out of bed and hiding in
closet.

Reves, Robbie

Films:
Shadowzone (1989) . . . . .James
0:16—Frontal nudity long shot.
• 0:26—Frontal nudity lying under plastic bubble.

Reynolds, Burt

Husband of actress Loni Anderson.
Films:
Operation C.I.A. (1965) . . . . Mark Andrews
Shark! (1969). . . . . .Caine
a.k.a. Maneaters!
Deliverance (1972). . . . . Lewis
Fuzz (1972) . . . . Detective Steve Carella
The Man Who Loved Cat Dancing (1973)
. . . . Jay Grobart
White Lightning (1973) . . . . Gator McKlusky
The Longest Yard (1974) . . . . Paul Crewe
Hustle (1975) . . . . Lieutenant Phil Gaines
Gator (1976) . . . . Gator McKlusky
Semi-Tough (1977) . . . . Billy Clyde Puckett
Smokey and the Bandit (1977). . . . . Bandit
The End (1978) . . . . Sonny Lawson
Hooper (1978). Sonny Hooper
Starting Over (1979) . . . . Phil Potter
Rough Cut (1980; British) . . . . .Jack Rhodes
Smokey and the Bandit II (1980) . . . . Bandit
The Cannonball Run (1981). . . . . J. J. McClure
Paternity (1981). . . . . Buddy Evans
Sharky's Machine (1981) . . . . Sharky

Best Friends (1982) . . . . .Richard Babson
The Best Little Whorehouse in Texas (1982) . . . . Ed Earl
The Man Who Loved Women (1983)
. . . . David Fowler
  •• 1:25—Brief buns, while chiseling a statue after making love with Julie Andrews.
Smokey and the Bandit III (1983) . . . . . .The Real Bandit
Stroker Ace (1983) . . . . Stroker Ace
Cannonball Run II (1984) . . . . J. J. McClure
City Heat (1984) . . . . Mike Murphy
Stick (1985) . . . . Stick
Heat (1987) . . . . Mex
Malone (1987) . . . . Richard Malone
Rent-a-Cop (1988) . . . . Church
Breaking In (1989) . . . . .Ernie Mullins
Physical Evidence (1989). . . . . Joe Paris
Modern Love (1990) . . . . Colonel Parker
TV:
Riverboat (1959-60) . . . . .Ben Frazer
Gunsmoke (1962-65) . . . . Quint Asper
Hawk (1966). .Lt. John Hawk
Dan August (1970-71) . . . . Det. Lt. Dan August
B. L. Stryker (1989-90) . . . . B. L. Stryker
Evening Shade (1990-) . . . . Wood Newton
Magazines:
Cosmopolitan (Apr 1972) . . . . Centerfold

• Ribeiro, Marcelo
Films:
Love Strange Love (1982; Brazilian). . . . Hugo (Child)
  • 0:20—Brief frontal nudity between his legs in bathtub.

• Rice, Randy
Films:
Pumping Iron II: The Women (1985) . . . . . .Himself
  • 0:08—Buns in G-string, while dancing in women's club.

Rios, Javier
Films:
Q & A (1990) . . . . Boat Lover
  • 1:44—Brief buns, while on boat, getting pulled out of bed by Nick Nolte.

• Rivals, Jean Luc
Films:
The Passion of Beatrice (1988; French) . . . . . . Jehan
  • 0:57—Brief frontal nudity, getting dried off.

Robbins, Tim
Significant Other of actress Susan Sarandon.
Films:
Toy Soldiers (1983) . . . . .Bean
No Small Affair (1984). . . . . Nelson
Fraternity Vacation (1985). . . . . . . Larry "Mother" Tucker
The Sure Thing (1985) . . . . .Gary Cooper
Howard the Duck (1986) . . . . Phil Blumburtt

Bull Durham (1988) . . . Ebby Calvin "Nuke" La Loosh
  • 0:03—Buns, while in locker room making love with Millie when the coach sees them.
Five Corners (1988) . . . . .Harry
Tapeheads (1988) . . . . Josh Tager
Erik the Viking (1989; British) . . . . Erik
Miss Firecracker (1989) . . . . Delmount Williams
Cadillac Man (1990) . . . . Larry
Jacob's Ladder (1990). . . . . Jacob Singer
  •• 0:40—Buns, twice in bathroom, while getting ready for ice bath.
Jungle Fever (1991) . . . . .Jerry
Bob Roberts (1992) . . . . .Bob Roberts
The Player (1992). . . . . .Griffin Mill

Roberts, Eric
Films:
King of the Gypsies (1978). . . . . Dave
Raggedy Man (1981) . . . . Teddy
Star 80 (1983) . . . . Paul Snider
  • 1:39—Buns, lying dead on floor, covered with blood after shooting Dorothy, then himself.
The Pope of Greenwich Village (1984) . . . . Paulie
The Coca-Cola Kid (1985; Australian). . . . . Becker
Nobody's Fool (1986) . . . . Riley
Slow Burn (1986). . . . . .Jacob Asch
Blood Red (1988). . . . . Marco Cologero
Rude Awakening (1989). . . . . .Fred
A Family Matter (1990) . . . . Shaun McGinnis
Lonely Hearts (1991) . . . . n.a.
Final Analysis (1992) . . . . Jimmy Evans
Made for Cable Movies:
Descending Angel (1990; HBO) . . . . .Michael Rossi
The Lost Capone (1990). . . . . .Al
Made for TV Movies:
Fugitive Among Us (1992) . . . . .Cal Harper

Robinson, David
Films:
Revenge of the Cheerleaders (1976) . . . . Jordan
  • 0:13—Buns when Tish plays with him while she's under the counter.
Mephisto (1981; German) . . . . n.a.

• Rose, Michael
Films:
Breakfast in Bed (1990) . . . . Jonathan Maxwell
Private Screenings.
  • 1:16—Half of buns, while lying in bed with Marilyn Chambers.

Ross, Chelchie
Films:
On the Right Track (1981) . . . . Customer
One More Saturday Night (1986) . . . . . Dad Lundahl
  • 0:39—Buns, squished against the car window in back seat with Moira Harris.
The Untouchables (1987). . . . . Reporter
Above the Law (1988) . . . . Nelson Fox

The Long Walk Home (1990) . . . . .n.a.
Bill and Ted's Bogus Journey (1991) . . . . .Colonel Oats
The Last Boy Scout (1991) . . . . Senator Baynard
Made for Cable Movies:
Rainbow Drive (1990; Showtime) . . . . .Tom Cutter
Made for Cable TV:
Tales From the Crypt: Four Sided Triangle (1990)
. . . . George Yates
Miniseries:
The Burden of Proof (1992). . . . . Dr. Nate Cawley

Ross, Willie
Films:
The Cook, The Thief, His Wife & Her Lover (1990)
. . . . .Roy
    0:03—Buns, while on ground covered with dog fe-
    ces getting urinated on by Albert. (Talk about a bad
    day!)
    • 0:07—Buns, kneeling on ground while dogs walk
    around.
    • 0:09—Buns, while standing up.
Strike it Rich (1990). . . . . .Man at Theater

Rossi, Leo
Films:
Grand Theft Auto (1977). . . . . Sal
Halloween II (1981) . . . . Budd
    • 0:48—Buns, while getting out of the whirlpool bath
    to check the water temperature.
Heart Like a Wheel (1983). . . . . .Jack Muldowney
River's Edge (1987) . . . . Jim
The Accused (1988) . . . . Cliff "Scorpion" Albrect
Leonard, Part 6 (1988) . . . . Chef
Relentless (1989). . . . . Sam Dietz
Fast Getaway (1990). Sam
Maniac Cop 2 (1990) . . . . .Turkell
Too Much Sun (1990) . . . . George Bianco
Relentless 2: Dead On (1991) . . . . .Sam Dietz
We're Talkin' Serious Money (1991) . . . . Charlie
TV:
Partners in Crime (1984). . . . . .Lt. Ed Vronsky
Tour of Duty (1988-90). . . . . Jake Bridger

Rossovich, Rick
Films:
The Lords of Discipline (1983). . . . . Pig
Streets of Fire (1984). . . . . Officer Cooley
The Terminator (1984) . . . . Matt
Warning Sign (1985). Bob
The Morning After (1986). . . . . Detective
Top Gun (1986) . . . . .Ron Kenner
Roxanne (1987) . . . . .Chris McDonell
Spellbinder (1988) . . . . .Derek Clayton
Paint It Black (1989) . . . . Jonathan Dunbar
    • 0:48—Upper half of buns while getting out of bed
    with Julie Carmen.
Navy SEALS (1990) . . . . Leary

Made for Cable TV:
Tales From the Crypt: The Switch (1990; HBO)
. . . . Hans
    (Available on *Tales From the Crypt, Volume 3*.)
    •• 0:23—Buns, while standing in front of mirror after
    being transformed into a younger Carlton.
Made for TV Movies:
Deadly Lessons (1983). . . . . .n.a.
TV:
MacGruder & Loud (1985) . . . . Geller
Sons and Daughters (1990-91) . . . . Spud Lincoln

• Rourke, Mickey
Husband of actress/model Carré Otis.
Films:
1941 (1979). . . . . .Reese
Fade to Black (1980) . . . . n.a.
Heaven's Gate (1980). n.a.
Body Heat (1981). . . . . .Teddy Lewis
Diner (1982) . . . . .Boogie
Eureka (1983; British). . . . . .Aurelio
Rumble Fish (1983) . . . . Motorcycle Boy
The Year of the Dragon (1985). . . . . Stanley White
9 1/2 Weeks (1986) . . . . John
Angel Heart (1987) . . . . Harry Angel
    (Original Unedited Version reviewed.)
    •• 1:28—Buns, while in bed with Lisa Bonet. Don't see
    his face. It gets kind of bloody.
Barfly (1987) . . . . Henry
A Prayer for the Dying (1987) . . . . Martin Fallon
Homeboy (1988) . . . . Johnny Walker
Johnny Handsome (1989) . . . . John Sedley
Desperate Hours (1990). . . . . Michael Bosworth
Wild Orchid (1990) . . . . .James Wheeler
Harley Davidson and The Marlboro Man (1991)
. . . . Harley Davidson
White Sands (1992) . . . . .German Lennox
Magazines:
Playgirl (Nov 1987) . . . . Raw Footage
    35—Buns in stills from *Angel Heart*.

Rowlatt, Michael
Films:
Spaced Out (1980; British). . . . . .Cliff
    • 0:42—Buns, while getting out of bed trying to get
    away from Partha.

Rubbo, Joe
Films:
The Last American Virgin (1982) . . . . .David
    • 0:45—Buns, in bed making love with Carmilla while
    his buddies watch through the key hole.
Hot Chili (1985). .Arney
    • 0:24—Brief buns while getting whipped by Brigitte.

• Russ, Tim
Films:
Crossroads (1986) . . . . Robert Johnson
Spaceballs (1987). Trooper

Eve of Destruction (1991) . . . . Carter
Night Eyes 2 (1991) . . . . Jesse Younger
•• 0:07—Buns, while getting out of bed and putting
his pants on.
Made for Cable Movies:
Fire With Fire (1986; Showtime) . . . . Jerry
TV:
Highwayman (1987-88) . . . . .D.C. Montana

Russell, Kurt

Significant Other of actress Goldie Hawn.
Ex-husband of actress Season Hubley.
Films:
The Horse in the Gray Flannel Suit (1968)
. . . . Ronnie Gardner
The Computer Wore Tennis Shoes (1969) . . . . . . Dexter
The Barefoot Executive (1971) . . . . .Steven Post
Fool's Parade (1971) . . . . .Johnny Jesus
Now You See Him, Now You Don't (1972)
. . . . Dexter Riley
Charley & the Angel (1973) . . . . Ray Ferris
Superdad (1973). . . . . Bart
The Strongest Man in the World (1975) . . . . Dexter
Used Cars (1980) . . . . .Rudy Russo
• 1:04—Very brief buns while putting on red under-
wear.
Escape from New York (1981) . . . . .Snake Pliskin
The Thing (1982) . . . . .MacReady
Silkwood (1984) . . . . Drew Stephens
Swing Shift (1984) . . . . Lucky Lockhart
The Mean Season (1985) . . . . Malcolm Anderson
The Best of Times (1986). . . . . Reno Hightower
Big Trouble in Little China (1986) . . . . .Jack Burton
Overboard (1987). . . . . .Dean Proffitt
Tequila Sunrise (1988). . . . . Lt. Nick Frescia
Tango & Cash (1989) . . . . .Cash
•• 0:31—Brief buns while walking into the prison
shower room with Sylvester Stallone.
Winter People (1989) . . . . .Wayland Jackson
Backdraft (1991). . . . . .Stephen McCaffrey
Captain Ron (1992). . . . . Captain Ron
Unlawful Entry (1992). . . . . .Michael Carr
Made for TV Movies:
The Quest (1976) . . . . Morgan

• Russo, James

Films:
Fast Times at Ridgemont High (1982) . . . . Robber
A Stranger is Watching (1982) . . . . . Ronald Thompson
Vortex (1982) . . . . .Anthony Demmer
Exposed (1983). . . . . Nick
Beverly Hills Cop (1984) . . . . Mikey Tandino
The Cotton Club (1984) . . . . .Vince Hood
Once Upon a Time in America (1984) . . . . Bugsy
(Long version reviewed.)
Extremities (1986). . . . . .Joe
China Girl (1987) . . . . Alby
The Blue Iguana (1988). . . . . .Reno
Freeway (1988). . . . . Frank Quinn

We're No Angels (1989). . . . . Bobby
Cold Heaven (1990). . . . . Daniel Corvin
• 0:02—Buns, while standing at window, putting on
underwear. Long shot.
• 1:15—Brief buns while in bed with Theresa Russell.
Illicit Behavior (1991). . . . . Bill Tanner
(Unrated version reviewed.)
A Kiss Before Dying (1991). . . . . Dan Corelli
My Own Private Idaho (1991) . . . . .Richard Waters
Made for Cable Movies:
Intimate Strangers (1991; Showtime). . . . . . Nick Ciccini

Rust, Richard

Films:
The Student Nurses (1970) . . . . .Les
a.k.a. Young LA Nurses
• 0:43—Buns, while lying in sand with Barbara Leigh.
The Last Movie (1971) . . . . Pisco
Kid Blue (1973) . . . . Train Robber
The Great Gundown (1976). . . . . .Joe Riles

• Ryan, Eric

Films:
The Bikini Carwash Company (1992). . . . . . Stanley
(Unrated version reviewed.)
• 1:15—Buns, when Sunny yanks his short pants
down.

Rydell, Christopher

Films:
Gotcha! (1985) . . . . Bob Jensen
Mask (1985). . . . . High School Student
The Sure Thing (1985). . . . . .Charlie
The Check is in the Mail (1986) . . . . . . .Drunken Sailor
Blood and Sand (1989; Spanish). . . . . .Juan
• 0:15—Buns, while running away after fighting bull.
Dark, long shot.
•• 0:18—Buns, seen between shower curtain when
Sharon Stone watches.
• 1:05—Buns, while on top of Stone. Long shot.
How I Got Into College (1989). . . . . Oliver
Listen to Me (1989) . . . . Tom Lloynd
Under the Boardwalk (1989) . . . . .Tripper
Side Out (1990). . . . . Wiley Hunter
For the Boys (1991) . . . . Danny

Sadler, William

Films:
Die Hard 2 (1990) . . . . Colonel Stuart
•• 0:02—Buns, while exercising in hotel room before
leaving for the airport.
Hard to Kill (1990) . . . . Vernon Trent
The Hot Spot (1990) . . . . Frank Sutton
Bill and Ted's Bogus Journey (1991)
. . . . .Grim Reaper/English Family Member
Rush (1991). . . . . Monroe

Sador, Daniel

Films:
Sugar Cookies (1973) . . . . .Gus
    0:37—Buns while in bed with Dola, then running
    around.

Sands, Julian

Films:
The Killing Fields (1984) . . . . Swain
Oxford Blues (1984) . . . . Colin
The Doctor and the Devils (1985) . . . . Dr. Murray
Gothic (1986; British) . . . . Shelley
  •• 0:17—Buns, while standing on roof in the rain.
A Room with a View (1986; British) . George Emerson
  ••• 1:05—Nude running around with Freddy and Mr.
    Beebe in the woods. Lots of frontal nudity.
Siesta (1987). . . . . Kit
Vibes (1988) . . . . Dr. Harrison Steele
Arachnophobia (1990) . . . . Dr. James Atherton
Warlock (1990). . . . . Warlock
Husbands and Lovers (1991; Italian). . . . . .Stefan
  (Unrated version reviewed.)
  ••• 0:32—Frontal nudity, in the shower and getting out.
  ••• 0:35—Frontal nudity, getting into bed.
  ••• 1:13—Nude, taking a shower then getting out.
  •• 1:17—Very brief frontal nudity after making love
    with Joanna.
Naked Lunch (1991) . . . . .Yves Cloquet
Made for Cable Movies:
Crazy in Love (1992; TNT) . . . . .n.a.
Made for TV Movies:
Murder by Moonlight (1989) . . . . .n.a.
Magazines:
Playboy (Nov 1986) . . . . Sex in Cinema 1986
  • 128—Buns, in photo from *A Room with a View*. Kind
  of blurry.

Sanville, Michael

Films:
The First Turn-On! (1983) . . . . Mitch
  • 1:18—Buns, while in cave orgy scene on top of Annie.

• Sarafian, Deran

Films:
10 to Midnight (1983). . . . . Dale Anders
  • 0:08—Buns, while making love in van with Betty.

Sarandon, Chris

Ex-husband of actress Susan Sarandon.
Films:
Dog Day Afternoon (1975) . . . . .Leon
Lipstick (1976) . . . . Gordon Stuart
  •• 0:50—Buns, while standing in his studio talking to
  Margaux Hemingway on the telephone.
The Sentinel (1977). . . . . Michael Lerman
Cuba (1979). . . . . .Juan Polido
The Osterman Weekend (1983) . . . . . . Joseph Cardone
Protocol (1984). . . . . Michael Ransome

Fright Night (1985) . . . . .Jerry Dandridge
The Princess Bride (1987). . . . . Prince Humperdinck
Child's Play (1988) . . . . Mike Norris
Collision Course (1989) . . . . Madras
Slaves of New York (1989) . . . . .Victor Okrent
Whispers (1989). . . . . .Detective Tony
The Resurrected (1991)
  . . . . .Charles Dexter Ward/Joseph Curwen
Made for TV Movies:
Mayflower Madam (1987) . . . . n.a.
A Murderous Affair: The Carolyn Warmus Story (1992) .
  n.a.

Savage, John

Films:
The Killing Kind (1973) . . . . Terry Lambert
  • 0:00—Upper half of buns when other guys pull his
  shorts down during rape of girl.
  •• 0:58—Buns while in shower when Mrs. Lambert
  opens the curtains to take a picture.
The Deer Hunter (1978). . . . . Steven
Hair (1979) . . . . .Claude
The Beat (1986) . . . . Frank Ellsworth
Hotel Colonial (1988). . . . . Marco Venieri
Do the Right Thing (1989). . . . . .Clifton
Hunting (1990; Australian). . . . . Michael Bergman
Primary Motive (1992). n.a.

Schneider, John

Films:
Eddie Macon's Run (1983) . . . . Eddie Macon
  • 0:15—Brief left side view of buns when beginning to
  cross the stream. Dark, hard to see.
Cocaine Wars (1986) . . . . Cliff
The Curse (1987). Carl Willis
Ministry of Vengeance (1989) . . . . .David Miller
Speed Zone (1989) . . . . .Cannonballer
Made for TV Movies:
Dream House (1981) . . . . Charlie Cross
Highway Heartbreaker (1992) . . . . n.a.
TV:
The Dukes of Hazzard (1979-85) . . . . Bo Duke

Schott, Bob

Films:
The Working Girls (1973) . . . . Roger
  • 0:07—Buns, while getting out of bed to meet Hon-
  ey.
Force Five (1981) . . . . Carl
Bloodfist III: Forced to Fight (1991) . . . . Weird Willy

Schwarzenegger, Arnold

Husband of Kennedy clan member/news reporter Maria
  Shriver.
Films:
Hercules in New York (1969) . . . . Hercules
  a.k.a. Hercules Goes Bananas
The Long Goodbye (1973). . . . . Hoods
Stay Hungry (1976) . . . . .Joe Santo

Pumping Iron (1977) . . . . .n.a.
The Villain (1979) . . . . Handsome Stranger
Conan the Barbarian (1982) . . . . Conan
Conan the Destroyer (1984) . . . . Conan
The Terminator (1984) . . . . .The Terminator
••• 0:03—Buns, while kneeling by garbage truck, walking to look at the city and walking toward the three punks at night.
Commando (1985) . . . . Matrix
Red Sonja (1985) . . . . Kalidor
Raw Deal (1986) . . . . Mark Kaminsky
Predator (1987) . . . . .Major Dutch Schaefer
The Running Man (1987) . . . . .Ben Richards
Red Heat (1988) .Ivan Danko
•• 0:02—Buns while in the sauna and outside fighting in the snow.
Twins (1988) . . . . Julius Benedict
Kindergarten Cop (1990) . . . . Kimble
Total Recall (1990) . . . . Doug Quaid
Terminator 2: Judgement Day (1991)
. . . . The Terminator
Made for TV Movies:
The Jayne Mansfield Story (1980) . . . . .n.a.

Scorpio, Bernie

Identical twin brother of Lennie Scorpio.
Films:
Video Vixens (1973) . . . . Turnip Twin
••• 1:05—Frontal nudity standing next to his identical twin brother after their trial.

Scorpio, Lennie

Identical twin brother of Bernie Scorpio.
Films:
Video Vixens (1973) . . . . Turnip Twin
•• 1:03—Frontal nudity, then buns while on top of victim in bed.
••• 1:05—Frontal nudity standing next to his identical twin brother after their trial.

• Scott, Campbell

Films:
Five Corners (1988) . . . . Cop
Longtime Companion (1990) . . . . Willy
The Sheltering Sky (1990) . . . . .Turner
Dead Again (1991) . . . . Doug
Dying Young (1991) . . . . .Victor Geddes
• 1:04—Brief buns, after running out of the house wrapped in a blanket and tossing it off. Long shot.
Singles (1992) . . . . Steve
Made for TV Movies:
The Perfect Tribute (1991) . . . . .n.a.

Scuddamore, Simon

Films:
Slaughter High (1986) . . . . Marty
• 0:05—Nude in girl's shower room when his classmates pull a prank on him.

Segado, Alberto

Films:
Two to Tango (1988) . . . . .Lucky Lara
• 0:29—Buns while on top of Adrienne Sachs, making love with her in bed.

Selby, David

Films:
Night of Dark Shadows (1971)
. . . . .Quentin/Charles Collins
Up the Sandbox (1972) . . . . Paul Reynolds
The Girl in Blue (1973; Canadian) . . . . Scott
a.k.a. U-turn
• 0:10—Brief buns while getting out of bed and putting on pants. Dark.
0:44—Left half of buns while in shower.
•• 1:14—Buns, while walking into the bathroom.
Super Cops (1974) . . . . Bob Hantz
Rich Kids (1979) . . . . Steve Sloan
Raise the Titanic (1980; British) . . . . . Dr. Gene Seagram
Rich and Famous (1981) . . . . Doug Blake
Dying Young (1991) . . . . Richard Geddes
Made for TV Movies:
Grave Secrets: The Legacy of Hilltop Drive (1992)
. . . . Shag Williams
TV:
Flamingo Road (1981-82) . . . . Michael Tyrone
Falcon Crest (1982-86) . . . . Richard Channing

Selleck, Tom

Films:
The Seven Minutes (1971) . . . . .Phil Sanford
Terminal Island (1973) . . . . .Dr. Norman Milford
Coma (1978) . . . . Sean
High Road to China (1983) . . . . O'Malley
Lassiter (1984) . . . . Lassiter
• 1:00—Buns, while getting out of bed after making love with Lauren Hutton.
Runaway (1984) . . . . Ramsay
Three Men and a Baby (1987) . . . . Peter
Her Alibi (1989) . . . . Phil Blackwood
An Innocent Man (1989) . . . . Jimmy Rainwood
Quigley Down Under (1990) . . . . . . .Matthew Quigley
Three Men and a Little Lady (1990) . . . . Peter
The Shadow Riders (1991) . . . . n.a.
Christopher Columbus: The Discovery (1992)
. . . . King Ferdinand
Folks! (1992) . . . . n.a.
Miniseries:
The Sacketts (1979) . . . . n.a.
Made for TV Movies:
Bunco (1977) . . . . n.a.
TV:
The Rockford Files (1979-80) . . . . .Lance White
Magnum P.I. (1980-88) . . . . Thomas Magnum

Serbedzija, Rade
Films:
Hanna's War (1988) . . . . Captain Ivan
Manifesto (1988) . . . . Emile
• 0:18—Buns, while under sheet and getting out of bed.

Serna, Pepe
Films:
The Student Nurses (1970) .Luis
a.k.a. Young LA Nurses
Group Marriage (1972) . . . . Ramon
The New Centurions (1972) . . . . .Young Mexican
Hangup (1974) . . . . .Enrique
The Day of the Locust (1975) . . . . Miguel
• 2:01—Buns while on top of Karen Black, then buns while jumping out of bed.
The Killer Inside Me (1975) . . . . Johnny Lopez
• 0:15—Brief upper half of buns, twice, getting strip searched at police station.
•• 0:16—Very, very brief frontal nudity getting restrained by policemen.
Car Wash (1976) . . . . Chuco
Swashbuckler (1976) . . . . Street Entertainer
The Jerk (1979) . . . . Punk #1
Walk Proud (1979) . . . . Cesar
Honeysuckle Rose (1980) . . . . .Rooster
Inside Moves (1980) . . . . Herrada
Vice Squad (1982) . . . . Pete Mendez
Deal of the Century (1983) . . . . Vardis
Heartbreaker (1983) . . . . .Loco
Scarface (1983) . . . . Angel
The Adventures of Buckaroo Banzai, Across the 8th Dimension (1984) . . . . Reno Nevada
Red Dawn (1984) . . . . Aardvark's Father
Fandango (1985) . . . . .Gas Station Mechanic
Silverado (1985) . . . . Scruffy
Out of Bounds (1987) . . . . Murano
Postcards from the Edge (1990) . . . . Raoul
The Rookie (1990). . . . . Lt. Ray Garcia
Only You (1992) .Dock Official

Shane, Michael Jay
Films:
Click: Calendar Girl Killer (1989) . . . . Jessie
Savage Beach (1989) . . . . .Shane Abeline
•• 0:08—Buns, while getting out of pool.
Guns (1990) .Shane Abilene
Do or Die (1991) . . . . .Shane Abeline
••• 1:10—Buns, while making love with Atlanta, outside at night.
Magazines:
Playgirl (Sep 1988) . . . . Man for September 44-51—Frontal nudity, side view of buns.

Shannon, George
Films:
Sugar Cookies (1973) . . . . Max
•• 0:14—Buns, while on top of Mary Woronov in bed.

Sharkey, Ray
Films:
The Lords of Flatbush (1974) . . . . Student
Trackdown (1976) . . . . Flash
Stunts (1977) . . . . Pauley
Paradise Alley (1978) . . . . .Legs
Who'll Stop the Rain? (1978) . . . . Smitty
Heart Beat (1979) . . . . Ira
The Idolmaker (1980) . . . . .Vince Vacarddi
Love and Money (1980). . . . . Byron Levin
Willie and Phil (1980). Phil
•• 1:45—Buns, while getting into the hot tub. (He's on the right.)
Some Kind of Hero (1982) . . . . Vinnie
Body Rock (1984) . . . . Terrence
Hellhole (1985) . . . . Silk
Wise Guys (1986) . . . . Marco
Private Investigations (1987) . . . . n.a.
Scenes from the Class Struggle in Beverly Hills (1989) . . . . .Frank
• 1:10—Brief buns while sleeping in bed with Zandra.
Act of Piracy (1990) . . . . Jack Wilcox
• 0:33—Brief side view of buns while on top of Laura in bed.
•• 0:35—Brief buns, while getting out of bed and putting on robe.
The Rain Killer (1990). . . . . .Vince Capra
Relentless 2: Dead On (1991). . . . . Kyle Volsone
Round Trip to Heaven (1992) . . . . Stoneface
Made for TV Movies:
The Revenge of Al Capone (1989) . . . . Al Capone
TV:
Wiseguy (1987) . . . . .Sonny Steelgrave
Man in the Family (1991). . . . . .Sal

Shea, John
Films:
Hussy (1980; British) . . . . Emory
•• 0:29—Buns while making love with Helen Mirren in bed. Half of lower frontal nudity when she rolls off him.
Missing (1982). . . . . .Charles Horman
Windy City (1984) . . . . Danny Morgan
Unsettled Land (1987) . . . . n.a.
A New Life (1988) . . . . .Doc
Harlequin Romance: Magic Moments (1989) . . . . Troy Gardner
Freejack (1992) . . . . .Morgan
Made for Cable Movies:
Ladykiller (1992; USA) . . . . Jack Packard
Notorious (1992; Lifetime). . . . . n.a.
Made for Cable TV:
The Hitchhiker: Minuteman . . . . .Jeremy

Sheen, Martin

Father of actors Emilio Estevez and Charlie Sheen.

Films:

Rage (1972) . . . . Major Holliford
Badlands (1973) . . . . Kit
The Cassandra Crossing (1977; British) . . . . Navarro
Eagle's Wing (1978; British) . . . . Pike
Apocalypse Now (1979) . . . . Captain Willard
  • 0:07—Brief buns, while in bedroom after opening
    door for military guys.
The Final Countdown (1980) . . . . Warren Lasky
Enigma (1982) . . . . Alex Holbeck
Gandhi (1982) . . . . Walker
That Championship Season (1982) . . . . Tom Daley
The Dead Zone (1983) . . . . Greg Stillson
Man, Woman and Child (1983) . . . . Bob Beckwith
Firestarter (1984) . . . . Capt. Hollister
The Believers (1987) . . . . Dr. Cal Jamison
Siesta (1987) . . . . Del
Wall Street (1987) . . . . Carl Fox
Beverly Hills Brats (1989) . . . . Dr. Jeffrey Miller
Cold Front (1989; Canadian) . . . . John Hyde
The Maid (1990) . . . . Anthony Wayne
Cadence (1991) . . . . Sergeant Otis V. McKinney

Made for Cable Movies:

The Guardian (1984; HBO) . . . . n.a.

Made for TV Movies:

The Little Girl Who Lives Down the Lane
  (1976; Canadian) . . . . Frank Hallet
Samaritan: The Mitch Snyder Story (1986) . . . . n.a.
Shattered Spirits (1986) . . . . n.a.

Sheffer, Craig

Films:

Voyage of the Rock Aliens (1985) . . . . Frankie
  a.k.a. When the Rains Begin to Fall
Split Decisions (1988) . . . . Eddie McGuinn
Blue Desert (1990) . . . . Randall Atkins
Instant Karma (1990) . . . . Zane Smith
  • 1:15—Brief buns while on top of Penelope. Don't
    see his face.
  1:18—Very brief buns again in flashback.
Night Breed (1990) . . . . Boone
Eye of the Storm (1991) . . . . Ray

Made for Cable Movies:

Fire With Fire (1986; Showtime) . . . . Joe Fisk

TV:

The Hamptons (1983) . . . . Brian Chadway

Shellen, Steve

Films:

Gimme an "F" (1981) . . . . Tommy Hamilton
  0:56—Dancing in his underwear in the boy's shower
    room while the girls peek in at him.
  • 0:57—Brief upper half of buns.
Burglar (1987) . . . . Christopher Marshall
  • 0:26—Buns, while in front of closet that Whoopi
    Goldberg is hiding in. Don't see his face, but proba-
    bly him.

Modern Girls (1987) . . . . Brad
The Stepfather (1987) . . . . Jim Ogilvie
Talking Walls (1987) . . . . Paul Barton
  •• 0:58—Buns, while taking off his clothes and running
    down railroad tracks.
American Gothic (1988) . . . . Paul
Casual Sex? (1988) . . . . Nick
Murder One (1988; Canadian) . . . . Wayne Coleman
Damned River (1990) . . . . Ray

Made for Cable TV:

The Hitchhiker: Love Sounds . . . . Kerry
  •• 0:15—Brief buns, while making love in the house
    with Belinda Bauer.
  •• 0:22—Buns, while making love in the boat with Bau-
    er.
Tales From the Crypt: Lover Come Hack To Me
  (1989; HBO) . . . . Charles
  • 0:10—Buns, while getting undressed with his new-
    lywed wife in a strange house.

Shirin, Moti

Films:

The Little Drummer Girl (1984) . . . . Michel
  •• 1:07—Nude, in a prison cell when Diane Keaton
    looks at his scars.
Unsettled Land (1987) . . . . Salim

• Shore, Pauly

Films:

Phantom of the Mall: Eric's Revenge (1988)
  . . . . Buzz
  •• 1:06—Buns, while mooning security guard on B&W
    surveillance monitor.
Wedding Band (1989) . . . . Nicky

TV:

Totally Pauly . . . . Host

Sibbit, John

Films:

Love Circles Around the World (1984) . . . . Jack
  • 0:06—Very brief frontal nudity pulling his under-
    wear down and getting into bed.
  •• 0:19—Buns, while trying to run away from Brigid af-
    ter she yanks his underwear off.

Siegel, David

Films:

Private Passions (1983) . . . . Toni
  • 0:29—Buns, with Laura. Don't see his face.

• Sills, David

Films:

Breakfast in Bed (1990) . . . . Henry Huntley
  Private Screenings.
  •• 0:25—Buns, while in bed with Wendy.
  •• 0:35—Brief buns, while standing up in boat with
    Wendy.

• Simione, Dan

TV:
General Hospital . . . . .n.a.
Magazines:
Playgirl (Sep 1989) . . . . The Natural
36-43—Upper half of buns, partial pubic hair.

• Simon, Mark

Video Tapes:
Inside Out 4 (1992) . . . . .William/What Anna Wants...
(Unrated version reviewed.)
• 1:09—Buns and very brief frontal nudity, making out
with Claudia while Anna takes photos.

• Simons, Alan

Films:
Auditions (1978) . . . . Alan Cole
• 0:18—Nude, undressing and caressing himself dur-
ing his audition.
•• 0:37—Buns, when his underwear is pulled down.

Singer, Marc

Brother of actress Lori Singer.
Films:
Go Tell the Spartans (1978). . . . . Captain Al Olivetti
The Beastmaster (1982) . . . . Dar
If You Could See What I Hear (1982). . . . . .Tom Sullivan
Born to Race (1988) . . . . Kenny Landruff
In the Cold of the Night (1989) . . . . Ken Strom
Beastmaster 2: Through the Portal of Time (1990)
. . . . Dar
Body Chemistry (1990) . . . . Dr. Tom Redding
• 0:18—Buns, standing up in hallway holding Claire
while making love. Long shot.
Dead Space (1990) . . . . Steve Krieger
A Man Called Serge (1990). . . . . Von Kraut
Watchers II (1990). . . . . .Paul Ferguson
The Berlin Conspiracy (1991) . . . . Harry Spangler
Ultimate Desires (1991). . . . . Jonathan Sullivan
Miniseries:
V (1983) . . . . Mike Donovan
V: The Final Battle (1984) . . . . Mike Donovan
TV:
V: The Series (1984-85). . . . . Mike Donovan
Dallas (1986-87) . . . . Matt Cantrell

Singleton, Andrew

Films:
Death Merchant (1990). . . . . McKinley
• 0:47—Brief buns, while pulling up his pants, getting
up out of bed with Natasha.

Skarsgard, Stellan

Films:
The Unbearable Lightness of Being (1988)
. . . . The Engineer
• 2:18—Buns, while making love with Tereza in his
apartment.

• Skerritt, Tom

Films:
Fuzz (1972) . . . . .Detective Bert Kling
Big Bad Mama (1974). . . . . Fred Diller
• 1:18—Brief buns, while lying down with Angie Dick-
inson in barn.
Thieves Like Us (1974) . . . . .Dee Mobley
The Devil's Rain (1975; U.S./Mexican) . . . . Tom Preston
The Turning Point (1977). . . . . Wayne Rogers
Up in Smoke (1978). . . . . .Strawberry
Alien (1979). . . . . Dallas
Ice Castles (1979). . . . . .Marcus Winston
Fighting Back (1982) . . . . John D'Angelo
The Dead Zone (1983). . . . . Sheriff Bannerman
Opposing Force (1986) . . . . Logan
a.k.a. Hell Camp
• 0:33—Very brief buns, while getting sprayed with
water and dusted with white powder.
•• 1:11—Brief buns, while jumping out of tree to knock
out Tuan.
The Big Town (1987) . . . . Phil Carpenter
Maid to Order (1987) . . . . .Charles Montgomery
Poltergeist III (1988). . . . . Bruce Gardner
Steel Magnolias (1989) . . . . Drum Eatenton
The Rookie (1990) . . . . Eugene Ackerman
Big Man on Campus (1991). . . . . Dr. Webster
Poison Ivy (1992). . . . . n.a.
Wild Orchid II: Two Shades of Blue (1992) . . . . Ham
Made for TV Movies:
In Sickness and in Health (1992) . . . . n.a.
TV:
Ryan's Four (1983) . . . . Dr. Thomas Ryan
Picket Fences (1992-) . . . . Sheriff Jimmy Brock

Slater, Christian

Films:
The Legend of Billie Jean (1985). . . . . .Binx
The Name of the Rose (1986) . . . . Adso of Melk
• 0:48—Buns, while making love with The Girl in the
monastery kitchen.
Tucker: The Man and His Dream (1988) . . . . Junior
Gleaming the Cube (1989) . . . . .Brian Kelly
Heathers (1989). . . . . J.D.
The Wizard (1989) . . . . .Nick Woods
Pump Up the Volume (1990) . . . . Mark Hunter
Tales From the Darkside, The Movie (1990) . . . . . . Andy
Young Guns II (1990). . . . . . . .Arkansas Dave Rudbaugh
Mobsters (1991) . . . . .Charlie "Lucky" Luciano
a.k.a. Mobsters—The Evil Empire
0:45—Very, very brief buns during love scene. Don't
see his face.
Robin Hood: Prince of Thieves (1991) . . . . . Will Scarlett
Star Trek VI: The Undiscovered Country (1991)
. . . . Excelsior Communications Officer
Kuffs (1992) . . . . George Kuffs

Sloane, Lance

Films:

The Big Bet (1985) . . . . .Chris
- •• 0:38—Buns, while taking off robe and getting into bed with Angela Roberts after visiting Mrs. Roberts.
- •• 0:52—Buns, while on elevator floor with Monique Gabrielle during his daydream.
- • 1:07—Buns, while getting into tub with Kimberly Evenson during video tape fantasy. Long shot.

Smith, Charlie Martin

Films:

The Culpepper Cattle Co. (1972) . . . . Tim Slater
Fuzz (1972) . . . . Baby
American Graffiti (1973) . . . . Terry the Toad
Pat Garrett and Billy the Kid (1973) . . . . .Bowdre
Rafferty and the Gold Dust Twins (1975) . . . . Alan
No Deposit, No Return (1976) . . . . .Longnecker
The Buddy Holly Story (1978) . . . . Ray Bob
More American Graffiti (1979) . . . . . . Terry the Toad
Herbie Goes Bananas (1980) . . . . D. J.
Never Cry Wolf (1983) . . . . Tyler
- • 0:32—Buns while warming himself and drying his clothes after falling through the ice.
- • 1:18—Very brief frontal nudity running and jumping off a rock into the pond.
- • 1:20—Buns while running in meadow with the caribou.
- • 1:23—Brief silhouette of lower frontal nudity while scampering up a hill. More buns when chasing the caribou.

Starman (1984) . . . . Shermin
The Untouchables (1987) . . . . Oscar Wallace
The Hot Spot (1990) . . . . Lon Gulick
Made for Cable Movies:
Boris and Natasha (1992; Showtime) . . . . . . Hotel Clerk

Smits, Jimmy

Films:

Running Scared (1986) . . . . Julio Gonzales
Terror on the Blacktop (1987) . . . . Bo
Old Gringo (1989) . . . . Arroyo
- • 1:26—Half of his buns while on bed with Jane Fonda. Long shot, don't see his face.

Vital Signs (1989) . . . . Dr. David Redding
Fires Within (1991) . . . . Nestor
Switch (1991) . . . . .Walter Stone
- ••• 1:21—Buns, while stretching after waking up in the morning. A bit on the dark side.

Made for TV Movies:
The Broken Cord (1992) . . . . David Moore
TV:
L.A. Law (1986-91) . . . . .Victor Sifuentes

• Sommer, Robert

Films:

Auditions (1978) . . . . .Frank Murphy
- ••• 0:33—Nude, during dungeon scene.
- • 1:07—Buns during orgy scene.

Hanna K. (1984) . . . . Court President
Saving Grace (1986) . . . . Mr. Carver

Spader, James

Films:

Tuff Turf (1984) . . . . Morgan Hiller
Pretty in Pink (1986) . . . . Steff McKee
Baby Boom (1987) . . . . Ken Arrenberg
Jack's Back (1987) . . . . John/Rick Wesford
Less than Zero (1987) . . . . .Rip
Mannequin (1987) . . . . .Richards
The Rachel Papers (1989; British) . . . . .De Forest
sex, lies and videotape (1989) . . . . Graham Dalton
Bad Influence (1990) . . . . .Michael Boll
White Palace (1990) . . . . .Max Baron
- •• 0:38—Buns, while taking off clothes and getting into bed with Susan Sarandon. Don't see his face.

True Colors (1991) . . . . Tim Garrity
TV:
The Family Tree (1983) . . . . .Jake Nichols

Spanjer, Maarten

Films:

Spetters (1980; Dutch) .Jeff
- ••• 0:35—Frontal nudity, measuring and comparing his manlihood with his friends in the auto shop.
- • 1:12—Buns while climbing into bed in trailer with Reneé Soutendijk.

Spano, Joe

Films:

American Graffiti (1973) .Vic
Roadie (1980) . . . . Ace
Terminal Choice (1985; Canadian) . . . . Frank Holt
- ••• 0:34—Buns, taking off towel and getting dressed in locker room while talking to Anna.
- • 0:49—Buns, while making love in bed with Anna. Long shot, don't see his face.

Made for Cable Movies:
Fever (1991; HBO) . . . . Junkman
Made for TV Movies:
The Girl Who Came Between Them (1990) . . . . .Jim
TV:
Hill Street Blues (1981-87) . . . . Henry Goldblume

Spano, Vincent

Films:

Over the Edge (1979) . . . . Mark
Baby, It's You (1983) . . . . Sheik
The Black Stallion Returns (1983) . . . . .Raj
Rumble Fish (1983) . . . . Steve
Alphabet City (1984) .Johnny
Creator (1985) . . . . Boris
- • 0:28—Brief buns, while in shower room with David Ogden Stiers after working out in a gym.
- • 0:57—Brief buns, before taking a shower.

Maria's Lovers (1985) . . . . Al Griselli
Good Morning, Babylon (1987; Italian/French)
. . . . .Nicola Bonnano

And God Created Woman (1988) . . . . Billy Moran
(Unrated version.)
City of Hope (1991) . . . . Nick
Oscar (1991). . . . . .Anthony Rossano, C.P.A.
Made for Cable Movies:
Blood Ties (1986; Italian; Showtime). . . . . .n.a.
Afterburn (1992; HBO) . . . . Ted Harduvel

Spechtenhauser, Robert Egon
Films:
Bizarre (1986; Italian) . . . . .Edward
  • 0:29—Partial buns, while taking a shower when Laurie peeks in at him.
  • 0:31—Brief buns, while on top of Laurie in the water.
  •• 0:36—Buns, while on bed with Laurie. (He's made up to look like a woman.)

Springfield, Rick
Singer.
Films:
Hard to Hold (1984). . . . . .James Roberts
  • 0:06—Buns, while running down the hall getting chased by a bunch of young girls.
  •• 0:15—Buns, while lying in bed sleeping.
Made for TV Movies:
Battlestar Gallactica (1978) . . . . Lieutenant Zac
Nick Knight (1989) . . . . Nick
TV:
The Human Target (1992). . . . . Christopher Chance

Stallone, Sylvester
Ex-husband of actress Brigitte Nielsen.
Adult Films:
The Italian Stallion (1970) . . . . Stud
X-rated film that Stallone did before he got famous. Originally called *A Party at Kitty and Stud's*. Re-titled and re-released in 1985. He has lots of nude scenes in this film.
Films:
The Lords of Flatbush (1974). . . . . .Stanley Rosiello
Capone (1975) . . . . Frank Nitti
(Not available on video tape.)
Death Race 2000 (1975) . . . . . Machine Gun Joe Viterbo
Farewell, My Lovely (1975; British) . . . . Kelly/Jonnie
Cannonball (1976; U.S./Hong Kong). . . . . .n.a.
Rocky (1976). . . . . Rocky Balboa
F.I.S.T. (1978) .Johnny Kouak
Paradise Alley (1978). . . . . Cosmo Carboni
Rocky II (1979) . . . . Rocky Balboa
Nighthawks (1981). . . . . Deke De Silva
Victory (1981). Robert Hatch
First Blood (1982) . . . . Rambo
Rocky III (1982). . . . . Rocky Balboa
Rhinestone (1984). . . . . Nick
Rambo: First Blood, Part II (1985) . . . . Rambo
Rocky IV (1985). . . . . Rocky Balboa
Cobra (1986) . . . . Marion Cobretti
Over the Top (1987) . . . . Lincoln Hawk
Lock Up (1989). . . . . Frank

Tango & Cash (1989) . . . . Ray Tango
  •• 0:31—Brief buns while walking into the prison shower room with Kurt Russell.
Rocky V (1990) . . . . .Rocky Balboa
  • 0:03—Side view of buns, while standing in the shower. Long shot.
Oscar (1991) . . . . .Angelo "Snaps" Provolone
Stop! Or My Mom Will Shoot (1992)
  . . . . Joe Bomowski
  • 0:22—Upper half of buns behind shower door when his mom talks to him in the bathroom.
Made for Cable TV:
Dream On: The Second Greatest Story Ever Told
(1991; HBO). . . . . Himself
Magazines:
Playboy (Feb 1980) . . . . The Year in Sex
  • 159—Partial buns in still from *The Italian Stallion*.

• Staskel, James
Films:
An Innocent Man (1989) . . . . n.a.
Video Tapes:
Inside Out 3 (1992). . . . . .Tom/The Houseguest
  •• 1:04—Buns, while getting into bathtub to get cleaned up by Marilyn Hassett.

• Steiner, John
Films:
Beyond the Door II (1977; Italian) . . . . Bruno
  • 0:12—Brief buns, while making love with Dora on the sofa. Dark.
Yor: The Hunter from the Future (1983) . . . . . . Overlord
Cut and Run (1985; Italian) . . . . .Vlado

Stern, Daniel
Films:
Breaking Away (1979) . . . . Cyril
Starting Over (1979) . . . . Student 2
It's My Turn (1980) . . . . Cooperman
A Small Circle of Friends (1980) . . . . .Crazy Kid
  • 1:22—Brief buns, while dropping his pants with several other guys for Army draft inspection.
Stardust Memories (1980) . . . . .Actor
Honky Tonk Freeway (1981). . . . . n.a.
I'm Dancing as Fast as I Can (1981) . . . . .Jim
Diner (1982) . . . . Shrevie
Blue Thunder (1983) . . . . .Lymangood
Get Crazy (1983) . . . . .Neil
C.H.U.D. (1984). . . . . The Reverend
Frankenweenie (1984) . . . . Ben Frankenstein
Key Exchange (1985). . . . . Michael
The Boss' Wife (1986) . . . . .Joel Keefer
Born in East L.A. (1987) . . . . Jimmy
D.O.A. (1988) . . . . Hal Petersham
The Milagro Beanfield War (1988) . . . . Herbie Platt
Friends, Lovers & Lunatics (1989). . . . . Mat
Little Monsters (1989) . . . . Glen Stevenson
Coupe de Ville (1990) . . . . Marvin Libner
Home Alone (1990) . . . . Marv

My Blue Heaven (1990) . . . . Will Stubbs
City Slickers (1991) . . . . Phil Berquist
Made for Cable Movies:
The Court-Martial of Jackie Robinson (1990)
. . . . William Cline
TV:
Hometown (1985) . . . . Joey Nathan

Stevens, Andrew

Son of actress Stella Stevens.
Films:
Massacre at Central High (1976) . . . . .Mark
Vigilante Force (1976) . . . . Paul Sinton
The Boys in Company C (1978) . . . . .Billy Ray Pike
The Fury (1978) . . . . Robin Sandza
Death Hunt (1981) . . . . .Alvin
The Seduction (1982) . . . . Derek
10 to Midnight (1983) . . . . Paul McAnn
Deadly Innocents (1988) . . . . Bob Appling
Red Blooded American Girl (1988)
. . . . Owen Augustus Urban III
The Terror Within (1988) . . . . David
Down the Drain (1989) . . . . Victor Scalia
Night Eyes (1990) . . . . .Will
(Unrated version reviewed.)
••• 1:11—Buns while in the shower.
••• 1:26—Side view of buns with Tanya Roberts seen
through a window.
Night Eyes 2 (1991) . . . . Will Griffith
• 1:07—Partial buns, in mirror, while lying on the floor
with Shannon Tweed.
The Terror Within II (1992) . . . . .David Pennington
TV:
Code Red (1981-82) . . . . Ted Rorchek
Emerald Point N.A.S. (1983-84)
. . . . Lieutenant Glenn Matthews
Dallas (1987-89) . . . . Casey Denault

• Stevenson, Parker

Husband of actress Kirstie Alley.
Films:
Lifeguard (1975) . . . . .Chris
Stroker Ace (1983) . . . . Aubrey James
Stitches (1985) . . . . Bobby Stevens
• 0:04—Brief buns, while chasing people down hall-
way. Don't see face. (He's in the last one.)
Made for Cable TV:
The Hitchhiker: Best Shot (1987; HBO) . . . . .Brett
Miniseries:
North and South, Book II (1986) . . . . Billy Hazard
TV:
The Hardy Boys Mysteries (1977-79) . . . . . . Frank Hardy
Falcon Crest (1984-85) . . . . .Joel McCarthy
Probe (1988) . . . . .Austin James
Baywatch (1989-90) . . . . Craig Pomeroy

• Stewart, Robin

Films:
Damn the Defiant! (1962; British) . . . . .Pardoe
Cromwell (1970; British) . . . . Prince of Wales
Horror House (1970; British) . . . . Henry
The Adventures of a Private Eye (1974; British)
. . . . Scott West
• 0:23—Buns, dancing around after getting caught in
a mousetrap.
• 0:35—Buns, while in boat on top of Clarissa
•• 0:36—Brief full frontal nudity, getting up and diving
off boat.
• 0:58—Buns, while on couch with the Inspector's
Wife.
• 1:17—Buns, while standing in bathroom at Lisa's
place.
Pacific Banana (1980) . . . . n.a.

Sting

Singer with *The Police* and on his own.
Husband of actress Trudi Styler.
Films:
Quadrophenia (1979; British) . . . . The Ace Face
Brimstone and Treacle (1982; British)
. . . . Martin Taylor
• 1:19—Buns, while making love with Suzanna Hamil-
ton on her bed. Dark, hard to see.
Dune (1984) . . . . .Feyd Rautha
The Bride (1985) . . . . Frankenstein
Plenty (1985) . . . . Mick
Julia and Julia (1987; Italian) . . . . Daniel
(This movie was shot using a high-definition video sys-
tem and then transferred to film.)
•• 1:11—Buns, while sleeping in bed when Kathleen
Turner leaves. Don't see his face very well.
Stormy Monday (1988) . . . . Finney

• Stockwell, Guy

Films:
Tobruk (1966) . . . . Lt. Max Mohnfeld
Airport 1975 (1974) . . . . Col. Moss
It's Alive (1974) . . . . Clayton
Santa Sangre (1989; Italian/Spanish) . . . . Orgo
•• 0:38—Buns, several times, when Concha catches
him with the tattooed lady. (He's a heavy guy.)
• 0:39—Buns, lying dead on the ground after he cuts
his own throat.
TV:
Adventures in Paradise (1959-62) . . . . Chris Parker

Stockwell, John

Films:
So Fine (1981) . . . . .Jim
Losin' It (1982) . . . . Spider
Christine (1983) . . . . .Dennis
Eddie and the Cruisers (1983) . . . . Keith
City Limits (1984) . . . . Lee
My Science Project (1985) . . . . Michael Harlan

Dangerously Close (1986) . . . . .Randy McDevill
  • 0:33—Brief buns while in steamy locker room.
Top Gun (1986) . . . . Cougar
Millions (1990) . . . . David Phipps
Miniseries:
North and South (1985) . . . . Billy Hazard

Stokes, Barry
Films:
Happy Housewives . . . . Bob
  • 0:31—Brief buns, while running away from Mrs. Elgin and her daughter in the barn.
Spaced Out (1980; British) . . . . Oliver
  • 0:54—Buns, while undressing to get in bed with
  Prudence.
Alien Prey (1984; British) . . . . Anders
  •• 1:19—Buns, while getting on top of Glory Annen in
  bed.

Stoltz, Eric
Films:
Fast Times at Ridgemont High (1982) . . . . . . Stoner Bud
Surf II (1984). . . . . Chuck
The Wild Life (1984) . . . . Bill Conrad
Code Name: Emerald (1985). . . . . .Andy Wheeler
Mask (1985) . . . . Rocky Dennis
The New Kids (1985) .Mark
Lionheart (1987). . . . . .Robert Nerra
Sister Sister (1987) . . . . Matt Rutledge
Some Kind of Wonderful (1987) . . . . .Keith Nelson
Haunted Summer (1988). . . . . .Percy Shelley
  ••• 0:09—Nude, under the waterfall and walking
  around in the river. Long scene.
Manifesto (1988) . . . . Christopher
  • 1:16—Buns, while helping Camilla unroll Emile in
  the rug.
The Fly II (1989) . . . . Martin
Say Anything (1989) . . . . Vahlere
Memphis Belle (1990). . . . . Danny Daily
The Waterdance (1992) . . . . .Joel
Made for TV Movies:
Paper Dolls (1982) . . . . Steve

Stone, Christopher
Husband of actress Dee Wallace Stone.
Films:
The Grasshopper (1970) . . . . .Jay Rigney
  a.k.a. The Passing of Evil
  0:26—Buns, seen through shower door when Jac-
  queline Bisset comes in to join him.
  • 1:17—Brief buns while lying in bed talking to Bisset.
The Howling (1981) . . . . R. William "Bill" Neill
  • 0:48—Brief buns, rolling over while making love
  with Elizabeth Brooks in front of a campfire.
Cujo (1983) . . . . Steve
The Annihilators (1985). . . . . Bill Esker
Blue Movies (1988). Brad
Miniseries:
Blue and the Gray (1982) . . . . .Major Fairbairn

TV:
The Interns (1970-71) . . . . Dr. Pooch Hardin
Spencer's Pilots (1976) . . . . .Cass Garrett
Harper Valley P.T.A. (1981-82) . . . . Tom Meechum
Dallas (1984) . . . . Dave Stratton

Street, Elliot
Films:
Honky (1971). . . . . n.a.
Welcome Home, Soldier Boys (1972) . . . . .Fat Back
The Harrad Experiment (1973). . . . . .Wilson
  •• 0:44—Frontal nudity taking off clothes and getting
  into the swimming pool.

• Strohmyer, Scott
Films:
The Bikini Carwash Company (1992). . . . .Big Bruce
  (Unrated version reviewed.)
  •• 0:18—Buns, while walking on beach with Rita.

• Sullivan, William Bell
Films:
Diamond Run (1988; Indonesian) . . . . .Nicky
  a.k.a. Java Burn
  •• 0:08—Buns, while lying in bed, then getting up.
The Hunt for Red October (1990)
  . . . . Lt. Cmdr. Mike Hewitt

Sutherland, Donald
Films:
Die, Die, My Darling (1965) . . . . .Joseph
Dr. Terror's House of Horrors (1965). . . . . . . Bob Carroll
The Dirty Dozen (1967) . . . . .Vernon Pinkley
Kelly's Heroes (1970) . . . . .Oddball
M*A*S*H (1970) . . . . Hawkeye Pierce
Start the Revolution Without Me (1970)
  . . . . Charles Coupe/Pierre De Sisi
Johnny Got His Gun (1971) . . . . Jesus Christ
Klute (1971). . . . . John Klute
Don't Look Now (1973) . . . . John Baxter
  • 0:27—Buns, while in the bathroom with Julie
  Christie.
Steelyard Blues (1973) . . . . Jesse Veldini
The Day of the Locust (1975). . . . . .Homer
1900 (1976; Italian) . . . . Attila
The Disappearance (1977). . . . . .Jay
The Eagle Has Landed (1977; British) . . . . . . Liam Devlin
Kentucky Fried Movie (1977) . . . . Clumsy
Animal House (1978) . . . . Dave Jennings
  • 1:22—Buns, while reaching up in kitchen to get
  something when his sweater goes up. Out of focus.
Invasion of the Body Snatchers (1978)
  . . . . Matthew Bennell
The Great Train Robbery (1979). . . . . .Agan
Murder by Decree (1979). . . . . Robert Lees
Bear Island (1980; British/Canadian) . . . . Frank Lansing
Nothing Personal (1980; Canadian)
  . . . . Professor Roger Keller
Ordinary People (1980) . . . . Calvin

Eye of the Needle (1981) .... Faber
Gas (1981; Canadian) .... Nick the Noz
Max Dugan Returns (1983) .... Brian
Threshold (1983; Canadian) .... Dr. Vrain
Crackers (1984)........................ Weslake
Ordeal by Innocence (1984) .... Arthur Calgary
Heaven Help Us (1985) .... Brother Thadeus
Revolution (1986) .... Sergeant Major Peasy
The Rosary Murders (1987) .... Father Koesler
Lock Up (1989) .... Warden Drumgoole
Lost Angels (1989) .... Dr. Charles Loftis
Backdraft (1991) .... Ronald Bartel
Eminent Domain (1991) .... Joseph
JFK (1991)....................... Colonel "X"
Buffy The Vampire Slayer (1992) .... n.a.

Swayze, Patrick

Films:
Skatetown, U.S.A. (1979) ....Ace
The Outsiders (1983) .... Darrel
Uncommon Valor (1983)....................Scott
Grandview, U.S.A. (1984) .... Ernie "Slam" Webster
Red Dawn (1984) .... Jed
Youngblood (1986)................... Derek Sutton
Dirty Dancing (1987) .... Johnny Castle
Steel Dawn (1988) ....Nomad
Tiger Warsaw (1988).......... Chuck "Tiger" Warsaw
Next of Kin (1989) .... Truman Gates
Roadhouse (1989) .... Dalton
  ••• 0:30—Brief buns getting out of bed while Kathleen
    Wilhoite watches.
Ghost (1990) ....Sam Wheat
Point Break (1991) .... Bodhi
City of Joy (1992) .... Max
Miniseries:
North and South (1985) ....Orry Main
North and South, Book II (1986)...........Orry Main
TV:
Renegades (1983).......................Bandit

Tabor, Erin

Films:
I Spit on Your Grave (1978) .... Johnny
  (Uncut, unrated version reviewed.)
  • 0:25—Buns, while undressing to rape Jennifer.
  • 1:20—Buns, while undressing at gun point.

Taylor, Zach

Films:
Group Marriage (1972)....................Phil
  •• 0:43—Buns, while walking on beach with Jan.

Tepper, William

Films:
Drive, He Said (1972) .... Hector
Breathless (1983) .... Paul
Bachelor Party (1984) .... Dr. Stan Gassko

Miss Right (1987; Italian).............Terry Bartell
  • 0:47—Buns, while jumping out of bed with Karen
    Black when the bed catches fire.

Terrell, John Canada

Films:
Recruits (1986; Canadian) ....Winston
She's Gotta Have It (1987).......... Greer Childs
  •• 0:27—Buns and very brief frontal nudity, while get-
    ting into bed with Nola. More quick shots of buns in
    bed.
Rooftops (1989).....................Junkie Cop
Def by Temptation (1990) .... Bartender #1
  •• 0:09—Nude, running through house trying to get
    away from The Temptress.
The Return of Superfly (1990) ...... Detective Loomey
The Five Heartbeats (1991) .... Michael "Flash" Turner

Terry, Nigel

Films:
The Lion in the Winter (1968; British)...... Prince John
Excalibur (1981; British) .... King Arthur
Deja Vu (1984) .... Michel/Greg
  • 1:17—Very brief buns, while jumping out of bed
    when Jaclyn Smith tries to kill him with a knife.
Sylvia (1985; New Zealand) .... Aden Morris
TV:
Covington Cross (1992-).................... Gray

Thompson, Jack

Films:
Libido (1973; Australian) .... Ken
Jock Petersen (1974; Australian) ...... Tony Petersen
  a.k.a. Petersen
  ••• 0:13—Buns, while making love with Wendy Hughes
    on the floor.
  ••• 0:20—Frontal nudity under tarp with Moira during
    protest.
  • 0:22—Buns while in bed with Suzy.
  •• 0:44—Nude running around the beach with Hugh-
    es.
  •• 0:50—Frontal nudity undressing, then buns while ly-
    ing in bed.
Mad Dog Morgan (1976)....... Detective Manwaring
Breaker Morant (1979; Australian) ...Major J. F. Thomas
The Earthling (1980) .... Ross Daley
The Man from Snowy River (1982; Australian) ...Clancy
Merry Christmas, Mr. Lawrence (1983; Japanese/British)
  .... Hicksley-Ellis
Sunday Too Far Away (1983; Australian)........ Foley
Burke and Wills (1985; Australian)
  .... Robert O'Hara Burke
Flesh + Blood (1985) .... Hawkwood
Ground Zero (1988; Australian) .... Trebilcock
Turtle Beach (1992) .... n.a.

Thomsen, Kevin

Films:

Cleo/Leo (1989) . . . . .Bob Miller
   • 1:07—Brief frontal nudity, then buns while making
   love with Jane Hamilton on bed.
Enrapture (1989). . . . . .Keith

Tierney, Aidan

Films:

Family Viewing (1987; Canadian) . . . . .Van
   •• 0:26—Brief buns, while getting up out of bed and
   putting on his underwear.

• Tobias, Oliver

Films:

Romance of a Horse Thief (1971) . . . . . Zanvill Kradnick
'Tis a Pity She's a Whore (1972; Italian) . . . . . . .Giovanni
The Stud (1978; British) . . . . Tony Blake
   • 1:06—Buns, running away from the pool.
The Wicked Lady (1983; British) . . . . Kit Locksby
   • 0:58—Buns, with Caroline in living room.
Mata Hari (1985) . . . . .Ladoux

Torgl, Mark

Films:

The First Turn-On! (1983) . . . . Dwayne
   • 1:02—Buns, while dropping his pants for Michelle.

Torn, Rip

Films:

Payday (1972). . . . . .Maury Dann
   • 1:21—Brief buns while getting up out of bed.
Slaughter (1972). . . . . Hoffo
The Man Who Fell to Earth (1976; British). Nathan Bryce
   (Uncensored version reviewed.)
Coma (1978) . . . . Dr. George
The Seduction of Joe Tynan (1979) . . . . . Senator Kittner
Heartland (1980) . . . . Clyde
One Trick Pony (1980) . . . . Walter Fox
The Beastmaster (1982) . . . . Maax
A Stranger is Watching (1982) . . . . .Artie Taggart
Cross Creek (1983) . . . . Marsh Turner
Flashpoint (1984) . . . . Sheriff Wells
Summer Rental (1985) . . . . Scully
Beer (1986). . . . . Buzz Beckerman
Extreme Prejudice (1987) . . . . . . .Sheriff Hank Pearson
Silence Like Glass (1989). . . . . .Dr. Markowitz
Defending Your Life (1991) . . . . .Bob Diamond
Dolly Dearest (1992) .n.a.
Made for Cable Movies:
Laguna Heat (1987; HBO). . . . . .n.a.
Another Pair of Aces (1991). . . . . Capt. Jack Parsons
   (Video tape includes nude scenes not shown on cable
   TV.)
Made for TV Movies:
Death Hits the Jackpot (1991). . . . . .Leon Lamarr
TV:
The Larry Sanders Show (1992-) . . . . .n.a.

Tovatt, Patrick

Films:

On the Nickel (1980) . . . . n.a.
Ellie (1984) . . . . .Art
   • 1:19—Brief blurry buns while falling down the stairs.

Tubb, Barry

Films:

The Legend of Billie Jean (1985). . . . . Hubie
Mask (1985). . . . . .Dewey
Top Gun (1986) . . . . Henry Ruth
Valentino Returns (1988). . . . . .Wayne Gibbs
   •• 1:15—Buns, while fighting two other guys after skinny dipping with Jenny Wright at night. Very, very
   brief, blurry frontal nudity after getting hit and rolling into the water.
Warm Summer Rain (1989). . . . . Guy
   •• 0:23—Lower frontal nudity getting off Kelly Lynch in
   bed.
   0:25—Side view of buns while dreaming in bed.
   •• 0:58—Frontal nudity kneeling on floor and behind
   the table while washing Lynch.
   • 1:00—Buns while getting washed by Lynch.
   • 1:07—Brief buns while making love with Lynch.
   Quick cuts.
   ••• 1:09—Nude picking up belongings and running out
   of burning house with Lynch.
Guilty by Suspicion (1991). . . . . Jerry Cooper
TV:
Bay City Blues (1983). . . . . Mickey Wagner

• Turturro, John

Films:

Exterminator 2 (1984) . . . . Guy No. 1
The Flamingo Kid (1984) . . . . Ted From Pinky's
Desperately Seeking Susan (1985) . . . . Ray
Gung Ho (1985) . . . . .Willie
To Live and Die in L.A. (1985) . . . . Carl Cody
The Color of Money (1986) . . . . .Julian
Hannah and Her Sisters (1986). . . . . Writer
Off Beat (1986) . . . . Neil Pepper
The Sicilian (1987) . . . . Aspanu Pisciotta
   (Director's uncut version reviewed.)
Five Corners (1988) . . . . Heinz Sabantino
Backtrack (1989) . . . . Pinella
   a.k.a. Catch Fire
Do the Right Thing (1989). . . . . Dino
Men of Respect (1990) . . . . Mike Battaglia
   0:21—Side view of buns, lying in bed with Ruthie.
   • 0:25—Brief upper half of buns, putting on robe and
   leaving room.
   •• 0:45—Buns, while washing blood off himself in
   bathroom with Ruthie's help.
Miller's Crossing (1990) . . . . .Bernie Bernbaum
Mo' Better Blues (1990) . . . . .Moe Flatbush
State of Grace (1990). . . . . .Nick
Barton Fink (1991) . . . . Barton Fink
Brain Donors (1992). . . . . Roland T. Flakfizer

Tyson, Richard
Films:
Three O'Clock High (1987) . . . . .Buddy Revell
Two Moon Junction (1988) . . . . .Perry
- 0:58—Very, very brief buns while wrestling with April in a motel room. Dark, hard to see.

Kindergarten Cop (1990) . . . . .Crisp
Made for Cable TV:
Red Shoe Diaries: Talk To Me (1992; Showtime) . . . Bud
TV:
Hardball (1989-90) . . . . Joe "Kaz" Kaczierowski

Underwood, Jay
Films:
The Boy Who Could Fly (1986) . . . . Eric
The Invisible Kid (1988) . . . . Grover Dunn
- 0:27—Brief buns while running around the school halls after becoming visible with his friend, Milton.

Uncle Buck (1989) . . . . Bug
The Gumshoe Kid (1990) . . . . .Jeff Sherman
To Die For 2 (1991). . . . . Danny
Made for Cable Movies:
Not Quite Human (1987; Disney) . . . . .Chip
Not Quite Human II (1989; Disney). . . . . .Chip
Still Not Quite Human (1992; Disney). . . . . .Chip

Valentine, Scott
Films:
Deadtime Stories (1985) . . . . .Peter
- 0:19—Buns, while getting out of bath.

My Demon Lover (1987). Kaz
Write to Kill (1990) . . . . Clark Sanford
- 1:03—Very brief partial frontal nudity, leaping out of bed.

Homicidal Impulse (1992). . . . . .Tim Casey
a.k.a. Killer Instinct
(Unrated version reviewed.)
Made for Cable Movies:
After the Shock (1990) . . . . .Shannon
The Secret Passion of Robert Clayton (1992; USA)
. . . . Robert Clayton, Jr.
Made for TV Movies:
Perry Mason: The Case of the Fatal Framing (1992)
. . . . .Damian Blakely
TV:
Family Ties (1985-89) . . . . Nick Moore

Van Damme, Jean-Claude
Films:
No Retreat, No Surrender (1986) . . . . . Ivan the Russian
Bloodsport (1987) . . . . Frank
- 0:50—Brief buns while putting underwear on after spending the night with Janice.

Cyborg (1989) . . . . .Gibson Rickenbacker
Kick Boxer (1989) .Kurt Sloane
Death Warrant (1990). . . . . .Louis Burke
Lionheart (1990) . . . . Lyon
- 0:47—Buns, while putting on robe after getting out of bed.

Double Impact (1991). . . . . Chad/Alec
- 1:11—Very brief buns, while making love with Danielle. Dark.

Universal Soldier (1992). . . . . n.a.

Van Hetenryck, Kevin
Films:
Basket Case (1982) . . . . .Duane Bradley
- • 1:21—Frontal nudity, twice, running around at night.

Basket Case 2 (1989) . . . . .Duane Bradley
- 0:34—Buns while standing in front of mirror looking at the large scar on the side of his body.

Basket Case 3: The Progeny (1991) . . . . .Duane Bradley

Van Hoffman, Brant
Films:
Police Academy (1984) . . . . .Kyle Blankes
The Further Adventures of Tennessee Buck (1987)
. . . . .Ken Manchester
- 0:38—Brief buns, behind a mosquito net while making love with his disinterested wife.

Guilty by Suspicion (1991). . . . . Stanley

• Van Patten, Nels
Films:
Lunch Wagon (1981) . . . . Scotty
The Young Warriors (1983; U.S./Canadian) . . . . . Roger
One Last Run (1990) .Charlie
Mirror Images (1991) . . . . .Joey Zoom
- • 0:08—Buns, while in bed and getting out of bed with Shauna.
- • 0:29—Buns, while on top of Kaitlin.

Live Wire (1992). . . . . Racquetball Player

Van Tongeren, Hans
Films:
Spetters (1980; Dutch) . . . . .Ron Hartman
- ••• 0:35—Frontal nudity, measuring and comparing his manlihood with his friends in the auto shop.

Summer Lovers (1982). . . . . Jan Tolin

• Vazquez, Yul
Made for Cable TV:
Tales From the Crypt: On a Dead Man's Chest
(1992; HBO). . . . . Danny
- ••• 0:06—Buns, while making love on top of Sherrie Rose, then getting out of bed.

Ventura, Clyde
Films:
Bury Me an Angel (1972). . . . . Bernie
Gator Bait (1973). . . . . n.a.
Terminal Island (1973) . . . . Dillon
- •• 0:42—Buns, while taking off pants in front of Phyllis Davis, then covered with honey and bees, then running to jump into a pond.

Serial (1980) . . . . Donald

Villard, Tom

Films:

Parasite (1982) . . . . Zeke
Surf II (1984). . . . . Jacko O'Finlay
Heartbreak Ridge (1986) . . . . Profile
The Trouble with Dick (1986) . . . . Dick Kendred
  0:30—Side view of buns, while leaving Haley's room.
  • 0:58—Buns from under his shirt, getting out of bed to open the door.
Weekend Warriors (1986) . . . . Mort Seblinsky
My Girl (1991) . . . . Justin
Popcorn (1991). . . . . Toby
Whore (1991) . . . . Hippy
  a.k.a. If you're afraid to say it... Just see it
TV:
We Got It Made (1983-84) . . . . Jay Bostwick

Vincent, Jan-Michael

Films:

Going Home (1971) . . . . Jimmy Graham
The Mechanic (1972) . . . . .Steve McKenna
The World's Greatest Athlete (1973) . . . . Nanu
Buster and Billie (1974) . . . . .Buster Lane
  ••• 1:06—Frontal nudity taking off his underwear and walking to Billie. Buns, in slow motion, while swinging into the water.
Bite the Bullet (1975) . . . . .Carbo
White Line Fever (1975) . . . . .Carrol Jo Hummer
Baby Blue Marine (1976). . . . . Marion Hedgepeth
Vigilante Force (1976). . . . . Ben Arnold
Damnation Alley (1977) . . . . Tanner
Big Wednesday (1978) . . . . Matt
Hooper (1978) . . . . Ski
Defiance (1980) . . . . .Tommy
The Return (1980). Deputy
Hard Country (1981) . . . . Kyle Richardson
Born in East L.A. (1987). . . . . McCalister
Enemy Territory (1987) . . . . .Parker
Deadly Embrace (1989). . . . . .Stewart Morland
Alienator (1990) . . . . Commander
Demonstone (1990) . . . . Andrew Buck
Hangfire (1990) . . . . .Hawks
Haunting Fear (1990) . . . . .James Trent
The Divine Enforcer (1991) . . . . Father Thomas
Raw Nerve (1991). . . . . Bruce Ellis
Xtro 2, The Second Encounter (1991)
  . . . . Dr. Ron Shepherd
Miniseries:
The Winds of War (1983) . . . . Byron Henry
TV:
The Survivors (1969-70) . . . . .Jeffrey Hastings
Airwolf (1984-86) . . . . .Stringfellow Hawke
Magazines:
Playboy (Nov 1974) . . . . Sex in Cinema 1974
  • 154—Frontal nudity in very blurry still from *Buster and Billie.*
Playboy (Dec 1974). . . . . Sex Stars of 1974
  ••• 210—Full frontal nudity.

• Vogel, Jack

Films:

Demon Wind (1990) . . . . Stacey
Presumed Guilty (1990) . . . . .Jessie Weston
  •• 0:19—Buns, while getting out of the shower.
Lock n' Load (1991). . . . . Paul McMillan

Voight, Jon

Films:

Midnight Cowboy (1969). . . . . Joe Buck
  • 0:00—Very brief side view of buns, picking up bar of soap from the shower floor.
  • 0:20—Brief buns, while running into bedroom and jumping onto bed with Sylvia Miles.
  • 0:50—Very brief buns, during struggle with a group of men. More buns when they hold his legs.
  • 1:32—Buns, while in bed with Brenda Vaccaro.
Catch-22 (1970) . . . . Milo Minderbinder
Deliverance (1972). . . . . Ed
The All-American Boy (1973) . . . . .Vic Bealer
Conrack (1974) . . . . Pat Conroy
The Odessa File (1974; British). . . . . Peter Miller
Coming Home (1978) . . . . .Luke Martin
  (Academy Award for Best Actor.)
The Champ (1979) . . . . .Bill
Table for Five (1983) . . . . J. P. Tannen
Runaway Train (1985) . . . . .Manny
Desert Bloom (1986) .Jack
Made for Cable Movies:
The Last of His Tribe (1992; HBO) . . . . Dr. Kroeber

Vu-An, Eric

Films:

The Sheltering Sky (1990) . . . . Belqassim
  • 1:59—Buns, while rolling over in bed with Debra Winger. Long shot, don't see his face.

• Wallace, Eric

Video Tapes:

Intimate Workout For Lovers (1992)
  . . . . Romantic Relaxation
  ••• 0:01—Nude, in bedroom, in bathtub and in bed.

Walsh, M. Emmet

Films:

Alice's Restaurant (1969) . . . . .Group W Sergeant
Serpico (1973) . . . . .Gallagher
Slap Shot (1977) .Dickie Dunn
Straight Time (1978) . . . . .Earl Frank
  • 0:47—Buns, while handcuffed to fence in the middle of the road with his pants down.
The Fish That Saved Pittsburgh (1979)
  . . . . Wally Cantrell
The Jerk (1979) . . . . Madman
Fast Walking (1981) . . . . Sgt. George Sager
  • 0:59—Frontal nudity standing in the doorway of Evie's mobile home yelling at James Woods after he interrupts Walsh making love with Evie.
Blade Runner (1982) . . . . Bryant

Scandalous (1983) . . . . Simon Reynolds
Blood Simple (1984) . . . . .Private Detective
Missing in Action (1984) . . . . Tuck
Fletch (1985) . . . . Dr. Dolan
Back to School (1986) . . . . .Coach Turnbull
The Best of Times (1986) . . . . Charlie
Critters (1986) . . . . Harv
Wildcats (1986) . . . . .Coes
Harry and the Hendersons (1987) . . . . George, Sr.
Clean and Sober (1988) . . . . Richard Dirks
The Milagro Beanfield War (1988) . . . . Governor
Sunset (1988) . . . . .Chief Dibner
Catch Me... If You Can (1989) . . . . . .Johnny Phatmun
The Mighty Quinn (1989) . . . . Miller
Red Scorpion (1989) . . . . .Dewey Ferguson
Sundown: The Vampire in Retreat (1989) . . . . . . .Mort
Thunderground (1989) . . . . Wedge
Chattahoochee (1990) . . . . .Morris
Narrow Margin (1990) . . . . . . Sergeant Dominick Benti
Killer Image (1991) . . . . .John Kane
White Sands (1992) . . . . Bert Gibson
Made for Cable Movies:
The Fourth Story (1990; Showtime) . . . . Harry
Miniseries:
The Right of the People (1986) . . . . .Mayor
Brotherhood of the Rose (1989) . . . . Hardy
Made for TV Movies:
Love & Lies (1990) . . . . .Clyde Wilson
TV:
The Sandy Duncan Show (1972) . . . . Alex Lembeck
Dear Detective (1979) . . . . Capt. Gorcey
East of Eden (1981) . . . . Sheriff Quinn
UNSUB (1989) . . . . Ned

• Walter, Tracey
Films:
Goin' South (1978) . . . . Coogan
Hardcore (1979) . . . . Main Teller
The Hunter (1980) . . . . Rocco Mason
Honkytonk Man (1982) . . . . .Pooch
Timerider (1983) . . . . Carl Dorsett
Conan the Destroyer (1984) . . . . Malak
Repo Man (1984) . . . . Miller
At Close Range (1986) . . . . Patch
Something Wild (1986) . . . . The Country Squire
Malone (1987) . . . . Calvin Bollard
Batman (1989) . . . . .Bob the Goon
Homer & Eddie (1989) . . . . Tommy Dearly
Under the Boardwalk (1989) . . . . Bum
Delusion (1990) . . . . .Bus Ticket Cashier
Pacific Heights (1990) . . . . .Exterminator
Silence of the Lambs (1990) . . . . .Lamar
The Two Jakes (1990) . . . . .Tyrone Otley
Young Guns II (1990) . . . . Beever Smith
City Slickers (1991) . . . . Cookie
  • 1:16—Very brief buns, mooning everybody while
    riding stagecoach. Happy face painted on his rear.
    Hard to tell if it's him.
Liquid Dreams (1992) .Cecil

Warburton, Patrick
Films:
Master of Dragonard Hill (1987) . . . .Richard Abdee
  0:07—Very brief buns in mirror. Hard to see.

Ward, Fred
Films:
Escape from Alcatraz (1979) . . . . .John Anglin
Southern Comfort (1981) . . . . .Reece
The Right Stuff (1983) . . . . Gus Grissom
Timerider (1983) . . . . Lyle Swann
Uncommon Valor (1983) . . . . Wilkes
Silkwood (1984) . . . . Morgan
Swing Shift (1984) . . . . Biscuits Toohey
Remo Williams: The Adventure Begins (1985)
. . . . .Remo Williams
Secret Admirer (1985) . . . . .Lou Fimple
Big Business (1988) . . . . .Roone Dimmick
Off Limits (1988) . . . . Dix
The Prince of Pennsylvania (1988) . . . . Gary
Backtrack (1989) . . . . Pauling
a.k.a. Catch Fire
Tremors (1989) . . . . Eal Bass
Henry & June (1990) . . . . .Henry Miller
  ••• 1:39—Buns, twice, while making love with Maria de
    Madeiros.
Miami Blues (1990) . . . . Sergeant Hoke Moseley
The Player (1992) . . . . n.a.
Thunderheart (1992) . . . . Jack Milton
Made for Cable Movies:
Cast a Deadly Spell (1991; HBO) . . . .H. Phillip Lovecraft
Made for Cable TV:
The Hitchhiker: Dead Heat (1987; HBO) . . . . Luther

Ward, Wally
Films:
Weird Science (1985) .A Weenie
Thunder Run (1986) . . . . .Paul
The Chocolate War (1988) . . . . Archie
The Invisible Kid (1988) . . . . .Milton McClane
  • 0:27—Brief buns while running around the school
    halls after becoming visible with his friend, Grover.
TV:
Fast Times (1986) .Mark Ratner

Warden, Jack
Films:
You're in the Army Now (1951) . . . . Morse
The Man Who Loved Cat Dancing (1973) . . . . . . Dawes
Shampoo (1975) . . . . .Lester Carr
All the President's Men (1976) . . . . Harry Rosenfeld
Death on the Nile (1978; British) . . . . Dr. Bessner
Heaven Can Wait (1978) . . . . Max Corkle
...and Justice for All (1979) . . . . Judge Rayford
Being There (1979) . . . . President Bobby
Beyond the Poseidon Adventure (1979)
. . . . Harold Meredith
The Champ (1979) . . . . .Jackie
Used Cars (1980) . . . . Roy L. Fuchs/Luke Fuchs

Chu Chu and the Philly Flash (1981) . . . . . . Commander
So Fine (1981) . . . . Jack
The Verdict (1982) . . . . Mickey Morrissey
Crackers (1984). . . . . Garvey
Problem Child (1990) . . . . "Big" Ben Healy
• 1:07—Buns, on TV in bar, mooning into the camera
when he doesn't know it is on. (Yes, it is him.)
Problem Child II (1991). . . . . "Big" Ben Healy
Passed Away (1992) . . . . .n.a.
TV:
The Bad News Bears (1979-80) . . . . Morris Buttermaker
Crazy Like a Fox (1984-86) . . . . Harry Fox

Warren, Michael

Films:
Butterflies Are Free (1972). . . . . .Roy
Drive, He Said (1972). . . . . .Easly Jefferson
• 0:09—Buns and very brief frontal nudity in the
shower room with the other basketball players.
Cleopatra Jones (1973) .Andy
Fast Break (1979) . . . . Preacher
Heaven is a Playground (1991) . . . . Byron Harper
TV:
Sierra (1974). . . . . Ranger P.J. Lewis
Paris (1979-80) . . . . Willie Miller
Hill Street Blues (1981-87). . . . . Officer Bobby Hill

• Washington, Denzel

Films:
Carbon Copy (1981). Roger
A Soldier's Story (1984). . . . . .Pfc. Peterson
Power (1986) . . . . Arnold Billings
Cry Freedom (1987; British) . . . . .Steve Biko
• 1:05—Side view of buns, while lying on the floor af-
ter getting beat up. Dark, hard to see anything.
• 1:07—Buns again. Dark.
1:26—Buns in B&W photo. Supposed to be him, but
probably not. Don't see face.
Glory (1989). . . . . .Trip
The Mighty Quinn (1989). . . . . .Xavier
Heart Condition (1990). . . . . Napoleon Stone
Mo' Better Blues (1990) . . . . .Bleek Gilliam
Ricochet (1991) . . . . Nick Styles
• 0:13—Very brief frontal nudity in locker room when
Lindsay Wagner comes to talk.
Mississippi Masala (1992) . . . . .Demetrius
TV:
St. Elsewhere (1982-88) . . . . .Dr. Phillip Chandler

• Wass, Ted

Films:
Curse of the Pink Panther (1983). . . . . Clifton Sleigh
Oh God, You Devil! (1984) . . . . Bobby Shelton
Sheena (1984). . . . . Vic Casey
• 1:48—Buns, after getting pulled out of the ground
after tribal healing ceremony.
Long Shot (1986) . . . . Stump
Made for TV Movies:
Pancho Barnes (1988) . . . . Frank Clarke

TV:
Soap (1977-81) . . . . Danny Dallas
Men (1989) . . . . .Dr. Steven Ratajkowski
Blossom (1991-) . . . . .Nick Russo

Wasson, Craig

Films:
Rollercoaster (1977). . . . . Hippie
The Boys in Company C (1978) . . . . .Dave Bisbee
Go Tell the Spartans (1978)
. . . . .Corporal Stephen Courcey
Carny (1980) . . . . .Mickey
Schizoid (1980) . . . . .Doug
Four Friends (1981) . . . . .Danilo Prozor
Ghost Story (1981) . . . . .Don/David
•• 0:08—Brief frontal nudity falling out the window,
then buns, while landing next to the pool.
• 0:41—Buns, while making love with Alice Krige in
bedroom.
Second Thoughts (1983) . . . . Will
Body Double (1984). . . . . .Jake
The Men's Club (1986) . . . . .Paul
A Nightmare on Elm Street 3: The Dream Warriors
(1987) . . . . Dr. Neil Goldman
Made for TV Movies:
Skag (1980) . . . . David Skagska
Why Me? (1984) . . . . n.a.
TV:
Phyllis (1977). . . . . Mark Valenti

Waters, John

Films:
The Adventures of Eliza Fraser (1976; Australian)
. . . . Dave Bracefell
• 0:27—Side view of buns, while undressing and getting into bed.
•• 0:29—Nude, walking around outside. Buns, while
standing in doorway.
•• 0:32—Brief pubic hair, then buns while getting off
bed to hide under it.
0:34—Upper half of buns, while in bed on top of Susannah York.
•• 0:38—Buns, while jumping on York, then getting
pushed out the door.

Waterston, Sam

Films:
Savages (1972) . . . . .James
The Great Gatsby (1974) . . . . Nick Carraway
Rancho Deluxe (1975) . . . . Cecil Colson
Capricorn One (1978) . . . . .Peter Willis
Eagle's Wing (1978; British) . . . . White Bull
Interiors (1978) . . . . Mike
Heaven's Gate (1980). . . . . Canton
Hopscotch (1980) . . . . Cutter
Sweet William (1980; British) . . . . William
• 0:27—Buns, seen through a window in the door,
standing on balcony with Jenny Agutter.
The Killing Fields (1984). . . . . .Sydney Schanberg

411

Warning Sign (1985)....................Cal Morse
Just Between Friends (1986)......... Harry Crandall
September (1987)........................Peter
Welcome Home (1989)................... Woody
The Man in the Moon (1991)........ Matthew Trant
Mindwalk (1991) ....Jack Edwards
Made for Cable Movies:
Finnegan Begin Again (1985)....................n.a.
The Nightmare Years (1989)................William
Miniseries:
Q.E.D. (1982)................. Quentin E. Deverill
TV:
I'll Fly Away (1991-).................Forrest Bedford

Waybill, John "Fee"
Lead singer of *The Tubes.*
Films:
Ladies and Gentlemen, The Fabulous Stains (1982)
...................................Lou Corpse
(Not available on video tape.)
Video Tapes:
Red Hot Rock (1984)....................Himself
••• 0:13—Nude, getting dressed in locker room during "Sports Fans" by The Tubes.
• 0:29—Buns, in G-string S&M outfit during "Mondo Bondage" by The Tubes.

Weaving, Hugo
Films:
The Right Hand Man (1987)............ Ned Devine
...Almost (1990; Australian).................. Jake
0:52—Very brief out of focus buns when he drops his pants in front of Rosanna Arquette. Don't see his face. Note in the very next scene, he's wearing underwear!

Wehe, Oliver
Films:
Erendira (1983; Brazilian)................. Ulysses
• 1:24—Buns, while getting into bed with Erendira.

• Welker, Michael
Films:
Drop Dead Fred (1991)........ Waiter at Wine Gala
• 1:12—Buns, when toga falls off while he's carrying trays.

Weller, Peter
Films:
Just Tell Me What You Want (1980)
.... Steven Routledge
Shoot the Moon (1982)........... Frank Henderson
Of Unknown Origin (1983; Canadian).... Bart Hughes
The Adventures of Buckaroo Banzai, Across the 8th Dimension (1984)............... Buckaroo Banzai
Firstborn (1984)........................ Sam
Robocop (1987)............ Alex Murphy/Robocop
The Tunnel (1987)................ Juan Pablo

Cat Chaser (1988)................George Moran
•• 0:24—Very, very brief frontal nudity, twice when he is kneeling and takes his pants off. Buns, while making love on top of Kelly McGillis.
Shakedown (1988)................... Roland Dalton
Leviathan (1989)..................... William Beck
Robocop 2 (1990)...........Alex Murphy/Robocop
Naked Lunch (1991)....................Bill Lee
Road to Ruin (1992)................. Jack Sloan
Made for Cable Movies:
Apology (1986; HBO)..............Rad Hungare
• 1:04—Brief buns, while putting pants on, getting out of bed to chase after intruder at night.
Rainbow Drive (1990; Showtime)...... Mike Gallagher
Women & Men: Stories of Seduction (1990; HBO)
.... Hobie

Welsh, Kenneth
Films:
Covergirl (1982; Canadian)....... Harrison Chandler
• 1:23—Brief buns, while seen on video tape used to get him in trouble. Long shot.
Of Unknown Origin (1983; Canadian).........James
Falling In Love (1984) ....Doctor
Heartburn (1986)..................... Dr. Appel
The House on Carroll Street (1988)......... Hackett
Physical Evidence (1989) ....Harry Norton
The Freshman (1990)...........Dwight Armstrong
The Big Slice (1991)..................Lt. Bernard

Weston, Jack
Films:
Fuzz (1972)................ Detective Meyer Meyer
Gator (1976)................... Irving Greenfield
The Ritz (1976)............... Gaetano Proclo
Can't Stop the Music (1980)......... Benny Murray
Four Seasons (1981)............. Danny Zimmer
• 0:48—Brief buns in water while skinny dipping with Rita Moreno.
High Road to China (1983) ....Struts
Dirty Dancing (1987).............. Max Kellerman
Ishtar (1987) ....Marty Freed
Short Circuit 2 (1988)............... Oscar Baldwin

Whiting, Leonard
Films:
Romeo and Juliet (1968) ....Romeo
•• 1:34—Buns, while in bed with Juliet, then getting out to stretch. Long scene.

• Wilborn, Carlton
Films:
Without You I'm Nothing (1990)....... Ballet Dancer
Truth or Dare (1991) .... Dancer
1:39—Frontal nudity showing himself to Madonna. Dark, hard to see. B&W.
1:43—Very brief frontal nudity getting into bed with Madonna. Too dark to see anything. B&W.
• 1:45—Brief buns, while in bed with Madonna. B&W.

Wilby, James

Films:

Maurice (1987; British) . . . . Maurice Hall
A Handful of Dust (1988) . . . . Tony Last
A Summer Story (1988) . . . . Frank Ashton
   • 0:08—Buns, in creek with Mr. Garten while skinny
    dipping.
Made for TV Movies:
Masterpiece Theatre: Adam Bede (1992)
   .Capt. Arthur Donnithorne

Wilder, Gene

Films:

The Producers (1968) . . . . Leo Bloom
Quackser Fortune has a Cousin in the Bronx (1970; Irish)
   . . . . Quackser Fortune
Start the Revolution Without Me (1970)
   . . . . Claude Coupe/Philippe De Sisi
Willy Wonka and the Chocolate Factory (1971)
   . . . . Willy Wonka
Blazing Saddles (1974) . . . . Jim
The Little Prince (1974; British) . . . . The Fox
Young Frankenstein (1974) . . . . Dr. Frankenstein
The Adventure of Sherlock Holmes' Smarter Brother
  (1975) . . . . Sigerson Holmes
Silver Streak (1976) . . . . George Caldwell
The World's Greatest Lover (1977) . . . . . Rudy Valentine
The Frisco Kid (1979) . . . . Avram Belinsky
Stir Crazy (1980) . . . . Skip Donahue
Hanky Panky (1982) . . . . Michael Jordon
The Woman in Red (1984) . . . . Theodore Pierce
   • 1:15—Side view of buns while getting back into bed
    with Kelly Le Brock after getting out to take his un-
    derwear off the lamp.
Haunted Honeymoon (1986) . . . . Larry Abbot
See No Evil, Hear No Evil (1989) . . . . .Dave
Funny About Love (1990) . . . . Duffy Bergman
Another You (1991)
   . . . . George Washington/Abe Fielding

• Wilder, James

Films:

Zombie High (1987) . . . . .Barry
Murder One (1988; Canadian) . . . . .Carl Isaacs
Scorchers (1992) . . . . .n.a.
Made for Cable Movies:
Prey of the Chameleon (1992; Showtime) . . . . . .J.D.
   • 0:32—Upper half of buns, while getting out of bed.
TV:
Equal Justice (1990-91) . . . . .Christopher Searls

Williams, Jason

Films:

Time Walker (1982) . . . . Jeff
Down and Out in Beverly Hills (1986) . . . . Lance
Danger Zone II: Reaper's Revenge (1988)
   . . . . Wade
   •• 0:06—Buns, while getting out of bed and putting
    pants on.

Vampire at Midnight (1988) . . . . .Detective Roger Sutter
Danger Zone III: Steel Horse War (1991)
   . . . . .Wade Olsen

• Williams, Robin

Films:

Can I Do It 'Til I Need Glasses? (1976) . . . . n.a.
Popeye (1980) . . . . Popeye
World According to Garp (1982) . . . . .T.S. Garp
The Survivors (1983) . . . . Donald Quinelle
Moscow on the Hudson (1984) . . . . Vladimir Ivanoff
The Best of Times (1986) . . . . Jack Dundee
Club Paradise (1986) . . . . Jack Moniker
Good Morning, Vietnam (1987) . . . . . . Adrian Cronauer
The Adventures of Baron Munchausen (1989)
   . . . . King of the Moon
Dead Poets Society (1989) . . . . John Keating
Cadillac Man (1990) . . . . Joey O'Brien
Awakenings (1991) . . . . Dr. Malcolm Sayer
Dead Again (1991) . . . . Dr. Cozy Carlisle
The Fisher King (1991) . . . . Parry
   ••• 0:58—Nude, dancing around in the park at night
    with Jeff Bridges.
Hook (1991) . . . . Peter Pan/Peter Banning
TV:
Mork & Mindy (1978-82) . . . . Mork

Williams, Treat

Films:

The Ritz (1976) . . . . .Michael Brick
The Eagle Has Landed (1977; British)
   . . . . Captain Happy Clark
1941 (1979) . . . . .Sitarski
Hair (1979) . . . . Berger
   • 0:57—Buns, while taking off clothes and diving into
    pond with Hud and Woof.
Why Would I Lie? (1980) . . . . Cletus
Prince of the City (1981) . . . . Daniel Ciello
Pursuit of D.B. Cooper (1981) . . . . .Meade
Flashpoint (1984) . . . . Ernie
   •• 0:03—Buns, putting on pants in locker room while
    talking to Kris Kristofferson.
Once Upon a Time in America (1984) . Jimmy O'Donnell
  (Long version reviewed.)
Smooth Talk (1985) . . . . .Arnold Friend
The Men's Club (1986) . . . . Terry
Dead Heat (1988) . . . . Roger Mortis
Heart of Dixie (1989) . . . . Hoyt
Sweet Lies (1989) . . . . Peter
   0:52—Side view of buns while in bed with Joanna
    Pacula. Very, very brief, blurry frontal nudity getting
    out of bed. Don't really see anything.
Made for Cable Movies:
Third Degree Burn (1989; HBO) . . . . Scott Weston
   • 0:43—Brief buns while taking off his robe with Vir-
    ginia Madsen in his bedroom.
The Water Engine (1992; TNT) . . . . Dave Murray

Made for Cable TV:
Tales From the Crypt: None but the Lonely Heart
(1992; HBO) . . . . .n.a.
TV:
Eddie Dodd (1991) . . . . Eddie Dodd

• Williamson, Fred

Films:
Black Caesar (1973) . . . . .Tommy Gibbs
Hell Up in Harlem (1973) . . . . .Tommy Gibbs
••• 0:42—Buns, while in bed making love with Marga-
ret Avery.
That Man Bolt (1973) . . . . Jefferson Bolt
Boss*(1974). . . . . Boss Nigger
a.k.a. Boss Nigger
Three the Hard Way (1974). . . . . .Jagger Daniels
Adios Amigo (1975) . . . . .Ben
Bucktown (1975) . . . . .Duke
Take a Hard Ride (1975; U.S./Italian). . . . . Tyree
Mean Johnny Barrows (1976) . . . . Johnny Barrows
One Down, Two to Go (1982) . . . . Cal
The Big Score (1983) . . . . Frank Hooks
The Bronx Warriors (1983; Italian). . . . . The Ogre
Vigilante (1983) . . . . Nick
Foxtrap (1986; U.S./Italian). . . . . Thomas Fox
The Messenger (1987; Italian). . . . Jake Sebastian Turner
Delta Force Commando 2 (1991) . . . . . Capt. Sam Beck
Miniseries:
Wheels (1978). . . . . Leonard Wingate
TV:
Julia (1970-71) .Steve Bruce
Half Nelson (1985) . . . . Chester Long

• Wilson, Dorien

Made for Cable TV:
Dream On: Come and Knock On Our Door...
(1992; HBO) . . . . Eddie Charles
•• 0:16—Buns, while getting out of bed in hotel room
with Martin.

Wilson, Lambert

Films:
Chanel Solitaire (1981) . . . . .n.a.
Sahara (1984). . . . . .Jaffar
Red Kiss (1985; French). . . . . Stephane
Rendez-Vous (1986; French). . . . . Quentin
• 0:22—Very brief buns, while falling with Juliet onto
net during play.
The Belly of an Architect (1987; British/Italian)
. . . . Caspasian Speckler
•• 0:56—Buns, several time in room with Chloe Webb
while Brian Dennehy watches through keyhole.
• 1:04—Upper half of buns, while lying in bed with
Webb. Long shot.

Wilson, Robert Brian

Films:
Silent Night, Deadly Night (1984). . . . . . . Billy at 18
• 0:30—Sort of buns while in bed with Pamela.

Wilson, Roger

Husband of model Christy Turlington.
Films:
Blow Out (1981) . . . . Coed Lover
Porky's (1981; Canadian) . . . . .Mickey
Thunder Alley (1985). . . . . Richie
Second Time Lucky (1986). . . . . Adam Smith
•• 0:13—Buns, while in the Garden of Eden.
•• 0:30—Buns, while standing out in the rain.
TV:
Seven Brides for Seven Brothers (1982-83)
. . . . Daniel McFadden

Winchester, Jeff

Films:
Olivia (1983) . . . . Richard
a.k.a. A Taste of Sin
• 1:17—Buns, while getting stuffed into trunk by Olivia. Dark.

Winn, David

Films:
My Therapist (1983) . . . . .Mike Jenner
•• 0:19—Buns, while making love with Marilyn Chambers in bed.

• Wolf, Axel

Video Tapes:
Sexy Lingerie III (1991) . . . . Additional Cast
Intimate Workout For Lovers (1992)
. . . . .Sensual Exercise
••• 0:11—Nude, exercising in living room and exercise
room.

Woltz, Randy

Films:
The Young Warriors (1983; U.S./Canadian)
. . . . "Brick Test" Frank
• 0:16—Dropping his pants in a room during pledge
at fraternity.

Wood, Timothy

Films:
Love Circles Around the World (1984) . . . . Michael
•• 1:29—Frontal nudity, lying in bed with Jill after making love while video taping it.

Woods, James

Films:
Hickey and Boggs (1972). . . . . Lt. Wyatt
The Visitors (1972). . . . . Bill Schmidt
The Way We Were (1973). . . . . Frankie McVeigh
The Gambler (1974) . . . . Bank Officer
Distance (1975). . . . . Larry
Night Moves (1975). . . . . .Quentin
The Choirboys (1977) . . . . Bloomguard
The Onion Field (1979). . . . . Gregory Powell
•• 1:33—Buns, while taking a shower in the prison.
The Black Marble (1980) . . . . .Fiddler

Eyewitness (1981) . . . . Aldo
Fast Walking (1981) . . . . Fast-Walking Miniver
Split Image (1982) . . . . Prattt
Videodrome (1983; Canadian) . . . . .Max Renn
Against All Odds (1984) . . . . Jake Wise
Once Upon a Time in America (1984) . . . . Max
　(Long version reviewed.)
Cat's Eye (1985) . . . . .Morrison
Joshua Then and Now (1985; Canadian)
　. . . . . Joshua Shapiro
Salvador (1986) . . . . Richard Boyle
Best Seller (1988) . . . . Cleve
Cop (1988). . . . . .Lloyd Hopkins
The Boost (1989) . . . . Lenny Brown
Immediate Family (1989) . . . . Michael Spector
True Believer (1989) . . . . Eddie Dodd
The Hard Way (1991) . . . . .John Moss
Diggstown (1992). . . . . .n.a.
Straight Talk (1992). . . . . Jack
Made for Cable Movies:
Women & Men: Stories of Seduction (1990; HBO)
　. . . . . Robert
Citizen Cohn (1992; HBO) . . . . .Roy Marcus Cohn
Miniseries:
Holocaust (1978) . . . . Karl Weiss
Made for TV Movies:
My Name is Bill W. (1989). . . . . .Bill Wilson
The Boys (1991) .Walter Farmer

Woods, Michael

Films:
Lady Beware (1987). . . . . Jack Price
　•• 0:43—Buns, while lying down in Diane Lane's bed.
FX 2 (1991). . . . . Second Mobster
Made for Cable TV:
Red Shoe Diaries: Double Dare (1992; Showtime)
　. . . . . .n.a.
Made for TV Movies:
Double Edge (1992) . . . . Paul
TV:
Bare Essence (1983) . . . . .Sean Benedict
Our Family Honor (1985-86). . . . . . . Jerry Cole (Danzig)
Capital News (1990) . . . . Clay Gibson

Wright, Dorsey

Films:
Hair (1979) . . . . Hud
　• 0:57—Buns, while taking off clothes and diving into
　　pond with Treat Williams and Woof.
Ragtime (1981). . . . . .n.a.
The Hotel New Hampshire (1984). . . . . Junior Jones

• Wright, Edward

Films:
Necromancer (1988) . . . . Carl Caulder
　• 0:41—Buns, while taking off his towel and walking
　　into shower.

• Wright, Ken

Films:
Skatetown, U.S.A. (1979). . . . . .n.a.
Opposing Force (1986). . . . . .Conway
　a.k.a. Hell Camp
　• 0:33—Brief buns, while getting his poncho after be-
　　ing sprayed with water and dusted with white pow-
　　der.
The Hanoi Hilton (1987) . . . . Kennedy

Wright, Patrick

Films:
Young Lady Chatterley (1977)
　. . . . . Flash Back Gardener
　••• 0:02—Nude, washing himself, outside while Lady
　　Frances Chatterley watches.
　• 0:05—Buns, while in house with Lady Chatterley.
　• 0:06—More buns, while on the floor.
　• 0:33—Buns, with Lady Chatterley by the pond.

• Yaari, Yossi

Films:
Auditions (1978) . . . . Moshe Mitzvah
　• 1:10—Buns, while taking off his clothes during orgy
　　scene.

• Young Evans, Mitchell

Video Tapes:
Inside Out 4 (1992) . . . . .Dave/Video Mate
　(Unrated version reviewed.)
　• 1:17—Buns, with Sharon Kane in his living room in
　　fast speed.

• Young, Aden

Films:
Black Robe (1991; Canadian/Australian) . . . . . . Daniel
　• 0:18—Brief side view of buns, while hanging his rear
　　end over the side of the canoe.
　• 1:04—Buns, while standing in Iroquois hut.

Youngs, Jim

Films:
The Wanderers (1979) . . . . Buddy
Footloose (1984) . . . . Chuck
Out of Control (1984). . . . . .Cowboy
　• 0:54—Buns, while making love with Claudia Udy.
Hot Shot (1986). . . . . n.a.
Nobody's Fool (1986) . . . . Billy
Youngblood (1986) . . . . Kelly Youngblood
You Talkin' To Me (1987) . . . . Bronson Green

Yurasek, John

Films:
Less than Zero (1987). . . . . Naked Man
　• 1:22—Brief buns while standing up when Andrew
　　McCarthy discovers him with Robert Downey, Jr.

Zane, Billy

Husband of actress Lisa Zane.

Films:

Back to the Future (1985) . . . . .Match
Critters (1986) . . . . Steve Elliot
Back to the Future, Part II (1989). . . . . .Match
Dead Calm (1989) . . . . Hughie Warriner
  • 1:01—Buns, while walking around on the boat.
Femme Fatale (1990) . . . . Elijah Hooper
Memphis Belle (1990). . . . . "Val" Valentine
Millions (1990) . . . . Maurizo Ferreti
Blood & Concrete: A Love Story (1991) . . . . . Joey Turks

Made for TV Movies:

The Case of the Hillside Strangler (1989)
. . . . Kenneth Bianchi

TV:

Twin Peaks (1990-91) . . . . .John Justice Wheeler

Zelnicker, Michael

Films:

Pick-Up Summer (1979; Canadian) . . . . .Greg
  • 0:04—Brief buns, while hanging a B.A. out the back
    window of the van.
Hog Wild (1980; Canadian). . . . . Pete
Touch and Go (1984) . . . . McDonald
Bird (1988) . . . . Red Rodney
Naked Lunch (1991). . . . . Martin
Queens Logic (1991). . . . . .n.a.

Titles

10 (1979)
Julie Andrews . . . . Sam
Brian Dennehy . . . . Bartender
Bo Derek . . . . Jennifer Hanley
   1:18—In yellow swimsuit running in slow motion.
- 1:27—Brief buns and topless taking off towel and putting on robe when Moore visits her. Long shot, hard to see.
- 1:34—Brief topless taking off dress trying to seduce Moore. Dark, hard to see.
- 1:35—Topless, lying in bed. Dark, hard to see.
- •• 1:39—Topless, going to fix the skipping record. Long shot, hard to see.

Sam Jones . . . . David Hanley
Dudley Moore . . . . George Webber
- 0:47—Buns, while at neighbor's party just before Julie Andrews sees him through a telescope.

Dee Wallace Stone . . . . Mary Lewis

10 to Midnight (1983)
Gene Davis . . . . Warren Stacy
- •• 0:08—Nude, running after girl in the woods.
- •• 0:28—Buns, in Betty's bedroom, while attempting to get her diary.
- •• 1:31—Buns, lots of times, while attacking the girls in their apartment.
- •• 1:36—Buns and very brief frontal nudity leaving the apartment at the top of the stairs.
- •• 1:37—Nude, running after Lisa Eilbacher in the street.

Lisa Eilbacher . . . . Laurie Kessler
Kelly Preston . . . . Doreen
Ola Ray . . . . Ola
- 1:30—Very brief buns and very brief left breast, taking off robe and getting into the shower.
- •• 1:31—Topless in the shower.
- •• 1:32—More topless in the shower.
- 1:39—Very brief topless, dead, covered with blood in the shower.

Cynthia Reams . . . . Hooker
- ••• 1:25—Topless in hotel room with killer when he tries to elude Charles Bronson.
- 1:26—Brief right breast, lying in bed, covered with sheet.

Deran Sarafian . . . . Dale Anders
- 0:08—Buns, while making love in van with Betty.

Andrew Stevens . . . . Paul McAnn
Patti Tippo . . . . Party Girl
- •• 0:52—Topless, making love with a guy in the laundry room at a party.

Jeana Tomasina . . . . Karen
   0:26—In white body suit, changing in bedroom while the killer watches from inside the closet.

18 Again! (1988)
Connie Gauthier . . . . Artist's Model
- •• 0:29—Very brief topless, then buns taking her robe off during art class.

Anita Morris . . . . Madeline
Jennifer Runyon . . . . Robin

1900 (1976; Italian)
Robert De Niro . . . . Alfredo Berlinghieri
- 1:59—Very brief buns while making love with Dominique Sanda in the hay. Don't see his face.

Gérard Depardieu . . . . Olmo Dalco
- 1:36—Brief frontal nudity sitting at table with Robert De Niro. Again when walking into the bedroom.
- ••• 1:40—Nude getting out of bed after the girl has a seizure.

Roberto Maccanti . . . . Olmo as a Child
- 0:53—Frontal nudity undressing and showing the young Alfredo his penis.

Dominique Sanda . . . . Ada
- •• 2:12—(0:05 into tape 2.) Full frontal nudity under thin fabric dancing with Robert De Niro for photographer.

Stefania Sandrelli . . . . Anita Foschi
Donald Sutherland . . . . Attila

1984 (1984)
Suzanna Hamilton . . . . Julia
- •• 0:38—Full frontal nudity taking off her clothes in the woods with John Hurt.
- ••• 0:52—Nude in secret room standing and drinking and talking to Hurt. Long scene.
- 1:11—Side view of left breast kneeling down.
- •• 1:12—Topless after picture falls off the view screen on the wall.

John Hurt . . . . Winston Smith
- 1:11—Buns, while walking from the bed to the window next to Suzanna Hamilton.

2020 Texas Gladiators (1983; Italian)
Sabrina Siani . . . . Maida
- •• 0:07—Left breast, in open white dress after gang rape.
- 0:34—Topless during rape.

3:15—The Moment of Truth (1986)
Wendy Barry . . . . Lora
Deborah Foreman . . . . Sherry Havilland
   0:26—Very brief blurry buns and side view of left breast jumping out of bed when her parents come home. Long shot, hard to see anything.

Gina Gershon . . . . One of the Cobrettes
Wings Hauser . . . . Mr. Havilland

48 Hrs. (1982)
Greta Blackburn . . . . Lisa
- •• 0:13—Topless and buns in bathroom in hotel room with James Remar.

Denise Crosby . . . . Sally
   0:47—Very, very brief side view of half of left breast, while swinging baseball bat at Eddie Murphy.
- 1:24—Very brief side view of right breast when James Remar pushes her onto bed.
- 1:25—Very brief topless then very brief side view of right breast attacking Nick Nolte.

Sandy Martin . . . . Policewoman
Chris Mulkey . . . . Cop
Nick Nolte . . . . Jack Cates

Annette O'Toole . . . . Elaine
Ola Ray . . . . .Vroman's Dancers
Suzanne M. Regard. . . . . Cowgirl Dancer
    0:39—Dancer in red-neck bar wearing silver star
    pasties.
Brenda Venus . . . . Hooker

52 Pick-Up (1986)

Ann-Margret. . . . . .Barbara Mitchell
Vanity . . . . .Doreen
  ••• 0:47—Topless, stripping in room while Roy Scheider
     takes Polaroid pictures.
  • 0:52—Topless under sheer purple nightgown. Par-
    tial buns in G-string underneath also.
Ron Jeremy . . . . Party Goer
Amber Lynn . . . . Party Goer
  • 0:23—Topless opening her blouse while being video
    taped at party.
  • 0:24—Topless and buns on TV. B&W.
  • 0:26—Left breast, then topless being video taped
    with another woman.
Kelly Preston . . . . Cini
  • 0:09—Brief buns in video tape made by blackmail-
    ers.
  • 0:36—Topless, tied to chair on video tape made by
    blackmailers.
    0:39—Very brief topless covered with blood after
    being shot.

8 Million Ways to Die (1986)

Rosanna Arquette . . . . Sarah
    1:00—In a bra in Jeff Bridges' apartment.
Jeff Bridges .Matthew Scudder
Alexandra Paul . . . . .Sunny
  •• 0:24—Full frontal nudity, standing in bathroom
    while Jeff Bridges watches.

9 1/2 Ninjas (1990)

Andee Gray. . . . . .Lisa Thorne
  •• 1:02—Topless making love with Joe in the rain.
  • 1:19—Brief topless during flashback.
Sharon Lee Jones. . . . . Zelda
  • 0:52—Topless eating Chinese food in the shower
    with Joe.

9 1/2 Weeks (1986)

Kim Basinger. . . . . .Elizabeth
  • 0:27—Blindfolded while Mickey Rourke plays with
    an ice cube on her. Brief right breast.
    0:36—Masturbating while watching slides of art.
    0:41—Playing with food at the refrigerator with
    Rourke. Messy, but erotic.
  • 0:54—Very brief left breast, while rolling over in bed.
    0:58—Making love with Rourke in clock tower.
  ••• 1:11—In wet lingerie, then topless making love in a
    wet stairwell with Rourke.
  • 1:19—Doing a sexy dance for Rourke in a white slip.
  • 1:22—Buns, showing off to Rourke on building.
  • 1:44—Brief buns, putting on pants and getting out
    of bed.

Mickey Rourke . . . . John
Margaret Whitton . . . . .Molly
Karen Young . . . . Sue

976-EVIL II: The Astral Factor (1991)

Deborah Dutch . . . . .Commerical Wife
George "Buck" Flower . . . . Turrell
Monique Gabrielle . . . . Miss Lawlor
Karen Mayo-Chandler . . . . Laurie
  •• 0:00—Topless in shower room, then putting on wet
    T-shirt.
    0:01—Running around the school hallways wearing
    white panties and wet, white T-shirt.
Brigitte Nielsen. . . . . Agnes

A Nos Amours (1984; French)

Sandrine Bonnaire . . . . .Suzanne
  • 0:17—Brief topless, pulling dress top down to put
    on nightgown.
  •• 0:34—Topless sitting up in bed talking to Bernard.
    Brief side view of buns.
  • 0:42—Very brief side view of left breast while waking
    up in bed.
  • 0:57—Very brief lower frontal nudity, while getting
    out of bed with Martine and her boyfriend. Long
    shot of buns, while hugging Bernard in the back-
    ground (out of focus).
Maïté Maillé . . . . Martine
Pierre-Loup Rajot . . . . Bernard
  • 0:56—Brief buns, while walking around in the back-
    ground. Long shot. Out of focus.
  • 0:58—Partial frontal nudity, lying in bed talking to
    Sandrine Bonnaire.

About Last Night... (1986)

Rob Lowe. . . . . Danny
  •• 0:52—Buns and almost frontal nudity when he
    opens the refrigerator with Demi Moore.
Demi Moore. . . . . Debbie
    0:32—In white bra getting dressed.
  • 0:34—Brief upper half of right breast in the bathtub
    with Rob Lowe.
    0:35—In white bra getting dressed.
  • 0:50—Side view of right breast, then very brief top-
    less.
  ••• 0:51—Buns and topless in bed with Lowe, arching
    her back, then lying in bed when he rolls off her.
  •• 0:52—Topless and buns in kitchen with Lowe.
Elizabeth Perkins . . . . .Joan

The Abyss (1989)

Michael Biehn . . . . Lieutenant Coffey
Ed Harris . . . . .Virgil "Bud" Brigman
Mary Elizabeth Mastrantonio . . . . Lindsey Brigman
  • 1:41—Topless during C.P.R. scene.

The Accused (1988)

Steve Antin. . . . . Bob Joiner
  • 1:29—Buns, while raping Jodi Foster on the pinball
    machine.

Woody Brown. . . . . Danny
  • 1:28—Buns, while raping Jodi Foster on the pinball machine.
Jodie Foster. . . . . Sarah Tobias
  • 1:27—Brief topless a few times during rape scene on pinball machine by Dan and Bob.
Kelly McGillis. . . . . Kathryn Murphy
Leo Rossi. . . . . Cliff "Scorpion" Albrect

Act of Piracy (1990)
Belinda Bauer . . . . Sandy Andrews
Nancy Mulford . . . . Laura Warner
  • 0:11—Very brief left breast under Gary Busey in bed. Dark, hard to see.
  0:12—In white lingerie, walking around on the boat shooting everybody.
  • 0:34—Brief, upper half of left breast, in bed with Ray Sharkey.
  0:35—In white nightgown.
Ray Sharkey. . . . . Jack Wilcox
  • 0:33—Brief side view of buns while on top of Laura in bed.
  •• 0:35—Brief buns, while getting out of bed and putting on robe.

Action Jackson (1988)
Vanity . . . . Sydney Ash
  •• 0:29—Topless in bed with Craig T. Nelson.
Susan Lentini. . . . . VW Driver
Ed O'Ross . . . . Stringer
Melissa Prophet. Newscaster
Sharon Stone . . . . Patrice Dellaplane
  •• 0:34—Topless in a steam room. Hard to see because of all the steam.
  • 0:56—Brief right breast, dead, on the bed when police view her body.

The Adultress (1973)
Tyne Daly . . . . Inez
  • 0:21—Brief side view of right breast in room with Carl. Brief out of focus topless in bed.
  •• 0:51—Topless outside with Hank.
  ••• 0:53—Topless on a horse with Hank.

The Adventures of Eliza Fraser (1976; Australian)
Abigail . . . . Buxom Girl
  • 0:01—Topless when Martin pulls the sheets off her.
John Waters . . . . Dave Bracefell
  • 0:27—Side view of buns, while undressing and getting into bed.
  •• 0:29—Nude, walking around outside. Buns, while standing in doorway.
  •• 0:32—Brief pubic hair, then buns while getting off bed to hide under it.
  0:34—Upper half of buns, while in bed on top of Susannah York.
  •• 0:38—Buns, while jumping on York, then getting pushed out the door.
Susannah York . . . . Elisa Fraser
  • 1:10—Brief topless twice during ceremony. Paint on her face while running from hut.

Affairs of the Heart (1992)
Private Screenings.
John Altamura . . . . Jock #1
Amy Lynn Baxter . . . . Josie Hart
  •• 0:00—Topless during opening credits.
  •• 0:02—Topless and buns in G-string, while posing for photos.
  ••• 1:09—Topless posing in santa cap during photo session.
  •• 1:13—Topless with Richard during smoky dream scene.
Cody Carmack. . . . . Itchy
  ••• 0:45—Topless taking off her bikini top with her husband.
Lorna Courtney . . . . Jane
  ••• 1:04—Topless, making love in front of a fire in sleeping bag with Dick.
Isabelle Fortea . . . . Karen
  ••• 1:06—Topless making love in cabin with Tom.
Melissa Leigh . . . . Jealous Woman
  ••• 0:38—Buns, then topless with the Jealous Man.
Jospeh E. Mauro. . . . . Jealous Man
  • 0:38—Buns in G-string, walking into room with the Jealous Woman.
Michael Montana. Richard
  •• 1:13—Buns, with Amy Lynn Baxter during smoky dream scene.
Beckie Mullen. . . . . Pool Girl
  ••• 0:52—Topless, after taking off her bikini top, then diving into pool.
  •• 0:53—Topless, lying on towel on diving board, then turning over.
Angela Nicholas . . . . Dreamgirl
  •• 0:14—In bra, then left breast while in bed with the Geek.

After Dark, My Sweet (1990)
Bruce Dern. . . . . Uncle Bud
Jeanie Moore . . . . Nanny
Jason Patric . . . . Kevin "Collie" Collins
  •• 1:19—Buns, while taking off pants and getting into bed with Rachel Ward. More brief buns on top of her.
Rachel Ward. . . . . Fay Anderson
  • 1:22—Very, very brief half of right breast under Jason Patric in bed when he moves slightly.

After Hours (1985)
Rosanna Arquette. . . . . Marcy
  0:48—In bed, dead, in panties. Arm covers breasts.
Henry Judd Baker . . . . Jett
Linda Fiorentino. . . . . Kiki
  0:11—In black bra and skirt doing paper maché.
  •• 0:19—Topless taking off bra in doorway while Griffin Dunne watches.
Teri Garr. . . . . Julie
John Heard. . . . . Bartender
Richard "Cheech" Marin . . . . Neil

After School (1987)

Renee Coleman. . . . . September Lane
- •• 0:35—Topless and buns getting into bathtub. Almost lower frontal nudity.

Sherrie Rose . . . . First Tribe Member

Age of Consent (1969; Australian)

Clarissa Kaye-Mason . . . . Meg
- • 0:05—Brief topless, crawling on the bed to watch TV.

Jack MacGowran. . . . . Nat Kelly
- • 1:01—Brief buns, while running into the ocean when Miss Marley sees him.
- •• 1:02—Buns, running away from her to the cabin while holding a dog to cover up his private parts.

Helen Mirren. . . . . Cora
- • 0:48—Topless several times in the mirror. Brief lower frontal nudity, kneeling on the floor.
- •• 0:55—Brief topless and buns quite a few time, snorkeling under water.
- ••• 1:20—Topless and half of buns, posing in the water for James Mason. Then getting out.

Alamo Bay (1985)

Ed Harris . . . . .Shang

Amy Madigan . . . . Glory
- •• 0:28—Topless lying in motel bed with Ed Harris.
- •• 0:30—Topless sitting up in the bed.
- 0:40—Walking in parking lot in a wet T-shirt.

Albino (1976)

a.k.a. *Night of the Askari*

Sybil Danning . . . . Sally
- • 0:19—Topless, then full frontal nudity getting raped by the Albino and his buddies.

Alexa (1988)

Ruth Corrine Collins . . . . Marshall
- • 0:01—Topless a couple of times taking blue dress off and putting it on again. Long shot.

Christine Moore . . . . Alexa
- 0:04—In red slip in bedroom.
- 0:06—In black bra, on bed with Tommy.
- 0:11—In black lingerie talking on phone in bed.
- •• 0:24—Topless lying in bed with Anthony while reminiscing.
- •• 1:08—Topless in bed with Anthony again.

Alien Prey (1984; British)

Glory Annen . . . . .Jessica
- • 0:22—Topless unbuttoning blouse to sunbathe.
- •• 0:34—Topless taking off top, getting into bed with Josephine, then making love with her.
- 0:36—Buns, rolling on top of Josephine.
- ••• 0:38—More topless when Josephine is playing with her.
- 0:39—More buns in bed. Long shot.
- • 0:46—Left breast and buns standing up in bathtub.
- •• 1:05—Topless getting out of bed and putting a dress on.

- •• 1:19—Topless in bed with Anders. Brief buns when he rips her panties off.

Sally Faulkner . . . . .Josephine
- • 0:32—Very, very brief left breast taking off top.
- 0:36—Buns, in bed with Glory Annen.
- • 0:37—Topless on her back in bed with Annen.

Barry Stokes . . . . .Anders
- •• 1:19—Buns, while getting on top of Glory Annen in bed.

Alien Space Avenger (1988)

Vicki Darnell. . . . . .Bordello Lady

Kirk Fairbanks Fogg . . . . Matt
- • 0:22—Buns, while walking out of apartment after Ginny.

Jamie Gillis . . . . Businessman

Gina Mastrogiacomo . . . . Ginny
- ••• 0:19—Topless in bed, making love with Matt. Topless and buns, getting out and getting dressed.

Angela Nicholas . . . . Doris
- • 0:56—Brief topless making whoopee with Jaimie Gillis.
- ••• 0:57—More topless making love on top of Gillis while killing him.

Miriam Zucker . . . . .Bordello Reporter

Alien Warrior (1985)

Tally Chanel. . . . . Barbara
- •• 0:46—In white lingerie, then topless and buns while undressing in room with the Police Captain.
- • 1:03—Brief topless and buns in flashback of 0:46 scene.

Brett Clark . . . . Buddy
- •• 0:03—Buns, while walking naked after getting transported to Earth.

Lydia Finzi . . . . Beverly

All That Jazz (1979)

Leah Ayres-Hamilton . . . . .Nurse Capobianco

Sandahl Bergman. . . . . .Sandra
- •• 0:52—Topless dancing on scaffolding during a dance routine.

Vicki Frederick .Menage Partner

Deborah Geffner . . . . Victoria
- • 0:17—Brief topless taking off her blouse and walking up the stairs while Roy Scheider watches. A little out of focus.

Jessica Lange . . . . Angelique

John Lithgow . . . . Lucas Sergeant

Sue Paul. . . . . Stacy
- • 1:18—Brief right breast in bed with Roy Scheider at the hospital.

K.C. Townsend. . . . . Stripper
- • 0:21—Topless backstage getting Joey excited before he goes on stage. Lit by red light.

...All the Marbles (1981)

a.k.a. *The California Dolls*

Angela Aames . . . . Louise
- •• 0:20—Topless in Peter Falk's motel room talking with Iris, then sitting on the bed.

Peter Falk . . . . Harry
Vicki Frederick. . . . . Iris
  • 1:03—Brief side view of left breast, while crying in
    the shower after fighting with Peter Falk.
Laurene Landon . . . . Molly
Tracy Reed . . . . Diane

All The Right Moves (1983)
Tom Cruise . . . . .Stef
  •• 1:00—Very brief frontal nudity getting undressed in
    his bedroom with Lea Thompson.
Christopher Penn . . . . .Brian
Lea Thompson . . . . .Lisa
  ••• 1:00—Topless and brief buns and lower frontal nu-
    dity, getting undressed and into bed with Tom
    Cruise in his bedroom.

Alley Cat (1982)
Karen Mani . . . . Billie
  • 0:01—Brief topless in panties taking night gown off
    during opening credits.
  0:17—In two piece swimsuit sitting by the pool.
  ••• 0:38—Brief side view of right breast and buns get-
    ting into the shower. Full frontal nudity in the show-
    er.
  ••• 0:48—Topless in women's prison shower room
    scene. Long scene.
Moriah Shannon . . . . Sam

...Almost (1990; Australian)
Rosanna Arquette . . . . Wendy
Susan Lyons . . . . Caroline
Hugo Weaving . . . . Jake
  0:52—Very brief out of focus buns when he drops
  his pants in front of Rosanna Arquette. Don't see his
  face. Note in the very next scene, he's wearing underwear!

Almost Pregnant (1992)
(Unrated version reviewed.)
Steve Adell . . . . Muscle Man
  • 0:04—Buns, while making love in bed with Tanya
    Roberts.
  •• 0:20—Buns, while on top of Roberts during Jeff Con-
    away's dream.
John Calvin . . . . Gordon Mallory
  •• 1:11—Buns, while on top of Tanya Roberts in bed.
Jeff Conaway. Charlie Alderson
  ••• 0:10—Buns, while making love on top of Tanya Rob-
    erts in bed.
  •• 1:12—Buns in bed in alternate scenes with Roberts
    and Joan Severance.
Lezlie Deane . . . . Party Girl
Tanya Roberts . . . . Linda Alderson
  ••• 0:04—Topless and buns, in bed with a guy. Long
    scene.
  • 0:10—Brief right breast, while under Conaway in
    bed.
  • 0:18—Brief left breast, while in bed with another
    guy during Conaway's dream.

0:40—Very brief side view of buns, in lingerie, walking down stairs.
  • 1:08—Buns, lying in bed while Gordon writes.
  ••• 1:11—Topless and buns in bed.
  ••• 1:12—Nude with Conaway.
Joan Severance. . . . . Maureen Mallory
  ••• 0:58—In belly dancer outfit in bedroom with Jeff
    Conaway, then topless.
  •• 1:06—In black leather outfit, then topless and buns
    in G-string. Her hair gets in the way a lot.
  •• 1:09—Brief topless and buns in various sexual posi-
    tions in bed with Conaway.

Alpine Fire (1985; Swiss)
Thomas Nock. . . . . Bob
  • 0:08—Brief buns, while outside taking a bath.

Altered States (1980)
Blair Brown . . . . .Emily Jessup
  • 0:10—Brief left breast making love with William Hurt
    in red light from an electric heater.
  •• 0:34—Topless lying on her stomach during Hurt's
    mushroom induced hallucination.
  1:39—Buns, sitting in hallway with Hurt after the
    transformations go away.
William Hurt. . . . . .Eddie Jessup
  0:46—Brief pubic hair twice when Charles Haid and
  Bob Balaban help him out of isolation tank.
  • 0:54—Very brief buns, while standing in the shower
    when he starts transforming. More buns standing
    near door and walking to bed.

Alvin Purple (1973; Australian)
Abigail . . . . Girl in See-Through
  0:01—On bus in see-through top. Hard to see any-
    thing.
Graeme Blundell .Alvin Purple
  •• 0:21—Brief nude, while painting Samantha's body.
  •• 0:22—Buns and brief frontal nudity in bedroom with
    the Kinky Lady.
  • 0:25—Brief buns with Mrs. Warren—who turns out
    to be a man.
  • 0:26—Very brief frontal nudity running out of room,
    then buns going down the stairs.
  ••• 0:33—Nude, undressing and taking a shower. Shot
    at fast speed.
  •• 1:04—Nude, running away from the girl during
    showing of movie.
  • 1:21—Buns, while getting chased by a group of
    women down the street.
Lynette Curran. . . . . .First Sugar Girl
  •• 0:02—Brief full frontal nudity when Alvin opens the
    door.
Kris McQuade . . . . Samantha
  ••• 0:21—Topless and buns, while painting Alvin's body.
Debbie Nankervis. . . . . Girl in Blue Movie
  •• 1:04—Nude, running after Alvin in bedroom during
    showing of movie.
Elke Neidhardt . . . . Woman in Blue Movie
  •• 1:07—In red bra, then full frontal nudity in bedroom
    with Alvin during showing of film.

Anne Pendlebury. . . . . .Woman with Pin
•• 0:48—Right breast and lower frontal nudity, while
lying in bed, talking with Alvin.
Jacki Weaver . . . . .Second Sugar Girl
•• 0:33—Brief full frontal nudity, lying in bean bag
chair.

Alvin Rides Again *(1974; Australian)*
Abigail . . . . Mae
••• 0:12—Topless in store with Alvin.
Graeme Blundell . . . . Alvin Purple
• 0:06—Buns, while running out of the office after he's
awakened. Blurry.
Chantal Contouri . . . . Boobs La Touche
• 1:15—Very brief lower frontal nudity, putting panties on in the car. Brief topless, putting red dress on.
Kris McQuade . . . . Mandy
••• 0:48—Full frontal nudity, taking off red dress and
getting into bed with Alvin. More topless lying in
bed. Long scene.
Debbie Nankervis . . . . Woman Cricketer
Candy Raymond . . . . Girl in Office
• 0:05—Lower frontal nudity and buns, in office with
Alvin.
Judy Stevenson . . . . .Housewife
•• 0:01—Full frontal nudity, dropping her towel while
Alvin washes her window.

Amazon Women on the Moon *(1987)*
Corinne Alphen. . . . . .Shari
••• 1:13—In black bra, then topless on TV while Ray
watches.
Rosanna Arquette . . . . Karen
Belinda Balaski. . . . . Bernice Pitnik
Ed Begley, Jr.. . . . . .Griffin
• 0:54—Buns, while walking around as the Son of the
Invisible Man. This section is in B&W.
Lana Clarkson . . . . Alpha Beta
Sybil Danning . . . . .Queen Lara
Monique Gabrielle . . . . Taryn Steele
••• 0:05—Nude during Penthouse Video sketch. Long
sequence of her nude in unlikely places.
Steve Guttenberg . . . . Jerry Stone
Tracey E. Hutchinson. . . . . Floozie
1:18—Brief right breast, while hitting balloon while
Carrie Fisher talks to a guy. This sketch is in B&W and
appears after the first batch of credits.
Michelle Pfeiffer . . . . .Brenda Landers
Kelly Preston . . . . Violet
Angel Tompkins . . . . First Lady
1:00—In white nightgown, then black bra, panties,
garter belt and stockings.

Amazons *(1986)*
Danitza Kingsley . . . . Tshingi
••• 0:30—Topless and buns quite a few times with Colungo out of and in bed.
Windsor Taylor Randolph . . . . Dyala
•• 0:22—Topless skinny dipping then getting dressed
with Tashi.

•• 0:24—Brief topless getting her top opened by bad
guys then fighting them.
Penelope Reed . . . . Tashi
• 0:22—Topless and buns undressing to go skinny
dipping. More topless getting dressed.
• 0:24—Brief topless getting top opened by bad guys.

The Ambassador *(1984)*
Ellen Burstyn . . . . Alex Hacker
••• 0:06—Topless opening her robe to greet her lover.
••• 0:07—Brief topless making love in bed.
••• 0:29—Topless in a movie while her husband, Robert
Mitchum, watches.
Iftach Katzur. . . . . n.a.
Zachi Noy . . . . n.a.

Ambition *(1991)*
Katherine Armstrong . . . . .Roseanne
••• 1:13—Buns in G-string, then topless in Clancy
Brown's apartment.
Clancy Brown. . . . . Albert
Karen Landry . . . . Woman in Bookstore
Celeste Yarnall . . . . Beverly Hills Shopper

The American Angels, Baptism of Blood *(1989)*
Jan MacKenzie . . . . Luscious Lisa
0:07—Buns in G-string on stage in club. More buns
getting lathered up for wrestling match.
• 0:11—Topless and buns when a customer takes her
top off. She's covered with shaving cream.
•• 0:12—Topless taking a shower when Diamond Dave
looks in to talk to her.
• 0:56—Right breast, while in wrestling ring with
Dave.

American Flyers *(1985)*
Rae Dawn Chong . . . . .Sarah
Kevin Costner. . . . . Marcus
• 0:53—Brief, upper half of buns, while riding bicycles
when his pants get yanked down by David.
David Grant. . . . . .David
• 0:05—Brief buns and very, very brief frontal nudity
taking off his shorts and walking to bathroom.
Katherine Kriss . . . . .Vera
Alexandra Paul. . . . . .Becky
• 0:50—Very brief right breast, then very brief half of
left breast changing tops with David Grant. Brief
side view of right breast. Dark.
•• 1:13—Brief topless in white panties getting into bed
with David Grant.

American Gigolo *(1980)*
Michele Drake . . . . 1st Girl on Balcony
• 0:03—Topless on the balcony while Richard Gere
and Lauren Hutton talk.
Richard Gere . . . . Julian
•• 0:39—Buns and frontal nudity. Long shot, so it's
hard to see anything.
Linda Horn. . . . . .2nd Girl on Balcony
• 0:03—Topless on the balcony while Richard Gere
and Lauren Hutton talk.

Lauren Hutton . . . . Michelle
- • 0:37—Left breast, making love with Richard Gere in bed in his apartment.

American Nightmare (1981; Canadian)
Alexandra Paul . . . . Isabelle Blake/Tanya Kelly
- ••• 0:02—Left breast while smoking in bed. Topless before getting killed. Long scene.

Lora Staley . . . . Louise Harmon
- •• 0:44—Topless and buns in G-string dancing on stage.
- ••• 0:54—Topless making love in bed with Eric.
- • 0:59—Brief right breast, then topless auditioning in TV studio.

Claudia Udy . . . . Andrea
- ••• 0:08—Buns, then topless dancing on stage.
- • 0:22—Buns getting into bathtub. Topless during struggle with killer.

Lenore Zann . . . . Tina
- ••• 0:25—Topless and buns dancing on stage.
- •• 1:05—Topless and buns dancing on stage again.

The American Success Company (1979)
Belinda Bauer . . . . Sarah
Jeff Bridges . . . . Harry
Bianca Jagger . . . . Corinne
- • 0:35—Topless under see-through black top while sitting on bed.

An American Werewolf in London (1981)
Jenny Agutter . . . . Alex Price
- • 0:41—Brief right breast in bed with David Naughton. Dark, hard to see.

Linzi Drew . . . . Brenda Bristols
- • 1:26—Side view of left breast in porno movie while David Naughton talks to his friend, Jack.
- • 1:27—Brief topless in movie talking on the phone.

David Naughton . . . . David Kessler
- • 0:24—Very brief buns while running naked through the woods.
- • 0:58—Buns, during his transformation into a werewolf.
- •• 1:09—Brief frontal nudity and buns after waking up in wolf cage at the zoo. Long shot, hard to see anything. More buns, while running around the zoo.

The Amityville Horror (1979)
Margot Kidder . . . . Kathleen Lutz
- • 0:21—Brief right breast in reflection in mirror while doing dance streching exercises in the bedroom. Hard to see because of the pattern on the mirror tiles.
- • 0:22—Cleavage in open blouse while talking to James Brolin.
- • 0:23—Very brief partial right breast, on the floor, kissing Brolin.

Helen Shaver . . . . Carolyn
Amy Wright . . . . Jackie

Amityville II: The Possession (1982)
Diane Franklin . . . . Patricia Montelli
- • 0:41—Half of right breast, while sitting on bed talking to her brother.

Amor Ciego (1980; Mexican)
Apollonia . . . . Patty
- • 0:32—Topless getting out of hammock.
- ••• 0:52—Right breast, standing up, then topless kissing Daniel. More topless in bed.
- ••• 0:59—Buns, making love in bed, then topless afterwards.
- •• 1:11—Topless, taking off her towel and putting Daniel's hand on her left breast.
- •• 1:15—Topless, turning over, then lying in bed.

Jaime Moreno . . . . Daniel
- ••• 0:51—Frontal nudity standing up from bed, then buns when Apollonia hugs him.
- • 0:53—Buns, while making love in bed with Apollonia.

And God Created Woman (1988)
(Unrated version.)
Rebecca De Mornay . . . . Robin
- •• 0:06—Brief Left breast and buns in gymnasium with Vincent Spano. Brief right breast making love.
- • 0:53—Brief buns and topless in the shower when Spano sees her.
- •• 1:02—Brief left breast with Langella on the floor.
- ••• 1:12—Topless making love with Spano in a museum.

Pat Lee . . . . Inmate
Vincent Spano . . . . Billy Moran

...and God created woman (1957; French)
Brigitte Bardot . . . . Juliette
- • 0:40—Very brief side view of right breast getting out of bed.

Andy Warhol's Frankenstein
(1974; Italian/German/French)
Dalila Di'Lazzaro . . . . The Girl
- •• 0:09—Topless lying on platform in the lab.
- • 0:37—Close up of left breast while the Count cuts her stitches. (Pretty bloody.)
- 0:43—Topless, covered with blood, strapped to table
- • 0:49—Topless on table, all wired up.
- • 1:03—Right breast lying on table. Long shot.
- • 1:05—More right breast, long shot.
- •• 1:06—More topless on table, then standing in the lab.
- •• 1:20—Brief right breast when Otto pulls her top down.
- •• 1:23—Topless on table again, then walking around. (Scar on chest.) Lower frontal nudity when Otto pulls her bandage down, then more gross topless when he removes her guts.

Monique Van Vooren . . . . Katherine
- •• 0:47—Topless in bed with Nicholas. Brief lower frontal nudity twice when he rolls on top of her.

- 1:21—Left breast letting Sascha, the creature, caress her breast
- 1:26—Topless, dead, when her breasts pop out of her blouse.

Angel (1983)

Josh Cadman . . . . Spike
John Diehl . . . . Crystal
- 0:35—Buns, while washing blood off himself. Dark, hard to see. Long scene.

Elaine Giftos . . . . Patricia Allen
Donna McDaniel . . . . Crystal
- 0:19—Brief topless, dead in bed when the killer pulls the covers down.

Graem McGavin . . . . Lana
•• 0:31—Topless standing in hotel bathroom talking to her John.

Susan Tyrrell . . . . Selly Mosler
Donna Wilkes . . . . Angel/Molly

Angel Heart (1987)

(Original Unedited Version reviewed.)
Lisa Bonet . . . . Epiphany Proudfoot
0:53—In wet top, talking with Mickey Rourke.
- 1:01—Brief left breast, twice, in open dress during vodoo ceremony.
••• 1:27—Topless in bed with Rourke. It gets kind of bloody.
- 1:32—Topless in bathtub.
- 1:48—Topless in bed, dead. Covered with a bloody sheet.

Robert De Niro . . . . Louis Cyphre
Charlotte Rampling . . . . Margaret Krusemark
- 1:10—Brief left breast, lying dead on the floor, covered with blood.
- 1:46—Very brief left breast during flashback of the dead-on-the-floor-covered-with-blood scene.

Mickey Rourke . . . . Harry Angel
•• 1:28—Buns, while in bed with Lisa Bonet. Don't see his face. It gets kind of bloody.

Elizabeth Whitcraft . . . . Connie
•• 0:33—Topless in bed talking with Mickey Rourke while taking off her clothes.

Angel III: The Final Chapter (1988)

Maud Adams . . . . Nadine
Laura Albert . . . . Nude Dancer
- 0:00—Brief topless dancing in a casino. Wearing red G-string.
- 0:01—Brief topless dancing in background.
- 0:06—Side view of left breast and buns, while yelling at Molly for taking her picture.

Toni Basil . . . . Hillary
Barbara Hammond . . . . Video Girl #2
- 0:34—Topless (on the right) on video monitor during audition tape talking with her roommate.

Tyronne Granderson Jones . . . . L.A. Pimp
•• 0:32—Buns, while standing in alley after Angel pushes him out of the car.

Mitzi Kapture . . . . Molly Stewart
Roxanne Kernohan . . . . White Hooker

Kim McKamy . . . . Video Girl #1
Julie Kristen Smith . . . . Darlene
••• 0:40—Topless during caveman shoot with a brunette girl.
••• 0:44—Topless again dancing in caveman shoot.

Cheryl Starbuck . . . . Video Girl #3

Angel in Red

See: Uncaged.

Angel of H.E.A.T. (1981)

a.k.a. The Protectors, Book I
Marilyn Chambers . . . . Angel Harmony
•• 0:15—Full frontal nudity making love with an intruder on the bed.
- 0:17—Topless in a bathtub.
- 0:40—Topless in a hotel room with a short guy.
•• 0:52—Topless getting out of a wet suit.
•• 1:01—Topless sitting on floor with some robots.
- 1:29—Topless in bed with Mark.

Remy O'Neill . . . . Andrea Shockley
•• 0:43—Topless, wearing a blue swimsuit, wrestling in the mud with Mary Woronov.

Mary Woronov . . . . Samantha Vitesse
••• 0:11—Frontal nudity changing clothes on a boat dock after getting out of the lake.
•• 0:43—Topless wrestling in the mud after wearing white bathing suit.

Angel of Passion (1991)

Tuscany . . . . Ellen
••• 0:36—Buns and topless making love with a guy on a boat.

Venus De Light . . . . Carol
•• 0:15—Topless taking a shower.
••• 0:19—Topless and buns in G-string dancing outside next to pool at a birthday party.
••• 0:23—Topless and buns in red lingerie in camper, then topless making love on top of Will.

Sonny Falconeti . . . . Will
- 0:22—Buns frolicking in the surf with Carol while wearing a G-string.

Pamela Jackson . . . . Eileen
••• 1:13—Topless and upper half of buns while on bed with Eric making love.

Kathleen Kane . . . . Suzette
•• 1:08—Topless posing for Marty in the house.

Ingrid Vold . . . . Vanessa
- 1:01—Brief topless posing on the couch for the photographer.

Angels Hard as They Come (1971)

Scott Glenn . . . . Long John
Gilda Texter . . . . Astrid
- 0:26—Brief topless several times when bad guys try to rape her. Dark.

Janet Wood . . . . Vicki
•• 1:09—Topless taking off her top, dancing with Clean Sheila at the biker's party.
•• 1:16—Topless outside when the General rips her blouse open.

Animal House (1978)

Karen Allen . . . . Katherine "Katy" Fuller
   1:21—Brief buns putting on shirt when Boone visits.
Kevin Bacon . . . . Chip Diller
James Daughton . . . . Greg Marmalard
Sarah Holcomb . . . . .Clorette DePasto
  •• 0:56—Brief topless lying on bed after passing out in
   Tom Hulce's bed during toga party.
Sunny Johnson . . . . Otter's Co-Ed
Tim Matheson. . . . . .Eric "Otter" Stratton
  • 0:08—Buns, changing clothes in his bedroom while
   talking to Boone.
Bruce McGill . . . . .D-Day
Martha Smith . . . . Babs Jansen
Donald Sutherland . . . . .Dave Jennings
  • 1:22—Buns, while reaching up in kitchen to get
   something when his sweater goes up. Out of focus.
Mary Louise Weller . . . . .Mandy Pepperidge
  ••• 0:38—In white bra, then topless in bedroom while
   John Belushi watches on a ladder through the window.

Anna (1987)

Sally Kirkland. . . . . .Anna
  •• 0:28—Topless in the bathtub talking to Daniel.

Another 48 Hrs. (1990)

Bernie Casey . . . . Kirkland Smith
Page Leong. . . . . Angel Lee
  • 1:00—Brief topless getting out of bed with Willie.
David Anthony Marshall . . . . .Willie Hickok
  • 0:57—Buns, while putting pants on after getting out
   of bed.
Francesca "Kitten" Natividad. . . . . .Girl in Movie
  • 1:04—Brief topless on movie screen when two mo-
   torcycles crash through it.
Yana Nirvana. . . . . CHP Officer
Nick Nolte. .Jack Cates
Ed O'Ross . . . . Frank Cruise

Another Chance (1989)

Vanessa Angel. . . . . Jacky Johanssen
  • 0:26—Sort of topless under water in spa. Hard to see
   because of the bubbles.
Leslee Bremmer. . . . . Girl in Womanizer's Meeting
Barbara Edwards . . . . .Diana the Temptress
  ••• 0:38—Topless in trailer with Johnny.
Bruce Greenwood . . . . .n.a.
Karen Witter . . . . Nancy Burton
  • 0:44—Brief side view of right breast and buns getting out of bed.
   0:45—In two piece swimsuit.

Another Pair of Aces (1991; Made for Cable Movie)

(Video tape includes nude scenes not shown on cable
TV.)
Kris Kristofferson . . . . Capt. Elvin Metcalf
Joan Severance . . . . Susan Davis
  •• 1:00—Brief topless several times, making love with
   Kris Kristofferson in bed.
Rip Torn . . . . Capt. Jack Parsons

Any Man's Death (1989)

Nancy Mulford. . . . . .Tara
Mia Sara. . . . . Gerlind
  • 0:50—Brief right nipple when John Savage undoes
   her top. Don't see her face.
Claudia Udy . . . . .Laura

Aphrodite (1982; German/French)

Catherine Jourdan . . . . .Valerie
  • 0:34—Brief upper half of breasts in bathtub.
Valerie Kaprisky . . . . Pauline
  ••• 0:12—Nude, washing herself off in front of a two-
   way mirror while a man on the other side watches.

Apocalypse Now (1979)

Sam Bottoms . . . . .Lance
Colleen Camp . . . . Playmate
Linda Carpenter . . . . Playmate
  • 1:01—Topless in centerfold photo, hung up for dis-
   play. Long shot.
Scott Glenn . . . . Civilian
Martin Sheen . . . . Captain Willard
  • 0:07—Brief buns, while in bedroom after opening
   door for military guys.
Cyndi Wood. . . . . Playmate of the Year

Apology (1986; Made for Cable Movie)

Peter Weller . . . . Rad Hungare
  • 1:04—Brief buns, while putting pants on, getting
   out of bed to chase after intruder at night.

Appassionata (1979; Italian)

Eleonora Giorgi . . . . Nicola
  • 0:14—Very brief left breast in open blouse with Emilio in his dentist office. Topless several times.
  •• 0:41—Full frontal nudity in bedroom when Emilio
   comes in. Dark.
  ••• 0:54—Nude in office with Emilio in stockings and
   garter belt.
  • 1:35—Brief right breast in bed with Emilio. Dark.
Ornella Muti. . . . . Virginia
  • 0:32—Brief topless in bathroom when her father rips
   open her T-shirt while looking for hickies.
   0:57—Partial left breast, leaning over to tempt her
   father.
   1:07—In white bra, changing clothes during party.
   1:21—In white bra, giving herself hickies.
   1:25—In white bra in bed, showing her father her
   pubic hair.
  • 1:35—Buns, getting out of bed with her father. Brief
   side of left breast when leaving the room.

Appointment with Fear (1988)

Pamela Bach . . . . Samantha
  • 0:56—Topless getting into the spa. Long shot, hard
   to see.
Michele Little . . . . Carol
Deborah Voorhees . . . . Ruth
  • 0:21—Very, very brief side view of left breast taking
   off bra to go swimming, then very brief topless getting out of the pool.

Apprentice to Murder (1987)
Mia Sara . . . . Alice
- 0:29—Left side view topless making love with Chad Lowe.

Aria (1988; U.S./British)
Beverly D'Angelo. . . . . Gilda
Linzi Drew . . . . Girl
- 1:09—Topless on operating table after car accident. Hair is all covered with bandages.
- •• 1:10—Topless getting shocked to start her heart.

Sandrine Dumas . . . . .n.a.
Bridget Fonda . . . . Girl Lover
- ••• 0:59—Brief right breast, then buns and topless lying down on bed in hotel room in Las Vegas.
- •• 1:02—Topless in the bathtub with her boyfriend.

Elizabeth Hurley . . . . Marietta
- 0:46—Brief topless, turning around while singing to a guy.
- 0:47—Buns while standing and hugging him.

John Hurt . . . . The Actor
James Mathers. . . . . Boy Lover
- •• 1:00—Brief dark outline of frontal nudity in hotel room, then buns while making love with Bridget Fonda.
- 1:02—Frontal nudity under water in the bathtub with her.

Anita Morris . . . . .Phoebe
Theresa Russell . . . . King Zog

Arizona Heat (1988)
Denise Crosby. . . . . .Jill Andrews
- 1:13—Brief upper half of left breast in shower with Larry.

Armed and Dangerous (1986)
Christine Dupree. . . . . .Peep Show Girl
- 0:58—Very, very brief topless shots behind glass dancing in front of John Candy and Eugene Levy.

Eugene Levy . . . . Norman Kane
- 1:02—Cheeks of his buns through the back of leather pants while dressed in drag with John Candy to escape from the bad cops.

Steve Railsback . . . . The Cowboy
Meg Ryan . . . . Maggie Cavanaugh
K.C. Winkler . . . . Vicki

Armed Response (1986)
Michelle Bauer . . . . Stripper
- 0:41—Topless, dancing on stage.

Bobbie Bresee. . . . . .Anna
David Carradine . . . . .Jim Roth
Laurene Landon . . . . .Deborah
Dawn Wildsmith . . . . Thug

The Arrogant (1987)
Teresa Gilmore-Capps. . . . . Charlotte
- 0:23—Brief topless, making love in a barn.

Gary Graham . . . . .Giovanni
Sylvia Kristel . . . . Julie
- 0:14—In wet blouse, in lake.

- 0:22—In wet blouse again, walking out of the lake.
- 0:44—Brief topless several times, in gaping dress.

The Art of Dying (1991)
Wings Hauser. . . . . Jack
- •• 0:28—Buns, while standing in kitchen making love with Kathleen Kinmont.

Kathleen Kinmont. . . . . Holly
- 0:28—Brief left breast, making love with Wings Hauser in the kitchen. Brief topless when he pours milk on her.
- •• 0:33—Topless in bathtub with Hauser. Intercut with Janet getting stabbed.

Ona Simms Wiegers . . . . Frances Warner

Assault of the Killer Bimbos (1988)
Elizabeth Kaitan . . . . .Lulu
- •• 0:41—Brief topless during desert musical sequence, opening her blouse, then taking off her shorts, then putting on a light blue dress. Don't see her face.

Christina Whitaker . . . . .Peaches

Assault of the Party Nerds (1989)
Michelle Bauer . . . . Muffin
- 0:16—Side view of left breast kissing Bud.
- ••• 0:20—Topless lying in bed seen from Bud's point of view, then sitting up by herself.
- 1:15—Brief right breast, then topless in bed with Scott.

Linnea Quigley. . . . . Bambi
- ••• 0:25—Topless straddling Cliff in bed.

At Play in the Fields of the Lord (1991)
Kathy Bates . . . . Hazel Quarrier
- 2:22—(0:52 into tape 2) Nude, covered with mud and leaves, going crazy outside after her son dies.

Tom Berenger . . . . .Lewis Moon
- •• 0:45—Buns, while taking off his clothes after parachuting into the jungle.
- ••• 0:46—Nude, arriving at the Niaruna village.
- 0:47—Very brief buns and frontal nudity.
- 0:50—Buns, while entering hut.
- ••• 0:52—Brief frontal nudity while standing up, then buns, while walking.
- •• 0:54—Buns, while wearing G-string.
- ••• 0:55—More buns, wearing G-string, while walking in the forest.
- •• 0:56—More buns, with Pindi.
- 1:31—(0:01 into tape 2) Buns, in G-string.
- ••• 2:14—(0:44 into tape 2) Buns, in G-string, with Pindi.
- 2:47—(1:17 into tape 2) Buns, outside in G-string.
- •• 2:50—(1:20 into tape 2) Buns, in G-string when the white men in the helicopter fire bomb the village.

Daryl Hannah. Andy Huben
2:09—(0:39 into tape 2) Brief buns, swimming in water.
- ••• 2:10—(0:40 into tape 2) Buns, getting out and resting by tree. Long shot, then excellent closer shot. Very brief top of lower frontal nudity. (Skip tape 1 and fast forward to this!)

•• 2:11—(0:41 into tape 2) Brief buns, running away after kissing Tom Berenger.

John Lithgow . . . . Leslie Huben

Aidan Quinn . . . . Martin Quarrier

Atlantic City (1981; French/Canadian)

Susan Sarandon . . . . Sally

•• 0:50—Left breast cleaning herself with lemon juice while Burt Lancaster watches through window.

Auditions (1978)

Cory Brandon . . . . Van Scott

•• 0:32—Frontal nudity when Tracy undresses him.

Rick Cassidy . . . . Charlie White

••• 0:04—Nude, undressing for his audition.

•• 0:29—Buns, during sex scene with a woman.

• 1:07—Buns in bed during orgy scene.

• 1:13—Nude on kneeling on bed.

Marita Ditmar . . . . Frieda Volker

•• 1:05—Topless and partial buns with another woman and a guy.

Mara Lutra . . . . Jenny Marino

•• 0:58—Nude during her audition.

•• 1:07—Topless and buns during orgy scene.

Rick Lutze . . . . Ron Wilson

• 1:00—Nude during audition.

William Margold . . . . Larry Krantz

•• 0:23—Frontal nudity during his audition.

•• 0:26—Frontal nudity during audition with Linnea Quigley and Harry.

•• 0:30—Frontal nudity, tied up on table.

Adore O'Hara . . . . Adore O'Hara

•• 0:47—Nude, while singing opera.

Harry Osbon . . . . Harry Boran

••• 0:26—Nude during audition with Linnea Quigley and Larry.

•• 0:30—Frontal nudity, getting whipped while standing up, chained at the wrists.

Rhonda Petty . . . . Patty Rhodes

•• 0:26—Topless during audition.

•• 0:30—Topless, standing next to Larry and full frontal nudity straddling him on the table.

Linnea Quigley . . . . Sally Webster

••• 0:06—Topless and buns, undressing and dancing during her audition.

••• 0:26—Full frontal nudity, acting with two guys.

Alan Simons . . . . Alan Cole

• 0:18—Nude, undressing and caressing himself during his audition.

•• 0:37—Buns, when his underwear is pulled down.

Robert Sommer . . . . Frank Murphy

••• 0:33—Nude, during dungeon scene.

• 1:07—Buns during orgy scene.

Sally Swift . . . . Melinda Sale

••• 0:21—Full frontal nudity, undressing and masturbating during her audition.

•• 0:30—Topless and buns, whipping Harry.

Idy Tripoldi . . . . Bonnie Tirol

••• 1:01—Full frontal nudity, taking off sweater.

•• 1:07—Topless and buns during orgy scene.

Bonnie Werchan. . . . . Tracy Matthews

••• 0:02—Topless, then full frontal nudity, undressing for her audition.

••• 0:31—Nude, undressing herself and Van.

•• 0:33—Buns and side of right breast, making love with Van.

•• 1:07—Topless and buns during orgy scene.

Yossi Yaari . . . . Moshe Mitzvah

• 1:10—Buns, while taking off his clothes during orgy scene.

Autumn Born (1979)

Dorothy Stratten . . . . Tara

0:03—In dressing room in beige bra, panties, garter belt and stockings changing clothes. Long, close-up lingering shots.

0:16—Unconscious in beige lingerie, then conscious, walking around the room.

0:21—In bra and panties getting her rear end whipped while tied to the bed.

•• 0:26—Left breast taking bath, then right breast getting up, then topless dressing.

• 0:30—Side view of left breast, then topless climbing back into bed.

0:35—In beige bra and panties in the shower with her captor.

0:43—Quick cuts of various scenes.

••• 0:46—In white bra and panties, side view of left breast and buns, then topless in bathtub. Long scene.

• 0:50—Side view of left breast and buns getting undressed. Nice buns shot. Right breast lying down in chair.

• 1:03—Brief topless shots during flashbacks.

Roberta Weiss. . . . . Melissa

0:07—Buns, wearing panties and bending over desk to get whipped.

Avanti! (1973)

(Not available on video tape. Shown on *The Arts and Entertainment Channel* periodically. Scenes are listed as 0:00 since I can't time correctly with the commercials.)

Jack Lemmon . . . . Wendell Armbruster

• 0:00—Buns, while standing up in bathtub talking to Juliet Mills.

Juliet Mills . . . . Pamela Piggott

0:00—Buns, climbing out of the water onto a rock.

• 0:00—Side view of right breast lying on rock talking to Jack Lemmon.

••• 0:00—Brief topless waving to fishermen on a passing boat.

0:00—Brief buns putting something up in the closet in Jack Lemmon's hotel room.

Avenging Angel (1985)

Laura Burkett . . . . Blonde Hooker

Charlene Jones . . . . Hooker

Karen Mani . . . . Janie Soon Lee

••• 0:06—Nude taking a shower, right breast in mirror drying herself off, then in bra getting dressed.

Betsy Russell . . . . Angel/Molly Stewart

Susan Tyrrell . . . . Selly Mosler
Deborah Voorhees . . . . Roxie
Lynda Wiesmeier. . . . . Debbie

Ay, Carmela! (1991; Spanish)
Carmen Maura . . . . Carmela
- •• 0:42—Showing her left breast to the Lieutenant to explain why she had a Republican flag. Subtitles get in the way.
- •• 1:38—Topless taking off flag on stage during play. Subtitles get in the way again.

Baby Love (1969)
Linda Hayden . . . . Luci
- 0:32—Buns, standing in room when Nick sneaks in.
- 0:34—Very brief right breast, white throwing doll at Robert.
- • 0:39—Topless in mirror taking a bath. Long shot. Brief left breast hidden by steam.
- • 0:52—Brief topless taking off her top to show Nick while sunbathing.
- 1:25—Brief topless calling Robert from window. Long shot.
- 1:27—Very brief topless sitting up while talking to Robert.
- • 1:28—Topless in open robe struggling with Robert.
Derek Lamden. . . . . Nick
- 1:29—Brief buns while in shower when Luci opens the door.

The Baby Maker (1970)
Scott Glenn. . . . . .Tad
- • 1:30—Buns while in bed with Charlotte.
Barbara Hershey . . . . Tish
- • 0:14—Side view of left breast taking off dress and diving into the pool. Long shot and dark. Buns in water.
- 0:23—Left breast (out of focus) under sheet in bed.
Helena Kallianiotes . . . . Wanda
- • 1:30—Brief topless when Barbara Hershey sees her in bed with Tad.
Brenda Sykes. . . . . Francis

Baby, It's You (1983)
Rosanna Arquette . . . . .Jill
- •• 1:17—Left breast, making love in bed with Vincent Spano.
Robert Downey, Jr. . . . . .Stewart
Richard Kantor . . . . Curtis
Marta Kober . . . . Debra
Matthew Modine . . . . Steve
Vincent Spano. . . . . Sheik

Bachelor Party (1984)
Angela Aames .Mrs. Klupner
Toni Alessandrini. . . . . . . Woman Dancing with Donkey
Monique Gabrielle . . . . Tracey
- •• 1:11—Full frontal nudity in the hotel bedroom with Tom Hanks as his bachelor party gift.
Annie Gaybis. . . . . Arab Dressed Hooker
Rosanne Katon . . . . Bridal Shower Hooker

Tawny Kitaen. . . . . .Debbie Thompson
Rebecca Perle. . . . . Screaming Woman
Robert Prescott. . . . . Richard Chance
- • 1:18—Buns, after being hung out the window tied up with sheets by Tom Hanks and his friends.
William Tepper. . . . . Dr. Stan Gassko

Back In the U.S.S.R. (1992)
Natalya Negoda. . . . . Lena
- •• 0:46—Side view of left breast, making love with Sloan in the bathtub. Brief right breast when Dimitri comes into the bathroom.

Back to Back (1990)
Apollonia . . . . .Jesse Duro
Susan Anspach. Madeline Hix
Todd Field . . . . Todd Brand
- •• 0:33—Buns, while walking to and jumping into swimming pool.
Bill Paxton . . . . Bo Brand

Back to School (1986)
Adrienne Barbeau. Vanessa
Robert Downey, Jr. . . . . .Derek
Leslie Huntly. . . . . Coed #1
- •• 0:14—Brief topless in the shower room when Rodney Dangerfield first arrives on campus.
Sally Kellerman. . . . . .Diane
Becky LeBeau . . . . Bubbles, the Hot Tub Girl
M. Emmet Walsh . . . . Coach Turnbull

Backdraft (1991)
William Baldwin . . . . .Brian McCaffrey
- •• 0:33—Brief buns (on the left) in the shower room with Jason Gedrick.
Rebecca De Mornay. . . . . Helen McCaffrey
Robert De Niro. . . . . .Donald Rimgale
Jason Gedrick. . . . . .Tim Krizminski
- •• 0:33—Brief buns (on the right) in the shower room with William Baldwin.
Scott Glenn. . . . . John Adcox
Jennifer Jason Leigh . . . . Jennifer Vaitkus
- • 1:16—Very, very brief left breast on back of fire truck with William Baldwin. (Right after someone knocks open a door with an axe.)
Kurt Russell . . . . Stephen McCaffrey
Donald Sutherland. . . . . .Ronald Bartel

Backfire (1987)
Karen Allen. . . . . Mara
- • 0:48—Lots of buns, then brief topless with Keith Carradine in the bedroom.
- • 1:00—Brief topless in the shower.
Keith Carradine . . . . Clinton James
Bernie Casey . . . . Clinton James
Jeff Fahey. . . . . Donnie
- • 0:22—Brief, partial buns while taking a shower, then very brief, out of focus frontal nudity in shower when blood starts to gush out of the shower head.

Backstab (1990)
June Chadwick. . . . . Mrs. Caroline Chambers

Meg Foster . . . . .Sara Rudnick
Isabelle Truchon . . . . .Jennifer
- •• 0:08—In bra, then topless in back seat of car with James Brolin.
- • 0:16—Buns, black panties and stockings while on the floor with Brolin. Brief right breast.
- • 0:18—Brief buns in front of fireplace. Side view of right breast. Buns, while walking into the other room.

Backstreet Dreams (1990)
Maria Celedonio . . . . Maria M.
Sherilyn Fenn . . . . Lucy
- • 0:00—Right breast while sleeping in bed with Dean. Medium long shot.
Brooke Shields. . . . . .Stephanie "Stevie" Bloom

Backtrack (1989)
a.k.a. Catch Fire
Jodie Foster . . . . Anne Benton
- • 0:50—Topless behind textured shower door.
- ••• 0:51—Topless, leaning out of the shower to get her towel. Very, very brief side of left breast and buns, while drying herself off in bedroom. Side of left breast and buns, while putting on slip.
Dennis Hopper . . . . Milo
Helena Kallianiotes . . . . .Grace Carelli
John Turturro . . . . .Pinella
Fred Ward. . . . . .Pauling

Bad Boys (1983)
Clancy Brown . . . . Viking Lofgren
Sean Penn. . . . . Mick O'Brien
- • 0:10—Brief buns while getting up off the floor with Ally Sheedy.
- •• 0:46—Buns while taking a shower.
Ally Sheedy . . . . J. C. Walenski
- • 0:12—Very, very brief left breast, while kneeling on floor next to bed when Sean Penn leaves. A little blurry and a long shot.

Bad Girls from Mars (1990)
Jasaé. . . . . .Terry
- ••• 0:03—Topless taking off her top.
- •• 0:05—More topless going into dressing room.
Dana Bentley Konkel . . . . Martine
- •• 0:28—Topless taking off her blouse in office.
- •• 0:59—Topless several times wrestling with Edy Williams.
Sherri Graham. . . . . Swimmer
- •• 0:22—Very brief topless diving into, then climbing out of pool.
Brinke Stevens. . . . . .Myra
- • 0:11—Brief side of left breast, then topless getting massaged on diving board.
Edy Williams . . . . .Emanuelle
- •• 0:17—Topless several times changing in back of convertible car.
- ••• 0:23—Topless changing out of wet dress in bathroom.
- ••• 0:30—Topless taking off blouse to get into spa.

- • 0:32—Topless in back of Porsche and getting out.
- ••• 0:35—Topless in store, signing autograph for robber.
- • 0:46—Buns in G-string, then topless taking off her top again.
- ••• 0:58—Topless in T.J.'s office. More topless when wrestling with Martine.
- • 1:05—Topless tied up.
- • 1:07—Topless again.
- •• 1:17—Topless taking off her outfit during outtakes.

Bad Influence (1990)
Charisse Glenn . . . . .Stylish Eurasian Woman
- ••• 1:26—Topless and partial lower frontal nudity making love on Rob Lowe.
- • 1:28—Very brief left breast in bed with the blonde woman.
Rob Lowe. . . . . .Alex
- ••• 1:27—Buns, while going into the bathroom.
James Spader . . . . .Michael Boll
Lisa Zane . . . . .Claire
- • 0:39—Brief topless on video tape seen on TV at party.

Bad Manners (1989)
Karen Black . . . . Mrs. Fitzpatrick
Kimmy Robertson. . . . . Sarah Fitzpatrick
- •• 0:38—Topless and buns taking off robe and getting into the shower when Mouse takes a picture of her. 1:16—In white bra when Piper rips her blouse open while she's tied up on the piano. 1:18—Briefly on piano again.
Edy Williams. . . . . .Mrs. Slatt

Bad Timing: A Sensual Obsession (1980)
Art Garfunkel . . . . Alex Linden
- • 0:55—Buns, while making love with Theresa Russell on stairwell. Don't see his face.
- • 0:57—Buns (Sort of see his balls through his legs), while on top of Russell when visited by Harvey Keitel. 1:48—Side view of buns while in bed with an unconscious Russell.
Harvey Keitel . . . . Inspector Netusil
Theresa Russell . . . . Milena Flaherty
- 0:14—Buns and topless under short, sheer blouse. 0:17—Almost brief right breast in bed during Art Garfunkel's flashback. Very brief left breast kneeling on bed with him.
- • 0:31—Full frontal nudity in bed with Garfunkel. Intercut with tracheotomy footage. Kind of gross.
- •• 0:32—Right breast, while sitting in bed talking to Garfunkel.
- • 0:41—Brief topless several times on operating table.
- • 0:55—Full frontal nudity making love on stairwell with Garfunkel. Quick cuts.
- • 0:56—Brief topless twice after stairwell episode while throwing a fit.
- •• 1:45—In bra, then topless passed out on bed while Garfunkel cuts her clothes off. Brief full frontal nudity.

•• 1:48—More topless cuts while Garfunkel makes love to her while she's unconscious from an overdose of drugs.

The Bagdad Café *(1988)*
Marianne Sägebrecht . . . . Jasmin
•• 1:09—Right breast slowly lowering her top, posing while Jack Palance paints.
•• 1:12—More topless posing for Palance.

Baja Oklahoma *(1988; Made for Cable Movie)*
Alice Krige. . . . . Patsy Cline
Karen Laine . . . . Girl at Drive-In
• 0:04—Left breast, in truck with a jerk guy. Dark, hard to see anything.
Julia Roberts . . . . Candy

The Ballad of Cable Hogue *(1970)*
Stella Stevens . . . . Hildy
1:12—Buns changing into nightgown in bedroom.
• 1:14—Brief top half of breasts in outdoor tub, then buns running into cabin when stagecoach arrives.

The Banker *(1989)*
Robert Forster . . . . Dan
Duncan Regehr . . . . Osbourne
• 0:03—Buns, while getting out of bed with Teri Weigel. Don't see his face.
Debi Richter . . . . Melanie
Christina Walker . . . . Girl
• 0:18—Topless on bed with Jeff Conaway
Teri Weigel . . . . Jaynie
••• 0:02—Taking off dress, then in lingerie, then topless making love with Osbourne in bed. More topless after.

Barbarella *(1968; French/Italian)*
Jane Fonda . . . . Barbarella
•• 0:04—Topless getting out of space suit during opening credits in zero gravity. Hard to see because the frame is squeezed so the lettering will fit.
Anita Pallenberg . . . . The Black Queen

Barbarian Queen *(1985)*
Lana Clarkson . . . . Amethea
•• 0:38—Brief topless during attempted rape.
••• 0:48—Topless being tortured with metal hand then raped by torturer.
Dawn Dunlap . . . . Taramis
• 0:00—Topless, in the woods getting raped.
Katt Shea . . . . Estrild
• 0:31—Brief topless getting top torn off by guards.

Barfly *(1987)*
Faye Dunaway. . . . . Wanda Wilcox
• 0:58—Brief upper half of breasts in bathtub talking to Mickey Rourke.
Alice Krige. . . . . Tully
Sandy Martin . . . . Janice
Mickey Rourke. . . . . Henry

Basic Training *(1984)*
Angela Aames . . . . Cheryl
• 0:19—Brief topless in bathtub.
Erika Dockery . . . . Salesgirl 2
• 0:00—Brief topless standing behind the desk.
Ann Dusenberry . . . . Melinda Griffin
••• 1:13—Topless in Russian guy's bedroom.
Barbara Peckinpaugh . . . . Salesgirl 1
• 0:00—Topless on desk with another salesgirl.
Rhonda Shear. . . . . Debbie
• 0:07—Topless making love with Mark.
0:15—In bra, making love on Mark's desk.

Basket Case *(1982)*
Kevin Van Hetenryck . . . . Duane Bradley
•• 1:21—Frontal nudity, twice, running around at night.

Basket Case 2 *(1989)*
Heather Rattray . . . . Susan
• 1:20—Brief right breast twice, when white blouse gapes open in bedroom with Duane. Special effect scar on her stomach makes it a little unappealing looking.
Annie Ross . . . . Granny Ruth
Kevin Van Hetenryck . . . . Duane Bradley
• 0:34—Buns while standing in front of mirror looking at the large scar on the side of his body.

Basket Case 3: The Progeny *(1991)*
Carla Morrell . . . . Twin #1
•• 0:41—Topless in bed with her twin sister and Duane's brother.
• 1:29—Brief breast, lying in bed with her twin sister and Duane's brother after the end credits.
Carmen Morrell . . . . Twin #2
•• 0:41—Topless in bed with her twin sister and Duane's brother.
• 1:29—Brief breast, lying in bed with her twin sister and Duane's brother after the end credits.
Heather Rattray . . . . Susan
Annie Ross . . . . Granny Ruth
Kevin Van Hetenryck . . . . Duane Bradley

Bay Boy *(1985; Canadian)*
Isabelle Mejias . . . . Mary McNeil
•• 1:28—Brief topless in her bedroom with Kiefer Sutherland, then brief topless in bed with him.

Beach Balls *(1988)*
Leslie Danon . . . . Kathleen
• 1:06—In bra, then brief topless in car with Doug.

The Beach Girls *(1982)*
Debra Blee. . . . . Sarah
••• 1:22—Brief topless opening her swimsuit top on the beach.
Corinne Bohrer. . . . . Champagne Girl
James Daughton . . . . Scott
• 0:33—Buns and very brief frontal nudity while taking off clothes and running into the ocean.
Tessa Richarde . . . . Doreen

Catherine Mary Stewart . . . . Surfer Girl
Jeana Tomasina. . . . . .Ducky
- •• 0:12—Topless and buns, lying on the beach with Ginger, while a guy looks through a telescope.
- ••• 0:54—Topless on a sailboat with a guy.
- • 0:55—Brief topless on the beach after being "saved" after falling off the boat.
- •• 1:12—Topless in sauna with Ginger and an older guy.

Beaks The Movie (1987)
Christopher Atkins. . . . . .Peter
Michelle Johnson. . . . . Vanessa
- • 0:26—Brief topless covered with bubbles after taking a bath. Don't see her face.
- • 0:31—Brief topless covered with bubbles after getting out of bathtub with Christopher Atkins. Don't see her face.

The Beast Within (1982)
Bibi Besch . . . . Caroline MacCleary
- •• 0:06—Topless, getting her blouse torn off by the beast while she is unconscious. Dark, hard to see her face.
Kitty Moffat. . . . . Amanda Platt
- •• 1:32—Topless, getting her dress torn off by the beast while she is unconscious. Don't see her face, could be a body double.

The Beastmaster (1982)
Tanya Roberts. . . . . Kiri
- ••• 0:35—Topless in a pond while Marc Singer watches, then topless getting out of the water when his pet ferrets steal her towel.
Marc Singer . . . . .Dar
Linda Smith. . . . . .Kiri's Friend
- • 0:35—Topless in a pond with Tanya Roberts.
Rip Torn . . . . Maax

Bedroom Eyes
(1985; Made for Cable Movie; Canadian)
Dayle Haddon. . . . . .Alixe
    1:06—Getting undressed in tap pants and white camisole top while Harry watches in the mirror.
Barbara Law . . . . Jobeth
- • 0:02—Topless taking off clothes while Harry watches through the window.
- •• 0:07—Topless and buns, kissing a woman.
- • 0:14—Topless during Harry's flashback when he talks to the psychiatrist.
- •• 0:23—Topless and buns dancing in bedroom.
- •• 0:57—Topless with Mary, kissing on floor.
    1:17—In beige bra, panties, garter belt and stockings in bed with Harry.
- • 1:23—Brief topless on top of Harry.

Bedroom Eyes II (1989)
Linda Blair. . . . . Sophie Stevens
    0:31—Buns, in bed with Wings Hauser.
- • 0:33—Brief left breast under bubbles in the bathtub. Don't see her face.

Jennifer Delora. . . . . Gwendolyn
- •• 0:04—Undressing in hotel room with Vinnie. Topless, then making love.
Jane Hamilton . . . . JoBeth McKenna
- • 0:50—Topless knifing Linda Blair, then fighting with Wings Hauser.
Wings Hauser. . . . . Harry Ross
Kathy Shower. . . . . Carolyn Ross
- •• 0:22—Topless in the artist's studio fighting with her lover while Wings Hauser watches through the window.
Kimberly Taylor . . . . .Michelle

The Bedroom Window (1987)
Brad Greenquist. .Henderson
- • 0:35—Buns, turning off the light while Steve Guttenberg spies on him.
Steve Guttenberg . . . . Terry Lambert
- •• 0:05—Buns, while getting out of bed and walking to the bathroom.
Isabelle Huppert. . . . . Sylvia Wentworth
- •• 0:06—Briefly nude while looking out the window at attempted rape.
Elizabeth McGovern. .Denise
    1:25—Topless silhouette on shower curtain when Steve Guttenberg peeks in the bathroom.

The Believers (1987)
Helen Shaver .Jessica Halliday
- • 0:38—Brief glimpse of right breast while lying in bed with Martin Sheen.
    1:17—Buns, getting out of bed.
Martin Sheen . . . . Dr. Cal Jamison

The Bell Jar (1979)
Roxanne Hart. . . . . n.a.
Marilyn Hassett . . . . .Esther Greenwood
- • 0:10—In bra, then brief topless in bed with Buddy. Dark, hard to see.
- •• 1:09—Topless taking off her clothes and throwing them out the window while yelling.
Jameson Parker. . . . . Buddy
- • 0:09—Frontal nudity silhouette standing in bedroom with Marilyn Hassett, then buns. Dark, hard to see.
Mary Louise Weller. Doreen

The Belly of an Architect (1987; British/Italian)
Stefania Casini . . . . .Flavia Speckler
- ••• 1:15—Lower frontal nudity, in open robe with Brian Dennehy. Then buns and topless on couch. Kind of a long shot.
Brian Dennehy. . . . . .Stourley Kraclite
- ••• 0:12—Buns, while taking off underwear and getting into bed with Chloe Webb. Kind of a long shot.
Chloe Webb. . . . . Louisa Kracklite
- •• 0:01—Very brief right breast, making love on train with Brian Dennehy. Brief side view of right breast sitting up and putting camisole top on.
- • 0:56—Brief buns in room with Lambert Wilson.
- • 1:07—Brief buns, lying in bed with Wilson.

1:27—Topless B&W photos of a pregnant woman. Supposedly her, but probably not.

Lambert Wilson . . . . Caspasian Speckler
- •• 0:56—Buns, several time in room with Chloe Webb while Brian Dennehy watches through keyhole.
- • 1:04—Upper half of buns, while lying in bed with Webb. Long shot.

Best Friends (1982)

Goldie Hawn .Paula McCullen
- • 0:18—Very, very brief side view of right breast getting into the shower with Burt Reynolds.
- • 1:14—Upper half of left breast in the shower, twice.

Burt Reynolds .Richard Babson

The Best of Sex and Violence (1981)

Elvira . . . . Katya
- •• 0:40—Brief topless dancing on stage in scene from *Working Girls*.

Vanity . . . . Tanya
- • 0:24—Buns and topless in various scenes from *Tanya's Island*.

Angela Aames . . . . Little Bo Peep
- • 0:18—Brief topless in scene from *Fairytales*.
- • 0:20—Brief right breast in scene from *Fairytales*.

Phyllis Davis . . . . Sugar/Joy
- •• 0:56—Topless after bath and in bed in scenes from *Sweet Sugar*.
- ••• 0:59—Topless and buns walking out of lake in scene from *Terminal Island*.

Uschi Digard . . . . Truck Stop Woman
- • 0:47—Topless getting chased by policeman in parking lot in scene from *Truck Stop Women*.

Laura Gemser . . . . .Emanuelle
- • 0:23—Side of left breast while getting clothes taken off by a guy. Long shot. Scene from *Emanuelle Around the World*.

Claudia Jennings . . . . Rose
- •• 0:46—Topless taking off her blouse in scene from *Truck Stop Women*.

Laura Jane Leary . . . . Girl Victim
- • 0:00—Getting clothes ripped off, then in bra and panties, then topless.

Joan Prather . . . . Herself
- •• 0:38—Topless getting her breasts squeezed by an attacker. Dark.

Cheryl Smith . . . . .Cinderella
- • 0:14—Topless taking a bath in scene from *Cinderella*.

Edy Williams . . . . Herself
- •• 0:46—Topless in various scenes from *Dr. Minx*.

The Betsy (1978)

Jane Alexander . . . . Alicia Hardeman
Kathleen Beller . . . . Betsy Hardeman
- ••• 0:12—Brief nude getting into swimming pool.
- •• 1:14—Topless in bed with Tommy Lee Jones.

Lesley-Anne Down . . . . Lady Bobby Ayres
- • 0:38—Brief left breast with Tommy Lee Jones.
- • 0:57—Very brief left breast in bed with Jones.

Tommy Lee Jones . . . . .Angelo Perino
Katharine Ross . . . . Sally Hardeman

Betty Blue (1986; French)

Jean-Hughes Anglade . . . . Zorg
- ••• 0:09—Frontal nudity.
- •• 1:03—Nude trying to sleep in living room.
- •• 1:39—Frontal nudity walking to the bathroom.
- •• 1:45—Frontal nudity talking on the telephone.

Béatrice Dalle . . . . Betty
- ••• 0:01—Topless making love in bed with Zorg. Long sequence.
- ••• 0:30—Nude on bed having sex with boyfriend.
- ••• 1:03—Nude trying to sleep in living room.
- ••• 1:21—Topless in white tap pants in hallway.
- ••• 1:29—Topless lying down with Zorg.
- ••• 1:39—Topless sitting on bathtub crying & talking.

Between the Lines (1977)

Allison Argo . . . . Dancer
- • 0:28—Topless dancing on stage.

Jeff Goldblum . . . . .Max
John Heard . . . . Harry
- •• 1:17—Buns, while putting his pants on.

Marilu Henner . . . . .Danielle
0:27—Dancing on stage wearing pasties.

Bruno Kirby . . . . .David
Gwen Welles . . . . .Laura
- •• 0:32—Buns and topless drying off with a towel in front of a mirror.

Beverly Hills Cop II (1987)

Rebecca Ferratti . . . . .Playboy Playmate
Kymberly Herrin . . . . .Playboy Playmate
Venice Kong . . . . .Playboy Playmate
Luann Lee .Playboy Playmate
Carrie Leigh . . . . Herself
Brigitte Nielsen . . . . Karla Fry
Kym Paige .Playboy Playmate
Jürgen Prochnow . . . . Maxwell Dent
Ola Ray . . . . .Playboy Playmate
Judge Reinhold . . . . Detective Billy Rosewood
Teal Roberts . . . . Stripper
- •• 0:45—Topless and buns, wearing G-string at the 385 North Club.

Peggy Sands . . . . Stripper
- • 0:48—Very brief topless, dancing at the 385 North Club.

Alana Soares . . . . .Playboy Playmate
Kari Whitman . . . . .Playboy Model

Beverly Hills Vamp (1989)

Michelle Bauer . . . . Kristina
- • 0:12—Buns and brief side view of right breast in bed biting a guy.
0:33—In red slip, with Kyle.
- •• 0:38—Topless trying to get into Kyle's pants.
1:09—In black lingerie attacking Russell in bed with Debra Lamb and Jillian Kesner.
1:19—In black lingerie enticing Mr. Pendleton into bedroom.
1:22—In black lingerie, getting killed as a vampire by Kyle.

Britt Ekland . . . . Madam Cassandra
Greta Gibson. . . . . Screen Test Starlet
•• 0:53—Topless and brief buns in G-string lying on Mr. Pendleton's desk.
Jillian Kesner . . . . Claudia
   0:06—In white lingerie riding a guy like a horse.
   0:33—In white slip with Brock.
   0:42—Almost topless in bed with Brock. Too dark to see anything.
   1:09—In white nightgown attacking Russell in bed with Debra Lamb and Michelle Bauer.
   1:17—In white nightgown, getting killed as a vampire by Kyle.
Debra Lamb . . . . Jessica
   0:33—In black slip, with Russell.
••• 0:36—Topless and buns in red G-string posing for Russell while he photographs her.
••• 0:41—More topless posing on bed.
   1:09—In white nightgown attacking Russell in bed with Michelle Bauer and Jillian Kesner.
   1:19—In white nightgown, getting killed as a vampire by Kyle.
Dawn Wildsmith . . . . Sherry Santa Monica

Beyond Erotica (1979)
Andrea Rau . . . . Lola
  • 0:26—Topless, undressing in her bedroom.
 •• 0:30—Nude, undressing, then lying in bed, then trying on bunny costume.
  • 0:47—Left breast, while lying on the floor.
  • 0:56—Brief buns, running around in her cell.
  • 0:57—Brief nude, behind wall with holes in it.
  • 0:59—Left breast, seen though hole in the wall.
 •• 1:10—Topless in her bedroom.
  • 1:23—Left breast, in flashback to 0:47 scene.

Beyond Obsession (1982)
Tom Berenger . . . . Matthew
Eleonora Giorgi . . . . Nina
 •• 0:01—Topless, taking off her top and getting into the shower with Tom Berenger.
  • 0:59—Right breast in bed with Marcello Mastroianni, brief right breast after.

Beyond the Door II (1977; Italian)
Daria Nicolodi . . . . Dora
  • 0:30—Buns, in the shower.
  • 0:47—Brief left breast in gaping nightgown, sitting up in bed.
John Steiner . . . . Bruno
  • 0:12—Brief buns, while making love with Dora on the sofa. Dark.

Beyond the Limit (1983)
Elpidia Carrillo . . . . Clara
 •• 0:31—Topless making love with Richard Gere. Long scene.
 •• 1:08—Topless talking to Gere. Another long scene.
Richard Gere . . . . Dr. Eduardo Plarr
  • 0:21—Buns.

Big Bad Mama (1974)
Angie Dickinson . . . . Wilma McClatchie
   0:38—Buns, making love in bed with Tom Skerritt.
••• 0:48—Topless in bed with William Shatner.
••• 1:18—Topless and brief full frontal nudity putting a shawl and then a dress on.
Sally Kirkland . . . . Barney's Woman
 •• 0:13—Topless and buns waiting for Barney then throwing shoe at Billy Jean.
Robin Lee . . . . Polly McClatchie
  • 0:09—Brief left breast in open dress in car when cops try to pull her car over.
   0:22—In see-through slip on stage with her sister and a stripper.
  • 0:32—Brief topless running around the bedroom chasing her sister.
Joan Prather . . . . Jane Kingston
 •• 1:15—Topless and buns in the bathroom with Tom Skerritt.
Susan Sennet . . . . Billy Jean
  • 0:49—Topless and buns with Tom Skerritt.
 •• 0:51—Topless and buns in bed with Skerritt.
Tom Skerritt . . . . Fred Diller
  • 1:18—Brief buns, while lying down with Angie Dickinson in barn.

Big Bad Mama II (1987)
Danielle Brisebois . . . . Billy Jean McClatchie
••• 0:12—Topless with Julie McCullough playing in a pond underneath a waterfall.
   0:36—In a white slip standing at the door talking to McCullough, then talking to Angie Dickinson.
Robert Culp . . . . Daryl Pearson
Angie Dickinson . . . . Wilma McClatchie
  • 0:48—Very brief full frontal nudity putting on her shawl scene from *Big Bad Mama* superimposed over a car chase scene.
 •• 0:52—Topless and brief buns (probably a body double) in bed with Robert Culp. You don't see her face with the body.
Kelli Maroney . . . . Willie McClatchie
Julie McCullough . . . . Polly McClatchie
 •• 0:12—Topless with Danielle Brisebois playing in a pond underneath a waterfall.
 •• 0:36—In lingerie, then topless sitting on Jordan who is tied up in bed.
Linda Shayne . . . . Bank Teller

The Big Bet (1985)
Stephanie Blake . . . . Mrs. Roberts
••• 0:04—Topless sitting on bed, then making love with Chris.
 •• 0:37—Nude on bed with Chris. Shot at fast speed, he runs between bedrooms.
 •• 0:59—Full frontal nudity in bed again. Shot at fast speed.
Elizabeth Cochrell . . . . Sister in Stag Film
••• 1:05—Topless and buns, undressing and getting into bathtub in a video tape that Chris is watching.

•• 1:08—Topless again on video tape, when Chris
   watches it on TV at home.
Kim Evenson . . . . Beth
•• 0:36—Right breast, sitting on couch with Chris.
•• 0:45—Brief topless, twice, taking off swimsuit top.
•• 0:54—Brief topless three times in elevator when
   Chris pulls her sweater up.
•• 1:06—Nude when Chris fantasizes about her being
   in the video tape that he's watching. Long shot.
••• 1:19—In white bra and panties, then nude while undressing for Chris.
Monique Gabrielle . . . . Fantasy Girl in Elevator
••• 0:51—In purple bra, then eventually nude in elevator with Chris.
Sylvia Kristel . . . . Michelle
• 0:07—Left breast in open nightgown while Chris
   tries to fix her sink.
•• 0:20—Topless dressing while Chris watches through
   binoculars.
•• 0:28—Topless undressing while Chris watches
   through binoculars.
••• 0:40—Topless getting out of the shower and drying
   herself off.
• 1:00—Topless getting into bed while Chris watches
   through binoculars.
••• 1:13—Topless in bedroom with Chris, then making
   love.
Lance Sloane . . . . .Chris
•• 0:38—Buns, while taking off robe and getting into
   bed with Angela Roberts after visiting Mrs. Roberts.
•• 0:52—Buns, while on elevator floor with Monique
   Gabrielle during his daydream.
• 1:07—Buns, while getting into tub with Kimberly
   Evenson during video tape fantasy. Long shot.
Jill Terashita . . . . .Koko

The Big Bird Cage (1972)
Teda Bracci . . . . Bull Jones
• 0:15—Topless in front of the guard, Rocco.
• 0:51—Very brief right breast, then left breast during
   fight with Pam Grier. Brief left breast standing up.
Anitra Ford . . . . .Terry
• 0:15—Left breast and buns taking shower. Brief low-
   er frontal nudity after putting shirt on when leaving.
0:19—Brief lower frontal nudity turing around.
• 0:44—Brief left breast during gang rape.
1:14—Brief left breast in gaping dress. Dark.
Pam Grier . . . . Blossom
Candice Roman . . . . .Carla
• 0:16—Buns, while in the shower.

The Big Chill (1983)
Tom Berenger . . . . Sam
Glenn Close . . . . Sara
• 0:27—Topless sitting down in the shower crying.
Jeff Goldblum . . . . Michael
William Hurt . . . . Nick
Kevin Kline . . . . Harold
Meg Tilly . . . . Chloé
JoBeth Williams . . . . Karen

The Big Doll House (1971)
Roberta Collins . . . . Alcott
••• 0:33—Topless in shower. Seen through blurry win-
   dow by prison worker, Fred. Blurry, but nice.
• 0:34—Brief left breast, while opening her blouse for
   Fred.
Pam Grier . . . . .Grear
• 0:28—Very brief most of right breast rolling over in
   bed.
•• 0:32—Topless getting her back washed by Collier.
   Arms in the way a little bit.
• 0:44—Left breast covered with mud sticking out of
   her top after wrestling with Alcott.
Brooke Mills . . . . .Harrad
• 0:28—Side of right breast, while lying in bed before
   rolling over.
Christiane Schmidtmer . . . . Miss Dietrich
Pat Woodell . . . . .Bodine
• 0:27—Brief topless hung by wrists and whipped by
   a guard. Hair covers most of her breasts.

The Big Easy (1987)
Ellen Barkin . . . . Anne Osborne
0:21—White panties in lifted up dress in bed with
   Dennis Quaid.
0:32—Brief buns jumping up in kitchen after pinch-
   ing a guy who she thinks is Quaid.
Dennis Quaid . . . . Remy McSwain
• 0:24—Brief buns when Ellen Barkin pulls his underwear down in bed.
••• 0:51—Buns, while putting underwear on after getting out of bed.

The Big Man (1991; British)
a.k.a. Crossing the Line
Julie Graham . . . . Melanie
•• 1:09—Topless when Liam Neeson undresses her and
   starts to make love with her.
Liam Neeson . . . . .Danny Scoular

The Big Sleep (1978; British)
Candy Clark . . . . Camilla Sternwood
••• 0:18—Topless, sitting in a chair when Robert
   Mitchum comes in after a guy is murdered.
• 0:30—Brief topless in a photograph that Mitchum is
   looking at.
0:38—Topless in the photos again. Out of focus.
•• 0:39—Topless sitting in chair during recollection of
   the murder.
•• 1:03—Very brief full frontal nudity in bed, throwing
   open the sheets for Mitchum.
1:05—Very, very brief buns, getting up out of bed.
Joan Collins .Agnes Lozelle
Edward Fox . . . . .Joe Brody
Sarah Miles . . . . Charlotte Sternwood
Diana Quick .Mona Grant
Oliver Reed . . . . Eddie Mars

The Big Town (1987)
Suzy Amis . . . . .Aggie Donaldson
Lolita Davidovich . . . . .Black Lace Stripper

Bruce Dern . . . . Mr. Edwards
Lee Grant . . . . Ferguson Edwards
Tommy Lee Jones . . . . George Cole
Diane Lane . . . . Lorry Dane
       0:51—Doing a strip routine in the club wearing a G-string and pasties while Matt Dillon watches.
    ••• 1:17—Topless making love on bed with Dillon in hotel room.
       1:27—Brief left breast wearing pasties walking into dressing room while Dillon plays craps.
Tom Skerritt . . . . .Phil Carpenter

The Bikini Carwash Company (1992)
(Unrated version reviewed.)
Suzanne Browne . . . . Sunny
    • 0:15—Brief topless when Stanley steals her bikini top.
    •• 0:25—Topless, washing windshield and side window.
    ••• 0:26—More topless while window washing.
    •• 0:30—Topless during water fight.
    •• 0:31—Topless at car wash.
    •• 0:35—Topless running after a guy who stole her bikini top.
    ••• 0:46—Topless and buns in G-string, hand washing a customer with Rita.
    ••• 0:47—Topless and buns, dancing inside car wash.
    ••• 0:53—Topless outside at car wash.
    ••• 1:02—Nude, soaped up in car wash with Melissa and Rita.
    ••• 1:12—Topless, posing for photos.
    •• 1:15—Topless when Stanley takes her top off.
Matthew Cary Dunn . . . . Donovan Drake
    ••• 0:44—Buns, while making love with Amy.
Jennifer Irwin . . . . .Awesome Beach Girl
    •• 0:00—Buns, on beach in a very small swimsuit.
    ••• 0:02—Brief right breast, turning over, then topless while yelling at Jack.
Eric Ryan . . . . Stanley
    • 1:15—Buns, when Sunny yanks his short pants down.
Scott Strohmyer . . . . Big Bruce
    •• 0:18—Buns, while walking on beach with Rita.

Bikini Summer (1991)
Melinda Armstrong . . . . .Cheryl
    • 0:07—Very brief topless and partial buns, in bathroom when Chet interrupts her.
       0:25—Close-up of buns, bending over while wearing a swimsuit.
    ••• 0:35—Nude in swimming pool and talking to Burt. Nice, long scene.
    •• 0:49—Topless and buns, trying on swimsuits, then having a water fight with Shelley Michelle.
       0:51—Buns, in swimsuit at the beach.
    ••• 1:17—Full frontal nudity in swimming pool flashback.
Lori Jo Hendrix . . . . Smart Girl on Beach
Jennifer Irwin . . . . .Mindy
Kelli Konop . . . . Rene

Shelley Michelle . . . . Jazz
    •• 0:33—Topless and buns in the shower while Max peeks through hole.
    •• 0:49—Topless and buns, trying on swimsuits, then having a water fight with Cheryl.

Bilitis (1982; French)
Patti D'Arbanville . . . . Bilitis
    ••• 0:25—Topless copying Melissa undressing.
    •• 0:27—Topless on tree.
    ••• 0:31—Full frontal nudity taking off swimsuit with Melissa.
       0:36—Buns, cleaning herself in the bathroom.
    •• 0:59—Topless and buns making love with Melissa.
Catherine Leprince . . . . .Helene
    •• 0:13—Topless taking off dress and getting into bed with Bilitis.

Billy Bathgate (1991)
Dustin Hoffman . . . . Dutch Schultz
Nicole Kidman . . . . .Drew Preston
    •• 0:42—Briefly nude, throwing off towel in front of a vanity with three mirrors.
    •• 0:52—Very brief full frontal nudity underwater. Brief full frontal nudity getting out of water and putting on dress.

Bio-Hazard (1984)
Angelique Pettijohn . . . . Lisa Martyn
    •• 0:30—Partial left breast on couch with Mitchell. In beige bra and panties talking on telephone, breast almost falling out of bra.
    ••• 1:15—Left breast, on couch with Mitchell, in outtake scene during the end credits.
    • 1:16—Upper half of left breast on couch again during a different take.

Bird on a Wire (1990)
David Carradine . . . . Eugene
Mel Gibson . . . . Rick Jarmin
    •• 1:01—Brief close-up of buns when Rachel operates on his gunshot wound. Don't see his face, but it is him.
Goldie Hawn . . . . Marianne Graves
    • 0:31—Buns, in open dress climbing up ladder with Mel Gibson.
    • 1:18—Very brief top of right breast rolling over on top of Gibson in bed. Don't see her face.
Joan Severance . . . . Rachel Varnay

Birdy (1985)
Sandra Beall . . . . Shirley
Nicholas Cage . . . . Al Columbato
Bruno Kirby . . . . Renaldi
Matthew Modine . . . . Birdy
    • 1:25—Buns, while squatting on the end of his bed, thinking he's a bird.
    • 1:29—Buns, while sitting on the bed. Longer shot.
    •• 1:33—Buns, while walking around naked in his bedroom.

• 1:42—Buns, after waking up when Nicholas Cage comes into his bedroom.

Elizabeth Whitcraft . . . . Rosanne

Maude Winchester . . . . Doris Robinson
　•• 1:32—Topless in car letting Mathew Modine feel her.

Karen Young . . . . Hannah Rourke

The Bitch (1979; British)

Joan Collins . . . . Fontaine Khaled
　0:01—In long slip getting out of bed and putting a bathrobe on.
　• 0:03—Brief topless in the shower with a guy.
　•• 0:24—Brief topless taking black corset off for the chauffeur in the bedroom, then buns getting out of bed and walking to the bathroom.
　0:39—Making love in bed wearing a blue slip.
　• 1:01—Left breast after making love in bed.

Sue Lloyd . . . . Vanessa Grant
　• 1:12—Side view of left breast and topless in the swimming pool.

Pamela Salem . . . . Lynn
　•• 0:46—Topless in bed making love with a guy after playing at a casino.

Bits and Pieces (1985)

Sandy Brooke . . . . Mrs. Talbot
　••• 1:03—Topless in bathtub washing herself before the killer drowns her. Very brief right breast when struggling.
　• 1:09—Brief topless under water in bathtub, dead.

Tally Chanel . . . . Jennifer
　0:58—In the woods with the killer, seen briefly in bra and panties before and after being killed.

Sheila Lussier . . . . Tanya
　•• 0:07—In bra, tied down by Arthur, then brief topless as he cuts her bra off before he kills her. Brief right breast several times with blood on her.

Bizarre (1986; Italian)

Florence Guerin . . . . Laurie
　•• 0:03—Topless on bed with Guido. Lower frontal nudity while he molests her with a pistol.
　••• 0:18—Nude after taking off her clothes in hotel room with a guy. Nice.
　••• 0:30—Full frontal nudity making love with Edward in the water.
　• 0:34—Brief side of right breast, taking off robe in bathroom with Edward. (He's made himself up to look like a woman.)
　••• 0:36—Topless in white panties making love with Edward.
　•• 0:40—Topless and brief lower frontal nudity in Guido's office with him.
　••• 0:45—Nude, playing outside with Edward, then making love with his toe.
　•• 0:47—Topless getting out of bed and putting a blouse on.
　•• 0:49—Topless with Edward when Guido comes in.
　• 1:11—Topless sitting in chair talking to Edward.

• 1:20—Lower frontal nudity, putting the phone down there.
• 1:28—Buns and lower frontal nudity on bed when Guido rips her clothes off and rapes her.

Robert Egon Spechtenhauser . . . . Edward
　• 0:29—Partial buns, while taking a shower when Laurie peeks in at him.
　• 0:31—Brief buns, while on top of Laurie in the water.
　••• 0:36—Buns, while on bed with Laurie. (He's made up to look like a woman.)

Black Belt (1992)

Sean'a Arthur . . . . Reporter

Deirdre Imershein . . . . Shanna
　••• 1:08—Topless in bed, making love with Don "The Dragon" Wilson.

Mia M. Ruiz . . . . Hooker
　••• 0:04—Topless sitting on bed.
　0:16—Topless, dead on bed, covered with blood.

Black Emanuelle (1976)

Laura Gemser . . . . Emanuelle
　• 0:00—Brief topless daydreaming on airplane.
　• 0:19—Left breast in car kissing a guy at night.
　•• 0:27—Topless in shower with a guy.
　••• 0:30—Full frontal nudity making love with a guy in bed.
　••• 0:37—Topless taking pictures with Karin Schubert.
　•• 0:41—Full frontal nudity lying on bed dreaming about the day's events while masturbating, then full frontal nudity walking around.
　•• 0:49—Topless in studio with Johnny.
　••• 0:52—Brief right breast making love on the side of the road. Full frontal nudity by the pool kissing Gloria.
　•• 1:00—Nude, taking a shower, then answering the phone.
　•• 1:04—Topless on boat after almost drowning.
　•• 1:08—Full frontal nudity dancing with African tribe, then making love with the leader.
　•• 1:14—Full frontal nudity taking off clothes by waterfall with Johnny.
　•• 1:23—Topless making love with the field hockey team on a train.

Karin Schubert . . . . Anne Danielli
　• 0:06—Brief topless adjusting a guy's tie.
　••• 0:14—Topless making love in gas station with the gas station attendant.
　••• 0:37—Nude, running in the jungle while Laura Gemser takes pictures of her.
　• 0:40—Topless, kissing Gemser.
　• 0:44—Right breast, making love with Johnny in bed.

Black Moon Rising (1986)

Linda Hamilton . . . . Nina
　• 0:50—Brief left breast, while making love in bed with Tommy Lee Jones.

Tommy Lee Jones . . . . Quint

Black Rainbow (1989; British)

Rosanna Arquette . . . . Martha Travis
   0:48—In black bra, panties, garter belt and stockings in while talking to Tom Hulce.
  ••• 0:50—Topless in bed with Hulce, then walking to bathroom.

Black Venus (1983)

José Antonio Ceinos . . . . Armand
  • 0:14—Buns, while making love with Venus in bed.
Monique Gabrielle . . . . Ingrid
  ••• 0:03—Nude in Sailor Room at the bordello.
  ••• 1:01—Topless and buns, taking off clothes for Madame Lilli's customers.
Florence Guerin . . . . Louise
  •• 0:45—Nude talking, then making love with Venus in bed.
  ••• 1:16—Nude frolicking on the beach with Venus.
  ••• 1:18—Nude in bedroom getting out of wet clothes with Venus.
  • 1:21—Buns in bed with Jacques and Venus.
Josephine Jaqueline Jones . . . . Venus
  •• 0:05—Topless in Jungle Room.
  ••• 0:11—Nude, in bedroom, posing for Armand while he sketches.
  • 0:14—Topless and buns making love with Armand in bed.
  •• 0:17—Nude, posing for Armand while he models in clay, then on the bed, kissing him.
  • 0:21—Brief nude getting dressed.
  ••• 0:38—Nude, making love in bed with Karin Schubert.
  0:45—Nude, talking and then making love in bed with Louise.
  •• 0:50—Topless when Pierre brings everybody in to see her.
  •• 0:57—Topless in silhouette while Armand fantasizes about his statue coming to life.
  ••• 1:04—Nude.
  ••• 1:07—Nude with the two diplomats on the bed.
  ••• 1:16—Nude frolicking on the beach with Louise.
  ••• 1:18—Topless in bedroom getting out of wet clothes with Louise.
  •• 1:21—Topless in bed with Jacques.
  •• 1:24—Full frontal nudity getting out of bed.
Karin Schubert . . . . Marie
  •• 0:38—Nude in bed with Venus, making love.

Black Widow (1987)

Sam Frey. . . . . Paul
  •• 1:18—Buns, while walking into swimming pool.
Dennis Hopper . . . . Ben
Terry O'Quinn. . . . . Bruce
Theresa Russell . . . . Catherine
  • 0:28—Briefly nude, making love in cabin.
  •• 1:18—Nude in pool with Paul.
Debra Winger . . . . Alexandra

Blackout (1989)

Michael Keyes Hall . . . . Alan Boyle
  • 1:19—Buns and balls viewed from the rear while stabbing Richard in bed.
Carol Lynley. . . . . Esther Boyle
  •• 1:01—Brief topless leaning against the wall while someone touches her left breast.

Blade Runner (1982)

Joanna Cassidy. . . . . Zhora
  •• 0:54—Topless getting dressed after taking a shower while talking with Harrison Ford.
Daryl Hannah. . . . . Pris
Rutger Hauer . . . . Roy Batty
Edward James Olmos . . . . Gaff
M. Emmet Walsh . . . . Bryant
Sean Young . . . . Rachael

Blame It on Rio (1984)

Michelle Johnson . . . . Jennifer Lyons
  •• 0:19—Topless on the beach greeting Michael Caine and Joseph Bologna with Demi Moore, then brief topless in the ocean.
  • 0:26—Topless taking her clothes off for Caine on the beach. Dark, hard to see.
  •• 0:27—Topless seducing Caine. Dark, hard to see.
  ••• 0:56—Full frontal nudity taking off robe and sitting on bed to take a Polaroid picture of herself.
  • 0:57—Very brief topless in the Polaroid photo showing it to Caine.
  • 1:02—Brief topless taking off her top in front of Caine while her dad rests on the sofa.
Demi Moore. . . . . Nicole Hollis
  • 0:19—Very brief right breast turning around to greet Michael Caine and Joseph Bologna.

Blaze (1989)

Lolita Davidovich . . . . Blaze Starr
  0:09—In bra doing her first strip routine. Very brief side views of left breast under hat.
  0:15—Strip tease routine in front of Paul Newman. At the end, she takes off bra to reveal pasties.
  0:42—In black bra and panties with Newman.
  •• 0:48—Topless on top of Newman, then side view of left breast.

Blind Date (1984)

(Not the same 1987 Blind Date with Bruce Willis.)
Kirstie Alley . . . . Claire Parker
  • 0:12—Brief topless making love in bed with Joseph Bottoms. Dark, hard to see anything.
Joseph Bottoms . . . . Jonathon Ratcliffe
Lana Clarkson. . . . . Rachel
  • 0:52—Brief topless rolling over in bed when Joseph Bottoms sneaks in. Dark, hard to see.
  1:11—In two piece swimsuit during a modeling assignment.
  1:18—In two piece swimsuit by pool.
James Daughton . . . . David

Valeria Golino . . . . Girl in Bikini
Marina Sirtis . . . . Hooker
••• 0:21—Topless walking to and lying in bed just before taxi driver kills her.

Blind Vision (1990)
Deborah Shelton . . . . Leanne Dunaway
••• 0:25—Topless, making love with her boyfriend on the floor.

Blindside (1988; Canadian)
Lolita Davidovich . . . . Adele
•• 0:32—Topless dancing on stage.
0:39—Sort of buns bending over and pointing a gun through her legs in front of mirror.
Lori Hallier . . . . Julie
Harvey Keitel . . . . Gruber

Blood & Concrete: A Love Story (1991)
Jennifer Beals . . . . Mona
• 0:10—Buns, in pulled up slip on bed with Billy Zane. Brief, out-of-focus shot of her left breast. Don't see her face.
James Le Gros . . . . Lance
Billy Zane . . . . Joey Turks

Blood and Sand (1989; Spanish)
Christopher Rydell . . . . Juan
• 0:15—Buns, while running away after fighting bull. Dark, long shot.
•• 0:18—Buns, seen between shower curtain when Sharon Stone watches.
• 1:05—Buns, while on top of Stone. Long shot.
Sharon Stone . . . . Doña Sol
0:57—Very brief upper half of right breast, making love on table with Juan.
•• 0:58—Left breast, making love in bed with Juan. Don't see her face well.
••• 1:04—Topless quite a few times, making love with Juan in the woods.

Blood Diner (1987)
Cynthia Baker . . . . Cindy
••• 0:44—Nude outside by fire with her boyfriend, then fighting a guy with an axe.
Carl Crew . . . . George Tutman
• 1:02—Buns, while mooning Sheeba through the passenger window of a van.
Tanya Papanicolas . . . . Sheetar & Bitsy
• 0:15—Brief topless as photographer during topless aerobics photo shoot.
• 0:24—Topless, dead on operating table, then dead, standing up.

Blood Link (1983)
Sarah Langenfeld . . . . Christine
•• 1:01—Topless in bed taking off her top in bed with Craig.
• 1:04—Topless in bed with Keith.
Penelope Milford . . . . Julie Warren
•• 0:22—Topless in bed with Craig. Very brief left breast grabbing pillow.

•• 1:24—In black bra in greenhouse with Keith, then topless, then brief right breast.
••• 1:35—Topless in bedroom with Keith.
Martha Smith . . . . Hedwig
•• 0:41—Topless, wearing black panties while in bed with Keith.
• 0:50—Topless getting slapped around by Keith.
••• 0:51—Topless sitting up in bed when Craig and Keith meet each other for the first time.
• 1:13—Topless, wearing red panties, in bed with Keith.

Blood Relations (1989)
Lydie Denier . . . . Marie
•• 0:07—Left breast making love with Thomas on stairway.
• 0:44—Brief left breast in bed with Thomas' father. Very brief cuts of her topless in B&W.
0:47—Getting out of swimming pool in a one piece swimsuit.
••• 0:54—Full frontal nudity undressing for the Grandfather.
Carrie Leigh . . . . Thomas' Girlfriend

Blood Sisters (1986)
Amy Brentano . . . . Linda
••• 0:12—Topless, getting out of bed.
•• 0:14—Topless, walking around. Right breast, in bed with Russ. Brief upper half of buns.
Ruth Corrine Collins . . . . Prostitute
Gretchen Kingsley . . . . Ellen
•• 0:32—Topless, changing clothes to go to sleep in bedroom.
••• 0:50—Topless in bed with Jim.
Maria Machart . . . . Marnie
•• 0:45—In bra, then brief topless putting on nightgown and caressing herself.

Blood Ties (1986; Made for Cable Movie; Italian)
Maria Conchita Alonso . . . . Caterina
•• 0:35—Brief topless when Vincent Spano rips her dress off.
Brad Davis . . . . n.a.
Barbara De Rossi . . . . Luisa
• 0:58—Brief topless on couch when bad guy rips her clothes off.
Vincent Spano . . . . n.a.

Bloodbath at the House of Death (1985; British)
Pamela Stephenson . . . . Barbara Coyle
• 0:50—Very brief topless getting clothes ripped off by an unseen being.

Bloodfist III: Forced to Fight (1991)
Jeannie Bell . . . . TNT Jackson
•• 0:55—Topless several times in movie *TNT Jackson* that the inmates watch while Diddler gets stabbed to death.
Bob Schott . . . . Weird Willy

Bloodsport (1987)
Leah Ayres-Hamilton . . . . Janice
Jean-Claude Van Damme . . . . Frank
•• 0:50—Brief buns while putting underwear on after spending the night with Janice.

Bloodstone (1988)
Laura Albert . . . . Kim Chi
• 0:05—Very brief side view of left breast turning around in pool to look at a guy.

Bloody Birthday (1980)
Julie Brown . . . . Beverly
••• 0:13—Dancing in red bra, then topless while two boys peek through hole in the wall, then buns. Nice, long scene.
0:48—In bedroom wearing red bra.
1:03—In bedroom again in the red bra.
Erica Hope. . . . . Annie
• 0:04—Brief topless in cemetery, making out with Duke.
Susan Strasberg. . . . . .Miss Davis
Sylvia Wright. . . . . .n.a.

Bloody Friday (1973)
a.k.a. Single Girls
Robyn Hilton. . . . . Denise
Chéri Howell . . . . .Shannon
• 1:01—Topless and buns after "accidentally" dropping her towel in front of Bud.
Claudia Jennings . . . . Allison
• 0:40—Topless, taking off her dress to sunbathe on rock at the beach. Long shot. Side view of right breast, putting dress back on when George talks to her.
•• 0:57—Topless, drying herself off after shower.
Joan Prather . . . . Lola
•• 1:06—Topless, acting out her fantasy with Blue just before getting killed. Dark.

Bloody Trail (1972)
Rickey Richardson . . . . Miriam
1:01—Peek at left breast in torn blouse.
• 1:05—Right breast while sleeping, dark, hard to see.

Blow Out (1981)
Nancy Allen. . . . . Sally
• 0:58—Brief upper half of right breast with the sheet pulled up in B&W photograph that John Travolta examines.
Amanda Cleveland . . . . .Coed Lover
• 0:02—Left breast in room while someone watches from the outside.
Missy Cleveland . . . . Shower Victim
•• 0:02—Topless in shower and on TV monitor while killer stalks outside.
John Lithgow . . . . Burke
Cindy Manion . . . . Dancing Coed
Missy O'Shea . . . . Dancing Coed
0:00—Dancing in sheer nightgown while a campus guard watches from outside the window.

Robin Sherwood. . . . . .Screamer
Roger Wilson . . . . Coed Lover

Blue Desert (1990)
Courteney Cox. . . . . Lisa Roberts
0:52—Silhouette of right breast, standing up with Steve. Probably a body double. Very, very brief right nipple between Steve's arms lying in bed. Dark, hard to see.
•• 0:53—Left breast, lying in bed under Steve. A little hard to see her face, but it sure looks like her to me!
1:14—Buns and part of left breast getting towel. Looks like a body double.
Craig Sheffer . . . . Randall Atkins

Blue Lagoon (1980)
Christopher Atkins . . . . Richard
•• 0:27—Nude swimming underwater after growing up from little children.
• 0:29—Buns, while underwater.
•• 1:03—Nude swimming under water.
• 1:05—Buns, while kissing Brooke Shields.
•• 1:09—Very brief frontal nudity in water slide with Shields.
Brooke Shields . . . . Emmeline
0:27—Nude swimming underwater after growing up from little children.
0:43—More underwater swimming.
1:00—Topless body double lying on a rock.
1:09—Right breast of body double in hammock.
1:24—Body double breast feeding the baby.

Blue Movies (1988)
Vickie Benson. . . . . .Andrea
Lucinda Crosby . . . . Randy Moon
• 0:10—Topless in a spa, in a movie.
•• 0:11—Topless, kneeling on a table, shooting a porno movie.
••• 0:32—Topless auditioning for Buzz.
• 1:02—Topless on desk in a movie.
Steve Levitt . . . . Buzz
•• 0:46—Buns, while walking around naked when Randy and Kathy make him and Cliff take their clothes off.
Darian Mathias. . . . . .Kathy
• 0:37—Very brief topless twice acting for the first time in a porno film.
0:39—Topless from above during screening of movie. Hard to see.
Christopher Stone . . . . Brad

Blue Steel (1989)
Clancy Brown. . . . . .Nick Mann
• 1:27—Upper half of buns, while lying on the bathroom floor. Don't see his face, so it could be anybody.
Jamie Lee Curtis . . . . Megan Turner
1:27—Very, very brief buns twice when rolling out of bed, trying to get her gun. Dark.
Elizabeth Peña . . . . Tracy Perez

Blue Velvet (1986)

Laura Dern . . . . Sandy Williams
Brad Dourif . . . . Raymond
Dennis Hopper . . . . Frank Booth
Kyle MacLachlan . . . . Jeffrey
- •• 0:41—Buns and very brief frontal nudity while running to closet in Isabella Rossellini's apartment.

Isabella Rossellini . . . . Dorothy
- • 1:08—Brief topless in apartment.
- • 1:40—Nude, standing on porch, bruised.

Bluebeard (1972)

Agostina Belli . . . . Caroline
- • 1:31—Brief left breast lying on grass getting a tan.
- •• 1:32—Topless taking off clothes and lying on the couch.

Sybil Danning . . . . The Prostitute
- • 1:08—Brief topless kissing Nathalie Delon showing her how to make love to her husband.
- • 1:09—Brief left breast, lying on the floor with Delon just before Richard Burton kills both of them.

Nathalie Delon . . . . Erika
- • 1:03—Topless in bed, showing Richard Burton her breasts.
- • 1:09—Brief right breast lying on the floor with Sybil Danning just before Richard Burton kills both of them.

Joey Heatherton . . . . Anne
- • 0:25—Topless under black see-through nightie while Richard Burton photographs her. Very brief right breast.
- ••• 1:46—Brief topless opening her dress top to taunt Richard Burton.

Karin Schubert . . . . Greta
- • 1:43—Brief topless, spinning around, unwrapping herself from a red towel for Richard Burton.

Marilu Tolo . . . . Brigitt
- • 1:25—Topless in sheer blue blouse arguing with Richard Burton.
- •• 1:27—Topless getting whipped by Burton.

Blume in Love (1973)

Susan Anspach . . . . Nina Blume
Kris Kristofferson . . . . Elmo
Marsha Mason . . . . Arlene
- • 0:22—Side view of right breast, then brief topless lying in bed with George Segal.
- • 0:35—Very brief right breast reaching over the bed.
- •• 0:54—Brief topless twice, reaching over to get a pillow while talking to Segal.

Erin O'Reilly . . . . Cindy
- • 0:40—Topless and buns, getting out of bed with George Segal.

Boarding School (1978; German)

a.k.a. Virgin Campus
a.k.a. Passion Flower Hotel
Nastassia Kinski . . . . Deborah Collins
- • 0:15—Brief topless in the shower with her roommates. Hard to tell who is who.

- • 1:11—Left breast, then topless in the shower (She's the second from the right) consoling Marie-Louise.
- • 1:16—Topless under sheer nightie.
- ••• 1:32—Topless making love with Sinclair.

Fabiana Udenio . . . . Gina

Bobbie Jo and the Outlaw (1976)

Belinda Balaski . . . . Essie Beaumont
- ••• 0:29—Topless in pond with Marjoe Gortner and Lynda Carter.
- • 0:43—Very brief topless, when Gortner pushes her into a pond.

Lynda Carter . . . . Bobbie Jo Baker
- 0:10—Partial side of left breast, changing blouses in her bedroom.
- ••• 0:17—Left breast, several times, while making love with Marjoe Gortner.
- •• 0:27—Brief left breast, making love with Gortner again at night.
- • 0:31—Very brief left breast, then very brief topless in pond with Gortner experimenting with mushrooms.

Body and Soul (1981)

Azizi Johari . . . . Pussy Willow
- ••• 0:31—Topless sitting on bed with Leon Isaac Kennedy, then left breast, while lying in bed.

Rosanne Katon . . . . Melody
- • 0:04—Left breast several times making love in restroom with Leon Isaac Kennedy.

Perry Lang . . . . Charles Golphin
Ola Ray . . . . Hooker #1
- • 0:54—Brief topless sitting on top of Leon Isaac Kennedy in bed with two other hookers.

Laurie Senit . . . . Hooker #3
- • 0:54—Brief topless lying next to Leon Isaac Kennedy in bed with two other hookers.

Body Chemistry (1990)

Lisa Pescia . . . . Claire
- ••• 0:18—Topless making love with Marc Singer standing up, then at foot of bed.
- 0:35—In purple bra in van with Singer.
- 0:55—Buns, standing in hallway. Long shot.

Marc Singer . . . . Dr. Tom Redding
- • 0:18—Buns, standing up in hallway holding Claire while making love. Long shot.

Body Chemistry 2: Voice of a Stranger (1991)

Maria Ford . . . . Uncredited Victim
- •• 0:37—Topless in bed during flashback. (This scene is from *Naked Obsession*.)

Monique Gabrielle . . . . Brunette in Flashback
- • 0:19—Very brief buns and left breast in bed.

Gregory Harrison . . . . Dan
- ••• 0:45—Buns on stairs when Brenda finds him in the morning.

Lisa Pescia . . . . Claire Archer
- • 0:42—Brief buns and side of left breast, making love on stairs with Dan.
- ••• 0:52—Topless and buns, in bathtub, standing up, sitting back down while talking with Dan.

- 1:07—Buns, in leather outfit in radio control booth with Morton Downey Jr.
- 1:18—Very brief buns and left breast on the stairs in flashback.

Body Double (1984)

Barbara Crampton . . . . Carol Sculley
- •• 0:04—Brief right breast, while making love in bed with another man when her husband walks in.

Alexandra Day. . . . . Girl in Bathroom #1
Melanie Griffith . . . . Holly Body
- •• 0:20—Topless in brunette wig dancing around in bedroom while Craig Wasson watches through a telescope.
- • 0:28—Topless in bedroom again while Wasson and the Indian welding on the satellite dish watch.
- •• 1:12—Topless and buns on TV that Wasson is watching.
- •• 1:13—Topless and buns on TV after Wasson buys the video tape.
- • 1:19—Brief buns in black leather outfit in bathroom during filming of movie.
- • 1:20—Brief buns again in the black leather outfit.

Barbara Peckinpaugh. . . Girl #2 (Holly Does Hollywood)
Windsor Taylor Randolph . . . . .Mindy
- ••• 1:50—Topless in the shower during filming of movie with Craig Wasson made up as a vampire.

Linda Shaw . . . . .Linda Shaw
- • 1:11—Left breast on monitor while Craig Wasson watches TV.

Deborah Shelton. . . . . Gloria
Brinke Stevens. . . . . Girl in Bathroom #3
- • 1:12—Topless sitting in chair in adult film preview that Craig Wasson watches on TV.

Craig Wasson . . . . Jake

Body Heat (1981)

William Hurt . . . . .Ned Racine
Mickey Rourke. Teddy Lewis
Kathleen Turner . . . . Maddy Walker
- • 0:22—Brief side view of left breast in bed with William Hurt.
- •• 0:24—Topless in a shack with Hurt.
  0:32—Buns, getting dressed. Long shot, hard to see.
- • 0:54—Brief left breast in bathtub. Long shot, hard to see.

Body Waves (1991)

Sean'a Arthur . . . . Dream Girl
- •• 0:02—Brief buns in swimsuit, walking into office.
- ••• 0:03—Topless, taking off her bathing suit top during Rick's dream.
- •• 0:07—Topless and side view of buns in swimsuit bottom, during Dooner's fantasy.

Sherrie Rose . . . . Suzanne
Sándra Wild . . . . .Anita
- ••• 0:39—Topless under sheer white robe, then topless with Larry on chair.
- ••• 1:12—Topless in bedroom with Larry.

Bolero (1984)

Ian Cochran . . . . .Robert Stewart
- • 1:26—Buns, while making love with Catalina.

Olivia D'Abo. . . . . Paloma
- • 0:38—Nude covered with bubbles taking a bath.
- • 1:05—Brief topless in the steam room with Bo.
- • 1:32—Topless in the steam room talking with Bo. Hard to see because it's so steamy.

Bo Derek . . . . Ayre McGillvary
- • 0:04—Brief topless, stripping to panties, outside after graduating from school.
- ••• 0:19—Topless making love with Arabian guy covered with honey, messy.
- ••• 0:58—Topless making love in bed with Angel.
- ••• 1:38—Topless during fantasy love making session with Angel in fog.

Ana Obregon . . . . Catalina Terry
- • 1:32—Brief topless making love with Robert.

Andrea Occhipinti . . . . Angel the Bullfighter
- •• 0:57—Buns, while lying in bed with Bo Derek, then making love with her.
- • 1:39—Side view of buns, during fantasy love making session with Bo in fog.

Bonnie's Kids (1973)

Tiffany Bolling . . . . Ellie
- •• 0:21—Topless, modeling in office.
- • 1:16—Brief right breast making love in bed.

Robin Mattson . . . . Myra
- • 0:05—Brief side view of right breast, changing in bedroom while two men watch from outside.
- ••• 0:07—Topless washing herself in the bathroom.

The Boost (1989)

James Woods . . . . Lenny Brown
Sean Young . . . . Linda Brown
- • 0:16—Very, very brief topless jumping into the swimming pool with James Woods. Very, very brief side view of right breast and buns, twice, getting out of the pool, sitting on edge, then getting pulled back in by James Woods.
- •• 0:17—Left breast, while in pool talking to Woods. Right breast visible under water.
  0:48—Brief topless under water in spa with Woods.

The Border (1982)

Elpidia Carrillo . . . . .Maria
- • 1:19—Right breast, opening her blouse in shack with Jack Nicholson.

Harvey Keitel . . . . .Cal
Jack Nicholson . . . . .Charlie
Valerie Perrine . . . . Marcy

Border Heat (1988)

Darlanne Fluegel . . . . .Peggy Martin
  0:23—In black bra straddling Ryan in the bedroom.
Michael J. Moore . . . . .J. C. Ryan
- • 0:14—Buns, while taking off his clothes and getting into spa with Darlanne Fluegel.

Born on the Fourth of July (1989)
Tom Berenger . . . . Recruiting Sergeant
Tom Cruise . . . . Ron Kovic
- • 0:47—Very brief buns, sort of, while in bed at hospital when his rear end is sticking through the bottom of a bed.
Willem Dafoe . . . . Charlie
Vivica Fox . . . . Hooker
- • 0:50—Brief right breast, while taking off bra on top of patient in hospital. Dark.
Jason Gedrick . . . . Martinez
Cordelia Gonzalez . . . . .Maria Elena
- ••• 1:43—Topless in black panties, then full frontal nudity in bed with Tom Cruise.
Andrew Lauer . . . . Vet
Mark Moses . . . . Optomistic Doctor
Billie Neal . . . . Nurse Washington
David Neidorf . . . . Patient
Kyra Sedgwick . . . . Donna
Lili Taylor . . . . .Jamie Wilson

Born to Race (1988)
Joseph Bottoms . . . . Al Pagura
- • 0:55—Brief buns, while taking off bathrobe on deck and jumping into the lake.
La Gena Hart . . . . Jenny
Marla Heasley . . . . .Andrea Lombardo
- • 0:52—Buns, outside at night while kissing Joseph Bottoms.
Marc Singer . . . . Kenny Landruff

The Boss' Wife (1986)
Arielle Dombasle . . . . Mrs. Louise Roalvang
- • 1:01—Brief topless getting a massage by the swimming pool.
- ••• 1:07—Topless trying to seduce Daniel Stern at her place.
- •• 1:14—Brief topless in Stern's shower.
Melanie Mayron . . . . Janet Keefer
Daniel Stern . . . . Joel Keefer

Boxcar Bertha (1972)
David Carradine . . . . Big Bill Shelly
- • 0:54—Buns, while putting pants on after hearing a gun shot.
Bernie Casey . . . . Von Morton
Barbara Hershey . . . . Bertha Thompson
- •• 0:10—Topless making love with David Carradine in a railroad boxcar, then brief buns walking around when the train starts moving.
- • 0:52—Nude, side view in house with David Carradine.
- 0:54—Buns, putting on dress after gun shot.

A Boy and His Dog (1976)
Suzanne Benton . . . . Quilla June
- •• 0:29—Nude, getting dressed while Don Johnson watches.
- • 0:45—Right breast lying down with Johnson after making love with him.
Don Johnson Vic

The Boy in Blue (1986; Canadian)
Melody Anderson . . . . Dulcie
- • 0:07—Brief cleavage while making love with Nicholas Cage, then very brief top half of right breast when a policeman scares her.
Nicholas Cage . . . . Ned Hanlan
Kim Coates . . . . .McCoy Man No. 2
Cynthia Dale . . . . Margaret
- ••• 1:15—Topless standing in a loft kissing Nicholas Cage.
David Naughton . . . . .Bill

Boys N the Hood (1991)
Cuba Gooding, Jr. . . . . .Tre Styles
- • 0:42—Buns, in bed with Tisha. Don't see his face, but it is him.
Tammy Hansen . . . . Rosa
Nia Long . . . . Brandi
- 1:16—In bra, lying in bed with Tre.
- • 1:17—Left breast, while in bed with Tre. Don't see her face, but it is her.

Boys Night Out (1987)
Teri Lynn Peake . . . . Maid
- ••• 0:25—Buns in G-string, then topless doing a strip routine. Long scene.

The Brain (1988)
Christine Kossack . . . . Vivian
- •• 0:24—Topless on monitor, then topless in person during Jim's fantasy.
- •• 1:11—Topless again in the basement during Jim's hallucination.

Brain Damage (1988)
Vicki Darnell . . . . Blonde in Hell Club
Joe Gonzales . . . . .Guy in Shower
- • 0:54—Buns, while taking a shower.

Brainwaves (1983)
Corinne Alphen . . . . .Lelia Adams
- • 0:03—Brief side of right breast, reaching out to turn off the water faucets in the bathtub.
- • 0:05—Full frontal nudity, getting electrocuted in the bubble bath.
- • 0:50—Brief right breast, during Kaylie's vision.
Suzanna Love . . . . Kaylie Bedford

Breakfast in Bed (1990)
Private Screenings.
Marilyn Chambers . . . . .Marilyn Valentine
- •• 0:04—Full frontal nudity, getting out of bubble bath and drying herself off while talking to her manager.
- ••• 0:21—Topless, taking off swimsuit top and sunbathing. Nude, swimming underwater.
- •• 0:53—In bra, then topless making love.
- 1:01—In black bra and panties, undressing in her room.
- •• 1:16—Full frontal nudity, getting out of bed, putting on robe, then getting back in with Jonathan.

Courtney James. . . . . .Mitzi
  ••• 0:36—Topless, walking into the pool. Also seen from
    under water.
  ••• 0:37—Topless and bun in G-string, getting out of
    pool.
  • 0:39—Topless on the beach with Mr. Stewart.
Michael Rose. . . . . .Jonathan Maxwell
  • 1:16—Half of buns, while lying in bed with Marilyn
    Chambers.
David Sills . . . . Henry Huntley
  •• 0:25—Buns, while in bed with Wendy.
  •• 0:35—Brief buns, while standing up in boat with
    Wendy.

Breathless (1983)
Richard Gere. . . . . Jesse
  •• 0:11—Frontal nudity dancing and singing in the
    shower. Hard to see because of the steam.
  •• 0:52—Buns, while taking his pants off to get into the
    shower with Valerie Kaprisky, then more buns in
    bed. Very brief frontal nudity. Dark, hard to see.
  • 0:53—Very, very brief top of frontal nudity popping
    up when Kaprisky gets out of bed.
Valerie Kaprisky. . . . . Monica Poiccard
  0:23—Brief side view of left breast in her apartment.
    Long shot, hard to see anything.
  ••• 0:47—Topless in her apartment with Richard Gere
    kissing.
  •• 0:52—Brief full frontal nudity standing in the shower
    when Gere opens the door, afterwards, buns in bed.
  •• 0:53—Topless, holding up two dresses for Gere to
    pick from, then topless putting the black dress on.
  • 1:23—Topless behind a movie screen with Gere. Lit
    with red light.
William Tepper . . . . Paul

A Breed Apart (1984; Made for Cable Movie)
Jane Bentzen. . . . . Reporter
  ••• 0:55—Left breast in bed with Powers Booth, then
    full frontal nudity getting out of bed and putting her
    clothes on.
Rutger Hauer. . . . . .Jim Malden
Kathleen Turner . . . . Stella Clayton
  •• 1:12—Topless in bed with Rutger Hauer, then left
    breast.

Breeders (1986)
LeeAnne Baker . . . . Kathleen
  ••• 0:28—Nude, undressing from her nurse outfit in the
    kitchen, then taking a shower.
  • 0:59—Brief topless in alien nest. (She's the blonde in
    front.)
  •• 1:08—Topless in alien nest.
  •• 1:09—Topless in alien nest again. (Behind Alec.)
  • 1:11—Topless behind Alec again. Then long shot
    when nest is electrocuted. (On the left.)
Amy Brentano. . . . . .Gail
  • 0:59—Long shot of buns, getting into the nest.
  • 1:07—Topless in nest, throwing her head back.
  •• 1:08—Brief topless, writhing around in the nest,
    then topless, arching her back.

  • 1:11—Topless, long shot, just before the nest is de-
    stroyed.
Adriane Lee . . . . .Alec
  •• 0:49—Topless, undressing while talking on the
    phone.
  • 1:07—Brief topless, covered with goop, in the alien
    nest.
  • 1:08—Brief topless in nest behind Frances Raines.
  • 1:09—Brief topless behind Raines again.
  • 1:11—Topless, lying back in the goop, then long
    shot topless.
Natalie O'Connell. . . . . .Donna
  • 0:02—Very brief left breast, getting her blouse
    ripped by creature.
  •• 0:44—Topless, sitting up in hospital bed, then buns,
    walking down the hall.
  ••• 0:47—More topless and buns, walking around out-
    side.
  • 1:10—Brief topless, standing up in the alien nest.
Frances Raines . . . . .Karinsa Marshall
  ••• 0:12—Nude stretching and exercising in photo stu-
    dio.
  • 0:16—Brief full frontal nudity, getting attacked by
    the creature.
  ••• 0:53—Topless and buns, taking off her blouse and
    walking down the hall and into the basement. Long
    scene.
  • 1:07—Very brief right breast in the alien nest with
    the other women.
  • 1:10—Brief topless standing up.

Brewster McCloud (1970)
William Baldwin . . . . Bernard
Shelley Duvall. . . . . .Suzanne
Sally Kellerman. . . . . Louise
  0:43—Brief back side of right breast giving a boy a
    bath.
  •• 1:07—Topless, playing in a fountain.
Jennifer Salt . . . . Hope

Bride of Re-Animator (1989)
Kathleen Kinmont . . . . Gloria/The Bride
  • 0:58—Brief topless several times with her top pulled
    down to defibrillate her heart.
  1:17—Topless under gauze. Her body has gruesome
    looking special effects appliances all over it.
  1:22—More topless under gauze.
  1:24—More topless. Pretty unappealing.
  1:27—Brief buns, when turning around after ripping
    out her own heart.
Fabiana Udenio . . . . .Francesca Danelli
  0:45—Most of her left breast in bed with Dan. His
    hand covers it most of the time.

Bright Angel (1990)
Valerie Perrine . . . . Alleen
Lili Taylor . . . . Lucy
  • 0:26—Brief top of breasts under water, taking a bath
    in a pond.
  •• 0:27—Topless, walking out of the pond.

Brimstone and Treacle (1982; British)
Sting . . . . Martin Taylor
- 1:19—Buns, while making love with Suzanna Hamilton on her bed. Dark, hard to see.

Suzanna Hamilton . . . . Patricia Bates
- •• 0:47—Topless in bed when Sting opens her blouse and fondles her.
- •• 1:18—Topless in bed when Sting fondles her again.
- • 1:20—Brief lower frontal nudity writhing around on the bed after Denholm Elliott comes downstairs.

Bring Me the Head of Alfredo Garcia (1974)
Kris Kristofferson . . . . Paco
Isela Vega . . . . Elita
- • 0:25—Brief right breast a couple of times, then brief topless in bed with Warren Oaks.
- ••• 0:44—Topless when Kris Kristofferson rips her top off. Long scene.
- •• 0:52—Topless sitting in shower with wet hair.
- •• 1:49—Still from shower scene during credits.

Broadcast News (1987)
Lois Chiles . . . . Jennifer Mack
William Hurt . . . . Tom Grunik
- •• 0:59—Brief buns when getting up from bed after making love with Jennifer. Shadow of semi-erect penis on the wall when she notices it.

Brubaker (1980)
Jane Alexander . . . . Lillian
Linda Haynes . . . . Carol
- • 1:03—Topless getting dressed with Huey in bedroom when Robert Redford comes in.

David Keith . . . . Larry Lee Bullen
Yaphet Kotto . . . . Dickie Coombes

Bull Durham (1988)
Kevin Costner . . . . Crash Davis
David Neidorf . . . . Bobby
Tim Robbins . . . . Ebby Calvin "Nuke" La Loosh
- • 0:03—Buns, while in locker room making love with Millie when the coach sees them.

Susan Sarandon . . . . Annie Savoy
1:39—Brief right breast peeking out from under her dress after crawling on the kitchen floor to get a match.

Bulletproof (1988)
Lydie Denier . . . . Tracy
- •• 0:14—Topless in Gary Busey's bathtub.
0:20—Brief buns, putting on shirt after getting out of bed. Very, very brief side view of left breast.

Darlanne Fluegel . . . . Devon Shepard

Bullies (1985)
Olivia D'Abo . . . . Becky Cullen
- •• 0:39—In wet white T-shirt swimming in river while Matt watches.

Burglar (1987)
Steve Shellen . . . . Christopher Marshall
- • 0:26—Buns, while in front of closet that Whoopi Goldberg is hiding in. Don't see his face, but probably him.

Bury Me an Angel (1972)
Dan Haggerty . . . . Ken
- • 1:17—Brief buns, while making love with Dag in bed. Lit with red light. Kind of a long shot, don't see his face very well.

Dixie Lee Peabody . . . . Dag
0:11—Very brief silhouette of left breast, while getting into bed.
- • 0:13—Very brief right breast, while getting back into bed.
- ••• 0:41—Nude, skinny dipping in river and getting out.
- • 1:16—Topless making love in bed with Dan Haggerty. Lit with red light.

Clyde Ventura . . . . Bernie

Bushido Blade (1979; British/U.S.)
Laura Gemser . . . . Tomoe
- • 1:08—Brief right breast taking off her top in bedroom with Captain Hawk.

Buster and Billie (1974)
Joan Goodfellow . . . . Billie
0:33—Brief topless in truck with Jan-Michael Vincent. Dark, hard to see.
- • 1:06—Buns, then brief topless in the woods with Vincent.
- • 1:25—Brief left breast getting raped by jerks.

Pamela Sue Martin . . . . n.a.
Jan-Michael Vincent . . . . Buster Lane
- ••• 1:06—Frontal nudity taking off his underwear and walking to Billie. Buns, in slow motion, while swinging into the water.

Butterfly (1982)
Pia Zadora . . . . Kady
0:15—Silhouette changing while Stacey Keach watches.
- •• 0:33—Topless and buns getting into the bath.
- ••• 0:35—Topless in bathtub when Stacey Keach is giving her a bath.

Buying Time (1987)
Laura Cruikshank . . . . Jessica
- •• 0:52—Topless several times making love with Ron on pool table.

By Dawn's Early Light (1990; Made for Cable Movie)
Rebecca De Mornay . . . . Cindy Moreau
Randal Patrick . . . . O'Toole
- • 0:14—Brief buns while in shower room getting dressed during red alert.

By Design (1982; Canadian)
Sara Botsford. . . . . Angie
- 0:23—Full frontal nudity in the ocean. Long shot, hard to see anything.
- 1:08—Brief side view of left breast making love in bed while talking on the phone.

Patty Duke . . . . Helen
- • 0:49—Left breast, lying in bed.
- • 1:05—Brief left breast sitting on bed.
- • 1:06—Brief left breast, then brief right breast lying in bed with the photographer.

Bye Bye Baby (1989; Italian)
Carol Alt . . . . Sandra
0:09—Part of right breast, while in the shower.
0:22—Wearing a white bra, while taking off her blouse in the doctor's office.

Luca Barbareschi . . . . Paulo
- 0:20—Brief buns, while on top of Brigitte Nielsen in bed.

Brigitte Nielsen . . . . Lisa
- 0:20—Brief side view of right breast, while lying on a guy in bed. Nice buns shot also.

C.O.D. (1983)
Corinne Alphen . . . . Cheryl Westwood
- 0:21—Brief topless changing clothes in dressing room while talking to Zacks.
- 1:25—Brief topless taking off her blouse in dressing room scene.
1:26—In green bra, talking to Albert.
1:28—In green bra during fashion show.

Carole Davis . . . . Contessa Bazzini
- 1:25—Brief topless in dressing room scene in black panties, garter belt and stockings when she takes off her robe.
1:29—In black top during fashion show.

Samantha Fox . . . . Female Reporter
Teresa Ganzel . . . . .Lisa Foster
- 0:46—Right breast hanging out of dress while dancing at disco with Zack.
- 1:25—Brief side view of left breast taking off purple robe in dressing room scene. Then in white bra talking to Albert.
1:29—In white bra during fashion show.

Marilyn Joi. . . . . Debbie Winter
- • 1:16—Topless during photo session.
- 1:25—Brief topless taking off robe wearing red garter belt during dressing room scene.
1:26—In red bra, while talking to Albert.
1:30—In red bra during fashion show.

Olivia Pascal . . . . Holly Fox
1:30—In white top during fashion show.

Caddyshack (1980)
Sarah Holcomb . . . . Maggie O'Hooligan
Cindy Morgan. . . . . Lacey Underall
0:50—Very, very brief side view of left breast sliding into the swimming pool. Very blurry.
- • 0:58—Topless in bed with Danny three times.

Cadillac Man (1990)
Fran Drescher. Joy Munchack
- 0:07—Very brief right breast several times while in bed with Robin Williams.

Lori Petty . . . . Lila
Pamela Reed . . . . .Tina
Tim Robbins. . . . . Larry
Annabella Sciorra . . . . .Donna
Robin Williams . . . . Joey O'Brien

Caged Fury (1984)
Taaffe O'Connell . . . . .Honey
- • 0:17—Topless on bed with a guard. Mostly left breast.
0:40—Very, very brief tip of left breast peeking out between arms in shower.
- 1:06—Very brief topless getting blouse ripped open by a guard in the train.

Caged Fury (1989)
Blake Bahner . . . . .Buck Lewis
April Dawn Dollarhide . . . . .Rhonda Wallace
0:33—In white bra in open blouse on couch with Jack Carter.
- • 0:41—Topless undressing to enter prison with other topless women.

Janine Lindemulder .Lulu
0:14—Dancing in bar in black bra and G-string.
- 0:16—Brief topless dancing in front of Erik Estrada.

Sandra Margot. Crazy Daisy
1:13—Buns in G-string and bra dancing for some men.
- • 1:15—Topless taking off bra.

Roxanna Michaels . . . . Katherine "Kat" Collins
Melissa Moore . . . . Gloria
Windsor Taylor Randolph . . . . .Warden Sybil Thorn
- • 0:55—Topless and buns undressing for bath, then in the bathtub.

Elena Sahagun . . . . Tracy Collins
0:54—In bra when Buck holds her hostage.
- • 1:01—Left breast while taking a shower.

Caged Heat (1974)
a.k.a. Renegade Girls
Juanita Brown. . . . . Maggie
- 0:25—Topless in shower scene.

Deborah Clearbranch. . . . . Debbie
Roberta Collins. . . . . Belle
- 0:11—Very brief topless getting blouse ripped open by Juanita.
- • • 1:01—Topless while the prison doctor has her drugged so he can take pictures of her.

Erica Gavin . . . . .Jacqueline Wilson
- 0:08—Buns, getting strip searched before entering prison.
- • 0:25—Topless in shower scene.
- 0:30—Brief side view of left breast in another shower scene.

Cheryl Smith. . . . . Lauelle
- 0:04—Brief left breast, dreaming in her jail cell that a guy is caressing her through the bars.
- 0:25—Topless in the shower scene.
- 0:50—Brief nude in the solitary cell.

Cal (1984; Irish)
John Lynch . . . . Cal
- 1:20—Buns, while getting into bed with Helen Mirren.
Helen Mirren. . . . . Marcella
1:18—In a white bra and slip.
- 1:20—Brief frontal nudity taking off clothes and getting into bed with Cal in his cottage, then right breast making love.

California Casanova (1991)
Michelle Johnston . . . . Laura
- 0:18—Brief topless under sheer black top in front of a guy.

California Dreaming (1978)
Kirsten Baker. . . . . Karen
John Calvin . . . . Rick
Glynnis O'Connor . . . . Corky
- 0:11—Topless pulling her top over her head when T.T. is using the bathroom.
1:12—In white bra, in bed with T.T.
- 1:14—Topless in bed with T.T.
Tanya Roberts . . . . Stephanie
Dorothy Tristan . . . . Fay
0:05—In braless white top, jogging on the beach with Glynnis O'Connor.
- 0:20—Brief topless changing clothes while a group of boys peek through a hole in the wall.

California Suite (1978)
Jane Fonda . . . . Hannah Warren
Sheila Frazier. . . . . Bettina Panama
Denise Galik . . . . .Bunny
Maggie Smith . . . . Diana Barrie
- 1:05—Very brief side of left breast, putting nightgown on over her head.

Caligula (1980)
(X-rated, 147 minute version.)
Adrianna Asti. . . . . Ennia
- 0:27—Topless at side of bed with Malcolm McDowell when he feels her breasts.
- 0:54—Topless lying down surrounded by slaves. Mostly her right breast.
Mirella D'Angelo. . . . . Livia
- 1:08—Buns and topless in kitchen with Malcolm McDowell. Full frontal nudity on table when he rapes her in front of her husband-to-be.
Anneka di Lorenzo . . . . Messalina
- 1:16—Nude, making love with Lori Wagner. Long scene.
Malcolm McDowell. . . . . Caligula
- 0:05—Buns, while rolling around in bed with Drusilla.

- 0:36—Brief buns, while taking ring off of Peter O'Toole.
- 0:46—Very brief buns while running to bed.
0:51—Buns, while putting Drusilla down in bed.
- 1:14—Nude walking around outside in the rain. Dark, long shot.
2:23—Very brief buns while under his white robe.
Helen Mirren . . . . Caesonia
1:02—Side view of buns with Malcolm McDowell
- 1:13—Brief topless several times getting out of bed to run after McDowell. Dark.
1:15—Very brief left breast taking off her dress to dry McDowell off.
Donato Placido . . . . .Proculus
- 1:11—Frontal nudity taking his robe off for Malcolm McDowell. Buns, while getting raped by McDowell's fist.
Theresa Ann Savoy. . . . . Druscilla
- 0:01—Nude, running around in the forest with Malcolm McDowell.
- 0:05—Buns, rolling in bed with McDowell. Very brief topless getting out of bed.
- 0:26—Left breast several times in bed.
- 0:46—Brief right breast in bed with McDowell again.
- 1:15—Left breast with McDowell and Helen Mirren.
- 1:22—Very brief left breast getting up in open dress.
- 1:45—Full frontal nudity, then buns when dead and McDowell tries to revive her.
Lori Wagner. . . . . Agrippina
- 1:16—Nude, making love with Anneka Di Lorenzo. Long scene.

Call Me (1988)
Patricia Charbonneau. Anna
- 1:18—Brief left breast making love in bed with a guy, then topless putting blouse on and getting out of bed.
Patti D'Arbanville . . . . Coni

Can She Bake a Cherry Pie? (1983)
Karen Black . . . . Zee
0:40—Sort of left breast squished against a guy, while kissing him in bed.
- 1:02—Very brief upper half of left breast in bed when she reaches up to touch her hair.
Frances Fisher. . . . . Louise
Michael Margotta . . . . Larry

Candy Stripe Nurses (1974)
Kimberly Hyde . . . . April
Robin Mattson . . . . Dianne
- 0:22—Nude in gym with the basketball player.
- 0:40—Nude in bed with the basketball player.
Candice Rialson . . . . Sandy
- 0:05—Topless in hospital linen closet with a guy.
- 0:08—Topless smoking and writing in bathtub.
- 0:14—Topless in hospital bed.

Carmen (1983; Spanish)
Laura Del Sol . . . . Carmen
- 1:14—Left breast, while lying in bed with Antonio.
- 1:27—Brief partial left breast, standing up when Antonio catches her in wardrobe room with another dancer.

Carnal Crimes (1991)
Jasaé . . . . Christa
- ••• 0:19—Full frontal nudity in lingerie, making love with a guy while Linda Carol secretly watches.

Linda Carol . . . . Elise
- 0:01—Very brief left breast, while rolling over in bed.
- 0:05—In wet lingerie and very brief side view of right breast in shower fantasy.
- 0:07—Topless in B&W photo collage.
- 0:09—Full frontal nudity under sheer nightie, trying to get Stanley into bed.
- 0:11—Topless in B&W photo again.
- 0:24—Brief right breast outside window opening her top while watching Renny & Mia make out.
- 0:26—Brief upper half of right breast when bum molests her.
- ••• 0:28—Topless posing for Renny with Mia.
- ••• 0:29—Full frontal nudity making love with Renny and Mia.
- 0:30—Brief buns, sleeping in bed.
- ••• 0:38—Topless making love with the baker. Long scene.
- 0:49—Topless in B&W photo again.
- 1:02—Brief side view of right breast in gaping blouse.
- 1:33—Side view of buns in dominatrix outfit.

Sherri Graham . . . . Party Girl #1
Martin Hewitt . . . . Renny
- •• 0:29—Buns, while making love with Linda Carol and Mia.

Deirdre Morrow . . . . Leggy Girl
- 1:22—Buns, in G-string, leaning over to talk to Renny and Stanley.

Julie Strain . . . . Ingrid
- ••• 0:55—Topless and partial buns, wearing black garter belt and stockings, making love with Renny in restroom. Long scene.

Paula Trickey . . . . Jasmine

Carnal Knowledge (1971)
Ann-Margret . . . . Bobbie
- •• 0:48—Topless and buns making love in bed with Jack Nicholson, then getting out of bed and into shower with Jack.
- 1:07—Brief side view of left breast putting a bra on in the bedroom.

Candice Bergen . . . . Susan
Art Garfunkel . . . . Sandy
Carol Kane . . . . Jennifer
Jack Nicholson . . . . Jonathan

Carrie (1976)
Nancy Allen . . . . Chris Hargenson
- •• 0:01—Nude, in slow motion in girls' locker room behind Amy Irving.

William Katt . . . . Tommy Ross
P.J. Soles . . . . Norma
Sissy Spacek . . . . Carrie White
- •• 0:02—Nude, taking a shower, then having her first menstrual period in the girls' locker room.
- 1:25—Brief topless taking a bath to wash all the pig blood off her after the dance.

Cartel (1990)
Miles O'Keeffe . . . . Chuck Taylor
Suzanne Slater . . . . Nancy
- 0:28—In red two piece swimsuit modeling on motorcycle.
- 0:35—Brief bra and panties on bed during struggle.
- 0:36—Topless during brutal rape/murder scene.

Castaway (1986)
Frances Barber . . . . Sister Saint Winifred
Amanda Donohoe . . . . Lucy Irvine
- •• 0:32—Nude on beach after helicopter leaves.
- •• 0:48—Full frontal nudity lying on her back on the rocks at the beach.
- ••• 0:51—Topless on rock when Reed takes a blue sheet off her, then catching a shark.
- ••• 0:54—Nude yelling at Reed at the campsite, then walking around looking for him.
- ••• 1:01—Topless getting seafood out of a tide pool.
- •• 1:03—Topless lying down at night talking with Reed in the moonlight.
- ••• 1:18—Topless taking off bathing suit top after the visitors leave, then arguing with Reed.
- ••• 1:22—Topless talking to Reed.

Virginia Hey . . . . Janice
Oliver Reed . . . . Gerald Kingsland
- •• 1:46—Nude, doing things around the hut during the storm.

Casualties of War (1989)
John Leguizamo . . . . Diaz
- 0:53—Buns, while pulling his pants down to rape Oahn.

Sean Penn . . . . Sergeant Meserve

Cat Chaser (1988)
Tony Bolano . . . . Corky
- •• 1:16—Nude, undressing in bathroom with Andres, before getting shot by Charles Durning.

Kelly McGillis . . . . Mary De Boya
- ••• 0:23—Topless on the floor with Peter Weller. Long scene.
- ••• 1:04—Full frontal nudity taking off her slip and getting raped by her husband's pistol. Kind of dark.
- •• 1:06—Brief buns, getting pushed around the house. Right breast while signing a paper.

Tomas Milian . . . . Andres De Boya
- •• 1:16—Full frontal nudity, undressing in bathroom with Corky, before getting shot by Charles Durning.

Adrianne Sachs . . . . Anita De Boya
Peter Weller. . . . . George Moran
- •• 0:24—Very, very brief frontal nudity, twice when he is kneeling and takes his pants off. Buns, while making love on top of Kelly McGillis.

Cat in the Cage (1978)
Colleen Camp. . . . . Gilda Riener
- • 0:36—Very brief left breast twice, while making love in bed with Bruce.

Sybil Danning . . . . Susan Khan
- • 0:24—Brief topless getting slapped around by Ralph.
- • 0:25—Brief left breast several times smoking and talking to Ralph, brief left breast getting up.
- •• 0:30—Full frontal nudity getting out of the pool.
- • 0:52—Black bra and panties undressing and getting into bed with Ralph. Brief left breast and buns. 1:02—In white lingerie in bedroom. 1:10—In white slip looking out window. 1:15—In black slip.
- • 1:18—Very brief right breast several times, struggling with an attacker on the floor.

Cat People (1982)
Ed Begley, Jr. . . . . Joe Creigh
John Heard . . . . Oliver Yates
- • 1:37—Very brief side view of buns, while taking off his pants and sitting on bed next to Kinski.
- •• 1:50—Buns, while making love with Nastassia Kinski in bed in a cabin.

Nastassia Kinski . . . . Irena Gallier
- ••• 1:03—Nude at night, walking around outside chasing a rabbit.
- •• 1:35—Topless taking off blouse, walking up the stairs and getting into bed.
- • 1:37—Brief right breast, lying in bed with John Heard.
- •• 1:38—Topless getting out of bed and walking to the bathroom.
- •• 1:40—Brief buns, getting back into bed. Topless in bed.
- •• 1:47—Full frontal nudity, walking around in the cabin at night.
- • 1:49—Topless, tied to the bed by Heard.

Lynn Lowry . . . . Ruthie
- • 0:16—In black bra in Malcolm McDowell's hotel room, then brief topless when bra pops open after crawling down the stairs.

Malcolm McDowell. . . . . Paul Gollier
- • 1:06—Side view of buns, while lying on the bathroom floor. Partial lower frontal nudity when he gets up.

Annette O'Toole . . . . Alice Perrin
- ••• 1:30—In a bra, then topless undressing in locker room.
- • 1:31—Some topless shots of her in the pool. Distorted because of the water.
- • 1:33—Brief right breast, after getting out of the pool.

Tessa Richarde . . . . Billie
- •• 1:00—Topless in bed with Malcolm McDowell trying to get him excited.

Catch-22 (1970)
Alan Arkin . . . . Captain Yossarian
- • 0:52—Buns, while standing wearing only his hat, talking to Dreedle. Don't see his face.

Richard Benjamin. . . . . Major Danby
Suzanne Benton. . . . . Dreedle's WAC
Olimpia Carlisi . . . . Luciana
- • 1:04—Topless lying in bed talking with Alan Arkin.

Art Garfunkel . . . . Captain Nately
Paula Prentiss . . . . Nurse Duckett
- • 0:22—Full frontal nudity in water throwing her dress to Alan Arkin who is swimming in the water during his dream. Long shot, over exposed, hard to see.

Jon Voight . . . . Milo Minderbinder

Catherine & Co. (1975; French)
Jane Birkin . . . . Catherine
- • 0:07—Topless, standing up in the bathtub to open the door for another woman.
- •• 0:09—Side view of left breast, while taking off her blouse in bed.
- ••• 0:10—Topless, sitting up and turning the light on, smoking a cigarette.
- •• 0:17—Right breast, while making love in bed.
- •• 0:24—Topless taking off her dress, then buns jumping into bed.
- • 0:36—Buns and left breast posing for a painter.
- • 0:45—Topless taking off dress, walking around the house. Left breast, inviting the neighbor in.

Patrick Dewaere . . . . Francois

Catherine Cherie (1982)
Ajita Wilson . . . . Dancer/Miss Ajita
- • 0:23—Topless and buns dancing in club. Covered with paint. Long shot. 0:24—Brief buns, greeting Carlo after the show.
- •• 0:43—Full frontal nudity in room with Carlo.

Cave Girl (1985)
Jasaé . . . . Locker Room Student
- •• 0:05—Topless with four other girls in the girls' locker room undressing, then running after Rex. She's sitting on a bench, wearing red and white panties.

Michelle Bauer . . . . Locker Room Student
- •• 0:05—Topless with four other girls in the girls' locker room undressing, then running after Rex. She's the first to take her top off, wearing white panties, running and carrying a tennis racket.

Susan Mierisch . . . . Locker Room Student
- •• 0:05—Topless with four other girls in the girls' locker room undressing, then running after Rex. She's blonde, wearing red panties and a necklace.

Cynthia Ann Thompson . . . . Eba
- •• 1:04—Topless making love with Rex.

Cellar Dweller (1987)
Pamela Bellwood . . . . Amanda
Cheryl-Ann Wilson . . . . Lisa
- •• 0:59—Brief right breast, then topless taking a shower.

The Centerfold Girls (1974)
Jennifer Ashley . . . . Charly
- • 0:34—Topless taking off blouse while changing clothes.
- •• 0:49—Topless and buns posing for photographer outside with Glory.

Jaime Lyn Bauer . . . . Jackie
- •• 0:04—Topless getting out of bed and walking around the house.
- ••• 0:14—Topless getting undressed in the bathroom.
- •• 0:15—Brief topless and buns putting on robe and getting out of bed, three times.

Tiffany Bolling . . . . Vera
- • 1:02—Brief topless in photograph.
- ••• 1:12—Topless in the shower.
- • 1:21—Brief topless in motel bed getting raped by two guys after they drug her beer.

Teda Bracci . . . . Rita
- • 0:18—Topless taking off her clothes in the living room in front of everybody.

Kitty Carl . . . . Sandi
- •• 0:45—Topless taking off her top while sitting on the bed with Perry.
- 0:51—Topless on the beach, dead. Long shot, hard to see.

Talie Cochrane . . . . Donna
Anneka di Lorenzo . . . . Pam
Ruthy Ross . . . . Glory
- ••• 0:49—Topless and buns posing for photographer outside with Charly.

Connie Strickland . . . . Patsy
- •• 1:07—Topless in bathroom washing her halter top just before getting killed.

Janet Wood . . . . Linda
- • 0:14—Topless putting on robe and getting out of bed.

Certain Fury (1985)
Nicholas Campbell . . . . Sniffer
- •• 0:38—Buns, while getting undressed to rape Irene Cara.

Irene Cara . . . . Tracy
- 0:32—Getting undressed to take a shower. Very brief side views of left breast.
- 0:35—Very brief topless in shower after Tatum O'Neal turns on the kitchen faucet. Hard to see because of the shower door.
- •• 0:36—Frontal nudity and side view of buns, behind shower door while Sniffer comes into the bathroom.
- •• 0:39—Topless several times when Sniffer tries to rape her and she fights back.
- • 0:41—Buns, kneeling on floor. Overhead view.

Tatum O'Neal . . . . Scarlet

A Certain Sacrifice (1981)
Madonna . . . . Bruna
- ••• 0:22—Topless during weird rape/love scene with one guy and two girls.
- • 0:40—Brief right breast in open top lying on floor after getting attacked by guy in back of restaurant.
- • 0:57—Brief topless during love making scene, then getting smeared with blood.

Chained Heat (1983; U.S./German)
Jennifer Ashley . . . . Grinder
Greta Blackburn . . . . Lulu
Linda Blair . . . . Carol
- ••• 0:30—Topless in the shower.
- •• 0:56—In bra, then topless in the Warden's office when he rapes her.

Christina Cardan . . . . Miss King
Sybil Danning . . . . Erika
- ••• 0:30—Topless in the shower with Linda Blair.

Monique Gabrielle . . . . Debbie
- ••• 0:08—Nude, stripping for the Warden in his office.
- ••• 0:09—Nude, getting into the spa with the Warden.

Sharon Hughes . . . . Val
- •• 0:30—Brief topless in the shower with Linda Blair.
- •• 0:51—Buns, in lingerie, stripping for a guy.
- •• 1:04—Topless in the spa with the Warden.

Marcia Karr . . . . Twinks
- ••• 0:30—Topless, getting soaped up by Edy Williams in the shower.
- • 0:37—Brief topless, taking off her top in bed with Edy Williams at night.
- •• 0:40—Topless in cell getting raped by the guard.

Louisa Moritz . . . . Bubbles
Stella Stevens . . . . Taylor
Kate Vernon . . . . Cellmate
Edy Williams . . . . Paula
- •• 0:30—Full frontal nudity in the shower, soaping up Twinks.
- •• 0:36—Topless at night in bed with Twinks.

The Challenge (1982)
Donna Kei Benz . . . . Akiko
- • 1:23—Topless making love with Scott Glenn in motel room. Could be a body double. Dark, hard to see anything.

Scott Glenn . . . . Rich

A Change of Seasons (1980)
Bo Derek . . . . Lindsey Routledge
- •• 0:00—Topless in hot tub during the opening credits.
- • 0:25—Side view of left breast in the shower talking to Anthony Hopkins.

Shirley MacLaine . . . . Karen Evans

Chattahoochee (1990)
Dennis Hopper . . . . Walker Benson
- • 0:32—Brief buns, while leaving the shower room after talking to Gary Oldman.

Gary Oldman . . . . Emmett Foley
- • 1:17—Brief buns, standing while guards search his clothes. Very, very brief frontal nudity turning around to get a high-pressure enema. Long shot, don't really see anything.

Pamela Reed . . . . Earlene

M. Emmet Walsh. . . . . Morris

Chatterbox (1977)
Perry Bullington . . . . .Ted
- • 0:02—Buns, while stumbling around the room.

Candice Rialson. . . . . Penny
- •• 0:01—Left breast, in bed with Ted, then topless getting out of bed.
  0:10—In white bra wrestling on couch with another woman.
- ••• 0:15—Side view of right breast then topless during demonstration on stage.
- ••• 0:26—Topless in bed talking on phone.
  0:32—In open dress letting her "chatterbox" sing during talk show. Something covers pubic area.
- •• 0:35—Topless during photo shoot.
- •• 0:38—Topless again for more photos while opening a red coat.
- •• 0:43—Topless in bed with Ted.
- ••• 0:55—Topless taking off white dress, walking up the stairs and opening the door.
- •• 1:09—Topless opening her raincoat for Ted.

Cheech & Chong's Nice Dreams (1981)
Shelby Chong . . . . .Body Builder

Evelyn Guerrero . . . . Donna
- • 0:43—Brief left breast sticking out of her spandex outfit, sitting down at table in restaurant.
  0:56—In burgundy lingerie in her apartment with Cheech Marin.

Richard "Cheech" Marin . . . . Himself
- • 0:57—Brief buns when climbing over railing to escape Donna's husband, Animal.

Linnea Quigley . . . . .Blondie Group #2

Roselyn Royce . . . . Beach Girl #3
- • 0:29—Brief topless on the beach with two other girls. Long shot, unsteady, hard to see.

Victoria Wells . . . . Beach Girl #1
- • 0:29—Brief topless on the beach with two other girls. Long shot, unsteady, hard to see.

Cheerleader Camp (1987)
a.k.a. Bloody Pom Poms

Vickie Benson . . . . .Miss Tipton
- • 0:27—Brief topless undressing in her bedroom.

Rebecca Ferratti. . . . . .Theresa Salazar

George "Buck" Flower. .Pop

Travis McKenna. . . . . Timmy Moser
  0:05—Buns, while hanging a B.A. out the van window. He's a very heavy guy.

Krista Pflanzer . . . . Suzy
- •• 0:11—Topless several times sunbathing on the rocks.
- • 0:14—Brief topless in flashback.

- • 0:17—Topless on TV in Timmy's video tape of sunbathing on the rocks.

Betsy Russell. . . . . Alison Wentworth

Teri Weigel. . . . . Pam Bently
- •• 0:12—Topless taking off her swimsuit top while sunbathing.

Chickboxer (1992)
Michelle Bauer . . . . Greta "Chickboxer" Holtz
  0:39—In sexy pink outfit.
- ••• 0:57—Full frontal nudity, making love with a guy in bed.

Chinatown (1974)
Faye Dunaway . . . . Evelyn
- • 1:26—Very brief right breast, in bed talking to Jack Nicholson.
- • 1:28—Very brief right breast in bed talking to Nicholson. Very brief flash of right breast under robe when she gets up to leave the bedroom.

Jack Nicholson . . . . J.J.
- • 1:28—Very brief buns, while putting pants on and getting out of bed after making love with Faye Dunaway.

Chopping Mall (1986)
Angela Aames . . . . Miss Vanders

Barbara Crampton . . . . Suzie
- •• 0:22—Brief topless taking off top in furniture store in front of her boyfriend on the couch.

Kelli Maroney. . . . . Alison

Toni Naples . . . . Bathing Beauty

Suzanne Slater . . . . .Leslie
- •• 0:28—Brief topless in bed showing breasts to Mike.
  0:31—Walking around the mall in panties and a blouse.

Mary Woronov. . . . . Mary Bland

Cinderella (1977)
Linda Gildersleeve . . . . .Farm Girl (redhead)
- ••• 0:21—Topless and buns with her brunette sister in their house making love with the guy who is looking for Cinderella.
- •• 1:24—Full frontal nudity with her sister again when the Prince goes around to try and find Cinderella.

Elizabeth Halsey . . . . .Farm Girl (brunette)
- ••• 0:21—Nude with her redhead sister in their house making love with the guy who is looking for Cinderella.
- • 1:24—Topless with her sister again when the Prince goes around to try and find Cinderella.

Yana Nirvana . . . . .Drucella
- • 0:02—Topless taking off clothes with her sister Maribella to let Cinderella wash.
- • 0:06—Brief topless sitting up in bed with Maribella.

Mariwin Roberts. . . . . Trapper's Daughter
- ••• 0:11—Frontal nudity getting a bath outside by her blonde sister. Long scene.

Cheryl Smith . . . . Cinderella
- •• 0:03—Topless dancing and singing.

••• 0:30—Frontal nudity getting "washed" by her sisters for the Royal Ball.

•• 0:34—Topless in the forest during a dream.

••• 0:41—Topless taking a bath. Frontal nudity drying herself off.

• 1:16—Brief topless with the Prince.

• 1:30—Brief left breast after making love with the Prince to prove it was her.

• 1:34—Brief side view of left breast making love in the Prince's carriage.

Cinderella Liberty *(1973)*
Dabney Coleman . . . . Executive Officer
Bruno Kirby. . . . . Alcott
Sally Kirkland. . . . . Fleet Chick
Marsha Mason . . . . Maggie Paul
    0:09—Brief panties shot leaning over pool table when James Caan watches.

•• 0:17—Side view of left breast in room with Caan. Brief right breast sitting down on bed.

••• 0:38—Topless sitting up in bed, yelling at Caan.

• 0:54—Very brief left breast turning over in bed and sitting up.

Circle of Two *(1980)*
Tatum O'Neal . . . . Sarah Norton
•• 0:56—Topless standing behind a chair in Richard Burton's studio talking to him.

City Limits *(1984)*
Kim Cattrall. . . . . Wickings
•• 1:02—Right breast, while sitting up in bed with a piece of paper stuck to her.
Rae Dawn Chong . . . . Yogi
John Diehl. . . . . Whitey
John Stockwell . . . . Lee

City Slickers *(1991)*
Bruno Kirby. . . . . Ed Furillo
Helen Slater. . . . . Bonnie Rayburn
Yeardley Smith . . . . Nancy
Daniel Stern . . . . Phil Berquist
Tracey Walter . . . . Cookie
• 1:16—Very brief buns, mooning everybody while riding stagecoach. Happy face painted on his rear. Hard to tell if it's him.

Clash of the Titans *(1981)*
Ursula Andress. . . . . Aphrodite
Claire Bloom . . . . Hera
Judi Bowker. . . . . Andromeda
• 1:41—Buns and partial side view of right breast getting out of bath. Don't see her face.
Harry Hamlin. . . . . Perseus
Maggie Smith . . . . Thetis
Vida Taylor . . . . Danae
• 0:11—Right breast while breast feeding her baby. Buns, walking on beach.

Class *(1983)*
Jacqueline Bisset . . . . Ellen
Candace Collins . . . . Buxom Girl

Lolita Davidovich . . . . 1st Girl (motel)
Rob Lowe. . . . . Skip
Virginia Madsen . . . . Lisa
•• 0:20—Brief left breast when Andrew McCarthy accidentally rips her blouse open at the girl's school.
Andrew McCarthy . . . . Jonathan

Class of Nuke 'Em High *(1986)*
Janelle Brady . . . . Chrissy
•• 0:26—Topless sitting on bed with Warren.
• 0:31—Brief topless scene from 0:26 superimposed over Warren's nightmare.

Clean and Sober *(1988)*
Henry Judd Baker . . . . Xavier
•• 0:15—Buns, when going crazy in drug rehabilitation room.
Brian Benben . . . . Martin Laux
Claudia Christian . . . . Iris
Harley Jane Kozak. . . . . Ralston Receptionist
Stephanie Menuez . . . . Ticket Agent
Rachel Ryan . . . . Uncredited Dead Girlfriend
• 0:02—Buns, lying dead in Michael Keaton's bed. Don't see her face, but it's her.
M. Emmet Walsh . . . . Richard Dirks

Cleo/Leo *(1989)*
Ginger Lynn Allen . . . . Karen
••• 0:39—Full frontal nudity getting out of the shower, getting dried with a towel by Jane Hamilton, then in nightgown.
••• 0:57—Full frontal nudity getting out of the shower and dried off again.
Scott Baker. . . . . Leo Blockman
• 0:09—Very brief buns after getting his butt kicked.
Ruth Corrine Collins. . . . . Sally
••• 0:08—Topless getting dress pulled off by Leo.
Jennifer Delora . . . . Bernice
Jane Hamilton . . . . Cleo Clock
•• 0:13—Nude undressing in front of three guys.
• 0:21—Topless changing in dressing room.
••• 0:22—Topless changing in dressing room with the Store Clerk.
    0:40—In bra and panties.
•• 1:07—Left breast and lower frontal nudity making love with Bob on bed.
Kimberly Taylor . . . . Store Clerk
••• 0:22—Topless in white panties, changing in dressing room with Jane Hamilton. Very nice!
Kevin Thomsen . . . . Bob Miller
• 1:07—Brief frontal nudity, then buns while making love with Jane Hamilton on bed.

A Climate for Killing *(1990)*
Steven Bauer . . . . Paul McGraw
John Diehl . . . . Wayne Paris
Sherrie Rose . . . . Rita Paris
•• 1:30—Topless in bed while Wayne recollects his crime to John Beck.
Katharine Ross . . . . Grace Hines
Mia Sara. . . . . Elise Shipp

A Clockwork Orange (1971)

Adrienne Corri. . . . . Mrs. Alexander
- •• 0:11—Breasts through cut-outs in her top, then full frontal nudity getting raped by Malcolm McDowell and his friends.

Malcolm McDowell. . . . . Alex
- • 0:27—Very brief nude having sex with two women in his bedroom. Shot at fast speed.
- 0:52—Upper half of frontal nudity getting admitted to jail.

Close My Eyes (1991; British)

Helen FitzGerald . . . . Scottish Girl
- •• 0:08—Nude, lying down, then getting up in room with Richard.

Clive Owen. . . . . Richard
- •• 0:09—Brief frontal nudity, then buns, while getting up from the floor and talking on the telephone.
- 0:29—Side view of buns, while lying on floor with Natalie.
- ••• 0:30—Buns, while getting up and walking around.
- •• 0:32—Very brief frontal nudity, rolling over. Out of focus buns, lying on his stomach.
- •• 0:46—Buns, while lying in bed with Natalie.
- •• 0:56—Buns, while getting out of bed and walking to the window.

Saskia Reeves. . . . . Natalie Gillespie
- •• 0:29—Very brief right breast, twice, then topless twice in room with Richard.
- ••• 0:31—Full frontal nudity, getting up and getting dressed.
- ••• 0:45—In white bra, then topless standing, then lying on the floor with Richard.
- •• 0:46—Buns, while lying in bed with Richard. Nude, getting out of bed and putting on robe.
- • 0:56—Right breast, while lying in bed.

Club Extinction (1990)

a.k.a. Doctor M

Alan Bates. . . . . Dr. Marsfeldt
Jennifer Beals. . . . . Sonja Vogler
- • 1:16—Brief side of left breast rolling over in bed with Hartmann. Don't see her face, but probably her.
- •• 1:17—Brief topless in bed with Hartmann when he kisses her right breast, then brief right breast.

Andrew McCarthy. . . . . The Assassin

Coach (1978)

Michael Biehn. . . . . Jack
- • 1:11—Upper half of buns, while in shower with Cathy Lee Crosby.

Cathy Lee Crosby . . . . Randy
- • 0:31—Very brief side view of left breast when Michael Biehn opens the door while she's putting on her top.
- 0:52—In wet white T-shirt at the beach and in her house with Biehn.
- 1:11—Very, very brief topless in shower room with Biehn. Blurry, hard to see anything.

Brent Huff. . . . . .Keith

Rosanne Katon. . . . . Sue
- • 0:10—Very brief topless flashing her breasts along with three of her girlfriends for their four boyfriends.

Lenka Novak . . . . Marilyn
- • 0:10—Very brief topless flashing her breasts along with her girlfriends for their boyfriends.

The Coca-Cola Kid (1985; Australian)

Kris McQuade . . . . Juliana
Eric Roberts . . . . Becker
Greta Scacchi. . . . . .Terri
- ••• 0:49—Nude taking a shower with her daughter.
- •• 1:20—Brief topless wearing a Santa Claus outfit while in bed with Eric Roberts.

Cocaine Wars (1986)

John Schneider. . . . . Cliff
Kathryn Witt. . . . . .Janet
- • 0:36—Brief topless and buns making love in bed with John Schneider.

Cocktail (1988)

Bryan Brown . . . . Doug Coughlin
Tom Cruise .Brian Hanagan
Gina Gershon. . . . . Coral
- • 0:31—Very, very brief right breast romping around in bed with Tom Cruise.

Kelly Lynch. Kerry Coughlin
- 0:45—Buns, wearing a two piece swimsuit at the beach.
- 1:01—Buns, in string bikini swimsuit on boat with Tom Cruise and Bryan Brown.

Elisabeth Shue . . . . Jordan Mooney
- 0:52—Side view of left breast while standing up in waterfall with Tom Cruise when she takes off her swimsuit top.

Coffy (1973)

Pam Grier. . . . . .Coffy
- • 0:05—Upper half of right breast in bed with a guy.
- 0:19—Buns, walking past the fireplace, seen through a fish tank.
- •• 0:25—Topless in open dress getting attacked by two masked burglars.
- ••• 0:38—Buns and topless undressing in bedroom. Wow!
- • 0:42—Brief right breast when breast pops out of dress while she's leaning over. Dark, hard to see.
- 0:49—In black bra and panties in open dress with a guy in the bedroom.

Cold Comfort (1988)

Jayne Eastwood . . . . Mrs. Brocket
Margaret Langrick . . . . Dolores
- •• 0:16—In tank top and panties, then topless undressing in front of Stephen.
- • 0:19—Very brief side of left breast and buns getting robe.
- •• 0:41—Doing strip tease in front of her dad and Stephen. In black bra and panties, then topless.
- • 0:42—Very brief topless jumping into bed.

Cold Feet (1989)
Keith Carradine......................... Monte
Sally Kirkland................... Maureen Linoleum
- 0:56—In black bra and panties taking off her dress in bedroom with Keith Carradine. Brief right breast pulling bra down.
- 0:58—Brief side view of right breast sitting up in bed talking to Carradine.

Cold Steel (1987)
Brad Davis.......................Johnny Modine
Sharon Stone .... Kathy Conners
- 0:33—Brief left breast making love in bed with Brad Davis. Dark, hard to see. Brief topless turning over after making love.

Coldfire (1990)
Lisa Axelrod.......................... Dancer
- •• 0:11—Topless, twice, dancing on stage.
- 0:13—Brief topless, getting pushed off the stage.
Darcy De Moss .... Maria
- ••• 0:27—Partial right breast and buns, lying in bed with Nick. Left breast, then topless making love with him.
- •• 0:30—Topless in bathtub with Nick.
Wings Hauser .... Lars

Collector's Item (1988)
a.k.a. The Trap
Laura Antonelli .... Marie Colbert
- 0:18—In white lingerie with Tony Musante.
- 0:20—Lower frontal nudity, then right breast making love with Musante.
- 0:37—In black bra, garter belt and stockings in open robe undressing for Musante.
- 0:41—In the same lingerie again dropping robe and getting dressed.
Blanca Marsillach ....Jacqueline
- •• 0:52—In white bra cleaning up Tony Musante in bed, then topless.
- 1:04—Lower frontal nudity while watching Musante and Laura Antonelli making love in bed.
- 1:18—Topless getting dressed. A little dark.
- •• 1:22—Topless changing clothes in bedroom while Antonelli talks to her.
Cristina Marsillach...................Young Marie
- •• 0:12—Right breast in elevator with Tony Musante.
- •• 0:36—Topless in open blouse, then full frontal nudity in hut with Musante.

The Color of Money (1986)
Tom Cruise ....Vincent
Mary Elizabeth Mastrantonio.............. Carmen
- 0:41—Brief topless in bathroom mirror drying herself off while Paul Newman talks to Tom Cruise. Long shot, hard to see.
Helen Shaver..........................Janelle
John Turturro .... Julian

Colors (1988)
Maria Conchita Alonso.............. Louisa Gomez
- ••• 0:48—Topless making love in bed with Sean Penn.
Sean Penn ....Danny McGavin

The Comfort of Strangers (1991)
Rupert Everett .... Colin
- •• 0:47—Buns, while walking around the room, looking for his clothes.
- 1:05—Buns, while making love with Natasha Richardson on bed. Lit with blue light.
Helen Mirren ....Caroline
Natasha Richardson .... Mary
- ••• 0:45—Topless sleeping in bed. Long shot. Then closer topless after waking up. Long scene.
- •• 1:05—Topless making love with Colin. Lit with blue light.
- •• 1:06—Right breast, lying in bed with Colin. Lit with blue light.

Coming Home (1978)
Bruce Dern................... Captain Bob Hyde
- •• 2:03—Buns, while taking off his clothes at the beach and running into the ocean.
Jane Fonda.......................... Sally Hyde
- •• 1:26—Making love in bed with Jon Voight. Topless only when her face is visible. Buns and brief left breast when you don't see a face is a body double.
Penelope Milford .... Viola Munson
- 1:19—Doing strip tease in room with Jane Fonda and two guys. Sort of right breast peeking out between her arms when she changes her mind.
Jon Voight ....Luke Martin

Coming to America (1988)
Victoria Dillard .... Bather
- •• 0:04—Topless, standing up in royal bathtub to announce "The royal penis is clean, Your Highness."
Cuba Gooding, Jr. ....Boy Getting Haircut
Bianca McEachin .....Uncredited Miss Black Awareness
- 0:37—Buns, wearing pink sequined, two piece swimsuit on stage during Black Awareness meeting.

Coming Together (1978)
a.k.a. A Matter of Love
Jeff Alin .... Frank Hughes
- 1:05—Buns, while putting pants on with Richard.
Marc Anderson................... Richard Duncan
- •• 0:13—Buns, while kneeling and kissing Angie, then more buns making love.
- 0:58—Buns, while making love with Vicky.
- 1:05—Buns, while putting pants on with Frank.
Christy Neal ....Vicky Hughes
- 0:12—In bra and panties, in bedroom with Frank.
- 0:30—Brief right breast in shower with Angie.
- 0:37—Topless and buns making love standing up in front of sliding glass door with Frank. Quick cuts.
- 0:49—Brief topless again during flashbacks.
- •• 0:57—Topless with Angie and Richard.
- 1:05—Topless on beach with Angie. Long shot.

Commando (1985)

Ava Cadell . . . . Girl in Bed
- • 0:46—Very brief topless three times in bed when Arnold Schwarzenegger knocks a guy through the motel door into her room.

Rae Dawn Chong . . . . Cindy
Chelsea Field . . . . Stewardess
Bill Paxton . . . . Intercept Officer
Arnold Schwarzenegger . . . . Matrix

Common Bounds (1991)

Rae Dawn Chong . . . . Ilene Curtis
Brad Dourif . . . . Johnny
Tasmin Kelsey . . . . Ginger
- • 0:04—Topless in hotel room with the cop when Michael Ironside bursts into the room. Long shot. More out of focus topless shots in the mirror.

The Company of Wolves (1985)

Danielle Dax . . . . Wolfgirl
- • 1:26—Brief buns and topless running around outside. Her hair is in the way a lot.

Con el Corazón en la Mano (1988; Mexican)

Maria Conchita Alonso . . . . .n.a.
- • 0:38—Very, very brief right breast, while turning over in bed with her husband.
- • 0:39—Topless several times, taking a bath.
- •• 1:15—Topless ripping off her dress. Long shot, side view, standing while kissing a guy.

Conan the Barbarian (1982)

Sandahl Bergman . . . . Valeria
- •• 0:49—Brief left breast making love with Arnold Schwarzenegger.

Valerie Quennessen . . . . The Princess
Arnold Schwarzenegger . . . . Conan

The Concrete Jungle (1982)

Greta Blackburn . . . . Lady in Bar
Sondra Currie . . . . Katherine
Aimée Eccles . . . . Spider
Marcia Karr . . . . Marcy
Camille Keaton . . . . Rita
- • 0:41—In black bra, then topless getting raped by Stone. Brief lower frontal nudity sitting up afterwards.

Convoy (1978)

Kris Kristofferson . . . . .Rubber Duck
Ali MacGraw . . . . Melissa
Cassie Yates . . . . Violet
- • 0:21—Very brief left breast, while in truck sleeper with Kris Kristofferson.

The Cook, The Thief, His Wife & Her Lover (1990)

Alan Howard . . . . Michael
- •• 0:32—Buns, while then brief frontal nudity with Helen Mirren.
- • 0:42—Buns, while on top of Mirren.
- • 1:11—Buns, with Mirren in kitchen.

- ••• 1:14—Buns, while getting into meat truck. Frontal nudity getting hosed off and walking around with Mirren.

Helen Mirren . . . . Georgina Spica
0:22—In black bra in restroom performing fellatio on Michael.
- •• 0:32—In lingerie undressing, then lower frontal nudity, buns and left breast in kitchen with Michael.
- • 0:42—Buns and right breast, while making love with Michael again.
- •• 0:57—Topless sitting and talking with Michael.
1:01—Buns, kneeling on table.
- • 1:05—Brief topless, while leaning back on table with Michael.
1:07—Lower frontal nudity opening her coat for Michael.
- • 1:11—Buns and topless in kitchen.
- ••• 1:14—Buns, getting into meat truck. Full frontal nudity in truck and walking around with Michael.

Willie Ross . . . . Roy
0:03—Buns, while on ground covered with dog feces getting urinated on by Albert. (Talk about a bad day!)
- • 0:07—Buns, kneeling on ground while dogs walk around.
- • 0:09—Buns, while standing up.

Cool Blue (1990)

Judie Aronson . . . . Cathy
- •• 1:03—Topless in bed on top of Woody Harrelson.
Ely Pouget . . . . Christiane
- •• 0:18—Side view of right breast, then topless with Woody Harrelson.

Corporate Affairs (1990)

Ria Coyne . . . . Mistress
- •• 0:10—Left breast several times in back of car with Arthur.
Stephen Davies . . . . .Ukranian #2
Kim Gillingham . . . . .Ginny Malmquist
- • 1:09—Topless, climbing out of cubicle.
Lisa Moncure . . . . .Carolyn Bean
- • 1:07—Very, very brief left breast, while kicking Douglas out of cubicle.
Elena Sahagun . . . . Stacy
Jeanne Sal . . . . Sandy
- • 0:38—Left breast in open dress while sneaking around the office with Buster.
Christina Veronica . . . . Tanning Woman
0:47—Side of right breast, getting tanned.

Corvette Summer (1978)

Annie Potts . . . . Vanessa
- • 0:51—Silhouette of right breast in van with Mark Hamill. Out of focus topless washing herself in the van while talking to him. Don't really see anything.

Cousin, Cousine (1975; French)

Marie-Christine Barrault . . . . Marthe
- •• 1:05—Topless in bed with her lover, cutting his nails.

- 1:07—Brief side view of right breast, while giving him a bath.
- ••• 1:16—Topless with penciled tattoos all over her body.
  1:33—Braless in see-through white blouse saying "good bye" to everybody.
Guy Marchand . . . . Pascal
Marie-France Pisier .Karine

Covergirl (1982; Canadian)
Jeff Conaway . . . . T. C. Sloane
- •• 0:43—Very brief lower frontal nudity getting out of bed.
Irena Ferris . . . . .Kit Paget
- •• 0:19—Brief topless taking off robe and getting into bathtub with Dee.
- • 0:43—Very brief right breast sticking out of nightgown.
- • 0:46—Upper half of left breast during modeling session.
- • 0:47—Topless in mirror in dressing room.
  0:49—Brief topless getting attacked by Joel.
- • 0:53—Brief left breast, putting another blouse on.
- • 0:53—Brief left breast, putting on blouse.
Roberta Leighton . . . . .Dee Anderson
  0:16—Almost topless, while making love dressed like a nun.
Michele Scarabelli . . . . .Snow Queen
Kenneth Welsh . . . . .Harrison Chandler
- • 1:23—Brief buns, while seen on video tape used to get him in trouble. Long shot.

Crack House (1989)
Heidi Thomas . . . . Annie
- • 1:09—Brief left breast and buns in a G string, on table getting raped by a gang.
- • 1:14—Topless in bathtub, dead.
Angel Tompkins . . . . Mother

Crazy Mama (1975)
Sally Kirkland. . . . . Ella Mae
Linda Purl . . . . .Cheryl
  0:05—In pink, two piece swimsuit at the beach.
- • 0:52—Very brief buns, then brief topless when Snake and Donny Most keep opening the door after she has taken a shower. Long shot, hard to see.

Creator (1985)
Mariel Hemingway . . . . Meli
  0:38—Brief topless cooling herself off by pulling up T-shirt in front of a fan.
- • 1:10—Brief topless flashing David Ogden Stiers during football game to distract him.
Virginia Madsen . . . . .Barbara
  0:53—Walking on beach in a blue one piece swimsuit with Vincent Spano.
- ••• 0:58—Nude in shower with Spano.
Vincent Spano. . . . . .Boris
- • 0:28—Brief buns, while in shower room with David Ogden Stiers after working out in a gym.
- • 0:57—Brief buns, before taking a shower.

Creature (1985)
Klaus Kinski . . . . Hans Rudy Hofner
Marie Laurin. Susan Delambre
- •• 0:41—Topless and brief buns with blood on her shoulders, getting Jon to take his helmet off.

Creatures the World Forgot (1971; British)
Julie Ege. . . . . Nala, The Girl
  0:56—Very brief topless several times (it looks like a stunt double) fighting in cave with The Dumb Girl. Hard to see.
- • 1:32—Very, very brief half of right breast when fighting a snake that is wrapped around her face.
Marcia Fox . . . . .The Dumb Girl
- • 0:51—Right breast, then brief topless turning around by the pool.
- • 0:58—Brief topless fighting with Julie Ege.
- • 1:20—Very brief right breast when The Dark Boy gets his leg cut.

Creepozoids (1987)
Ken Abraham . . . . .Butch
- •• 0:16—Side view of buns, while standing in shower with Linnea Quigley.
Kim McKamy . . . . .Kate
Linnea Quigley. . . . . .Blanca
- •• 0:15—Topless taking off her top to take a shower.
- •• 0:16—Right breast, while standing in shower with Butch.
- • 0:24—Right breast several times while sleeping in bed with Butch.

Creepshow 2 (1987)
Lois Chiles . . . . Annie Lansing
- •• 0:59—Brief topless getting out of boyfriend's bed, then getting dressed.

Cries and Whispers (1972; Swedish)
a.k.a. Viskingar Och Rop
Ingrid Thulin . . . . Karin
- •• 0:57—Topless and buns, undressing and getting ready for bed. Something covers lower frontal nudity.

Crime Lords (1990)
Susan Byun . . . . .Monahan
- •• 1:06—Left breast, then right breast, while making out with Wayne Crawford on the couch.
Martin Hewitt. . . . . Peter Russo
- •• 0:50—Buns, while getting back into bed with two Chinese girls.
Kimberleigh Stark. . . . . Lieutenant Sylvestri

Crime Zone (1989)
David Carradine. . . . . .Jason
Sherilyn Fenn . . . . .Helen
  0:16—In black lingerie and stockings in bedroom.
- •• 0:23—Topless wearing black panties making love with Bone. Dark, long shot.

Crimes of Passion (1984)
(Unrated version reviewed.)
John Laughlin . . . . Bobby Grady
- 0:50—Buns, while getting dressed after having sex with Kathleen Turner. (Viewed through peep hole by Anthony Perkins.)

Annie Potts . . . . Amy Grady
Kathleen Turner . . . . Joanna Crane/China Blue
- ••• 0:45—Topless, wearing black panties and stockings, in bed with Bobby. Shadows of them making love on the wall.
- 1:00—Right breast in back of a limousine with a rich couple.

1:22—In blue bra and panties.

1:27—Right breast in bed with Bobby.

Criminal Law (1989)
Kevin Bacon . . . . Martin Thiel
Gary Oldman . . . . Ben Chase
- 1:21—Very, very brief blurry frontal nudity in bed with Ellen.

Karen Young . . . . Ellen Falkner
- 1:21—Very brief buns, then brief topless in bed with Ben.

Critters 2: The Main Course (1988)
Roxanne Kernohan . . . . Lee
- •• 0:37—Brief topless after transforming from an alien into a Playboy Playmate.

Crooked Hearts (1991)
Marg Helgenberger. Jennetta
Jennifer Jason Leigh. Harriet
- •• 1:10—In black bra, then topless in bathtub with Tom.

Cindy Pickett. . . . . Jill

Cross Country (1983; Canadian)
Nina Axelrod. . . . . Lois Hayes
0:28—Brief buns and sort of topless, getting fondled by Richard.
1:05—Very, very brief topless fighting outside the motel in the rain with Johnny.
Roberta Weiss . . . . Alma Jean
- •• 0:59—Topless on bed with two other people.

Cross My Heart (1987)
Annette O'Toole . . . . Kathy
0:44—In pink bra standing in bedroom with Martin Short.
- •• 0:46—Left breast, in bed with Short.
- •• 0:48—Topless in bed when Short heads under the covers.
- •• 0:49—Brief topless again getting her purse.
- 1:05—Brief topless and buns, dressing after Short finds out about her daughter.

Crossover (1980; Canadian)
a.k.a. Mr. Patman
Fionnula Flanagan. Abadaba
- 0:27—Brief topless opening her robe and flashing James Coburn.

Tabitha Harrington. . . . . Montgomery
- 0:11—Brief right breast, then brief full frontal nudity lying in bed, then struggling with James Coburn in her room. Wearing white makeup on her face.
- •• 0:29—Nude walking in to room to talk with Coburn, then topless and brief buns leaving.

Michael Kirby. . . . . Dr. Turley
Kate Nelligan . . . . Peabody

Cry Freedom (1987; British)
Kevin Kline. . . . . .Donald Woods
John Matshikiza .Mapetla
Denzel Washington . . . . Steve Biko
- 1:05—Side view of buns, while lying on the floor after getting beat up. Dark, hard to see anything.
- 1:07—Buns again. Dark.
1:26—Buns in B&W photo. Supposed to be him, but probably not. Don't see face.

Cry of a Prostitute: Love Kills (1975; Italian)
Barbara Bouchet. .Margie
- 0:30—Brief left breast, lying in bed with Rico.
- 0:31—Brief topless in bed, with Rico when he starts making love with her.
- •• 0:50—Topless in panties and robe, walking angrily around her room.
0:56—In braless blouse in Bedroom with Tony.

Crystal Heart (1987)
Tawny Kitaen . . . . Alley Daniels
- •• 0:46—Topless and buns, while "making love" with Lee Curreri through the glass.
- •• 0:50—Nude, crashing through glass shower door, covered with blood during her nightmare.
- 1:14—Brief topless making love with Curreri in and falling out of bed.

Marina Saura . . . . Justine

Curse III: Bloody Sacrifice (1990)
Jenilee Harrison . . . . Elizabeth Armstrong
- ••• 0:43—Topless sitting in bathtub. Almost side of right breast when wrapping a towel around herself.

Jennifer Steyn. . . . . Cindy
- 0:35—Side of left breast, kissing Roger while at the beach inside a tent. Upper half of left breast when blade tears through tent.
0:40—Topless, covered with blood when Geoff looks in the tent.

Cut and Run (1985; Italian)
Karen Black . . . . Karin
Lisa Blount . . . . Fran Hudson
Valentina Forte. . . . . Ana
- ••• 0:29—Brief left breast being made love to in bed. Then topless sitting up in bed and left side view and buns taking a shower.

John Steiner . . . . .Vlado

Cutter's Way (1981)
a.k.a. Cutter and Bone
Jeff Bridges. . . . . Richard Bone
Julia Duffy . . . . Young Girl

Ann Dusenberry . . . . Valerie Duran
Lisa Eichhorn. . . . . Maureen "Mo" Cutter
- 1:07—Brief right breast, wearing bathrobe, lying on lounge chair while Jeff Bridges looks at her.
John Heard . . . . Alex Cutter

Cyborg *(1989)*
Dayle Haddon . . . . Pearl Prophet
Debi Richter . . . . Nady Simmons
0:28—Buns, after taking off clothes and running into the ocean.
- 0:30—Brief left breast by the fire showing herself to Jean-Claude Van Damme.
Jean-Claude Van Damme . . . . .Gibson Rickenbacker

Cyclone *(1986)*
Michelle Bauer . . . . Uncredited Shower Girl
- 0:06—Very brief buns and side of left breast walking around in locker room. (Passes several times in front of camera.)
Martine Beswick . . . . Waters
Ashley Ferrare . . . . .Carla Hastings
0:04—Working out at health club with Heather Thomas.
Pamela Gilbert . . . . Uncredited Shower Girl
0:06—Buns and topless brunette in the showers. Long shot.
Heather Thomas . . . . .Teri Marshall
Dawn Wildsmith . . . . Henna

D.C. Cab *(1983)*
Irene Cara . . . . Herself
John Diehl. . . . . .Kidnapper
Jill Schoelen. . . . . Claudette
Moriah Shannon . . . . .Venus Club Passenger
- • 0:16—In bra, then topless, undressing in back seat of cab.
- • 0:17—Topless when Albert tries to get his fare.
- • 0:18—Topless, then buns when Gary Busey takes her money. Buns and very brief lower frontal nudity running out of the club after him.

Daddy's Boys *(1988)*
Laura Burkett. . . . . .Christie
- • • 0:17—Topless in room with Jimmy.
- • • 0:20—Left breast, while making love with Jimmy in bed again.
- • 0:21—Brief topless during Jimmy's nightmare.
- • 0:43—Brief topless in bed again, then getting dressed.
- • 0:53—Brief topless in bed consoling Jimmy.
- • 1:11—Left breast, while in bed with Jimmy.
Daryl Haney . . . . .Jimmy
- • 0:17—Buns, while getting undressed in room with Christie.
Linda Shayne. . . . . Nanette

The Damned *(1969; German)*
Helmut Berger. . . . . .Martin Von Essenbeck
- • 2:03—Buns, while walking up to his mother and ripping her dress off. Dark, don't see his face.

Charlotte Rampling . . . . Elizabeth Thallman
Ingrid Thulin . . . . Sophie Von Essenbeck
- • • 1:23—Topless in bed with Frederick. Long scene for a 1969 film.
- • 2:03—Left breast in bed with Martin (her son in the film).

Damned River *(1990)*
Lisa Aliff . . . . .Anne
0:28—Silhouette topless undressing in tent.
- • 0:32—Very, very brief top of right breast in open blouse, then half of right breast in wet blouse washing her hair.
- • 0:50—Very brief topless struggling with Ray when he rips her top open. Don't see her face.
Steve Shellen . . . . Ray

Dance of the Damned *(1988)*
Starr Andreeff. . . . . Jodi
- • • 0:03—Topless dancing in black bikini bottoms on stage in a club.
  1:06—In black bra, panties, garter belt and stockings dancing in bar just for the vampire.
- • • 1:08—Topless in the bar with the vampire.
Maria Ford . . . . Teacher
- • 0:11—Brief topless during dance routine in club wearing black panties, garter belt and stockings.
Deborah Ann Nassar . . . . .La Donna
- • 0:07—Brief topless during dance routine in club.
Cyril O'Reilly . . . . .Vampire

Dance with Death *(1991)*
Sean'a Arthur . . . . Sherilyn
- • 0:42—Buns, while dancing on stage with Lola.
Tracey Burch . . . . .Whitney
- • • • 0:03—Topless and buns in G-string, dancing on stage.
- • • • 0:05—More topless and buns while dancing.
Maxwell Caulfield. . . . . Shaughnessy
- • 1:01—Brief side view of buns, while making love in bed with Kelly.
Catya Sassoon . . . . Jodie
- • • • 0:29—Topless and buns in G-string, while dancing on stage.
- • • • 0:37—Topless and buns, dancing on stage. Her body is painted gold.
- • • • 0:38—More topless and buns.
Barbara Alyn Woods. . . . . Kelly
- • • • 0:16—In black bra, panties and stockings, doing strip tease on stage. Topless and buns in G-string.
- • • 0:24—Topless, dancing in red bra and panties.
- • • • 0:46—Topless and buns in G-string, dancing on stage.
- • 0:47—Brief side view of left breast, while changing back stage. Buns seen in mirror.
- • • • 0:59—Topless and buns, doing strip tease routine in Marilyn Monroe outfit.
- • • • 1:01—Topless, making love in bed with Maxwell Caulfield.

Dances with Wolves (1990)

Kevin Costner . . . . Lt. John Dunbar
- •• 0:37—Brief buns, while washing his clothes in the pond.
- ••• 0:40—Buns, while standing by himself after scaring away Kicking Bird.

Danger Zone II: Reaper's Revenge (1988)

Stephanie Blake. . . . . Tattooed Topless Dancer
- ••• 0:47—Topless, dancing on stage in bikini bottoms.

Alisha Das . . . . Francine
Jane Higginson . . . . Donna
- •• 0:17—Topless unconscious on sofa while the bad guys take Polaroid photos of her.
- • 0:18—Brief topless in the photo that Wade looks at.
- • 0:22—Brief left breast adjusting her blouse outside. Long shot.
- • 0:34—Left breast in another Polaroid photograph.
  0:45—In black bra, panties and stockings posing on motorcycle for photograph.

Jason Williams . . . . Wade
- •• 0:06—Buns, while getting out of bed and putting pants on.

Dangerous Game (1988; Australian)

Kathryn Walker . . . . Kathryn
- • 1:19—Very, very brief topless when her black top is pulled up while struggling with Murphy.

Dangerous Liaisons (1988)

Glenn Close . . . . Marquise de Merteuil
Michelle Pfeiffer . . . . Madame de Tourvel
Uma Thurman. . . . . Cécile de Volanges
- ••• 0:59—Topless taking off her nightgown in her bedroom with John Malkovich.

Dangerous Love (1988)

Teri Austin. . . . . Dominique
Brenda Bakke . . . . Chris
Collin Bernsen. . . . . Brooks
Eloise Broady. . . . . Bree
- ••• 0:06—Topless changing into lingerie in the mirror.

Nicole Picard. . . . . Jane
Brenda Swanson . . . . Felicity

Dangerous Obsession (1990; Italian)

Corrine Clery. . . . . Carol Simpson
- • 0:14—Right breast sticking out of lingerie while lying in bed.
- •• 0:36—Full frontal nudity lying in bed waiting for her husband, then with him, then getting out of bed.

Blanca Marsillach . . . . Jessica
- • 0:02—Left breast, getting fondled by Johnny in recording studio. Lower frontal nudity when he pulls down her panties.
- •• 0:05—Topless opening her blouse while Johnny plays his saxophone.
- • 0:17—Lower frontal nudity on the stairs with Johnny, then brief topless.
- • 0:29—Brief topless in video tape on T.V.
- •• 0:40—Topless changing blouses.

- ••• 0:56—Full frontal nudity masturbating while looking at pictures of Johnny. Buns, then more full frontal nudity getting video taped.
- ••• 0:58—Topless in bed with a gun. Nude walking around the house. Long scene.
- • 1:05—Brief topless on beach taking off sweater and burying a dog.
- • 1:06—Brief full frontal nudity during video taping session.
- • 1:07—Topless cleaning up Dr. Simpson.
- ••• 1:13—Topless taking chains off Dr. Simpson, then lying in bed. Full frontal nudity making love with him.

Dangerously Close (1986)

Carey Lowell . . . . Julie
John Stockwell . . . . Randy McDevill
- • 0:33—Brief buns while in steamy locker room.

Angel Tompkins. . . . . Mrs. Waters
Karen Witter. . . . . Betsy

Dark Obsession (1989; British)

Gabriel Byrne . . . . Hugo
Amanda Donohoe . . . . Ginny
- •• 0:01—Topless getting felt by a pair of hands.
- ••• 0:41—Left breast, topless, brief lower frontal nudity while making love with Gabriel Byrne.
- • 0:47—In black bra and panties, then full frontal nudity getting into tub. Right breast while in tub.

Sadie Frost . . . . Rebecca
- • 0:22—Very brief right breast in bed after she rolls off Jamie.
- ••• 0:33—Topless several times while making love with Jamie when Gabriel Byrne interrupts them.

Dark Side of the Moon (1989)

Wendy MacDonald . . . . Alex
- • 0:54—In bra, then brief topless having it torn off. Don't see her face.

Camilla More . . . . Lesli

Daughter of Death (1982)

a.k.a. Julie Darling
Sybil Danning . . . . Susan
- •• 0:36—Topless in bed with Anthony Franciosa.
- • 0:38—Brief right breast under Franciosa.

Cindy Girling . . . . Irene
- •• 0:12—Topless in bathtub and getting out.

Isabelle Mejias . . . . Julie

The Day After Halloween (1978; Australian)

a.k.a. Snapshot
Chantal Contouri . . . . Madeline
Sigrid Thornton . . . . Angela
- • 0:04—Very brief topless in ad photos on wall.
- •• 0:19—Topless modeling at the beach.
- ••• 0:21—More topless at the beach.
- • 0:37—Topless in magazine ad several times.
- • 0:43—Brief right breast in magazine ad.
- • 0:46—Topless in ad again.
- • 1:18—Entering room covered with the ad.
  1:20—In beige bra in room with weirdo guy.

The Day of the Cobra (1980)
Sybil Danning . . . . Brenda
  • 0:41—Buns and side view of right breast getting out of bed and putting robe on with Lou. Long shot.
Franco Nero . . . . n.a.

The Day of the Locust (1975)
Karen Black . . . . Faye
Pepe Serna . . . . Miguel
  • 2:01—Buns while on top of Karen Black, then buns while jumping out of bed.
Donald Sutherland . . . . Homer

Dead Aim (1987)
Ed Marinaro . . . . .Malcolm "Mace" Douglas
  • 0:52—Buns, while in bed making love with Amber. Dark, hard to see.
Lynn Whitfield .Sheila Freeman

Dead and Buried (1981)
Melody Anderson . . . . .Janet
Lisa Blount . . . . Girl on the Beach
  • 0:06—Brief topless on the beach getting her picture taken by a photographer.

Dead Calm (1989)
Nicole Kidman . . . . .Rae Ingram
  • 0:59—Brief buns and topless with the attacker.
Sam Neill . . . . .John Ingram
Billy Zane .Hughie Warriner
  • 1:01—Buns, while walking around on the boat.

Dead Ringers (1988)
Genevieve Bujold . . . . Claire Niveau
  •• 0:49—Very brief right breast in bed with Jeremy Irons, then brief topless reaching for pills and water. Dark, hard to see.
Heidi Von Palleske . . . . Cary
  • 0:45—Brief left breast sticking out of bathrobe, while talking to Jeremy Irons in the bathroom.

Dead Solid Perfect (1988; Made for Cable Movie)
Corinne Bohrer . . . . Janie Rimmer
  ••• 0:31—Nude, getting out of bed to get some ice for Randy Quaid. Nice scene!
Kathryn Harrold . . . . Beverly T. Lee

Dead Space (1990)
Marc Singer . . . . Steve Krieger
Laura Tate . . . . Marissa Salinger
  •• 0:33—Topless in bed with Marc Singer during her dream.

The Dead Zone (1983)
Brooke Adams .Sarah Bracknell
Martin Sheen .Greg Stillson
Tom Skerritt . . . . Sheriff Bannerman
Roberta Weiss . . . . Alma Frechette
  • 0:49—Briefly in beige bra, then brief topless when the killer rips her blouse open during Christopher Walken's vision.

Dead-End Drive-In (1986; Australian)
Natalie McCurry . . . . .Carmen
  •• 0:19—Topless in red car with Ned Manning.

Deadline (1988)
John Hurt . . . . .Granville Jones
Imogen Stubbs . . . . .Lady Romy-Burton
  0:42—Doing handstands in a bikini top.
  • 0:44—Brief left breast, while getting out of bed with John Hurt. Full frontal nudity turning toward bed, brief topless getting back into bed.

Deadly Blessing (1981)
Lisa Hartman Black . . . . Faith
  1:31—It looks like brief left breast after getting hit with a rock by Maren Jensen, but it's a special-effect appliance over her breasts because she's supposed to be a male in the film.
Maren Jensen . . . . Martha
  •• 0:27—Topless and buns changing into a nightgown while a creepy guy watches through the window. 0:52—Buns, getting into the bathtub. Kind of steamy and hard to see.
  • 0:56—Brief topless in bathtub with snake. (Notice that she gets into the tub naked, but is wearing black panties in the water).
Colleen Riley . . . . Melissa
Sharon Stone . . . . Lana

Deadly Companion (1979)
Susan Clark . . . . .Paula West
  • 0:19—Brief left breast, while consoling Michael Sarrazin in bed, then brief side view of left breast.
  • 0:20—Brief topless sitting up in bed.
Pita Oliver . . . . .Lorraine
  • 0:14—Very brief left breast, then very brief topless sitting up in bed during Michael Sarrazin's daydream. Dark.
  1:32—Brief full frontal nudity, dead on bed when Susan Clark comes into the bedroom.

Deadly Dreams (1988)
Juliette Cummins .Maggie Kallir
  • 0:25—Topless on bed, taking off her blouse and kissing Alex.
  ••• 0:55—Topless and brief buns, making love with Jack in bed.
Stacey Travis . . . . Librarian

Deadly Embrace (1989)
Ken Abraham . . . . Chris Thompson
  •• 0:17—Buns, while taking a shower.
  • 1:01—Brief buns, while making love on top of Linnea Quigley.
Michelle Bauer . . . . .Female Spirit of Sex
  •• 0:22—Topless caressing herself during fantasy sequence.
  ••• 0:28—Topless taking off tube top and caressing herself.
  ••• 0:40—Topless and buns kissing blonde guy. Nice close up of him kissing her breasts.

- 0:42—Side of left breast lying down with the guy.
- 1:03—Buns and side of right breast with the guy.

Ruth Corrine Collins . . . . .Dede Magnolia
Linnea Quigley . . . . Michelle Arno
- •• 0:15—In white lingerie, then topless and buns during Chris' fantasy.
- •• 0:34—Topless and buns caressing herself.
- •• 0:43—Topless again.
- 0:46—Brief topless.
- •• 0:50—Topless and buns undressing.
- ••• 0:58—Topless in bed on top of Chris, then making love.
- 1:02—Topless and buns on top of Chris while Charlotte watches on T.V.
- 1:11—Topless in Chris' fantasy.
- 1:12—Topless and buns in playback of video tape.

Windsor Taylor Randolph . . . . Charlotte Morland
- 0:19—In yellow one piece swimsuit by the pool.
- 0:27—In wet, white T-shirt in the kitchen with Chris.
- •• 0:28—Topless taking off her top. Mostly side view of left breast.
- • 0:29—More left breast, while in bed with Chris.
- ••• 0:30—Topless, making love in bed with Chris.
- • 1:10—Brief right breast, on T.V. when she replays video tape for Linnea Quigley.

Jan-Michael Vincent . . . . .Stewart Morland

Deadly Eyes (1982; Canadian)
Sara Botsford. . . . . Kelly Leonard
- • 0:42—Topless several times, making love with Paul.

Lisa Langlois . . . . Trudy

Deadly Force (1983)
Marilyn Chambers. . . . . Actress in Video Tape
- • 0:25—Topless in adult video tape on projection TV.

Gina Gallego . . . . Maria
Wings Hauser . . . . Stoney Cooper
- •• 0:44—Very brief buns, leaping out of bathtub when gunman starts shooting. More buns, while lying on the floor.
- •• 0:49—Buns, while in hammock, lying on top of Joyce Ingalls.

Joyce Ingalls . . . . Eddie Cooper
- •• 0:48—Topless, making out with Wings Hauser on hammock.

The Deadly Games (1980)
Colleen Camp. . . . . .Randy
Denise Galik . . . . .Mary
- • 1:13—Left breast, twice, making love on top of Roger in bed.

Jo Ann Harris. . . . . .Keegan
- • 0:48—Topless in the shower. Hard to see because of the pattern on the glass.

Alexandra Morgan . . . . Linda
- •• 0:03—In bra, standing in doorway at night, then topless. Dark.
- • 0:04—Very brief left breast and lots of cleavage in open blouse talking on the phone.
- 0:05—Most of right breast, standing up.

Steve Railsback . . . . Billy

Deadly Innocents (1988)
Zag Dorison . . . . .Crazy Norm
- • 0:04—Buns, while standing on top of van and mooning the paramedics.

Andrew Stevens . . . . Bob Appling
Amanda Wyss . . . . Andy/Angela
- •• 0:12—Topless, taking off T-shirt and putting on lingerie.
- ••• 1:29—Right breast, twice, with Andrew Stevens.

Deadly Passion (1985)
Ingrid Boulting. . . . . Martha Greenwood
- • 0:46—Brief buns taking off clothes and jumping into pool. Long shot.
- •• 0:47—Topless getting out of pool and kissing Brent Huff. Right breast in bed.
- • 0:54—Topless in whirlpool bath with Huff.
- ••• 1:02—Topless, wearing white panties and massaging herself in front of a mirror.
- •• 1:31—Topless taking off clothes and jumping into bed with Huff.

Brent Huff . . . . Sam Black
Susan Isaacs. . . . . .Trixie
- •• 0:02—Topless sitting up in bed talking to Brent Huff.

Deadly Strangers (1974; British)
Hayley Mills . . . . Belle
- 1:02—Buns in bathtub when her uncle watches her.
- 1:05—In black bra, garter belt and panties while Steven fantasizes as he sees her through a keyhole.
- ••• 1:13—In white bra and panties while Steven watches through keyhole, then topless taking off bra and reading a newspaper.
- 1:15—In white bra, getting dressed.

Deadly Survailance (1991; Made for Cable Movie)
Susan Almgren. . . . . Rachel
- 0:00—Very, very brief right breast, while getting dressed. Don't see her face. B&W.
- • 0:12—Topless in the shower. Long shot.
- •• 0:34—Topless in the shower with Nickels.
- ••• 0:54—Buns, in black panties and bra, then topless in room with Michael Ironside.

Christopher Bondy. .Nickels
- • 0:31—Buns, while dropping his towel to run after Michael.

David Carradine. .Lieutenant

Deadly Vengeance (1985)
(Although the copyright on the movie states 1985, it looks more like the 1970's.)
Grace Jones .Slick's Girlfriend
- ••• 0:06—Right breast, then topless in bed with Slick.
- •• 0:13—Left breast, when Slick sits up in bed, then full frontal nudity after he gets up.

Deadtime Stories (1985)
Cathryn De Prume . . . . Goldi-lox
- •• 1:08—Topless taking a shower, quick cuts.

Nicole Picard. . . . . .Rachel (Red Riding Hood)
- 0:48—Very brief right breast in shack with boy-friend.

Scott Valentine . . . . .Peter
- 0:19—Buns, while getting out of bath.

Death Feud (1989)

Greta Blackburn . . . . Jenny
0:29—In sexy black dress talking to Frank Stallone.
1:04—In black lingerie on couch.

Lisa Loring. . . . . Roxey
0:06—Dancing in club with feathery pasties. Later, wearing the same thing under a sheer negligee.
0:41—Dancing again with the same pasties.
1:20—Dancing with red tassel pasties.

Karen Mayo-Chandler. . . . . .Anne
0:26—In lingerie with a customer.
- - 0:36—In white lingerie, then topless several times outside taking off robe.

Erika Nann . . . . Hooker

Gail Thackray . . . . .Harry's Girl Friend
- - 1:12—Topless on bed with Harry.
1:16—In black lingerie on boat with Harry.

Death Game, The Seducers (1977)

a.k.a. Mrs. Manning's Weekend

Colleen Camp. . . . . Donna
0:16—Buns, in spa with Sondra Locke trying to get George in with them.
- 0:47—Brief topless jumping up and down on the bed while George is tied up.
- - 1:16—Topless behind stained glass door taunting George. Hard to see.

Sondra Locke . . . . .Jackson
0:16—Buns and brief right breast in spa with Colleen Camp trying to get George in with them.
- 0:48—Brief topless running around the room trying to keep George away from the telephone.

Death of a Soldier (1985)

Nikki Lane. . . . . Stripper in bar
- - 0:49—Nude, dancing on stage.

Death Race 2000 (1975)

David Carradine .Frankenstein

Roberta Collins . . . . .Matilda the Hun
- - 0:27—Topless being interviewed and arguing with Calamity Jane.

Simone Griffeth. . . . . Annie Smith
- 0:32—Side view of left breast, while holding David Carradine. Dark, hard to see.
- - - 0:56—Topless and buns getting undressed and lying on bed with Carradine.

Martin Kove . . . . Nero the Hero

Louisa Moritz . . . . .Myra
- 0:28—Topless and buns getting a massage and talking to David Carradine.

Sylvester Stallone . . . . Machine Gun Joe Viterbo

Mary Woronov . . . . Calamity Jane
- 0:27—Brief topless arguing with Matilda the Hun.

Death Wish (1974)

Jeff Goldblum. . . . . Freak 1
- 0:10—Brief buns, while standing with pants down in living room raping Carol with his two punk friends.

Christopher Guest . . . . .Patrolman Reilly

Kathleen Tolan. . . . . .Carol Toby
- 0:09—Brief topless and buns getting raped by three punks.

Death Wish II (1982)

Roberta Collins. . . . . .Woman at Party

Silvana Gallardo . . . . Rosario
- 0:11—Buns, on bed getting raped by gang. Brief topless on bed and floor.
- 0:13—Nude, trying to get to the phone. Very brief full frontal nudity, lying on her back on the floor after getting hit.

Ava Lazar . . . . Girl in TV Soap Opera

Robin Sherwood. . . . . Carol Kersey
- 0:15—Topless after getting raped by gang member in their hideout.

Death Wish III (1985)

Marina Sirtis. . . . . .Maria
- 0:42—Topless getting blouse ripped open next to a car by the bad guys.
- 0:43—More topless on mattress at the bad guy's hangout.

Deathrow Game Show (1988)

Esther Alise. . . . . .Groupie
- - 0:08—Topless in bed with Chuck.

Debra Lamb. . . . . .Shanna Shallow
- - - 0:23—Topless dancing in white G-string and garter belt during the show.

Deathstalker (1983)

Barbi Benton . . . . .Codille
- - 0:39—Topless struggling while chained up and everybody is fighting.
- 0:47—Right breast, struggling on the bed with Deathstalker.

Lana Clarkson. . . . . Kaira
- - 0:26—Topless when her cape opens, while talking to Deathstalker and Oghris.
- - - 0:29—Topless lying down by the fire when Deathstalker comes to make love with her.
- 0:49—Brief topless with gaping cape, sword fighting with a guard.

Deathstalker II (1987)

Monique Gabrielle . . . . Reena the Seer/Princess Evie
- 0:57—Brief topless getting dress torn off by guards.
- - - 1:01—Topless making love with Deathstalker.
- 1:24—Topless, laughing during the blooper scenes during the end credits.

Toni Naples . . . . Sultana
- 0:55—Brief topless in strobe lights making love with the bad guy. Hard to see because of blinking lights. Might be a body double, don't see her face.

Maria Socas. . . . . .Amazon Queen
    0:50—In see-through nightgown after telling
    Deathstalker she is going to marry him.

Deathstalker III: The Warriors From Hell (1988)
Carla Herd. . . . . .Carlisa/Elizena
- 0:20—Side view of right breast, while making love in
tent when guard looks in.
- •• 0:46—Topless taking a bath.

Terri Treas. . . . . Camlearde

Deceptions (1990; Made for Cable Movie)
Harry Hamlin. . . . . Nick Gentry
Nicollette Sheridan . . . . .Adrienne Erickson
- 0:35—Very, very brief silhouette of breasts, while
hugging Harry Hamlin when the camera tilts down
from her head to her buns.

The Deep (1977)
Jacqueline Bisset . . . . Gail Berke
- ••• 0:01—Scuba diving underwater in a wet T-shirt.
- 0:08—More wet T-shirt, getting out of water, onto
boat.

Nick Nolte. . . . . .David Sanders

The Deer Hunter (1978)
Robert De Niro . . . . Michael
- •• 0:50—Nude, running in street, then more nude by
basketball court. Brief frontal nudity getting covered
by Christopher Walken's jacket. Long shot.

John Savage . . . . Steven
Meryl Streep . . . . Linda
Amy Wright . . . . Bridesmaid

Def by Temptation (1990)
John Canada Terrell. . . . . Bartender #1
- •• 0:09—Nude, running through house trying to get
away from The Temptress.

Deja Vu (1984)
Claire Bloom . . . . n.a.
Nigel Terry . . . . .Michel/Greg
- 1:17—Very brief buns, while jumping out of bed
when Jaclyn Smith tries to kill him with a knife.

Delinquent School Girls (1974)
George "Buck" Flower. .Earl
Sharon Kelly . . . . Greta
- 0:05—Left breast in mirror when she practices ma-
trial arts.

Delta Fox (1977)
Priscilla Barnes. . . . . Karen
    0:36—Left breast undressing in room for David. Very
dark, hard to see.
- 0:38—Very brief topless struggling with a bad guy
and getting slammed against the wall.
    0:39—Very brief blurry left breast running in front of
the fireplace.
- 0:40—Topless sneaking out of house. Brief topless
getting into Porsche.

- 0:49—Brief right breast reclining onto bed with David. Side view of left breast several times while making love.
    1:29—Very brief side view of left breast in David's
flashback.

Delusion (1990)
Barbra Horan . . . . Carly
Tamara Landry. . . . . Arabella
Jennifer Rubin. . . . . .Patti
- 0:34—Brief buns, pulling her panties down to moon
the guys before entering the lake.
    0:37—Walking out of the lake in red bra and panties.
More in red bra while playing with her lizard.
    0:46—Very briefly in wet bra, coming up for air from
the water. Slow motion.
- ••• 1:07—Topless in motel bathroom, drying her hair.
More topless in the motel room with George.
- 1:12—Right breast, in open blouse, while sitting on
the bed, talking with George.

Tracey Walter. . . . . Bus Ticket Cashier
Barbara Alyn Woods. .Julie

Demon of Paradise (1987)
Leslie Huntly. . . . . .Gobby
- •• 0:51—Topless taking off her top on a boat, then
swimming in the ocean.

Kathryn Witt. . . . . .Annie

Demon Seed (1977)
Julie Christie. .Susan Harris
- 0:25—Side view of left breast, getting out of bed.
- •• 0:30—Topless and buns getting out of the shower
while the computer watches with its camera.

Demon Wind (1990)
Eric Larson . . . . Cory
- •• 0:10—Buns, while standing outside at gas station.
Don't see his face.

Sandra Margot. . . . . Beautiful Demon
- •• 0:50—Topless trying to tempt Stacy and Chuck out
of the cabin.

Mia M. Ruiz . . . . Reana
Jack Vogel . . . . Stacey

Demonwarp (1988)
Michelle Bauer . . . . Betsy
- •• 0:41—Topless, taking off her T-shirt to get a tan in
the woods.
- •• 0:43—Left breast, lying down, then brief topless
getting up when the creature attacks.
- •• 0:47—Topless putting blood-stained T-shirt back on.
- •• 1:19—Topless, strapped to table, getting ready to
be sacrificed.
- 1:22—Topless on stretcher, dead.

Pamela Gilbert . . . . Carrie Austin
- ••• 0:20—In bra, then topless in bed with Jack.
- ••• 0:22—Right breast, then topless lying in bed, making love with Jack.
- •• 1:23—Topless, strapped to table.
- 1:24—Topless several more times on the table.

•• 1:25—Topless getting up and getting dressed.
Colleen McDermott . . . . Cindy
•• 0:23—Topless and buns drying herself off after taking a shower.
• 0:24—Very brief lower frontal nudity, under her towel, trying to run up the stairs.

Deranged (1987)
Jerry Butler . . . . Frank
Jennifer Delora . . . . Maryann
• 1:09—Topless in bed with Frank. Long shot.
Bob Fitzpatrick . . . . .Valet
Jamie Gillis . . . . .Eugene
• 1:06—Buns, while getting into bed with Jane Hamilton.
Nancy Groff . . . . Teacher
Jane Hamilton . . . . Joyce
• 0:29—Buns, getting undressed to take a shower. Side of left breast.
• 0:37—Side view of left breast, taking off towel and putting blouse on. Long shot.
• 1:01—Topless, changing blouses in her bedroom.
• 1:05—Topless in bedroom, taking off her blouse with Jamie Gillis.
• 1:07—Topless in bed when Jennifer wakes her up.

Descending Angel (1990; Made for Cable Movie)
Diane Lane . . . . Irina Stroia
• 0:01—Brief right breast, while making love with Eric Roberts on train during opening credits.
•• 0:44—In white camisole top with Roberts, then topless lying in bed with him.
Eric Roberts . . . . Michael Rossi

Desert Hearts (1986)
Patricia Charbonneau . . . . Cay Rivvers
••• 1:09—Brief topless making love in bed with Helen Shaver.
Denise Crosby. . . . . Pat
Helen Shaver. . . . . .Vivian Bell
• 1:05—Brief topless in bed in hotel room.
••• 1:09—Topless making love in bed with Patricia Charboneau.
Gwen Welles. . . . . Gwen

Desperate Hours (1990)
Kelly Lynch . . . . .Nancy Breyers
• 0:10—Brief topless, walking on sidewalk with Mickey Rourke when her breasts pop out of her suit.
• 1:19—Brief topless, getting wired with a hidden microphone in bathroom.
Mimi Rogers . . . . .Nora Cornell
Mickey Rourke. . . . . .Michael Bosworth

Desperately Seeking Susan (1985)
Madonna . . . . Susan
0:09—Briefly in black bra taking off her blouse in bus station restroom.
1:16—In black bra getting out of pool and lying down on lounge chair.

Rosanna Arquette. . . . . .Roberta Glass
• 0:46—Topless getting dressed when Aidan Quinn sees her through the fish tank. Long shot, hard to see.
Anne Carlisle . . . . Victoria
Ann Magnuson .Cigarette Girl
Aidan Quinn. . . . . Dez
John Turturro. . . . . Ray

Devil in the Flesh (1986; French/Italian)
Maruschka Detmers . . . . Giulia Dozza
• 0:20—Very brief side view of left breast and buns going past open door way to get a robe.
••• 0:27—Nude, talking to Andrea's dad in his office.
• 0:55—Topless putting a robe on. Dark.
•• 0:57—Topless and buns in bedroom with Andrea.
•• 1:09—Topless in hallway with Andrea.
1:19—Performing fellatio on Andrea. Dark, hard to see.
••• 1:22—Full frontal nudity holding keys for Andrea to see, brief buns.
1:42—Lower frontal nudity dancing in living room in red robe.
Fredrico Pitzalis . . . . .Andrea
• 0:57—Brief buns while in bed with Maruschka Detmers.
• 1:19—Frontal nudity when Detmers performs fellatio on him. Dark, hard to see.

Devonsville Terror (1983)
Suzanna Love. . . . . .Jessica Scanlon
•• 0:30—Topless as an aparition getting Mr. Gibbs attention.
• 0:36—Brief topless during flashback to 0:30 scene.
• 0:43—Brief right breast during Ralph's past-life recollection.

Dial Help (1988)
Charlotte Lewis . . . . .Jenny Cooper
1:06—Black panties and bare back dressing in black corset top and stockings. Yowza!
•• 1:09—Brief right breast while rolling around in the bathtub.

Diamond Run (1988; Indonesian)
a.k.a. Java Burn
Ava Lazar . . . . Samantha
•• 0:07—Brief topless, several times, making love in bed with Nicky. Hard to see her face.
William Bell Sullivan . . . . .Nicky
•• 0:08—Buns, while lying in bed, then getting up.

Diary of a Mad Housewife (1970)
Richard Benjamin. . . . . Jonathan Balser
Peter Boyle. . . . . Man in Group Therapy Session
Carrie Snodgress .Tina Balser
••• 0:01—Topless taking off nightgown and getting dressed, putting on white bra while Richard Benjamin talks to her.
0:36—Buns and brief side view of left breast, while kissing Frank Langella.

- 0:41—Very brief topless lying on floor when Langella pulls the blanket up.
- 0:54—Topless lying in bed with Langella.
  1:03—In white bra and panties getting dressed in Langella's apartment.
  1:10—In white bra and panties in Langella's apartment again.
- ••• 1:21—Topless in the shower with Langella, then drying herself off.

Diary of Forbidden Dreams *(1973; Italian)*
Sydne Rome . . . . The Girl
- ••• 0:06—Brief topless taking off torn T-shirt in a room, then topless sitting on edge of bed.
- ••• 0:09—Nude getting out of shower, drying herself off and getting dressed.
- 0:20—Brief side view of right breast, while talking to Marcello Mastroianni in her room.
- •• 0:22—Brief topless putting shirt on.
- 1:28—Topless outside on stairs fighting for her shirt.
- 1:30—Brief buns and topless climbing onto truck.

Die Hard *(1988)*
Cheryl Baker .Woman with Man
- 0:22—Brief topless in office with a guy when the terrorists first break into the building.
Bonnie Bedelia . . . . Holly McClane
Terri Lynn Doss . . . . Girl at Airport
Kym Malin . . . . Hostage

Die Hard 2 *(1990)*
Bonnie Bedelia . . . . Holly McClane
Tony Ganios . . . . Baker
John Leguizamo . . . . Burke
Franco Nero . . . . Esperanza
William Sadler . . . . Colonel Stuart
- •• 0:02—Buns, while exercising in hotel room before leaving for the airport.

A Different Story *(1979)*
(R-rated version reviewed.)
Linda Carpenter . . . . Chastity
- 1:33—Very brief topless in shower, shutting the door when Meg Foster discovers her with Perry King.
Meg Foster . . . . Stella
  0:12—In white bra and panties exercising and changing clothes in her bedroom.
- •• 0:53—Topless sitting on Perry King, rubbing cake all over each other on bed.
- 0:59—Brief buns and side view of right breast, while getting into bed with King.
Perry King . . . . Albert
- 1:33—Buns, through shower door, then brief buns while getting out of the shower to talk to Meg Foster.

Diplomatic Immunity *(1991)*
Robert Forster . . . . Stonebridge
Meg Foster . . . . .Gerta Hermann

Fabiana Udenio . . . . Teresa
- •• 1:06—Topless in panties, on the floor with her hands tied behind her back when Klaus rips her blouse open to photograph her.

Dirty Hands *(1975; French)*
Romy Schneider . . . . .Julie
- 0:01—Buns and right breast getting a tan, lying on the grass after a man's kite lands on her.
- •• 0:09—Side view of right breast, while lying in bed with a man, then topless.
- 1:04—Topless lying on floor, then brief topless sitting up and looking at something on the table.

Diva *(1982; French)*
Thuy Ann Luu . . . . .Alba
- 0:13—Topless in B&W photos when record store clerk asks to see her portfolio.
- 0:15—More of the B&W photos on the wall.
  1:27—Very brief upper half of left breast taking off top, seen through window. Long shot.

The Divine Nymph *(1977; Italian)*
Laura Antonelli . . . . Manoela Roderighi
- •• 0:10—Full frontal nudity reclining in chair.
- 0:18—Right breast in open blouse sitting in bed. Lower frontal nudity while getting up.

Diving In *(1990)*
Yolanda Jilot . . . . Amanda Lansky
  0:32—In red, one piece swimsuit, getting out of the pool to talk to Wayne.
  0:54—In blue, one piece swimsuit, getting out of the pool.
- 0:55—Brief topless, in open blouse, getting dressed while talking to Burt Young.
Matt Lattanzi . . . . Jerome Colter

Dixie Lanes *(1987)*
Karen Black . . . . Zelma
Pamela Springsteen . . . . .Judy
- •• 1:00—Topless, turning around in pond, while talking to Everett at night.

Do or Die *(1991)*
Cynthia Brimhall . . . . Edy Stark
- 0:31—Most of buns, wearing white lingerie outfit, singing and dancing at night.
- ••• 0:36—Topless and buns, making love with Lucas on floor in front of fire.
William Bumiller . . . . .Lucas
Ava Cadell . . . . Ava
- •• 0:20—Buns and brief topless, getting dressed in motor home. Lots of buns shots, wearing swimsuit.
Carolyn Liu . . . . Silk
- ••• 0:14—Topless, getting up off massage table and putting robe on.
- •• 1:04—Topless in bed with Pat Morita.
Stephanie Schick . . . . Atlanta Lee
- ••• 1:09—Topless making love with Shane outside at night.

- 1:15—Brief topless in background, getting dressed. Out of focus.

Michael Jay Shane . . . . Shane Abeline
- ••• 1:10—Buns, while making love with Atlanta, outside at night.

Dona Speir . . . . Donna Hamilton
  - • 0:06—Brief topless taking off towel and getting into spa.
  - •• 0:32—Topless, mostly right breast, changing clothes in back of airplane.
  - ••• 1:21—Topless and buns, in swimming pool with Erik Estrada.

Roberta Vasquez . . . . Nicole Justin
  - 0:06—Sort of topless under water in spa.
  - •• 0:56—Topless, making love with Bruce, outside.

Doc Hollywood (1991)
Bridget Fonda . . . . Nancy Lee
Woody Harrelson . . . . .Hank
Julie Warner . . . . Lou
  - • 0:15—Silhouette of left breast in water while Michael J. Fox sleeps.
  - ••• 0:16—Topless several times, skinny dipping in lake, then getting out while Fox watches.

Doctor's Wives (1971)
Anthony Costello . . . . #31 Mike Traynor
  - • 0:52—Brief buns, while getting tape recorder and running back to bed.

Domino (1989)
Brigitte Nielsen . . . . Domino
  - • 0:05—Right breast, lying down next to swimming pool, topless getting out.
  - ••• 1:04—Right breast, caressing herself in a white lingerie body suit, wearing a black wig.

Don't Answer the Phone (1979)
Pamela Jean Bryant .Sue Ellen
  - •• 0:28—Topless in the killer's photo studio when he rips her jacket off and kills her.

Denise Galik . . . . Lisa
Flo Gerrish. . . . . Dr. Lindsay Gale
  - • 1:05—Very brief topless rolling over in bed with McCabe. Brief topless when he pulls the covers down.
  - 1:19—Side view of right breast, several times, while taking off blouse and putting nightgown on.

Suzanne Severeid . . . . Hooker
  - • 0:43—Very brief right breast in open blouse after the killer strangles her.

Don't Go Near the Park (1979)
Linnea Quigley . . . . .Bondi's Mother
  - 0:08—Full frontal nudity, behind shower door.
  - • 0:09—Brief left breast, while wrapping a towel around herself.
  - ••• 0:19—Left breast, while lying in bed with Mark.

Don't Look Now (1973)
Julie Christie . . . . Laura Baxter
  - • 0:27—Brief topless in bathroom with Donald Sutherland.

- • 0:30—Topless making love with Sutherland in bed.

Donald Sutherland . . . . John Baxter
  - • 0:27—Buns, while in the bathroom with Julie Christie.

Dona Flor and Her Two Husbands (1978; Brazilian)
Sonia Braga . . . . Flor
  - • 0:13—Buns and brief topless with her husband.
  - •• 0:15—Topless lying on the bed.
  - 0:17—Buns, getting out of bed.
  - ••• 0:54—Topless making love on the bed with her husband.
  - •• 0:57—Topless lying on the bed.
  - ••• 1:41—Topless kissing her first husband.

Doom Asylum (1987)
Ruth Corrine Collins . . . . .Tina
  - •• 0:19—Topless pulling up her top while yelling at kids below.

Patty Mullen. . . . . Judy LaRue/Kiki LaRue

The Doors (1991)
Josie Bissett . . . . Robby Krieger's Girlfriend
Bill Landrum
  . . . . .Choreographer/Body Double for Val Kilmer
  - •• 1:04—Buns, while making love in bed with Kathleen Quinlan.

Andrew Lauer. UCLA Student
Kyle MacLachlan . . . . Ray Manzarek
Michael Madsen. .Tom Baker
Annie McEnroe. . . . . Secretary
Mark Moses . . . . Jac Holzman
Kathleen Quinlan . . . . Patricia Kenneaiy
  - ••• 1:00—Brief left breast, while in bed with Val Kilmer, topless (while wearing glasses) out of bed.
  - • 1:02—Left breast, while crawling on the floor.
  - ••• 1:03—Nude, dancing around her apartment with Kilmer.

Mimi Rogers. . . . . Magazine Photographer
Jennifer Rubin. . . . . Edie
Meg Ryan . . . . Pamela Courson
  - •• 1:06—Right breast, while lying in bed with Val Kilmer.

Charlie Spradling . . . . .CBS Girl Backstage

Double Exposure (1983)
Pamela Hensley . . . . Sergeant Fontain
Victoria Jackson . . . . .Racetrack Model #1
Sally Kirkland . . . . Hooker
  - •• 0:26—Topless in alley getting killed.

Terry Moore. Married Woman
Joanna Pettet . . . . Mindy Jordache
  - •• 0:55—Topless, making love in bed with Adrian.

Misty Rowe . . . . Bambi
Kathy Shower. . . . . .Mudwrestler #1
Jeana Tomasina . . . . Renee
  - • 0:20—Very brief glimpse of left breast under water in swimming pool.

Double Impact (1991)

Julie Strain. . . . . Student
- • 0:09—Brief buns, lying on floor in pink leotard in exercise class.

Jean-Claude Van Damme . . . . Chad/Alec
- • 1:11—Very brief buns, while making love with Danielle. Dark.

Down and Out in Beverly Hills (1986)

Nick Nolte. . . . . .Jerry Baskin
- • 0:28—Buns, while changing out of wet clothes on patio.
- • 1:37—Brief buns, while changing out of Santa Claus outfit.

Elizabeth Peña. . . . . Carmen
Jason Williams . . . . Lance

Down the Drain (1989)

Teri Copley . . . . Kathy Miller
- 0:04—Full frontal nudity making love on couch with Andrew Stevens. Looks like a body double.
- 0:31—In two piece swimsuit, then body double nude doing strip tease for Stevens. Notice body double isn't wearing earrings.
- 0:33—Buns, (probably the body double) on top of Stevens.
- 1:21—In black bra in motel room when bad guy opens her blouse.

Andrew Stevens . . . . Victor Scalia
Stella Stevens . . . . Sophia
- 0:45—In black lingerie yelling at Dino in the bathroom.

Downtown (1990)

Anthony Edwards . . . . .Alex Kearney
- • 0:19—Buns, while outside after getting his police uniform ripped off.

Dr. Alien (1989)

a.k.a. I Was a Teenage Sex Mutant

Laura Albert . . . . Rocker Chick #3
- ••• 0:21—Topless in black outfit during dream sequence with two other rocker chicks.

Ginger Lynn Allen . . . . Rocker Chick #1
- ••• 0:21—Topless in red panties during dream sequence with two other rocker chicks.

Michelle Bauer . . . . .Coed #1
- ••• 0:53—Topless taking off her top (she's on the left) in the women's locker room after another coed takes hers off in front of Wesley.

Julie Gray . . . . .Karla
- ••• 0:44—In white bra, then topless in Janitor's room with Wesley.

Elizabeth Kaitan. Waitress
Linnea Quigley . . . . Rocker Chick #2
- ••• 0:21—Topless in white outfit during dream sequence with two other rocker chicks.

Karen Russell. . . . . .Coed #2
- ••• 0:53—Topless taking off her top (she's on the right) in the women's locker room before another coed takes her's off in front of Wesley.

Edy Williams. . . . . .Buckmeister
- ••• 0:54—Topless taking off her top in the women's locker room in front of Wesley.

Dr. Caligari (1989)

Laura Albert . . . . Mrs. Van Houten
- ••• 0:05—Topless taking off yellow towel, then sitting in bathtub.
- •• 0:07—Lying down, making love with guy wearing a mask.
- ••• 0:10—Topless taking orange bra off, then lying back and playing with herself.
- •• 0:11—More topless, lying on the floor.
- •• 0:12—More topless, lying on the floor again.
- • 0:30—Brief left breast with big tongue.

Catherine Case. . . . . Patient with Extra Hormones
Debra De Liso . . . . Grace Butter

Dr. Jekyll and Sister Hyde (1971)

Martine Beswick. Sister Hyde
- • 0:25—Topless, opening her blouse and examining her breasts after transforming from a man.
- • 0:27—Left breast, feeling herself.
- • 0:44—Brief buns, taking off coat to put on a dress.

Dracula's Widow (1988)

Rachel Jones. . . . . .Jenny
- • 0:54—Brief left breast, then brief topless, twice, lying in the bathtub, getting stabbed by Sylvia Kristel.

Sylvia Kristel . . . . Vanessa

Dragonard (1988)

Oliver Reed . . . . Captain Shanks
Annabel Schofield . . . . Honore
- • 0:26—Brief side view of left breast, brief topless lying down, then left breast again in stable with Abdee.

Claudia Udy. . . . . .Arabella
- •• 1:11—Topless dressed as Cleopatra dancing a routine in front of a bunch of guys.

Dragonslayer (1981)

Caitlin Clarke . . . . Valerian
- 0:27—Body double's very brief side of left breast from under water.

Peter McNichol . . . . .Galen
- • 0:27—Very brief buns while diving into pond. Sort of frontal nudity swimming under water. Hard to see because the water is so murky.

Dream Lover (1986)

Kristy McNichol . . . . Kathy Gardner
- • 0:17—Very, very brief right breast getting out of bed, then walking around in a white top and underwear.
- 0:21—Walking around in the white top again. Same scene used in flashbacks at 0:34, 0:46 and 0:54.

The Dream Team (1989)

Peter Boyle. . . . . Jack
- •• 0:05—Buns, while getting up out of chair.

Christopher Lloyd. . . . . Henry

Dressed to Kill (1980)

Nancy Allen.........................Liz Blake
  1:21—In black bra, panties and stockings in Michael Caine's office.
  • 1:36—Topless (from above), buns and brief right breast in shower.
Angie Dickinson....................Kate Miller
  • 0:01—Brief side view behind shower door. Long shot, hard to see.
  0:02—Frontal nude scene in shower is a body double, Victoria Lynn Johnson.
  0:24—Brief buns getting out of bed after coming home from museum with a stranger.
Victoria Lynn Johnson
  .... Body Double for Angie Dickinson
  •• 0:02—Frontal nudity in the shower body doubling for Angie Dickinson.

The Drifter (1988)

Timothy Bottoms ....Arthur
Kim Delaney.......................Julia Robbins
  • 0:11—Brief topless making love with Miles O'Keeffe on motel floor.
  •• 0:21—Topless in bed talking with Timothy Bottoms.
Miles O'Keeffe.........................Trey
  • 0:11—Brief upper half of buns while on the motel floor with Kim Delaney.

Drive, He Said (1972)

Karen Black............................Olive
  • 1:05—Brief topless screaming in the bathtub when she gets scared when a bird flies in.
  1:19—Brief lower frontal nudity running out of the house in her bathrobe.
June Fairchild .... Sylvie
  • 0:16—Buns and brief topless walking around in the dark while Gabriel shines a flashlight on her.
  • 1:01—Topless, then brief nude getting dressed while Gabriel goes crazy and starts trashing a house.
Michael Margotta.....................Gabriel
  •• 1:21—Running nude across the grass and up some stairs, then trashing a biology room at the university.
William Tepper ....Hector
Michael Warren....................Easly Jefferson
  • 0:09—Buns and very brief frontal nudity in the shower room with the other basketball players.

Drop Dead Fred (1991)

Phoebe Cates ....Elizabeth
Marsha Mason ....Polly
Tim Matheson.........................Charles
Michael Welker .... Waiter at Wine Gala
  • 1:12—Buns, when toga falls off while he's carrying trays.

Drowning by Numbers (1988; British)

Trevor Cooper........................Hardy
  •• 0:12—Full frontal nudity, lying in bed sleeping.
Bernard Hill.........................Madgett
  •• 0:35—Buns, getting out of bed to throw papers out the window.

David Morrissey ....Bellamy
  • 0:43—Buns, while on couch with Joely Richardson.
  •• 1:24—Nude, getting drowned in the swimming pool.
Bryan Pringle ....Jake
  • 0:04—Buns, while undressing with Nancy.
  • 0:06—Nude, in the tub, drunk.
Joely Richardson................. Cisse Colpitts 3
  • 0:28—Topless, taking off swimsuit and drying herself off. Long shot.
  ••• 0:43—Topless and buns, making love on couch with Bellamy.
  • 1:23—Topless under water in pool with Bellamy.
  •• 1:24—Topless getting out of pool.
  ••• 1:25—Topless standing up and putting swimsuit back on.
  •• 1:37—Left breast, while in car with Madgett.
Juliet Stevenson .... Cisse Colpitts 2
  • 0:57—Lower frontal nudity and left breast, while trying to entice Hardy. Long shot.

Drum (1976)

Pam Grier...........................Regine
  • 0:58—Very brief topless getting undressed and into bed with Maxwell.
Paula Kelly ....Rachel
Yaphet Kotto ....Blaise
  • 1:02—Buns, while getting hung upside down in barn and spanked along with Ken Norton.
Fiona Lewis .... Augusta Chauvet
  ••• 0:57—Topless taking a bath, getting out, then having Pam Grier dry her off.
Ken Norton ....Drum
  • 1:02—Buns, while getting hung upside down in barn and spanked along with Yaphet Kotto.
Cheryl Smith .... Sophie Maxwell
  •• 0:54—Topless in the stable trying to get Yaphet Kotto to make love with her.
Brenda Sykes ....Calinda
  • 0:19—Topless standing next to bed with Ken Norton.
Isela Vega...........................Marianna
  • 0:04—Topless in bed with the maid, Rachel.
  •• 0:22—Brief topless standing next to the bed with Maxwell.

Duet for One (1987)

Julie Andrews .... Stephanie Anderson
  • 0:28—Very brief left breast in gaping blouse in bathroom splashing water on her face because she feels sick, then wet T-shirt.
  ••• 1:06—Topless stretching, lying in bed.
  • 1:07—Very brief buns and very brief right breast, when she rolls off the bed onto the floor.
  1:30—In wet white blouse from perspiring after taking an overdose of pills.
Alan Bates .... David Cornwallis
Rupert Everett .... Constantine Kassanis
Cathryn Harrison .... Penny Smallwood

Liam Neeson. . . . . Totter
- 1:07—Buns, while behind shower door, getting out of shower. Very, very brief buns, falling into bed when robe flies up. Long shot.

Dune Warriors (1990)
David Carradine . . . . Michael
Maria Isabel Lopez . . . . Miranda
- •• 0:25—Topless in underground lake with Val.
- ••• 0:43—Topless making love with a guy in bed.

Jillian McWhirter . . . . Val
- 0:25—Brief right breast with Miranda in underground lake. (Her hair is in the way of her left breast.)

Dust (1985; French/Belgian)
Jane Birkin. . . . . Magda
- 1:17—Brief topless and buns, taking off robe and pounding the wall. Very dark.

John Matshikiza. . . . . Hendrik
- 0:38—Buns, while on top of a girl, trying to rape her.

Dying Young (1991)
Ellen Burstyn. . . . . .Mrs. O'Neil
Julia Roberts . . . . .Hilary O'Neil
Campbell Scott. .Victor Geddes
- 1:04—Brief buns, after running out of the house wrapped in a blanket and tossing it off. Long shot.

David Selby. . . . . Richard Geddes

Easy Money (1983)
Sandra Beall . . . . Maid of Honor
Jennifer Jason Leigh. . . . . Allison Capuletti
Kimberly McArthur . . . . .Ginger Jones
- •• 0:47—Topless sunbathing in the backyard when seen by Rodney Dangerfield.

Easy Rider (1969)
Toni Basil . . . . .Mary
- 1:24—Brief right breast (her hair gets in the way) and very, very brief buns, taking off clothes in graveyard during hallucination sequence.
  1:26—Very brief buns, climbing on something (seen through fish-eye lens).
- 1:27—Buns, while lying down (seen through fish-eye lens).

Karen Black. . . . . Karen
Dennis Hopper . . . . Billy
Jack Nicholson . . . . George Hanson

Easy Wheels (1989)
Eileen Davidson. . . . . .She Wolf
Mike Leinert . . . . .Meatball
- 0:52—Brief buns, while putting his pants on.

Karen Russell. . . . . .Candy
Roberta Vasquez . . . . Tondalco

Eating Raoul (1982)
Ed Begley, Jr.. . . . . Hippie
Robert Beltran. . . . . Raoul

Mary Woronov. . . . . Mary Bland
- ••• 0:46—Topless on the couch struggling with Ed Begley, Jr. More topless while Raoul counts money on her stomach. Long scene.
- 0:53—Buns and side view of right breast in hospital room with Raoul. A little dark.

The Ebony Tower (1985)
Greta Scacchi. . . . . .Mouse
- 0:38—Topless having a picnic.
- 0:43—Brief nude walking into the lake.

Echo Park (1986)
Elvira . . . . Sheri
Michael Bowen . . . . .August
Susan Dey . . . . Meg "May" Greer
- 1:17—Brief glimpse of right breast, while doing a strip tease at a party.

Richard "Cheech" Marin . . . . .Sid

Ecstasy (1932)
Hedy Lamarr . . . . The Wife
- 0:25—Brief topless starting to run after a horse in a field.
- 0:26—Long shot running through the woods, side view naked, then brief topless hiding behind a tree.

Eddie Macon's Run (1983)
Leah Ayres-Hamilton . . . . Chris
Kirk Douglas. . . . . .Marazack
John Schneider. . . . . Eddie Macon
- 0:15—Brief left side view of buns when beginning to cross the stream. Dark, hard to see.

Edge of Sanity (1988)
Glynnis Barber .Elisabeth Jekyll
Sarah Maur-Thorp . . . . .Susannah
- 0:00—Left breast pulling down top to show the little boy in the barn.
- •• 0:09—Topless talking to the two doctors after they examine her back.
- •• 0:50—Topless in red room with Anthony Perkins and Johnny.
- 0:56—Very brief topless in nun outfit.
- 1:10—Brief topless in Perkins' hallucination at Flora's whorehouse.

Claudia Udy . . . . Liza

The Eiger Sanction (1975)
Clint Eastwood. . . . . .Jonathan Hemlock
Candice Rialson . . . . Art Student
Brenda Venus. . . . . George
- 0:50—Very brief topless opening her blouse to get Clint Eastwood to climb up a hill.
- 1:06—Topless taking off her clothes in Eastwood's room, just before she tries to kill him. Dark, hard to see.

Eleven Days, Eleven Nights (1988; Italian)
Joshua McDonald. . . . . .Michael
- 0:33—Buns, when Sarah removes his underwear.

Jessica Moore . . . . Sarah Asproon
- 0:03—Topless opening her raincoat on boat for Michael, then making love.
- 0:11—Buns, taking off robe in front of Michael.
- • 0:16—Right breast, on T.V., then side of breast.
- • 0:29—Topless with Michael, changing clothes with him in restroom.
- • 0:33—Topless in motel room with Michael, then making love.
- 0:44—Brief topless and buns when leaving Michael all tied up.
- • 0:51—Topless and buns in recording studio with Michael.
- 1:17—Topless in flashbacks.
- • • 1:19—Nude, making love with Michael on bed.

Ellie (1984)
Edward Albert . . . . Tom
Sheila Kennedy . . . . Ellie May
- • 0:29—Full frontal nudity posing for Billy while he takes pictures of her just before he falls over a cliff.
0:38—In white bra and panties, in barn loft with Frank.
0:58—In white bra and panties struggling to get away from Edward Albert.
- 1:16—In bra and panties taking off dress with Art. Topless taking off bra and throwing them on antlers. Brief topless many times while frolicking around.
Patrick Tovatt . . . . Art
- 1:19—Brief blurry buns while falling down the stairs.

Emanuelle in Bangkok (1977)
Laura Gemser . . . . Emanuelle
- • 0:07—Topless making love with a guy.
- • 0:12—Full frontal nudity changing in hotel room.
- • • 0:17—Full frontal nudity getting a bath, then massaged by another woman.
- • 0:35—Topless during orgy scene.
- • 0:53—Topless in room with a woman, then taking a shower.
- • 1:01—Topless in tent with a guy and woman.
- • 1:08—Full frontal nudity dancing in a group of guys.
- • 1:16—Full frontal nudity taking a bath with a woman.
- • 1:18—Topless on bed making love with a guy.

Emanuelle the Seductress (1979; Greek)
Laura Gemser . . . . Emanuelle
- 0:01—Full frontal nudity lying in bed with Mario.
- 0:02—Brief topless riding horse on the beach.
- • 0:42—Topless making love then full frontal nudity getting dressed with Tommy.
- • • 0:48—Topless undressing in bedroom, then in white panties, then nude talking to Alona.
- • 0:54—Topless walking around in a skirt.
- • 1:02—Topless outside taking a shower, then on lounge chair making love with Tommy.

Emanuelle's Amazon Adventure (1977)
Laura Gemser . . . . Emanuelle
- 0:17—Brief left breast in flashback sequence in bed with a man.
- 0:21—Brief topless making love in bed.
- 0:25—Brief topless in the water with a blonde woman.
- • 1:10—Full frontal nudity painting her body.
- 1:11—Brief topless in boat.
- 1:13—Nude walking out of the water trying to save Isabelle.
- 1:14—Brief topless getting into the boat with Isabelle.

Embryo (1976)
Barbara Carrera . . . . Victoria
0:36—Almost topless meeting Rock Hudson for the first time. Hair covers breasts.
1:09—In see through top in bedroom with Hudson.
- • 1:10—Brief buns and topless in the mirror after making love with Hudson.
- 1:11—Left breast sticking out of bathrobe.

The Emerald Forest (1985)
Tetchie Agbayani . . . . Caya
- 1:48—Topless in the river when Kachiri is match making all the couples together.
Charley Boorman . . . . Tommy
- 0:23—Brief buns, while running through camp.
- 0:24—Brief buns, while running from waterfall and diving into pond.
- 0:30—Buns, during ceremony.
- 0:45—Buns, while running away from the Fierce People with his dad.
- 1:02—Buns while running on the rocks, then bun in hut.
- • 1:31—Buns while climbing up the building.
- 1:35—Buns while running down the hall to save Kachiri.
Meg Foster . . . . Jean Markham
Dira Paes . . . . Kachiri
- • 0:24—Brief buns while running from waterfall and diving into the pond.
- 0:33—Topless in water talking to Tomme.
- 0:56—Left breast in courtyard when Tomme proposes marriage to her.
- 0:57—Left breast in forest with Tomme. Long shot.
- • 1:01—Topless by the river.
- • 1:04—Topless and buns during wedding ceremony.
- • 1:16—Topless with the other tribe women after being captured by the fierce people.
- 1:18—Topless with the other girls being herded into the building.
- • 1:38—Topless in forest taking off clothes.
- 1:40—Buns, returning to the forest.
- 1:48—Topless in the river.

Emily (1976; British)

Sarah Brackett . . . . Margaret
  • 0:09—Buns, while looking out the window at Koo Stark.
Jeannie Collings . . . . Rosalind
  • 1:05—Brief topless on the couch with Gerald while Richard watches.
Jane Hayden . . . . Rachel
  •• 1:09—Topless in bed with Billy.
Ina Skriver . . . . Augustine
  ••• 0:43—Topless getting into the shower with Koo Stark to give her a massage.
Koo Stark . . . . Emily
  •• 0:08—Topless, lying in bed caressing herself while fantasizing about James.
  ••• 0:30—Topless in studio posing for Augustine, then kissing her.
  ••• 0:42—Buns and topless taking a shower after posing for Augustine.
  •• 0:56—Left breast, under a tree with James.
  • 1:16—Topless in the woods seducing Rupert.

Emmanuelle (1974)

(R-rated version reviewed.)
Christine Boisson . . . . Marie-Ange
  •• 0:16—Full frontal nudity diving into swimming pool. Also buns, under water.
  ••• 0:19—Topless outside in hanging chair with Sylvia Kristel.
Marika Green . . . . Bee
  • 0:46—Nude, undressing outside with Sylvia Kristel. Brief full frontal nudity, when leaving blanket.
  •• 0:47—Topless, getting dressed.
  • 0:50—Upper half of buns, while lying down, talking to Kristel.
Sylvia Kristel . . . . Emmanuelle
  • 0:00—Very brief left breast in robe, while sitting on bed.
  • 0:02—Topless in B&W photos.
  • 0:10—Topless and buns, making love in bed with her husband under a net.
  • 0:13—Brief topless taking off bikini top by swimming pool.
  ••• 0:14—Topless getting up from chair, then full frontal nudity while talking to Ariane.
  ••• 0:15—Nude, swimming under water. Nice.
  • 0:18—Partial left breast, while sleeping in bed.
  •• 0:24—Topless, making love with a stranger on an airplane.
  •• 0:31—Topless with Ariane in the squash court.

Emmanuelle IV (1984)

Sophie Berger . . . . Maria
  •• 0:46—Full frontal nudity putting on robe.
  0:49—Buns, taking off robe in front of Mia Nygren.
Sylvia Kristel . . . . Sylvia
  •• 0:00—Topless in photos during opening credits.
Mia Nygren . . . . Emmanuelle IV
  0:13—Buns, lying on table after plastic surgery.

  ••• 0:15—Full frontal nudity walking around looking at her new self in the mirror.
  • 0:20—Brief topless a couple of times making love on top of a guy getting coached by Sylvia Kristel in dream-like sequence.
  •• 0:22—Full frontal nudity taking off blouse in front of Dona.
  0:25—Almost making love with a guy in bar.
  ••• 0:30—Nude undressing in front of Maria.
  •• 0:39—Full frontal nudity taking her dress off and getting covered with a white sheet.
  ••• 0:40—Full frontal nudity lying down and then putting dress back on.
  • 0:45—Full frontal nudity during levitation trick.
  0:49—Right bra cup reclining on bed.
  • 0:52—Brief topless in stable.
  ••• 0:54—Topless taking off black dress in chair. Brief lower frontal nudity.
  0:57—Brief lower frontal nudity putting on white panties.
  • 1:00—Brief topless when Susanna takes her dress off.
  • 1:03—Brief right breast making love on ground with a boy.
  ••• 1:07—Topless walking on beach.
  • 1:09—Topless with Dona. Dark.
Deborah Power . . . . Dona
  • 1:09—Buns, while lying down and getting a massage from Mia Nygren.
Brinke Stevens . . . . Uncredited Dream Girl
  ••• 0:19—Topless, getting coached by Sylvia Kristel during dream-like sequence on how to get a guy aroused.

Emmanuelle, The Joys of a Woman (1975)

Laura Gemser . . . . Massage Woman
Sylvia Kristel . . . . Emmanuelle
  • 0:18—Topless making love with her husband in bedroom.
  •• 0:22—Topless, then full frontal nudity, undressing in bedroom, then making love with her husband.
  ••• 0:32—Topless with acupuncture needles stuck in her. More topless masturbating while fantasizing about Christopher.
  • 0:53—Right breast, while making love with polo player in locker room.
  ••• 0:58—Nude, getting massaged by another woman.
  ••• 1:14—Right breast in bedroom in open dress, then topless with Jean in bed. Flashback of her with three guys in a bordello.

Endgame (1983)

Laura Gemser . . . . Lilith
  • 1:10—Brief topless a couple of times getting blouse ripped open by a gross looking guy.

Endless Love (1981)

Tom Cruise . . . . Billy
Jami Gertz . . . . Patty

Martin Hewitt . . . . David
- • 0:22—Buns when seen in front of fireplace in living room with Brooke Shields. Long shot.
- • 0:27—Very brief buns in bedroom when Shields closes the door. Another long shot.
- •• 0:28—Buns, while jumping into bed with Shields.
- • 0:38—Buns, while lying on top of Shields in bed.

Shirley Knight . . . . .Anne
Penelope Milford. Ingrid
Brooke Shields. . . . . Jade
    0:37—Body double, side view of right breast in bed with David.
    1:08—Body double very brief left breast, in bed with another guy during David's dream.

Endless Night (1977)
Britt Ekland . . . . Greta
- • 1:21—Brief topless several times with Michael.

Hayley Mills. . . . . .Ellie

Enemies, A Love Story (1989)
Anjelica Huston. . . . . .Tamara
Lena Olin . . . . Masha
- •• 0:16—In white bra, then brief topless several times in bed with Ron Silver. Topless again after making love and starting to make love again.

Enigma (1982)
Brigitte Fossey. . . . . Karen
- • 0:39—Brief topless after undressing in jail cell. Very brief lower frontal nudity and buns, shielding herself from the light.
- • 0:40—Topless getting interrogated.

Sam Neill . . . . .Dimitri Vasilkov
Martin Sheen . . . . Alex Holbeck

Enrapture (1989)
Deborah Blaisdell . . . . .Martha
- ••• 0:10—Topless undressing in her apartment with Keith.
- •• 0:17—Left breast, in bed with Keith, then brief topless.

Jamie Gillis . . . . James
Jane Hamilton . . . . Annie
Felicia Peluso . . . . Ingenue
Ona Simms Wiegers . . . . .Chase Webb
- •• 0:13—In red bra, panties, garter belt and stockings. Buns in G-string, then topless undressing when she doesn't know Keith is watching.
- •• 0:17—Topless when Keith fantasizes about her while he's making love with Martha.
- •• 0:21—Topless in back of limousine with a lucky guy.
- ••• 1:08—Full frontal nudity making love on top of Keith in bed.

Kevin Thomsen . . . . .Keith

Enter the Dragon (1973)
Ahna Capri . . . . Tania
- • 0:47—Very brief left breast three times in open blouse in bed with John Saxon.

The Entity (1983)
George Coe . . . . Dr. Weber
Barbara Hershey. . . . . Carla Moran
- • 0:33—Topless and buns getting undressed before taking a bath. Don't see her face.
    0:59—"Topless" during special effect when The Entity fondles her breasts with invisible fingers while she sleeps.
- • 1:32—"Topless" again getting raped by The Entity while Alex Rocco watches helplessly.

Entre Nous (1983; French)
a.k.a. Coup de Foudre
Miou-Miou. . . . . Madeleine
Isabelle Huppert. . . . . Helen Webber
- • 1:01—Brief topless in shower room talking about her breasts with Miou-Miou.

Guy Marchand. . . . . .Michel

Equus (1977)
Jenny Agutter. . . . . .Jill Mason
- ••• 2:00—Nude in loft above the horses in orange light, then making love with Alan.

Peter Firth . . . . Alan Strang
- • 1:19—Frontal nudity standing in a field with a horse.
- ••• 2:00—Nude in loft above the horses in orange light with Jenny Agutter. Long scene.

Erendira (1983; Brazilian)
Blanca Guerra . . . . Ulysses' Mother
Claudia Ohana. . . . . .Erendira
- • 0:14—Topless getting fondled by a guy against her will.
- •• 0:26—Topless lying in bed sweating and crying after having to have sex with an army of men.
- ••• 1:04—Topless lying in bed sleeping.
    1:08—Brief topless getting out of bed. Long shot, hard to see.
- •• 1:24—Topless and buns on bed with Ulysses.

Oliver Wehe. . . . . .Ulysses
- • 1:24—Buns, while getting into bed with Erendira.

Erotic Images (1983)
Alexandra Day . . . . Logan's Girlfriend
- •• 0:37—Topless getting out of bed while Logan talks on the phone to Britt Ekland.

Britt Ekland . . . . Julie Todd
- • 0:16—Brief side view of left breast in bed with Glenn.
- ••• 0:29—In bra, then topless in bed with Glenn.
    0:33—In bra, in open robe looking at herself in the mirror.
    1:27—In black bra, talking to Sonny.

Alexandra Morgan . . . . .Emily Stewart
- •• 0:57—In black lingerie, then topless on the living room floor with Glenn.
- • 1:05—Topless in bed, making love with Glenn.
- ••• 1:12—Topless in the kitchen with Glenn.
- •• 1:21—Right breast, on couch with Glenn.

Remy O'Neill. . . . . .Vickie Coleman
- ••• 0:04—Topless sitting in chaise lounge talking to Britt Ekland about sex survey. Long scene.
- • 0:06—Topless in bed with Marvin. Brief lower frontal nudity.
- •• 0:07—Brief left breast in spa with TV repairman, then brief topless.

Julia Parton . . . . Marvin's Nurse
- • 0:08—Brief topless in office with Marvin. Dark, hard to see.

Barbara Peckinpaugh. . . . . Cheerleader
- • 0:07—Topless dancing in an office with another cheerleader.

Eternity (1989)

Eileen Davidson. . . . . .Dahlia/Valerie
0:33—In black bra and panties in dressing room. Brief buns standing in bathtub during Jon Voight's flashback.
- • 0:52—Brief left breast, then topless, in bed with Voight. Don't see face.

Eureka (1983; British)

Rutger Hauer. . . . . Claude Maillot Van Horn
Emma Relph . . . . Mary (blue dress)
- • 1:17—Brief topless during African voodoo ceremony.

Mickey Rourke. . . . . Aurelio
Theresa Russell . . . . Tracy
0:38—In lingerie talking to Rutger Hauer.
- • 0:40—Right breast, lying in bed with Hauer.
- • 1:04—Very brief left breast in bed with Hauer, then brief lower frontal nudity and brief buns when Gene Hackman bursts into the room.
- •• 1:09—Topless on a boat with Hauer.
- • 1:41—Left breast peeking out from under black top while lying in bed.
- ••• 1:59—Full frontal nudity kicking off sheets in the bed.

Ann Thornton . . . . .Jane (red dress)
- • 1:17—Brief topless during African voodoo ceremony.

Europa Europa (1991; German)

Julie Delpy. . . . . Leni
Marco Hofschneider . . . . Young Salomon Perel
- ••• 0:03—Buns, while taking off underwear to take a bath.
- • 0:05—Very, very brief frontal nudity, getting into tub.
- ••• 0:06—Nude, getting out of the bathtub and running to hide in a barrel.
- •• 0:45—Nude, running around in barn, trying to get away from his fellow German officer.
- • 1:19—Brief, discolored frontal nudity, after he tries to "create" a foreskin.

Eve of Destruction (1991)

Gregory Hines. . . . . .Jim McQuade
Tim Russ . . . . .Carter

Reneé Soutendijk . . . . .Dr. Eve Simmons/Eve VIII
0:17—Left breast, while on table as a robot, with half her skin removed. Possibly a special-effect body.
- • 0:22—Brief topless in bathroom (as a robot), fixing her wound. Topless sitting on bed, butting a large bandage over the wound.

An Evening with Kitten (1983)

Francesca "Kitten" Natividad . . . . .Herself
- •• 0:02—Topless busting out of her blouse.
- •• 0:09—Topless in miniature city scene.
- •• 0:11—Brief topless on stage.
- • 0:20—Left breast, in bed with a vampire.
- ••• 0:21—Topless and buns in G-string during dance in large champagne glass prop. Long scene.
- ••• 0:24—Topless on beach in mermaid costume with little shell pasties.
- ••• 0:25—Topless in the glass again.
- •• 0:28—Topless in and out of glass.
- •• 0:29—Brief topless during end credits.

Every Time We Say Goodbye (1986)

Cristina Marsillach . . . . .Sarah
1:00—In white slip in her bedroom.
1:03—In white slip again.
- •• 1:09—Right breast, then brief topless lying in bed with Tom Hanks.

Everybody's All-American (1988)

Timothy Hutton . . . . Donnie
Jessica Lange . . . . Babs
0:32—Brief breasts under sheer nightgown in bedroom with Dennis Quaid.
- • 0:54—Buns and very, very brief side view of left breast by the campfire by the lake with Timothy Hutton at night. Might be a body double.

Dennis Quaid. . . . . .Gavin

The Evil Below (1991)

Sheri Able. . . . . .Tracy
- • 0:10—Buns, in two piece swimsuit on boat.
0:16—In wet T-shirt getting on boat after diving.
- • 0:21—Right breast, with Max behind curtain. Hard to see.

June Chadwick. . . . . Sarah Livingston
- • 0:08—Very, very brief left breast, while on the floor with Max after he takes off her bra.
0:39—In red, one piece swimsuit on boat.
- • 0:45—Very brief left breast, while on the floor with Max. Different angle from 0:08.

Evil Laugh (1986)

Kim McKamy . . . . Connie
Myles O'Brien. . . . . Mark
0:30—Sort of buns and brief lower frontal nudity rolling over on top of Tina in bed. Very, very brief frontal nudity when she takes the sheet away from him.

Evil Spawn (1987)

Bobbie Bresee . . . . Lynn Roman
    0:14—Very brief half of right breast in bed with a guy.
    0:26—In red one piece swimsuit.
    ••• 0:36—Topless in bathroom looking at herself in the mirror, then taking a shower.
Pamela Gilbert . . . . .Elaine Talbot
    ••• 0:46—Nude taking off black lingerie and going swimming in pool. Hubba, hubba!
    ••• 0:49—Topless in the pool, then full frontal nudity getting out.
Dawn Wildsmith . . . . Evelyn Avery

Evil Toons (1991)

Suzanne Ager . . . . .Terry
    ••• 0:31—Topless and buns in G-string, taking off clothes to put on her pajamas.
    •• 1:09—Right breast, while on the floor getting her pajamas ripped open by Roxanne.
    •• 1:10—Brief topless when Roxanne rips the pajamas all the way down.
Michelle Bauer . . . . Mrs. Burt
    •• 0:48—Topless opening her lingerie for Burt. Buns, while walking away in G-string.
David Carradine . . . . .Gideon Fisk
Barbara Dare. . . . . Jan
    ••• 0:30—Topless, taking off robe and putting on red nightgown.
    •• 1:06—Topless when her top is pulled down by Roxanne.
Monique Gabrielle . . . . Megan
    0:21—In bra in open blouse when Roxanne tries to get her to do a strip tease.
    ••• 0:25—In bra, then topless undressing in front of mirror.
Madison Stone . . . . Roxanne
    ••• 0:20—Buns in G-string, then topless doing a strip routine in front of her girlfriends.
    ••• 0:33—Topless, taking off blouse and putting on bra and panties. Buns in sheer panties.
    •• 0:36—Topless on the floor, getting attacked by the monster.
    ••• 0:38—Topless walking around, covered with blood, talking with Megan.
    •• 0:41—Topless putting blouse on.
    • 0:42—Topless on couch with Biff.
    • 0:55—Left breast in open blouse, seducing Burt.
    • 0:59—Brief topless several times, dead, when the other girls discover her.

Evil Town (1987)

Lynda Wiesmeier. . . . . Dianne
    ••• 0:09—Topless on top of Tony outside while camping.
    •• 0:11—Right breast while making out with boyfriend outside. Topless getting up.
    • 0:13—Topless in open blouse running from bad guy. Nice bouncing action.
    •• 0:15—Topless getting captured by bad guys.

    •• 0:17—Topless getting out of car and brought into the house.
    •• 0:23—Topless tied up in chair.

Excalibur (1981; British)

Katrine Boorman . . . . Igrayne
    • 0:14—Right breast, then topless in front of the fire when Uther tricks her into thinking that he is her husband and makes love to her.
Gabriel Byrne. . . . . .Uther
Nicholas Clay. . . . . .Lancelot
    •• 1:13—Buns, while fighting with himself in a suit of armor.
    • 1:31—Brief buns, while running into the woods after waking up. Long shot, hard to see.
Cherie Lunghi . . . . .Guenevere
    • 1:25—Brief topless in the forest kissing Lancelot.
Helen Mirren . . . . Morgana
    • 1:31—Side view of left breast under a fishnet outfit climbing into bed.
Liam Neeson . . . . Gawain
Nigel Terry. . . . . King Arthur

The Executioner's Song (1982)

(European Version reviewed.)
Rosanna Arquette. . . . . Nicole Baker
    ••• 0:30—Brief topless in bed, then getting out of bed. Buns, walking to kitchen.
    ••• 0:41—Topless in bed with Tommy Lee Jones.
    ••• 0:48—Topless on top of Jones making love.
    •• 1:36—Right breast and buns, standing up getting strip searched before visiting Jones in prison.
Tommy Lee Jones. . . . . Gary Gillmore
    •• 0:48—Buns, while walking to kitchen after hitting Rosanna Arquette.

Exposed (1983)

Iman . . . . Model
Bibi Andersson. . . . . Margaret
Pierre Clementi Vic
Janice Dickinson. . . . . Model
Harvey Keitel . . . . Rivas
Nastassia Kinski . . . . .Elizabeth Carlson
    •• 0:54—Topless in bed with Rudolf Nureyev.
Rudolf Nureyev . . . . Daniel Jelline
    ••• 0:54—Buns, while in bed with Nastassia Kinski.
James Russo . . . . .Nick

Extreme Prejudice (1987)

Maria Conchita Alonso. . . . . .Sarita Cisneros
    •• 0:27—Brief topless in the shower while Nick Nolte is in the bathroom talking to her.
Clancy Brown. . . . . Sgt. Larry McRose
Rip Torn. . . . . Sheriff Hank Pearson

Extremities (1986)

Farrah Fawcett . . . . .Marjorie
    • 0:37—Brief side view of right breast when Joe pulls down her top in the kitchen. Can't see her face, but reportedly her.
Michael Hennessy . . . . Pizza Man

Sandy Martin . . . . .Officer Sudow
James Russo . . . . Joe

Eye of the Needle *(1981)*
Christopher Cazenove. David
Kate Nelligan . . . . Lucy
•• 0:52—Brief left breast, while drying herself off in the
bathroom when Donald Sutherland accidentally
sees her.
1:15—Top half of buns, making love in bed with
Sutherland.
• 1:26—Topless making love in bed with Sutherland
after he killed her husband. Dark, hard to see.
Donald Sutherland . . . . Faber

Eyes of a Stranger *(1981)*
Jennifer Jason Leigh. . . . . Tracy
• 1:15—Very brief topless lying in bed getting attacked by rapist.
•• 1:19—Left breast, while cleaning herself in bathroom.

Eyes of Fire *(1983)*
Karlene Crockett. . . . . Leah
• 0:44—Brief topless sitting up in the water and scar-
ing Mr. Dalton.
• 1:16—Topless talking to Dalton who is trapped in a
tree. Brief topless again when he pulls the creature
out of the tree.

The Fabulous Baker Boys *(1989)*
Jeff Bridges . . . . .Jack Baker
Michelle Pfeiffer . . . . Susie Diamond
Terri Treas. . . . . Girl in Bed
• 0:00—Brief upper half of right breast when sheet
falls down when she leans over in bed.

Fade to Black *(1980)*
Linda Kerridge. . . . . .Marilyn
• 0:44—Topless in the shower.
Mickey Rourke. . . . . .n.a.
Marya Small . . . . .Doreen

Fair Game *(1985; Australian)*
Cassandra Delaney . . . . .Jessica
• 0:15—Buns and brief side of left breast, taking off
her outfit and lying on bed.
• 0:16—Topless rolling over in bed.
0:19—Brief, out of focus buns, in Polaroid photograph taped to inside of the refrigerator.
• 0:32—Brief left breast, taking off outfit to take a
shower.
•• 0:48—Brief topless when the bad guys cut her
blouse open. Topless several times, while tied to
front of truck.
• 0:49—Brief left breast while getting up off the
ground.
0:50—Half of right breast, while sitting in the shower. Dark.

Fair Game *(1988; Italian)*
Trudie Styler. . . . . Eva
0:14—Very, very brief blurry top of right breast in
gaping blouse, while standing up after changing
clothes.
• 0:37—Brief buns, kneeling in bathtub. Very brief
buns in the mirror several times putting on robe and
getting out of the bathtub.

Fairytales *(1979)*
Angela Aames . . . . Little Bo Peep
••• 0:14—Nude with The Prince in the woods.
Nai Bonet. . . . . Sheherazade
• 0:29—Buns and very brief left breast doing a belly
dance and rubbing oil on herself.
Marita Ditmar . . . . S & M Dancer
• 0:38—Topless wearing masks with two other S&M
Dancers.
Lindsay Freeman . . . . Jill
•• 0:24—Nude on hill with Jack.
Annie Gaybis . . . . .Snow White
••• 0:21—Nude in room with the seven little dwarfs
singing and dancing.
Evelyn Guerrero . . . . S & M Dancer
•• 0:38—Topless wearing masks with two other blonde
S&M Dancers.
•• 0:56—Full frontal nudity dancing with the other
S&M Dancers again.
Linnea Quigley. .Dream Girl
•• 1:07—Topless waking up after being kissed by The
Prince.
Mariwin Roberts. . . . . Elevator Operator
• 0:20—Brief full frontal nudity in the elevator.
• 0:23—Topless again, closer shot.
Idy Tripoldi. . . . . .Naked Girl
••• 0:06—Nude, dancing in bedroom and getting in
and out of bed with The Prince.

Fame *(1980)*
Irene Cara . . . . Coco
1:16—In leotard, dancing and talking to Hillary.
• 1:57—Brief topless during "audition" on a B&W TV
monitor.
Meg Tilly . . . . Principal Dancer

A Family Matter *(1990)*
Carol Alt. . . . . Nancy
•• 1:08—Buns, in panties. Brief side view of left breast
with Eric Roberts.
Eric Roberts . . . . Shaun McGinnis

Family Viewing *(1987; Canadian)*
Gabrielle Rose . . . . .Sandra
• 0:27—Brief left breast, lying down with Stan. Seen
on TV that Van watches.
• 0:29—Same 0:27 scene again.
Aidan Tierney. . . . . Van
•• 0:26—Brief buns, while getting up out of bed and
putting on his underwear.

Famous T & A (1982)
(No longer available for purchase, check your video store for rental.)

Elvira .... Katya
- ••• 0:28—Topless scene from *Working Girls*.

Vanity .... Tanya
- • 1:02—Topless scenes from *Tanya's Island*.

Angela Aames .... Little Bo Peep
- •• 0:50—Topless scene from *Fairytales*.

Ursula Andress .... Herself
- ••• 0:15—Full frontal nudity scenes from *Slave of the Cannibal God*.

Brigitte Bardot .... Joan
- • 0:25—Buns, then brief topless in scene from *Ms. Don Juan*.

Jacqueline Bisset .... Jenny
- ••• 0:31—Topless scene from *Secrets*.

Timothy Brown .... Mojo
- • 1:05—Buns in outtake from *Sweet Sugar*.

Pamela Collins .... Dolores
- ••• 1:05—Topless in scenes and outtakes from *Sweet Sugar*.

Sybil Danning .... Hostess
- • 0:00—Brief side view of buns and partial left breast, getting dressed.

Phyllis Davis .... Joy/Sugar
- ••• 0:02—Nude in lots of great out-takes from *Terminal Island*. Check this out if you are a Phyllis Davis fan!
- ••• 0:51—Topless in scenes from *Sweet Sugar*. Includes more out-takes.
- ••• 1:04—More out-takes from *Sweet Sugar*.

Uschi Digard .... Truck Stop Woman
- •• 0:44—Topless scenes from *Harry, Cherry & Raquel* and *Truck Stop Women*.

Ella Edwards .... Simone
- •• 1:07—Buns and topless in outtakes from *Sweet Sugar*.

Laura Gemser .... Emanuelle
- ••• 0:55—Topless scenes from *Emanuelle Around the World*.

Claudia Jennings .... Rose
- •• 0:26—Topless scenes from *Single Girls* and *Truck Stop Women*.

Laura Jane Leary .... Motorcycle Rider
- • 0:29—Lower nudity, riding a motorcycle with only a jacket on.

Barbara Leigh .... Bunny Campbell
- ••• 0:45—Topless scene from *Terminal Island*. Includes additional takes that weren't used.

Ornella Muti .... Lisa
- •• 0:07—Topless in scenes from *Summer Affair*. Nude underwater and running around the beach.

Joan Prather .... Herself
- •• 0:49—Brief topless in scene from *Bloody Friday*.

Victoria Thompson .... Beth Hillyer
- • 1:07—Brief topless and bun scene from *The Harrad Experiment*.
- • 1:12—Brief nude, getting up from the floor with Don Johnson.

Idy Tripoldi .... Bonnie Tirol
- ••• 0:35—Full frontal nude scene from *Auditions*.

Laurie Walters .... Sheila Grove
- • 1:08—Topless scene from *The Harrad Experiment*.
- •• 1:11—Nude pool scene from *The Harrad Experiment*.

Edy Williams .... Herself
- •• 0:39—Topless and bun scenes from *Dr. Minx*.

The Fanatasist (1986; Irish)
Moira Harris .... Patricia Teeling
- • 1:24—Brief topless and buns climbing onto couch for the weird photographer.
- • 1:28—Brief right breast leaning over to kiss the photographer.
- • 1:31—Very brief side view of left breast in bathtub.

Gabrielle Reidy .... Kathy O'Malley
- • 0:03—Topless getting attacked in a room.

Fanny Hill (1981; British)
Lisa Raines Foster .... Fanny Hill
- •• 0:09—Nude, getting into bathtub, then drying herself off.
- • 0:10—Full frontal nudity getting into bed.
- ••• 0:12—Full frontal nudity making love with Phoebe in bed.
- ••• 0:30—Nude, making love in bed with Charles.
- ••• 0:49—Topless, whipping her lover, Mr. H., in bed.
- •• 0:53—Nude getting into bed with William while Hannah watches through the keyhole.
- ••• 1:26—Nude, getting out of bed, then running down the stairs to open the door for Charles.

Fantasies (1974)
a.k.a. *Once Upon a Love*
Bo Derek .... Anastasia
- • 0:03—Left breast, in bathtub.
- •• 0:15—Topless taking off top, then right breast, in bathtub.
- • 0:43—Topless getting her dress top pulled down.
- • 0:59—Brief topless in the water. Very brief full frontal nudity walking back into the house.
- • 1:00—Buns and left breast several times outside the window.
- • 1:17—Upper left breast, in bathtub again.

Peter Hooten .... Damir
- • 1:06—Buns, while dropping his towel in front of Bo Derek. Long shot, don't see his face.
- • 1:18—Buns again. Same shot from 1:06.

Far and Away (1992)
Tom Cruise .... Joseph Donelly
- 1:02—Upper half of buns, bending over to fix his bedding while Nicole Kidman peeks through hole in room divider.

Michelle Johnson .... Grace
Nicole Kidman .... Shannon Christie
- 1:03—Back half of right breast, seen through sheer room divider when she changes clothes.

Far From Home (1989)
Susan Tyrrell . . . . Agnes Reed
- 0:29—Very, very brief right breast in bathtub getting electrocuted.

Teri Weigel . . . . Woman in Trailer
- •• 0:16—Topless making love when Drew Barrymore peeks in window.

Farewell, My Lovely (1975; British)
Charlotte Rampling . . . . Velma
Cheryl Smith . . . . Doris
- 0:56—Frontal nudity in bedroom in a bordello with another guy before getting beaten by the madam.

Sylvester Stallone . . . . Kelly/Jonnie

Fast Times at Ridgemont High (1982)
Phoebe Cates . . . . Linda Barrett
- ••• 0:50—Topless getting out of swimming pool during Judge Reinhold's fantasy.

Lana Clarkson . . . . Mrs. Vargas
Anthony Edwards . . . . Stoner Bud
Ava Lazar . . . . Playmate
Jennifer Jason Leigh . . . . Stacy Hamilton
- 0:18—Left breast, while making out with Ron in a dugout.
- ••• 1:00—Topless in poolside dressing room.

Kelli Maroney . . . . Cindy
Tom Nolan . . . . Dennis Taylor
Sean Penn . . . . Jeff Spicoli
Judge Reinhold . . . . Brad Hamilton
James Russo . . . . Robber
Eric Stoltz . . . . Stoner Bud
Lori Sutton . . . . Playmate
Amanda Wyss . . . . Lisa

Fast Walking (1981)
Kay Lenz . . . . Moke
- 0:26—Brief topless closing the door after pulling James Woods into the room.
- 0:42—Caressing herself under her dress while in prison visiting room, talking to George.
- ••• 1:27—Right breast in store. Topless getting hosed down and dried off outside by James Woods.
- 1:32—Brief left breast, making love with Woods.

Susan Tyrrell . . . . Evie
M. Emmet Walsh . . . . Sgt. George Sager
- 0:59—Frontal nudity standing in the doorway of Evie's mobile home yelling at James Woods after he interrupts Walsh making love with Evie.

James Woods . . . . Fast-Walking Miniver

Fatal Attraction (1987)
Anne Archer . . . . Ellen Gallagher
- 0:51—In white bra, sitting in front of mirror, getting ready for a party.

Glenn Close . . . . Alex Forrest
- •• 0:17—Left breast when she opens her top to let Michael Douglas kiss her. Then very brief buns, falling into bed with him.
- 0:20—Brief right breast in freight elevator with Douglas.

- ••• 0:32—Topless in bed talking to Douglas. Long scene, sheet keeps changing positions between cuts.

Michael Douglas . . . . Dan Gallagher
- •• 0:16—Brief buns, while pulling his pants down to make love with Glenn Close on the kitchen sink.
- 0:17—Very brief buns while falling into bed with Close.
- 0:22—Brief buns, while taking a shower.

Fatal Attraction (1981; Canadian)
a.k.a. Head On
Sally Kellerman . . . . Michelle Keys
- 0:46—Brief topless in building making out with a guy. Dark, hard to see.
- 1:19—Brief half of left breast, after struggling with a guy.

Fatal Charm (1992; Made for Cable Movie)
Christopher Atkins . . . . Adam Brenner
Tracy Dali . . . . Dream Girl
- •• 0:11—Topless in van with Christopher Atkins. Lots of diffusion.
- 0:20—Brief topless in van during Amanda Peterson's fantasy.

Fatal Games (1984)
Angela Bennett . . . . Sue Allen Baines
- •• 0:21—Full frontal nudity in the sauna with Teal Roberts.
- 0:23—Nude, running around the school, trying to get away from the killer. Dark.

Sally Kirkland . . . . Diane Paine
Melissa Prophet . . . . Nancy Wilson
- 0:14—Buns and side view of left breast in shower with other girls. Long shot. (She's wearing a white towel on her head.)

Linnea Quigley . . . . Athelete
Teal Roberts . . . . Lynn Fox
- ••• 0:08—Topless on bed and floor when Frank takes her clothes off, more topless in shower.
- •• 0:21—Topless in sauna with Sue.

Brinke Stevens . . . . Uncredited Shower Girl
- 0:14—Brief, out of focus side of left breast and upper half of buns, taking a shower in the background while two girls talk. (She's wearing a light blue towel around her hair.)

Fatal Instinct (1991)
(Unrated version reviewed.)
Laura Johnson . . . . Catherine Merrims
- 0:45—Brief left breast in open robe, getting out of bed.
- ••• 0:47—Topless in bed talking with Michael Madsen, then making love.
- ••• 0:51—Topless in the bathtub when Bill comes in. Partial lower frontal nudity when standing up.
- •• 0:52—Brief buns and topless getting dressed in bedroom.
- 0:59—In wet T-shirt in pool. Brief buns, underwater, more when getting out.

Michael Madsen . . . . Cliff Burden
- 0:43—Half of buns, while lying in bed.
- •• 0:48—Upper half of buns, while making love in bed with Laura Johnson.

Kim McKamy . . . . Frank Stegner's Girlfriend
- •• 0:01—Topless, opening her towel in front of Frank at night before he gets shot.

Fatal Mission (1990)
Tia Carrere . . . . Mai Chang
- 0:22—Side view of right breast while changing tops. Dark.

Fatal Pulse (1987)
Roxanne Kernohan . . . . Ann
- 0:58—Brief topless in yellow outfit before getting thrown out of the window.

Christie Mucciante . . . . Karen
- •• 0:52—Topless, getting dressed for bed.

Fear (1991; Made for Cable Movie)
Michelle Foreman . . . . Gale the Stripper
- 0:50—Topless and buns dancing in bar. Hard to see because seen through the killer's eyes.

Lauren Hutton. Jessica Moreau
Ally Sheedy . . . . .Cayce Bridges

Fear City (1984)
Maria Conchita Alonso . . . . Silver Chavez
Tom Berenger. . . . . .Matt Rossi
Rae Dawn Chong . . . . Leila
- ••• 0:26—Topless and buns, dancing on stage.
- 0:50—Brief topless in the hospital getting a shock to get her heart started.

Emilia Crow. . . . . .Bibi
- •• 0:16—Topless, dancing at the Metropole club.
- •• 1:00—Topless, dancing on the stage.

Melanie Griffith. . . . . Loretta
- 0:04—Buns, in blue G-string, dancing on stage.
- •• 0:07—Topless, dancing on stage.
- ••• 0:23—Topless dancing on stage wearing a red G-string.

Tracy Griffith. . . . . .Sandra Cook
Janet Julian . . . . .Ruby
Joy Michael. . . . . Metropole Dancer
Joe Palese . . . . .Tony
Ola Ray. . . . . .Honey Powers

Fearless (1978)
Joan Collins . . . . Bridgitte
- 0:01—In bra and panties, then brief right breast during opening credits.
- •• 0:41—Topless after doing a strip tease routine on stage.
- 1:17—Undressing in front of Wally in white bra and panties, then right breast.
- 1:20—Brief right breast lying dead on couch.

The Fearless Hyena, Part II (1984; Chinese)
Jackie Chan. . . . . Chan Lung
- 0:06—Brief buns, jumping up in the water while trying to catch a fish. Don't see his face clearly.

The Fearless Vampire Killers (1967)
Fiona Lewis . . . . Maid
Sharon Tate . . . . Sarah Shagal
- 0:24—Very, very brief topless struggling in bathtub with vampire. Hard to see.

Felicity (1978; Australian)
Glory Annen. . . . . .Felicity
- •• 0:02—Topless taking off leotard in girl's shower room, then nude taking a shower.
- 0:05—Buns, then left breast, then right breast undressing to go skinny dipping.
- •• 0:10—Topless and buns at night at the girl's dormitory.
- •• 0:15—Topless undressing in room with Christine.
- 0:16—Left breast, while touching herself in bed.
- ••• 0:20—Lots of lower frontal nudity trying on clothes, bras and panties in dressing room. Brief topless.
- ••• 0:25—Buns and topless taking a bath. Full frontal nudity when Steve peeks in at her.
- 0:31—Brief full frontal nudity losing her virginity on car with Andrew.
- ••• 0:38—Full frontal nudity in bath with Mei Ling and two other girls. Long scene.
- ••• 0:58—Full frontal nudity in bed with Miles.
- ••• 1:13—Full frontal nudity with Mei Ling making love on bed. Long scene.
- 1:20—Left breast, while making love standing up.
- •• 1:21—Topless and buns making love with Miles.
- •• 1:27—Nude making love again with Miles.
- 1:29—Buns, in the water with Miles.

Fellow Traveller (1989; Made for Cable Movie)
Imogen Stubbs. . . . . Sarah Aitchison
- 0:54—Topless in bed with Asa. Very, very brief right breast when he rolls off her.

Sarah Trigger . . . . Gloria
- •• 0:02—Topless, sitting up in bed, stretching, then getting out.

Femme Fatale (1990)
Lisa Blount . . . . .Jenny
Suzanne Snyder . . . . .Andrea
- ••• 0:08—Topless, nonchalantly taking off her top and posing for Billy Zane's painting. (She sometimes has a bag over her head.)
- •• 0:46—Topless posing again with the bag on and off her head.

Billy Zane. . . . . .Elijah Hooper
Lisa Zane . . . . Cynthia

Fever (1991; Made for Cable Movie)
Teresa Gilmore-Capps . . . . Jeanine
Marcia Gay Harden . . . . .Lacy
- 0:18—Brief topless making love in bed with Sam Neill.
- •• 1:31—In bra in bed with bad guy, then topless when he opens her bra. Kind of dark.

Joe Spano. . . . . Junkman

Fever Pitch (1985)
Catherine Hicks............................ Flo
- 0:11—Brief left breast, while sitting on bed in hotel room talking with Ryan O'Neal.

Cherie Michan..................... Rose O'Sharon
Ryan O'Neal ....Taggart

The Fifth Floor (1978)
John David Carson .... Ronnie Denton
Patti D'Arbanville .... Cathy Burke
Dianne Hull...................... Kelly McIntyre
- •• 0:29—Topless and buns in shower while Carl watches, then brief full frontal nudity running out of the shower.
- •• 1:09—Topless in whirlpool bath getting visited by Carl again, then raped.

The Fifth Monkey (1990)
Vera Fischer......................... Mrs. Watts
Ben Kingsley ....Kunda
- 1:04—Brief buns, while standing under waterfall. Don't see his face and water is in the way.

The Final Alliance (1990)
David Hasselhoff .... Will Colton
Jeanie Moore............................. Carrie
- 1:03—Brief topless getting into bed with David Hasselhoff, then brief right breast twice in bed with him. A little dark.

Fiona (1978; British)
Linda Regan .... Secretary
Fiona Richmond .... Fiona Richmond
- •• 0:23—Topless on boat with a blonde woman rubbing oil on her.
- •• 0:27—In a bra, then frontal nudity stripping in a guy's office for an audition.
- •• 0:35—Topless, then frontal nudity lying down during photo session.
- • 0:51—Topless walking around her apartment in boots.
- •• 1:00—Topless with old guy ripping each other's clothes off.
- •• 1:08—Frontal nudity taking off clothes for a shower.

Fire Birds (1990)
a.k.a. Wings of the Apache
Nicholas Cage....................... Jake Preston
Tommy Lee Jones .... Brad Little
Sean Young......................Billie Lee Guthrie
- • 0:52—Very, very brief right breast twice in bed with Nicholas Cage.

Firehouse (1987)
Ruth Corrine Collins .... Bubbles
Gianna Rains.....................Barrett Hopkins
- ••• 0:33—Topless taking a shower, then drying herself just before the fire alarm goes off.
- •• 0:56—Topless making love with the reporter on the roof of a building.

Fires Within (1991)
Greta Scacchi...........................Isabel
- • 0:18—Upper half of buns, very brief topless in bed.
  0:19—In bra, changing clothes.
- • 0:38—Very brief topless in bed.

Jimmy Smits.......................... Nestor

First Love (1977)
Beverly D'Angelo ....Shelley
  0:05—Very, very brief half of left breast when her jacket opens up while talking to William Katt.
  0:11—In white bra and black panties in Katt's bedroom.
- • 1:10—Brief topless taking off her top in bedroom with Katt.

Susan Dey .... Caroline Hedges
- ••• 0:31—Topless making love in bed with William Katt. Long scene.
- • 0:51—Topless taking off her top in her bedroom with Katt.

John Heard.............................David
William Katt .... Elgin Smith

The First Nudie Musical (1979)
Leslie Ackerman .... Susie
Alexandra Morgan .... Mary La Rue
- • 0:54—Topless, singing and dancing during dancing dildo routine.
- ••• 1:04—Full frontal nudity in bed trying to do a take.
  1:07—Topless in bed with a guy with a continuous erection.
- •• 1:17—Topless in bed in another scene.

The First Turn-On! (1983)
Georgia Harrell.................... Michelle Farmer
- ••• 1:17—Topless and brief buns in cave with everybody during orgy scene.

Sheila Kennedy...................... Dreamgirl
- • 0:52—In red two piece swimsuit, then topless when the top falls down during Danny's daydream.
- • 0:59—Right breast, while in bed with Danny.

Michael Sanville .... Mitch
- • 1:18—Buns, while in cave orgy scene on top of Annie.

Mark Torgl............................Dwayne
- • 1:02—Buns, while dropping his pants for Michelle.

A Fish Called Wanda (1988)
John Cleese .... Archie
- • 1:13—Very brief upper half of buns, in house when he's surprised by the returning family. Looks like very, very brief frontal nudity when he stands up after pulling his underwear down.

Jamie Lee Curtis ....Wanda
  0:21—In black bra and panties changing in the bedroom talking to Kevin Kline.
  0:35—In black bra sitting on bed getting undressed.

Kevin Kline............................. Otto

The Fisher King (1991)

Jeff Bridges . . . . Jack
Michael Jeter. . . . . Homeless Cabaret Singer
Robin Williams . . . . .Parry
••• 0:58—Nude, dancing around in the park at night with Jeff Bridges.

Five Easy Pieces (1970)

Susan Anspach . . . . Catherine Van Oost
Toni Basil . . . . .Terry Grouse
Karen Black . . . . Rayette Dipesto
0:48—In sheer black nightie in bathroom, then walking to bedroom with Jack Nicholson.
Helena Kallianiotes . . . . Palm Apodaca
Jack Nicholson . . . . Robert Dupea
Sally Struthers . . . . .Betty
0:15—In a bra sitting on a couch in the living room with Jack Nicholson and another man and a woman.
•• 0:34—Brief topless a couple of times making love with Nicholson. Lots of great moaning, but hard to see anything.

A Flash of Green (1984)

Blair Brown . . . . Catherine "Kat" Hubble
• 1:30—Very brief right breast moving around in bed with Ed Harris.
Joan Goodfellow . . . . .Mitchie
Ed Harris . . . . Jimmy Wing

Flashdance (1983)

Belinda Bauer . . . . Katie Hurley
Jennifer Beals. . . . . Alex
Malcolm Danare . . . . Cecil
Marine Jahan
. . . . Uncredited Dance Double for Jennifer Beals
Sunny Johnson .Jennie Szabo
• 1:28—Topless on stage with other strippers.
Dirga McBroom . . . . Heels
Michael Nouri . . . . .Nick Hurley

Flashpoint (1984)

Kris Kristofferson . . . . .Logan
Rip Torn . . . . Sheriff Wells
Treat Williams . . . . .Ernie
•• 0:03—Buns, putting on pants in locker room while talking to Kris Kristofferson.

Flesh + Blood (1985)

Nancy Cartwright . . . . .Kathleen
• 0:28—Brief topless showing Jennifer Jason Leigh how to make love. Long shot.
Rutger Hauer. . . . . Martin
• 1:35—Buns, while in a jock strap running up stairs after everybody throws their clothes into the fire.
Jennifer Jason Leigh. .Agnes
• 0:45—Brief right breast, while being held down.
•• 1:05—Full frontal nudity getting into the bath with Rutger Hauer and making love.
••• 1:16—Full frontal nudity getting out of bed with Hauer and walking to the window.
•• 1:35—Nude throwing clothes into the fire.

Blanca Marsillach . . . . Clara
•• 0:11—Full frontal nudity on bed having convulsions after getting hit on the head with a sword.
Marina Saura . . . . Polly
• 0:59—Brief left breast during feast in the castle.
• 1:09—Topless on balcony of the castle with everybody during the day.
Jack Thompson . . . . Hawkwood
Susan Tyrrell. . . . . Celine
• 1:35—Right breast sticking out of her dress when everybody throws their clothes into the fire.

The Fly (1986)

Joy Boushel . . . . .Tawny
• 0:54—Very brief topless viewed from below when Jeff Goldblum pulls her by the arm to get her out of bed.
Geena Davis. .Veronica Quaife
0:40—Brief almost side view of left breast getting out of bed.
Jeff Goldblum. . . . . Seth Brundle

For Your Love Only (1979; German)

Nastassia Kinski . . . . Zena
•• 0:04—Topless, twice, in the woods with her teacher, Victor, while Michael watches through the bushes.
• 0:15—Brief right breast, in the woods with Michael.
•• 0:58—Partial left breast, sitting up in bed with Victor. Topless walking around and putting on robe.

Forbidden World (1982)

Michael Bowen . . . . .Jimmy Swift
June Chadwick . . . . Dr. Barbara Glaser
•• 0:29—Topless in bed making love with Jesse Vint.
•• 0:54—Topless taking a shower with Dawn Dunlap.
Dawn Dunlap. Tracy Baxter
• 0:27—Brief topless getting ready for bed.
••• 0:37—Nude in steam bath.
•• 0:54—Topless in shower with June Chadwick.

Forbidden Zone (1980)

Gisele Lindley. . . . . .The Princess
••• 0:21—Topless in jail cell.
••• 0:39—Topless turning a table around.
••• 0:45—Topless bending over, making love with a frog.
•• 0:51—Topless in a cave.
•• 0:53—More topless scenes.
•• 1:06—Even more topless scenes.
Susan Tyrrell. . . . . Queen Doris
•• 0:19—Left breast sticking out of dress, sitting on big dice with Herve Villechaize.
•• 1:02—Left breast sticking out of dress after fighting with the Ex-Queen.

Force Ten from Navarone (1978)

Barbara Bach . . . . Maritza
• 0:32—Brief topless taking a bath in the German officer's room.
Edward Fox . . . . .Miller

Forced Entry (1975)
Nancy Allen . . . . Hitchhiker
- 0:44—Topless and buns tied up by Carl on the beach.

Tanya Roberts . . . . Nancy Ulman
0:57—In white bra and panties walking around the house.

Forced Vengeance (1982)
Mary Louise Weller . . . . Claire Bonner
- 1:04—Brief topless, struggling with the bad guy.
- 1:08—Very brief right breast then left breast, while lying dead on the floor.

Foreign Body (1986; British)
Amanda Donohoe. . . . . Susan
0:37—Undressing in her bedroom down to lingerie. Very brief side view of right breast, then brief left breast putting blouse on.
- • 0:40—Topless opening her blouse for Ram.

Anna Massey. . . . . Miss Furze
Sinitta Renet . . . . Lovely Indian Girl
- 0:06—Buns, then topless in bedroom.

Forever Lulu (1987)
Deborah Harry . . . . Lulu
Hanna Schygulla . . . . Elaine
- 1:03—Brief topless in and getting out of bubble bath.

The Forgotten One (1989)
Elisabeth Brooks . . . . .Carla
Kristy McNichol. . . . . Barbara Stupple
0:06—Jogging in braless pink top, then talking to Terry O'Quinn.
1:33—In pink top, lying in bed.

Terry O'Quinn. . . . . .Bob Anderson
- 1:11—Brief buns while turning over in bed with Evelyn.

Rebecca Wood-Sharkey. . . . . Barmaid

Fort Apache, The Bronx (1981)
Kathleen Beller . . . . .Theresa
Pam Grier . . . . Charlotte
Rachel Ticotin . . . . .Isabelle
- 1:25—Brief upper half of breasts in bathtub while Paul Newman pours bubble bath in.

Fortress (1985; Made for Cable Movie)
Rachel Ward . . . . Sally Jones
- 0:38—Swimming in a sheer bra underwater.

Four Friends (1981)
Jodi Thelen . . . . Georgia
- • 0:17—Left breast in open blouse three times with her three male friends.
0:58—In pink bra taking off her blouse.

Craig Wasson . . . . Danilo Prozor

Four Seasons (1981)
Bess Armstrong . . . . Ginny Newley
0:26—In two piece swimsuit on boat putting lotion on herself.
- 0:38—Brief buns twice skinny dipping in the water with Nick.
0:40—In one piece swimsuit.

Jack Weston . . . . Danny Zimmer
- 0:48—Brief buns in water while skinny dipping with Rita Moreno.

The Fourth Man (1984; Dutch)
Thom Hoffman. . . . . Herman
- 1:00—Frontal nudity on cross when Gerard pulls his red trunks down. Long shot.
- • 1:10—Nude in bathroom when Gerard comes in.
- • • 1:11—Buns making love on bed with Christine while Gerard watches through keyhole.

Jeroen Krabbé . . . . .Gerard
- • • 0:03—Frontal nudity getting out of bed and walking down the stairs.
- • 0:26—Frontal nudity drying himself off and getting into bed.
- 0:33—Buns, while getting out of bed.

Reneé Soutendijk . . . . Christine
- • • 0:27—Full frontal nudity removing robe, brief buns in bed, side view left breast, then topless in bed with Gerard.
- 0:32—Brief left breast in bed with Gerard after he hallucinates and she cuts his penis off.
- • • 0:53—Left breast, then right breast in red dress when Gerard opens her dress.
- 1:11—Topless making love with Herman while Gerard watches through keyhole.

The Fourth Protocol (1987; British)
Pierce Brosnan . . . . Petrofsky
Joanna Cassidy. . . . . Vassilieva
- 1:39—Brief left breast. She's lying dead in Pierce Brosnan's bathtub.
- 1:49—Same thing, different angle.

The Fourth Story (1990; Made for Cable Movie)
Mark Harmon. .David Shepard
- • • 0:53—Buns, while getting out of bed with Mimi Rogers. More buns, while walking outside and around the house.

Mimi Rogers. . . . . Valerie McCoughlin
M. Emmet Walsh . . . . Harry

Foxtrap (1986; U.S./Italian)
Beatrice Palme . . . . .Marianna
- • 0:41—Brief breasts and buns in bed with Fred Williamson, then more breasts making love.

Fred Williamson .Thomas Fox

Foxy Brown (1974)
Juanita Brown. . . . . Claudia
Pam Grier. . . . . Foxy Brown
- 0:05—Topless, getting out of bed and taking off nightgown.

• 0:40—Brief left breast, while getting dressed.
    1:04—Upper half of breasts, while tied to bed.
••• 1:05—Right breast, then topless rolling over in bed.
Kimberly Hyde . . . . Jennifer
Brenda Venus . . . . Arabella

Frame Up (1990)
Frances Fisher . . . . Jo Westlake
•• 0:52—Topless, lying back in bed with Wings Hauser.
•• 0:54—Left breast, while lying in bed with Hauser.
Wings Hauser . . . . Ralph Baker

Frances (1982)
Anjelica Huston . . . . . Hospital Sequence: Mental Patient
Jessica Lange. . . . . Frances Farmer
• 0:41—Very brief upper half of left breast, while lying on bed and throwing a newspaper.
• 0:50—Brief full frontal nudity covered with bubbles standing up in bathtub and wrapping a towel around herself. Long shot, hard to see.
• 1:01—Brief buns and right breast running into the bathroom when the police bust in. Very, very brief full frontal nudity, then buns closing the bathroom door. Reportedly her, even though you don't see her face clearly.

Frank and I (1983)
Sophie Favier. . . . . Maud
• 0:16—Nude, undressing then topless lying in bed with Charles.
• 0:40—Brief topless in bed with Charles.
Jennifer Inch . . . . Frank/Frances
    0:10—Brief buns, getting pants pulled down for a spanking.
••• 0:22—Nude getting undressed and walking to the bed.
• 0:24—Brief nude when Charles pulls the sheets off her.
    0:32—Brief buns, getting spanked by two older women.
••• 0:38—Full frontal nudity getting out of bed and walking to Charles at the piano.
•• 0:45—Full frontal nudity lying on her side by the fireplace. Dark, hard to see.
•• 1:09—Brief topless making love with Charles on the floor.
••• 1:11—Nude taking off her clothes and walking toward Charles at the piano.

Frankenhooker (1990)
Lia Chang . . . . Crystal
• 0:38—Buns, when Jeffrey draws a check mark on her.
• 0:40—Brief buns, fighting with the other girls over the drugs.
Vicki Darnell . . . . Sugar
• 0:36—Brief middle part of each breast through slit bra during introduction to Jeffrey.
•• 0:37—Breasts, sticking out of black lingerie while getting legs measured.
• 0:38—Right breast, while sitting in chair.

• 0:39—Topless through slit lingerie three times while folding clothes.
    0:40—Buns, fighting over drugs.
••• 0:41—Very brief right breast, sitting on bed (on the right) enjoying drugs. Topless dancing with the other girls.
Jennifer Delora. . . . . .Angel
• 0:36—Brief topless during introduction to Jeffrey.
••• 0:41—Topless dancing in room with the other hookers. (Nice tattoos!)
Charlotte J. Helmcamp. . . . . Honey
•• 0:26—Topless yanking down her top outside of Jeffrey's car window.
Heather Hunter .Chartreuse
• 0:36—Brief topless during introduction to Jeffrey.
• 0:37—Brief topless bending over behind Sugar.
••• 0:41—Brief topless and buns, running in front of bed. A little blurry. Then topless and buns dancing with the other girls.
• 0:43—Topless dodging flying leg with Sugar.
•• 0:44—Topless, crawling on the floor.
Patty Mullen. . . . . Elizabeth
•• 1:01—Topless and buns in garter belt and stockings, in room with a customer.
Susan Napoli . . . . Anise
• 0:42—Brief left breast on bed with Amber, taking off her top. Brief topless after Angel explodes.
• 0:43—Topless, kneeling on bed screaming before exploding.
Kimberly Taylor . . . . Amber
• 0:36—Brief left breast in green top during introduction to Jeffrey.
•• 0:37—Brief topless during exam by Jeffrey. Then topless getting breasts measured with calipers.
• 0:41—Brief right breast, twice, enjoying drugs.
•• 0:42—Topless, getting off bed and onto another bed with Anise.
• 0:43—Topless kneeling in bed screaming before exploding.

Frankenstein General Hospital (1988)
Rebunkah Jones . . . . Elizabeth Rice
•• 1:05—Topless in the office letting Mark Blankfield examine her back.
Kathy Shower. . . . . .Dr. Alice Singleton
    0:35—In white lingerie outfit pacing around office.
• 1:15—Brief topless running out of her office after the monster, putting her lab coat on.

Frankenstein Unbound (1990)
Myriam Cyr . . . . Information Officer
Bridget Fonda . . . . Mary
John Hurt. . . . . Buchanan
Raul Julia . . . . Victor Frankenstein
Jason Patric . . . . .Lord Byron
Catherine Rabett . . . . Elizabeth
    1:10—Very brief left breast, while lying dead after getting shot by Frankenstein. Unappealing looking because of all the gruesome makeup.
Terri Treas . . . . Computer Voice

Frantic (1988)

Emmanuelle Seigner . . . . Michelle
- 1:02—Brief side view of right breast, while changing blouses in bedroom.

Tina Sportolaro . . . . TWA Clerk

Alexandra Stewart . . . . Edie

Fraternity Vacation (1985)

Barbara Crampton . . . . Chrissie
- ••• 0:16—Topless and buns in bedroom with two guys taking off her swimsuit.

Cameron Dye . . . . Joe Gillespie

Kathleen Kinmont . . . . Marianne
- ••• 0:16—Topless and buns taking off her swimsuit in bedroom with two guys.

Julie Payne . . . . Naomi Tvedt

Tim Robbins . . . . Larry "Mother" Tucker

Sheree J. Wilson . . . . Ashley Taylor
- 0:43—In white leotard at aerobics class.
- 0:47—Topless and buns of her body double in the bedroom (Roberta Whitewood) when the guys photograph her with a telephoto lens.
  1:01—In white leotard exercising in living room with Leigh McCloskey.

Freddy's Dead: The Final Nightmare (1991)

Lezlie Deane . . . . Tracy

Johnny Depp . . . . Glen Lantz

Yaphet Kotto . . . . Doc

Linnea Quigley . . . . Soul from Freddy's Chest
- 1:25—Brief topless, struggling in Freddy's stomach during the end credits special-effects review.

Lisa Zane . . . . Maggie Burroughs

Free Ride (1986)

Tally Chanel . . . . Candy
- 0:57—Brief topless in bedroom with Dan.

Elizabeth Cochrell . . . . Nude Girl #1
- 0:25—Brief buns taking a shower with another girl.

Rebecca Lynn . . . . Nude Girl #2
- 0:25—Brief buns taking a shower with another girl.

Renée Props . . . . Kathy
- 0:13—Brief topless in the shower while Dan watches.

Mamie Van Doren . . . . Debbie Stockwell

Freeway (1988)

Darlanne Fluegel . . . . Sarah "Sunny" Harper
- 0:27—In bra in bathroom taking a pill, then very, very brief right breast, getting into bed.
- 0:28—Brief left breast putting on robe and getting out of bed.

Joe Palese . . . . Gomez

James Russo . . . . Frank Quinn

French Postcards (1979)

George Coe . . . . Mr. Weber

David Grant . . . . Alex

Mandy Patinkin . . . . Sayyid

Marie-France Pisier . . . . Madame Tessier
- •• 0:16—In white bra, then topless in dressing room while a guy watches without her knowing.

Valerie Quennessen . . . . Toni

Debra Winger . . . . Melanie

French Quarter (1978)

Lindsay Bloom . . . "Big Butt" Annie/Policewoman in Bar

Susan Clark . . . . Bag Stealer/Sue

Alisha Fontaine
. . . . Gertrude "Trudy" Dix/Christine Delaplane
- 0:12—Dancing on stage for the first time. Buns in G-string. Topless in large black pasties.
- 0:47—Brief left breast several times, posing for Mr. Beloq.
- 0:49—Left breast again.
- •• 1:13—Topless during auction.
- •• 1:18—Brief topless, then buns making love with Tom, then topless again.
- 1:26—Brief topless getting her top pulled down during party.
- 1:31—Brief topless getting tied down during voodoo ceremony.
- •• 1:32—More topless tied down during ceremony.

Ann Michelle
. . . . . "Coke Eye" Laura/Policewoman in French Hotel
- 0:42—Right breast, when Josie wakes her up.
- ••• 0:43—Topless in bed, caressing Josie's breasts.
- •• 0:58—Topless during voodoo ceremony. Close ups of breasts with snake.
- 1:19—Brief topless, sitting in bed.
- ••• 1:20—More topless sitting in bed, talking to a customer. Long scene.

Laura Misch Owens . . . . "Ice Box" Josie/Girl on Bus
- 0:41—Topless under sheer white nightgown.
- ••• 0:43—Full frontal nudity taking off nightgown, wearing garter belt. Getting into bed with Laura.

The French Woman (1979)

a.k.a. Madame Claude

Dayle Haddon . . . . Elizabeth
- 0:15—Very, very brief topless in dressing room.
- •• 0:49—Topless on bed with Madame Claude.
- 0:55—Topless kissing Pierre, then buns while lying on the floor.
  1:10—In two piece swimsuit on sailboat.
- 1:11—Left breast, then buns at the beach with Frederick.

Frenzy (1972; British)

Barbara Leigh-Hunt . . . . Brenda Blaney
- 0:31—Left breast, while sitting in chair with the necktie killer. Don't see her face.

Anna Massey . . . . Babs Milligan
- •• 0:45—Topless getting out of bed and then buns, walking to the bathroom. Most probably a body double.

Friday Foster (1975)
Pam Grier . . . . Friday Foster
- ••• 0:29—Topless, several times, while taking a shower while Carl Weathers stalks around in her apartment.
- ••• 1:12—Upper half of breast, while in bubble bath with Blake. Topless in bed with him.

Yaphet Kotto. . . . . Colt Hawkins

Friday the 13th (1980)
Kevin Bacon . . . . Jack
- • 0:39—Close up of buns when Marci squeezes them.

Friday the 13th, Part II (1981)
Kirsten Baker. . . . . .Terry
- •• 0:45—Topless and buns taking off clothes to go skinny dipping.
- • 0:47—Very brief topless jumping up in the water.
- • 0:48—Full frontal nudity and buns getting out of the water. Long shot.

Marta Kober . . . . Sandra

Friday the 13th, Part IV—The Final Chapter (1984)
Judie Aronson . . . . Samantha
- • 0:26—Brief topless and very brief buns taking clothes off to go skinny dipping.
- • 0:29—Brief topless under water pretending to be dead.
- •• 0:39—Topless and brief buns taking off her T-shirt to go skinny dipping at night.

Kimberly Beck . . . . .Trish

Alan Hayes . . . . Paul
- • 0:26—Brief buns, while swinging on a rope and jumping into the lake.

Barbara Howard . . . . Sara
  - 0:52—In white bra and panties putting on a robe in the bedroom getting ready for her boyfriend.
- • 1:01—Buns, through shower door.

Camilla More . . . . Tina
- • 0:26—Very brief topless in the lake jumping with her twin sister to show they are skinny dipping.
- • 0:48—Left breast, in bed with Crispin Glover.

Carey More. . . . . Terri
- • 0:26—Very brief topless in the lake jumping up with her twin sister to show they are skinny dipping.

Friday the 13th, Part V—A New Beginning (1985)
Juliette Cummins. . . . . Robin
- ••• 1:01—Topless, wearing panties getting undressed and climbing into bed just before getting killed.
  - 1:05—Very brief topless, covered with blood when Reggie discovers her dead.

Melanie Kinnaman . . . . Pam Roberts
  - 1:08—In wet white blouse coming back into the house from the rain.

Deborah Voorhees . . . . Tina
- ••• 0:41—Topless after making love with Eddie, then lying down and relaxing just before getting killed.
- • 0:43—Buns and brief left breast when Eddie turns her over and discovers her dead.

Rebecca Wood-Sharkey . . . . Lana
- • 0:33—Brief topless opening her dress while changing to go out with Billy.

Friday the 13th, Part VII: The New Blood (1988)
Elizabeth Kaitan . . . . .Robin
- • 0:53—Brief left breast in bed making love with a guy.
- • 0:55—Brief topless sitting up in bed after making love and the sheet falls down.
- •• 1:00—Brief topless again sitting up in bed and putting a shirt on over her head.

Heidi Kozak . . . . .Sandra
- • 0:36—Buns, while taking off clothes to go skinny dipping. Brief topless under water just before getting killed by Jason.

Friendly Favors (1983)
a.k.a. Six Swedes on a Pump
Private Screenings.
Brigitte Lahaie . . . . .Greta
- •• 0:02—Full frontal nudity riding a guy in bed. (She's wearing a necklace.)
- ••• 0:39—Full frontal nudity having fun on "exercise bike."
- ••• 0:46—Full frontal nudity taking off clothes and running outside with the other girls. Nice slow motion shots.
- •• 0:53—Topless, making love with Kerstin.
- ••• 1:01—Full frontal nudity in room with the Italian.
- ••• 1:15—Full frontal nudity in room with guy from the band.

From Beyond (1986)
Barbara Crampton . . . . Dr. Katherine McMichaels
- •• 0:44—Brief topless after getting blouse torn off by the creature in the laboratory.
  - 0:51—Buns getting on top of Jeffrey Combs in black leather outfit.

The Funhouse (1981)
Elizabeth Berridge . . . . .Amy
- •• 0:03—Brief topless taking off robe to get into the shower, then very brief topless getting out to chase Joey.

Sylvia Miles . . . . .Madame Zena

The Further Adventures of Tennessee Buck (1987)
Kathy Shower. . . . . .Barbara Manchester
  - 0:22—In white lingerie in her hut getting dressed.
- ••• 0:57—Topless getting rubbed with oil by the cannibal women. Nice close up shots.
- •• 1:02—Topless in a hut with the Chief of the tribe.

Brant Van Hoffman. . . . . .Ken Manchester
- • 0:38—Brief buns, behind a mosquito net while making love with his disinterested wife.

The G.I. Executioner (1971)
Angelique Pettijohn...................... Bonnie
- •• 0:16—Doing a strip routine on stage. Buns in G-string, very brief side view of right breast, then topless at end.
- •• 0:40—Topless, lying asleep in bed.
- ••• 0:58—Topless and buns, undressing in front of Dave, getting into bed, fighting an attacker and getting shot. Long scene.
- • 1:14—Topless, lying shot in rope net.

Gabriela (1984; Brazilian)
Sonia Braga......................... Gabriela
- •• 0:26—Topless leaning back out the window making love on a table with Marcello Mastroianni.
- ••• 0:27—Nude, taking a shower outside and cleaning herself up.
- • 0:32—Right breast in bed.
- •• 0:38—Nude, making love with Mastroianni on the kitchen table.
- •• 0:45—Nude, getting in bed with Mastroianni.
  1:13—Full frontal nudity, on bed with another man, then getting beat up by Mastroianni.
- ••• 1:17—Nude, changing clothes in the bedroom.
- •• 1:32—Topless and buns making love outside with Mastroianni. Lots of passion!

Gaby, A True Story (1987)
Robert Beltran...........................Luis
Rachel Levin .... Gaby
- • 0:56—Right breast, then topless on the floor making love with another handicapped boy, Fernando.

Galaxy of Terror (1981)
Edward Albert.........................Cabren
Taaffe O'Connell...................... Damelia
- •• 0:42—Topless getting raped by a giant alien slug. Nice and slimy.
  0:46—Buns, covered with slime being discovered by her crew mates.

Gallipoli (1981)
Mel Gibson.........................Frank Dunne
- •• 1:18—Buns, while running into the water. (He's the guy on the left.)
Mark Lee........................ Archy Hamilton
- •• 1:18—Buns, while running into the water with Mel Gibson. (Mark is the guy on the right.)

Games That Lovers Play (1970)
Private Screenings.
Penny Brahms........................ Constance
- •• 0:08—Topless outside with a customer.
- •• 0:10—Topless again putting dress back on.
Joanna Lumley .... Fanny
- •• 0:17—Nude, getting out of bed and putting on robe.
- • 0:50—Right breast, while in bed with Jonathan.
- •• 1:18—Topless sitting in bed, talking on the phone.

- •• 1:29—Brief topless several times in bed with Constance and a guy. Topless after and during the end credits.

The Garden of the Finzi-Continis (1971; Italian/German)
Helmut Berger .... Alberto
Dominique Sanda ....Micol
- 0:24—In braless wet white T-shirt after getting caught in a rainstorm.
- • 1:12—Topless sitting on a bed after turning a light on so the guy standing outside can see her.

Gator Bait (1973)
Janit Baldwin .... n.a.
- •• 0:27—Topless and buns walking into a pond, then getting out and getting dressed.
- • 0:35—Very brief right breast, twice, popping out of her dress when the bad guys hold her.
- • 0:40—Brief left breast struggling against two guys on the bed.
Claudia Jennings .... Desiree
- • 0:06—Brief left and right breasts during boat chase sequence.
Clyde Ventura .... n.a.

Gator Bait II—Cajun Justice (1988)
Jan MacKenzie .... Angelique
  0:13—Most of right breast while kissing her husband.
  0:29—Most of right breast while in bed.
- •• 0:34—Buns and side view of left breast, taking a bath outside. Brief topless a couple of times while the bad guys watch.
- • 0:41—Brief side view of left breast taking off towel in front of the bad guys.
  1:05—Brief buns occasionally when her blouse flaps up during boat chase.

The Gauntlet (1977)
Clint Eastwood..................... Ben Shockley
Sondra Locke .... Gus Mally
- •• 1:10—Brief right breast, then topless getting raped by two biker guys in a box car while Clint Eastwood is tied up.

Gemini Affair (1974)
Kathy Kersh .... Jessica
  0:10—In white bra and black panties changing in front of Marta Kristen.
- •• 0:11—Nude getting into bed with Kristen.
- • 0:12—Brief topless turning over onto her stomach in bed.
- •• 0:17—Nude, standing up in bed and jumping off.
- ••• 0:57—Nude in bed with Kristen.
- •• 1:04—Left breast sitting up in bed after Kristen leaves.
Marta Kristen............................Julie
- ••• 0:32—Topless wearing beige panties talking with Jessica in the bathroom.

- 0:56—Very, very brief left breast and lower frontal nudity standing next to bed with a guy. Very brief left breast in bed with him.
- ••• 0:59—Topless and buns making love in bed with Jessica. Wowzers!

Genuine Risk (1989)
Michelle Johnson. . . . . Girl
- 0:27—In black bra in room with Henry.
- 0:29—In bra in open top coming out of the bathroom.
- 0:43—On bed in black bra and panties with Henry. Left breast peeking out of the top of her bra.

Get Out Your Handkerchiefs (1978)
Gérard Depardieu . . . . Raoul
Carole Laure . . . . Solange
- •• 0:21—Topless sitting in bed listening to her boyfriend talk.
- •• 0:31—Topless sitting in bed knitting.
- • 0:41—Upper half of left breast in bed.
- •• 0:47—Left breast, while sitting in bed and the three guys talk.
- • 1:08—Brief right breast when the little boy peeks at her while she sleeps.
  1:10—Lower frontal nudity while he looks at her some more.
- ••• 1:17—Full frontal nudity taking off nightgown while sitting on bed for the little boy.

The Getaway (1972)
Ali MacGraw . . . . Carol McCoy
  0:16—In wet white blouse after jumping in pond with Steve McQueen.
- • 0:19—Very brief left breast lying back in bed kissing McQueen.
Sally Struthers . . . . Fran Clinton
  1:15—In black bra getting out of bed and leaning over injured bad guy to get something.

Getting It Right (1989)
Helena Bonham-Carter . . . . Minerva Munday
- •• 0:18—Topless a couple of times in bed talking to Gavin. It's hard to recognize her because she has lots of makeup on her face.
Jane Horrocks . . . . Jenny
Bryan Pringle. . . . . Mr. Lamb
Lynn Redgrave . . . . Joan
- •• 0:46—Brief right breast, then brief topless on couch seducing Gavin. More right breast shot when wrestling with him.

Ghost Story (1981)
Alice Krige. . . . . Alma/Eva
- • 0:41—Brief topless making love in bedroom with Craig Wasson.
- •• 0:44—Topless in bathtub with Wasson.
- •• 0:46—Topless sitting up in bed.
- ••• 0:49—Buns, then topless standing on balcony turning and walking to bedroom talking to Wasson.

Craig Wasson . . . . .Don/David
- •• 0:08—Brief frontal nudity falling out the window, then buns, while landing next to the pool.
- • 0:41—Buns, while making love with Alice Krige in bedroom.

Ghosts Can't Do It (1989)
Leo Damian . . . . Fasto
- • 1:31—Brief, lower buns while sliding down stack of hay. Long shot.
Bo Derek . . . . .Kate
- ••• 0:26—In one piece swimsuit on beach, then full frontal nudity taking it off. Brief buns covered with sand on her back. Long scene.
- ••• 0:32—Topless, sitting and washing herself. Very brief buns, jumping into tub.
- •• 0:48—Full frontal nudity taking a shower.
- • 0:49—Very, very brief topless and buns jumping into pool. Long shot. Full frontal nudity under water.
  0:52—Very, very brief partial topless pulling a guy into the pool
  1:00—In wet dress, dancing sexily in the rain.
- •• 1:12—Topless behind mosquito net with her boyfriend.
Julie Newmar . . . . .Angel

The Gift (1982; French)
Clio Goldsmith. . . . . Barbara
- •• 0:39—Brief topless several times in the bathroom, then right breast in bathtub.
- • 0:49—Topless lying in bed sleeping.
- 0:51—Very brief left breast turning over in bed.
- • 0:52—Brief right breast then buns, reaching for phone while lying in bed.
  1:16—Very brief left breast getting out of bed. Dark, hard to see.

Gimme an "F" (1981)
Daphne Ashbrook . . . . .Phoebe Willis
Jennifer Cooke . . . . Pam Bethlehem
  1:10—Wearing United States flag pasties frolicking with Dr. Spirit. Nice bouncing action.
  1:38—Still of pasties scene during end credits.
Darcy De Moss. . . . . One of the "Ducks"
Julie Gray . . . . Falcon Marsha
Valerie McIntosh . . . . One of the "Vikings"
Steve Shellen . . . . Tommy Hamilton
  0:56—Dancing in his underwear in the boy's shower room while the girls peek in at him.
- • 0:57—Brief upper half of buns.
Cindy Silver . . . . .One of the "Ducks"

Ginger Ale Afternoon (1989)
Yeardley Smith. . . . . .Bonnie Cleator
- • 0:53—Brief upper half of left breast, taking off top in trailer with Hank.

The Girl from Petrovka (1974)
Goldie Hawn. . . . . Oktyabrina
  1:30—Very, very brief topless in bed with Hal Holbrook. Don't really see anything—it lasts for about one frame.
Hal Holbrook. . . . . Joe
  • 0:40—Brief buns, while getting out of bed, putting on a robe and talking to Goldie Hawn.

The Girl in a Swing (1989; U.S./British)
Meg Tilly. . . . . Karin Foster
  •• 0:44—In white bra, then topless and buns.
  •• 0:50—Nude, swimming under water.
  ••• 1:14—Topless sitting on swing, then making love.
  1:18—In white bra, sitting in front of a mirror.
  ••• 1:44—Topless at the beach.

The Girl in Blue (1973; Canadian)
a.k.a. U-turn
Maud Adams. . . . . .Paula/Tracy
  • 1:16—Side view of right breast, while sitting on bed with Scott.
  1:19—In two piece swimsuit getting out of lake.
Gay Rowan . . . . Bonnie
  • 0:06—Left breast, in bed with Scott.
  • 0:31—Brief topless in bathtub.
  • 0:48—Right breast, while in shower talking to Scott. Brief topless (long shot) on balcony throwing water down at him.
  • 1:21—Brief right breast and buns getting out of bed and running out of the room.
David Selby. . . . . .Scott
  • 0:10—Brief buns while getting out of bed and putting on pants. Dark.
  0:44—Left half of buns while in shower.
  •• 1:14—Buns, while walking into the bathroom.

Girl on a Motorcycle (1968; French/British)
a.k.a. Naked Under Leather
Marianne Faithfull. Rebecca
  •• 0:05—Nude, getting out of bed and walking to the door.
  • 0:38—Brief side view of left breast putting nightgown on.
  • 1:23—Brief topless while lying down and talking with Alain Delon.
  • 1:30—Very brief right breast a couple of times making love with Delon.
Catherine Jourdan. . . . . Catherine

A Girl to Kill For (1989)
Karen Medak. . . . . Sue
  ••• 0:17—Topless showering at the beach after surfing with Chuck.
  0:38—In bra lying on desk in office with Chuck.
  •• 1:08—Topless in spa when Chuck takes her shirt off. Then miscellaneous shots making love.

Girlfriend from Hell (1989)
James Daughton . . . . David
Lezlie Deane . . . . Diane

Christina Veronica . . . . Dancer
  ••• 1:17—Topless dancing on stage in club.

Girlfriends (1978)
Christopher Guest . . . . Eric
  • 1:04—Buns, while running after Melanie Mayron in her apartment, then hugging her.
Melanie Mayron. . . . . .Susan Weinblatt
  • 0:14—Buns, very brief lower frontal nudity and brief left breast getting dressed in bathroom.
Anita Skinner . . . . Anne Munroe
Amy Wright . . . . Ceil
  • 0:42—Brief topless getting out of bed to talk to Melanie Mayron.

Glitch (1988)
Laura Albert . . . . Topless
  • 0:35—Brief topless auditioning for two guys by taking off her top.
Christina Cardan . . . . Non SAG
  • 0:47—Brief topless in spa taking off her swimsuit top.
Teri Weigel. . . . . Lydia
  0:41—In pink bathing suit talking to blonde guy.
  • 0:54—Very brief side view of right breast in bathtub with dark haired guy.

Gnaw: Food of the Gods II (1988; Canadian)
Eduardo Castillo. . . . . Carlos
  • 0:46—Buns, while walking through bushes to take a leak. More buns, while running away from the giant rats.

God's Gun (1977)
a.k.a. A Bullet from God
Sybil Danning . . . . .Jenny
  • 1:09—Right breast popping out of dress with a guy in the barn during flashback.
Robert Lipton. . . . . n.a.

The Godfather (1972)
Marlon Brando. . . . . .Don Vito Corleone
Diane Keaton . . . . .Kay Adams
Simonetta Stefanelli . . . . .Apollonia
  •• 1:50—Topless in bedroom on honeymoon night.

Goin' All the Way (1981)
Josh Cadman . . . . .Bronk
  • 1:05—Buns, while in the shower talking to Boom Boom.
Gina Calabrese. . . . . n.a.
  •• 0:12—Left breast, in the girls' locker room shower. Standing on the left.
Eileen Davidson . . . . .BJ
  ••• 0:12—Topless in the girls' locker room shower. Standing next to Monica.
  ••• 0:22—Exercising in her bedroom in braless pink T-shirt, then topless talking on the phone to Monica.
Sherrie Miller . . . . Candy
  0:47—Brief right breast getting out of bubble bath.
  •• 0:49—Topless with Artie during his fantasy.

Going Places (1974; French)

Miou-Miou . . . . .Marie-Ange
- ••• 0:14—Topless sitting in bed, filing her nails. Full frontal nudity standing up and getting dressed.
- •• 0:48—Topless in bed with Pierrot and Jean-Claude.
- • 0:51—Left breast under Pierrot.
- ••• 0:52—Buns in bed when Jean-Claude rolls off her. Full frontal nudity sitting up with the two guys in bed.
- •• 1:21—Brief topless opening the door. Topless and panties walking in after the two guys.
- • 1:27—Partial left breast taking off dress and walking into house.
  - 1:28—Very brief topless closing the shutters.
- •• 1:31—Full frontal nudity in open dress running after the two guys. Long shot. Full frontal nudity putting her wet dress on.
- • 1:41—Topless in back of car. Dark.

Gérard Depardieu . . . . Jean-Claude
- • 0:42—Upper half of buns and pubic hair, while talking to Pierrot.
- •• 0:49—Buns while in bed, then more buns making love to Miou-Miou. Nice up and down action.
- • 0:50—Brief buns while switching places with Pierrot.
- • 0:51—Brief frontal nudity getting out of bed. Dark, hard to see. Subtitles get in the way.

Patrick Dewaere . . . . Pierrot
- • 0:42—Upper half of buns while starting to leave the room. Surgical tape on his buns.
- •• 0:48—Buns while in bed with Marie-Ange.
- • 0:50—Brief buns, while switching places with Jean-Claude.
  - 1:41—Sort of buns, while making love in back seat of car. Dark.
- • 1:42—Buns, while getting out of car and pulling up his pants.

Brigitte Fossey. . . . . Young Mother
- ••• 0:32—In bra, then topless in open blouse on the train when she lets Pierrot suck the milk out of her breasts.

Isabelle Huppert . . . . .Jacqueline
- • 1:53—Brief upper half of left breast making love with Jean-Claude.

Good Morning, Babylon (1987; Italian/French)

Desiree Becker. . . . . .Mabel
- • 1:06—Brief topless in the woods making love.

David Brandon . . . . Grass

Greta Scacchi . . . . .Edna
- •• 1:05—Topless in the woods making love with Vincent Spano.

Vincent Spano. . . . . Nicola Bonnano

The Good Mother (1988)

Tracy Griffith. . . . . .Babe
- • 0:06—Brief topless opening her blouse to show a young Anna what it's like being pregnant.

Diane Keaton . . . . .Anna

The Good Wife (1987; Australian)

a.k.a. The Umbrella Woman

Bryan Brown . . . . Sonny Hills

Helen Jones . . . . Rosie Gibbs

Clarissa Kaye-Mason. . . . . Mrs. Jackson

Susan Lyons . . . . Mrs. Fielding
- • 1:22—Very brief topless coming in from the balcony.

Sam Neill . . . . Neville Gifford

Rachel Ward. . . . . Marge Hills

Goodbye Emmanuelle (1977)

Olga Georges-Picot . . . . n.a.

Sylvia Kristel . . . . .Emmanuelle
- •• 0:03—Full frontal nudity in bath and getting out.
- •• 0:04—Full frontal nudity taking off dress.
- ••• 0:06—Full frontal nudity in bed with Angelique.
- ••• 0:26—Topless with photographer in old house.
  - 0:42—Brief side view of right breast, in bed with Jean.
- ••• 1:03—Full frontal nudity on beach with movie director.
- •• 1:06—Full frontal nudity lying on beach sleeping.
- •• 1:28—Side view of left breast lying on beach with Gregory while dreaming.

Alexandra Stewart . . . . .Dorothee

Goodbye, Columbus (1969)

Richard Benjamin. . . . . .Neil
- • 1:11—Brief buns, while walking into the bathroom. Very, very brief frontal nudity. Blurry, hard to see anything.

Ali MacGraw . . . . .Brenda
- • 0:50—Very brief side view of left breast, taking off dress before running and jumping into a swimming pool. Brief right breast jumping into pool.
- • 1:11—Very brief side view of right breast in bed with Richard Benjamin. Brief buns, getting out of bed and walking to the bathroom.

Goodbye, Norma Jean (1975)

Patch Mackenzie . . . . Ruth Latimer

Misty Rowe . . . . Norma Jean Baker
  - 0:02—In white bra putting makeup on.
- •• 0:08—In white bra and panties, then topless.
- • 0:14—Brief topless in bed getting raped.
  - 0:31—Very, very brief silhouette of right breast, in bed with Rob.
- ••• 0:59—Topless during shooting of stag film, then in B&W when some people watch the film.
  - 1:14—In white bra and panties undressing.

Gorky Park (1983)

Brian Dennehy. . . . . William Kirwill

William Hurt. . . . . .Arkady Renko

Joanna Pacula. . . . . .Irina
- •• 1:20—Brief topless in bed making love with William Hurt.

Gotcha! (1985)

Nick Corri . . . . Manolo

Anthony Edwards. . . . . .Jonathan Moore

Linda Fiorentino . . . . Sasha
•• 0:53—Brief topless getting searched at customs.
Kari Lizer. . . . . Muffy
Christopher Rydell. . . . . Bob Jensen

Gotham (1988; Made for Cable Movie)
a.k.a. The Dead Can't Lie
Tommy Lee Jones . . . . Eddie Mallard
• 0:50—Buns, while walking over to Virginia Madsen.
Dark, hard to see anything.
Virginia Madsen . . . . Rachel Carlyle
• 0:50—Brief topless in the shower when Tommy Lee
Jones comes over to her apartment, then topless lying on the floor.
•• 1:12—Topless, dead, in the freezer when Jones
comes back to her apartment, then brief topless on
the bed.
• 1:18—Topless in the bathtub under water.

Gothic (1986; British)
Gabriel Byrne . . . . Byron
Myriam Cyr. . . . . Claire
•• 0:53—Left breast, then topless lying in bed with
Gabriel Byrne.
• 0:55—Brief left breast lying in bed. Long shot.
• 1:02—Topless sitting on pool table opening her top
for Julian Sands. Special effect with eyes in her nip-
ples.
• 1:12—Buns and brief topless covered with mud.
Natasha Richardson. . . . . .Mary
Julian Sands. . . . . Shelley
•• 0:17—Buns, while standing on roof in the rain.

Graduation Day (1981)
Erica Hope. . . . . Diane
• 1:02—Brief topless in open blouse running away
from the killer.
Patch Mackenzie. . . . . .Anne Ramstead
Linnea Quigley . . . . .Dolores
•• 0:36—Topless by the piano in classroom with Mr.
Roberts unbuttoning her blouse.
Vanna White. . . . . .Doris

Grand Canyon (1991)
Sharon Lee Jones. . . . . Studio Girl
Kevin Kline . . . . Mack
Mary-Louise Parker . . . . Dee
• 1:00—Topless, pulling sheet down, while lying in
bed during dream sequence.
Sarah Trigger . . . . Vanessa

Grandview, U.S.A. (1984)
Jamie Lee Curtis . . . . Michelle "Mike" Cody
••• 1:00—Left breast, lying in bed with C. Thomas How-
ell.
C. Thomas Howell. . . . . Tim Pearson
Jennifer Jason Leigh. . . . . .Candy Webster
Patrick Swayze . . . . Ernie "Slam" Webster

The Grasshopper (1970)
a.k.a. The Passing of Evil
Jacqueline Bisset. . . . . Christine Adams
0:21—In flesh colored Las Vegas-style showgirl costume. Dark, hard to see.
0:27—More showgirl shots.
1:14—In black two piece swimsuit.
1:16—Almost left breast while squished against Jay
in the shower.
Christopher Stone . . . . Jay Rigney
0:26—Buns, seen through shower door when Jac-
queline Bisset comes in to join him.
• 1:17—Brief buns while lying in bed talking to Bisset.

Graveyard Shift (1987)
Sugar Bouche. . . . . Fabulous Frannie
••• 0:12—Topless doing a stripper routine on stage.
• 0:24—Brief topless in the shower.
Kim Cayer . . . . Suzy
•• 0:06—In black bra, then brief left breast when vampire rips the bra off.
• 0:53—Brief topless in junk yard with garter belt,
black panties and stockings.
Silvio Oliviero. . . . . Stephen Tsepes
• 0:09—Buns, while climbing into his coffin.

The Grifters (1990)
Annette Bening .Myra Langtry
•• 0:36—In bra and panties in her apartment, then
topless lying in bed "paying" her rent. Kind of dark.
••• 1:06—Nude, walking down the hall to the bedroom
and into bed.
1:30—Very brief right breast, dead in morgue. Long
shot.
Anjelica Huston . . . . Lilly Dillon

Grim Prairie Tales (1990)
Brad Dourif . . . . .Farley
Lisa Eichhorn . . . . Maureen
Michelle Joyner . . . . .Jenny
• 0:35—Very brief right breast, then left breast while
making love with Marc McClure. Kind of dark.

The Groove Tube (1974)
Jennifer Wells .The Geritan Girl
•• 0:21—Dancing nude around her husband, Chevy
Chase.

Group Marriage (1972)
Aimée Eccles . . . . Chris
0:15—Buns, getting into bed.
• 1:15—Brief side view of left breast and buns getting
into the shower.
Claudia Jennings . . . . .Elaine
••• 1:02—Topless under mosquito net in bed with Phil.
Long scene.
Pepe Serna. . . . . .Ramon
Zach Taylor . . . . Phil
•• 0:43—Buns, while walking on beach with Jan.

Victoria Vetri . . . . Jan
- ••• 0:28—Buns and topless getting into bed with Dennis, Sander and Chris. More topless sitting in bed. Long scene.
- • 1:19—Brief side view of right breast in lifeguard booth.

The Guardian (1990)
Dwier Brown . . . . Phil
   0:37—Soft of buns, while in bed with Carey Lowell. Don't see his face.
Carey Lowell . . . . Kate
- •• 0:37—Right breast twice, in bed with Phil.
Jenny Seagrove . . . . Camilla
- ••• 0:21—Side view of left breast, while in bathtub with the baby. Right breast, then topless.
   0:23—Buns, drying herself off. Long shot.
- •• 0:38—Topless, mostly left breast on top of Phil. Don't see her face, probably a body double.
   0:46—Buns, skinny dipping. Long shot.
- •• 0:47—Topless healing her wound by a tree. Side view of right breast.
- • 1:18—Very brief topless under sheer gown in forest just before getting hit by a Jeep.
   1:24—Very briefly topless scaring Carey Lowell. Body is painted all over.

Gulag (1985)
David Keith . . . . Mickey Almon
- •• 1:26—Buns, while standing outside with Malcolm McDowell in the snow being hassled by guards.
Malcolm McDowell . . . . Englishman
- •• 1:26—Buns, while standing outside with David Keith in the snow being hassled by guards.
Nancy Paul . . . . Susan
- •• 0:42—Buns, then topless taking a shower while David Keith daydreams while he's on a train.

The Gumshoe Kid (1990)
Tracy Scoggins . . . . Rita Benson
   0:33—In two piece white swimsuit. Nice bun shot while Jay Underwood hides in the closet.
- ••• 1:10—Side view of left breast in the shower with Underwood. Excellent slow motion topless shot while turning around. Brief side view of right breast in bed afterwards.
Pamela Springsteen . . . . Mona Krause
Jay Underwood . . . . Jeff Sherman

Guns (1990)
Cynthia Brimhall . . . . Edy Stark
   0:26—Buns, in G-string singing and dancing at club.
- •• 0:27—Topless in dressing room.
   0:53—Buns, in black one piece outfit and stockings, singing in club. Nice legs!
William Bumiller . . . . Lucas
Allegra Curtis . . . . Robyn
Phyllis Davis . . . . Kathryn Hamilton
Devin De Vasquez . . . . Cash
- • 1:12—Brief side view of right breast and buns undressing for bath.

Liv Lindeland . . . . Ace
Lisa London . . . . Rocky
Kym Malin . . . . .Kym
   0:27—Oil wrestling with Hugs.
- ••• 0:28—Showering (in back) while talking to Hugs (in front).
Michael Jay Shane . . . . Shane Abilene
Donna Spangler . . . . Hugs Huggins
   0:27—Oil wrestling with Kym.
   0:28—Showering (in front) while talking to Kym (in back).
Dona Speir . . . . Donna Hamilton
- ••• 1:00—Topless and buns in black G-string getting dressed in locker room. Then in black lingerie.
Roberta Vasquez . . . . Nicole Justin
- •• 0:50—Right breast while making love on motorcycle with her boyfriend.

H.O.T.S. (1979)
Angela Aames . . . . Boom-Boom Bangs
- • 0:21—Topless parachuting into pool.
- • 0:39—Topless in bathtub playing with a seal.
- • 1:33—Topless playing football.
Lindsay Bloom . . . . Melody Ragmore
- • 0:28—Very brief right breast on balcony.
- • 1:34—Brief topless during football game throwing football as quarterback.
Steve Bond . . . . John
- • 0:32—Buns, while trapped in van with K. C. Winkler.
Pamela Jean Bryant . . . . Teri Lynn
- • 1:33—Topless during football game.
Sandy Johnson . . . . Stephanie
- •• 0:27—Topless on balcony in red bikini bottoms.
- •• 1:34—Topless during football game during huddle with all the other girls.
Susan Lynn Kiger . . . . Honey Shayne
- • 0:00—Topless in shower room with the other girls.
- •• 0:33—Topless in pool making love with Doug.
- • 1:33—Topless in football game.
Lisa London . . . . Jennie O'Hara
- • 1:22—Topless changing clothes by the closet while a crook watches her.
- • 1:33—Topless playing football.
K.C. Winkler . . . . Cynthia
- • 0:27—Topless in blue bikini bottom on balcony.
- •• 0:31—Topless in van making love, then arguing with John.

Hair (1979)
Beverly D'Angelo . . . . Sheila
- • 0:59—In white bra and panties, then topless on rock near pond. Medium long shot.
- ••• 1:01—Topless in panties getting out of the pond.
- • 1:38—Side view of right breast changing clothes in car with George.
Don Dacus . . . . Woof
- • 0:57—Buns, while taking off clothes and diving into pond with Treat Williams and Hud.
Michael Jeter . . . . Woodrow Sheldon
- • 1:06—Buns while in front of Army guys.

491

John Savage . . . . Claude
Treat Williams . . . . Berger
- • 0:57—Buns, while taking off clothes and diving into pond with Hud and Woof.
Dorsey Wright. . . . . Hud
- • 0:57—Buns, while taking off clothes and diving into pond with Treat Williams and Woof.

Half Moon Street (1986)
a.k.a. Escort Girl
Vincent Lindon . . . . Sonny
- • 1:04—Buns, while getting out of bed with Sigourney Weaver.
Janet McTeer. . . . . Van Arkady's Ambassador
Sigourney Weaver . . . . Lauren Slaughter
- • 0:05—Brief topless in the bathtub.
- •• 0:11—Brief topless in the bathtub again.
- • 0:18—Brief buns and side view of right breast putting on makeup in front of the mirror. Wearing a black garter belt and stockings.
- ••• 0:39—Topless riding exercise bike while being photographed, then brief topless getting out of the shower.
  0:46—Very, very brief topless wearing a sheer black blouse with no bra during daydream sequence.
- • 0:50—Brief topless in bed with Michael Caine, then left breast.
  1:16—In braless, wet, white blouse in bathroom after knocking a guy out.

Halloween (1978)
Jamie Lee Curtis . . . . Laurie
Sandy Johnson . . . . Judith Meyers
  0:06—Very brief topless covered with blood on floor after Michael stabs her to death.
P.J. Soles . . . . Lynda
- • 1:04—Brief right breast, sitting up in bed after making love in bed with Bob.
- • 1:07—Brief topless getting strangled by Michael in the bedroom.

Halloween II (1981)
Jamie Lee Curtis . . . . Laurie
Leo Rossi. . . . . Budd
- • 0:48—Buns, while getting out of the whirlpool bath to check the water temperature.
Pamela Susan Shoop. . . . . Karen
- ••• 0:48—Topless getting into the whirlpool bath with Budd in the hospital.

Hamburger—The Motion Picture (1986)
Debra Blee . . . . Mia Vunk
  0:25—Briefly in wet dress in the swimming pool.
Randi Brooks. . . . . Mrs. Vunk
- •• 0:52—Brief topless in helicopter with a guy.
Karen Mayo-Chandler. . . . . Dr. Victoria Gotbottom
- • 0:03—Brief topless in her office trying to help, then seduce Russell.
Maria Richwine . . . . Conchita
- •• 0:49—Topless trying to seduce Russell in a room.

The Hand (1981)
Annie McEnroe. . . . . Stella Roche
- •• 0:51—Topless undressing for Michael Caine.
Bruce McGill . . . . Brian Ferguson
Tracey Walter . . . . Cop

A Handmaid's Tale (1990)
David Dukes. . . . . Doctor
Faye Dunaway . . . . Serena Joy
Elizabeth McGovern . . . . Moira
Aidan Quinn. . . . . Nick
Natasha Richardson . . . . Kate
- •• 0:30—Topless twice at the window getting some fresh air.
- • 0:59—Topless making love with Aidan Quinn.
- ••• 1:00—Topless after Quinn rolls off her.
Victoria Tennant. . . . . Aunt Lydia

Hanover Street (1979)
Lesley-Anne Down . . . . Margaret Sallinger
- • 0:22—In bra and slip, then brief topless in bedroom with Harrison Ford.
Patsy Kensit . . . . Sarah Sallinger

The Happy Hooker (1975)
Denise Galik. . . . . Cynthia
Anita Morris . . . . Linda Jo/Mary Smith
- • 0:59—Topless lying on table while a customer puts ice cream all over her.
- • 1:24—Topless covered with whipped cream getting it sprayed off with champagne by another customer.
Lynn Redgrave . . . . Xaviera Hollander
  0:43—In black bra and panties doing a strip tease routine in a board room while Tom Poston watches.

The Happy Hooker Goes Hollywood (1980)
Martine Beswick. . . . . Xaviera Hollander
- •• 0:05—Brief topless in bedroom with Policeman.
- ••• 0:22—Brief buns, jumping into the swimming pool, then topless next to the pool with Adam West.
- • 0:27—Topless in bed with West, then topless waking up.
Lindsay Bloom . . . . Chris
Tanya Boyd . . . . Sylvie
- • 0:39—Brief topless in jungle room when an older customer accidentally comes in.
Liz Glazowski . . . . Liz
Kim Hopkins. . . . . Young Xaviera
Susan Lynn Kiger . . . . Susie
- • 0:42—Topless, singing "Happy Birthday" to a guy tied up on the bed.
- ••• 0:43—Topless, wearing a red garter belt playing pool with K.C. Winkler.
Lisa London . . . . Laurie
Alexandra Morgan . . . . Max
K.C. Winkler. . . . . Amber
- •• 0:41—Topless in cowboy outfit on bed with a guy.
- ••• 0:43—Topless, wearing a blue garter belt playing pool with Susan Kiger.

The Happy Hooker Goes to Washington (1977)
Dawn Clark . . . . Candy
- 1:18—Topless, covered with spaghetti in a restaurant.

Cissie Colpitts-Cameron . . . . Miss Goodbody
- 0:29—Very brief topless when her top pops open during the senate hearing.

Raven De La Croix . . . . Uncredited Ice Cream Girl
- 0:31—Brief topless, while lying on table, getting her rear end covered with ice cream.

Linda Gildersleeve . . . . Honeymoon Wife
- 0:35—Brief topless in a diner during the filming of a commercial.

Joey Heatherton . . . . Xaviera Hollander
Joyce Jillson . . . . Herself
Marilyn Joi . . . . Sheila
- 0:09—Left breast while on a couch.
- 0:47—Brief topless during car demonstration.
- • 1:14—Topless in military guy's office.

Bonnie Large . . . . Carolyn (Model)
- 0:06—Topless during photo shoot.

Louisa Moritz . . . . Natalie Naussbaum
- 0:39—Brief topless and buns, lying down on top of Larry Storch in tennis court.

Pamela Zinszer . . . . Linda
- 1:19—Brief topless in raincoat flashing in front of congressional panel.

Happy Housewives (British)
Ava Cadell . . . . Schoolgirl
0:39—Buns, getting caught by the Squire and getting spanked.

Jeannie Collings . . . . Mrs. Wain
- 0:16—Very, very brief right breast with the Newsagent's Daughter and Bob in the bathtub.

Sue Lloyd . . . . The Blonde
Nita Lorraine . . . . Jenny Elgin
- 0:31—Brief side view of left breast and buns in barn chasing after Bob.
- 0:32—Brief topless in open dress talking to policeman.

Helli Louise . . . . Newsagent's Daughter
- • 0:16—Topless with Mrs. Wain and Bob in the bathtub.

Penny Meredith . . . . Margaretta
- 0:02—Brief right breast, while talking on the telephone while Bob makes love with her.
- • 0:19—Topless standing up in bathtub talking to Bob.
- 0:34—In sheer black lingerie.
- 1:05—Brief topless pulling her top down when interrupted by the policeman at the window.

Barry Stokes . . . . Bob
- 0:31—Brief buns, while running away from Mrs. Elgin and her daughter in the barn.

Happy Together (1988)
Patrick Dempsey . . . . Christopher "Chris" Wooden
Helen Slater . . . . Alexandra "Alex" Page
- •• 0:17—Brief right breast changing clothes while talking to Patrick Dempsey. Unfortunately, she has a goofy expression on her face.
0:57—In red lingerie tempting Dempsey. Later, panties under panty hose when Dempsey pulls her dress up while she's on roller skates.
1:07—Very brief panties under panty hose again straddling Dempsey in the hallway.
1:14—Panties under white stockings while changing in the closet.

Hard Choices (1986)
Margaret Klenck . . . . Laura
- •• 1:10—Left breast, then topless making love with Bobby. Nice close up shot.
- • 1:11—Very brief half of left breast and lower frontal nudity getting back into bed. Long shot.

Gary McCleery . . . . Bobby
- •• 1:11—Buns, while making love on top of Laura.

Hard Rock Zombies (1985)
Annabelle Larsen . . . . Groupie
Lisa Toothman . . . . Elsa
- • 0:01—Buns, undressing to go skinny dipping. Topless long shot.
- ••• 0:32—Buns, while getting into the shower. Topless and buns in the shower behind clear plastic curtain.

Hard Ticket to Hawaii (1987)
Cynthia Brimhall . . . . Edy
- •• 0:47—Topless changing out of a dress into a blouse and pants.
- •• 1:33—Topless during the end credits.

Hope Marie Carlton . . . . Taryn
- •• 0:07—Topless taking a shower outside while talking to Dona Speir.
- ••• 0:23—Topless in the spa with Speir looking at diamonds they found.
- ••• 0:40—Topless and buns on the beach making love with her boyfriend, Jimmy John.
- • 1:33—Topless during the end credits.

Patty Duffek . . . . Patticakes
- • 0:48—Topless talking to Michelle after swimming.

Dona Speir . . . . Donna
- • 0:01—Topless on boat kissing her boyfriend, Rowdy.
- ••• 0:23—Topless in the spa with Hope Marie Carlton looking at diamonds they found.
- ••• 1:04—Topless and buns with Rowdy after watching a video tape.
- •• 1:33—Topless during the end credits.

Hard to Hold (1984)
Janet Eilber . . . . Diana Lawson
Monique Gabrielle . . . . Wife #1
Sharon Hughes . . . . Wife
Charlene Jones . . . . Wife

Rick Springfield . . . . James Roberts
  • 0:06—Buns, while running down the hall getting
    chased by a bunch of young girls.
  •• 0:15—Buns, while lying in bed sleeping.

Hardbodies (1984)

Julie Always . . . . Photo Session Hardbody
  •• 0:40—Topless with other girls posing topless getting
    pictures taken by Rounder. She's wearing blue dress
    with a white belt.
Leslee Bremmer . . . . Photo Session Hardbody
  • 0:02—Topless in the surf when her friends take off
    her swimsuit top during the opening credits.
  •• 0:40—Topless with other topless girls posing for
    photographs taken by Rounder. She takes off her
    dress and is wearing a black G-string.
Roberta Collins . . . . Lana
Grant Cramer . . . . Scotty
  • 0:03—Brief buns, while getting out of bed after
    making love with Kristi.
Darcy De Moss . . . . Dede
  ••• 0:55—Topless in the back seat of the limousine with
    Rounder.
Erika Dockery . . . . Hardbody in Car
Jackie Easton . . . . Girl in Dressing Room
  •• 0:27—Topless taking off dress to try on swimsuit.
  •• 0:40—Topless with other topless girls posing for
    photographs taken by Rounder. She's wearing a
    white skirt.
Kathleen Kinmont . . . . Pretty Skater
Teal Roberts . . . . Kristi Kelly
  •• 0:03—Topless in bed after making love with Scotty,
    then putting her sweater on.
  ••• 0:47—Topless standing in front of closet mirrors
    talking about breasts with Kimberly.
  ••• 0:56—Topless making love with Scotty on the
    beach.
  •• 1:22—Topless on fancy car bed with Scotty.
Cindy Silver . . . . Kimberly
  •• 0:07—Brief topless on beach when a dog steals her
    bikini top.
  ••• 0:47—Topless standing in front of closet mirrors
    talking about breasts with Kristi.
Kristi Somers . . . . Michelle
  •• 0:53—Nude, dancing on the beach while Ashley
    plays the guitar and sings.

Hardbodies 2 (1986)

Brenda Bakke . . . . Morgan
  •• 0:34—Buns, getting into bathtub, then topless, tak-
    ing a bath.
Roberta Collins . . . . Lana Logan
Fabiana Udenio . . . . Cleo/Princess

Hardcore (1979)

Leslie Ackerman . . . . Felice
  • 0:44—Topless in porno house with George C. Scott.
Ed Begley, Jr. . . . . Soldier
Bibi Besch . . . . Mary
Peter Boyle . . . . Andy Mast

Season Hubley . . . . Niki
  • 0:27—Topless acting in a porno movie.
  ••• 1:05—Full frontal nudity talking to George C. Scott
    in a booth. Panties mysteriously appear later on.
Linda Smith . . . . Hope (Mistress Victoria)
Gigi Vorgan . . . . Teenage Girl
  • 0:32—Topless on sofa in Peter Boyle's apartment.
Tracey Walter . . . . Main Teller

Hardware (1990)

Stacey Travis . . . . Jill
  • 0:21—Almost topless in shower. Brief left breast in
    bed with Moses. Lit with blue light.
  0:38—Brief topless in bedroom seen by a guy
    through telescope. Infrared-looking effect.

Harem (1985; French)

Rosanne Katon . . . . Judy
Ben Kingsley . . . . Selim
Nastassia Kinski . . . . Diane
  • 0:14—Topless getting into swimming pool.
  •• 1:04—Topless in motel room with Ben Kingsley.

The Harrad Experiment (1973)

Don Johnson . . . . Stanley Cole
  •• 0:18—Brief frontal nudity after getting out of the
    shower while Laurie Walters watches.
Bruno Kirby . . . . Harry Schacht
  • 0:41—Brief frontal nudity, getting into the swim-
    ming pool with Beth, Don Johnson and Laurie
    Walters.
Elliot Street . . . . Wilson
  •• 0:44—Frontal nudity taking off clothes and getting
    into the swimming pool.
Sharon Taggart . . . . Barbara
Victoria Thompson . . . . Beth Hillyer
  0:08—Buns, in the bathroom while talking to Harry.
  • 0:10—Brief topless getting into bed.
  •• 0:21—Topless in nude encounter group.
  • 0:41—Topless getting into the swimming pool with
    Don Johnson and Laurie Walters.
  0:49—Buns, getting dressed after making love with
    Johnson.
Laurie Walters . . . . Sheila Grove
  • 0:29—Topless in white panties with Don Johnson.
  • 0:40—Nude taking off blue dress and getting into
    the swimming pool with Johnson.

The Harrad Summer (1974)

a.k.a. Student Union
Sherry Miles . . . . Dee
Robert Reiser . . . . Stanley
  • 0:57—Buns, while getting out of bed and hiding in
    closet.
Patrice Rohmer . . . . Marcia
  • 0:33—Brief topless, starting to take off her blouse in
    motel room with Harry.
Victoria Thompson . . . . Beth Hillyer
  •• 0:57—Buns and brief topless running down hallway
    and jumping into bed, pretending to be asleep.
  1:03—Buns, lying on inflatable lounge in the pool.

1:04—Buns, lying face down on lounge chair.

Laurie Walters . . . . Sheila Grove

0:02—Topless undressing in bathroom. Long shot, out of focus.

•• 1:04—Topless lying on lounge chair, then buns and more topless getting up and pushing Harry into the pool.

Harry and Tonto (1974)

Ellen Burstyn . . . . Shirley

Melanie Mayron . . . . Ginger

• 0:57—Very brief topless in motel room with Art Carney taking off her towel and putting on blouse. Long shot, hard to see.

Haunted Summer (1988)

Alice Krige. . . . . Mary Godwin

Eric Stoltz . . . . Percy Shelley

••• 0:09—Nude, under the waterfall and walking around in the river. Long scene.

Haunting Fear (1990)

Karen Black . . . . Dr. Julia Harcourt

Sherri Graham. Visconti's Girl

• 0:45—Buns in swimming pool. (Breasts seen under water.)

• 0:47—Topless, giving Visconti a massage while he talks on the phone.

Delia Sheppard . . . . Lisa

••• 0:13—Topless on desk, making love with Terry.

••• 1:10—Full frontal nudity, making love in bed with Terry. Long scene.

Brinke Stevens. . . . . Victoria

••• 0:10—Full frontal nudity, taking a bath and getting out.

•• 0:22—Topless changing into nightgown in bedroom.

••• 0:32—Topless on Coroner's table.

Jan-Michael Vincent . . . . James Trent

The Haunting of Morella (1989)

Lana Clarkson . . . . Coel Deveroux

••• 0:17—Topless, taking a bath, then getting out and wrapping a towel around herself.

••• 1:00—Topless in white panties, standing under a waterfall.

Deborah Dutch . . . . Serving Girl

••• 0:14—Topless and buns, taking off pink tap pants and getting into bath.

• 0:15—Buns, lying dead on the floor, covered with blood.

Nicole Eggert . . . . Morella/Lenora

• 0:16—Topless taking a bath in blood. Don't see her face, probably a body double.

0:47—Buns, on top of Guy in bed. Note the body double has different colored hair.

0:48—Side view of right breast in bed with Guy. Body double again.

Maria Ford . . . . Diane

••• 1:00—Topless taking off nightgown and swimming in pond, then walking to waterfall.

Gail Thackray . . . . Ilsa

•• 0:38—Topless in bed with Niles. Buns also when getting out and getting dressed.

Havana (1990)

Alan Arkin . . . . Joe Volpi

Lise Cutter . . . . Patty

• 0:44—Most of side of left breast with Robert Redford. Very, very brief part of right breast while he turns her around. Very brief left breast when Redford puts a cold glass on her chest. Dark, hard to see.

Lena Olin . . . . Bobby Duran

Karen Russell . . . . Dancer #2

He Knows You're Alone (1980)

Elizabeth Kemp . . . . Nancy

••• 1:12—Topless, taking off robe and taking a shower.

Patsy Pease. . . . . Joyce

• 0:42—Very, very brief left breast in open blouse when she turns around to turn off the lights.

he said, she said (1991)

Kevin Bacon . . . . .Dan Hanson

Elizabeth Perkins . . . . .Lorie Bryer

• 1:15—Brief topless getting into the shower with Kevin Bacon.

Sharon Stone . . . . Linda

Heart Beat (1979)

Stephen Davies . . . . Bob Bendix

Ann Dusenberry . . . . Stevie

•• 0:41—Full frontal nudity frolicking in bathtub with Nick Nolte.

John Heard. . . . . Jack Kerouac

Nick Nolte . . . . .Neal Cassady

Ray Sharkey . . . . Ira

Sissy Spacek . . . . Carolyn Cassady

Heart of Midnight (1988)

Jennifer Jason Leigh . . . . Carol

• 0:27—Very brief side view of right breast, while reaching for soap in the shower.

Brenda Vaccaro . . . . Betty

Heart of the Stag (1983; New Zealand)

Terence Cooper .Robert Jackson

• 0:03—Buns, while making love in bed on top of his daughter. Don't see his face.

Bruno Lawrence . . . . Peter Daley

Mary Regan . . . . Cathy Jackson

• 0:03—Brief right breast twice, very brief lower frontal nudity in bed with her father.

•• 1:06—Topless in bed, ripping her blouse open while yelling at her father.

Heartbreak Ridge (1986)

Clint Eastwood. . . . . Highway

Marsha Mason . . . . .Aggie

Rebecca Perle. . . . . Student in Shower

• 1:48—Very brief topless getting out of shower when the Marines rescue the students.

Tom Villard . . . . Profile

Heartbreaker (1983)

Apollonia. . . . . Rose
Dawn Dunlap . . . . Kim
- 0:49—Topless putting on dress in bedroom.
  0:51—Very, very brief right breast in open dress during rape attempt. Dark.
- • 1:02—Left breast, lying on bed with her boyfriend. Long scene.
Pepe Serna . . . . Loco

Heartbreakers (1984)

Kathryn Harrold . . . . Cyd
  0:02—In black bra and panties changing clothes in Peter Coyote's studio.
Carole Laure . . . . Liliane
- 0:56—Brief topless making love in car with Nick Mancuso. Dark, hard to see.
- 1:25—In sheer black dress, then brief right breast making love in art gallery with Peter Coyote.
Jamie Rose. . . . . Libby
- ••• 0:09—Topless in bed talking with Nick Mancuso and Peter Coyote.
Carol Wayne . . . . Candy
  0:22—In black wig and bra posing for Peter Coyote in his studio.
- ••• 0:41—In white bra and panties, then brief topless in the mirror stripping in front of Coyote and Nick Mancuso. Then brief topless lying in bed with Coyote.

Hearts and Armour (1983)

Barbara De Rossi . . . . Bradamante
- •• 1:05—Topless while sleeping with Ruggero.
Tanya Roberts . . . . Angelica

Heat and Dust (1982)

Christopher Cazenove. . . . . Douglas Rivers
- •• 1:25—Buns while lying in bed with Greta Scacchi under a mosquito net.
Julie Christie . . . . .Anne
Greta Scacchi . . . . Olivia Rivers
- •• 1:25—Buns, lying in bed under a mosquito net with Douglas, then topless rolling over.

The Heat of Desire (1982; French)

a.k.a. Plein Sud
Patrick Dewaere . . . . .Serge Laine
- 0:17—Buns, while getting out of bed and going into Carol's "house" that she has made out of sheets.
  0:20—Pubic hair, while lying on his back.
- 0:21—Side view of buns, while on the floor with Carol.
  0:57—Brief side view of buns, while getting out of bed and putting on pants.
- 1:02—Buns, while getting into bed with Carol. Very, very brief frontal nudity hidden by subtitles.
- 1:14—Buns, while taking off pants and getting into bed.
Clio Goldsmith . . . . Carol
- 0:09—Topless and buns, getting out of bed in train to look out the window. Dark.

- 0:12—Brief topless in bathroom mirror when Serge peeks in.
- •• 0:19—Full frontal nudity in the bathtub.
- •• 0:20—Nude, sitting on the floor with Serge's head in her lap.
- •• 0:21—Buns, lying face down on floor. Very brief topless. A little dark. Then topless sitting up and drinking out of bottle.
- 0:22—Right breast, in gaping robe sitting on floor with Serge.
- 0:24—Partial left breast consoling Serge in bed.
- 0:25—Topless sitting on chair on balcony, then walking inside. Dark.
- 0:56—Topless walking from bathroom and getting into bed. Dark.
- 0:57—Brief right breast, while on couch with Guy Marchand.
- •• 0:58—Topless getting dressed while Serge is yelling.
Guy Marchand. . . . . .Max

Heated Vengeance (1984)

Cameron Dye. . . . . Bandit
Richard Hatch . . . . Hoffman
- ••• 0:38—Buns, while making love in bed with Michelle during his dream.
- •• 0:40—Buns, while getting up out of bed and walking to bathroom.

Heaven's Gate (1980)

Jeff Bridges. . . . . John
Isabelle Huppert. . . . . Ella
- •• 1:10—Nude running around the house and in bed with Kris Kristofferson.
- ••• 1:18—Nude, taking a bath in the river and getting out.
- 2:24—Very brief left breast getting raped by three guys.
John Hurt. . . . . .Irvine
Kris Kristofferson . . . . Averill
Terry O'Quinn . . . . Captain Minardi
Mickey Rourke . . . . n.a.
Sam Waterston. . . . . Canton

Heavenly Bodies (1985)

Jo Anne Bates . . . . Girl in Locker Room
Sugar Bouche. . . . . Stripper
- 0:16—Topless doing stripper-gram for Steve.
Cynthia Dale . . . . Samantha Blair
- 0:30—Brief topless fantasizing about making love with Steve while doing aerobic exercises.
Laura Henry . . . . Debbie
- 0:46—Brief topless making love while her boyfriend, Jack, watches TV.

The Heavenly Kid (1985)

Jason Gedrick. . . . . Lenny
- •• 0:31—Brief buns, while in clothing store when Bobby magically dresses him in better looking clothes.
Nancy Valen. . . . . Melissa

The Heist *(1989; Made for Cable Movie)*
Pierce Brosnan . . . . Bobby Skinner
Wendy Hughes . . . . Susan
- • 0:52—Very brief side view of right breast making love in bed with Pierce Brosnan.

Hell Comes to Frogtown *(1987)*
Sandahl Bergman . . . . Spangle
Suzanne Solari . . . . Runaway Girl
Kristi Somers . . . . Arabella
Cec Verrell . . . . Centinella
- •• 0:19—Topless taking off her blouse and getting into sleeping bag with Roddy Piper. Brief topless again after he throws her off him.

Hell High *(1989)*
Karen Russell . . . . .Teen Girl
- •• 0:04—Topless in shack with Teen Boy while little girl watches through a hole in the wall.

Hell Up in Harlem *(1973)*
Margaret Avery . . . . Sister Jennifer
- ••• 0:42—Topless in bed, while making love with Fred Williamson.
Gloria Hendry . . . . Helen Bradley
Fred Williamson . . . . .Tommy Gibbs
- ••• 0:42—Buns, while in bed making love with Margaret Avery.

Hellhole *(1985)*
Lamya Derval . . . . Jacuzzi Girl
- ••• 1:08—Topless (she's on the right) sniffing glue in closet with another woman.
- ••• 1:12—Full frontal nudity in Jacuzzi room with Mary Woronov.
Terry Moore .Sidnee Hammond
Ray Sharkey . . . . Silk
Dyanne Thorne . . . . .Chrysta
Pamela Ward . . . . Tina
Edy Williams . . . . Vera
- ••• 0:22—Topless on bed posing for Silk.
- ••• 0:24—Topless in white panties in shower, then fighting with another woman.
- ••• 1:03—Topless in mud bath with another woman. Long scene.
Mary Woronov .Dr. Fletcher

Hello Again! *(1987)*
Corbin Bernsen . . . . Jason Chadman
Gabriel Byrne . . . . .Kevin Scanlon
Shelley Long . . . . Lucy Chadman
- • 0:58—Brief buns, in hospital gown, walking down hallway.

Hellraiser *(1987)*
Clare Higgins . . . . Julia
- • 0:17—Very, very brief left breast and buns making love with Frank.
  1:10—In white bra in bedroom putting necklace on.

Hellraiser II—Hellbound *(1988)*
Catherine Chevalier . . . . Tiffany's Mother

Clare Higgins . . . . Julia
- • 0:20—Very, very brief right breast, lying in bed with Frank. Scene from *Hellraiser.*

Hellroller *(1992)*
Michelle Bauer . . . . Michelle Novak
  0:26—Undressing in motel room down to white body suit, then exercising.
- ••• 0:30—Topless taking a bath.
  0:35—Dead in bathroom, covered with blood and with her guts hanging out.
Ruth Corrine Collins . . . . Eugene's Mother
Elizabeth Kaitan . . . . Lizzy
Hyapatia Lee . . . . Dancer
- ••• 0:43—Topless, dancing in room by herself.
- ••• 0:45—Topless and buns, while taking a shower.

Henry & June *(1990)*
Maria De Medeiros . . . . .Anais Nin
- • 0:50—Brief right breast, popping out of dress top.
- •• 0:52—Topless lying in bed with Richard E. Grant.
- •• 1:13—Topless in bed with Fred Ward, buns getting out. Right breast standing by the window.
- ••• 1:31—Topless in bed with Brigitte Lahaie.
  1:37—Nude under sheer black patterned dress.
- •• 1:43—Close up of right breast as Ward plays with her.
- •• 2:01—Left breast, then topless after taking off her top in bed with Uma Thurman.
Richard E. Grant . . . . .Hugo
Brigitte Lahaie . . . . Harry's Whore
- •• 0:23—Brief buns and topless under sheer white dress going up stairs with Fred Ward.
- •• 1:22—Topless in sheer white dress again. Nude under dress walking up stairs.
- ••• 1:23—Topless and buns making love with another woman while Anais and Hugo watch.
- • 1:31—Topless in bed with Anais. Intercut with Uma Thurman, so hard to tell who is who.
Maïté Maillé . . . . Frail Prostitute
- • 1:22—In black see-through dress.
- • 1:23—Topless making love with Brigitte Lahaie in front of Anais and Hugo.
Uma Thurman . . . . .June Miller
Fred Ward . . . . .Henry Miller
- ••• 1:39—Buns, twice, while making love with Maria de Madeiros.

Hide and Go Shriek *(1988)*
Donna Baltron . . . . Judy Ramerize
- •• 0:56—Topless after undressing in front of her boyfriend.
Brittain Frye . . . . Randy Flint
- • 0:51—Brief buns, while undressing and getting into bed. Long shot.
- • 0:52—Brief buns, while putting on his pants after getting out of bed.
- • 0:58—Very brief buns, while pulling up his pants. Dark.

Rebunkah Jones . . . . Bonnie Williams
- •• 0:27—Topless taking off her blouse. More topless sitting in bed.

Annette Sinclair . . . . Kim Downs
- • 0:51—Brief topless and buns, undressing and getting into bed. Long shot.
- •• 0:57—Topless, getting up and out of bed, then getting dressed.
- • 1:02—Topless and buns, tied up on top of freight elevator.
- • 1:05—Topless on top of elevator.
- • 1:17—Topless on top of elevator fighting with the killer. Lit with red light.

Hider in the House *(1989)*

Rebekka Armstrong . . . . .Attractive Woman
- • 0:47—Brief topless in bed with Mimi Roger's husband when she surprises them.

Mimi Rogers . . . . .Julie Dreyer

The High Country *(1980; Canadian)*

Timothy Bottoms . . . . Jim
- • 1:19—Buns, while walking into the pond with Linda Purl.
- • 1:24—Buns, while pulling underwear on after getting out of sleeping bag.

Linda Purl . . . . Kathy
- • 1:03—Brief buns, while taking a shower in the waterfall.

High Heels *(1980)*

Laura Antonelli . . . . Martine
- 0:35—Topless undressing while Jean-Paul Belmondo watches. Long, long shot.
- • 0:36—Briefly nude when Belmondo watches through opera glasses.
- ••• 0:53—Topless and buns, getting out of bed and walking around.
- • 0:55—Buns, getting a shot while lying on examination table.
- •• 0:56—Topless, twice, sitting naked on examination table.
- • 1:30—Brief side of right breast during flashback of 0:56 scene.
- 1:31—Brief full frontal nudity, running around her house while Mia Farrow watches. Long shot.

Mia Farrow . . . . Christine Du Pont

High Season *(1988; British)*

Jacqueline Bisset . . . . .Katherine Shaw
- • 0:56—Brief topless doing the backstroke in the water with Rick, then left breast while lying down. Hard to see, everything is lit with blue light.

Kenneth Branagh . . . . Rich Lamb
- • 0:56—Buns, while putting a wrap around Jacqueline Bisset after they fool around in the water.

High Stakes *(1989)*

Kathy Bates . . . . .Jill
Maia Danziger . . . . .Veronica

Sally Kirkland . . . . .Melanie "Bambi" Rose
- • 0:01—In two piece costume, doing a strip tease routine on stage. Buns in G-string, then very, very brief topless flashing her breasts.
- 1:11—In black bra cutting her hair in front of a mirror.

Higher Education *(1987; Canadian)*

Lori Hallier . . . . Nicole Hubert
- • 0:44—Right breast, twice, while making love with Andy in bed.

Jennifer Inch . . . . Gladys/Glitter
Isabelle Mejias . . . . Carrie Hanson

Highlander *(1986)*

Clancy Brown . . . . .Kuragan
Roxanne Hart . . . . .Brenda Wyatt
- • 1:30—Brief topless making love with Christopher Lambert. Dark, hard to see.

Christopher Lambert . . . . .Conner MacLeod
- • 1:30—Buns while making love with Roxanne Hart.

The Hills Have Eyes, Part II *(1989)*

Robert Houston . . . . Bobby
Penny Johnson . . . . Sue
- • 0:49—Brief topless in bus, trying to get Foster's attention.

John Laughlin . . . . .Hulk
Colleen Riley . . . . .Jane
- • 0:55—Very brief left breast, twice, while taking a shower outside when Foster talks to her.

Hired to Kill *(1990)*

Cynthia Lee . . . . .Armwrestler
Michelle Moffett . . . . Ana
- • 0:46—Left breast in dress, then topless when Oliver Reed lowers her top.
- •• 0:47—More topless in open dress top.
- •• 1:04—Very, very brief tip of right breast, lying on table when Brian Thompson rips her blouse open. More topless, lying on the table. Dark.

Oliver Reed . . . . Bartos
Penelope Reed . . . . .Katrina

The Hitchhikers *(1971)*

Misty Rowe . . . . Maggie
- • 0:00—Brief side view of left breast getting dressed.
- • 0:17—Very brief topless getting dress ripped open, then raped in van.
- • 0:48—Brief right breast while getting dressed.
- • 1:09—Left breast, making love with Benson.
- • 1:10—Brief topless taking a bath in tub.
- • 1:13—Very brief right breast in car with another victim.

Hitz *(1992)*

a.k.a. Judgment

Karen Black . . . . Tiffany Powers
Emilia Crow . . . . Chelsea Walker
- ••• 0:27—Topless and very brief upper half of lower frontal nudity, making love in bed with Jimmy. Lit with red light.

Hollywood Boulevard (1976)
Candice Rialson. . . . . Candy Wednesday
- •• 0:29—Topless getting her blouse ripped off by actors during a film.
- ••• 0:32—Topless sunbathing with Bobbi and Jill.
- •• 0:45—Brief topless in the films she's watching at the drive-in. Same as 0:29.

Tara Stromeir . . . . .Jill McBain
- •• 0:00—Topless getting out of van and standing with film crew.
- • 0:31—Silhouette of breasts, making love with P.G.
- ••• 0:32—Topless sunbathing with Bobbi and Candy.
- ••• 0:33—Topless acting for film on hammock. Long scene.

Mary Woronov . . . . Mary McQueen

Hollywood Boulevard II (1989)
Ginger Lynn Allen . . . . Candy Chandler
- •• 0:33—Topless in screening room with Woody, the writer.

Michelle Moffett . . . . Mary Randolf
Windsor Taylor Randolph
. . . . .Amazon Warrior from Brooklyn
Penelope Reed . . . . Amazon Warrior with Crystal
Maria Socas. .Amazon Queen
Lynn Theel . . . . .Ann Gregory

Hollywood Chainsaw Hookers (1988)
Esther Alise . . . . .Lisa
- ••• 0:25—Topless playing with a baseball bat while a John photographs her.

Michelle Bauer . . . . Mercedes
- ••• 0:09—Nude in motel room with a John just before chainsawing him to pieces.

Tricia Brown . . . . Ilsa
- •• 0:37—Topless while Jack is tied up in bed.

Linnea Quigley . . . . Samantha
- •• 0:32—Topless, dancing on stage.
- • 1:02—Topless, (but her body is painted) dancing in a ceremony.

Dawn Wildsmith . . . . .Lori

Hollywood Hot Tubs (1984)
Becky LeBeau . . . . Veronica
- •• 0:49—Topless changing in the locker room with other girl soccer players while Jeff watches.
- • 0:54—Topless in hot tub with the other girls and Shawn.

Donna McDaniel. . . . . Leslie Maynard
Remy O'Neill. .Pam Landers
- • 1:00—Brief right breast in hot tub with Jeff.

Katt Shea . . . . Dee-Dee
- • 0:21—Topless with her boyfriend while Shawn is working on the hot tub.

Jewel Shepard . . . . Crystal Landers
Edy Williams . . . . Desiree
- ••• 0:26—Topless, trying to seduce Shawn while he works on a hot tub.
- 1:26—In black lingerie outfit in the hallway.

- • 1:30—Partial topless with breasts sticking out of her bra while she sits by hot tub with Jeff.
- •• 1:32—Topless in hot tub room with Shawn.
- • 1:38—Topless again in the hot tub lobby.

Hollywood Hot Tubs 2—Educating Crystal (1989)
Martina Castle . . . . .Hardie
Tally Chanel . . . . Mindy Wright
Dori Courtney . . . . Hot Tub Girl
- •• 1:00—Topless stuck in the spa and getting her hair freed.

Bob Garrison . . . . Billy "Derrick" Dare
- • 0:53—Buns, while running up to hot dog stand.

Remy O'Neill . . . . Pam Landers
0:57—Swinging tassels on the tips of her belly dancing top.

Jewel Shepard . . . . Crystal Landers
0:38—In white slip during Gary's fantasy.
- • 1:12—Brief left breast, while lying down, kissing Gary.

The Hollywood Knights (1980)
Dawn Clark . . . . Pom Pom Girl
- •• 0:01—Topless sunbathing outside with Fran Drescher and another Pom Pom Girl.
- • 0:11—In bra, then brief topless, changing clothes at night.
- • 0:20—Topless in B&W Polaroid photograph. Long shot.

Michele Drake . . . . .Cheerleader
- • 0:28—Brief lower nudity in raised cheerleader outfit doing cheers in front of school assembly.

Fran Drescher. . . . . .Sally
Debra Feuer . . . . .Cheetah
Gary Graham . . . . Jimmy Shine
Kim Hopkins. Pom Pom Girl
- • 0:01—Topless, sunbathing outside with her two girlfriends.

Joyce Hyser . . . . Brenda Weintraub
Michelle Pfeiffer . . . . .Suzi Q.
Carol Ann Williams. .Jane
- • 0:51—Very brief topless, opening her blouse to distract Dudley. Don't see her face.

Holocaust 2000 (1978)
Agostina Belli . . . . .Sara Golen
- •• 0:50—Topless in bed making love with Kirk Douglas.

Kirk Douglas. Robert Caine
- •• 0:52—Buns, during nightmare sequence. Long shots, hard to tell it's him.

Homework (1982)
Michelle Bauer . . . . Uncredited Dream Groupie
- ••• 1:01—Topless with two other groupies, groping Tommy while he sings. (She has a flower in her hair and is the only brunette.)

Joan Collins . . . . .Diane
Wings Hauser. . . . . Reddog

Joy Michael
.........Diane, Age 16/Body Double for Joan Collins
- •• 0:39—In bra, then topless in car making out with her boyfriend.
- •• 1:18—Topless, taking off her bra and making love with Tommy. (Supposed to be Joan Collins.)
Barbara Peckinpaugh. . . . .Uncredited Magazine Model
- ••• 0:01—Brief topless in magazine layout. In lingerie, then topless in Tommy's photo session fantasy.
Carrie Snodgress. . . . . .Dr. Delingua
Betty Thomas . . . . .Reddog's Secretary

Honey (1980; Italian)
Clio Goldsmith . . . . Annie
- •• 0:05—Nude kneeling in a room.
- •• 0:20—Nude getting into the bathtub.
- •• 0:42—Nude getting changed.
- ••• 0:44—Nude while hiding under the bed.
- •• 0:58—Nude getting disciplined, taking off clothes, then kneeling.

Honky (1971)
Elliot Street . . . . .n.a.
Brenda Sykes. . . . . Sheila Smith
- ••• 0:42—Topless with her boyfriend, making love on the floor.
- • 1:22—Brief topless several times getting raped by two guys.

Horror Planet (1980; British)
a.k.a. Inseminoid
Jennifer Ashley. . . . . .Holly
Stephanie Beacham. . . . . Kate
Judy Geeson . . . . Sandy
- •• 0:31—Brief topless on the operating table.
- • 0:37—Same scene during brief flashback.
Victoria Tennant . . . . .Barbara

Hospital Massacre (1982)
a.k.a. X-Ray
Barbi Benton. . . . . Susan Jeremy
   0:29—Undressing behind a curtain while the Doctor watches her silhouette.
- ••• 0:31—Topless getting examined by the Doctor. First sitting up, then lying down.
- ••• 0:34—Great close up shot of breasts while the Doctor uses stethoscope on her.

Hostile Takeover (1988; Canadian)
a.k.a. Office Party
Jayne Eastwood. Mrs. Talmage
Cindy Girling. . . . . Mrs. Gayford
Kate Vernon . . . . Sally
- • 0:35—Very brief, left breast undressing in office with John Warner. Dark.
- •• 0:39—Right breast, turning over in her sleep, then playing with the chain.

Hot Blood (1989; Spanish)
Robert Case. . . . . .Ricardo
- •• 1:20—Buns, with Alicia in stable.

Sylvia Kristel . . . . .Sylvia
- • 0:44—Buns, getting molested by Dom Luis.
Alicia Moro. . . . . Alicia
- • 0:00—Buns and lower frontal nudity in stable with Ricardo. Long shot.
- • 0:06—In bra and panties with Julio, then buns and topless. Looks like a body double because hair doesn't match.

Hot Bodies (1988)
Sara Costa . . . . .Herself
- ••• 0:00—Nude, dancing on stage. Long scene. Dancing with a big boa snake.
- ••• 0:04—Topless and buns in G-string.
Venus De Light. . . . . .Herself
- •• 0:22—Topless, dancing and taking off dress.
- ••• 0:24—Nude in large champagne glass prop.
- ••• 0:27—Nude dancing on stage.
- ••• 0:47—Topless and buns in G-string stripping in nurse uniform.
- ••• 0:49—Topless and buns on hospital gurney.
- ••• 0:52—Topless and buns dancing with a life-size dummy prop.
Glenda Moore . . . . .Herself
- ••• 0:37—Topless, dancing with a sword. Sort of buns, under skirt.
- ••• 0:40—Dancing without the sword. Buns in G-string.
- ••• 0:44—Topless and buns dancing with sword again.

The Hot Box (1972)
Andrea Cagan . . . . Bunny
- •• 0:16—Topless cleaning herself off in stream behind Ellie and getting out.
- • 0:21—Topless sleeping in hammock. (She's the third girl from the front, stretching.)
- ••• 0:45—Topless in stream while bathing with the other three girls.
Margaret Markov. . . . . .Lynn Forrest
- • 0:12—Topless when bad guy cuts her swimsuit top open.
- •• 0:16—Topless in stream consoling Bunny.
- • 0:21—Topless in the furthest hammock from camera. Long shot.
- ••• 0:45—Topless bathing in stream with the other girls.
Rickey Richardson. . . . . Ellie St. George
- •• 0:16—Topless cleaning herself off in stream and getting out.
- • 0:21—Topless sleeping in hammocks. (She's the second one from the front.)
- • 0:26—Topless getting accosted by the People's Army guys.
- ••• 0:43—Full frontal nudity making love with Flavio.
- ••• 0:45—Topless in stream bathing with the other three girls.
- • 1:01—Topless taking off top in front of soldiers.
Laurie Rose. . . . . Sue
- •• 0:16—Topless cleaning herself off in stream and getting out.
- •• 0:21—Topless sleeping in hammocks. (She's the first one from the front.)

- 0:26—Topless getting accosted by the People's Army guys.
- ••• 0:45—Topless in stream bathing with the other three girls.
- 0:58—Full frontal nudity getting raped by Major Dubay.

Hot Child in the City (1987)

Leah Ayres-Hamilton . . . . Rachel
    0:38—In braless white T-shirt walking out by the pool and inside her sister's house.
- 1:12—Very brief topless in the shower with a guy. Long shot, hard to see anything.

Shari Shattuck . . . . Abby

Hot Chili (1985)

Victoria Barrett . . . . Victoria Stevenson
- 0:55—Very brief close up shot of right breast when it pops out of her dress. Don't see her face.

Bea Fiedler . . . . The Music Teacher
- •• 0:08—Topless, while playing the cello and being fondled by Ricky.
    0:29—Buns, while playing the violin.
- •• 0:34—Nude during fight in restaurant with Chi Chi. Hard to see because of the flashing light.
- ••• 0:36—Topless lying on inflatable lounge in pool, playing a flute.
- ••• 0:43—Left breast, while playing a tuba.
- ••• 1:01—Topless and buns, while dancing in front of Mr. Lieberman.
- 1:07—Buns, then right breast while dancing with Stanley.

Flo Gerrish . . . . Mrs. Baxter

Katherine Kriss . . . . Allison Baxter
- ••• 0:56—Topless getting out of the pool and talking to Ricky.
- 1:09—Buns and side view of left breast, while lying down and kissing Ricky.

Louisa Moritz . . . . Chi Chi
    0:06—Brief buns turning around in white apron after talking with the boys.
- •• 0:34—Nude during fight in restaurant with the Music Teacher. Hard to see because of the flashing light.

Taaffe O'Connell . . . . Brigitte
- ••• 0:21—Topless lying on the bed. Shot with lots of diffusion.
- 0:30—Brief topless playing the drums.
- 1:11—Brief topless in bed making love with Ernie, next to her drunk husband.

Joe Rubbo . . . . Arney
- 0:24—Brief buns while getting whipped by Brigitte.

Hot Dog... The Movie (1984)

David Naughton . . . . Dan

Crystal Smith . . . . Motel Clerk
- •• 0:10—Nude getting out of spa and going to the front desk to sign people in.

Shannon Tweed . . . . Sylvia Fonda
- ••• 0:42—Topless getting undressed, then making love in bed and in hot tub with Harkin.

Hot Moves (1984)

Monique Gabrielle . . . . Babs
- 0:29—Nude on the nude beach.
- •• 1:07—Topless on and behind the sofa with Barry trying to get her top off.

Gayle Gannes . . . . Jamie
- 1:09—Topless, taking off her white blouse and getting in bed with Joey.

Suzi Horne . . . . Hooker #1

Debi Richter . . . . Heidi
    0:06—Brief left bun, pulling pink swimsuit bottom aside for the boys at the beach.
- 0:29—Topless on nude beach.
- ••• 1:09—Topless, taking off her red dress in bed with Michael.

Jill Schoelen . . . . Julie Ann

Hot Resort (1984)

Victoria Barrett . . . . Jane

Dana Kaminsky . . . . Melanie
- •• 1:02—Topless taking off her white dress in a boat.

Linda Kenton . . . . Mrs. Geraldine Miller
- 0:11—Very brief right breast, while in back of car with a guy.
- 0:16—Right breast, while passed out in closet with a bunch of guys.
- 0:24—Brief upper half of right breast, while on boat with a guy.
- 0:46—Brief topless in Volkswagen.
- 0:51—Brief topless in bathtub with Bronson Pinchot.
- 1:24—Brief topless making love on a table while covered with food.

Cynthia Lee . . . . Alice
- 1:08—Topless in the bathtub.

The Hot Spot (1990)

Debra Cole . . . . Irene Davey
- 1:26—Topless sunbathing next to Jennifer Connelly at side of lake. Long shot.
- •• 1:27—Topless talking with Connelly some more.

Jennifer Connelly . . . . Gloria Harper
    1:01—In black bra and panties walking out of lake with Don Johnson.
    1:26—Buns, lying next to Irene next to lake. Long shot.
- ••• 1:27—Topless, talking to Irene next to lake. Wow!

Don Johnson . . . . Harry Madox
- •• 0:41—Brief buns, while pulling up his underwear, talking to Virginia Madsen.
- 1:17—Buns, while undressing to go swimming with Madsen.
- 1:18—Buns, while getting out of the water. Long shot.

Virginia Madsen . . . . Dolly Harshaw
- 0:41—Side view of left breast while sitting on bed talking to Don Johnson.
- 0:47—Tip of right breast when Johnson kisses it.
- •• 1:16—Buns, undressing for a swim outside at night. Topless hanging on rope.

- 1:18—Buns, getting out of water with Johnson. Long shot.
- 1:21—Left breast when robe gapes open while sitting up.
  1:23—Brief lower frontal nudity and buns in open robe after jumping off tower at night.
  1:24—Topless at bottom of hill with Johnson. Long shot.
  1:45—Nude, very, very briefly running out of house. Very blurry, could be anybody.

William Sadler . . . . Frank Sutton
Charlie Martin Smith . . . . Lon Gulick

Hot T-Shirts (1980)

Corinne Alphen . . . . Judy
  0:55—In braless T-shirt as a car hop.
- 1:10—In yellow outfit dancing in wet T-shirt contest. Brief topless flashing her breasts at the crowd.

Hot Target (1985)

Simone Griffeth . . . . Christine Webber
- • 0:09—Topless taking off top for shower, then topless and brief frontal nudity taking shower.
- • • 0:19—Topless in bed after making love with Steve Marachuck.
- • 0:21—Buns, getting out of bed and walking to bathroom.
- • 0:23—Topless in bed with Marachuck again.
- 0:34—Topless in the woods with Marachuck while cricket match goes on.

House of the Rising Sun (1987)

Jamie Barrett . . . . Janet
- 1:04—Very brief topless making love with Louis.
James Daughton . . . . n.a.

The House on Carroll Street (1988)

Jeff Daniels . . . . Cochran
Kelly McGillis . . . . Emily
- 0:39—Brief topless reclining into the water in the bathtub.
Mandy Patinkin . . . . Ray Salwen
Kenneth Welsh . . . . Hackett

House on Sorority Row (1983)

Eileen Davidson . . . . Vicki
- • 0:16—Topless and buns in room making love with her boyfriend.
  0:19—In white bikini top by the pool.
Harley Jane Kozak . . . . Diane
Kate McNeil . . . . Katherine

The House on Straw Hill (1976; British)

a.k.a. Exposé
Linda Hayden . . . . Linda Hindstatt
- 0:28—Topless getting undressed in her room.
- • • 0:47—Topless, masturbating in bed.
- • 1:06—Right breast, in bed with Fiona Richmond.
Karl Howman . . . . Small Youth
- • 0:36—Buns, raping Linda Hayden in a field, while his friend holds a gun.

Fiona Richmond . . . . Suzanne
- • • 0:05—Buns and topless undressing and getting into bed and making love with Udo Kier.
- • 0:56—In black bra, then topless undressing in front of Kier.
- • • 1:00—Topless in bedroom, then making love with Kier.
  1:03—Brief buns, lying on Linda's bed.
  1:05—Buns, lying on Linda's bed.
- • 1:06—Right breast, in bed with Linda.
- • 1:07—Topless in bed with Linda.
- 1:09—Buns and side of left breast getting up from bed.
- 1:11—Full frontal nudity, getting stabbed in the bathroom. Covered with blood.

House Where Evil Dwells (1985)

Edward Albert . . . . Ted
- 1:00—Very brief, upper half of buns, while making love with Susan George on the floor.
Susan George . . . . Laura
- • • 0:21—Topless in bed making love with Edward Albert.
- • 0:59—Topless making love again.

Housewife (1972)

Yaphet Kotto . . . . Bone
Joyce Van Patten . . . . Bernadette
- 0:46—Topless and buns on pool table getting attacked by Yaphet Kotto. Probably a body double, don't see her face.
  1:04—Most of left breast getting on top of Kotto. In side view, you can see black tape over her nipple.
- 1:05—Brief side of right breast under Kotto's arm several times after she falls on the floor with him.

How Funny Can Sex Be? (1973)

Laura Antonelli . . . . Miscellaneous Personalities
- 0:01—Brief topless taking off swimsuit.
- 0:04—Brief topless in bathtub covered with bubbles.
  0:13—Lying in bed in sheer nightgown.
  0:18—Lying in bed again.
- 0:26—Topless getting into bed.
- 0:36—Topless making love in elevator behind frosted glass. Shot at fast speed.
- 1:08—In sheer white nun's outfit during fantasy sequence. Brief topless and buns. Nice slow motion.
  1:16—In black nightie.
- 1:24—In black bra and panties, then topless while changing clothes.

How to Beat the High Cost of Living (1980)

Richard Benjamin . . . . Albert
Dabney Coleman . . . . Jack Heintzel
Jane Curtin . . . . Elaine
  1:28—In pink bra, distracting everybody in the mall so her friends can steal money.
- 1:29—Close up topless, taking off her bra. Probably a body double.
Sybil Danning . . . . Charlotte
Jessica Lange . . . . Louise

How to Get Ahead in Advertising (1988)
Sean Bean . . . . Carry Frisk
Richard E. Grant . . . . Bagley
- 0:19—Brief buns, while wearing apron in kitchen all covered with food. Brief buns again talking with Rachel Ward at top of stairs.

Jacqueline Pearce . . . . Maud
Rachel Ward . . . . Julia

How to Seduce a Woman (1973)
Alexandra Hay . . . . .Nell Brinkman
- 1:05—Brief right breast in mirror taking off black dress.
- 1:06—Topless posing for pictures. Long scene.
- 1:47—Topless during flashback. Lots of diffusion.

Angel Tompkins . . . . Pamela
1:28—In bra and panties for a long time getting a massage in bedroom.

The Howling (1981)
Belinda Balaski. . . . . .Terry Fisher
Elisabeth Brooks . . . . Marsha
- • 0:46—Full frontal nudity taking off her robe in front of a campfire.
- 0:48—Topless sitting on Bill by the fire.

Christopher Stone . . . . R. William "Bill" Neill
- 0:48—Brief buns, rolling over while making love with Elizabeth Brooks in front of a campfire.

Dee Wallace Stone . . . . Karen White

Howling IV: The Original Nightmare (1988)
Lamya Derval . . . . .Elanor
- • 0:32—Brief left breast, then topless making love with Richard. Nice silhouette on the wall.

Suzanne Severeid . . . . Janice
Romy Windsor . . . . Marie

Howling V (1989)
Elizabeth Shé. . . . . .Mary Lou Summers
- 0:33—Buns and side view of right breast getting into pool with Donovan.
- 0:36—Very brief full frontal nudity climbing out of pool with Donovan.

Mary Stavin. . . . . .Anna
- • 1:09—Topless three times drying herself off while Richard watches in the mirror. Possible body double.

Humanoids from the Deep (1980)
Denise Galik . . . . Linda Beale
Lisa Glaser . . . . Becky
- • • 0:34—Full frontal nudity, undressing in tent with Billy and his ventriloquist dummy.
- 0:35—Nude, running on the beach at night, trying to escape the humanoids.

Linda Shayne. Miss Salmon
- 1:06—Topless after getting bathing suit ripped off by a humanoid.

Lynn Theel . . . . Peggy Larsen
- 0:22—Very, very brief half of right breast, when fight in parking lot startles her and her boyfriend in back of truck.

- 0:30—Brief topless getting raped on the beach by a humanoid.
- 0:51—Brief topless, dead, lying on the beach all covered with seaweed.

Humongous (1982; Canadian)
Janit Baldwin . . . . Carla Simmons
Joy Boushel . . . . Donna Blake
- • • 0:09—Topless looking out the window. More topless in the room in the mirror.
- 0:48—Topless undoing her top to warm up Bert.

Shay Garner . . . . Ida Parsons
- 0:05—Brief left breast and brief lower frontal nudity getting her clothes ripped off by a guy. Don't see her face.

Janet Julian. . . . . Sandy Ralston

Hundra (1983)
Laurene Landon . . . . Hundra
- 0:29—Very brief topless, several times, riding her horse in the surf. Partial buns. Blurry.

The Hunger (1983)
David Bowie. . . . . John
Catherine Deneuve .Miriam
- 0:08—Brief topless taking a shower with David Bowie. Probably a body double, you don't see her face.

Ann Magnuson . . . . .Young Woman from Disco
- 0:05—Brief topless in kitchen with David Bowie just before he kills her.

John Pankow . . . . 1st Phone Booth Youth
Susan Sarandon . . . . Sarah Roberts
- • • • 0:59—In a wine stained white T-shirt, then topless during love scene with Catherine Deneuve.

Hurricane (1979)
Timothy Bottoms . . . . .Jack Sanford
Mia Farrow. . . . . .Charlotte Bruckner
- 0:39—Brief left breast in open dress top while crawling under bushes at the beach.

Hurricane Smith (1990)
Cassandra Delaney. .Julie
- • • 0:45—Topless, while making love with Carl Weathers in bed.

Jürgen Prochnow . . . . Charlie Dowd

Husbands and Lovers (1991; Italian)
(Unrated version reviewed.)
Joanna Pacula. . . . . .Helena
- • • • 0:03—Topless, making love on top of Julian Sands in bed. Left breast, while lying in bed after.
- • • • 0:10—Nude, walking around and getting into bed with Sands.
- • • • 0:18—Topless in bathroom, brushing her teeth, then getting dressed.
- • • • 0:32—Buns and topless, getting into the shower with Sands.
- 0:35—Brief topless getting into bed.
- • • 0:37—Topless in white panties, putting on stockings.
- • • 0:59—Buns, getting spanked by Paolo.

••• 1:17—Buns, then topless making love in bed with Sands. Nude getting out of bed.
• 1:19—Brief topless, putting on stockings, then white bra and panties.
• 1:21—Buns, in greenhouse with Paolo when he beats her.
Julian Sands..........................Stefan
••• 0:32—Frontal nudity, in the shower and getting out.
••• 0:35—Frontal nudity, getting into bed.
••• 1:13—Nude, taking a shower then getting out.
•• 1:17—Very brief frontal nudity after making love with Joanna.
Lara Wendel ....Louisa
••• 0:47—In bra and panties with Julian Sands, then topless making love with him.

Hussy (1980; British)
Helen Mirren...........................Beaty
•• 0:22—Left breast, then side of right breast, while lying in bed with John Shea.
••• 0:29—Nude, making love in bed with Shea.
•• 0:31—Full frontal nudity in bathtub.
John Shea ....Emory
•• 0:29—Buns while making love with Helen Mirren in bed. Half of lower frontal nudity when she rolls off him.

Hustle (1975)
Catherine Bach ....Peggy Summers
Eileen Brennan ....Paula Hollinger
Catherine Deneuve ....Nicole Britton
Sharon Kelly ....Gloria Hollinger
• 0:12—Brief topless several times getting rolled out of freezer, dead.
• 1:03—In pasties, dancing behind curtain when Gloria's father imagines the dancer is Gloria.
• 1:42—In black lingerie, brief buns and side views of breast in bed in film.
Burt Reynolds ....Lieutenant Phil Gaines
Patrice Rohmer ....Linda (Dancer)
• 1:03—In pasties, dancing on stage behind beaded curtain. Buns in G-string.

I Love N.Y. (1987)
Scott Baio ....Mario Colone
• 1:19—Brief, upper half of buns, while getting out of bed. Dark, hard to see.

I Love You (1982; Brazilian)
a.k.a. Eu Te Amo
Sonia Braga ....Maria
••• 0:34—Full frontal nudity making love with Paulo.
•• 0:36—Topless sitting on the edge of the bed.
• 0:49—Topless running around the house teasing Paulo.
•• 0:50—Brief nude in blinking light. Don't see her face.
• 0:53—Topless eating fruit with Paulo.
••• 0:54—Topless wearing white panties in front of windows with Paulo. Long scene.
• 1:03—Left breast standing talking to Paulo.

• 1:10—Left breast talking to Paulo.
• 1:15—Very brief full frontal nudity, several times, in Paulo's flashback in blinking light scene.
••• 1:23—Topless with Paulo during an argument. Dark, but long scene.
•• 1:28—Topless walking around Paulo's place with a gun. Dark.
•• 1:33—Various topless scenes.
Vera Fischer ....Barbara Bergman
••• 0:31—Left breast while in front of TV and in chair with Paulo.
•• 0:46—Left breast sticking out of nightgown. Topless silhouette getting up. Full frontal nudity taking off nightgown.
••• 0:47—Nude in bed with Paulo.
••• 1:05—Topless on couch with Paulo.
• 1:09—Topless on TV while opening her dress.
Paulo Cesar Pereio ....Paulo
• 0:35—Brief side view of buns and frontal nudity, while kneeling on the floor with Sonia Braga.
• 0:38—Buns, in mirror, while walking in hallway.
•• 0:59—Buns and part of frontal nudity covered with paint with Braga.
• 1:36—Side view of buns, while making love on top of Braga.
• 1:37—Brief buns while lying on floor with Braga. Lit with neon lights.

I Love You to Death (1990)
Phoebe Cates...............Uncredited Girl in Bar
William Hurt..........................Harlan
Victoria Jackson ....Lacey
Michelle Joyner ....Donna Joy
Kevin Kline...........................Joey
• 0:10—Buns, while wearing an apron walking from the bedroom in Victoria Jackson's apartment.
Keanu Reeves ....Marlon James

I Never Promised You a Rose Garden (1977)
Bibi Andersson ....Dr. Fried
Jeff Conaway ....Lactamaeon
Kathleen Quinlan ....Deborah
• 0:27—Topless changing in a mental hospital room with the orderly.
• 0:52—Brief topless riding a horse in a hallucination sequence. Blurry, hard to see. Then close up of left breast (could be anyone's).
Susan Tyrrell..........................Lee

I Posed for Playboy (1991)
a.k.a. Posing: Inspired by Three Real Stories
(Shown on network TV without the nudity.)
Josie Bissett ....Claire Baywood
• 0:09—Close-up of left breast, while on couch with Nick. Don't see her face.
Lynda Carter ....Meredith Lanahan
Brittany York ....Herself
••• 0:20—Right breast, then topless on motorcycle during photo shoot.
••• 0:22—In T-shirt, then topless during second photo shoot.

I Spit on Your Corpse (1974)

Talie Cochrane . . . . .Hitchhiker
- • 0:47—Brief right breast, then topless getting shot. More topless, dead, covered with blood.

Mikel James. . . . . Laura

Susan McIver. . . . . Donna
- ••• 0:24—Topless undressing for a guy. More topless and buns making love in bed with him, then getting out of bed.

Georgina Spelvin. . . . . Sandra
- • 0:38—Flashing her left breast to get three guys to stop their car.
- ••• 0:39—Topless, fighting with the three guys.
- • 0:47—Brief right breast in gaping blouse.
- ••• 0:53—Topless outside, de-virginizing the backwoods kid.
- •• 1:08—Topless, close-up view, showing her breasts to him.
- • 1:10—Buns, in lowered pants and left breast in open blouse.

I Spit on Your Grave (1978)

(Uncut, unrated version reviewed.)

Camille Keaton . . . . .Jennifer
- • 0:05—Topless undressing to go skinny dipping in lake.
- •• 0:23—Left breast sticking out of bathing suit top, then topless after top is ripped off. Right breast several times.
- • 0:25—Topless, getting raped by the jerks.
- • 0:27—Buns and brief full frontal nudity, crawling away from the jerks.
- • 0:29—Nude, walking through the woods.
- • 0:32—Topless, getting raped again.
- • 0:36—Topless and buns after rape.
- • 0:38—Buns, walking to house.
- • 0:40—Buns and lower frontal nudity in the house.
- • 0:41—More topless and buns on the floor.
- • 0:45—Nude, very dirty after all she's gone through.
- • 0:51—Full frontal nudity while lying on the floor.
- • 0:52—Side of left breast while in bathtub.
- •• 1:13—Full frontal nudity seducing Matthew before killing him.
- ••• 1:23—Full frontal nudity in front of mirror, then getting into bathtub. Long scene.

Gunter Kleemann . . . . .Andy
- • 0:33—Buns, while raping Jennifer.

Richard Pace . . . . .Matthew
- • 0:42—Buns, while undressing in the house to rape Jennifer.
- 1:15—Silhouette of penis while getting hung (by the neck) by Jennifer.

Erin Tabor. . . . . Johnny
- • 0:25—Buns, while undressing to rape Jennifer.
- • 1:20—Buns, while undressing at gun point.

I, the Jury (1982)

Corinne Bohrer . . . . .Soap Opera Actress

Bobbi Burns . . . . Sheila Kyle

Barbara Carrera . . . . .Dr. Charolette Bennett
- ••• 1:02—Nude on bed making love with Armand Assante. Very sexy.
- • 1:46—Brief topless in hallway kissing Assante.

Lee Anne Harris . . . . .1st twin
- ••• 0:48—Topless on bed talking to Armand Assante.
- • 0:52—Full frontal nudity on bed wearing red wig, talking to the maniac.

Lynette Harris. . . . . .2nd twin
- ••• 0:48—Topless on bed talking to Armand Assante.
- • 0:52—Full frontal nudity on bed wearing red wig, talking to the maniac.

Laurene Landon . . . . .Velda

Iced (1988)

Debra De Liso . . . . Trina
- • 0:11—In a bra, then brief nude making love with Cory in hotel room.

Elizabeth Gorcey . . . . .Diane

Joseph Alan Johnson. . . . . .Alex
- • 0:46—Brief buns while in bathtub reminiscing about making love with a girl.

Ron Kologie . . . . Carl
- • 0:39—Buns, while in bathroom snorting cocaine.

Lisa Loring . . . . .Jeanette
- • 0:46—Brief left breast in bathtub.
- • 0:53—Buns and brief right breast in bathtub with Alex.
- •• 1:05—Brief lower frontal nudity and buns, while getting into hot tub. Topless in hot tub just before getting electrocuted.
- •• 1:13—Full frontal nudity lying dead in the hot tub.
- • 1:18—Brief full frontal nudity lying dead in the hot tub again.

If Looks Could Kill (1987)

Bob Fitzpatrick. . . . . .Doorman
- ••• 0:18—Buns, while undressing and getting into bed with the maid.

Jamie Gillis . . . . Jack Devonoff

Jane Hamilton . . . . Mary Beth

Gretchen Kingsley . . . . Elizabeth

Jeanne Marie . . . . .Jeannie Burns
- •• 0:06—Topless taking off her robe and kissing George.

Sharon Moran . . . . Madonna Maid
- •• 0:17—Full frontal nudity after Laura leaves the apartment.

Illicit Behavior (1991)

(Unrated version reviewed.)

Sondra Currie. . . . . .Yolanda

Jenilee Harrison . . . . Charlene Lernoux

James Russo . . . . Bill Tanner

Joan Severance. . . . . .Melissa Yarnell
- • 0:12—Buns, while making love standing up in the kitchen with Jack Scalia. Don't see face.
- ••• 0:13—Topless on table making love with Scalia. Don't see her face.
- •• 0:54—Right breast and buns, while taking off stockings, panties and bra in bathtub. Don't see face.

•• 1:10—Topless and buns in car with Davi. (Sometimes you see her face with her breasts, sometimes not.)
•• 1:16—Right breast, while lying in bed and talking to Davi.

Ilsa, She Wolf of the S.S. (1974)
Gregory Knoph . . . . Wolfe
• 0:31—Buns, while in bed with Ilsa.
• 0:32—More buns, while in bed with Ilsa.
••• 0:46—Buns, while in bed with the two blonde female guards.
Dyanne Thorne . . . . Ilsa
•• 0:00—Buns, then topless making love in bed.
••• 0:01—Topless taking a shower.
••• 0:29—Buns and topless in bed with Wolfe.
•• 0:32—Right breast several times in bed with Wolfe.
••• 0:48—In white bra, then topless undressing for Wolfe.
•• 0:50—Right breast, while lying in bed.
1:18—In black bra, panties, garter belt and stockings, tied to the bed.

The Image (1990; Made for Cable Movie)
Marsha Mason . . . . Jean Cromwell
• 0:08—Two brief side views of left breast standing in bathroom after Albert Finney gets out of the shower.

Images (1972; Irish)
Cathryn Harrison . . . . Susannah
Susannah York . . . . Cathryn
• 0:59—Brief lower frontal nudity, then right breast lying on the bed.
1:38—Brief buns in the shower.

Imagine: John Lennon (1988)
John Lennon . . . . Himself
• 0:43—Nude in B&W photos from his White Album.
0:57—Brief frontal nudity of album cover again during interview.
Yoko Ono . . . . Herself
• 0:43—Nude in B&W photos from John Lennon's White Album.
0:57—Brief full frontal nudity from album cover again during an interview.
1:27—Almost topless in bed with Lennon.

Immortalizer (1990)
Rebekka Armstrong . . . . June
• 0:16—Topless getting blouse taken off by nurse.
••• 0:29—Topless when a worker fondles her while she's asleep.
Raye Hollitt . . . . Queenie

Impulse (1989)
Jeff Fahey . . . . Stan
Theresa Russell . . . . Lottie
•• 0:37—Left breast, making love with Stan in bed.

Impulse (1984)
Tim Matheson . . . . Stuart
• 0:17—Buns, when getting out of bed with Meg Tilly.

Bill Paxton . . . . Eddie
Sherri Stoner . . . . Young Girl
Meg Tilly . . . . Jenny
0:58—In wet red swimsuit in photograph, then topless in B&W photograph (don't see her face) when Tim Matheson looks at photos.

In Harm's Way (1965)
Barbara Bouchet . . . . Liz Eddington
• 0:05—Very, very brief right breast waving to a guy from the water.
Kirk Douglas . . . . Paul Eddington
Paula Prentiss . . . . Bev

In Praise of Older Women (1978; Canadian)
Tom Berenger . . . . Andras Vayda
• 0:32—Buns, while in bed with Karen Black (seen in mirror). Long shot.
•• 1:04—Buns, while rolling off Susan Strasberg. Kind of dark.
•• 1:07—Very brief lower frontal nudity three times, standing up and picking up Strasberg.
1:20—Very brief frontal nudity turning over in bed waiting for Alexandra Stewart.
1:23—Very, very brief blurry frontal nudity turning over in bed after getting mad at Alexandra Stewart.
••• 1:42—Buns, while undressing with Helen Shaver. Very brief balls.
Karen Black . . . . Maya
•• 0:35—Topless in bed with Tom Berenger.
Michael Kirby . . . . n.a.
Marilyn Lightstone . . . . Klari
• 0:45—Left breast, twice, while on floor with Tom Berenger before being discovered by Karen Black.
Marianne McIssac . . . . Julika
•• 0:23—Topless and buns, getting into bed with Tom Berenger.
Helen Shaver . . . . Ann MacDonald
••• 1:40—Blue bra and panties, then topless with Tom Berenger.
•• 1:42—Nude lying in bed with Berenger, then getting out and getting dressed.
Alexandra Stewart . . . . Paula
•• 1:21—Topless in bed with Tom Berenger.
•• 1:23—Nude, in and out of bed with Berenger.
Susan Strasberg . . . . Bobbie
•• 1:03—Left breast, while making love in bed with Tom Berenger.
••• 1:04—Topless in bed after Berenger rolls off her.
Alberta Watson . . . . Mitzi
•• 0:51—Topless sitting in chair talking with Tom Berenger, then more topless lying in bed. Long scene.

In Search of the Perfect 10 (1986)
Blondi . . . . Perfect Girl #3
••• 0:14—Topless in back of car.
Lois Ayer . . . . Perfect Girl #2
••• 0:08—In swimsuit, then topless exercising by the pool.

Michelle Bauer .Perfect Girl #10
••• 0:53—In yellow outfit stripping in office. Topless and
buns in G-string bottom.
Iris Condon . . . . .Perfect Girl #6/Jackie
••• 0:37—Topless (she's the blonde) playing Twister
with Rebecca Lynn. Buns in G-string.
Venus De Light .Perfect Girl #4
••• 0:18—Topless talking on the phone and buns in G-
string seen through the Nude-Cam.
••• 0:21—In two piece swimsuit, then topless taking it
off in the doorway.
Rebecca Lynn . . . . Perfect Girl #7/Ellen
••• 0:37—Topless (she's the redhead) playing Twister
with Iris Condon. Buns in G-string.
Heidi Paine . . . . .Perfect Girl #8
••• 0:45—Brief topless pulling down her top outside of
car.
Teri Lynn Peake .Perfect Girl #9
••• 0:47—Buns and topless taking a shower.
Gail Thackray .Perfect Girl #5
••• 0:31—Topless and buns trying on all sorts of lingerie
in dressing room.

In the Cold of the Night (1989)
Melinda Armstrong . . . . .Laser Model 2
Tammy Hansen . . . . Model 2
Jeff Lester . . . . Scott Bruin
• 0:05—Very brief buns, whhile rolling over to stran-
gle Shannon Tweed.
Shelley Michelle . . . . Model 3
Adrianne Sachs . . . . Kimberly Shawn
••• 0:52—Buns and topless in shower, then making love
with Scott. Long, erotic scene.
• 0:59—Brief topless in outdoor spa.
•• 1:06—Topless making love on Scott's lap in bed.
Marc Singer . . . . Ken Strom
Shannon Tweed . . . . Lena
• 0:02—Right breast while making love with Scott.

In the Heat of Passion (1991)
(Unrated version reviewed.)
Nick Corri . . . . Charlie
Sally Kirkland . . . . Dr. Lee Adams
••• 0:21—In black bra, then topless making love with
Charlie while her husband is downstairs.
• 0:23—Brief topless in the shower when her husband
opens the shower curtain.
•• 0:29—Topless with Charlie in stall in women's restroom.
••• 0:42—Topless teasing Charlie from the bathroom.
• 0:45—Right breast, then topless in bed with Charlie.
• 1:11—Very brief buns, while on the couch with
Charlie.

In the Shadow of Kilimanjaro (1985)
Timothy Bottoms . . . . .Jack Ringtree
•• 0:18—Buns, three times, while in bedroom with
Irene Miracle.
• 0:21—Brief buns, in mirror, while putting towel
around himself.

Irene Miracle . . . . Lee Ringtree
• 0:18—Brief topless in bed with Timothy Bottoms.
Kind of hard to see anything because it's dark.

In the Spirit (1990)
Peter Falk . . . . .Roger Flan
•• 0:17—Buns, three times while standing up, a little
embarrassed, talking to Crystal.
Melanie Griffith . . . . .Lureen

Incoming Freshman (1979)
Alice Barrett . . . . Boxing Student
•• 0:43—Topless answering a question during Profes-
sor Bilbo's fantasy.
• 0:55—Topless in another of Bilbo's fantasy.
• 1:18—Topless during end credits.
Georgia Harrell . . . . Student
Marilyn Faith Hickey . . . . Sargeant Laverne Finterplay
• 0:06—Topless and buns when Professor Bilbo fantasizes about her.
• 0:56—Topless and buns during Bilbo's fantasy.
• 1:18—Topless during end credits.
Al Nazario . . . . Mooner
• 0:44—Buns, while mooning Professor Bilbo during
his daydream.
• 0:56—Buns again during Bilbo's daydream.
• 1:19—Buns, during end credits.

An Indecent Obsession (1985)
Wendy Hughes . . . . .Honour Langtry
0:32—Possibly Wendy topless, could be Sue because
Luce is fantasizing about Wendy while making love
with Sue. Dark, long shot, hard to see.
•• 1:10—Left breast, making love in bed with Wilson.
Bruno Lawrence . . . . Matt Sawyer
Richard Moir . . . . .Luce Daggett
• 0:31—Buns when at the beach with his pals. Don't
see his face.

The Inheritance (1978; Italian)
Adrianna Asti .Teta Ferramonti
Dominique Sanda . . . . Irene
•• 0:18—Full frontal nudity getting undressed and lying on the bed with her new husband.
••• 0:37—Full frontal nudity lying in bed with her lover.
• 1:19—Very brief right breast, while undoing top for
Anthony Quinn.
••• 1:22—Left breast, lying in bed. Full frontal nudity
jumping out of bed after realizing that Quinn is
dead.

Inhibition (1984; Italian)
Cesare Barro . . . . n.a.
Ilona Staller . . . . Anna
••• 0:08—Nude taking a shower with Carol.
• 0:43—Brief full frontal nudity getting out of swimming pool.
••• 0:55—Topless making love in the water with Robert.
••• 1:00—Full frontal nudity getting disciplined by Carol.

Inner Sanctum (1991)

Suzanne Ager . . . . Maureen

Michelle Bauer . . Body Double for Margaux Hemingway
- • 0:09—Left breast, body double in office for Margaux Hemingway.
- •• 0:23—Topless body double for Hemingway, while in bed with Joseph Bottoms.

Joseph Bottoms . . . . Baxter Reed
- • 0:10—Lower half of buns, while in office with Margaux Hemingway.
- ••• 0:43—Buns, while on sofa with Tanya Roberts.

Brett Clark . . . . Neil Semple

Margaux Hemingway . . . . Anna Rawlins
- • 0:09—Brief buns and tip of left breast in office with Joseph Bottoms.
- ••• 0:23—In bra with Bottoms, then topless, while in bed. (When you don't see her face, it's Michelle Bauer doing the body double work.)

Tanya Roberts . . . . Lynn Foster
- • 0:35—Right breast, several times, while looking out the window.
- ••• 0:40—Buns in lingerie on sofa with Joseph Bottoms, then topless while making love.
- ••• 0:57—In black lingerie under trench coat, stripping for Bret Clark. Buns, then topless making love.

Valerie Wildman . . . . Jennifer Reed
- 0:05—Wearing transparent light blue nightgown, getting out of bed, into wheelchair.
- •• 0:11—Right breast, while sitting on bed with Joseph Bottoms.

Innerspace (1987)

Fiona Lewis . . . . Dr. Margaret Canker

Dennis Quaid . . . . Tuck Pendleton
- •• 0:08—Buns, while standing naked in the street as taxi drives off with his towel. Kind of a long shot.

Meg Ryan . . . . Lydia

The Innocent (1976; Italian)

Laura Antonelli . . . . Julianna
- ••• 0:41—Topless in bed with her husband.
- ••• 0:53—Full frontal nudity in bed when her husband lifts her dress up.

Innocent Sally (1973)

a.k.a. The Dirty Mind of Young Sally

Angela Carnon . . . . n.a.

George "Buck" Flower . . . . Toby
- • 0:50—Brief frontal nudity, changing places with Sally.
- ••• 0:53—Buns, while making love on top of Sally in back of van.

Sharon Kelly . . . . Sally
- ••• 0:35—Topless, undressing in back of van. Long scene.
- ••• 0:37—Full frontal nudity, on pillow in back of van while caressing herself. Another long scene.
- ••• 0:39—More full frontal nudity in van.
- ••• 0:47—Right breast, then full frontal nudity, making love with Toby in van. Long scene.

- ••• 1:05—Topless, making love in bed with another guy. Long scene.
- ••• 1:10—Full frontal nudity, making more love. Long scene.
- ••• 1:19—Topless, after making love.
- ••• 1:23—Full frontal nudity, while making love with a guy.

Robyn Whitting . . . . n.a.

Innocent Victim (1988)

Peter Firth . . . . Terence

Paul McGann . . . . Barry

Helen Shaver . . . . Benet Archdale
- • 1:05—Very brief side of left breast on top of a guy in bed.

Inserts (1976)

Veronica Cartwright . . . . Harlene
- •• 0:16—Topless sitting on bed with Richard Dreyfuss.
- ••• 0:31—Nude on bed with Stephen Davies making a porno movie for Dreyfuss. Long scene.

Stephen Davies . . . . Rex
- •• 0:31—Buns and balls, while on bed with Veronica Cartwright, making a porno movie for Richard Dreyfuss.

Jessica Harper . . . . Cathy Cake
- ••• 1:15—Topless in garter belt and stockings, lying in bed for Richard Dreyfuss. Long scene.

Instant Karma (1990)

Rebekka Armstrong . . . . Jamie

Hedy Lamarr . . . . Movie Goddess

Craig Sheffer . . . . Zane Smith
- • 1:15—Brief buns while on top of Penelope. Don't see his face.
- 1:18—Very brief buns again in flashback.

Annette Sinclair . . . . Amy

Internal Affairs (1990)

Victoria Dillard . . . . Kee

Richard Gere . . . . Dennis Peck

Faye Grant . . . . Penny
- • 0:50—Right breast, while straddling Richard Gere while she talks on the telephone.

Billie Neal . . . . Dorian's Wife

Nancy Travis . . . . Kathleen Avila
- • 0:38—Side view of left breast when Raymond opens the shower door to talk to her.

Into the Fire (1988)

a.k.a. Legend of Lone Wolf

Susan Anspach . . . . Rosalind Winfield
- •• 0:22—Left breast, under trench coat when she first comes into the house, briefly again in the kitchen.
- •• 0:31—Topless in bedroom standing up with Wade.

Olivia D'Abo . . . . Liette
- 0:07—Very, very brief silhouette of left breast in bed.
- •• 0:32—Topless on bed with Wade. A little bit dark and hard to see.
- •• 1:10—Topless in the bathtub. (Note her panties when she gets up.)

Into the Night (1985)

David Bowie . . . . Colin Morris
Sue Bowser . . . . Girl on Boat
•• 0:24—Topless taking off blouse with Jake on his boat after Michelle Pfeiffer leaves.
Jeff Goldblum . . . . Ed Okin
Kathryn Harrold . . . . Christie
Tracey E. Hutchinson. . . . . Federal Agent
Michelle Pfeiffer . . . . Diana
• 0:27—Buns and very brief side nudity in her brother's apartment getting dressed. Long shot, hard to see.
Peggy Sands . . . . Shameless Woman
• 0:43—Topless putting dress on after coming out of men's restroom stall after a man leaves the stall first.

Invasion of the Bee Girls (1973)

Anna Aries. . . . . Cora Kline
•• 0:55—Buns and topless getting transformed into a Bee Girl.
••• 1:00—Topless getting out of the bee transformer.
Anitra Ford . . . . Dr. Susan Harris
••• 0:47—Topless and buns undressing in front of a guy in front of a fire.
Susan Player Jarreau . . . . Girl
Beverly Powers . . . . Harriet Williams
• 1:14—In white bra and panties, then right breast and buns, taking off her clothes for her husband.
Victoria Vetri . . . . Julie Zorn
• 0:30—Brief topless getting molested by jerks.
••• 1:19—Topless in the bee transformer, then brief buns getting rescued.

Invasion of the Body Snatchers (1978)

Brooke Adams . . . . Elizabeth Driscoll
0:49—All covered in pod gunk in her bedroom when Donald Sutherland discovers her. Don't really see anything.
•• 1:43—Brief topless behind plants when Sutherland sees her change into a pod person. Hard to see because plants are in the way.
• 1:48—Topless walking through the pod factory pointing out Sutherland to everybody. Long shot, hard to see.
Veronica Cartwright . . . . Nancy Bellicec
Jeff Goldblum . . . . Jack Bellicec
Donald Sutherland . . . . Matthew Bennell

The Invisible Kid (1988)

Karen Black. . . . . Mom
Jay Underwood . . . . Grover Dunn
• 0:27—Brief buns while running around the school halls after becoming visible with his friend, Milton.
Wally Ward . . . . Milton McClane
• 0:27—Brief buns while running around the school halls after becoming visible with his friend, Grover.

Invisible Maniac (1990)

Dana Bentley Konkel . . . . Newscaster
• 1:22—Brief topless on monitor doing the news.

Stephanie Blake . . . . Mrs. Cello
•• 0:42—Topless opening her blouse for Chet.
•• 0:52—Topless in her office trying to seduce Dr. Smith. Nice close up of right breast.
Debra Lamb. . . . . Betty
• 0:21—Buns and very brief side view of right breast in the shower with the other girls.
••• 0:43—In bra, then topless and buns standing on the left in the locker room with the other girls.
• 0:44—Buns and brief topless in the shower with the other girls.
•• 0:56—In bra, then topless getting killed by Dr. Smith.
• 0:58—Brief topless, dead, discovered by April and Joan.
Melissa Moore . . . . Bunny
• 0:21—Buns in shower with the other girls.
••• 0:43—In bra, then topless sitting with yellow towel in locker room with the other girls.
• 0:44—Topless in shower with the other girls.
••• 1:09—In bra, then topless making out in Principal's Office with Chet. Long scene.
Tracy Walker . . . . Telescope Gal
•• 0:01—Nude, taking off clothes during opening credits. Nice dancing.
Shannon Wilsey . . . . Vicky
• 0:21—Buns and very, very brief side of left breast in the shower with the other girls.
• 0:33—Right breast covered with bubbles.
••• 0:43—In bra, then topless and lots of buns in locker room with the other girls.
•• 0:44—Buns and left breast in the shower with the other girls.
••• 1:04—Undressing in locker room in white bra and panties, then topless. More topless taking a shower and getting electrocuted.

Ironweed (1987)

Carroll Baker . . . . Annie Phelan
Jack Nicholson . . . . Francis Phelan
Meryl Streep . . . . Helen
Margaret Whitton . . . . Katrina
•• 1:19—Full frontal nudity leaving the house and walking down steps while young Francis brushes a horse.

Irreconcilable Differences (1984)

Dana Kaminsky . . . . Woman in Dress Shop
Ryan O'Neal. Albert Brodsky
Sharon Stone . . . . Blake Chandler
•• 0:56—Topless lowering her blouse in front of Ryan O'Neal during film test.

Isadora (1968; British)

James Fox. . . . . Gordon Craig
Vanessa Redgrave. . . . . Isadora Duncan
0:47—Brief glimpses of topless and buns dancing around in her boyfriend's house at night. Hard to see anything.
• 2:19—Very brief topless dancing on stage after coming back from Russia.

Ishtar (1987)

Isabelle Adjani. . . . . Shirra Assel
- 0:27—Very brief left breast flashing herself to Dustin Hoffman at the airport while wearing sunglasses.

Warren Beatty. . . . . Lyle Rogers
Dustin Hoffman. . . . . Chuck Clarke
Carol Kane . . . . Carol
Jack Weston . . . . Marty Freed

The Island (1980)

Angela Punch McGregor. . . . . Beth
- • 0:45—Topless taking off poncho to make love with Michael Caine in hut after rubbing stuff on him.
  0:50—Braless under poncho walking towards Caine.

Island of 1000 Delights (German)

Bea Fiedler . . . . Julia
- • 0:25—Full frontal nudity washing herself in bathtub, then nude taking off her towel for Michael.
- • 0:27—Topless lying on floor after making love, then buns walking to chair.
- • 0:46—Full frontal nudity taking off her dress and kissing Howard.
- • 0:50—Topless in white bikini bottoms coming out of the water to greet Howard.
- ••• 1:06—Topless sitting in the sand near the beach, then nude talking with Sylvia.
- ••• 1:17—Right breast (great close up) making love with Sylvia.
- ••• 1:18—Topless above Sylvia.

Scarlett Gunden . . . . Francine
- ••• 0:02—Topless on beach dancing with Ching. Upper half of buns sitting down.
  0:20—Dancing braless in sheer brown dress.
- • • 0:44—Full frontal nudity getting tortured by Ming.
- • 1:16—Topless on beach after Ching rescues her.

Olivia Pascal . . . . Peggy
- • • 0:16—Topless, tied up while being tortured by two guys. Upper half lower frontal nudity.
- • • 0:23—Full frontal nudity lying in bed, then buns running out the door. Full frontal nudity running up stairs, nude hiding in bedroom.
  0:33—In braless black dress.
- ••• 0:57—Nude, taking off her clothes in shower with Michael.
- • 1:26—Brief topless running on the beach with Michael.

It's My Turn (1980)

Jill Clayburgh . . . . Kate Gunzinger
- • 1:10—Brief upper half of left breast in bed with Michael Douglas after making love.

Michael Douglas. . . . . Ben Lewin
Jennifer Salt. . . . . Maisie
Daniel Stern . . . . Cooperman

Jackson County Jail (1976)

Marciee Drake . . . . Candy (David's Girlfriend)
- • 0:04—Brief topless wrapping towel around herself, in front of Howard Hessman. Long shot.

Tommy Lee Jones . . . . Coley Blake

Yvette Mimieux . . . . Dinah Hunter
- • 0:39—Topless in jail cell getting raped by policeman.

Patrice Rohmer. Cassie Anne
Betty Thomas. . . . . Waitress
Mary Woronov. . . . . Pearl

Jacob's Ladder (1990)

Perry Lang . . . . Jacob's Assailant
Billie Neal. . . . . Della
Elizabeth Peña . . . . Jezzie
- • 0:14—Side view of right breast taking off robe and getting into shower with Tim Robbins.
- ••• 0:16—Topless several times opening dress and putting pants on. Then in black bra.
- • • 0:31—Very, very brief topless in bed with Robbins, then left breast a lot. Dark.

Tim Robbins. . . . . Jacob Singer
- • • 0:40—Buns, twice in bathroom, while getting ready for ice bath.

Jakarta (1988)

Sue Francis Pai . . . . Esha
- • 1:01—Brief right breast, while making love in the courtyard with Falco.
  1:13—Brief side of right breast while kissing Falco.
- • • 1:13—Side view of right breast, then brief topless twice, making love under a mosquito net with Falco. Hard to see her face clearly.

James Joyce's Women (1983)

Fionnula Flanagan . . . . Molly Bloom
- • 0:48—Brief topless getting out of bed.
- ••• 0:56—Topless getting back into bed.
- ••• 1:02—Full frontal nudity masturbating in bed talking to herself. Very long scene—9 minutes!

The January Man (1988)

Harvey Keitel . . . . Frank Starkey
Kevin Kline. . . . . Nick Starkey
Mary Elizabeth Mastrantonio . . . . Bernadette Flynn
- • 0:40—Topless in bed with Kevin Kline. Side view of left breast squished against Kline.
- ••• 0:42—Topless after Kline gets out of bed. Brief shot, but very nice!

Billie Neal. . . . . Gwen
Susan Sarandon . . . . Christine Starkey

Jekyll & Hyde... Together Again (1982)

Elvira . . . . Busty Nurse
- • 0:56—Brief right breast, peeking out from smock in operating room. (She's wearing a surgical mask.)

Bess Armstrong . . . . Mary
Krista Errickson. . . . . Ivy
  0:31—In red bra and panties in bedroom with Mark Blankfield.

Noelle North . . . . Student

Jessi's Girls (1976)

Regina Carroll . . . . Claire
- • • 0:58—Topless and buns in hay with Indian guy. Don't see her face.

Sondra Currie . . . . Jessica
- 0:02—Nude in water cleaning up, then brief left breast getting dressed.
- 0:07—Topless getting raped by four guys. Fairly long scene.
- 0:37—Topless kissing Clay under a tree. Hard to see because of the shadows.

Ellen Stern. . . . . Kana
••• 1:10—Left breast, then topless in bed with a guy.

Jesus of Montreal (1990; French/Canadian)

Lothaire Bluteau . . . . Daniel Coulombe
- 0:43—Buns, getting whipped while tied to a tree during a play. Long shot.
- 0:44—Buns, during crucifixion during play.
- 1:13—Upper half of frontal nudity when police arrest him during play.
- 1:36—Very brief frontal nudity when the cross he's on falls over.

Isabelle Truchon . . . . Richard's Girlfriend
Catherine Wilkening . . . . Mireille Fontaine
- 1:08—Brief topless starting to take off her sweatshirt during an audition.

Jezebel's Kiss (1990)

Katherine Barrese . . . . Jezebel
•• 0:36—Full frontal nudity washing herself off in kitchen after having sex with the sheriff.
- 0:42—Brief buns, going for a swim in the ocean. Dark.
••• 0:48—Topless taking off her robe in front of Hunt, then making love with him.
- 0:58—Brief right breast and buns while Malcolm McDowell watches through slit in curtain. Long shot.
- 1:09—Right breast and buns getting undressed. Long shot. Closer shot of buns, putting robe on.
••• 1:12—Topless making love with McDowell. More topless after.

Meg Foster . . . . Amanda Faberson
Malcolm McDowell . . . . Benjamin J. Faberson
•• 1:12—Buns, while making love with Jezebel.

The Jigsaw Murders (1988)

Laura Albert . . . . Blonde Stripper
••• 0:19—Topless and buns in black G-string, stripping during bachelor party in front of a group of policemen.

Michelle Bauer . . . . Cindy Jakulski
0:20—Brief buns on cover of puzzle box during bachelor party.
- 0:21—Brief topless in puzzle on underside of glass table after the policemen put the puzzle together.
- 0:29—Very brief topless when the police officers show the photographer the puzzle picture.
- 0:43—Very brief topless long shots in some pictures that the photographer is watching on a screen.

Catherine Case . . . . Stripper #2
- 0:27—Brief topless in black peek-a-boo bra posing for photographer.

Michelle Johnson . . . . Kathy DaVonzo
0:51—Posing in leotards in dance studio.
1:07—Posing in lingerie on bed.
1:20—In light blue dance outfit.
1:27—Posing in blue swimsuit.

Yaphet Kotto . . . . Dr. Fillmore
Brinke Stevens . . . . Stripper #1
- 0:28—Very, very brief topless posing for photographer in white bra and panties when camera passes between her and the other stripper.

Jo Jo Dancer, Your Life Is Calling (1986)

Tanya Boyd . . . . Alicia
Wings Hauser. . . . . Cliff
Paula Kelly . . . . Satin Doll
0:26—Doing a strip tease in the night club wearing gold pasties and a gold G-string.

Richard Pryor . . . . Jo Jo Dancer/Alter Ego
•• 0:06—Buns, while walking naked out of the hospital waiting for the limousine.

Barbara Williams. . . . . Dawn

Jock Petersen (1974; Australian)
a.k.a. Petersen

Belinda Giblin. . . . . Moira Winton
•• 0:21—Left breast several times, under a cover with Jock, then buns when cover is removed.

Wendy Hughes . . . . Patricia Kent
••• 0:12—Topless in her office with Tony.
- 0:13—Topless making love with Tony on the floor.
•• 0:44—Nude running around the beach with Tony.
•• 0:50—Nude in bed making love with Tony.
- 1:24—Full frontal nudity when Tony rapes her in her office.

Anne Pendlebury . . . . Peggy
Jack Thompson . . . . Tony Petersen
••• 0:13—Buns, while making love with Wendy Hughes on the floor.
••• 0:20—Frontal nudity under tarp with Moira during protest.
- 0:22—Buns while in bed with Suzy.
•• 0:44—Nude running around the beach with Hughes.
•• 0:50—Frontal nudity undressing, then buns while lying in bed.

Jacki Weaver. . . . . Susie Petersen
••• 0:01—Full frontal nudity lying in bed with Jock.

Joe (1970)

Peter Boyle. . . . . Joe Curran
Susan Sarandon . . . . Melissa Compton
- 0:02—Topless and very brief lower frontal nudity taking off clothes and getting into bathtub with Frank.

Johnny Handsome (1989)

Ellen Barkin . . . . Sunny Boyd
Elizabeth McGovern. . . . . Donna McCarty
•• 0:47—Right breast, while in bed with Mickey Rourke.

Mickey Rourke . . . . John Sedley

The Josephine Baker Story
(1991; Made for Cable Movie)
David Dukes . . . . Jo Bouillon
Lynn Whitfield. . . . . Josephine Baker
- 0:00—Topless dancing during opening credits. Slow motion.
- 0:13—Topless taking off her dress top for the French painter.
- 0:14—Topless in the mirror and dancing with the painter after making love. Nice. Dancer doing splits looks like a body double.
  0:16—Brief buns, in wet dress, getting out of swimming pool.
- 0:31—Topless on stage doing the Banana Dance.
- 0:33—Topless some more, doing the Banana Dance.
- 2:02—Brief topless dancing during flashback.

Joy *(1983; French/Canadian)*
Nancy Cser . . . . Unidentified
Jeffrey Kime. . . . . .Helmut
Claudia Udy . . . . Joy
- 0:11—Nude, undressing, getting into bath then into and out of bed.
- 0:14—Nude in bed with Marc.
- 0:31—In swimsuits, posing for photos, then full frontal nudity.
- 0:54—Topless sitting with Bruce at encounter group.
- 1:04—Buns and topless getting into bathtub.

The Joy of Flying *(1979)*
Olivia Pascal . . . . Maria
- 0:39—Topless wearing panties, in bedroom with George, then nude.
- 0:46—Nude with George in bathroom.
Ajita Wilson. Madame Gaballi
- 1:20—Full frontal nudity undressing for George.
- 1:23—Topless, making love on top of George.
- 1:25—Left breast, while in bed with George.

Joy: Chapter II *(1985; French)*
a.k.a. Joy and Joan
Brigitte Lahaie. . . . . Joy
- 0:01—Left breast in coat during photo session.
- 0:11—Nude, getting into bubble bath and out with Bruce.
- 0:20—Topless, lying in bed after party.
- 0:22—Topless, talking on the phone.
- 0:27—Nude, getting a massage from Milaka. Nice.
- 0:32—Topless changing clothes.
- 0:45—In bra, then topless changing clothes with Joanne.
- 0:47—Full frontal nudity, masturbating in bed. Medium long shot.
- 0:54—Nude, making love with Joanne on train. Nice, long scene!
- 1:03—Topless in the water with Joanne.
- 1:08—Topless, getting molested by a bunch of guys in the shower.
- 1:10—Right breast, lying next to a pool.

- 1:17—Nude in bubble bath with Joanne and getting out.
- 1:23—Buns, dancing with Joanne.
- 1:27—Nude, making love with Joanne and Mark.
Maria Isabel Lopez . . . . Milaka
- 0:10—Topless, showing Joy her breasts at Bruce's request.
- 0:27—Topless, taking off her robe and massaging Joy.

Joyride *(1977)*
Melanie Griffith . . . . Susie
- 0:05—Topless in back of station wagon with Robert Carradine, hard to see anything.
- 0:59—Brief topless in spa with everybody.
- 1:11—Brief topless in shower with Desi Arnaz, Jr.
Anne Lockhart . . . . Cindy
- 0:59—Brief topless in the spa with everybody.
- 1:00—Topless, standing in the kitchen kissing Desi Arnaz Jr.

Joysticks *(1983)*
Corinne Bohrer. . . . . Patsy Rutter
John Diehl . . . . Arnie
Erin Halligan. . . . . Sandy
- 1:08—Right breast, then topless in bed with Jefferson surrounded by candles.
Becky LeBeau . . . . Liza
Kym Malin . . . . Lola
- 0:03—Topless with Alva showing a nerd their breasts by pulling their blouses open.
- 0:18—Topless during strip-video game with Jefferson, then in bed with him.
- 0:57—Topless during fantasy sequence, lit with red lights, hard to see anything.
- 1:02—Brief topless in slide show in courtroom.
Lynda Wiesmeier . . . . Candy

Julia *(1974; German)*
Ekkhardt Belle . . . . Patrick
- 1:01—Very brief buns, while in bed with Terry.
Peter Berling . . . . Alex Lovener
- 0:12—Brief buns, while playing the piano outside on the dock.
Gisela Hahn . . . . .Miriam
- 0:12—Topless tanning herself outside.
- 1:14—Brief topless sitting in the rain.
Sylvia Kristel . . . . .Julia
  0:23—Brief topless in the lake.
- 0:25—Topless on deck in the lake.
- 0:28—Brief topless changing clothes at night. Long shot.
- 0:34—Topless on boat with two boys.
- 0:42—Topless taking off her towel.
- 1:12—Topless on tennis court with Patrick.

Julia and Julia (1987; Italian)
(This movie was shot using a high-definition video system and then transferred to film.)
Sting . . . . .Daniel
- •• 1:11—Buns, while sleeping in bed when Kathleen Turner leaves. Don't see his face very well.
Gabriel Byrne . . . . Paolo
Kathleen Turner . . . . Julia
- ••• 0:32—Topless making love in bed with her husband.
- ••• 1:08—Topless, then right breast making love in bed with Sting.

Julia Has Two Lovers (1990)
David Duchovny . . . . .Daniel
- • 0:42—Frontal nudity, standing outside during Julia's fantasy. Hard to see because vertical blinds get in the way. Upper half of buns, while in bed with her (in B&W).
- • 0:54—Brief side view of buns, getting out of bed and putting underwear on. Long shot.
Daphna Kastner . . . . Julia
- • 0:11—Brief topless, changing blouses while talking on the telephone.
- • 0:25—Partial left breast, while in bubble bath.
- • 0:29—Right breast, while in bubble bath.
- • 0:30—Topless in mirror, getting out of bath tub.
- • 0:53—Left breast, while lying in bed with David Duchovny. Long shot.

Jungle Fever (1991)
Brad Dourif . . . . Leslie
Gina Mastrogiacomo. . . . . .Louise
Lonette McKee . . . . Drew
- •• 0:04—Left breast while making love with Wesley Snipes in bed.
- • 2:03—Brief left breast in bed with Snipes again.
Tim Robbins . . . . Jerry
Annabella Sciorra .Angie Tucci
0:32—In black bra

Jungle Warriors (1985)
Ava Cadell. . . . . .Didi Belair
- • 0:50—Brief topless getting yellow top ripped open by a bad guy.
Sybil Danning . . . . Angel
0:53—Buns, getting a massage while lying face down.
Suzi Horne . . . . Pam Ross
- • 0:51—Brief topless twice during jail scene. Wearing a white blouse, with a yellow shirt underneath. Brief buns. Don't see her face.
Louisa Moritz . . . . Laura McCashin

Just Before Dawn (1980)
Jamie Rose. . . . . Megan
0:33—Topless in pond. Long shot.
- • 0:34—Brief topless in pond, closer shot.
- •• 0:36—Brief upper half of left breast, then brief topless several times splashing in the water.
- • 0:37—Topless getting out of the water.

Just One of the Guys (1986)
Sherilyn Fenn . . . . Sandy
Joyce Hyser . . . . Terry Griffith
0:10—In two piece swimsuit by the pool with her boyfriend.
- •• 1:27—Brief topless opening her blouse to prove that she is really a girl.

Just Tell Me What You Want (1980)
Leslie Easterbrook. . . . . .Hospital Nurse
Ali MacGraw .Bones Burton
- •• 0:16—Topless getting dressed in her bedroom.
- •• 1:26—Brief topless in bathroom getting ready to take a shower.
Peter Weller . . . . .Steven Routledge

Just the Way You Are (1984)
Kaki Hunter . . . . Lisa
Kristy McNichol . . . . .Susan
- • 0:50—Very brief left breast showing her friend that she's not too hot because there is nothing under her white coat. Medium long shot.
Michael Ontkean . . . . Peter
Alexandra Paul . . . . .Bobbie

Just You and Me, Kid (1979)
Brooke Shields . . . . .Kate
- • 0:07—Brief buns, running down stairs after her towel gets caught in fence.

Justine
Koo Stark . . . . .Justine
- •• 0:09—Topless getting fondled by a nun.
- • 0:16—Topless getting attacked by a nun.
- • 0:57—Topless in open dress getting attacked by old guy.
- ••• 1:00—Topless getting bathed, then lower frontal nudity.
- • 1:28—Right breast and buns taking off clothes, then brief full frontal nudity getting dressed again.
- • 1:32—Topless getting thrown in to the water.

K2 (1991)
Michael Biehn . . . . .Taylor Brooks
- • 0:43—Brief buns, while standing up in pool outside.
Patricia Charbonneau. . . . . Jacki Metcalfe
Julia Nickson-Soul. . . . . Cindy
- • 0:26—Briefly nude, getting up out of bed and putting robe on.

Kandyland (1987)
Sandahl Bergman. . . . . Harlow Divine
Catlyn Day. . . . . .Diva
- ••• 0:50—Topless wearing pasties doing strip routine.
- • 1:06—Brief topless talking on the telephone in dressing room.
- • 1:12—Brief topless during dance routine with the other girls.
Kim Evenson . . . . .Joni
0:26—In purple bra and white panties practicing dancing on stage.
- ••• 0:31—Topless doing first dance routine.

•• 0:45—Brief topless during another routine with bubbles floating around.

Alan Popper . . . . Heckler

Kangaroo (1986; Australian)

Judy Davis . . . . Harriet Somers
Colin Friels . . . . Richard Somers
•• 1:08—Buns, while running into the ocean.
• 1:09—Frontal nudity walking towards Judy Davis. Long shot, hard to see anything.

Katie's Passion (1978; Dutch)

Rutger Hauer . . . . Dandy
• 1:12—Buns seen through torn pants while he is kneeling on the floor.
•• 1:15—Brief frontal nudity getting out of bed.

Monique Van De Ven . . . . Katy
0:38—Brief buns when guy rips her panties off.
•• 0:45—Topless in hospital when a group of doctors examine her.
0:50—Left breast a couple of times talking to a doctor. Brief buns sitting down.
1:12—Buns, getting into bed.
••• 1:18—Nude burning all her old clothes and getting into bathtub.

The Keep (1983)

Gabriel Byrne . . . . Kaempffer
Scott Glenn . . . . Glaeken Trismegestus
Jürgen Prochnow . . . . Woorman
Alberta Watson . . . . Eva Cuza
• 0:59—Very brief topless making love with Scott Glenn, then brief lower frontal nudity.

Keeper of the City (1991; Made for Cable Movie)

Gina Gallego . . . . Elena
• 0:19—Brief half of left breast, getting out of bed and putting on black bra. Wearing black panties.

Reneé Soutendijk . . . . Vickie Benedetto
Barbara Williams . . . . Grace

Kentucky Fried Movie (1977)

Uschi Digard . . . . Woman in Shower
•• 0:09—Topless getting breasts massaged in the shower, then squished breasts against the shower door.

Marilyn Joi . . . . Cleopatra
• 1:11—Topless in bed with Schwartz.

Lenka Novak . . . . Linda Chambers
• 0:09—Topless sitting on a couch with two other girls.

Tara Stromeir . . . . Girl
•• 1:16—In bra, then topless making love on couch with her boyfriend while people on the TV news watch them.

Donald Sutherland . . . . Clumsy

The Key (1983; Italian)

Stefania Sandrelli . . . . Teresa
••• 0:31—Nude when Nino examines her while she's passed out. Long scene.

•• 0:42—Full frontal nudity in bathtub while Nino peeks in over the door.
•• 1:04—In lingerie, then topless and buns, undressing sexily in front of Nino.
•• 1:16—Left breast, sticking out of nightgown so Nino can suck on it.
••• 1:19—Topless and buns making love in bed with Laszlo.
•• 1:21—Topless and buns getting up and cleaning herself.
•• 1:28—Topless sitting in bed talking to Nino.
••• 1:30—Nude, getting on top of Nino in bed.

Key Exchange (1985)

Brooke Adams . . . . Lisa
0:10—Nude on bicycle with her boyfriend, but you can't see anything because of his strategically placed arms.
• 0:45—Very brief right breast getting into the shower with her boyfriend, then hard to see behind the shower curtain.

Kerry Armstrong . . . . The Beauty
Sandra Beall . . . . Marcy
••• 1:14—Topless on bed taking off her clothes and talking to Daniel Stern.

Terri Garber . . . . Amy
Daniel Stern . . . . Michael

Kidnapped (1986)

Barbara Crampton . . . . Bonnie
0:35—In white bra and panties in hotel room.
••• 0:37—Topless getting tormented by a bad guy in bed.
•• 1:12—Topless opening her pajamas for David Naughton.
•• 1:14—Topless in white panties getting dressed.

Kim Evenson . . . . Debbie
• 0:25—Right breast in bed talking on the phone. Long shot, hard to see.
0:30—In blue nightgown in room.
••• 1:28—Topless getting her arm prepared for a drug injection. Long scene.
••• 1:30—Topless acting in a movie. Long shot, then close up. Wearing a G-string.

David Naughton . . . . Vince McCarthy

Kill Crazy (1989)

Danielle Brisebois . . . . Libby
•• 0:39—Topless taking off top to go skinny dipping with Rachel.

Rachelle Carson . . . . Rachel
•• 0:39—Topless taking off top to go skinny dipping with Libby.
• 0:46—Very brief right breast, while lying on ground with a bad guy while getting raped. Buns, getting turned over before being shot.

The Killer Inside Me (1975)

Pepe Serna . . . . Johnny Lopez
• 0:15—Brief upper half of buns, twice, getting strip searched at police station.

•• 0:16—Very, very brief frontal nudity getting restrained by policemen.

Susan Tyrrell . . . . Joyce Lakeland
•• 1:27—Very brief left breast, then very brief topless (both breasts!) in bed with Stacy Keach during flashback scene.

Killer Workout (1987)
a.k.a. Aerobi-Cide

Marcia Karr . . . . .Rhonda
    1:03—Topless, opening her jacket to show the policeman her scars. Unappealing.
    1:12—Topless in locker room, killing a guy. Covered with the special effects scars.

Teresa Vander Woude . . . . Jaimy
•• 0:43—Topless in locker room with Tommy during his nightmare.

Killing Cars (1986)
Senta Berger . . . . Marie
Jürgen Prochnow . . . . Ralph Korda
• 0:48—Buns, while getting up from bed to look at cigarette lighter. Slightly out of focus. Don't see his face well.

Killing Heat (1981)
Karen Black . . . . Mary Turner
•• 0:41—Full frontal nudity giving herself a shower in the bedroom.

The Killing Kind (1973)
Sue Bernard . . . . Tina
• 0:00—Topless during gang rape.
• 0:19—Topless again during flashback.
• 1:12—Brief topless again several times during flashbacks.

John Savage . . . . Terry Lambert
• 0:00—Upper half of buns when other guys pull his shorts down during rape of girl.
•• 0:58—Buns while in shower when Mrs. Lambert opens the curtains to take a picture.

The Killing of Sister George (1968)
Susannah York . . . . Alice McNaught
    0:19—Topless under sheer blue nightgown.
    0:59—In black bra and panties.
    1:45—In black bra and panties getting undressed.
•• 2:07—(0:09 into tape 2) Topless lying in bed with another woman.

Killing Streets (1991)
Michael Paré . . . . Chris/Craig Brandt
Jennifer Runyon . . . . Sandra Ross
• 1:00—In white lingerie then brief topless taking off lingerie in bed with Michael Paré. Hard to see.

King David (1985)
Richard Gere . . . . David
Alice Krige . . . . .Bathsheba
•• 1:16—Full frontal nudity getting a bath outside at dusk while Richard Gere watches.

Cherie Lunghi . . . . .Michal
•• 0:28—Topless lying in bed with Richard Gere. (Her hair is in the way a little bit.)

King Kong Lives! (1986)
Linda Hamilton . . . . Amy Franklin
• 0:47—Very, very brief right breast getting out of sleeping bag after camping out near King Kong.

Brian Kerwin . . . . Hank Mitchell

King of Marvin Gardens (1972)
Ellen Burstyn . . . . .Sally
• 0:50—Brief topless, while kneeling on the floor and turning around to shoot squirt guns.

Bruce Dern . . . . Jason Staebler
Jack Nicholson .David Staebler

King of New York (1990)
Ariane . . . . .Dinner Guest
Vanessa Angel . . . . British Female
Paul Calderon . . . . .Joey Dalesio
Janet Julian . . . . Jennifer
• 0:26—Very brief left breast, standing in subway car kissing Christopher Walken. Don't see her face.

Phoebe Légerè . . . . Bordello Woman

King of the Gypsies (1978)
Danielle Brisebois . . . . .Young Tita
Annette O'Toole . . . . .Sharon
Annie Potts . . . . Persa
Eric Roberts . . . . Dave
Susan Sarandon . . . . Rose
• 0:49—Brief right breast during fight with Judd Hirsch.

Brooke Shields . . . . Tita

King of the Kickboxers (1990)
Sherrie Rose . . . . .Molly
• 1:05—Very brief buns in G-string and partial side of left breast, while getting into tub with Jake.

The Kiss (1988)
Céline Lomez . . . . Aunt Irene
Joanna Pacula . . . . .Felice
•• 0:49—Side view topless making love with a guy. Intercut with Meredith Salenger seeing a model of a body spurt blood.
• 0:57—Topless covered with body paint doing a ceremony in a hotel room.
•• 1:24—Brief right breast, while making love with a guy on bed while Salenger is asleep in the other room.

A Kiss Before Dying (1991)
Lia Chang . . . . .Shoe Saleslady
Joie Lee . . . . Cathy
Billie Neal . . . . Nurse
James Russo . . . . Dan Corelli
Sean Young . . . . Ellen/Dorothy Carlsson
•• 0:31—Brief topless making love in bed with Matt Dillon. Kind of dark.

- 0:35—Brief side view or right breast in shower with Dillon. Don't see her face.
  1:11—Very brief partial left breast in gaping pajama top when she leans over to turn off the light.

Kiss of the Beast
See: Meridian.

The Kitchen Toto (1987; British)
Edwin Mahinda........................ Mwangi
- 0:24—Nude, getting a bath outside.

Klute (1971)
Rosalind Cash .... Pat
Jane Fonda .... Bree Daniel
- 0:27—Side view of left and right breasts stripping in the old man's office.
Donald Sutherland ....John Klute
Dorothy Tristan .... Arlyn Page

Knightriders (1981)
Ed Harris............................. Billy Davis
- 0:01—Buns, while kneeling in the woods. Long shot, hard to see.
- 1:51—Upper half of buns, while standing in a pond doing something with a stick.
Amy Ingersoll ....Linet
- 0:00—Very brief left breast, while lying down, then sitting up in woods next to Ed Harris.
Patricia Tallman........................... Julie
- 0:46—Brief topless in the bushes in moonlight talking to her boyfriend while a truck driver watches.

Kramer vs. Kramer (1979)
Jane Alexander .... Margaret Phelps
Iris Alhanti................................n.a.
George Coe .... Jim O'Connor
Dustin Hoffman......................Ted Kramer
Meryl Streep.................... Joanna Kramer
JoBeth Williams .... Phyllis Bernard
- 0:45—Buns and brief topless in the hallway meeting Dustin Hoffman's son.

L'Annee Des Meduses (1987; French)
Caroline Cellier .... Claude, Chris' Mother
- •• 0:02—Topless taking off top at the beach.
- •• 0:56—Topless on boat at night with Romain.
- •• 1:06—Topless on the beach with Valerie Kaprisky.
- • 1:14—Left breast, lying on beach with Romain at night.
Valerie Kaprisky...........................Chris
- •• 0:06—Topless pulling down swimsuit at the beach.
- ••• 0:24—Full frontal nudity while taking off dress with older man.
- ••• 0:42—Topless walking around the beach talking to everybody.
- •• 0:46—Topless on the beach taking a shower.
- ••• 1:02—Topless on the beach with her mom.
- ••• 1:37—Nude dancing on the boat for Romain.
- •• 1:42—Topless walking from the beach to the bar.
- •• 1:43—Topless in swimming pool.

L.A. Bounty (1989)
Sybil Danning .... Ruger
Wings Hauser....................... Cavanaugh
Lenore Kasdorf..................... Kelly Rhodes
Maxine Wasa .... Model
- 0:07—Right breast while posing for Wings Hauser while he paints. Left breast, getting up. Long shot.
- 0:26—Left breast while posing on couch for Hauser.
- •• 0:38—Topless lying on couch again.

L.A. Story (1991)
Iman .... Cynthia
Cheryl Baker............... Changing Room Woman
- 0:18—Brief topless in dressing room, when Steve Martin sees her.
Frances Fisher............................June
Richard E. Grant.........................Roland
Marilu Henner .... Trudi
Victoria Tennant.......................... Sara

La Bamba (1987)
Elizabeth Peña .... Rosie Morales
- 0:06—Brief side view of right breast taking a shower outside when two young boys watch her from a water tower. Long shot, hard to see.

La Cicala (The Cricket) (1983)
Barbara De Rossi ....Saveria
- •• 0:39—Nude swimming under waterfall with Clio Goldsmith.
- •• 0:43—Topless undressing in room with Goldsmith.
- • 0:57—Brief right breast changing into dress in room.
- • 1:05—In wet white lingerie in waterfall with a guy, then in a wet dress.
  1:26—Very brief buns in bed with Anthony Franciosa.
- •• 1:28—Topless in bathroom with Franciosa.
- • 1:36—Brief right breast making love with trucker.
Clio Goldsmith......................... Cicala
- •• 0:26—Nude when Wilma brings her in to get Anthony Franciosa excited again.
- •• 0:39—Nude swimming under waterfall with Barbara de Rossi.
- ••• 0:43—Full frontal nudity undressing in room with de Rossi.

La Lectrice (1989; French)
a.k.a. The Reader
Miou-Miou.................... Constance/Marie
  1:06—Making love with a guy while reading to him in bed.
- • 1:18—Full frontal nudity lying in bed. Close-up pan shot from lower frontal nudity, then left breast, then right breast.
- • 1:20—Very brief right breast, then lower frontal nudity getting dressed.
Maria De Medeiros................... Silent Nurse

The Lacemaker (1977; French)
Yves Beneyton. . . . . François
- 0:57—Buns, while walking to bed. Dark.

Isabelle Huppert . . . . Beatrice
- 0:50—Briefly nude while getting into bed.
- 0:57—Topless under shawl, then nude while getting into bed.
- •• 0:58—Topless, lying in bed.
- 1:04—Nude, in her apartment.
- ••• 1:22—Nude, in her apartment with François.

Lady Avenger (1991)
Michelle Bauer . . . . Annalee
- ••• 0:30—Topless, making love in bed on top of J.C.
- 0:52—Topless, making love in bed on top of Ray.

Billy Frank . . . . .Arnie
Peggy Sands . . . . .Maggie
- ••• 0:18—Topless in bed with Kevin.

Lady Beware (1987)
Diane Lane . . . . Katya Yarno
  0:10—Walking around in her apartment in a red silk teddy getting ready for bed.
  0:14—Lying down in white semi-transparent pajamas after fantasizing.
  0:24—In black bra in apartment.
- ••• 0:46—Topless in her apartment and in bed making love with Mack.
- •• 0:52—Brief topless during Jack's flashback when he is in the store.
- •• 0:59—Brief side view topless in bed with Mack again during another of Jack's flashbacks.
  1:02—Very brief topless in bed with Mack.
  1:06—Brief topless lying in bed behind thin curtain in another of Jack's flashbacks.

Michael Woods. . . . . Jack Price
- •• 0:43—Buns, while lying down in Diane Lane's bed.

Lady Chatterley's Lover (1981; French/British)
Nicholas Clay . . . . .Oliver Mellors (The Gardener)
- ••• 0:21—Nude, washing himself while Sylvia Kristel watches from the trees.

Sylvia Kristel . . . . Constance Chatterley
- •• 0:25—Nude in front of mirror.
- 0:59—Brief topless with the Gardener.
- 1:04—Brief topless.
- ••• 1:16—Nude in bedroom with the Gardener.

Lady Cocoa (1974)
Lola Falana . . . . Coco
- 0:45—Left breast lying on bed, pulling up yellow towel. Long shot, hard to see.
- ••• 1:23—Topless on boat with a guy.

The Lady in Red (1979)
Christopher Lloyd . . . . Frognose
Pamela Sue Martin . . . . Polly Franklin
- 0:07—Right breast, while in bedroom with a guy clutching her clothes.
- ••• 0:20—Topless in jail with a group of women prisoners waiting to be examined by a nurse.

Francesca "Kitten" Natividad . . . . .Uncredited Partygoer
- 0:39—Brief topless outside during party.

Mary Woronov. . . . . .Woman Bankrobber

Lady Jane (1987; British)
Helena Bonham-Carter. . . . . Lady Jane Grey
- 1:19—Topless kneeling on the bed with Guilford.
- 2:09—Side view of right breast and very, very brief topless sitting by fire with Guilford.

Cary Elwes . . . . .Guilford Dudley
- 1:19—Brief buns, while getting out of bed.

Sara Kestelman. Frances Grey

Lady on the Bus (1978; Brazilian)
Sonia Braga . . . . n.a.
- 0:11—Brief left breast.
- ••• 0:12—Topless, then buns, then full frontal nudity in bed getting her slip torn off by her newlywed husband. Long struggle scene.
- •• 0:39—Right breast standing with half open dress, then topless lying in bed, then getting into the pool.
- ••• 0:48—Topless and buns on the beach after picking up a guy on the bus.
- 0:54—Brief topless in bed dreaming.
- 1:02—Brief topless in waterfall with bus driver.
- •• 1:05—Topless in cemetery after picking up another guy on the bus.
- 1:13—Topless on the ground with another guy from a bus.
- 1:16—Left breast sitting on sofa while her husband talks.

Laguna Heat (1987; Made for Cable Movie)
Harry Hamlin . . . . .Tom Shephard
- 0:50—Buns, while walking into the ocean with Catherine Hicks.

Catherine Hicks . . . . Jane Algernon
- •• 0:50—Topless and buns, running around the beach with Harry Hamlin.
- •• 1:05—Brief topless in bed making love with Harry Hamlin, having her head hit the headboard.

Rip Torn. . . . . n.a.

The Lair of the White Worm (1988; British)
Sammi Davis-Voss . . . . Mary Trent
Amanda Donohoe . . . . Lady Sylvia Marsh
- 0:52—Nude, opening a tanning table and turning over.
- 0:57—Brief left breast licking the blood off a phallic-looking thing.
- 1:19—Brief topless jumping out to attack Angus, then walking around her underground lair (her body is painted for the rest of the film).
- 1:22—Topless walking up steps with a large phallic thing strapped to her body.

Linzi Drew . . . . Maid/Nun
Tina Shaw . . . . Maid/Nun

Lassiter (1984)

Lauren Hutton. . . . . Kari Von Fursten
- • 0:18—Brief topless over-the-shoulder shot making love with a guy on the bed just before killing him.

Belinda Mayne . . . . .Helen Boardman
- ••• 0:06—In bra then topless letting Tom Selleck undress her while her husband is in the other room.

Tom Selleck. . . . . Lassiter
- • 1:00—Buns, while getting out of bed after making love with Lauren Hutton.

Jane Seymour . . . . Sara
- • 0:10—Buns and brief side view of right breast lying on stomach on bed with Tom Selleck.

Jane Wood . . . . Mary Becker

The Last American Virgin (1982)

Steve Antin . . . . Rick
Diane Franklin. . . . . Karen
- ••• 1:06—Topless in room above the bleachers with Jason.
- •• 1:17—Topless and almost lower frontal nudity taking off her panties in the clinic.

Louisa Moritz . . . . Carmela
- ••• 0:42—Topless and buns in her bedroom with Rick.

Brian Peck. . . . . Victor
- • 0:20—Buns, during penis measurement in boy's locker room. Don't see his face.

Tessa Richarde. . . . . Brenda
- •• 0:15—Brief topless walking into the living room when Gary's parents come home.

Kimmy Robertson . . . . Rose
Joe Rubbo. . . . . David
- • 0:45—Buns, in bed making love with Carmilla while his buddies watch through the key hole.

Last Call (1990)

Crisstyn Dante. . . . . Hooker
William Katt . . . . .Paul Avery
- ••• 0:29—Buns, while on floor with Shannon Tweed.
- • 0:41—Brief buns, while getting up from bed and putting his pants on.
- • 1:02—Brief buns, while in bed with Tweed.

Stella Stevens . . . . .Betty
- 0:52—Very brief left nipple popping out of black lingerie top while making love with Jason on a pool table.

Shannon Tweed . . . . Cindy/Audrey
- • 0:12—In black body stocking, dancing on stage. Topless and buns in G-string underneath.
- •• 0:29—Right breast, on the floor with William Katt.
- •• 0:39—Brief buns, rotating in chair with Katt. Topless leaning against column.
- • 0:40—Topless on stair railing.
- • 1:01—Left breast, while leaning against column and kissing Katt.
- • 1:02—Left breast in bed with Katt.
- ••• 1:05—Topless making love on roof with Katt.

The Last Detail (1973)

Nancy Allen . . . . Nancy
Carol Kane . . . . Young Whore
- • 1:02—Brief topless sitting on bed talking with Randy Quaid. Her hair is in the way, hard to see.

Michael Moriarty . . . . .Marine Duty Officer
Jack Nicholson . . . . .Buddusky
Randy Quaid . . . . .Meadows

The Last Embrace (1979)

Janet Margolin . . . . .Ellie "Eva" Fabian
- • 1:10—Brief topless in bathtub with Bernie, before strangling him.
- •• 1:14—Right breast, while reaching for the phone in bed with Roy Scheider.
- • 1:20—Left breast in photo that Scheider is looking at with a magnifying glass (it's supposed to be her grandmother).
- 1:22—Almost topless in the shower talking to Scheider.

Mandy Patinkin . . . . .Commuter

The Last Emperor (1987)

Joan Chen . . . . Wan Jung
Jade Go . . . . Ar Mo
- • 0:10—Right breast in open top after breast feeding the young Pu Yi.
- • 0:20—Right breast in open top telling Pu Yi a story.
- • 0:29—Right breast in open top breast feeding an older Pu Yi. Long shot.

Last Exit to Brooklyn (1990)

Maia Danziger . . . . .Mary Black
- 0:10—Out of focus buns and right breast taking off her slip.
- • 0:12—Very brief topless making love with Harry. Topless after.

Jennifer Jason Leigh .Tralata
- •• 1:28—Topless, opening her blouse in bar after getting drunk.
- • 1:33—Topless getting drug out of car, placed on mattress, then basically raped by a long line of guys. Long, painful-to-watch scene.
- • 1:35—Topless lying on mattress when Spook comes to save her.

The Last Hour (1990)

a.k.a. Concrete War

Raye Hollitt . . . . Adler
Michael Paré . . . . .Jeff
Robert Pucci. . . . . Eric
- • 0:05—Brief buns, while making love in bed with Shannon Tweed.

Shannon Tweed. .Susan
- •• 0:05—Topless in bed, making love with Eric.
- • 0:07—Brief buns and side of left breast, in the shower.

The Last Innocent Man
(1987; Made for Cable Movie)

Ed Harris . . . . n.a.

Roxanne Hart . . . . .n.a.
  ••• 1:06—Topless in bed making love, then sitting up
    and arguing with Ed Harris in his apartment.

The Last Married Couple in America *(1980)*
Priscilla Barnes. . . . . Helena Dryden
Richard Benjamin . . . . Marv Cooper
Sondra Currie . . . . Lainy
  •• 1:32—Topless taking off her clothes in bedroom in
    front of Natalie Wood, George Segal and her hus-
    band.
Catherine Hickland . . . . Rebecca

The Last Picture Show *(1971)*
Sam Bottoms . . . . Billy
  • 0:41—Brief buns, after falling out of car with Jimmy
    Sue.
Timothy Bottoms . . . . Sonny Crawford
Eileen Brennan . . . . .Genevieve
Jeff Bridges . . . . Duane Jackson
Gary Brockette . . . . Bobby Sheen
  • 0:36—Upper frontal nudity and buns, while getting
    out of pool and greeting Randy Quaid and Cybill
    Shepherd. More buns, getting back into the pool.
Ellen Burstyn. . . . . .Lois Farrow
Kimberly Hyde . . . . Annie-Annie Martin
  •• 0:36—Full frontal nudity, getting out of pool to
    meet Randy Quaid and Cybill Shepherd.
  • 0:37—Topless several times, sitting at edge of pool
    with Bobby.
  • 0:38—More topless, sitting on edge of pool in back-
    ground.
Randy Quaid. . . . . .Lester Marlow
  • 0:38—Very brief frontal nudity jumping into pool af-
    ter Cybill Shepherd jumps in.
Cybill Shepherd. . . . . .Jacy Farrow
  •• 0:37—Undressing on diving board. Very brief left
    breast falling onto diving board. Brief topless tossing
    bra aside.
  • 0:38—Brief left breast jumping into the water.
  ••• 1:05—Topless and buns in motel room with Jeff
    Bridges.
Sharon Taggart. . . . . Charlene Duggs
  •• 0:11—In bra, then topless making out in truck with
    Timothy Bottoms.

Last Resort *(1985)*
Brenda Bakke . . . . Veroneeka
  •• 0:36—Topless in the woods with Charles Grodin.
William Bumiller . . . . .Etienne
Brett Clark. . . . . Manuello
Steve Levitt . . . . Pierre

Last Rites *(1988)*
Tom Berenger. . . . . Michael
Robert Corbo . . . . .Gino
  • 0:03—Buns and frontal nudity in a room with
    Daphne Zuniga just before getting caught by anoth-
    er woman and shot.
Anne Twomey. . . . . .Zena Pace

Daphne Zuniga . . . . .Angela
  • 0:04—Very brief topless running into the bathroom
    to escape from being shot. Covered with blood,
    don't see her face. Very brief right breast reaching
    for a bathrobe. Don't really see anything.
  0:40—Buns, behind a shower door.
  0:50—Buns, getting out of bed and standing in front
    of Tom Berenger.

Last Summer *(1969)*
Catherine Burns . . . . Rhoda
  • 1:31—Very brief topless struggling with Stacy, Peter
    and Dan. Long shot.
Barbara Hershey. . . . . Sandy
  • 0:19—Topless after taking off her swimsuit top on
    sailboat with Richard Thomas. Hair is in the way.
  • 1:30—Very brief right breast, after taking off her top
    in the woods.

Last Tango In Paris *(1972)*
(X-rated, letterbox version.)
Marlon Brando. . . . . .Paul
  • 1:59—Brief buns, while pulling his pants down to
    moon a woman at a dance.
Maria Schneider. . . . . .Jeanne
  • 0:15—Lower frontal nudity and very brief buns, roll-
    ing on the floor.
  • 0:44—Topless in jeans, walking around apartment.
  •• 0:53—Left breast, while lying down, then walking to
    Marlon Brando, then topless.
  ••• 0:55—Topless, kneeling while talking to Brando.
  • 0:56—Side of left breast.
  • 0:57—Topless, rolling off the bed, onto the floor.
  •• 1:01—Right breast, in bathroom. Topless in mirror.
  • 1:03—Brief topless in bathroom with Brando while
    she puts on makeup.
  ••• 1:04—Nude, in bathroom with Brando, then sitting
    on counter.
  • 1:27—Brief lower frontal nudity, pulling up her dress
    in elevator.
  • 1:30—Topless in bathtub with Brando.
  ••• 1:32—Nude, standing up in bathtub while Brando
    washes her. More topless, getting out. Long scene.

The Last Temptation of Christ *(1988)*
David Bowie. . . . . .Pontius Pilate
Willem Dafoe . . . . Jesus Christ
  • 1:56—Buns, getting beaten and whipped.
  • 1:57—Buns, while getting crown of thorns placed
    on his head.
  2:02—Side view of buns, while hanging on cross.
Leo Damian . . . . Person in Crowd
Andre Gregory. . . . . .John the Baptist
Barbara Hershey. . . . . Mary Magdelene
  • 0:16—Brief buns behind curtain. Brief right breast
    making love, then brief topless.
  0:17—Buns, while sleeping.
  •• 0:20—Topless, tempting Jesus.
  • 2:12—Brief tip of left breast, lying on ground.
  • 2:13—Left breast while caressing her pregnant belly.
Harvey Keitel . . . . Judas

The Last Warrior (1989)
Gary Graham . . . . Gibb
- 0:07—Brief buns, while taking off his towel when he sees a ship.

Maria Holvöe . . . . Katherine
- 1:24—Right breast, after the Japanese warrior removes her dress.

The Last Winter (1983; Israeli)
Yona Elian . . . . Maya
- 0:48—Topless taking off her robe to get into pool.
  0:49—Buns, lying on marble slab with Kathleen Quinlan.

Kathleen Quinlan . . . . Joyce
- 0:48—Brief side view of left breast taking off her robe and diving into pool Very brief buns.
  0:49—Buns, lying on marble slab, talking with Maya.
  0:50—Very brief right breast sitting up. Long shot, hard to see.

Laura (1979)
a.k.a. Shattered Innocence
Maud Adams . . . . Sarah
Dawn Dunlap . . . . Laura
- 0:20—Brief side view of left breast and buns talking to Maud Adams, then brief side view of right breast putting on robe.
- 0:23—Nude, dancing while being photographed.
- 1:15—Nude, letting Paul feel her so he can sculpt her, then making love with him.
  1:22—Buns, putting on panties talking to Maud Adams.

Maureen Kerwin . . . . Martine
- 0:03—Brief full frontal nudity getting out of bed and putting white bathrobe on.

The Lawnmower Man (1992)
Pierce Brosnan . . . . Lawrence Angelo
Jeff Fahey . . . . Jobe Smith
Jenny Wright . . . . Marnie Burke
- 1:04—Brief right breast, while in bed with Jeff Fahey.

Left for Dead (1978)
Cindy Girling . . . . Pauline Corte
- 0:19—Nude, taking off shirt in bedroom.

Elke Sommer . . . . Magdalene Krushcen
- 0:38—Left breast, while posing for photographer.
- 0:39—Very brief left breast in B&W photo.
  0:58—Buns and topless when police officers lift her up to put plastic under her. Covered with blood, can't see her face.
- 1:09—Very brief left breast in B&W photo.

Legal Tender (1991)
Wendy MacDonald . . . . Verna Wheeler
  0:22—Brief buns in lingerie in Morton Downey Jr.'s office. Don't see her face.
- 1:20—Long shot of buns and side of left breast taking off robe in front of Downey. Topless on bed with him.

Jacqueline Palmer . . . . Mal's Girl
- 0:24—Topless in bubble bath with blonde girl and Morton Downey Jr.
- 0:31—Topless outside by the swimming pool.

Tanya Roberts . . . . Rikki Rennick
- 0:41—Buns and topless making love with Robert Davi. Don't see her face.

Shannon Wilsey . . . . Mal's Girl
- 0:24—Topless in bubble bath with brunette girl and Morton Downey Jr.
- 0:31—Topless and buns in G-string bringing phone to Downey.

The Legend of Hell House (1973; British)
Pamela Franklin . . . . Florence Tanner
- 1:03—Topless silhouette taking off nightgown and getting into bed.

Lenny (1974)
Dustin Hoffman . . . . Lenny Bruce
Valerie Perrine . . . . Honey Bruce
  0:04—Doing a strip tease on stage down to pasties and buns in a G-string. No nudity, but still nice.
- 0:14—Topless in bed when Dustin Hoffman pulls the sheet off her then makes love.
- 0:17—Topless sitting on the floor in a room full of flowers when Hoffman comes in.
  0:24—Left breast wearing pastie doing dance in flashback.
- 0:43—Right breast with Kathryn Witt.

Kathryn Witt . . . . Girl
- 0:43—Right breast with Valerie Perrine while Dustin Hoffman watches.

Less than Zero (1987)
Robert Downey, Jr. . . . . Julian
  1:22—Very brief blurry buns in bedroom with another guy when Andrew McCarthy discovers them.

Jami Gertz . . . . Blair
Andrew McCarthy . . . . Clay
- 0:03—Very brief buns when getting out of bed to answer the phone.

James Spader . . . . Rip
John Yurasek . . . . Naked Man
- 1:22—Brief buns while standing up when Andrew McCarthy discovers him with Robert Downey, Jr.

Lethal Obsession (1987)
a.k.a. The Joker
Tahnee Welch . . . . Daniela Santini
  0:14—Buns, putting on robe after talking to John on the phone.
- 0:15—Half of left breast, taking off coat to hug John in the kitchen.
  0:16—Sort of left breast, in bed with John. Too dark to see anything.
  1:16—Buns, getting an injection.

Lethal Persuit (1989)
Blake Bahner . . . . Warren

Mitzi Kapture . . . . Debra J.
•• 0:32—Topless in motel shower, then getting out. (You can see the top of her swimsuit bottom.)
0:47—In wet tank top talking with Warren.

Lethal Weapon (1987)
Cheryl Baker . . . . Girl in Shower #1
Terri Lynn Doss . . . . Girl in Shower #2
Mel Gibson . . . . Martin Riggs
••• 0:06—Buns, while getting out of bed and walking to the refrigerator.
Ed O'Ross . . . . Mendez
Jackie Swanson . . . . Amanda Huntsacker
•• 0:01—Brief topless standing on balcony rail getting ready to jump.

Lethal Weapon 2 (1989)
Mel Gibson . . . . Martin Riggs
Patsy Kensit . . . . Rika Van Den Haas
•• 1:15—Right breast lying in bed with Mel Gibson.
•• 1:19—Topless in bed with Gibson.

Lethal Woman (1988)
Robert Lipton . . . . Major Derek Johnson
• 1:02—Very brief frontal nudity in the ocean with Shannon Tweed, when the water goes down.
• 1:05—Brief buns while in the water on the beach with Tweed.
Adrienne Pearce . . . . Trudy
Shannon Tweed . . . . Tory
••• 1:01—Topless at the beach with Derek. Brief buns in white bikini bottom.
Merete Van Kamp . . . . Diana/Christine
• 1:23—Very brief side view of left breast, reaching for towel after bath. Hard to see.

Letter to Brezhnev (1986; British)
Peter Firth . . . . Peter
Alexandra Pigg . . . . Elaine
•• 0:57—Brief topless in bed with a guy.

Letters to an Unknown Lover (1985)
Andrea Ferréol . . . . Julia
Cherie Lunghi . . . . Helene
0:40—In white slip in her bedroom.
Mathilda May . . . . Agnes
• 0:43—Upper half of breasts in bathtub when Gervais opens the door.
••• 0:58—Buns and topless taking off her robe in Gervais' room.

Liebestraum (1991)
(Unrated Director's cut reviewed.)
Pamela Gidley . . . . Jane Kessler
0:37—Caressing her right breast during dream. Don't see anything.
• 1:07—Buns, while taking a shower. Almost topless, but her arm gets in the way.
Catherine Hicks . . . . Mary Parker

Lies (1984; British)
Miriam Byrd-Nethery . . . . n.a.

Ann Dusenberry . . . . Robyn Wallace
•• 0:10—Topless opening the shower curtain in front of her boyfriend.
• 0:11—Right breast while kissing her boyfriend.

Life is Sweet (1991; British)
Jane Horrocks . . . . Nicola
• 0:50—Topless in bed with her boyfriend. Hard to see because she has chocolate all over her chest.

Lifeforce (1985)
Peter Firth . . . . Caine
Emma Jacobs . . . . Crew Member
Mathilda May . . . . Space Girl
• 0:08—Full frontal nudity in glass case upside down.
• 0:13—Topless, lying down in space shuttle. Blue light.
••• 0:16—Topless sitting up in lab to suck the life out of military guard. Brief full frontal nudity.
•• 0:17—Topless again in the lab.
•• 0:19—Topless walking around, then buns.
••• 0:20—Topless walking down the stairs. Brief nude fighting with the guards.
•• 0:44—Topless with Steve Railsback in red light during his nightmare.
• 1:10—Brief topless in space shuttle with Railsback.
Steve Railsback . . . . Carlsen
• 1:26—Buns, while standing with Mathilda May after he stabs her with the sword. Surrounded by special effects.

Lifeguard (1975)
Anne Archer . . . . Cathy
• 1:04—Very brief nipple while kissing Sam Elliott. Need to crank the brightness on your TV to the maximum. It appears in the lower right corner of the screen as the camera pans from right to left.
Sharon Clark . . . . Tina
• 0:07—Brief side view of right breast undressing and getting into the shower.
• 0:08—Buns and brief topless wrestling with Sam Elliott on the bed.
Kathleen Quinlan . . . . Wendy
Parker Stevenson . . . . Chris

Link (1986)
Elisabeth Shue . . . . Jane Chase
• 0:50—Brief right breast and buns, side view of a body double, standing in bathroom getting ready to take a bath while Link watches.

Lionheart (1990)
Jean-Claude Van Damme . . . . Lyon
••• 0:47—Buns, while putting on robe after getting out of bed.

Lipstick (1976)
Margaux Hemingway . . . . Chris McCormick
•• 0:10—Brief topless opening the shower door to answer the telephone.
•• 0:19—Brief topless during rape attempt, including close-up of side view of left breast.

0:24—Buns, lying on bed while rapist runs a knife up her leg and back while she's tied to the bed.
•• 0:25—Brief topless getting out of bed.
Mariel Hemingway . . . . .Kathy McCormick
Perry King . . . . Steve Edison
Chris Sarandon . . . . Gordon Stuart
•• 0:50—Buns, while standing in his studio talking to Margaux Hemingway on the telephone.

Listen to Me (1989)
Christopher Atkins. . . . . Bruce Arlington
Jami Gertz. . . . . Monica Tomanski
Christopher Rydell. . . . . Tom Lloynd
Annette Sinclair. . . . . .Fountain Girl
Yeardley Smith . . . . Cootz
Nancy Valen . . . . .Mia
• 0:06—Very, very brief left breast in bed with Garson when Kirk Cameron first meets him.

Lisztomania (1975; British)
Nell Campbell. . . . . .Olga
••• 1:04—Topless in bed several times with Roger Daltrey when Ringo Starr comes in.
•• 1:06—Topless in bed, sitting up and drinking.
••• 1:07—More topless in bed with a gun after Starr leaves.
Roger Daltrey . . . . .Franz Liszt
• 0:01—Brief buns while standing on bed tying a sheet to make some pants. Dark, don't see his face.
Anulka Dziubinska. . . . . Lola Montez
•• 0:08—Topless sitting on Roger Daltrey's lap, kissing him. Nice close up.
• 0:21—Topless, backstage with Daltrey after the concert.
• 0:39—Topless, wearing pasties, during Daltrey's nightmare/song and dance number.
Sara Kestelman . . . . Princess Carolyn
Fiona Lewis . . . . .Countess Marie
•• 0:00—Topless in bed getting breasts kissed by Roger Daltrey to the beat of a metronome.
• 0:01—Brief topless swinging a chandelier to Daltrey.
•• 0:03—Brief topless and buns while running from chair (long shot). Brief topless when catching a candle on the bed.
•• 0:04—Brief left breast when her dress top is cut down. Left breast, sitting inside a piano with Daltrey.

Little Darlings (1980)
Krista Errickson . . . . Cinder
Kristy McNichol. . . . . Angel
Tatum O'Neal . . . . Ferris
• 0:35—Very, very brief half of left nipple, sticking out of swimsuit top when she comes up for air after falling into the pool to get Armand Assante's attention.

The Little Drummer Girl (1984)
Sam Frey. . . . . Khalil
Diane Keaton . . . . Charlie
Klaus Kinski . . . . Kurtz

Moti Shirin. . . . . .Michel
•• 1:07—Nude, in a prison cell when Diane Keaton looks at his scars.

Little Nikita (1988)
Loretta Devine . . . . Verna McLaughlin
• 1:03—Very brief left breast in bed after Sidney Poitier jumps out of bed when River Phoenix bursts into their bedroom.

The Little Thief (1989; French)
a.k.a. La Petite Voleuse
Nathalie Cardone. . . . . .Mauricette
•• 1:19—Topless in convent arguing with a nun, then getting a shot.
Simon De La Brosse . . . . .Raoul
• 1:07—Very brief buns and frontal nudity while jumping into bed (seen in mirror).
Charlotte Gainsbourg. . . . . .Janine Castang
•• 0:41—Topless twice, taking off blouse in bedroom with Michel.

Little Vera (1988; U.S.S.R.)
Natalya Negoda. . . . . .Vera
0:15—Very brief topless and buns getting dressed. Dark, hard to see.
••• 0:50—Topless making love with Sergei.
•• 1:05—Topless taking off her dress in the kitchen.

Live Wire (1992)
Pierce Brosnan . . . . Danny O'Neill
•• 1:02—Brief buns in bed with Lisa Eilbacher.
Lisa Eilbacher . . . . Terry O'Neill
•• 1:01—Brief topless several times and partial buns, in bath tub and in bed with Pierce Brosnan.
Tracy Tweed . . . . Rolls Royce Girl
Nels Van Patten . . . . Racquetball Player

The Living Daylights (1987)
Maryam D'Abo. . . . . Kara Milovy
Virginia Hey . . . . Rubavitch (Colonel Pushkin's girlfriend)
• 1:10—Brief side view of left breast when James Bond uses her to distract bodyguard.
Catherine Rabett . . . . n.a.

Living to Die (1990)
Rebecca Barrington . . . . Married Woman
• 0:23—In red bra, blindfolded and tied to a lounge chair, then topless while getting photographed.
• 0:27—Topless in chair when Wings Hauser talks to her.
Darcy De Moss. . . . . .Maggie Sams
0:11—Taking off clothes to white bra, panties, garter belt and stockings in hotel room with a customer.
• 0:32—Buns, getting out of spa while Wings Hauser watches without her knowing.
0:33—Buns, in long shot when Hauser fantasizes about dancing with her.
••• 0:56—In black bra, then topless and buns making love with Hauser.
• 1:20—Topless in mirror taking off black top for the bad guy.

Wings Hauser . . . . Nick Carpenter
Wendy MacDonald . . . . Rookie Policewoman

Loaded Guns (1975)
Ursula Andress. . . . . Laura
  0:32—Buns, lying in bed with a guy.
 ••• 0:33—Topless and buns getting out of bed. Full
     frontal nudity in elevator.
 •• 0:40—Nude getting out of bed and putting dress
     on.
 ••• 0:48—Nude getting into bathtub, topless in tub,
     nude getting out and drying herself off.
     1:00—Buns while getting undressed and hopping in
     to bed.
 • 1:02—Brief side view of right breast while getting
     dressed.

Logan's Run (1976)
Jenny Agutter . . . . Jessica
 • 1:05—Very brief topless and buns changing into fur
     coat in ice cave with Michael York.
Farrah Fawcett . . . . Holly

The Lonely Guy (1983)
Lamya Derval . . . . One of "The Seven Deadly Sins"
Robyn Douglass . . . . Danielle
 • 0:05—Upper half of right breast in sheer nightgown
     in bed with Raoul while talking to Steve Martin.
     Great nightgown!
     0:33—In sheer beige negligee lying on couch talk-
     ing to Martin on the phone.
 • 1:03—Very, very brief peek at left nipple when she
     flashes it for Martin so he'll let her into his party.
Marie Laurin . . . . One of "The Seven Deadly Sins"
Julie Payne . . . . Rental Agent

Lonely Hearts (1983; Australian)
Wendy Hughes . . . . Patricia
 • 1:05—Brief topless getting out of bed and putting a
     dress on. Dark, hard to see.
Norman Kay . . . . Peter
 • 1:03—Buns, while getting out of bed. Very brief
     frontal nudity.
Kris McQuade . . . . Rosemarie

The Lonely Lady (1983)
Glory Annen . . . . Marion
 • 0:07—Brief left breast in back seat of car with Joe.
     Dark, hard to see.
Bibi Besch . . . . Veronica
Joseph Cali . . . . Vincent Dacosta
 • 1:05—Buns, while near pool table and walking
     around the house with Pia Zadora.
Carla Romanelli. . . . . Carla Maria Peroni
 •• 1:10—Brief topless taking off her top to make love
     with Pia Zadora while a guy watches.
Pia Zadora. . . . . JeniLee Randall
 • 0:12—Brief topless getting raped by Joe, after get-
     ting out of the pool.
 •• 0:22—Brief topless, then left breast, while making
     love with Walter.

 •• 0:28—Side view topless lying in bed with Walter.
 •• 0:44—Buns and side view of left breast taking a
     shower.
 • 0:46—Very brief right breast, in bed with George.
 •• 1:05—Left breast, then brief topless making love
     with Vinnie.

Looker (1981)
Donna Kei Benz . . . . Ellen
Randi Brooks . . . . Girl in Bikini
Pamela Jean Bryant. . . . . Reston Girl
Ashley Cox. . . . . Candy
Susan Dey . . . . Cindy
     0:28—In white one piece swimsuit shooting a com-
     mercial at the beach.
 • 0:36—Buns, then brief topless in computer imaging
     device. Topless in computer monitor.
Melissa Prophet . . . . Commercial Script Girl
Lori Sutton. . . . . Reston Girl
Leigh Taylor-Young . . . . Jennifer Long
Jeana Tomasina . . . . Suzy
Terri Welles . . . . Lisa
 • 0:02—Brief topless getting photographed for opera-
     tion. In black bra and panties in her apartment a lot.
Vanna White . . . . Reston Girl
Kathryn Witt. . . . . Tina Cassidy
     0:17—In beige lingerie undressing in her room.

Looking for Mr. Goodbar (1977)
Tom Berenger . . . . Gary
Richard Gere . . . . Tony
 •• 1:00—Buns, while on Diane Keaton's floor doing
     push-ups, then running around in his jock strap.
Caren Kaye. . . . . Rhoda
Diane Keaton . . . . Theresa
 •• 0:11—Right breast in bed making love with her
     teacher, Martin, then putting blouse on.
 • 0:31—Brief left breast over the shoulder when the
     Doctor playfully kisses her breast.
 •• 1:04—Brief topless smoking in bed in the morning,
     then more topless after Richard Gere leaves.
 ••• 1:17—Topless making love with Gere after doing a
     lot of cocaine.
 • 1:31—Brief topless in the bathtub when James
     brings her a glass of wine.
     2:00—Getting out of bed in a bra.
 •• 2:02—Topless during rape by Tom Berenger, before
     he kills her. Hard to see because of strobe lights.

Loose Shoes (1977)
Louisa Moritz. . . . . Margie
Misty Rowe . . . . Louise
Robin Sherwood. . . . . Biker Chic #2
Betty Thomas. . . . . Biker Chick #1
 • 0:02—Brief right breast dancing on the table during
     the *Skateboarders from Hell* sketch.
Susan Tyrrell. . . . . Boobies

Lost Angels (1989)
Frances Fisher . . . . Judith Loftis
Nina Siemaszko . . . . Merilee
- • 0:38—Brief topless and buns, running through courtyard. Long shot, don't really see anything.
- • 0:45—Buns, sitting at table outside, undressing and rubbing feces (yuck!) on herself.

Donald Sutherland . . . . Dr. Charles Loftis

The Lost Empire (1983)
Angela Aames . . . . Heather McClure
- ••• 0:31—Topless and buns taking a shower while Angel and White Star talk to her.

Deborah Blaisdell . . . . Girl Recruit
Raven De La Croix . . . . White Star
- ••• 1:05—Topless with a snake after being drugged by the bad guy.
- •• 1:07—Topless lying on a table.

Annie Gaybis . . . . n.a.
Angelique Pettijohn . . . . Whiplash
0:29—In a sexy, black leather outfit fighting in prison with Heather.

Linda Shayne . . . . Cindy Blake

Loulou (1980; French)
Gérard Depardieu . . . . Loulou
- • 0:07—Brief buns, while getting out of bed after it breaks. Dark.
- •• 0:36—Buns, while lying in bed with Isabelle Huppert.

Isabelle Huppert . . . . Nelly
- • 0:06—Very, very brief topless leaning over in bed.
- • 0:18—Brief topless getting out of bed.
- • 0:27—Brief topless turning over in bed.
- •• 0:36—Topless lying in bed talking on phone. Mostly right breast.
- • 0:40—Lower frontal nudity and buns taking off panties and getting into bed.
- •• 0:59—Left breast in bed with André, then topless taking him to the bathroom.

Guy Marchand . . . . André
- •• 0:59—Buns, while getting out of bed with Isabelle Huppert.

Love Child (1982)
Amy Madigan . . . . Terry Jean Moore
- • 0:08—Brief side view of right breast and buns taking a shower in jail while the guards watch.
- •• 0:53—Brief topless and buns, making love with Beau Bridges in a room at the women's prison.

Margaret Whitton . . . . Jacki Steinberg

Love Circles Around the World (1984)
Sophie Berger . . . . Dagmar
- ••• 0:38—Topless in women's restroom in casino making love with a guy in a tuxedo.
- ••• 0:43—Topless in steam room wearing a towel around her waist, then making love.

Josephine Jaqueline Jones . . . . Brigid
- •• 0:18—Topless, then nude running around her apartment chasing Jack.

- • 0:30—Topless, making love with Count Crispa in his hotel room.

John Sibbit . . . . Jack
- • 0:06—Very brief frontal nudity pulling his underwear down and getting into bed.
- •• 0:19—Buns, while trying to run away from Brigid after she yanks his underwear off.

Timothy Wood . . . . Michael
- •• 1:29—Frontal nudity, lying in bed with Jill after making love while video taping it.

Love Crimes (1991)
(Unrated version reviewed.)
Patrick Bergin . . . . David Hanover
- • 1:02—Buns, during love scene with Sean Young. Lit with red light, don't see his face.

Fern Dorsey . . . . Colleen Dells
- ••• 0:03—Topless, getting photographed by Patrick Bergin.

Arnetia Walker . . . . Maria Johnson
Sean Young . . . . Dana Greenway
- •• 0:20—Almost left breast, getting out of bathtub. Buns and partial lower frontal nudity, getting dressed.
- •• 0:55—Topless in open blouse, yelling at Patrick Bergin.
- • 0:57—Brief right breast, on bed in open blouse.
- ••• 0:59—Nude in bathtub.
- ••• 1:01—Topless, making love with Bergin. Lit with red light.
- ••• 1:03—Full frontal nudity, getting covered with a towel.
- • 1:08—Full frontal nudity, in Polaroid that Maria looks at.
- • 1:11—More full frontal nudity in Polaroid.
- 1:21—Partial right breast, while taking a shower.
- • 1:23—Brief topless in the shower.
- 1:25—Very brief right breast in gaping robe.
- • 1:27—Full frontal nudity in burning Polaroid.

A Love in Germany (1984; French/German)
Marie-Christine Barrault . . . . Maria Wyler
- • 0:23—Right breast, in bed with her lover when Pauline peeks from across the way.
- •• 0:28—Right breast in bedroom with Karl. Very brief lower frontal nudity getting back into bed. Long scene.
- ••• 0:43—Topless in bedroom with Karl. Subtitles get in the way! Long scene.

Gerard Desarthe . . . . Karl Wyler
- • 0:28—Buns, while lying in bed with Maria.

Hanna Schygulla . . . . Pauline Kropp

Love Letters (1984)
Jamie Lee Curtis . . . . Anna Winter
- ••• 0:31—Topless in bathtub reading a letter, then topless in bed making love with James Keach.
- • 0:36—Brief topless in lifeguard station with Keach.
- ••• 0:44—Brief topless admiring a picture taken of her by Keach.

••• 0:46—Topless and buns in bedroom undressing with Keach.
• 0:49—Topless in black and white Polaroid photographs that Keach is taking.
1:02—In white slip in her house with Keach.
• 1:07—Right breast, sticking out of slip, then right breast, while sleeping in bed with Keach.

Sally Kirkland. . . . . Hippie
Amy Madigan . . . . Wendy

Love Lust and Ecstasy
Ajita Wilson. . . . . Sara
•• 0:02—Nude taking a shower and getting into bed with an old guy.
•• 0:04—Nude making love with a young guy.
•• 0:17—Topless in bathtub, then making love on bed.
•• 0:22—Topless making love in a swimming pool, in a river, by a tree.
•• 0:26—Nude getting undressed and taking a shower.
•• 0:35—Full frontal nudity changing clothes.
••• 0:54—Full frontal nudity making love in bed.

The Love Machine (1971)
Madeleine Collinson . . . . Sandy
•• 1:22—Topless in shower with Robin and her sister when Dyan Cannon discovers them all together. Can't tell who is who.
Mary Collinson . . . . Debbie
•• 1:22—Topless in shower with Robin and her sister when Dyan Cannon discovers them all together. Can't tell who is who.
Alexandra Hay. . . . . .Tina St. Claire
• 0:34—Brief topless in bed with Robin.
• 0:38—Brief topless coming around the corner putting blue bathrobe on.
Claudia Jennings . . . . .Darlene

Love Scenes (1984)
a.k.a. Ecstacy
Tiffany Bolling . . . . Val
•• 0:01—Side view of left breast in bed with Peter.
••• 0:06—Topless getting photographed by Britt Ekland in the house.
• 0:09—Brief topless opening her bathrobe to show Peter.
• 0:12—Topless in bathtub with Peter.
••• 0:19—Topless lying in bed talking with Peter, then making love.
• 0:43—Topless acting in a movie when Rick opens her blouse.
•• 0:57—Nude behind shower door, then topless getting out and talking to Peter.
•• 0:59—Topless making love tied up on bed with Rick during filming of movie.
•• 1:07—Topless, then full frontal nudity acting with Elizabeth during filming of movie.
•• 1:17—Full frontal nudity getting out of pool.
•• 1:26—Topless with Peter on the bed.
Britt Ekland . . . . Annie

••• 1:11—Full frontal nudity making love with Rick on bed.
Julie Newmar . . . . Belinda

Love Strange Love (1982; Brazilian)
Xuxa . . . . Tamara
•• 0:26—Topless standing on table, getting measured for outfit.
••• 0:29—Topless again when Hugo watches. Long scene.
•• 0:58—Right breast when she lets Hugo caress it. (Film is reversed since mole above her right breast appears over the left.)
• 1:00—More right breast.
•• 1:09—Topless, stripping out of bear costume during party.
••• 1:13—Topless several times undressing in room. Long scene.
•• 1:27—Side view of left breast in bed with Hugo.
Vera Fischer . . . . Anna
•• 0:23—Brief topless and lower frontal nudity in bathtub. Topless and buns, getting out.
•• 0:38—Topless making love with Dr. Osmar.
• 0:39—Brief buns, while lying in bed.
•• 1:19—Topless in bed with Dr. Osmar when Hugo watches.
Marcelo Ribeiro . . . . Hugo (Child)
• 0:20—Brief frontal nudity between his legs in bathtub.

Lovers Like Us (1975)
a.k.a. The Savage
Catherine Deneuve . . . . Nelly
• 1:06—Brief left upper half of left breast in bed with Yves Montand. Dark.
••• 1:09—Topless sitting up in bed.

The Loves of a French Pussycat (1976)
Sybil Danning . . . . .Andrea
••• 0:18—Topless dancing with her boss, then in bed.
•• 0:24—Topless and buns in swimming pool.
0:40—In sheer white bra and panties doing things around the house. Long sequence.
• 0:46—Topless in bathtub with a guy.
• 1:03—Left breast sticking out of bra, then topless.

The Loves of a Wall Street Woman (1989)
Private Screenings.
Tara Buckman . . . . Brenda Baxter
• 0:00—Topless taking a shower, opening the door and getting a towel.
•• 0:06—Topless changing clothes in locker room in black panties. Nice legs!
••• 0:18—Topless in bed making love with Alex.
•• 0:31—Topless in bed with Alex making love.
•• 0:40—Topless in black panties dressing in locker room.
• 0:46—Brief topless lying in bed, talking to her lover, side view of buns. Long shot.
••• 1:16—Topless making love in bed with Alex.

Lower Level (1990)

Elizabeth Gracen . . . . Hillary
- • 0:11—Topless in back seat of BMW making love with Craig. Long shot.
- 0:12—Very, very brief partial left breast afterwards.
- • 0:13—Brief right breast and lower frontal nudity getting dressed. Then in black lingerie.
- 0:14—In wet black lingerie under fire sprinkler in parking garage.
- •• 0:23—In black lingerie, then brief topless changing in her office while Sam secretly watches.

Shari Shattuck . . . . Dawn Simms

Lunch Wagon (1981)

Pamela Jean Bryant . . . . Marcy
- •• 0:04—Topless changing tops in room in gas station with Rosanne Katon while a guy watches through key hole.
- • 0:55—Left breast, several times, in van with Bif.

Rosanne Katon . . . . Shannon
- • 0:01—Brief topless getting dressed.
- • 0:04—Brief side view of left breast changing tops in room in gas station with Pamela Bryant while a guy watches through key hole.
- •• 0:10—Topless changing again in gas station.

Candy Moore . . . . Diedra
- •• 0:53—Topless under sheer robe, then topless on couch with Arnie.

Louisa Moritz . . . . Sunshine
- • 0:37—Topless in spa taking off her swimsuit top.

Nels Van Patten . . . . Scotty

Lurkers (1987)

Ruth Corrine Collins . . . . Jane (Model)
- 0:12—Undressing in white bra (on the right) with another model.
- •• 0:13—Topless, changing clothes with the other model.

Nancy Groff . . . . Rita
- • 1:07—Partial right breast in bathroom with another woman while Cathy talks.

Christine Moore . . . . Cathy
- ••• 0:19—Topless in bed, making love with her boyfriend.
- • 0:42—Brief topless in bubble bath during hallucination scene with her mother.

Lust for a Vampire (1970; British)

Yutte Stensgaard . . . . Mircalla
- ••• 0:19—Topless, three times, getting a massage from another school girl.
- 0:22—Very, very brief full frontal nudity while diving into the water. Long shot, don't see anything.
- •• 0:53—Topless outside with Lestrange. Left breast when lying down.
- • 0:58—Topless during Lestrange's dream.

Luther the Geek (1988)

Stacy Haiduk . . . . Beth
- 0:24—In bra and panties after undressing to take a shower.

- ••• 0:26—Topless with Rob in the shower. Wow!
- ••• 0:28—Topless taking off her robe in bed, then making love with Rob.

Thomas Mills . . . . Rob
- • 0:27—Very brief buns when Stacey Haiduk gooses him.

M*A*S*H (1970)

Sally Kellerman . . . . Margaret "Hot Lips" Houlihan
- • 0:42—Very, very brief left breast opening her blouse for Frank in her tent.
- • 1:11—Very, very brief buns and side view of right breast during shower prank. Long shot, hard to see.
- • 1:54—Very brief topless in a slightly different angle of the shower prank during the credits.

Donald Sutherland . . . . Hawkeye Pierce

Made in Heaven (1987)

Ellen Barkin . . . . Lucille
Timothy Hutton . . . . Mike Shea/Elmo Barnett
- •• 0:08—Buns, while standing in a room when he first gets to heaven.

Kelly McGillis . . . . Annie Packert/Ally Chandler
Debra Winger . . . . Emmett
Mare Winningham . . . . Brenda Carlucci

Made in U.S.A. (1988)

Judy Baldwin . . . . Dorie
Adrian Pasdar . . . . Dar
- • 0:12—Buns, while walking to sit down at the laundromat when he washes all his clothes with Christopher Penn.

Christopher Penn . . . . Tuck
- • 0:12—Buns, while walking to sit down at the laundromat when he washes all his clothes with Adrian Pasdar.

Lori Singer . . . . Annie
- • 0:26—Brief left breast and very brief lower frontal nudity in the back of a convertible with Dar at night.
- 0:44—In white, braless tank top talking to a used car salesman.

Magic (1978)

Ann-Margret . . . . Peggy Ann Snow
- ••• 0:44—Right breast, lying on her side in bed talking to Anthony Hopkins.

Magnum Force (1973)

Margaret Avery . . . . Prostitute
Clint Eastwood . . . . Harry Callahan
Hal Holbrook . . . . Lieutenant Briggs
Tim Matheson . . . . Sweet
Suzanne Somers . . . . Uncredited Pool Girl
- •• 0:26—In blue swimsuit getting into a swimming pool, brief topless a couple of times before getting shot, brief topless floating dead.

Maiden Quest (1972)

a.k.a. The Long Swift Sword of Siegfried
Private Screenings.
Lance Boyle . . . . Siegfried
- •• 0:24—Buns, during orgy scene.

Sybil Danning . . . . Kriemhild
- 0:02—Topless in bath, surrounded by topless blonde servants.
- 0:04—Topless in the bath again.
- ••• 0:10—Nude in tub surrounded by topless servant girls.
- ••• 0:12—Topless on bed, getting rubbed with ointment by the servant girls.
- •• 0:35—Topless while in bed with Siegfried.
- 1:00—Topless in bed with Siegfried.
- ••• 1:19—Topless in bed with Siegfried.

Major League (1989)
Tom Berenger . . . . Jake Taylor
Corbin Bernsen . . . . Roger Dorn
- 0:58—Brief buns, while running in locker room to cover himself with a towel when Rachel comes in to talk to the team.
Margaret Whitton . . . . Rachel Phelps

Malibu Beach (1978)
James Daughton . . . . Bobby
- 0:32—Buns, while running into the ocean with his friends.
Kim Lankford. . . . . Dina
0:32—Buns, running into the ocean.
- 0:34—Brief right breast getting out of the ocean.
- 1:16—Right breast on beach at night with boyfriend.
- 1:19—Brief topless at top of the stairs.
- •• 1:20—Brief topless when her parent's come home.
- 1:21—Topless in bed with her boyfriend.
Michael Luther . . . . Paul
- 0:32—Buns, while running into the ocean with his friends.
Susan Player Jarreau . . . . Sally
- 0:28—Side view of left breast with boyfriend at night on the beach. Long shot.
0:32—Buns, running into the ocean with her two male friends.
0:33—Brief side view of left breast in water. Long shot.
- 0:34—Brief topless in the ocean, then topless by the fire getting dressed.
Tara Stromeir . . . . Glorianna
- 0:08—Topless kissing her boyfriend at the beach when someone steals her towel.

The Malibu Bikini Shop (1985)
Debra Blee . . . . Jane
Bruce Greenwood . . . . Todd
Barbra Horan. . . . . Ronnie
- 0:33—In wet tank top during Alan's fantasy.
- 1:13—Most of side of left breast, while kissing Alan in the spa.
Rita Jenrette . . . . Aunt Ida
Jeana Loring . . . . Margie Hill
- •• 0:43—Topless, dancing on stage during bikini contest (Contestant #4).
Gretchen Palmer. . . . . Woman

Bobbi Pavis. . . . . Stunning Girl
- •• 0:19—Topless trying on bikini behind two-way glass.
Allene Simmons . . . . Milinda Riley

Malibu Express (1984)
Sybil Danning . . . . Countess Luciana
- 0:13—Brief topless making love in bed with Cody.
Barbara Edwards . . . . May
- •• 0:10—Topless taking a shower with Kimberly McArthur on the boat.
- •• 1:05—Topless serving Cody coffee while he talks on the telephone.
Robyn Hilton . . . . Maid Marian
Darby Hinton . . . . Cody Abilene
- 0:08—Brief buns, while taking a shower on his boat.
Kimberly McArthur. . . . . Faye
- •• 0:10—Topless taking a shower on the boat with Barbara Edwards.
Lorraine Michaels. . . . . Liza Chamberlin
- ••• 0:23—Topless in the shower making love with Shane, while getting photographed by a camera.
Shelly Taylor Morgan . . . . Anita Chamberlain
- 0:22—Topless doing exercises on the floor.
- •• 0:26—Topless making love with Shane in bed while being video taped. Then right breast while standing by door.
Suzanne M. Regard . . . . Sexy Sally
- 0:50—Brief topless talking on the telephone.
- 1:06—Topless talking on the telephone.
Lori Sutton. . . . . Beverly
- ••• 0:54—Topless and buns, making love in bed with Cody.
Lynda Wiesmeier . . . . June Khnockers
- •• 0:04—Topless in locker room taking jumpsuit off.
- 1:16—Topless leaning out of racing car window while a helicopter chases her and Cody.

Malibu Hot Summer (1981)
a.k.a. Sizzle Beach
(*Sizzle Beach* is the re-released version with Kevin Costner featured on the cover. It is missing all the nude scenes during the opening credits before 0:06.)
Terry Congie . . . . Dit McCoy
- 0:02—Side view of right breast, while on floor during opening credits.
0:39—In bra, taking off her blouse in front of her drama class.
- •• 0:45—Topless in front of fireplace with Kevin Costner. Side view of right breast.
Kevin Costner. . . . . John Logan
Roselyn Royce . . . . Cheryl Rielly
- •• 0:15—On exercise bike, then topless getting into bed.
- ••• 0:16—Topless sitting up in bed, buns going to closet to get dressed to go jogging.
0:26—In pink two piece swimsuit running to answer the phone.
- •• 0:52—Topless on boat with Brent.

Sylvia Wright. .Actress at Party
- •• 0:01—Nude, standing up during opening credits.
- ••• 1:07—Topless fixing her hair in front of mirror, then full frontal nudity talking to Howard.
- • 1:09—Topless on top of Howard.

Malicious (1974; Italian)
Laura Antonelli . . . . Angela
- • 1:14—Topless after undressing while two boys watch from above.
- •• 1:27—Topless, undressing under flashlight. Hard to see because the light is moving around a lot.
- • 1:29—Topless and buns running around the house.

The Mambo Kings (1992)
Antonio Banderas . . . . Nestor Castillo
- • 0:48—Buns, while in bed on top of Maruschka Detmers.
- • 1:10—Upper half of buns, sitting on side of bed, while putting his pants on.
Stephanie Blake. . . . . Stripper
Maruschka Detmers . . . . Dolores Fuentes
- •• 0:47—Topless several times, making love in bed with Antonio Banderas.
Valerie McIntosh . . . . .Tracy Blair
- •• 1:10—Topless, getting her bathing suit after Armand Assante discovers her with Antonio Banderas.

A Man for Sale (1982)
Ajita Wilson. . . . . Dancer/Model
- • 0:02—Topless several times posing for photographer with another model.
- • 0:26—Topless and buns, dancing in an erotic ballet show.

A Man in Love (1987)
Jamie Lee Curtis . . . . Susan Elliot
Greta Scacchi . . . . Jane Steiner
- ••• 0:31—Topless with Peter Coyote.
- •• 1:04—Buns and left breast in bed with Coyote.
- 1:10—Brief side view topless, putting black dress on.
- • 1:24—Brief topless in bed.

The Man Who Fell to Earth (1976; British)
(Uncensored version reviewed.)
David Bowie . . . . Thomas Jerome Newton
- 0:58—Brief buns, while turning over in bed with Candy Clark.
- 1:56—Frontal nudity and brief buns in bed with Clark. Don't see his face.
Bernie Casey. . . . . Peters
- • 1:42—Buns, while getting out of swimming pool during a black and white dream sequence.
Candy Clark . . . . Mary-Lou
- •• 0:42—Topless in the bathtub, washing her hair and talking to David Bowie.
- •• 0:55—Topless sitting on bed and blowing out a candle.
- ••• 0:56—Topless in bed with Bowie.
- ••• 1:26—Full frontal nudity climbing into bed with Bowie after he reveals his true alien self.

1:56—Nude with Bowie making love and shooting a gun.
Claudia Jennings . . . . Uncredited Girl by the Pool
- • 1:42—Topless, standing by the pool and kissing Bernie Casey.
Rip Torn. . . . . .Nathan Bryce

The Man Who Loved Women (1983)
Julie Andrews . . . . .Marianna
Jennifer Ashley . . . . David's Mother
Kim Basinger . . . . .Louise "Lulu"
Jill Carroll . . . . Sue the Baby Sitter
Denise Crosby . . . . .Enid
Cindi Dietrich. . . . . Darla
Marilu Henner . . . . Agnes Chapman
- •• 0:18—Brief topless in bed with Burt Reynolds.
Sharon Hughes . . . . Nurse
Burt Reynolds . . . . David Fowler
- •• 1:25—Brief buns, while chiseling a statue after making love with Julie Andrews.
Tracy Vaccaro. . . . . .Legs

The Man Who Wasn't There (1983)
Vincent Baggetta . . . . Riley
- • 0:23—Buns, while lying on the floor after fighting with the other guys.
Deborah Dutch . . . . Miss Dawson
Steve Guttenberg. . . . . Sam Cooper
- ••• 0:54—Buns, while dropping his pants in office with three other men.
- • 1:46—Brief buns, while kissing Cindy during their wedding ceremony.
Lisa Langlois. . . . . Cindy Worth
- •• 0:58—Nude running away from two policemen after turning visible.
- ••• 1:08—Topless in white panties dancing in her apartment with an invisible Steve Guttenberg.
- 1:47—Very, very brief upper half of left breast, while throwing bouquet at wedding.
Brinke Stevens . . . . .Nymphet
- • 0:45—Buns and brief topless in the girls' shower, when she gets shampoo from an invisible Steve Guttenberg.

The Man with Two Brains (1983)
Randi Brooks . . . . .Fran
- •• 1:11—Brief topless showing Steve Martin her breasts in front of the hotel. Buns, changing in the hotel room, then wearing black see-through negligee.
Kathleen Turner . . . . Dolores Benedict
- • 0:08—Right breast when Steve Martin is operating on her in the operating room.
- 0:22—In sheer lingerie in bedroom with Steve Martin, teasing him and driving him crazy.
- • 0:36—Buns, in hotel room with a guy about to squeeze her buns when Steve Martin walks in.

Mandingo (1975)
Susan George. . . . . Blanche
- • 1:36—Brief topless in bed with Ken Norton.

Perry King . . . . Hammond
   •• 0:17—Frontal nudity walking to bed to make love
      with Dite.
Debbi Morgan . . . . Dite
   • 0:17—Topless in bed talking to Perry King.
Ken Norton . . . . Mede
   •• 1:36—Buns, while standing in bed with Susan
      George. More buns when making love with her.
Brenda Sykes . . . . Ellen
   • 0:58—Topless in bed with Perry King.

Maniac Cop 2 (1990)
Claudia Christian . . . . Susan Riley
Laurene Landon . . . . Teresa Mallory
Leo Rossi . . . . Turkell
Paula Trickey . . . . Cheryl
   •• 0:41—In orange two piece swimsuit on stage, then
      topless and buns in G-string.

Manifesto (1988)
Simon Callow . . . . Police Chief Hunt
Svetozar Cvetkovic . . . . Rudi
Rade Serbedzija . . . . Emile
   • 0:18—Buns, while under sheet, getting out of bed.
Camilla Søeberg . . . . Svetlana
   ••• 0:15—Nude, in bathtub and bedroom with Emile.
      Long scene.
   • 0:19—Brief left breast when Emile cuts off her hair.
   •• 1:04—Left breast, several times when Emile is in her
      room. More left breast cleaning up after Emile acci-
      dentally dies.
   • 1:15—Brief side of left breast, while making love
      with Eric Stoltz. Dark. Buns, getting out of bed.
   •• 1:16—Topless and buns unrolling Emile in the rug.
   •• 1:23—Topless sitting in bed with puppies.
Eric Stoltz . . . . Christopher
   • 1:16—Buns, while helping Camilla unroll Emile in
      the rug.

Manon of the Spring (1987; French)
Emmanuelle Béart . . . . Manon
   • 0:11—Brief nude dancing around a spring playing a
      harmonica.

Marathon Man (1976)
Dustin Hoffman . . . . Babe
   •• 1:09—Buns, getting out of the bathtub and putting
      some pajamas on while someone lurks outside the
      bathroom.
Marthe Keller . . . . Elsa
   •• 0:42—Topless lying on the floor after Dustin Hoff-
      man rolls off her.

Maria's Lovers (1985)
Keith Carradine . . . . Clarence Butts
Nastassia Kinski . . . . Maria Bosic
   0:59—In a black bra.
   • 1:12—Brief right breast, while looking at herself in
      the mirror.
Anita Morris . . . . Mrs. Wynic
Vincent Spano . . . . Al Griselli

The Marilyn Diaries (1990)
Private Screenings.
John Altamura . . . . Frankie
   • 0:13—Buns, while in hall after Marilyn Chambers
      takes his sheet away.
Tara Buckman . . . . Jane
   •• 0:53—Topless and buns, taking off robe and getting
      into bathtub. Left breast, in tub reading diary.
   •• 0:54—Topless in and getting out of tub. Very brief
      lower frontal nudity.
   •• 1:27—Topless in bathtub talking with John.
Marilyn Chambers . . . . Marilyn
   •• 0:02—Topless in bathroom with a guy during party.
   •• 0:26—In bra and panties in Istvan's studio, then top-
      less.
   ••• 0:27—Topless in panties when Istvan opens her
      blouse.
   •• 0:45—Topless in trench coat, opening it up to give
      the Iranian secret documents.
   • 0:47—Topless when the Rebel Leader opens her
      trench coat.
   • 0:48—Topless with Colonel South.
   •• 0:57—Topless opening her top for Hollywood pro-
      ducer.
   • 1:10—In swimsuit, then topless with Roger.
   ••• 1:13—In black lingerie, then topless making love
      with Chet.
   • 1:19—Left breast, in flashback with Roger.
   •• 1:25—In slip, then right breast, then topless with
      Chet.

Marked for Death (1990)
Tracey Burch . . . . Sexy Girl #1
   • 0:39—Brief topless on bed with Jimmy when Steven
      Seagal bursts into the room. (She's the blonde.)
Leslie Danon . . . . Girl #1
Elizabeth Gracen . . . . Melissa
   0:45—Very brief part of right breast in gaping
      blouse, while crawling on the floor.
Joanna Pacula . . . . Leslie
Elena Sahagun . . . . Carmen
   • 0:06—Topless in room, shooting Steven Seagal's
      partner.
Teri Weigel . . . . Sexy Girl #2
   • 0:39—Brief topless on bed with Jimmy when Steven
      Seagal bursts into the room. (She's the brunette.)

Married to the Mob (1988)
Matthew Modine . . . . Mike Downey
Michelle Pfeiffer . . . . Angela de Marco
Nancy Travis . . . . Karen Lutnig
   • 0:15—Buns and brief side view of right breast, with
      Tony in hotel room. Brief topless in the bathtub.

Mary, Mary, Bloody Mary (1975)
Cristina Ferrare . . . . Mary
   •• 0:07—Brief topless making love with some guy on
      the couch just before she kills him.
   ••• 0:41—Topless when Greta helps pull down Ferrare's
      top to take a bath.

1:12—Bun and brief silhouette of left breast getting out of bed and getting dressed.

Helena Rojo. . . . . Greta
- 0:42—Buns and brief topless getting into bathtub with Cristina Ferrare.

Mascara (1987; French/Belgian)
Derek De Lint . . . . Chris Brine
Charlotte Rampling. Gaby Hart
- 1:03—Brief topless putting on sweater when Michael Sarrazin watches through binoculars.
- 1:18—Right breast, while making love with Chris.

Alexandra Vandernoot. . . . . Euridice

Masquerade (1988)
Kim Cattrall. . . . . Mrs. Brooke Morrison
••• 0:04—Topless in bed with Rob Lowe.
   0:47—In white teddy after having sex with Lowe.
Rob Lowe . . . . Tim Whalen
••• 0:04—Buns, while getting up from bed with Kim Cattrall.
•• 0:30—Buns, while making love with Meg Tilly in bed.
Meg Tilly. Olivia Lawrence
   0:55—In pink nightgown in bedroom.

Massacre at Central High (1976)
Kimberly Beck. . . . . Theresa
- 0:32—Nude romping in the ocean with David. Long shot, dark, hard to see anything.
•• 0:42—Topless on the beach making love with Andrew Stevens after a hang glider crash.
Steve Bond . . . . Craig
Derrel Maury. . . . . David
- 0:32—Buns, while romping around in the ocean with Kimberly Beck. Dark, long shot. Hard to see anything.
Lani O'Grady. . . . . Jane
••• 1:09—Topless walking out of a tent and getting back into it with Rainbeaux Smith and Robert Carradine.
Cheryl Smith. . . . . Mary
- 0:27—Brief topless in a classroom getting attacked by some guys.
••• 1:09—Nude walking around on a mountain side with Robert Carradine and Lani O'Grady.
Andrew Stevens . . . . Mark

Master of Dragonard Hill (1987)
Patrick Dewee. . . . . Calabar
•• 0:14—Buns, while getting out of bed after being discovered in bed with Claudia Udy by her father.
Oliver Reed . . . . Captain Shanks
Kimber Sissons . . . . Jane Abdee
•• 0:08—Topless making love in bed with Richard.
Claudia Udy . . . . Arabella
••• 0:11—Nude, undressing to seduce Calabar. More topless and buns while kissing him.
•• 0:14—Silhouette topless while making love with Calabar, then topless.

- 0:58—Brief buns and side of right breast during flash back. Brief right breast when she gets out of bed.
Patrick Warburton . . . . Richard Abdee
   0:07—Very brief buns in mirror. Hard to see.

Masterblaster (1986)
Tracey E. Hutchinson . . . . Lisa
••• 0:57—Topless taking a shower (wearing panties).
Kari Whitman. . . . . Jennifer

Mata Hari (1985)
Christopher Cazenove . . . . . . Captain Karl Von Byerling
Derek De Lint. . . . . Handsome Traveler
Sylvia Kristel . . . . Mata Hari
••• 0:11—Topless making love with a guy on a train.
•• 0:31—Topless standing by window after making love with the soldier.
- 0:35—Topless making love in empty house by the fireplace.
•• 0:52—Topless masturbating in bed wearing black stockings.
•• 1:02—Topless having a sword fight with another topless woman.
•• 1:03—Topless in bed smoking opium and making love with two women.
Oliver Tobias . . . . Ladoux

Matador (1986; Spanish)
Antonio Banderas. . . . . Angel
Nacho Martinez. . . . . Diego Montes
••• 0:29—Buns, while making love with Eva in bed.
Carmen Maura. . . . . Julie
Assumpta Serna . . . . Maria Cardinal
- 0:03—Topless taking off wrap and making love with a guy just before she kills him.
••• 1:38—Topless on floor with Diego. Long shot, hard to see. Topless in front of the fire.
- 1:41—Brief topless making love with Diego.
- 1:43—Topless lying on floor dead.

Mausoleum (1983)
Bobbie Bresee . . . . Susan Farrell
••• 0:25—Topless and buns wrapping a towel around herself in her bedroom.
•• 0:26—Topless on the balcony showing herself to the gardener.
- 0:29—Topless in the garage with the gardener. Brief, dark, hard to see.
- 0:32—Brief left breast, while kissing Marjoe Gortner.
- 1:10—Topless in the bathtub talking to Gortner. Long shot.

Me & Him (1988; West German)
Carey Lowell . . . . Janet Anderson
- 0:37—Very brief upper half of right breast sticking out of nightgown after turning over in bed with Griffin Dunne.

The Mean Season (1985)
Mariel Hemingway. . . . . Christine Connelly
•• 0:15—Topless taking a shower.
Kurt Russell . . . . Malcolm Anderson

Mean Streets (1973)

Jeannie Bell . . . . Diane
- 0:07—Topless dancing on stage with pasties on.
- 1:00—Topless backstage wearing pasties.

David Carradine . . . . Drunk
Robert De Niro . . . . Johnny Boy
Harvey Keitel . . . . Charlie

Meatballs III (1987)

Caroline Arnold . . . . Ida (Girl in VW Bug)
Patrick Dempsey . . . . Rudy
- • 0:19—Buns, while in the shower when first being visited by Sally Kellerman.

Sally Kellerman . . . . Roxy Du Jour
Isabelle Mejias . . . . Wendy
Shannon Tweed . . . . The Love Goddess

Medium Cool (1969)

Peter Boyle . . . . Gun Clinic Manager
Robert Forster . . . . John
- • 0:36—Nude, running around the house frolicking with Ruth.

Mariana Hill . . . . Ruth
- 0:18—Close-up of breast in bed with John.
- • 0:36—Nude, running around the house frolicking with John.

Meet the Applegates (1989)

Ed Begley, Jr. . . . . Dick Applegate
- 0:46—Buns, while runnning around nuclear power plant after his pile of clothes are taken away by the janitor.

Dabney Coleman . . . . Aunt Bea
Savannah Smith Bouchér . . . . Dottie

Melanie (1982)

Don Johnson . . . . Carl
Glynnis O'Connor . . . . Melanie
- 0:08—Very brief right breast, while turning over in bed next to Don Johnson.
- • 0:09—Topless, while sitting up and putting on a T-shirt, then getting out of bed.

Melody in Love (1978)

Wolf Goldan . . . . Octavio
- 1:14—Buns, while making love in bed with Rachel and Angela.

Scarlett Gunden . . . . Angela
- ••• 0:17—Full frontal nudity taking off dress and dancing in front of statue.
- ••• 0:50—Nude with a guy on a boat.
- •• 0:53—Topless on another boat with Octavio.
- •• 0:59—Buns and topless in bed talking to Rachel.
- •• 1:12—Full frontal nudity getting a tan on boat with Rachel.
- • 1:14—Topless making love in bed with Rachel and Octavio.

Sascha Hehn . . . . Alain
- •• 1:08—Buns while outside with Melody. Very brief erect penis under covers.

- 1:16—Buns, twice while making love with Melody near an erupting volcano.

Melvin and Howard (1980)

Martine Beswick . . . . Real Estate Woman
Dabney Coleman . . . . Judge Keith Hayes
Denise Galik . . . . Lucy
Pamela Reed . . . . Bonnie Dummar
Mary Steenburgen . . . . Lynda Dummar
- •• 0:31—Topless and buns, ripping off barmaid outfit and walking out the door.

Men of Respect (1990)

Peter Boyle . . . . Duffy
John Turturro . . . . Mike Battaglia
0:21—Side view of buns, lying in bed with Ruthie.
- 0:25—Brief upper half of buns, putting on robe and leaving room.
- •• 0:45—Buns, while washing blood off himself in bathroom with Ruthie's help.

The Men's Club (1986)

Penny Baker . . . . Lake
- •• 1:13—Topless in bed with Treat Williams.

David Dukes . . . . Phillip
Ann Dusenberry . . . . Page
- •• 1:05—Topless lying in bed after making love with Roy Scheider.

Gina Gallego . . . . Felicia
Marilyn Jones . . . . Allison
- •• 1:21—Topless wearing gold panties standing in bedroom talking to Harvey Keitel.

Harvey Keitel . . . . Sully
- 1:22—Buns, while getting up off the bed to talk to Allison.

Jennifer Jason Leigh . . . . Teensy
Cindy Pickett . . . . Hannah
Helen Shaver . . . . Sahra (uncredited)
Craig Wasson . . . . Paul
Gwen Welles . . . . Redhead
Treat Williams . . . . Terry

The Mephisto Waltz (1971)

Jacqueline Bisset . . . . Paula Clarkson
- 0:48—Very brief right and side view of left breast in bed with Alan Alda.
  1:36—Sort of left breast getting undressed for witchcraft ceremony. Long shot side views of right breast, but you can't see her face.
- •• 1:45—Very brief topless twice under bloody water in blood covered bathtub, dead. Discovered by Kathleen Widdoes.

Barbara Parkins . . . . Roxanne
- 1:26—Left breast, while kissing Alan Alda during witchcraft sequence.

Kathleen Widdoes . . . . Maggie West

Meridian (1989)
a.k.a. Kiss of the Beast
a.k.a. Phantoms
Sherilyn Fenn . . . . Catherine
- •• 0:23—White bra and panties, getting clothes taken off by Lawrence. Then topless.
- ••• 0:28—Topless in bed with Oliver.
- •• 0:51—Topless getting her blouse ripped open lying in bed.
  1:11—Briefly in white panties and bra putting red dress on.
Charlie Spradling. . . . . Gina
- •• 0:22—Topless getting her blouse torn off by Lawrence while lying on the table.
- ••• 0:28—Topless standing next to fireplace, then topless on the couch. Hot!

Metamorphosis (1989)
Laura Gemser . . . . Prostitute
- • 0:37—Very brief topless several times in Peter's flashback.
- • 0:43—Very brief topless in flashback again.

Miami Blues (1990)
Martine Beswick . . . . Noira
Jennifer Jason Leigh. . . . . Susie Waggoner
  0:07—Very brief upper half of right breast, while changing clothes behind Alec Baldwin.
- ••• 0:10—Topless in panties, taking off red dress and getting into bed.
  0:24—Very, very brief half of right breast while taking a bath. Long shot.
- • 0:33—Topless making love with Baldwin in the kitchen.
Fred Ward . . . . Sergeant Hoke Moseley

Midnight (1989)
Kathleen Kinmont . . . . .Party
Lynn Redgrave . . . . Midnight
Karen Witter . . . . Missy Angel
- • 0:32—In bed with Mickey. Nice squished breasts against him, but only a very brief side view of left breast.
  0:48—In two piece swimsuit, going into the pool.
  0:58—In nightgown, walking around with lots of makeup on her face.

Midnight Cowboy (1969)
Dustin Hoffman. . . . . Ratso
Sylvia Miles . . . . Cass
- • 0:20—Brief buns, running into bedroom and jumping onto bed with Jon Voight. More when changing the TV channel with the remote control. Most of her right breast in bed under Voight.
Jennifer Salt. . . . . Annie
- • 0:31—Very brief buns, while running away from some bad guys in flashback.
- • 0:42—Brief left breast on bed with Voight in flashback.

- • 0:49—Very brief topless in car in B&W flashback. More brief topless and buns in car and running on porch.
Brenda Vaccaro . . . . Shirley
- • 1:30—Very, very brief out of focus left breast in open fur coat, lying down with Jon Voight.
- • 1:31—Very brief left breast when falling back onto bed with Voight.
- •• 1:32—Brief right breast, while rolling in bed with Voight.
Jon Voight . . . . Joe Buck
- • 0:00—Very brief side view of buns, picking up bar of soap from the shower floor.
- • 0:20—Brief buns, while running into bedroom and jumping onto bed with Sylvia Miles.
- • 0:50—Very brief buns, during struggle with a group of men. More buns when they hold his legs.
- • 1:32—Buns, while in bed with Brenda Vaccaro.

Midnight Crossing (1988)
Kim Cattrall . . . . .Alexa Schubb
  0:39—In wet white blouse, arguing in the water with her husband.
Crisstyn Dante . . . . Body Double for Kim Cattrall
- • 0:29—Brief left breast making love on small boat, body double for Kim Cattrall.
Faye Dunaway . . . . Helen Barton
John Laughlin. Jeffrey Schubb

Midnight Dancer (1987; Australian)
a.k.a. Belinda
Robyn Moase . . . . .Brenda
- • 0:43—Brief topless putting her black top on.
Mary Regan . . . . .Crystal
- •• 0:29—Topless in dressing room, undressing and rubbing makeup on herself.
- •• 0:56—In bra, then topless in panties, changing clothes and getting into bed.
Kathryn Walker. . . . . .Kathy

Midnight Express (1978; British)
Brad Davis . . . . Billy Hayes
- • 0:12—Buns, while standing naked in front of guards after getting caught trying to smuggle drugs.
John Hurt. . . . . .Max
Irene Miracle . . . . .Susan
- •• 1:39—Topless in prison visiting booth showing her breasts to Brad Davis so he can masturbate.
Randy Quaid . . . . Jimmy Booth

Mike's Murder (1984)
Kym Malin . . . . .Beautiful Girl #1
Debra Winger . . . . Betty
- • 0:26—Brief left breast in bathtub.

Millions (1990)
Carol Alt. . . . . .Beta
Catherine Hickland . . . . Connie
- • 0:36—Buns, getting out of bed to open safe. Don't see her face, probably a body double because the hair is too dark.

• 1:20—Buns, walking away from John Stockwell. Very brief back side of right breast, when she bends over to pick up blouse. Don't see her face.

Lauren Hutton........................Christina

Alexandra Paul .... Julia

   0:19—In black stockings and body suit, changing clothes.

  ••• 0:44—Topless while making love in bed with Billy Zane.

  • 0:59—Topless in bed with Zane.

John Stockwell .... David Phipps

Billy Zane .... Maurizo Ferreti

Mirror Images (1991)

Lee Anne Beaman .... Rebecca

  ••• 1:11—Buns in G-string, then topless in conference room, undressing in front of Jeff Conaway and Carter.

Jeff Conaway...........................Jeffrey

George "Buck" Flower..................Wolfman

Michael Meyer .... Georgio

  •• 0:15—Buns, while getting out of bed with Shauna.

Deirdre Morrow .... Slave Girl

  ••• 0:58—Buns in G-string, then topless with masked guy.

  ••• 1:00—Topless on bed with masked guy and Julie Strain.

Delia Sheppard .... Kaitlin/Shauna

  •• 0:07—Right breast, while undressing in front of vanity mirror.

  •• 0:08—More topless. Topless as Shauna in bed.

   0:12—Buns, while dancing on stage with a band, wearing a sexy outfit.

  ••• 0:14—Topless in bed with Georgio.

  ••• 0:27—Topless and buns in G-string, making love with Joey. Long scene.

  ••• 0:33—Buns in black bra and panties, walking around her sister's apartment. Long scene.

  •• 0:39—Right breast, while with a guy with a mask.

  ••• 0:41—Nude, taking a shower. Great!

  ••• 0:43—Topless in bedroom after her shower.

  ••• 0:48—Left breast, while making love in bed with Julie Strain.

  ••• 1:29—Topless in bed in lingerie with the policeman.

Julie Strain............................. Gina

  •• 0:48—Buns and right breast, making love in bed with Kaitlin.

  •• 0:49—Buns in black bra and panties.

  • 0:57—Buns in black body suit.

  ••• 0:58—Topless lying on bed, watching the slave girl and guy with the mask make love.

Nels Van Patten..................... Joey Zoom

  •• 0:08—Buns, while in bed and getting out of bed with Shauna.

  •• 0:29—Buns, while on top of Kaitlin.

Mirror Mirror (1990)

Karen Black........................Mrs. Gordon

Charlie Spradling .... Charleen Kane

  • 1:05—Very, very brief side of left breast, after taking of swimsuit in locker room.

  • 1:06—Buns, taking a shower. Brief topless a couple of times when the hot water pipes break.

   1:09—Buns, lying on the floor, dead, covered with blisters.

The Misadventures of Mr. Wilt (1990)

Griff Rhys Jones .... Henry Wilt

  • 0:34—Sort of buns, while naked and tied to inflatable doll.

  • 0:36—More buns, while up on balcony. Long shot.

Diana Quick..............................Sally

Mischief (1985)

Jami Gertz .... Rosalie

Doug McKeon .... Jonathan

  • 0:56—Brief buns, while putting on his underwear after making love with Kelly Preston.

Terry O'Quinn .... Claude Harbrough

Kelly Preston .... Marilyn McCauley

  ••• 0:56—In a bra, then topless and brief buns, while making love with Doug McKeon in her bedroom.

Catherine Mary Stewart .... Bunny

Miss Right (1987; Italian)

Karen Black ....Amy

  • 0:47—Brief topless jumping out of bed and running to get a bucket of water to put out a fire.

Dalila Di'Lazzaro.................... Art Student

Clio Goldsmith.......................... n.a.

Margot Kidder .... Juliet

Marie-France Pisier....................... Bebe

  •• 0:07—Topless in open top dress when the reporter discovers her in a dressing room behind a curtain.

William Tepper....................... Terry Bartell

  • 0:47—Buns, while jumping out of bed with Karen Black when the bed catches fire.

Missing in Action (1984)

Lenore Kasdorf ....Ann

  • 0:41—Very brief topless when Chuck Norris sneaks back in room and jumps into bed with her.

M. Emmet Walsh .... Tuck

Mission Manila (1989)

Tetchie Agbayani ....Maria

Maria Isabel Lopez ....Jessie

  • 0:22—Brief right breast several times in bed while Harry threatens her with knife.

Mo' Better Blues (1990)

Tracy Camilla Johns .... Club Patron

Joie Lee .... Indigo Downes

  •• 1:06—Right breast while in bed with Bleek.

  • 1:08—Very, very brief right breast while pounding the bed and yelling at Bleek.

John Turturro......................Moe Flatbush

Denzel Washington .... Bleek Gilliam

Cynda Williams .... Clarke Betancourt

  •• 0:24—Topless, then left breast after kissing Bleek.

••• 1:07—Topless on bed when Bleek accidentally calls her "Indigo."
•• 1:28—Left breast while making love in bed with Wesley Snipes.

Mob Boss (1990)
Jasaé . . . . Bar Girl
•• 0:46—Topless serving drinks to the guys at the table.
Suzanne Ager . . . . Pool Girl
Dori Courtney. . . . . Kathryn
••• 0:31—In black bra, talking with Eddie Deezen, then topless. Nice close-up. Long scene.
Morgan Fairchild. . . . . Gina
Sherri Graham . . . . Bar Girl
•• 0:46—Topless and buns, dancing on stage. Medium long shot.
Debra Lamb . . . . Janise
Tamara Landry . . . . .n.a.
Karen Russell. . . . . .Mary
Brinke Stevens. . . . . Sara

Modern Love (1990)
Robby Benson. . . . . Greg Frank
•• 0:35—Brief buns while running out of room after finding out he's going to be a father.
0:36—Long shot of buns, while standing on roof of house yelling the good news to the world.
Burt Reynolds . . . . Colonel Parker

Modern Problems (1981)
Dabney Coleman . . . . .Mark
••• 1:09—Buns, while taking off towel in front of Patti D'Arbanville.
Patti D'Arbanville . . . . Darcy
• 0:48—Very brief right breast in bed after Chevy Chase has telekinetic sex with her.

Modern Romance (1981)
Kathryn Harrold . . . . Mary Harvard
• 0:46—Very brief topless and buns taking off robe and getting into bed with Albert Brooks.
1:05—In pink lingerie opening her blouse to undo her skirt while talking to Brooks.
Bruno Kirby. . . . . Jay

The Moderns (1988)
Genevieve Bujold . . . . .Libby Valentin
Keith Carradine. . . . . Nick Hart
•• 1:17—Buns, while walking into bathroom with Linda Fiorentino.
Geraldine Chaplin . . . . Nathalie de Ville
Linda Fiorentino .Rachel Stone
• 0:40—Topless sitting in bathtub while John Lone shaves her armpits.
• 0:41—Right breast while turning over onto stomach in bathtub.
•• 1:18—Topless getting out of tub while covered with bubbles to kiss Keith Carradine.

Mondo New York (1987)
Phoebe Légerè . . . . Singer
0:01—On stage, singing "Marilyn Monroe." Buns and most of lower frontal nudity while writhing on stage in a mini-skirt.
Ann Magnuson . . . . Poetry Reader
Annie Sprinkle .Model/Performer
• 0:17—Nude, painted body with other models during "Rapping & Rocking" segment.

Monkey Shines: An Experiment in Fear (1988)
Jason Beghe . . . . Allan Mann
• 0:01—Side view of buns while on the floor, stretching to go running.
Kate McNeil . . . . .Melanie Parker
• 1:07—Brief upper half of right breast, while making love with Allan. Dark, hard to see anything.
John Pankow . . . . Geoffrey Fisher
Patricia Tallman . . . . Party Guest and Stunts
Janine Turner . . . . .Linda Aikman
0:01—Side view of buns, lying in bed when Jason Beghe wakes up. Don't really see anything.
Joyce Van Patten . . . . .Dorothy Mann

Monsignor (1982)
Genevieve Bujold . . . . Clara
••• 1:05—Topless getting undressed and climbing into bed while talking to Christopher Reeve.
Pamela Prati . . . . .1st Roman Girl
• 1:22—Brief topless (on the left, wearing necklaces) next to a guy sitting in a chair, with another Roman girl on the right.

Montenegro (1981; British/Swedish)
Susan Anspach. .Marilyn Jordan
•• 1:08—Full frontal nudity taking a shower.
• 1:28—Right breast making love with Montenegro.
Svetozar Cvetkovic . . . . Montenegro
••• 1:07—Frontal nudity taking a shower while Susan Anspach watches.

Monty Python's Jabberwocky (1977)
Deborah Fallender . . . . .The Princess
• 0:56—Buns and brief full frontal nudity in bath when Michael Palin accidentally enters the room.
0:57—Topless under sheer white robe.
Bryan Pringle . . . . Second Gate Guard

Monty Python's Life of Brian (1979; British)
Graham Chapman . . . . Brian Called Brian
••• 1:03—Buns before opening window, frontal nudity after opening window and being surprised by his flock of followers, buns while putting clothes on. Funniest frontal nude scene.
John Cleese . . . . Third Wise Man

Moon 44 (1990; West German)
Lisa Eichhorn . . . . Terry Morgan
John March . . . . Moose Haggerty
• 0:43—Brief buns while in shower room. (Sort of see frontal nudity through grating in the shower divider.)

Malcolm McDowell. . . . . Major Lee
Michael Paré . . . . Felix Stone

Moon in Scorpio (1987)

Donna Kei Benz. . . . . Nurse Mitchell
Britt Ekland . . . . Linda
Jillian Kesner . . . . Claire
- •• 0:39—Topless sitting on deck of boat with bathing suit top down.

April Wayne . . . . Isabel
- • 0:32—Brief right breast in bed with a guy.
- • 0:35—Brief topless putting bathing suit on in a bathroom on a boat when a guy opens the door.

Moontrap (1989)

Leigh Lombardi. . . . . .Mera
- •• 1:08—Topless with Walter Koenig in moon tent.

The Morning After (1986)

Kathy Bates . . . . Woman on Mateo Street
Jeff Bridges . . . . Turner
Jane Fonda . . . . Alex Sternbergen
- • 1:08—Brief topless making love with Jeff Bridges.

Raul Julia . . . . Joaquin Manero
Rick Rossovich . . . . Detective

Mortal Passions (1989)

Michael Bowen . . . . Burke
- • 0:42—Brief buns, while on top of Adele.

Krista Errickson . . . . Emily
- •• 0:08—Brief topless in bed with Darcy, while tied to the bed. Topless getting untied and rolling over.
- • 0:11—Very brief right breast, rolling back on top of Darcy.
- ••• 0:40—Topless after dropping her sheet for Burke, then making love with him.
- •• 0:46—Topless getting into bed with her husband.

Sheila Kelley . . . . Adele

Mortuary Academy (1988)

Rebekka Armstrong. Nurse
Christopher Atkins. . . . . Sam Grimm
Vickie Benson . . . . Salesgirl
Laurie Ann Carr. . . . . Nurse
Lynn Danielson . . . . .Valerie Levitt
James Daughton . . . . Yuppie at Car Lot
Perry Lang. . . . . Max Grimm
Kym Paige. . . . . Nurse
Bobbi Pavis . . . . Sexy Dancer
Dona Speir . . . . Nurse
Cheryl Starbuck. . . . . Linda Hollyhead
- • 1:08—Topless, dead, in morgue when Paul Bartel tries to make love with her.

Karen Witter . . . . Christie Doll
Mary Woronov . . . . Mary Purcell

Moscow on the Hudson (1984)

Maria Conchita Alonso . . . . Lucia Lombardo
- •• 1:17—Topless in bathtub with Robin Williams.

Robin Williams . . . . Vladimir Ivanoff

Motel Hell (1980)

Nina Axelrod . . . . Terry
- 0:58—In wet white T-shirt, tubin' with Ida.
- •• 1:01—Topless sitting up in bed to kiss Vincent.
- • 1:04—Very brief topless in tub when Bruce breaks the door down, then getting out of tub.

Rosanne Katon. . . . . Suzi
Monique St. Pierre . . . . Debbie

Mountains of the Moon (1989)

Patrick Bergin. . . . . .Richard Burton
Richard E. Grant. Oliphant
Bernard Hill . . . . Dr. David Livingstone
Anna Massey . . . . .Mrs. Arundell
Fiona Shaw . . . . .Isabel
- •• 0:33—Topless and very brief lower frontal nudity letting Patrick Bergin wax the hair off her legs.
- •• 1:43—Topless in bed with Bergin.

Ms. Don Juan (1973)

Brigitte Bardot . . . . .Joan
- • 0:19—Left breast in bathtub.
- •• 1:19—Topless through fish tank. Buns and left breast, then brief topless in mirror with Paul.

Jane Birkin . . . . Clara
- 0:58—Lower frontal nudity lying in bed with Brigitte Bardot.
- 1:00—Brief topless in bed with Bardot. Long shot.
- •• 1:01—Full frontal nudity getting dressed. Brief topless in open blouse.

Mugsy's Girls (1985)

Ken Norton . . . . Branscombe
Darcy Nychols . . . . .Madame Antoinette
Kristi Somers . . . . Laurie
- • 0:15—Brief topless several times while mud wrestling.
- • 0:29—Topless and buns in bathtub on bus.
- • 0:34—Brief topless holding up sign to get truck driver to stop.

Murder Weapon (1989)

Michelle Bauer . . . . Girl in Shower on TV
- • 1:00—Brief left breast on TV that the guys are watching. Scene from Nightmare Sisters.

Linnea Quigley. . . . . Dawn
- • 0:08—Buns and very brief side of left breast walking into shower. Long shot.
- •• 0:40—Topless taking off her top in car.
- •• 0:48—Topless and buns taking off her top.
- ••• 0:50—Topless in bed on top of a guy. Excellent long scene. Brief buns, getting out of bed.

Karen Russell . . . . .Amy
- ••• 0:05—Topless in bed with a guy after taking off her swimsuit top, then making love on top of him. Long scene.
- • 0:34—Brief topless in shower.
- 0:58—In black bra and panties in bedroom.

Brinke Stevens . . . . Girl in Shower on TV
- • 1:00—Brief left breast on TV that the guys are watching. Scene from Nightmare Sisters.

Murderers Among Us: The Simon Wiesenthal Story
(1989; Made for Cable Movie)
Ben Kingsley . . . . Simon Wiesenthal
•• 0:27—Buns and brief frontal nudity standing in and leaving a line in a concentration camp.
Reneé Soutendijk. . . . . Cyla

Murphy's Law *(1986)*
Leigh Lombardi. Stewardess
Teri Lynn Peake. . . . . .n.a.
Carrie Snodgress. . . . . Joan Freeman
Angel Tompkins . . . . Jan
• 0:19—Topless doing a strip routine on stage while Charles Bronson watches.
• 0:27—Brief topless doing another routine.

Murphy's Romance *(1985)*
Sally Field . . . . Emma Moriarity
Brian Kerwin . . . . Bobbie Jack Moriarity
•• 0:55—Brief buns while walking into the bathroom.

My Beautiful Laundrette *(1985; British)*
Daniel Day-Lewis. . . . . Johnny
Rita Wolf . . . . Tania
•• 0:15—Topless holding blouse up, showing off her breasts outside window to Omar.

My Best Friend's Girl *(1984; French)*
a.k.a. La Femme du Mon Ami
Isabelle Huppert . . . . Vivian Arthund
• 0:40—Brief left breast peeking out of bathrobe walking around in living room.
1:00—Buns, making love with Thierry Lhermitte while his friend watches.
Thierry Lhermitte . . . . Pascal Saulnier

My Chauffeur *(1986)*
Cindy Beal. . . . . .Beebop
Vickie Benson . . . . Party Girl
Jeannine Bisignano . . . . Party Girl
• 1:23—Topless, several times, taking off her white blouse in the back of the limousine. (She's the only brunette.)
Leslee Bremmer. Party Girl
1:19—Dancing in yellow outfit at a club. Most of buns.
• 1:24—Buns and brief topless in back of the limousine, taking off her yellow outfit.
• 1:25—Topless sleeping when Penn and Teller leave the limousine.
Sam Jones. . . . . Battle
••• 0:42—Buns, while running around the park naked.
Sheila Lussier. . . . . Party Girl
• 1:23—Brief topless taking off her blue blouse in the back of the limousine.
Darian Mathias . . . . .Dolly

My Father's Wife *(1976; Italian)*
Carroll Baker . . . . Lara
• 0:03—Right breast making love in bed with her husband, Antonio.

•• 0:06—Topless standing in front of bed talking to Antonio.
••• 0:18—Topless kneeling in bed, then getting out and putting a robe on while wearing beige panties.
Cesare Barro. . . . . Claudio
• 0:52—Buns, while bringing Patricia champagne.

My First Wife *(1985)*
Wendy Hughes . . . . .Helen
1:00—Brief topless and lower frontal nudity under water during husband's dream. Don't see her face.
•• 1:08—In bra, then topless on the floor with her husband.
•• 1:10—Topless in bed lying down, then fighting with her husband. A little dark.
Anna-Maria Monticelli . . . . Hillary

My Man Adam *(1986)*
Veronica Cartwright . . . . .Elaine Swit
• 1:09—Side view of right breast lying on tanning table when Adam steals her card keys. Long shot, hard to see.
Lydia Finzi . . . . Sunbather
• 0:32—Brief topless sunbathing by the swimming pool when Adam jumps into the pool and angers her.

My Pleasure is My Business *(1974)*
Jayne Eastwood . . . . Isabella
• 1:16—Topless in bed trying to get His Excellency's attention.
• 1:28—Topless sitting up in bed with blonde guy.
Xaviera Hollander. . . . . .Gabriele
•• 0:14—Full frontal nudity in everybody's daydream.
•• 0:39—Topless sitting up in bed and putting on a blouse.
•• 0:40—Topless getting back into bed.
••• 0:59—Topless and buns taking off clothes to go swimming in the pool, swimming, then getting out.
•• 1:09—Topless, buns and very brief lower frontal nudity, underwater in indoor pool with Gus.
• 1:31—Buns and very brief side view of right breast, undressing at party.
Michael Kirby. . . . . Gus
• 0:41—Brief buns while making love with Xaviera Hollander.

My Therapist *(1983)*
Marilyn Chambers . . . . .Kelly Carson
•• 0:01—Topless in sex therapy class.
•• 0:07—Topless, then full frontal nudity undressing for Rip. Long scene.
••• 0:10—Topless undressing at home, then full frontal nudity making love on couch. Long scene. Nice. Then brief side view of right breast in shower.
• 0:18—Topless on sofa with Mike.
•• 0:21—Topless taking off and putting red blouse on at home.
••• 0:26—Nude in bedroom by herself masturbating on bed.

••• 0:32—Topless exercising on the floor, buns in bed with Mike, topless in bed getting covered with whipped cream.

•• 0:41—Left breast and lower frontal nudity fighting with Don while he rips off her clothes.

•• 1:08—Topless and brief buns in bed.

1:12—In braless pink T-shirt at the beach.

Danielle Martin . . . . Francine

•• 0:29—In bra, garter belt, stockings and panties, then topless in room with Rip.

David Winn . . . . Mike Jenner

•• 0:19—Buns, while making love with Marilyn Chambers in bed.

My Tutor (1983)

Caren Kaye . . . . Terry Green

•• 0:25—Topless walking into swimming pool.

•• 0:52—Topless in the pool with Matt Lattanzi.

••• 0:55—Right breast, lying in bed making love with Lattanzi.

Matt Lattanzi . . . . Bobby Chrystal

Graem McGavin . . . . Sylvia

••• 0:21—In white bra, then topless in back seat of a car in a parking lot with Matt Lattanzi.

Shelly Taylor Morgan . . . . Louisa

Francesca "Kitten" Natividad . . . . Anna Maria

••• 0:10—Topless in room with Matt Lattanzi, then lying in bed.

Katt Shea . . . . Mud Wrestler

• 0:48—Brief topless when a guy rips her dress off.

Jewel Shepard . . . . Girl in Phone Booth

• 0:40—Brief left breast in car when Matt Lattanzi fantasizes about making love with her.

Nails (1992; Made for Cable Movie)

Anne Archer . . . . Mary Niles

•• 0:16—Topless and buns, several times during love scene with Dennis Hopper. Probably a body double because you never see her face.

Teresa Crespo . . . . Elena Hernandez

•• 0:44—Topless, taking off her top in room with Dennis Hopper.

Dennis Hopper . . . . Harry "Nails" Niles

••• 0:39—Buns, while getting out of the bathtub and running outside after the guy who shot at him.

• 0:40—Very, very brief frontal nudity, dropping towel to drape on his shoulder.

Shelley Michelle . . . . Stunt Player

•• 0:16—Topless and buns, several times body double for Anne Archer during love scene with Dennis Hopper.

The Naked Cage (1985)

Lucinda Crosby . . . . Rhonda

Flo Gerrish . . . . Mother

Leslie Huntly . . . . Peaches

Lisa London . . . . Abbey

•• 0:22—Topless in S&M costume with Angel Tompkins.

•• 0:38—Left breast making out in bed with Angel Tompkins.

Valerie McIntosh . . . . Ruby

••• 0:24—Topless and buns in infirmary, then getting attacked by Smiley. Brief lower frontal nudity.

• 0:28—Topless, hanging by rope dead.

Stacey Shaffer . . . . Amy

••• 1:03—Nude in shower room getting hassled by the other girls.

Shari Shattuck . . . . Michelle

•• 0:42—Buns and topless in shower, then getting slashed by Rita during a dream.

•• 1:00—Left breast getting attacked by Smiley in jail cell, then fighting back.

1:28—In panties, during fight with Rita.

Angel Tompkins . . . . Diane Wallace

•• 0:22—In lingerie, then topless with Abbey.

• 0:38—Brief right breast, in bed with Abbey.

Christina Whitaker . . . . Rita

••• 0:08—Topless in bed with Willy.

• 0:55—Brief topless in gaping sweatshirt during fight with Sheila.

1:28—Panties during fight with Shari Shattuck.

1:29—Sort of left breast in gaping dress.

Naked Obsession (1990)

Ria Coyne . . . . Cynthia

•• 0:11—Topless on stage, dancing in black lingerie.

• 0:13—Buns in G-string while dancing.

•• 0:14—More topless and buns while dancing.

Maria Ford . . . . Lynne Hauser

0:16—Dancing on stage doing strip tease. Wearing bra, panties, garter belt and stockings.

••• 0:18—Buns in G-string.

••• 0:20—Topless and buns in G-string, dancing on stage in front of William Katt. Long scene.

••• 0:23—Nude, dancing with Katt's necktie.

•• 0:34—Nude, on stage at end of dance routine.

•• 0:44—Topless in her apartment with Katt.

••• 0:45—Topless and buns on top of Katt in bed while he gently strangles her with his necktie for oxygen deprivation.

•• 0:47—Topless in bed after making love with Katt.

Sherri Graham . . . . Waitress

William Katt . . . . Franklyn Carlyle

• 0:46—Very, very brief buns, while turning over in bed with Maria Ford. Long shot.

Wendy MacDonald . . . . Saundra Carlyle

••• 0:28—In black bra, panties and stockings on the dining table during William Katt's fantasy, then topless.

Elena Sahagun . . . . Becky

1:07—Dancing on stage in white outfit (She's got a mask over her face).

••• 1:10—In white bra, panties, garter belt and stockings while wearing the mask. Topless and buns in G-string.

Madison Stone . . . . Jezebel

•• 0:35—In black leather outfit. Buns in G-string and topless.

•• 0:37—More topless and buns.

• 0:38—More.

•• 0:39—Brief full frontal nudity.

Naked Warriors (1973)

a.k.a. The Arena

Pam Grier . . . . Mamawi
- •• 0:08—Brief left breast, then lower frontal nudity and side view of right breast getting washed down in court yard.
- ••• 0:52—Topless getting oiled up for a battle. Wow!

Lucretia Love. . . . . Deidre
- • 0:07—Brief topless getting clothes torn off by guards.
- •• 0:08—Brief nude getting washed down in court yard.
- 1:08—Brief buns, while bent over riding a horse.

Margaret Markov . . . . Bodicia
- • 0:07—Brief topless getting clothes torn off by guards.
- • 0:13—Topless getting her dress ripped off, then raped during party.
- • 0:19—Brief left breast, on floor making love, then right breast and buns.
- 0:45—In sheer white dress consoling Septimus, then walking around.
- • 0:52—Brief topless sitting down, listening to Cornelia.

A Name for Evil (1973)

Robert Culp. . . . . John Blake
- •• 0:52—Frontal nudity running through the woods with a woman.
- • 1:07—Buns, while going skinny dipping. Lots of bun shots underwater.

Samantha Eggar . . . . Joanna Blake
- • 0:42—Very brief topless turning over in bed with Robert Culp. Dark, hard to see.

Sheila Sullivan . . . . Luanna Baxter
- • 0:51—Full frontal nudity dancing in the bar with everybody.
- • 0:54—Topless while Robert Culp makes love with her.
- • 0:56—Topless getting dressed.
- • 1:17—Nude, skinny dipping with Culp.

The Name of the Rose (1986)

Christian Slater . . . . Adso of Melk
- • 0:48—Buns, while making love with The Girl in the monastery kitchen.

Valentina Vargas . . . . The Girl
- ••• 0:46—Topless and buns making love with Christian Slater in the monastery kitchen.

Nashville (1975)

Karen Black. . . . . Connie White
Timothy Brown . . . . Tommy Brown
Keith Carradine. Tom Frank
- • 0:47—Buns, while sitting on floor after getting out of bed.

Geraldine Chaplin. . . . . Opal
Shelley Duvall . . . . L.A. Jane
Scott Glenn. . . . . Glenn Kelly
Jeff Goldblum . . . . Tricycle Man

Cristina Raines . . . . Mary
Gwen Welles . . . . Sueleen Gay
- •• 2:09—In bra singing to a room full of men, then topless doing a strip tease, buns walking up the steps and out of the room.

National Lampoon's Class Reunion (1982)

Misty Rowe . . . . Cindy Shears
- • 0:37—Very brief topless running around school stage in Hawaiian hula dance outfit.

Marya Small. . . . . Iris Augen

National Lampoon's Vacation (1983)

Beverly D'Angelo . . . . Ellen Griswold
- •• 0:18—Brief topless taking a shower in the motel.
- • 1:19—Brief topless taking off shirt and jumping into the swimming pool.

John Diehl . . . . Assistant Mechanic
Eugene Levy. Car Salesman
Randy Quaid . . . . Cousin Eddie

Naughty Nymphs (1972; German)

a.k.a. Passion Pill Swingers

a.k.a. Don't Tell Daddy

Sybil Danning . . . . Elizabeth
- ••• 0:21—Nude taking a bath while yelling at her two sisters.
- • 0:30—Topless and buns throwing Nicholas out of her bedroom.
- •• 0:38—Full frontal nudity running away from Burt.

Sascha Hehn . . . . n.a.

The Naughty Stewardesses (1978)

Donna Desmond . . . . Margie
- •• 0:12—Topless leaning out of the shower.

Mikel James . . . . Diane
- •• 0:34—Topless in bed waiting for Ben then in bed with him.

Tracey Ann King. Barbara
- •• 0:56—Topless dancing by the pool in front of everybody.

Necessary Roughness (1991)

Michael Dolan . . . . Eric "Samurai" Hanson
- • 1:09—Buns, while taking a shower, kind of hard to see. (He's the guy in the middle.)

Marcus Giamatti. . . . . Sargie
- • 1:09—Buns, while taking a shower. (He's the tall guy on the left.)

Harley Jane Kozak. . . . . Suzanne Carter
Andrew Lauer. . . . . Charlie Banks
- • 1:09—Buns, while taking a shower. (He's the brunette guy on the far right.)

Necromancer (1988)

Carla Baron . . . . Gail
- • 0:42—Brief topless getting out of bed with Paul. Dark.

Stan Hurwitz . . . . Paul DuShane
- • 0:46—Brief buns, when Julie pulls his underwear down. Don't see his face.

Elizabeth Kaitan.....................Julie Johnson
•• 0:41—Topless in the shower with Carl.
• 0:45—Very brief side view of right breast, taking off dress in front of Paul.
1:01—In red and black lingerie.
Edward Wright .... Carl Caulder
• 0:41—Buns, while taking off his towel and walking into shower.

Necropolis (1987)

LeeAnne Baker .... Eva
• 0:04—Right breast, while dancing in skimpy black outfit during vampire ceremony.
• 0:38—Brief topless in front of three evil things. (Before she has special make up to make it look like she has six breasts).
Adriane Lee....................... Cult Member

Neon Maniacs (1985)

Alan Hayes .... Steven
Marta Kober .... Lorraine
Susan Mierisch .... Young Lover
• 0:07—Very brief upper half of right breast while kissing her boyfriend at night.

Network (1976)

Faye Dunaway.................Diana Christensen
• 1:10—Brief left breast twice, taking off clothes in room with William Holden.

Nevada Heat (1982)

a.k.a. Stake Out
Camelia Kath..........................Voice #4
Anastassia Stakis ....Wooly
• 0:13—Topless in the shower room scene.
Pia Zadora........................... Bobbi
• 0:14—Very brief partial right breast and brief buns, in the showers.
• 0:47—Side of left breast, while in bubble bath with Desi Arnaz, Jr.

Never Cry Wolf (1983)

Brian Dennehy ....Rosie
Charlie Martin Smith......................Tyler
• 0:32—Buns while warming himself and drying his clothes after falling through the ice.
• 1:18—Very brief frontal nudity running and jumping off a rock into the pond.
• 1:20—Buns while running in meadow with the caribou.
• 1:23—Brief silhouette of lower frontal nudity while scampering up a hill. More buns when chasing the caribou.

Never on Tuesday (1988)

Claudia Christian....................... Tuesday
• 0:43—Brief side view of right breast in the shower with Eddie during his fantasy.

Never Too Young to Die (1986)

Vanity .... Donja Deering
0:25—In white bra in the kitchen with John Stamos while he tends to her wounded arm.
• 1:04—Wearing a bikini swimsuit, putting on suntan lotion. Brief topless in quick cuts making love with John in a cabin bedroom.
Tara Buckman .... Sacrificed Punkette

New Jack City (1991)

Eek-A-Mouse .... Fat Smitty
• 0:15—Buns, when Nino holds a gun to his head and makes him walk nude outside.
Tracy Camilla Johns .... Unigua
• 0:40—Buns, while dancing in red bra, panties, garter belt and stockings.
• 0:53—Buns and right breast in bed with Nino.

New Year's Evil (1981)

Teri Copley .... Teenage Girl
• 0:48—Brief right breast in the back of the car with her boyfriend at a drive-in movie. Breast is half sticking out of her white bra. Dark, hard to see anything.
Grant Cramer..................... Derek Sullivan

New York Nights (1981)

Corinne Alphen .... The Debutante
•• 0:10—Topless, making love in the back seat of a limousine with the rock star.
••• 1:38—Topless dancing in the bedroom while the Financier watches from the bed.
Bobbi Burns .... The Authoress
•• 0:16—Topless on the couch outside with the rock star, then topless in bed.
Cynthia Lee ....The Porn Star
•• 1:15—Topless in the steam room talking to the prostitute.
••• 1:26—Topless in office with the financier and making love on his desk.
Missy O'Shea ....The Model
0:30—In white bra in restroom making love with the photographer.
•• 0:37—in black bra, panties, garter belt and stockings then topless taking off bra and getting into bed.
•• 0:40—Topless on floor when the photographer throws her on the floor and rips her bra off.
••• 0:41—Full frontal nudity putting bathrobe on.
• 0:44—Topless standing in front of a mirror with short black hair and a moustache getting dressed to look like a guy.

New York's Finest (1988)

John Altamura .... Brian Morrison
Ruth Corrine Collins................. Joy Sugarman
• 0:04—Brief topless with a bunch of hookers.
• 0:36—Topless with her two friends doing push ups on the floor.
•• 1:02—Topless making love on top of a guy talking about diamonds.
Jennifer Delora .... Loretta Michaels
• 0:02—Brief topless pretending to be a black hooker.

539

- 0:04—Brief topless with a bunch of hookers.
- 0:36—Topless with her two friends doing push ups on the floor.

Jane Hamilton . . . . Bunny
Heidi Paine . . . . Carley Pointer
- 0:04—Brief topless with a bunch of hookers.
- 0:36—Topless with her two friends doing push ups on the floor.

Denise Torek . . . . Hooker #2
Miriam Zucker . . . . Mrs. Rush

Next Year if All Goes Well (1983; French)
Isabelle Adjani . . . . Isabelle
- 0:27—Brief right breast, lying in bed with Maxime.

Thierry Lhermitte . . . . Maxime

Nickel Mountain (1985)
Brian Kerwin . . . . George
Heather Langencamp . . . . Callie
- ••• 0:24—Topless in bed lying with Willard.
- 0:29—Side view of left breast and brief topless falling on bed with Willard.
- 0:29—In white panties, peeking out the window.

Nicole (1972)
a.k.a. The Widow's Revenge
Catherine Bach . . . . Sue
- •• 1:01—Brief topless, twice, undressing to put on nightgown on boat. Nice shots, but too brief.
- •• 1:10—Very brief side view of breasts, three times, getting felt by Leslie Caron. Don't see either Bach's or Caron's face.

Night Angel (1989)
Linden Ashby . . . . Craig
- 1:22—Buns, while kneeling down to pick up picture. Don't see his face.

Lisa Axelrod . . . . Double
Karen Black . . . . Rita
Debra Feuer . . . . Kirstie
- 0:46—Brief side of left breast. Dark.

Night Breed (1990)
Catherine Chevalier . . . . Rachel
- 1:12—Topless in police jail, going through a door and killing a cop.

Craig Sheffer . . . . Boone

Night Call Nurses (1972)
a.k.a. Young LA Nurses 2
Patti T. Byrne . . . . Barbara
- •• 0:59—Topless several times in bed with the Doctor.

Alana Collins . . . . Janis
- •• 0:12—Topless in bed with Zach.
- 0:24—In white two piece swimsuit on boat.
- •• 0:28—Topless and buns on bed with Kyle.
- 0:52—Brief right breast twice in shower with Kyle.

Lynne Guthrie . . . . Cynthia
- 0:00—Topless on hospital roof taking off robe and standing on edge just before jumping off.

Mitte Lawrence . . . . Sandra
- •• 0:49—Topless in bed with a guy.

Dixie Lee Peabody . . . . Robin
- •• 0:35—Topless taking off clothes in encounter group.
- 0:39—Brief topless in Barbara's flashback.

Night Club (1989)
Nicholas Hoppe . . . . Nick
- 0:27—Brief buns, while making love on roof with stripper. Long shot.
- ••• 0:37—Frontal nudity, getting up off the floor.
- ••• 0:47—Buns, while making love with Elizabeth Kaitan.

Elizabeth Kaitan . . . . Beth/Liza
- •• 0:31—Left breast, while pulling down blouse and caressing herself.
- •• 0:33—Left breast in pulled down blouse on stairwell with Nick.
- ••• 0:36—Topless on warehouse floor with Nick.
- ••• 0:46—Full frontal nudity, taking off her dress in front of Nick.
- ••• 1:03—Topless, making love with another guy in front of Nick.

Night Eyes (1990)
(Unrated version reviewed.)
Yvette Buchanan . . . . Baby Doll
- 0:07—Brief left breast, then topless making love in bathroom with Ronee.

Barbara Ann Klein . . . . Sleeping Woman
- 0:02—Brief topless struggling with burglar/rapist.

Stephen Meadows . . . . Michael Vincent
- 0:27—Buns and balls in bed with Tanya Roberts while Andrew Stevens watches on monitor.

Tanya Roberts . . . . Nikki
- 0:18—In white one piece swimsuit by the pool.
- 0:20—Side view of left breast, while getting dressed while sitting on bed.
- 0:25—In white lingerie, making love in bed with Michael.
- 0:30—Repeat of last scene on TV when Andrew Stevens brings the video tape home to watch.
- 0:55—Making love with Stevens. Don't see anything, but still steamy. Bubble covered left breast in tub with Stevens.
- ••• 1:09—Topless giving Stevens a massage, then making love. Nice! Buns and left breast, while in the shower making love.
- 1:27—Buns, making love with Stevens in a chair.

Andrew Stevens . . . . Will
- ••• 1:11—Buns while in the shower.
- ••• 1:26—Side view of buns with Tanya Roberts seen through a window.

Night Eyes 2 (1991)
Tim Russ . . . . Jesse Younger
- •• 0:07—Buns, while getting out of bed and putting his pants on.

Lisa Saxton . . . . Car Rental Girl
- ••• 0:05—Topless and buns, making love in bed with Jesse.
- 0:09—Buns, on TV when video tape is played back.

Andrew Stevens . . . . Will Griffith
- • 1:07—Partial buns, in mirror, while lying on the floor with Shannon Tweed.

Shannon Tweed . . . . Marilyn Mejenes
- ••• 0:49—Buns and topless making love with Andrew Stevens in bed.
- ••• 1:06—Topless, making love with Stevens (nice use of raspberries).

Night Force (1986)
Linda Blair. . . . . n.a.
Claudia Udy . . . . Christy Hanson
- •• 0:07—Topless making love in the stable with Steve during her engagement party.
- ••• 0:10—Nude, fantasizing in the shower.

Night Game (1989)
Karen Young. . . . . Roxy
- 0:02—In white slip with Roy Scheider.
- • 0:06—Right breast, while in bed with Scheider after he answers the phone.

Night Games (1980)
Joanna Cassidy . . . . Julie Miller
- 0:44—Buns, skinny dipping in the pool with Cindy Pickett.
- •• 0:45—Brief full frontal nudity sitting up.

Gene Davis . . . . Timothy
Cindy Pickett. . . . . Valerie St. John
- •• 0:05—Brief topless getting scared by her husband in the shower.
- • 0:45—Buns and topless by and in the swimming pool with Joanna Cassidy.
- 0:46—Topless in sheer blue dress during fantasy sequence with Cassidy.
- •• 0:48—Brief full frontal nudity getting out of the pool, then topless lying down with Cassidy.
- 1:03—Dancing at night in a see through nightgown.
- ••• 1:14—Full frontal nudity standing up in bathtub, then topless during fantasy with a guy in gold.
- •• 1:18—Topless getting out of pool at night.
- ••• 1:24—Topless sitting up in bed and stretching.

A Night in Heaven (1983)
Christopher Atkins. . . . . Rick
- • 1:03—Very brief frontal nudity when he pulls down his pants in hotel room with Leslie Ann Warren.
- • 1:15—Brief buns while on boat with Leslie Ann Warren's angry husband.

Sandra Beall . . . . Slick
- • 1:09—Brief close up of left breast in shower with Christopher Atkins.

Veronica Gamba . . . . Tammy
Rose McVeigh . . . . Alison
Carrie Snodgress. . . . . Mrs. Johnson

Night Moves (1975)
Susan Clark. . . . . Ellen
- • 1:09—Brief topless in bed with Gene Hackman.

Melanie Griffith . . . . Delly Grastner
- • 0:42—Brief topless changing tops outside while talking with Gene Hackman.
- • 0:46—Nude, saying "hi" from under water beneath a glass bottom boat.
- • 0:47—Brief side view of right breast getting out of the water.

Jennifer Warren . . . . Paula
- •• 0:56—Topless in bed with Gene Hackman.
- • 0:57—Right breast after making love in bed with Hackman.

James Woods . . . . Quentin

Night of the Creeps (1986)
Suzanne Snyder . . . . Lisa
Jill Whitlow. . . . . Cynthia Cronenberg
- 0:31—In bra and panties taking off sweater.
- • 0:33—Brief topless putting nightgown on over her head in her bedroom.

Night of the Cyclone (1990)
Marisa Berenson. Francoise
Alla Korot. . . . . Angelique
- • 0:21—Right breast, then brief topless getting out of the shower.

Kris Kristofferson . . . . Stan
Jeffrey Meek. . . . . Adam
- • 1:07—Brief buns, while putting on his pants, when he's interrupted in bed with Angelique. Long shot.

Kimberleigh Stark. Venna
- • 0:01—Brief left breast while posing for the painter.
- • 0:40—Topless on the boat, fighting with the businessman. Topless on the floor, dead.

Jennifer Steyn. . . . . Celeste

Night of the Demons (1987)
(Unrated version reviewed.)
Cathy Podewell . . . . Judy
- • 0:06—Brief buns, while changing clothes and talking on the phone.
- 0:07—In white bra taking off her sweater.

Linnea Quigley. . . . . Suzanne
- •• 0:52—Topless twice, opening her dress top while acting weird. Pushes a tube of lipstick into her left breast. (Don't try this at home kids!)
- 0:56—Lower frontal nudity, lifting her skirt up for Jay.

Jill Terashita . . . . Frannie
- •• 0:57—Topless making love with her boyfriend in a coffin.

Night of the Living Babes (1987)
Blondi . . . . Mondo Zombie Girl Darlene
- ••• 0:12—Topless wearing dark purple wig and long gloves, with the other Mondo Zombie Girls.
- ••• 0:16—More topless and buns in bed with Buck.
- • 0:50—Topless on the couch with the other Zombie Girls.
- • 0:52—Topless on the couch again.

Michelle Bauer. . . . . Sue
- •• 0:44—Topless chained up with Chuck and Buck.

••• 0:46—More topless chained up.

• 0:50—Topless getting rescued with Lulu.

Louis Bonanno . . . . Buck

Teri Lynn Peake. . . . . Vesuvia

••• 0:25—Topless and buns in G-string, dancing in front of Chuck and Buck. Long scene.

Connie Woods . . . . Lulu

• 0:46—Topless and buns in lingerie, in a cell with Buck.

••• 0:48—More topless in cell with Buck.

• 0:50—Topless getting rescued with Michelle Bauer.

Night of the Warrior (1991)

Bridget Carney . . . . Sarah

Kathleen Kinmont. . . . . Katherine Pierce

0:29—Very brief upper half of right breast, leaning out of the shower to get a towel.

0:46—Very, very brief part of buns, lifting her leg up while kissing Lorenzo Lamas at the art gallery.

• 1:10—Brief right breast, while making love with Lamas on motorcycle.

Teal Roberts . . . . Still Model

Night of the Wilding (1990)

Julie Austin . . . . .Betty

0:13—In bra and panties, undressing in bedroom.

•• 0:14—Side of left breast, taking off bra in bathroom. Topless in shower.

• 0:16—More topless in the shower.

0:17—Topless behind shower door.

Night Patrol (1985)

Linda Blair. . . . . .Sue

• 1:19—Brief left breast, in bed with The Unknown Comic.

Francesca "Kitten" Natividad. . . . . Hippie Woman

•• 1:01—Topless in kitchen with Pat Paulsen, the other police officer and her hippie boyfriend.

Lori Sutton . . . . .Edith Hutton

••• 0:47—In white bra, panties, garter belt and stockings, then topless three times taking off bra in bedroom with the Police officer.

The Night Porter (1974; *Italian/U.S.*)

Charlotte Rampling. . . . . .Lucia

•• 0:11—Side nudity being filmed with a movie camera in the concentration camp line.

• 0:13—Nude running around a room while a Nazi taunts her by shooting his gun near her.

••• 1:12—Topless doing a song and dance number wearing pants, suspenders and a Nazi hat. Long scene.

Night Rhythms (1992)

(Unrated version reviewed.)

David Carradine . . . . .Vincent

Deborah Driggs . . . . Cinnamon

••• 1:15—Left breast, then topless and lower frontal nudity, making love with Martin Hewitt in bed.

••• 1:19—Topless, sitting on bed and talking to Hewitt.

Martin Hewitt. . . . . Nick West

•• 0:29—Buns, while making love with Tracy Tweed.

••• 0:31—Buns, while making love with Tweed.

• 0:33—Partial buns, while getting up off the floor.

••• 1:18—Buns, while making love on top of Deborah Driggs in bed.

Sam Jones . . . . Jackson

Erika Nann . . . . .Alex

••• 1:00—Buns in G-string and bra, then topless, undressing in front of Martin Hewitt and making love with him.

Kristine Rose. . . . . Marilyn

••• 0:17—Taking off her blouse at bar with Martin Hewitt, then nude, making love on the bar with him.

Delia Sheppard . . . . Bridget

••• 1:25—Full frontal nudity, making love with Kit in bed. Long scene.

Julie Strain . . . . .Linda

••• 0:03—In white bra, then left breast, while talking on the phone and playing with herself.

Tracy Tweed . . . . Honey

••• 0:28—Topless making love with Martin Hewitt in radio station. Nice, long scene.

••• 0:31—Nude, getting up after changing positions.

•• 0:33—Topless, lying dead on the floor.

Night School (1980)

Rachel Ward. . . . . Elanor

• 0:24—In sheer white bra and panties, taking off clothes to take a shower. Topless taking off bra. Hard to see because she's behind a shower curtain.

0:28—Buns, when her boyfriend rubs red paint all over her in the shower.

Night Shift (1982)

Brett Clark . . . . .Nick "The Dick"

Kevin Costner. . . . . Frat Boy #1

Ashley Cox. . . . . Jenny Lynn

Dawn Dunlap. . . . . Maxine

Monique Gabrielle . . . . Tessie

• 0:55—Brief topless on college guy's shoulders during party in the morgue.

Ava Lazar . . . . .Sharon

Shelley Long . . . . Belinda Keaton

0:20—In black teddy and robe talking to Henry Winkler in the hallway.

0:37—In panties, socks and tank top cooking breakfast in Winkler's kitchen.

Ola Ray . . . . Dawn

K.C. Winkler. . . . . Cheryl

Robbin Young . . . . Nancy

Night Visitor (1989)

Shannon Tweed. . . . . Lisa Grace

Teresa Vander Woude . . . . Kelly Fremont

Teri Weigel. . . . . Victim in Cellar

• 0:50—Brief out of focus topless changing tops in the cellar.

• 0:55—Right breast, during ceremony. Very brief topless just before being stabbed.

Night Warning (1982)
Julia Duffy . . . . .Julie Linden
    0:44—Upper half of left breast.
- 0:46—Brief topless when her boyfriend pulls the sheets down.
- - 0:47—Brief topless when Susan Tyrrell opens the bedroom door.

Susan Tyrrell . . . . Cheryl Roberts
- 0:17—Left breast, sticking out of dress just before she stabs the TV repairman.

The Nightcomers (1971; British)
Stephanie Beacham . . . . Miss Margaret Jessel
- 0:13—Brief left breast lying in bed having her breasts fondled.
- - - 0:30—Topless in bed with Marlon Brando while a little boy watches through the window.
- - 0:55—Topless in bed pulling the sheets down.

Marlon Brando . . . . .Peter Quint
    0:30—Looks like you can see something between his legs, but most of his midsection is hidden by bed post.

Nightfall (1988)
Andra Millian . . . . .Anna
- 0:12—Very brief topless making love with David Birney.
- 0:41—Very brief topless making love in front of a fire.
    0:58—Same scene in a flashback while the guy is talking to another woman.

Nightmare at Shadow Woods (1983)
a.k.a. Blood Rage
Jane Bentzen . . . . Julie
    0:38—In red lingerie, black stockings and garter belt in her apartment with Phil.

Chad Montgomery . . . . .Gregg
- 0:52—Brief buns, while making love with Andrea on diving board just before getting killed.

A Nightmare on Elm Street 4: The Dream Master (1988)
Hope Marie Carlton . . . . Pin-Up Girl
- 0:21—Brief topless swimming in a waterbed.

Linnea Quigley . . . . Soul from Freddy's Chest
- 1:23—Brief topless twice, trying to get out of Freddy's body. Don't see her face clearly.

The Nightmare on Elm Street 5: The Dream Child (1989)
Erika Anderson . . . . Greta
Crisstyn Dante. . . . . Body Double for Alice

Nightmare Sisters (1987)
Michelle Bauer . . . . Mickey
- - - 0:39—Topless standing in panties with Melody and Marci after transforming from nerds to sexy women.
- - - 0:40—Topless in the kitchen with Melody and Marci.

- - - 0:44—Full frontal nudity in the bathtub with Melody and Marci. Excellent, long scene.
- - - 0:47—Topless in the bathtub. Nice close up.
- - - 0:48—Still more topless in the bathtub.
- - 0:53—Topless in bed with J.J.

Sandy Brooke . . . . .Amanda Detweiler
Matthew Phelps . . . . J.J.
- - 0:53—Buns, while taking off his pants and getting into bed with Michelle Bauer.

Linnea Quigley . . . . Melody
- - - 0:39—Topless standing in panties with Mickey and Marci after transforming from nerds to sexy women.
- - - 0:40—Topless in the kitchen with Mickey and Marci.
- - - 0:44—Topless in the bathtub with Mickey and Marci. Excellent, long scene.
- - - 0:46—Topless in the bathtub. Nice close up.
- - - 0:48—Still more topless in the bathtub.
- - - 0:55—Topless dancing and singing in front of Kevin. Long scene.
- - 0:57—Topless on the couch with Bud.

Brinke Stevens . . . . .Marci
- - - 0:39—Topless standing in panties with Melody and Mickey after transforming from nerds to sexy women.
- - - 0:40—Topless in the kitchen with Melody and Mickey.
- - - 0:44—Nude in the bathtub with Melody and Mickey. Excellent, long scene.
- - - 0:47—Topless in the bathtub. Nice close up.
- - - 0:48—Still more buns and topless in the bathtub.

Nights in White Satin (1987)
Kim Waltrip . . . . Stevie Hughes
    0:37—In white wig, bra, panties, garter belt and stocking during photo session.
    0:39—Brief side view of left breast in black slip during photo session.
- 0:53—Topless in bathtub with Walker. Out of focus, hard to see.

The Nightstalker (1987)
Tally Chanel . . . . .Brenda
- 0:54—Brief frontal nudity lying dead in bed covered with paint. Long shot, hard to see anything.

Joan Chen . . . . Mai Wong
Lydie Denier . . . . First Victim
- - - 0:03—Topless making love with big guy.

Ola Ray . . . . .Sable Fox
Diane Sommerfield . . . . .Lonnie Roberts
- 0:35—Side view of right breast lying dead in morgue.

Nightwish (1988)
(Unedited version reviewed.)
Alisha Das . . . . Kim
- - 1:09—Brief topless, then left breast in open dress caressing herself while lying on the ground.

Elizabeth Kaitan . . . . .Donna
- 0:04—In wet T-shirt, then brief topless taking it off during experiment. Long shot.
- 1:10—Briefly in braless, see-through purple dress.

Ninja Academy (1990)

Michele Burger . . . . Nudist
Becky LeBeau . . . . Nudist
•• 0:26—Nude, carrying plate, then going to swing at nudist colony. Then playing volleyball (she's the first one to hit the ball).
Bonnie Paine. . . . . Nudist
• 0:26—Brief buns and topless playing volleyball. (She's the second blonde on the far side of the net who misses the ball.)

No Small Affair (1984)

Judy Baldwin . . . . Stephanie
••• 0:36—In white bra, panties and garter belt, then topless in Jon Cryer's bedroom trying to seduce him.
Elizabeth Daily. . . . . Susan
Demi Moore . . . . Laura
• 1:34—Very, very brief side view of left breast in bed with Jon Cryer.
Tim Robbins . . . . Nelson

No Way Out (1987)

Iman. . . . . Nina Beka
Kevin Costner . . . . Lt. Cmdr. Tom Farrell
Sean Young . . . . Susan Atwell
0:11—In black stockings, garter belt & corset in love scene in back of limousine with Kevin Costner.
••• 0:13—Side view of left breast, then brief right breast, going into Nina's apartment with Costner.
0:21—In bed in pink lingerie and a robe talking on telephone when Costner is in Manila.
0:31—In corset and stockings with garter belt in bathroom talking to Costner.

Nomads (1986)

Pierce Brosnan . . . . .Pommier
• 0:56—Buns, while taking his pants off by the window. Kind of dark, hard to see.
Lesley-Anne Down . . . . Flax
Anna-Maria Monticelli. Niki
• 0:57—Left breast, making love in bed with Pierce Brosnan. Dark, hard to see anything.
Mary Woronov .Dancing Mary

North Dallas Forty (1979)

Peter Boyle . . . . Emmett
Mac Davis. . . . . Maxwell
• 0:53—Brief buns while getting a can of Coke in the locker room.
Dayle Haddon. . . . . Charlotte
Nick Nolte. . . . . Phillip Elliott
• 0:49—Brief buns, while pulling down underwear to get into whirlpool bath in locker room.
Savannah Smith Bouchér . . . . Joanne
• 0:27—Very brief topless in bed tossing around with Nick Nolte.

Not of This Earth (1988)

Ava Cadell. Second Hooker
•• 0:41—Topless in cellar with Paul just before getting killed with two other hookers. Wearing a gold dress.

Monique Gabrielle . . . . Agnes
Roxanne Kernohan . . . . Lead Hooker
••• 0:41—Topless in cellar with Paul just before getting killed with two other hookers. Wearing a blue top.
Becky LeBeau . . . . .Happy Birthday Girl
••• 0:47—Topless doing a Happy Birthday stripper-gram for the old guy.
Traci Lords. . . . . Nadine
•• 0:25—Buns and side view of left breast drying herself off with a towel while talking to Jeremy.
0:27—In blue swimsuit by swimming pool.
•• 0:42—Topless in bed making love with Harry.
0:46—Walking around the house in white lingerie.
Kelli Maroney. . . . . Nurse Mary Oxford
Taaffe O'Connell . . . . .Damelia
• 0:04—Brief topless and buns from Galaxy of Terror during the opening credits.
Rebecca Perle. . . . . Alien Girl
0:53—In black swimsuit wearing sunglasses.
Cynthia Ann Thompson . . . . . Third Hooker (black dress)

Not Quite Paradise (1986; British)

a.k.a. Not Quite Jerusalem
Joanna Pacula. . . . . Gila
• 1:04—Left breast, lying in bed with Sam Robards.

Novel Desires (1991)

Monica Akesson . . . . Model
••• 0:17—Buns, then topless while making love outside during story.
••• 0:18—Topless making love on picnic table with Eric.
Tyler Gains . . . . .Brian/Eric
• 0:18—Buns, as Eric, making love with the Model on picnic table.
Lysa Hayland . . . . Linda

Nowhere to Hide (1987)

Amy Madigan .Barbara Cutter
• 1:04—Brief side view of right breast taking off towel to get dressed in cabin. Long shot, hard to see.

Nudity Required (1989)

Pamela Bach . . . . Dee Dee
Billy Frank . . . . Buddy
••• 0:32—Buns, while walking around bathtub and talking to Scammer, then jumping into tub.
• 0:57—Side view of buns, behind textured shower door with Julie Newmar.
Becky LeBeau . . . . Melanie
•• 0:35—Topless, taking off pink swimsuit.
•• 0:36—Brief topless (third girl) standing in line.
• 0:37—Topless, standing behind Scammer.
• 0:39—Very brief topless.
•• 0:41—Topless while sitting next to Scammer by the pool.
Brooke Moore . . . . .Bikini Girl
Julie Newmar . . . . .Irina
• 0:57—Side of left breast and side view of buns behind textured shower door with Buddy.
Heidi Paine. . . . . .Jane
Windsor Taylor Randolph . . . . .Brenda

Gail Thackray . . . . .Midge
- •• 0:36—Topless, asking Buddy a question. Brief topless (tenth girl) standing in line.
- ••• 0:37—Topless doing her song and tap dance audition.
- • 0:44—Topless while playing in pool.

Edy Williams . . . . Isabella
- ••• 1:05—Topless with whip, while acting in movie.
- •• 1:07—More topless in movie.
- •• 1:09—More right breast.
- •• 1:13—Topless during screening of the movie.

Nudo di Donna (1984; Italian)
a.k.a. Portrait of a Woman, Nude
Eleonora Giorgi . . . . Laura
- • 0:11—Very brief left breast, while taking off robe. Subtitles get in the way.
- • 0:12—Right breast, while in the shower, getting consoled.
- • 0:13—Brief upper half topless, getting into bed.
- •• 0:14—Topless in bed.
- •• 0:36—Nude, mostly buns, sleeping in bed when Sandro pulls back the covers.
- • 1:12—Brief right breast, while in bed with Sandro.
- 1:13—Right breast under sheer dress.

Object of Desire (1991)
Private Screenings.
Tara Buckman . . . . Angie
- • 0:12—Topless, leaning up on massage table.
- ••• 0:14—Topless, getting dressed so Derrick can see.
- •• 0:23—Topless, making love with Derrick in her dressing room.
- ••• 0:28—Topless in bathtub with Derrick.
- • 0:43—Right breast, while making love in bed.
- • 0:50—Side view of buns, while lying in bed.
- •• 0:51—Right breast, while sitting up in bed, then full frontal nudity.
- ••• 0:55—Topless, opening her blouse in Steve's office in front of him.
- ••• 1:09—Full frontal nudity, posing for photographer in studio. Also side view of his buns.
- • 1:12—Brief topless in magazine photos.
- ••• 1:18—Topless changing clothes in dressing room.

Laura Gemser . . . . Uncredited Photographer

Obsession: A Taste For Fear (1987)
Virginia Hey . . . . Diane
- • 0:04—Buns and very brief side view of right breast dropping towel to take a shower.
- •• 0:14—Brief right breast in bed when sheet falls down.
- • 0:38—Topless lying down, wearing a mask, while talking to a girl.
- ••• 1:03—Topless waking up in bed.
- ••• 1:17—Topless in hallway with Valerie.
- • 1:19—Brief lower frontal nudity and right breast in bed with Valerie, then buns in bed.
- ••• 1:20—Topless getting dressed, walking and running around the house when Valerie gets killed.
- • 1:26—Topless tied up in chair.

The Octagon (1980)
Carol Bagdasarian . . . . Aura
- • 1:18—Brief side view of right breast, while sitting on bed next to Chuck Norris and taking her blouse off.

Karen Carlson. . . . . Justine
Kim Lankford . . . . Nancy

Of Unknown Origin (1983; Canadian)
Jennifer Dale . . . . Lorrie Wells
Shannon Tweed. Meg Hughes
- • 0:00—Brief side view of right breast taking a shower.

Peter Weller . . . . .Bart Hughes
Kenneth Welsh. . . . . .James

Off Limits (1988)
Woody Brown . . . . .Co-Pilot
Willem Dafoe. . . . . .Bud McGriff
Scott Glenn . . . . .Colonel Dexter Armstrong
Thuy Ann Luu . . . . Lanh
- •• 0:48—Topless dancing on stage in a nightclub.

Fred Ward . . . . Dix

Off the Wall (1982)
Rosanna Arquette. . . . . .Pam
Roselyn Royce . . . . .Buxom Blonde
- • 0:35—Left breast, while kissing an inmate in visiting room while the guards watch.
- •• 0:51—Left breast again, while kissing inmate through bars while the guards watch.

An Officer and a Gentleman (1982)
Lisa Blount . . . . Lynette Pomeroy
- 1:25—In a red bra and tap pants in a motel room with David Keith.

Lisa Eilbacher . . . . Casey Seeger
Richard Gere . . . . .Zack Mayo
David Keith . . . . Sid Worley
John Laughlin. . . . . .Troy
Debra Winger. Paula Pokrifki
- ••• 1:05—Brief side view of right breast, then topless making love with Richard Gere in a motel.

The Offspring (1986)
Martine Beswick. . . . . .Katherine White
Miriam Byrd-Nethery . . . . Eileen Burnside
- • 0:26—Topless in bathtub filled with ice while her husband tries to kill her with an ice pick.
- • 0:29—Very brief right breast, dead in bathtub while her husband is downstairs.

Susan Tyrrell. . . . . Beth Chandler

Oh, Alfie! (1975; British)
a.k.a. Alfie Darling
Minah Bird. . . . . Gloria
Joan Collins . . . . Fay
- 0:28—In white bra and panties, running to answer the phone, then talking to Alfie.
- ••• 1:00—Topless lying in bed after Alfie rolls off her.

Patsy Kensit . . . . Penny
Rula Lenska . . . . Louise
- •• 0:12—Topless, then left breast in bed after making love with Alfie.

Alan Price . . . . Alfie Elkins
  •• 0:14—Buns washing himself off in the kitchen while talking to Louise's husband.
Annie Ross. . . . . Claire
  •• 1:34—Topless on top of Alfie in open black dress while he's lying injured in bed.
Sheila White . . . . Norma

Old Gringo (1989)
Jane Fonda . . . . Harriet Winslow
  • 1:24—Side of left breast, while undressing in front of Jimmy Smits. Sort of brief right breast, while lying in bed and hugging him.
Jimmy Smits . . . . Arroyo
  • 1:26—Half of his buns while on bed with Jane Fonda. Long shot, don't see his face.

Olivia (1983)
a.k.a. *A Taste of Sin*
Suzanna Love . . . . Olivia
  •• 0:34—Buns and topless making love in bed with Mike.
  •• 0:58—Topless and buns making love with Mike in the shower.
  • 1:08—Very brief full frontal nudity getting into bed with Richard. Dark, long shot.
  •• 1:09—Buns, lying in bed. Dark. Full frontal nudity getting out of bed and going to the bathroom.
Jeff Winchester . . . . Richard
  • 1:17—Buns, while getting stuffed into trunk by Olivia. Dark.

The Omega Man (1971)
Anna Aries. . . . . Woman in Cemetary Crypt
Rosalind Cash . . . . Lisa
  •• 1:09—Side view of left breast and upper half of buns getting out of bed. Buns and topless sitting in bed.
  • 1:21—Side view topless in beige underwear while trying on clothes.
Charlton Heston . . . . Neville

On the Edge (1985)
(Unrated version reviewed.)
Bruce Dern . . . . Wes
  • 0:52—Brief buns, seen from below while floating in a pond.
Pam Grier . . . . Cora
  0:18—In leotards, leading an aerobics dance class.
  •• 0:42—Topless in the mirror, then full frontal nudity making love with Bruce Dern standing up. Then brief left breast. A little dark.

On the Line (1984; Spanish)
Victoria Abril . . . . Engracia
  ••• 0:16—Topless getting undressed to make love with Mitch.
  • 0:29—Very brief topless, making love in bed with Mitch.
  0:54—In white lingerie getting dressed.

David Carradine. . . . . Bryant
  • 0:11—Buns, while lying on a table, getting a massage by three women.

Once Bitten (1985)
Lauren Hutton . . . . Countess
Skip Lackey . . . . Russ
  • 1:11—Brief buns while in the school showers trying to see if Mark got bitten by a vampire.
Carey More . . . . Moll Flanders Vampire

Once is Not Enough (1975)
Kirk Douglas. . . . . Mike Wayne
David Janssen. . . . . Tom Colt
  • 1:22—Buns, while taking off clothes and walking to the bathroom.
Brenda Vaccaro . . . . Linda

Once Upon a Time in America (1984)
(Long version reviewed.)
Jennifer Connelly . . . . Young Deborah
Robert De Niro. . . . . Noodles
Darlanne Fluegel . . . . Eve
Olga Karlatos . . . . Woman in the Puppet Theatre
  •• 0:11—Right breast twice when bad guy pokes at her nipple with a gun.
Elizabeth McGovern. . . . . Deborah
  • 2:33—(0:32 into tape 2) Brief glimpses of left breast when Robert De Niro tries to rape her in the back seat of a car.
James Russo . . . . Bugsy
Treat Williams . . . . Jimmy O'Donnell
James Woods . . . . Max

One Deadly Summer (1984; French)
Isabelle Adjani . . . . Eliane
  •• 0:21—Brief topless changing in the window for Florimond.
  ••• 0:32—Nude, walking in and out of the barn.
  • 0:36—Brief left breast lying in bed when Florimond gets up.
  • 0:40—Buns and topless taking a bath.
  • 1:41—Part of right breast, getting felt up by an old guy, then right breast then brief topless.
  •• 1:47—Topless in bedroom with Florimond.
  1:49—In white bra and panties talking with Florimond.

One Flew Over the Cuckoo's Nest (1975)
Brad Dourif . . . . Billy
  •• 1:50—Buns in hallway, putting on his pants after getting caught with Candy.
Christopher Lloyd. . . . . Taber
Louisa Moritz . . . . Rose
Jack Nicholson . . . . R. P. McMurphy
Marya Small. . . . . Candy
  • 1:00—Very brief side view of left breast, bending over to pick up her clothes on boat.

One from the Heart (1982)
Teri Garr . . . . Frannie
- •• 0:09—Brief topless getting out of the shower.
  0:10—In a bra, getting dressed in bedroom.
- •• 0:40—Side view of right breast changing in. bedroom while Frederic Forrest watches.
- ••• 1:20—Brief topless in bed when standing up after Forrest drops in though the roof while she's in bed with Raul Julia.

Raul Julia . . . . Ray
- • 1:20—Very brief buns while getting out of bed with Teri Garr when Frederic Forrest crashes through the ceiling.

Nastassia Kinski . . . . Leila
- • 1:13—Brief topless in open blouse when she leans forward after walking on a ball.

One Man Force (1989)
Blueberry . . . . Santiago's Girlfriend
Maria Celedonio . . . . Maria
- • 0:30—Brief topless, twice, hiding John Matuzak in her apartment. Long shot.

Sam Jones . . . . Pete

One More Saturday Night (1986)
Moira Harris . . . . Peggy
Bess Meyer . . . . Tobi
- • 1:02—Brief topless in bed with Tom Davis.

Chelchie Ross . . . . Dad Lundahl
- • 0:39—Buns, squished against the car window in back seat with Moira Harris.

Nina Siemaszko . . . . Karen Lundahl

One Night Only (1984; Canadian)
Wendy Lands . . . . Jane
- •• 0:36—Topless taking a bath while Jamie watches through keyhole.
- •• 0:38—Brief left breast in open robe.
- • 1:15—Brief topless in bed with policeman.

Helene Udy . . . . Suzanne
- • 0:50—Buns and right breast in bed talking with a guy.
- • 1:12—Over the shoulder, brief left breast on top of a guy in bed.

Lenore Zann . . . . Anne
- •• 0:20—Topless getting dressed in bedroom with Jamie.
- • 1:04—Right breast in bedroom with Jamie.
- ••• 1:19—Topless and buns making love with Jamie.

One Trick Pony (1980)
Blair Brown . . . . Marion
Joan Hackett . . . . Lonnie Fox
- ••• 1:21—Nude getting out of bed and getting dressed while talking to Paul Simon.

Rip Torn . . . . Walter Fox
Mare Winningham . . . . McDeena Dandridge
- •• 0:14—Topless in the bathtub with Paul Simon, smoking a cigarette. Long scene.

One Woman or Two (1986; French)
a.k.a. *Une Femme Ou Deux*
Zabou . . . . Constance
- •• 0:28—Brief topless pulling up her blouse for Gerard Depardieu.

Sigourney Weaver . . . . Jessica
  1:30—In braless white blouse.
- •• 1:31—Very brief side view of left breast in bed with Gerard Depardieu.

The Onion Field (1979)
James Woods . . . . Gregory Powell
- •• 1:33—Buns, while taking a shower in the prison.

Open House (1987)
Adrienne Barbeau . . . . Lisa Grant
- • 0:27—In black lace lingerie, then very brief half of left breast making love with Joseph Bottoms on the floor.
- • 1:15—Brief side view of right breast getting out of bed at night to look at something in her briefcase.
- ••• 1:16—Brief topless taking off bathrobe and getting back into bed. Kind of dark.

Tiffany Bolling . . . . Judy Roberts
Mary Stavin . . . . Katie Thatcher

Opposing Force (1986)
a.k.a. *Hell Camp*
Lisa Eichhorn . . . . Lieutenant Casey
- • 0:17—Wet T-shirt after going through river.
- ••• 0:33—Topless getting sprayed with water and dusted with white powder.
- •• 1:03—Topless after getting raped by Anthony Zerbe in his office, while another officer watches.
- ••• 1:05—Topless and buns, getting dressed.

Jay Louden . . . . Stevenson
- • 0:31—Buns, while getting yanked out of the line by Becker.
- • 0:32—Buns, while getting sprayed with water and dusted with white powder. He's the first guy through.

Tom Skerritt . . . . Logan
- • 0:33—Very brief buns, while getting sprayed with water and dusted with white powder.
- •• 1:11—Brief buns, while jumping out of tree to knock out Tuan.

Ken Wright . . . . Conway
- • 0:33—Brief buns, while getting his poncho after being sprayed with water and dusted with white powder.

Ordeal by Innocence (1984)
Faye Dunaway . . . . Rachel Argyle
Sarah Miles . . . . Mary Durrant
Diana Quick . . . . Gwenda Vaughn
Cassie Stuart . . . . Maureen Clegg
- •• 1:14—Topless in bed talking to Donald Sutherland.

Donald Sutherland . . . . Arthur Calgary

The Osterman Weekend (1983)

Meg Foster . . . . Ali Tanner
    0:14—Very, very brief tip of right breast after getting nightgown out of closet.
Rutger Hauer. . . . . John Tanner
Dennis Hopper . . . . .Richard Tremayne
John Hurt . . . . .Lawrence Fassett
  • 0:01—Buns, while getting out of bed and walking to the shower.
Chris Sarandon . . . . Joseph Cardone
Helen Shaver. . . . . .Virginia Tremayne
  •• 0:24—Topless in an open blouse yelling at her husband in the bedroom.
  • 0:41—Topless in the swimming pool when everyone watches on the TV.
Merete Van Kamp. . . . . Zuna Brickman
  •• 0:01—Topless and brief buns in bed on a TV monitor, then topless getting injected by two intruders.
  • 0:35—Brief topless on video again while Rutger Hauer watches in the kitchen on TV.
  • 1:30—Topless again on video during TV show.
Cassie Yates. . . . . Betty Cardone
  •• 0:48—Topless getting into bed with Chris Sarandon while Rutger Hauer watches on TV.
  • 0:51—Right breast, making love with Sarandon.

Other Side of Midnight (1977)

Marie-France Pisier . . . . Noëlle Page
  • 0:10—Very brief topless in bed with Lanchon.
  0:28—Buns, in bed with John Beck. Medium long shot.
  0:45—In white bra, in dressing room talking to Henri.
  0:50—Topless in bathtub, giving herself an abortion with a coat hanger. Painful to watch!
  •• 1:11—Topless wearing white slip in room getting dressed in front of Henri.
  ••• 1:17—Full frontal nudity in front of fireplace with Armand, rubbing herself with oil, then making love with ice cubes. Very nice!
  • 1:35—Full frontal nudity taking off dress for Constantin in his room.
Susan Sarandon . . . . Catherine Douglas
  • 1:10—Topless in bedroom with John Beck. Long shot, then right breast while lying in bed.
  2:18—In wet white nightgown running around outside during a storm.

The Other Woman (1992)

(Unrated version reviewed.)
Lee Anne Beaman . . . . Jessica Mathews
  ••• 0:17—Nude, undressing and getting into the shower.
  •• 0:40—Topless in the bathtub.
  •• 0:51—Buns, while lying in bed in the fetal position.
  ••• 1:09—Nude, on the floor making love with Traci. Interesting camera angles.
  ••• 1:13—Nude, getting up and out of bed, taking a shower, then making love with Carl. Long scene.

  •• 1:23—Topless on floor with Traci during video playback on TV.
  ••• 1:34—Buns, in long shot, taking off robe to greet Zmed. Topless and buns in bed with him.
Billy Bradshaw . . . . Scott
  • 0:52—Half of buns, making love with Sally in the office screening room.
Sam Jones . . . . .Mike Florian
Melissa Moore . . . . .Elysse
  •• 0:58—Topless, taking off her blouse while taking pictures during photo shoot.
Daniel Moriarity. . . . . Carl
  • 0:59—Buns, during photo shoot.
  ••• 1:15—Buns, while in the shower with Jessica.
Jenna Persaud . . . . .Traci Collins
  •• 0:21—Topless under sheer black top in her apartment with her boyfriend.
  ••• 0:22—Topless taking off her top and getting milk poured on her.
  ••• 0:23—Topless and buns, making love in kitchen while Jessica secretly watches.
  •• 0:31—Topless posing with Sheila at the the beach for Elysse.
  ••• 0:32—Full frontal nudity at the beach some more.
  • 0:33—Topless and buns, running in the surf. Long shot.
  •• 0:40—Topless with the milk and at the beach during Jessica's flashbacks.
  ••• 0:53—Nude, taking a shower, drying herself off and putting on robe.
  ••• 0:57—Topless posing with Carl during photo shoot.
  •• 0:59—More topless during photo shoot.
  ••• 1:09—Topless and buns, on the floor making love with Jessica. Interesting camera angles.
  1:23—Topless on floor with Jessica during video playback on TV.

Out Cold (1989)

Lisa Blount . . . . Phyllis
Tom Byrd. . . . . .Mr. Holstrom
  • 0:10—Brief frontal nudity getting out of bed with Teri Garr when her husband comes home.
Teri Garr. . . . . Sunny Cannald
Debra Lamb. . . . . Panetti's Dancer
  • 1:04—Brief topless dancing in G-string on stage. Don't see her face.
John Lithgow . . . . Dave Geary
Bruce McGill . . . . Ernie Cannald
  •• 0:12—Frontal nudity, while opening the shower door, talking to Teri Garr. Brief buns, when putting on underwear.
Randy Quaid . . . . Lester Atlas

Out for Justice (1991)

Gina Gershon. . . . . Patti Modono
John Leguizamo . . . . Boy in Alley
Julie Strain . . . . Roxanne Ford
  • 0:53—Brief side view of right breast in Polaroid photograph that Steven Seagal looks at.

- 1:06—Brief side view of right breast in Polaroid again.
- 1:11—Brief right breast, twice, dead in bed when discovered by Seagal.
- 1:12—Briefly in Polaroid again.

Out of Control (1984)
Cindi Dietrich . . . . Robin
- 0:29—Topless taking off her red top. Long shot.
Sherilyn Fenn . . . . .Katie
   0:19—In wet white T-shirt in pond with the other girls.
Martin Hewitt . . . . .Keith
Richard Kantor . . . . Gary
- 0:29—Buns, while pulling his underwear down during a game of strip spin the bottle.
Betsy Russell . . . . .Chrissie
   0:19—In white corset and panties in the pond.
•• 0:29—Topless taking off her top while playing Strip Spin the Bottle.
   0:30—Buns, taking off her panties.
Claudia Udy . . . . Tina
   0:19—In leopard skin pattern bra and panties.
- 0:28—In leopard bra and panties playing Strip Spin the Bottle, then very brief topless taking off her top. Long shot.
- 0:47—Brief left breast getting raped by bad guy on the boat.
- 0:54—Brief left breast, then right breast making love with Cowboy.
Jim Youngs . . . . Cowboy
- 0:54—Buns, while making love with Claudia Udy.

Out of the Dark (1988)
Starr Andreeff . . . . .Camille
Karen Black. . . . . Ruth
Teresa Crespo . . . . Debbie
Lynn Danielson . . . . .Kristi
- 0:09—Brief topless getting out of bed. More topless outside getting photographed.
•• 1:01—Topless in motel room making love with Kevin.
- 1:06—Left breast, while getting out of bed.
Cameron Dye . . . . Kevin Silver/Bobo
- 0:32—Brief buns when Kristi yanks his underwear down while he is throwing a basketball. Don't see his face.
Silvana Gallardo . . . . McDonald
Karen Mayo-Chandler .Barbara
- 0:16—Brief topless pulling red dress down wearing black stocking in Kevin's studio.
••• 0:17—Topless and buns posing during photo shoot.
Karen Witter . . . . Jo Ann

Out on Bail (1988)
Adrienne Pearce . . . . .Maggie
Kathy Shower . . . . .Sally Anne
- 1:01—Brief topless in shower with Robert Ginty.

The Outing (1987)
Mark Mitchell. . . . . Mike Daley
- 1:08—Buns when his friend gets killed, then very brief frontal nudity sitting up.
Michelle Watkins . . . . Faylene
•• 0:12—Topless taking off her top, standing by the edge of the swimming pool, then running topless through the house with panties on.

The Outlaw Josey Wales (1976)
Sam Bottoms . . . . .Jamie
Clint Eastwood. . . . . Josey Wales
Sondra Locke . . . . .Laura Lee
•• 1:20—Briefly nude in rape scene.

Overexposed (1990)
Karen Black . . . . Mrs. Trowbridge
William Bumiller. . . . . Hank
- 0:54—Brief buns, while taking off his pants to get into bed with Catherine Oxenberg.
Shelley Michelle . . Body Double for Catherine Oxenberg
•• 0:54—Left breast several times, buns when taking off panties, lower frontal nudity while in bed with Hank. Wearing a wig with wavy hair.
David Naughton . . . . Phillip

Pacific Heights (1990)
Beverly D'Angelo . . . . .Ann
- 0:01—Sort of topless in reflection on TV screen, then right breast, in bed with Michael Keaton.
   0:03—Very brief buns, turning over on bed when two guys burst in to the house.
Melanie Griffith . . . . Patty Parker
Matthew Modine . . . . Drake Goodman
Tracey Walter. . . . . Exterminator

Paint It Black (1989)
Sally Kirkland . . . . Marion Easton
   0:05—Most of left breast, while sitting in bed talking to Rick Rossovich.
Rick Rossovich . . . . .Jonathan Dunbar
- 0:48—Upper half of buns while getting out of bed with Julie Carmen.
Monique Van De Ven .Kyla Leif

Paperback Hero (1973; Canadian)
Elizabeth Ashley . . . . .Loretta
••• 0:37—Nude in shower with Keir Dullea. Long scene.
••• 0:39—Topless, straddling Dullea in the shower.
Dayle Haddon . . . . .Joanna
   0:31—Lower half of buns, under T-shirt while standing behind a bar with Keir Dullea.

Paradise (1981)
Willie Aames. . . . . .David
   0:42—Buns, while walking into the ocean with a fishing net. Dark, hard to see anything.
•• 1:12—Nude swimming with Phoebe Cates under water.
Phoebe Cates. . . . . .Sarah
•• 0:23—Buns and topless taking a shower in a cave while Willie Aames watches.

0:36—In wet white dress in a pond with Aames.
- 0:40—Very brief left breast caressing herself while looking at her reflection in the water.
- 0:43—Buns, getting out of bed to check out Aames' body while he sleeps.
- 0:46—Buns, washing herself in a pond at night.
- •• 0:55—Side view of her silhouette at the beach at night. Nude swimming in the water, viewed from below.
- •• 1:10—Topless making love with Aames. It looks like a body double. Don't see her face.
- ••• 1:12—Nude swimming under water with Aames.
- •• 1:16—Topless making love with Aames again. It looks like the body double again.

Paradise (1991)
Melanie Griffith . . . . .Lily Reed
Don Johnson . . . . Ben Reed
Sarah Trigger . . . . .Darlene
- 0:14—Brief topless ironing her clothes in open window while Willard and Billie watch from their tree house. Long shot after. Hard to see her face.

Paradise Motel (1985)
Leslee Bremmer . . . . Uncredited Girl Leaving Room
- 0:38—Topless buttoning her pink sweater, leaving motel room.
Gary Hershberger . . . . Sam
- •• 0:33—Buns, while running away from the Coach's house.
Colleen McDermott . . . . Debbie
- •• 0:24—Topless in motel room with Mic, when Sam lets them use a room.
Laurie Smith . . . . Honeymoon Wife
- ••• 0:02—Left breast, then topless in Honeymoon Suite with her new husband, then making love in bed.

Parasite (1982)
Cherie Currie . . . . Dana
Demi Moore . . . . .Patricia Welles
Cheryl Smith . . . . Captive Girl
- •• 0:08—Topless tied by wrists in kitchen.
- •• 0:12—Topless knocking gun out of guy's hands standing behind fence.
Tom Villard . . . . .Zeke

The Park is Mine (1985; Made for Cable Movie)
Tommy Lee Jones . . . . Mitch
Yaphet Kotto . . . . Eubanks
Helen Shaver . . . . .Valery Weaver
- 0:46—Very brief topless undressing then very, very brief left breast, while catching clothes from Tommy Lee Jones.

Partners (1982)
Iris Alhanti . . . . Jogger
- •• 0:21—Topless in the shower when Ryan O'Neal opens the shower curtain.
Jennifer Ashley . . . . Secretary

Robyn Douglass . . . . Jill
- •• 1:00—Brief topless taking off her top and getting into bed with Ryan O'Neal.
Denise Galik . . . . Clara
John Hurt . . . . Kerwin
Ryan O'Neal . . . . Benson
- •• 0:48—Buns, while wearing Indian outfit for photo session with Robyn Douglass. Don't see his face.

Party Camp (1987)
Jewel Shepard . . . . .Dyanne Stein
- ••• 0:57—In white bra and panties, then topless playing strip poker with the boys.
April Wayne . . . . .Nurse Brenda

Party Favors (1987)
Blondi . . . . .Bobbi
- •• 0:04—Topless in dressing room, taking off red top and putting on black one.
- 0:23—Brief topless when blouse pops off while delivering pizza.
- ••• 0:27—Topless and buns in G-string doing a strip routine outside.
- 0:31—Brief topless flapping her blouse to cool off.
- ••• 1:04—Topless doing a strip routine in a little girl outfit. Buns, in G-string. More topless after.
- 1:16—Nude taking off swimsuit next to pool during final credits.
April Dawn Dollarhide . . . . n.a.
George "Buck" Flower . . . . Pop
Jill Johnson . . . . .Trixie
- •• 0:04—Topless in dressing room, taking off blue dress and putting on red swimsuit.
- ••• 0:35—Topless in doctors office taking off her clothes.
- ••• 1:03—Topless doing strip routine in cowgirl costume. More topless after.
- 1:16—Topless taking off swimsuit next to pool during final credits.
Gail Thackray . . . . Nicole
- 0:04—Topless in dressing room with the other three girls changing into blue swimsuit.
- 0:11—Brief left breast in the swimsuit during dance practice.
- 0:12—Topless during dance practice.
- 0:17—More topless during dance practice.
- •• 0:42—Topless doing strip routine at anniversary party. Great buns in G-string shots.
- ••• 1:01—Topless and buns in G-string after stripping from cheerleader outfit. Lots of bouncing breast shots. Mingling with the men afterwards.
- 1:16—Nude by the swimming pool during the final credits.

Party Incorporated (1989)
a.k.a. Party Girls
Marilyn Chambers . . . . .Marilyn Sanders
- ••• 0:56—In lingerie, then topless in bedroom with Weston. Nice!
- 1:11—Brief topless on the beach when Peter takes her swimsuit top off.

Ruth Corrine Collins . . . . .Betty
- 0:07—Topless on desk with Dickie. Long shot.
- 1:08—Topless in bed with Weston when Marilyn Chambers comes in.

Susan Napoli. . . . . .n.a.

Kimberly Taylor. . . . . .Felicia
- 0:26—Topless shaking her breasts trying an outfit on.
- 0:39—Topless and buns in G-string in the bar with the guys.

Christina Veronica. . . . . .Christina
- 0:52—Buns and topless dancing in front of everybody at party.

Party Plane (1988)

Laura Albert . . . . Uncredited Auditioning Woman
- 0:30—Topless, taking off blue dress during audition. She's wearing a white ribbon in her ponytail.

Michele Burger . . . . .Carol
- 0:31—Topless, squirting whipped cream on herself for her audition.
- 0:38—Topless doing a strip tease routine on the plane.
- 1:02—Topless mud wrestling with Renee on the plane.
- 1:09—Topless in the cockpit, covered with mud.
- 1:17—Topless in serving cart.

Iris Condon. . . . . Renee
- 0:29—Buns, in white lingerie during audition.
- 0:48—Topless plane doing a strip tease routine.
- 1:02—Topless on plane mud wrestling with Carol.
- 1:12—Left breast, covered with mud, holding the Mad Bomber.
- 1:17—Left breast, then topless in trunk with the Doctor.

Jill Johnson . . . . Laurie
- 0:06—Topless and buns changing clothes and getting into spa with her two girlfriends. (She's wearing a black swimsuit bottom.)
- 0:11—Topless getting out of spa.
- 0:16—Topless in pool after being pushed in and her swimsuit top comes off.
- 0:20—In bra and panties, then topless on plane doing a strip tease.

Jacqueline Palmer . . . . .Suzie
- 0:06—Topless and buns changing clothes and getting into spa with her two girlfriends. (She's the dark haired one.)
- 0:11—Topless again, getting out of spa.
- 0:23—In bra, then topless doing strip tease routine on plane.
- 0:35—Topless doing another routine on the plane.

Renee Way . . . . .Andy
- 0:01—Topless taking off her blouse to fix the plane.
- 0:06—Topless sitting on edge of spa.
- 0:11—Topless again, getting out of spa.
- 0:12—Brief topless dropping her towel while talking to Tim.

Pascali's Island (1988; British)

Ben Kingsley. . . . . Basil Pascali

Helen Mirren .Lydia Neuman
- 1:00—Left breast, lying in bed with Charles Dance. Long shot.

The Passion of Beatrice (1988; French)

Erick Bernard . . . . .L'amant
- 0:06—Brief buns, in bed with François' mother when discovered by François.

Julie Delpy . . . . Béatrice
- 0:13—Full frontal nudity, wiping her crotch and burning her clothes.
- 0:58—Left breast, then topless getting out of bed.
- 1:11—Side view of right breast, holding dress after getting raped by her father. Nude, running to the door and barricading it with furniture.
- 1:12—More nude, arranging furniture.
- 1:36—More of right breast, when her father puts soot on her face.
- 1:37—Brief left breast, then topless and brief buns standing with soot on her face. Long shot.
- 1:44—Topless taking a bath. Subtitles get in the way a bit.

Maïté Maillé. . . . . .La Noiraude
- 1:24—Brief left breast, showing Béatrice how she was abused.

Isabelle Nanty . . . . La Nourrice
- 1:53—Right breast, offering her breast milk to Arnaud.

Jean Luc Rivals . . . . .Jehan
- 0:57—Brief frontal nudity, getting dried off.

Tina Sportolaro . . . . Mère de François Enfant
- 0:06—Brief topless when the young François discovers her in bed with another man and kills him.

Pat Garrett and Billy the Kid (1973)

Rita Coolidge . . . . .Maria
- 1:34—Brief right breast getting undressed to get into bed with Kris Kristofferson.

Kris Kristofferson . . . . Billy the Kid
- 0:37—Buns, while getting into bed with a girl after Harry Dean Stanton gets out. Long shot, hard to see.

Charlie Martin Smith . . . . Bowdre

Patricia (1984)

Private Screenings.

José Antonio Ceinos. . . . . n.a.

Sascha Hehn . . . . Harry Miller
- 0:41—Lower half of buns, while scratching his butt in the hallway.

Anne Parillaud . . . . Patricia Cook
- 0:25—Topless, opening her jumpsuit top to get attention while trying to hitchhike.
- 0:30—Topless in white panties, running around at a seminary, trying to get away from a group of guys.
- 0:31—Topless in confessional booth.
- 0:32—Running around some more.
- 0:37—Nude making love with Priscilla on bed.

0:46—Sort of briefly topless running around in skimpy costume.

••• 0:49—Dancing in two piece swimsuit, then topless.

•• 0:50—Topless while lying on her stomach.

• 0:52—Brief topless running into the ocean.

• 0:53—Brief topless under water.

• 0:55—More brief topless shots under the water.

••• 0:56—Nude, getting out of the ocean and lying down on the beach.

•• 1:09—Topless taking off her dress and playing bull-fight with Harry.

•• 1:10—Nude, dancing in her room. Hard to see because the curtains get in the way.

• 1:24—Brief buns while making love with Harry.

• 1:26—Brief topless while making love with Harry.

••• 1:27—Full frontal nudity making love on top of Harry in bed.

The Patriot (1986)

Jeff Conaway..........................Mitchell

Simone Griffeth...........................Sean

•• 0:46—Brief topless lying in bed, making love with Ryder.

Patti Rocks (1988)

John Jenkins ....Eddie

• 1:07—Buns, while making love with Patti in bed.

Karen Landry.............................Patti

0:48—Buns, walking from bathroom to bedroom and shutting the door. Long shot.

• 0:48—Very brief right breast in shower with Billy.

•• 1:04—Topless in bed with Eddie while Billy is out in the living room.

Chris Mulkey.............................Billy

•• 0:24—Nude in restroom with Eddie, undressing and putting on underwear.

Patty Hearst (1989)

Frances Fisher ....Yolanda

Natasha Richardson.................Patricia Hearst

•• 0:13—Topless, blindfolded in the bathtub while talking to a woman member of the S.L.A.

Pauline at the Beach (1983; French)

Simon De La Brosse......................Sylvain

Arielle Dombasle........................Marion

• 0:24—Brief topless lying in bed with a guy when her cousin looks in the window.

•• 0:43—Brief topless in house kissing Henri, while he takes her white dress off.

•• 0:59—Topless walking down the stairs in a white bikini bottom while putting a white blouse on.

Payback (1988)

Michele Burger ....Laura

• 0:08—Brief topless sitting up in bed just before getting shot, then brief topless twice, dead in bed.

Jean Carol ....Donna Nathan

••• 0:24—Topless opening her pink robe for Jason while reclining on couch.

Payback (1991)

Corey Michael Eubanks ....Clinton

• 0:49—Brief buns, while putting his pants on after jerks tip his trailer over.

Payday (1972)

Ahna Capri............................Mayleen

• 0:20—Left breast in bed sleeping, then right breast with Rip Torn.

••• 0:21—Topless sitting up in bed smoking a cigarette and talking to Torn. Long scene.

Rip Torn...........................Maury Dann

• 1:21—Brief buns while getting up out of bed.

Payoff (1991; Made for Cable Movie)

Keith Carradine ....Peter "Mac" MacAlister

• 0:01—Sort of buns, while in shower, seen from above, looking down.

Pennies from Heaven (1981)

Josh Cadman...............................n.a.

Jessica Harper............................Joan

• 0:43—Brief topless opening her nightgown for Steve Martin.

Perfect (1985)

Jamie Lee Curtis ....Jessie Wilson

0:14—No nudity, but doing aerobics in leotards.

0:26—More aerobics in leotards.

0:40—More aerobics, mentally making love with John Travolta while leading the class.

1:19—More aerobics when photographer is shooting pictures.

1:32—In red leotard after the article comes out in *Rolling Stone*.

Chelsea Field ....Randy

Marilu Henner...........................Sally

0:13—Working out on exercise machine.

Charlene Jones.........................Shotsy

• 0:17—Topless stripping on stage in a club. Buns in G-string.

Mathew Reed............................Roger

• 1:01—Buns, while dancing in a jock strap at Chippendale's.

Perfect Strangers (1984)

Anne Carlisle ....Sally

• 0:34—Left breast, while making love in bed with Johnny.

Ann Magnuson ....Maida

Perfect Timing (1984)

Jo Anne Bates...........................Karen

••• 0:21—Nude, getting ready to get her picture taken.

Paul Boretski.............................Joe

•• 0:11—Brief frontal nudity and buns, while rolling over on the bed.

• 0:29—Frontal nudity on the roof in the snow with Bonnie.

• 0:35—Buns, while on bed getting slapped on the behind.

• 0:50—Buns, while in bed with Judy.

•• 1:03—Brief frontal nudity on TV with Judy while he and Bonnie watch.

Nancy Cser . . . . Lacy
0:54—In white lingerie, taking off clothes for Harry and posing.

••• 0:56—Topless getting photographed by Harry.

• 0:58—Topless, making love with Harry.

• 1:01—Topless.

Alexandra Innes. . . . . Salina

•• 1:06—Right breast and buns, posing for Harry.

Stephen Markle. . . . . Harry

• 0:58—Buns, while making love with Lacy.

Mary Beth Rubens . . . . Judy

• 0:04—In a bra, then topless in bedroom with Joe.

•• 0:05—Nude, walking to kitchen, then talking with Harry.

• 0:08—Left breast seen through the camera's view finder.

• 0:10—Nude, getting dressed in bedroom.
0:49—In red bra and panties.

•• 0:50—Nude, in bed with Joe.

••• 1:00—Nude, discovering Joe's hidden video camera, then going downstairs.

Michele Scarabelli . . . . Charlotte

•• 1:11—Brief buns, then topless in bed with Harry.

• 1:18—Topless in bed with Harry during the music video.

Perfect Victims (1988)

Deborah Shelton. . . . . Liz Winters
0:55—Very brief, upper half of breasts, lying back in bubble bath.

Jackie Swanson . . . . Carrie Marks

•• 0:13—In bra, then left breast, while changing clothes by closet.

• 0:23—Brief left breast, while lying on sofa when Brandon opens her robe while she's drugged out. Brief right breast and lower frontal nudity when he rips off her panties.
0:25—Right breast several more times, while lying on sofa while Brandon torments her.

••• 1:15—Left breast and buns, seen through clear shower door. Nice shot for bun lovers!

• 1:16—Brief buns in the shower, seen from above.

Performance (1970)

James Fox . . . . Chas

• 0:00—Very brief frontal nudity and buns while making love with a woman. Don't see his face.

• 0:02—Buns, while getting up next to his girlfriend.

• 0:24—Brief buns, while getting roughed up by bad guys.

Mick Jagger. . . . . Turner
0:48—Side view of buns, while getting out of bathtub.

Anita Pallenberg . . . . .Pherber

• 0:44—Side view of left breast, while in bed with Mick Jagger.

••• 0:47—Topless and buns, while in bathtub with Lucy and Jagger.

• 0:50—Buns, injecting herself with drugs.

•• 1:20—Right breast, while lying on the floor. Then topless and buns, in bed with Chas.

Ann Sidney. . . . . Dana

• 0:01—Very brief topless and buns.

• 0:24—Brief topless with Chas in flashbacks.

The Perils of Gwendoline in the Land of the Yik Yak (1984; French)

Zabou . . . . Beth

•• 0:36—Topless in the rain in the forest, taking off her blouse.

•• 0:57—Topless in torture chamber getting rescued by Tawny Kitaen.

•• 1:04—Topless after Kitaen escapes.

• 1:11—Buns, in costume during fight.

Brent Huff . . . . .Willard

• 0:51—Brief buns, in G-string while wearing costume.

•• 0:52—Buns, in G-string, walking around with Tawny Kitaen in costumes.

•• 0:54—More buns, after the women realize he's a man.

••• 0:56—Buns, in jail while wearing only the G-string.

Tawny Kitaen . . . . .Gwendoline

••• 0:36—Topless in the rain in the forest, taking off her top. More topless with Willard.

•• 0:52—Buns, while walking around with Willard in costumes.

• 0:55—Buns, falling into jail cell, then in jail cell in costume.

• 0:57—Buns, while rescuing Beth in torture chamber.

•• 1:01—Topless in S&M costume in front of mirrors.

• 1:04—Brief topless escaping from chains.

• 1:07—Buns, in costume while riding chariot and next to wall.

• 1:09—Buns, while standing up.

•• 1:11—Buns, in costume during fight. Wearing green ribbon.

•• 1:18—Topless making love with Willard.

Personal Best (1982)

Patrice Donnelly. Tory Skinner

•• 0:16—Full frontal nudity after making love with Mariel Hemingway.

•• 0:30—Full frontal nudity in steam room.
1:06—Topless in shower.

Scott Glenn . . . . .Terry Tingloff

Mariel Hemingway. . . . . Chris Cahill

•• 0:16—Brief lower frontal nudity getting examined by Patrice Donnelly, then topless after making love with her.

•• 0:30—Topless in the steam room talking with the other women.

Kenny Moore. . . . . .Denny Stiles

•• 1:31—Nude, getting out of bed and walking to the bathroom.

Personal Services (1987)
Julie Walters . . . . Cynthia Payne
- 0:21—Very brief side view of left breast, while reaching to turn off radio in the bathtub. Her face is covered with cream.

Pets (1974)
Joan Blackman . . . . Geraldine Mills
- 0:46—Brief side view of left breast, while getting out of bed after making love with Bonnie.
Candice Rialson. . . . . Bonnie
- • 0:26—Topless dancing in field while Dan is watching her while he's tied up.
- • • 0:33—Topless making love on top of Dan while he's still tied up.
  0:35—Running through woods in braless orange top.
- • 0:40—Topless getting into bath at Geraldine's house.
- 0:45—Topless posing for Geraldine.
  0:54—In black and red lingerie outfit getting ready for bed.
- • • 1:02—Topless taking off lingerie in bed with Ron, then making love with him.
  1:34—Almost topless, getting whipped by Vincent.

Phantom Empire (1987)
Michelle Bauer . . . . Cave Bunny
  0:32—Running around in the cave a lot in two piece loincloth swimsuit.
- • 1:13—Finally topless after losing her top during a fight, stays topless until Andrew puts his jacket on her.
Tricia Brown . . . . Cavegirl
Sybil Danning . . . . The Alien Queen
Dawn Wildsmith . . . . Eddy Colchilde

Phantom of the Mall: Eric's Revenge (1988)
Crisstyn Dante. . . . . Body Double for Ms. Whitman
- • 0:25—Topless in bed about five times with Peter.
Morgan Fairchild. . . . . .Karen Wilton
Pauly Shore. . . . . Buzz
- • 1:06—Buns, while mooning security guard on B&W surveillance monitor.
Kimber Sissons . . . . .Suzie
  0:14—Briefly in bra, in dressing room on B&W security monitor.
Brinke Stevens. . . . . .Girl in Dressing Room
- 0:14—Topless in dressing room and on B&W monitor several times (second room from the left).
Kari Whitman . . . . Melody Austin

Picasso Trigger (1989)
Steve Bond . . . . .n.a.
Cynthia Brimhall. . . . . Edy
- • 0:59—Topless in weight room with a guy.
Hope Marie Carlton. Taryn
  0:17—In white lingerie on boat with Dona Speir.
- • • 0:56—Topless and buns in spa with a guy.
Patty Duffek . . . . Patticakes
- • 1:04—Topless taking a Jacuzzi bath.

Liv Lindeland . . . . .Inga
Kym Malin . . . . .Kym
- • 1:04—Topless taking a shower.
Dona Speir. . . . . Donna
  0:17—In white lingerie on boat with Hope Marie Carlton.
- • • 0:49—Topless and buns standing, then making love in bed.
Roberta Vasquez. . . . . Pantera

Pick-Up Summer (1979; Canadian)
Joy Boushel . . . . .Sally
- • • 0:56—Topless playing pinball, then running around.
Carl Marotte . . . . Steve
- 0:18—Side view of buns, while hanging a B.A. out passenger window at Rod.
Karen Stephen. . . . . .Donna
- 0:25—Very brief lower half of breast, pulling her T-shirt up to distract someone.
  0:34—Very, very brief topless when the boys spray her and she jumps up.
Helene Udy . . . . Suzy
  0:34—Very, very brief topless when the boys spray her and she jumps up.
Michael Zelnicker. . . . . Greg
- 0:04—Brief buns, while hanging a B.A. out the back window of the van.

Pin (1988)
David Hewlett . . . . Leon
Terry O'Quinn . . . . Dr. Linden
Helene Udy . . . . Marcia Bateman
- • • 1:03—Topless in bedroom with Leon.

Pink Floyd The Wall (1982)
Nell Campbell . . . . .Groupie
Jenny Wright . . . . American Groupie
- • • 0:41—Topless backstage in back of a truck doing a strip tease dance in front of some people.

A Place Called Today (1972)
Cheri Caffaro . . . . .Cindy Cartwright
- • 0:14—Full frontal nudity covered with oil or something writhing around on the bed.
- 1:21—Brief side view of right breast undressing in the bathroom.
- 1:23—Brief full frontal nudity getting kidnapped by two guys.
- • 1:30—Nude when they take off the blanket.
- 1:35—Brief topless just before getting killed.
Lana Wood. .Carolyn Scheider
- • • 0:40—Side view of left breast, then topless lying down talking to Ron.

Planet of the Apes (1968)
Jeff Burton . . . . .Dodge
- 0:26—Very brief buns while taking off clothes to go skinny dipping. (Guy on the right.)
Robert Gunner. . . . . Landon
- 0:26—Very brief buns while taking off clothes to go skinny dipping. (Guy on the left.)

Charlton Heston . . . . .George Taylor
- 0:26—Buns, seen through a waterfall and while walking on rocks. Long shots.
- 1:04—Buns while standing in middle of the room when the apes tear his loin cloth off.

Play Misty for Me *(1971)*
Clint Eastwood . . . . Dave Garland
Donna Mills. . . . . Tobie
- 1:10—Brief side view of right breast hugging Clint Eastwood in a pond near a waterfall. Long shot, hard to see.
Jessica Walter . . . . .Evelyn
- 0:13—Very brief right breast in bed with Clint Eastwood. Lit with blue light. Hard to see anything.

Playbirds *(1978; British)*
Pat Astley . . . . Doreen Hamilton
- • 0:00—Topless posing for photo session.
Suzy Mandel . . . . Lena
- • 0:12—Nude stripping in Playbird office.

Playroom *(1989)*
a.k.a. Schizo
Lisa Aliff. . . . . Jenny
- • 0:23—Topless making love on top of Christopher.
James Purcell. . . . . Paul
- • 0:25—Buns, while making love with Jamie Rose on a chair.
Jamie Rose. . . . . Marcy

Point Blank *(1967)*
Angie Dickinson . . . . .Chris
  0:46—In white slip when John Vernon opens her dress.
- 0:51—Topless in background putting dress on. Kind of a long shot.

Point Break *(1991)*
Debra Lamb . . . . .Uncredited Flame Blower at Party
James Le Gros . . . . .Roach
- 0:07—Brief buns, twice, while mooning the bank security camera. Wearing Richard Nixon mask. Could be anybody.
- 0:11—Buns, on B&W monitor in the FBI office.
- 0:59—Buns, mooning his friends while riding surfboard. Can't see his face clearly.
Julie Michaels . . . . .Freight Train
- 0:53—Brief topless in the shower.
- 0:54—Nude, beating up Keanu Reeves in the bathroom during shootout. Full frontal nudity while stabbing an FBI agent.
Lori Petty. . . . . .Tyler
- 1:14—Very brief buns, running out of Keanu Reeves' bedroom.
Keanu Reeves .Johnny Utah
- 1:14—Very brief buns, while standing up to run after Tyler.
Patrick Swayze . . . . Bodhi

Police *(1985; French)*
Sandrine Bonnaire . . . . Lydie
- ••• 0:49—Full frontal nudity, undressing in front of Gérard Depardieu, then getting out of the shower.
Gérard Depardieu . . . . Mangin
Jonathan Leina. . . . . Simon
- •• 0:11—Upper half of buns and brief frontal nudity in police station. Typewriter gets in the way.
Sophie Marceau . . . . .Noria
- 0:10—Brief left breast in window during police strip search.
- 1:36—Right and left breasts several times, while in bed with Gérard Depardieu

Police Academy II: Their First Assignment *(1985)*
Julie Brown. . . . . Chloe
Colleen Camp . . . . .Kirkland
Steve Guttenberg. . . . . .Carey Mahoney
Art Metrano. . . . . Lt. Mauser
- 0:39—Buns, while in the locker room after the guys put epoxy resin in his shampoo.

Popcorn and Ice Cream *(1978; West German)*
Ursula Buchfellner . . . . Yvonne
- ••• 0:30—Nude with the hotel manager, Vivi and Bea.
- 0:40—Topless in open dress at the disco.
Bea Fiedler . . . . .Policewoman
- ••• 0:47—Full frontal nudity getting dressed.
- ••• 1:13—Right breast, then topless in bed with a lover.
- ••• 1:14—Full frontal nudity in bed some more.
Zachi Noy . . . . .Johnny
Olivia Pascal Vivi
- 0:26—Full frontal nudity (she's on the right), covered with soap, taking a shower with Bea.

Porky's *(1981; Canadian)*
Rod Ball . . . . Steve
- 0:18—Brief frontal nudity sitting on bench in the cabin.
- 0:21—Very brief frontal nudity, following Meat out the front door of the cabin, then buns, while in front of the house.
Kim Cattrall . . . . Honeywell
- 0:58—Brief buns, then very brief lower frontal nudity after removing skirt to make love in the boy's locker room.
Susan Clark . . . . .Cherry Forever
Tony Ganios. . . . . Meat
- •• 0:21—Brief buns, while running out of the cabin during practical joke.
Kaki Hunter . . . . .Wendy
- 1:02—Brief full frontal nudity, then brief topless in the shower scene.
Wyatt Knight . . . . Tommy Turner
Pat Lee. . . . . .Stripper
- 0:33—Brief topless dancing on stage at Porky's showing her breasts to Pee Wee.
Dan Monahan . . . . Pee Wee
- 0:22—Buns, while running down the road at night. Long shot.

Jack Mulcahy. . . . . Frank Bell
- • 0:21—Very brief frontal nudity, getting up from bench. Then buns while in front of the cabin.

Cyril O'Reilly. . . . . .Tim
- • 0:21—Very, very brief frontal nudity, getting up from bench. Then buns, while in front of the cabin.

Allene Simmons . . . . Jackie
- • 1:02—Topless in the shower scene.

Jill Whitlow . . . . .Mindy

Roger Wilson. . . . . Mickey

Porky's II: The Next Day *(1983; Canadian)*

Rod Ball. . . . . Steve

Cissie Colpitts-Cameron . Graveyard Gloria/Sandy Le Toi
- 0:26—Buns in G-string at carnival.
- •• 0:39—Topless and buns in G-string, stripping for Pee Wee at cemetery.
- •• 0:40—More topless, pretending to die.
- • 0:42—Topless, being carried by Meat.

Kaki Hunter. . . . . Wendy

Dan Monahan. . . . . Pee Wee
- • 0:39—Buns while at cemetery with Graveyard Gloria, then upper half of lower frontal nudity when he's holding her.
- • 0:40—Upper half of lower frontal nudity when he drops Gloria.
- • 0:42—Nude, trying to hide Steve.
- ••• 0:44—Nude when guys with shotguns shoot at him.

Jack Mulcahy. . . . . Frank Bell

Cyril O'Reilly. . . . . .Tim

Porky's Revenge *(1985; Canadian)*

Kim Evenson . . . . Inga
- •• 0:02—Right breast, while opening her graduation gown during Pee Wee's dream.
- •• 1:27—Topless showing Pee Wee that she doesn't have any clothes under her graduation gown.

Tony Ganios . . . . .Meat
- •• 0:16—Buns, while getting out of swimming pool (the fifth guy getting out). More buns running around.

Mark Herrier . . . . Billy
- •• 0:16—Buns, while getting out of swimming pool (the second guy getting out). More buns running around.

Kaki Hunter. . . . . Wendy
- 1:22—In white bra and panties taking off her clothes to jump off a bridge.

Wyatt Knight. . . . . Tommy Turner
- •• 0:16—Buns, while getting out of swimming pool (the first guy getting out). More buns running around.
- • 0:54—Buns, getting his underwear pulled down while trying to escape from a motel room from Balbricker.

Rose McVeigh. . . . . Miss Webster
- ••• 0:39—In black bra, panties, garter belt and stockings then topless in her apartment with Mr. Dobish while Pee Wee and his friends secretly watch.

Dan Monahan . . . . Pee Wee
- •• 0:02—Buns, when his graduation gown gets accidentally torn off during a dream.
- •• 0:16—Buns, while getting out of swimming pool (the fourth guy getting out). More buns while running around.
- •• 1:27—Buns, while getting his graduation gown town off.

Nancy Valen. . . . . Ginger

Portfolio *(1983)*

Carol Alt. . . . . .Herself
- • 0:28—Brief right breast, while adjusting black, see-through blouse.
- 0:31—Brief side view of a little bit of right breast while changing clothes backstage at a fashion show.

Kelly Lynch. . . . . Elite Model

Shari Shattuck . . . . Elite Model

Posed for Murder *(1988)*

Charlotte J. Helmcamp. . . . . .Laura Shea
- • 0:00—Topless in photos during opening credits.
- ••• 0:22—Posing for photos in sheer green teddy, then topless in sailor's cap, then great topless shots wearing just a G-string.
- 0:31—Very brief right breast in photo on desk.
- 0:44—In black one piece swimsuit.
- ••• 0:52—Topless in bed making love with her boyfriend.

Possession *(1981; French/German)*

Isabelle Adjani .Anna/Helen
- • 0:04—Topless in bed.
- • 0:16—Topless lying in bed when Sam Neill pulls the covers over her.
- ••• 0:47—Right breast, then topless lying in bed with Neill.
- • 1:08—Right breast, while lying on the floor with Neill, then sitting up.

Sam Neill . . . . Marc

The Postman Always Rings Twice *(1981)*

Anjelica Huston . . . . .Madge
- • 1:30—Brief side view left breast sitting in trailer with Jack Nicholson.

Jessica Lange . . . . Cora Papadakis
- 0:17—Making love with Jack Nicholson on the kitchen table. No nudity, but still exciting.
- 0:18—Pubic hair peeking out of right side of her panties when Nicholson grabs her crotch.
- 1:03—Very, very brief topless, then very, very brief right breast twice, when Nicholson rips her dress down to simulate a car accident.
- 1:26—Brief lower frontal nudity when Nicholson starts crawling up over her in bed.

Jack Nicholson . . . . Frank Chambers
- • 1:25—Buns, while lying across the bed.

Powwow Highway *(1988; U.S./British)*

Gary Farmer . . . . Philbert Bono
- •• 1:00—Buns, while in bedroom getting out of bed to wake up Buddy.

Amanda Wyss . . . . Rabbit Layton

Predator 2 *(1990)*

Maria Conchita Alonso . . . . Leona
Elpidia Carrillo. . . . . .Anna
Nick Corri . . . . Detective
Bill Paxton. . . . . Jerry
Corey Rano. . . . . .Ramon Vega
- • 0:23—Buns, while hanging upside down several times.
- • 0:26—Nude, hanging upside down, dead.

Teri Weigel . . . . Columbian Girl
- • 0:22—Brief topless making love on bed. More topless several times being held on the floor, brief full frontal nudity getting up when the Predator starts his attack.

Preppies *(1984)*

Nitchie Barrett. . . . . Roxanne
- • 0:11—Brief topless changing into waitress costumes with her two friends.

Sharon Kane . . . . Exotic Dancer
Cindy Manion. . . . . Jo
- • 0:11—Brief topless changing into waitress costumes with her two friends.
- • 0:44—Topless during party with the three preppie guys.

Katt Shea . . . . .Margot
- ••• 0:20—Topless teasing Richard through the glass door of her house.
- 0:54—In bra and panties with Trini, practicing sexual positions on the bed.
- 1:07—Brief topless after taking off bra in bed.

Lynda Wiesmeier. . . . . Trini
- 0:54—In bra and panties, practicing sexual positions on beds with Margot.
- ••• 1:06—Topless on bed with Mark.

Presumed Guilty *(1990)*

Holly Floria . . . . Mary Austin
- • 1:02—Side view of left breast, very brief lower frontal nudity and buns, while making love with Jessie.

Jack Vogel. . . . . Jessie Weston
- •• 0:19—Buns, while getting out of the shower.

Presumed Innocent *(1990)*

Bonnie Bedelia . . . . Barbara Sabich
Brian Dennehy . . . . Raymond Horgan
Raul Julia. . . . . Sandy Stern
Greta Scacchi . . . . .Carolyn Polhemus
- • 0:46—Left breast, while making love on desk with Harrison Ford.
- • 0:53—Buns, lying in bed on top of Ford.

Pretty Baby *(1978)*

Keith Carradine . . . . Bellocq
Susan Sarandon . . . . Hattie
- 0:12—Feeding a baby with her left breast, while sitting by the window in the kitchen.
- • 0:24—Brief side view, taking a bath.
- ••• 0:39—Topless on the couch when Keith Carradine photographs her.

Brooke Shields . . . . .Violet
- • 0:57—Topless and buns taking a bath.
- • 1:26—Topless posing on couch for Keith Carradine.
- • 1:28—Buns, getting thrown out of the room, then trying to get back in.

Pretty Maids All in a Row *(1971)*

Joy Bang . . . . Rita
- • 0:57—Brief topless in car with Rock Hudson.
- • 1:01—Right breast, in car with Hudson. Dark. More right breast, while getting dressed.

Gretchen Burrell. . . . . .Marjorie
- • 0:05—Partial side of right breast, in office with Rock Hudson.
- • 0:07—Topless on the couch in Hudson's office.

Joanna Cameron . . . . Yvonne
John David Carson . . . . Ponce
- • 1:04—Very brief buns, sticking out from under sheet when he uses it to cover Angie Dickinson in bed.

Angie Dickinson . . . . .Miss Smith
- • 1:04—Buns, in long shot, while lying on bed with Ponce.

Aimée Eccles . . . . Hilda
- • 1:06—Partial buns while sitting on desk in Rock Hudson's office. Her hair covers most of her right breast.

June Fairchild . . . . Sonya "Sonny" Swingle
- • 1:10—Brief topless and lower frontal nudity, taking Polaroid photos of herself in Rock Hudson's office.

Barbara Leigh. . . . . .Jean McDrew
- • 0:30—Brief partial side view of right breast when she leans over chess board on bed to touch Rock Hudson.

Margaret Markov. . . . . Polly
Brenda Sykes .Pamela Wilcox

Pretty Smart *(1986)*

Julie Kristen Smith . . . . .Samantha Falconwright
- •• 0:20—Nude in her room when Daphne sees her.
- •• 0:26—Topless in bed talking to Jennifer.
- •• 0:40—Topless in bed.
- •• 0:52—Topless sitting in lounge by the pool.
- • 0:57—Brief left breast, while brushing teeth.
- • 1:10—Brief right breast, while making love with boyfriend in bed.
- • 1:13—More brief right breast.
- ••• 1:14—Nude, sitting on pillow on top of her boyfriend in bed.

Kim Waltrip . . . . .Sara Gentry (the teacher)
- •• 0:53—Topless sunbathing with her students.

Pretty Woman *(1990)*

Judy Baldwin . . . . Susan
John David Carson . . . . .Mark
Lucinda Crosby . . . . .Olsen Sister
Richard Gere . . . . Edward Lewis
Shelley Michelle . . . . Body Double for Julia Roberts
    0:04—In black panties and bra, waking up and getting dressed.
Julia Roberts . . . . Vivian Ward
    • 1:30—Very, very brief tip of left breast, then right breast, then left breast seen through head board, in bed with Gere. It's her—look especially at the vertical vein that pops out in the middle of her forehead whenever her blood pressure goes up.

The Prey *(1980)*

Steve Bond . . . . .Joel
Gayle Gannes . . . . .Gail
    • 0:36—Brief topless putting T-shirt on before the creature attacks her.

Prey of the Chameleon *(1992; Made for Cable Movie)*

Linda Carol . . . . Nurse
    • 0:00—Topless several times, making love with a guy in restroom. Dark.
Lisa London . . . . Alice
Michelle McBride . . . . Leslie
Alexandra Paul . . . . Carrie
James Wilder . . . . .J.D.
    • 0:32—Upper half of buns, while getting out of bed.
Daphne Zuniga . . . . .Patricia/Elizabeth Burrows
    0:08—Buns, of dead body, lying on ground. Don't see face.

Priceless Beauty *(1989; Italian)*

Christopher Lambert . . . . Monroe
Diane Lane . . . . China/Anna
    •• 0:34—Topless in bed with Christopher Lambert.
    • 0:35—Brief left breast, then side of right breast on top of Lambert.
Claudia Ohana . . . . .Lisa

Prime Cut *(1972)*

Janit Baldwin . . . . Violet
    • 0:25—Very brief nude, being swung around when Gene Hackman lifts her up to show to Lee Marvin.
    • 0:41—Brief topless putting on a red dress.
Sissy Spacek . . . . .Poppy
    • 0:25—Brief side view of left breast lying in hay, then buns when Gene Hackman lifts her up to show to Lee Marvin.
    ••• 0:30—Topless sitting in bed, then getting up to try on a dress while Marvin watches.
    0:32—Close up of breasts though sheer black dress in a restaurant.
Angel Tompkins . . . . Clarabelle
    • 1:03—Very brief left breast sitting up in bed to talk to Lee Marvin.
    1:04—Very brief back side view of left breast jumping out of bed.

Prime Evil *(1987)*

Amy Brentano . . . . Brett
    ••• 1:13—Topless removing her gown (she's in the middle) with Cathy and Judy.
Ruth Corrine Collins . . . . Cathy
    ••• 0:15—Topless making love with her boyfriend in bed.
    • 0:16—More topless sitting up and getting out of bed.
    ••• 0:27—Topless, sitting up while the priest talks to her.
    •• 1:13—Left breast, while removing her gown (she's on the left) with Brett and Judy.
Jeanne Marie . . . . .Judy
    1:13—Topless removing her gown (she's on the right) with Cathy and Brett.
Christine Moore . . . . Alexandra Parkman
    0:09—In white bra in locker room.
Miriam Zucker . . . . .Nancy Deans
    •• 0:03—Topless several times, during sacrificial ceremony.

The Prime of Miss Jean Brodie *(1969)*

Pamela Franklin . . . . Sandy
    •• 1:21—Topless posing as a model for Teddy's painting. Brief right breast, while kissing him. Long shot of buns, while getting dressed.
Maggie Smith . . . . Jean Brodie

Prime Target *(1991)*

Jenilee Harrison . . . . Kathy Bloodstone
    ••• 0:12—Topless, lying back in bed with David Heavener. Short, but sweet!
    • 0:13—Partial right breast, under Heavener's arm.
Sandra Margot . . . . Girl in Shower
    ••• 0:52—Side view of left breast and buns, taking a shower.
    • 0:53—Buns, in hotel room after getting out of the shower.

The Prince of Pennsylvania *(1988)*

Bonnie Bedelia . . . . Pam Marshetta
    0:12—In black bra in open blouse in kitchen. Long scene.
Amy Madigan . . . . Carla Headlee
    • 0:37—Left breast and buns, while getting out of bed with Keanu Reeves and putting on a robe.
Dan Monahan . . . . Tommy Rutherford
Fred Ward . . . . Gary

Prison Stories, Women on the Inside
(1990; Made for Cable Movie)

Rae Dawn Chong . . . . Rhonda
    • 0:26—Very brief right breast several times in prison shower with Annabella Sciorra.
Lolita Davidovich . . . . Lorretta
Silvana Gallardo . . . . .Mercedes
Annabella Sciorra . . . . Nicole
Rachel Ticotin . . . . Iris
    0:07—Brief buns, squatting while getting strip searched in jail. Don't see her face.

Private Lessons *(1981)*

Ed Begley, Jr. . . . . Jack Travis
Pamela Jean Bryant . . . . Joyce
- • 0:03—Very brief right breast, changing in the house while Billy and his friend peep from outside.
Sylvia Kristel . . . . Mallow
- • 0:20—Very brief topless sitting up next to the pool when the sprinklers go on.
- • 0:24—Topless and buns, stripping for Billy. Some shots might be a body double.
- •• 0:51—Topless in bed when she "dies" with Howard Hessman.
- • 1:28—Topless making love with Billy. Some shots might be a body double.

Private Passions *(1983)*

Gavin Brannan . . . . Mark
- • 1:19—Buns, while lying in bed on top of Sybil Danning.
Sybil Danning . . . . Katherine
David Siegel . . . . Toni
- • 0:29—Buns, with Laura. Don't see his face.

Private Popsicle *(1982)*

Bea Fiedler . . . . Eva
- •• 0:04—In black bra with Bobby. Upper half of left breast, very brief side of right breast, then topless.
- ••• 0:06—Full frontal nudity with Bobby in bed.
- •• 0:07—More topless with Bobby.
- ••• 0:08—Topless on bed with Hughie.
- •• 0:09—More topless when her husband gets into bed.
Iftach Katzur . . . . Benji
- •• 1:26—Buns, while walking around after Rena steals his clothes.
Zachi Noy . . . . Hughie
- • 0:09—Buns while in bed with Eva.

Private Resort *(1985)*

Vickie Benson . . . . Bikini Girl
- • 0:28—In blue two piece swimsuit, showing her buns, then brief topless with Reeves.
- 1:11—Buns, in locker room, trying to slap Reeves.
Johnny Depp . . . . Jack
- •• 0:12—Buns, while in hotel room with Leslie Easterbrook.
Leslie Easterbrook . . . . Bobbie Sue
- •• 0:14—Very brief buns taking off swimsuit, then topless under sheer white nightgown.
Lisa London. . . . . Alice
- 0:51—In beige bra and panties several times with Ben and Jack while she's drunk.
Rob Morrow . . . . Ben
- • 0:36—Brief buns while standing with Hillary Shapiro worshiping Baba Rama.
- •• 0:39—Buns while getting caught naked by Mrs. Rawlins, then more buns, while running through the halls.

Hilary Shepard . . . . Shirley
- ••• 0:36—Topless, then buns, taking off her dress in front of Ben.

Private Road *(1987)*

Mitzi Kapture . . . . Helen Milshaw
- 0:50—Wearing a white bra during a strip-spin-the-bottle game.
- •• 1:29—Topless, making love in bed with Greg Evigan.

Private School *(1983)*

Phoebe Cates . . . . Christine
- 1:21—Brief buns lying in sand with Mathew Modine.
- 1:24—Upper half of buns flashing with the rest of the girls during graduation ceremony.
Sylvia Kristel . . . . Ms. Copuletta
- 0:57—In wet white dress after falling in the pool.
Steve Levitt . . . . Bellboy
Kari Lizer . . . . Rita
- • 0:30—Very brief left breast popping out of cheerleader's outfit along with the Coach.
Matthew Modine . . . . Jim
Julie Payne . . . . Coach Whelan
- • 0:30—Very, very brief left breast popping out of cheerleader's outfit along with Rita.
Betsy Russell . . . . Jordan Leigh-Jensen
- 0:02—Taking a shower behind a frosted door.
- • 0:04—Very, very brief right breast and buns when Bubba takes her towel off through window.
- ••• 0:19—Topless riding a horse after Kathleen Wilhoite steals her blouse.
- 0:35—In jogging outfit stripping down to black bra and panties, brief upper half of buns.
- 1:15—In white bra and panties, in room with Bubba.
- 1:24—Upper half of buns flashing with the rest of the girls during graduation ceremony.
Brinke Stevens . . . . Uncredited School Girl
- •• 0:42—Brief topless and buns in shower room scene. She's the brunette wearing a pony tail who passes in front of the chalkboard.
Lynda Wiesmeier . . . . School Girl
- ••• 0:42—Nude in shower room scene. First blonde in shower on the left.

Prizzi's Honor *(1985)*

Anjelica Huston . . . . Maerose Prizzi
Jack Nicholson . . . . Charley Partanna
- 2:05—Buns, sort of. Viewed from above while he takes a shower. Hard to see anything.
Kathleen Turner . . . . Irene Walker
- • 0:30—Very brief left breast making love with Jack Nicholson on bed.

Problem Child *(1990)*

Jack Warden . . . . "Big" Ben Healy
- • 1:07—Buns, on TV in bar, mooning into the camera when he doesn't know it is on. (Yes, it is him.)

Programmed to Kill (1987)
a.k.a. The Retaliator
Sandahl Bergman . . . . Samira
- • 0:11—Brief side view of right breast taking off T-shirt and leaning over to kiss a guy. Don't see her face.

Project: Alien (1990)
Maxwell Caulfield . . . . George Abbott
Darlanne Fluegel. . . . ."Bird" McNamara
- • 0:18—Buns, getting out of bed and putting on a kimono.
Michael Nouri . . . . Jeff Milker

Prom Night (1980)
Jamie Lee Curtis . . . . Kim
Pita Oliver . . . . Vicki
- •• 0:35—Brief buns, mooning Mr. Sykes outside of tennis court.
Mary Beth Rubens . . . . Kelly
- • 0:59—Very brief right breast making out with Drew in the locker room.
- • 1:02—Brief upper half of breasts, standing up to put dress on. Dark.

Prom Night III (1989)
Tim Conlon . . . . Alex
- • 0:15—Brief buns and very brief balls when the flag he's wearing falls off.

Promised Land (1988)
Debi Richter . . . . Pammie
Meg Ryan . . . . Beverly
- • 0:22—Very brief side view of left breast in bed with Kiefer Sutherland.

Promises, Promises (1963)
Jayne Mansfield . . . . Sandy Brooks
0:02—Bubble bath scene.
- ••• 0:04—Topless drying herself off with a towel. Same shot also at 0:48.
- ••• 0:06—Topless in bed. Same shot also at 0:08, 0:39 and 0:40.
- ••• 0:59—Buns, kneeling next to bathtub, right breast in bathtub, then topless drying herself off.

Psycho III (1986)
Juliette Cummins. . . . . .Red
- ••• 0:39—Topless making love with Duke in his motel room, then getting thrown out.
Jeff Fahey . . . . Duane
Katt Shea . . . . .Patsy
Brinke Stevens. . . . . Body Double for Diana Scarwid
- •• 0:30—Brief topless and buns getting ready to take a shower, body doubling for Diana Scarwid.

Psycho IV: The Beginning
(1990; Made for Cable Movie)
Olivia Hussey. .Norma Bates
- •• 0:49—Topless in motel room mirror while young Norman, watches through peephole.

Pucker Up and Bark Like a Dog (1989)
Iris Condon . . . . Stretch Woman
Robert Culp . . . . .Gregor
Wendy O. Williams. . . . . .Butch
Lisa Zane . . . . Taylor Phillips
- •• 0:52—Topless in shower with Max. Left breast, while in bed.

Pump Up the Volume (1990)
Samantha Mathis . . . . Nora Diniro
- •• 1:13—Topless taking off sweater on patio with Christian Slater.
Christian Slater. Mark Hunter

The Punisher (1989)
Jeroen Krabbé . . . . Gianni Franco
Dolph Lundgren. .Frank Castle
- • 0:06—Upper half of buns, while kneeling in his underground hideout. Don't see his face.
- • 1:23—Same shot at 00:06 used again.
Bryan Marshall . . . . Dino Moretti

Puppet Master (1989)
Barbara Crampton . . . . Woman at Carnival
Irene Miracle . . . . Dana Hadley
Kathryn O'Reilly . . . . Carissa Stamford
- • 0:41—Left breast in bathtub, covered with bubbles.
- • 0:43—Brief left breast getting out of tub. Nipple covered with bubbles.
0:50—Riding on Frank in bed. Don't see anything, but still exciting. Very brief buns under sheer nightgown when she gets off Frank.
1:11—Right breast under sheer black nightgown, dead sitting at the table. Blood on her face.

Puppet Master II (1990)
Collin Bernsen . . . . .Michael
- •• 1:10—Buns, while putting out fire on the bed.
George "Buck" Flower . . . . Matthew
Charlie Spradling . . . . .Wanda
- •• 1:04—Topless getting out of bed and adjusting her panties.

Puppet Master III: Toulon's Revenge (1990)
Michelle Bauer Lili
- • 0:15—Brief topless bringing the phone to the General while he takes a bath.
- • 0:43—Topless, twice, making love on top of the General.

Purgatory (1988)
Adrienne Pearce . . . . Janine
- •• 0:51—Brief topless in shower scene with Kirsten.
Tanya Roberts . . . . Carly Arnold
- • 0:29—Nude, getting into the shower.
- • 0:42—Very brief topless in bed with the Warden. 0:43—In white lingerie in whorehouse.
- •• 0:57—Left breast, then brief topless in bed talking to Tommy.

Purple Hearts *(1984)*
Annie McEnroe . . . . .Hallaway
- •• 1:23—Brief topless coming out of the bathroom surprising Ken Wahl and Cheryl Ladd.
Cyril O'Reilly . . . . Zuma

Purple Rain *(1984)*
Apollonia. . . . . Apollonia
- •• 0:20—Brief topless taking off jacket before jumping into lake.
- 0:41—In lingerie making love with Prince.
- 1:06—In black lingerie and stockings singing on stage.

Pyrates *(1991)*
Kevin Bacon . . . . Ari
- • 0:06—Brief side view of buns several times while making love with Kyra Sedgwick. Long shot.
- •• 0:22—Buns in jock strap, while horsing around in bed with Sedgwick.
Kyra Sedgwick. . . . . Sam
- ••• 0:19—In sheer lingerie on top of Kevin Bacon in bed, then topless.
- 0:21—Partial buns, bouncing in bed with Bacon.
- • 0:22—Brief buns, lying on top of Bacon.
- • 0:26—Topless under water in hot tub with Bacon.
Petra Verkaik. . . . . .Basia

Q *(1982)*
Bobbi Burns . . . . .Sunbather
- •• 0:06—Topless taking off swimsuit top and rubbing lotion on herself.
David Carradine . . . . Detective Shepard
Candy Clark . . . . Joan
Michael Moriarty. . . . . Jimmy Quinn
Mary Louise Weller . . . . .Mrs. Pauley

Q & A *(1990)*
Paul Calderon . . . . Roger Montalvo
- • 1:50—Brief buns, while on floor of boat, getting strangled by Nick Nolte.
Timothy Hutton . . . . .Al Rielly
Nick Nolte. . . . . Mike Brennan
Javier Rios . . . . Boat Lover
- • 1:44—Brief buns, while on boat, getting pulled out of bed by Nick Nolte.

Quackser Fortune has a Cousin in the Bronx
(1970; Irish)
Margot Kidder. . . . . Zazel
- •• 1:03—Topless undressing on a chair, then brief right, then breasts when Gene Wilder kisses her.
- • 1:05—Side view of left breast, then buns, getting out of bed.
Gene Wilder . . . . Quackser Fortune

Quartet *(1981; British/French)*
Isabelle Adjani . . . . Marya Zelli
- •• 1:06—Topless in bed with Alan Bates.
Alan Bates. . . . . .H.J. Heidler
Pierre Clementi . . . . .Theo

Jeffrey Kime . . . . .James
- •• 0:49—Nude, posing with two women for the pornographer.
Maggie Smith . . . . Lois

Quest For Fire *(1981)*
Joy Boushel . . . . Tribe Member
Rae Dawn Chong. . . . . .Ika
- 0:37—Topless and buns, running away from the bad tribe.
- 0:40—Topless and buns, following the three guys.
- 0:41—Brief topless behind rocks.
- • 0:43—Brief side view of left breast, healing Noah's wound.
- • 0:50—Right breast, while sleeping by the fire.
- 0:53—Long shot, side view of left breast after making love.
- • 0:54—Topless shouting to the three guys.
- • 1:07—Topless standing with her tribe.
- • 1:10—Topless and buns, walking through camp at night.
- • 1:18—Topless in a field.
- • 1:20—Left breast, turning over to demonstrate the missionary position. Long shot.
- • 1:25—Buns and brief left breast running out of bear cave.

The Quiet Earth *(1985; New Zealand)*
Bruno Lawrence. . . . . .Zac Hobson
- •• 0:02—Brief frontal nudity lying on the bed.
- •• 0:04—Brief nude getting back into bed.
- • 0:33—Very brief frontal nudity jumping out of the ocean. Blurry, hard to see anything.
- •• 1:01—Frontal nudity during flashback lying in bed.
Alison Routledge . . . . .Joanne
- 0:49—Brief buns, after making breakfast for Zac.
- • 1:24—Topless in guard tower making love with Api.

R.P.M. *(1970)*
Ann-Margret . . . . Rhoda
- •• 0:07—Brief left breast and buns getting out of bed talking with Anthony Quinn.
- 0:30—In fishnet top.
Teda Bracci . . . . n.a.

R.S.V.P. *(1984)*
Jane Hamilton . . . . .Mrs. Ellen Edwards
Tamara Landry. . . . . Vicky
- •• 0:43—Topless sitting in van taking top off.
- •• 0:48—Topless making love in the van with two guys.
Suzanne Remey Lawrence . . . . Stripper
- •• 0:56—Topless dancing in a radio station in front of a D.J.
Harry Reems. .Grant Garrison
Laurie Senit . . . . Sherry Worth
- •• 1:00—Topless in the shower with Harry Reems.
- •• 1:06—Topless again.
Katt Shea . . . . Rhonda Rivers
- • 0:31—Side view of left breast, making love in bed with Jonathan.

Allene Simmons . . . . .Patty De Fois Gras
•• 0:13—Topless taking off red top behind the bar with the bartender.
•• 0:38—Topless in bed with Mr. Edwards, then buns running to hide in the closet.
•• 0:41—Frontal nudity in room with Mr. Anderson.
••• 0:51—Topless talking to Toby in the hallway trying to get help for the Governor.
Lynda Wiesmeier. . . . . .Jennifer Edwards
•• 0:11—Topless diving into the pool while Toby fantasizes about her being nude.
• 0:19—Topless in kitchen when Toby fantasizes about her again.
••• 1:21—Nude getting out of the pool and kissing Toby, when she really is nude.

Rabid (1977; Canadian)
Marilyn Chambers. . . . . Rose
•• 0:14—Topless in bed.
•• 1:04—Topless in closet selecting clothes.
•• 1:16—Topless in white panties getting out of bed.

The Rachel Papers (1989; British)
Dexter Fletcher . . . . .Charles Highway
• 0:58—Very brief buns, while jumping into bed with Ione Skye.
Ione Skye . . . . Rachel
•• 0:58—Topless getting undressed and into bed with Charles. Long shot, then topless in bed.
••• 1:03—Brief topless in three scenes. From above in bathtub, in bed and in bathtub again.
•• 1:04—Left breast, making love sitting up with Charles.
• 1:06—Brief topless sitting up in bathtub.
• 1:08—Brief topless long shot getting dressed in Charles' room.
• 1:28—Brief topless kissing Charles in bed during his flashback.
James Spader . . . . De Forest

Racing with the Moon (1984)
Nicholas Cage. . . . . Nicky
Barbara Howard . . . . Gatsby Girl
Carol Kane . . . . Annie
Michael Madsen . . . . Frank
Elizabeth McGovern . . . . Caddie Winger
• 0:45—Upper half of breast in pond with Sean Penn.
Sean Penn. . . . . Henry "Hopper" Nash

A Rage in Harlem (1991)
Robin Givens. . . . . Imabelle
••• 0:32—Buns, while lying in bed with Forest Whitaker.
Gregory Hines. . . . . Goldy

Ragtime (1981)
Jeff Daniels . . . . .O'Donnell
Brad Dourif . . . . .Younger Brother
Michael Jeter. . . . . .n.a.
Elizabeth McGovern . . . . Evelyn Nesbit
••• 0:52—Topless in living room sitting on couch and arguing with a lawyer. Very long scene.

Mandy Patinkin . . . . .Tateh
Mary Steenburgen . . . . Mother

The Rain Killer (1990)
Woody Brown . . . . .Jordan Rosewall
••• 0:39—Buns, while getting into bed, kneeling next to bed, then getting into bed with Satin. Long scene.
Maria Ford . . . . Satin
•• 0:29—Nude, dancing on stage in club. Backlit too much.
••• 0:37—Topless in bedroom with Jordan, taking off her clothes, getting tied to bed. Long scene.
• 0:41—Topless lying on her back on bed, dead.
• 0:48—Same scene from 0:41 when Rosewall looks at B&W police photo.
Ray Sharkey . . . . .Vince Capra

Rain Man (1988)
Tom Cruise . . . . .Charlie Babbitt
Valeria Golino. . . . . .Suzanna
• 0:35—Very brief left breast four times and very, very brief right breast once with open blouse fighting with Tom Cruise after getting out of the bathtub.
Dustin Hoffman . . . . .Raymond Babbitt
Gigi Vorgan . . . . .Voice-Over Actress

The Rainbow (1989)
Sammi Davis-Voss . . . . .Winifred Inger
••• 0:21—Topless and buns with Amanda Donohoe undressing, running outside in the rain, jumping into the water, then talking by the fireplace.
•• 0:30—Topless and buns posing for a painter.
• 1:33—Brief right breast and buns getting out of bed.
••• 1:44—Nude running outside with Donohoe.
Amanda Donohoe . . . . .Winifred Inger
••• 0:21—Nude with Sammi Davis undressing, running outside in the rain, jumping into the water, then talking by the fireplace.
••• 0:43—Full frontal nudity taking off nightgown and getting into bed with Davis, then right breast.
••• 1:44—Nude running outside with Davis.
Glenda Jackson. . . . . .Anna Brangwen
Paul McGann . . . . Anton Skrebensky
•• 1:30—Buns, while opening a bottle of wine in room with Sammi Davis.
• 1:44—Very brief frontal nudity and buns when running up a hill with Amanda Donohoe.

Rainbow Drive (1990; Made for Cable Movie)
Kathryn Harrold . . . . Christine
David Neidorf . . . . Bernie Maxwell
• 1:16—Buns, while in shower room when Peter Weller is interrogating him.
Chelchie Ross . . . . Tom Cutter
Peter Weller . . . . Mike Gallagher

Rambling Rose (1991)
Laura Dern. . . . . Rose
•• 0:23—Right breast several times, while lying on bench with Robert Duvall while Lucas Haas peeks in.
John Heard. . . . . Willcox Hillyer

The Rapture (1991)

Carole Davis . . . . Angie
- 0:20—Buns, on top of Vic in bed. Most of side of her right breast.
- 0:21—Very brief right breast, then very brief topless while turning around to talk.

David Duchovny . . . . Randy
- ••• 0:24—Buns and brief frontal nudity getting out of bed in Mimi Roger's bedroom.

James Le Gros . . . . Tommy

Stephanie Menuez . . . . Diane
- ••• 0:06—Topless in furniture store with Mimi Rogers, Vic and Randy.

Mimi Rogers . . . . Sharon
- 0:08—Most of her left breast, while lying in bed with Randy
- •• 0:36—Very brief side view of right breast, dropping nightgown and walking into closet.

Raw Force (1981)

Jennifer Holmes. . . . . Ann Davis

Camille Keaton . . . . Girl in Toilet
- •• 0:28—Topless in bathroom with a guy.
- •• 0:29—Topless in bathroom again with the guy.
- 0:31—Topless in bathroom again when he rips her pants off.

Jillian Kesner . . . . Cookie Winchell

Jewel Shepard . . . . Drunk Sexpot
- 0:31—Topless in black swimsuit, when a guy adjusts her straps and it falls open.

The Razor's Edge (1984)

Stephen Davies . . . . Malcolm

Catherine Hicks. . . . . Isabel
- 0:43—Brief upper half of left breast, in bed after seeing a cockroach.

Theresa Russell . . . . Sophie

Re-Animator (1985)

(Unrated version reviewed.)

Barbara Crampton . . . . Megan Halsey
- •• 0:10—Brief buns putting panties on, then topless, putting bra on after making love with Dan.
- •• 1:09—Full frontal nudity, lying unconscious on table getting strapped down.
- 1:10—Topless getting her breasts fondled by a headless body.
- 1:19—Topless on the table.

Real Men (1987)

Mark Herrier . . . . Bradshaw

Travis McKenna. . . . . Oaf

Suzanne Slater . . . . Woman in Bed
- 0:07—Brief left breast, in bed with James Belushi.

Dyanne Thorne. . . . . Dad

Rebel (1985; Australian)

Bryan Brown. . . . . Tiger Kelly

Cassandra Delaney . . . . All-Girl Band Member

Rainee Skinner. . . . . Prostitute in bed
- 0:37—Brief topless sitting up in bed.

Reborn (1978)

Dennis Hopper. . . . . Rev. Tom Harley

Michael Moriarty . . . . Mark
- 0:38—Brief buns, while rolling off Maria in bed.

Antonella Murgia . . . . .Maria
- 0:35—Topless in bed with Michael Moriarty.
- •• 0:37—More topless in bed with Moriarty.
- ••• 0:38—Nude, getting out of bed.
- ••• 0:39—Nude, walking around in bedroom.

Reckless (1984)

Daryl Hannah. . . . . Tracey Prescott
- 0:48—In a white bra fighting in gymnasium with Johnny then in pool area in bra and panties.
- ••• 0:52—Topless in furnace room of school making love with Johnny. Lit with red light.

Toni Kalem. . . . . .Donna

Aidan Quinn. Johnny Rourke
- 1:03—Very brief frontal nudity and buns while running into Daryl Hannah's brother's room when her parents come home early.
- 1:12—Side view nude, taking a shower.

Pamela Springsteen . . . . Karen Sybern

Recruits (1986; Canadian)

Lolita Davidovich . . . . .Susan
- 0:19—Very brief topless when Steve bumps into her in the shower room.
- •• 0:54—Right breast, then topless making out with Steve in car.
- •• 0:56—Topless, twice, while driving around in car with Steve, the Governor and his wife.
- •• 0:58—Topless, getting out of the car.

Dominique St. Croix. . . . . n.a.

John Canada Terrell .Winston

Red Blooded American Girl (1988)

Kim Coates. . . . . .Dennis
- 0:01—Buns, while giving Rebecca a glass in bed.
- 0:30—Very brief buns, while getting into bathtub.

Lydie Denier. Rebecca Murrin
- ••• 0:00—Topless in bed wearing panties, garter belt and stockings. Buns, rolling over. Long scene.

Andrew Stevens . . . . .Owen Augustus Urban III

Heather Thomas. . . . . Paula Bukowsky
- 1:19—Lower half of right breast when Andrew Stevens is on top of her. Very, very brief silhouette of right breast. Probably a body double.

Red Heat (1987; U.S./German)

Linda Blair . . . . Chris Carlson
- 0:09—In blue nightgown in the bedroom with her boyfriend, almost topless.
- ••• 0:56—Topless in shower room scene.
- ••• 1:01—Brief topless getting raped by Sylvia Kristel while the male guard watches.

Sue Kiel . . . . Hedda
- 0:56—Brief topless in shower room scene (third girl behind Linda Blair). Long shot, hard to see.

Sylvia Kristel . . . . Sofia
- 0:23—In red lingerie.

•• 0:56—Topless in shower room scene.
• 1:01—Brief topless raping Linda Blair.

Red Heat (1988)
Gina Gershon . . . . .Cat Manzetti
Ed O'Ross . . . . Viktor Rostavili
Gretchen Palmer. . . . . Hooker
• 1:20—Topless and buns in hotel during shoot out.
Arnold Schwarzenegger . . . . .Ivan Danko
•• 0:02—Buns while in the sauna and outside fighting
in the snow.
Gigi Vorgan. . . . . Audrey

Red Sonja (1985)
Sandahl Bergman . . . . Queen Gedren
Brigitte Nielsen . . . . Red Sonja
• 0:01—Half of right nipple through torn outfit, while
sitting up.
Arnold Schwarzenegger . . . . Kalidor

Reform School Girls (1986)
Michelle Bauer . . . . Uncredited Shower Girl
•• 0:25—Topless, then nude in the shower.
Leslee Bremmer. . . . . Uncredited Shower Girl
•• 0:25—Brief topless in the shower three times. Walking from left to right in the background, full frontal
nudity by herself with wet hair, topless walking from
left to right.
Linda Carol . . . . Jennifer Williams
•• 0:05—Nude in the shower.
• 0:56—Topless in the back of a truck with Norton.
•• 1:13—Topless getting hosed down by Edna.
Sybil Danning . . . . Warden Sutter
Darcy De Moss . . . . .Knox
Sherri Stoner. . . . . .Lisa
• 1:03—Very brief topless and buns, lying on stomach
in the restroom, getting branded by bad girls.
Wendy O. Williams . . . . Charlie
•• 0:26—Topless talking to two girls in the shower.

The Reincarnation of Peter Proud (1975)
Margot Kidder. . . . . Marcia Curtis
• 1:29—Brief topless sitting in bathtub masturbating
while remembering getting raped by husband.
Cornelia Sharpe. .Nora Hayes
•• 0:03—Topless in bed with Michael Sarrazin, then
buns when getting out of bed.

Relentless 2: Dead On (1991)
Shelby Chong . . . . Waitress
Meg Foster . . . . Carol Dietz
Barbara Ann Klein . . . . Realtor
Perry Lang. . . . . .Ralph Bashi
Miles O'Keeffe. . . . . Gregor
••• 0:17—Buns, while putting ice cubes into bathtub,
then getting in.
Leo Rossi. . . . . .Sam Dietz
Ray Sharkey. . . . . .Kyle Volsone

Remember My Name (1978)
Geraldine Chaplin . . . . Emily
• 1:23—Very brief left breast, lying in bed, then right
breast, with Anthony Perkins.
Jeff Goldblum. Mr. Nadd

Rendez-Vous (1986; French)
Juliette Binoche . . . . Anne "Nina" Larrieu
• 0:07—Brief topless in dressing room when Paulot
surprises her and Fred.
••• 0:25—Side of left breast, then topless and buns in
empty apartment with Paulot.
•• 0:32—Full frontal nudity in bed with Quentin.
•• 0:35—Buns, then brief topless in bed with Paulot
and Quentin. Full frontal nudity getting out.
•• 1:08—Topless taking off her top in front of Paulot in
the dark, then topless lying on the floor.
• 1:11—Right breast, making love on the stairs. Dark.
Olimpia Carlisi . . . . n.a.
Caroline Faro . . . . .Juliette
• 0:22—Buns, walking up stairs, then full frontal nudity on second floor during play. Buns, while hugging
Romeo and falling back into a net.
Lambert Wilson. .Quentin
• 0:22—Very brief buns, while falling with Juliet onto
net during play.

Rented Lips (1988)
Robert Downey, Jr.. . . . . .Wolf Dangler
• 0:01—Buns, while wearing fishnet shorts in S&M
outfit during porno movie shoot.
• 0:22—Buns, while through shorts again during playback of the film.
Edy Williams. .Heather Darling
• 0:22—Topless in bed, getting fondled by Robert
Downey, Jr. during porno movie shoot.

Repo Jake (1990)
Dana Bentley Konkel . . . . .Jenny
Dan Haggerty . . . . .Jake
Bonnie Paine . . . . R.V. Girl
•• 0:28—Topless (mostly left breast) while in R.V. with
her boyfriend.
•• 0:29—More topless, making love with him.
Jacqueline Palmer. Porn Gal
••• 0:47—Topless and buns, while on bed, acting in a
movie.

Repossessed (1990)
Belle Avery . . . . Gym Receptionist
Linda Blair . . . . .Nancy Aglet
Charlotte J. Helmcamp. . . . . Incredible Girl
Melissa Moore . . . . Bimbo Student
•• 0:05—Topless pulling her top down in classroom in
front of Leslie Nielsen.

Return (1985)
Karlene Crockett . . . . .Diana
• 0:46—Topless sitting up and getting out of bed.
Long shot.
Lenore Zann. . . . . .Susan

The Return of the Living Dead (1985)
Linnea Quigley . . . . Trash
- ••• 0:05—Topless and buns, strip tease and dancing in cemetery. (Lower frontal nudity is covered with some kind of make-up appliance).
- • 1:08—Topless, walking out of the cemetery to eat someone.

Jewel Shepard . . . . Casey

Return to Horror High (1987)
Darcy De Moss . . . . Sheri Haines
- • 0:21—Very brief left breast when her sweater gets lifted up while she's on some guy's back.

Brendan Hughes . . . . Steven Blake
Maureen McCormick . . . . Officer Tyler
Remy O'Neill. Esther Molvania
Kristi Somers . . . . Ginny McCall

A Return to Salem's Lot (1988)
Katja Crosby . . . . Cathy
- •• 0:36—Topless making love in bed with Joey.
- • 0:48—Side view of right breast kissing Joey outside next to a stream.

Michael Moriarty. . . . . Joey

Return to the Blue Lagoon (1991)
Milla Jovovich Lilli
- • 0:49—Brief upper half topless in front of mirror.
- • 1:07—Very brief topless under water with Richard. Brief topless under waterfall with Richard.
  1:09—Brief partial left breast on hilltop with Richard. Necklace gets in the way.
- • 1:20—Briefly in wet beige blouse, standing up in pond.
- • 1:26—Side view of right breast three times, washing make up off her face in the pond.
- •• 1:28—Side view of right breast again. Very brief left breast, while picking up her top off rock.
  1:30—Side of left breast, lying on bed while held down.

Reuben, Reuben (1983)
E. Katherine Kerr . . . . Lucille Haxby
- • 0:51—Brief left breast in bedroom, undressing in front of Tom Conti.

Kelly McGillis. . . . . Geneva Spofford

Revenge (1990)
Kevin Costner . . . . Cochran
- •• 1:14—Brief buns while getting out of bed and wrapping a sheet around himself.

Sally Kirkland. . . . . Rock Star
John Leguizamo . . . . Ignacio
Madeleine Stowe . . . . Miryea
  0:44—Side view of buns when Kevin Costner pulls up her dress to make love with her.
  0:52—In white slip talking to Costner in bedroom.
- • 1:00—Buns, making love with Costner in jeep. Very brief topless coming out of the water.
- • 1:07—Very brief topless when Costner is getting beat up.

Revenge of the Cheerleaders (1976)
David Hasselhoff . . . . Boner
- • 0:28—Buns in shower room scene.
- ••• 0:30—Frontal nudity in shower room scene while soaping Gail.

David Robinson . . . . Jordan
- • 0:13—Buns when Tish plays with him while she's under the counter.

Patrice Rohmer. . . . . Sesame
- • 0:28—Brief topless and buns in the boys shower room.

Cheryl Smith . . . . Heather
- • 0:00—Brief topless changing tops in back of car. (Blonde on the far right.)
  0:28—Buns, in shower room scene.
  0:36—Full frontal nudity, but covered with bubbles.

Jerii Woods. . . . . Gail
- • 0:00—Topless changing in front left seat of car.
  0:05—Lower frontal nudity taking off cheerleader skirt in girl's restroom and putting on panties.
- • 0:26—Brief right breast, while sitting in bleachers with the other cheerleaders.
- ••• 0:28—Nude in boy's shower room scene.
- •• 0:37—Topless sitting up in sleeping bag.
- • 0:44—Brief topless in front seat of car with David Hasselhoff.
- ••• 0:53—Nude with Leslie and hiker guy while frolicking in the woods.
- •• 0:55—Nude some more making out with the hiker guy with Leslie.
- ••• 0:57—Nude walking down road with Leslie when stopped by a policeman.
- ••• 1:23—Topless during Hawaiian party.

Revenge of the Nerds (1984)
Bernie Casey . . . . U. N. Jefferson
Anthony Edwards. . . . . Gilbert
Julie Montgomery . . . . Betty
- •• 0:49—Frontal nudity getting ready for a shower.
- • 1:10—Topless in the pie pan.

Lisa Welch . . . . Suzy

Revenge of the Ninja (1983)
Ashley Ferrare. . . . . Cathy
  0:33—In white lingerie sitting on couch with Dave.
- • 0:48—Brief topless getting attacked by the Sumo Servant in the bedroom.
  1:13—In wet white tank top talking on the phone.

Rich and Famous (1981)
Candice Bergen . . . . Merry Noel Blake
Jacqueline Bisset. . . . . Liz Hamilton
Matt Lattanzi . . . . The Boy, Jim
- ••• 1:10—Buns, while making love with Jacqueline Bisset.

Meg Ryan . . . . Debbie at 18 years
David Selby . . . . Doug Blake

Richard's Things (1980)
Amanda Redman . . . . Josie
- •• 0:51—Topless, lying in bed talking to Liv Ullman.

Ricochet (1991)
Victoria Dillard . . . . Alice
Linda Doná . . . . Wanda
- •• 1:03—Topless, undoing her dress, then buns, getting on bed to make love with Denzel Washington while he's drugged.
- • 1:16—Buns, on top of Washington during video playback.

Susan Lentini . . . . Reporter
John Lithgow . . . . Earl Talbot Blake
Heidi Thomas . . . . Reporter
Denzel Washington . . . . Nick Styles
- • 0:13—Very brief frontal nudity in locker room when Lindsay Wagner comes to talk.

Rikky & Pete (1988; Australian)
Tetchie Agbayani . . . . Flossie
- • 0:58—Brief upper half of left breast in bed with Pete when Rikky accidentally sees them in bed.
- ••• 1:30—Topless in black panties dancing outside the jail while Pete watches from inside.

Bruno Lawrence . . . . Sonny

Risky Business (1983)
Cynthia Baker . . . . Test Teacher
Tom Cruise . . . . Joel
Rebecca De Mornay . . . . Lana
- • 0:28—Brief nude standing by the window with Tom Cruise.

River's Edge (1987)
Danyi Deats . . . . Jamie
- • 0:03—Topless, dead lying next to river with her killer. (All the shots of her topless in this film aren't exciting unless you like looking at dead bodies).
- • 0:15—Close up topless, then full frontal nudity when Crispin Glover pokes her with a stick.
  0:16—Full frontal nudity when the three boys leave.
  0:22—Full frontal nudity when all the kids come to see her body. (She's starting to look very discolored).
  0:24—Right breast when everybody leaves.
  0:30—Right breast when they come to dump her body in the river.

Dennis Hopper . . . . Feck
Keanu Reeves . . . . Matt
Leo Rossi . . . . Jim
Ione Skye . . . . Clarissa

Roadhouse (1989)
Jasaé . . . . Strip Joint Girl
Laura Albert . . . . Strip Joint Girl
- •• 0:45—Topless and buns dancing on stage, wearing a hat.

Lisa Axelrod . . . . Party Girl
Cheryl Baker . . . . Well-Endowed Wife
Sylvia Baker . . . . Table Dancer
Michele Burger . . . . Strip Joint Girl
Terri Lynn Doss . . . . Cody's Girlfriend
Kymberly Herrin . . . . Party Girl
Pamela Jackson . . . . Strip Joint Girl
Susan Lentini . . . . Bandstand Babe

Kelly Lynch . . . . Doc
- •• 1:04—Topless and buns getting out of bed with a sheet wrapped around her.

Kym Malin . . . . Party Girl
Julie Michaels . . . . Denise
- ••• 1:18—Topless dancing on stage in club in front of Patrick Swayze.

Heidi Paine . . . . Party Girl
Jacqueline Palmer . . . . Party Girl
Patrick Swayze . . . . Dalton
- ••• 0:30—Brief buns getting out of bed while Kathleen Wilhoite watches.

Patricia Tallman . . . . Bandstand Babe
Christina Veronica . . . . Strip Joint Girl

Roadhouse 66 (1984)
Willem Dafoe . . . . Johnny Harte
- •• 1:02—Buns, standing up while kissing Jesse.

Kaaren Lee . . . . Jesse Duran
- •• 1:00—Topless, taking off her top to go skinny dipping with Willem Dafoe. Dark.

Judge Reinhold . . . . Beckman Hallsgood, Jr.
Kate Vernon . . . . Melissa Duran
- • 1:03—Brief topless in back of car with Judge Reinhold. Dark.

Robin Hood: Prince of Thieves (1991)
Kevin Costner . . . . Robin of Locksley
   1:14—Body double's buns, while bathing under waterfall when Marian sees him. Hard to see because of the falling water. Body double was used because the water was so cold.

Mary Elizabeth Mastrantonio . . . . Marian
Christian Slater . . . . Will Scarlett

Robot Jox (1990)
Gary Graham . . . . Achilles
- • 0:32—Very brief buns, getting dressed in his room while talking to Athena.

Anne-Marie Johnson . . . . Athena
- •• 0:35—Buns, walking to the showers after talking to Achilles and Tex.

The Rocky Horror Picture Show (1975; British)
Nell Campbell . . . . Columbia
- • 1:17—Top of breasts popping out of her blouse during song and dance on stage.

Patricia Quinn . . . . Magenta
Susan Sarandon . . . . Janet Weiss
Koo Stark . . . . Bridesmaid

Roller Blade (1986)
Michelle Bauer . . . . Bod Sister
- • 0:11—Topless, being held by Satacoy's Devils.
- ••• 0:13—More topless and buns in G-string during fight. Long scene.
- • 0:16—Brief topless twice, getting saved by the Sisters.
- •• 0:33—Topless during ceremony with the other two Bod Sisters. Buns also.

••• 0:35—Full frontal nudity after dip in hot tub. (Second to leave the tub.)

•• 0:40—Nude, on skates with the other two Bod Sisters. (She's on the left.)

Barbara Peckinpaugh. . . . . Bod Sister

•• 0:33—Topless during ceremony. Cut on her throat is unappealing.

••• 0:35—Full frontal nudity after dip in hot tub with the other two Bod Sisters. (She's the first to leave.)

•• 0:40—Nude, on skates with the other two Bod Sisters. (She's in the middle.)

Suzanne Solari. . . . . Sister Sharon Cross

0:04—Buns, in G-string, lying in bed.

• 1:21—Brief upper half of right breast, taking off suit. Buns in G-string.

The Romantic Englishwoman *(1975; British/French)*

Helmut Berger. . . . . Thomas

• 1:08—Upper half of buns, while sitting at edge of pool talking to Glenda Jackson.

Nathalie Delon . . . . Miranda

Glenda Jackson . . . . .Elizabeth

• 0:30—Brief full frontal nudity outside, taking robe off in front of Michael Caine.

• 0:31—Buns, walking back into the house.

• 1:08—Side view of right breast sitting at edge of pool talking to Thomas.

• 1:45—Very, very brief topless in bed talking with Thomas.

Kate Nelligan . . . . Isabel

Romeo and Juliet *(1968)*

Olivia Hussey. . . . . .Juliet

• 1:37—Very brief topless rolling over and getting out of bed with Romeo.

Leonard Whiting . . . . Romeo

•• 1:34—Buns, while in bed with Juliet, then getting out to stretch. Long scene.

A Room with a View *(1986; British)*

Helena Bonham-Carter . . . . Lucy Honeychurch

Simon Callow . . . . .The Reverend Mr. Beebe

• 1:04—Frontal nudity taking off clothes and jumping into pond.

••• 1:05—Nude running around with Freddy and George in the woods. Lots of frontal nudity.

Daniel Day-Lewis. . . . . .Cecil Vyse

Rupert Graves . . . . Freddy Honeychurch

••• 1:05—Nude running around with Mr. Beebe and George in the woods. Lots of frontal nudity.

Julian Sands. . . . . .George Emerson

••• 1:05—Nude running around with Freddy and Mr. Beebe in the woods. Lots of frontal nudity.

Maggie Smith . . . . Charlotte Bartlett

Roots of Evil *(1991)*

(Unrated version reviewed.)

Jasaé. . . . . Subway Hooker

••• 1:05—Topless taking off her top in subway stairwell, then getting killed by the bad guy.

Yvette Buchanan. . . . . Hooker

Daphne Cheung . . . . .Tina

••• 0:09—Topless in alley with a customer.

Jillian Kesner. . . . . .Brenda

••• 0:27—Topless, giving Alex Cord a back massage in bed.

• 0:30—Brief topless, getting up out of bed.

Deanna Lund . . . . Marissa

• 0:19—Most of left breast, then brief right breast, while making love in bed with Johnny.

•• 0:20—More right breast, while making love.

•• 0:21—Still more right breast.

••• 1:33—Right breast, then topless while lying in bed with Brinke Stevens.

Jewel Shepard . . . . .Wanda

• 1:31—Brief right breast, a couple of times, when it pops out of her blouse while she's in police station.

Delia Sheppard . . . . Monica

••• 0:04—Topless and buns in G-string, dancing on stage.

• 0:07—Topless and buns, while on stage when wounded guy disturbs her act.

••• 0:38—Buns in outfit, then topless dancing on stage.

••• 0:41—More buns and topless in bed, making love with Johnny. Long scene.

Donna Spangler. Scarlett

•• 0:04—Topless, getting attacked by the crazy guy, then killed.

• 0:07—Brief topless, dead, covered with blood when Alex Cord discovers her.

Brinke Stevens . . . . Candy

•• 1:33—Right breast, then topless while sitting on bed talking to Deanna Lund.

The Rosebud Beach Hotel *(1985)*

Julie Always . . . . Bellhop

•• 0:22—Topless, in open blouse, undressing with two other bellhops. She's the blonde on the left.

•• 0:44—Topless, playing spin the grenade, with two guys and the two other bellhops. She's on the left.

Colleen Camp . . . . .Tracy

0:07—In white lingerie in hotel room with Peter Scolari.

0:28—In black one piece swimsuit on lounge chair, then walking on the beach.

Cherie Currie . . . . Cherie

1:13—Singing with her twin sister in braless pink T-shirt on the beach.

Fran Drescher. . . . . .Linda

Monique Gabrielle . . . . .Lisa

•• 0:22—Topless and buns undressing in hotel room with two other girls. She's on the right.

•• 0:44—Topless taking off her red top in basement with two other girls and two guys.

• 0:56—In black see-through nightie in hotel room with Peter Scolari.

Dirga McBroom. . . . . Bellhop

• 0:49—Buns, then topless, standing with the other bell hops, outfitted with military attire. (She's the one at the far end, furthest from the camera.)

Julia Parton . . . . Bellhop
- •• 0:49—Buns, then topless, standing in line. Second from the camera.

Rosemary's Baby (1968)
Mia Farrow . . . . Rosemary Woodhouse
- • 0:10—Brief left breast in room in new apartment on floor with John Cassavetes. Hard to see anything.
- • 0:43—Brief close up of her breasts while she's sitting on a boat during a nightmare.
- •• 0:44—Buns walking on boat, then breasts during impregnation scene with the devil.

Round Trip to Heaven (1992)
Tara Buckman. . . . . Phyllis
Julie McCullough. . . . . Lucille
Kristine Rose . . . . Tina
Ray Sharkey. . . . . Stoneface
Amy-Rochelle Weiss . . . . Yvette
- ••• 0:19—In black bra and G-string in bedroom with Corey Feldman, then topless and buns on top of him in bed.

Runaway (1984)
Kirstie Alley . . . . Jackie
- 1:04—Briefly in white bra getting scanned at the police station for bugging devices.
Tom Selleck. . . . . Ramsay
Cec Verrell . . . . Hooker
- •• 0:44—Topless in hotel bathroom while Tom Selleck sneaks into her room.

Running Out of Luck (1986)
Rae Dawn Chong . . . . Slave Girl
- •• 0:42—Left breast, while hugging Mick Jagger, then again while lying in bed with him.
- •• 1:12—Left breast painting some kind of drug laced solution on herself.
- •• 1:14—Right breast, while in prison office offering her breast to the warden.
- • 1:21—Buns and left breast, in bed with Jagger during a flashback.
Jerry Hall . . . . Herself
Dennis Hopper . . . . Video Director
Mick Jagger . . . . Himself
- • 0:42—Brief buns in mirror in room with Rae Dawn Chong lying in bed. Another buns long shot in bed on top of Chong.

Running Scared (1986)
Steven Bauer. . . . . Frank
Darlanne Fluegel. . . . . Anna Costanzo
Gregory Hines. . . . . Ray Hughes
Tracy Reed . . . . Maryann
- • 0:18—Brief buns.
- • 1:30—Very brief topless in bed with Gregory Hines.
Jimmy Smits . . . . Julio Gonzales

Rush (1991)
Jennifer Jason Leigh. . . . . Kristen Cates
- • 1:09—Brief buns, when Jason Patric takes off her pajama bottoms and forces himself on her.

Jason Patric . . . . Jim Raynor
William Sadler . . . . Monroe

Rush Week (1989)
Laura Burkett . . . . Rebecca Winters
- •• 0:43—Topless in the shower, talking to Jonelle.
- • 0:55—Brief topless getting dressed after modeling session.
David Denney . . . . Greg Ochs
Kathleen Kinmont . . . . Julie Ann McGuffin
- • 0:07—Brief topless several times during modeling session. Buns in G-string getting dressed. Long shot.

Ruthless People (1986)
Jeannine Bisignano . . . . Hooker in Car
0:17—Topless, hanging out of the car. Long, long shot, don't see anything.
- • 0:40—Topless in the same scene three times on TV while Danny De Vito watches.
- • 0:49—Left breast hanging out of the car when the Chief of Police watches on TV. Closest shot.
1:15—Same scene again in department store TV's. Long shot, hard to see.
Laura Cruikshank . . . . n.a.
Anita Morris. . . . . Carol
Judge Reinhold. . . . . Ken Kessler
Helen Slater . . . . Sandy Kessler

S.A.S. San Salvador (1982)
Sybil Danning . . . . Countess Alexandra
- • 0:07—Brief left breast, while lying on the couch and kissing Malko.
Miles O'Keeffe . . . . Prince Malko

S.O.B. (1981)
Julie Andrews . . . . Sally Miles
- •• 1:19—Topless pulling the top off her red dress during the filming of a movie.
Rosanna Arquette. . . . . Babs
- • 0:21—Brief topless taking off white T-shirt on the deck of the house. Long shot, hard to see.
Marisa Berenson. . . . . Mavis
- •• 1:20—Topless in bed with Robert Vaughn.
Corbin Bernsen . . . . n.a.
Gisele Lindley. . . . . n.a.
James Purcell . . . . n.a.
Gay Rowan. . . . . n.a.

The Sailor Who Fell From Grace with the Sea (1976)
Kris Kristofferson . . . . Jim Cameron
Sarah Miles . . . . Anne Osborne
- • 0:18—Topless sitting at the vanity getting dressed while her son watches through peephole.
- •• 0:23—Topless, fantasizing about her husband.
- •• 0:42—Nude, making love with Kris Kristofferson.
- • 1:15—Brief right breast, in bed with Kristofferson.

Salome's Last Dance (1987)
Linzi Drew . . . . 1st Slave
- •• 0:08—Topless in black costume around a cage.
- •• 0:52—Topless during dance number.

Dougie Howes .Phoney Salome
- 1:05—Very brief frontal nudity at the end of a dance routine when you think he's a female Salome.

Glenda Jackson . . . . Herodias/Lady Alice

Tina Shaw . . . . 2nd Slave
- •• 0:08—Topless in black costume around a cage.
- •• 0:52—Topless during dance number.

Salvador (1986)

Elpidia Carrillo. . . . . Maria
- 0:21—Very brief right breast, lying in a hammock with James Woods.

Cynthia Gibb . . . . Cathy Moore

James Woods . . . . Richard Boyle

Santa Sangre (1989; Italian/Spanish)

Blanca Guerra . . . . .Concha
- 0:34—Half of buns, in sexy circus outfit.

Axel Jodorowsky . . . . Fenix
- •• 0:00—Buns, in room in an asylum.

Guy Stockwell . . . . Orgo
- •• 0:38—Buns, several times, when Concha catches him with the tattooed lady. (He's a heavy guy.)
- 0:39—Buns, lying dead on the ground after he cuts his own throat.

Satan's Princess (1989)

Lydie Denier . . . . Nicole St. James
- 0:27—Full frontal nudity, getting out of pool.
- ••• 0:28—Full frontal nudity, next to bed and in bed with Karen.
- ••• 0:45—Topless and buns, making love in bed with Robert Forster.

Robert Forster . . . . .Lou Cherney

Leslie Huntly . . . . Karen Rhodes
- ••• 0:27—Topless sitting on bed and in bed with Nicole.

Marilyn Joi. . . . . Hooker

Caren Kaye . . . . Leah

Debra Lamb . . . . Fire Eater/Dancer
- •• 0:23—Topless in G-string doing a fire dance in club.
- 0:25—Topless, doing more dancing. Long shot.

Saturday Night Fever (1977)

(R-rated version reviewed.)

Joseph Cali . . . . Joey

Paul Pepe . . . . Double J.
- 0:22—Buns, while making love in back seat of car with a girl.

Saturn 3 (1980)

Kirk Douglas . . . . Adam
- 0:57—Brief buns while fighting with Harvey Keitel, more brief buns sitting down in bed with Farrah Fawcett.

Farrah Fawcett . . . . Alex
- •• 0:17—Brief right breast taking off towel and running to Kirk Douglas after taking a shower.

Harvey Keitel. . . . . Benson

Savage Attraction (1983; Australian)

Kerry Mack. Christine Maresch
- ••• 0:10—Topless, getting out of shower and putting on robe.
- 0:11—Topless behind shower door, making love with Walter.
- •• 0:17—Topless sitting at the end of the bed.
- •• 0:59—Topless undressing in bedroom, then in bathtub with Walter.
- ••• 1:04—Topless getting her blouse unbuttoned, then topless in bed with Walter.
- 1:19—On boat, in semi-sheer white blouse.

Savage Beach (1989)

Hope Marie Carlton . . . . .Taryn
  0:06—Almost topless in spa with the three other women.
- 0:32—Topless changing clothes in airplane with Dona Speir.
- •• 0:48—Nude, going for a swim on the beach with Speir.

Patty Duffek . . . . Patticakes
- 0:06—Topless in spa with Lisa London, Dona Speir and Hope Marie Carlton.
- •• 0:50—Topless changing clothes.

Lisa London . . . . Rocky
- 0:06—Topless in spa with Patty Duffek, Dona Speir and Hope Marie Carlton.
- •• 0:50—Topless changing clothes.

Michael Jay Shane . . . . Shane Abeline
- •• 0:08—Buns, while getting out of pool.

Dona Speir. . . . . .Dona
  0:06—Almost topless in spa with the three other women.
- 0:32—Topless changing clothes in airplane with Hope Marie Carlton.
- •• 0:48—Nude, going for a swim on the beach with Carlton.

Maxine Wasa . . . . .Sexy Beauty
- ••• 0:08—Side view of left breast, in pool with Shane, then topless getting out of pool.
- ••• 0:10—Topless while Shane talks on the phone.

Teri Weigel. . . . . Anjelica
- ••• 0:33—Topless taking off black teddy and getting into bed to make love.
- •• 0:47—Topless making love in the back seat of car.

Savage Streets (1985)

Linda Blair . . . . .Brenda
- ••• 1:05—Topless sitting in the bathtub thinking.

Debra Blee . . . . .Rachel
  0:20—In a bra in the girls locker room.

Marcia Karr . . . . Stevie

Rebecca Perle. . . . . Cindy Clark
  0:24—In bra and panties, fighting with Brenda in the locker room.
- •• 0:53—Brief topless in biology class getting her top torn off by Linda Blair.

Linnea Quigley. . . . . Heather
- 0:28—Topless getting raped by the jerks.

Suzanne Slater . . . . Uncredited
•• 0:09—Topless being held by jerks when they yank
  her tube top down.
Kristi Somers . . . . Valerie
  0:24—In bra and panties in the locker room.

Scandal (1989)
(Unrated version reviewed.)
Britt Ekland . . . . Mariella Novotny
•• 0:31—Topless lying on table with John Hurt.
• 0:51—Right breast talking with Hurt and Christine.
Bridget Fonda . . . . Mandy Rice-Davis
• 0:20—Brief topless dressed as an Indian dancing
  while Christine tries to upstage her.
  0:54—In white lingerie, then lower frontal nudity in
  sheer nightgown in room with a guy.
  1:05—Brief buns walking back into bedroom. Long
  shot.
John Hurt . . . . Stephen Ward

Scarecrow (1973)
Eileen Brennan . . . . Darlene
• 0:27—Brief topless in bed when Gene Hackman
  takes off her bra and grabs her breasts.
Dorothy Tristan . . . . Coley

Scarface (1983)
Angela Aames . . . . Woman at the Babylon Club
Steven Bauer . . . . Manny Ray
Lana Clarkson . . . . Woman at the Babylon Club
Emilia Crow . . . . Echevera
Mary Elizabeth Mastrantonio . . . . Gina
• 2:36—(0:39 into tape 2) Very, very brief left breast
  when she gets shot and her nightgown opens up
  when she gets hit.
Shelly Taylor Morgan . . . . . Woman at the Babylon Club
Michelle Pfeiffer . . . . Elvira
Pepe Serna . . . . Angel
Katt Shea . . . . Woman at the Babylon Club

Scenes from the Class Struggle in Beverly Hills (1989)
Ed Begley, Jr. . . . . Peter
Robert Beltran . . . . Juan
• 1:34—Brief buns, when his shorts are pulled down
  by Frank.
Jacqueline Bisset . . . . Clare
Ray Sharkey . . . . Frank
• 1:10—Brief buns while sleeping in bed with Zandra.
Arnetia Walker . . . . To-Bel
• 0:37—Topless making love with Frank on the sofa.
•• 1:10—Topless in bed waking up with Howard.
••• 1:23—Topless making love on top of Ed Begley, Jr.
  on the floor.
Mary Woronov . . . . Lizabeth
••• 1:06—In black lingerie, then topless in bedroom,
  then in bed with Juan.

Schizoid (1980)
Flo Gerrish . . . . Pat
Mariana Hill . . . . Julie
  0:58—Left breast, while making love in bed with
  Klaus Kinski. Dark, hard to see.
Klaus Kinski . . . . Dr. Peter Fales
Christopher Lloyd . . . . Gilbert
Craig Wasson . . . . Doug
Donna Wilkes . . . . Allison Foles
  0:12—Topless taking off her bra in bathroom while
  Klaus Kinski watches. Buns, getting into the shower.
  Out of focus shots.
•• 0:13—Side view topless getting into the shower.

School Spirit (1985)
Leslee Bremmer . . . . Sandy
• 1:18—Topless on a guy's shoulder in pool. (She's on
  the right, wearing red swimsuit bottoms.)
Linda Carol . . . . Hogette
Roberta Collins . . . . Helen Grimshaw
Jackie Easton . . . . Hogette
Julie Gray . . . . Kendall
Marlene Janssen . . . . Sleeping Princess
•• 0:16—Topless in shower room, shaving her legs.
•• 0:42—Topless and buns, sleeping when old guy
  goes invisible to peek at her.
Marta Kober . . . . Ursula
Becky LeBeau . . . . Hogette
• 1:07—Topless sliding down water slide at dance,
  wearing black and white swimsuit bottoms.
Tom Nolan . . . . Billy Batson
• 0:17—Buns in open hospital smock. More buns
  while running up stairs.
• 1:29—Brief buns, in hospital gown, while leaving
  Judy's room.
Pamela Ward . . . . Girl in Sorority Room
••• 0:15—Buns, then topless in her room while Billy is
  invisible.
••• 0:16—More topless and buns with other women in
  shower room.

Scissors (1990)
Vicki Frederick . . . . Nancy Leahy
Steve Railsback . . . . Alex Morgan/Cole Morgan
Sharon Stone . . . . Angela Anderson
  0:04—Upper half of left breast sitting up after attack
  in elevator.
•• 0:12—Topless changing clothes.
  0:36—In bra with Steve Railsback. Brief upper half of
  left breast. Dark.

Scorchy (1971)
Connie Stevens . . . . Jackie Parker
•• 0:23—Open blouse, revealing left bra cup while talking on the telephone. Brief topless swimming in the
  water after taking off bathing suit top.
•• 0:52—Side view left breast, taking a shower.
••• 0:56—Brief right breast making love in bed with
  Greg Evigan. Topless getting tied to the bed by the

thieves. Kind of a long shot and a little dark and hard to see.
- 1:00—Brief topless getting covered with a sheet by the good guy.

Scream Dream (1989)

Melissa Moore .Jamie Summers
- ••• 0:39—Topless in black panties in room with Derrick. Then straddling him.
- •• 0:58—Topless in dressing room pulling her top down during transformation into monster.

Screen Test (1986)

Michelle Bauer . . . . Dancer/Ninja Girl
- •• 0:04—Topless dancing on stage.
- ••• 0:42—Nude, with Monique Gabrielle, making love in a boy's dream.

Deborah Blaisdell . . . . Dancer
- • 1:20—Brief topless, twice, dancing on stage. Long shot.

Monique Gabrielle . . . . Roxanne
- •• 0:06—Topless taking off clothes in back room in front of a young boy.
- ••• 0:42—Nude, with Michelle Bauer, seducing a boy in his day dream.
- •• 1:20—Topless taking off her top for a guy.

Screwball Hotel (1988)

Corinne Alphen. . . . . .Cherry Amour
- • 0:46—Buns, in black outfit on bed with Norman.

Gianna Amore. .Mary Beth
Lisa Bradford-Aiton . . . . Punk Singer
Andi Bruce . . . . Bobbi Jo
Lori Deann Pallett . . . . .Candy
- ••• 0:26—Topless in the shower while Herbie is accidentally in there with her.

Reneé Shugart. . . . . Blue Bell

Screwballs (1983)

Kim Cayer. . . . . Brunette Cheerleader
Alan Daveau . . . . Howie Bates
- • 1:00—Buns, after losing at strip bowling.

Raven De La Croix . . . . Miss Anna Tomical
- ••• 1:08—Topless during strip routine in nightclub.

Linda Shayne. . . . . Bootsie Goodhead
- ••• 0:43—Right breast, while in back of van at drive-in theater, then topless.

Season of Fear (1989)

Clancy Brown .Ward St. Clair
Clare Wren .Sarah Drummond
    0:23—Topless in bed with Mick. Long shot, hard to see.
    0:25—Brief silhouette, behind shower door.
- • 0:42—Side view of left breast, on top of Mick. Very, very brief left breast, turning over when they hear a noise outside.

Second Time Lucky (1986)

Diane Franklin. . . . . Eve
    0:07—In white bra and panties in frat house bedroom taking off her wet dress.

- •• 0:13—Topless a lot during first sequence in the Garden of Eden with Adam.
- ••• 0:28—Brief full frontal nudity running to Adam after trying an apple.
- • 0:41—Left breast, while taking top of dress down.
- ••• 1:01—Topless, opening her blouse in defiance, while standing in front of a firing squad.

Roger Wilson . . . . Adam Smith
- •• 0:13—Buns, while in the Garden of Eden.
- •• 0:30—Buns, while standing out in the rain.

Secret Admirer (1985)

C. Thomas Howell . . . . .Michael Ryan
Kelly Preston . . . . Deborah Anne Fimple
- •• 0:53—Brief topless in car with C. Thomas Howell.
- • 1:17—Very brief topless in and out of bed.

Leigh Taylor-Young . . . . Elizabeth Fimple
Dee Wallace Stone . . . . Connie Ryan
Fred Ward . . . . .Lou Fimple

Secret Fantasy (1981)

Laura Antonelli. . . . . Costanza Vivaldi
- ••• 0:16—In black bra in Doctor's office, then left breast, then topless getting examined.
- •• 0:18—In black bra and panties in another Doctor's office. Topless and buns.
- •• 0:19—Topless getting X-rayed. Brief topless lying down.
- •• 0:32—Topless and buns when Nicolo drugs her and takes Polaroid photos of her.
- •• 0:49—Topless and buns posing around the house for Nicolo while he takes Polaroid photos.
- •• 0:53—Topless and buns during Nicolo's dream.
- ••• 1:12—Topless in Doctor's office.
- •• 1:14—Topless and buns in room with another guy.
- • 1:16—Topless on train while workers "accidentally" see her.
- •• 1:20—Topless on bed after being carried from bathtub.
- •• 1:25—Topless dropping dress during opera.
- •• 1:27—More topless scenes from 0:49.

Secret Games (1991)

(Unrated version reviewed.)
Michele Brin. . . . . .Julianne
- •• 0:03—Left breast, while lying in bed with Billy Drago.
- ••• 0:08—Topless and buns, while taking a shower.
- ••• 0:09—Topless under sheer white robe, trying to entice Drago.
- ••• 0:34—Topless, sunbathing with the other girls. (She's wearing brown framed sunglasses.)
- ••• 0:38—Topless in bed, making love with Martin Hewitt.
- ••• 0:43—Buns and topless making love in bed with Drago.
- ••• 0:48—Topless, while tied to the bed.
- ••• 0:54—In white bra and panties, then nude taking them off and putting new ones on.
- ••• 1:10—Topless, while lying in bed with Hewitt.

- ••• 1:13—Topless and buns, making love with Hewitt in bathtub.
- •• 1:15—Topless under sheer robe.
- •• 1:32—Buns in G-string, then topless, getting into bed and making love with Drago.

Martin Hewitt . . . . .Eric
- • 0:38—Brief side view of buns, while in bed with Julianne.
  0:48—Almost buns, on top of Julianne in bed. (Her foot gets in the way.)

Monique Parent . . . . Robin
- • 0:33—Right breast, buns and crotch, while in bed with Julianne.

Catya Sassoon. . . . . Sandra
- ••• 0:21—Topless during modeling session with the other girls. (She's the only brunette.)
- ••• 0:26—Topless, making love in bed with Emil.
- •• 0:34—Topless in yellow bikini bottoms, sunbathing with the other girls.
- ••• 0:40—Topless, getting out of the swimming pool and lying on lounge chair.

Delia Sheppard . . . . Celeste
- • 0:38—Topless under sheer black body suit.
  0:45—Buns, under sheer robe.
- •• 0:48—Topless with her lover, while watching Julianne and Eric on TV.

The Secret of My Success (1987)
John Pankow. . . . . .Fred Melrose
Helen Slater. . . . . Christy
Margaret Whitton . . . . Vera Prescott
- • 0:31—Very brief topless taking off swimsuit top in swimming pool with Michael J. Fox.

Secrets (1971)
Jacqueline Bisset . . . . Jenny
  0:49—Very brief lower frontal nudity, putting panties on while wearing a black dress.
- ••• 1:02—Brief buns and a lot of topless on bed making love with Raoul.

The Secrets of Love—Three Rakish Tales (1986)
Marc Legein . . . . Luke
- • 0:18—Buns, while in the hay with the Weaver's wife.
- • 0:24—More buns.

Tina Shaw. The Weaver's Wife
- ••• 0:10—Topless in bed with Luke.
- ••• 0:17—Topless in the barn.

The Seduction (1982)
Colleen Camp. . . . . Robin
Morgan Fairchild. . . . . Jamie
- • 0:02—Brief topless under water, swimming in pool.
- • 0:05—Very brief left breast, getting out of the pool to answer the telephone.
  0:13—In white bra changing clothes while listening to telephone answering machine.
  0:50—In white lingerie in her bathroom while Andrew Stevens watches from inside the closet.
- •• 0:51—Topless pinning her hair up for her bath, then brief left breast in bathtub covered with bubbles.

- • 1:21—Topless getting into bed. Kind of dark, hard to see anything.

Andrew Stevens . . . . .Derek

See No Evil, Hear No Evil (1989)
Richard Pryor . . . . .Wally
Joan Severance. . . . . Eve
- •• 1:08—Topless in and leaning out of the shower while Gene Wilder tries to get her bag.

Gene Wilder. . . . . Dave

Senior Week (1987)
Vicki Darnell. . . . . Everett's Dream Teacher
- •• 0:03—Topless during classroom fantasy.

Miriam Zucker . . . . .Princeton Dream Girl
- •• 0:42—Topless during dream.

Seniors (1978)
Priscilla Barnes . . . . .Sylvia
- •• 0:18—Topless at the top of the stairs while Arnold climbs up the stairs while the rest of the guys watch.

Dennis Quaid. . . . . .Alan

Sensations (1988)
Blake Bahner . . . . Brian Ingles
- •• 0:10—Very, very brief lower frontal nudity pushing the covers off the bed, then buns, while getting out of bed.

Jennifer Delora. Della Randall
- • 0:11—Brief topless talking to Jenny to wake her up.
- • 0:13—Brief topless a couple of times in open robe.
- •• 0:38—Topless making love with a guy on bed.

Jane Hamilton . . . . .Tippy
Rebecca Lynn . . . . Jenny Hunter
- • 0:11—Topless, sleeping on couch.
- •• 0:23—Topless talking on the telephone.
- •• 1:09—Topless making love in bed with Brian.

Jacqueline Palmer. . . . . .Tess
Denise Torek . . . . Phone Girl #2
- • 0:23—Topless talking on the phone sex line.

Miriam Zucker . . . . Cookie Woman
- • 0:06—Topless on couch making love with a guy while Jenny and Brian watch.

Sensual Response (1992)
(Unrated version reviewed.)
Emile Levisetti . . . . Edge
- ••• 0:31—Buns, while standing and looking out the window, then sitting on the bed.
- ••• 0:43—Buns, while making love with Shannon Tweed.

Shannon Tweed. . . . . Eve
- ••• 0:25—Topless in studio with Edge, while he checks her out.
- ••• 0:29—Topless, making love with him. Long scene.
- ••• 0:31—Full frontal nudity, lying in bed, then sitting up.
- ••• 0:43—Topless, while making love in her house with Edge.
- ••• 0:51—Topless in pool at night with Edge.

•• 0:52—Nude, getting up out of bed and putting robe on.

•• 0:55—Topless in study with Edge.

••• 1:07—Topless and buns, while taking a shower. Nude, getting out and drying herself off.

The Sensuous Nurse (1975; Italian)
Ursula Andress. . . . . .Anna
- •• 0:16—Topless and buns in bed after making love with Benito.
- •• 0:22—Nude swimming in pool while Adonais watches.
- ••• 0:50—Nude slowly stripping and getting in bed with Adonais.
- ••• 1:10—Nude getting into bed.

Luciana Paluzzi . . . . .n.a.
- •• 0:20—Topless in room, ripping off her clothes and reluctantly making love with Benito.

Carla Romanelli. . . . . Tosca
- •• 0:06—Topless, then nude standing in the winery, then running around.
- •• 0:41—Nude, in basement, playing army, then making love with bearded guy.

The Sentinel (1977)
Tom Berenger. . . . . .Man at End
Beverly D'Angelo. . . . . Sandra
- 0:25—Masturbating in red leotard and tights on couch in front of Cristina Raines.
- • 0:33—Brief topless playing cymbals during Raines' nightmare (in B&W).
- 1:24—Brief topless long shot with zombie make up, munching on a dead Chris Sarandon.

Jeff Goldblum . . . . Jack
Sylvia Miles . . . . Gerde
- • 0:33—Brief left breast, three times, standing behind Beverly D'Angelo. Right breast, ripping dress of Christina Raines. B&W dream.
- 1:23—Brief topless, three times, with D'Angelo made up to look like zombies, munching on a dead Chris Sarandon.
- 1:27—Very brief right breast during zombie scene.
- • 1:28—Brief topless when the zombies start dying.

Cristina Raines. . . . . .Alison Parker
- • 0:18—Briefly in sheer beige bra, putting her blouse on.
- • 0:33—Very, very brief left breast immediately after Sylvia Miles rips her dress off. B&W dream sequence.

Chris Sarandon . . . . Michael Lerman

Separate Vacations (1985)
Susan Almgren . . . . Helene Gilbert
- •• 1:05—Topless and buns before getting into bed and then in bed with David Naughton.
- • 1:07—Topless in bathroom with Naughton.

Nancy Cser . . . . Stewardess
Jennifer Dale. . . . . .Sarah Moore
- • 0:17—Brief right breast in bed with her husband after son accidentally comes into their bedroom.
- 0:20—In a bra and slip showing the baby sitter the house before leaving.

•• 1:14—Topless on the cabin floor with Jeff after having a fight with her husband.

• 1:19—Brief right breast, in bed with her husband.

Blanca Guerra . . . . Alicia
- • 0:56—Topless on the bed with David Naughton when she turns out to be a hooker.

Laura Henry . . . . Nancy
Sherrie Miller . . . . Sandy
David Naughton . . . . .Richard Moore

Separate Ways (1979)
Karen Black . . . . Valentine Colby
- • 0:04—Topless and in panties changing while her husband talks on the phone, then in bra. Long shot.
- •• 0:18—Topless in bed, while making love with Tony Lo Bianco.
- •• 0:36—Topless taking a shower, then getting out.

Pamela Jean Bryant. . . . . Cocktail Waitress
Sybil Danning . . . . Mary
David Naughton . . . . Jerry Lansing

Serial (1980)
Pamela Bellwood . . . . Carol
Sally Kellerman. . . . . Martha
- ••• 0:03—Topless sitting on the floor with a guy.

Patch Mackenzie . . . . Stella
- • 0:59—Brief topless in mirror in swinger's club with Martin Mull.

Robin Sherwood. . . . . Woman
Clyde Ventura . . . . Donald

The Serpent and the Rainbow (1988)
Cathy Tyson. . . . . Dr. Marielle Duchamp
- • 0:41—Brief topless making love with Dennis. Probably a body double, don't see her face.

The Serpent of Death (1989)
Jeff Fahey . . . . Jake Bonner
Camilla More . . . . Rene
- •• 0:15—Brief topless in bed with Jeff Fahey.
- •• 1:22—Brief left breast while in bed, then topless and buns, getting out of bed (in mirror).

Serpico (1973)
Cornelia Sharpe . . . . Leslie
- •• 0:41—Topless in bathtub with Al Pacino.

M. Emmet Walsh . . . . .Gallagher

The Seventh Sign (1988)
Michael Biehn . . . . .Russell Quinn
Demi Moore. . . . . .Abby Quinn
- • 1:03—Brief topless, taking off bathrobe to take a bath. Her pregnant belly is not real—it's a full body prosthetic.

A Severed Head (1971; British)
Claire Bloom . . . . Honor Klein
- • 1:10—Topless leaning up then right beast while sitting up in bed with Richard Attenborough.

Jennie Linden . . . . .Georgie Hands
- 0:02—Buns, rolling over on the floor with Ian Holm.

Sex Appeal (1986)
Louis Bonanno . . . . Tony
Philip Campanaro . . . . Ralph
Tally Chanel . . . . Corinne
  • 1:22—Brief topless at the door of Tony's apartment
    when he opens the door while fantasizing about her.
Samantha Fox . . . . Sheila
  ••• 1:14—In black lingerie, then topless and buns in
    black G-string with Rhonda. Long scene.
Jane Hamilton . . . . Monica
  ••• 0:58—Topless dancing on the bed with Tony in his
    apartment. Long scene.
Kim Kafkaloff . . . . Stephanie
  •• 0:29—Buns, in G-string in Tony's bachelor pad. Top-
    less dancing and on bed.
Marcia Karr . . . . Christina
  • 1:12—Brief left breast, then in bra and panties on
    bed with her boyfriend.
Taija Rae . . . . Rhonda
  •• 1:14—In black lingerie, then topless in black push-
    up teddy with Sheila.

Sex on the Run (1979; German/French/Italian)
a.k.a. Some Like It Cool
a.k.a. Casanova and Co.
Jeannie Bell . . . . Slave Girl
  ••• 0:01—Topless, reading book in large bath with
    Marisa Berenson.
  ••• 0:24—Topless, giving Berenson a back massage.
Marisa Berenson . . . . n.a.
    1:23—Almost right breast, while in bed with Tony
    Curtis when she rolls over him.
Britt Ekland . . . . Countess Trivulsi
  • 0:44—Left breast while making love in bed with
    Tony Curtis (don't see her face).
Andrea Ferréol . . . . Beatrice
Sylva Koscina . . . . Jelsamina
  ••• 0:28—Topless and brief buns dropping her top for
    Tony Curtis, then walking around with the "other"
    Tony Curtis.
  •• 1:20—Topless talking to her husband.
Marisa Mell . . . . Francesca
  • 0:52—Very, very brief left breast, while getting out
    of bed with Tony Curtis.
    1:12—Braless in white nightgown.
Lillian Müller . . . . Angela
  ••• 0:15—Second woman (blonde) to take off her
    clothes with the other two women, nude. Long
    scene.
Olivia Pascal . . . . Convent Girl
  ••• 0:15—First woman (brunette) to take off her clothes
    with the other two women, full frontal nudity. Long
    scene.

Sex with a Smile (1976; Italian)
Barbara Bouchet . . . . "One for the Money" segment
  ••• 0:50—Topless sitting up in bed with a guy in bed,
    then lying down, wearing glasses.

Edwige Fenech . . . . Dream Girl
  •• 0:03—Topless tied to bed with two holes cut in her
    red dress top.
    0:09—Buns, in jail cell in court when the guy pulls
    her panties down with his sword.
  • 0:13—Brief topless in bed with Dracula taking off
    her top and hugging him.
  • 0:16—Topless in bathtub. Long shot.
Dayle Haddon . . . . The Girl
  •• 0:23—Topless, covered with bubbles in the bathtub.
  • 0:43—Buns, taking off robe to take a shower, then
    brief topless with Marty Feldman.
Sydne Rome . . . . "A Dog's Day" segment

Sexpot (1986)
Ruth Corrine Collins . . . . Ivy Barrington
  •• 0:09—Topless on table, taking her dress off for Phil-
    lip.
  • 0:41—Buns, in Damon's arms.
  •• 0:51—Left breast, while in shower talking to Boop-
    sie.
Jennifer Delora . . . . Barbara
  ••• 0:28—In bra, then topless with her two sisters when
    their bras pop off. (She's in the middle.)
  •• 0:36—Topless on bed with Gorilla.
  • 1:32—Topless during outtakes of 0:28 scene.
Jane Hamilton . . . . Beth
  ••• 0:28—In bra, then topless with her two sisters when
    their bras pop off. (She's on the right.)
  • 1:32—Topless during outtakes of 0:28 scene.
Christina Veronica . . . . Betty
  ••• 0:28—In bra, then topless with her two sisters when
    their bras pop off. (She's on the left.)
  • 0:46—Topless taking off her top in boat with Gorilla.
  • 0:54—Topless lying on the grass with Gorilla.
  • 1:28—Topless during outtakes of 0:28 scene.

Shadow Play (1986)
Ron Kuhlman . . . . John Crown
  • 1:06—Buns, while standing and holding Dee Wal-
    lace in his arms.
Dee Wallace Stone . . . . Morgan Hanna
  • 1:06—Brief topless making love with Ron Kuhlman.
    Kind of dark and hard to see.

Shadows Run Black (1981)
Terry Congie . . . . Lee Faulkner
  •• 0:22—Topless, going for a swim in pool at night.
  • 0:23—Topless under water.
Kevin Costner . . . . Jimmy Scott
Barbara Peckinpaugh . . . . Sandy
  ••• 0:57—Full frontal nudity, undressing in bedroom.
  •• 0:58—Buns and very, very brief topless getting into
    the shower.
  ••• 0:59—Full frontal nudity, drying herself off. Nude,
    walking around the house. Long scene.
  •• 1:01—Nude, in the bathroom, trying to avoid the
    killer.

Shadowzone (1989)
Maureen Flaherty . . . . Jenna
- •• 0:13—Topless lying under plastic cover.
- • 0:18—Topless on table getting operated on.
- •• 1:11—Topless again under plastic cover several times.
- •• 1:17—Brief topless again, then full frontal nudity.
- • 1:24—Topless alive under the plastic cover.

Robbie Reves. . . . . James
- 0:16—Frontal nudity long shot.
- • 0:26—Frontal nudity lying under plastic bubble.

Shawn Weatherly . . . . Dr. Kidwell

The Shaming (1979)
a.k.a. Good Luck, Miss Wyckoff
a.k.a. The Sin
Anne Heywood . . . . Evelyn Wyckoff
- ••• 0:49—Right breast, then topless in open blouse after being raped by Rafe in her classroom.
- 0:52—Topless on classroom floor, making love with Rafe.

John Lafayette . . . . Rafe
- •• 0:43—Very brief frontal nudity, taking off his jumpsuit in classroom with Anne Heywood.
- • 0:52—Buns, while making love on top of Heywood in classroom.

Shampoo (1975)
Warren Beatty . . . . George
- • 0:42—Upper half of buns with pants a little bit down in the bathroom with Julie Christie.
- • 1:24—Buns, while making love with Christie when Goldie Hawn discovers them. Long shot, hard to see.

Julie Christie . . . . Jackie
Lee Grant . . . . Felicia
- • 0:03—Brief topless in bed sitting up and putting bra on talking to Warren Beatty. Long shot, hard to see.

Goldie Hawn . . . . Jill
Sharon Kelly . . . . Painted Lady
- • 1:17—Brief topless covered with tattoos all over her body during party. Lit with strobe light.

Susan McIver . . . . Customer
Jack Warden . . . . Lester Carr

Shattered (1991)
Tom Berenger . . . . Dan Merrick
Corbin Bernsen . . . . Jeb Scott
Greta Scacchi . . . . Judith Merrick
- •• 0:14—Topless, turning over in bed.
- • 0:16—Topless in a strip of B&W photos that Tom Berenger looks at.
- • 0:36—Topless in B&W photos in Bob Hoskins' office. Brief topless in flashback.
- •• 1:24—Topless during love-making flashback.

She (1983)
Sandahl Bergman . . . . She
- •• 0:22—Topless getting into a pool of water to clean her wounds after sword fight.

David Brandon . . . . Pretty Boy

She'll be Wearing Pink Pyjamas (1985; British)
Maureen O'Brien . . . . Joan
- • 0:46—Brief topless making love in bed. Dark.

Julie Walters . . . . Fran
- ••• 0:07—Full frontal nudity taking a shower with the other women. Long scene.
- •• 0:58—Nude, undressing and going skinny dipping in mountain lake, then getting out. Nice bun shot walking into the lake.

Jane Wood . . . . Jude
- • 0:07—Nude, shaving her legs in the women's shower room.

She's Gotta Have It (1987)
Tracy Camilla Johns . . . . Nola Darling
- ••• 0:05—Topless, making love in bed with Jamie.
- •• 0:25—Brief left breast taking off leotard with Greer. More topless waiting for him to undress.
- •• 0:27—Topless and buns in bed with Greer.
- • 0:38—Topless, close up of breast, while making love with Spike Lee.
- •• 0:41—Left breast, while lying in bed with Lee.
- •• 1:05—Topless, twice, in bed masturbating.

Joie Lee . . . . Clorinda Bradford
John Canada Terrell . . . . Greer Childs
- •• 0:27—Buns and very brief frontal nudity, while getting into bed with Nola. More quick shots of buns in bed.

Sheba, Baby (1975)
Pam Grier . . . . Sheba Shayne
- • 0:26—Side view of left breast, while lying in bed with Brick.

Sheena (1984)
Nancy Paul . . . . Betsy Ames
Tanya Roberts . . . . Sheena
- •• 0:18—Topless and buns taking a shower under a waterfall. Full frontal nudity (long shot), diving into the water.
- ••• 0:54—Nude taking a bath in a pond.

Ted Wass . . . . Vic Casey
- • 1:48—Buns, after getting pulled out of the ground after tribal healing ceremony.

The Sheltering Sky (1990)
John Malkovich . . . . Port
- ••• 0:32—Frontal nudity and half of buns, while getting out of bed and opening door.

Campbell Scott . . . . Turner
Eric Vu-An . . . . Belqassim
- • 1:59—Buns, while rolling over in bed with Debra Winger. Long shot, don't see his face.

Debra Winger . . . . Kit Moresby
- 0:13—Upper half of lower frontal nudity in open robe when John Malkovich caresses her stomach.
- 0:24—Buns, getting out of bed.
- • 0:41—Very brief topless grabbing sheets and getting out of bed with Tunner.
- 1:58—Lower frontal nudity and sort of buns, getting undressed with Belqassim.

Shining Through (1992)
Michael Douglas . . . . Ed Leland
Melanie Griffith . . . . Linda Voss
  •• 0:22—Topless, making love in bed on top of Michael
    Douglas.
Liam Neeson . . . . .Franz-Otto Dietrich
Joely Richardson . . . . .Margrete von Eberstien

Shirley Valentine (1989; British)
Pauline Collins . . . . .Shirley Valentine
  • 0:13—Brief left breast giving Joe a shampoo in the
    bathtub.
  •• 1:17—Topless jumping from the boat into the water
    in slow motion. Very brief topless in the water.
  •• 1:19—Buns, hugging Tom Conti, left breast several
    times kissing him.
Bernard Hill . . . . .Joe Bradshaw
Joanna Lumley . . . . Marjorie

Shock 'Em Dead (1990)
Suzanne Ager . . . . .Groupie 3
Kathleen Kane. . . . . Pizza Girl 2
Traci Lords . . . . Lindsay Roberts
Jackie Moen . . . . .Groupie 4
  •• 1:05—Topless, taking off her top to tempt Martin.
Karen Russell. . . . . Michelle
  •• 0:16—In lingerie, then topless twice with Martin.

The Shout (1979)
Alan Bates . . . . Charles Crossly
John Hurt . . . . Anthony Fielding
Susannah York . . . . Rachel Fielding
  •• 0:53—Brief topless changing from a bathrobe to a
    blouse in bedroom.
  • 1:02—Brief nude in upstairs room getting ready to
    make love with Alan Bates.
    1:05—Brief buns, standing at end of hallway.
    1:09—In white slip inside and outside house.
    1:11—Topless in bathtub with John Hurt.
  • 1:18—Brief topless getting up from bed with Bates.
    Long shot, hard to see anything.

Showdown in Little Tokyo (1991)
Tia Carrere . . . . .Minako
  • 0:50—Buns and side view of left breast, taking off
    robe and getting into outdoor tub with Dolph
    Lundgren. Don't see her face.
  • 0:52—Left breast, while making love in bed with
    Lundgren. Don't see her face again.
Dolph Lundgren . . . . Detective Kenner
  ••• 0:53—Buns, while getting out of bed to check on
    noise outside.

The Sicilian (1987)
(Director's uncut version reviewed.)
Christopher Lambert . . . . .Salvatore Giullano
  •• 1:02—Buns, when the Duchess yanks his underwear
    down. Don't see his face, but probably him.
Barbara Sukowa . . . . Camilia Duchess of Crotone
  •• 0:05—Buns and brief topless taking a bath, three
    times.

  • 0:07—Brief right breast reading Time magazine. Full
    frontal nudity in the mirror standing up in the tub.
  • 0:08—Brief right breast standing at the window
    watching Christopher Lambert steal a horse.
  ••• 1:01—In bra, then topless in bedroom with Lam-
    bert. More topless, then nude. Long scene.
John Turturro . . . . Aspanu Pisciotta

Sid and Nancy (1986; British)
Gary Oldman . . . . .Sid Vicious
Patti Tippo . . . . Tanned and Sultry Blonde
Chloe Webb. . . . . Nancy
  • 0:21—Left breast, under Sid's arm in bed with him.
    Covered up, hard to see.
  •• 0:44—Topless in bed after making love, then argu-
    ing with Sid.

Side Out (1990)
Hope Marie Carlton . . . . Vanna
C. Thomas Howell . . . . Monroe Clark
Harley Jane Kozak. . . . . Kate Jacobs
  • 0:53—Brief left breast, then out of focus left breast,
    while in bed with Peter Horton.
Christopher Rydell . . . . Wiley Hunter

Side Roads (1988)
Ingrid Vold. . . . . Bonnie Velasco
  • 0:29—Brief topless in motel room, getting un-
    dressed and carried into bed by Joe.
    0:30—In white lingerie, talking with Joe. Long
    scene.
    0:56—In white bra and panties, changing clothes.
  • 1:45—Brief topless in mirror, getting out of bed.

Siesta (1987)
Ellen Barkin . . . . .Diane
  ••• 0:03—Brief full frontal nudity long shot taking off
    red dress, topless, brief buns standing up, then full
    frontal nudity lying down.
    1:22—Right nipple sticking out of dress while imag-
    ining she's with Gabriel Byrne instead of the reality
    of getting raped by taxi driver.
  • 1:23—Brief lower frontal nudity, very brief silhouette
    of a breast, then brief buns some more while with
    Byrne. Dark, hard to see.
  • 1:24—Lower frontal nudity, with torn dress while ly-
    ing in bed after the taxi driver gets up.
    1:26—Very brief lower frontal nudity, while running
    down road and her dress flies up as police cars pass
    by.
    1:28—Very brief side view of right breast putting on
    dress in bed just before Isabella Rossellini comes into
    the bedroom to attack her. Long distance shot.
Gabriel Byrne . . . . Augustine
  • 1:28—Brief buns and frontal nudity, while getting
    out of bed. Long shot, hard to see.
Jodie Foster . . . . Nancy
    0:47—In a black slip combing Ellen Barkin's hair.
    0:50—In a slip again in bedroom with Barkin.
Grace Jones . . . . Conchita
Isabella Rossellini . . . . .Marie

Julian Sands. . . . . Kit
Martin Sheen . . . . Del
Anastassia Stakis . . . . Desdra

Silent Night, Deadly Night (1984)
Tara Buckman. Mother (Ellie)
- 0:12—Brief right breast twice when the killer dressed as Santa Claus, rips her blouse open. Topless lying dead with slit throat.
- 0:18—Very, very brief topless during Billy's flashback.
- 0:43—Brief topless a couple of times again in another of Billy's flashbacks.

Toni Nero . . . . Pamela
- 0:30—Brief right breast twice just before Billy gets stabbed during fantasy scene.
- 0:42—Topless in stock room when Andy attacks her.
- 0:44—Topless in stock room struggling with Billy, then getting killed by him.

Linnea Quigley . . . . Denise
- ••• 0:52—Topless on pool table with Tommy, then putting on shorts and walking around the house. More topless, impaled on antlers.

Robert Brian Wilson . . . . Billy at 18
- 0:30—Sort of buns while in bed with Pamela.

Silent Night, Deadly Night, Part 2 (1986)
Tara Buckman. . . . . .Mother
- 0:09—Very brief right breast, with Santa Claus during flashback.
- 0:14—Very brief topless on ground during flashback.
- 0:22—Very, very brief blurry topless during flashback.
- 0:47—Very, very brief topless during flashback.

Elizabeth Kaitan. . . . . .Jennifer
0:58—Most of right breast, then buns, kissing Ricky.

Toni Nero . . . . Pamela
- •• 0:22—Topless in back of toy store in flashback from *Silent Night, Deadly Night.*

Linnea Quigley . . . . Denise
- ••• 0:26—Topless on pool table and getting dressed flashback from *Silent Night, Deadly Night.*

Silent Night, Deadly Night III: Better Watch Out! (1989)
Robert Culp. . . . . .Lt. Connely
Laura Herring . . . . .Jerri
- ••• 0:48—Topless in bathtub with her boyfriend Chris.

Silent Night, Deadly Night 4: Initiation (1990)
Maud Adams. . . . . .Fima
Tommy Hindley . . . . .Hank
- 0:03—Brief buns, while carrying Kim onto bed.

Marjean Holden . . . . Jane
Neith Hunter. . . . . Kim
- 0:03—Brief topless several times in bed with Hank.
- 0:47—Brief topless during occult ceremony when a worm comes out of her mouth.
- 1:05—Right breast, while lying on floor. Long shot.

1:06—Topless, covered with gunk, transforming into a worm.
- 1:07—Very brief side of right breast, while sitting up.

The Silent Partner (1978)
Gail Dahms . . . . Louise
- 0:31—Right breast in bathroom with another guy when Elliott Gould surprises them.

Michael Kirby. . . . . Packard
Céline Lomez . . . . .Elaine
- 1:05—Side view of left breast, then topless, then buns with Elliott Gould.

Susannah York . . . . .Julie
- 0:38—Very brief right breast pulling her dress back up with Elliott Gould.

Silent Rage (1982)
Toni Kalem. . . . . Alison Halman
- •• 0:22—Side view of left breast, then topless, while in bed with Chuck Norris.
- •• 0:46—Right breast, while lying in bed with Norris.
1:01—Briefly in bra, undressing in bedroom to take a shower.

Silk 2 (1989)
Monique Gabrielle . . . . Jenny "Silk" Sleighton
- ••• 0:27—Topless, then full frontal nudity taking a shower while killer stalks around outside.
0:28—Very, very brief blurry right breast in open robe when she's on the sofa during fight.
- 0:29—Brief topless doing a round house kick on the bad guy. Right breast several times during the fight.
- ••• 0:55—Topless taking off her blouse and making love on bed. Too much diffusion!

Silkwood (1984)
E. Katherine Kerr . . . . Gilda Schultz
Bruce McGill . . . . Mace Hurley
Kurt Russell . . . . Drew Stephens
Meryl Streep . . . . Karen Silkwood
- 0:24—Very brief glimpse of upper half of left breast when she flashes it in nuclear reactor office.

Fred Ward . . . . .Morgan

Simply Irresistible (1983)
(R-rated version. *Irresistible* is the X-rated version.)
Nicole Black . . . . Mata Hari
1:07—Pulling up her dress, then stripping in front of two guys in prison.
- •• 1:14—Full frontal nudity tied to a chair.

Samantha Fox . . . . .Arlene Brooks
- 1:20—In see-through white nightgown, then brief peeks at right breast when nightgown gapes open.

Sinbad and the Eye of the Tiger (1977; U.S./British)
Taryn Power. . . . . Dione
1:16—Very brief buns, skinny dipping in pond with Jane Seymour. Long shot, but still pretty amazing for a G-rated film.
1:18—Very brief partial side view of right breast, running away from the troglodyte.

Jane Seymour . . . . Farah
    1:16—Very brief buns, skinny dipping in pond with
    Taryn Power. Long shot, but still pretty amazing for
    a G-rated film.
    1:17—Very brief partial right breast (arm covers
    most of it) screaming when scared by the troglo-
    dyte.

Sincerely Charlotte (1986; French)
Caroline Faro. . . . . Irene the Baby Sitter
Isabelle Huppert . . . . Charlotte
    0:20—Brief topless in bathtub. Long shot, out of fo-
    cus.
    1:07—Very brief left breast changing into red dress
    in the back seat of the car.
  •• 1:15—Topless in bed with Mathieu. Kind of dark.
Tina Sportolaro . . . . .n.a.

Sister Sister (1987)
Jennifer Jason Leigh. . . . . Lucy Bonnard
  •• 0:01—Topless making love during a dream.
    0:52—In lingerie talking with Eric Stoltz.
  •• 0:53—Left breast, while making love with Stoltz in
    her bedroom.
  • 0:58—Topless in bathtub surrounded by candles.
Eric Stoltz . . . . Matt Rutledge

Sisters (1973)
Margot Kidder. . . . . .Danielle Breton
  • 0:11—Very brief left breast, undressing while walk-
    ing down hallway. Long shot.
  • 0:14—Topless opening her robe on couch for her
    new boyfriend. Shadows make it hard to see.
Jennifer Salt. . . . . .Grace Collier

Ski School (1990)
Ava Fabian . . . . .Victoria
  ••• 0:53—In white bra and panties, then topless making
    love with Johnny.
Charlie Spradling. . . . . Paulette
Darlene Vogel . . . . .Lori
  • 1:03—Topless in bed with Johnny.

Skin Deep (1989)
Denise Crosby. Angie Smith
Chelsea Field . . . . Amy
Raye Hollitt . . . . Lonnie
  • 0:26—Brief side view topless and buns getting un-
    dressed and into bed with John Ritter.
Heidi Paine . . . . Tina
  • 0:01—Brief side view topless sitting on John Ritter's
    lap while Denise Crosby watches.
Brenda Swanson . . . . Emily

Slam Dance (1987)
Virginia Madsen . . . . Yolanda Caldwell
Mary Elizabeth Mastrantonio. . . . . .Helen Drood
Lisa Niemi . . . . .Ms. Schell
  ••• 0:54—Nude in Tom Hulce's apartment.
  • 1:00—Topless, dead, lying on the floor in Hulce's
    apartment.

Slammer Girls (1987)
Louis Bonanno . . . . Cubby
Philip Campanaro . . . . Gary
  • 0:48—Buns, while dancing in G-string in front of the
    girls in their prision cell.
  • 0:49—More buns in G-string, while wrestling with
    Melody.
Tally Chanel . . . . .Candy Treat
  • 0:56—Buns, in G-string, doing a dance routine
    wearing feathery pasties for the Governor in the hos-
    pital.
Samantha Fox . . . . .Mosquito
  •• 0:17—Topless in the shower hassling Melody with
    Tank.
Jane Hamilton . . . . Miss Crabapples
Devon Jenkin . . . . Melody Campbell
    0:08—In lingerie in her bedroom, then in jail.
  • 0:12—Brief topless getting lingerie ripped off by the
    prison matron.
  • 0:16—Brief topless getting blouse ripped off by Tank
    in the shower.
Kim Kafkaloff . . . . Ginny
  • 0:23—Brief topless changing clothes under table in
    the prison cafeteria.
Sharon Kane. . . . . Rita
  • 0:23—Brief topless changing clothes under table in
    the prison cafeteria.
  •• 1:01—Topless walking around an electric chair try-
    ing to distract a prison guard.
Sharon Kelly. . . . . .Professor
  • 0:23—Brief topless changing clothes under table in
    the prison cafeteria.
  •• 0:34—Topless squishing breasts against the window
    during prison visiting hours.
  •• 0:36—Topless with an inflatable male doll.
Adriane Lee . . . . Dead Convict
Maria Machart . . . . Hooker
  •• 0:06—Topless, getting fondled by a cop.
Darcy Nychols . . . . Tank
  • 0:17—Topless ripping blouse open while hassling
    Melody.

Slap Shot (1977)
Melinda Dillon . . . . .Suzanne
  ••• 0:30—Right breast, lying in bed with Paul Newman,
    then topless sitting up and talking. Nice, long scene.
Michael Ontkean . . . . .Ned Braden
  •• 1:56—Brief buns while wearing a jock strap, while
    skating off the hockey rink and carrying a trophy.
M. Emmet Walsh .Dickie Dunn
Jennifer Warren . . . . Francine Dunlop

The Slasher (1975)
Sylva Koscina . . . . Barbara
  •• 0:17—Left breast lying down getting a massage.
  •• 1:18—Topless undressing and putting a robe on at
    her lover's house. Left breast after getting stabbed.

Slaughter (1972)
Marlene Clark . . . . Kim Walker
- 0:11—Very brief buns and right breast, getting thrown out of room by Jim Brown.

Stella Stevens . . . . Ann
- 0:47—Left breast, several times in bed with Jim Brown.
- 0:55—Left breast, making love in bed with Brown again. Dark.
- 0:57—Brief right breast, in bed afterwards. Close up shot.
- 1:14—Buns and topless taking a shower and getting out. This is her best nude scene.

Rip Torn . . . . Hoffo

Slaughter High (1986)
Billy Hartman . . . . Frank
- 1:00—Brief buns while in bed with Stella.

Caroline Munro. . . . . Carol
0:19—Walking around her house in lingerie and a robe.

Simon Scuddamore. Marty
- 0:05—Nude in girl's shower room when his classmates pull a prank on him.

Slaughterhouse Five (1972)
Perry King. . . . . Robert Pigrim
Ron Liebman. . . . . Paul Lazzaro
Valerie Perrine . . . . Montana Wildhack
- 0:39—Topless in Playboy magazine as a Playmate.
- 0:43—Topless getting into the bathtub.
- 1:27—Topless in a dome with Michael Sacks.

Slaughterhouse Rock (1988)
Toni Basil . . . . Sammy Mitchell
Hope Marie Carlton. . . . . Krista Halpern
- 0:09—Brief right breast, taking off her top in bedroom with her boyfriend.
- 0:49—Topless, getting raped by Richard as he turns into a monster.

Slave of the Cannibal God (1979; Italian)
Ursula Andress. . . . . n.a.
- 0:33—Topless taking off shirt and putting on a T-shirt.
- 1:07—Nude getting tied to a pole by the Cannibal People and covered with red paint.
1:20—Brief peek at buns under her skirt when running away from the Cannibal People.

Slavegirls from Beyond Infinity (1987)
Cindy Beal. . . . . Tisa
0:25—Walking around in white bra and panties.
- 0:36—Topless on beach wearing white panties.
- 1:05—Left breast leaning back on table while getting attacked by Zed.

Elizabeth Kaitan. . . . . Daria
- 0:38—Topless undressing and jumping into bed with Rik.

Brinke Stevens . . . . Shala
0:29—Chained up wearing black lingerie.
- 0:31—Brief side view of left breast on table. Nice pan from her feet to her head while she's lying face down.

Slavers (1977)
Britt Ekland . . . . Anna
- 0:40—Topless undressing in front of Ron Ely.

Slaves of New York (1989)
Nick Corri . . . . Marley Mantello
Adam Coleman Howard. . . . . Stash
- 1:15—Buns, while putting on his pants and silhouette of penis. Dark, hard to see.

Madeleine Potter . . . . Daria
- 1:14—Topless making love with Stash on chair. Mostly see left breast. Dark.

Chris Sarandon. . . . . Victor Okrent

Sleepaway Camp II: Unhappy Campers (1988)
Susan Marie Snyder . . . . Mare
- 0:08—Brief topless lifting up her T-shirt.
- 0:24—Brief topless flashing in boy's cabin.
- 0:33—Topless in Polaroid photograph that Angela confiscates from the boys.

Pamela Springsteen . . . . Angela

Sleepaway Camp III: Teenage Wasteland (1989)
Tracy Griffith . . . . Marcia Holland
Pamela Springsteen . . . . Angela Baker
Jill Terashita . . . . Arab
- 0:16—Topless putting sweatshirt on.

The Sleeping Car (1990)
Judie Aronson. . . . . Kim
- 0:42—Brief topless on top of David Naughton making love. Brief topless three times after he hallucinates.

Jeff Conaway . . . . Bud Sorenson
Sandra Margot . . . . 19-Year Old Girl
- 0:00—Brief topless shots taking off clothes then making love with a guy. Left breast while making love.

Dani Minnick. . . . . Joanne
David Naughton . . . . Jason McCree

Sloane (1984)
Debra Blee. . . . . Cynthia Thursby
- 0:15—Very brief topless during attempted rape.

Ann Milhench . . . . Janice Thursby
- 0:02—Topless and buns getting out of shower and being held by kidnappers.

Slow Burn (1986)
Beverly D'Angelo . . . . Laine Fleischer
- 1:01—Topless making love with Eric Roberts. Don't see her face. Part of lower frontal nudity showing tattoo.

Eric Roberts . . . . Jacob Asch

Slumber Party '57 (1976)

Bridget Holloman . . . . Bonnie May
- 0:10—Topless with her five girl friends during swimming pool scene. Hard to tell who is who.
- 0:26—Left breast in truck with her cousin Cal.

Joyce Jillson . . . . Gladys

Janice Karman . . . . .Hank
- • 1:06—Topless, sitting watching Smitty and David make love in the stable.

Noelle North . . . . Angie
- • 0:37—Buns, then topless in bed with a party guest of her parents.

Cheryl Smith . . . . .Sherry

Debra Winger . . . . Debbie
- 0:10—Topless with her five girl friends during swimming pool scene. Hard to tell who is who.
- • • 0:53—Topless three times, lying down, making out with Bud.

Janet Wood . . . . .Smitty
- 0:10—Topless with her five girl friends during swimming pool scene. Hard to tell who is who.
- • • 1:06—Left breast, then topless in stable with David while his sister watches.

The Slumber Party Massacre (1982)

Debra De Liso . . . . Kim
- 0:08—Very brief topless getting soap from Trish in the shower.
- • • 0:29—In beige bra and panties, then topless putting on a U.S.A. shirt while changing with the other girls.

Joseph Alan Johnson . . . . Neil

Michele Michaels . . . . Trish
- • • 0:01—Topless in white panties while getting dressed.
- • • 0:08—Buns, then brief topless passing the soap to Kim.
- • • 0:29—Topless in white panties putting shirt on while two boys watch from outside.

Brinke Stevens . . . . Linda
- • • 0:07—Buns, then topless taking a shower during girls locker room scene.

Slumber Party Massacre II (1987)

Juliette Cummins . . . . Sheila
- • • 0:24—In black bra, then topless in living room during a party with her girlfriends.

Heidi Kozak . . . . Sally

Kimberly McArthur . . . . Amy

A Small Circle of Friends (1980)

Karen Allen . . . . .Jessica
- 0:47—Brief topless in bathroom with Brad Davis. Don't see her face.
- 0:48—Very brief topless, pushing Davis off her. Then very, very brief half of left breast turning around to walk to the mirror.

Brad Davis . . . . Leo DaVinci
- • • 1:22—Brief buns, while dropping his pants with several other guys for Army draft inspection.

Shelley Long . . . . .Alice

Jameson Parker . . . . Nick Baxter

Daniel Stern . . . . .Crazy Kid
- • 1:22—Brief buns, while dropping his pants with several other guys for Army draft inspection.

Smash Palace (1981; New Zealand)

Bruno Lawrence . . . . .Al Shaw
- • • • 0:39—Buns while in bed after arguing, then making up with Jacqui.

Anna-Maria Monticelli . . . . .Jacqui Shaw
  0:21—Silhouette of right breast changing while sitting on the edge of the bed.
- • • • 0:39—Topless in bed after arguing, then making up with Bruno Lawrence.

Smile (1974)

Colleen Camp . . . . .Connie Thompson
  0:47—Side profile of right breast and buns in dressing room while Little Bob is outside taking pictures.

Bruce Dern . . . . Big Bob

Melanie Griffith . . . . .Karen Love
  0:07—Brief glimpse at panties, bending over to pick up dropped box.
- 0:34—Very, very brief side view of right breast in dressing room, just before passing behind a rack of clothes.
- 0:47—Very brief side view of right breast, then side view of left breast when Little Bob is outside taking pictures.
- 0:48—Very brief topless as Polaroid photograph that Little Bob took develops.
- 1:51—Topless in the same Polaroid in the policeman's sun visor.

Annette O'Toole . . . . .Doria Houston
  0:34—In white bra and panties in dressing room.
  1:06—In white bra and slip talking to Joan Prather in bedroom.

Joan Prather . . . . .Robin
- 0:47—Brief buns in dressing room, while taking off pants while Little Bob is outside taking pictures. (She's wearing a pink ribbon in her hair.)

Smoke Screen (1988)

Kim Cattrall .Odessa Muldoon
  0:31—Brief half of right breast sitting in bed with sheet pulled up on her.
- • • 1:16—Topless in bed on top of Gerald.
- • • • 1:17—Topless lying in bed under Gerald while he kisses her breasts.

Smoothtalker (1990)

Suzanne Ager . . . . .Candy (The 976-GIRL)
- 0:23—Left breast and partial buns, while lying on the floor dead.
- 0:24—More left breast, while lying dead on the floor. Lit with red light.
- 0:35—Left breast, while lying dead on the floor. Very brief buns in G-string.

Julie Austin . . . . Ms. Weston

Soft Touch (1987; Made for Cable Movie)
(Shown on *The Playboy Channel* as *Birds in Paradise*.)
Jennifer Inch .Tracy Anderson
  • 0:01—Full frontal nudity during the opening credits.
  • 0:02—Topless with her two girlfriends during the opening credits.
  ••• 0:17—Topless exercising on the floor, walking around the room, the lying on bed. Long scene.
  • 0:20—Full frontal nudity getting out of bed.
  •• 0:23—Topless in bed.
  ••• 0:50—Topless sunbathing on boat with Carrie.
  •• 1:01—Full frontal nudity, sitting on towel, watching Carrie.
  • 1:02—Full frontal nudity, waving to a dolphin.
  •• 1:04—Topless at night by campfire with Carrie.
  ••• 1:05—Brief left breast, then topless putting on skirt and walking around the island.
  •• 1:13—Topless in hut with island guy.
  • 1:19—Topless in stills during the end credits.
Jeanine Louise . . . . Carrie Crawford
  • 0:00—Topless during opening credits.
  • 0:02—Topless with her two girlfriends during the opening credits.
  • 0:03—Brief topless getting out of the shower.
  • 0:17—Topless seen in mirror, while taking a shower.
  •• 0:19—Full frontal nudity during pillow fight on bed.
  •• 0:23—Topless in bed with the other two girls.
  • 0:27—Topless in T-shirt, leaning over to wash car.
  • 0:32—Topless with Neill in open dress.
  ••• 0:35—Dancing on stage in red lingerie, then topless and buns in G-string.
  •• 0:41—Full frontal nudity walking in water with a guy.
  ••• 0:50—Topless sunbathing on the boat with Tracy.
  • 1:01—Nude, swinging into water. Long shot.
  • 1:02—Buns, waving to a dolphin.
  • 1:04—Topless at night by campfire with Tracy.
  • 1:05—Brief left breast, while sleeping.
  • 1:06—Topless when Tracy wakes her up.
  • 1:19—Topless in stills during the end credits.
Sue Morrow . . . . .Ashley Keyes
  • 0:01—Topless during opening credits.
  • 0:02—Topless with her two girlfriends during the opening credits.
  •• 0:19—Topless taking off her T-shirt in bed. More topless sleeping, then waking up.
  • 0:20—Topless getting out of bed.
  •• 0:22—Topless making love with a guy.
  • 0:23—Topless in bed.
  •• 0:53—Topless on bed with Ensign Landers.
  ••• 0:59—Topless and buns in play pool with Landers.
  • 1:19—Topless in stills during end credits.
Jennifer Wyhl. . . . . .Nancy
  • 0:00—Topless during opening credits.

Soft Touch II (1987; Made for Cable Movie)
(Shown on *The Playboy Channel* as *Birds in Paradise*.)
Jennifer Inch .Tracy Anderson
  • 0:01—Topless during opening credits.
  • 0:02—Topless with her two girlfriends during opening credits.
  •• 0:14—Topless dancing in Harry's bar by herself.
  • 0:27—Full frontal nudity on stage at Harry's after robbers tell her to strip.
  • 0:29—Side of left breast tied to Neill on bed.
  • 0:31—Topless tied up when Ashley and Carrie discover her.
  •• 0:52—Full frontal nudity during strip poker game, then covered with whipped cream.
  • 0:57—Full frontal nudity getting out of bed.
Jeanine Louise . . . . Carrie Crawford
  • 0:00—Topless during opening credits.
  • 0:02—Topless with her two girlfriends during opening credits.
  •• 0:24—Topless in bed feeling herself.
  •• 0:41—Full frontal nudity undressing and putting swimsuit on.
  • 0:51—Topless with her diving instructor.
Sue Morrow . . . . Ashley Keyes
  • 0:01—Topless during opening credits.
  • 0:02—Topless with her two girlfriends during the opening credits.
  •• 0:26—Topless sitting and sunbathing on boat.
  • 0:50—Brief topless in the water.
  • 0:52—Topless during strip poker game, then covered with whipped cream.
  •• 0:56—Full frontal nudity getting out of bed.
Jennifer Wyhl . . . . Nancy
  • 0:01—Topless during opening credits.
  • 0:05—Topless in bed with Neill.
  • 0:18—Topless undressing for robbers. Brief full frontal nudity.
  • 0:57—Topless in bed with Neill.
  • 1:01—Full frontal nudity in bed with Neill.

Soldier of Orange (1977; Dutch)
Derek De Lint. . . . . .Alex
Edward Fox . . . . .Col. Rafelli
Rutger Hauer . . . . Erik Lanshoff
Jeroen Krabbé . . . . Gus
Susan Penhaligon. . . . . .Susan
  • 1:34—Brief topless kissing her boyfriend when Rutger Hauer sees them through the window. Medium long shot.
  ••• 1:36—Topless in bed with her boyfriend and Hauer.

Sole Survivor (1982)
Anita Skinner . . . . .Denise Watson
  • 0:29—Very, very brief right breast in bed with Dr. Richardson. Brief side view of right breast when he jumps out of bed.
  1:13—In bra, zipping up pants.
Brinke Stevens . . . . Jennifer
  •• 0:45—In bra playing cards, then topless.

Some Call It Loving (1972)
Tisa Farrow . . . . Jennifer
••• 1:17—Topless in bed with Troy.
Brandy Herred . . . . Cheerleader
••• 1:12—Nude dancing in a club doing a strip tease
dance in a cheerleader outfit.
Richard Pryor . . . . Jeff

Some Girls (1988)
Jennifer Connelly . . . . Gabriella
Patrick Dempsey . . . . Michael
• 0:34—Brief frontal nudity, then buns while running
all around the house chasing Jennifer Connelly.
Andre Gregory . . . . Mr. D'Arc
• 1:24—Buns, while standing in the study looking at a
book. Very brief frontal nudity when he turns around
to sit at his desk.
Sheila Kelley . . . . Irenka
• 0:13—Topless and buns getting something at the
end of the hall while Michael watches. Long shot,
hard to see.
• 1:01—Topless in window while Michael watches
from outside. Long shot, hard to see.
1:17—In black slip seducing Michael after funeral.

Something Wild (1986)
Jeff Daniels . . . . Charles Driggs
•• 0:16—Buns, while lying in bed after making love
with Melanie Griffith.
Melanie Griffith . . . ."Lulu"/Audrey Hankel
••• 0:16—Strips to topless in bed with Jeff Daniels.
• 0:24—Buns and brief topless, while looking out the
window.
Tracey Walter . . . . .The Country Squire

Sorceress (1982)
Lee Anne Harris . . . . Mira
••• 0:11—Topless (on the left) greeting the creature
with her sister. Upper half of buns, getting dressed.
•• 0:29—Topless (she's the second one) undressing
with her sister in front of Erlick and Baldar.
Lynette Harris . . . . .Mara
••• 0:11—Topless (on the right) greeting the creature
with her sister.
•• 0:29—Topless (she's the first one) undressing with
her sister in front of Erlick and Baldar.
Bob Nelson . . . . .Erlick
• 0:43—Brief buns, just before being put to death.
•• 0:45—Buns, while getting massaged.

Sorority Babes in the Slimeball Bowl-O-Rama (1988)
Carla Baron . . . . Frankie
Michelle Bauer . . . . .Lisa
0:07—In panties getting spanked with Brinke
Stevens.
••• 0:12—Topless brushing herself in the front of mirror
while Stevens takes a shower.
• 0:14—Brief full frontal nudity when the three nerds
fall into the bathroom.

0:33—In black bra, panties, garter belt and stockings asking for Keith.
0:35—Wearing the same lingerie, on top of Keith in
the locker room.
••• 0:40—Topless taking off her bra.
••• 0:43—More topless undoing garter belt.
•• 0:46—More topless in locker room.
•• 0:47—More topless taking off stockings.
• 1:04—Full frontal nudity sitting on the floor by herself.
•• 1:05—Full frontal nudity getting up after the lights
go out. Kind of dark.
George "Buck" Flower . . . . Janitor
Linnea Quigley . . . . Spider
Brinke Stevens . . . . Taffy
0:07—In panties getting spanked with Michelle Bau-
er.
••• 0:12—Nude showering off whipped cream in bathtub while talking to a topless Michelle Bauer. Excellent long scene!

Sorority Girls and the Creature from Hell (1990)
Dori Courtney . . . . Belinda
•• 0:06—Topless, drying herself off after shower.
(Wearing panties.)
••• 0:08—More topless, still drying herself off.
• 0:12—Brief right breast, while in car with J.J.
••• 0:35—Topless in spa with J.J.
• 0:37—Buns, then left breast, while in spa during
Gerald's fantasy.
••• 0:41—Topless taking off her top by stream while J.J.
gets killed.
•• 0:43—Topless, running around at night getting
chased by the creature.
Vicki Darnell . . . . Dancer
0:17—Topless in bar in open blouse, dancing on
stage. Lit with red light.
• 0:24—More topless dancing on stage.
Deborah Dutch . . . . .Mary Anne
0:08—Very brief, side of left breast changing clothes
in background.
• 0:32—Lower half of left breast, dancing in cabin.
Kelli Lee . . . . .Nude Double for Dori Courtney
• 0:23—Topless in bedroom with J.J.
• 0:36—Topless getting playfully strangled by Skip in
the spa. Buns, getting out.
Ashley St. Jon . . . . Bar Patron

Sorority House Massacre (1987)
Joe Nassi . . . . Craig
• 0:50—Buns, while running away from the killer that
has just killed his girlfriend Tracy in a tepee.
Nicole Rio . . . . Tracy
•• 0:20—In a sheer bra changing clothes with two oth-
er girls in a bedroom.
•• 0:49—Topless in a tepee with her boyfriend, Craig,
just before getting killed.

Sorority House Massacre 2 (1990)

Dana Bentley Konkel . . . . Janey
- ••• 0:23—Topless in bedroom talking to Suzanne and looking in the mirror. Buns, while getting dressed in black bodysuit.
- 0:48—Left breast, sticking out of bodysuit, covered with blood, when the girls discover her dead.

Bridget Carney . . . . .Candy
- ••• 0:40—Topless and buns in G-string, dancing in club.

Melissa Moore. . . . . .Jessica
- ••• 0:22—Topless, talking to Kimberly, then taking a shower.
- 0:50—In wet lingerie.
- • 0:53—Buns, while going up the stairs.

Gail Thackray . . . . Linda
- •• 0:25—In bra and panties, then topless while changing clothes.
- 0:50—In wet lingerie.

Shannon Wilsey. . . . . Satana
- •• 0:43—Topless and buns in G-string, dancing in club.

Stacia Zhivago . . . . .Kimberly
- ••• 0:21—Nude, taking a shower.
- 0:50—In wet lingerie.
- • 0:53—Buns, while going up the stairs.
- 0:55—Brief buns, while going up the stairs.
- • 1:00—Brief topless, sitting up in bathtub filled with bloody water to strangle Linda.

South of Reno (1987)

Lisa Blount . . . . Anette Clark
- 1:02—In black bra getting blouse torn open while lying down.

Danitza Kingsley . . . . .Louise

Julie Montgomery . . . . Susan
- • 1:22—Brief topless kissing Martin. Dark, hard to see.
- 1:25—In motel room wearing black top and panties, then pink spandex top with the panties.

Spaced Out (1980; British)

Glory Annen . . . . Cosia
- ••• 0:23—Topless talking to the other two space women. Long scene.
- • 0:31—Very brief topless changing clothes while dancing.
- •• 0:43—Topless in bed with Willy.
- ••• 1:08—Topless lying down.

Ava Cadell. . . . . .Partha
- •• 0:41—Left breast making love on bed with Cliff.
- •• 0:42—Nude wrestling on bed with Cliff.
- • 0:43—Brief left breast lying in bed alone.
- •• 1:08—Topless sitting on bed.

Kate Ferguson . . . . Skipper
- • 1:07—Brief topless making love with Willy in bed. Lit with red light.

Tony Maiden. . . . . .Willy
- • 0:38—Buns, while getting examined by Cosia.

Michael Rowlatt . . . . Cliff
- • 0:42—Buns, while getting out of bed trying to get away from Partha.

Barry Stokes . . . . Oliver
- • 0:54—Buns, while undressing to get in bed with Prudence.

Speaking Parts (1989; Canadian)

Gabrielle Rose . . . . .Clara
- •• 0:41—Right breast, on TV monitor, masturbating with Lance. Then topless getting dressed.

Special Effects (1984)

Eric Bogosian . . . . .Neville
- • 0:21—Buns, while fighting with Zoe Tamerlis in bed. Medium long shot.

Zoe Tamerlis . . . . .Amelia/Elaine
- 0:01—Side view of right breast, wearing pasties during photo session.
- • 0:16—Brief topless sitting by pool with Eric Bogozian.
- •• 0:19—Topless getting into bed and in bed with Bogozian.
- • 0:22—Topless, dead in spa while Bogozian washes her off.
- 0:44—Brief topless in moviola that Bogozian watches.
- •• 1:12—Topless making love on bed with Keefe.
- • 1:17—Topless getting into bed during filming of movie. Brief topless during Bogozian's flashbacks. 1:20—More left breast shots on moviola getting strangled.
- ••• 1:33—Topless with Bogozian when he takes her dress off.
- • 1:35—Topless sitting on bed kissing Bogozian. More topless and more flashbacks.
- • 1:40—Brief topless during struggle. Dark.

The Specialist (1975)

Ahna Capri. . . . . .Londa Wyeth
- ••• 0:10—Topless, while in bed, talking on the phone.
- ••• 0:28—Topless on couch, posing for Bert.
- •• 1:09—Topless, sitting up in bed and putting robe on.

Christiane Schmidtmer. . . . . Nude Model
- ••• 0:12—Topless, posing for artist, then buns when she gets up to leave.

Spellbinder (1988)

Alexandra Morgan . . . . Pamela

Kelly Preston . . . . Miranda Reed
- ••• 0:19—Topless in bed making love with Timothy Daly.
- 1:26—Dancing around in a sheer white gown with nothing underneath during cult ceremony at the beach.

Rick Rossovich . . . . Derek Clayton

Spetters (1980; Dutch)

Toon Agterberg . . . . Hans
- ••• 0:35—Frontal nudity, measuring and comparing his manlihood with his friends in the auto shop.
- • 1:21—Buns, getting gang raped by gay guy he has been stealing money from.

Rutger Hauer..........................Witkamp
Jeroen Krabbé.......................Henkhof
Reneé Soutendijk.....................Fientje
•• 1:12—Topless making love in trailer with Jeff.
Maarten Spanjer..........................Jeff
••• 0:35—Frontal nudity, measuring and comparing his manlihood with his friends in the auto shop.
• 1:12—Buns while climbing into bed in trailer with Reneé Soutendijk.
Hans Van Tongeren...................Ron Hartman
••• 0:35—Frontal nudity, measuring and comparing his manlihood with his friends in the auto shop.

Spirits (1991)
Michelle Bauer......................Sister Mary
••• 0:21—Topless, taking off nun's habit, trying to seduce Erik Estrada. Brief lower frontal nudity and buns also. Long scene.
Carol Lynley.......................Sister Jillian
Sandra Margot.....................Nun Demon
Brinke Stevens....................Amy Goldwyn

Splash (1984)
Daryl Hannah.......................Madison
• 0:27—Brief right breast, swimming under water, entering the sunken ship.
• 0:28—Buns, walking around the Statue of Liberty.
• 1:26—Brief right, then left breast in tank when Eugene Levy looks at her.
• 1:44—Brief right breast, under water when frogman grabs her from behind.
Amy Ingersoll.......................Reporter
Ron Kuhlman.....................Man with Date
Eugene Levy.................Walter Kornbluth
Valerie Wildman..................Wedding Guest

Split Second (1992)
Kim Cattrall........................Michelle
•• 0:43—Topless in the shower.
•• 0:45—Topless in the shower, when Rutger Hauer opens the curtains.
Rutger Hauer.........................Stone
Tina Shaw...................Nightclub Stripper
•• 0:07—Topless, dancing in club in black S&M outfit, wearing a mask over her head.

The Spring (1989)
Shari Shattuck.......................Dyanne
• 0:00—Nude, several times, swimming under the water. Shot from under water.
• 0:50—Topless and buns, swimming under water.
•• 0:51—Topless, getting out of the water.
•• 0:59—Brief topless, turning over in bed with Dack Rambo.
• 1:05—Standing up in wet lingerie, then swimming under water.

Spring Break (1983; Canadian)
Corinne Alphen........................Joan
0:32—Taking a shower in a two piece bathing suit in an outdoor shower at the beach.

Sheila Kennedy.........................Carla
•• 0:49—Topless during wet T-shirt contest.
Perry Lang............................Adam
• 0:27—Brief buns while opening his towel in the shower, mooning his three friends.

Spring Fever USA (1988)
a.k.a. Lauderdale
Amy Lynn Baxter..............Amy (Car Wash Girl)
Mark Levine........................Duke Dork
• 1:17—Buns, twice, while in boat hallway with his skinny brother after being tricked.
Janine Lindemulder.............Heather Lipton
•• 0:14—Taking off her stockings, then brief topless undressing for bath, then taking a bath.
Cari Mayor.....................Girl on Campus
Robert Moss.........................Dick Dork
• 1:17—Buns, twice, while in boat hallway with his heavy brother after being tricked.
Anne Marie Oliver.................Rita Durango
•• 1:02—Topless during wet T-shirt contest.
Sherrie Rose...................Vinyl Vixen #1
Reneé Shugart....................Beach Beauty

Spring Symphony (1983)
Nastassia Kinski........................Clara
0:29—Brief left breast, when it pops out of her corset when she tries on a dress.

Squeeze Play (1979)
Jim Harris.............................Wes
•• 0:39—Buns, tied up in a room while people walking by look in through open door.
Jennifer Hetrick.....................Samantha
•• 0:00—Topless in bed after making love.
• 0:26—Right breast, brief topless with Wes on the floor.
0:37—In bra, in bedroom with Wes.

Stacey (1973)
Anitra Ford............................Tish
•• 0:13—Topless in bed making love with Frank.
Cristina Raines.......................Pamela
Anne Randall.....................Stacey Hansen
••• 0:01—Topless taking off her driving jump suit.
••• 0:12—Topless changing clothes.
••• 0:39—Topless in bed with Bob.

Star 80 (1983)
Carroll Baker..................Dorothy's Mother
Lonnie Chin...............Playboy Mansion Guest
Deborah Geffner........................Billie
Tabitha Harrington.....................Blonde
Mariel Hemingway..............Dorothy Stratten
•• 0:00—Topless in still photos during opening credits.
• 0:02—Topless lying on bed in Paul's flashbacks.
••• 0:22—Topless during Polaroid photo session with Paul
• 0:25—Topless during professional photography session. Long shot.
• 0:36—Brief topless during photo session.

- 0:57—Right breast, in centerfold photo on wall.
- 1:04—Upper half of breasts, in bathtub.
- 1:05—Brief topless in photo shoot flashback.
- 1:17—Brief topless during layout flashbacks.
- 1:20—Very brief topless in photos on the wall.
- •• 1:33—Topless undressing before getting killed by Paul. More brief topless layout flashbacks.

Lorraine Michaels . . . . Paul's Party Guest
Eric Roberts . . . . Paul Snider
- 1:39—Buns, lying dead on floor, covered with blood after shooting Dorothy, then himself.

Cathy St. George . . . . Playboy Mansion Guest
Kathryn Witt . . . . Robin

Star Slammer—The Escape *(1986)*
Bobbie Bresee . . . . Marai
Sandy Brooke . . . . Taura
- ••• 0:21—Topless in jail putting a new top on. In braless white T-shirt for most of the rest of the film.
- •• 1:09—Topless changing into a clean top.

Dawn Wildsmith . . . . Muffin

Starman *(1984)*
Karen Allen . . . . Jenny Hayden
Jeff Bridges . . . . Scott/Starman
- 0:11—Brief buns, while standing up after growing from DNA to a man.

Pat Lee . . . . Bracero Wife
Charlie Martin Smith . . . . Shermin

Stars and Bars *(1988)*
Ingrid Buxbaum . . . . Photographer
Daniel Day-Lewis . . . . Henderson Bores
- •• 1:21—Brief buns, while trying to open the window. Very, very brief frontal nudity when he throws the statue out the window. Blurry and dark. More buns, climbing out the window and into a trash dumpster.

Starting Over *(1979)*
Candice Bergen . . . . Jessica Potter
1:01—In a sheer blouse sitting on couch talking to Burt Reynolds.
- 1:29—Very, very brief left breast in bed with Reynolds when he undoes her top. You see her breast just before the scene dissolves into the next one. Long shot, hard to see.

Jill Clayburgh . . . . Marilyn Holmberg
- 0:45—Very brief upper half of breasts taking a shower while Burt Reynolds waits outside.

Burt Reynolds . . . . Phil Potter
Daniel Stern . . . . Student 2

State of Grace *(1990)*
Sandra Beall . . . . Steve's Date
Ed Harris . . . . Frankie
Gary Oldman . . . . Jackie
Sean Penn . . . . Terry
John Turturro . . . . Nick
Robin Wright . . . . Kathleen
- •• 0:38—Topless making love standing up with Sean Penn in the hall. Dark.

1:01—In bra on bed with Penn, than walking around while talking to him.
- 1:58—Brief side of right breast taking off towel and putting on blouse.

State Park *(1988; Canadian)*
Crisstyn Dante . . . . Blond in Net
- 0:45—Very, very brief left breast putting swimsuit top back on after being rescued from net by the guy in the bear costume.

Jennifer Inch . . . . Linnie
- 0:34—Brief right breast, undoing swimsuit top while sunbathing.
- 0:39—Brief topless, taking off swimsuit top while cutting Raymond's hair.

Isabelle Mejias . . . . Marsha

Stateline Motel *(1975; Italian)*
a.k.a. Last Chance for a Born Loser
Ursula Andress . . . . Michelle Nolton
- ••• 0:34—Left breast, then topless on bed with Oleg.

Barbara Bach . . . . Emily

Staying Together *(1989)*
Sean Astin . . . . Duncan McDermott
Melinda Dillon . . . . Eileen McDermott
Sheila Kelley . . . . Beth Harper
Tom Quill . . . . Brian McDermott
- 0:03—Brief buns while getting out of bed with Stockard Channing. Hard to see because of the reflections in the window.

Daphne Zuniga . . . . Beverly Young
- •• 0:56—Buns, lying in bed with Kit. Nice, long buns scene.

The Steagle *(1971)*
Richard Benjamin . . . . Harold Weiss
Susan Tyrrell . . . . Louise
- 0:48—Brief left breast twice, lying on bed with Richard Benjamin.

Stealing Heaven *(1988; British/Yugoslavian)*
Victoria Burgoyne . . . . Prostitute
- 0:28—Left breast, taking off her top. Side view of right breast and buns.
- •• 0:29—Topless lying in bed.

Derek De Lint . . . . Abelard
- ••• 0:47—Brief frontal nudity taking off his shirt. Then buns, while in bed making love with Kim Thomson.
1:07—Brief side view of buns under Kim. Long shot.

Cassie Stuart . . . . Petronilla
Kim Thomson . . . . Heloise
- 0:42—Side of left breast kneeling on floor with steam. Long shot.
- •• 0:43—Closer view of left breast.
- ••• 0:47—Topless and very brief lower frontal nudity lying in bed with Abelard. More left breast afterwards.
- 1:07—Nude, left side view on top of Abelard in bed. Long shot.

Steaming (1985; British)

Felicity Dean . . . . Dawn
- •• 1:12—Topless painting on herself.

Patti Love . . . . Josie
- • 0:08—Frontal nudity, getting undressed.
- • 0:45—Brief topless.
- • 1:30—Topless, jumping around in the pool.

Sarah Miles . . . . Sarah
- •• 0:23—Topless getting into pool with Vanessa Redgrave.
- •• 0:49—Topless getting undressed.
- •• 1:31—Nude lying down next to pool.

Vanessa Redgrave . . . . Nancy
- • 1:32—Buns and brief side view of right breast getting into pool.

Steel and Lace (1990)

Cindy Brooks. . . . . Girl in T-bird
Stacy Haiduk. . . . . Alison
David Naughton . . . . Dunn
Brenda Swanson . . . . Miss Fairweather
- •• 0:58—Topless in lunchroom, opening her blouse in front of one of the bad guys on the table.

Clare Wren . . . . Gally

The Stepfather (1987)

Terry O'Quinn. . . . . Jerry Blake
- ••• 0:02—Buns, while getting undressed, frontal nudity in mirror as he gets into the shower.

Gabrielle Rose . . . . Dorothy
Jill Schoelen . . . . Stephanie Maine
- •• 1:16—Buns and brief side of right breast, while getting into the shower. Topless in the shower.

Steve Shellen. . . . . Jim Ogilvie

Stepfather III: Father's Day (1992)

Priscilla Barnes. Christine Davis
- • 1:27—Very brief buns, sitting down in bubble bath.

Season Hubley . . . . Jennifer Ashley
Brenda Strong. . . . . Crime Search Reporter

Steppenwolf (1974)

Pierre Clementi . . . . Pablo
- • 1:40—Very brief frontal nudity, sleeping on floor with Dominique Sanda.

Carla Romanelli. . . . . Maria
- ••• 0:59—Topless sitting on bed with John Huston. Long scene.

Dominique Sanda . . . . Hermine
- 1:40—Brief lower frontal nudity, sleeping with a guy.
- • 1:41—Very brief left breast, waking up and rolling over to hug John Huston.

Stewardess School (1987)

Sandahl Bergman . . . . Wanda Polanski
Corinne Bohrer . . . . Cindy Adams
Vicki Frederick. . . . . Miss Grummet
Leslie Huntly . . . . Alison Hanover
- •• 0:46—Topless, doing a strip tease on a table at a party at her house.

Julie Montgomery . . . . Pimmie Polk

Still of the Night (1982)

Sara Botsford . . . . Gail Phillips
Meryl Streep . . . . Brooke Reynolds
- 0:22—Side view of right breast and buns taking off robe for a massage. Long shot, don't see her face.

Stitches (1985)

Lucinda Crosby . . . . Nurse #5
Bob Dubac. . . . . Al Rosenberg
- • 0:03—Very brief buns, while walking around in classroom. Made up to look like a bald corpse.
- 0:04—Brief buns, while chasing people down hallway. Don't see face. (He's in the middle, holding a beer can.)

Deborah Fallender . . . . Nurse #1
Daniel Greene . . . . Ted Fletcher
- • 0:45—Brief buns, twice, while pulling his pants down in front of visiting medical students.

Tommy Koenig . . . . Barfer Bogan
- • 0:03—Brief buns, while getting off gurney. Made up to look like a bald corpse. Something is covering his frontal nudity. Brief buns, while walking in classroom.
- • 0:04—Brief buns, while chasing people down hallway. Don't see face. (He's in front.)

Rebecca Perle. Bambi Belinka
- ••• 0:33—Topless during female medical student's class where they examine each other.
- • 1:00—Brief topless on bed with Parker Stevenson when discovered by Nancy.

Parker Stevenson . . . . Bobby Stevens
- • 0:04—Brief buns, while chasing people down hallway. Don't see face. (He's in the last one.)

Stone Cold (1991)

Laura Albert . . . . Joe's Girlfriend
- • 0:11—Buns, in bed when waking up. Very brief right breast.

Tracey E. Hutchinson . . . . Pool Playing Chick
- • 0:25—Brief topless, playing pool with the guys.

Stop! Or My Mom Will Shoot (1992)

Vanessa Angel . . . . Stewardess
Marjean Holden . . . . Stewardess
Sylvester Stallone . . . . Joe Bomowski
- • 0:22—Upper half of buns behind shower door when his mom talks to him in the bathroom.

JoBeth Williams . . . . Gwen Harper

Stormy Monday (1988)

Sting . . . . Finney
Sean Bean . . . . Brendan
- •• 0:37—Buns, putting on his underwear while Melanie Griffith watches.

Catherine Chevalier . . . . Cosmo's Secretary
Melanie Griffith . . . . Kate
- 0:03—Buns and side of right breast, behind shower door. Don't see anything because of the glass.
- • 1:11—Very brief left breast, while making love in bed with Brendan.

Tommy Lee Jones. . . . . Cosmo

The Story of "O" (1975; French)
Corrine Clery. . . . . O
- •• 0:09—Topless in bedroom with two women.
- •• 0:12—Topless being made love to.
- •• 0:20—Frontal nudity making love with two men.
- •• 0:29—Topless taking a bath while a man watches.
- ••• 0:42—Buns, on a sofa while her boyfriend lifts her dress up, then topless while another man plays with her, then nude except for white stockings.
- •• 0:51—Brief topless chained by wrists and gagged.
- ••• 1:22—Nude making love with a young guy.

The Story of "O" Continues (1981; French)
a.k.a. Les Fruits de la Passion
Arielle Dombasle . . . . Nathalie
- • 0:17—Brief left breast, lying on her stomach in bed with Klaus Kinski.
- ••• 0:40—Full frontal nudity on bed, making love in front of O.
- • 1:00—Very, very brief left breast, while grabbing her blouse out of Kinski's hands.

Isabelle Illiers . . . . O
- ••• 0:06—Topless in chair, getting made up.
- •• 0:08—Topless and buns, walking up stairs.
- • 0:10—Topless sitting in bed.
- •• 0:11—Topless sitting in bed putting up Klaus Kinski's picture on the wall.
- •• 0:12—Topless and buns getting out of bed and walking around the room.
- • 0:13—Tip of right breast, while looking out the window.
- •• 0:18—Topless looking out the window.
- • 0:24—Brief left breast, under her dress.
- • 0:26—Tips of breasts, sticking out of dress top.
- • 0:27—Topless and buns in chair, more in room with a customer.
- • 0:35—Topless, sitting while looking at Kinski.
- •• 0:36—Brief left breast, then full frontal nudity lying on bed during fantasy.
- 0:40—Full frontal nudity, getting chained up by Kinski.
- •• 0:58—Full frontal nudity running in slow-motion during boy's fantasy.
- •• 1:02—Topless in room with the boy.
- •• 1:04—Topless making love with the boy.

Klaus Kinski . . . . Sir Stephen
- • 0:40—Very, very brief part of buns while making love on bed with Arielle Dombasle.

The Story of Fausta (1988; Brazilian)
Betty Faria. . . . . .Fausta
- • 1:10—Left breast, while leaning out of the shower to talk to Lourdes.

Straight Time (1978)
Kathy Bates . . . . Selma Darin
Dustin Hoffman. . . . . Max Dembo
- 0:38—Very, very brief tip of penis in jail shower scene after getting sprayed by guard. Don't really see anything.

Theresa Russell . . . . .Jenny Mercer
- ••• 1:00—Left breast, while in bed with Dustin Hoffman. Don't see her face.

M. Emmet Walsh . . . . .Earl Frank
- • 0:47—Buns, while handcuffed to fence in the middle of the road with his pants down.

The Stranger (1986)
Bonnie Bedelia . . . . Alice Kildee
- • 0:15—Brief right breast sticking up from behind her lover's arm making love in bed during flashback sequence (B&W).
- • 0:19—Brief left breast turning over in hospital bed when a guy walks in. Long shot, hard to see.
- •• 0:38—Right breast again making love (B&W).

Straw Dogs (1972)
Susan George. . . . . .Amy
- •• 0:32—Topless taking off sweater, tossing it down to Dustin Hoffman, then looking out the door at the workers.
- ••• 1:00—Topless on couch getting raped by one of the construction workers.

Dustin Hoffman . . . . .David

Street Hunter (1990)
John Leguizamo . . . . .Angel
Susan Napoli . . . . Eddie's Girl
- •• 0:40—Topless in bed with Eddie (she's on the left, wearing white panties).

Streets of Fire (1984)
Ed Begley, Jr. . . . . Ben Gunn
Willem Dafoe . . . . Raven
Elizabeth Daily . . . . .Baby Doll
Marine Jahan . . . . "Torchie's" Dancer
- 0:28—Buns in G-string dancing in club.
- 0:34—More dancing.
- • 0:35—Very brief right breast under body stocking, then almost topless under stocking when taking off T-shirt.

Diane Lane. . . . . .Ellen Aim
Amy Madigan . . . . McCoy
Michael Paré . . . . Tom Cody
Bill Paxton . . . . .Clyde
Rick Rossovich . . . . Officer Cooley

Streetwalkin' (1985)
Samantha Fox . . . . Topless Dancer
- • 0:22—Topless, dancing on stage in nightclub (She's the one wearing a headband).
- • 0:27—More topless, dancing on stage.
- • 0:29—More topless, dancing on stage.
- • 0:56—Topless, giving Antonio Fargas a massage at the bar.

Melissa Leo . . . . .Cookie
- • 0:05—Brief topless taking off red blouse in front of mirror.
- •• 0:15—Topless, stripping and taking off her top for a customer.

- 0:18—Brief right breast, having sex with her pimp on the floor.
- 0:44—Topless, taking off her top and sitting on bed with a customer (long shot seen in mirror).
  0:53—Buns, in body suit, in hotel room with customer.

Julie Newmar . . . . Queen Bee

Stripes (1981)

Sue Bowser . . . . Mud Wrestler
Dawn Clark . . . . Mud Wrestler
John Diehl . . . . Cruiser
Roberta Leighton . . . . .Anita
- 0:07—Topless, wearing blue panties, while putting her shirt on and talking to Bill Murray.

Bill Paxton . . . . .n.a.
Judge Reinhold . . . . .Elmo
P.J. Soles . . . . Stella
Sean Young. . . . . Louise Cooper

Stripped to Kill (1987)

Michelle Foreman . . . . Angel
••• 0:02—Topless dancing on stage for Norman Fell.
Debra Lamb . . . . Amateur Dancer
Kay Lenz . . . . Cody Sheehan
•• 0:23—Topless dancing on stage.
• 0:47—Topless dancing in white lingerie.
Deborah Ann Nassar . . . . Dazzle
••• 0:07—Topless wearing a G-string dancing on stage with a motorcycle prop.

Stripped to Kill II (1988)

Jeannine Bisignano . . . . .Sonny
  0:06—Buns, while wearing a black bra in dressing room.
••• 0:38—Topless and buns during strip dance routine in white lingerie.
Maria Ford . . . . .Shady
•• 0:21—Topless, dancing on table in front of the detective. Buns, walking away.
• 0:40—Brief upper half of left breast in the alley with the detective.
•• 0:52—Topless and buns during dance routine.
Lisa Glaser. . . . . .Victoria
•• 0:01—Topless and buns in G-string doing a strip dance routine during Shadey's nightmare.
Marjean Holden . . . . .Something Else
•• 0:17—Topless during strip dance routine.
Debra Lamb . . . . Mantra
•• 0:04—Topless during strip dance routine.
••• 0:42—Topless in black lingerie during strip dance routine.
Karen Mayo-Chandler . . . . .Cassandra
  0:06—Black bra and panties in dressing room.
•• 0:18—Topless taking off her top for a customer.

Stripper (1985)

Sara Costa . . . . Herself
••• 0:16—Topless doing strip dance routine.
••• 0:46—Topless and buns dancing on stage in a G-string.

••• 1:12—Topless doing another strip routine.
Venus De Light. . . . . .Herself
• 0:59—Brief topless, on stage, blowing fire.
••• 1:07—Topless and buns in black G-string, doing routine on stage, using fire.
Suzanne Primeaux . . . . Herself
•• 0:03—Topless dancing on stage, kneeling on her left knee. Very brief buns in G-string.

The Stud (1978; British)

Minah Bird . . . . .Molly
•• 0:26—Topless in bed when Tony is talking on the telephone.
Joan Collins . . . . Fontaine
• 0:10—Brief left breast making love with Tony in the elevator.
  0:27—Brief buns in panties, stockings and garter belt in Tony's apartment.
  0:58—Brief black bra and panties under fur coat in back of limousine with Tony.
• 1:03—Brief topless taking off dress to get in pool.
• 1:04—Nude in the pool with Tony.
Emma Jacobs . . . . Alexandra
•• 0:44—In bra, then topless taking bra off in bedroom.
• 0:48—Close up of breasts making love with Tony in his dark apartment.
• 1:14—Topless in bed with Tony, yelling at him.
Sue Lloyd . . . . .Vanessa
• 1:04—Topless in the swimming pool with Joan Collins and Tony.
Oliver Tobias . . . . .Tony Blake
• 1:06—Buns, running away from the pool.

Student Affairs (1987)

Jim Abele . . . . Andrew Armstrong
• 1:07—Buns, when his friends play a practical joke on him in the shower.
Deborah Blaisdell . . . . Kelly
••• 0:26—Topless sitting up in bed talking to a guy.
Louis Bonanno . . . . Louie Balducci
Jane Hamilton . . . . Veronica
•• 0:48—Topless changing in dressing room, showing herself off to a guy.
• 0:51—Brief topless in a school room during a movie.
•• 0:56—In black lingerie outfit, then topless in bedroom while she tape records everything.
Jeanne Marie . . . . Robin Ready
• 0:35—Brief topless wearing black panties in bed trying to seduce a guy.
••• 0:41—Topless making love with another guy, while banging her back against the wall.
• 0:44—Very brief topless in VW with a nerd.
• 1:09—Very brief topless falling out of a trailer home filled with water.

The Student Body (1975)

June Fairchild . . . . .Mitzi Mashall
• 0:15—Brief topless and buns, running and jumping into the pool during party. Brief long shot topless, while in the pool.

•• 0:21—Topless getting into bed.
Peter Hooten . . . . Carter Blalock
Jillian Kesner . . . . Carrie Rafferty
  •• 0:29—Left breast, making out with Carter in the car.

Student Confidential (1987)

Corwyn Anthony . . . . Greg
  • 1:26—Buns, while getting into bed with Susan.
Katherine Kriss . . . . Elaine's Friend
Susie Scott . . . . Susan Bishop
  • 0:02—Lying in bed covered with a gold sheet. Sort
   of right breast through her hair.
  •• 1:26—Full frontal nudity standing in front of Greg.

The Student Nurses (1970)

a.k.a. Young LA Nurses
Karen Carlson . . . . Phred
  • 0:08—Topless in bed with the wrong guy.
  0:19—In bra, on sofa with Dr. Jim Casper.
  ••• 0:50—In bed with Jim, topless and buns getting out,
   then topless sitting in chair. Long scene.
  • 1:02—Brief topless in bed.
Lawrence Casey . . . . Dr. Jim Casper
  •• 0:52—Buns, while walking to Karen Carlson to talk.
Elaine Giftos . . . . Sharon
  • 1:14—Brief topless undressing and getting into bed
   with terminally ill boy. Dark, hard to see.
Barbara Leigh . . . . Priscilla
  ••• 0:43—Topless on the beach with Les. Long scene.
Richard Rust . . . . Les
  • 0:43—Buns, while lying in sand with Barbara Leigh.
Pepe Serna . . . . Luis

The Stunt Man (1980)

Barbara Hershey . . . . Nina
  • 1:29—Buns and side view of left breast in bed in a
   movie within a movie while everybody is watching
   in a screening room.
Steve Railsback . . . . Cameron

Submission (1976; Italian)

Andrea Ferréol . . . . Juliet
  •• 0:43—Topless in room with Franco Nero and Elaine.
Lisa Gastoni . . . . Elaine
  0:28—Lower frontal nudity on the floor behind the
   counter with Franco Nero.
  • 0:30—Left breast, while talking on the phone with
   her husband while Nero fondles her.
  •• 0:32—Topless and buns, making love on bed with
   Nero. Slightly out of focus.
  •• 0:33—Topless getting out of bed to talk to her
   daughter.
  ••• 0:43—Topless in room with Juliet and Nero. Long
   scene.
  ••• 0:45—More topless on the floor yelling at Nero.
  0:54—Brief lower frontal nudity in slip, sitting on
   floor with Nero.
  ••• 0:57—Left breast, while wearing slip, walking in
   front of pharmacy. Then full frontal nudity while
   wearing only stockings. Long scene.

  •• 1:00—Topless in pharmacy with Nero, singing and
   dancing.
  •• 1:28—Topless when Nero cuts her slip open. Nice
   close up.
  •• 1:29—Topless getting up out of bed.
Franco Nero . . . . Armond
  • 0:32—Brief side view of buns when making love
   with Lisa on the bed.

Subspecies (1990)

Michelle McBride . . . . Lillian
  • 0:34—Left breast, while sleeping in bed when the
   vampire comes to get her.
Laura Tate . . . . Michelle

Sudden Impact (1983)

Clint Eastwood . . . . Harry Callahan
Sondra Locke . . . . Jennifer Spencer
Lisa London . . . . Young Hooker
  •• 1:04—Topless in bathroom, walking to Nick in the
   bed.

Sugar Cookies (1973)

Maureen Byrnes . . . . Dola
  •• 0:37—Right breast while Gus is on top of her, then
   topless and buns.
Lynn Lowry . . . . Alta/Julie
  ••• 0:03—Brief topless falling out of hammock, then
   topless on couch with Max, then nude. Long scene.
   (Brunette wig as Alta.)
  • 0:14—Left breast on autopsy table.
  • 0:20—Topless in movie.
  •• 0:52—Topless taking off clothes for Mary Woronov.
   Topless on bed. (Blonde as Julie.)
  ••• 1:00—Topless and buns with Woronov in bedroom,
   nude while wrestling with her.
  • 1:04—Topless with Woronov in bathtub.
  ••• 1:06—Nude in bed with Woronov. Long scene.
  •• 1:11—Right breast outside displaying herself to
   Max.
  • 1:16—Right breast, then topless making love with
   Woronov.
  ••• 1:20—Nude with Woronov and Max. Long scene.
Daniel Sador . . . . Gus
  0:37—Buns while in bed with Dola, then running
   around.
George Shannon . . . . Max
  •• 0:14—Buns, while on top of Mary Woronov in bed.
Monique Van Vooren . . . . Helene
Jennifer Wells . . . . Max's Secretary
  • 0:28—Topless in red panties in Max's office while he
   talks on the phone, then lower frontal nudity.
  •• 0:56—Full frontal nudity getting dressed.
Mary Woronov . . . . Camila
  ••• 0:10—Topless in bathtub, then wearing white panties exercising topless on the floor. Long scene.
  • 1:04—Topless with Julie in the bathtub.
  • 1:07—Brief topless, then left breast, making love
   with Julie.
  • 1:17—Brief right breast when Lynn Lowry yanks her
   dress up.

Summer Affair (1979)
Ornella Muti . . . . Lisa
- 0:44—Topless silhouette in cave by the water.
- 1:00—Brief topless getting chased around in the grass and by the beach.

Summer Heat (1987)
Kathy Bates . . . . Ruth Stanton
Miriam Byrd-Nethery . . . . Aunt Patty
Anthony Edwards . . . . Aaron Walston
Lori Singer. . . . . Roxy
- •• 0:36—Topless in bed with Jack. Kind of dark and hard to see.

Summer Job (1989)
Amy Lynn Baxter. . . . . Susan
- •• 0:10—Topless changing in room with the other three girls. More topless sitting on bed.
  0:15—In white bra, looking at herself in mirror.
- 0:34—Brief topless when her swimsuit top pops off after saving a guy in swimming pool.
- 0:45—In white lingerie, brief topless on stairs, flashing her breasts (wearing curlers).
  1:00—Brief buns in two piece swimsuit turning around.
- 1:23—Topless pulling her top down talking to Mr. Burns.
Kirt Earhar. . . . . Tom
- 0:30—Buns in black G-string bikini when his swim trunks get ripped off.
- 0:43—Buns in G-string underwear getting out of bed and going to the bathroom.
Chona Jason . . . . Beautiful Lady
Cari Mayor . . . . Donna
- 0:10—Brief topless twice, taking off her top before and after Herman comes into the room.
George O . . . . Herman
- 0:17—Buns, while getting his underwear torn off by five angry women, then running back to his room.
Anne Marie Oliver . . . . Kathy's Friend #2
Sherrie Rose . . . . Kathy Shields
  0:25—In bed wearing white bra and panties talking to Bruce. Long scene.
  0:52—Buns, walking around in swimsuit and jacket.
- •• 0:53—Topless taking off swimsuit top kneeling by the phone, then brief buns standing up.
  1:15—In yellow two piece swimsuit walking on the beach.
- •• 1:24—Brief topless taking off her yellow top on the beach talking to Bruce.
Reneé Shugart. . . . . Karen
  0:15—In lingerie reading a magazine.
- 0:42—Topless taking off her top. Long shot, dark.
- 0:45—In white lingerie, standing on stairs, then very brief left breast flashing.

Summer Lovers (1982)
Peter Gallagher . . . . Michael Pappas
- 0:22—Buns, while running into the water after Valerie Quennessen.

- 0:54—Frontal nudity getting ready to dive off a rock while Daryl Hannah and Quennessen watch. Long shot, hard to see anything.
Daryl Hannah. . . . . Cathy Featherstone
- 0:07—Very brief topless getting out of bed.
  0:17—In a two piece swimsuit.
  0:54—Buns, lying on rock with Valerie Quennessen watching Michael dive off a rock.
  0:56—In a swimsuit again.
- 1:03—Brief right breast sweeping the balcony.
Valerie Quennessen . . . . Lina
- 0:12—Topless on balcony.
- ••• 0:19—Nude on the beach with Michael.
- 0:23—Brief topless in a cave with Michael.
- •• 0:30—Topless lying on the floor with Michael.
  0:54—Buns, lying on a rock with Daryl Hannah watching Michael dive off a rock.
- 1:03—Left breast in bed.
- •• 1:05—Topless dancing on the balcony.
  1:09—Topless on the beach.
Hans Van Tongeren . . . . Jan Tolin

Summer Night (1987; Italian)
Mariangela Melato. . . . . Signora Bolk
- •• 0:26—Topless behind gauze net over bed making love with a German guy.
- •• 1:02—Topless on the bed making love with the prisoner.
- •• 1:09—Topless again.
- ••• 1:13—Buns, walking out of the ocean, then topless with wet hair.

Summer School (1987)
Kirstie Alley . . . . Robin Bishop
Mark Harmon. Freddy Shoop
Ken Olandt . . . . Larry
- •• 0:48—Brief buns while wearing a red G-string in a male stripper club.
Fabiana Udenio . . . . Anna-Maria

Summer School Teachers (1975)
Pat Anderson . . . . Sally
- •• 0:52—Topless and buns, posing for photos, then in bed with Bob.
- 1:05—Side view of right breast in photo in magazine.
Rhonda Leigh Hopkins . . . . Denise
- 0:45—Topless making love with a guy. Close up of a breast.
Candice Rialson . . . . Conklin T.
- 0:14—Breasts and buns when Mr. Lacy fantasizes about what she looks like. Don't see her face, but it looks like her.
- ••• 0:38—Topless outside with other teacher, kissing on the ground.

A Summer Story (1988)
Imogen Stubbs. Megan David
- •• 0:36—Left breast several times, then right breast while making love with Frank in barn.

0:41—Very, very brief buns, frolicking in pond at night with Frank.

1:03—Very brief silhouette of left breast during Frank's flashback sequence.

James Wilby . . . . Frank Ashton
  • 0:08—Buns, in creek with Mr. Garten while skinny dipping.

Susannah York . . . . Mrs. Narracrombe

Summer's Games (1987)

Amy Lynn Baxter . . . . Boxer/Girl from Penthouse
  •• 0:04—Topless opening her swimsuit top after contest. (1st place winner.)
  • 0:18—Topless during boxing match.

Andi Bruce . . . . News Anchor
  0:12—Brief right breast, while turning around to look at monitor.
  • 0:42—Topless turning around to look at the monitor.

Lori Deann Pallett . . . . Torch Carrier
  • 0:00—Half topless running in short T-shirt carrying torch.
  •• 0:04—Topless opening her swimsuit top after contest. (2nd place winner.)

Teri Lynn Peake . . . . Penthouse Girl

Sunset Heat (1991)

(Unrated version reviewed.)

Daphne Ashbrook . . . . Julie
  • 1:06—Brief topless silhouette, making love with Michael Paré. Dark.
  •• 1:07—More topless, on top of Paré, then lying down.

Bridget Butler . . . . Lady in New York
  • 0:00—Buns, lying in bed.
  • 0:01—Buns, when Michael Paré takes off her shirt. Buns and partial left breast lying on him in bed.

Tracy Dali . . . . Carl's Pool Girl
  •• 1:08—Topless in pool with Dennis Hopper. Topless and buns, getting out of pool while wearing a G-string.

Dennis Hopper . . . . Carl Madson

Michael Paré . . . . Eric Wright
  • 0:00—Buns, while standing and looking out the window.
  ••• 0:22—Buns, while standing on stairs with Tracy Tweed, then making love with her on the floor.
  • 0:24—Buns, while standing up and walking up the stairs.

Elena Sahagun . . . . Brandon's Model

Julie Strain . . . . Carl's Breakfast Girl/Party Statuette
  •• 0:51—Topless, covered with silver paint, made up to look like a statue at the party.

Tracy Tweed . . . . Lena
  ••• 0:19—Topless making love with Michael Paré. Nice, long scene.
  ••• 0:22—Topless and buns, making love with Paré on stairs, sofa and the floor.

••• 0:24—Topless, lying on the floor when the bad guys come in. Brief partial right breast, standing up and covering herself with a jacket.

Sunset Strip (1992)

Bridget Butler . . . . Candice

Jeff Conaway . . . . Tony

Michelle Foreman . . . . Heather
  •• 0:29—In black bra and G-string, practicing her dance routine in her living room.
  0:42—Brief back side of left breast, while in the shower.
  0:46—In black bra and G-string, practicing some more.
  •• 1:24—Buns in G-string, while dancing during contest.
  •• 1:28—Topless in the shower with Jeff Conaway. Don't see her face well, but it looks like her.
  ••• 1:30—Buns in G-string dancing on stage and topless (finally!) at the end.

Lori Jo Hendrix . . . . Tammy
  •• 0:54—Topless, taking off her swimsuit top for Crystal's video camera.
  ••• 1:12—Topless and buns in G-string, doing strip routine on stage.
  • 1:16—Topless in music video.

Shelley Michelle . . . . Veronica

Superchick (1978)

Uschi Digard . . . . Mayday
  ••• 0:42—Buns and topless getting whipped acting during the making of a film, then talking to three people.

Flo Gerrish . . . . Funky Jane

Joyce Jillson . . . . Tara B. True/Superchick
  • 0:03—Brief upper half of right breast leaning back in bathtub.
  • 0:06—Topless in bed throwing cards up.
  • 0:16—Brief topless under net on boat with Johnny.
  • 0:29—Brief right breast several times in airplane restroom with a Marine.
  1:12—Buns, frolicking in the ocean with Johnny. Don't see her face.
  • 1:27—Close up of breasts (probably body double) when sweater pops open.

Candy Samples . . . . Lady on Boat
  ••• 0:08—Topless in bed with Johnny on boat.

Superfly (1972)

Sheila Frazier . . . . Georgia
  •• 0:40—Topless and buns, making love in the bathtub with Superfly.

Surf Nazis Must Die (1986)

Bobbie Bresee . . . . Smeg's Mom

Dawn Wildsmith . . . . Eva
  • 0:25—Topless being fondled at the beach wearing a wet suit by Adolf. Mostly right breast.

Surfacing (1980)

Kathleen Beller . . . . Kate
- 0:22—Very brief buns, pulling down pants to change. Dark, hard to see.
- 0:23—Very brief right breast undressing. Dark, hard to see.
- • 0:24—Very, very brief topless turning over in bed.
- 0:25—Buns, standing next to bed.
- ••• 1:23—Topless washing herself in the water. One long shot, one side view of right breast.

Joseph Bottoms . . . . Joe
- • 0:23—Buns, while in bed with Kathleen Beller.

The Surrogate (1984; Canadian)

Carole Laure . . . . Anouk Vanderlin
- • 0:48—Very brief topless when Frank rips her blouse open in his apartment.

Barbara Law . . . . .Maggie Simpson
Marilyn Lightstone . . . . Dr. Harriet Forman
Shannon Tweed . . . . Lee Wake
- ••• 0:03—Topless taking a Jacuzzi bath.
- • 0:42—Brief topless changing in bedroom, then in bra getting dressed. Long shot.
- ••• 1:02—Topless in sauna talking with Frank. Long scene.

Survivor (1987)

Sue Kiel . . . . The Woman
- ••• 0:33—Right breast, then topless and buns making love with Survivor in hammock. Long scene.

Suzanne (1980; Canadian)

Jennifer Dale . . . . Suzanne
- •• 0:29—Topless when boyfriend lifts her sweatshirt up when she's sitting on couch doing homework.
- •• 0:53—Topless with Nicky on the floor.

Suzanne (1973)

a.k.a. The Second Coming of Suzanne
(Suzanne has nudity in it, The Second Coming of Suzanne has the nudity cut out.)

Sondra Locke . . . . Suzanne
- •• 0:27—Topless sitting, looking at a guy. Brief left breast several times lying down.
- ••• 0:29—Topless lying down.

Swamp Thing (1981)

Adrienne Barbeau . . . . Alice Cable
- • 1:03—Side view of left breast washing herself off in the swamp. Long shot.

Karen Price . . . . Messenger

Swann in Love (1984; French/German)

a.k.a. Un Amour de Swann

Marie-Christine Barrault . . . . .Madame Verdunn
Jeremy Irons . . . . Charles Swann
Ornella Muti .Odette de Crécy
- •• 1:15—Brief left breast, making love with Jeremy Irons.
- ••• 1:28—Topless sitting on bed talking to Irons.

Swashbuckler (1976)

Peter Boyle. . . . . .Lord Durant
Genevieve Bujold . . . . Jane Barnet
- • 1:00—Very brief side view nude, diving from the ship into the water. Long shot, don't really see anything.
- • 1:01—Buns and brief side of left breast seen from under water.

Anjelica Huston . . . . Woman of Dark Visage
Pepe Serna. . . . . .Street Entertainer
Dorothy Tristan . . . . Alice
Brenda Venus. . . . . Bath Attendant

Sweet Country (1985)

Jane Alexander. . . . . Anna
- • 1:39—Brief side view of left breast after getting out of bed.

Carole Laure. . . . . Eva
- •• 0:31—Topless changing in apartment while Randy Quaid watches.
- • 0:43—Nude in auditorium with other women prisoners.
- ••• 1:13—Nude in bed with Quaid.

Joanna Pettet . . . . Monica

Sweet Revenge (1987)

Nancy Allen . . . . .Jillian Grey
Gina Gershon. . . . . .K.C.
- • 0:41—Brief topless in water under a waterfall with Lee.

Michele Little . . . . Lee
- • 0:41—Brief topless in water under a waterfall with K.C.

Sweet Sixteen (1982)

Steve Antin. . . . . Hank Burke
Aleisa Shirley .Melissa Morgan
- • 0:16—Side view of body, nude, taking a shower.
- • 1:11—Topless undressing to go skinny dipping with Hank. Dark, hard to see.
- • 1:13—Topless, getting out of the water.

Susan Strasberg . . . . Joanne Morgan

Sweet Sugar (1972)

Timothy Brown . . . . Mojo
Pamela Collins . . . . Dolores
- • 0:26—Brief topless when doctor tears her bra off.
- ••• 0:50—Topless in the shower with Phyllis Davis.

Phyllis Davis . . . . .Sugar
- ••• 0:34—Topless in bed with a guard.
- ••• 0:50—Topless in the shower with Dolores.
- •• 0:57—Brief topless in the bathroom.

Ella Edwards. . . . . Simone
- • 0:58—Topless in bed with Mojo.

Jackie Giroux . . . . .Fara
- •• 0:33—Topless, skinny dipping in stream with Dolores.

Sweet William *(1980; British)*

Jenny Agutter . . . . Ann
     0:27—Buns, while standing on balcony with Sam
     Waterston.
   •• 0:28—Topless sitting on edge of the bed while talk-
     ing with Waterston.
   • 0:44—Brief left breast when Waterston takes her
     blouse off in the living room.
Anna Massey. . . . . Edna
Sam Waterston . . . . William
   • 0:27—Buns, seen through a window in the door,
     standing on balcony with Jenny Agutter.

Swept Away *(1975; Italian)*

a.k.a. Swept Away...by an unusual destiny in the blue sea of
august
Mariangela Melato . . . . Raffaela Lenzetti
   •• 1:10—Topless on the sand when Giancarlo Giannini
     catches her and makes love with her.

The Swindle *(1991)*

Jasaé . . . . Nina
   ••• 0:28—Nude, posing for Tom while he video tapes
     her. Long scene.
   ••• 0:31—Nude, making love with Tom.
   ••• 0:36—Topless in back of limousine with Dude.
Monica Akesson . . . . Tom's Last Hurrah
   ••• 1:17—Topless, then full frontal nudity, posing on
     couch for Tom.

Swing Shift *(1984)*

Alana Collins. . . . . Frankie Parker
     0:11—Buns in B&W photo that Christine Lahti
     shows to Fred Ward. Possible photo composite.
Ed Harris . . . . Jack Walsh
   • 0:03—Very brief frontal nudity when he sits down in
     chair wearing a towel around his waist.
Goldie Hawn. . . . . Kay Walsh
Penny Johnson . . . . Genevieve
Kurt Russell . . . . Lucky Lockhart
Fred Ward . . . . Biscuits Toohey

The Swinging Cheerleaders *(1974)*

Colleen Camp. . . . . Mary Ann
Sandra Dempsey. . . . . 1st Girl at Tryout
Rosanne Katon . . . . Lisa
   •• 0:25—Topless taking off her blouse in her teacher's
     office. Half of right breast while he talks on the
     phone.
Cheryl Smith. . . . . Andrea
   •• 0:12—Topless taking off her bra and putting sheer
     blouse on.
   • 0:17—Left breast, several times, sitting in bed with
     Ross.

Switch *(1991)*

Lysette Anthony . . . . Liz
   • 0:05—Brief topless in spa with JoBeth Williams and
     Felicia, trying to kill Steve.
Ellen Barkin . . . . Amanda Brooks/Steve
Linda Doná . . . . Gay Club Patron

Perry King . . . . Steve Brooks
John Lafayette . . . . Sgt. Phillips
Karen Medak . . . . Saleswoman
Jackie Moen . . . . Girl at City Grille
Jimmy Smits. . . . . Walter Stone
   ••• 1:21—Buns, while stretching after waking up in the
     morning. A bit on the dark side.
JoBeth Williams . . . . Margo Brofman
Rebecca Wood-Sharkey . . . . Gay Club Patron

Switchblade Sisters *(1975)*

Marlene Clark. . . . . Muff
Janice Karman . . . . Bunnie
Robin Lee. . . . . Lace
   • 0:48—Topless sitting up in bed to talk to Dominic.
     Dark.
Joanne Nail . . . . Maggie
   • 0:21—Very, very brief right breast in ripped blouse
     when she tries to rip Dominic's shirt off.
Jerii Woods. . . . . Toby

The Sword and the Sorcerer *(1982)*

Kathleen Beller. . . . . Alana
   • 0:54—Side view of buns, lying face down getting oil
     rubbed all over her.
Shelly Taylor Morgan . . . . Bar-Bra
   • 0:54—Brief topless when Lee Horsley crashes
     through the window and almost lands on her.

Sylvester *(1985)*

Melissa Gilbert-Brinkman . . . . Charlie
   • 0:23—Very, very brief topless struggling with a guy
     in truck cab. Seen through a dirty windshield.
   •• 0:24—Very brief left breast after Richard Farnsworth
     runs down the stairs to help her. Seen from the open
     door of the truck.

Taffin *(1988; U.S./British)*

Pierce Brosnan . . . . Mark Taffin
Alison Doody . . . . Charlotte
   • 0:14—Very, very brief side view of right breast when
     Pierce Brosnan rips her blouse open. Long shot, hard
     to see.
Tina Shaw . . . . Lola the Stripper
   •• 1:04—Topless doing routine in a club.

Tai-Pan *(1986)*

Bryan Brown . . . . Dirk Struan/"Tai-Pan"
Joan Chen . . . . May May
     0:55—In sheer top sitting on bed talking to Bryan
     Brown.
   • 0:56—Brief left breast washing herself, hard to see
     anything.
     1:14—Sheer top again.
     1:30—Sheer top again.
Kyra Sedgwick . . . . Tess
Janine Turner . . . . Shevaun

Tainted

Shari Shattuck. . . . . Cathy
- •• 0:09—Buns, while lying on top of Frank.
- ••• 0:27—Topless in bubble bath, getting up, drying herself off, then putting on white bra while wearing panties.
- 0:28—In white bra and panties, masturbating on chair.
- 0:30—Briefly in white bra and panties, getting attacked by rapist.
- ••• 0:49—Topless taking a shower.
- • 0:51—Brief side view of left breast in the shower again.

Take Two *(1988)*

Grant Goodeve . . . . .Barry Griffith/Frank Bentley
- • 0:31—Buns, while in bed with Robin Mattson.
- ••• 0:46—Buns, while getting into bed with Mattson again.

Robin Mattson . . . . Susan Bentley
- 0:21—Exercising in yellow outfit while Frank Stallone plays music.
- •• 0:25—Brief topless taking a shower.
- 0:26—Showing Grant Goodeve her new two piece swimsuit.
- ••• 0:29—Topless in bed with Goodeve.
- ••• 0:45—Right breast in shower, then topless getting into bed.
- • 0:47—Brief topless getting out of bed and putting an overcoat on.
- 0:51—One piece swimsuit by the swimming pool.
- 1:12—In two piece swimsuit at the beach.
- ••• 1:28—Topless taking a shower after shooting Goodeve in bed.

Karen Mayo-Chandler. . . . . Dorothy
- •• 1:17—Brief topless on bed when her gold dress is pulled down a bit.

Suzanne Slater . . . . Sherrie
- •• 0:11—Topless in office talking with Grant Goodeve, wearing panties, garter belt and stockings.
- • 1:00—Topless undressing to get into hot tub wearing black underwear bottom.

Takin' It All Off *(1987)*

Becky LeBeau . . . . Becky
- •• 0:16—Topless and brief full frontal nudity getting introduced to Allison.
- ••• 0:23—In black bra and panties, then nude doing a strip routine outside.
- • 0:35—Brief full frontal nudity pushing Elliot into the pool.
- • 0:36—Brief topless in studio with Allison again.
- • 0:36—Brief left breast in dance studio with Allison.
- •• 1:23—Nude, dancing with all the other women on stage.

Francesca "Kitten" Natividad. . . . . Betty Bigones
- ••• 0:12—Nude, washing herself in the shower.
- •• 0:39—Nude, on stage in a giant glass, then topless backstage in her dressing room.
- •• 0:42—Topless in flashbacks from *Takin' It Off*.

- 0:46—Topless in group in the studio.
- ••• 0:53—Nude, dancing on the deck outside. Some nice slow motion shots.
- •• 1:16—Topless on stage in club.
- ••• 1:23—Nude, dancing with all the other women on stage.

Jean Poremba. . . . . Allison
- 0:36—In pink bra and G-string.
- ••• 0:49—In white lingerie, then topless, then nude dancing.
- ••• 0:58—Topless, dancing outside when she hears the music.
- ••• 0:59—Nude dancing in a park.
- •• 1:01—Nude dancing in a laundromat.
- ••• 1:03—Nude dancing in a restaurant.
- ••• 1:07—Nude in shower with Adam.
- •• 1:13—Topless dancing for the music in a studio.
- ••• 1:23—Nude dancing with all the other women on stage.

Gail Thackray . . . . Hannah

Takin' It Off *(1984)*

Francesca "Kitten" Natividad . . . . .Betty Bigones
- •• 0:01—Topless dancing on stage.
- ••• 0:04—Topless and buns dancing on stage.
- •• 0:29—Topless in the Doctor's office.
- ••• 0:32—Nude dancing in the Psychiatrists' office.
- ••• 0:39—Nude in bed with a guy during fantasy sequence playing with vegetables and fruits.
- •• 0:49—Topless in bed covered with popcorn.
- • 0:51—Nude doing a dance routine in the library.
- ••• 1:09—Nude splashing around in a clear plastic bathtub on stage.
- •• 1:20—Nude at a fat farm dancing.
- •• 1:24—Nude running in the woods in slow motion.

Angelique Pettijohn . . . . .Anita Little
Ashley St. Jon. . . . . .Sin
- ••• 0:20—Topless and buns doing two dance routines on stage.
- •• 0:53—Nude, stripping and dancing in the library.

Taking Care of Business *(1990)*

Jill Johnson . . . . Tennis Court Girl
Loryn Locklin . . . . Jewel
- • 0:42—Buns and very brief side view, twice, seen through door, changing by the pool. Then in black two piece swimsuit.

Tales From the Darkside, The Movie *(1990)*

Rae Dawn Chong. . . . . Carola
- • 1:09—Left breast in blue light, twice, with James Remar. Don't see her face.

Deborah Harry. . . . . Betty
Christian Slater. . . . . Andy

Talking Walls *(1987)*

Judy Baldwin . . . . n.a.
Sybil Danning . . . . Bathing Beauty
Sally Kirkland . . . . Hooker
Marie Laurin. . . . . .Jeanne

Steve Shellen. . . . . .Paul Barton
•• 0:58—Buns, while taking off his clothes and running down railroad tracks.
June Wilkinson . . . . Blonde
• 0:13—Brief left breast, in car room, getting green towel yanked off.
0:14—Very, very brief left breast in car room again. Dark.
•• 1:08—Brief topless, getting green towel taken off.

The Tall Guy (1990)

Jeff Goldblum . . . . Dexter King
0:34—Brief right cheek of buns, while rolling around on the floor with Kate. Don't see his face.
Neil Hamilton . . . . Naked George
•• 0:04—Buns, while walking around apartment talking to Jeff Goldblum. Brief frontal nudity (out of focus).
• 0:06—More buns, when getting introduced to Goldblum.
• 1:22—Brief buns, during end credits.
Anna Massey. . . . . .Mary
Emma Thompson . . . . Kate
••• 0:33—Very brief right breast, brief buns, then topless during funny love making scene with Jeff Goldblum.

Tango & Cash (1989)

Dori Courtney. . . . . .Dressing Room Girl
• 1:06—Topless, sitting in chair looking in the mirror in the background. Long shot.
Michael Jeter. . . . . Skinner
Roxanne Kernohan . . . . .Dressing Room Girl
• 1:06—Brief topless in dressing room with three other girls. She's the second one in the middle.
Tamara Landry . . . . Girl in Bar
Christie Mucciante . . . . .Dressing Room Girl
• 1:06—Brief topless in dressing room. (She's the first topless blonde.)
Kurt Russell . . . . .Cash
•• 0:31—Brief buns while walking into the prison shower room with Sylvester Stallone.
Sylvester Stallone . . . . Ray Tango
•• 0:31—Brief buns while walking into the prison shower room with Kurt Russell.

Tanya's Island (1980; Canadian)

Vanity . . . . Tanya
0:04—Very brief topless and buns covered with paint during B&W segment.
••• 0:07—Nude caressing herself and dancing during the opening credits.
•• 0:09—Nude making love on the beach.
0:11—Brief right breast, while talking to Lobo.
•• 0:19—Brief topless on the beach with Lobo, then more topless while yelling at him.
• 0:28—Mostly topless in flimsy halter top exploring a cave.
• 0:33—Full frontal nudity undressing in tent.
• 0:35—Left breast sleeping. Dark, hard to see.
0:37—Buns while sleeping.

• 0:40—Topless superimposed over another scene.
0:48—Brief buns swimming in the ocean.
•• 0:51—Full frontal nudity walking out of the ocean and getting dressed.
• 0:53—Brief topless in open blouse.
•• 1:08—Topless in middle of compound when Lobo rapes her in front of Blue.
• 1:16—Full frontal nudity running through the jungle in slow motion. Brief buns.

Target (1985)

Ilona Grubel. . . . . .Carla
• 1:12—Brief topless in bed with Matt Dillon.

Tarzan, The Ape Man (1981)

Bo Derek . . . . .Jane
••• 0:43—Nude taking a bath in the ocean, then in a wet white dress.
• 1:35—Brief topless painted all white.
• 1:45—Topless washing all the white paint off in the river with Tarzan.
•• 1:47—Topless during the ending credits playing with Tarzan and the orangutan. (When I saw this film in a movie theater, the entire audience actually stayed to watch the credits!)
Richard Harris. . . . . Parker
Miles O'Keeffe . . . . .Tarzan
• 0:45—Sort of buns, under loin cloth in the surf. Lots of other semi-bun shots in the loin cloth throughout the rest of the film.
1:09—Buns, while in loin cloth at side of lake with Bo Derek.
• 1:48—Buns, while in loin cloth, wrestling with orangutan during end credits.

Tattoo (1981)

Maud Adams . . . . .Maddy
• 0:22—Very brief topless taking off clothes and putting a bathrobe on.
•• 0:23—Topless opening bathrobe so Bruce Dern can start painting.
•• 0:25—Brief topless getting into the shower to take off body paint.
•• 0:58—Brief topless and buns getting out of bed.
•• 1:04—Topless, knocked out on table before Dern starts tattooing her.
••• 1:07—Topless looking at herself in the mirror with a few tattoos on.
•• 1:24—Topless lying on table masturbating while Dern watches through peep hole in the door.
••• 1:36—Full frontal nudity taking off robe then making love with Dern (her body is covered with tattoos).
Bruce Dern. . . . . Karl Kinski
•• 1:36—Buns, while making love with Maud Adams before she kills him.

The Teacher (1974)

Angel Tompkins .Diane Marshall
••• 0:09—Topless on a boat taking off her swimsuit.
••• 0:12—More topless on the boat getting a suntan.

••• 0:36—Topless taking off her top in bedroom, then buns and topless taking a shower.

• 0:41—Brief right breast lying back on bed.

•• 0:43—Brief topless opening her bathrobe for Jay North.

•• 0:47—Side view of right breast lying on bed, then right breast from above.

•• 0:52—Topless in boat after making love.

Teachers (1984)

Laura Dern . . . . Diane
Lee Grant . . . . Dr. Burke
Julia Jennings. . . . . The Blonde

•• 0:05—Brief left breast, while sitting up in bed with Nick Nolte.

Nick Nolte. . . . . Alex
JoBeth Williams . . . . Lisa

• 1:39—Brief topless taking off clothes and running down school hallway yelling at Nick Nolte.

Teen Lust (1978)

a.k.a. Girls Next Door
Kirsten Baker. . . . . Carol Hill

• 0:45—Brief side view of left breas, while changing clothes in her bedroom.

Perry Lang. . . . . .Terry

• 0:01—Buns in jock strap getting his pants pulled down while he does pull ups.

The Tempest (1982)

Raul Julia. . . . . Kalibanos
Susan Sarandon . . . . Aretha

0:58—In braless white tank top washing clothes with Molly Ringwald in the ocean.

1:53—In wet white T-shirt on balcony during rainstorm with Jason Robards and Raul Julia.

1:55—In wet white T-shirt on the beach.

• 1:57—Brief right, then left breasts in open T-shirt saving someone in the water.

Terminal Choice (1985; Canadian)

Teri Austin. . . . . Lylah Crane

0:14—Full frontal nudity, covered with blood on operating table. Long shot.

0:21—Right breast, on table being examined by Ellen Barkin. Dead, covered with dried blood.

0:26—Very brief left breast under plastic on table, hard to see.

Ellen Barkin . . . . Mary O'Connor
Joe Spano . . . . .Frank Holt

••• 0:34—Buns, taking off towel and getting dressed in locker room while talking to Anna.

• 0:49—Buns, while making love in bed with Anna. Long shot, don't see his face.

Diane Venora . . . . .Anna

0:44—In lingerie, talking to Frank.

• 0:48—Brief left breast, making love in bed with Frank. Don't see her face.

Sandra Warren . . . . Nurse Tipton
Cheryl-Ann Wilson . . . . Nurse Fields

Terminal Entry (1986)

Barbara Edwards . . . . Lady Electric

••• 0:05—Topless taking a shower and getting a towel during video game scene.

Jill Terashita . . . . Gwen

Terminal Exposure (1988)

Tara Buckman . . . . n.a.
Hope Marie Carlton . . . . Christie

••• 1:11—Topless in bathtub licking ice cream off a guy.

Ava Fabian . . . . Bruce's Girl
Luann Lee . . . . Bruce's Girl
Nicole Rio . . . . Hostage Girl

Terminal Island (1973)

Phyllis Davis . . . . .Joy Lange

••• 0:39—Topless and buns in a pond, full frontal nudity getting out, then more topless putting blouse on while a guy watches.

Marta Kristen . . . . .Lee Phillips
Barbara Leigh. . . . . Bunny Campbell

••• 0:22—Topless and buns undressing in room while Bobbie watches from the bed.

Tom Selleck .Dr. Norman Milford
Clyde Ventura . . . . Dillon

•• 0:42—Buns, while taking off pants in front of Phyllis Davis, then covered with honey and bees, then running to jump into a pond.

The Terminator (1984)

Michael Biehn . . . . Kyle Reese

• 0:06—Side view of buns after arriving from the future. Brief buns running down the alley. A little dark.

Linda Hamilton . . . . Sarah Connor

•• 1:18—Brief topless about four times making love on top of Michael Biehn in motel room.

Bill Paxton . . . . .Punk Leader
Rick Rossovich . . . . Matt
Arnold Schwarzenegger . . . . The Terminator

••• 0:03—Buns, while kneeling by garbage truck, walking to look at the city and walking toward the three punks at night.

Terror at the Opera (1989; Italian)

Cristina Marsillach . . . . Betty

• 0:23—Brief left breast during nightmare. Brief topless, sitting up in bed and screaming.

Daria Nicolodi . . . . Mira

Terror in the Aisles (1984)

Nancy Allen . . . . Hostess
Kirsten Baker . . . . Terry

•• 1:03—Topless and buns, undressing to go skinny dipping from Friday the 13th, Part II.

Morgan Fairchild . . . . .Jamie

•• 1:06—Topless in mirror in scene from The Seduction.

• 1:08—Brief left breast, getting out of pool from The Seduction.

Sandy Johnson . . . . Judith Meyers

• 0:15—Brief topless in scene from Halloween.

Victoria Lynn Johnson
. . . . Body Double for Angie Dickinson
- • 1:07—Topless in shower from Angie Dickinson's shower scene in *Dressed to Kill*.

David Naughton . . . . David Kessler
- • 0:17—Brief buns during transformation into a werewolf from *An American Werewolf in London*.

P.J. Soles . . . . Lynda
- • 0:24—Brief topless in scene from *Halloween*.

The Terror on Alcatraz (1986)
Sandy Brooke . . . . Mona
- • 0:05—Right breast on bed getting burned with a cigarette by Frank.

Alisa Wilson . . . . Clarissa
- • 1:14—Brief topless opening her blouse to distract Frank, so she can get away from him.

Terror Train (1980; Canadian)
Vanity . . . . Merry
Joy Boushel . . . . Pet
- •• 0:49—Topless wearing panties in sleeper room on train with Mo.

Jamie Lee Curtis . . . . Alena

Tess (1979; French/British)
Arielle Dombasle . . . . Mercy Chant
Peter Firth . . . . Angel Clare
Suzanna Hamilton . . . . Izz
Nastassia Kinski . . . . Tess Durbeyfield
- • 0:47—Brief left breast, opening blouse in field to feed her baby.

Texas Detour (1977)
Priscilla Barnes . . . . Claudia Hunter
- ••• 1:03—Topless, changing clothes and walking around in bedroom. This is her best topless scene.
- • 1:11—Topless sitting up in bed with Patrick Wayne.

Lindsay Bloom . . . . Sugar McCarthy

That Cold Day in the Park (1969)
Suzanne Benton . . . . Nina
- • 0:38—Side view of left breast putting top on.
- • 1:05—Topless taking off her clothes and getting into the bathtub. Another long shot.

That Obscure Object of Desire
(1977; French/Spanish)
Carole Bouquet . . . . Conchita
- ••• 0:53—Topless in bedroom.
- ••• 1:01—Topless in bed with Fernando Rey.

Angela Molina . . . . Conchita
- • 0:53—Brief topless in bathroom.
- •• 1:20—Nude dancing in front of a group of tourists.
- • 1:29—Brief topless behind a gate taunting Fernando Rey.

There Was a Crooked Man (1970)
Michael Blodgett . . . . Coy Cavendish
Jeanne Cooper . . . . Prostitute
- • 0:18—Brief left breast trying to seduce the sheriff, Henry Fonda, in a room.

Kirk Douglas . . . . Paris Pitman, Jr.
- • 0:11—Brief upper half of buns, while leaving bedroom wearing only his gun belt.
- •• 1:09—Brief buns and balls, while jumping into a barrel to take a bath in prison.

Lee Grant . . . . Mrs. Bullard
Pamela Hensley . . . . Edwina
- • 0:12—Very brief left breast lying on pool table with a guy.

There's a Girl in My Soup (1970)
Christopher Cazenove . . . . Nigel
Gabrielle Drake . . . . Julia Halford-Smythe
- • 0:09—In beige bra with Peter Sellers, brief left breast in bed with him. Don't see her face well, but it is her.

Goldie Hawn . . . . Marion
- • 0:37—Buns and very brief right side view of her body getting out of bed and walking to a closet to get a robe. Long shot.

Geraldine Sherman . . . . Caroline
- •• 0:43—Topless in bed, then getting out after Goldie Hawn splashes water on her.

They Bite (1991)
Ron Jeremy . . . . Darryl
Susie Owens . . . . Kate
- • 1:01—Right breast, while lying on the beach after getting attacked.
- ••• 1:02—Topless and buns, while in bed on top of a guy before killing him.

Blake Pickett . . . . Model
- 0:00—Posing for photographer in two piece swimsuit.
- ••• 0:03—Left breast, then topless and buns, taking off swimsuit for the photographer. More topless in the water, struggling with the monster.

Christina Veronica . . . . Tammy
- ••• 0:20—Topless in bed during porno movie shoot.
- ••• 0:55—Topless, sunbathing on the beach while a guy rubs suntan lotion on her.
- • 1:03—Topless on the beach during playback of film.
- •• 1:08—Topless on boat, getting attacked by monster.
- • 1:09—Topless in water, struggling with the monster.
- • 1:10—Brief topless on beach during playback of film.

They're Playing with Fire (1984)
Sybil Danning . . . . Diane Stevens
- 0:04—In two piece swimsuit on boat. Long scene.
- ••• 0:08—Topless and buns making love on top of Jay in bed on boat. Nice!
- ••• 0:10—Topless and buns getting out of shower, then brief side view of right breast.
- 0:43—In black bra and slip, in boat with Jay.
- •• 0:47—In black bra and slip, at home with Michael, then panties, then topless and buns getting into shower.
- ••• 1:12—In white bra and panties in room with Jay then topless.

Thief of Hearts (1984)

(Special Home Video Version reviewed.)
Steven Bauer........................ Scott Muller
•• 0:53—Brief side view of buns, carrying Barbara Williams into bed.
Annette Sinclair.................... College Girl #1
Barbara Williams .... Mickey Davis
• 0:46—Right breast in bathtub when her husband comes in and tries to read her diary.
••• 0:53—Topless making love with Steven Bauer in his condo.
Romy Windsor ....Nicole
••• 0:12—Full frontal nudity with Steven Bauer getting dressed.

Thieves of Fortune (1989)

Michael Nouri..........................Juan Luis
• 0:57—Buns, while taking a shower outside. Long shot.
Claudia Udy ....Marissa
Shawn Weatherly ....Peter
• 1:09—Brief topless several times, taking a shower (while wearing beard and moustache disguise).
••• 1:21—Topless in white panties distracting tribe so she can get away.

Things are Tough all Over (1982)

Evelyn Guerrero .... Donna
Richard "Cheech" Marin ....Mr. Slyman
• 0:21—Buns while in the laundromat dryer.

Third Degree Burn (1989; Made for Cable Movie)

Virginia Madsen .... Anne Scholes
Treat Williams .... Scott Weston
• 0:43—Brief buns while taking off his robe with Virginia Madsen in his bedroom.

Those Lips, Those Eyes (1980)

Steve Levitt .... Westervelt
Glynnis O'Connor...................... Ramona
• 0:37—Left breast in car with Tom Hulce. Dark, hard to see.
•• 1:12—Topless and buns on bed with Tom Hulce. Dark.

Threshold (1983; Canadian)

Jeff Goldblum .... Aldo Gehring
Donald Sutherland ....Dr. Vrain
Mare Winningham .... Carol Severance
• 0:56—Brief full frontal nudity, lying on operating table, then side view of left breast getting prepped.

Thrilled to Death (1988)

Rebecca Lynn ....Elaine Jackson
• 0:01—Topless twice when Baxter opens her blouse.
•• 0:31—Topless in locker room talking to Nan.
Christine Moore .... Nan Christie
••• 0:38—Topless in office with Mr. Dance just before killing him.
Christina Veronica........................Satin
•• 0:33—Topless talking to Cliff during porno film shoot.

Thumb Tripping (1972)

Bruce Dern............................. n.a.
Meg Foster........................... Shay
• 1:19—Very, very brief topless leaning back in field with Jack. Long shot.
• 1:20—Topless at night. Face is turned away from the camera.
Mariana Hill .... Lynn
• 1:14—In black bra, then very, very brief left breast when Jack comes to cover her up.
• 1:19—Topless frolicking in the water with Gary.
1:20—In white swimsuit, dancing in bar.

Thunder Alley (1985)

Clancy Brown.........................Weasel
Melanie Kinnaman .... Star
• 0:52—Brief topless under water in pool talking to a guy.
• 1:14—Topless and buns making love on bed and getting out.
Susan McIver .... Redhead
Jill Schoelen .... Beth
Roger Wilson .... Richie

Thunderbolt and Lightfoot (1974)

Catherine Bach......................... Melody
Jeff Bridges.........................Lightfoot
Clint Eastwood......... John "Thunderbolt" Doherty
June Fairchild .... Gloria
• 0:20—Very brief right breast getting dressed in the bathroom after making love with Clint Eastwood.
Leslie Oliver ....Teenager
•• 1:16—Brief topless in bed when robbers break in and George Kennedy watches her.
Luanne Roberts .... Suburban Housewife
• 0:57—Brief full frontal nudity standing behind a sliding glass door tempting Jeff Bridges.

Tie Me Up! Tie Me Down! (1990; Spanish)

Victoria Abril .... Marina Osorio
••• 0:24—Full frontal nudity playing with a frogman toy in the bathtub.
• 0:34—Buns and brief side of right breast, getting dressed.
• 0:44—Topless changing clothes, then on TV while Maximo watches.
•• 1:09—Topless changing clothes.
••• 1:16—Right breast, then topless in bed making love with Ricky.
Antonio Banderas......................... Ricky
• 1:17—Buns in mirror on ceiling, while making love with Victoria Abril. Long shot.

Tiffany Jones (British)

Anouska Hempel .... Tiffany Jones
• 0:02—Brief topless walking in from the surf in wet white dress.
•• 0:13—Topless in bath. Buns also, getting out.
• 0:18—Brief left breast, taking off her top in front of bright light.

- 0:23—Topless, several times, changing clothes in her bedroom.
- •• 0:24—Topless walking around her apartment in white panties.
- 0:31—Topless in bubble bath.
- 0:32—Brief left breast, wrapping an orange towel around herself.
- ••• 0:39—Lying on table in black and red bra, then topless. More right breast.
- 0:41—Side view topless, covered with sweat.
- •• 0:55—Topless, partial lower frontal nudity, taking a shower.
- 1:26—Topless, running outside in a field when guys rip off her dress.

A Tiger's Tale (1988)
Ann-Margret . . . . Rose
- 0:45—Side view of left breast in bra, then topless jumping up after fire ants start biting her. Brief buns running along a hill. Long shot, probably a body double.

C. Thomas Howell . . . . Bubber Drumm
- 0:38—Upper half of buns getting undressed in bedroom while Ann-Margret changes in the bathroom.

Leigh Lombardi . . . . Marcia
Kelly Preston . . . . Shirley
- •• 0:03—Topless in the car, letting C. Thomas Howell open her blouse and look at her breasts.

Angel Tompkins . . . . La Vonne

Tigers in Lipstick (1979)
Ursula Andress . . . . The Stroller and The Widow
0:02—In black bra, panties and garter belt and stockings opening her fur coat to cause an accident.
0:48—In slip posing for photographer.
- 0:50—Very brief topless when top of slip accidentally falls down.
- 0:51—More topless with the photographer.

Laura Antonelli . . . . The Pick Up
0:24—In brown lingerie lying in bed, then getting dressed.
0:34—In same lingerie, getting undressed, then in bed.

Sylvia Kristel . . . . The Girl
0:04—Topless in photograph on the sand.
0:06—Braless in sheer nightgown lying in bed.
- •• 0:09—Topless lying in bed with The Arab.
- •• 0:16—Lying in bed in red lingerie, then left breast for awhile.

Tightrope (1984)
Randi Brooks . . . . Jamie Cory
- ••• 0:20—Topless taking off her robe and getting into the spa.
0:24—Buns, dead in the spa while Clint Eastwood looks at her.

Genevieve Bujold . . . . Beryl Thibodeaux
Clint Eastwood . . . . Wes Block
- 0:33—Buns, while on the bed on top of Becky. Slow pan, red light, covered with sweat.

Margaret Howell . . . . Judy Harper
- 0:44—Brief left breast viewed from above in a room with Clint Eastwood.

Rebecca Perle . . . . Becky Jacklin
Jamie Rose . . . . Melanie Silber
0:07—Buns, lying face down on bed, dead.

Till Marriage Do Us Part (1974; Italian)
Laura Antonelli . . . . Eugenia
- •• 0:58—Topless in the barn lying on hay after guy takes off her clothes.
- •• 1:02—Full frontal nudity standing up in bathtub while maid washes her.
- •• 1:07—Right breast with chauffeur in barn.
- •• 1:36—Topless surrounded by feathers on the bed while priest is talking.

Karin Schubert . . . . Evelyn

A Time to Die (1991)
Nitchie Barrett . . . . Sheila
- 0:12—Buns, getting out of bed.
- •• 0:16—Topless making love in bed with Sam.

Daphne Cheung . . . . Sunshine
Jeff Conaway . . . . Frank
Traci Lords . . . . Jackie
Nicole Picard . . . . Patti

Time Walker (1982)
Nina Axelrod . . . . Susie
Greta Blackburn . . . . Sherri
Melissa Prophet . . . . Jennie
- 0:27—Brief topless putting bra on while a guy watches from outside the window.
1:17—Very, very brief right breast in shower when the mummy comes to get the crystal.

Allene Simmons . . . . Nurse
Jason Williams . . . . Jeff

Timebomb (1990)
Michael Biehn . . . . Eddy Kay
Julie Brown . . . . Uncredited Waitress at Al's Diner
Robert Culp . . . . Mr. Phillips
Patsy Kensit . . . . Dr. Anna Nolmar
- •• 1:15—Topless, mostly left breast, making love with Michael Biehn in bed. Partial buns also.

Tracy Scoggins . . . . Ms. Blue

Tintorera (1977)
Jennifer Ashley . . . . n.a.
Priscilla Barnes . . . . n.a.
- 1:12—Very brief topless dropping her beer into the water.
- 1:14—Topless, on the beach after the shark attack (on the left).

Andres Garcia . . . . Miguel
- 0:41—Very brief frontal nudity in boat kitchen with Susan George and Steve.
- •• 0:42—Nude, picking up George and throwing her overboard.

Susan George . . . . Gabriella
- 0:42—Very brief topless waking up Steve.

Fiona Lewis . . . . Patricia
    0:20—Side view of left breast in silhouette. Long
    shot, hard to see. Nude swimming under water just
    before getting eaten by a shark. Don't see her face.

To Die For (1988)
Steve Bond . . . . Tom
Eloise Broady. . . . . Girl at Party
Ava Fabian . . . . Franny
Brendan Hughes . . . . Vlad Tepish
  • 1:13—Buns, while making love with Kate.
Remy O'Neill. . . . . Jane
Amanda Wyss . . . . Celia Kett

To Die For 2 (1991)
Rosalind Allen . . . . Nina
  • 0:37—Topless a few times in bed, making love with
    Max.
Steve Bond . . . . Tom
Remy O'Neill. . . . . Jane
Jay Underwood . . . . Danny
Amanda Wyss . . . . Celia

To Kill a Clown (1971)
Blythe Danner. Lily Frischer
  • 1:10—Side view of left breast sitting on bed talking
    to Alan Alda. Hair covers breast, hard to see. Buns,
    getting up and running out of the house.

To Live and Die in L.A. (1985)
Willem Dafoe . . . . Eric Masters
    0:58—Side view of buns, while kneeling on floor,
    burning counterfeit money.
    0:59—Lower half of buns, while making love in bed
    with Debra Feuer in bed. Seen on TV.
  • 1:06—Buns, while sitting on bench in locker room,
    changing clothes.
Debra Feuer . . . . Bianca Torres
    0:58—Side view of buns, lying on bed while watch-
    ing Willem Dafoe burn the counterfeit money. Long
    shot.
  • 1:47—Brief topless on video tape being played back
    on TV in empty house, hard to see anything.
Darlanne Fluegel . . . . Ruth Lanier
  •• 0:44—Brief topless and buns, in bed when William
    Petersen comes home.
    1:29—In stockings on couch with Petersen.
  • 1:50—Very brief topless on bed with Petersen in a
    flashback.
Jackie Giroux. Claudia Leith
John Pankow. John Vukovich
  •• 1:06—Buns, while changing in the locker room.
William L. Petersen . . . . Richard Chance
  • 0:44—Brief frontal nudity, but hard to see anything
    because it's dark.
John Turturro . . . . Carl Cody

To Protect and Serve (1992)
Lezlie Deane. . . . . Harriet
  • 0:47—Brief topless in front of fireplace with C. Tho-
    mas Howell. Hard to see because candles get in the
    way.
  • 0:51—Brief topless, getting up off the floor.
  • 1:18—Brief side view of left breast in mirror in bath-
    room. Long shot.
C. Thomas Howell . . . . Egan
  ••• 0:07—Buns, while getting out of bed to get dressed.
    Don't see his face.

To the Devil, a Daughter (1976)
Nastassia Kinski . . . . Catherine Beddows
  ••• 1:24—Full frontal nudity, taking off her robe outside
    and walking towards Richard Widmark in slow mo-
    tion.

The Tomb (1987)
Michelle Bauer . . . . Nefartis
Sybil Danning . . . . Jade
Francesca "Kitten" Natividad . . . . Stripper
  ••• 0:19—Topless and buns in G-string dancing on
    stage.
  • 0:21—Brief topless again.
Dawn Wildsmith . . . . Anna Conda
  ••• 0:54—Topless taking off robe in room with Michelle
    Bauer, then getting pushed onto a bed full of snakes.

Tomboy (1985)
Jerry Dimone . . . . Randy Star
  •• 0:59—Buns, while making love with Betsy Russell in
    the exercise room.
Betsy Russell . . . . Tomasina "Tommy" Boyd
  •• 0:44—In wet T-shirt, then brief topless after landing
    in the water with her motorcycle.
  •• 0:59—Topless making love with the race car driver
    in an exercise room.
Kristi Somers . . . . Seville Ritz
  •• 0:14—Topless taking a shower while talking to Betsy
    Russell.
  • 0:53—Brief topless stripping at a party.
Cynthia Ann Thompson . . . . Amanda
  • 0:23—Brief right breast getting out of car in auto re-
    pair shop.
  •• 1:02—Topless delivering drinks to two guys in the
    swimming pool.

Too Hot To Handle (1975)
Cheri Caffaro . . . . Samantha Fox
  •• 0:06—Topless wearing a black push-up bra and
    buns in black G-string.
  • 0:13—Full frontal nudity lying on boat.
  ••• 0:39—Topless making love in bed with Dominco.
  ••• 0:55—Full frontal nudity taking off clothes and lying
    in bed.
  • 1:06—Brief left breast in bed with Dominco.
Aharon Ipalé. . . . . Dominco de la Torres
  • 0:39—Buns, while in bed with Cheri Caffaro. Dark,
    hard to see.

The Toolbox Murders (1978)
Marciee Drake . . . . Debbie
- •• 0:09—In wet blouse, then topless taking it off and putting a dry one on.

Evelyn Guerrero . . . . Maria
Kelly Nichols . . . . .Victim

Top Model (1989; Italian)
Laura Gemser . . . . Dorothy/Eve
- • 0:44—Brief right breast and buns, frolicking with the cowboy.

Jessica Moore . . . . Sarah Asproon/Gloria
- ••• 0:03—Nude, posing for photographer customer in his loft with mannequins, then talking on the phone.
- • 0:08—Topless in dressing room, when seen by Cliff.
- •• 0:23—Buns and brief side of right breast, undressing in front of a customer.
- •• 0:24—Topless, rubbing oil on him.
- •• 0:30—Full frontal nudity, in her bedroom when Peter blackmails her.
- ••• 0:35—Nude in photographer customer's loft again.
- • 0:40—Brief buns, turning over in bed.
- •• 0:43—Topless on couch, making love (disinterestedly) with cowboy.
- • 0:56—Buns and partial right breast, while getting dressed.
- ••• 1:00—Topless making love with Cliff on sofa, then sleeping afterward.
- •• 1:04—Nude, undressing and walking down hallway.
- ••• 1:08—Nude, in hotel room, making love with Cliff.
- ••• 1:19—Buns, with Cliff in stairwell. Topless and buns in bathroom with him.

Total Exposure (1991)
Martina Castle . . . . .Cissy
- • 1:06—Topless in spa being questioned by a guy with a gun.

Jeff Conaway . . . . Peter Keynes
Deborah Driggs . . . . Kathy
- ••• 0:08—Topless dancing in front of Jeff Conaway, then making love in bed with him. Long scene.
- • 0:22—Brief side view topless in B&W photos that Conaway looks at.
- • 0:24—Brief buns in black G-string and side of right breast changing clothes in locker room.
- •• 0:25—Topless and buns, trying to beat up Season Hubley.

Season Hubley . . . . Andi Robinson
0:07—Buns, getting into hot tub. Probably a body double.

Michael Nouri . . . . Dave Murphy
Kristine Rose . . . . .Rita

Totally Exposed (1991)
Tina Bockrath . . . . Lillian Tucker
- •• 0:00—Buns and topless, turning over on tanning table during opening credits.
- • 0:01—Brief full frontal nudity, lying on tanning table.

- •• 0:03—Brief nude, getting out of bed and putting on towel while talking to Bill.
- ••• 1:01—Full frontal nudity, turning over in tanning table. Full frontal nudity, dropping her towel in reception area.
- ••• 1:02—Buns, walking back to the room. Nude, taking off towel and lying on massage table.
- ••• 1:04—Nude, sitting up on table and standing up with Bill.

Kelli Konop . . . . Sue
- • 0:18—Undressing to take a shower. Brief right breast, bending over to take off panties. Brief side view of left breast, while getting into the shower.
- • 0:19—Sort of topless, while washing herself in the shower. Her arms get in the way.
- 1:12—In white bra, making out with Bill.

The Touch (1971; U.S./Swedish)
Bibi Andersson . . . . Karen Vergerus
- • 0:31—Topless in bed with Elliott Gould.
- ••• 0:56—Topless kissing Gould.
- 1:13—Very, very brief right breast washing Gould's hair in the sink.

Tough Guys (1986)
Kirk Douglas . . . . .Archie Long
- • 1:36—Buns, while standing on moving train, mooning Charles Durning.

Darlanne Fluegel . . . . Skye Foster
- • 0:47—Very brief side view of right breast, leaning over to kiss Kirk Douglas.

Lisa Pescia . . . . Customer #1
Hilary Shepard . . . . Sandy

Tough Guys Don't Dance (1987)
Frances Fisher . . . . .Jessica Pond
Wings Hauser . . . . Regency
Ryan O'Neal . . . . Tim Madden
Isabella Rossellini . . . . Madeleine
Debra Sandlund . . . . Patty Lareine
- •• 1:24—Topless ripping her blouse off to kiss the policeman after they have killed and buried another woman.
- • 1:24—Very brief left breast, twice, in bed with Ryan O'Neal. Long shot.

The Toxic Avenger (1985)
Cindy Manion . . . . .Julie
0:14—In two piece swimsuit in locker room with Melvin.
- ••• 0:15—Topless, after untying her swimsuit top in front of Melvin.

The Toxic Avenger: Part II (1988)
John Altamura . . . . Toxic Avenger
Phoebe Légerè . . . . .Claire
- • 0:31—Brief right breast, while caressing herself while making out with the Toxic Avenger.

Toy Soldiers (1983)
Terri Garber . . . . Amy
- 0:18—Brief right breast taking off her tank top when the army guys force her. Her head is down.

Tim Robbins . . . . Bean
Tracy Scoggins . . . . .Monique

Toy Soldiers (1991)
Sean Astin . . . . Billy Tepper
- 1:08—Brief buns, while taking off his wet clothes after coming in through the window.

Track 29 (1988; British)
Sandra Bernhard . . . . .Nurse Stein
Colleen Camp . . . . .Arlanda
Christopher Lloyd . . . . Henry Henry
- 0:34—Very brief side view of his buns, while lying in the hospital getting spanked by Sandra Bernhard.

Gary Oldman . . . . Martin
- 1:24—Buns, while holding onto Christopher Lloyd and stabbing him.

Theresa Russell . . . . Linda Henry

The Tracker (1988; Made for Cable Movie)
Kris Kristofferson . . . . Noble Adams
Mark Moses . . . . Tom Adams
- •• 0:35—Buns, while getting out of the river after washing himself, then getting hassled by some bandits.

Tracks (1977)
Dennis Hopper . . . . Sgt. Jack Falen
- •• 0:58—Frontal nudity running through the train. Long scene.

Sally Kirkland. . . . . Uncredited
Taryn Power . . . . .Stephanie
- 0:32—Brief side view of right breast changing in her room on the train. Don't see her face.
- 1:15—Brief left breast making love with Dennis Hopper in a field.

Trading Places (1983)
Jamie Lee Curtis . . . . Ophelia
- ••• 1:00—Topless in black panties after taking red dress off in bathroom while Dan Aykroyd watches.
- ••• 1:09—Topless and black panties taking off halter top and pants getting into bed with a sick Aykroyd.

Transformations (1988)
Michael Hennessy . . . . Stephens
- 1:07—Brief, partial buns, while pulling his pants down.

Ann Margaret Hughes. . . . . .Myra
- 0:42—Right breast, then topless under Rex Smith in bed.
- 0:43—More topless, dead in bed.

Lisa Langlois . . . . Miranda
Pamela Prati .Woman Succubus
- ••• 0:05—Topless and buns making love on top of Rex Smith in bed. She starts transforming into a creature.
- 0:21—Brief topless again during Smith's flashback.

- 0:24—Brief topless again, while transforming.
- 0:26—Brief topless again, while transforming.

Cec Verrell . . . . Antonia

Traveling Man (1989; Made for Cable Movie)
Ingrid Buxbaum . . . . .Uncredited Salesgirl
- ••• 0:05—Topless and buns while wearing G-string, dancing during sales meeting.

John Lithgow . . . . Ben Cluett
- 0:48—Brief buns, while trying to get the VCR away from Mona in her living room.

Traxx (1988)
Priscilla Barnes . . . . Mayor Alexandria Cray
Gwendolyn Hajek. . . . . Playmate
Suzanne Primeaux . . . . Hooker #1
- •• 0:37—Topless, dancing on stage while wearing a mask.

Trick or Treat (1986)
Marc Price . . . . Eddie Weinbauer
- •• 0:04—Buns, while lying on the floor and also kneeling at boys' locker room door when the bullies leave him outside where the girls can see him.
- 0:12—Brief buns, in Polaroid photo of the previous incident.

Tropical Snow (1989)
David Carradine. . . . . .Oskar
Nick Corri . . . . Tavo
- •• 0:11—Buns while in bed with Madeleine Stowe.
- •• 0:44—Buns, while standing naked in police station.

Madeleine Stowe . . . . .Marina
- 0:05—Very brief side view of left breast putting red dress on.
- 0:11—Buns, lying in bed. Very brief right breast sitting up. (I wish they could have panned the camera to the right!)
- •• 0:24—Topless in mirror putting red dress on. 0:32—Buns, lying on top of Tavo in bed.
- 0:54—Brief topless making love in the water with Tavo. Then buns, lying on the beach (long shot.) 1:22—Long shot side view of right breast in water with Tavo.

Trouble in Mind (1986)
Genevieve Bujold . . . . .Wanda
Keith Carradine . . . . .Coop
Kris Kristofferson . . . . .Hawk
Lori Singer . . . . Georgia
- 1:01—Very brief left breast, in bed with Kris Kristofferson.

The Trouble with Dick (1986)
Susan Dey . . . . .Diane
Elaine Giftos. . . . . Sheila
Elizabeth Gorcey . . . . .Haley
- 0:13—Very brief left breast in gaping T-shirt while she lies on bed, plays with a toy and laughs. 0:26—Lower half of buns under robe on sofa with Dick. 0:27—Half of right breast on top of Dick in bed.

Tom Villard . . . . Dick Kendred
 0:30—Side view of buns, while leaving Haley's
 room.
 • 0:58—Buns from under his shirt, getting out of bed
 to open the door.

Truck Stop Women (1974)
Uschi Digard . . . . Truck Stop Woman
 •• 0:18—Topless getting arrested in the parking lot by
 the police officer, then buns and topless getting
 frisked in a room.
Claudia Jennings . . . . Rose
 • 0:27—Brief topless taking off blouse and getting
 into bed.
 0:48—Brief side view of right breast in mirror, getting dressed.
 • 1:10—Brief topless wrapping and unwrapping a
 towel around herself.

True Blood (1989)
Jeff Fahey . . . . Raymond Trueblood
Sherilyn Fenn . . . . Jennifer Scott
 • 1:22—Very brief right breast in closet trying to stab
 Spider with a piece of mirror.

True Love (1989)
Al Juliano. . . . . Male Stripper
 • 0:43—Buns while in G-string dancing on stage in a
 club.
Annabella Sciorra . . . . Donna

Truth or Dare (1991)
Madonna . . . . Herself
 ••• 0:44—Brief topless changing clothes backstage.
 B&W.
 1:16—Wearing a bra, in a store, trying on earrings.
 B&W.
 1:35—Very brief half of left breast, while wearing
 robe and jumping up. B&W.
 1:43—Sort of topless in bed with her dancers. Her
 hands cover her breasts. B&W.
Antonio Banderas . . . . Himself
Warren Beatty . . . . Himself
Sandra Bernhard . . . . Herself
Carlton Wilborn . . . . Dancer
 1:39—Frontal nudity showing himself to Madonna.
 Dark, hard to see. B&W.
 1:43—Very brief frontal nudity getting into bed with
 Madonna. Too dark to see anything. B&W.
 • 1:45—Brief buns, while in bed with Madonna. B&W.

Tuff Turf (1984)
Robert Downey, Jr. . . . . Jimmy Parker
Kim Richards. . . . . Frankie Croyden
 1:07—In black lingerie getting dressed.
 • 1:29—Brief topless supposedly of a body double
 (Fiona Morris) in bedroom with James Spader but I
 have heard from a very reliable source that it really
 was her.
Catya Sassoon. . . . . Feather
James Spader . . . . Morgan Hiller

The Tunnel (1987)
Jane Seymour. . . . . Maria
 • 0:29—Very brief left breast, while in bed with Peter
 Weller when the sheet is pulled down.
 •• 0:44—Brief right beast, while getting dressed,
 throwing off her robe.
Peter Weller . . . . Juan Pablo

Turkish Delight (1974; Dutch)
Rutger Hauer . . . . Erik
 ••• 0:01—Brief nude walking around his apartment talking to a woman he has just picked up.
 • 0:04—Buns, while in bed (covered with a sheet),
 then very brief frontal nudity throwing another girl
 out.
 •• 0:36—Frontal nudity getting up to answer the door
 with flowers.
 •• 1:12—Frontal nudity lying in bed depressed.
 •• 1:16—Buns, while making love with Olga in bed.
Monique Van De Ven . . . . Olga
 •• 0:24—Topless when Rutger Hauer opens her blouse,
 then nude on the bed.
 •• 0:27—Topless, waking up in bed.
 ••• 0:33—Topless on bed with Hauer, then nude getting
 up to fix flowers.
 0:42—Buns, with Hauer at the beach.
 •• 0:46—Topless modeling for Hauer, then brief nude
 running around outside.
 •• 0:54—Topless in bed with open blouse with flowers.
 • 1:04—In wet T-shirt in the rain with Hauer, then
 brief topless coming down the stairs.

Tusks (1990)
Lucy Gutteridge . . . . Micah Hill
 •• 0:23—Topless in tub taking a bath.

Twelfth Night (1988; Italian)
Carlo de Meijo . . . . Orsino
 • 0:00—Buns, while standing up after bath. Out of focus.
 • 0:49—Half of buns, while sitting on rock, talking to
 Viola.
Viju Krim . . . . Maria
 •• 1:09—Topless, dancing in tavern in open top.
Ajita Wilson . . . . Antonia
 •• 0:50—Buns, taking off her dress and walking into
 stream with a guy.
 • 0:51—Very brief topless, making love with him in
 the stream.
 •• 1:11—Right breast, hanging out of black dress,
 dancing in tavern.

Twenty-One (1991)
Patsy Kensit . . . . Katie
 ••• 1:17—Topless in reflection in bathroom mirror undressing, then dressing.

Twice a Woman (1979)
Bibi Andersson . . . . Laura
 • 0:05—Topless taking off her bra and putting a
 blouse on.

- 0:06—Brief side view of left breast, getting into bed, brief left breast lying back in bed.

Sandrine Dumas . . . . Sylvia
- 0:06—Topless, kneeling on the bed, then more brief topless in bed with Bibi Andersson.
- ••• 0:47—Brief right breast, then topless in bed with Andersson. Long scene.
- 1:15—Left breast, lying in bed with Anthony Perkins. Long shot.
- ••• 1:23—Topless with Andersson.

Twice Dead (1989)
Charlie Spradling. . . . . Tina
- •• 1:11—Topless taking off jacket next to bed.
- ••• 1:14—Topless making love with her boyfriend in bed.
- 1:18—Brief topless dead in bed.

Jill Whitlow . . . . Robin/Myrna
0:27—In white slip, getting ready for bed, then walking around the house.

Twins of Evil (1971)
Madeleine Collinson . . . . Freida Gelhorn
- •• 1:07—Right breast, then brief topless undoing dress, then full frontal nudity after turning into a vampire in bedroom.

Mary Collinson . . . . Maria Gelhorn

The Twist (1976)
Ann-Margret . . . . Charlie Minerva
0:24—Left breast when Claire daydreams someone is sticking a pin into Ann-Margret's breast. A little bloody. Body double.
1:24—Very, very brief left breast during Bruce Dern's daydream. Seen from above, body double again.

Sybil Danning . . . . .Jacques' Secretary
- •• 1:24—Brief topless sitting next to Bruce Dern during his daydream.

Bruce Dern . . . . William
- •• 0:45—Buns, while taking off his clothes and walking onto stage during a play. Long shot.

Sydne Rome . . . . Nathalie

Twisted Justice (1990)
Julie Austin . . . . Andrea Leyton
Karen Black . . . . Mrs. Granger
Bonnie Paine. . . . . Hooker
- •• 0:11—Topless in black panties and stockings, getting photographed.

Tanya Roberts . . . . Secretary
Shannon Tweed .Hinkle

Two Moon Junction (1988)
Sherilyn Fenn . . . . April
- ••• 0:07—Topless taking a shower in the country club shower room.
- •• 0:27—Brief topless on the floor kissing Perry.
- •• 0:42—Topless in gas station restroom changing camisole tops with Kristy McNichol.
- 0:54—Brief topless making love with Perry in a motel room.

- ••• 1:24—Nude at Two Moon Junction making love with Perry. Very hot!
- 1:40—Brief left breast and buns in the shower with Perry.

Kristy McNichol .Patti Jean
- •• 0:42—Topless in gas station restroom changing camisole tops with Sherilyn Fenn.

Richard Tyson . . . . Perry
- 0:58—Very, very brief buns while wrestling with April in a motel room. Dark, hard to see.

Two to Tango (1988)
Adrianne Sachs. Cecilia Lorca
- •• 0:29—Side of left breast and buns in bedroom with Lucky Lara. More left breast while Dan Stroud watches through camera.
- •• 0:59—Topless and buns in bed with Dan Stroud.

Alberto Segado . . . . Lucky Lara
- 0:29—Buns while on top of Adrienne Sachs, making love with her in bed.

Ultimate Desires (1991)
Sheri Able. . . . . Carlos' Girlfriend
Tracy Scoggins. . . . . Samantha Stewart
0:44—In white bra and panties, dancing sexily in her house, while two guys watch from outside.
0:53—Getting dressed in white bra and panties. Don't see her face.
- 0:59—Very brief buns and side of left breast taking off her dress and walking out of the room.
1:07—In black bra, panties, garter belt and stockings with Marc Singer.
- ••• 1:10—Topless, several times, in bed with Singer.

Marc Singer .Jonathan Sullivan

The Unbearable Lightness of Being (1988)
Juliette Binoche . . . . Tereza
0:22—In white bra in Tomas' apartment.
- 1:33—Brief topless jumping onto couch.
1:36—Buns, sitting in front of fire being photographed, then running around, trying to hide.
- 2:18—Left breast in The Engineer's apartment.

Daniel Day-Lewis . . . . Thomas
Derek De Lint. . . . . Franz
Lena Olin . . . . Sabina
- •• 0:03—Topless in bed with Tomas looking at themselves in a mirror.
0:17—In black bra and panties looking at herself in a mirror on the floor.
1:21—In black bra, panties, garter belt and stockings.
- •• 1:29—Topless and buns while Tereza photographs her. Long shots, hard to see.
- 1:43—Very brief left breast, in bed with Tomas.
2:32—Brief topless in B&W photo found in a drawer by Tomas.

Stellan Skarsgard . . . . The Engineer
- 2:18—Buns, while making love with Tereza in his apartment.

The Unborn (1991)
Brooke Adams. . . . . .Virginia Marshall
* 1:12—Right breast, while breast feeding her baby creature.

Daryl Haney . . . . .Policeman

Under Cover (1987)
David Denney. . . . . .Hassie Pearl
* 0:43—Brief buns while walking around boy's locker room wearing his jock strap.

Jennifer Jason Leigh. . . . . Tanille Lareoux

Under the Gun (1989)
Sam Jones . . . . Braxton
* 0:41—Brief buns, while taking a shower at Vanessa Williams place. Don't see his face.

Vanessa Williams . . . . Samantha Richards

Under the Volcano (1984)
Anthony Andrews . . . . Hugh Firmin
Jacqueline Bisset . . . . Yvonne Firmin
Albert Finney. .Geoffrey Firmin
* * * 0:49—Buns and brief frontal nudity in bathroom with Jacqueline Bisset and Anthony Andrews when they try to give him a shower.
* * 0:52—Buns and very brief frontal nudity, putting on his underwear.

The Underachievers (1987)
Edward Albert . . . . Danny Warren
Barbara Carrera . . . . Katherine
Carl Crew . . . . Thug 2
Becky LeBeau .Ginger Bronsky
* * * 0:40—Topless in swimming pool playing with an inflatable alligator after her exercise class has left.

Jewel Shepard . . . . Sci-Fi Teacher
* 0:27—Topless ripping off her Star Trek uniform when someone enters her classroom. Dark, hard to see.

Susan Tyrrell . . . . Mrs. Grant

Unfaithfully Yours (1984)
Nastassia Kinski. . . . . Daniella Eastman
* 0:37—Topless and buns in the shower.

Dudley Moore. . . . . Claude Eastman
Cassie Yates. Carla Robbins

The Unholy (1988)
Jill Carroll . . . . Millie
* 1:10—Very brief upper half of left breast, while talking in the courtyard with Ben Cross.

Hal Holbrook. . . . . .Archbishop Mosley

An Unmarried Woman (1978)
Alan Bates. . . . . Saul
Jill Clayburgh . . . . Erica
0:05—Dancing around the apartment in white long sleeve T-shirt and white panties.
* * 0:12—Brief topless getting dressed for bed, kind of dark and hard to see.
* * 1:10—In bra and panties in guy's apartment, then brief topless lying on bed.

The Unnameable (1988)
Laura Albert . . . . Wendy Barnes
* * 0:46—Left breast while lying on floor kissing John, then brief buns when he pulls her panties down.

Until September (1984)
Karen Allen. Mo Alexander
* * 0:41—Topless in bed making love with Thierry Lhermitte.
* * 1:13—Topless and buns walking from bed to Lhermitte.
* 1:25—Brief topless jumping out of bathtub.

Christopher Cazenove . . . . .Philip
Maryam D'Abo. . . . . .Nathalie
Marika Green . . . . Banker
Thierry Lhermitte . . . . .Xavier de la Pérouse
* * 0:43—Buns, after making love with Karen Allen.
0:53—Almost frontal nudity getting out of bathtub.

Until the End of the World (1991)
Lois Chiles . . . . Elsa Farber
Solveig Dommartin . . . . Claire Tourneur
* * * 0:34—Left breast, then topless, then full frontal nudity in bedroom with William Hurt and Winter.

William Hurt. . . . . Sam Farber/Trevor McPhee
Sam Neill . . . . Eugene Fitzpatrick

Up 'n' Coming (1987)
(R-rated version reviewed, X-rated version available.)
Marilyn Chambers . . . . Cassie
* * * 0:01—Nude, getting out of bed and taking a shower.
* * 0:08—Topless making love in bed with the record producer.
* 0:30—Brief topless in bed with two guys.
* * 0:47—Full frontal nudity getting suntan lotion rubbed on her by another woman.
* 0:55—Topless taking off her top at radio station.

Lisa De Leeuw . . . . Altheah Anderson
* 0:33—Very brief topless by the pool when her robe opens.
* 0:48—Brief topless walking around the house when her robe open.
* * 0:49—Left breast talking with a guy, then topless walking into the bedroom.

Monique Gabrielle . . . . .Boat Girl #1
* 0:39—Topless wearing white shorts on boat. Long shot.
* 0:40—More brief nude shots on the boat.

Loni Saunders . . . . .Dixanne
* 0:19—Topless kissing a guy on the bus.

Up the Creek (1984)
Tim Matheson . . . . Bob McGraw
Dan Monahan . . . . .Max
Julie Montgomery . . . . .Lisa
Tom Nolan. . . . . .Whitney
Jennifer Runyon . . . . Heather Merriweather
Lori Sutton. . . . . Cute Girl
* 0:40—Brief topless pulling up her T-shirt to get the crowd excited while cheerleading the crowd.

Jeana Tomasina........................... Molly
Peggy Trentini........................... Co-Ed
Romy Windsor .... Corky

Used Cars (1980)
Cheryl Rixon .... Margaret
- •• 0:29—Topless after getting her dress torn off during a used car commercial.

Kurt Russell .... Rudy Russo
- • 1:04—Very brief buns while putting on red underwear.

Betty Thomas ....Bunny
0:37—Dancing on top of a car next to Kurt Russell wearing pasties to attract customers (wearing a brunette wig).

Jack Warden .... Roy L. Fuchs/Luke Fuchs

Valentino Returns (1988)
Veronica Cartwright .... Pat Gibbs
- ••• 0:33—Topless sitting in bed with Frederic Forrest. Fairly long scene.

Barry Tubb .... Wayne Gibbs
- •• 1:15—Buns, while fighting two other guys after skinny dipping with Jenny Wright at night. Very, very brief, blurry frontal nudity after getting hit and rolling into the water.

Jenny Wright.......................Sylvia Fuller

Valley Girl (1983)
Michael Bowen ....Tommy
Nicholas Cage........................ Randy
Colleen Camp .... Sarah Richman
Elizabeth Daily......................... Loryn
- •• 0:16—In bra through open jumpsuit, then brief topless on bed with Tommy.

Cameron Dye .... Fred
Deborah Foreman....................... Julie
Joyce Hyser .... Joyce

Valley of the Dolls (1967)
Patty Duke .... Neely O'Hara
Lee Grant .... Miriam
Barbara Parkins .... Anne Welles
- • 0:28—Very brief silhouette of a breast, taking off nightgown and getting into bed.

Sharon Tate.......................Jennifer North
- • 1:21—In bra, acting in a movie. Very, very brief left breast in bed with a guy (curtain gets in the way).
- • 1:23—Very brief side view of right breast, while sitting up in bed.

The Vals (1982)
Tiffany Bolling........... Valley Attorney and Parent
Gina Calabrese .... Annie
- • 0:04—Topless changing clothes in bedroom with three of her friends. Long shot, hard to see.
- • 0:15—Right breast, while making love with a guy at a party.
0:32—In black bra with her friends in a store dressing room.

Jill Carroll .... Sam

Vampire at Midnight (1988)
Esther Alise....................... Lucia Giannini
- ••• 1:01—In black lingerie, then topless and buns while taking off clothes to wish Roger a happy birthday.

Barbara Hammond......................... Kelly
- •• 0:07—Topless and buns, getting out of the shower and drying herself off.
- • 0:16—Left breast, dead, in Victor's car trunk. Blood on her.

Jeanie Moore ....Amalia
- •• 0:32—Topless getting up to run an errand.

Christina Whitaker .... Ingrid
Jason Williams ....Detective Roger Sutter

Vampire Cop (1990)
Melissa Moore....................Melanie Roberts
- ••• 0:46—Topless in bed with the Vampire Cop.
- •• 0:51—Right breast, sitting in bed talking with Hans.
- • 1:21—Right breast, in bed on the phone during end credits.

Vampire Hookers (1979)
Lenka Novak .... Suzy
0:22—In sheer green dress getting into coffin.
0:33—In sheer green dress again.
0:45—In sheer green dress again.
- •• 0:51—Topless in bed during the orgy with the guy and the other two Vampire Hookers.

Vampire Lovers (1970; British)
Ingrid Pitt................... Marcilla/Carmilla
- •• 0:32—Topless and buns in the bathtub and reflection in the mirror talking to Emma.

Madeline Smith .... Emma
- •• 0:32—Topless trying on a dress in the bedroom after Carmilla has taken a bath.
- • 0:49—Topless in bed, getting her top pulled down by Carmilla.

Vampire's Kiss (1989)
Maria Conchita Alonso.....................Alva
0:47—In white bra, ironing her clothes in her living room.
0:59—In white bra getting attacked by Nicholas Cage.

Elizabeth Ashley .... Dr. Glaser
Jennifer Beals .... Rachel
0:14—Almost topless in bed with Nicholas Cage. Squished left breast against Cage while she bites him. In one shot, you can see the beige pastie she put over her left nipple.
0:27—In bed again with Cage.
0:41—In black lingerie taking her dress off for Cage.

Nicholas Cage.......................Peter Loew
Kasi Lemmons .... Jackie
- •• 0:05—In black bra and panties, then topless in living room with Nicholas Cage.

Vampyres (1974; British)
Murray Brown .... Ted
- •• 0:22—Buns, while making love in bed with Fran.

- 0:56—Buns, while falling into bed.

Brian Deacon .... John
Anulka Dziubinska .... Miriam
- 0:00—Brief full frontal nudity in bed with Fran, kissing each other before getting shot.
- 0:43—Topless taking a shower with Fran.
- ••• 0:58—Topless and buns in bed with Fran, drinking Ted's blood. Brief lower frontal nudity.

Sally Faulkner .... Harriet
- 1:14—Side of left breast, partial buns, then right breast while making love with John in the trailer.
- •• 1:22—Full frontal nudity getting her clothes ripped off by Fran and Miriam in the wine cellar before being killed.

Vanessa *(1977)*

Olivia Pascal .... Vanessa
- ••• 0:08—Nude undressing, taking a bath and getting washed by Jackie. Long scene.
- ••• 0:16—Buns, then full frontal nudity getting a massage.
- 0:26—Topless getting fitted for new clothes.
- 0:47—Full frontal nudity when Adrian rips her clothes off.
- ••• 0:56—Full frontal nudity on beach with Jackie.
- ••• 1:05—Nude making love with Jackie in bed. Nice close up of left breast.
- •• 1:19—Full frontal nudity lying on the table.
- •• 1:27—Topless in white panties, garter belt and stockings shackled up by Kenneth.

Vanishing Point *(1971)*

Gilda Texter .... Nude Rider
- 1:17—Topless riding motorcycle.
- ••• 1:19—Topless riding motorcycle and walking around without wearing any clothes. Long scene.

Velvet Dreams *(Italian)*

Alicia Moro .... n.a.
Kathy Shower .... Laura
- •• 0:15—Left breast, while making love with Paul in the dressing room.
- 0:35—Brief buns, while getting a massage.
- •• 0:42—Topless, tied to a tree during her writing fantasy.

The Velvet Vampire *(1971)*

Michael Blodgett .... Lee Ritter
- •• 0:21—Buns, getting up out of bed during desert dream scene.
- ••• 0:42—Buns, in desert dream scene.
- •• 0:46—Buns, while on floor with Diane.

Sherry Miles .... Susan Ritter
- 0:08—Brief topless in bed with Lee.
- ••• 0:18—Topless sitting up in bed, then making love with Lee.
- 0:21—Topless in bed in desert during dream scene.
- ••• 0:22—Topless sitting up in bed and turning on the light.
- 0:42—Topless in bed during desert dream scene, long shot.

- 0:55—Topless in bed during desert dream scene.
- ••• 0:56—Topless in bed in desert scene, closer shot with Diane.
- 1:19—Brief topless in desert scene during flashback.

Celeste Yarnall .... Diane Le Fanu
- 0:32—Brief topless, zipping up her blouse after trying to seduce Lee.
- •• 0:42—Topless in desert scene when Lee pulls her blouse down.
- ••• 0:45—Topless on the floor, making love with Lee.
- •• 0:55—Topless in desert scene with Lee.
- 0:57—Side view of buns, lying on top of someone in a coffin.
- •• 1:02—Topless in bed with Lee.

Vendetta *(1986)*

Roberta Collins .... Miss Dice
Marta Kober .... Sylvia
- 1:10—Very brief, dark, right breast in open blouse, in her prison cell with the guard.

Sandy Martin .... Kay Butler
- 0:34—Brief left breast, while making love with her boyfriend. Don't see her face.

Dirga McBroom .... Willow
Marianne Taylor .... Star

Vengeance... One by One

Romy Schneider .... n.a.
  0:02—In black slip getting dressed.
- 0:28—Very brief left breast when a soldier rips her bra open during struggle.
  1:14—In black lingerie in her husband's flashback.

Vice Academy *(1988)*

Ken Abraham .... Dwayne
Ginger Lynn Allen .... Holly
  1:20—Buns, in white lingerie outfit when graduation robe gets torn off.

Stephanie Bishop .... Desiree/Redhead
Linnea Quigley .... Didi
- ••• 0:45—Topless making love with Chuck while he's handcuffed.

Karen Russell .... Shawnee
- •• 0:09—Topless exposing herself to Duane to disarm him.
- •• 1:13—Topless pulling her top down to distract a bad guy.

Vice Academy, Part 2 *(1990)*

Toni Alessandrini .... Aphrodisia
- 0:33—Topless in dressing room.
- ••• 0:34—Topless and buns in G-string, dancing in club.

Ginger Lynn Allen .... Holly
- 0:44—Buns in black bra, panties, garter belt and stockings.
- •• 1:04—Buns in G-string, then topless dancing with Linnea Quigley on stage at club.

Scott Layne .... Petrolino
- 0:49—Buns, twice, while in men's locker room when Linnea Quigley and Ginger Lynn Allen come in.

Melissa Moore .... Glaze

Linnea Quigley . . . . Didi
- •• 1:04—Buns in G-string, then topless dancing with Ginger Lynn Allen on stage at club.

Vice Academy, Part 3 *(1991)*
Toni Alessandrini. . . . . Stripper
- •• 0:26—Topless taking off dress on stage.
- •• 0:27—More topless on stage (about five times).
- • 0:28—More topless giving away her money.
- • 0:34—Buns in G-string, dancing on stage.

Ginger Lynn Allen . . . . .Holly
Darcy De Moss . . . . .Samantha (uncredited)
Elizabeth Kaitan. . . . . .Candy
- ••• 0:12—Topless in back of van with her boyfriend.

Steve Mateo . . . . Professor Dirk Kaufinger
- •• 0:47—Buns, when Ginger Lynn Allen and Elizabeth Kaitan come into his lab.

Julia Parton . . . . Melanie/Malathion
- •• 0:44—Topless, opening her blouse after seeing all the money.

Video Vixens *(1973)*
Angela Carnon . . . . .Mrs. Gordon
- •• 1:13—Full frontal nudity making love with Mr. Gordon in bed in various positions. Shot at fast speed.

Sandra Dempsey. . . . . Actress
- •• 0:05—Full frontal nudity, lying down getting make up put on.

Marva Farmer . . . . .Girl
- •• 0:59—Full frontal nudity in the swimming pool with three other women during commercial.

George "Buck" Flower. . . . . .Rex Boorski
- •• 0:52—Frontal nudity taking off his pants, then buns in bed with actress during filming of a movie. In B&W.

Robyn Hilton. . . . . Inga
- •• 1:18—Topless, opening her top in a room full of reporters.

Kimberly Hyde . . . . .Claudine
Terri Johnson. . . . . .Anita
- •• 0:43—Full frontal nudity, talking with her mother in bedroom during commercial.

Marius Mazmanian . . . . Psychiatrist
- •• 0:42—Buns and balls from behind, while frolicking on couch with his patient. In B&W.

Bernie Scorpio. . . . . Turnip Twin
- ••• 1:05—Frontal nudity standing next to his identical twin brother after their trial.

Lennie Scorpio . . . . Turnip Twin
- •• 1:03—Frontal nudity, then buns while on top of victim in bed.
- ••• 1:05—Frontal nudity standing next to his identical twin brother after their trial.

Cheryl Smith. . . . . Twinkle Twat Girl
- ••• 0:24—Full frontal nudity doing a commercial, sitting next to pool.

Robyn Whitting. . . . . Patient and Virginia
- •• 0:40—Topless, then nude on couch in psychiatrist's office. In B&W.

- •• 0:52—Full frontal nudity acting in bed with Rex for a film. In B&W.

Linda York . . . . Dial-A-Snatch Girl
- •• 0:34—Nude on a turntable during a commercial, getting felt by four blindfolded guys.

Videodrome *(1983; Canadian)*
Deborah Harry . . . . Nicki Brand
- •• 0:16—Topless rolling over on the floor when James Woods is piercing her ear with a pin.
- 0:22—In black bra, sitting on couch with James Woods.

James Woods . . . . Max Renn

Vindicator *(1986; Canadian)*
a.k.a. Frankenstein '88
Caroline Arnold . . . . Lisa
- •• 0:40—Topless in bed with a jerk, then putting her blouse on.

Teri Austin . . . . Lauren Lehman
- • 0:30—Very brief left breast and buns in mirror getting out of the bubble bath covered with bubbles. Long shot, hard to see anything.

Pam Grier. . . . . .Hunter

Violets Are Blue *(1986)*
Bonnie Bedelia. Ruth Squires
Kevin Kline. . . . . Henry Squires
- • 1:02—Brief buns, while standing up and putting on his shorts, on island with Sissy Spacek.

Sissy Spacek . . . . Gussie Sawyer

Virgin High *(1990)*
Michelle Bauer . . . . Miss Bush
Tracy Dali. . . . . .Christy
- •• 0:04—Brief topless several times when her blouse and bra pop open while talking to her parents.

Linnea Quigley. . . . . Kathleen
- •• 0:24—Topless, nonchalantly making love on top of Derrick.
- •• 0:55—Brief topless several times on top of Derrick, then topless.
- • 1:21—Topless in photo during party.

Visionquest *(1985)*
Madonna. . . . . Nightclub Singer
Linda Fiorentino. . . . . Carla
Matthew Modine. . . . . Louden Swain
- • 1:29—Very brief buns while taking off underwear to get weighed for wrestling match.

Daphne Zuniga .Margie Epstein

Vital Signs *(1989)*
Diane Lane. . . . . .Gina Wyler
- ••• 1:11—In white bra, then topless making love with Michael in the basement.

Adrian Pasdar. . . . . Michael Chatham
- 1:11—Upper half of buns, with his pants partially down in basement with Diane Lane.

Jimmy Smits. . . . . .Dr. David Redding
Gigi Vorgan . . . . Nell

W. B., Blue and the Bean (1988)

a.k.a. Bail Out

Linda Blair..............................Nettie
David Hasselhoff.................... White Bread
Debra Lamb ....Motel Clerk
- 0:42—Full frontal nudity opening door in motel to talk to David Hasselhoff.

Wall Street (1987)

Michael Douglas................... Gordon Gekko
Daryl Hannah .... Darian Taylor
Hal Holbrook.....................Lou Mannheim
Annie McEnroe................. Muffie Livingston
Sylvia Miles........................... Realtor
Suzen Murakoshi................... Girl in Bed
- 0:13—Brief full frontal nudity getting out of bed and walking past the camera in Charlie Sheen's bedroom (slightly out of focus).

Martin Sheen .... Carl Fox
Monique Van Vooren ....n.a.
Sean Young........................Kate Gekko

The War of the Roses (1989)

Sean Astin.........................Josh, Age 17
Michael Douglas..................... Oliver Rose
1:36—Almost buns, while cleaning himself in the bi-det.
Susan Isaacs .... Auctioneer's Assistant
Marianne Sägebrecht .... Susan
Kathleen Turner ....Barbara Rose
0:06—In braless white blouse walking around on the sidewalk with Michael Douglas.
- 0:12—Brief left breast, while in bed with Michael Douglas.

Warlords (1988)

Michelle Bauer .... Harem Girl
••• 0:14—Topless, getting her top ripped off, then shot by a bad guy.
David Carradine ....Dow
Greta Gibson....................... Harem Girl
•• 1:05—Topless in tent with the other harem girls. Holding a snake.
•• 1:09—Topless again.
Debra Lamb .... Harem Girl
••• 0:14—Topless, getting her blouse ripped off by a bad guy, then kidnapped.
••• 0:17—Topless in harem pants while shackled to an-other girl.
Brinke Stevens.....................Dow's Wife
Dawn Wildsmith .... Danny

Warm Summer Rain (1989)

Kelly Lynch .... Kate
- 0:03—Brief topless and side view of buns in B&W ly-ing on floor during suicide attempt. Quick cuts top-less getting shocked to start her heart.
•• 0:23—Full frontal nudity when Guy gets off her in bed.
•• 0:24—Side view of right breast in bed, then topless.

••• 0:58—Buns then topless, getting washed by Guy on the table.
••• 1:07—Brief buns making love. Quick cuts full frontal nudity spinning around. Side view of left breast with Guy.
••• 1:09—Nude picking up belongings and running out of burning house with Guy.
Barry Tubb................................Guy
•• 0:23—Lower frontal nudity getting off Kelly Lynch in bed.
0:25—Side view of buns while dreaming in bed.
•• 0:58—Frontal nudity kneeling on floor and behind the table while washing Lynch.
- 1:00—Buns while getting washed by Lynch.
- 1:07—Brief buns while making love with Lynch. Quick cuts.
••• 1:09—Nude picking up belongings and running out of burning house with Lynch.

The Warrior and the Sorceress (1984)

David Carradine............................Kain
Maria Socas .... Naja
••• 0:15—Topless wearing robe and bikini bottoms in room with Zeg. Sort of brief buns, leaving the room.
•• 0:22—Topless standing by a wagon at night.
•• 0:27—Topless in room with David Carradine. Dark. Most of buns when leaving the room.
• 0:31—Topless and buns climbing down wall.
- 0:34—Brief topless, then left breast with rope around her neck at the well.
- 0:44—Topless when Carradine rescues her.
- 0:47—Topless walking around outside.
- 0:57—More topless outside.
- 1:00—Topless watching a guy pound a sword.
- 1:05—Topless under a tent after Carradine uses the sword. Long shot.
- 1:09—Topless during big fight scene.
- 1:14—Topless next to well. Long shot.

Warrior Queen (1987)

Tally Chanel............................ Vespa
••• 0:09—Topless hanging on a rope, being auctioned.
••• 0:20—Topless and buns with Chloe.
•• 0:37—Nude, before attempted rape by Goliath.
•• 0:58—Topless during rape by Goliath.
Sybil Danning .... Berenice
Samantha Fox .... Philomena/Augusta
••• 0:31—Nude, doing a dance with a snake during orgy scene.
- 1:03—Brief right breast after unsuccessfully trying to seduce Marcus.
Josephine Jaqueline Jones................... Chloe
••• 0:20—Topless making love with Vespa.

Watchers II (1990)

Irene Miracle .... Sarah Ferguson
••• 0:40—Side view in black bra, then topless a few times in the bathtub.
Tracy Scoggins.................... Barbara White
Marc Singer...................... Paul Ferguson
Mary Woronov..................... Dr. Glatman

We're No Angels (1989)
Robert De Niro . . . . Ned
Bruno Kirby . . . . Deputy
Demi Moore . . . . Molly
   • 0:18—One long shot, then two brief side views of
      left breast when Robert De Niro watches from out-
      side. Reflections in the window make it hard to see.
Sean Penn . . . . Jim
James Russo . . . . Bobby

A Wedding (1978)
Geraldine Chaplin . . . . Rita Billingsley
Mia Farrow . . . . Buffy Brenner
   ••• 1:10—Topless posing in front of a painting, while
      wearing a wedding veil.
Lauren Hutton . . . . Florence Farmer

Weeds (1987)
Nick Nolte . . . . Lee Umstetter
   •• 0:51—Buns, while getting out of bed and putting
      his pants on.

Weekend Pass (1984)
Sara Costa . . . . Tuesday Del Mundo
   ••• 0:07—Buns in G-string, then topless during strip
      dance routine on stage.
Graem McGavin . . . . Tawny Ryatt
Valerie McIntosh . . . . Etta
Hilary Shepard . . . . Cindy Hazard
   •• 1:05—In red bra, then topless taking off bra.
   • 1:07—Buns and topless getting into bathtub.
Annette Sinclair . . . . Maxine
Ashley St. Jon . . . . Xylene B-12
   •• 0:13—Topless dancing on stage.

Weekend Warriors (1986)
Monique Gabrielle . . . . Showgirl on plane
   •• 0:51—Brief topless taking off top with other show-
      girls.
Daniel Greene . . . . Phil McCracken
Brenda Strong . . . . Danny El Dubois
   • 0:44—Topless, lit from the side, standing in the dark.
Tom Villard . . . . Mort Seblinsky

Weird Science (1985)
Judie Aronson . . . . Hilly
Robert Downey, Jr. . . . . Ian
Kelly Le Brock . . . . Lisa
   0:12—In blue underwear and white top baring her
      midriff for the two boys when she is first created.
   1:29—In blue leotard and grey tube top gym clothes
      to teach boy's gym class.
Kym Malin . . . . Girl Playing Piano
   • 0:55—Brief topless several times as her clothes get
      torn off by the strong wind and she gets sucked up
      and out of the chimney.
Bill Paxton . . . . Chet
   •• 0:30—Buns, while taking off towel to give to his
      younger brother in the kitchen.
Renée Props . . . . One of The Weenies
Suzanne Snyder . . . . Deb

Wally Ward . . . . A Weenie
Jill Whitlow . . . . Perfume Salesgirl

Welcome Home Roxy Carmichael (1990)
Jeff Daniels . . . . Denton Webb
Ava Fabian . . . . Roxy Carmichael
   • 0:10—Buns in water in swimming pool, then more
      while getting out.
Frances Fisher . . . . Rochelle Bossetti

Welcome to 18 (1986)
Mariska Hargitay . . . . Joey
   • 0:26—Buns, taking a shower when video camera is
      taping her.
   0:43—Watching herself on the videotape playback.

Welcome to Arrow Beach (1973)
a.k.a. Tender Flesh
Meg Foster . . . . Robbin Stanley
   0:12—Buns and brief side view of right breast get-
      ting undressed to skinny dip in the ocean. Don't see
      her face.
   •• 0:40—Topless getting out of bed.
Joanna Pettet . . . . Grace Henry

Welcome to L.A. (1977)
Keith Carradine . . . . Carroll Barber
Geraldine Chaplin . . . . Karen Hood
   •• 1:28—Full frontal nudity standing in Keith Car-
      radine's living room.
Lauren Hutton . . . . Nora Bruce
   • 0:56—Very brief, obscured glimpse of left breast un-
      der red light in photo darkroom.
Harvey Keitel . . . . Ken Hood
Sally Kellerman . . . . Ann Goode
Sissy Spacek . . . . Linda Murray
   •• 0:51—Brief topless after bringing presents into Keith
      Carradine's bedroom.

Wetherby (1985; British)
Suzanna Hamilton . . . . Karen Creasy
   0:42—In white lingerie top and bottom.
   1:03—In white lingerie getting into bed and lying
      down.
   1:06—In white lingerie, fighting with John.
Richard Harris . . . . Sir Thomas
Vanessa Redgrave . . . . Jean Travers
Joely Richardson . . . . Young Jean Travers
   •• 1:10—Topless in room with Jim when he takes off
      her coat.

When a Stranger Calls (1979)
Tony Beckley . . . . Curt Duncan
   • 1:07—Side view of buns, while kneeling in restroom.
Carol Kane . . . . Jill Johnson

Where the Heart Is (1990)
Suzy Amis . . . . Chloe McBain
   • 0:08—Topless during her art film. Artfully covered
      with paint, with a bird. Topless again in the third
      segment.

- 0:09—Topless during the film again. Hard to see because of the paint. Last segment while she narrates.

Joanna Cassidy . . . . Jean McBain

Dabney Coleman . . . . Stewart McBain

David Hewlett . . . . .Jimmy
- 0:56—Buns, while walking around the hall in an angel costume.

Sheila Kelley . . . . Sheryl

Uma Thurman . . . . Daphne McBain
- 0:08—Topless during art film, but her entire body is artfully painted to match the background paintings. The second segment.

0:40—More topless with body painted posing for her sister. Long shot.

1:16—In slide of painting taken at 0:40.

1:43—Same painting from 0:40 during the end credits.

Where's Poppa? (1970)

Ron Liebman . . . . Sidney Hocheiser
- 0:45—Buns while running across the street, then in front of door in hall, then brief buns leaving George Segal's apartment.

Whispers (1989)

Chris Sarandon . . . . Detective Tony

Victoria Tennant . . . . .Hilary Thomas
- 0:43—Buns and side of right breast getting into bathtub. Long shot, looks like a body double (the ponytail in her hair changes position).
- 0:44—Buns and brief topless running down the stairs. Looks like the same body double.

White Light (1990)

Martin Kove . . . . Sean Craig

1:23—Upper half of buns, while on the floor with Rachel.
- 1:24—Very brief buns, while getting out of bed.

James Purcell . . . . Bill Dockerty

Heidi Von Palleske . . . . Debra Halifax

White Men Can't Jump (1992)

Woody Harrelson . . . . .Billy Hoyle
- 0:21—Very, very brief half of buns, while getting into shower.
- 0:37—Very, very brief half of buns, while getting out of bed.

Rosie Perez . . . . Gloria Clemente
- 0:36—Topless in shower and making love in bed with Woody Harrelson.
- 0:39—Brief right breast, while sitting up in bed.
- 0:40—Very brief side of right breast, three times, while getting out of bed quickly.

White Mischief (1988)

Geraldine Chaplin . . . . Nina

John Hurt . . . . Colville

Sarah Miles . . . . Alice

Jacqueline Pearce . . . . .Idina
- 0:07—Topless standing up in the bathtub while several men watch.

Greta Scacchi .Diana Broughton
- 0:16—Topless taking a bath while an old man watches through a peephole in the wall.
- 0:24—Brief topless in bedroom with her husband.
- 0:29—Brief topless taking off bathing suit top in the ocean in front of Charles Dance.
- 0:30—Topless lying in bed talking to Dance.

White Palace (1990)

Kathy Bates . . . . .Rosemary Powers

Eileen Brennan . . . . .Judy

Barbara Howard . . . . Sherri Klugman

Rachel Levin . . . . Rachel

Susan Sarandon . . . . Nora Baker
- 0:28—Topless on top of James Spader. Great shots of right breast.
- 0:38—Topless on bed with Spader.

James Spader . . . . .Max Baron
- 0:38—Buns, while taking off clothes and getting into bed with Susan Sarandon. Don't see his face.

White Sands (1992)

Willem Dafoe . . . . Ray Dolezal

John Lafayette . . . . Demott

Mary Elizabeth Mastrantonio . . . . .Lane Bodine
- 1:11—Brief left breast in shower with Willem Dafoe. You see her face, so this shot is really her.

Mimi Rogers . . . . .Uncredited Molly Dolezal

Mickey Rourke . . . . .German Lennox

Tera Tabrizi . . . .

Body Double for Mary Elizabeth Mastrontonio
- 1:10—Left breast and upper half of buns in the shower undressing with Willem Dafoe. Don't see face, so it's probably Tera.

M. Emmet Walsh . . . . Bert Gibson

Who's That Knocking at My Door? (1968)

Harvey Keitel . . . . .J.R.
- 0:42—Buns, several times, while in bed and standing up. Quick cuts.

Whore (1991)

a.k.a. If you're afraid to say it... Just see it

Ginger Lynn Allen . . . . Wounded Girl

Stephanie Blake . . . . Stripper in Big T's
- 0:35—Buns, in G-string on stage.
- 0:36—Topless, dancing on stage in a club.

Dori Courtney . . . . Topless woman on TV
- 0:14—Brief topless on TV in old folks home in a scene from *Mob Boss*.

John Diehl . . . . Derelict

Theresa Russell . . . . Liz
- 0:13—Topless and buns in G-string outfit, taking off her coat.
- 0:25—In black bra, doing sit ups. Topless making love in spa with Blake.
- 1:18—Brief buns, in open skirt in back of car with a customer.

Tom Villard . . . . Hippy

Whose Life Is It, Anyway? (1981)
Janet Eilber . . . . .Patty
- •• 0:30—Nude, ballet dancing during B&W dream sequence.
- • 1:13—Very brief side of left breast when her back is turned while changing clothes.

Kaki Hunter. . . . . .Mary Jo
Lissa Layng . . . . Nurse

The Wicked Lady (1983; British)
Glynnis Barber. . . . . Caroline
- ••• 0:58—Topless and buns making love with Kitt in the living room. Possible body double.

Alan Bates. . . . . Jerry Jackson
Faye Dunaway. . . . . Barbara Skelton
Marina Sirtis . . . . Jackson's Girl
- ••• 1:06—Full frontal nudity in and getting out of bed when Faye Dunaway discovers her in bed with Alan Bates.
- ••• 1:20—Topless getting whipped by Dunaway during their fight during Bates' hanging.

Oliver Tobias. . . . . Kit Locksby
- • 0:58—Buns, with Caroline in living room.

Wicked Stepmother (1989)
Colleen Camp. . . . . Jenny
Barbara Carrera. . . . . Priscilla
- • 1:14—Very, very brief upper half of right breast peeking out of the top of her dress when she flips her head back while seducing Steve.

Laurene Landon . . . . Vanilla

The Wicker Man (1973; British)
Britt Ekland . . . . Willow
- ••• 0:58—Topless in bed knocking on the wall, then more topless and buns getting up and walking around the bedroom. Long scene.

Lorraine Peters . . . . Girl on Grave
- • 0:22—Side view of right breast sitting on grave, crying. Dark, long shot, hard to see.

Ingrid Pitt . . . . .Librarian
- •• 1:11—Brief topless in bathtub seen by Edward Woodward.

Wifemistress (1977; Italian)
Laura Antonelli . . . . .Antonia De Angelis
- 0:50—In lacy nightgown in her bedroom.
- 1:22—Brief upper half of left breast in bed with Clara and her husband.
- 1:25—In sheer lacy nightgown leaning out the window.
- 1:29—Almost right breast making love with a guy in bed.

Olga Karlatos . . . . Miss Paula Pagano, M.D.
- •• 0:42—Topless undressing in room with Laura Antonelli. Right breast and part of left breast lying in bed with Marcello Mastroianni.
- • 0:46—Brief topless in bed with Mastroianni and Clara.

Wild at Heart (1990)
Lisa Ann Cabasa . . . . Reindeer Dancer
- •• 0:30—Topless standing while Mr. Reindeer talks on the phone. More topless dancing in front of him.

Nicholas Cage . . . . Sailor
Willem Dafoe . . . . Bobby Peru
Laura Dern. . . . . Lula
- ••• 0:07—Topless putting on black halter top.
- •• 0:26—Left breast, then topless sitting on Nicholas Cage's lap in bed.
- ••• 0:35—Topless wriggling around in bed with Cage.
- • 0:41—Brief topless several times making love with Cage. Hard to see because it keeps going overexposed. Great moaning, though.

Sherilyn Fenn . . . . Girl in Accident
Isabella Rossellini . . . . Perdita
Mia M. Ruiz . . . . Mr. Reindeer's Resident Valet #1
- •• 0:32—Topless standing next to Mr. Reindeer on the right, holding a tray. Long scene.

Charlie Spradling . . . . Irma
- •• 0:40—Brief topless in bed during flashback.

The Wild Life (1984)
Michael Bowen . . . . .Vince
Sherilyn Fenn . . . . Penny Hallin
Tracey E. Hutchinson . . . . Poker Girl #2
- • 1:23—Brief topless in a room full of guys and girls playing strip poker when Lea Thompson looks in.

Leigh Lombardi . . . . Stewardess
Francesca "Kitten" Natividad . . . . Stripper #2
- ••• 0:50—Topless doing strip routine in a bar just before a fight breaks out.

Christopher Penn . . . . Tom Drake
Randy Quaid . . . . .Charlie
Ashley St. Jon . . . . Stripper #1
- ••• 0:47—Topless and brief buns doing strip tease routine in front of Christopher Penn and his friends.

Eric Stoltz. . . . . .Bill Conrad
Lea Thompson . . . . Anita
- 0:38—In bra and panties putting body stocking on.

Jenny Wright . . . . .Eileen
- •• 0:22—In bra and panties, then topless changing in her bedroom while Christopher Penn watches from the window.

Wild Man (1988)
Ginger Lynn Allen . . . . Dawn Hall
- •• 0:24—Topless taking off her dress in front of Eric, then making love with him.

Michelle Bauer . . . . Trisha Collins
- 1:02—In sheer white lingerie with Eric. Buns also.
- ••• 1:06—Topless on couch making love with Eric. Brief lower frontal nudity.

Jeanie Moore . . . . Lady at Pool

Wild Orchid (1990)
Jacqueline Bisset. . . . . Claudia
- 1:21—Dancing in braless white tank top during carnival.

Bruce Greenwood . . . . Jermone McFarland
- •• 1:02—Buns, while in room with Carré Otis.

Carré Otis . . . . Emily Reed
- •• 0:51—Left breast in mirror looking at herself while getting dressed.
- ••• 1:01—Topless when a guy takes off her dress while Mickey Rourke watches.
- ••• 1:02—Right breast, then topless on the floor with Jerome.
- • 1:31—Brief topless in flashback with Jerome.
- • 1:42—Topless opening her blouse for Rourke.
- ••• 1:44—Nude making love with Rourke. Nice and sweaty.

Jens Peter . . . . Voleyball Player
- ••• 1:29—Buns, while in room with Jacqueline Bisset and Carré Otis.

Mickey Rourke. James Wheeler

Assumpta Serna . . . . Hanna
- ••• 0:39—Topless at the beach and in the limousine. Very erotic.

Wild Orchid II: Two Shades of Blue (1992)

Lydie Denier . . . . Dominique
- ••• 0:28—Topless, undressing from lingerie while Blue and Elle watch.

Wendy Hughes . . . . Elle

Nina Siemaszko. . . . . Blue
- ••• 0:27—Topless and buns, getting undressed in front of Wendy Hughes.
- •• 0:43—Topless and buns in steam room with a customer.
- •• 0:58—Topless in panties, garter belt and stockings while undressing for Josh.
- ••• 1:06—Topless while humiliating J. J. in front of everyone at a party.

Tom Skerritt . . . . Ham

Wild Zone (1989)

Edward Albert. . . . . Colonel Lavera

Cristobel D'Ortez . . . . Mary
- •• 1:19—Topless in the brush, getting molested by a bad guy.

Carla Herd. . . . . Nicole Laroche

Wildcats (1986)

Woody Harrelson . . . . Krushinski

Goldie Hawn. . . . . Molly
- • 0:30—Brief topless in bathtub.

Bruce McGill . . . . Dan Darwill

M. Emmet Walsh. . . . . Coes

Wildest Dreams (1987)

Deborah Blaisdell . . . . Joan Peabody
- • 1:10—Brief topless during fight on floor with two other women.

Ruth Corrine Collins . . . . Stella
- ••• 0:22—Topless wearing panties in bedroom on bed with Bobby.
- • 1:10—Brief topless fighting on floor with two other women.

Jane Hamilton . . . . Ruth Delaney

Jill Johnson . . . . Rachel Richards
- •• 0:51—Topless on bed underneath Bobby in a net.
- • 1:10—Brief topless during fight with two other women.

Jeanne Marie . . . . Isabelle
- •• 0:35—Topless in panties in bedroom with Bobby.

Susan Napoli . . . . .Punk #4
- • 0:21—Brief left breast, leaning backwards on couch with her boyfriend.

Angela Nicholas . . . . Claudia
- •• 1:01—Topless typing on computer doing Bobby's book keeping.

Heidi Paine. . . . . Dancee
- • 0:23—Topless in the arms of a gladiator in Bobby's bedroom.

Miriam Zucker . . . . Customer

Wilding, The Children of Violence (1990)

Catlyn Day. .Officer Breedlove

Jackie Moen . . . . .Car Rape Victim
- • 0:23—Very brief right breast in back of car with her boyfriend when the gang of kids terrorizes them.

Karen Russell . . . . Cathy
- •• 0:20—Topless in bedroom when Wings Hauser pulls her lingerie down.

Willie and Phil (1980)

Kristine DeBell . . . . Rena

Jerry Hall . . . . .Karen
- • 0:05—Brief topless getting dressed in bedroom with Phil.

Kaki Hunter .Patti Sutherland

Margot Kidder . . . . .Jeanette Sutherland
- • 0:36—Brief topless in bed when Phil opens up her blouse. Long shot.
- • 0:47—Brief topless playing in a lake with Willie and Phil.
- • 1:36—Topless on the beach (mostly silhouette). Brief side of left breast.

Michael Ontkean . . . . .Willie
- •• 1:36—Buns, while taking off his swimsuit at the beach and jumping around.
- •• 1:45—Buns, while getting into the hot tub. (He's on the left.)

Ray Sharkey . . . . Phil
- •• 1:45—Buns, while getting into the hot tub. (He's on the right.)

Wimps (1987)

Jim Abele . . . . Charles Conrad

Deborah Blaisdell . . . . Roxanne Chandless
- • 1:22—Brief topless and buns taking off clothes and getting into bed with Francis in bedroom.

Louis Bonanno . . . . .Francis
- • 1:13—Buns, while running into a restaurant kitchen.

Jane Hamilton . . . . Tracy
- • 0:40—Lifting up her sweater and shaking her breasts in the back of the car with Francis. Too dark to see anything.
- •• 0:44—Topless and buns taking off sweater in a restaurant.

Gretchen Kingsley . . . . Debbie
Jeanne Marie. . . . . Janice
•• 0:20—Topless in bed taking off top with Charles.
Annie Sprinkle. . . . . Head Stripper
•• 1:12—Topless on stage with two other strippers,
teasing Francis.

Wings of Desire (1987)
a.k.a. Der Himmel Uber Berlin
Solveig Dommartin . . . . Marion
• 0:34—Brief side of left breast, while putting robe on.
(The film changes from B&W to color.)
Peter Falk . . . . Himself

Winter Kills (1979)
Belinda Bauer . . . . Yvette Malone
•• 0:46—Topless making love in bed with Jeff Bridges,
then getting out of bed.
• 1:25—Topless, dead as a corpse when sheet uncov-
ers her body.
Jeff Bridges . . . . Nick Kegan
•• 0:50—Buns, while getting dressed after making love
with Belinda Bauer.
Tisa Farrow . . . . Nurse Two
Amanda Jones . . . . Beautiful Woman Seven
Candice Rialson. . . . . Second Blonde Girl

Winter of Our Dreams (1981)
Bryan Brown . . . . Reb
• 0:48—Brief buns while falling into bed with Judy
Davis.
Judy Davis. . . . . Lou
• 0:19—Brief left breast sticking out of yellow robe in
bed with Pete.
• 0:26—Very brief side view of left breast taking off
top to change. Long shot.
•• 0:48—Topless taking off top and getting into bed
with Bryan Brown, then brief right breast lying
down with him.
Cathy Downes . . . . Gretel
• 0:41—Brief right breast putting top on while talking
to Judy Davis.
•• 1:04—Topless sitting up in bed at night.
• 1:11—Topless sitting up in bed while Bryan Brown
and Davis talk.

Witchboard (1987)
Tawny Kitaen . . . . Linda
• 1:26—Nude, stuck in the shower and breaking the
glass doors to get out.

Witchcraft II: The Temptress (1989)
Mia M. Ruiz. . . . . Michelle
• 0:27—Brief topless several times making love with a
guy on the floor during William's hallucination.
Delia Sheppard . . . . Dolores
•• 1:20—Brief topless several times with William.

Witchcraft III: The Kiss of Death (1991)
Leana Hall . . . . Roxy
•• 1:08—Topless on bed with William making love
when Charlotte gets trapped in the room.

Lisa Toothman . . . . Charlotte
•• 1:02—Buns and topless in shower with Louis while
William has a bad dream.
•• 1:12—Left breast, while on bed with Louis, against
her will.

Witchcraft IV: Virgin Heart (1992)
Julie Strain . . . . Belladonna
• 0:25—Buns, while dancing on stage in a red bra and
red G-string.
••• 0:27—Topless, dancing on stage.
•• 0:46—Topless on the floor with Santara.
• 0:49—Brief topless in open dress on couch with Will.
• 1:15—Topless, lying on couch in her dressing room
while Will tries to talk to her.

Witchfire (1986)
Vanessa Blanchard . . . . Liz
•• 0:52—Brief topless in bed and then the shower.

The Witching (1983)
a.k.a. Necromancy
(Originally filmed in 1971 as *Necromancy*, additional
scenes were added and re-released in 1983.)
Sue Bernard . . . . Nancy
• 1:03—Brief topless in bed with Michael Ontkean.
Pamela Franklin . . . . Lori
•• 0:38—Topless lying in bed during nightmare.
0:46—Partial right breast, tied to a stake. Flames
from fire are in the way.
• 1:07—Brief topless putting on black robe.
• 1:17—Brief topless in several quick cuts.
Annie Gaybis . . . . Spirit
Michael Ontkean . . . . Frank Brandon
Barbara Peckinpaugh . . . . Jennie
••• 0:02—Topless and buns in open gown during occult
ceremony. Brief full frontal nudity holding a doll up.
Laurie Senit . . . . Witches Coven
Brinke Stevens . . . . Black Sabbath Member

Witchtrap (1989)
Linnea Quigley. . . . . Ginger Kowowski
••• 0:34—Nude taking off robe and getting into the
shower.
•• 0:36—Topless just before getting killed when the
shower head goes into her neck.

Without You I'm Nothing (1990)
Steve Antin. . . . . Steve Antin
Sandra Bernhard . . . . Miscellaneous Characters
••• 1:20—Dancing in very small pasties and very small
G-string on stage for a long time. Rear shots of her
buns.
Carlton Wilborn . . . . Ballet Dancer

Witness (1985)
Kelly McGillis . . . . Rachel
••• 1:18—Topless taking off her top to take a bath while
Harrison Ford watches.
Viggo Mortensen . . . . Moses Hochleitner

Wolf Lake (1978)
a.k.a. Survive the Night at Wolf Lake
Robin Mattson . . . . Linda
- 0:54—Brief full frontal nudity during rape in cabin. Dark.
- 0:55—Brief topless afterwards.

Wolfen (1981)
Max M. Brown . . . . Christopher Van der Veer
- 0:21—Brief frontal nudity, lying dead as a corpse on the coroner's table. Don't see his face.

Albert Finney. .Dewey Wilson
Gregory Hines. . . . . Whittington
- 1:24—Buns, twice when he moons Albert Finney, who is looking through a green-tinted night vision scope.

Edward James Olmos . . . . .Eddie Holt
- 1:04—Buns, while lapping water, then nude, running around the beach. Dark.
- •• 1:05—Very brief frontal nudity, leaping off pier in front of Albert Finney.
- 1:12—Very brief frontal nudity, running under pier during Finney's vision.

Diane Venora . . . . Rebecca Neff

The Woman in Red (1984)
Kelly Le Brock . . . . Charlotte
0:02—Wearing the red dress, dancing over the air vent in the car garage while Gene Wilder watches.
- 1:13—Brief right breast, getting into bed. Too far to see anything.
1:15—Brief lower frontal nudity getting out of bed when her husband comes home. Very brief left breast, but it's blurry and hard to see.

Gene Wilder . . . . Theodore Pierce
- 1:15—Side view of buns while getting back into bed with Kelly Le Brock after getting out to take his underwear off the lamp.

Women & Men: Stories of Seduction
(1990; Made for Cable Movie)
Melanie Griffith. . . . . Hadley
Elizabeth McGovern . . . . Vicki
0:18—In white lingerie in train car with Beau Bridges.
- ••• 0:22—Topless when Bridges takes her top off when she lies back in bed.

Peter Weller. . . . . Hobie
James Woods . . . . Robert

Women in Love (1971)
Alan Bates . . . . Rupert
- 0:25—Buns and brief frontal nudity walking around the woods rubbing himself with everything.
- 0:50—Buns, while making love with Ursula after a boy and girl drown in the river.
- ••• 0:54—Nude fighting with Oliver Reed in a room in front of a fireplace. Long scene.

Glenda Jackson . . . . Gudrun Brangwen
- ••• 1:20—Topless taking off her blouse on the bed with Oliver Reed watching her, then making love.

- •• 1:49—Brief left breast making love with Reed in bed again.

Jennie Linden . . . . Ursula Bragwen
- 0:38—Brief topless skinny dipping in the river with Glenda Jackson.
- 1:11—Brief topless in a field with Alan Bates. Scene is shown sideways.

Oliver Reed . . . . Gerald Crich
- ••• 0:54—Nude, fighting with Alan Bates in a room in front of a fireplace. Long scene.

The Women's Club (1987)
Maud Adams . . . . Angie Blake
0:17—In black panties, garter belt and stockings making out with Michael Paré.

Michael Paré . . . . .Patrick
1:05—Brief buns, during nightmare. Hard to see because of fog.
- 1:06—Buns, while standing in hallway during nightmare. Long shot.

Pamela Ward . . . . Fashion Show Woman

Working Girl (1989)
Melanie Griffith . . . . Tess McGill
0:08—In bra, panties, garter belt and stockings in front of a mirror.
0:32—In black bra, garter belt and stockings trying on clothes.
0:43—In black bra, garter belt and stockings getting out of bed.
1:15—In white bra, taking off her blouse with Harrison Ford.
- 1:18—Very, very brief right breast turning over in bed with Ford.
- 1:20—Topless, vacuuming. Long shot seen from the other end of the hall.

Sigourney Weaver . . . . Katherine Parker
1:22—In white lingerie, sitting in bed, then talking to Harrison Ford.

Elizabeth Whitcraft. . . . . Doreen DiMucci
- •• 0:29—Topless on bed on Alec Baldwin when Melanie Griffith opens the door and discovers them.

The Working Girls (1973)
Elvira . . . . .Katya
0:18—Dancing in a G-string on stage in a club.
- ••• 0:20—Topless, dancing on stage.

Lynne Guthrie . . . . Jill
- ••• 0:43—Topless, dancing on stage at club.
- •• 0:48—Topless in swimming pool with Nick.

Laurie Rose. . . . . .Denise
Bob Schott. . . . . Roger
- 0:07—Buns, while getting out of bed to meet Honey.

Working Girls (1987)
Roger Babb . . . . .Paul
- 1:18—Frontal nudity with Molly.

World According to Garp (1982)
Glenn Close . . . . Jenny Fields
John Lithgow . . . . .Roberta
Robin Williams . . . . T.S. Garp
Jenny Wright. . . . . Curbie
- •• 0:33—Brief topless behind the bushes with Robin Williams giving him "something to write about."

The World is Full of Married Men (1979; British)
Carroll Baker . . . . Linda Cooper
- • 0:19—Brief left breast, while sitting up in bathtub covered with bubbles.

The Wraith (1986)
Vickie Benson . . . . Waitress
- • 0:59—Topless in bed with Packard when Loomis interrupts them.

Sherilyn Fenn . . . . .Keri
- • 0:13—Very brief topless when Packard's gang catches her in bed with Jamie.
- • 1:02—Brief topless during flashback when caught in bed by Packard's gang.
- • 1:03—Very brief right breast, pulling her swimsuit top off in pond with Charlie Sheen.

Randy Quaid. .Sheriff Loomis

Write to Kill (1990)
Joan Severance .Belle Washburn
- 0:59—Wearing purple bra in house with Scott Valentine.
- ••• 1:01—Topless, making love in bed with Valentine.
- • 1:04—Very brief, blurry topless when Valentine tosses her a blouse.

Scott Valentine . . . . Clark Sanford
- • 1:03—Very brief partial frontal nudity, leaping out of bed.

Xtro (1982)
Maryam D'Abo . . . . Analise
- ••• 0:25—Topless making love with her boyfriend on the floor in her bedroom.
- •• 0:56—Brief topless with her boyfriend again.

Yanks (1979)
Lisa Eichhorn. . . . . Jean Moreton
- • 1:48—Brief topless in bed when Richard Gere rolls off her.

Richard Gere. . . . . Matt
Vanessa Redgrave . . . . Helen
- • 1:25—Brief side of left breast and buns, taking off robe and getting into bed.

Annie Ross. Red Cross Lady

The Year of the Dragon (1985)
Ariane. . . . . Tracy Tzu
- • 0:59—Very brief topless when Mickey Rourke rips her blouse off in her apartment.
- •• 1:14—Nude, taking a shower in her apartment.
- •• 1:18—Topless straddling Rourke, while making love on the bed.

Mickey Rourke. . . . . Stanley White

Year of the Gun (1991)
Valeria Golino. . . . . Lia Spinelli
- ••• 0:17—Topless, making love in bed with Andrew McCarthy.
- • 0:25—Half of buns and side of right breast, lying in bed with McCarthy.

Andrew McCarthy . . . . David Raybourne
John Pankow . . . . .Italo Bianchi
Sharon Stone . . . . Alison King
- • 1:00—Brief left breast, standing against the door, with Andrew McCarthy. Long shot.
- • 1:01—Side of left breast, making love on bed.

Yentl (1983)
Mandy Patinkin . . . . Avigdor
- •• 0:49—Buns, after taking off his clothes to go skinny dipping.
- • 0:51—Brief buns while sitting down next to Barbra Streisand, the brief buns, while standing up.
- • 0:52—Buns, while walking around and sitting down. Long shot.

You Can't Hurry Love (1984)
Bridget Fonda . . . . Peggy
Sally Kellerman. . . . . Kelly Bones
Danitza Kingsley. . . . . Tracey
Kristy McNichol . . . . Rhonda
David Packer . . . . .Eddie
- • 0:59—Buns, in store taking his pants off while people watch him from the sidewalk.

Jean Poremba. . . . . Model in Back
- • 0:05—Topless posing in the backyard getting photographed.
- •• 0:48—Nude in backyard again getting photographed.

Kimber Sissons. . . . . .Brenda
- 0:48—Partial side of right breast in open shirt, bending over to pick up her bra off the coffee table.

Merete Van Kamp . . . . Monique

Young Doctors in Love (1982)
Jaime Lyn Bauer. . . . . Cameo
Ed Begley, Jr. . . . . Young Simon's Father
Dabney Coleman. . . . . Dr. Joseph Prang
Kimberly McArthur. . . . . .Jyll Omato
- •• 0:58—Topless in front of Dabney Coleman after taking off her Santa Claus outfit in his study.

Pamela Reed . . . . Norine Sprockett
Tessa Richarde . . . . Rocco's Wife
Peggy Trentini . . . . Christmas Elf
- •• 0:55—Brief topless greeting visitors to the party.
- • 0:57—Topless again sitting on couch.

Janine Turner . . . . Cameo
Sean Young . . . . Dr. Stephanie Brody
- 0:48—In white panties and camisole top in the surgery room with Michael McKean.

Young Einstein (1989; Australian)
Glenn Butcher. . . . . Ernest Rutherford
- 0:56—Buns, while standing in front of sink when Marie comes to rescue Einstein. (He's the one on the left.)

Warren Coleman. . . . . .Lunatic Professor
- 0:55—Buns while in Lunatic Asylum, taking a shower.
- 0:56—More buns while standing in front of sink when Marie comes to rescue Einstein. (He's the one on the right.)
- 0:58—Brief buns while crowding into the shower stall with the other Asylum people.

Young Guns (1988)
Emilio Estevez . . . . William H. Bonney (Billy the Kid)
- 1:19—Brief buns while standing up in the bathtub.

Pat Lee . . . . Janey
Terry O'Quinn. . . . . Alex McSween

Young Guns II (1990)
Ginger Lynn Allen . . . . Dove
Tom Byrd . . . . .Pit Inmate
Emilio Estevez . . . . William H. Bonney (Billy the Kid)
- •• 1:00—Buns, while getting up out of bed, putting his pants on.

Balthazar Getty . . . . Tom O'Folliard
Viggo Mortensen . . . . John W. Poe
William L. Petersen . . . . Pat Garrett
Christian Slater . . . . Arkansas Dave Rudbaugh
Tracey Walter . . . . Beever Smith
Jenny Wright. . . . . Jane Greathouse
- 1:07—Buns, taking off her clothes, getting on a horse and riding away. Hair covers breasts.
- 1:38—Buns, walking down stairs during epilogue.

Young Lady Chatterley (1977)
Lindsay Freeman . . . . Sybil (light-duty maid)
- 1:35—Brief left breast, while on the floor, covered with cake.

Michael Hearne. . . . . .Hitchhiker
- ••• 0:52—Buns, several times in back of car with Harlee McBride.
- 0:54—Brief buns when he's let out of the car.

Ray Martin . . . . .Ronnie (stable boy)
- •• 1:35—Frontal nudity, covered with cake during cake orgy.

Harlee McBride . . . . Cynthia Chatterley
- •• 0:19—Nude masturbating in front of mirror.
- 0:28—Brief topless with young boy.
- ••• 0:41—Nude in bathtub while maid washes her.
- ••• 0:52—Nude in back of car with the hitchhiker while the chauffeur is driving.
- ••• 1:03—Nude in the garden with the sprinklers on making love with the Gardener.
- ••• 1:31—Topless and buns in bed with the gardener.

Ann Michelle. . . . . Gwen (roommate)
Peter Ratray. . . . . Paul (young gardener)
- 0:37—Very brief buns, while pulling his pants up after getting caught with Janette.

- 1:03—Buns, while making love with Harlee McBride in the rain.
- •• 1:32—Buns, while in bed with McBride.

Patrick Wright . . . . Flash Back Gardener
- ••• 0:02—Nude, washing himself, outside while Lady Frances Chatterley watches.
- 0:05—Buns, while in house with Lady Chatterley.
- 0:06—More buns, while on the floor.
- 0:33—Buns, with Lady Chatterley by the pond.

Young Lady Chatterley II (1986)
Wendy Barry . . . . Sybil "Maid in Hot House"
- 0:12—Topless in hot house with the Gardener.

Brett Clark . . . . Thomas "Gardener"
- •• 0:15—Brief buns, while pulling up his pants after getting caught with Monique Gabrielle in the woods by Adam West.
- 0:16—Very brief buns, when Monique pulls his pants down again.

Sybil Danning . . . . Judith Grimmer
- ••• 1:02—Topless in the hut on the table with the Gardener.

Alexandra Day . . . . Jenny "Maid in Hut"
- ••• 0:06—Topless and buns in hut on the bed with the Gardener.
- ••• 0:28—Topless taking bath with Harlee McBride.

Monique Gabrielle . . . . Eunice "Maid in Woods"
- • 0:15—Topless in the woods with the Gardener.
- ••• 0:43—Topless in bed with Virgil.

Stephen Kean Mathews . . . . Robert Downing
- 0:59—Buns, while making love with Cynthia Chatterley outside on the grass.

Harlee McBride . . . . .Cynthia Chatterley
- •• 0:20—Topless getting a massage with Elanor.
- •• 0:22—Full frontal nudity during flashback to the first time she made love with Robert.
- ••• 0:28—Topless taking a bath with Jenny.
- ••• 0:35—Topless in library seducing Virgil.
- ••• 0:50—Topless in back of the car with the Count.
- ••• 0:58—Topless in the garden with Robert.

Allene Simmons . . . . Marta "Maid in Bed"

Young Nurses in Love (1987)
John Altamura . . . . n.a.
Jennifer Delora. . . . . Bunny
Jamie Gillis . . . . Dr. Spencer
Jane Hamilton . . . . .Franchesca
- •• 1:05—Topless on top of a guy on a gurney.

Jeanne Marie . . . . Nurse Ellis Smith
- 0:31—Brief side view of left breast in mirror with Dr. Riley.
- •• 1:09—Topless in panties, getting into bed with Dr. Riley.

Sharon Moran .Bambi/Bibi
Annie Sprinkle . . . . .Twin Falls
- •• 0:23—Topless getting measured by Dr. Spencer.

The Young Warriors (1983; U.S./Canadian)
John Alden . . . . Jorge
- 0:16—Dropping his pants in a room during pledge at fraternity.

Anne Lockhart. . . . . Lucy
- • 0:42—Topless and buns making love with Kevin on the bed. Looks like a body double.

Jimmy Patterson . . . . "Ice Test" Monty
- 0:14—Buns, while dropping pants and sitting on a block of ice during pledge at fraternity.

Linnea Quigley . . . . Ginger
- 0:05—Nude in and getting out of bed in bedroom.

Nels Van Patten. . . . . Roger
Randy Woltz . . . . "Brick Test" Frank
- 0:16—Dropping his pants in a room during pledge at fraternity.

Youngblood (1986)
Fionnula Flanagan. . . . . .Miss McGill
Cynthia Gibb . . . . Jessie Chadwick
- 0:50—Brief topless and buns making love with Rob Lowe in his room.

Rob Lowe . . . . Dean Youngblood
- • • 0:16—Buns, standing in hallway in jockstrap and walking around while Cindy Gibb watches.

Keanu Reeves . . . . Hoover
Patrick Swayze . . . . Derek Sutton
Jim Youngs . . . . Kelly Youngblood

Your Ticket is No Longer Valid (1982)
Jennifer Dale . . . . Laura
- • • 0:27—In black panties, then topless when her husband fantasizes, then makes love with her.
- 1:23—Left breast in bed with Montoya, then sitting, waiting for Richard Harris.

Richard Harris . . . . Jason
- 1:19—Buns, while taking off robe and sitting on the floor.

Winston Reckert . . . . Antonio Montoya
- 1:24—Buns, while in bed with Jennifer Dale.

Zandalee (1991)
Erika Anderson . . . . Zandalee Martin
- • • • 0:02—Nude, taking off robe and dancing around the room.
- • • • 0:21—Nude, undressing, then in bed with Judge Reinhold. Long scene.
- • • 0:30—Right breast, then topless making love in bed with Nicholas Cage.
- • • 0:32—Topless as Cage paints on her with his finger.
- • • • 0:45—Left breast, then topless and lower frontal nudity on floor with Cage.
- • • 0:47—Nude, getting massaged by Cage with an oil and cocaine mixture.
- 0:48—Brief topless getting into bed with Reinhold. Slightly out of focus.
- • • 1:09—Topless opening her dress for Reinhold while lying on a river bank, then making love with him at night in bed.

Nicholas Cage . . . . Johnny Collins
- • • 0:30—Buns, while making love in bed with Zandalee.

Judge Reinhold. Thierry Martin
- • • • 0:21—Buns while in bed with Zandalee.
- 0:23—Upper half of buns, while standing by the window.

Zapped! (1982)
Willie Aames. . . . . .Peyton
Scott Baio. . . . . .Barney
Corinne Bohrer. . . . . Cindy
Rosanne Katon . . . . Donna
Jewel Shepard . . . . Uncredited Girl in Car
- 0:39—Brief topless after red and white top pops off when Scott Baio uses his Telekinesis on her.

Marya Small . . . . Mrs. Springboro
Heather Thomas. . . . . Jane Mitchell
- 0:20—Brief open sweater, wearing a bra when Scott Baio uses telekinesis to open it.
- 1:28—Body double, very, very brief topless in photo that Willie Aames gives to Robby.
- 1:29—Body double brief topless when Baio drops her dress during the dance.

Zardoz (1974; British)
Sara Kestelman. . . . . .May
- 1:04—Left breast, in open blouse, under sheet with Sean Connery.
- 1:05—Very brief topless grabbing Connery from behind during struggle.

Charlotte Rampling .Consuella
- 0:29—Topless under yellow net blouse.
- 1:05—Very brief left breast, when Sean Connery grabs her during struggle.
- 1:26—Wearing yellow blouse, trying to kill Connery.
- 1:44—Very brief right breast feeding her baby in time lapse scene at the end of the film.

A Zed and Two Noughts (1985; British)
Frances Barber . . . . Venus de Milo
- • • • 0:22—Topless, sitting in bed, talking to Oliver, then nude while getting thrown out of his place.

Brian Deacon . . . . Oswald Deuce
- 1:12—Buns (he's on the right), getting into bed with Alba and Oliver.
- • • 1:25—Nude (on the right), walking to chair and sitting down while Oliver does the same.
- • • • 1:27—Frontal nudity, standing up.
- • • • 1:50—Nude, injecting himself and lying down to time lapse photograph himself decay with Oliver.

Eric Deacon . . . . Oliver Deuce
- • • 0:24—Buns in bed, then nude while throwing Venus out, then her clothes.
- • • • 0:30—Frontal nudity, sitting on bathroom floor.
- 1:12—Buns (he's on the left), getting into bed with Alba and Oswald.
- • • 1:25—Nude (on the left), walking to chair and sitting down while Oswald does the same.

••• 1:27—Frontal nudity, standing up.
••• 1:50—Nude, injecting himself and lying down to time lapse photograph himself decay with Oswald.

Andrea Ferréol. . . . . Alba Bewick
Guusje Van Tilborgh . . . . .Caterina Bolnes
- 0:42—Brief lower frontal nudity when Oliver lifts her skirt up in restroom to check to see what kind of panties she's wearing.
- 0:51—Lower frontal nudity, then very brief topless while posing for photo by Van Meegeren.

Zombie *(1980)*
Tisa Farrow . . . . .Anne Bolles
Olga Karlatos . . . . .Mrs. Menard
- 0:40—Topless and buns taking a shower.

Zombie Island Massacre *(1984)*
Rita Jenrette . . . . .Sandy
••• 0:01—Topless taking a shower while Joe sneaks up on her. Topless in bed with Joe.
•• 0:10—Brief right breast with open blouse, in boat with Joe. Left breast with him on the couch.

OTHER SOURCES

Back issues of *Playboy* magazine can be purchased through *The Playboy Catalog*. Their catalog is free by calling 1-800-345-6066. They have a large assortment of *Playboy* magazine back issues from the 1960's to the present. They also sell *Playboy* Video Magazines, *Playboy* Video Centerfolds and other video tapes listed in this book such as *Nudity Required* and the *Mermaid* series.

Penthouse magazine runs the Book & Video Society. They sell adult video tapes and books in addition to old issues of *Penthouse* magazine. 15 times a year, you receive an announcement describing the featured Selection, plus other offerings. If you wish to receive the Selection, you don't have to do anything—it's shipped to you automatically. If you don't want the Selection, you can order something else or nothing at all.

> Penthouse Book & Video Society
> P.O. Box 941
> Hicksville, NY 11802-0941

If you can't find the video tapes listed in *The Bare Facts Video Guide* for rent at your local video tape rental stores, an excellent source for purchasing video tapes is *Movies Unlimited*. Their catalog costs $7.95 plus $3.00 shipping, but you get a $5.00 credit voucher to use on your order. The address is:

> Movies Unlimited
> 6736 Castor Avenue
> Philadelphia, PA 19149
> (800) 4-MOVIES

Another source for locating hard to find video tapes is *Critic's Choice*. Their catalog is free by calling 1-800-544-9852. They have over 2,300 video tapes for sale. They also have a Video Search Line that operates Monday through Friday, from 9 a.m. to 5 p.m. EST. Their phone number is 1-900-370-6500. The cost is $1.95 for the first minute and $.95 for each additional minute. They will research your request and call you back within 1 to 2 weeks. The decision to buy—or not to buy—is yours.

Video Oyster has a catalog of hard to find video tapes called *Pearls Magazine*. Issue #3 is $4.00 or an 11 issue subscription is $30.00. The issues come out about two per year. Video Oyster will also search for a video tape for free. Tell them The Bare Facts sent you.

> Video Oyster
> 62 Pearl Street
> New York, NY 10004
> (212) 480-2440

If you are interested in writing to your favorite actor or actress to get an autograph or ask a question, you'll want to purchase *Celebrity Access—The Directory*. The book lists thousands of celebrity addresses. The cost is $21.95, plus $2.50 for shipping and handling. (California residents add 7.25% sales tax.) For Foreign countries the cost is $30.00 (postage included). Write or call:

> Celebrity Access Publications
> 20 Sunnyside Avenue, Suite A241
> Mill Valley, CA 94941
> (415) 389-8133

Another source for celebrity addresses is the *V.I.P. Address Book* by James M. Wiggins. It costs $89.95 and is available from:

> Associated Media Companies
> P.O. Box 10190
> Marina del Rey, CA 90295-8864
> (213) 821-2011

Brinke Steven's *Private Collection* video tape can be purchased directly from her (she also has a fan club). Write to her at:

> Brinke Stevens Fan Club
> 8033 Sunset Boulevard, Suite 557
> Hollywood, CA 90046

Becky LeBeau's video tapes and still photos can be purchased directly from her (she also has a fan club). Call or write:

> Soft Bodies
> 505 S. Beverly Drive, Suite 973
> Beverly Hills, CA 90212
> (800) 622-9920
> (310) 652-3520 Outside the United States

An excellent magazine that you should definitely check out is *Celebrity Sleuth*. In it, you'll find photographs of many celebrities that don't or won't do nudity for video tapes. People like Jackie Onassis, Deidre Hall and Caroline Munro are featured in various issues of *Celebrity Sleuth*.

Celebrity Sleuth
P.O. Box 273
West Redding, CT 06896

Drive-in film critic, Joe Bob Briggs, publishes a weekly newsletter, *We Are the Weird*. He writes a humorous column and reviews a movie in each edition. The movies he reviews are usually the type that are destined for inclusion in *The Bare Facts Video Guide*. It costs $35.00 for 52 issues. His address is:

We Are the Weird
P.O. Box 2002
Dallas, TX 75221

Perfect 10 Video sells hundreds of video tapes, photos and calendars. Their selection includes video tapes with nudity such as *Dermopathies*, *Becky Bubbles* and *In Search of the Perfect 10* plus a large selection of bikini contests. Call or write for their catalog ($2.00). Tell them The Bare Facts sent you.

Perfect 10 Video
11684 Ventura Blvd., Suite 589
Studio City, CA 91604
(800) GIRL-USA

Hot Body International video tapes may be purchased from Artists View Entertainment. Tell them The Bare Facts sent you. Call them at:

(800) 336-4321

Video Sports Ltd. carries a large selection of nude female wrestling and boxing video tapes featuring Jasaé, Venus de Light and others. Tell them The Bare Facts sent you. They can be reached at:

Video Sports Ltd.
1525 Aviation Blvd., Suite A199
Redondo Beach, CA 90278
(800) 926-2284

If you are interested in viewing the Rob Lowe video tape that he accidentally made in 1989, you can purchase it from Al Goldstein, publisher of *Screw* magazine. His New York cable TV show, *Midnight Blue*, showed some of the footage on show #672. The cost is $29.95, you need to specify VHS or Beta. Contact:

Media Ranch, Inc.
P.O. Box 432
Old Chelsea Station
New York, NY 10013

REFERENCES

Books:

Bowker's Complete Video Directory 1990
  R. R. Bowker, 1990

The Complete Actors' Television Credits, 1948–1988, Second Edition
  Volume 1: Actors and Volume 2: Actresses
  James Robert Parish and Vincent Terrace
  The Scarecrow Press, Inc., 1990

The Complete Directory to Prime Time Network TV Shows, 1946–Present
  Tim Brooks and Earle Marsh
  Ballantine, 1988

Halliwell's Film Guide, Seventh Edition
  Leslie Halliwell
  HarperPerennial, 1990

HBO's Guide to Movies on Videocassette and Cable TV 1991
  Daniel Eagan
  Harper & Ross, 1990

Leonard Maltin's TV Movies and Video Guide, 1992 Edition
  Leonard Maltin
  Signet, 1991

The Motion Picture Guide (1984 through 1992 editions)
  Baseline II, 1992

Movies on TV and Videocassette, 1991–1992
  Steven H. Scheuer
  Bantam Books, 1991

Movies Unlimited catalog
  Movies Unlimited, 6736 Castor Avenue, Philadelphia, PA 19149
  Various catalogs from 1987-1992

Roger Ebert's Movie Home Companion 1991 Edition
  Roger Ebert
  Andrews and McMeel, 1990

Russ Meyer—The Life and Films
  David K. Fraiser
  McFarland & Company, Inc., 1990

Video Movie Guide 1992
  Mick Martin and Marsha Porter
  Ballantine, 1990

The Blue Guide to Adult Film Stars—1990 Edition
  FD Enterprises, 1990

MORE REFERENCES

Periodicals:

Adult Video News magazine
   8600 West Chester Pike, Suite 300, Upper Darby, PA 19082
   Various issues from 1990–1992

Entertainment Weekly magazine
   Entertainment Weekly Inc., 1675 Broadway, New York, NY 10019
   Various issues from 1990–1992

Playboy magazine
   919 North Michigan Avenue, Chicago, IL 60611
   Various issues from 1972–1992

Penthouse magazine
   1965 Broadway, New York, NY 10023-5965
   Various issues from 1980–1992

Premiere magazine
   Premiere Publishing, 2 Park Avenue, New York, New York 10016
   Various issues from 1987–1992

The San Jose Mercury News newspaper
   750 Ridder Park Drive, San Jose, CA 95190
   Various issues from 1987–1992

Sight and Sound magazine
   21 Stephen Street, London W1P 1PL, England
   Various issues from 1990–1992

TV Guide magazine
   Triangle Publications, Inc., 100 Matsonford Road, Radnor, PA 19088
   Various issues from 1987–1992

We Are the Weird newsletter
   Joe Bob Briggs, P.O. Box 2002, Dallas, TX 75221
   Various issues from 1990–1992

ABOUT THE AUTHOR

Craig Hosoda is a Software Engineer. He grew up in Silicon Valley, California, then went to the University of California at Berkeley where he graduated with a B.S. degree in Electrical Engineering and Computer Science. After graduation, he worked at Hewlett-Packard for two years before getting a programming job at Industrial Light and Magic, George Lucas' special effects division of Lucasfilm Ltd. (Craig's film credits can be found in *The Golden Child*, *The Goonies* and **batteries not included*.)

While working at ILM, the seeds for *The Bare Facts Video Guide* were planted during a casual conversation one day with his friend, Marty Brenneis. While working on the film, *Howard the Duck*, Marty asked Craig about Lea Thompson's film credits. When Marty didn't know about her nude scene in *All the Right Moves*, Craig thought, "There should be a book that lists this type of important information in one place..."

After returning to Silicon Valley in 1987 to raise a family with his wife, he began research for the book during the evenings while working as a software engineer during the day. Unfortunately, it was difficult to balance a full-time job, work on *The Bare Facts* and have time for his family, so in July 1990, he quit his regular job to devote his life to uncovering the bare facts.

HOW THIS BOOK WAS CREATED

This book was published using the latest in database publishing techniques on an Apple Macintosh IIci computer. A custom ACIUS *4th Dimension* database was created to keep track of the data. An export module was written in *4th Dimension* that outputs the information with *FrameMaker* format tags into a text file. The text file was read into Frame Technology's *FrameMaker* and cleaned up a bit. Camera-ready copy was printed on an Apple Personal LaserWriter, then sent to the book printer.